STRATEGIC MANAGEMENT

Text, Readings, and Cases

FOURTH EDITION

STRATEGIC MANAGEMENT

Text, Readings, and Cases

Paul W. Beamish

Royal Bank Professor of International Business
Western Business School
The University of Western Ontario

C. Patrick Woodcock

Assistant Professor
Faculty of Administration
University of Ottawa

Represented in Canada by:

 **Times Mirror**
Professional Publishing Ltd.

IRWIN

Toronto • Chicago • Bogotá • Boston • Buenos Aires
Caracas • London • Madrid • Mexico City • Sydney

To our wives: Maureen and Trish

Irwin Book Team

Publisher: *Roderick T. Banister*
Sponsoring editor: *Evelyn Veitch*
Developmental editor: *Karen Conlin*
Marketing manager: *Murray Moman*
Production supervisor: *Lara Feinberg*
Project editor: *Mary Conzachi*
Assistant director, art and design: *Keith McPherson*
Cover designer: *Stuart Paterson*
Assistant manager, graphics: *Charlene R. Perez*
Compositor: *Bi-Comp, Inc.*
Typeface: *10/12 Times Roman*
Printer: *R. R. Donnelley & Sons Company*

Times Mirror
Higher Education Group

ISBN: 0-256-18674-X
Library of Congress Catalog Number: 95-78248

Printed in the United States of America
1 2 3 4 5 6 7 8 9 DO 2 1 0 9 8 7 6 5

ABOUT THE AUTHORS

Paul Beamish is the Royal Bank professor of International Business at the the Richard Ivey School of Business, The University of Western Ontario. Since 1992, he has served as editor-in-chief of the *Journal of International Business Studies (JIBS)*. He is the author or co-author of 13 books, over 40 articles or contributed chapters, and 50 case studies. His articles have appeared in such journals as *Strategic Management Journal, JIBS,* and *Columbia Journal of World Business*. His consulting and management training activities have been in both the public and private sector for such organizations as The World Bank, the Canadian Foreign Service Institute, Northern Telecom, and Valmet. He has received best research awards from the Academy of Management, the European Foundation for Management Development, and the Administrative Sciences Association of Canada. He worked for the Procter and Gamble Company of Canada and Wilfrid Laurier University before joining Western's faculty in 1987.

Patrick Woodcock is an assistant professor at the University of Ottawa where he teaches Strategic Management and International Business Strategy. He is author or co-author of a number of articles, some of which have appeared in *Business Quarterly, Group Decision and Negotiations,* and *The Journal of International Business Studies*. Prior to entering the academic world, he worked for over a decade as a mergers and acquisitions analyst and consultant. Some of the large multinational companies he worked with include Steetley Plc., Holderbank Corporation, and St. Lawrence Cement. He has received business research awards from the Academy of Management in the United States, the Canadian Exporter's Association, and the Administrative Sciences Association of Canada.

TO THE STUDENT

"Why are textbook prices so high?"

This is, by far, the most frequently asked question heard in the publishing industry. There are many factors that influence the price of your new textbook. Here are just a few:

- **Author Royalties:** Authors are paid based on a percentage of new book sales and **do not** receive royalties on the sale of a used book. They are also deprived of their rightful royalties when their books are illegally photocopied.

- **The Cost of Instructor Support Materials:** Your instructor may be making use of a teaching supplement such as an instructor's manual. This supplement is designed as part of a learning package to enhance your educational experience.

- **Developmental Costs:** These are costs associated with the extensive development of your textbook. Expenses include permissions fees, manuscript review costs, artwork, typesetting, printing and binding costs, and more.

- **Marketing Costs:** Instructors need to be made aware of new textbooks. Marketing costs include academic conventions, remuneration of the publisher's representatives, promotional advertising pieces, and the provision of instructor's examination copies.

- **Bookstore Markups:** In order to stay in business, your local bookstore must cover its costs. A textbook is a commodity, just like any other item your bookstore may sell, and bookstores are the most effective way to get the textbook from the publisher to you.

- **Publisher Profits:** In order to continue to supply students with quality textbooks, publishers must make a profit to stay in business. Like the authors, publishers **do not** receive any compensation from the sale of a used book or the illegal photocopying of their textbooks.

We at Times Mirror Professional Publishing hope you will find this information useful and that it addresses some of your concerns. We also thank you for your purchase of this new textbook. If you have any questions that we can answer, please fax us at:

905-470-0050

PREFACE AND ACKNOWLEDGMENTS

As with the previous three editions, this book was made possible only through the academic and intellectual support from colleagues at The University of Western Ontario (UWO), University of Ottawa, and others across the country. The primary stimulus for this book was our own ongoing need for new, high-quality Canadian material.

Having made the decision to produce a book of Canadian cases in strategic management, a number of other decisions were made: (1) to bring together Canadian cases written not only by ourselves, but by faculty across North America; (2) to include only decision-oriented cases, which we believe provide the best training for future managers; (3) to include cases dealing with international business, service industries, not-for-profit industries, and business ethics; (4) to provide text material including a basic conceptual framework for use with all of the cases; and (5) to include a section on how to do case and financial analysis.

We solicited and received much useful feedback on the third edition from colleagues at the more than 40 institutions in Canada and the United States where the third edition has been used. From this feedback, we retained the basic structure of the third edition, but have changed the majority of the cases and updated the text material where appropriate. This edition contains 18 new cases and several new readings. In addition, 4 cases have been revised or condensed.

We are indebted to several groups of people for assisting in the preparation of this book. First, we are grateful to the case contributors from UWO, Wilfrid Laurier University, University of Ottawa, and other institutions. At UWO, we wish to thank Mary Crossan, Ann Frost, Tony Frost, Nick Fry, John Hulland, Bud Johnston, John Kennedy, Peter Killing, Kerry McLellan, Don Thain, and Rod White; the doctoral and research assistants Azimah Ainuddin, Fred Chan, Garnet Garven, Jennifer McNaughton, Detlev Nitsch, Doug Reid, and Ian Sullivan. Finally more than anyone else, we would like to thank Mark Baetz, from Wilfrid Laurier University, for his contributions that have been carried over from previous editions and for his cooperation in helping us produce this edition.

Cases were also contributed by colleagues from other institutions:

Julian Birkenshaw, *Stockholm School of Economics*

Bill Blake, *Memorial University*

Bruce Buchan, *Queens University*

Jonathan Calof, *University of Ottawa*

Brooke Dobni, *University of Saskatchewan*

Louis Hebert, *Concordia University*

Diane Hogan, *Memorial University*

Andrew Inkpen, *Thunderbird; AGSIM*

Louise Jones, *Memorial University*

David Leighton, *NCMRD*

Mathew Fischer, *City of London*

Raymond Gaudette, *Concordia University*

Mike Geringer, *California Polytechnic State Univ.*

Walter Good, *University of Manitoba*

R.K. Gupta, *Memorial University*

Barb Marcolin, *University of Calgary*

Allen Morrison, *Thunderbird: AGSIM*

Thomas Poynter, *Transitions Group*

M.D. Skipton, *Memorial University*

From the above list it is clear that the effort to produce the book has been both a national and international effort.

With regard to the textual material, the footnotes at the end of each chapter indicate the source of the material in the chapter. We wish to acknowledge, in particular, the assistance of Art Thompson and A.J. Strickland on Chapters 2, 8, and 10; Ken Harling on Chapters 5 and 6; and Ray Suutari on Chapter 6 and the reading on "Doing Business in the United States, and a Comparison of Location Sensitive Operating Costs in Canadian and U.S. Cities."

Others who provided helpful comments on the outline of the fourth edition include Jack Ito, University of Regina; A. Scott Carson, Saint Mary's University; and Brooke Dobni, University of Saskatchewan.

We are indebted to the strategy area teaching groups, past and present, at UWO and Wilfrid Laurier University. At Wilfrid Laurier, our special thanks to Larry Agranove, John Banks, Ruth Cruikshank, Elliott Currie, Tom Diggory, Ken Harling, Peter Kelly, and Ray Suutari.

We are also grateful for the secretarial assistance. At Western, we wish to thank Jeannette Weston.

Another group that was instrumental in the preparation of this book was the group of reviewers used by our publisher. These include the following colleagues from across the country:

James W. Alsop	Stephen Drew	Greg Libitz
R.W. Archibald	Dwight Dyson	Rich Mimick
Michael Bellas	Gordon Fullerton	Wojciech Nasierowski
Bob Blunden	Christopher Gadsby	John Oldland
Pierre Brunet	George Gekas	Vicky Paine-Mantha
Donald Buskas	Barry Gorman	David Pringate
James Butler	Ann Gregory	Bob Sexty
Mick Carney	Louis Hebert	Reza Sina
John Charmard	G.V. Hughes	Michael Skipton
Ron Correll	John Knox	John Usher

Financial assistance for some of the case writing at Western was received through the Plan for Excellence.

In addition, we wish to thank the various executives who gave us the required access to complete the cases in this book. Finally, we wish to recognize our students on whom we tested the cases for classroom use. Some students served as research assistants; their contributions are duly noted in each case.

Any errors or omissions in this book remain our responsibility. We look forward to feedback from its various users.

Paul W. Beamish
C. Patrick Woodcock

CONTENTS

SECTION II

READINGS

SECTION III

CASES

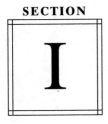

SECTION

I

CHAPTERS

STRATEGIC MANAGEMENT
An Overview

Nothing energizes an individual or a company more than clear goals and a grand purpose. Nothing demoralizes more than confusion and lack of content.

Tony O'Reilly, *CEO of H.J. Heinz Co. (1994)*

On McDonalds Restaurants' dominance in the fast food business—*Never have I seen a company more focused. . . . The company is an army with one objective that has never strayed.*

Don Kenough, *Member of the Board of Directors, McDonalds Corp., and retired President of Coca Cola. (1994)*

Businesses are successful for a variety of reasons. Some are the first to do something. Some do a very good job on the one or two things that are most critical to their success. And some have developed complex skills, technologies, and systems to support their success. Yet, how do managers consistently develop successful business plans and implement them effectively? The study of strategic management attempts to formalize concepts and approaches that have been observed to produce business success over the long term. These strategic approaches are not a substitute for hard work or functional skills. Rather, they are general management tools aimed at improving a firm's long-term prosperity.

Does strategic planning result in higher performance? Many studies have examined this relationship and the majority of studies have concluded that firms which have a formal strategic planning process outperform those that do not. Furthermore, firms taking a proactive strategic approach have better performance than those taking a reactive strategic approach. This evidence demonstrates the usefulness and, in fact, necessity of having a formal, proactive strategic planning process in a firm, whether it be large or small.

The Strategic Management Process Defined

The study of strategic management has been steadily evolving. Original emphasis was on the functions of the general manager—still an integral part of the field. More recently, the strategic management field has broadened to include the study *"of the organizational systems and processes used to establish overall organizational goals and objectives and to formulate, implement, and control the strategies and policies necessary to achieve these goals and objectives."*[1]

The common element in discussions of strategic management is an emphasis on strategy. Derived from the ancient Greek *strategos,* "the art of the general,"[2] strategy has military roots. In fact, not surprisingly, strong similarities exist between the responsibilities of the military general and the general manager of an organization. Their definitions of strategy often overlap as well. In a military context, strategy has been defined as "the employment of the battle as the means to gain the end of the war."[3] In a corporate setting, strategy can be defined as the implementable management scheme for achieving corporate ends. Alternately, corporate strategy has been viewed as "the pattern in the organization's important decisions and actions, and consists of a few key

---

EXHIBIT 1–1   Some Major Subfields of Strategic Management/Business Policy

---

Groups
- Board of directors
- General management
- Stakeholder analysis

Conceptualizing strategic management
- The strategy–structure–performance linkage
- Corporate-level strategy (including mergers, acquisitions, and divestiture)
- Business-level strategy

Elements of strategy formulation
- Organizational goals
- Corporate social policy and management ethics
- Macroenvironmental analysis
- Strategic decision making (choice of strategy)

Elements of strategy implementation and review
- The design of macro-organizational structure and systems
- Strategic planning and information systems
- Strategic control systems
- Organizational culture
- Leadership style for general managers

Organizations
- The strategic management of small businesses and new ventures
- The strategic management of not-for-profit organizations (including governments)
- The strategic management of international business

Source: Reprinted by permission from West Series in Strategic Management, Charles W. Hofer, consulting ed. (St. Paul, MN.: West Publishing, 1986). Copyright © 1986 by West Publishing Co. All rights reserved.

areas or things by which the firm seeks to distinguish itself."[4] In a broader context, strategy has been defined as "that which has to do with determining the basic objectives of an organization and allocating resources to their accomplishment."[5] A contemporary view of a strategic manager is a facilitator, coach, team builder, and motivator who establishes direction, builds the organization's capabilities, and implements change in the firm on a continuous basis.

To provide the student with a broader understanding of the strategic management concept, 18 major subfields are summarized in Exhibit 1–1.

The strategic management processes of planning and implementing strategy are complex and evolutionary. The dynamic nature of these processes are important to understand because they are not always completely planned. Rather, they are processes where managers attempt to plan and manage a firm's strategy in an ever-changing competitive environment. In this context, the firm's strategy evolves in a direction that is sometimes planned and other times influenced by unforeseen external competitive forces. Managers plan a strategy based on assumptions about their competitors and their own organizational capabilities. However, as various competitive and organizational influences depart from their expected course, managers must abandon part of the strategy (i.e., unrealized strategy) and adopt new strategies (i.e., emergent strategy). This process, shown in Exhibit 1–2, illustrates the dynamic nature of the strategic process—a process that requires continual learning, review, flexibility, and renewal to meet the needs of the ever-changing competitive environment. This continual evolution of strategy is necessary to produce a sustainable "realized strategy"—one that produces long-term success.

The Levels of Strategy

Several levels of strategy have been developed by business strategists. These levels, although intimately interwoven in reality, can be considered separately

EXHIBIT 1–2   The Strategy-Making Process

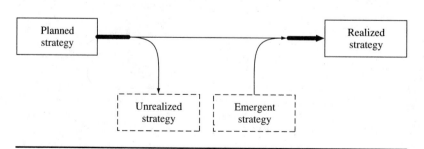

Source: Adapted from Henry Mintzberg and Alexandra Mchugh, "Strategy Formation in an Adhocracy," *Administrative Science Quarterly* 30, no. 2 (June 1985).

EXHIBIT 1–3   Levels of Strategies

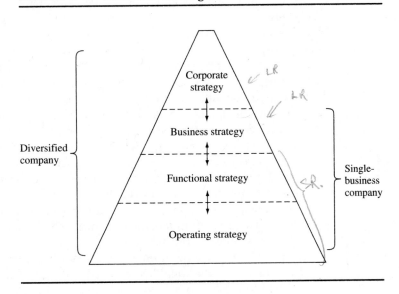

EXHIBIT 1–4   Description of Levels of Strategy

Level of Strategy	Level of Influence	Strategy Makers	Types of Decisions
Corporate strategy	Corporate strategies.	Corporate managers and board members.	Allocation of resources to businesses, and scope of business diversification.
Business strategy	Business strategies.	Top business managers in company or business division.	Types of products/markets to be in and the organizational and resource-specific attributes required to support the product/market focus.
Functional strategy	R&D, finance, marketing, manufacturing, human resource strategies/ functions.	Top functional managers within a business.	Type of operational technique, approaches, and resources that best support the overall business strategy.
Operational strategy	Plants, teams, sales groups, and individuals within functions.	Individuals within the functions that have responsibility for tasks or decision-making units.	Specific operational tactics, approaches, and resources that support the business and functional strategies.

for analytical purposes. The levels, illustrated in Exhibit 1–3, are differentiated based upon what decisions are taken, who makes and implements the decisions, and how the decisions impact on the overall firm. Exhibit 1–4 describes the various characteristics of these strategic levels.

Corporate strategy focuses on decisions related to which businesses a firm is in. For example, should the firm enter a new business or get out of old businesses, and to which of its businesses should it allocate resources (i.e., capital, equipment, skills, etc.) in the future? This level of strategy is most important for the diversified firm (i.e., a firm in several different businesses). The text addresses this strategic level using the same frameworks as are discussed at the business strategy level. However, the pertinent decisions and relationships to corporate strategy are described in the relevant chapters.

Business strategy focuses on decisions about how a specific business competes in its particular market for product or service emphasis. This strategy is the principal strategic concern of a firm that is in only one business, or of a single business unit in a diversified firm. The business-level strategy will be the primary focus of this book.

Functional and operational strategies are the strategies occurring in the functional and operational levels of the business. They provide critical input into the formulation of a business strategy and are important tools for implementing the business strategy at the functional and operational levels within the firm. These latter two strategies will not actively be studied because they are normally covered more thoroughly elsewhere in the business school curriculum. However, the student must understand these strategies because it is at this level that managers must eventually translate the corporate and business strategies for effective implementation.

Another type of strategy, international strategy, is important both at the corporate and business levels. International strategy is concerned with where, when, what, and how to enter and develop businesses in international regions. International strategies are addressed throughout the text.

A Conceptual Framework for Strategic Management

The basic underlying paradigm in the strategic management area for over 30 years has been the strategy–structure–performance relationship.[6] This relationship tells us two things—one of which is immediately obvious and the other not. The first and obvious point is that strategy affects performance. Whether one is attempting to organize a fundraiser, increase sales, start a business, or allocate resources in a large organization—strategy matters.

The second, perhaps less obvious point is that organizational structure matters also, because it can support or hamper the strategy. To implement any strategy, certain organizational actions must be taken: tasks must be carried out; reward and information systems put in place; people hired, trained, and managed; and reporting relationships established. An unlimited number of potential organizational actions exist. However, they are not all equally

EXHIBIT 1–5   The Underlying Paradigm in Strategic Management

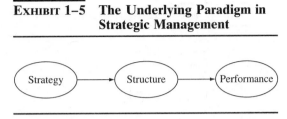

appropriate in all situations. Depending on the strategy chosen, some organizational structures are more appropriate than others. In fact, possibly the greatest challenge in the strategic management area is fitting an appropriate organization to the strategy that has been formulated.

A sports analogy can illustrate this second point most effectively. Any hockey team can put six players on the ice with a playing strategy; however, the organization of the players into three forwards, two defence men, and a goalie appears to be critical in enabling the team to strategically react both defensively and offensively in a balanced manner. Thus, it is the organization of the players that allows the various strategies to be carried out most effectively.

In the balance of this chapter, we review several well-accepted strategic management models that form the basis for the conceptual framework used in this text. Keep in mind that all of these models have as part of their origins the same underlying paradigm, depicted in Exhibit 1–5.

Exhibit 1–6 details one of the dozens of published models of strategic management. Like many approaches, this model is divided into sections on strategy formulation and implementation. Although formulation and implementation are inextricably linked, for analytic purposes they can be considered separately.

The major variables influencing strategy formulation are:

1. the preferences, personal values, and aspirations of top management.
2. the external environment, including competitive opportunities and risks.
3. the internal environment, which focuses on the organization's managerial, financial, and technical resources and capabilities.
4. organizational responsibility to society.

The conceptual framework used in this text includes the first three of these variables. The fourth variable is subsumed under managerial preferences and values.

In Exhibit 1–6 there are a large number of arrows between the variables used to illustrate the interrelationships that exist. Although in the general case, strategy influences structure, certainly in many instances the relationship can be in the other direction or, in fact, in both directions.

EXHIBIT 1–6   Strategic Management Process

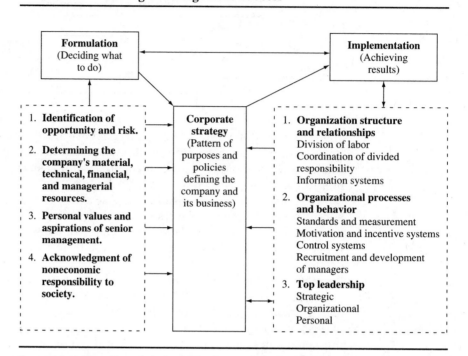

Source: Adapted from Kenneth Andrews, *The Concept of Corporate Strategy* rev. ed. (Burr Ridge, Ill. Richard D. Irwin 1980)

The strategy implementation half of the model in Exhibit 1–6 is composed of a separate group of variables. Typically, the major organization design variables are (a) information and control systems, (b) reward systems, (c) people, which includes leadership style, (d) organizational structure, and (e) resource allocation task. This last variable, task, is sometimes viewed as a bridge between formulation and implementation. In this text, all five of these variables are included as part of strategy implementation, although using a slightly different configuration. The role of these variables in the strategic management process will be discussed in detail in Chapters 7 and 8.

The above framework enunciates the differences between strategic formulation and implementation. Strategic formulation involves deciding what to do and where to do it, whereas strategic implementation involves doing it. However, students will be asked to describe recommendations and plans specific to both the strategic formulation and implementation issue. Exhibit 1–7 considers these two dimensions and their characteristics. In particular, the exhibit delineates the descriptive and planning questions that the student should focus on when considering strategic formulation versus implementation. In general, formulation is focused on the what and where questions, while implementation is focused on the when and how questions.

Exhibit 1–8 illustrates the conceptual framework and the key variables

EXHIBIT 1–7   Planning the Formulation and Implementation in Strategic Management

	Formulation	*Implementation*
Strategic Business Description	Deciding what to do.	Doing it and achieving results.
Planning Description	Planning a desired set of objectives, strategic position, and set of competitive advantages that are consistent with the forecasted competitive environment and management preferences, as well as developing the appropriate resources, organizational systems, processes, and structure.	Planning how and when to implement the desired strategy in a logical and doable manner.
Basic Planning Questions	What business or market/product/ service emphasis should the firm take; what competitive advantages does it have to take such an emphasis; and where should it take such an emphasis?	How and when to implement strategic positions, advantages, components, and tactics?
Examples of Detailed Planning Questions to Be Focused on	What products should the business focus on? What type of customers should the business focus on? What geographic market should the business focus on? What competitive advantages or skills, capabilities, etc., should the business attempt to develop?	When should various aspects of the strategic change be implemented? How will the managers overcome political resistance and get employees to embrace the change? How should the company develop? How should the resistance to change be handled? How does the firm control and review strategic action?

used in this text. The environment is largely an uncontrollable influence in this framework, whereas the other influences or components are more managerially controllable. Therefore, managers, in the short term, must exert influence on the other components in this framework and position themselves in the environment so as to maximize performance. It is for this reason that strategic analysis normally begins with the environmental analysis.

The Major Components of Strategy

Every firm has a strategy. Implicit or explicit, effective or ineffective, as intended or not—whenever a firm allocates the resources of people or capital, it is making a statement about its strategy.

Three components are present in a strategy: (1) mission/objectives, (2) competitive position (i.e., market/product/service emphasis), and (3) competitive advantage (i.e., basis of competition).

EXHIBIT 1–8   Strategic Management Process: Basic Conceptual Framework

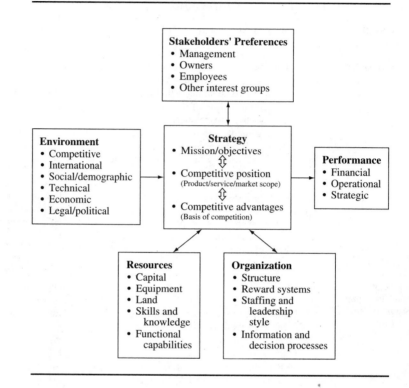

Mission/Objectives

In many of the more successful organizations there is a clear sense of "who we are and where we are going." In deriving a notion of mission or purpose, managers must confront questions such as: What kind of organization/business is it? What do they want it to be? What should it be, given their strategic capabilities? As such, a firm's mission and objectives are influenced considerably by managers' preferences as well as the preferences and values of its other stakeholders including the owners, customers, and employees.

The organization's mission or purpose can be translated into specific measurable performance targets. These objectives typically relate to profitability, growth, return on investment, market share, technological strength, and so forth. In addition, there are "soft" goals and objectives. These might include such things as benefits to society, employee welfare, and management autonomy. Knowledge of the existence of a "soft" counterpart to "hard" terms is essential if one is to have a more complete understanding of an organization.

A firm's mission and objectives are intimately linked to the other strategic variables because the mission and objectives describe the desired strategic

---

EXHIBIT 1–9   Example

Genuine Door Manufacturing Co.

Mission/Objectives: Genuine Door's objective is to maintain its position as the largest
standard frame door manufacturer in Canada. Its annual revenue growth objective is 10
percent and it has return on investment objectives of over 20 percent annually.

⇕

Competitive Position: The market and products that Genuine focuses on is the standard house
door in both steel and wood throughout Canada. Its products are the lowest priced in the
market, and are relatively plain in presentation, coming in only five colours. Genuine
services its doors through an on-site 10-year warranty policy, which is standard in the
industry.

⇕

Competitive Advantages: The competitive advantages that allow Genuine to hold this market
position are its economies of scale and production capabilities. Genuine's economies of scale
(or large size) allow it to buy steel and wood in volume discounts that other door
manufacturers cannot match. This size also gives Genuine access to the most efficient and
effective distribution channels and the largest dealers because it can provide advertising
assistance to dealers. Genuine also has developed a highly automated manufacturing process
that minimizes production costs, material waste, quality rejections, and production time.
Finally, Genuine's supplier and dealer ordering and billing is done by computer connection,
thus minimizing the delivery times and inventory quantities.

---

results, yet the other strategic variables govern which objectives can be at-
tained, how, and when. An example of a firm's objectives is described in
Exhibit 1–9.

A clear strategic mission is particularly important to a not-for-profit organization because such an organization is driven by its mission to the community
and to society. Therefore, it is vital that all employees, volunteers, donators,
and customers understand and agree with the mission statement and objectives
of the organization.

Competitive Position

A second component of strategy is a firm's competitive position, or positions (if
the firm is diversified into several businesses). *Competitive position* is defined as
the firm's market/product/service emphasis and it can be described as the
location and type of customer it services, the product and service attributes
its customers value, and its market/product/service emphases relative to its
competitors. A firm's competitive position relative to its competitors will be
discussed further in Chapter 3.

Business research suggests that there are three generic competitive positions that firms can profitably seek in a market. They are customer focus, low
cost, and differentiation. All of these strategies are aimed at focusing the
strategy on a specific competitive position so that you can use your resources

and organizational capabilities efficiently and effectively. Very few companies can be everything to everybody in a market. A *customer focus strategy* entails having a competitive position that focuses on specific customers. An example would be a travel agency that focuses on high-risk adventures or skin divers. A *low-cost strategy* naturally focuses the firm to be competitively positioned in the low-cost market of the industry. Examples of firms with low-cost strategies are Wal-Mart, the Price Club, and Costco. Firms that take a *differentiation strategy* are attempting to provide the customer with valued, yet distinctive products or services that their competitors are not providing. Examples of this strategic approach are Holt Renfrew, Birks Jewelry Stores, and the Concorde air service between New York and London.

The term *market* refers to both geographic and customer groups. *Geographic markets* can be local, regional, national, or international in scope. *Customer groups,* which are defined in terms of customer scope and focus, are an important characterization of a firm's business and focus.[7] Specifically, a business can be defined in terms of (1) customer groups (who is being satisfied?), (2) customer needs (what is being satisfied?), and (3) alternative technologies (how are customer needs satisfied?). This, then, describes the competitive position of the firm in the eyes of the customers. Therefore, competitive position is a description of the firm's strategy in relation to its environment, as shown in Exhibit 1–8.

The example in Exhibit 1–9 defines Genuine's competitive position in terms of both geographic and customer group focus. The geographic market encompasses all of Canada, and the pertinent attributes that define the customer group are the low price, limited designs, material choice (i.e., steel and wood), and warranty period and service.

The firm's objectives and competitive position are linked because managers must decide whether the firm's competitive position (i.e., market/product/service emphasis) is going to provide it with the desired growth and performance levels. If the competitive position is not going to provide such growth, then either the objectives must be changed or the competitive position must be changed. Both the existing and potential range and focus of market/product/service alternatives must be considered in analysing possible competitive positions. Exhibit 1–10 delineates some of the alternative market and product/service emphasis one should examine when considering possible new competitive positions.

Competitive Advantages

The third component of strategy is the firm-specific competitive advantages that enable the company to compete effectively in a specific product/market position. These advantages represent the bases upon which a firm competes in its industry and market. Clearly these advantages are important because they allow the firm to occupy a competitive position. However, these advantages also are important because they characterize how easily and quickly a firm will be able to meet its strategic objectives. A firm with stronger competitive advantages will be able to achieve more challenging strategic objectives than a company with relatively weak competitive advantages. In this context, competitive advantages are relative. However, examples of strong competitive advantages might be highly valued product patents, highly trained managers and workers, or a mix of competitive advantages providing synergies that other companies have not been able to duplicate. The competitive advantages in a company originate from the resources and organizational capabilities and design, as is illustrated in Exhibit 1–8.

The example in Exhibit 1–9 describes Genuine Door's intrinsic competitive advantages. These are principally related to economies of scale. More specifically, they are automated, high-volume mass production, volume purchasing discounts, access to efficient and effective distribution channels, and a computer-automated supplier/buyer ordering system. These advantages all allow Genuine to be the largest, low-cost door manufacturer in Canada (i.e., its competitive position). These advantages will, hopefully, allow the firm to achieve its desired growth and profitability objectives.

The five elements of competitive advantage pertinent to industry structure, discussed in greater detail in Chapter 3 (see Exhibit 3–1), show that the competitive forces that shape strategy not only arise from internal industry competition rivalry,[8] but also arise from competitive forces generated by suppliers,[9] customers,[10] substitute products, and potential new entrants. This framework for analysing competitors (and industries) is useful for understanding how a firm competes now and in the future.

Some of the questions related to the various levels of strategic decision making at the corporate, business, and international levels are described in Exhibit 1–11. These questions attempt to illustrate the practical decision-making emphasis both from a competitive position and from a competitive-advantages perspective at these various levels.

EXHIBIT 1–10   Competitive Position Growth Alternatives

		Market alternatives			
		Reduced Market	Existing Market	Expanded Market	New Market
Product/service alternatives	Reduced Product/services				
	Existing Products/services				
	Modified Products/services				
	New Product/services				

EXHIBIT 1–11   **The Relationship between Strategic Variables and Strategic Level**

Level of Strategy	Questions Related to Competitive Position	Questions Related to Competitive Advantages
Corporate strategy	Is the firm's competitive position(s) good from an investment perspective? Will the portfolio of competitive positions satisfy the corporate objectives? Should they consider either investing or divesting in a business?	Do the competitive advantages in the various businesses that the firm holds provide synergy to one another? Can the firm provide corporate-level competitive advantages such as financial acumen to the individual businesses?
Business strategy	Would the business's performance be enhanced if the competitive position were changed? Does the business competitive position satisfy the firm's objectives?	Do the competitive advantages support the business's competitive position? Can the firm improve its business competitive advantages?
International strategy	When entering a new country, what competitive position should the firm be seeking? Does the new international competitive position satisfy the firm's objectives?	Does the firm have adequate home-based competitive advantages to move into international markets? Does the firm have enough international competitive advantages, such as organizational control capabilities and market and cultural knowledge, to enter an international market?

Evaluating Strategic Performance

The ultimate evaluation of a firm's strategy is its performance over the long term. This is illustrated in Exhibit 1–7. Thus, when assessing a firm's strategy, performance outcomes should be examined because they can provide strong evidence of the quality of strategy formulation and implementation in a firm.

There are three basic types of performance indicators: financial, operational, and other strategic indicators. Exhibit 1–12 describes these various performance indicators. Financial indicators are broad performance measures that provide one with an indication of how the firm is doing financially. Operational performance indicators allow the analyst to focus on evaluating and comparing specific strategically critical operational aspects of the firm that are relevant to its operational competitive advantage. For example, a service firm depends upon the efficiency and effectiveness of its people. Therefore, sales per employee may be an important operational indicator to examine. Furthermore, it is critical to look at both static comparative indicators and their trends over time. Other strategic (non-numerical) indicators involve subjective examination of information provided to the manager. This information could be in the form of dissatisfied customers, unhappy employees, or strategic changes or misalignments. This information usually requires subjective assessment, yet it is useful because it is often a precursor to financial or operational performance deterioration.

EXHIBIT 1–12   Performance Indicators

Type of Performance Indicator	Measurement Tools
Financial indicators	Financial values and ratios based on standards or competitive comparisons. Examples: Debt-to-equity ratio, profitability ratios (see Chapter 2 for more).
Operational indicators	Operational measures are values and ratios that indicate the operational efficiency and effectiveness of the firm. These measures are often used to measure comparatively the firm's key operational competitive advantages relative to their prime competitors. Examples: Sales to employee, sales to assets, R&D expenses to sales, market share (see Chapter 2).
Other strategic indicators	Strategic measures and non-numerical measures are more abstract and subtle in nature. They involve such things as the perceived strategic fit between the various components by various experts in the field, the enthusiasm of employees or employee complaints, supplier or customer complaints, etc.

A relatively new and intensive business performance evaluation tool is benchmarking. Benchmarking is a technique that is being used by companies to evaluate their functional and operational level efficiencies and effectiveness relative to the best in the world. Establishing a benchmarking program involves locating a firm that has the best, for example, purchasing operation having similar requirements to yours and sending in your purchasing experts to compare their practices with yours. This type of program not only allows the firm to compare its performance with another's, but it also allows the firm to observe and learn about possible improvements.

Some other key questions that should be asked as part of the process of reviewing and evaluating a strategy are:

1. Is there internal consistency between the components of the strategy (i.e., do the goals/objectives, product/market scope, and basis of competition all fit together)?
2. Is the strategy appropriate in light of threats and opportunities in the environment?
3. Is the strategy appropriate in light of the available resources?
4. To what extent does the strategy satisfy managerial preferences and values?
5. What are the key tasks arising out of the strategy and has the organization been designed so that these tasks are performed?

The case studies in this text were chosen to illustrate the impact/role of some or all of the variables in the conceptual framework. They are all decision oriented, requiring students to analyse and make recommendations as to a course of action for the organization. Achievement of a defensible overall strategy for the organization means that errors in tactics (the specific means of exercising the strategy) may not be fatal. Although the perspective we employ here is that of the general manager, it is important to acknowledge that effective functional managers are also called upon to adopt a strategic orientation. All functions in an organization include both strategic and non-strategic activities (non-strategic activities would be made up of the more routinized activities that require little attention from the general manager or other senior managers). Wherever possible, the effective functional manager will approach tasks strategically rather than operationally. Exhibit 1–13 provides an example of how a particular function can be characterized as strategic rather than operational.

EXHIBIT 1–13   Purchasing as a Strategic Function

Characteristics	*Operational Approach*	*Strategy Approach*
Organization structure	Low visibility, lengthy reporting chain.	High visibility, direct reporting to top management.
Organization perception	Isolated, ineffective clerks. A necessary administrative expense.	Active, effective material supply managers. Possible source of additional profit.
Information access	Limited exposure to critical reports and meetings; added only occasionally to distribution lists of key material.	Access to library of material, some of which is generated at the request of purchasing.
Decision issues	Decisions based on price.	Provides expert analysis of forecasting, sourcing, price, availability, delivery, and supplier information. Even makes outsourcing recommendations.
Supplier network and relationships	Works superficially with many suppliers. Arm's-length, often adversarial, relationships.	Focuses on fewer suppliers. Cooperative relationships.
Frame of reference	Local, provincial, or at best, international.	International, with regular investigation of non-domestic sources
Strategic management	No direct input to the strategy process.	Provides critical input to strategy process.

Source: Adapted by P. W. Beamish from John N. Pearson and Karen J. Gritsmacher, "Integrating Purchasing into Strategic Management," *Long Range Planning,* 23, no. 3 (1990) pp. 91–99.

In Chapter 2, a detailed framework for conducting a case study analysis—including the financial analysis—is provided. This material is included in order to provide some direction in developing "better" case analyses.

Notes to Chapter 1

1. Hofer, Charles W., consulting ed. *West Series in Strategic Management*. St. Paul, MN.: West Publishing, 1986, p. xi.
2. Galbraith, Jay R., and Robert K. Kazanjian. *Strategy Implementation: Structure, Systems and Process*. 2nd ed. St. Paul, MN.: West Publishing, 1986, p. 3.
3. Clausewitz, Carl von. *On War,* Tr. Routledge and Kegan Paul, Ltd., 1908. Middlesex, England: Pelican Books, 1968. Originally published in 1832.
4. Kamis, Michael. *Strategic Planning for Changing Times*. Dayton, OH.: Cassette Recording Co., 1984.
5. Curry, William. "A Condensed Version of Business Policy," mimeographed Waterloo, ON.: Wilfrid Laurier University, 1980.
6. Chandler, Alfred D. *Strategy and Structure*. Cambridge, MA.: MIT Press, 1962.
7. Abell, Derek F. *Defining a Business: The Starting Point of Strategic Planning*. Englewood Cliffs, NJ.: Prentice Hall, 1980, p. 169.
8. Porter, Michael E. *Competitive Strategy: Techniques for Analyzing Industries and Competitors*. New York: Free Press, 1980.
9. Mintzberg, Henry. *The Nature of Managerial Work*. New York: Harper & Row, 1973, pp. 91–93.
10. Abell, Derek F. *Defining a Business: The Starting Point of Strategic Planning*. Englewood Cliffs, NJ.: Prentice Hall, 1980, p. 169.

Recommended Readings

Adkam, J. D., and S. S. Cowen. "Strategic Planning for Increased Profit in the Small Business." *Long Range Planning,* December 1990, pp. 63–79.

Hahn, D. "Strategic Management—Tasks and Challenges in the 1990s." *Long Range Planning,* February 1991, pp. 26–39.

Hitt, M. A.; R. E. Hoskisson; and J. S. Harrison. "Strategic Competitiveness in the 1990s: Challenges and Opportunities for U.S. Executives." *Academy of Management Executives,* May 1991, pp. 7–22.

McMillan, Ian C., and Patricia E. Jones. *Strategy Formulation: Power and Politics*. 2nd ed. St. Paul, MN.: West Publishing, 1986.

Mintzberg, Henry. *The Rise and Fall of Strategic Planning*. New York, The Free Press, 1994.

Some of these questions were derived from Tilles, Seymour. "How to Evaluate Corporate Strategy." *Harvard Business Review,* July–August 1963, pp. 111–21.

Tenaglia, Mason, and Alistair Davidson. "A Directory of Strategic Management Software Tools." *Planning Review,* July–August 1993, pp. 38–94.

Watson, Gregory H. "How Process Benchmarking Supports Corporate Strategy." *Planning Review,* January–February 1993, pp. 12–15.

CASE ANALYSIS*

Solve the problem or you don't have a business; solve it or you don't have a job.

Bob Woods, *President of Zeneca Agricultural Products (1994)*

Management is an action-oriented activity. It requires doing to achieve proficiency. Managers succeed or fail not so much because of what they know as because of what they do. A person cannot expect to succeed as a manager and become a "professional" simply by studying excellent books on management—no matter how thoroughly the text material is mastered, nor how many "A"s are earned at exam time. Just as a skater needs to practise at being a better skater, a person who aspires to become a manager can benefit from practising at being a manager.

Practising Management via Case Analysis

In academic programs of management education, students practise at being managers via case analysis. A case sets forth, in a factual manner, the events and organizational circumstances surrounding a particular managerial situation. It puts the readers at the scene of the action and familiarizes them with the situation which prevailed. A case can concern a whole industry, a single organization, or even just a part of an organization; the organization involved can be either profit seeking or not-for-profit. Cases about business organiza-

---

* This chapter has been adapted by the authors *or* incorporates material from Arthur A. Thompson and A. J. Strickland, *Strategic Management: Concepts and Causes* (Plano, TX.: Business Publications, 1984), pp. 272–289. Used with permission.

tions usually include descriptions of the industry and its competitive conditions, the organization's history and development, its products and markets, the backgrounds and personalities of the key people involved, the production facilities, the work climate, the organizational structure, the marketing methods, and the external environment, together with whatever pertinent financial, production, accounting, sales, and market information was available to management.

The essence of the student's role in the case method is to diagnose and size up the situation described in the case and to think through what, if any, actions need to be taken. The purpose is for the student, as analyst, to appraise the situation from a managerial perspective, asking: What factors have contributed to the situation? What problems are evident? How serious are they? What analysis is needed to probe for solutions? What actionable recommendations can be offered? What facts and figures support my position?

It should be emphasized that most cases are not intended to be examples of right and wrong, or good and bad management. The organizations concerned are selected neither because they are the best or the worst in their industry, nor because they present an interesting and relevant analytical situation. The important thing about a case is that it represents an actual situation where managers were obligated to recognize and cope with the problems as they were.

Why Use Cases to Practise Management?

Charles I. Gragg's classic article, "Because Wisdom Can't Be Told,"[1] illustrates that the mere act of listening to lectures and sound advice about management does little for anyone's management skills. He contended it was unlikely that accumulated managerial experience and wisdom could effectively be passed on by lectures and readings alone. Gragg suggested that if anything has been learned about the practice of management, it is that a storehouse of ready-made answers does not exist. Each managerial situation has unique aspects, requiring its own diagnosis and understanding as a prelude to judgment and action. In Gragg's view and in the view of other case-method advocates, cases provide aspiring managers with an important and valid kind of daily practice in wrestling with management problems.

The case method is, indeed, *learning by doing.* The pedagogy of the case method of instruction is predicated on the benefits of acquiring managerial "experience" by means of simulated management exercises (cases). The best justification for cases is that few, if any, students during the course of their university education have an opportunity to come into direct personal contact with different kinds of companies and real-life managerial situations. Cases offer a viable substitute by bringing a variety of industries, organizations, and management problems into the classroom and permitting students to assume the manager's role. Management cases, therefore, provide students with a kind of experiential exercise in which to test their ability to apply their textbook knowledge about management.

Objectives of the Case Method

As the foregoing discussion suggests, using cases as an instructional technique is intended to produce four student-related results[2]:

1. Helping you to acquire the skills of putting textbook knowledge about management into practice.
2. Getting you out of the habit of being a receiver of facts, concepts, and techniques and into the habit of diagnosing problems, analysing and evaluating alternatives, and formulating workable plans of action.
3. Training you to work out answers and solutions for yourself, as opposed to relying upon the authoritative crutch of the professor or a textbook.
4. Providing you with exposure to a range of firms and managerial situations (which might take a lifetime to experience personally), thus offering you a basis for comparison when you begin your own management career.

If you understand that those are the objectives of the case method of instruction, then you are less likely to be bothered by something that puzzles some students: "What is the answer to the case?" Being accustomed to textbook statements of fact and supposedly definitive lecture notes, students often find that discussions and analyses of managerial cases do not produce any hard answers. Instead, issues in the case are discussed pro and con. Various alternatives and approaches are evaluated. Usually, a good argument can be made for more than one course of action. If the class discussion concludes without a clear consensus on what to do and which way to go, some students may, at first, feel frustrated because they are not told "what the answer is" or "what the company actually did."

However, cases where answers are not clear-cut are quite realistic. Organizational problems whose analysis leads to a definite, single-pronged solution are likely to be so oversimplified and rare as to be trivial or devoid of practical value. In reality, several feasible courses of action may exist for dealing with the same set of circumstances. Moreover, in real-life management situations when one makes a decision or selects a particular course of action, there is no peeking at the back of a book to see if you have chosen the best thing to do. No book of probable correct answers exists; in fact, the first test of management action is *results*. The important thing for a student to understand in case analysis is that it is the managerial exercise of identifying, diagnosing, and recommending that counts rather than discovering the right answer or finding out what actually happened.

To put it another way, *the purpose of management cases is not to learn authoritative answers to specific managerial problems but to become skilled in the process of designing workable action plans through evaluation of the prevailing circumstances.* The aim of case analysis is not for you to try to guess what the instructor is thinking or what the organization did but, rather, to see whether you can support your views against the counterviews of the group or, failing to do so, join in the sense of discovery of different approaches and perspectives. Therefore, *in case analysis, you are expected to hear the strains of thinking actively, of making managerial assessments that may be vigorously challenged, of offering your analysis, and of proposing action plans—this is how you are provided with meaningful practice at being a manager.*

Analysing the case yourself is what initiates you in the ways of thinking "managerially" and exercising responsible judgment. At the same time, you can use cases to test the rigour and effectiveness of your own approach to the practice of management and to begin to evolve your own management philosophy and management style.

Use of the Socratic method of questioning–answering–questioning–answering, where there is no single correct answer but always another question, is at the heart of the case process. A good case can be used with student groups of varying qualifications. With the more highly experienced qualified groups, the other questions become tougher.

Preparing a Case for Class Discussion

Given that cases rest on the principle of learning by doing, their effectiveness hinges upon you making *your* analysis and reaching *your* own decisions and then in the classroom participating in a collective analysis and discussion of the issues. If this is your first experience with the case method, you may have to reorient your study habits. Since a case assignment emphasizes student participation, it is obvious that the effectiveness of the class discussion depends upon each student having studied the case *beforehand.* Consequently, unlike lecture courses where there is no imperative of specific preparation before each class and where assigned readings and reviews of lecture notes may be done at irregular intervals, *a case assignment requires conscientious preparation before class.* You cannot, after all, expect to get much out of hearing the class discuss a case with which you are totally unfamiliar.

Unfortunately, though, there is no nice, neat, proven procedure for conducting a case analysis. There is no formula, no fail-safe, step-by-step technique that we can recommend beyond emphasizing the sequence: *identify, evaluate, consider alternatives,* and *recommend.* Each case is a new situation and has its own set of issues, analytical requirements, and action alternatives.

A first step in understanding how the case method of teaching/learning works is to recognize that it represents a radical departure from the lecture/discussion/problem classroom technique. To begin with, members of the class do most of the talking. The instructor's role is to solicit student participation and guide the discussion. Expect the instructor to begin the class with such questions as: What is the organization's strategy? What are the strategic issues and problems confronting the company? What is your assessment of the company's situation? Is the industry an attractive one to be in? Is management doing a good job? Are the organization's objectives and strategies compatible with its skills and resources? Typically, members of the class will evaluate and test their opinions as much in discussions with each other as with the instructor. But irrespective of whether the discussion emphasis is instructor–student or student–student, members of the class carry the burden for analysing the situation and for being prepared to present and defend their analyses in the classroom. Thus, you should expect an absence of professorial "here's how to do it," "right answers," and "hard knowledge for our notebook"; instead, be prepared for a discussion involving your size-up of the situation, what actions you would take, and why you would take them.[3]

Begin preparing for class by reading the case once for familiarity. An initial reading should give you the general flavor of the situation and make possible preliminary identification of issues. On the second reading, attempt to gain full command of the facts. Make some notes about apparent organizational objectives, strategies, policies, symptoms of problems, root problems, unresolved issues, and roles of key individuals. Be alert for issues or problems that are lurking beneath the surface. For instance, at first glance it might appear that an issue in the case is whether a product has ample market potential at the current selling price; on closer examination, you may see that the root problem is that the method being used to compensate salespeople fails to generate adequate incentive for achieving greater unit volume. Strive for a sharp, clear-cut size-up of the issues posed in the case situation.

To help diagnose the situation, put yourself in the position of some manager or managerial group portrayed in the case and get attuned to the overall environment facing management. Try to get a good feel for the condition of the company, the industry, and the economics of the business. Get a handle on how the market works and on the nature of competition. This is essential if you are to come up with solutions that will be both workable and acceptable in light of the prevailing external constraints and internal organizational realities. Do not be dismayed if you find it impractical to isolate the problems and issues into distinct categories that can be treated separately. Very few significant strategy management problems can be neatly sorted into mutually exclusive areas of concern. Furthermore, expect the cases (especially those in this book) to contain several problems and issues, rather than just one. Guard against making a single, simple statement of the problem unless the issue is very clear-cut. Admittedly, there will be cases where issues are well defined and the main problem is figuring out what to do; but in most cases you can expect a set of problems and issues to be present, some of which are related and some of which are not.

Next, you must move toward a solid evaluation of the case situation, based on the information given. Developing an ability to evaluate companies and size up their situations is the core of what strategic analysis is all about. The cases in this book, of course, are all strategy related, and they each require some form of strategic analysis, that is, analysis of how well the organization's strategy has been formulated and implemented. Uppermost in your efforts, strive for defensible arguments and positions. Do not rely upon just your opinion; support it with evidence! Analyse the available data and make whatever relevant accounting, financial, marketing, or operations calculations are necessary to support your assessment of the situation. Crunch the numbers! If your instructor has provided you with specific study questions for the case, by all means make some notes as to how you would answer them. Include in your notes all the reasons and evidence you can muster to support your diagnosis and evaluation.

Last, when information or data in the case are conflicting and/or various opinions are contradictory, decide which is more valid and why. Forcing you to make judgments about the validity of the data and information presented in the case is both deliberate and realistic. It is deliberate because one function of the case method is to help you develop your powers of judgment and inference. It is realistic because a great many managerial situations entail conflicting points of view.

Once you have thoroughly diagnosed the company's situation and weighed the pros and cons of various alternative courses of action, the final step of case analysis is to decide what you think the company needs to do to improve its performance. Draw up your set of recommendations on what to do and be prepared to give your action agenda. This is really the most crucial part of the process; diagnosis divorced from corrective action is sterile. But bear in mind that proposing realistic, workable solutions and offering a hasty, ill-conceived "possibility" are not the same thing. Don't recommend anything you would not be prepared to do yourself if you were in the decision maker's shoes. Be sure you can give reasons that your recommendations are preferable to other options that exist.

On a few occasions, some desirable information may not be included in the case. In such instances, you may be inclined to complain about the lack of facts. A manager, however, uses more than facts upon which to base his or her decision. Moreover, it may be possible to make a number of inferences from the facts you do have. So be wary of rushing to include as part of your recommendations the need to get more information. From time to time, of course, a search for additional facts or information may be entirely appropriate, but you must also recognize that the organization's managers may not have had any more information available than that presented in the case. Before recommending that action be postponed until additional facts are uncovered, be sure that you think it will be worthwhile to get them and that the organization can afford to wait. In general, though, try to recommend a course of action based upon the evidence you have at hand.

Again, remember that rarely is there a "right" decision or just one "optimal" plan of action or an "approved" solution. Your goal should be to develop what you think is a pragmatic, defensible course of action based upon a serious analysis of the situation and appearing to you to be right in view of your assessment of the facts. Admittedly, someone else may evaluate the same facts in another way and thus have a different right solution, but since several good plans of action can normally be conceived, you should not be afraid to stick by your own analysis and judgment. One can make a strong argument for the view that the right answer for a manager is the one that he or she can propose, explain, defend, and make work when it is implemented. This is the middle ground we support between the "no right answer" and "one right answer" schools of thought. Clearly, some answers are better than others.

The Classroom Experience

In experiencing class discussion of management cases, you will, in all probability, notice very quickly that you will not have thought of everything in the case that your fellow students think of. While you will see things others did not, they will see things you did not. Do not be dismayed or alarmed by this. It is normal. As the old adage goes, "Two heads are better than one." So it is to be expected that the class as a whole will do a more penetrating and searching job of case analysis than will any one person working alone. This is the power of group effort, and one of its virtues is that it will give you more insight into the variety of approaches and how to cope with differences of opinion. Second, you will see better why sometimes it is not managerially wise to assume a rigid position on an issue until a full range of views and information has been assembled. And, undoubtedly, somewhere along the way, you will begin to recognize that neither the instructor nor other students in the class have all the answers, and even if they think they do, you are still free to present and hold to your own views. The truth in the saying, "there's more than one way to skin a cat" will be seen to apply nicely to most management situations.

For class discussion of cases to be useful and stimulating, you need to keep the following points in mind:

1. The case method enlists a maximum of individual participation in class discussion. It is not enough to be present as a silent observer; if every student took this approach, then there would be no discussion. (Thus, do not be surprised if a portion of your grade is based on your participation in case discussions.)

2. Although you should do your own independent work and independent thinking, don't hesitate to discuss the case with other students. Managers often discuss their problems with other key people.

3. During case discussions, expect and tolerate challenges to the views expressed. Be willing to submit your conclusions for scrutiny and rebuttal. State your views without fear of disapproval and overcome the hesitation of speaking out.

4. In orally presenting and defending your ideas, strive to be convincing and persuasive. Always give supporting evidence and reasons.

5. Expect the instructor to assume the role of extensive questioner and listener. Expect to be cross-examined for evidence and reasons by your instructor or by others in the class. Expect students to dominate the discussion and do most of the talking.

6. Although discussion of a case is a group process, this does not imply conformity to group opinion. Learning respect for the views and approaches of others is an integral part of case analysis exercises. But be willing to "swim against the tide" of majority opinion. In the practice of management, there is always room for originality, unorthodoxy, and uniqueness of personality.

7. In participating in the discussion, make a conscious effort to *contribute* rather than just talk. There is a big difference between saying something that builds the discussion and offering a long-winded, off-the-cuff remark that leaves the class wondering what the point was.

8. Effective case discussion can occur only if participants have the facts of the case well in hand; rehashing information in the case should be held to a minimum except as it provides documentation, comparisons, or support for your position. In making your point, assume that everyone has read the case and knows what "the case says."

9. During the discussion, new insights provided by the group's efforts are likely to emerge. Don't be alarmed or surprised if you and others in the class change your mind about some things as the discussion unfolds. Be alert for how these changes affect your analysis and recommendations (in case you are called on to speak).

10. Although there will always be situations in which more technical information is imperative to the making of an intelligent decision, try not to shirk from making decisions in the face of incomplete information. Wrestling with imperfect information is a normal condition managers face and is something you should get used to.

Preparing a Written Case Analysis

From time to time, your instructor may ask you to prepare a written analysis of the case assignment. Preparing a written case analysis is much like preparing a case for class discussion, except that your analysis, when completed, must be reduced to writing. Just as there was no set formula for preparing a case for oral discussion, there is no iron-clad procedure for doing a written case analysis. With a bit of experience, you will arrive at your own preferred method of attack in writing up a case, and you will learn to adjust your approach to the unique aspects that each case presents.

Your instructor may assign you a specific topic around which to prepare your written report. Common assignments include answering questions such as the following:

1. How would you identify and evaluate company X's corporate strategy?
2. In view of the opportunities and risks you see in the industry, what is your assessment of the company's position and strategy?
3. How would you size up the strategic situation of company Y?
4. What recommendation would you make to company Z's top management?
5. What specific functions and activities does the company have to perform especially well in order for its strategy to succeed?

Alternatively, you may be asked to do a comprehensive written case analysis. It is typical for a comprehensive written case analysis to emphasize four things:

1. Identification.
2. Analysis and evaluation.
3. Discussion of alternatives.
4. Presentation of recommendations.

You may wish to consider these pointers in preparing a comprehensive written case analysis.[4]

Identification

It is essential that your paper reflect a sharply focused diagnosis of strategic issues and key problems and, further, that you demonstrate good business judgment in sizing up the company's present situation. Make sure you understand and can identify the firm's strategy (see Chapters 1, 3, 4, and 5). You would probably be well advised to begin your paper by sizing up the company's situation, its strategy, and the significant problems and issues that confront management. State problems/issues as clearly and precisely as you can. Unless it is necessary to do so for emphasis, avoid recounting facts and history about the company (assume your professor has read the case and is familiar with the organization!).

Analysis and Evaluation

Very likely, you will find this section the hardest part of the report. Analysis is hard work! Study the tables, exhibits, and financial statements in the case carefully. Check out the firm's financial ratios, its profit margins and rates of return, and its capital structure, and decide how strong the firm is financially. (Exhibit 2–1 contains a summary of various financial ratios and how they are calculated.) Similarly, look at marketing, production, managerial competence, and so on, and evaluate the factors underlying the organization's successes and failures. Decide whether it has a distinctive competence and, if so, whether it is capitalizing upon it. Check out the quality of the firm's business portfolio.

Check to see if the firm's strategy at all levels is working and determine the reasons why or why not. An initial analytical tool that can be used is "SWOT analysis," which involves appraising the firm's internal *strengths* and *weaknesses* and assessing external *opportunities* and *threats;* see Exhibit 2–2 for suggestions of what to look for. An analysis should also possibly incorporate a competitive analysis of the competitive forces impinging on the firm (you may want to draw up a strategic group map as in Exhibit 3–3 and/or do an industry analysis as in Exhibit 3–1, in Chapter 3). Decide whether and why the firm's competitive position is getting stronger or weaker. Subsequent chapters develop more detailed and specialized analytical tools to assess many of the relationships. Review those chapters to see if you have overlooked some aspect of strategy evaluation. Try to decide whether the main problems revolve around a need to revise strategy, a need to improve strategy implementation, or both.

In writing your analysis and evaluation, bear in mind:

1. You are obliged to offer supporting evidence for your views and judgments. Do not rely upon unsupported opinions, overgeneralizations, and platitudes as a substitute for a tight, logical argument backed up with facts and figures.

2. If your analysis involves some important quantitative calculations, then you should use tables and charts to present the data clearly and efficiently. Don't just tack the exhibits on at the end of your report and let the reader figure out what they mean and why they were included. Instead, in the body of your report, cite some of the key numbers and summarize the conclusions to be drawn from the exhibits and refer the reader to your charts and exhibits for more details.

3. You should indicate that you have command of the economics of the business and the key factors that are crucial to the organization's success or failure. Check to see that your analysis states what the company needs to concentrate on in order to be a higher performer.

4. Your interpretation of the evidence should be reasonable and objective. Be wary of preparing a one-sided argument that omits all aspects not favorable to your conclusion. Likewise, try not to exaggerate or overdramatize. Endeavor to inject balance into your analysis and to avoid emotional rhetoric. Strive to display good business judgment.

EXHIBIT 2–1   A Summary of Key Financial Ratios, How They Are Calculated, and What They Show

Ratio	*How Calculated*	*What It Shows*
Profitability Ratios		
1. Gross profit margin	$$\frac{\text{Sales} - \text{cost of goods sold}}{\text{Sales}}$$	An indication of the total margin available to cover operating expenses and yield a profit.
2. Operating profit margin	$$\frac{\text{Profit before taxes and before interest}}{\text{Sales}}$$	An indication of the firm's profitability from current operations without regard to the interest charges accruing from the capital structure (helps to assess impact of different capital structures).
3. Net profit margin (or return on sales)	$$\frac{\text{Profits after taxes}}{\text{Sales}}$$	After-tax profits per dollar of sales. Subparprofit margins indicate that the firm's sales prices are relatively low or that its costs are relatively high or both.
4. Return on total assets	$$\frac{\text{Profits after taxes}}{\text{Total assets}}$$ or $$\frac{\text{Profits after taxes} + \text{interest}}{\text{Total assets}}$$	A measure of the return on total investment in the enterprise. It is sometimes desirable to add interest to after-tax profits to form the numerator of the ratio since total assets are financed by creditors as well as by stockholders; hence, it is accurate to measure the productivity of assets by the returns provided to both classes of investors.
5. Return on stockholders' equity (or return on net worth)	$$\frac{\text{Profits after taxes}}{\text{Total stockholders' equity}}$$	A measure of the rate of return on stockholders' investment in the enterprise.
6. Return on common equity	$$\frac{\text{Profits after taxes} - \text{preferred stock dividends}}{\text{Total stockholders' equity} - \text{Par value of preferred stock}}$$	A measure of the rate of return on the investment that the owners of common stock have made in the enterprise.
7. Earnings per share	$$\frac{\text{Profits after taxes} - \text{preferred stock dividends}}{\text{Number of shares of common stock outstanding}}$$	The earnings available to the owners of common stock.

Exhibit 2–1   *(Continued)*

Ratio	How Calculated	What It Shows
Liquidity Ratios		
1. Current ratio	$$\frac{\text{Current assets}}{\text{Current liabilities}}$$	The extent to which the claims of short-term creditors are covered by assets expected to be converted to cash in a period roughly corresponding to the maturity of the liabilities.
2. Quick ratio (or acid-test ratio)	$$\frac{\text{Current assets} - \text{inventory}}{\text{Current liabilities}}$$	A measure of the firm's ability to pay off short-term obligations without relying upon the sale of its inventories.
3. Inventory to net working capital	$$\frac{\text{Inventory}}{\text{Current assets} - \text{current liabilities}}$$	A measure of the extent to which the firm's working capital is tied up in inventory.
Leverage Ratios		
1. Debt-to-assets ratio	$$\frac{\text{Total debt}}{\text{Total assets}}$$	A measure of the extent to which borrowed funds have been used to finance the firm's operations.
2. Debt-to-equity ratio	$$\frac{\text{Total debt}}{\text{Total stockholders' equity}}$$	Another measure of the funds provided by creditors versus the funds provided by owners.
3. Long-term debt-to-equity ratio	$$\frac{\text{Long-term debt}}{\text{Total stockholders' equity}}$$	A widely used measure of the balance between debt and equity in the firm's long-term capital structure.
4. Times-interest-earned (or coverage) ratios	$$\frac{\text{Profits before interest and taxes}}{\text{Total interest charges}}$$	A measure of the extent to which earnings can decline without the firm becoming unable to meet its annual interest costs.
5. Fixed-charge coverage	$$\frac{\text{Profits before taxes and interest} \div \text{lease obligations}}{\text{Total interest charges} \div \text{lease obligations}}$$	A more inclusive indication of the firm's ability to meet all of its fixed-charge obligations.
Activity Ratios		
1. Inventory turnover	$$\frac{\text{Sales}}{\text{Inventory of finished goods}}$$	When compared to industry averages, it provides an indication of whether a company has excessive or inadequate finished goods inventory.

EXHIBIT 2–1 *(Concluded)*

Ratio	How Calculated	What It Shows
2. Fixed-assets turnover	$\dfrac{\text{Sales}}{\text{Fixed assets}}$	A measure of the sales productivity and utilization of plant and equipment.
3. Total-assets turnover	$\dfrac{\text{Sales}}{\text{Total assets}}$	A measure of the utilization of all the firm's assets. A ratio below the industry average indicates that the company is not generating a sufficient volume of business given the size of its asset investment.
4. Accounts-receivable turnover	$\dfrac{\text{Annual credit sales}}{\text{Accounts receivable}}$	A measure of the average length of time it takes the firm to collect the sales made on credit.
5. Average collection period	$\dfrac{\text{Accounts receivable}}{\text{Total sales} \div 365}$ or $\dfrac{\text{Accounts receivable}}{\text{Average daily sales}}$	The average length of time the firm must wait after making a sale before it receives payment.

Other Ratios

Ratio	How Calculated	What It Shows
1. Dividend yield on common stock	$\dfrac{\text{Annual dividends per share}}{\text{Current market price per share}}$	A measure of the return to owners received in the form of dividends.
2. Price-earnings ratio	$\dfrac{\text{Current market price per share}}{\text{After-tax earnings per share}}$	Faster growing or less risky firms tend to have higher price-earnings ratios than slower growing or more risky firms.
3. Dividend-payout ratio	$\dfrac{\text{Annual dividends per share}}{\text{After-tax earnings per share}}$	The percentages of profits paid out as dividends.
4. Cash flow per share	$\dfrac{\text{After-tax profits} + \text{depreciation}}{\text{Number of common shares outstanding}}$	A measure of the discretionary funds over and above expenses available for use by the firm.
5. Break-even analysis	$\dfrac{\text{Fixed costs}}{\text{Contribution margin/unit}}$ (Selling price/unit − variable cost/unit)	A measure of how many units must be sold to begin to make a profit; to demonstrate the relationship of revenue, expenses, and net income.

Note: Industry-average ratios against which a particular company's ratios may be judged are available in the following:

1. Statistics Canada, Corporation Financial Statistics (15 ratios for 182 industries).
2. *Key Business Ratios,* published by Dun and Bradstreet Canada (11 ratios for 166 lines of business).
3. *Market Research Handbook,* published by Statistics Canada (7 ratios for 23 industries).
4. The Financial Post, Industry Reports (35 ratios for 19 industries and latest quarterly results for top public firms in industry).
5. Almanac of Business and Industry Financial Ratios (14 ratios, 13 trend indicators, and 23 average balance sheet and income statement values, for over 180 industries)

Exhibit 2–2   The SWOT Analysis, with Suggestions of What to Look For

---

Internal

Strengths
- Adequate financial resources?
- Well thought of by buyers?
- An acknowledged market leader?
- Well-conceived functional area strategies?
- Access to economies of scale?
- Insulated (at least somewhat) from strong competitive pressure?
- Proprietary technology?
- Cost advantages?
- Product innovation abilities?
- Proven management?
- Other?

Weaknesses
- No clear strategic direction?
- Obsolete facilities?
- Lack of managerial depth and talent?
- Missing any key skills or competencies?
- Poor track record in implementing strategy?
- Plagued with internal operating problems?
- Falling behind in R & D?
- Too narrow a product line?
- Weak market image?
- Below-average marketing skills?
- Unable to finance needed changes in strategy?
- Other?

External

Opportunities
- Serve additional customer groups?
- Enter new markets or segments?
- Expand product line to meet broader range of customer needs?
- Diversify into related products?
- Add complementary products?
- Vertical integration?
- Ability to move to better strategic group?
- Complacency among rival firms?
- Faster market growth?
- Other?

Threats
- Likely entry of new competitors?
- Rising sales of substitute products?
- Slower market growth?
- Adverse government policies?
- Growing competitive pressures?
- Vulnerability to recession and business cycle?
- Growing bargaining power of customers or suppliers?
- Changing buyer needs and tastes?
- Adverse demographic changes?
- Other?

Discussion of Alternatives

There are typically many more alternatives available than a cursory study of the case reveals. A thorough case analysis should include a discussion of all major alternatives. It is important that meaningful differences exist between alternatives. In addition, the discussion of alternatives must go beyond the following:

- Do nothing.
- Something obviously inappropriate.
- The alternative to be recommended.

Each alternative discussed should be analyzed in terms of the associated pros and cons.

Recommendations

The final section of the written case analysis should consist of a set of definite recommendations and a plan of action. Your set of recommendations should address all of the problems/issues you identified and analysed. If the recommendations come as a surprise, or do not follow logically from the analysis, the effect is to weaken greatly your suggestions of what to do. Obviously, your recommendations for action should offer a reasonable prospect of success. State what you think the consequences of your recommendations will be and indicate how your recommendations will solve the problems you identified. *Be sure that the company is financially able to carry out what you recommend.* Also check to see if your recommendations are workable in terms of acceptance by the persons involved, the organization's competence to implement them, and prevailing market and environmental constraints. Unless you feel justifiably *compelled* to do so, do not qualify, hedge, or weasel on the actions you believe should be taken.

Furthermore, state your recommendations in sufficient detail to be meaningful—get down to some operational-level details. Avoid such unhelpful statements as "the organization should do more planning" or "the company should be more aggressive in marketing its products." State *specifically* what should be done and *make sure your recommendations are operational and provide the manager with specific considerations that he or she can implement.* For instance, do not stop with saying, "The firm should improve its market position." Continue on with exactly how you think this should be done. And, finally, you should say something about how your plan should be implemented. Here you may wish to offer a definite agenda for action, stipulating a timetable and sequence for initiating actions, indicating priorities, and suggesting who should be responsible for doing what. For example, "Manager X should take the following steps: (1) _____, (2) _____, (3) _____, and (4) _____." One way to organize your recommendations is in a one-page summary according to the chart in Exhibit 2–3.

A key element in the recommendation summary is to assess the financial implications of each recommendation. Any proposed strategy must be feasible, which means, among other things, that the organization must be able to afford it. In addition, when there are major uncertainties, particularly in the medium to long term, contingency plans should be specified, that is, "If such and such transpires, then do X."

In preparing your plan of action, remember there is a great deal of difference between being responsible, on the one hand, for a decision that may be costly if it proves in error and, on the other hand, expressing a casual opinion as to some of the courses of action that might be taken when you do not have to bear the responsibility for any of the consequences. A good rule to follow in making your recommendations is to avoid recommending anything you would not yourself be willing to do if you were in management's shoes. The importance of learning to develop good judgment in a managerial situation is indicated by the fact that while the same information and operating data

EXHIBIT 2–3   Organizing Recommendations

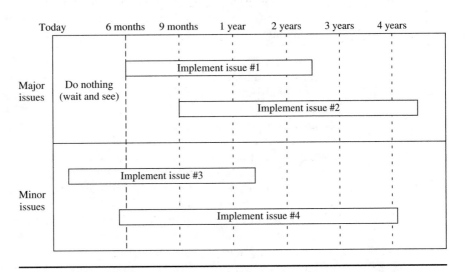

How to Use This Framework. After dividing the major issues from the minor issues, each issue is plotted according to timing. The closed hollow bar indicates over which period this issue will be resolved. Inside each hollow bar should be noted the title of the issue and the cost (financial, managerial, and so forth) of implementation. This framework allows us to assess on one page the reasonableness of whatever organizational recommendations are being made.

may be available to every manager or executive in an organization, the quality of the judgments about what the information means and what actions need to be taken do vary from person to person.[5] Developing good judgment is thus essential.

It should go without saying that your report should be organized and written in a manner that communicates well and is persuasive. Great ideas amount to little unless others can be convinced of their merit—this takes effective communication.

Keeping Tabs on Your Performance

Every instructor has his or her own procedure for evaluating student performance; so, with one exception, it is not possible to generalize about grades and the grading of case analyses. The one exception is that grades on case analyses (written or oral) almost never depend entirely on how you propose to solve the organization's difficulties. The important elements in evaluating student performance on case analysis consist of:

1. the care with which facts and background knowledge are used.
2. demonstration of the ability to state problems and issues clearly.
3. use of appropriate analytical techniques.

4. evidence of sound logic and argument.
5. consistency between analysis and recommendations.
6. ability to formulate reasonable and feasible recommendations for action.

Remember, a hard-hitting, incisive, logical approach will almost always triumph over a seat-of-the-pants opinion, emotional rhetoric, and platitudes.

One final point. You may find it hard to keep a finger on the pulse of how much you are learning from cases. This contrasts with lecture/problem/discussion courses where experience has given you an intuitive feeling for how well you are acquiring substantive knowledge of theoretical concepts, problem-solving techniques, and institutional practices. But in a case course, where analytical ability and the skill of making sound judgments are less apparent, you may lack a sense of solid accomplishment, at least at first. Admittedly, additions to one's managerial skills and powers of diagnosis are not as noticeable or as tangible as a loose-leaf binder full of lecture notes. But this does not mean they are any less real or that you are making any less progress in learning how to be a manager.

To begin with, in the process of hunting around for solutions, very likely you will find that considerable knowledge about types of organizations, the nature of various businesses, the range of management practices, and so on has rubbed off. Moreover, you will be gaining a better grasp of how to evaluate risks and cope with the uncertainties of enterprise. Likewise, you will develop a sharper appreciation of both the common and the unique aspects of managerial encounters. You will become more comfortable with the processes whereby objectives are set, strategies are initiated, organizations are designed, methods of control are implemented and evaluated, performance is reappraised, and improvements are sought. Such processes are the essence of strategic management, and learning more about them through the case method is no less an achievement just because there is a dearth of finely calibrated measuring devices and authoritative crutches on which to lean.

Notes to Chapter 2

1. Gragg, Charles I. "Because Wisdom Can't Be Told." In *The Case Method at the Harvard Business School.* ed. M. P. McNair. New York: McGraw-Hill, 1954, p. 11.
2. Ibid., pp. 12–14; and Schoen, D. R., and Philip A. Sprague. "What Is the Case Method?" In *The Case Method at the Harvard Business School.*, ed. M. P. McNair. New York: McGraw-Hill, 1954, pp. 78–79.
3. Schoen and Sprague. "What Is the Case Method?" p. 80.
4. For some additional ideas and viewpoints, you may wish to consult Raymond, Thomas J. "Written Analysis of Cases." In *The Case Method at the Harvard Business School.* ed M. P. McNair. New York: McGraw-Hill, 1954, pp. 139–63.

In Raymond's article is an actual case, a sample analysis of the case, and a sample of a student's written report on the case.

5. Gragg. "Because Wisdom Can't Be Told," p. 10.

Recommended Readings

Reid, Beverly. *Essentials of Business Writing and Speaking: A Canadian Guide.* Mississauga, ON.: Copp Clark Pitman, 1989.

Treece, Malra, and Larry Hartman. *Effective Reports for Managerial Communication.* 3rd ed. Boston, MA.: Allyn & Bacon, 1991.

Strategy Formulation and Environment

3

On General Motors' strategic misdirection during the last decade—*We lost touch with the customer would be the kindest way of saying it.*
Jack Smith, *Chairman of General Motors Co. (1994)*

On evolving competition in the software business, specifically Lotus Notes—*I would be insane to say that Microsoft won't be competitive with us. It is an awesome force in American capitalism.*
Jim Manzi, *CEO of Lotus Development Corp. (1994)*

On environmental changes surrounding the aero-defence industry—*Our market isn't declining. It is truly collapsing.*
Norman Augustine, *President of Lockheed Martin Co. (1994)*

Making strategic decisions or choices is the critical function of the general manager. In formulating a strategy, the effective general manager makes strategic choices that are consistent with environmental threats and opportunities, organizational resources, and managerial preferences and values. This chapter will consider the influences that the environment has on formulating a strategy.

The Influence of Environment on Formulation

All managers must understand the environment in which they are doing business. An environmental analysis must examine both the industry environment and the macro environment that the firm is facing. The industry environment represents all of the industry-specific competitive influences impinging on the firm, whereas the macro environment represents more general threats or opportunities to the firm. Specifically, macro environmental influences include such things as the economy, technological changes, legal and political influences, international differences, and social and demographic changes. This chapter will initially examine the industry competitive environment.

The Industry Environment

When analysing the industry competitive environment the student must consider two strategic notions: the firm's *competitive position* and the firm's *competitive advantages*. Normally, it is advantageous to initially examine and fully describe a firm's competitive position. Then the competitive analysis can be completed by examining the competitive advantages of the industry and firm, as well as the competitive forces impinging on them. This section will adhere to this stepwise competitive analysis approach.

Analysing a Firm's Competitive Position

In Chapter 1, the competitive position of a firm was described in terms of its customers' wants. However, a full analysis of competitive position must also consider the competitors' positions. Generic dimensions for a firm's competitive position have been defined as customer focus, low cost, and differentiation. These generic dimensionalizations are worthwhile starting points in the process of understanding a firm's competitive position, as will be explained in Chapter 4. However, a manager, in reality, must understand the firm's competitive position in much more detail. There are a variety of ways in which one can assess a firm's competitive position in an industry. Two of the most common techniques are the *competitive position matrix* and the *strategic group map*.

The competitive position matrix compares the competitors in an industry, highlighting each firm's relevant competitive dimensions. To develop a matrix, we must first discern what are the important competitive dimensions that add value and are important to the customer. These dimensions could be price, product/service characteristics, product/service scope, or geographic scope. In addition, many managers also consider competitive advantages that differentiate the competitors. These competitive advantage dimensions are used to further differentiate the firms in the industry. Exhibit 3–1 provides an example of a competitive position matrix for part of the Canadian newspaper industry.

When an industry has many firms, it is often more useful to combine the firms into groups having similar competitive characteristics and market positions. These groups are called strategic groups and they represent firms that compete in the same market, for many of the same customers, and using many of the same competitive advantages.

The second approach, a strategic group map, serves the same purpose as the competitive position matrix. However, it describes the competitive positions graphically, a technique that is often easier to understand, and thus more forceful in a presentation. Exhibit 3–2 provides an example of a strategic group map using the Canadian retail furniture industry. It should be noted

---

Exhibit 3–1   Competitive Position Matrix:
A Sample of the Canadian Newspaper Industry (1994)

Competition	Geographic Scope	Price	Delivery Schedule	Editorial Policy	Customer Focus
Toronto Star	National	$0.75	Daily–Morning	Liberal	Broad
Globe & Mail	National	$0.75	Daily–Morning	Conservative	Broad, business
Vancouver Sun	Regional–B.C	$0.65	Daily–Morning	Very liberal	Broad, blue collar
Ottawa Citizen	Regional–Ottawa region	$0.65	Daily–Morning	Conservative, regional and local news	Broad, regional and local readers
Oshawa Times	Regional/ local–Oshawa region	$0.65	Daily–Evening	Conservative, regional and local news	Broad, regional and local readers
The Penny Saver	Regional	Free	Weekly	Advertisements	Buyers of new and used goods and services
University Students Gazette	University campus	Free	Weekly	Very liberal	Young–students
Computing Times	National	Free	Monthly	Computer focus	Computer users and literate

that because there are many competitors the industry has been broken into strategic groups.

One constraint of the strategic groups map is that only two dimensions can be represented simultaneously. This limits the descriptive capacity of this approach and it means the analyst must carefully select the dimensions in the map to represent the key strategic dimensions in the industry. The competitive dimensions that were deemed to be important in the Canadian retail furniture business were price/quality and product/service scope.

Once a manager has defined the competitive position of the firm, he or she should attempt to delineate some of the fundamental characteristics of the customers being served in that competitive position. Some of the important characteristics would be the size of the market, the firm's market share, the market growth, and the buying characteristics and desires of the customers being serviced in that competitive position. The manager may also want to look at some of the characteristics of "nearby" competitive positions to see if a movement in some direction might improve their performance.

After having described the competitive position of the firm and its competitors, we should have a good understanding of the business/market focus of the firm and its competitors. It is important to have this understanding before analysing the competitive influences and pressures in the industry.

EXHIBIT 3–2   Illustrative Strategic Group Map of Competitors in Canadian Retail Furniture Business

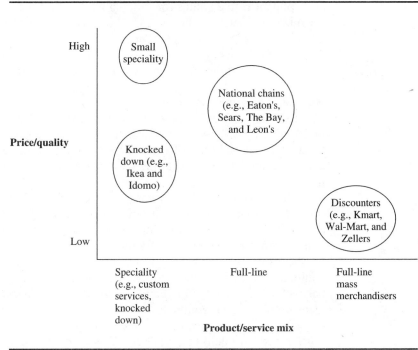

Not-for-Profit Organizational Competitive Position Analysis

Analysing a not-for-profit organization's market and competitors is a little different from a for-profit organization because the former faces competition from two directions, customers and fund-raising. Customer needs (e.g., community needs) may be satisfied by a number of organizations. Hence, the not-for-profit organization has to find a unique set of needs that it can satisfy most effectively in the community. Often a market analysis, called a *needs assessment*, is completed prior to setting up new programs. A needs assessment uses community focus groups, interviews, and questionnaires to evaluate the community's needs in specific areas such as health care or social assistance. During this process, it is important to clearly describe the needs that other organizations satisfy that may overlap or make redundant the need being assessed. The managers can then decide if there is a viable market position that has not been satisfied in the community. Another possible alternative is for the competing organizations to cooperate and, thus, improve the delivery and content of needs provision to the community.

Competition for fund-raising is also an issue for competitive position. Some organizations are privately funded whereas others are largely publicly funded by the government. In addition, organizations take on different marketing approaches. Certain not-for-profit programs rely on the community members' philanthropic values for funding while other more entertainment-based organizations, such as theatres, tend to rely on advertising and the quality of the product and service to get funding. Whether it be a value-based or product/service-based pitch, a manager must clearly map out various funding sources and attempt to target new sources, using new fund-raising pitches.

Analysing a Firm's Competitive Advantages

The first step in assessing a firm's competitive advantage is to develop an understanding of how it operationally does business in its industry compared to its competitors. One of the most effective techniques for developing this understanding is to draw an activity chain or value-chain for the firm and industry.

Porter's value-chain contains primary activities (inbound logistics, operations, outbound logistics, marketing and sales, and service) and secondary activities (firm infrastructure, human resource management, technology development, and procurement). Organizations can and do compete at any place on the value-chain. Firms can attempt to attain competitive advantage by adding value at one or more locations, or in terms of certain dimensions within particular activities. Value can be defined as attainable selling price and is measured by total revenue. Profits can result when the attainable selling price exceeds product/service costs (that is, when a margin exists).

An activity chain (or value-chain) is defined as the path that the product or service moves along as value is added, until it finally reaches the end consumer. An example of an industry activity chain is illustrated in Exhibit 3–3. This example shows how the product moves from purchasing right through to servicing of the rugs after the sale has been completed. It is important that all of the various channels of supply, product flow, and distribution be identified in an industry because different companies in an industry may use different channels to gain competitive advantage.

EXHIBIT 3–3   A Generic Activity Chain for the Retail Oriental Carpet Industry

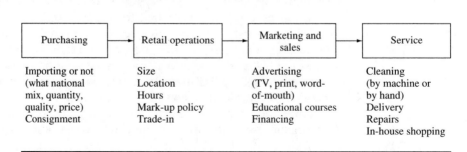

Purchasing	Retail operations	Marketing and sales	Service
Importing or not (what national mix, quantity, quality, price) Consignment	Size Location Hours Mark-up policy Trade-in	Advertising (TV, print, word-of-mouth) Educational courses Financing	Cleaning (by machine or by hand) Delivery Repairs In-house shopping

Some of the more fundamental questions to be considered when developing and examining the activity chain are the following:

1. Where is the power located in the activity chain?
2. What are the most efficient and effective channels to use in the industry?
3. Are specific channels more effective and efficient for targeting specific customers (i.e., competitive positions in the marketplace)?
4. Have any of the firms vertically integrated into different activities in the activity chain and will this provide an advantage or disadvantage?

A more generic activity or value-chain-analysis approach has been developed by Michael Porter (see Exhibit 3–4). Porter's generic value-chain contains primary activities (inbound logistics, operations, outbound logistics, marketing and sales, and service) and support activities (firm infrastructure, human resource management, technology development, and procurement). Organizations can and do compete at any place on the value-chain by adding value at one or more locations, or in terms of certain dimensions within particular activities. *Value* is defined as improving the worth of the product or service to the customer either through lowering the price or increasing the product or service characteristics. The critically important issue for the manager is to increase the value to the customer while minimizing the costs to the firm—this would of course maximize the profits to the firm. (Note: in the case of a not-for-profit business the manager's goal is not to gain profitability but to maximize the satisfaction of targeted customers—whether they be the sick or amateur theatre audiences—while controlling costs.)

Not all firms strive for cost leadership in their quest for profits. Some firms emphasize differentiation as a means of achieving greater profitability. For example, automakers will deliberately add a vast array of "options" to the cars they produce in the hope that customers will pay for these high-margin items. These options will normally increase the attainable selling price (value). The important question managers must ask themselves is: Is there an activity that could be added to their firm's value-chain that increases the value of the product or service to the customer more than it increases the cost to the company, or is there an activity that can be deleted from the value-chain that the customers do not value and that has associated costs to the firm? This relationship between activity cost and customer value illustrates how competitive advantage is intrinsically linked to a firm's competitive position and focus in the marketplace.

Competitive advantage is how a firm manages to provide this value to its customers for a lower cost than its competitors. For a company to be competitively successful, its costs and value must be in line with those of rival producers. The need to be cost competitive is not so stringent as to *require* the costs of every firm in the industry to be *equal*, because value is an important

EXHIBIT 3–4   Generic Activity or Value-Chain in an Industry

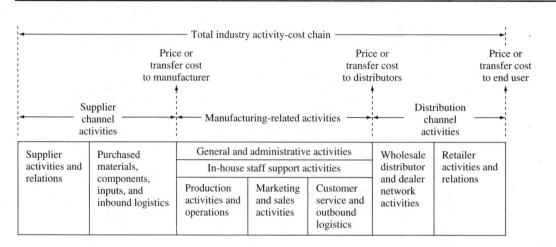

Activity	Specific Cost Activities and Cost Elements	Activity	Specific Cost Activities and Cost Elements
Supplier channel activities	• Managing and controlling suppliers • Ingredient raw materials and component parts supplied by outsiders • Energy • Inbound shipping • Inbound materials handling • Inspection • Warehousing	**Production activities and operations**	• Facilities and equipment • Processing, assembling & packaging • Labor • Maintenance • Process and product design and testing • Quality control and inspection • Inventory management • Internal materials handling • Manufacturing supervision
Marketing and sales activities	• Sales force operations • Advertising and promotion • Market research • Technical literature • Travel and entertainment • Dealer/distributor relations	**Customer service and outbound logistics**	• Service representatives • Order processing • Service manuals and training • Spare parts • Transportation services • Other outbound logistics costs • Scheduling
In-house staff support activities	• Payroll and benefits • Recruiting and training • Internal communications • Computer services • Procurement functions • R&D • Safety and security • Supplies and equipment • Union relations	**General and administrative activities**	• Finance and accounting • Legal services • Public relations • General management • Interest on borrowed funds • Tax-related costs • Regulatory compliance
Distribution channel activities	• Includes all of the activities, associated costs, and markups of distributors, wholesale dealers, retailers, and any other forward channel allies whose efforts are used to get the product into the hands of end-users/customers		

way in which firms can differentiate from the low-cost producer. Prospective customers buy based on value, which is the relationship of product or service features to cost. For example, some car buyers may value a convertible top, but most buyers will appreciate a lower price. Thus, when a firm is concentrating on providing increased value to its customers relative to its competitors (i.e., differentiating itself), it must be certain that the added product characteristics and/or services are valued by the customers. Thus, each activity in a firm's value-chain must be considered from both of these dimensions, cost and value.

Strategic value analysis focuses on a firm's relative value position vis-à-vis its rivals. The analytical approach must combine an analysis of the firm's total industry value-chain and the firm's competitive position. The manager must appreciate the relationship between the firm's competitive position (i.e., its customers that are served by that competitive position) and the value provided to these customers by the various activities in the firm's value-chain. The analysis must include value provided by assets possibly not owned and controlled by the firm, including such things as the quality of service provided by their chosen retail distribution channels and the quality of raw materials provided by suppliers. All of these factors may influence customer value.

Strategic cost analysis focuses on a firm's relative cost position vis-à-vis its rivals. The primary analytical tool of strategic cost analysis is the construction of a total industry value-chain showing the makeup of costs all the way from the inception of raw materials and components production to the end price paid by ultimate customers.[1] The activity-cost chain thus includes more than just a firm's own internal cost structure; it includes the buildup of cost (and thus the "value" of the product) at each stage in the whole market chain of getting the product into the hands of the final user, as shown in Exhibit 3–4. Constructing an integrated activity-cost chain is more revealing than restricting attention to just a firm's own internal costs. This is because a firm's overall ability to furnish end-users with its product at a competitive price can easily depend on cost factors originating either *backward* in the supplier's portion of the activity-cost chain or *forward* in the distribution channel portion of the chain.

Benchmarking, a technique described in Chapter 1, is a very effective tool used by companies to assess the costs and effectiveness of activities in its value-chain relative to other firms that are considered very cost effective in a specific activity.

The task of constructing a complete cost chain is not easy. It requires breaking a firm's own historical cost accounting data out into several principal cost categories and developing cost estimates for the backward and forward channel portions of getting the product to the end-user as well. And it requires estimating the same cost elements for one's rivals and estimating their cost chains—an advanced art in competitive intelligence in itself. But despite the tedium of the task and the imprecision of some of the estimates, the payoff in exposing the cost competitiveness of one's position and the attendant strategic alternatives make it a valuable analytical tool.

In Exhibit 3–4 observe that there are three main areas in the cost chain where important differences in the *relative* costs of competing firms can occur: in the suppliers' part of the cost chain, in their own respective activity segments, or in the forward channel portion of the chain. To the extent that the reasons for a firm's lack of cost competitiveness lie either in the backward or forward sections of the cost chain, its job of reestablishing cost competitiveness may well have to extend beyond its own in-house operations. When a firm has a cost disadvantage in the area of purchased inputs and inbound logistics, five strategic options quickly emerge for consideration:

1. Negotiate more favorable prices with suppliers.
2. Integrate backward to gain control over material costs.
3. Use lower priced substitute inputs.
4. Search out sources of savings in inbound shipping and materials logistics costs.
5. Make up the difference by initiating cost savings elsewhere in the overall cost chain.

When a firm's cost disadvantage occurs in the forward end of the cost chain, there are three corrective options:

1. Push for more favorable terms with distributors and other forward channel allies.
2. Change to a more economical distribution strategy, including the possibility of forward integration.
3. Make up the difference by initiating cost savings earlier in the cost chain.

It is likely, of course, that a substantial portion of any relative cost disadvantage lies within the activity-cost structures of rival firms. Here, five options for restoring cost parity emerge:

1. Initiate internal budget-tightening measures aimed at using fewer inputs to generate the desired output (cost-cutting retrenchment).
2. Invest in cost-saving technological improvements.
3. Innovate around the troublesome cost components as new investments are made in plant and equipment.
4. Redesign the product or service to achieve cost reductions.
5. Make up the internal cost disadvantage by achieving cost savings in the backward and forward portions of the cost chain.

The construction of value-chains is a worthwhile tool for competitive diagnosis because of what it reveals about a firm's overall cost/value competitiveness and the relative cost/value positions of firms in the industry. Examining the makeup of one's own value-chain and comparing it against the chains of important rival firms indicates who has how much of a cost/value advantage/

disadvantage vis-à-vis major competitors, and pinpoints which cost/value components in the cost chain are the source of advantage or disadvantage. Strategic cost/value analysis adds much to the picture of the competitive environment, particularly concerning who the low-cost producers are, who is in the best position to compete on the basis of value, and who may be vulnerable to attack because of a poor relative cost/value position.

Once the various types of competitive channels and activities have been delineated in an industry, other tools can be used to further describe the competitive advantages and structure of an industry. One of the most fundamental tools for assessing competitive advantages is Porter's five-forces model, shown in Exhibit 3–5. This model describes five forces that influence the competitive pressures a firm experiences given its competitive position and advantages. These five competitive forces are: (1) the threat of new entrants, (2) the threat of substitutes, (3) the bargaining power of buyers, (4) the bargaining power of suppliers, and (5) internal industry competition and rivalry. Each of these forces, in turn, can be broken down into various intrinsic elements of competition, as outlined in Exhibit 3–6. For example, entry barriers in the industry, which can be broken into elements such as economies of scale, brand identity, and government policy, determine the extent to which new entrants are a threat to the firm, strategic group, and industry.

Exhibit 3–7 also illustrates how one can quickly evaluate various competitive advantages as they relate to the competitive pressures in an industry, and thus on a firm. To use this worksheet, select the applicable elements of competition and then rate their competitive advantage (strength) or disadvantage (threat) as either high or low (e.g., from 1 to 5). Then each competitive force can be assessed as to the competitive pressure that it exerts on the firm or industry over the long term.

EXHIBIT 3–5   **Competitive Forces in an Industry Structure**

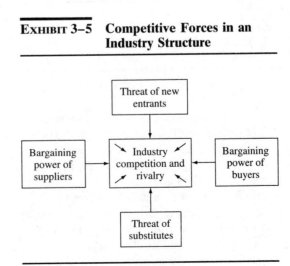

EXHIBIT 3–6   **Worksheet for Competitive Forces in an Industry**

Elements	Competitiveness Rating					Elements	Competitiveness Rating				
Determinants of entry barriers (threat of new competitors)	Low				High	**Determinants of supplier power**	Low				High
						1. Differentiation of inputs	1	2	3	4	5
1. Economies of scale	1	2	3	4	5	2. Switching costs of suppliers and firms in					
2. Proprietary; product differences	1	2	3	4	5	the industry	1	2	3	4	5
3. Brand identity	1	2	3	4	5	3. Presence of substitute inputs or suppliers	1	2	3	4	5
4. Switching costs	1	2	3	4	5	4. Supplier concentration	1	2	3	4	5
5. Capital requirements	1	2	3	4	5	5. Importance of volume to supplier	1	2	3	4	5
6. Access to distribution	1	2	3	4	5	6. Cost relative to total purchases in the					
7. Absolute cost advantages						industry	1	2	3	4	5
Proprietary learning curve	1	2	3	4	5	7. Impact of inputs on cost or differentiation	1	2	3	4	5
Access to necessary inputs	1	2	3	4	5	8. Threat of forward integration relative to					
Proprietary low-cost product design	1	2	3	4	5	threat of backward integration by firms in					
8. Government policy	1	2	3	4	5	the industry	1	2	3	4	5
9. Expected retaliation	1	2	3	4	5						
Determinants of industry internal competitive rivalry	Low				High	**Determinants of buying power** Bargaining Leverage	Low				High
1. Stage of industry growth	1	2	3	4	5	1. Buyer concentration versus firm					
2. Fixed (or storage) costs/value added	1	2	3	4	5	concentration	1	2	3	4	5
3. Intermittent overcapacity and fixed costs of						2. Buyer volume	1	2	3	4	5
capacity	1	2	3	4	5	3. Buyer switching costs relative to firm					
4. Product/service differences or differentiation	1	2	3	4	5	switching costs	1	2	3	4	5
5. Brand identity and reputation	1	2	3	4	5	4. Buyer information	1	2	3	4	5
6. Costs of switching brands to the customer	1	2	3	4	5	5. Ability to backward integrate	1	2	3	4	5
7. Number of competitors and quality of						6. Substitute products	1	2	3	4	5
competitive advantages	1	2	3	4	5	7. Pull-through marketing	1	2	3	4	5
8. Difficulty of knowing about competitors	1	2	3	4	5	8. Price/total purchases	1	2	3	4	5
9. Diversity of competitors	1	2	3	4	5	9. Product differences	1	2	3	4	5
10. Corporate risk and stakes	1	2	3	4	5	10. Brand identity	1	2	3	4	5
11. Exit barriers	1	2	3	4	5	11. Impact on quality/performance	1	2	3	4	5
						12. Buyer profits	1	2	3	4	5
						13. Decision makers incentives	1	2	3	4	5
Determinants of substitution threat	Low				High						
1. Relative price performance of substitutes	1	2	3	4	5						
2. Switching costs of customers to substitutes	1	2	3	4	5						
3. Buyer propensity to substitute	1	2	3	4	5						

Source: Adapted from Michael E. Porter, *Competitive Advantage: Creating and Sustaining Superior Performance* (New York: The Free Press, a Division of Macmillan, Inc., 1985)

Another major element of the industry environment is the product/market life cycle, which assumes that all products, and, therefore, industries, move through stages of growth and decline. The cycle begins at the development stage, moving to a growth stage, then maturity, and finally, the decline stage. Although sales revenues follow these stages, the cash flow and profits are likely to follow somewhat different patterns. Furthermore, the major strategic concerns and competitive pressures at each stage vary quite considerably. For example, at the emerging or embryonic stage, the concerns are the ultimate potential demand and the scale and timing of commitment, whereas at the decline stage, the concerns are milking resources to employ elsewhere, timing of a possible exit, and emphasis on substitutes (see Exhibit 3–7).

EXHIBIT 3–7   Product/Service/Market Life-Cycle Stages

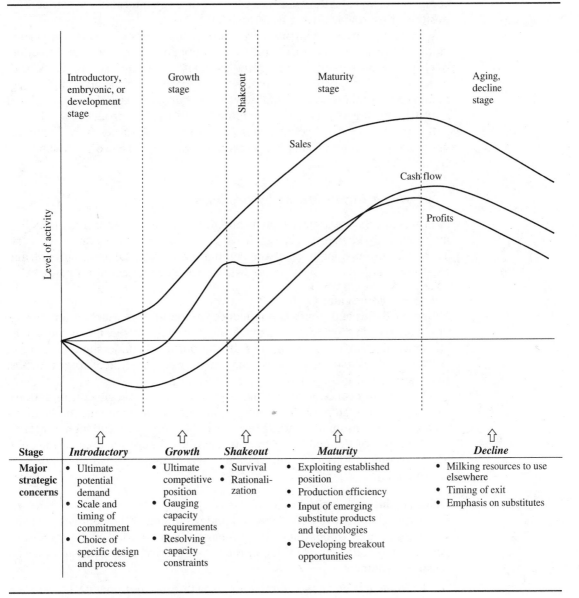

Stage	*Introductory*	*Growth*	*Shakeout*	*Maturity*	*Decline*
Major strategic concerns	• Ultimate potential demand • Scale and timing of commitment • Choice of specific design and process	• Ultimate competitive position • Gauging capacity requirements • Resolving capacity constraints	• Survival • Rationalization	• Exploiting established position • Production efficiency • Input of emerging substitute products and technologies • Developing breakout opportunities	• Milking resources to use elsewhere • Timing of exit • Emphasis on substitutes

International Competitive Advantage

In analysing an industry, it is also useful to determine if the industry has international competitors. Often managers focus on local competition and neglect international competitors who may be changing competitive advantages and positions to the detriment of the local firm. Tracking international competition may also be beneficial if a firm is developing, as most should, an international strategy itself. Research has indicated that a strong home-country competitive advantage is usually necessary before an international competitive position will provide strong performance.[1]

Some industries are intrinsically international. These industries are called global industries and competitors require global operations to compete effectively.[2] An industry can be considered global if the product/service has worldwide demand, production economies of scale exist, there is no complex segmentation within markets, and few trade barriers exist. Firms in global industries must generally be true multinationals (that is, production and marketing in several foreign countries) in order to compete successfully. Examples of globally oriented Canadian firms are Northern Telecom, Alcan, and Bombardier.

Analysing a Firm's Macro Environment

A firm is also facing a macro environment that includes other influences that may indirectly change the competitive forces and pressures in an industry. These include economic, social and demographic, technical, international, and legal/political forces. These forces will be briefly commented on below:

Economic Trends and Cycles
Economic cycles and trends can influence competitive pressures dramatically. For example, in a recession many firms have to become much more cost efficient due to lower levels of sales. It is important to understand short-term economic cycles and the influence they might have on strategic plans such as fund-raising and increasing plant capacity.

Long-term economic trends are also important strategic considerations. In Canada, our high public debt may create long-term economic implications such as lower consumer spending because of high tax rates, and higher interest rates because of the need to attract foreign investment to support our debt. These considerations may influence a firm's strategy both in Canada and internationally.

Demographic and Social Forces
Every firm should have a fundamental understanding of the demographic and social forces and trends that are impinging on its market and competitive position. The following are some of the key concerns in the demographic and social environment:

1. Demographics (e.g., population growth rates and unequal distribution of population, aging workforce in industrialized countries, high education requirements).

2. Quality of life (e.g., safety, health care, education, standard of living).

3. Moral issues (e.g., volunteerism, charities, ecology, community needs).

As with all of the various environments, one of the tasks of the general manager is the ability to identify significant environmental forces, to understand them in the context of the organization, and to create (when necessary) responses to these pressures and opportunities. The relationship between the demographic and social environment and any organization's viability is increasingly intertwined.

It is fundamental that managers understand the demographic trends that affect their firm's market and competitive position. Future strategic moves to new competitive positions involving new competitive advantages must be based upon a thorough analysis of the future demographic trends that will influence the nature of demand in the newly desired competitive position. In addition, a manager must be aware of the other social issues that concern the firm's various stakeholders such as owners, customers, employees, etc.

Technological Trends

Technological developments have reshaped the ability of many firms to compete. The key concerns in the technological environment involve building the organizational capability to (1) forecast and identify relevant developments—both within and beyond the industry, (2) assess the impact of these developments on existing operations, and (3) define opportunities. Development of such an organizational capability should result in the eventual creation of a technological strategy. Technological strategy deals with "choices in technology, product design and development, sources of technology and R&D management and funding."[3]

International Considerations

The sixth and final environment relevant to firms in Canada is the international environment. Given Canada's open economy, high levels of foreign ownership, and small domestic market, Canadian firms, as seen in many of the cases in this book, are forced to be aware of the trends and market opportunities in countries outside Canada, particularly the United States. For 200 large U.S. and European multinational enterprises (MNEs), higher performance is associated with a greater degree of internationalization.[4] The implication of this for many Canadian firms is that internationalization is something that can be welcomed rather than feared.

Some of the many differences between the environment in Canada and the international environment concern such variables as currencies (which differ in value and stability), political and economic stability, data availability and its reliability, types of regulatory (legal and accounting) systems, market homogeneity, stage of economic development, and language and cultural mores.

The Legal and Political Considerations

The legal and political environment of Canadian business is particularly important given the scale and scope of government activity in Canada.[5] Governments act in a wide variety of ways to create both opportunities and threats for business. Among the most important government actions are:

1. *Regulation,* which can increase costs but also control competition or even give a competitive advantage (if firms have adapted to particularly stringent regulations in one location and are therefore better able to handle such regulations elsewhere).

2. *Taxation,* which can reduce returns but also increase competitive advantage if a firm faces lower taxation than its competitors.

3. *Expenditure,* which can create competitive disadvantage or advantage depending on whether government grants and subsidies received are larger than what competitors receive.

4. *Takeover,* creating a grown corporation, which can produce an unpredictable competitor but also a deep-pocket customer.

5. *Privatization,* which can increase competition but also result in a more level playing field.

6. *Consultation,* which can become an opportunity for business to influence government policy but also provides government an opportunity to manipulate (i.e., co-opt) business by using the consultative process to justify decisions already made.

There are, then, at least six environments that are important to strategic decision making in Canada: (1) industry, (2) competitive, (3) political/governmental/legal, (4) social, (5) technological, and (6) international. Each of these must be considered in making strategic choices because analysis of these environments will indicate various opportunities and threats facing the organization. The objective in assessing the various environments is to formulate a strategy that best fits these environments. This is an ongoing challenge, given that environments change continually.

Notes to Chapter 3

1. Porter, Michael. *The Competitive Advantage of Nations.* New York: The Free Press, 1990.

2. Porter, Michael. *Competitive Strategy: Techniques for Analyzing Industries and Competitors.* New York: The Free Press, 1980, chap. 11.

3. See Burgelman, R. A., and M. A. Maidique. *Strategic Management of Technology and Innovation.* Homewood, IL.: Richard D. Irwin, 1988.

4. See Geringer, J. M.; Paul W. Beamish; and R. da Costa. "Diversification Strategy and Internationalization: Implications for MNE Performance." *Strategic Management Journal* 10, no. 2 (March/April 1989), pp. 109–19.

5. See, for example, Baetz, Mark C., and Donald H. Thain. *Canadian Cases in Business-Government Relations.* Toronto: Methuen Publications, 1985.

Recommended Readings

The ins and outs of strategic cost analysis are discussed in greater length in Porter, Michael E. *Competitive Advantage: Creating and Sustaining Superior Performance.* New York: The Free Press, 1985, chap. 2. What follows is a distilled adaptation by Thompson and Strickland of the approach pioneered by Porter. See Thompson, Arthur A. Jr., and A. J. Strickland III, *Strategy Formulation and Implementation.* 3rd ed. Plano, TX.: Business Publications, 1986, pp. 135–37.

These categories are from Clarkson, Max B. "Defining, Evaluating and Managing Corporate Social Performance: The Stakeholder Management Model." In *Research in Corporate Social Performance and Policy,* vol. 12. Greenwich, CT.: JAI Press, 1991.

Mockler, Robert. "Strategic Intelligence Systems: Competitive Intelligence Systems to Support Strategic Management Decision Making." *SAM Advanced Management Journal,* Winter 1992, pp. 4–9.

Williams, Jeffrey. "How Sustainable Is Your Competitive Advantage?" *California Management Review,* Spring 1992, pp. 29–51.

Zahra, Shaker, and Sherry Chaples. "Blind Spots in Competitive Analysis." *Academy of Management Executive,* May 1993, pp. 7–28.

GENERIC BUSINESS STRATEGIES AND DECISIONS

If you stay on the same track, sooner or later you will get run over.
Louis Hughs, *President of General Motors Europe Division (1994)*

Our company believed for decades there was only one way for success: Don't talk to anyone else. Those days are over.
Helmut Werner, *President of Mercedes-Benz Co. (1994)*

Firms must strive continuously to improve their competitive position and advantages relative to their competition. This necessitates a constant search for new strategic directions and initiatives. Constant improvement, what the Japanese call the Kaizen Principle, is the only way a firm will sustain its long-term competitive advantage.

This chapter considers a variety of potential generic business strategic directions, and builds on the frameworks and relationships developed in the previous chapter. There are many ways of categorizing strategic decisions, and although we will look at some generic approaches, it must be remembered that firms in general must take an approach that is appropriate to their own unique conditions. Most managers in an industry know and understand the basic generic approaches. Managers, therefore, must create new twists to the generic strategies as well as implement their strategies creatively and skilfully to improve their competitive position.

Nevertheless, it is instructive to understand some generic strategies that have been used successfully in the past. This chapter concentrates specifically on situations where the firm's environment has created certain competitive pressures that must be addressed by the firm. These environmental situations arise because of high competitive pressures due to low barriers of entry, as well as changing competitive conditions due to life cycle transitions. In general, the firm must seek to intensify its competitive position focus by becoming a low-cost or differentiated producer or both. In doing so, the firm should attempt to enhance the competitive advantages that provide it with its competitive position in a manner that creates entry barriers and decreases the ability of competitors to replicate its approach.

Following from the work of Michael Porter,[1,2] among others, strategies can be viewed broadly as falling into three dimensions: (1) overall cost leadership, where the firm strives to be the price leader in the industry by using a range of functional policies compatible with industry economics; (2) differentiation, where the firm strives to be distinctive across the industry in some aspect of its products or services that is of value to the customer, such as quality, or style; (3) focus, where a firm concentrates its efforts on serving a distinctively defined market segment, which may include some combination of a portion of a product line, particular customer segment, limited geographic area, or particular distribution channel. The firm choosing a focus or niche strategy may be able to achieve either or both cost leadership or differentiation; however, it is very difficult to be the low-cost producer and differentiated producer simultaneously in an industry.

Each of three generic strategies involves risks. Cost leadership is vulnerable to imitation by competitors or technology changes (for example, "technological leapfrogging"). Differentiation will not be sustained if the bases for differentiation become less important to buyers or if competitors imitate. A focus strategy is vulnerable to imitation, or the target segment can become unattractive if demand disappears or if broadly targeted competitors overwhelm the segment. A critical element of both the low-cost and differentiation strategies is quality. According to Deming, improved quality can result in lower costs due to "less rework, fewer mistakes, fewer delays or snags, better use of machine time and materials."[3]

Highly Competitive or Fragmented Industries

Industries that have a large number of competitors are called fragmented industries because the market is fragmented by many small firms having very similar competitive positions and advantages. Competition in these industries is intense because of the number of competitors and the inability of competitors to differentiate from one another. Characteristically fragmented industries are easy to enter because of low entry barriers, as delineated by Porter's five-forces model (see Exhibit 3–6). Examples of highly competitive or fragmented industries are dry-cleaning, local bicycle couriers, coffee shops, and donut shops.

Approaches to competing in fragmented industries are often limited by the very nature of the industry. However, potentially effective strategic initiatives include the following:

• Very careful focus on low costs and process innovations that minimize costs. When a firm is expanding, it should apply a "formula" approach to duplicating plants and offices. This will minimize both the capital and operating costs of the expansion.

• Unrecognized market niches where customers are not having their needs met. A firm may be able to take a focused-differentiated or focused-low-cost approach to such a small market.

• Participation in smaller, less dense markets where competition is sometimes less intensive. It may be possible for a company to focus on these markets in an efficient and effective manner. This is one of the strategic approaches that Wal-Mart took in establishing itself as one of the top competitors in the very competitive general merchandise/retailing industry.

• A constant look-out for new trends in technology, government policies, international relations, etc., which may allow the firm to take advantage of a newly created market.

• A search for any alternative approaches to the business that would provide the company with a competitive advantage. Examine Porter's five-forces model and carefully review, periodically, whether there is a viable approach to lowering competitive pressures. Often firms in fragmented markets become lethargic and miss opportunities for competitive improvement. Such things as economies of scale, forward or backward integration, and economies of scope may enable a company to change the nature of the business and thus, the competitive forces. This approach often requires considerable creativity combined with certain environmental or industry-based changes that allow an aggressive firm to take advantage of a unique opportunity.

Life Cycle Generic Strategies

Emerging Industries

Emerging industries are recently formed industries and are a result of changes in the environment—technological changes, changes in customer needs, legal and political changes, etc. Characteristically, firms in an emerging industry are facing considerable uncertainty in key competitive advantages such as technology. If the environment conspires to change the nature of that competitive advantage and it is no longer effective, the firm loses its ability to support its competitive position. For example, a firm may have a strong technological advantage that is nullified when a new, better technology becomes available. Examples of emerging industries include the biotechnology industry, the value-added food processing industry, and specific growth sectors in the telecommunications industry.

Strategies for coping in an emerging industry include the following:

• Ensure that the firm has a strong technological, or political (or whatever other environmental uncertainty exists) capability. It is critical that top managers are knowledgeable and aware of the competitive advantages and associated environmental forces. This ensures rapid action if changes appear to be taking place. The firm may also want to supplement its in-house strengths with external forecasting capabilities.

• Concentrate initially on the competitive advantages that are vital to learning and creating better products and services for the customer. Avoid costs and investments that are not associated with the critical advantages and success factors in the industry if at all possible. For example, many technology companies avoid the costs of manufacturing. Rather, they concentrate all of their limited resources on product/service improvement. Manufacturing can be subcontracted to low-cost manufacturers in low-cost countries. It must be noted that this assumes that manufacturing process development is not a critical part of the emerging industry.

• Cooperate with other companies in the industry in an attempt to build a product or service standard and create customer awareness. Many emerging industries have successfully done this (e.g., the firms behind the VHS tape format and the original IBM PC).

• Strive for an early entry into an industry if there appear to be clear abilities to build strong competitive advantages or entry barriers. Otherwise, wait until the costs of uncertainty have been eliminated.

Maturing Industries

A maturing industry is an industry that is facing, for the first time, no or minimal market growth. As was delineated in Chapter 3, slower growth means that the industry evolves towards higher competition. Furthermore, the power in the value-chain often evolves forward to the distributor, retailer, or customer because they have a wider choice of producers and are experienced with the product/service attributes. International competition increases and the ability to differentiate oneself based on product attributes is declining. The critical strategic notion in this situation is that the firm must build competitive advantages that maximize the barriers to entry and minimize the competitive forces, as delineated by Porter's model in Chapter 3. An example of an industry in the early stages of the maturing process is the computer software industry. Firms in this industry are having to merge with other firms, others are attempting to reorganize themselves so they can compete in the changing environment, and a few are going bankrupt.

Some of the alternative strategic approaches to this environmental situation are the following:

• The firm must focus on low costs and improved customer service. This is a difficult transition because many of these activities, such as manufacturing and customer service, are not activities that the firm has concentrated upon in the past. The activities that it has concentrated upon in the past, such as R&D, are not required or are much less critical to the survival of the firm now. If a firm cannot make this transition in activities, possibly it should look to merge with a firm that has these capabilities.

• The firm may have to consider aggressively competing internationally to gain the economies of scale and scope that are necessary in a mature business.

• Management and the organization should be preoccupied with defining its strategy clearly, preferably as a low-cost strategy because differentiated niche strategies may slowly erode as the industry matures even further.

• The organization must evolve into a disciplined cost efficient and effective operation where managers focus on controlling costs, quality, and service—things that have become important to the customers. This change often is not easy because the organization, during the emerging and growth stages, has accumulated unnecessary departments, people, and managers.

• Recreate the growth cycle by adapting resources and capabilities to new market needs.

Declining Industries

A declining industry is an industry where the size of the market is decreasing. Competition in such an industry becomes extremely intense, particularly if high barriers to exit exist. A barrier to exit is defined as an impediment to the firm if it wants to get out of the industry. For example, if a firm has invested a lot of capital on production capacity, and this capacity is not useable in another industry, then the firm and its owners will be reticent about getting out of the industry and writing off the investment with no prospect of future returns. An example of a Canadian industry in decline is the east coast fisheries industry, which is facing low fish stocks and a moratorium on fishing in most areas.

In general, four alternative strategies are available to a firm in this situation. They are to (1) take a leadership position, (2) seek a niche position, (3) divest, or (4) harvest. A firm that takes a leadership position must decide it can capture the best competitive position using its competitive advantages in the market with possibly some additional investment and strategic changes. The leadership position must clearly put the firm in a low-cost or product/ service attribute leadership position relative to its competitors. Furthermore, the managers must be fairly certain that it can attain such a position; otherwise it is a very high-risk strategy. This strategy may also be effective if the managers feel the decline is not permanent and that demand will eventually stabilize. A vivid example of a firm using the industry leadership approach is the case of Fisheries Products International (FPI), where Vick Young, the CEO, completely redefined the company's competitive position in the industry by refocusing the company from a fish catcher to a value-added fish processing company. The company now concentrates on importing fish, processes the fish in a value-added manner, and then re-exports them.

Seeking a niche position is a good strategy for a firm that does not have a leadership position and its limited competitive advantages do not allow it to gain such a position. The critical nature of this strategy is that the firm must focus on a market niche that is small enough to be somewhat neglected by the firm(s) seeking leadership positions. This strategy is often combined with a harvest strategy.

A harvest strategy is one in which the firm has decided to eventually discontinue the business, particularly if the decline continues over the long term. However, in the short term the firm keeps its prices high, minimizes reinvestment costs, and allows its market share to slowly decline while maximizing its profits.

A divestment strategy is the most obvious strategic alternative. Yet, it is the most difficult strategy to implement effectively because it is difficult to sell a sinking firm. Furthermore, managers in a single business firm don't want to put themselves out of work. The task in this strategy is making the firm look good and finding a buyer.

Strategic Evolution in the Life Cycle Process

Businesses in maturing and declining industries may also be able to adapt their organizations, resources, and capabilities to new products, services, or markets. Such an action may create a growth stage by appealing to customers and needs that have not been fulfilled yet.

Exhibit 4–1 illustrates how institutions in the business education industry are attempting to create new segments in the industry that are in the emerging and growth stages. In this example, the institutions are evolving from a two-year standard MBA program, a service that is facing demographic and compet-

Exhibit 4–1   The Canadian Business Education Industry–1995

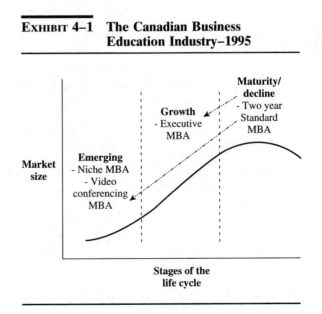

itive pressures, to executive MBAs, niche MBAs (e.g., high technology or international MBAs), and MBA video-conferencing programs.

The Exhibit illustrates how business schools are attempting to evolve into new life cycle stages by redefining their customer and service focus. They are altering their competitive position by refocusing their competitive advantages on these new markets and customers. However, in doing this firms must be aware of the difficulties that are present. First, a firm developing a new competitive position may lose its previous position because it has taken some competitive advantages away from supporting that position to refocus on the new position. This may leave the firm worse off if the new market segment does not develop as predicted. Second, often the new market segments require resources and capabilities that the entering firm does not have. This makes the firm less competitive in the new market segment. Therefore, firms must ensure that the market segment does not require it to spread its competitive advantages over two or more very different market positions requiring very new and different resources and capabilities.

Notes to Chapter 4

1. See Porter, Michael E. *Competitive Advantage: Creating and Sustaining Superior Performance.* New York: The Free Press, 1985, chap. 9.
2. See Porter, Michael E. *Competitive Strategy: Techniques for Analyzing Industries and Competitors.* New York: The Free Press, 1980, chap 11.
3. Deming, W. E. *Out of the Crisis.* Cambridge, MA: MIT Press, 1986, p. 31.

Recommended Readings

Adler, P. S.; D. W. McDonald; and E. MacDonald. "Strategic Management of Technical Functions." *Sloan Management Review,* Winter 1992, pp. 19–38.

Foster, John. "Scenario Planning for Small Businesses." *Long Range Planning,* February 1993, pp. 123–29.

Nutt, Paul, and Robert Backoff. "Transforming Public Organizations with Strategic Management and Strategic Leadership." *Journal of Management,* Summer 1993, pp. 299–348.

Waalewijn, Phillip, and Peter Segaar. "Strategic Management: The Key to Profitability in Small Companies." *Long Range Planning,* April 1993, pp. 24–30.

STRATEGY AND RESOURCES

The components of cost in a product today are largely R&D, intellectual assets, and services.

Edmund Jenkins, *Partner in Arthur Andersen and Chair of American Institute of Public Accountants Task Force on Non-financial Measures of Performance (1994)*

We operate in a global economy in which measures of quality, delivery, customer satisfaction and other operating factors are indicators of success as important as financial indicators. AMP is now investing hundreds of millions of dollars each year in new equipment, systems, services and training our employees. . . .

James E. Marley, *Chairman of AMP Corp. (1994)*

Analysis of resources is a crucial consideration when both formulating and implementing a strategy. If the strategy is not supported by the business's resources, the strategy will be unsuccessful. And when a strategy changes, accompanying changes in resources are usually necessary. The questions that then arise are whether these changes are possible and how they can best be brought about. In this chapter, the analysis of resources and their relationship with strategy are considered.

Strategy's Fit with Resources

The relationship between resources and strategy is two-way (Exhibit 5–1). Strategy affects resources and resources affect strategy, because certain strategies demand certain resources and certain resources are only applicable to certain strategies. In this manner, resources provide the firm with its inherent competitive advantages. Therefore, the selection and quality of resources is critical to the firm's competitive advantages and competitive position.

Two questions must be kept in mind when determining the specific resources required to pursue a strategy: Do the resources allow the strategy to

---

EXHIBIT 5–1   The Relationship between Strategy and Resources

---

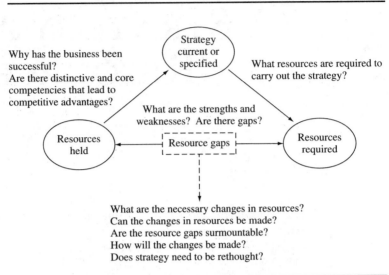

be implemented, and do they support a firm-specific competitive advantage? Starting with resources held, the strategist determines the unique characteristics of the firm's current resources—ones that differentiate it from its competitors. These broad-based differences are called *distinctive competencies*. A firm also has *core competencies,* which are resources that give a firm its clear leadership competitive position, in the eyes of its competitors and customers. More specifically, core competencies are the resources or capabilities in an organization that truly distinguish it from its competitors, and the performance of the company, both today and in the future, depends on these capabilities. The difference between distinctive and core competencies is subtle, but distinctive competencies are resources and capabilities that broadly differentiate it from the competitors, whereas core competencies are just a few vital resources and capabilities that provide the firm with its most consequential competitive advantage and, therefore, its superior competitive position. For example, Honda Motor Company has many distinctive competencies such as its trained workforce, plant location, and international skills. However, its core competency is its ability to design and manufacture engines. It has successfully employed this core competency to broaden its product scope into a wide variety of products from Formula 1 race cars to lawnmowers to portable motorized electrical generators. Having established what these competencies are, a strategy is then developed that makes good use of them. The overall resource requirements of this strategy are then examined.

EXHIBIT 5–2   An Overview of the Functional Perspective

Function	*A Partial List of Questions to Answer*
Finance	What is the apparent capacity of the firm to generate internal and external funds? What funds are required for each strategic alternative?
Research and development	How important is technology to the firm's processes and products? What percentage of the firm's resources are devoted to research and development?
Human resources	What is the ambition, depth, drive, loyalty, and skill of the managerial/administrative group in the firm?
Procurement	What is the cost, flexibility, motivation, productivity, and skill of the workforce? How important is the procurement function to the firm?
Operations	Does the firm have good relations with suppliers? What is the capacity, cost, and productivity of operations? What is the age, condition, and flexibility of the plant and equipment? What is the quality of the products produced?
Marketing	Does the firm command a premium price and, if so, why? How well does the firm know its customers and its competitors?

Resource gaps are the differences between the resources required and the resources held. If the gaps can be reduced, the strategy makes sense from the perspective of resources. If the gaps cannot be filled, the strategy has to be revised so that the gaps between resources required and those held are surmountable.

Evaluating Resources Held and Determining Resources Required

Resources can be evaluated from several different perspectives. The most prevalent way of evaluating them is *by functional areas:* finance, research and development, human resources, operations, marketing, and so forth. For each function, functionally related questions, samples of which appear in Exhibit 5–2, are answered. When a functional perspective is taken, the strategist also needs to consider the context within which the functions operate. The contribution of each function to the business's strategy needs to be addressed because some functions may be more important to the strategy than others. The interrelationships among the functions also need to be addressed because what is done in one function can have a bearing on what can or cannot be done in another function.

A second way of evaluating resources is *by type:* financial, physical, human, and organizational. Financial resources are the funds that the company has or can raise. They are the most basic and flexible resources of the business, and can be converted into other resources. Converting other resources into financial resources is less certain and more difficult. Physical resources are the buildings, raw material, and equipment that the company has to work with and what it can do with them. Human resources are the number and type of people in the firm and what they are able to do. Organizational resources are the procedures and techniques the firm has developed that are necessary for success in the business.

A third way of evaluating resources is in terms of their *tangibility. Tangible* resources, such as a plant or the number of employees, can be observed and measured. Less tangible resources are also important, although their characteristics and importance are harder to evaluate. Examples of less tangible resources are a recognized corporate name that may allow the company to command a premium price in the market, long-term contracts with suppliers that ensure availability of inputs, and the loyalty and dedication of employees that can determine their productivity.

A fourth way of evaluating resources is in terms of their *breadth.* A resource is essentially broad/wide when it is easily transferred to other situations and narrow/specialized when it is not. A sales staff with knowledge of many different products is an example of a broad resource, whereas specialized product knowledge is an example of a narrow resource. A broad resource base facilitates a business's expansion of its product, market, and industry scope, whereas a narrow resource base serves to limit the firm's ability to increase its scope.

A final way of evaluating resources is in terms of the *activity cost chain.* Within each activity, different kinds of resources are required as indicated by the different cost elements that were identified in Exhibit 3–5.

Resource Gaps

Rarely is the precise combination of resources needed to pursue a strategy in place. With a new strategy, resource requirements can be considerably different from current resources, thus creating resource gaps. When assessing the resource gaps, a useful approach is to construct a table with entries down the side for the various tasks or functions and with headings across the top for (1) current resources, (2) projected resources, (3) gaps between those two, and (4) how the gaps might be filled (Exhibit 5–3). The body of this table is then filled in with the analytical details.

A new strategy is not the only situation in which resource gaps occur. Just maintaining an ongoing strategy may create resource gaps. New resources must be developed when existing resources deteriorate, depreciate, or turn over. In addition, success with the existing strategy can create resource gaps when additional resources are required for growth. On occasion, more resources are generated than can be employed profitably in a business. Underutilization of existing resources is a form of resource gap that is unrecognized in many organizations. Another dilemma, for example, is when a firm generates

---

EXHIBIT 5–3   Assessing Resource Gaps

Functional Area	Current Resources	Required Resources	Resource Gaps	Filling the Gaps: Tactics and Risk
Finance				
R&D				
Human resources				
Procurement				
Operations				
Marketing				

---

more cash than it can use in the business and makes itself an attractive takeover target.

Identifying the Gaps

Resource gaps are identified through strength-and-weakness analysis as part of the SWOT analysis described in Chapter 2. Determination of strengths and weaknesses involves a relative comparison and must be done for each strategic alternative because each alternative has its own peculiar resource requirements. Tied to each strength or weakness is a gap between the resource held and the resource required to pursue the strategy. Each gap can be described in terms of magnitude, direction of change, and time by which it has to be reduced.

Reducing the Gaps

The ability of the business to reduce the gaps identified is influenced by the nature of the changes required and the ability of the business to make these changes. The gaps can be reduced by reallocating, developing, buying, and selling resources. Depending on how the gap is reduced, cost, ease, and timing will differ. Resources can be acquired from the outside, but their high market cost can make it more desirable to develop them internally. Developing resources is usually cheaper, but slower. It can have other positive benefits, however, such as providing for the development of managers. Moreover, development of resources may be required if sufficient quantities or qualities are not available, either elsewhere in the business or in the marketplace. Obviously, many tactical issues have to be addressed when considering how gaps might be filled.

It should also be noted that the ability to reduce a resource gap will depend on the particular country in which the firm is located. A firm's resource base is not simply a function of its own past investments but is also determined by the supply of resources such as capital and labour in the country.[1] In other words, there is an interaction between firm-level and country-level sources of competitive advantage.

Reducing gaps presents the business with risks. The risk associated with filling a gap is greater when the gap is larger, when the resource has to be increased rather than decreased, and when the gap has to be filled sooner. Risk is also greater when there are more gaps to be filled because it is less likely that the company will be able to fill them all. If the risk posed by the gaps is acceptable while the strategy appears effective, then a fit has been found between resources and strategy.

Resource Allocation in Corporate, Business, and Operational Strategy

Understanding the role of resource allocation in the strategic management process is critical. Resource allocations serve to interpret and apply the firm's strategy. In fact, the essence of the strategy of an organization is how and where it allocates resources.

A firm grasp of the resource allocation process is necessary to appreciate its role in the strategic management process. As the matrix in Exhibit 5–4 indicates, the resource allocation process has three phases and three sub-processes. The first phase is the initiating phase—where many product/market ideas and proposals originate. This is the level where many new business graduates will spend their first years of employment. The other two phases are corporate (senior management level) and integrating. It is through the integrating phase—or what might be called the middle-management level—that the goals and plans defined by corporate management will be conveyed down through the organization. It is also through the integrating phase that operational proposals (from the intiating phase) will be first screened and, if deemed promising, conveyed up through the organization to the corporate level.

The three subprocesses in the resource allocation process are definition, commitment, and organizational context. In the definition process, the under-lying economic and technical considerations of a proposed investment (re-source allocation) are determined. In order to understand how proposals that have already been defined move toward funding, the second of the three subprocesses—commitment or impetus—comes into play. It is at this stage that a senior manager must commit (or not) to sponsor a project. Because the general manager's reputation for good judgment may rise or fall depending on the outcome of the investment, the required commitment will be given only after careful consideration of the various demands at the corporate and operational levels. Not surprisingly, this second subprocess can be viewed primarily as a political one.[2]

The final subprocess is context, which is the set of organizational ele-ments—including formal structure information and control systems, and re-

Exhibit 5–4   The Resource Allocation Process

Phase	Process					
	Definition Goal/plan/result definition and measurement		*Commitment* Project/plan impetus		*Organization* Determination of organizational context	
Corporate (senior management)	Macro strategy Company environment aggregate system		Terminal decision yes or no		Design of corporate context Overall structure, personnel assignment, and development, incentive, and control systems style	
Integrating (middle management)	Financial aggregate goals Strategic thrust ⇩	⇧ Product market strategies	Filtered company needs (the company wants) ⇩	⇧ Filtered product/ market needs (the businesses wants)	Corporate needs Implementa- tion (differ- entiation integration) ⇩	⇧ Subunit needs Interpre- tation, adaptive needs
Initiating (operating level)	Product market strategies Operational plans and execution		Competing plans/proposals I've got a "great" idea		Product/market not served by structure	

Source: Adapted from Joseph L. Bower, *Managing the Resource Allocation Process* (Boston, MA: Harvard Business School Press, 1986), p. 80.

ward systems—which influence both definition and impetus. This flow from the definition or formulation of potential resource allocations through to commitment, and how it will ultimately affect and be affected by the organization, begins to move us toward an understanding of how the basic framework underlying strategy supports the management of resource development in the firm.

Summary

Finding an acceptable fit between the strategy and the resources available to the business is a major step in formulating strategy.[3] First, the resource situation must be examined in terms of what is available and what is needed. Resources can be evaluated in several ways: by functional area, by type, by tangibility, by breadth, and by activity costs. Resource gaps must be identified and evaluated to determine the likelihood of their being overcome. Whether they can be overcome depends on size of the gaps, their number, and nature; the ways in which the gaps can be reduced; and the time available. When the likelihood of filling the resource gaps poses too great a risk to be acceptable, the strategy has to be modified in order to bring its resource requirements closer to current resources.

Notes to Chapter 5

1. See Porter, M. E. *The Competitive Advantage of Nations.* New York: The Free Press, 1990.
2. Bower, Joseph L. *Managing the Resource Allocation Process.* Boston, MA: Harvard Business School Press, 1986, p. 80.
3. For more discussion on the analysis of resources, see Buchele, R. B. "How to Evaluate a Firm." *California Management Review,* Fall 1962; Grant, J. H., and W. R. King. *The Logic of Strategic Planning.* Boston, MA: Little, Brown, 1982, chaps. 4–7; Porter, M. E. *Competitive Advantage: Creating and Sustaining Superior Performance.* New York: The Free Press, 1985; Rothschild, W. E. *Putting It All Together: A Guide to Strategic Thinking.* New York: AMACOM, 1976, chap. 6; Sloma, R. S. *How to Measure Managerial Performance.* New York: Macmillan, 1980; and Stevenson, H. H. "Defining Corporate Strengths and Weaknesses," *Sloan Management Review,* Spring 1976, pp. 51–68.

Recommended Readings

Lado, Augustine; Nancy Boyd; and Peter Wright. "A Competency-Based Model of Sustainable Competitive Advantage: Toward a Conceptual Integration." *Journal of Management,* March 1992, pp. 77–92.

Stalk, George; P. Evans; and L. E. Shulman. "Competing on Capabilities: The New Rules of Corporate Strategy." *Harvard Business Review,* March-April 1992, pp. 57–69.

STRATEGY AND STAKEHOLDERS' PREFERENCES/VALUES

People working together with integrity and authenticity and collective intelligence are profoundly more effective as a business than people living together based on politics, game playing, and narrow self-interest.

Peter Senge, *Senior Lecturer at Sloan School of Business, MIT, and Corporate Consultant (1994)*

It is more than morale; it is a real feeling that people can make a difference. As big as this company is, you can always worry about people feeling they can have any impact. . .

Harry Pearce, *Executive Vice President of General Motors Corp. (1994)*

Strategy formulation may seem to be a highly rational and reasoned process of analysing environmental opportunities and threats, and resource strengths and weaknesses. However, managers and other persons associated with a business may have different assessments of the firm's environment and resource base. They may also use different criteria when evaluating strategic alternatives, and have different perceptions of the need for change. Or, the organization may have inherent preferences and value conflicts within it.

In this chapter, the role of stakeholder preferences and values in strategy formulation are considered. The chapter also describes the concept of corporate culture, corporate ethics, and stakeholder pressures because they influence, and are influenced by, managerial preferences and values.

Managerial Preferences and Values

Everybody has individual preferences that influence his or her thoughts and behaviour. Preferences are derived from the individual's basic needs and values. These needs and values are modified through a person's experience, personal goals, beliefs, attitudes, and competencies.[1] In this context, a manager's task is therefore to unify the preferences and values and, ultimately, the employees' behaviours, in a way that supports the competitive advantages and the strategic direction of the firm. To do this, a manager must confront two issues. First, managers must develop a shared set of preferences and behaviours for their organization; and second, they must ensure that the shared organizational preferences are appropriate for the strategic direction of the company.

Managing Organizationwide Preferences/Values and Behaviour

Personal preferences must be assimilated into group preferences if management is to have a consistent set of preferences to guide strategic decision making. Managers attempt to guide their organization's preferences and inform their stakeholders of their preferences, by developing a mission statement. A *mission statement* is a description of the firm's vision, corporate ethics, values, and a broad set of objectives. The goal of the mission statement is to provide all of the stakeholders with a general description of the company's vision, strategic direction and intent, and its values and preferences. In this way, the firm's strategic objectives can be set and the future strategy (i.e., competitive position and advantages) objectively sought by everybody in the firm.

Getting agreement on common and shared preferences by all individuals in an organization is not an easy task. This assimilation process is accomplished through a complex process in which power often plays an instrumental role.[2] Power enables certain individuals in management to dominate the formation of managerial preferences (should they so desire) such that the group's preferences closely reflect their personal preferences. For this reason, any assessment of managerial preferences must consider who the powerful people in the management team are, how they see the situation, and what they think should be done. This process and the participatory groups are described more thoroughly below in the sections on stakeholders and corporate ethics.

Stakeholders' Preferences and Values

Managers are increasingly expected to consider a growing number of stakeholders when formulating strategy. A stakeholder is an individual or a group with a personal interest in the business. Each stakeholder depends on the business in order to realize goals, while the business depends on them for something they provide to the business. Management is most likely to satisfy more influential stakeholders if it takes their preferences into account when formulating the strategy.

General classes of stakeholders who directly influence strategic decisions are shareholders, management, employees, financiers, suppliers, customers, community, and government. Indirectly, other interest groups can influence strategy. Illustrative preferences/values of these stakeholders and how they encourage managers to meet them are presented in Exhibit 6–1. Managers often reflect the preferences/values of stakeholders they see as important to the performance of their job. Thus, the marketing manager will tend to reflect customer interests, and the financial manager will tend to reflect financiers' interests. Stakeholders sometimes share certain common interests, as do shareholders and managers who hold stock options.

Some stakeholders are "self-appointed," yet they have the potential to reshape an entire company's or industry's status. For example, at the industry level, outside interest groups in Europe were able to convince politicians to ban selected fur imports from Canada which, in turn, eliminated the annual Canadian seal hunt.

Which stakeholders' preferences management seeks to satisfy involves difficult choices, sometimes including ethical issues; trade-offs need to be made among the competing preferences of stakeholders, and the decision is often

EXHIBIT 6–1   The Interests of Stakeholders

Stakeholder	*Preferences, Values, Expectations*	*Ways Stakeholders Exert Influence on the Business*
Shareholders	• Appreciation in the value of stock dividends • Social responsibility	• Buying and selling stock • Election of directors • Proxy fights • Public expression of satisfaction or discontent through the press or at annual meetings
Managers	• Participation in decisions • Authority/power • Compensation (salary, bonuses, benefits) • Opportunity for advancement • Job security	• Taking/leaving jobs in the firm • Commitment to work • Quality of work
Employees	• Compensation (wages, benefits, profit sharing) • Participation in workplace decisions • Safe working conditions • Opportunity for advancement • Job security	• Taking/leaving jobs in the home • Strikes • Absenteeism • Workplace grievances • Quality of work • Union activity
Financiers	• Orderly repayment of principal and interest • Further opportunities for sound investment of monies • Timely disclosure of events	• Willingness to lend additional funds • Covenants in the loan agreements • Enforcement of covenants • Credit rating interest rates charged
Suppliers	• Continued, consistent orders • Prompt payment	• Prices charged • Credit terms • Delivery performance • Willingness to meet special demands • Supply priority during periods of shortage • Technical assistance • Recommendations to other suppliers

---

EXHIBIT 6–1 *(Concluded)*

Stakeholder	Preferences, Values, Expectations	Ways Stakeholders Exert Influence on the Business
Customers	• Satisfactory products or services • Satisfactory price/quality relationship • Fair adjustment practices (warranties, responses, etc.)	• Amount purchased • Word-of-mouth advertising • Complaints, returns, claims • Product liability suits • New product ideas
Community	• Continuity of employment • Continuity of payment of taxes • Environmentally sound activities • Actions socially sound • Employee participation in community activities	• Boycotts, protests, demonstrations • Awards by community groups • Pressure on government
Government	• Continuity of employment • Continuity of payment of taxes • Environmentally sound activities • Advance national objectives (R&D, exports, job creation) • Satisfy regulations	• Subsidies, tax concessions • Regulations • Licences, permits • Awards by government • Enforcement of regulations
Other interest groups	• Interested in social, moral, environmental, cultural, and community issues	• Boycotts, protests, demonstrations • Educating the consumers and public

influenced by the stakeholders' power. Factors influencing the potential power of stakeholders are outlined in Exhibit 6–2. When top executives were asked, "who is really important to the business," customers were seen as most important, followed by themselves, subordinates, employees, and bosses. Those who were least important, in order of declining importance, were stockholders, elected public officials, government bureaucrats, and other interest groups.[3]

The following questions are relevant when determining the influence of stakeholder interests:

1. Which stakeholders' interests are most important?
2. Will any stakeholders be injured by the proposed decisions?
3. Should and can strategy be changed to accommodate stakeholder expectations?
4. Is it possible to negotiate a compromise?
5. Should and can certain stakeholders be replaced?

These questions also raise ethical considerations about "what is right" and "what is wrong,"[4] which are addressed later in the chapter.

Corporate Culture

Corporate culture is defined as the common preferences and values held by those working in the firm about the way things are done. It gives rise to norms,

EXHIBIT 6–2   Potential Power Held by Stakeholders When Seeking to Influence Strategic Decisions

	Degree of Potential Power	
Stakeholder	*Is High If*	*Is Low If*
Shareholders	• A controlling block of shares is held by shareholders with an active interest in the company. • Many shareholders have a common interest in what the company does. • Shareholders hold stock so they can exert influence over management decisions.	• Shares are widely held by uninterested shareholders. • Shares are widely held by shareholders with heterogeneous interests. • A dominant CEO strongly influences elections to the board.
Managers	• Management is led by a dominating CEO. • The management team has been in place for a long time. • Compensation is heavily influenced by performance-based bonuses.	• The board of directors dominates decision making.
Employees	• Employees belong to a strong union. • The company has a tradition of good employee relations.	• Employees make up an unskilled labour force. • There is high unemployment.
Financiers	• The company is highly leveraged. • The company has defaulted on the covenants in the loan agreements.	• The company generates the investment money it needs internally.
Suppliers	• Supply sources are limited. • Switching costs are high.	• Many alternative suppliers.
Customers	• Only a few possible customers. • A few customers buy a significant proportion of the output. • Customers possess a credible threat for backward integration.	• Many possible customers. • The company's product is unique.
Community	• A single-industry town.	• The company has facilities in many locations.
Government	• Regulations provide government with control over company activities. • Government approval is required for mergers and acquisitions. • The government can provide grants, licences, and special tax benefits.	• Firm is international with the ability to move operations outside of the country. • The country does not have any attractive resources or markets.
Other interest groups	• Can influence the actions of some of the other stakeholders such as customers and government.	• Cannot influence other stakeholders.

routines, and informal rules that people follow. It also provides them with a common understanding of what is considered important, and a standard for performance in areas that preserve the firm's distinctiveness (see box). The culture of an organization can be compared to a national culture, yet the organizational culture is within the bounds of an organization.

From the strategic perspective, a corporate culture closely linked to an effective business strategy can mean the difference between success and failure for a business.[5] The reason is that the culture often has a direct impact on how well a particular strategy is or can be implemented. Consequently, when the culture accounts for a business's success, strategy can be expected to build on it. And when the strategy requires a change in culture, pursuit of the strategy is constrained, sometimes to the extent that a strategy cannot be pursued. Exhibit 6–3 contrasts two very different business strategies and organizational cultures.

AT&T just recently acquired McCaw Communications Corp. and this merger provides a good contrast in company cultures, one that is often present between small entrepeneurially managed and larger bureaucratically managed firms. Fortune magazine stated that the companies were "so different that McCaw will be forever changed."[6]

One culture, AT&T, is very formal and conservative in nature, whereas the other culture, McCaw, is very informal and liberal in nature. It is also important to note how the organizational demographics, environment, culture (i.e., styles), and strategies are linked. For example, McCaw's informal and aggressive culture suits it well in its high-growth environment and strategic direction. This link between preferences and strategy will be considered in more detail in a subsequent section in this chapter.

Exhibit 6–3 also illustrates how various processes and components in an organization are linked to develop an organizational culture. For example, both AT&T and McCaw's organizational and leadership styles are supportive of each other in producing an organizational culture that is specific to that company.

Culture in an organization can range between strong and weak. A strong culture greatly influences the behaviour of organizational members. Evidence for the strength of a culture is found in Exhibit 6–4. In general, businesses with strong cultures are likely to have better performance[7]. However, a strong culture is not a sure road to success. A culture that has been a strength may become a weakness if it does not fit with the requirements of a new strategy. Nor is a strong culture necessarily self-sustaining. It can break down when rapid growth brings in new people faster than they can be socialized to the culture.

The compatibility between culture and strategy, sometimes called *cultural risk,* can be examined using a logical process. First, the key tasks arising from the strategy are determined. Next, the behaviour required to perform the tasks satisfactorily is determined. This is compared with the behaviour arising out of the current corporate culture. If required behaviour is similar to actual behaviour, culture poses no risk to the implementation of strategy. If it is

EXHIBIT 6–3   The Impact of Culture on Strategy and Implementation

Organizational Trait	AT&T	McCaw Communications
Demographics of organization	300,000 employees. 43 years–avg. employee age. 15 years–avg. length of service.	7,000 employees. 33 years–avg. employee age. 3 years–avg. length of service.
Organizational style	Hierarchical, staid, and steeped in boss fear (e.g., managers fearful of talking on the same topics that their bosses had previously talked about to the interviewer)	Fun and freewheeling (e.g., employees at all levels encouraged to contact CEO directly).
Leadership style	Career telephone executive who has a very formal style. Soft-spoken, but has remade himself into a forceful—sometimes bold—decision maker.	Informal and soft-spoken gentleman who is known for his innovative ideas and for piloting his own seaplane.
Management dress style	Formal—suit and tie.	Informal—open-neck shirt and slacks.
Decision-making style	Centralized. Bureaucratic: –good at making big decisions fast, but very slow when making smaller decisions made by lower level managers. –usually managers seek written authorization.	Decentralized. Entrepreneurial: –very fast at making decisions as the manager can either make the decision or consult the CEO who is only a phone call away. –verbal authorization is adequate.
Corporate strategy	Diversified into 24 different businesses.	Focused on one business.
Business strategy	80% of business is in the mature long distance telephone business. Critical competitive advantages are quality, service, and low cost. Administrative approach emphasizes control and army-like discipline.	Business is focused in the mobile telephone business, a growth industry. Critical strategy focus is expansion into more geographic markets. (Quality, service, and low cost are not absolutely critical.) Also trying to offer other wireless services.
Business Environment	Highly competitive.	Somewhat competitive, although geographic market areas are monopolies for the moment.
Performance	Profitable. Slow internal growth of sales revenue.	Marginally profitable. Very high internal growth of sales revenue (i.e., 30% annually).

EXHIBIT 6–4   Evidence of the Strength of a Culture

Character of the Culture	*Evidence of Character*
Strong	• Members share preferences or values about how to succeed. • Members show the activities the business must carry out well to be successful. • Standards of achievement are well established. • "Heroes" in the organization personify values and provide tangible role models to follow.
Weak	• Members have no clear preferences or values about how to succeed. • Members do not agree on the beliefs or values that are important. • Different parts of the business have different beliefs or values. • "Heroes" of the business are destructive or disruptive. • Rituals are disorganized, with organizational members either "doing their own thing" or working at cross-purposes.

---

different, culture can present so much risk that it is a barrier to the pursuit of a strategy.

The strategist can deal with cultural risk in several ways. One approach is to ignore culture and plunge ahead. Since a good fit is needed between culture and strategy, this approach nearly always invites disaster. Another approach is to manage around culture, either by performing the tasks in ways more in line with the current culture, or, more drastically, by modifying the strategy so that different tasks are required. A third approach is to change the selected components of culture that affect performance of specific tasks and which are identified as areas of risk. A simple example of a change in culture so that it meets the needs of a new strategy is as follows. A company facing a more competitive environment found that it needed to improve its relationships with customers. It reoriented the culture to fit its new strategy and environment by using the slogan "the customer is always right" and by training employees to respond courteously and promptly to customer requests.

Managing Business Ethics

Business ethics are related to societal and personal ethics, which of course are dependent upon a person's values and motivations. Some people know when they are acting unethically, yet they are motivated to do so by various rewards and incentives. In addition, often people have different values from others simply because of social or family background. A vivid example of an individual's values differing from society's values is the case of a hardened criminal.

Yet, what are ethics? Personal values are related but do not make up one's ethics because one can value exercise more than reading, or chocolate cake above apple pie, but neither of these are ethical decisions. In addition, legal rights do not necessarily define ethical rights because a legal judgment can also be very unethical, an example being when a criminal is freed because of an improperly served search warrant.

Ethical decisions are concerned with decisions that impact the welfare, personal rights, and justice of other people or things. Ethics, however, do depend upon one's values and what one thinks is right or wrong, and what is harmful or not.

Some national cultures can have different ethics from others. For example, in some countries giving ex gratia payments (i.e., what we call *bribes*) to various officials is an expected business practice, whereas in other countries it is both morally and criminally an offence. Therefore, managers must not only be aware of individual ethical differences, but national cultural differences.

Managing ethical behaviour in a company is not an easy task. One way in which large companies attempt to do this is through a *statement of ethical conduct or behaviour.* This statement is often a separate document from the mission statement and it clearly lays out appropriate behaviours for employees in the company. However, managers must also set an example on a day-to-day basis when interacting with employees and customers. Furthermore, they should be fully versed in the ethical principles of the firm so that they can provide guidance to employees when necessary. Consistent implementation and review of such guidelines, as well as punishment when appropriate for improper behaviour, is critical to the effectiveness of an ethics policy.

Formulating ethical guidelines is extremely difficult and somewhat situationally dependent. However, a good objective to strive for when formulating guidelines is to accommodate the ethical values of all of your stakeholders. For example, if your business is done in several countries, the most stringent ethical principles should be adopted—otherwise those stakeholders, including customers, owners, and employees, could take issue with your ethical standards, and business performance could suffer. Ultimately, all people must take responsibility for their actions and must consider the long-term consequences of their behaviours to their career, family, and personal prospects.[4]

Questions that should be asked when assessing a company's ethical guidelines are the following:

1. Would the manager like to have that behaviour done to him or her?
2. Is there evidence that any of the firm's stakeholders have adopted or oppose this ethical belief?
3. Is the reason the ethical principle has not been adopted one of short-term profitability, or have the long-term arguments been fully considered?
4. Are the committees and organizational processes that establish and control the ethical guidelines democratic?

Managing the Fit between Preferences/Values and Strategy

Preferences and values, at both the group and individual levels, are directly related to the components of strategy. Some organizations, such as not-for-profit organizations, have preferences and values related to warmth, kindness, and giving. Yet other organizations, particularly those in tough competitive situations, have preferences and values related to efficiency, effectiveness, getting the job done, and not giving competitors an inch. This notion of organizational values (i.e., culture) and their relationship to strategy is also illustrated in Exhibit 6–3, where McCaw has an informal, creative culture and its strategy is growth and new product development. AT&T, on the other hand, reportedly has preferences for formality and restraint, which correspond to its low-cost, low-growth strategy.

These differences are often due to managerial preferences and values. For example, an entrepreneur is a gambler who wants his company to grow at virtually all costs, often using highly risky strategies. However, a bureaucrat is risk averse and is more willing to curtail short-term growth and performance by taking strategies that maintain long-term stable growth and performance. In this context, the entrepreneur perceives the environment to be full of opportunities, whereas the bureaucrat sees mostly threats and danger. This difference in perceptions, preferences, and values can create a variety of problems. First, if the managers in a firm have different perceptions and preferences, considerable conflict can result. It is the top manager's responsibility to resolve this conflict. Second, when a consultant is advising various firms, each having top managers with uniquely different perceptions, preferences, and values, the consultant must consider these differences when formulating strategy and when presenting and implementing alternatives.

Managers also have preferences and values, and these influence the manager's strategic decisions. In fact, it is the top managers' preferences that tend to prevail over the other groups in the organization, particularly when a firm's strategy is being set. These managers also often attempt to convert the organization's preferences to theirs. Furthermore, top managers govern and direct the selection of both organizational preferences and organizational strategic direction. Therefore, they must ultimately be responsible to the "fit" between preferences and strategy. In fact, it is often the top managers' preferences that ultimately drive the strategic direction of the firm. An example of this is entrepreneurs, who tend to have preferences for high risk, optimism, and informality, which often translate into strategies involving high risk, high growth, instability, and aggressiveness. The question is whether such a strategy is appropriate for the firm's environment, resources, and organizational capabilities, or whether the top manager has hijacked the firm's strategy so that it corresponds to his or her preferences but does not correspond logically to the firm's environment, resources, and organizational capabilities.

Managers have preferences for the types and levels of goals, and where and how the company competes (i.e., competitive positions). Managerial preferences are important to strategy in other ways as well. Risk preferences influence the trade-off between risks and rewards, and determine the margin of safety sought to ensure competitive success, financial continuity, and organizational survival. Preferences about self-sufficiency influence the degree of independence sought from key stakeholders. And finally, preferences about how to lead and manage will influence the culture of the firm as these preferences shape decisions about how to keep employees committed, motivated, and loyal, and about how to best use employees' talents.

Advisers and consultants to top managers must understand the managers' preferences so that they can take into account these preferences when providing advice to them. Either the adviser should understand the manager's preferences and perspective of the firm's environment, resources, organizational capabilities, and strategic "fit," or the adviser should attempt to convince the top managers that their perspective and, therefore, preferences are errant. Changing a top manager's preferences and perspective is not easy. Often it is easier to change top managers than to convince the manager that a different preference would be appropriate.

The Relationship between Strategy and Managerial Preferences and Values

Managerial preferences and values influence strategy. For example, a preference for growth to satisfy a need for achievement or recognition can encourage managers to follow a strategy of diversification. However, the firm may lack the resources, or there may not be environmental opportunities to follow such a strategy. As a result, the managers' preferences and values are not satisfied. This leaves a gap between the preferences/values the manager holds and the preferences/values that can be satisfied (Exhibit 6–5).[8] Sometimes a gap arises

EXHIBIT 6–5   Preferences and Strategic Gap Analysis

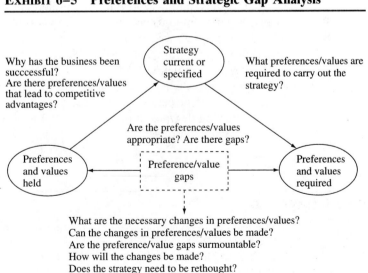

Why has the business been succcessful?
Are there preferences/values that lead to competitive advantages?

Strategy current or specified

What preferences/values are required to carry out the strategy?

Are the preferences/values appropriate? Are there gaps?

Preferences and values held

Preference/value gaps

Preferences and values required

What are the necessary changes in preferences/values?
Can the changes in preferences/values be made?
Are the preference/value gaps surmountable?
How will the changes be made?
Does the strategy need to be rethought?

from ethical standards. For example, some managers may be against the consumption of liquor because of religious background. They would likely face an ethical dilemma if asked to support or implement a strategic decision to acquire a liquor company.

When there is a major gap between the preferences/values held and preferences/values satisfied, a change in either strategy or preferences/values is required. However, it may be very difficult to close the gap. A change in strategy may not be possible without negatively affecting the strategy's fit with the environment and/or resources. A change in preferences/values may be resisted because of strongly held beliefs based on a particular educational, employment, or religious background. For example, in terms of employment background, managers who have worked most of their lives in a particular industry may have a preference for staying in that industry because they know and understand it. For such managers, a strategic decision to move into another industry is likely to create a gap between preferences/values held and preferences/values satisfied.

When a management group rather than an individual is setting a firm's strategy, there can be additional complications in assessing the fit between managerial preferences/values and strategy. In particular, when managers in the group have conflicting preferences, it becomes a problem of determining whose preferences are relevant. In most cases, the relevant preferences are those of the managers with the greatest power.

Summary

This chapter has emphasized the human element in the strategy formulation process. What seemed to be a highly rational and analytical process up to this point no longer seems so with the introduction of managerial preferences/ values, corporate culture, and stakeholder pressures. Corporate culture reflects preferences and values shared by all in the firm. A culture in which many preferences and values are shared is said to be a strong culture and may be a major source of success for the firm. Every firm has stakeholders who exert power in varying degrees in order to get the firm to satisfy their preferences, values, and expectations.

Notes to Chapter 6

1. Discussion of the personal system in relation to needs and behaviour is found in most texts dealing with organizational behaviour. One good example is Cohen, A. R.; S. L. Fink; H. Gadon; and R. Willets. *Effective Behaviour in Organizations,* 4th ed. Burr Ridge, IL.: Richard D. Irwin, 1988, chaps. 7 and 8.
2. Additional coverage of this topic can be found in MacMillan, I. C., and P. E.

Jones. *Strategy Formulation: Power and Politics.* 2nd ed. St. Paul, MN.: West Publishing, 1986.

3. Poster, B. Z., and W. H. Schmidt. "Values and the American Manager: An Update." *California Management Review,* Spring 1984, p. 206.

4. Additional sources of information on ethical questions are Freeman, R. E., and D. R. Gilbert, Jr. *Corporate Strategy and the Search for Ethics.* Englewood Cliffs, NJ.: Prentice Hall, 1988; Gellerman, S. W. "Why 'Good' Managers Make Bad Ethical Choices." *Harvard Business Review,* July–August 1986, pp. 85–90; and Nash, L. L. "Ethics without a Sermon." *Harvard Business Review,* November–December 1981, pp. 79–90.

5. The role of culture in successful business organizations has been popularized in Great Britain by Goldsmith, W., and D. Clutterback. *The Winning Streak.* Harmondsworth, Middlesex, England: Penguin Books, 1985, and in the United States by Peters, T., and R. H. Waterman. *In Search of Excellence.* New York: Harper & Row, 1982. Additional sources of information on corporate culture are Barney, J., "Organizational Culture: Can It Be a Source of Sustained Competitive Advantage?" *Academy of Management Review,* July 1986, pp. 656–65; Davis, S. *Managing Corporate Culture.* Cambridge, MA.: Ballinger, 1984; and Deal, T., and A. Kennedy. *Corporate Cultures.* Reading, MA.: Addison-Wesley, 1982.

6. The differences are described in greater detail in Kupfer, Andrew, and Kathleen C. Smyth. "AT&T's $12 Billion Cellular Dream." *Fortune,* December 12, 1994, pp. 100–12.

7. According to T. Deal and A. Kennedy, a strong culture has almost always been the driving force behind continuing success in American business. In *Corporate Cultures.* Reading, MA.: Addison-Wesley, 1982, p. 5.

8. Additional sources of information on managerial preferences are Donaldson, G., and J. W. Lorsch. *Decision Making at the Top.* New York: Basic Books, 1983, chaps. 5 and 6; Fry J. N., and J. P. Killing. *Strategic Analysis and Action.* 3rd ed. Scarborough, ON.: Prentice-Hall Canada, 1995, chap. 8; and Schwenk, C. R. "Management Illusions and Biases: Their Impact on Strategic Decisions." *Long Range Planning* 18, no. 5 (1985), pp. 74–80.

Recommended Readings

Badaracco, J. L. "Business Ethics: Four Spheres of Executive Responsibility." *California Management Review,* Spring 1992, pp. 64–79.

Morgan, Malcolm. "How Corporate Culture Drives Strategy." *Long Range Planning,* April 1993, pp. 110–18.

Savage, G. T.; T. Nix; C. J. Whitehead; and J. D. Blair. "Strategies for Assessing and Managing Organizational Stakeholders." *Academy of Management Executive,* May 1991, pp. 61–75.

Stark, Andrew. "What's the Matter with Business Ethics?" *Harvard Business Review,* May–June 1993, pp. 38–48.

7

GENERIC CORPORATE AND INTERNATIONAL STRATEGIES

On AT&T's takeover of McCaw Communications—*There's a sense of exhilaration, that we're in the middle of a whole new world and now we can't be beaten. But at the same time I feel a sense of grieving and loss . . . Do I have bureaucracy around me I didn't before? Damn right I do. I have already had meetings about logos and the position of the logos and the position of the fanciful AT&T globe. Yeah I'm frustrated. I can't just wake up in the morning and call Wayne and Craig. I have to make sure I'm not stepping on toes.*

Keith Grinstein, *President of Claircom, a Subsidiary of McCaw Communications (1994)*

While once we would have asked, "Why shouldn't we do that ourselves?" now more and more companies are asking, "Why should we do that ourselves?" Expertise and excellence come from specialization.

Michael Beer, *Professor at Harvard Business School and corporate consultant (1994)*

This chapter considers a variety of generic corporate and international strategies. There are dozens of ways of categorizing strategic decisions. Not all are appropriate for each organization. Nonetheless, there are typically more viable alternatives available than are actually considered by most managers.

Corporate Strategy

Corporate strategy focusses on the task of selecting what businesses to be in, what businesses not to be in, and what businesses to invest in further. Therefore, it really represents an investment or resource allocation strategy for the firm. This section describes the following basic categories of corporate strategic choices:

1. Diversification.
2. Integration.
3. Cooperation.
4. Retrenchment.

Diversification

Based on the extent of product line diversification, Leonard Wrigley identifies the following four types of firms: single-product, dominant-product, related-product, and unrelated-product. Each type represents a distinct corporate strategy, with measurable differences between the types in terms of their deviation from an original product technology or marketing emphasis.

In turn, the original product technology or marketing emphasis suggests an underlying skill base within the firm. This skill base or "core skill" is defined by Wrigley as "the collective knowledge, skills, habits of working together, as well as the collective experience of what the market will bear, that is required in the cadre of managerial and technical personnel if the firm is to survive and grow in a competitive market."[1]

Wrigley's four categories of firms are subdivided by Rumelt into a total of nine types, each of which is then related to performance. Significantly, firms adopting a single-business, dominant-constrained, related-constrained, or active-conglomerate strategy were observed to have above-average profitability. This held true in both a domestic context (United States, Canada) and an international context (United States multinational, European multinational).[2]

The higher performance associated with firms having a single-product, dominant-constrained, or related-constrained product diversification is intuitively consistent with the "core skill" concept. It has been frequently emphasized that successful firms "stick to their knitting."[3] The above-average profitability associated with active conglomerates—the exception to the core-skill concept—must be understood in their portfolio nature. Here, unrelated-product firms are actively bought and sold primarily on the basis of their short-term financial contribution to overall corporate profits. There are important implications for general managers of differences in the profitability levels associated with the degree of product diversification. Internally, whether a firm is considering an acquisition, a merger, or simply a change in product emphasis, the likely impact of the change upon profits can be now better assessed. External to the firm, product diversification strategy represents another tool that bankers, accountants, and investment dealers can use to assist them in assessing a firm's future profitability. The notion of relatedness of product/service has been combined with "newness" of market to produce a variety of strategic choices, as illustrated in Exhibit 7–1.

Two of these strategic directions are more related to business strategy and they were covered very briefly in that section. For completeness, this section will look at them more thoroughly. These two strategic directions are the formulation and implementation of market penetration and development strategies. The other strategic growth issues are essentially corporate strategy issues.

Market penetration involves seeking increased market share for present products or services in present markets through greater marketing efforts. It is appropriate when:[4]

EXHIBIT 7–1   Product/Market Strategic Choices

		Market Customer	
		Existing	*New*

Product/service	*Existing*
	Modified/improved
	New but related
	New and unrelated
		Market penetration
		Product
		Concentric
		Horizontal
		  diversification
			Market development
			Development
			Diversification
			Conglomerate
			  diversification

- Current markets are not saturated with the firm's particular product or service.
- The usage rate of present customers could be significantly increased.
- The market shares of major competitors have been declining while total industry sales have been increasing.
- The correlation between dollar sales and dollar marketing expenditures has historically been high.
- Increased economies of scale provide major competitive advantages.

Market development involves the introduction of present products or services into new geographic areas. It is appropriate when:

- New channels of distribution are available that are reliable, inexpensive, and of good quality.
- An organization is very successful at what it does.
- New untapped or unsaturated markets exist.
- An organization has the needed capital and human resources to manage expanded operations.
- An organization has excess production capacity.
- An organization's basic industry is rapidly becoming global in scope.

Product development involves seeking increased sales by improving or modifying present products or services, for either existing or new customers. This strategy is appropriate when:

- An organization has successful products that are in the maturity stage of their life cycles. The idea here is to attract satisfied customers to try new (improved) products as a result of their positive experience with the organization's present products or services.
- An organization competes in an industry that is characterized by rapid technological developments.
- Major competitors offer better quality products at comparable prices.
- An organization competes in a high-growth industry.

- An organization has especially strong research and development capabilities.

Concentric diversification involves the addition of new, but related, products or services for either existing or new customers. For example, Gillette's development of an array of shaving supplies and products to supplement its blade product strategy. This strategy is appropriate when:

- An organization competes in a no-growth or a slow-growth industry.
- Adding new, but related, products would significantly enhance the sales of current products.
- New, but related, products could be offered at highly competitive prices.
- New, but related, products have seasonal sales levels that counterbalance an organization's existing peaks and valleys.
- An organization's products are currently in the decline stage of their life cycles.

Horizontal diversification involves the addition of new, unrelated products or services for present customers. It is appropriate when:

- Revenues derived from an organization's current products or services would significantly increase by adding the new, unrelated products.
- An organization competes in a highly competitive and/or a no-growth industry, as indicated by low industry profit margins and returns.
- An organization's present channels of distribution can be used to market the new products to current customers.
- The new products have countercyclical sales patterns compared to an organization's present products.

Conglomerate diversification involves the addition of new, unrelated products or services for new customers. It is appropriate when:

- An organization's basic industry is experiencing declining annual sales and profits.
- An organization has the capital and managerial talent needed to compete successfully in a new industry.
- The organization has the opportunity to purchase an unrelated business that is an attractive investment opportunity.
- There exists financial synergy between the acquired and acquiring firm. Note that a key difference between concentric and conglomerate diversification is that the former should be based on some commonality in markets, products, or technology, whereas the latter should be based more on profit considerations.
- Existing markets for an organization's present products are saturated.

- An organization may have to consider new markets for growth if its market share in a specific product market is so high as to violate Canada's Competition Act.

To create shareholder wealth with any form of diversification, Porter[5] suggests the need to meet three essential tests:

1. *Industry Attractiveness Test.* The industry chosen for diversification must be an attractive one.
2. *Cost-of-Entry Test.* The cost of entry must not capitalize future profits.
3. *Better-Off Test.* Either the acquirer or acquired must gain competitive advantage.

Based on a sample of the diversification records of 33 large U.S. companies, Porter found that companies had ignored at least one or two of these tests, and "the strategic results were disastrous."[6] Most of the 33 companies had divested many more acquisitions than they had kept.

Integration

There are two basic types of integration: vertical and horizontal. Vertical integration involves a choice of integrating backward to the original supplier of goods or services, and/or integrating forward to the ultimate customer. Horizontal integration means seeking ownership or increased control over competitors in very similar markets.

Some advantages of vertical integration are to reduce vulnerability by securing supply and/or markets, or to reduce transaction costs and absorb more of the value in the chain of stages of integration. In general, vertical integration helps a business to protect profit margins and market share by ensuring access to consumers or material inputs. Some of the advantages and disadvantages of vertical integration are summarized in Exhibit 7–2.

Backward integration, that is, seeking ownership or increased control over suppliers, is appropriate when:

- An organization's present suppliers are especially expensive, unreliable, or incapable of meeting the firm's needs for parts, components, assemblies, or raw materials.
- The number of suppliers is few and the number of competitors is many.
- An organization competes in an industry that is growing rapidly; this is a factor because integrative-type strategies (forward, backward, and horizontal) reduce an organization's ability to diversify in a declining industry.
- An organization has both the capital and human resources needed to manage the new business of supplying its own raw materials.

Exhibit 7–2   Some Advantages and Disadvantages of Vertical Integration

Advantages	*Disadvantages*
Internal benefits: • Integration economies reduce costs by eliminating steps, reducing duplicate overhead, and cutting costs (technology-dependent). • Improved coordination of activities reduces inventory and other costs. • Time-consuming tasks, such as price shopping, communicating design details, or negotiating contracts, are avoided.	**Internal costs:** • Need for overhead to coordinate costs for vertical integration increases. • Burden of excess capacity from unevenly balanced minimum-efficient-scale plants (technology-dependent). • Poorly organized vertically integrated firms do not enjoy synergies that compensate for higher costs.
Competitive benefits: • Foreclosure to inputs, services, or markets is avoided. • Marketing or technological intelligence is improved. • Opportunity to create product differentiation (increased value-added). • Superior control of firm's economic environment (market power). • Credibility for new products is created. • Synergies could be created by coordinating vertical activities skilfully.	**Competitive dangers:** • Obsolete processes may be perpetuated. • Mobility (or exit) barriers created. • Links firm to sick adjacent businesses. • Access to information from suppliers or distributors is lost. • Synergies created through vertical integration may be overrated. • Managers integrated before thinking through the most appropriate way to do so.

Source: Adapted from Kathryn Rudie Harrigan, *Strategic Flexibility: A Management Guide for Changing Times* (Lexington, MA: Lexington Books, D. C. Heath and Company).

- The advantages of stable prices are particularly important. This is a factor because an organization can stabilize the cost of its raw materials and the associated price of its products through backward integration.
- Present suppliers have high profit margins, which suggests that the business of supplying products or services in the given industry is a worthwhile venture.
- An organization needs to acquire a needed resource quickly.

Forward integration, that is, gaining ownership or increased control over distributors or retailers, is appropriate when:

- An organization's present distributors are especially expensive, unreliable, or incapable of meeting the firm's distribution needs.
- The availability of quality distributors is so limited as to offer a competitive advantage to those firms that integrate forward.
- An organization competes in an industry that is growing and is expected to continue to grow markedly. This is a factor because forward integration reduces an organization's ability to diversify if its basic industry falters.

- An organization has both the capital and human resources needed to manage the new business of distributing its own products.
- The advantages of stable production are particularly high. This is a consideration because an organization can increase the predictability of the demand for its ouput through forward integration.
- Present distributors or retailers have high profit margins. This situation suggests that a company could profitably distribute its own products and price them more competitively by integrating forward.

Horizontal integration, that is, seeking ownership or increased control over competitors, is appropriate when:

- An organization can gain monopolistic characteristics in a particular area or region without being challenged by the federal government for "tending substantially" to reduce competition.
- An organization competes in a growing industry.
- Increased economies of scale provide major competitive advantages.
- An organization has both the capital and human talent needed to successfully manage an expanded organization.
- Competitors are faltering due to a lack of managerial expertise or a need for particular resources that your organization possesses; note that horizontal integration would not be appropriate if competitors are doing poorly because overall industry sales are declining.

A frequently observed method of horizontal integration is through acquisition or merger. In any acquisition or merger, four acquisition postures exist: rescues, collaborations, contested situations, and raids (see Exhibit 7–3). The most adversarial acquisition is the raid; the most cooperative, the rescue. The degree of resistance rises steadily from rescues through to raids. The need to consider carefully how to integrate a newly acquired business is often overlooked. Numerous stresses exist which, if not managed, can result in failure.

EXHIBIT 7–3   Four Acquisition Postures

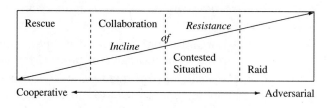

Source: Adapted from Price, Pritchett, Pritchett and Associates, Inc., *After the Merger, Managing the Shockwaves* (Burr Ridge, IL.: Dow-Jones Irwin, 1985).

Cooperation

One of the predominant trends in the past decade has been the increased use of cooperative strategies. Whether in the domestic or international market, more frequent use of joint ventures, licensing, counter trade, and technology/R&D collaboration has been observed. Characterizing these collaborative arrangements has been a willingness to either share or split managerial control in a particular undertaking.

Several opportunities for sharing can come from a cooperative strategy. These include sharing a sales force, advertising activities, manufacturing facilities, and management know-how.[7] A number of potential competitive advantages are associated with each type of opportunity for sharing, but sometimes the fit can be more illusory than real. For example, salespersons may not be as effective as expected in representing a new product. Despite the difficulties that can arise, a recent trend is the increase in cooperative arrangements between hitherto competing organizations.

Some cases in this book provide specific examples of cooperative strategies. These include cases on outsourcing (First Fidelity Bancorporation), joint ventures (Russki Adventures and Neilson Cadbury in Mexico), and technology sharing (IKEA).

The existence of so many potential cooperative strategies dramatically increases the opportunities available to Canadian businesses. There are conditions, however, that would suggest the use of one form of cooperation over another. Some of the considerations before deciding on the form of cooperation would include assessments of:

- Level of risk (e.g., creating a competitor).
- Synergies/complementary skills to be gained.
- Regulations influencing type of involvement.
- Managerial and financial resources available to go it alone.
- Speed of innovation required.

The advantages to be gained by *licensing* depend on the technology, firm size, product maturity, and extent of the firm's experience. A number of internal and external circumstances may lead a firm to employ a licensing strategy:

1. The licensee has existing products or facilities but requires technology, which may be acquired more cheaply or quickly from third parties (licensers) than by internal R&D; the need may be of limited extent or long duration.
2. The licenser wishes to exploit its technology in secondary markets that may be too small to justify larger investments; the required economies of scale may not be attainable.

3. The licensee wishes to maximize its own business by adding new technologies.

4. Host-country governments restrict imports and/or foreign direct investment (FDI), or the risk of nationalization or foreign control is too great.

5. Prospects of "technology feedback" are high (that is, the licenser has contractually assured itself of access to new developments generated by the licensee and based on licensed knowledge).

6. Licensing is a way of testing and developing a market that can later be exploited by direct investment.

7. The licensee is unlikely to become a future competitor.

8. The pace of technological change is sufficiently rapid that the licenser can remain technologically superior and ahead of the licensee, who is a potential competitor.

9. Opportunities exist for licensing auxiliary processes without having to license basic product or process technologies.

10. A firm lacks the capital and managerial resources required for exporting or FDI but wants to earn additional profits with minimum commitment.

Joint ventures are appropriate when:

- A privately owned organization is forming a joint venture with a publicly owned organization. There are some advantages of being privately held, such as close ownership; there are some advantages of being publicly held, such as access to stock issuances as a source of capital. Therefore, the unique advantages of being privately and publicly held may sometimes be synergistically combined.

- A domestic organization is forming a joint venture with a foreign company; joint venture can provide a domestic company with the opportunity for obtaining local management in a foreign country and the local managers' knowledge of the foreign economy, politics, and culture. This may also have the residual advantage of reducing risks such as expropriation and harassment by host country officials.

- The distinctive competencies of two or more firms complement each other especially well.

- Some project is potentially very profitable, but requires overwhelming resources and risks.

- Two or more smaller firms have trouble competing with a large firm.

- There exists a need to introduce a new technology quickly.

Outsourcing

A recent strategic alternative, from an investment perspective, is outsourcing. Outsourcing involves contracting out, on a long-term basis, critical competencies or tasks. An example of outsourcing is the contracting out of the computer and information services (CIS) by banks to companies specializing in these businesses. The banks realize that they do not have the expertise nor the strategic focus to provide CIS to their organization or customers. Therefore, they outsource the task to computer service firms such as IBM and EDS, which have core competencies in this particular business. In this case, outsourcing provides lower costs and better services. Critical issues to think about when considering the outsourcing option are the following:

- Is the competency or task being outsourced a core competency, and will it provide critical competitive advantages in the future?
- Will outsourcing allow the insourcer to compete with you more directly? (E.g., Intel is now competing with PC computer assemblers such as Compaq.)
- Will outsourcing provide lower costs and higher effectiveness or efficiency? Are these critical competitive advantages for the firm?
- Do the outsourcer and insourcer trust each other? How can this trust be established or built?

Retrenchment

As stated earlier, corporate and business strategy in reality cannot be separated. Here we look at how business strategies must be addressed when a corporate strategic decision to either divest or invest in a business has been taken. A corporate decision to harvest an ailing business (i.e., divest or liquidate) versus invest (i.e., retrench or turn around) is based upon the firm's competitive position and advantages as well as the future prospects for the industry. The retrenchment and turnaround strategies are based upon establishing stronger business-based competitive advantages and competitive positions. The alternatives are broadly delineated by the dimensional options discussed in Chapter 4—low cost, differentiation, and focus.

The four corporate/business strategies are discussed further below. When a business is in trouble—whether it be the result of such factors as strong, sometimes unexpected competition, technological turbulence, or escalating interest rates—a different set of strategic choices faces the general manager. An attempt can be made to turn the business around, or the business can be immediately divested or liquidated. The business can also be "harvested," which involves optimizing cash flows through such tactics as curtailing all new investments, cutting advertising expenditures, or increasing prices, until the business is sold or liquidated.

The decision of whether to attempt a turnaround depends on the kind of turnaround strategy that is likely to be successful and then whether the firm is willing to bear the risks, devote the resources, and make the management commitment associated with this particular turnaround strategy.

Turnaround strategies can be classified as follows:[8]

1. Efficiency oriented.
    a. Asset reduction (e.g., disposal of assets).
    b. Cost cutting (e.g., cutbacks in administrative, R&D, marketing expenses).
2. Entrepreneurial.
    a. Revenue generation (e.g., increase sales by product reintroduction, increased advertising, increased selling effort, lower prices).
    b. Product/market refocusing (e.g., shift emphasis into defensible or lucrative niches).

Turnarounds can follow definite stages: (1) change in management, (2) evaluation, (3) emergency, to "stop the bleeding" or "unload," (4) stabilization, emphasizing organization (i.e., building), and (5) return-to-normal growth.

Turnarounds are appropriate when an organization:

- Has a clearly distinctive competence, but has failed to meet its objectives and goals consistently over time.
- Is one of the weakest competitors in a given industry.
- Is plagued by inefficiency, low profitability, poor employee morale, and pressure from stockholders to improve performance.
- Has failed to capitalize on external opportunities, minimize external threats, take advantage of internal strengths, and overcome internal weaknesses over time; that is, when the organization's strategic managers have failed (and possibly have been replaced by more competent individuals).
- Has grown so large so quickly that major internal reorganization is needed.

Divestiture, that is, selling a division or part of an organization, is appropriate when:

- An organization has pursued a turnaround strategy and has failed to accomplish needed improvements.
- A division needs more resources to be competitive than the company can provide.
- A division is responsible for an organization's overall poor performance.
- A division is a misfit with the rest of an organization. This can result from radically different markets, customers, managers, employees, values, or needs.

- A large amount of cash is needed quickly and cannot be reasonably obtained from other sources.

Liquidation, that is, selling all of a company's assets, in parts, for their tangible worth, is appropriate when:

- An organization has pursued both a turnaround strategy and a divestiture strategy and neither has been successful.
- An organization's only alternative is bankruptcy; liquidation represents an orderly and planned means of obtaining the greatest possible cash for an organization's assets. A company can legally declare bankruptcy first and then liquidate various divisions to raise needed capital.
- The stockholders of a firm can minimize their losses by selling the organization's assets.

International Strategies and Modes of Entry

International strategic decisions cover a wide variety of problems and issues. However, some of the more basic international strategies are related to selecting an appropriate entry mode for entering a new international market, and defining how a regional strategy should be coordinated or managed relative to other regional strategies within the company.

International Strategies

Coordinating international strategies presents managers with problems that are specific to the international nature of business strategy. In general, there are two approaches to international strategic coordination, as shown in Exhibit 7–4.

The first approach requires managers to use, and thus coordinate, the same strategy in all of the firm's international regions to maximize the firm's global competitive advantage. Generally, this approach involves providing a standard product or service in all geographic regions. This approach is called a global strategy. An example of a global strategy would be a firm that designs its products in Japan because of the technical capabilities, manufactures the products in China because of the low cost of manufacturing, and sells the products in the United States and Europe where wealthy customers can most afford the products. Managers select a global strategy to try to maximize the overall global competitive advantage of the firm. A good example of global industries are the consumer electronic and computer industries where different parts of the value chain of companies are distributed throughout the world. The real challenge for a manager using this strategy is coordinating the different linked value chain entities around the world so that the firm's overall global competitive advantage is maximized.

EXHIBIT 7–4   International Strategic Positions and Coordination

---

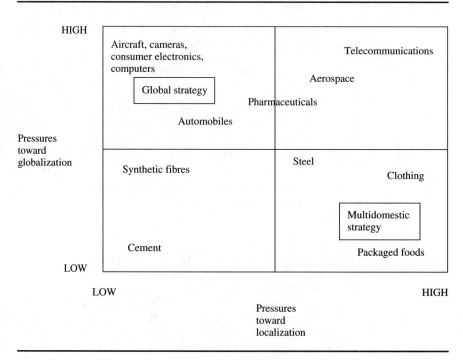

Source: Reprinted with permission. P. Beamish, P. Killing, D. Lecraw, and A. Morrison, *International Management: Text and Cases,* 2nd ed. (Burr Ridge, IL.: Irwin, 1994).

The second approach requires managers to coordinate and manage different strategies in different international regions. This approach, called a multidomestic strategy, emphasizes the different regional aspects of business and the marketplace. A manager would take a multidomestic approach if all of the firm's regional markets had different customer tastes, different distribution networks, different marketing approaches, and/or different product standards. In this situation, each region must be given the responsibility to carry out its own product development, manufacturing, and selling so that it most effectively meets the needs of the customers. A good example of this type of business is the packaged-processed food industry because the content, packaging, and distribution channels vary considerably between markets. The challenge facing a manager using this strategy is to coordinate the various international strategies so that the brand image is strongly supported, but to diversify decision making and primary value chain activities into the regions in an effective yet economic manner.

The forces that dictate whether a firm takes a multidomestic, global, or intermediate international strategic position depends upon the pressures of globalization and localization. Pressures for globalization are associated with

EXHIBIT 7–5   International Strategic Modes of Entry

Mode	Reasons for Taking Mode	Potential Risks of Using Mode
Licensing Agreement	• Requires few resources, particularly capital. • Potentially can get an agreement with a firm having the missing resources (e.g., manufacturing or sales force). • May be the only way for a small company to enter international markets if the product or service does not transport easily. • Circumvents import duties and quotes. • The licensing firm has minimal risk of income loss because the operational costs are being supported by the licenser.	• Neither party has complete long-term strategic control over the development of the product. • One party may put in more effort than the other party.
Exporting	• Requires more resources than licensing but fewer than joint venture and wholly owned subsidiary. • May be a good method for a small company to take if the product or service does transport easily.	• May incur extra costs associated with transporting, duties, or volume restrictions related to quotas.
Joint venture	• Requires more resources than licensing or exporting, but fewer than a wholly owned subsidiary. • The firm shares any income losses wth its partners. • The potential for learning from the partners is maximized.	• The relationship may not last because of differing long-term objectives or values. • Operational and capital losses can be higher than in the licensing and exporting options because of greater ownership and operational involvement. • The joint venture partner(s) and possibly future competitor(s) may have access to proprietary information and resources in your company.
Wholly owned subsidiary	• The firm has complete control of the product or service from inception through sales and distribution. • The firm captures all of the profit potential of the product or service.	• The firm risks income losses if the product or service does not do well.

industries that have extremely intense international competitive pressures, whose regional market characteristics are uniform, and whose regional competitive advantages provide a firm with international competitive advantages. Pressures for localization are where regional market characteristics are very different, and regional competitive advantages do not provide firms with strong international competitive advantages. Product, service, and knowledge transferability in the industry are also quite important in the global business position, because if you manufacture goods in Asia but cannot transport them effectively or efficiently to North America, then this strategy becomes less viable.

Some companies must take a dual strategic approach. An example of this is the telecommunications industry where firms must use global technological competitive advantages, yet cater to individual market tastes, product standards, and distribution requirements. This often puts extra pressure on the managers because they have to coordinate a much more complex set of strategic alternatives.

It must also be noted that the global and multidomestic strategies are associated with different types of international organizational structures. Such structures are delineated in Chapter 9.

International Strategic Mode Alternatives

Mode selection involves a complex trade-off decision between having enough new market knowledge, having sufficient resources to support the entry mode, preferring more ownership and management control, and minimizing financial risks. Some of the concerns specifically related to the various entry modes are delineated in Exhibit 7–5.

Notes to Chapter 7

1. Wrigley, Leonard, "Divisional Autonomy and Diversification." Doctoral dissertation, Harvard University, 1970.
2. For more details, see Geringer, J. M.; Paul W. Beamish; and R. da Costa. "Diversification Strategy and Internationalization: Implications for MNE Performance." *Strategic Management Journal* 10, no. 2 (March/April 1989), 109–19.
3. See Peters, Thomas J., and Robert H. Waterman. *In Search of Excellence.* New York: Harper & Row, 1982.
4. The conditions for the various strategic choices outlined in Exhibit 6–1 and in the integration, cooperation, and retrenchment sections of this chapter have been reprinted by permission from David, F. R. "How Do We Choose among Alternative Growth Strategies?" *Managerial Planning* 33, no. 4 (January–February 1985), pp. 14–17, 22.

5. For more details see Porter, Michael E. "From Competitive Advantage to Corporate Strategy." *Harvard Business Review,* May–June 1987, pp. 43–59.

6. Ibid., p. 46.

7. For more examples, see Porter, Michael E. *Competitive Advantage: Creating and Sustaining Superior Performance.* New York: The Free Press, 1985, chap. 9.

8. For a more complete analysis of these turnaround strategies, see Hambrick, Donald C., and Steven M. Schecter. "Turnaround Strategies for Mature Industrial Product Business Units." *Academy of Management Journal,* June 1983, pp. 231–48.

Recommended Readings

Beamish, Paul: Peter Killing; Donald Lecraw; and Allen Morrison. *International Management.* 2nd ed. Burr Ridge, IL., Irwin, 1994.

See Deming, W. E. *Out of the Crisis.* Cambridge, MA.: MIT Press, 1986, p. 31.

Hu, Yao-Su. "Global Corporations are National Firms with International Operations." *California Management Review,* Winter 1992, pp. 66–87.

See Porter, Michael E. *Competitive Strategy: Techniques for Analyzing Industries and Competitors.* New York: The Free Press, 1980, chap 11.

Sadtler, David R. "Brief Case: The Role of Today's Board in Corporate Strategy." *Long Range Planning,* August 1993, pp. 112–13.

8

ORGANIZATIONAL DESIGN

Those rules aimed at 1% of the employees handcuff the other 99%. Nobody can do all the stuff in the book, so people end up following just one official objective: Keep the boss happy . . . I make sure the reward system changes to support the key results. Ninety percent of all (organizational) cultural conflicts exist because of conflicts in measures and rewards.

Jerry Stead, *CEO of AT&T Global Information Solutions* (1994)

On customer ordering problems—I'd talk to every person who touched that order, looking for the person to kick. I'd talk to four people—and all four people did their job. After three trips of not being able to kick somebody I said this is crazy. It isn't the people.

Doug Cahill, *General Manager of Great Lakes Chemicals* (1994)

To implement any strategy, certain organizational actions must be taken. In this chapter, we review the major components for the design of organizations.

The major organization design variables significant in implementing strategy are structure, information and decision processes, reward systems, and staffing and leadership style (see Exhibit 8–1).

Structure

Structure can be viewed as "the design of organization through which the enterprise is administered."[1] Structure is more than an organizational chart. Here it is viewed as having three elements: division of labour (amount of role differentiation), shape (span of control and number of layers), and distribution of power (both vertical and horizontal, explicit and implicit).

Organizational structure is considered more fully in Chapter 9. However, a manager establishes an organizational structure that is appropriate for its strategy and most effectively allows the people in the organization to carry

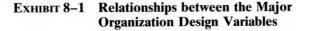

EXHIBIT 8–1   Relationships between the Major Organization Design Variables

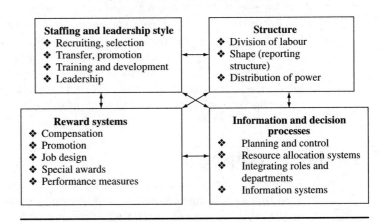

Source: Adapted from Jay Galbraith and Robert Kazanjian, *Strategy Implementation*, 2nd ed. (St. Paul, MN: West Publishing Company, 1986), p. 115.

out the necessary processes, activities, and decisions. This chapter will initially concentrate on considering the organizational processes and systems that a manager must consider.

Information and Decision Processes

"Across the structure, processes are overlaid to allocate resources and coordinate activities not handled by the department structure."[2] These information and decision processes include planning and control systems (for such things as budgets, schedules, and forecasts), integrating mechanisms (particularly necessary when the task context is one of high interdependence between the functional areas), and information systems (be they computerized, statistical, or informal). In any organization it is critically important that the information and knowledge pertinent to a specific decision be provided to the decision maker making that decision. This means that decision processes must either be decentralized or information processes must convey critical information to the individuals making the decisions.

Reward Systems

Perhaps the most easily understood element of organization design is reward systems. Decisions on compensation packages (however they are composed), on promotions (accompanied with any combination of such things are bigger offices, more status, a free parking space, increased holidays, a private secretary, and so forth), on ways of awarding outstanding performance, and on the design of jobs (and who gets the more interesting or high-profile assignments), all can be designed in such a way as to reinforce desired behaviour.

Managers design reward systems so that individuals and teams focus on the firm's strategic objectives. The eventual design must consider and support job efficiency and effectiveness, core competitive advantages and positions, and individual as well as group values, preferences, and expectations. Often these diverse needs are difficult to fulfill in a large, complex company that is facing ever-changing environmental and strategic forces. However, reward systems are critical indicators and motivators for employees in an organization.

Staffing and Leadership Style

People are critically important to an organization's success and long-term performance. Getting (recruiting and selecting), grooming (training and developing), and retaining (transferring or promoting) personnel are critical activities in every organization. All of these activities ensure that a company hires and retains the most motivated, skilled, and effective people in its organization because managers realize that an organization is only as good as the people in it over the long term.

Training and developing skills is becoming particularly important to firms because of the advent of new technology and processes. Pertinent skills for personnel in a firm range from general business skills, to industry-specific knowledge, firm-specific knowledge, and job- or task-specific knowledge and skills. As one moves higher in the organization, a broader spectrum of these skills is required, yet it is more task-specific skills that often have to be taught at the lower levels in an organization.

Top managers also have leadership styles that help motivate and direct employees to fulfill the firm's objectives. The classical leadership dimensions in the business literature are identified in Exhibit 8–2. These dimensions are structural, considerate, autocratic, democratic, transactional, and transformational. It should be noted that the styles of the first and third dimensions are not necessarily mutually exclusive. In other words, a leader can have qualities of both the structural and considerate styles or of the transactional and transformational styles simultaneously. The styles of the second dimension—autocratic and democratic—are mutually exclusive in that a leader must take a specific approach in a certain situation because being autocratic does not allow him or her to be democratic.

Other dimensions that are important to consider in leaders are their knowledge and experience in the industry and company, their risk preferences, their creativity, and their intrinsic motivation to get the job done. Since leadership styles are not easily changed, it is important for a firm to select an appropriate leadership style for its particular strategic situation and organizational characteristics.

EXHIBIT 8–2   Dimensions of Leadership Style

The Structural and the Considerate Leadership Dimension

A *structural leadership* dimension involves focusing on basic managerial functions such as planning, coordinating, and controlling. The focus is on achieving activity results. Typical behaviour includes emphasizing deadlines and the quantity and quality of work to be accomplished. Such an approach is particularly useful if employees know what they have to do, little interaction is required between tasks and the manager, the job can be objectively measured and evaluated, the task is mundane and repetitive, or the organizational culture and employees are very logical and structured in their social thinking and activity patterns.

A *considerate leadership* dimension involves focusing on building mutual trust with subordinates, respecting their ideas, and showing concern for their ideas. The leader is friendly towards subordinates, engages in two-way conversations, and expresses concern about their welfare. Such an approach can be appropriate when the task is very difficult to measure and evaluate, the employee is learning about the task and social structure in the organization, the task involves intimate contact with others including the manager, or when the organizational culture and employee are emotional in their social, thinking, and activity patterns.

The Autocratic versus the Democratic Leadership Dimension
(Note: most leadership styles fall somewhere between the two extremes)

An *autocratic leadership* dimension is where the leader tends to make unilateral decisions, dictate work methods, provide only short-term goals, and give feedback only when things go wrong. This type of leadership style is sometimes necessary when a firm faces a crisis and immediate action is required.

A *democratic leadership* dimension is where a leader involves group members in decision making and the determination of work methods, provides longer term objectives, and gives complete information feedback and coaching. A democratic leadership style is almost essential when the critical knowledge in the organization is dispersed throughout the employees in the organization. This is the case in law and consulting firms, for example.

The Transactional and the Transformational Motivational Leadership Dimension

The *transactional leadership* dimension involves motivating employees to perform to expected levels of performance by clarifying responsibilities and the means to achieve their goals, and by exchanging rewards for performance. This type of leadership style may be best suited to motivating employees who are involved with repetitive, mundane tasks and whose output is easily measured.

The *transformational leadership* dimension involves motivating employees to transcend expected levels of performance by articulating a compelling vision of the future that is consistent with their values, and inspiring them to focus on broader missions that go beyond their immediate self-interest. Transformational leaders provide subordinates or "followers" with individual consideration by engaging them in activities that are tailored to their individual needs and will contribute to their personal development. They stimulate followers intellectually by offering them new ideas and encouraging them to think in new ways about old problems. This type of leadership dimension may be particularly important for firms going through change or taking a leadership role in the development of their industry.

Source: Adapted from the personal notes of C. Shea, 1995.

Probably the greatest failing when organizations are designed is the lack of consistency between (a) the organization design variables themselves and (b) the strategy variables as formulated. Also, if the strategy changes, all of the design variables may need to be adjusted to maintain the desired consistency and fit.

Specific examples of recommended configurations of strategy and organi-

---

EXHIBIT 8–3   Strategy–Organization Fit

Strategy	*Dominant Business: Vertically Integrated*	*Unrelated Diversified: Growth through Acquisition*	*Related Diversified: Growth through Internal Development, Some Acquisition*
Strategic focus and task focus	Degree of integration Market share Product line breadth	Degree of diversity Types of business Resource allocation across discrete businesses Entry and exit businesses	Realization of synergy from related products, processes, technologies, markets Resource allocation Diversification opportunities
Structure and decision-making style	Centralized functional Top control of strategic decisions Delegation of operations through plans and procedures	Highly decentralized product divisions/profit centers Small corporate office No centralized line functions Almost complete delegation of operations and strategy within existing businesses Control through results, selection of management, and capital allocation	Multidivisional/profit centers Grouping of highly related business with some centralized functions within groups Delegated responsibility for operations Shared responsibility for strategy
Information and decision process	Coordination and integration through structure, rules, planning, and budgeting Use of integrating roles for project activity across functions	No integration across businesses Coordination and information flows between corporate and division levels around management information systems and budgets	Coordinate and integrate across businesses and between levels with planning, integrating roles, integrating departments
Rewards	Performance against functional objectives Mix of objective and subjective performance measures	Formula-based bonus on ROI or profitability of divisions Equity rewards Strict objective, impersonal evaluation	Bonus based on divisional and corporate profit performance Mix of objective and subjective performance measures
People and careers	Primarily functional specialists Some interfunctional movement to develop some general managers	Aggressive, independent general managers of divisions Career development opportunities are primarily intradivisional	Broad requirements for general managers and integrators Career developments cross functional, interdivisional, and corporate-divisional

Source: Reprinted with permission. Jay Galbraith and Robert Kazanjian, *Strategy Implementation* (St. Paul, MN: West Publishing Company, 1986), pp. 116–7.

zational variables that constitute a fit are shown in Exhibit 8–3 for three broad strategies: single or dominant business, related diversified, and unrelated diversified.

How Structure Evolves as Strategy Evolves: The Stages Models

In a number of respects, the strategist's approach to organization building is governed by the size and growth stage of the enterprise, as well as by the key success factors inherent in the organization's business. For instance, the type of organization structure that suits a small specialty steel firm relying upon a concentration strategy in a regional market is not likely to be suitable for a large, vertically integrated steel producer doing business in geographically diverse areas. The organization form that works best in a multiproduct, multi-technology, multibusiness corporation pursuing unrelated diversification is, understandably, likely to be different yet again. Recognition of this characteristic has prompted several attempts to formulate a model linking changes in organizational structure to stages in an organization's strategic development.[3]

The underpinning of the stages concept is that enterprises can be arrayed along a continuum running from very simple to very complex organizational forms and that there is a tendency for an organization to move along this continuum toward more complex forms as it grows in size, market coverage, and product-line scope and as the strategic aspects of its customer-technology/business portfolio become more intricate. Four distinct stages of strategy-related organization structure have been singled out.

Stage I.   A Stage I organization is essentially a small, single-business enterprise managed by one person. The owner-entrepreneur has close daily contact with employees and each phase of operations. Most employees report directly to the owner, who makes all the pertinent decisions regarding objectives, strategy, daily operations, and so on. As a consequence, the organization's strengths, vulnerabilities, and resources are closely allied with the entrepreneur's personality, management ability and style, and personal financial situation. Not only is a Stage I enterprise an extension of the interests, abilities, and limitations of its owner-entrepreneur but also its activities are typically concentrated in just one line of business. For the most part, Stage I enterprises are organized very simply with nearly all management decisions and functions being performed by the owner-entrepreneur.

Stage II.   Stage II organizations differ from Stage I enterprises in one essential respect: An increased scale and scope of operations create a pervasive strategic need for management specialization and force a transition from one-person management to group management. However, a Stage II enterprise, although run by a team of managers with functionally specialized responsibilities, remains fundamentally a single-business operation. This is not to imply, though, that the categories of management specialization are uniform among large, single-business enterprises. In practice, there is wide variation. Some Stage II organizations prefer to divide strategic responsibilities along classic functional lines—marketing, production, finance, personnel, control, engineering, public relations, procurement, planning, and so on. In vertically integrated Stage II companies, the main organization units are sequenced according to the flow from one vertical stage to another. For example, the organizational building blocks of a large oil company usually consist of exploration, drilling, pipelines, refining, wholesale distribution, and retail sales. In a process-oriented Stage II company, the functional units are sequenced in the order of the steps of the production process.

Stage III. Stage III embraces those organizations whose operations, although concentrated in a single field or product line, are large enough and scattered over a wide enough geographical area to justify having *geographically decentralized* operating units. These units all report to corporate headquarters and conform to corporate policies, but they are given the flexibility to tailor their unit's strategic plan to meet the specific needs of each respective geographic area. Ordinarily, each of the semi-autonomous operating units of a Stage III organization is structured along functional lines.

The key difference between Stage II and Stage III, however, is that while the functional units of a Stage II organization stand or fall together (in that they are built around one business and one end market), the operating units of a Stage III firm can stand alone (or nearly so) in the sense that the operations in each geographic unit are not rigidly tied to or dependent on those in other areas. Characteristic firms in this category would be breweries, cement companies, and steel mills having production capacity and sales organizations in several geographically separate market areas.

Stage IV. Stage IV is typified by large, multiproduct, multiunit, multimarket enterprises decentralized by line of business. Their corporate strategies emphasize diversification—related and/or unrelated. As with Stage III companies, the semi-autonomous operating units report to a corporate headquarters and conform to certain firm-wide policies, but the divisional units pursue their own respective line-of-business strategies. Typically, each separate business unit is headed by a general manager who has profit-and-loss responsibility and whose authority extends across all of the unit's functional areas except, perhaps, accounting and capital investment (both of which are traditionally subject to corporate approval). Both business-strategy decisions and operating decisions are thus concentrated at the line-of-business level rather than at the corporate level. The organization structure within the line-of-business unit may be along the lines of Stage I, II, or III types of organizations. A characteristic Stage IV company would be Canadian Pacific.

Movement through the Stages. The stages model provides useful insights into why organization structure tends to change in accordance with product/

customer-technology relationships and new directions in corporate strategy. As firms have progressed from small, entrepreneurial enterprises following a basic concentration strategy to more complex strategic phases of volume expansion, vertical integration, geographic expansion, and line-of-business diversification, their organizational structures have evolved from dysfunctional to functionally centralized to multidivisional, decentralized organizational forms. Firms that remain single-line businesses almost always have some form of a centralized functional structure. Enterprises predominantly in one industry but slightly diversified typically have a hybrid structure; the dominant business is managed via a functional organization, and the diversified activities are handled through a decentralized, divisionalized form. The more diversified an organization becomes, irrespective of whether the diversification is along related or unrelated lines, the more it moves toward some form of decentralized business units.

However, it is by no means imperative that organizations begin at Stage I and move in irreversible lock-step sequence toward Stage IV.[4] Some firms have moved from a Stage II organization to a Stage IV form without ever passing through Stage III. And some organizations exhibit characteristics of two or more stages simultaneously. Furthermore, some companies have found it desirable to revert to more centralized forms after decentralizing.

Still, it does appear that as the strategic emphasis shifts from a small, single-product business to large, dominant-product businesses and then on to broad diversification, a firm's organizational structure evolves, in turn, from one-person management to large group functional management to decentralized, line-of-business management. About 90 percent of the Fortune 500 firms (nearly all of which are diversified to one degree or another) have a divisionalized organization structure with the primary basis for decentralization being line-of-business considerations.

Exhibit 8–4 summarizes some of the common organizational changes required in the transition from Stage I to Stage IV.

One final lesson that the stages model teaches is worth iterating. A reassessment of organization structure and authority is always useful whenever strategy is changed.[5] A new strategy is likely to entail new or subtly different skills and key activities. If these changes go unrecognized, especially the subtle ones, the resulting mismatch between strategy and organization can pose implementation problems and curtail performance.

Organizational Reengineering

Organizational reengineering is a management technique that has been effective in increasing the efficiency of some organizations. Organizations that are particularly appropriate for reengineering include organizations that are large and bureaucratic, have not changed in many years, or where modern technological and business system changes have not been adopted. The objective of

---

EXHIBIT 8–4   Common Organizational Changes Required in Transitions

	Entrepreneurial Single Business-Stage I to Professional Single Business-Stage II	*Professional Single Business-Stage II to Professional Multibusiness-Stages III & IV*
Structure	Move from ill-defined functional specialization to well-articulated functions. Almost total centralization converted to substantial functional responsibility, authority. Integration by entrepreneur gives way to various integrating devices.	Move from functional to product/market (business unit) specialization. Development of corporate functions to manage business unit portfolio. Delegation of operating and some strategic discretion to units. Integration across units by corporate functions.
Business-decision processes	Move planning and resource allocation from an extension of entrepreneurial preferences to more objective processes. Increasing use of functional (sales, costs to budget) performance criteria.	Move planning and resource allocation focus from functional departments to business units. Strategic goals (market share, profits) used to assess and control businesses.
Personnel-decision processes	Move to more systematic procedures and objective criteria for staffing, training, and assessing individual performance. Rewards less subject to personal relationships, paternalism.	Further development of systematic procedures with broadening to emphasize the development of general managers. Rewards variable in relation to business unit performance.
Leadership style	Move from a personally oriented, hands-on domination of operations to a less obtrusive style emphasizing leadership and integration of functional units relative to strategic needs.	Senior management further distanced from operations. Symbolic and context-setting aspects of style become more critical. Leadership in relation to corporate business unit strategic needs.

Source: Adapted and used with permission. J. N. Fry and J. P. Killing, *Strategic Analysts and Action,* 2nd ed. (Scarborough, ON.: Prentice-Hall Canada, 1989), fig. 10.8, p. 226.

organizational reengineering is to make the organization more efficient and effective at focusing on the customers' needs and desires. Some of the characteristics of the reengineered organization can include the following:

- Customer satisfaction drives all processes in the organization.
- The company is organized around processes, not functions.
- The organization has a flatter structure.
- Interdisciplinary teams are used to manage many things across functional boundaries.
- Teams and personnel are rewarded based on process performance.
- Responsibility and appropriate training are provided to all members.

Many companies are now considering the organizational reengineering process in place of downsizing or just layoffs. The process for completing reengineering involves the following steps:

1. Get all of the top managers enthusiastically behind the move from a functional orientation to a process orientation. This is often one of the most difficult steps.

2. Analyse and identify key processes that support core competitive advantages and that support customer product and service desires. Each of the processes should be linked to a customer product or service outcome.

3. Organize the business around the processes, not functions. This means that the processes will normally be completed by multifunctional teams. All processes should be directly linked to the customer in some way.

4. Eliminate unnecessary activities or steps in these key processes, and eliminate unnecessary processes in the organization that do not support these objectives. This step will also hopefully cut the number of employees in functional and staff departments to a minimum, although key expertise should be preserved.

5. Appoint a manager as the "owner" of each key process, and empower employees by giving them the necessary information and allow them to have responsibility for changing the process and achieving the process's goals.

6. Revamp the reward system so that it supports the team that gets the process done most efficiently and effectively. Rewards should also be given for retraining, flexibility, and creativity in designing and accomplishing the process. Performance objectives must be set on a regular basis and they must be linked to customer satisfaction.

Notes to Chapter 8

1. Chandler, A. D., *Strategy and Structure*. Cambridge, MA.: MIT Press, 1962, p. 14.

2. Galbraith, Jay R. and Robert K. Kazanjian. *Strategy Implementation,* ed. St. Paul, MN.: West Publishing, 1986, p. 114.

3. See, for example, Salter, Malcolm S., "Stages of Corporate Development." *Journal of Business Policy*, Spring 1970, pp. 23–27; Thain, Donald H. "Stages of Corporate Development." *Business Quarterly*, Winter 1969, pp. 32–45; Scott, Bruce R. "The Industrial State: Old Myths and New Realities." *Harvard Business Review,* March-April 1973, pp. 133–48; and Chandler, *Strategy and Structure,* chap. 1.

4. For a more thorough discussion of this point, see Salter, "Stages of Corporate Development," pp. 34–35.

5. For an excellent documentation of how a number of well-known corporations revised their organizational structures to meet the needs of strategy changes and specific product/market developments, see Corey, E. R., and S. H. Star, *Organization Strategy*. Boston, MA.: Division of Research, Harvard University Graduate School of Business Administration, 1971, chap. 3.

Recommended Readings

Fry, Joseph N., and J. Peter Killing. *Strategic Analysis and Action.* Scarborough, ON.: Prentice-Hall Canada, 1986, p. 202.

Garvin, David. "Building a Learning Organization." *Harvard Business Review,* July-August 1993, pp. 78–91.

Ghoshal, Sumantra, and Christopher Bartlett. "Changing the Role of Top Management: Beyond Structure to Process." *Harvard Business Review*, Part I November-December 1994, and Part II January-February 1995.

Hammer, Michael, and James Champy. *Reengineering the Corporation.* New York: Harper Collins, 1993.

This section has been adapted in part from Thompson, Arthur A., Jr., and A. J. Strickland III. *Strategy Formulation and Implementation.* 3rd ed. Plano, TX.: Business Publications, 1986, pp. 330–34.

ORGANIZATIONAL FORMS

On effective organizational form—*An organization so flat you could stick it under the door.*

Doug Cahill, *General Manager of Great Lakes Chemicals (1994)*

On describing an ineffective organizational form—*Hierarchy is a prosthesis for trust.*

Warren Bennis, *Business Professor at USC and Corporate Consultant (1994)*

There are essentially four strategy-related approaches to organization: (1) functional specialization, (2) geographic organization, (3) decentralized business/product divisions, and (4) matrix structures featuring *dual* lines of authority and strategic priority. Each form relates structure to strategy in a different way and, consequently, has its own set of strategy-related pros and cons. Each of these forms will now be discussed.

The Functional Organization Structure

A functional organization structure tends to be effective in single-business units where key activities revolve around well-defined skills and areas of specialization. In such cases, in-depth specialization and focused concentration on performing functional area tasks and activities can enhance both operating efficiency and the development of a distinctive competence. Generally speaking, organizing by functional specialties promotes full utilization of the most up-to-date technical skills and helps a business capitalize on the efficiency gains to be had from using specialized personnel, facilities, and equipment. These are strategically important considerations for single-business organizations, dominant product enterprises, and vertically integrated firms, and account for why they usually have some kind of centralized, functionally specialized structure.

However, just what form the functional specialization will take varies according to customer–product–technology considerations. For instance, a technical instruments manufacturer may be organized around research and development, engineering, production, technical services, quality control, marketing, personnel, and finance and accounting. A municipal government may, on the other hand, be departmentalized according to purposeful function—fire, public safety, health services, water and sewer, streets, parks and recreation, and education. A university may divide up its organizational units into academic affairs, student services, alumni relations, athletics, buildings and grounds, institutional services, and budget control. Two types of functional organizational approaches are diagrammed in Exhibit 9–1.

EXHIBIT 9–1   Functional Organizational Structures

A. The building blocks of a "typical" functional organization structure

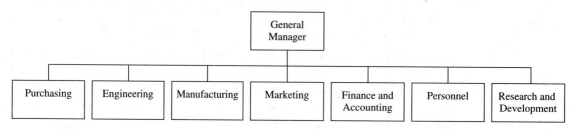

B. The building blocks of a process-oriented functional structure

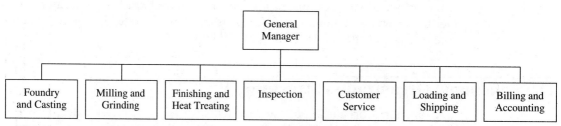

Advantages
- Enhances operating efficiency where tasks are routine and repetitive
- Preserves centralized control of strategic results
- Allows benefits of specialization and learning/experience curve effects to be fully exploited
- Simplifies training of management specialists
- Promotes high emphasis on craftsmanship and professional standards
- Well-suited to developing distinctive competencies in one or more functional areas
- Structure is tied to key activities within the business

Disadvantages
- Poses problems of functional coordination
- Can lead to interfunctional rivalry, conflict, and empire building
- May promote overspecialization and narrow management viewpoints
- Limited development of general managers
- Forces profit responsibility to the top
- Functional specialists often attach more importance to what is best for the functional area than to what is best for the whole business
- May lead to uneconomically small units or underutilization of specialized facilities and manpower
- Functional myopia often works against creative entrepreneurship, against adapting to change, and against attempts to restructure the activity-cost chain that threatens the status of one or more functional departments

The Achilles' heel of a functional structure is getting and keeping tight strategic coordination across the separated functional units. Functional specialists, partly because of how they are trained and the technical "mystique" of jobs, tend to develop their own mind-set and ways of doing things. The more functional specialists differ in their perspectives and their approaches to task accomplishment, the more difficult it becomes to achieve both strategic and operating coordination between them. They neither "talk the same language" nor have an adequate understanding of and appreciation for one another's strategic role, problems, and changed circumstances. Each functional group is more interested in its own "empire" and promoting its own strategic interest and importance (despite the lip service given to cooperation and "what's best for the company"). Tunnel vision and empire building in functional departments impose a time-consuming administrative burden on a general manager in terms of resolving cross-functional differences, enforcing joint cooperation, and opening lines of communication. In addition, a purely functional organization tends to be myopic when it comes to promoting entrepreneurial creativity, adapting quickly to major customer–market–technological changes, and pursuing opportunities that go beyond the conventional boundaries of the industry.

Geographic Forms of Organization

Organizing according to geographic areas or territories is a rather common structural form for large-scale enterprises whose strategies need to be tailored to fit the particular needs and features of different geographical areas. As indicated in Exhibit 9–2, geographic organization has its advantages and disadvantages, but the chief reason for its popularity is that, for one reason or another, it promotes improved performance.

In the private sector, a territorial structure is typically utilized by chain store retailers, power companies, cement firms, railroads, airlines, the larger paper-box and carton manufacturers, and large bakeries and dairy products enterprises. In the public sector, such organizations as the Canadian Red Cross and religious groups have adopted territorial structures in order to be directly accessible to geographically dispersed clienteles.

Decentralized Business Units

Grouping activities along business and product lines has been a clear-cut trend among diversified enterprises for the past half century, beginning with the pioneering efforts of Du Pont and General Motors in the 1920s. Separate business/product divisions emerged because diversification made a functionally specialized manager's job incredibly complex. Imagine the problems a manufacturing executive and his or her staff would have if put in charge of, say, 50 different plants using 20 different technologies to produce 30 different

EXHIBIT 9–2   A Geographic Organization Structure

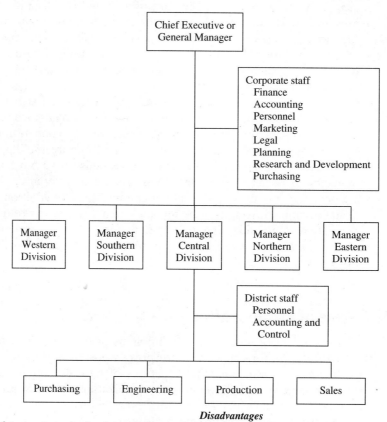

Advantages
- Allows tailoring of strategy to needs of each geographic market
- Delegates profit/loss responsibility to lowest strategic level
- Improves functional coordination within the target geographic market
- Takes advantage of economies of local operations
- Area units make an excellent training ground to higher level general managers

Disadvantages
- Greater difficulty in maintaining consistent and uniform companywide practices
- Requires a larger management staff, especially general managers
- Leads to duplication of staff services
- Poses a problem of headquarters control over local operations

products in 8 different businesses/industries. In a multibusiness enterprise, the needs of strategy virtually dictate that the organizational sequence be corporate to line of business to functional area within a business rather than corporate to functional area (aggregated for all businesses). The latter produces a nightmare in making sense out of business strategy and achieving functional area coordination for a given business.

EXHIBIT 9–3   A Decentralized Business Division Type of Organization Structure

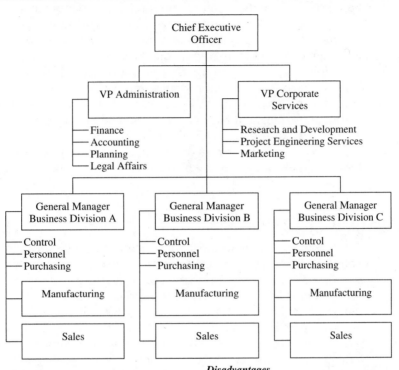

Advantages
- Offers a logical and workable means of decentralizing responsibility and delegating authority in diversified organizations
- Puts responsibility for business strategy in closer proximity to each business's unique environment
- Allows critical tasks and specialization to be organized to fit business strategy
- Frees CEO to handle corporate strategy issues
- Creates clear profit/loss accountability

Disadvantages
- Leads to proliferation of staff functions, policy inconsistencies between divisions, and problems of coordination of divisional operations
- Poses a problem of how much authority to centralize and how much to decentralize
- May lead to excessive divisional rivalry for corporate resources and attention
- Raises issue of how to allocate corporate-level overhead
- Business/division autonomy works against achieving coordination of related activities in different business units, thus blocking, to some extent, the capture of strategic fit benefits

From a business strategy implementation standpoint, it is far more logical to group all the different activities that belong to the same business under one organization roof, thereby creating line-of-business units (which, then, can be subdivided into whatever functional subunits suit the key activities/ critical tasks makeup of the business). The outcome not only is a structure that fits strategy but is also a structure that makes the jobs of managers more doable. The creation of separate business units (or strategic business units—SBUs—as they are sometimes called) is then accomplished by decentralizing authority over the unit to the business-level manager. The approach, very simply, is to put entrepreneurially oriented general managers in charge of the business unit, giving them enough authority to formulate and implement the business strategy that they deem appropriate, motivating them with incentives, and then holding them accountable for the results they produce. However, when a strong strategic fit exists across related business units, it can be tough to get autonomy-conscious business-unit general managers to cooperate in coordinating and sharing related activities; each GM tends to want to argue long and hard about "turf" and about being held accountable for activities not totally under his or her control.

A typical line-of-business organization structure is shown in Exhibit 9–3, along with the strategy-related pros and cons of this type of organization form.

Matrix Forms of Organization

A matrix form of organization is a structure with two (or more) channels of command, two lines of budget authority, two sources of performance and reward, and so forth. The key feature of the matrix is that product (or business) and functional lines of authority are overlaid (to form a matrix or grid), and managerial authority over the activities in each unit/cell of the matrix is shared between the product manager and the functional manager, as shown in Exhibit 9–4. In a matrix structure, subordinates have a continuing dual assignment: to the business/product line/project and to their base function.[1] The outcome is a compromise between functional specialization (engineering, R&D, manufacturing, marketing, or accounting) and product line or market segment or line-of-business specialization (where all of the specialized talents needed for the product line/market segment/line of business are assigned to the same divisional unit).

A matrix-type organization is a genuinely different structural form and represents a "new way of life." One reason is that the unit-of-command principle is broken; two reporting channels, two bosses, and shared authority create a new kind of organization climate. In essence, the matrix is a conflict resolution system through which strategic and operating priorities are negotiated, power is shared, and resources are allocated internally on a "strongest case for what is best overall for the unit" type basis.[2]

The impetus for matrix organizations stems from growing use of strategies that add new sources of diversity (products, customer groups, technology, and lines of business) to a firm's range of activities. Out of this diversity come product managers, functional managers, geographic-area managers, new venture managers, and business-level managers—all of whom have important *strategic* responsibilities. When at least two of several variables (product, customer, technology, geography, functional area, and market segment) have roughly equal strategic priorities, then a matrix theoretically can be an effective

Exhibit 9–4   A Matrix Organization Structure

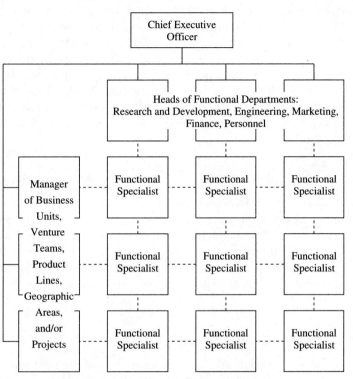

Advantages
- Permits more attention to each dimension of strategic priority
- Creates checks and balances among competing viewpoints
- Facilitates simultaneous pursuit of different types of strategic initiative
- Promotes making trade-off decisions on the basis of "what's best for the organization as a whole"
- Encourages cooperation, consensus building, conflict resolution, and coordination of related activities

Disadvantages
- Very complex to manage
- Hard to maintain balance between the two lines of authority
- So much shared authority can result in a transaction logjam and disproportionate amounts of time being spent on communications
- It is hard to move quickly and decisively without getting clearance from many other people
- Promotes an organizational bureaucracy and hamstrings creative entrepreneurship

structural form. A matrix arrangement promotes internal checks and balances among competing viewpoints and perspectives, with separate managers for different dimensions of strategic initiative. A matrix approach thus allows *each* of several strategic considerations to be managed directly and to be formally represented in the organization structure. In this sense, it helps middle managers make trade-off decisions from an organizationwide perspective.[3] Most applications of matrix organization are limited to certain important functions rather than spanning the whole of a large-scale diversified enterprise.

A number of companies shun matrix organization because of its chief weaknesses.[4] It is a complex structure to manage; people often end up confused over whom to report to and for what. Moreover, because the matrix signals that everything is important and, further, that everybody needs to communicate with everybody else, a "transactions logjam" can emerge. Actions turn into paralysis, since with shared authority it is hard to move decisively without first considering many points of view and getting clearance from many other people. Sizable transactions costs and communications inefficiency can arise, as well as delays in responding. Even so, there are situations where the benefits of conflict resolution and consensus building outweigh these weaknesses.

Combination and Supplemental Methods of Organization

A single type of structural design is not always sufficient to meet the requirements of strategy. When this occurs, one option is to mix and blend the basic organization forms, matching structure to strategy, requirement by requirement, and unit by unit. Another is to supplement a basic organizational design with special-situation devices such as project manager/project staff approaches, task force approaches, or venture teams.

International Organizational Forms

There are a variety of ways a manager can design for international activities in the firm. The most common approaches are described briefly below.[5]

International Division

The international division is an international business division that is simply added onto the domestic structure that now exists, as shown in Exhibit 9–5. This type of structure is typical of a firm that has a relatively simple structure such as a single business functional structure or a geographic structure in

EXHIBIT 9–5   The International Divisional Structure

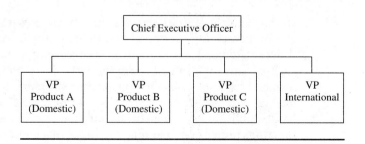

which one of the geographic regions encompasses international sales. This structure is appropriate for a firm that is not highly diversified from an international perspective. An international division is usually the first international structural form to be adopted by a firm that evolves into international markets. The formation of the international division is an acknowledgment that the international market has become important to the overall performance and strategy of the company. Managers are also acknowledging that they must establish an organizational form that links them more closely with their international customers.

Multidomestic Structure

A multidomestic structure is essentially an international geographical structure, as shown in Exhibit 9–6. This international structural form segments the regional markets based on the similarity of culture, language, product desires, distribution channels, etc. Divisions are then established in markets that have similar characteristics. It should also be noted that often activities such as product research and development, marketing, purchasing, and finance are relegated to the local divisional level. The objective of the multidomestic structure is to move the key functional processes and activities to a location close to the customer.

Managers use the multidomestic structure when they are using a multidomestic strategy, as described in Chapter 6. This structure allows the firm to carry out the decentralized multidomestic strategy in the most effective manner possible. The role of head office in the multidomestic structure is to provide management personnel, skills, and direction to the international divisions as well as to coordinate the sharing of technology and information between the divisions.

EXHIBIT 9–6   The Multidomestic Divisional Structure

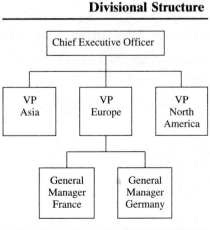

EXHIBIT 9–7   The Global Product-Division Structure

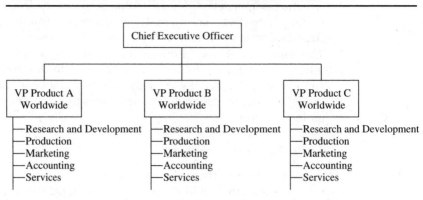

Global Product Structure

The global product structure is illustrated in Exhibit 9–7. In a global product-division structure the firm is focusing each of its product lines on a broad scope of international markets. This structure allows each business product-division to locate its value-chain activities in international locations that maximize the business's overall competitive advantages. Therefore, in one division, production may be done in Asia, R&D in North America, and marketing in various regions around the world. For example, in some global companies, parts are manufactured in one continent and the product is assembled in a completely different continent. The objective of this structure is to locate parts of the business where they will be most competitive globally.

The global product-division structure is applied to firms that are taking a global strategy internationally (see Chapter 6 for a description of global strategy).

Mini-case: Illustration of Structure-Strategy Linkages

The following mini-case can be used to assess alternative organizational structures. Suggested discussion questions follow this case.

T. G. BRIGHT AND CO., LIMITED—1986*

In 1977, T. G. Bright and Co., Limited (Brights), of Niagara Falls, Ontario, sold a wide range of wine products in Ontario in eight categories—sparkling, rosé, white table, port, sherry, appetizer, red table, and other (which included such diverse products as Muscatel, Mazel Tov, and sacramental wine). Through

---

*This case was prepared by Professor Paul W. Beamish as a basis for classroom discussion. Copyright © 1986 by Paul W. Beamish

wholly owned subsidiaries, Brights also offered additional selections in many of these eight categories in other provinces.

It was a small firm ($14 million in sales) with over half its sales volume in Ontario (see Exhibit 9–8), most of its manufacturing in Ontario, and a product line which had not digressed from wine. Its 1977 organization is reflected in Exhibit 9–9.

By 1980, Brights' organization was modified to include a second regional operations manager (see Exhibit 9–10). A third production facility in Quebec had been acquired in 1979. With this acquisition, the proportion of sales in Quebec—27 percent in 1979—was expected to increase so that Brights would have the largest non-government operation in Quebec.

Two other organization changes were made:

1. Hatch became chairman and Arnold became president, with the position of executive vice president dropped.

EXHIBIT 9–8   Percentage Share of Canadian Wine Market

	Ontario	Quebec	Rest of Country
Brights' Sales	55%	27%	18%
Total Canadian market	34	32	34

EXHIBIT 9–9   1977 Organization

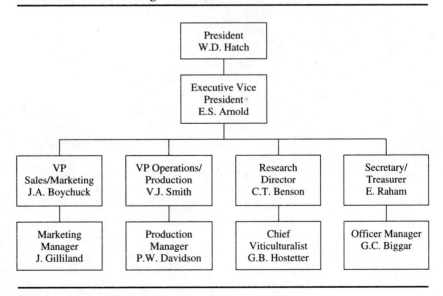

Source: Derived from list of officers and executives in the 1977 annual report.

EXHIBIT 9–10   1980 Organization

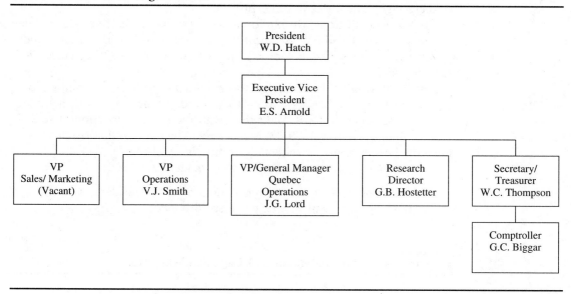

2. The position of vice president, sales/marketing, had been filled for a few months but of late had been vacant and was being managed by the president.

In late 1980, Brights formed a joint venture with the Inkameep Indian Band of Oliver, British Columbia, to establish a winery in B.C.'s Okanagan Valley. In 1984 and 1985, small winery operations were established in Manitoba and Nova Scotia, respectively. Sales in 1984 were nearly $38 million, net of excise and sales tax.

In 1985 a limited import operation in wines and spirits under the name of Wines of the Globe was established. (In 1984 the Province of Quebec modified its regulations to permit the bottling of imported wines by local wineries.)

Brights' non-restaurant sales were through provincial government outlets, small grocery stores (in Quebec), and company-owned retail outlets. The company operated over 20 retail outlets in Ontario, with perhaps half being located in Toronto.

In order to keep pace with changing consumer tastes, Brights' product mix had been steadily shifting away from fortified wines to those with lower alcohol levels. In addition, a greater proportion of sales was in white rather than red wines. With the purchase of a Quebec cider company in 1978, Brights acquired the ability and license to produce cider. Brights had also introduced a wine cooler, which combined specially fermented wine and pure spring water.

Grapes were supplied from three sources—company-owned vineyards, purchases from other grape growers, and concentrate and bulk purchases from other countries. Grapes purchased from local growers in Southern Ontario

EXHIBIT 9–11   1985 Organization

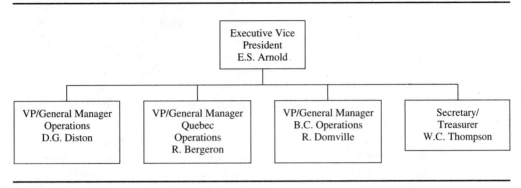

Source: List of officers and executives from the 1985 annual report.

(and, to a lesser extent, the Okanagan region in B.C.) were the primary source of supply.

By 1985, Brights had once again modified its organization structure (see Exhibit 9–11).

The chairman, W. D. Hatch, died in 1985. The chairman's position was not reflected in the 1985 annual report list of officers and executives. In lieu of a vice president, sales/marketing, a staff director of marketing was appointed to work with the regional vice presidents. The previous vice president/general manager of Quebec Operations had left the company. His replacement held the title of vice president/general manager Eastern Division.

In 1986, W. C. Thompson resigned and G. C. Biggar became secretary. The designation for the three vice presidents/general managers changed from being in charge of Operations, Quebec Operations, and B. C. Operations to being in charge of the Central Division, Eastern Division, and Western Division, respectively.

Carling O'Keefe, Limited, Toronto, Ontario, announced on June 26, 1986, that its wholly owned subsidiary, Jordan & Ste-Michelle Cellars, Ltd., had been sold (including substantially all of its assets) to T. G. Bright and Co., Limited.

The purchase price was approximately $30 million. It was estimated that the transaction resulted in a loss to Carling O'Keefe, Limited, of approximately $7,750,000 after tax, or 36 cents per common share. The business had been unprofitable in 1986.

Jordan & Ste-Michelle Cellars, Ltd., had wineries in St. Catharines, Ontario, and Surrey, British Columbia, and, until September 1985, had operated a winery in Calgary, Alberta. Except for 33 company-operated retail stores in Ontario, all sales were made through outlets operated by provincial liquor boards. The company had recently entered into a joint venture to manufacture and distribute cider products for the U.S. market.

At the time of the sale, the gross income for Jordan & Ste-Michelle Cellars, Ltd., was almost identical to that of Brights. The acquisition meant that Brights was now the largest winery in Canada by a large margin.

Discussion Questions

1. In 1986, Brights had a regional structure. What alternative forms could it have adopted?
   a. Why, then, did it adopt a regional structure?
   b. How big does a company have to be to justify a regional structure?
2. Why did Brights have a functional structure in 1977, given the arguments for a regional?
3. Why was the position of executive vice president eliminated in 1980? Why was the position of vice president, marketing, kept vacant in 1980/81? Why was the position of vice president, marketing, ultimately eliminated and replaced with a staff director of marketing?
4. What might occur now that the acquisition has occurred?

Notes to Chapter 9

The text in the first half of this chapter had been adapted in part from Thompson, Arthur A., Jr., and A. J. Strickland III. *Strategy Formulation and Implementation.* 3rd ed. Plano, TX.: Business Publications, 1986, pp. 334–45.

1. A more thorough treatment of matrix organization forms can be found in Galbraith, Jay R. "Matrix Organizational Designs." *Business Horizons,* February 1971, pp. 29–40.
2. An excellent critique of matrix organizations is presented in Davis, Stanley M., and Paul R. Lawrence. "Problems of Matrix Organizations." *Harvard Business Review,* May–June 1978, pp. 131–42.
3. Ibid., p. 132.
4. Peters, Thomas J., and Robert H. Waterman, Jr. *In Search of Excellence.* New York: Harper & Row, 1982, pp. 306–7.
5. Beamish, Paul; Peter Killing; Donald Lecraw; and Allen Morrison. *International Management.* 2nd ed. Burr Ridge, IL: Richard D. Irwin, Inc., 1994.

Recommended Readings

Bahrami, Homa. "The Emerging Flexible Organization." *California Management Review,* Summer 1992, pp. 33–52.

Krackhardt, David, and Jeffrey Hanson. "Informal Networks: The Company Behind the Chart." *Harvard Business Review,* July–August 1993, pp. 104–13.

Spitzer, Quinn, and Benjamin Tregoe. "Thinking and Managing Beyond the Boundaries." *Business Horizons,* January–February 1993, pp. 36–40.

MANAGING STRATEGIC CHANGE

If you're changing the circus and changing the clowns at the same time, that's a message that the organization hears loud and clear.

Dean Berry, *Senior Vice President of Gemini Consulting (1994)*

Transforming IBM is not something we can do in one or two years. The better we are at fixing some of the short-term things, the more time we have to deal with the long-term issues.

Lou Gerstner, *CEO of IBM Corp. (1994)*

If you do incremental change, you'll never get there. It's not just this wild industry (i.e., the computers & communications industry) where there's a real need to make enormous change quickly. Look at financial services, look at retailing. It's true of all industries.

Jerre Stead, *CEO of AT&T Global Information Solutions (1994)*

Organizations must constantly deal with change. Managers wishing to make changes in their organization must often be both effective champions and implementers of the particular change plan. The ability to commit to change and see that it is adopted is a highly valued skill. Such a skill may, however, be overvalued, for it neglects important steps in the change process. Such steps both precede and follow the commitment-adoption phase of strategic change.

The Three Phases of Strategic Change

In broad terms, the process of strategic change can be thought of as having three phases. The first phase is awareness and capability building; the second, commitment and adoption; and the third, reinforcement and recycling (see Exhibit 10–1). The most exciting phase for most managers, and certainly the

121

Exhibit 10–1   Achieving Readiness for and Implementing Strategic Change

---

Change Target Development	Potential Obstacles	Common Management Tactics
Awareness understanding: Establishing a general appreciation of the need for and direction of change Building a greater depth of knowledge of the situation, its consequences, and potential remedies	Ambiguous change requirements Inertial resistance Information bottlenecks Limited capacity to understand	Informal contact, lobbying Loosening up exercises—target exposure, involvement Short-term task forces
Capability: Developing capacity to perform new tasks	Personnel bottlenecks—inadequate training and experience Support systems bottlenecks Behavioural resistance	Training programs Support systems development Personnel changes Direct coaching
Commitment: Developing genuine agreement about and support for the required changes	Displacement of the problem Behavioural resistance Inadequacies, inconsistencies in support and incentive systems Weak position of power	Involvement activities Partial solutions and demonstrations Negotiations Coalition building Coercion Personnel changes
Adoption: Achieving change in behaviour, effective performance	Tangible risk Lagging resistance, support factors Poor readiness	Close monitoring Intensification and recycling of readiness efforts Mop-up action
Reinforcement: Sustaining effort and diligence in performing new tasks	Loss of commitment Resource and organizational inconsistencies	Rewards for new behaviour Adjustment of resource and organizational factors
Recycling: Defining and implementing improvements and new directions	Problems in linking a series of changes Complacency	Training and structuring for flexibility Continuous challenges for improvement

---

Source: Reprinted with permission. J. N. Fry and J. P. Killing, *Strategic Analysis and Action,* 2nd ed. (Scarborough, ON.: Prentice Hall Canada, 1989), figs. 13.5 and 13.6.

one that receives the greatest emphasis in the popular press, is the second one. Managing this phase well is necessary but not sufficient for overall organizational success.

Phase One: Awareness and Capability Building

The first phase in the strategic change process is awareness and capability building. Without widespread awareness of the need for change, most managers will resist the change. Such a reaction is both understandable and unfortunate.

Even when wide awareness of the need for change exists, there may not be a shared view of the appropriate direction of change. For example, everyone may be dissatisfied with the firm's performance and recognize the need for change. But should the solution be to retrench, or to take an aggressive, growth-oriented approach? Developing commitment to a particular change will be extremely difficult if the organization cannot first resolve fundamental questions about the firm's direction.

Assuming that widespread awareness of the need for, and agreement on the direction of, change does exist—and this is a big assumption—management can then proceed with examining whether it has (or can develop) the necessary capabilities to permit the change to take place. Building capabilities through staff or systems development can be a time-consuming and (in the short term) not immediately gratifying process. Nonetheless, it is absolutely essential. Just as a hockey coach needs players who know how to skate and who possess hockey sticks, managers must ensure that the organizational capability for change exists.

Phase Two: Commitment and Adoption

With the proper groundwork laid, the manager-as-change-agent can begin placing greater effort on the development of widespread support and enthusiasm for the proposed change. Organizational champions cannot enact changes themselves, particularly in larger firms. Through negotiations and coalition building they need to get other managers to "sign on," or if this is unsuccessful or too slow, they need to consider such tactics as coercion or personnel changes. As at many points in the strategic change process, resistance may exist.

Having developed wider commitment (and mitigated where possible the principal sources of resistance), managers can then turn their attention to the actual adoption of the change. Construction of a facility can begin, people can be hired or moved, money can be spent, people can agree to take on new responsibilities.

What characterizes the commitment and adoption phase is an escalating sense of irrevocability. Decisions are being made and acted upon. In contrast, during the awareness and capability phase—even though some resources were being allocated—management still had the option to change their mind, or slow the process.

Phase Three: Reinforcement and Recycling

Even with the change having been adopted, the change process does not end. Follow-up effort and reinforcement are typically required. It may be a less glamorous phase, but it is no less important. Just as a newly purchased automobile will subsequently require scheduled maintenance, service, and parts, so also does a company change require ongoing attention. This ongoing attention is necessary both to reinforce change and to ensure that the organization keeps pace with changes in the environment. Only through a process of ongoing reassessment can the organization improve overall prospects for success.

Types of Change

One of the most significant influences on the way in which the three phases of the change process are managed is the degree of urgency required. When the impact of urgency on change is considered, we are left with four principal types of change: imperative change, contrived crisis, responsive change, and foreseeable change (see Exhibit 10–2).

Imperative Change

When the necessity for change is urgent, comprehensive action is required, and little slack exists with respect to timing. Action is required now. Imperative

EXHIBIT 10–2   Pressure for Change

	Type of Change			
	Imperative	*Contrived Crisis*	*Responsive*	*Foreseeable*
Necessity for change	Pressing	Questionable	Tangible, but not pressing	Forecast
Action required	Comprehensive	Comprehensive	Diagnostic, plus some clear needs	Uncertain, but diagnostic at a minimum
Timing for required change	Immediate	Immediate	Soon	Uncertain
Range of options available	Limited	Limited	Mid-level	Wide

change may or may not constitute a crisis. A true crisis would be a situation where the viability of the organization, or a significant portion of it, is in jeopardy. For example, a competitor may have made a significant technological advance that threatens sales or the bank may be demanding immediate repayment.

Organizations may confront many imperative change situations that are not crises. With abrupt changes in legislative or competitive environments, opportunities may present themselves according to a timetable not of the company's making. Or perhaps an attractive acquisition candidate is suddenly available and requires a bid decision now. When such opportunities occur, the company's ability to move quickly will determine its success—or failure.

Contrived Crisis

"Of Boxes, Bubbles, and Effective Management,"[1] details the unique response of a group of Canadian managers to a true crisis. The issue for these managers was not so much one of opportunities, but of surviving. Three years after the crisis—when the crisis was no longer present—their proposed solution to avoid stagnant management was "if there isn't a crisis, we create one."

The use of a contrived crisis is inherently risky. The nature of crisis management—whether of a true or contrived crisis—is that rapid action, based on incomplete analysis, is required now. In a contrived crisis, however, the need for change may be questionable, and managerial resistance may develop. As well, the general manager who throws his or her organization into a crisis, and is seen to have contrived it, runs a serious risk of losing credibility. A contrived crisis may help to energize a tired or complacent workforce, test the quality of existing management, or "engage an entire organization"[2] toward a particular challenge. The risk is that because events happen so quickly in any crisis, it may not be possible to direct this pool of energy to where it is desired.

Responsive Change

Unlike with imperative change, in a responsive change situation the necessity for change is not as pressing. Action is clearly required, but sufficient time is available to permit the organization to respond to conditions in a more planned fashion. Abrupt realignments of a firm's strategy or organization are not required.

Foreseeable Change

The characteristics of foreseeable change are a forecast need for change but with the required actions and the timing both uncertain. This type of change tends to have the longest term perspective. Here one can identify the need for some sort of change in the future, but without knowing precisely the extent and timing. Nor surprisingly, it is sometimes more difficult to develop awareness and understanding around this type of change.

Given the uncertainty that surrounds it, the method of change tends to be incremental. Managers edge toward their goals with small steps.

There is a view in some circles that change typically results primarily from a long-range planning process—a process in which a presumably omniscient strategic planner lays out precisely what is needed. Omniscience is in short supply in all organizations, and most managers will readily admit their knowledge is finite. Realistically, then, change tends to take place in a more incremental fashion.

Most good managers recognize the value of gaining practice with change through small, logical incremental steps rather than major one-time realignments. As one writer noted:

> An organization that is used to continuous small changes and that has balanced strategic expertise at the top with operating expertise and entrepreneurship at the bottom is probably better prepared for a big leap than is any organization that has gone for several years without any change at all.[3]

Further, these managers recognize that dealing with change will always create some level of stress in an organization, and too much stress all at once can be fatal. The process of logical incrementalism[4] necessarily contains a large number of steps due to its contingent reinforcing behavioural nature.

The General Manager and Change

The general manager (GM) is the person most responsible for managing change. His or her task is influenced by:

- Experience in the organization and industry.
- Political position in the organization.
- Preferences and values.
- Style.
- Urgency.
- Available resources.

The obvious implication of such a complex list is that key stakeholders may very well hold different perceptions about what type of change situation exists. As Exhibit 10–3 suggests, by plotting an estimate of how each stakeholder may perceive the change situation, it is possible to focus on areas of potential disagreement. The specific type of change that is obvious to you may not be obvious to someone else, and vice versa. Further, others may not perceive the need for any change.

Exhibit 10–3   Key Stakeholder Perceptions of Type of Change Situation

Type of Change

Stakeholder	No Change	Foreseeable	Responsive	Contrived	Imperative
A					
B					
C					
D					

Tactics for Change

The general manager has a variety of tactics available for implementing change. These will depend in part on the level and preference for the use of power, and whether this power can or should be exerted directly or indirectly. Exhibit 10–4 lays out four basic tactics for change—giving orders, changing the context, persuasion, and opening channels. Each has advantages and disadvantages and unique characteristics.

Giving Orders

This approach is characterized by the forceful, top-down unambiguous issuance of orders. It has the advantage of being fast, and requires little senior management time. However, low organization commitment and high resistance may result from such an approach. In addition, it places heavy reliance on the abilities of the GM to have correctly surmised what change is needed. Not surprisingly, giving orders is a tactic frequently observed in an imperative change situation.

Persuasion

Persuasion is a less formal and more time-intensive tactic than giving orders. It involves negotiation and is more participative in nature. It is a tactic employed by GMs who either do not have a great deal of power, or prefer not to use it. In order to persuade, additional information may have to be collected in order to educate the target group on the advantages of the change. If the target groups or individuals see the change as being in their self-interest, greater motivation and commitment will result. The problems associated with this change tactic are that it may require a lot of GM time, is much slower than giving orders, and may require more compromise.

Opening Channels

The most subtle of the tactics for change has been called *opening channels*. It is characterized by a low use of power and by indirect actions. It is slow,

---

EXHIBIT 10–4   Tactics for Change

High Use of Power

Direct Action: Giving Orders	*Indirect Action: Changing Context*
Characteristics: • Forceful, top-down, unambiguous, power based	**Characteristics:** • Formal or informal, power driven; if the organization or resources are changed as a means of driving a change in direction or behaviour, great attention must be placed on implementation
Pros: • Fast • Desired direction clear • Requires little senior management time	**Pros:** • Fast (but not as quick as Giving Orders) • Useful approach when management power cannot be used directly on principal targets
Cons: • Low organization commitment • High resistance possible • Places heavy reliance on abilities of the GM	**Cons:** • High resistance possible • Risky since action is indirect but power driven • Timing important

Lower Use of Power

Direct Action: Persuasion	*Indirect Action: Opening Channels*
Characteristics: • Less formal; time-intensive, participative, negotiated; may require information to "educate" the employees and/or to permit employees to see that change is in their self-interest	**Characteristics:** • Subtle, evolutionary, informal; slower; consensus oriented
Pros: • Higher organization commitment likely • Greater motivation	**Pros:** • High commitment likely • Draws ideas from maximum number of people
Cons: • Slower implementation • Requires a lot of GM time for communications • May require compromise	**Cons:** • Very slow implementation • Requires a GM with foresight, patience, tolerance for ambiguity • Will require compromise

informal, consensus oriented, and takes an evolutionary approach. The objective is to open the channels of communication and interaction in such a way that employees are guided in a particular general direction. The task of the GM is to put in place the conditions (through resource means such as task forces and training programs) that will enable the organization to more openly consider a particular change.

Realistically, the GM will be unable to exert a great deal of control or precision over the pace at which the change occurs. This is not typically a problem, however, since here the GM has a longer term focus. Not surprisingly, this tactic for change is often associated with foreseeable change.

The principal benefits of opening channels are that high commitment is likely, and input will be received from the maximum number of people. It has the disadvantages of being slow and requiring a GM with foresight, patience, tolerance for ambiguity, and a willingness to compromise.

Changing Context

Changing context as a tactic for implementing change is characterized by high use of power and by indirect action. Changing the organization and/or resources are the principal methods employed. Some of the advantages of this tactic are that it is fast (but not as fast as giving orders) and useful when management power cannot be exerted directly on the change target. For example, a GM wishing to make an important acquisition may wish to make the acquisition with the support of senior management. Although the GM has wide support, he or she faces some resistance, particularly from one key head officer manager who would likely be involved if the acquisition were made. One organizational solution would be to transfer the resisting manager to an unrelated or distant division. Then, the acquisition can proceed with support of management. The GM exerts his or her power by moving the resisting manager, and by this indirect action achieves the GM's acquisition objective. Although moving a manager is a direct action, this tactic is considered indirect because it was not strictly a requirement of achieving the principal change—the acquisition. The organization context was changed so as to facilitate achievement of the prime change.

There are inherent risks to this tactic for change. Changing context may not eliminate all the intended resistance, and may create new sources of resistance. Consequently, the GM must give great attention to implementation and timing issues.

Conclusion

This chapter has provided an introduction to managing change. The process of a strategic change has three phases: awareness and capability building, commitment and adoption, and reinforcement and recycling. As Exhibit 10–1 noted, there are potential obstacles and common management tactics for each phase.

A significant influence on how the change process is managed is the degree of urgency required. In this context there are four main types of change: imperative change, contrived crisis, responsive change, and foreseeable change.

A strategy has not been implemented until the target behaviour has changed. In most instances, the task of installing the new strategy and seeing that the behaviour of people in the organization changes is a formidable one for the GM. Yet with creativity and determination it is possible.

The tactics available for implementing change will depend in part on the GM's status and degree of preference for the use of power, and on whether or not this power should be applied directly. Exhibit 10–2 noted four basic tactics for achieving change: giving orders, persuasion, opening channels, and changing the context.

Notes to Chapter 10

1. Hurst, David K. "Of Boxes, Bubbles and Effective Management." *Harvard Business Review,* May–June 1984, pp. 78–88.
2. Hamel, Gary, and C. K. Prahalad, "Strategic Intent." *Harvard Business Review,* May–June 1989, p. 67.
3. Hayes, Robert A. "Strategic Planning—Forward in Reverse?" *Harvard Business Review,* November–December 1985, p. 117.
4. For further discussion, see Quinn, James Brian. *Strategies for Change: Logical Incrementalism.* Homewood, IL.: Richard D. Irwin, 1980.

Recommended Readings

Berling, Robert. "The Emerging Approach to Business Strategy: Building a Relationship Advantage." *Business Horizons,* July–August 1993, pp. 16–27.

Brache, Alan. "Process Improvement and Management: A Tool for Strategy Implementation." *Planning Review,* September–October 1992, pp. 24–26.

Floyd, Steven W., and Bill Wooldridge. "Managing Strategic Consensus: The Foundation of Effective Implementation." *The Executive,* November 1992, pp. 27–39.

Fry, Joseph N., and J. Peter Killing. *Strategic Analysis and Action.* Scarborough, ON: Prentice Hall Canada Inc., 1995.

Pearson, Christine, and Ian Mitroff. "From Crisis Prone to Crisis Prepared: A Framework for Crisis Management." *The Executive,* February 1993, pp. 48–59.

Starr, Martin, "Accelerating Innovation." *Business Horizons,* July–August 1992, pp. 44–51.

Wilhelm, Warren. "Changing Corporate Culture—or Corporate Behavior? How to Change Your Company." *The Executive,* November 1992, pp. 72–77.

READINGS

A MANAGER'S GUIDE FOR EVALUATING COMPETITIVE ANALYSIS TECHNIQUES

John Prescott
John Grant

Virtually all managers acknowledge the importance of understanding their industries and their competitors. As a result, interest has grown rapidly in the use of various competitive analysis techniques to help formulate and implement strategy. However, managers who want to conduct competitive analyses are faced with perplexing choices among a wide variety of techniques with different strengths and weaknesses, an abundance of internal and external data sources, an array of computer software packages, and constraints in terms of time, money, information, and personnel. Many managers are asking, "Where do I start?"

The efficient selection of appropriate techniques for a particular situation depends on a three-phase process of awareness and choice. First, what relevant techniques are available and how do they relate to one another? Second, what is the focus and scope of the competitive arena of interest? Third, what constraints on time and other resources limit the extent of analyses that can be undertaken? Our extensive review of the literature and of applications in several industries can help managers and analysts complete these three phases effectively.

Source: Reprinted with permission. "A Manager's Guide for Evaluating Competitive Analysis Techniques." *Interfaces* 18, no. 3 (May–June 1988). Copyright © 1988. The Institute of Management Sciences, 290 Westminster Street, Providence, Rhode Island, 02903, USA.

Utilization Profiles

In order to assist managers to select and apply competitive analysis techniques, we developed a reference guide consisting in part of profiles describing various competitive analysis techniques (Exhibit 1). These profiles can assist managers in several ways. We chose a broad array of techniques to illustrate the increasing variety of analytical options available. The key characteristics of each technique have been highlighted along with their typical advantages and limitations. This should help managers to identify the techniques best suited to their situations. Few competitive analyses can be successfully completed using a single technique; the guide can help managers to choose the combination of techniques that will address the issue most effectively and efficiently. We provide references that present additional operational details for each technique.

Competitive Analysis Techniques

The utilization profiles array a diverse set of 21 techniques and evaluate them along 11 important dimensions. The techniques described below are sequenced beginning with broad industry-level techniques and moving to narrower functional area techniques. However, most of the techniques are applicable at either the corporate or the business-unit level. Detailed descriptions of the techniques can be found in Hax and Majluf [1984], Grant and King [1982], Porter [1980], and Prescott [1987].

Political and country risk analysis assesses the types (asset, operational, profitability, personnel) and extent of risks from operating in foreign countries.

Industry scenarios develop detailed, internally consistent descriptions of what various future structures of the industry may be like.

The economists' model of industry attractiveness analyzes the five basic forces (bargaining power of suppliers and customers, threat of substitute products, threat of entry, and industry rivalry) driving industry competition.

BCG industry matrix identifies the attractiveness of an industry based on the number of potential sources for achieving a competitive advantage and the size of the advantage that a leading business can achieve.

Industry segmentation identifies discrete pockets of competition within an industry. The bases of segment identification are often product variety, buyer characteristics, channels of distribution, and geography.

PIMS is an ongoing database of the Strategic Planning Institute which collects data describing business units' operating activities, their industries and competitors, their products and customers. The purpose is to assist planning efforts of the participating businesses.

A technological assessment develops an understanding of the technological relationships and changes occurring in an industry.

Multipoint competition analysis explores the implications of a situation in which diversified firms compete against each other in several markets.

EXHIBIT 1   **Utilization Profiles of Competitive Analysis Techniques. Twenty-one techniques are evaluated along 11 important dimensions. To use the table, locate the technique and evaluate dimension of interest. In the row and column intersection (cell), our assessment of a technique's characteristics as they apply to the dimension will be summarized.**

| *Dimensions* | Resource Needs | | | | Data Needs | | |
| | Time | | | | | | |
Techniques	*Development*	*Execution*	*Costs*	*Managerial Skills*	*Sources*	*Availability*	*Timeliness*
(1) Political and country risk analysis	Long	Long	High	Conceptual Analytical Diagnostic	Literature search Informants Personal interviews	From analysis	Historical Current
(2) Industry scenarios	Long	Long	High	Conceptual Analytical Diagnostic	Focus groups Literature search Personal interviews	Customized	Future
(3) Economists' model of industry attractiveness	Moderate	Long	Medium	Technical Conceptual Diagnostic	Case study Personal interviews Literature search	Off-the-shelf but basically derived from analysis	Current
(4) BCG industry matrix	Short	Moderate	Medium	Technical Conceptual Diagnostic	Literature search Personal interviews	From analysis	Current
(5) Industry segmentation	Moderate	Moderate	Medium	Conceptual Diagnostic Analytical	Case study Personal interviews Literature search	From analysis	Current
(6) PIMS	Moderate	Short	Medium	Technical Analytical	Databases	Off-the-shelf	Current
(7) Technological assessment	Long	Long	High	Technical Conceptual Analytical	Direct observation Participant observation Databases Documents	From analysis Sometimes Customized	Future

The techniques are arranged in descending order from a broad industry level to a narrower functional level. Multiple entries for the managerial skills and sources and evaluate dimensions are in descending order of importance and priority, respectively.

Accuracy Constraints	**Updating Requirements**		*Advantages*	*Limitations*	*References*
	Frequency	*Difficulty*			
Availability	Periodic	Reanalyze	Understand other cultures or political positions and potential problem areas	Often evaluated using own norms Language problems Data often difficult to evaluate and can change rapidly if power positions change	Desta [1985] Hofer and Haller [1980]
Assumption of sources	Ad hoc	Reconceptualize	Sensitize management to the need to adapt to industry evolution	Based upon assumptions subject to change Costs	Wack [1985a, b] Porter [1985]
Managerial skills	Ad hoc	Reconceptualize	Structured approach to examining industries Identifies competitors Basis for other in-depth analysis	Basic assumption that economic structure of industry is root of competition Drawing of industry boundaries	Porter [1980]
Managerial skills	Ad hoc	Reanalyze	Primarily a diagnostic tool for identifying profitable industry segments	Needs to be used in conjunction with other techniques such as industry analysis and CSFs	Pekar [1982]
Conceptual skills	Ad hoc	Reanalyze	Identifies pockets of opportunity Identifies pockets of future profits or areas under attack	Choosing segmentation dimensions Piecemeal approach to competition	Bonoma and Shapiro [1983] Porter [1985]
Representativeness of businesses in database	Periodic	Repetitive	Flexibility of use Variety of operations	Lack of organizational variables	Wagner [1984] Schoeffler, Buzzell, and Heaney [1974] Ramanujam and Venkatraman [1984]
Financial support	Continuous	Reconceptualize	Keep abreast of key technological drivers	Expensive, continuous, difficult process	Petrov [1982] Hayes and Wheelwright [1979a, b]

EXHIBIT 1 *(Continued)*

| Dimensions | Resource Needs | | | | Data Needs | | |
| Techniques | Time | | Costs | Managerial Skills | Sources | Availability | Timeliness |
	Development	Execution					
(8) Multipoint competition	Short	Moderate	Low to Medium	Conceptual Diagnostic	Literature search Personal interviews	From analysis	Current
(9) Critical success factors	Short	Moderate	Medium	Conceptual Diagnostic Analytical	Literature search Case study	From analysis	Current
(10) Strategic group analysis	Moderate	Short	Low	Conceptual Diagnostic	Literature search Personal interviews Case study	From analysis	Current
(11) Value-chain analysis and field maps	Short	Long	High	Technical Diagnostic	Case study Personal interviews Literature search	Customized	Current
(12) Experience curve	Short	Moderate	Medium	Technical Diagnostic	Documents Personal interviews Direct observation	From analysis	Current
(13) Stakeholder analysis and assumption surfacing and testing	Short	Moderate to High	Medium	Conceptual Diagnostic Analytical	Personal interviews Focus groups Literature search	Customized	Past Current
(14) Market signaling	Moderate to Long	Continuous	Low	Conceptual Diagnostic Analytical	Documents Personal interviews Direct observation	From analysis	Future
(15) Portfolio analysis	Moderate	Short	Low	Technical	Literature search Case study Personal interviews	From analysis	Current
(16) Strength and weakness analysis	Short	Long	High	Interpersonal Technical Diagnostic	Personal interviews Direct observation Case study	Customized	Current

EXHIBIT 1 *(Continued)*

Accuracy Constraints	Updating Requirements		Advantages	Limitations	References
	Frequency	*Difficulty*			
Sources	Ad hoc	Reanalyze	Identifies areas where a competitor may retaliate (vice versa)	Typically ignores motives, skills, etc., of competitor	Karnani and Wernerfelt [1985]
Managerial skills	Periodic	Reanalyze	Fast, inexpensive method for focusing efforts	Often is superficial	Rockart [1979] Leidecker and Bruno [1984]
Managerial skills	Periodic	Reanalyze	Fast, cheap, easy way to understand key competitors	Superficial; ignores firms outside industry	McGee and Thomas [1986] Porter [1980]
Sources	Ad hoc	Reanalyze	Best techniques for understanding operating details of a competitor or one's self	Data often difficult to obtain Slow, expensive	Kaiser [1984] Porter [1985]
Sources	Ad hoc	Repetitive	Provides an understanding of cost and thus pricing dynamics Gives a picture of whether to compete on basis of costs	Based upon history which may not carry through to future	Hall and Howell [1985] Hax and Majluf [1984]
Managerial skills	Periodic	Reanalyze	Introspection Attempts to get at underlying causes of behavior	Subject to misinterpretation	Freeman [1984] Rowe, Mason, and Dickel [1985]
Managerial skills	Continuous	Reconceptualize	Early warning indicator	Misinterpretation Get off in the wrong direction	Porter [1980]
Sources	Periodic	Reanalyze	Visual summary Requires managers to think systematically about industry and competitive position Heuristic method of decision making	Superficial Assumes cash flow/ profit drives decision	Hax and Majluf [1984] Grant and King [1982]
Sources	Ad hoc	Reanalyze	Provides in-depth understanding of entire business's capabilities Provides feedback for remedial action	Costly; long; cooperation of personnel essential Hierarchical position of manager influences perception	Stevenson [1985, 1976]

EXHIBIT 1   *(concluded)*

Dimensions	Resource Needs				Data Needs		
	Time			Managerial Skills			
Techniques	Development	Execution	Costs		Sources	Availability	Timeliness
(17) Synergy analysis	Moderate	Long	High	Technical Diagnostic Conceptual	Documents Case study Personal interviews	Customized	Current
(18) Financial statement analysis	Short	Short	Low	Technical Analytical	Documents Historical records Databases	Off-the-shelf From analysis	Historical
(19) Value-based planning	Long	Moderate to Long	Medium	Technical	Historical records Databases	From analysis	Historical
(20) Management profiles	Short	Short	Low	Interpersonal Technical	Personal interviews Informants Documents	From analysis	Current
(21) Reverse engineering	Short	Varies	Varies	Technical	Product purchasing	Off-the-shelf	Current

Critical success factor analysis identifies the few areas in which a business must do adequately in order to be successful.

A strategic group analysis identifies groups of businesses which follow similar strategies, have similar administrative systems, and tend to be affected by and respond to competitive moves and external events in similar ways.

A value chain analysis and field maps identify the costs, operating characteristics, and interrelationships of a business's primary activities (that is, inbound logistics, operations, outbound logistics, marketing and sales, service) and supporting activities (that is, firm infrastructure, human resource management, technological development, procurement).

EXHIBIT 1   *(concluded)*

Accuracy Constraints	Updating Requirements		Advantages	Limitations	References
	Frequency	*Difficulty*			
Sources	Ad hoc	Reanalyze	Shows cost or differentiation advantage as a result of sharing—staying power, exit decisions, response times	Data difficulties Time-consuming	Porter [1985]
Sources	Periodic	Repetitive	Fast, easy, cheap handle on financial picture	Data problems Usually limited to public corporations	Hax and Majluf [1984] Hofer and Schendel [1978]
Sources	Periodic	Repetitive	Simplicity—ability to compare alternatives and competitors	Basic assumption that maximizing stock price is primary goal Difficult to implement for individual business units of multidivision company (private firm)	Reimann [1986] Kaiser [1984] Fruhan [1979]
Recency of sources	Continuous	Repetitive	Development of management profiles and manpower (succession) charts Managers do not always act in a rational manner	Past is good predictor of future	Ball [1987]
Managerial skills	Ad hoc	Reanalyze	Best way to understand a competitor's product characteristics and costs	Can be time-consuming May not be critical success factor	—

Experience curves show that the costs of producing a product (service) decrease in a regular manner as the experience of producing it increases. The decrease in costs occurs over the total life of a product.

Stakeholder analysis and assumption surfacing and testing identify and examine any individual or group goals that affect or are affected by the realization of the businesses' goals.

Market signaling is any action by a competitor that provides a direct or indirect indication of its intentions, motives, goals, or internal situation.

Portfolio analysis locates a corporation's businesses along dimensions of industry attractiveness and competitive position to help managers to make resource allocation decisions and to evaluate future cash flows and profitability potential.

Strengths and weaknesses analysis identifies advantages and deficiencies in resources, skills, and capabilities for a business relative to its competitors.

Synergy analysis examines tangible (raw material, production, distribution) and intangible (management know-how, reputation) benefits of shared activities among business units.

Financial statement analysis assesses both the short-term health and long-term financial resources of a firm.

Value-based planning evaluates strategies and strategic moves in light of their probable stock market effects and financing implications. (It does not refer to managerial values in our usage.)

Management profiles examine the goals, backgrounds, and personalities of the individuals making strategic decisions in a competing firm or institution.

Reverse engineering is purchasing and dismantling a competitor's product to identify how it was designed and constructed so that costs and quality can be estimated.

Dimension Descriptions

For each of the 11 dimensions developed to evaluate the techniques, we selected criteria to enhance its meaningfulness. The criteria reflect our experience and understanding of what considerations are important for evaluating a particular technique. While firms often use external consultants for some aspects of competitive analysis, we assume that internal personnel will be conducting all phases of the analyses.

Time: The time required to implement a technique can be separated into development and execution phases. The developmental phase involves specifying objectives and determining any initial constraints that will be imposed on the project. The execution phase involves the collection of data, analysis, and dissemination of the findings to the appropriate individuals.

Financial Resources: The financial resources required to conduct an analysis with a given technique can be categorized as low (under $10,000), medium ($10,000 to $50,000), or high (over $50,000).

Managerial Skills: To complete an assignment a manager may need a number of specific skills; these may be classed in five groups: technical, interpersonal, conceptual, diagnostic, and analytic. Technical skills are those necessary to accomplish specialized activities. Interpersonal skills involve the ability to communicate with, understand, and motivate both individuals and groups. Conceptual skills are the abilities of a manager to think of the abstract and understand cause-and-effect relationships. Diagnostic skills allow a manager to study the symptoms of a problem and determine the underlying causes. Analytical skills involve the ability to identify the key variables in a situation, understand their interrelationships, and decide which should receive the most attention.

Sources: Sources are persons, products, written materials, anything from which information is obtained. Sources are of two primary types, "learning-curve" and "target" [Washington Researchers, 1983]. Learning-curve sources are those that provide general rather than specific knowledge; they are used when time is not critical and to prepare for a target source. For example, industry studies and books are typical learning-curve sources. Target sources, on the other hand, contain specific information and provide the greatest volume of pertinent information in the shortest period of time. Trade associations, company and competitor personnel are typical target sources. They are often one-shot sources that cannot be used repetitively.

The sites from which one obtains information can be classified as either "field" or "library." By combining the sources and sites of information, we developed a typology of data collection techniques. Exhibit 2 contains 15 data collection techniques that can be used for competitive analysis assignments [Miller, 1983]. For each, we have recommended the most appropriate sources. If a particular technique presents problems in availability or application, then nearby techniques in the exhibit should be considered. For example, if product purchasing is desired but is too expensive or unavailable, then direct observation or a literature search should be used.

Availability: While data can be obtained for almost any project for a price, the ease with which one can secure data can be classified. Three categories we have found useful are "off-the-shelf," "derived from analysis," and "customized." Off-the-shelf refers to data in the form the manager needs. If the essential raw data are available but require some analyses to put them in the desired form, then we classify the availability as "derived from analysis." When the information for a study must be developed, we call it "customized."

Timeliness: Data, analysis, and implications that deal primarily with the past are historical; those that address the present or future, we call current or future.

Accuracy Constraints: The value of a particular technique is limited by the quality of the resources and validity of the data used. Using the above dimensions, we identified the key constraint that would potentially hinder the usefulness of the given technique. This dimension is analogous to a warning label for the user.

Updating Requirements: Competitive analyses are seldom one-time phenomena. In order to understand the updating requirements for each technique, two useful dimensions are "frequency" and "difficulty." The frequency dimension can be divided into ad hoc (when the need arises), periodic (according to an established schedule), and continuous.

The difficulty dimension addresses the extent and nature of skills that may be required during an update. If the same analysis can be performed again with no modifications, then we have labeled it repetitive. If modifications must be made because the format or content of the information has changed, we describe it as reanalysis. If the assumptions of the analysis need to be challenged or changed, then the updating requires a reconceptualization.

EXHIBIT 2   A Typology of Data Collection Techniques

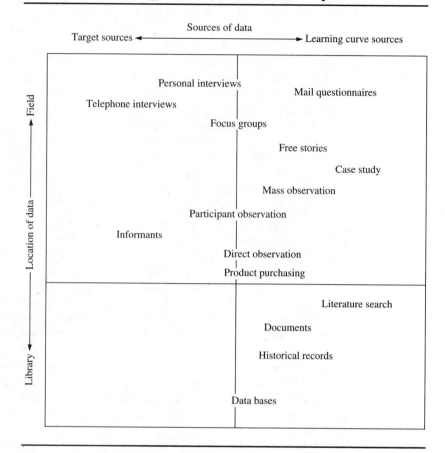

Note: The exhibit shows the options available for collecting data, given the desired source and location. A source of data can either provide specific target information or general learning-curve information. The location of the data can reside in a field setting or in a library.

Advantages and Limitations: The final two dimensions summarize the major advantages and limitations of the technique. While these assessments are implicit once the preceding criteria have been applied to a specific analytical assignment, they are intended to underscore special considerations. Examples of advantages could be insight into cultural constraints or an industry's evolution; whereas limitations could be communications difficulties or conflicting assumptions, either of which may lead to misunderstandings.

References: The publications chosen are from a much broader list of strategic management references. We based our choice on their availability, managerial orientation, and relative recency. Most contain bibliographies that further extend the resources.

While these evaluation dimensions vary in importance across competitive analysis assignments, recognizing them can greatly facilitate choices when groups of managers and analysts are working together.

Selecting and Using the Techniques

The transition from a description of techniques to their selection for application is best conveyed by an actual example.

The competitive environment of an electric utility company has recently been undergoing significant changes. A great many industrial customers, the utility's "bread-and-butter," have been closing or reducing operations. Other industrial and commercial customers have been threatening partial backward integration into cogeneration systems. Residential customers have been voicing concerns before the public utility board because they pay some of the highest rates in the country. Because of potentially low returns and increasingly high risks, the investment community seems less willing to finance the large capital expenditures necessary in this industry. The utility's geographic service area, vigorously engaged in attracting new businesses, is looking for high-technology and service businesses, which typically consume modest amounts of electricity.

To further complicate its competitive problems, a variety of governmental bodies is openly discussing the benefits of deregulation. Since electricity can be distributed cheaply over wide geographical areas, the need to restrict the boundaries of each utility is being questioned. Deregulation, some argue, would benefit consumers by allowing them to choose among a wider set of competitors.

The managers in the company are faced with an internal situation of severe financial constraints, top management's desire to take immediate corrective action, and a lack of skills in formal strategic planning. The newly hired planners charged with addressing the above issues need a method for organizing their competitive analysis efforts. They must choose techniques for understanding their industry and competitors.

Selecting Techniques

Many competitive analysis assignments begin when top executives become dissatisfied with their firm's prevailing emphasis and understanding of the competitive environment. This was the case in the electrical utility company described above. Management initiated a series of meetings which focused on the strategic planning efforts at the firm. One of the outcomes was an assignment to conduct an analysis of the industry and competitors. The planners, facing the constraints of a limited budget, perceived urgency, and after a series of meetings, an inexperienced support staff decided to focus on two fundamental issues: first, to understand the contemporary dynamics of the broadly defined electrical utility industry; second, to address the strategic position of the firm relative to its key existing and potential competitors. The managers needed to identify those competitive analysis techniques that would best answer their questions within their existing constraints. The outcome is shown in Exhibit 3.

Exhibit 3 also illustrates several important aspects of the process of initiating a competitive analysis assignment. Even the most basic assignments, like those described in the table, present the manager with a variety of choices. The firm in this case concentrated its efforts on basic analyses that would lay the foundation for later in-depth studies. As a result, several possible alternatives were rejected because they were too costly, time-consuming, complicated, or not relevant to the circumstances at that time. For example, industry scenarios were deferred for two interrelated reasons. The team needed to understand the industry better before it could address more sophisticated issues. Second, developing industry scenarios would have been too costly and time-consuming. Techniques, such as political and country risk analysis, multipoint competition, synergy analysis, and market signaling were viewed as not relevant to the immediate issues. The competitive analysis team examined each of the 21 techniques and chose those which best suited the assignment and the constraints imposed on the project.

The team applied three interrelated techniques in order to better understand the industry. First, the economists' model of industry attractiveness provided a comprehensive picture of the industry. It revealed that competition should be viewed from both a regional and a national perspective. Further, deregulation (a concern of top management) was not likely to occur for another three to five years, and then the transmission systems of electrical utilities would be the first area to be deregulated. Finally, while the bargaining power of electrical utilities is not strong, their profitability was expected to

---

EXHIBIT 3   A Competitive Analysis at an Electrical Utility Company

	Techniques	
Needs	*Chosen*	*Rejected/Deferred*
To understand the dynamics of the industry	Economists' model of industry attractiveness Strategic group analysis Critical success factors	Industry scenarios Industry segmentation Stakeholder analysis
To identify its strategic position relative to its key competitors	Financial analysis Management profiles Strengths and weaknesses analysis	Value-based planning Value-chain analysis

increase over the next five years due in part to a construction cycle coming to an end.

Second, using the industry analysis as a foundation, strategic group analysis identified those key competitors important in identifying the firm's relative position. Strategic groups were developed on a national level using publicly available operating and financial data for a set of about 70 firms. On a regional level, a group of eight electrical and gas utility firms were selected, which were either in the firm's transmission grid or which competed in their geographical territory.

Third, critical success factors (CSFs) were identified at two levels. During the industry analysis, CSFs were identified for the industry as a whole. Then CSFs were identified for the strategic groups. The layering or combining of techniques within an analysis allows managers to address multiple aspects of a question.

Having narrowed the field of competitors to a manageable number through the strategic group analysis, the team turned to the second issue. It sought to build profiles of the competitors to depict the relative positions of the firms. The choices were to conduct a financial analysis of the firms, to examine their management teams' profiles, and to analyze their strengths and weaknesses. These methods were chosen because the data were easily available, the time for the analysis was relatively short, and the result would be a set of reports that other managers in the firm could use easily. This last point was very important. Since most managers were not really convinced that it was necessary to consider the competition, the competitive analysis team felt it extremely important to choose those techniques that were understood by virtually all managers. When the managers saw the usefulness of these analyses, the team would then move to other analyses that were less familiar but which could provide additional intelligence. Most of the techniques rejected or deferred (Exhibit 3) fit in this category.

From this example, it is clear that even seemingly simple competitive analysis assignments pose important issues and questions. In this case, questions concerning the relative position of the firm could not be tackled until the managers understood the industry as a competitive arena. This new perspective on the environment required customer feedback, technical appraisals, and regulatory understanding.

The assignment in this case took approximately three months to complete, with approximately one-third of the time being spent on the developmental aspects of the study.

Conclusions

Growing competitiveness in many markets and along many combinations of dimensions is increasing the complexity of competitive analysis problems facing managers. Our descriptions of techniques, evaluation dimensions, and information types should provide managers with helpful guidance in making competitive analyses.

References

Ball, Richard. "Assessing your competitor's people and organization." *Long-Range Planning* 20, no. 2 (1987), pp. 32–41.

Bonoma, Thomas V., and Bensen P. Shapiro. *Segmenting the Industrial Market.* Lexington, MA: Lexington Books, 1983.

Desta, Asayehgn. "Assessing political risk in less developed countries." *Journal of Business Strategy* 5, no. 4 (1985), pp. 40–53.

Freeman, R. Edward. *Strategic Management: A Stakeholder Approach.* Boston, MA: Pitman Publishing Company 1984.

Fruhan, William E., Jr. *Financial Strategy: Studies in the Creation, Transfer and Destruction of Shareholder Value.* Homewood, IL: Richard D. Irwin, 1979.

Grant, John H., and William R. King. *The Logic of Strategic Planning.* Boston, MA: Little, Brown, 1982.

Hall, Graham, and Sydney Howell. "The experience curve from the economist's perspective." *Strategic Management Journal* 6, no. 2, (1985), pp. 197–212.

Hax, Arnoldo C., and Nicolas S. Majluf. *Strategic Management: An Integrative Perspective.* Englewood Cliffs, N.J. Prentice Hall, 1984.

Hayes, Robert H., and Steven C. Wheelwright. "The dynamics of process-product life cycles." *Harvard Business Review* 57, no. 2 (March–April 1979a), pp. 127–36.

Hayes, Robert H., and Steven C. Wheelwright. "Link manufacturing process and product life cycles." *Harvard Business Review* 57, no. 1 (January–February 1979b), pp. 133–40.

Hofer, Charles W., and Terry Haller, "Globescan: A way to better international risk assessment." *Journal of Business Strategy* 1, no. 2, (1980). pp. 41–55.

Hofer, Charles W., and Dan Schendel. *Strategy Formulation: Analytical Concepts,* St. Paul, MN: West Publishing, 1978.

Kaiser, Michael M. *Understanding the Competition: A Practical Guide to Competitive Analysis,* Washington, D.C.: Michael M. Kaiser Associates, Inc., 1984.

Karnani, Aneel, and Birger, Wernerfelt. "Multiple point competition." *Strategic Management Journal* 6, no. 1, (1985), pp. 87–96.

Leidecker, Joel K., and Albert V. Bruno. "Identifying and using critical success factors." *Long-Range Planning* 17, no. 1 (February 1984), pp. 23–32.

McGee, John, and Howard Thomas. "Strategic Groups: Theory, research and taxonomy." *Strategic Management Journal,* 7, no. 2, (1986), pp. 141–60.

Miller, Delbert C. *Handbook of Research Design and Social Measurement,* New York, NY: Longman, 1983.

Pekar, Peter P. "The strategic environmental matrix: A concept on trial," *Planning Review* 10, no. 5, 1982, pp. 28–30.

Petrov, Boris. "The advent of the technology portfolio." *Journal of Business Strategy* 3, no. 2, (1982), pp. 70–75.

Porter, Michael E. *Competitive Strategy.* New York, NY: Free Press, 1980.

Porter, Michael E. *Competitive Advantage: Creating and Sustaining Superior Performance.* New York, NY: Free Press, 1985.

Prescott, John E. "A process for applying analytic models in competitive analysis." In *Strategic Planning and Management Handbook,* eds. David I. Cleland and William R. King. New York, NY: Van Nostrand Reinhold, 1987, pp. 222–51.

Ramanujam, Vasudevan, and N. Venkatraman. "An inventory and critique of strategy research using the PIMS data base." *Academy of Management Review* 9, no. 1, (1984), pp. 138–51.

Reimann, B. C. "Strategy valuation in portfolio planning: Combining Q and VROI ratios." *Planning Review,* 14, no. 1 (1986), pp. 18–23, 42–45.

Rockart, John F. "Chief executives define their own data needs." *Harvard Business Review* 5, no. 2 (March–April 1979), pp. 81–92.

Rowe, Alan, J.; Richard O. Mason; and Karl E. Dickel. *Strategic Management and Business Policy.* 2nd ed., Reading, MA: Addison-Wesley Publishing, 1985.

Schoeffler, Sidney; Robert D. Buzzell; and Donald F. Heany. "Impact of strategic planning on profit performance." *Harvard Business Review* 52, no. 2, (1974), pp. 137–45.

Stevenson, Howard H. "Defining corporate strengths and weaknesses." *Sloan Management Review* 17, no. 3 (Spring, 1976), pp. 51–68.

Stevenson, Howard H. 1985, "Resource assessment: Identifying corporate strengths and weaknesses." In *Handbook of Business Strategy,* ed. William D. Guth. Boston, MA: Warren, Gorham and Lamont, chap. 5, pp. 1–30.

Wack, Pierre. "Scenarios: Shooting the rapids." *Harvard Business Review* 63, no. 6, (1985a), pp. 139–50.

Wack, Pierre. "Scenarios: Uncharted waters ahead." *Harvard Business Review* 63, no. 5, (1985b), pp. 73–89.

Wagner, Harvey M. "Profit wonders, investment blunders." *Harvard Busines Review* 62, no. 5, (1984), pp. 121–35.

Washington Researchers. *Company Information: A Model Investigation,* Washington, D.C.: Washington Researchers Ltd., 1983.

CRAFTING STRATEGY

Henry Mintzberg

Tracking Strategy

In 1971, I became intrigued by an unusual definition of strategy as a pattern in a stream of decisions (later changed to actions). I initiated a research project at McGill University, and over the next 13 years a team of us tracked the strategies of 11 organizations over several decades of their history. (Students at various levels also carried out about 20 other less comprehensive studies.) The organizations we studied were Air Canada (1937–1976), Arcop, an architectural firm (1953–1978), Asbestos Corporation (1912–1975), Canadelle, a manufacturer of women's undergarments (1939–1976), McGill University (1829–1980), the National Film Board of Canada (1939–1976), *Saturday Night* magazine (1928–1971), the *Sherbrooke Record*, a small daily newspaper (1946–1976), Steinberg Inc., a large supermarket chain (1917–1974), the U.S. military's strategy in Vietnam (1949–1973), and Volkswagenwerk (1934–1974).

As a first step, we developed chronological lists and graphs of the most important actions taken by each organization—such as store openings and closings, new flight destinations, and new product introductions. Second, we inferred patterns in these actions and labeled them as strategies.

Third, we represented graphically all the strategies we inferred in an organization so that we could line them up to see whether there were distinct periods in their development—for example, periods of stability, flux, or global change. Fourth, we used interviews and in-depth reports to study what appeared to be the key points of change in each organization's strategic history.

Finally, armed with all this strategic history, the research team studied each set of findings to develop conclusions about the process of strategy formation. Three themes guided us: the interplay of environment, leadership, and organization; the pattern of strategic change; and the processes by which strategies form. This article presents those conclusions.

Source: Reprinted with permission. Henry Mintzberg, "Crafting Strategy," *Harvard Business Review*, July–August 1987. Copyright © 1987 by the President and Fellows of Harvard College. All rights reserved.

Imagine some planning strategy. What likely springs to mind is an image of orderly thinking: a senior manager, or a group of them, sitting in an office formulating courses of action that everyone else will implement on schedule. The keynote is reason—rational control, the systematic analysis of competitors and markets, of company strengths and weaknesses, the combinations of these analyses producing clear, explicit, full-blown strategies.

Now imagine someone *crafting* strategy. A wholly different image likely results, as different from planning as craft is from mechanization. Craft evokes traditional skill, dedication, perfection through the mastery of detail. What springs to mind is not so much thinking and reason as involvement, a feeling of intimacy and harmony with the materials at hand, developed through long experience and commitment. Formulation and implementation merge into a fluid process of learning through which creative strategies evolve.

My thesis is simple: the crafting image better captures the process by which effective strategies come to be. The planning image, long popular in the literature, distorts these processes and thereby misguides organizations that embrace it unreservedly.

In developing this thesis, I shall draw on the experiences of a single craftsman, a potter, and compare them with the results of a research project that tracked the strategies of a number of corporations across several decades. Because the two contexts are so obviously different, my metaphor, like my assertion, may seem farfetched at first. Yet if we think of a craftsman as an organization of one, we can see that he or she must also resolve one of the great challenges the corporate strategist faces: knowing the organization's capabilities well enough to think deeply enough about its strategic direction. By considering strategy making from the perspective of one person, free of all the paraphernalia of what has been called the strategy industry, we can learn something about the formation of strategy in the corporation. For much as our potter has to manage her craft, so too managers have to craft their strategy.

At work, the potter sits before a lump of clay on the wheel. Her mind is on the clay, but she is also aware of sitting between her past experiences and her future prospects. She knows exactly what has and has not worked for her in the past. She has an intimate knowledge of her work, her capabilities, and her markets. As a craftsman, she senses rather than analyzes these things; her knowledge is "tacit." All these things are working in her mind as her hands are working the clay. The product that emerges on the wheel is likely to be in the tradition of her past work, but she may break away and embark on a new direction. Even so, the past is no less present, projecting itself into the future.

In my metaphor, managers are craftsmen and strategy is their clay. Like the potter, they sit between a past of corporate capabilities and a future of market opportunities. And if they are truly craftsmen, they bring to their work an equally intimate knowledge of the materials at hand. That is the essence of crafting strategy.

In the pages that follow, we will explore this metaphor by looking at how strategies get made as opposed to how they are supposed to get made. Throughout, I will be drawing on the two sets of experiences I've mentioned. One, described in the insert, is a research project on patterns in strategy formation that has been going on at McGill University under my direction since 1971. The second is the stream of work of a successful potter, my wife, who began her craft in 1967.

Strategies Are Both Plans for the Future and Patterns from the Past

Ask almost anyone what strategy is, and they will define it as a plan of some sort, an explicit guide to future behavior. Then ask them what strategy a competitor or a government or even they themselves have actually pursued. Chances are they'will describe consistency in *past* behavior—a pattern in action over time. Strategy, it turns out, is one of those words that people define in one way and often use in another, without realizing the difference.

The reason for this is simple. Strategy's formal definition and its Greek military origins notwithstanding, we need the word as much to explain past actions as to describe intended behavior. After all, if strategies can be planned and intended, they can also be pursued and realized (or not realized, as the case may be). And pattern in action, or what we call realized strategy, explains that pursuit. Moreover, just as a plan need not produce a pattern (some strategies that are intended are simply not realized), so too a pattern need not result from a plan. An organization can have a pattern (or realized strategy) without knowing it, let alone making it explicit.

Patterns, like beauty, are in the mind of the beholder, of course. But anyone reviewing a chronological lineup of our craftsman's work would have little trouble discerning clear patterns, at least in certain periods. Until 1974, for example, she made small, decorative ceramic animals and objects of various kinds. Then this "knickknack strategy" stopped abruptly, and eventually new patterns formed around waferlike sculptures and ceramic bowls, highly textured and unglazed.

Finding equivalent patterns in action for organizations isn't that much more difficult. Indeed, for such large companies as Volkswagenwerk and Air Canada, in our research, it proved simpler! (As well it should. A craftsman, after all, can change what she does in a studio a lot more easily than a Volkswagenwerk can retool its assembly lines.) Mapping the product models at Volkswagenwerk from the late 1940s to the late 1970s, for example, uncovers a clear pattern of concentration on the Beetle, followed in the late 1960s by a frantic search for replacements through acquisitions and internally developed new models, to a strategic reorientation around more stylish, water-cooled, front-wheel-drive vehicles in the mid-1970s.

But what about intended strategies, those formal plans and pronouncements we think of when we use the term *strategy?* Ironically, here we run into all kinds of problems. Even with a single craftsman, how can we know what her intended strategies really were? If we could go back, would we find expressions of intention? And if we could, would we be able to trust them? We often fool ourselves, as well as others, by denying our subconscious motives. And remember that intentions are cheap, at least when compared with realizations.

Reading the Organization's Mind

If you believe all this has more to do with the Freudian recesses of a craftsman's mind than with the practical realities of producing automobiles, then think again. For who knows what the intended strategies of a Volkswagenwerk really mean, let alone what they are? Can we simply assume in this collective context that the company's intended strategies are represented by its formal plans or by other statements emanating from the executive suite? Might these be just vain hopes or rationalizations or ploys to fool the competition? And even if expressed intentions exist, to what extent do others in the organization share them? How do we read the collective mind? Who is the strategist anyway?

The traditional view of strategic management resolves these problems quite simply, by what organizational theorists call attribution. You see it all the time in the business press. When General Motors acts, it's because Roger Smith has made a strategy. Given realization, there must have been intention, and that is automatically attributed to the chief.

In a short magazine article, this assumption is understandable. Journalists don't have a lot of time to uncover the origins of strategy, and GM is a large, complicated organization. But just consider all the complexity and confusion that gets tucked under this assumption—all the meetings and debates, the many people, the dead ends, the folding and unfolding of ideas. Now imagine trying to build a formal strategy-making system around that assumption. Is it any wonder that formal strategic planning is often such a resounding failure?

To unravel some of the confusion—and move away from the artificial complexity we have piled around the strategy-making process—we need to get back to some basic concepts. The most basic of all is the intimate connection between thought and action. That is the key to craft, and so also to the crafting of strategy.

Strategies Need Not Be Deliberate—They Can Also Emerge

Virtually everything that has been written about strategy making depicts it as a deliberate process. First we think, then we act. We formulate, then we implement. The progression seems so perfectly sensible. Why would anybody want to proceed differently?

Our potter is in the studio, rolling the clay to make a waferlike sculpture. The clay sticks to the rolling pin, and a round form appears. Why not make a cylindrical vase? One idea leads to another, until a new pattern forms. Action has driven thinking: a strategy has emerged.

Out in the field, a salesman visits a customer. The product isn't quite right, and together they work out some modifications. The salesman returns to his company and puts the changes through; after two or three more rounds, they finally get it right. A new product emerges, which eventually opens up a new market. The company has changed strategic course.

In fact, most salespeople are less fortunate than this one or than our craftsman. In an organization of one, the implementor is the formulator, so innovations can be incorporated into strategy quickly and easily. In a large organization, the innovator may be 10 levels removed from the leader who is supposed to dictate strategy and may also have to sell the idea to dozens of peers doing the same job.

Some salespeople, of course, can proceed on their own, modifying products to suit their customers and convincing skunk works in the factory to produce them. In effect, they pursue their own strategies. Maybe no one else notices or cares. Sometimes, however, their innovations do get noticed, perhaps years later, when the company's prevalent strategies have broken down and its leaders are groping for something new. Then the salesperson's strategy may be allowed to pervade the system, to become organizational.

Is this story farfetched? Certainly not. We've all heard stories like it. But since we tend to see only what we believe, if we believe that strategies have to be planned, we're unlikely to see the real meaning such stories hold.

Consider how the National Film Board of Canada (NFB) came to adopt a feature-film strategy. The NFB is a federal government agency, famous for its creativity and expert in the production of short documentaries. Some years back, it funded a filmmaker on a project that unexpectedly ran long. To distribute his film, the NFB turned to theaters and so inadvertently gained experience in marketing feature-length films. Other filmmakers caught onto the idea, and eventually the NFB found itself pursuing a feature-film strategy—a pattern of producing such films.

My point is simple, deceptively simple: strategies can *form* as well as be *formulated*. A realized strategy can emerge in response to an evolving situation, or it can be brought about deliberately, through a process of formulation followed by implementation. But when these planned intentions do not produce the desired actions, organizations are left with unrealized strategies.

Today we hear a great deal about unrealized strategies, almost always in concert with the claim that implementation has failed. Management has been lax, controls have been loose, people haven't been committed. Excuses abound. At times, indeed, they may be valid. But often these explanations prove too easy. So some people look beyond implementation to formulation. The strategists haven't been smart enough.

While it is certainly true that many intended strategies are ill conceived, I believe that the problem often lies one step beyond, in the distinction we make between formulation and implementation, the common assumption that thought must be independent of (and precede) action. Sure, people could be smarter—but not only by conceiving more clever strategies. Sometimes they can be smarter by allowing their strategies to develop gradually, through the organization's actions and experiences. Smart strategists appreciate that they cannot always be smart enough to think through everything in advance.

Hands and Minds

No craftsman thinks some days and works others. The craftsman's mind is going constantly, in tandem with her hands. Yet large organizations try to separate the work of minds and hands. In so doing, they often sever the vital feedback link between the two. The salesperson who finds a customer with an unmet need may possess the most strategic bit of information in the entire organization. But that information is useless if he or she cannot create a strategy in response to it or else convey the information to someone who can—because the channels are blocked or because the formulators have simply finished formulating. The notion that strategy is something that should happen way up there, far removed from the details of running an organization on a daily basis, is one of the great fallacies of conventional strategic management. And it explains a good many of the most dramatic failures in business and public policy today.

We at McGill call strategies like the NFB's that appear without clear intentions—or in spite of them—emergent strategies. Actions simply converge into patterns. They may become deliberate, of course, if the pattern is recognized and then legitimated by senior management. But that's after the fact.

All this may sound rather strange, I know. Strategies that emerge? Managers who acknowledge strategies already formed? Over the years, our research group at McGill has met with a good deal of resistance from people upset by what they perceive to be our passive definition of a word so bound up with proactive behavior and free will. After all, strategy means control—the ancient Greeks used it to describe the art of the army general.

Strategic Learning

But we have persisted in this usage for one reason: learning. Purely deliberate strategy precludes learning once the strategy is formulated; emergent strategy fosters it. People take actions one by one and respond to them, so that patterns eventually form.

Our craftsman tries to make a freestanding sculptural form. It doesn't work, so she rounds it a bit here, flattens it a bit there. The result looks better, but still isn't quite right. She makes another and another and another.

Eventually, after days or months or years, she finally has what she wants. She is off on a new strategy.

In practice, of course, all strategy making walks on two feet, one deliberate, the other emergent. For just as purely deliberate strategy making precludes learning, so purely emergent strategy making precludes control. Pushed to the limit, neither approach makes much sense. Learning must be coupled with control. That is why the McGill research group uses the word *strategy* for both emergent and deliberate behavior.

Likewise, there is no such thing as a purely deliberate strategy or a purely emergent one. No organization—not even the ones commanded by those ancient Greek generals—knows enough to work everything out in advance, to ignore learning en route. And no one—not even a solitary potter—can be flexible enough to leave everything to happenstance, to give up all control. Craft requires control just as it requires responsiveness to the material at hand. Thus deliberate and emergent strategy form the end points of a continuum along which the strategies that are crafted in the real world may be found. Some strategies may approach either end, but many more fall at intermediate points.

Effective Strategies Develop in All Kinds of Strange Ways

Effective strategies can show up in the strangest places and develop through the most unexpected means. There is no one best way to make strategy.

The form for a cat collapses on the wheel, and our potter sees a bull taking shape. Clay sticks to a rolling pin, and a line of cylinders results. Wafers come into being because of a shortage of clay and limited kiln space in a studio in France. Thus errors become opportunities, and limitations stimulate creativity. The natural propensity to experiment, even boredom, likewise stimulates strategic change.

Organizations that craft their strategies have similar experiences. Recall the National Film Board with its inadvertently long film. Or consider its experiences with experimental films, which made special use of animation and sound. For 20 years, the NFB produced a bare but steady trickle of such films. In fact, every film but one in that trickle was produced by a single person, Norman McLaren, the NFB's most celebrated filmmaker. McLaren pursued a *personal strategy* of experimentation, deliberate for him perhaps (though who can know whether he had the whole stream in mind or simply planned one film at a time?) but not for the organization. Then 20 years later, others followed his lead and the trickle widened, his personal strategy becoming more broadly organizational.

Conversely, in 1952, when television came to Canada, a *consensus strategy* quickly emerged at the NFB. Senior management was not keen on producing films for the new medium. But while the arguments raged, one filmmaker quietly went off and made a single series for TV. That precedent set, one by one his colleagues leapt in, and within months the NFB—and its management—found themselves committed for several years to a new strategy with an intensity unmatched before or since. This consensus strategy arose spontaneously, as a result of many independent decisions made by the filmmakers about the films they wished to make. Can we call this strategy deliberate? For the filmmakers perhaps; for the senior management certainly not. But for the organization? It all depends on your perspective, on how you choose to read the organization's mind.

While the NFB may seem like an extreme case, it highlights behavior that can be found, albeit in muted form, in all organizations. Those who doubt this might read Richard Pascale's account of how Honda stumbled into its enormous success in the American motorcycle market. Brilliant as its strategy may have looked after the fact, Honda's managers made almost every conceivable mistake until the market finally hit them over the head with the right formula. The Honda managers on site in America, driving their products themselves (and thus inadvertently picking up market reaction), did only one thing right: they learned, firsthand.[1]

Grass-Roots Strategy Making

These strategies all reflect, in whole or part, what we like to call a grass-roots approach to strategic management. Strategies grow like weeds in a garden. They take root in all kinds of places, wherever people have the capacity to learn (because they are in touch with the situation) and the resources to support that capacity. These strategies become organizational when they become collective, that is, when they proliferate to guide the behavior of the organization at large.

Of course, this view is overstated. But it is no less extreme than the conventional view of strategic management, which might be labeled the hothouse approach. Neither is right. Reality falls between the two. Some of the most effective strategies we uncovered in our research combined deliberation and control with flexibility and organizational learning.

Consider first what we call the *umbrella strategy*. Here senior management sets out broad guidelines (say, to produce only high-margin products at the cutting edge of technology or to favor products using bonding technology) and leaves the specifics (such as what these products will be) to others lower down in the organization. This strategy is not only deliberate (in its guidelines) and emergent (in its specifics), but it is also deliberately emergent in that the

---

[1] Richard T. Pascale, "Perspective on Strategy: The Real Story behind Honda's Success," *California Management Review*, May–June 1984, p. 47.

process is consciously managed to allow strategies to emerge en route. IBM used the umbrella strategy in the early 1960s with the impending 360 series, when its senior management approved a set of broad criteria for the design of a family of computers later developed in detail throughout the organization.[2]

Deliberately emergent, too, is what we call the *process strategy*. Here management controls the process of strategy formation—concerning itself with the design of the structure, its staffing, procedures, and so on—while leaving the actual content to others.

Both process and umbrella strategies seem to be especially prevalent in businesses that require great expertise and creativity—a 3M, a Hewlett-Packard, a National Film Board. Such organizations can be effective only if their implementors are allowed to be formulators because it is people way down in the hierarchy who are in touch with the situation at hand and have the requisite technical expertise. In a sense, these are organizations peopled with craftsmen, all of whom must be strategists.

Strategic Reorientations Happen in Brief, Quantum Leaps

The conventional view of strategic management, especially in the planning literature, claims that change must be continuous: the organization should be adapting all the time. Yet this view proves to be ironic because the very concept of strategy is rooted in stability, not change. As this same literature makes clear, organizations pursue strategies to set direction, to lay out courses of action, and to elicit cooperation from their members around common, established guidelines. By any definition, strategy imposes stability on an organization. No stability means no strategy (no course to the future, no pattern from the past). Indeed, the very fact of having a strategy, and especially of making it explicit (as the conventional literature implores managers to do), creates resistance to strategic change!

What the conventional view fails to come to grips with, then, is how and when to promote change. A fundamental dilemma of strategy making is the need to reconcile the forces for stability and for change—to focus efforts and gain operating efficiencies on the one hand, yet adapt and maintain currency with a changing external environment on the other.

Quantum Leaps

Our own research and that of colleagues suggest that organizations resolve these opposing forces by attending first to one and then to the other. Clear

---

[2] James Brian Quinn, "IBM (A) case," *The Strategy Process: Concepts, Contexts, Cases,* ed. James Brian Quinn, Henry Mintzberg, and Robert M. James (Englewood Cliffs, N.J.: Prentice Hall, 1988).

periods of stability and change can usually be distinguished in any organization; while it is true that particular strategies may always be changing marginally, it seems equally true that major shifts in strategic orientation occur only rarely.

In our study of Steinberg Inc., a large Quebec supermarket chain head-quartered in Montreal, we found only two important reorientations in the 60 years from its founding to the mid-1970s: a shift to self-service in 1933 and the introduction of shopping centers and public financing in 1953. At Volkswa-genwerk, we saw only one between the late 1940s and the 1970s, the tumultous shift from the traditional Beetle to the Audi-type design mentioned earlier. And at Air Canada, we found none over the airline's first four decades, following its initial positioning.

Our colleagues at McGill, Danny Miller and Peter Friesen, found this pattern of change so common in their studies of large numbers of companies (especially the high-performance ones) that they built a theory around it, which they labeled the quantum theory of strategic change.[3] Their basic point is that organizations adopt two distinctly different modes of behavior at different times.

Most of the time they pursue a given strategic orientation. Change may seem continuous, but it occurs in the context of that orientation (perfecting a given retailing formula, for example) and usually amounts to doing more of the same, perhaps better as well. Most organizations favor these periods of stability because they achieve success not by changing strategies but by exploiting the ones they have. They, like craftsmen, seek continuous improvement by using their distinctive competencies in established courses.

While this goes on, however, the world continues to change, sometimes slowly, occasionally in dramatic shifts. Thus gradually or suddenly, the organization's strategic orientation moves out of sync with its environment. Then what Miller and Friesen call a strategic revolution must take place. That long period of evolutionary change is suddenly punctuated by a brief bout of revolutionary turmoil in which the organization quickly alters many of its established patterns. In effect, it tries to leap to a new stability quickly to reestablish an integrated posture among a new set of strategies, structures, and culture.

But what about all those emergent strategies, growing like weeds around the organization? What the quantum theory suggests is that the really novel ones are generally held in check in some corner of the organization until a strategic revolution becomes necessary. Then as an alternative to having to develop new strategies from scratch or having to import generic strategies from competitors, the organization can turn to its own emerging patterns to find its new orientation. As the old, established strategy disintegrates, the seeds of the new one begin to spread.

---

[3] See Danny Miller and Peter H. Friesen, *Organizations: A Quantum View* (Englewood Cliffs, N.J.: Prentice Hall, 1984).

This quantum theory of change seems to apply particularly well to large, established, mass-production companies. Because they are especially reliant on standardized procedures, their resistance to strategic reorientation tends to be especially fierce. So we find long periods of stability broken by short disruptive periods of revolutionary change.

Volkswagenwerk is a case in point. Long enamored of the Beetle and armed with a tightly integrated set of strategies, the company ignored fundamental changes in its markets throughout the late 1950s and 1960s. The bureaucratic momentum of its mass-production organization combined with the psychological momentum of its leader, who institutionalized the strategies in the first place. When change finally did come, it was tumultuous: the company groped its way through a hodgepodge of products before it settled on a new set of vehicles championed by a new leader. Strategic reorientations really are cultural revolutions.

Cycles of Change

In more creative organizations, we see a somewhat different pattern of change and stability, one that's more balanced. Companies in the business of producing novel outputs apparently need to fly off in all directions from time to time to sustain their creativity. Yet they also need to settle down after such periods to find some order in the resulting chaos.

The National Film Board's tendency to move in and out of focus through remarkably balanced periods of convergence and divergence is a case in point. Concentrated production of films to aid the war effort in the 1940s gave way to great divergence after the war as the organization sought a new raison d'être. Then the advent of television brought back a very sharp focus in the early 1950s, as noted earlier. But in the late 1950s, this dissipated almost as quickly as it began, giving rise to another creative period of exploration. Then the social changes in the early 1960s evoked a new period of convergence around experimental films and social issues.

We use the label "adhocracy" for organizations, like the National Film Board, that produce individual, or custom-made, products (or designs) in an innovative way, on a project basis.[4] Our craftsman is an adhocracy of sorts too, since each of her ceramic sculptures is unique. And her pattern of strategic change was much like that of the NFB's, with evident cycles of convergence and divergence: a focus on knickknacks from 1967 to 1972; then a period of exploration to about 1976, which resulted in a refocus on ceramic sculptures;

---

[4] See Henry Mintzberg, "Organization Design: Fashion or Fit?" *Harvard Business Review*, January–February 1981, p. 103; also see Mintzberg, *Structure in Fives: Designing Effective Organizations* (Englewood Cliffs, N.J.: Prentice Hall, 1983). The term *adhocracy* was coined by Warren G. Bennis and Philip E. Slater in *The Temporary Society* (New York: Harper & Row, 1964).

that continued to about 1981, to be followed by a period of searching for new directions. More recently, a focus on ceramic murals seems to be emerging.

Whether through quantum revolutions or cycles of convergence and divergence, however, organizations seem to need to separate in time the basic forces for change and stability, reconciling them by attending to each in turn. Many strategic failures can be attributed either to mixing the two or to an obsession with one of these forces at the expense of the other.

The problems are evident in the work of many craftsmen. On the one hand, there are those who seize on the perfection of a single theme and never change. Eventually the creativity disappears from their work and the world passes them by—much as it did Volkswagenwerk until the company was shocked into its strategic revolution. And then there are those who are always changing, who flit from one idea to another and never settle down. Because no theme or strategy ever emerges in their work, they cannot exploit or even develop any distinctive competence. And because their work lacks definition, identity crises are likely to develop, with neither the craftsmen nor their clientele knowing what to make of it. Miller and Friesen found this behavior in conventional business too; they label it "the impulsive firm running blind."[5] How often have we seen it in companies that go on acquisition sprees?

To Manage Strategy Is to Craft Thought and Action, Control and Learning, Stability and Change

The popular view sees the strategist as a planner or as a visionary, someone sitting on a pedestal dictating brilliant strategies for everyone else to implement. While recognizing the importance of thinking ahead and especially of the need for creative vision in this pedantic world, I wish to propose an additional view of the strategist—as a pattern recognizer, a learner if you will—who manages a process in which strategies (and visions) can emerge as well as be deliberately conceived. I also wish to redefine that strategist, to extend that someone into the collective entity made up of the many actors whose interplay speaks an organization's mind. This strategist *finds* strategies no less than creates them, often in patterns that form inadvertently in its own behavior.

What, then, does it mean to craft strategy? Let us return to the words associated with craft: dedication, experience, involvement with the material, the personal touch, mastery of detail, a sense of harmony and integration. Managers who craft strategy do not spend much time in executive suites reading MIS reports or industry analyses. They are involved, responsive to their materials, learning about their organizations and industries through personal touch. They are also sensitive to experience, recognizing that while

---
[5] Danny Miller and Peter H. Friesen, "Archetypes of Strategy Formulation," *Management Science*, May 1978, p. 921.

individual vision may be important, other factors must help determine strategy as well.

Manage Stability

Managing strategy is mostly managing stability, not change. Indeed, most of the time senior managers should not be formulating strategy at all; they should be getting on with making their organizations as effective as possible in pursuing the strategies they already have. Like distinguished craftsmen, organizations become distinguished because they master the details.

To manage strategy, then, at least in the first instance, is not so much to promote change as to know *when* to do so. Advocates of strategic planning often urge managers to plan for perpetual instability in the environment (for example, by rolling over five-year plans annually). But this obsession with change is dysfunctional. Organizations that reassess their strategies continuously are like individuals who reassess their jobs or their marriages continuously—in both cases, people will drive themselves crazy or else reduce themselves to inaction. The formal planning process repeats itself so often and so mechanically that it desensitizes the organization to real change, programs it more and more deeply into set patterns, and thereby encourages it to make only minor adaptations.

So-called strategic planning must be recognized for what it is: a means, not to create strategy, but to program a strategy already created—to work out its implications formally. It is essentially analytic in nature, based on decomposition, while strategy creation is essentially a process of synthesis. That is why trying to create strategies through formal planning most often leads to extrapolating existing ones or copying those of competitors.

That is not to say that planners have no role to play in strategy formation. In addition to programming strategies created by other means, they can feed ad hoc analyses into the strategy-making process at the front end to be sure that the hard data are taken into consideration. They can also stimulate others to think strategically. And of course people called planners can be strategists too, so long as they are creative thinkers who are in touch with what is relevant. But that has nothing to do with the technology of formal planning.

Detect Discontinuity

Environments do not change on any regular or orderly basis. And they seldom undergo continuous dramatic change, claims about our "age of discontinuity" and environmental "turbulence" notwithstanding. (Go tell people who lived through the Great Depression or survivors of the siege of Leningrad during World War II that ours are turbulent times.) Much of the time, change is minor and even temporary and requires no strategic response. Once in a while there is a truly significant discontinuity or, even less often, a gestalt shift in the environment, where everything important seems to change at once. But these events, while critical, are also easy to recognize.

The real challenge in crafting strategy lies in detecting the subtle discontinuities that may undermine a business in the future. And for that, there is no technique, no program, just a sharp mind in touch with the situation. Such discontinuities are unexpected and irregular, essentially unprecedented. They can be dealt with only by minds that are attuned to existing patterns yet able to perceive important breaks in them. Unfortunately, this form of strategic thinking tends to atrophy during the long periods of stability that most organizations experience (just as it did at Volkswagenwerk during the 1950s and 1960s). So the trick is to manage within a given strategic orientation most of the time yet be able to pick out the occasional discontinuity that really matters.

The Steinberg chain was built and run for more than half a century by a man named Sam Steinberg. For 20 years, the company concentrated on perfecting a self-service retailing formula introduced in 1933. Installing fluorescent lighting and figuring out how to package meat in cellophane wrapping were the "strategic" issues of the day. Then in 1952, with the arrival of the first shopping center in Montreal, Steinberg realized he had to redefine his business almost overnight. He knew he needed to control those shopping centers and that control would require public financing and other major changes. So he reoriented his business. The ability to make that kind of switch in thinking is the essence of strategic management. And it has more to do with vision and involvement than it does with analytic technique.

Know the Business

Sam Steinberg was the epitome of the entrepreneur, a man intimately involved with all the details of his business, who spent Saturday mornings visiting his stores. As he told us in discussing his company's competitive advantage: "Nobody knew the grocery business like we did. Everything has to do with your knowledge. I knew merchandise, I knew cost, I knew selling, I knew customers. I knew everything, and I passed on all my knowledge; I kept teaching my people. That's the advantage we had. Our competitors couldn't touch us."

Note the kind of knowledge involved: not intellectual knowledge, not analytical reports or abstracted facts and figures (though these can certainly help), but personal knowledge, intimate understanding, equivalent to the craftsman's feel for the clay. Facts are available to anyone; this kind of knowledge is not. Wisdom is the word that captures it best. But wisdom is a word that has been lost in the bureaucracies we have built for ourselves, systems designed to distance leaders from operating details. Show me managers who think they can rely on formal planning to create their strategies, and I'll show you managers who lack intimate knowledge of their businesses or the creativity to do something with it.

Craftsmen have to train themselves to see, to pick up things other people miss. The same holds true for managers of strategy. It is those with a kind of peripheral vision who are best able to detect and take advantage of events as they unfold.

Manage Patterns

Whether in an executive suite in Manhattan or a pottery studio in Montreal, a key to managing strategy is the ability to detect emerging patterns and help them take shape. The job of the manager is not just to preconceive specific strategies but also to recognize their emergence elsewhere in the organization and intervene when appropriate.

Like weeds that appear unexpectedly in a garden, some emergent strategies may need to be uprooted immediately. But management cannot be too quick to cut off the unexpected, for tomorrow's vision may grow out of today's aberration. (Europeans, after all, enjoy salads made from the leaves of the dandelion, America's most notorious weed.) Thus some patterns are worth watching until their effects have more clearly manifested themselves. Then those that prove useful can be made deliberate and be incorporated into the formal strategy, even if that means shifting the strategic umbrella to cover them.

To manage in this context, then, is to create the climate within which a wide variety of strategies can grow. In more complex organizations, this may mean building flexible structures, hiring creative people, defining broad umbrella strategies, and watching for the patterns that emerge.

Reconcile Change and Continuity

Finally, managers considering radical departures need to keep the quantum theory of change in mind. As Ecclesiastes reminds us, there is a time to sow and a time to reap. Some new patterns must be held in check until the organization is ready for a strategic revolution, or at least a period of divergence. Managers who are obsessed with either change or stability are bound eventually to harm their organizations. As pattern recognizer, the manager has to be able to sense when to exploit an established crop of strategies and when to encourage new strains to displace the old.

While strategy is a word that is usually associated with the future, its link to the past is no less central. As Kierkegaard once observed, life is lived forward but understood backward. Managers may have to live strategy in the future, but they must understand it through the past.

Like potters at the wheel, organizations must make sense of the past if they hope to manage the future. Only by coming to understand the patterns that form in their own behavior do they get to know their capabilities and their potential. Thus crafting strategy, like managing craft, requires a natural synthesis of the future, present, and past.

Author's note: Readers interested in learning more about the results of the tracking strategy project have a wide range of studies to draw from. Works published to date can be found in Robert Lamb and Paul Shivastava, eds., *Advances in Strategic Management,* vol. 4 (Greenwich, CT.: JAI Press, 1986), pp. 3–41; *Management Science,* May 1978, p. 934; *Administrator Science Quarterly,* June 1985, p. 160; *Canadian Journal of Administrative Sciences,* June 1984, p. 1; *Academy of Management Journal,* September 1982, p. 465; Robert Lamb, ed., *Competitive Strategic Management* (Englewood Cliffs, N.J.: Prentice Hall, 1984).

DOING BUSINESS IN THE UNITED STATES

Ray Suutari
C. Patrick Woodcock

The United States is Canada's natural trading partner. Geographically close, with a similar culture and no barriers arising from a difference in the basic language of business, English, it is not surprising that approximately 75 percent of Canadian trade is with the United States. In 1994, Canadian exports to the United States totalled $137 billion. Canadian exports are, however, concentrated in resources, resource-based products, and automobiles, all of which have had virtually duty-free entry into the United States for some time.

The relatively low proportion of exports of nonresource-based goods, despite the natural advantage of exporting to the U.S. market, is not due to the existence of tariffs, because they have been relatively low. More likely, it is due to the Canadian attitude toward the need to export. Canada enjoys a relatively high standard of living, and as a result, there have been no overwhelming pressures to export. However, in the early 1990s this attitude has started to change as new markets have had to be found to offset increasing competition from U.S. companies entering the Canadian market. Further rationalization of production to a North American basis under the Free Trade Agreement (FTA) and the North American Free Trade Agreement (NAFTA) has resulted in some Canadian branch plants being closed, so that replacement customers have to be found.

Some Canadians are also concerned about their ability to compete. One tongue-in-cheek indication of Canadian perceptions of themselves is provided by a survey of attitudes reflected in Canadian business textbooks as shown in Exhibit 1. These perceptions are, of course, wrong. Canadians have no inherent barriers to doing business in the United States, provided that they recognize certain facts:

1. There are significant differences between Canadian and U.S. business arising from the Canadian environment. These must be understood.

EXHIBIT 1   Survey of Canadian Business Perceptions in Relation to the United States

---

1. The fact that Canada is not like the United States is cause for shame and sadness.
2. The fact that we have more government institutions than the United States is evidence that something is wrong with the country.
3. Canadians, Canadian managers, Canadian customers, and definitely Canadian entrepreneurs all compare poorly with their American counterparts.
4. The fact that we have many foreign-owned firms is evidence that there is something wrong with all of us personally as well as the country.
5. Our early resource-based economy is a thing to be ashamed of. It would have been better if we had big manufacturing industries in 1880. Why this did not occur is a mystery.
6. The government in Canada "controls" business.
7. Canadian firms that venture into the United States do so because there is something wrong with Canadians.
8. Foreign firms that set up business in Canada do so because there is something wrong with Canadians.
9. The fact that an American firm succeeds is always evidence of that management's superior personal qualities; it is never due solely to huge domestic markets.
10. There is no risk capital in Canada. All the capital in the United States is risk capital.
11. R&D is something Americans and Japanese do well all the time. R&D, if done in Canada, is always too little or just plain bad.
12. My colleagues will laugh at me if I write positive things about Canadian business.

Source: Reprinted with permission. John W. Redston, "The Canadian Business Context: Conclusions from a Survey of Canadian General Business Texts 1960–1987," Working Paper, (Winnipeg: Red River Community College, 1988).

---

2. These differences create both competitive advantages and disadvantages which must be recognized in developing export strategies.
3. Implementation requires considerable effort to establish distribution capability, as well as sensitivity to U.S. buying practices.

The sections to follow will review each of these aspects in more detail. Appendix I is a report comparing the costs of locating in London, Ontario, Canada versus several U.S. cities. Appendix II illustrates export pricing calculations.

The Canadian Environment

Canadian business structures, their strategies, attitudes, and practices have evolved in response to the Canadian environment. The differences in the Canadian environment from the United States must be recognized in order to understand the adjustments which must be made in order to successfully do business in the United States.

Some of the hurdles businesses face in the Canadian environment can be defined in terms of demographics, geography, the labour force, the commercial/industrial structure, and the role of the government. These can be summarized as follows:

1. Demographically, Canada has a small population which is culturally fragmented
2. Geographically, the Canadian population is broadly dispersed in a narrow band close to the U.S. border. Further, Canada has a relatively harsh climate.
3. The Canadian labour force is highly unionized, particularly in the public sector.
4. Overall business activity is concentrated in relatively few companies with a significant but declining degree of foreign control.
5. The governments, federal and provincial, play a significant role in the economy, though this intervention is frequently in favour of business.

Demographics

The Canadian demographic situation and the underlying reasons are shown in Exhibit 2.

The main implication of the small domestic market is the difficulty in achieving economies of scale, particularly in manufacturing. Diseconomies tend to be present at the product level (short production runs), plant level (smaller plants which cannot justify the use of highly productive, specialized machinery), and the corporate level (ability to afford R&D, product

---

EXHIBIT 2   Demographic Characteristics

Canadian Situation

Small domestic population of 29 million versus 261 million in the United States.

Culturally segmented, with a Francophone component constituting one quarter of the population.

Immigration patterns have changed. Far more new Canadians are of Asian descent than European descent.

Underlying Reasons

The United States has been the preferred destination of immigrants due to image, dynamic economy, climate, and so on. More recently, restrictive Canadian immigration policies have limited population growth.

Historic cultural segmentation centered in Quebec has been perpetuated and reinforced by special political status.

---

development, and specialized staff). These advantages in secondary manufacturing had been substantially offset by high tariffs which are now disappearing under free trade.

Cultural segmentation further fragments the relatively small market with special product needs and imposes the costs of bilingual labeling, instructions, and so on. The United States also has a substantial cultural segment in its Hispanic population. However, this is a smaller proportion of its population (officially 4.1 percent), is geographically dispersed, and it does not enjoy special political status protecting its culture.

The Canadian market is also regionally segmented by geography, different economic bases, and cultural traditions. However, the differences between Canadian regions are likely no greater than occur in the United States, where lifestyle and climate can create the differences as exist between the Northeast and the Southwest.

The relatively small Canadian market has resulted in some Canadian industries outgrowing the Canadian market. For example, Canadian banks are turning to the U.S. market for further growth and to develop international economies of scale.

Geography

In terms of population distribution, as set out in Exhibit 3, Canada is a country approximately 5000 km long by 200 km wide. In contrast, a distance of only 800 km along the Atlantic seaboard from Boston to Washington contains a population of 25 million in the major metropolitan centres alone. Of course, not all of the United States is this densely populated, but the major concentrations on the Atlantic, Midwest, and Pacific coast each are far larger than the total Canadian market. For example, the population of the New England and

---

EXHIBIT 3   Geographic Factors

Canadian Situation
- Long distances between population concentrations.
- Population concentrated along U.S. border.
- Relatively cold climate with well-defined seasons.

Underlying Reasons
- Distances between major population concentrations are the result of the breadth of the country and natural geographic barriers, such as the Gulf of St. Lawrence and the Rocky Mountains.
- Population concentration along the southern border results from historic transportation routes (St. Lawrence River and the Great Lakes), the location of the best agricultural land, and the more moderate climate.

Mid-Atlantic states alone (New York, New Jersey, Pennsylvania) totals over 50 million, almost twice the size of the Canadian domestic market.

The northern United States is also exposed to the same climate as Canada, but this area contains a relatively small proportion of the total population. A large proportion of the United States has the advantage of a more moderate climate.

The broad implications of Canadian geography as a consequence of the population distribution and climatic factors are as follows:

1. Many costs are higher.

- For manufacturing, buildings must be more substantial and heating costs incurred.
- Distribution distances are longer and frequently require regional warehousing.
- More government infrastructure is required for highways and their maintenance, postal service, and so on.
- Consumers face nondiscretionary costs for heating and clothing, reducing discretionary income.

2. Merchandising is fragmented by four well-defined seasons, which increases risks due to short selling periods. For example, a cool early summer can slow down apparel sales to the point that markdowns are required to dispose of inventory to make room for the next season due within several months.

3. The very large proportion of population living near the U.S. border is exposed to U.S. media and cultural influence by receipt of U.S. television signals. This has contributed to cultural similarity and standardization of consumer products between Canada and the United States. On the other hand, the U.S. population living within the reach of a Canadian TV signal (about 100 km) is relatively small, with only a few major cities such as Detroit and Cleveland within this area.

The implications of the Canadian geographic environment are not entirely negative. It is the basis for a major tourist industry, and the solutions to transportation and communications problems have placed Canada in the forefront of the telecommunications industry and railway operations.

Labour

The Canadian labour relations environment is occasionally confrontational due to the high degree of unionization, as indicated in Exhibit 4. As a result, the incidence of strikes and their duration is significantly higher than in the United States and among the worst of the seven major industrialized nations, except for Italy.

EXHIBIT 4   Labour Force Situation

Canadian Situation
• The non-agricultural labour force is highly unionized at 33 percent versus 16 percent in the United States.
• Canadian unions are especially prevalent in the public sector.

Underlying Reasons
• Labour laws (provincial) are favourable to union organization and certification. This has included unionization of the civil service, which contributes 6 percent to the overall Canadian unionization rate.
• There are no Canadian nonunion havens, as exist in the U.S. South and the "right-to-work" states.
• Canadian industry is more concentrated in large companies, which have been easier to unionize.
• Unions in Canada have direct political representation via the New Democratic Party. U.S. unions must moderate their views in order to remain compatible with the Democratic or Republican party platforms.

Another characteristic of the Canadian labour force is that its small size relative to the U.S. results in a shortage of some specialized skills, particularly during boom periods.

Industrial/Commercial Structure

The extent of industrial concentration in Canada is a natural consequence of the relatively small economy. There is, after all, only room for a limited number of large operations, and the Combines Act does not significantly inhibit mergers, as has the Sherman Anti-Trust Act in the United States (see Exhibit 5).

Canadians are often characterized as being averse to taking risks, leading to the high degree of foreign ownership. This is, however, unfair. A foreign company, drawing on its domestic resources, can start a branch operation at relatively little risk in comparison with a stand-alone Canadian plant. However, this foreign control does result in product designs being imported, limiting Canadian contribution opportunities, and research and development activities.

The overall implication of the degree of industrial concentration in Canada is that the level of competition is lower in Canada than the United States. For example, off-price retailing and merchandising and "factory outlet" malls have strong market representation in the United States, while only limited market representation in Canada. The high degree of buying power of the major companies has tended to inhibit competition across the economic spectrum. It must, however, be acknowledged that Free Trade and NAFTA appear to have increased the competition in a variety of industries. For example,

---

EXHIBIT 5 Industrial/Commercial Structure

Canadian Situation

- Economic activity is concentrated in a relatively smaller number of companies compared to the United States.
- Foreign control is extensive with 165 of the largest 500 industrial companies being foreign controlled.
- Ownership by Canadians is also highly concentrated. Companies controlled by the Bronfman, Weston, Thompson and Desmarais families have sales equivalent to about 7 percent of the Canadian gross domestic product. In contrast, the U.S. auto industry accounts for only about 4 percent of that country's GDP.
- The five largest banks control about 60 percent of the total assets of the 100 largest financial institutions in Canada. However, Canada's national banking system has been less prone to financial problems compared to the fragmented U.S. banking system.
- Deregulation is proceeding more slowly than in the United States.

Underlying Reasons

- The relatively small domestic market limits the number of competitive units that can have reasonable economies of scale.
- Relatively lenient combines laws have not discouraged concentration.
- The proximity of the United States and the absence of language barriers have made Canada the logical area for U.S. expansion.

---

large discount stores, including The Price Club, Costco, and Walmart, are now entrenched in the Canadian retail industry.

The Government Role

A broad illustration of the difference in the role of government between Canada and the United States is provided by their underlying national philosophies. For Canada, the role of government as set out in the British-North America Act is to provide "peace, order and good government." In the United States, the Declaration of Independence sets the goal as "life, liberty and the pursuit of happiness." In general, Canadians are more tolerant of government intervention than are Americans, and Canada is regarded as a more caring society with extensive social programs in such areas as medical care, unemployment insurance, and old age security.

The implication of government involvement is not necessarily bad for business as is generally believed (Exhibit 6). In certain cases it is quite favourable, such as in the reduction of fringe benefit costs made possible by the Medicare system and the availability of subsidies or loans for establishing major new plants. Some of these benefits are the following:

- The productivity in some industries is very high compared to the U.S., an example being the auto industry where many companies have located in Canada (i.e., 17 percent of the North American productive capacity in this industry is in Canada) because of the productivity benefits.

___

EXHIBIT 6   The Government Role

Canadian Situation
- Canadian governments (federal and provincial) actively intervene in the business sector via regulation, crown corporations, and subsidization. There has been and continues to be a trend in the Canadian government to do less intervening using these approaches because they cost money and inhibit efficiency.
- Six of the 50 largest industrial companies in Canada are crown corporations with Ontario Hydro, Hydro-Quebec, and Petro Canada ranking 7th, 11th, and 22nd, respectively (1994 figures). The federal government has indicated its willingness to divest itself of some of these corporations in the future.
- Government power is fragmented between the federal and provincial levels, with the provincial government having substantial jurisdiction.

Underlying Reasons
- The relatively small economy has forced government to provide infrastructure which would not support private initiatives, particularly in more remote areas. This has involved the governments in transportation (railway, airline) and in electric power.
- The relatively high degree of jurisdiction vested in the provinces was a condition of confederation in which relatively mature, established provinces required the dilution of the central government role.
- Existence of relatively undeveloped areas requires active subsidization of economic development under the government policy of equalizing social service standards between provinces.

___

- The government-based health care system is up to 10 times more expensive for U.S. companies than Canadian-based companies (see Appendix I). Furthermore, the health care system in Canada appears to be relatively effective as the life expectancy in Canada is 78.4 years versus 75.9 years in the U.S.

However, there are problems associated with the degree of government involvement in Canada. They are the following:

- The extent of provincial jurisdiction multiplies regulation and fragments certain industries such as brewing and trucking.
- Interprovincial non-tariff trade barriers make it more difficult to ship some products from one province to another than from the U.S. to the destination province.

Some Other Differences

The relatively large size of the U.S. market and the intensity of the competition have led to differences in consumer behaviour. Some key differences are:

- Shoppers are accustomed to a much wider range of choice than in Canada. Six or seven brands of a product are not unusual as compared with two or three in Canada.

• Retailing tends to be much more specialized than in Canada, with stores targeting specific market segments. This too is attributable to the large market which can support specialized chains of the size necessary to achieve economies of scale.

• Shopping malls and free-standing stores account for 48 percent of U.S. shoppers as compared with only 20 percent in Canada, where shopping centres are dominant.

The U.S. situation requires highly sophisticated marketing management. Retailers try to develop special relationships with their market segments in order to create and sustain a loyal customer following. Canadian retailers cannot therefore expect to enter the U.S. market by merely transplanting a concept which has been successful in Canada. Marketing at any level in the United States requires more specialized expertise.

Overall Conclusions

As indicated by the discussion of the various elements of the Canadian environment, the Canadian situation is, in many respects, substantially different from the United States. The major factors which must be recognized in the development of a strategy for doing business in the United States can be summarized as follows:

1. Canada is a relatively high-cost country. The combination of reasons creating this includes the small scale of operation, high labour rates, climatic factors, and distances in supply and distribution. The cost disadvantages may be partially or totally offset by currency exchange rates.

2. Canadians are generally conditioned to a slightly less competitive domestic environment than exists in the United States in virtually all areas of activity. However, Canadians have proportionately more experience than Americans when operating outside of North America.

3. Concepts which are effective in Canada cannot necessarily be successfully transplanted to the United States, and vice versa. This is due to the overall differences in the environments and applies particularly to retailing.

Successful entry into the U.S. market cannot therefore be undertaken on the basis that the markets are identical. To the contrary, an entry strategy must be planned on the basis that the environments are considerably different, with weaknesses to overcome, and strengths leveraged.

Entry Strategy

The U.S. market can be entered by way of direct investment in a U.S. facility or by exporting. The primary consideration in the decision is obviously the need to be cost competitive. Exporting is usually a logical first step as it usually requires less investment and can provide increased sales volume with a high marginal profit contribution.

Export Strategy

As a first step to planning an export program, the company's potential as an exporter should realistically be assessed by asking the questions provided in Exhibit 7.

Given that a company sees export potential for its products or services, an export strategy should contain the following elements:

1. Compete on the basis of "value," not "price." In the face of the high-cost Canadian environment, competing solely on the basis of price, while not impossible, is obviously difficult. The factor which reduces price sensitivity is "value," which can consist of:

   a. Superior performance or durability, either in general or in some specific function.
   b. More attractive or unique design or styling.
   c. Extended warranties.

EXHIBIT 7   Something to Sell: A Checklist to Assess Your Potential as an Exporter

---

Assess your potential as an exporter by realistically examining your products or services in a global framework. Begin by asking the following questions:

1. Who already uses your product or service? Is it in broad general use or is it limited to a particular group because of socioeconomic factors? Is is particularly popular with a certain age group?
2. What modifications are required for it to appeal to customers in a foreign market?
3. Is its use influenced or affected by climatic or geographic factors? If so, what are they?
4. What is its shelf life? Will it be affected by time in transit?
5. Does your product or service involve operating costs? If so, what complementary equipment or services must the customer buy?
6. Does it require professional assembly or other technical skills?
7. What special packaging or literature is required? These costs must be added to the unit cost to determine whether or not you can export at a competitive price.
8. What are the technical or regulatory requirements? They may differ from country to country.
9. What after-sales service is needed? Is it locally available or is it up to you to provide it? If you need to provide it, do you have the resources?
10. How easily can the product be shipped? Would shipping costs make competitive pricing a problem?
11. Will you be able to serve both your domestic customers and your new foreign clients?
12. If domestic demand increases, can you still handle the requirements of your export customers?

Source: Adapted from "How To Do Business in the U.S." Ministry of Industry, Trade and Technology, Province of Ontario, 1987.

2. Target specific rather than broad markets. This follows directly from the "value" approach, as differentiated products usually appeal only to specific market segments. These markets must be identified, and the product or approach tailored or modified to appeal to these markets. It is in this area where the basis of success in Canada must be reexamined in the context of the U.S. market in order to establish the extent to which it can be transplanted, or how it must be modified to be effective. While the niches may constitute only a relatively small proportion of the U.S. market, they are still large in comparison with the Canadian market, and being small may not be as intensely competitive as the mass markets.

3. Give close attention to distribution. Value must be sold, that is, the features which provide competitive advantage must be brought to the potential buyers' attention. This means that the distributor must be capable of providing this sales effort through the combination of direct selling, promotional material, follow-up, and so on. This requires the careful selection of the distribution channel and the organization which will be representing you in the United States, as well as the incentives necessary to do a good job.

4. Recognize that there are differences between Canadian and U.S. channels of distribution and selling practices. Specifically,

   a. U.S. manufacturers make greater use of independent sales representatives. About 70 percent of manufacturers use agents on a commission basis, which can be as low as 3 percent. In Canada, manufacturers rely on in-house sales forces with only 30 percent using independent representatives.

   b. The wholesale function is less important in the United States where its revenue equals 32.7 percent of GNP versus 41.1 percent in Canada. The smaller average size of the Canadian retailer and distribution distances likely account for the difference.

5. Exploit the Canadian image if possible. For example, the Canadian brewing industry has developed a substantial export market in the United States, assisted by the fact that Canadian beer has a favourable image. Similarly, Canadian winter recreational products such as snowmobiles, hockey equipment, and so on, have gained significant positions in the U.S. market. Where applicable, the ability to withstand and operate in a "Canadian" winter can be used to emphasize durability.

6. Support the strategy with adequate resources, both financial and management. The process of identifying markets, recruiting distributors, providing them with support material (catalogues, brochures), training the sales staff in your product's characteristics (seminars, plant visits), advertising, and even establishing inventories in regional warehouses can be expensive. If viewed solely as an expense, the effort may be incomplete and risk failure or disappointing results. It should be kept in mind that being established in any market with strong distributor relationships and customer base can provide consistency in sales volume and growth potential over a long time. This is an asset of enduring value and like all assets of enduring value, the outlays

and effort to establish it should be treated like an investment rather than an expense.

To summarize, strategies to export to the United States should be highly specific, that is, planned to capture highly targeted markets with well-defined appeals. This requires not only careful development of the strategy but close attention to implementation.

The implementation effort must also recognize that the U.S. market is different and that it must be approached with recognition of its characteristics and its sensitivities. The following suggestions are based upon exporters' experiences:

1. Where U.S. management or services are required, such as a regional sales manager or product managers, hire experienced U.S. people. Canadians sent to the United States must initially learn about the idiosyncrasies of the U.S. market, its regulations, tax structures, hiring and training, and so on, which distracts from the basic job, particularly in the very important early phase.

2. Set price on the basis of delivered cost including any duties (Delivered Duty Paid), or as a minimum, DDP at port of entry. This avoids the confusion and uncertainty of these items. The U.S. price list should be separate and not show prices in both U.S. and Canadian dollars. In pricing for the United States, it should be remembered that the Canadian Goods and Services Tax is not applicable on exported products. Imported raw materials used in manufacture are entitled to duty drawback. (Appendix II provides a summary of the components of export pricing.)

3. Catalogues, display, or promotional material should not emphasize Canadian content, unless there is a specific image advantage. In particular, bilingual (French/English) sales literature is not well received in the United States. American importers often believe that Canadian-made goods are better than those from offshore suppliers since they consider Canada to be part of the North American domestic economy. As a result, the appearance of "foreignness" should be de-emphasized. The image of proximity may be further enhanced by having a U.S. postal address (via a U.S. mail agency) and a toll-free 800 phone line.

4. The product must conform to American standards and requirements. This can include labelling for country of origin and "care" standards (not bilingual), flammability standards, Food and Drug Administration Standards for food and cosmetic products, electrical product approvals, and product liability requirements.

5. Use Canadian government assistance, which is readily available. The governments, both federal and provincial, have very active export promotion programs. The range of assistance available includes:
    a. Assistance in identifying potential markets from provincial departments and consulates in major U.S. cities.
    b. Publications and seminars on various export-related issues.

  c. Assistance in participating in trade missions, trade fairs, and exhibitions.

  d. Ensuring supplier credit programs via the Export Development program.

  e. Financing export development programs via grants or loans (varies from province to province).

In addition, the Canadian Manufacturers Association and Canadian Export Association provide assistance via various publications.

The principle underlying the implementation suggestions is "know your market," a basic axiom for both domestic and export marketing.

Direct Investment Strategy

When a market base has been established in the United States and expansion of capacity is required, the question as to where additional capacity should be built must be considered. This is mainly an issue of where costs are lowest, after recognizing costs arising from the duplication of infrastructures.

While U.S. wage rates and taxes are generally lower than in Canada, these may not be the only determinants of the economics of production. The following must also be taken into consideration:

- Certain energy costs, particularly electricity, are lower in Canada.
- The overall quality of labour tends to be low in the low-wage geographic areas of the United States as the result of low levels of education. Thus, both worker productivity and the ability to handle more sophisticated tasks may be limited.

Medical insurance if provided to employees as a fringe benefit is both expensive and highly variable in cost. As an indication of the level of cost, the major automobile manufacturers estimate that medical insurance costs are approximately six times higher in the U.S. than in Canada. In the United States, smaller companies trying to keep their costs down often place coverage with limited preferred risk pools if they qualify by way of the age and general health of the employees. However, it takes only a few serious illnesses on the part of the employees to drastically raise premiums, making year-to-year estimation of costs difficult.

Appendix I is a study comparing the costs of locating in several U.S. cities versus London, Ontario. It is a study that was completed by a large U.S. consulting firm, and it indicates how close costs actually are on a comparative basis.

In addition to operating cost advantages, financing for new plants may be available on better terms than in Canada. Counties and municipalities are able to offer attractive financing by way of locally-issued revenue bonds to attract new industry. These provide a combination of low interest rates and extended repayment terms, or are used to build a plant and lease it to the company. Many municipalities also offer tax concessions to the new company.

Summary

1. The United States is a natural export market for Canadian business because of its size, proximity, common language, and similarity of cultures.

2. Despite these advantages, there are substantial differences between the Canadian and U.S. environments which result in Canada being a relatively high-cost country with a less competitive environment. As a result of the differences, concepts successful in Canada may not be effective in the United States.

3. Strategies for exporting to the United States should be based on reducing price sensitivity by selling "value" to specific target markets via carefully chosen distributors. The high cost of entry on any significant scale should be regarded as an investment.

4. Implementation requires knowledge of the idiosyncrasies of the U.S. market, clear pricing, and meeting their product and labeling standards.

Government programs at both the federal and provincial levels are available to assist U.S. export development programs.

References

"Annual Report of the Ministry of Supply and Services Canada under the Corporations and Labour Unions Returns Act, Part II—Labour Unions, 1986." Statistics Canada 71–202.

Arnold, J. R. "Exporting to the United States—Costing Products" Appendix II, Selecting and Using Manufacturers Agents in the United States.

Brown, P. B. "Matters of Impact." *Inc.,* October 1988, pp. 115–8.

"Diversions." Report on Business Magazine, *The Globe and Mail,* July/August 1985.

Evans, W.; H. Lane; and S. O'Grady. *Border Crossings: Doing Business in the U.S.* Toronto: Prentice Hall Canada, 1992.

"The Financial Post 500." Financial Post Company Ltd., 1995.

"The Fortune 500." *Fortune,* April 25, 1988.

"How to Do Business in the U.S.," Ministry of Industry, Trade and Technology, Province of Ontario, (Queen's Printer for Ontario), 1987.

Kidd, Kenneth. "Price Gaps that Drive Canadians to U.S. Shops Start in the Far East." *The Globe and Mail,* April 23, 1991.

Leighton, David S. R. "Doing Business in the U.S.: Canada's Challenge." *Quarterly,* Fall 1987, pp. 80–84.

Marfels, Christian. "Aggregate Concentration in International Perspective: Canada, Federal Republic of Germany, Japan and the United States." In *Mergers, Corporate Concentration and Power in Canada,* ed. R. S. Khemani, D. M.

Shapiro, and W. T. Stanbury (Institute for Research on Public Policy), 1988, chap. 3.

Saffer, Morris. "Canadian Retailers: How to Succeed in U.S. Markets," *Business Quarterly,* Winter 1989, pp. 38–41.

Tigert, D. D. "Canada Versus the U.S.: The Growing Economic Gap." *The Financial Post,* March 21, 1984.

APPENDIX I
COST COMPARISON EXAMPLE OF LOCATING IN CANADA VERSUS THE U.S.

Executive Summary

A. Study Background and Objectives

On behalf of the Corporation Of The City Of London, KPMG Management Consulting has carried out an analysis of key location-sensitive costs for selected U.S. citites in comparison with London, Ontario. This report summarizes the results of our study.

This study builds on the work conducted by KPMG Management Consulting in a recent report entitled *"A Comparison Of Location-Sensitive Operating Costs In Canada And The United States,"* prepared for the Department of Foreign Affairs and International Trade of the Government of Canada. Our original report examined operating costs in 10 cities—5 in the U.S. and 5 in Canada. The analysis was based on the development of illustrative business cases and a computer-based financial model. We modeled typical operating costs for each business case from facility start-up to 10 years of operation, using current tax rates, cost factors, and exchange rates. We examined the total impact of key location-sensitive capital and operating costs, including land, building, labour, taxation, electricity, and interest costs, in three types of facilities.

In this study, we have adapted the model used in our previous work and expanded it to examine four types of facilitites. In addition, we have updated the tax rates and cost factors used. Transportation costs were excluded from our previous report because of the broad geographic disposition of the cities examined. Due to the narrower geographic scope of the cities examined in this analysis, transportation costs have been added. All costs within this report are expressed in U.S. dollars with an exchange rate of $0.75 U.S. per Canadian dollar.

Each model facility is assumed to have sales in excess of $10 million, and a minimum of 100 employees. The analysis focuses on the costs of establishing facilities on three- to five-acre sites in suburban areas zoned for light-to-medium industrial purposes. The four industries analyzed included:

1. A medical devices manufacturer.
2. A pharmaceuticals manufacturer.
3. An autoparts manufacturer.
4. A computer software development firm.

Source: Excerpts from a study prepared for the City of London by KPMG Management Consulting Co.

The five cities examined included:

United States	Canada
Rochester, New York	London, Ontario
Columbus, Ohio	
Manchester, New Hampshire	
Raleigh, North Carolina	

B. Rankings on the Basis of Key Location-Sensitive Costs

A summary of the rankings for the cities on the basis of key location–sensitive operating costs is shown in Exhibit I–1. The study results for each of the four model facilitites are shown graphically in Exhibits I–2 to I–5.

    The results of the analysis indicate that Raleigh and Manchester provide low-cost sites based on location-sensitive factors. In three of the four industry models examined, these cities provided the lowest operating costs.

    Operating costs in London are competitive with costs in the U.S. cities examined. London ranked third in three of the four industry models studied, and first in the computer software development facility model. In the three industries where London ranked third, a gap of only 3 percent separated London from the city with the lowest location-sensitive costs. Since these results are based on an exchange rate of $0.75 U.S. per $1 Canadian, and current exchange rates are in the $0.74 U.S. range, the gap in location-sensitive costs has been reduced to less than 2 percent.

C. Summary of Key Findings

    • **Raleigh and Manchester ranked first and second** in three of the four industry models studied, including medical devices, pharmaceuticals, and autoparts manufacturing.

    • **London competes effectively** against U.S. cities in terms of location-sensitive operating costs. London ranked first in terms of operating costs for the computer

---

EXHIBIT I–1   Rankings on the Basis of Location-Sensitive Operating Costs

	Industry Model			
City	*Medical Devices Mfg.*	*Pharmaceuticals Mfg.*	*Autoparts Mfg.*	*Software Development*
Raleigh, NC	1	1	1	2
Manchester, NH	2	2	2	4
Columbus, OH	4	4	4	3
Rochester, NY	5	5	5	5
London, Ont.	3	3	3	1

Note: A ranking of "1" indicates lowest costs.

EXHIBIT I–2   Location-Sensitive Operating Costs for Medical Devices Manufacturing Facility Model

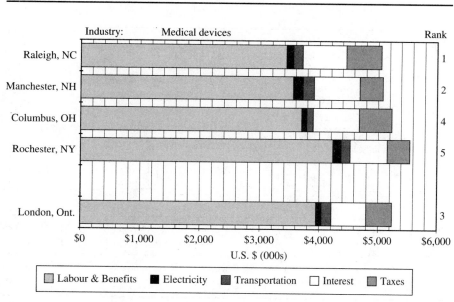

EXHIBIT I–3   Location-Sensitive Operating Costs for Pharmaceuticals Manufacturing Facility Model

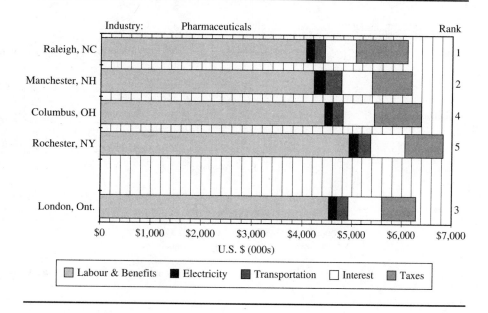

Exhibit I–4 **Location-Sensitive Operating Costs for Autoparts Manufacturing Facility Model**

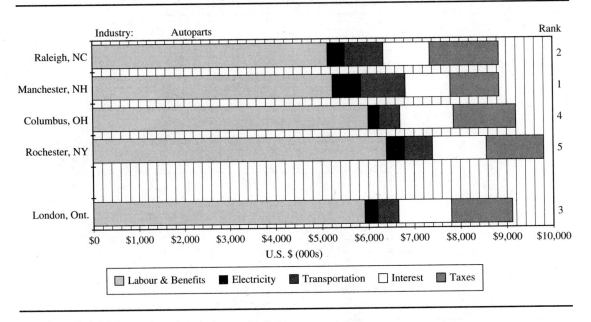

Exhibit I–5 **Location-Sensitive Operating Costs for Computer Software Development Facility Model**

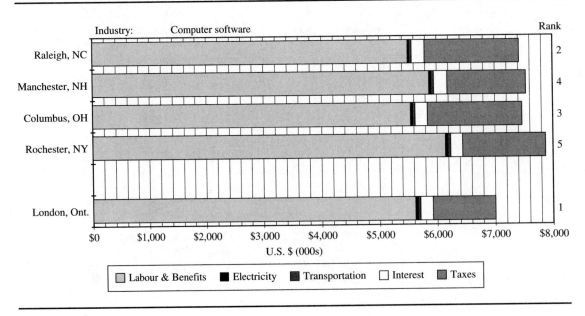

software development facility model, and third in the other industries examined. Where London placed third, a gap of only 3 percent in location-sensitive costs existed between London and the lowest cost cities.

• **Federal, regional, and local taxation rates** vary significantly between the cities examined. However, **income tax credits for research and development** in Canada provide a significant advantage over those provided in U.S. locations. In addition, income tax legislation in Canada allows capital assets associated with research and development to be depreciated at a faster rate in Canada than in the United States.

• **Electricity costs** for industrial users are 9 to 49 percent lower in London than in the U.S. cities examined.

• **Wage costs** in London for typical manufacturing and software development positions are competitive with those in the U.S. cities examined.

• **The costs of employer-sponsored benefits** in Canada are lower than those in the United States.

• **The costs of employer-paid statutory employee benefits and taxes** tend to be lower in Canada than in the United States, primarily because of the existence of a public-sponsored health care system in Canada and significantly lower workers' compensation costs.

• **Industrial land costs** in London are 10 to 20 percent lower than in Rochester and Raleigh, but 30 to 60 percent higher than in Columbus and Manchester.

• **Construction costs** in London are 6 to 37 percent higher than in the U.S. cities examined.

D. Recent Exchange Rate Trends Increase Canada's Competitiveness

All costs in this report are expressed in U.S. dollars, and are based on an exchange rate of $0.75 U.S. per $1 Canadian. As shown in Exhibit I–6, the value of the Canadian dollar has steadily declined against the U.S. dollar since late 1991. This trend provides a significant cost advantage for investment in Canada because the costs of labour, land, construction, and electricity have declined in terms of U.S. dollars. A drop of $0.01 U.S. below the $0.75 U.S. level results in a 1.3 percent increase in cost competitiveness for Canadian manufacturers.

E. Other Factors

The focus of this analysis is to assess the impact of site location of comparative business operating costs. These are the critical factors in a site location decision, but a number of other criteria are also important—such as the availability of a suitable workforce, quality of life, and transportation infrastructure.

Canadian cities, such as London, have advantages in these areas as well. For example, a recent study published by the United Nations Development Programme[1] ranked Canada number one in the world on the basis of factors contributing to quality of life, such as education, life expectancy, and availability of medical care. The United States ranked eighth in the same study.

Canada also ranked first in the United Nations comparison of post-secondary education enrollment.[2] The study compared the percentage of the population aged 20 to 24

---

[1] Human Development Report 1994, United Nations Development Programme, 1994.
[2] UNESCO, Statistical Yearbook 1991.

EXHIBIT I–6   Trends in the Value of the Canadian Dollar in Terms of U.S. Funds

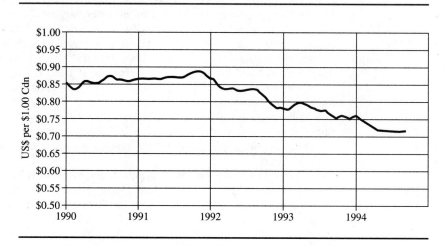

years that are enrolled in post-secondary education programs. The United States ranked second in this study.

In addition, Canada ranked first in a comparison of transportation infrastructure performed by the World Economic Forum (Geneva, Switzerland) and the Institute of Management Development (Lausanne, Switzerland).[1] The study measured the extent to which each country's transportation infrastructure is developed to meet the business needs of a company competing internationally, and the adequacy of roads, railroads, air transport, and port access. The United States ranked third in this study, behind Canada and Germany.

This study is based on current tax rates and cost factors, all of which are subject to change. While every effort has been made to ensure the accuracy of the information contained in this report, KPMG cannot accept liability for actions taken on the basis of the study. In addition, each investment decision requires a detailed investigation of many location-sensitive factors, such as workforce quality and availability, quality of life, as well as the factors examined in this study.

Study Scope And Methodology

A. The Comparison Focused on Location-Sensitive Factors

In designing this study, our objective was to assess the cost-competitiveness of London, Ontario, as a place to do business, relative to comparable cities in the U.S. Accordingly,

---

[1] World Competitive Report, 1993.

our analysis involved a comparison of 20 business cases, covering four industries and five cities.

For each of the business cases, a detailed analysis of key location-sensitive factors was performed. These factors included the cost of land, buildings, wages and salaries, benefits, electricity, transportation, interest, and federal, regional, and municipal taxes. While the broad scope of the analysis precluded inclusion of local licenses and fees, the major location-sensitive costs identified were analyzed and compared.

B. Four U.S. Cities Were Selected for Comparison with London, Ontario

Four U.S. cities were selected for comparison with London because they compete with London for economic development projects in the sectors examined. In addition, each city offers a diverse and dynamic economy with good access to the North American market, and each has received recognition as a good location for business investment.

The five cities examined included:

United States	**Canada**
Rochester, New York	London, Ontario
Columbus, Ohio	
Manchester, New Hampshire	
Raleigh, North Carolina	

EXHIBIT I–7   Locations of Cities Examined

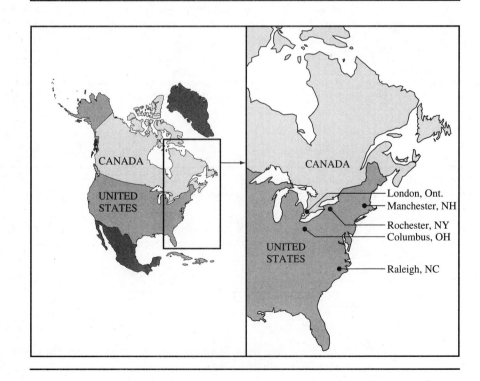

Exhibit I–8   City Populations and Major Employers

	Population	Major Manufactured Products	Major Employers
London, Ont.	299,000 City 379,000 MSA	Diesel vehicles, motor vehicles, beverages, chemical products, electrical products, foods, and printed materials	Ford Motor Co. Can. General Motors Can. Bell Canada 3M Canada Inc. CAMI Automotive Inc. Northern Telecom
Rochester, NY	232,000 City 1,062,000 MSA	Photographic equipment, optical equipment, graphic technologies, electronics, clothing, pharmaceutical equipment, industrial mixed fluids, gear cutting machinery, shoes, and communication equipment	Eastman Kodak Bausch and Lomb Mobile Chemical Corp. Xerox Corp. General Motors Corp. Rochester Gas and Electric
Columbus, OH	633,000 City 1,345,000 MSA	Fabricated metals, chemicals, refrigerators, communications and transportation equipment, machinery, technical instruments, and processed food.	Honda of America Limited Corporation American Electric Power Sears Roebuck & Co. Bank One of Columbus AT&T Network Systems
Manchester, NH	100,000 City 150,000 MSA	Electronics, paper and plastics, and automobile accessories.	General Electric Co. GTE Products SCI Manufacturing Raytheon Corp. Velcro USA New England Telephone
Raleigh, NC	208,000 City 886,000 MSA	Electronics, electrical equipment, metals, and processed foods.	IBM Corp. Northern Telecom Glaxo Carolina Power & Light Burroughs Wellcome Telex Computer Prod.

Note: MSA refers to Metropolitan Statistical Area.
Source: *The 1994 Geographic Reference Report,* BTA Economic Research Institute

The locations of these cities are shown in Exhibit I–7, and population and major employer information is presented in Exhibit I–8.

Location-Sensitive Cost Factors

We gathered data from a number of sources to compare the cost of doing business in each of the locations under study.

The location-sensitive factors examined include:

Industrial land costs

Construction costs

Labour costs

Electricity costs

Transportation costs

Federal, regional, and local taxes

A. Industrial Land Costs

Our analysis focused on the costs of establishing facilities in suburban areas zoned for light-to-medium industrial purposes. In October 1994, we gathered land cost data through interviews with representatives of the economic development offices and realty firms in each location. The costs quoted were based on a three- to five-acre site of fully serviced industrial land in a light-to-medium industrial park setting, with access to transportation infrastructure. Based on these quotes, an average range of land costs was developed for each city.

Our survey found the lowest costs in Manchester and Columbus, and the highest costs in Raleigh and Rochester. At $40,000 to $50,000 per acre, costs in Manchester and Columbus are up to 50 percent lower than costs in Raleigh and Rochester. The high costs in Raleigh reflect a recent increase in commercial and industrial investment speculation within the region.

At $50,000 to $65,000 per acre, industrial land costs in London are in the middle of the range, about 20 percent higher than those in Columbus and Manchester, but about 40 percent lower than the costs in Rochester.

Industrial land costs for the locations under examination are shown in Exhibit I–9.

B. Construction Costs

We assumed that our model businesses would establish "greenfield" facilities in the selected location. Construction costs for a one-story factory with 30,000 square feet in floor space are shown in Exhibit I–10.

Of the five cities examined, Raleigh provides the lowest construction costs, at $42 per square foot. Construction costs in Raleigh are 16 to 37 percent lower than in the other locations examined. The highest costs are found in London, where costs are $57 per square foot.

C. Labour Costs

In the industries examined, labour costs represent 25 to 30 percent of total operating costs. The labour costs examined were broken down into:

Wages and salaries

Employer-sponsored benefits

Employer-paid statutory benefits and taxes.

1. **Wage and salary costs.** Annual wage costs for three typical manufacturing positions are shown in Exhibit I–11. Wage costs in London for these positions are

EXHIBIT I–9   Industrial Land Costs in Suburban Areas of Selected Locations

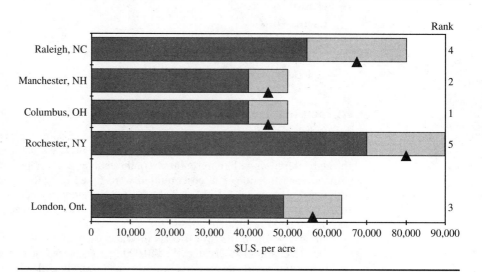

Note: Based on three to five acres of fully serviced, light-to-medium industrial land in suburban areas of each location, with access to transportation infrastructure.

Source: KPMG survey of realty firms in each city (October 1994).

EXHIBIT I–10   Construction Costs in Selected Locations

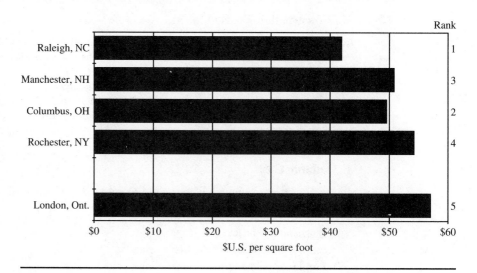

Source: Means Square Foot Construction Cost Data, 1994 adjusted to reflect exchange rate of $0.75 U.S. per $1 Canadian.

comparable to, if not lower than, those in the U.S. cities examined. For example:

- London has the lowest wages for machinists, $1,110 lower than in Raleigh and $7,420 lower than in Columbus.
- Median annual wages for machine tool operators are $1,830 lower in London than in Rochester, but $4,430 higher than in Manchester.
- Although London has the highest wages for electronics technicians, wages in London are within 3 percent of those in Manchester, Columbus, and Rochester.

2. **Employer-sponsored benefits.** A comparison of employer-sponsored benefits in Canada and the United States is shown in Exhibit I–12. The exhibit compares benefit costs as a percentage of gross annual payroll.

Employer-sponsored benefits in Canada are lower than in the United States. Costs for hospital, surgical, medical, and major medical insurance premiums are the prime reason for the difference in costs. These insurance premiums represent a cost of 7.9 percent of gross pay in the United States compared with 0.6 percent in Canada.

3. **Employer-paid statutory benefits and taxes.** Employer-paid statutory benefits and taxes based on wages include:

Unemployment insurance premiums
Medicare (U.S.) and medical plan premiums (Canada)

EXHIBIT I–11   Median Annual Wages in Selected Locations

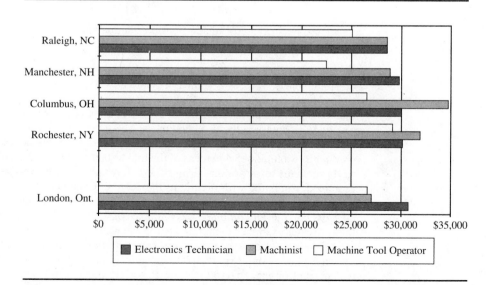

Source: The 1994 Geographic Reference Report, BTA Economic Research Institute. U.S. dollars.

Exhibit I–12   Employer-Sponsored Benefits in Canada and the United States

	United States[a] (%)	Canada[b] (%)
Overall	**26.9**	**25.1**
Payments for, or in lieu of, vacation	5.6	5.9
Payments for, or in lieu of, holidays	3.4	3.5
Self-insured short-term disability/sick leave pay	1.3	0.9
Other	2.8	3.6[c]
Payments for time not worked	**13.1**	**13.9**
Pension plan contributions, pension plan premiums (net) under insurance, administrative, and other costs	4.0	5.7
Life insurance and death benefits	0.5	0.4
Hospital, surgical, medical, and major medical insurance premiums	7.9[d]	0.6
Short-term disability, sickness, or accident insurance and long-term disability or wage continuation	0.5	2.8
Dental insurance premiums	0.6	0.7
Other (vision care, physical and mental fitness, etc.)	0.3	[e]
Other		1.0[f]
Employer-sponsored plans	**13.8**	**11.2**

[a] U.S. Source: Employee Benefits, 1990 prepared by the Research Centre, Economic Policy Division, The Chamber of Commerce of the United States.
[b] Canadian Source: KPMG Management Consulting.
[c] Canadian figures include rest periods, bereavement, jury duty, and other paid time off.
[d] Includes payments for retired employees.
[e] Canadian figures included in hospital, surgical, medical, etc.
[f] Figure includes the cost of thrift savings and share purchase plans.

Social Security and Canada Pension Plan payments

Other payroll taxes

A summary of labour wage rates and employer-paid statutory benefits and taxes in Canadian and U.S. cities is shown in Exhibit I–13.

Employer-paid social insurance premiums in the U.S. are higher than those in Canada. For example, premiums for a worker earning $30,000 in Canada represent a cost of $673, compared with $1,860 in the U.S.

In the U.S., premiums for state unemployment insurance are deductible from federal premiums to a limit of 5.4 percent of the first $7,000 paid to each employee. Employer-paid premiums for a worker earning $30,000 would amount to $434 in the U.S. cities examined, compared with premiums of $1,290 in Canada.

Ontario has a 1.95 percent payroll tax and a 4 percent medical insurance premium on gross payroll, for combined payroll taxes of 5.95%. In comparison, payroll taxes in the U.S. cities examined are limited to the Medicare tax of 1.45 percent of gross payroll.

A significant difference in workers' compensation premiums is evident between the five cities. For example, in the pharmaceuticals manufacturing sector, rates vary from 0.92 percent of gross payroll in Raleigh to 7.15 percent in Rochester. In the medical

Exhibit I–13   Labour Wage Rates, Statutory Benefits, and Taxes[a]

	Canada	United States			
	London, Ont.	*Rochester, NY*	*Columbus, OH*	*Manchester, NH*	*Raleigh, NC*
Median annual wages for selected positions[b]					
Electronics technician	$30,809	$30,228	$30,110	$29,827	$28,449
Machine tool operator	$27,029	$28,856	$27,055	$22,600	$25,201
Machinist	$27,418	$32,281	$34,836	$28,950	$28,532
Programmer	$31,512	$33,622	$30,771	$33,974	$32,262
Social insurance (% of gross pay)	2.60%	6.20%	6.20%	6.20%	6.20%
Base maximum	$25,865[c]	$60,600	$60,600	$60,600	$60,600
Unemployment insurance[d] (% of gross pay)					
Federal	4.30%	6.2%	6.2%	6.2%	6.2%
Base maximum	$30,496	$7,000	$7,000	$7,000	$7,000
Provincial/state	—	4.30%	3.00%	2.70%	2.25%
Base maximum		$7,000	$8,500	$7,000	$13,200
Payroll tax[e] (% of gross pay)	1.95%	1.45%	1.45%	1.45%	1.45%
	4.00%				
Workers' compensation[f] (% of gross pay)					
Medical devices mftg.	1.34%	2.95%	1.86%	2.78%	1.78%
Pharmaceuticals mftg.	1.46%	7.15%	2.84%	2.95%	0.92%
Autoparts Mftg.	4.92%	8.70%	7.53%	4.67%	4.26%
Computer software dev.	0.00%	1.46%	0.62%	0.63%	0.37%
Base maximum	$40,150	None	None	None	None

[a] All figures in U.S. dollars. Exchange rate: $0.75 U.S. per $1 CAN.
[b] Source: The 1994 Geographic Reference Report, BTA Economic Research Institute.
[c] In Canada: Canada Pension Plan (CPP), first $2,556 exempt.
   In U.S.: Federal Income Contribution Act (FICA).
[d] In U.S.: State unemployment insurance costs can be credited to federal costs to a maximum of 5.4% of the first $7,000 paid to each employee. Rates shown for state plans apply to new employers. Source: State Tax Handbook, CCH.
[e] In Ontario: The 4.00% payroll tax is for a medical insurance premium.
   In U.S.: The payroll tax represents the costs for the Medicare program.
[f] Source: Workers' Compensation Boards in each jurisdiction.

devices manufacturing sector, rates vary from 1.34 percent in London to 2.95 percent in Rochester. Rates in Rochester, which are the highest for all four industrial categories across the five cities, are about two to five times higher than the corresponding rates in London.

D. Electricity Costs

Electricity costs for industrial users are significantly lower in Canada than the United States. London has the lowest electricity rates for the five cities examined. Specifically, London's electricity rates are 8 percent lower than those in Columbus, and 21 to 48 percent lower than those in the three other cities. Electricity costs in Manchester and Rochester are significantly higher than in the other three cities. Users in these two cities pay rates 38 to 90 percent higher than in the other cities.

Exhibit I–14   Monthly Electricity Costs in Selected Locations

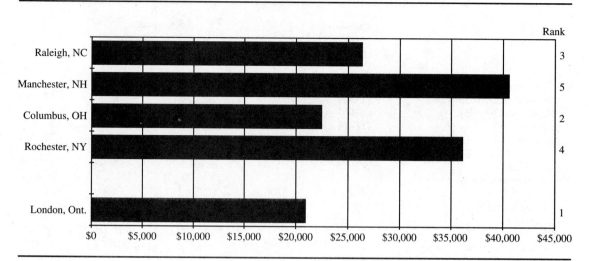

Notes: Rates quoted are for monthly consumption of 400,000 KWH and 1,000 KW demand load. Demand charges based on peak load are applied where required by the local utility. All figures expressed in U.S. dollars and do not include regional or local taxes.
Source: Edison Electric Institute, Summer 1994, London Hydro.

The monthly electricity costs for an example of an industrial user in each city are shown in Exhibit I–14. Based on this consumption level, an industrial user would pay an additional $235,000 annually, or 90 percent more, to operate in Manchester instead of London.

E. Federal, Regional, and Local Taxation Rates

Federal, regional, and local taxation rates vary significantly between the locations examined. In addition to, or in place of, federal and provincial or state income taxes, other types of taxation may apply, such as:

- Corporation Minimum Tax, based on alternative calculations of taxable income.
- Corporation Capital/Franchise Tax, based on the amount of paid-up capital.
- Business Taxes, based on the market value of property or total payroll.
- Sales of Use Taxes on purchases of goods or services.
- Property Tax, based on the market or assessed value of property.
- Real Property Transfer Tax, based on the purchase price of real property.

A summary of corporate taxes in each city is shown in Exhibit I–15.

The federal corporate tax rate for Canadian manufacturers is 21.84 percent of taxable income. In the U.S., a graduated scale of rates provides a maximum rate of 34 percent for taxable income in excess of $335,000·and below $10 million. In the U.S.,

EXHIBIT I–15   Corporate and Other Taxes

	Canada	United States			
	London, Ont.	Rochester, NY	Columbus, OH	Manchester, NH	Raleigh, NC
Corporation income tax (% of taxable income)					
Federal	21.84%[a]	30.57%[b]	30.97%[b]	31.62%[b]	31.34%[b]
Provincial/state	13.50%[a]	10.10%[c,g]	8.90%[d,e]	7.00%	7.83%[f]
Total	35.34%	40.67%	39.87%	38.62%	39.17%
Corporation minimum tax (% of alternative minimum taxable income)					
Federal	—	20.00%	20.00%	20.00%	20.00%
Provincial/State	2.00%[a]	5.63%[g]	—	—	—
Corporation capital/franchise tax	0.30%[h]	0.20%[g]	0.58%[e]	—	—
Business & occupation tax (% of property market value)	2.10%	—	—	—	—
Business enterprise tax	—	—	—	0.25%[i]	—
Sales tax (% of purchases)					
General	8.00%	8.00%	5.75%	—	6.00%
Electricity	—	—	—	—	3.00%
Property tax (% of market value)					
Land and Buildings	3.50%	2.23%	4.00%[j]	3.00%[k]	0.66%
Machinery & equipment	—	—	—	—	—
Real property transfer tax (% of purchase price)	2.00%[l]	0.40%	0.10%	0.50%	0.20%

[a] Rate for manufacturing and processing firms.
[b] Marginal tax rate applies if earnings exceed $335,000 and are less than $10 million. Rates shown reflect adjustments to federal marginal rate of 34.00% account for deduction of state taxes from federal taxable income.
[c] Based on 9% taxation rate and 12.5% surtax.
[d] Highest nominal tax rate applies if earnings exceed $50,000.
[e] Corporation pays the greater of Ohio Corporate Income Tax or Business Franchise tax. Business Franchise Tax is based on net worth.
[f] Includes 1.00% surtax.
[g] In New York, corporations pay the greater of: corporation tax on allocated net income (9%), business/investment capital tax (1.78 mills per dollar), alternative minimum tax (5%), or minimum flat rate tax. In addition, a surtax of 12.5% is applied.
[h] Corporation capital tax is based on paid-up capital.
[i] Credited against Corporate Income Tax liability. Based on compensation paid, interest paid or accrued, and dividends paid or accrued.
[j] Assessed value may not exceed 35% of market value.
[k] Most property is assessed at less than 100% of market value.
[l] Maximum rate. Lower rates apply for values less than $301,000.

state taxes are deductible from federal taxable income. Therefore, the effective federal tax rate is different for each state. The federal tax rates shown in Exhibit I–15 reflect adjustments for state taxes paid.

London has the lowest combined federal and state corporate income tax rate for the five cities examined. At 35.34 percent, corporate income tax rates in London are 3.3 to 5.3 percentage points lower than in the other cities. However, nominal income taxation rates should not be used as the sole measure of the impact of taxation in each location. Other factors, such as depreciation rates and the availability of investment incentives, have a significant impact on the amount of taxes paid.

Appendix II
How to Work out Export Prices
An Export Pricing Worksheet (C.I.F.)

Ref: 6243
Name of customer: Mr. Buyer, Importers Inc.
Address: 162 Overseas Blvd., Foreign Country
Product: Widget
Special terms or conditions quoted:
    Unit quoted: 1,000
    Goal weight: 64 kg.
    Cubic measure: 140 m³

Item	*(Can $)*
Cost and freight	
1. Cost of unit before profit	10,000
2. Profit at 10% (for example)	1,000
3. Overseas agent's commission at 7.5% (for example)	825
4. Exporting packing	75
5. Labeling cost	10
6. Stencil marking cost	0
7. Strapping cost	5
8. Cartage	2
9. Freight to seaboard cost: $6.00 per 1,000; type of carrier–rail	6
10. Unloading charges	2
11. Terminal charges	1
12. Long load or heavy load charges	0
13. Consular documents charges	N/A
14. Other charges (cable, phone)	4
15. Ocean freight cost	30
16. Forwarding agent's fee	10
17. Export credit insurance at 1% (for example)	100
18. Financing charges for credit sales	400
Total of cost and freight	12,470
Insurance	
19. Marine insurance (add 10% to total of cost and freight)	
Approximate premium 137	
Amount to be insured 13,854	
20. Type of insurance: All risks; Rate: 1%; Premium: 138.54	139
Grant Total (C.I.F.)	**12,609**
Convert Canadian $ to export market currency (1 Cdn. = 8.2646 F.C.)	**104,208 F.C.**

One of the early steps in campaigning for export markets is working out realistic export prices—or *costing,* as it is sometimes called. Too often, goods are priced for export merely on the basis of domestic price plus freight and insurance. Sometimes the resulting price is unrealistically high; occasionally it is too low. The would-be exporter should remember that foreign buyers usually have quotations from many countries to compare and will seek the best possible prices. Export quotations should therefore be kept as low as possible commensurate with reasonable profit—and certainly a profit no higher than on domestic sales. Manufacturers who want eventually to make volume foreign sales should bear in mind that these will result from good quality offered at a fair price and should keep their profit to a minimum.

Federal sales tax does not apply to exports, and if any charge for advertising is made in domestic prices, it should be deducted from the base price before calculating export prices.

The worksheet on page 192 may serve as a sample guide to assist you in arriving at a realistic export price for your products.

More detailed information about exporting and export financing can be obtained from the Department of External Affairs or the provincial government.

4

CANADA AT THE CROSSROADS

The Reality of a New Competitive Environment

Michael E. Porter
Monitor Company

CANADA AND INTERNATIONAL COMPETITION: THEORY AND EVIDENCE

Setting the Context

The principal economic goal of a country is to provide a high and rising standard of living for its citizens. By this yardstick Canada's economy has performed well over the last 30 years. It has achieved one of the world's highest standards of living while creating and maintaining a generous and socially progressive state. Adjusted for purchasing power, Canada ranked second among Organization for Economic Cooperation and Development (OECD) countries in per capita gross domestic product (GDP) in 1989, up from fourth in 1960.

We believe, however, that Canada today is at an economic crossroads and that the core of its economic prosperity is at risk. Canada's rich natural resource endowments, its proximity to the United States, and a history of insulation from international competition have combined to allow Canadian industry to achieve an enviable economic performance. These same advantages, however, have led to an array of policies, strategies, and attitudes on the part of governments, business, labour, and individual Canadians that leave the economy in many respects ill-equipped to respond to a rapidly changing competitive environment.

Canadian industry now is undergoing a rapid structural change. As this process continues, signs are already accumulating that Canadian industry is

Source: Excerpts from a study prepared for the Business Council on National Issues and the government of Canada, October 1991, by Michael E. Porter, Harvard Business School, and Monitor Company.

encountering difficulties as it confronts a changed and more competitive environment. If the current trajectory continues, the standard of living of Canadians seems destined to fall behind. Yet there is nothing inevitable about this outcome; Canadians have in their own hands the power to change it.

Threats to Prosperity

The underpinning of competitiveness, and thus of a country's standard of living, is productivity. Productivity is the value of output produced by a day of work or a dollar of capital invested. In the long run, productivity determines the standard of living by setting wages, profits, and, ultimately, the resources available to meet social needs. To achieve sustained productivity growth, an economy must continually *upgrade* itself. An upgrading economy is one that relentlessly pursues greater productivity in existing industries by improving products, utilizing more efficient production processes, and migrating into more sophisticated and higher-value industry segments. It is also an economy that has the capability to compete in entirely new industries, absorbing the resources made available from improved productivity in existing industries. The capacity of an economy to upgrade—its competitive potential—depends on underlying structural and institutional characteristics, such as its work force, its infrastructure, its postsecondary educational institutions, and its public policies. Cyclical factors, such as shifts in world commodity prices or exchange rates, can create the illusion of prosperity, but in reality yield only temporary advantages.

The Changing Competitive Environment

Traditionally, Canadians have lived in a relatively insulated environment brought about by paternalistic government policies, a history of market protection, and the accumulated attitudes and experiences of both individuals and businesses.

This old economic order, as we call it, was a system where many prospered. However, because the old order generally provided insulation from external pressures and fostered limited internal pressures, many of the critical requirements for upgrading to more sophisticated and sustainable competitive advantages in Canadian industry have been missing or are only weakly present.

Increasing globalization of trade and investment, accelerating technological changes, rapidly evolving company and country strategies, and—more recently—the Free Trade Agreement with the United States, represent significant discontinuities in the nature of international competition confronting Canadian-based industry. Together, these forces are pushing Canada away from the "comfortable insularity" of the old order. They will both magnify long-standing competitive weaknesses and hasten the pace of structural adjustment to a new competitive reality. What is most troubling is the fact that in essential areas such as science, technology, education, and training, significant barriers stand in the way of effective upgrading.

Owing to Canada's extensive trading relationship with the United States and its unusually high degree of foreign ownership, the shifting character of international competition poses particularly daunting challenges for Canadian firms and public policymakers. Many companies are currently in the process of determining how to reconfigure their North American and international activities, including deciding where to locate what we describe as their "home bases" for individual product lines and even their entire corporate operation. Typically, a company's home base is where the best jobs reside, where core research and development is undertaken, and where strategic control lies. Home bases are important to an economy because they support high productivity and productivity growth. In the context of the changing global economy, we believe that Canada is in danger of losing much of its capacity to attract and retain home bases.

So far, many industries and sectors show few signs of upgrading. In addition, as we discuss below, macroeconomic indicators have begun to manifest the weaknesses that exist at the industry level. Though Canada's status as a wealthy country is not in doubt, the risk is of a slowly eroding standard of living over the coming years.

Worrisome Performance Trends

Over the 1980s, Canada's economy performed quite well. Real economic growth between 1983 and 1989 was second only to Japan among the seven leading industrial countries (the G7). Canada also enjoyed the second fastest rate of employment growth among the G7 over the same period (the United States was first). Yet despite these favourable macroeconomic indicators, there is mounting evidence that Canada suffers from underlying economic weaknesses that could undercut its ability to achieve a higher standard of living in the future.

• The most serious weakness is *low productivity growth*. Since the early 1970s, Canada has ranked near the bottom of all major industrial countries in productivity growth. From 1979 to 1989, total factor productivity (TFP)—which measures the growth in productivity of both labour and capital inputs—rose by a mere 0.4 percent per year, tying Canada with the United States as the worst performer among the G7 countries. Over the same period, manufacturing labour productivity growth in Canada was the lowest among the G7 countries, averaging only 1.8 percent per annum.

• A second and closely related concern is Canada's record in the area of *unit labour costs*. Unit labour costs measure labour costs adjusted for productivity. They are a key indicator of competitiveness, especially for industries and firms that produce tradeable goods and services. Between 1979 and

1989, Canada's unit labour costs in the manufacturing sector rose more quickly than those in most other industrialized countries, and increased more than twice as fast as costs in the United States, which is the most important competitive benchmark for Canadian industry.

• *Unemployment* is a third danger signal. Despite robust employment growth over the past two decades, the unemployment rate in Canada has exceeded that in most other industrialized countries. In recent years, long-term unemployment has become more of a problem, and the average duration of unemployment has risen. Although the unemployment trend is a separate issue from that of productivity growth, growing numbers of workers with marginal or intermittent attachments to the labour force, and the rising average duration of unemployment, point to underlying problems that could affect Canada's capacity to upgrade its economy and respond successfully to changes in technology and global markets.

• *Lagging investments in upgrading skills and technology.* Canada's poor record in productivity growth and unemployment is disturbing. More worrisome in many ways, however, is that the investments that will drive productivity and employment growth in the future have been lagging. While aggregate investment growth has been quite strong, Canada trails competitor countries in private sector investments linked directly to enhanced productivity. Between 1980 and 1989, investment in machinery and equipment as a percentage of GDP was lower in Canada than in most other major industrialized countries. Similarly, Canadian private sector investment in research and development as a percentage of GDP is the second lowest among the G7 countries (slightly ahead of Italy). Moreover, investments by Canadian firms in worker training fall well short of levels registered in the United States, Germany, Japan, and many other advanced countries.

• Finally, the *macroeconomic environment* is not sufficiently supportive of investment. The ability of government to create a stable macroeconomic environment is being hampered by chronic government deficits and rapidly growing public debt. Combined federal and provincial government debt has been growing more quickly than the economy for a decade and now exceeds 70 percent of GDP. Among the G7 countries, only Italy has a higher government debt level. Servicing these massive government debt obligations lowers Canadian income and places constraints on the ability of Canadian governments to maintain an environment that encourages investment and the upgrading efforts of Canadian industry.

Canada's Position in International Competition

This study provides a detailed examination of Canada's position in international competition between 1978 and 1989 and how this compares with the positions of other industrialized countries. Here, we can only summarize the key findings and conclusions that flow from this in-depth analysis.

Focus on the Traded Sector

A country's performance in the traded sector provides a unique window into the sources of national economic prosperity. The traded sector is a large and increasingly important component of the economies of all industrialized countries. It has particular leverage for productivity growth, especially in smaller and mid-size countries such as Canada, where the ability to trade frees productive local industries from the constraints of the domestic market. Thus freed, these industries can grow and absorb resources from less productive industries, whose products can then be imported. In addition, the traded sector is where firms from a multiplicity of countries compete. It is the place where one can best analyze the ways in which the economic context in different countries creates advantages or disadvantages for firms.

This study takes a detailed look at Canada's export sector. It explores Canada's position in international competition, both over time and relative to other industrialized countries. The basis for our statistical analysis is the United Nations Standard International Trade Classification (SITC) statistics. These trade statistics, which measure exports and imports in approximately 4,000 narrowly defined industries, allow us to compare the trade performance of many countries over time at the level of strategically distinct industries. The UN trade statistics were also used in the original 10-nation research reported in *The Competitive Advantage of Nations.*

The export sector is a vital component of Canada's economy, representing 25.2 percent of GDP in 1989. Among the G7 countries, Canada is second only to Germany in the importance of trade to its economy. Canada's share of world market economy exports has varied between 4 and 5 percent over the past three decades. The trend for the period as a whole has been one of slow decline. More important than the trend in Canada's world export share, however, is how the composition of Canadian exports has evolved.

The remainder of this section summarizes the main characteristics of Canada's exports—a subject explored at much greater length in the full study report.

Significant Natural Resource Dependence

Perhaps the most striking feature of Canada's export profile is the prominent role of natural resource-based exports. These accounted for 45.8 percent of Canada's total exports in 1989. In fact, Canada's share of world resource exports rose from 5.0 percent in 1978 to 8.3 percent in 1989. Of nine major trading countries, Canada has by far the largest share of country exports based on unprocessed and semiprocessed natural resources; these comprised more than one third of all Canadian exports in 1989, compared to 20 percent in the United States and 11 percent in Sweden.

Exports of natural resource-based products are by no means undesirable—indeed, they have done much to make Canada wealthy. However, a high proportion of exports concentrated in relatively *unprocessed* resources suggests that, on the whole, Canadian industry has failed to upgrade or extend its competitive advantage into processing technology and the marketing and support of more sophisticated resource-based products. Dependence on semi- and unprocessed resources also leaves Canada vulnerable to commodity price shifts, technology substitution, and the emergence of lower-cost competitors, often in less developed countries. Why this pattern exists and what it means for the future is therefore a critical issue.

Exports Concentrated in Five Broad Clusters

Understanding the underpinnings of Canada's competitive advantage is aided by examining the nature of its industry *clusters*. To do this, all export industries are grouped into distinct clusters defined by end-use applications. Each cluster contains a number of distinct industries (with forest products, for example, consisting of market pulp, newsprint, sawmilling, and many other industries related to the forest sector). *Upstream industries* produce inputs used by many other industries. Most upstream industries are resource-based, with the exception of semiconductors/computers. There are six broad sectors connected to *industrial and supporting functions.* Industries at this level typically compete on the basis of technology and are often the industrial core of the economy. Another six sectors are associated with *final consumption goods and services.* Industries at this level are connected to end consumer needs. Resource-rich countries typically begin at the top level of upstream industries, while resource-poor countries start from the bottom level of labour-intensive final consumption goods. Most gradually grow toward the middle (industrial and supporting) level as they upgrade and lay the foundation of an industrial core.

Canadian exports are highly concentrated in three of the 16 clusters—materials/metals, forest products, and transportation—which together account for nearly 62 percent of Canada's exports. These three clusters, along with petroleum/chemicals and food/beverages, represented more than 82 percent of total Canadian exports in 1989. Looked at by end-use application, Canadian exports are concentrated at the level of upstream industries, where three of the five main clusters are located. At the level of industrial and supporting goods, Canadian exports consist largely of transportation equipment. Here we see the effect of the Canada–United States Auto Pact, which has had a profound influence on Canada's manufacturing sector (and, especially, its manufacturing exports). In 1989, fully 79 percent of transportation sector exports were from industries related to the Auto Pact. (Other cluster exports included aircraft and related parts and urban mass transit equipment.) Final consumption goods and services represent a relatively small share of Canada's exports (15 percent in 1989), the most significant cluster being food/beverage products, which consists largely of minimally processed products such as fish and grain.

Key Role of Foreign-Controlled Companies

Foreign ownership is relatively high in Canada, although it has been declining since the 1960s. In the manufacturing sector, for example, approximately 45 percent of assets in Canada are foreign controlled. Foreign ownership is quite widespread in most of Canada's five leading export clusters. Exhibit 1 shows the share of corporate assets controlled by foreign firms in selected industries within the various clusters. Among Canada's five main export clusters, foreign ownership is highest in transportation equipment and lowest in forest products. Many of the strategic decisions in important Canadian sectors are made outside of Canada, based on the overall global strategies of parent companies. How the choices made by these parent companies with respect to the location of home base activities for all or segments of their businesses will evolve in response to changes in international competition is a critical issue for the Canadian economy.

Very Limited Machinery Exports

Canada has few internationally competitive machinery industries. In total, machinery exports accounted for just 3.4 percent of all Canadian exports in

EXHIBIT 1   Foreign-Controlled Share of Assets of Selected Canadian Industries, 1987

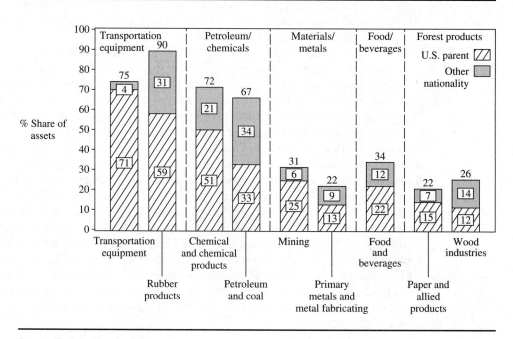

SOURCE: Statistics Canada; Calura

1989, up slightly from 3 percent in 1978, but substantially lower than in other major industrialized countries. In fact, Canada's share of competitive machinery exports fell from 1.3 percent of world exports in 1978 to 0.7 percent in 1989.[1] In addition, Canada's trade deficit in machinery increased 31 percent in real terms since 1978, to U.S. $3.3 billion.

Machinery industries are a sign of healthy economic upgrading. They give a country's core industries quicker access to and more control over fast-changing process technologies. Superiority in machinery and related and supporting industries can help to sustain competitive advantage in primary goods. Primary goods producers can often work closely with machinery firms located in their home country to upgrade and improve productivity. This relationship tends to be more difficult to build with foreign suppliers. In short, with few competitive machinery industries, many Canadian businesses are deprived of the dynamic interactions that foster process innovation and upgrading.

Principal Clusters Exhibit Limited Breadth or Depth

In looking in more detail, we find that even the most significant export clusters exhibit limited breadth or depth. For instance, in the forest products cluster, three industries—sawn wood, newsprint, and market pulp—account for 75 percent of total exports. There is almost no export position in more sophisticated segments such as fine paper. Most significantly, in analyzing the patterns of change in export composition from 1978–1989, we see little evidence to suggest exports have shifted into more sophisticated industry segments within these clusters.

Few Service Industries Are Internationally Competitive

Services represent about 68 percent of Canada's GDP and account for upwards of 70 percent of total employment. Among the G7 countries, Canada is second only to the United States in the relative size of the service sector. Although most services are not traded, they do represent a significant portion of the inputs of all goods exported by Canada. Uncompetitive domestic service industries can undermine the competitive position of a country's goods-producing sectors. The need for constant productivity improvements and upgrading thus applies equally to service industries, regardless of whether the output of such industries directly enters international trade.

International trade in services has been growing rapidly and now amounts to more than U.S. $700 billion per year (out of total world trade of $3.3 trillion). However, relatively few industries in the Canadian services sector

---

[1] The definition of international competitiveness employed in this study was consistent with that of the 10-nation study: a world export market share greater than Canada's overall share of market economy exports in 1989.

have reached international standing and Canada's service exports as a percentage of total exports are the lowest of the G7.

Deteriorating Trade Balances Outside of Resource Sectors

Canada's overall mix of exports has remained quite consistent in the recent past, with resource-dependent industries maintaining a 45–46 percent share of total exports between 1978 and 1989. Four out of Canada's five dominant export sectors enjoy positive trade balances—materials/metals, forest products, petroleum/chemicals, and food/beverages. Canada's strength in resource-based sectors is reflected in its growing positive trade balance in upstream industries, reaching $23 billion in 1989 (measured in U.S. dollars), up sharply from $9 billion in 1978. A rising trade surplus in the forest products sector (from $5.3 billion in 1978 to $16.4 billion in 1989) largely accounts for Canada's strengthening position in upstream industries.

Canada's trade balance is negative, however, in most of 16 industry clusters. Overall, Canada has recorded growing trade surpluses in resource-dependent goods, and rising trade deficits in nonresource sectors. Higher deficits in most nonresource industries point to weaknesses in Canada's competitive profile. Imports are fulfilling Canadian demand in a growing range of sophisticated industry segments. Canada remains extremely dependent on exports of resource-based products (and transportation equipment) to sustain its wealth and standard of living.

Export Economy Divided into Four Main Categories

Looking closely at Canada's trade patterns suggests another way of picturing the Canadian economy. In particular, it is possible to divide the export sector into four broad industry groupings:

1. *Resource-based industries.* These are industries in which Canadian exports are derived wholly or largely from natural resource advantages. Pulp and paper, lumber, and copper are examples.

2. *Market access-driven industries.* These consist of industries where Canadian exports come from plants established by foreign companies primarily to gain access to the Canadian market. Indicators used to identify such industries in our research were a high share of assets controlled by foreign companies and/or historically high tariffs. Auto Pact industries are the most important example and currently represent about 60 percent of all exports from market access-driven industries. Other industries in this category are rubber products, commercial refrigeration, office and business machines, electrical appliances, and some areas of industrial chemicals.

3. *Innovation-driven industries.* These are defined as either Canadian-owned indigenous industries or foreign-owned industries where competitiveness has been driven largely by Canadian-based innovation. Manufacturing

industries in this category include telecommunications equipment, aircraft and aircraft parts, and electronic components.

4. *Other industries.* These represent the balance of Canada's export sector. Industries falling into this group tend to be uncompetitive or marginally competitive based on world export share. Industries in this group consist mainly of foreign-controlled firms with modest exports or indigenous industries involved in trade solely with bordering states of the United States.

To approximate how Canadian exports are divided into these groups, we used UN trade data. Unfortunately, this data covers goods-producing industries but not services. Canadian goods-producing industries were classified using the above categories, and the industries in each category were then aggregated (as measured by shipments). Exhibit 2 displays the trends by category in terms of exports and balance of trade. (Note that exports are valued in 1989 U.S. dollars.) The estimates are crude, but they are consistent with earlier data. As shown, the most significant growth in Canadian exports

EXHIBIT 2   Canadian Goods-Producing Export Economy by Type of Industries

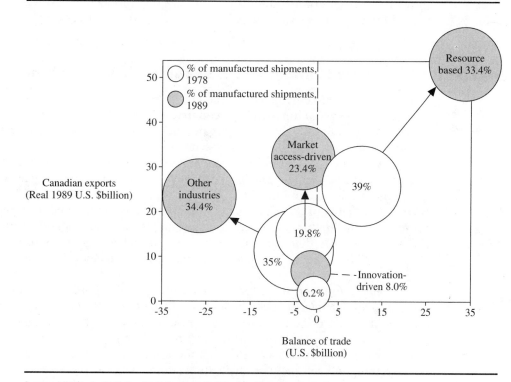

Source: UN Trade Statistics; Statistics Canada; Monitor Company Analysis.

of goods between 1978 and 1989 was in the resource sector, which markedly increased its exports and its trade surplus over the decade. In the innovation-driven industries, exports have increased slightly and the trade balance is slightly negative, while in the market access sector, exports are up and the trade balance relatively steady. However, the size and trajectory of the "other industries" category is troubling. It is a significant part of the economy but has been contributing to worsening trade balances. This again underscores the fact that the resource sector is the strongest part of the export economy.

Canada's International Competitive Position: Conclusion

This brief overview of Canada's position in international competition and its export economy highlights a number of real or potential weaknesses. Canada's high dependence on exports of relatively unprocessed natural resource-based products signals a lack of breadth even in the country's most prominent export clusters. Likewise, Canada's very weak position in machinery indicates a lack of depth within key industry clusters. Most importantly, our analysis found little evidence that either the breadth or the depth of Canada's major export clusters is increasing. Taken together, this evidence is consistent with the brief macroeconomic picture, previously presented, which points to an economy that shows limited signs of upgrading, and suggests that productivity growth—the critical driver of prosperity—may be increasingly difficult to achieve.

Determinants of National Competitive Advantage: The "Diamond"

Competitiveness has emerged as a preeminent issue for firms and government policymakers in every industrialized country. Most efforts to explain national competitiveness have taken an aggregate perspective, focusing on factor en-dowments, macroeconomic indicators, or government policies. Patterns of international trade have traditionally been explained within the framework of comparative advantage. The best-known variant of this theory begins with the premise that all countries employ equivalent technologies but differ in their endowments of so-called factors of production—land, labour, natural resources, and capital—which are the basic inputs of production. The traditional theory holds that particular countries gain advantage in those industries that make the most intensive use of the productive factors they have in abundance.

Recently, however, there has been a growing realization that traditional comparative advantage theory is no longer sufficient to understand the patterns of trade in modern international competition. Competition is becoming increasingly global in character. More and more firms are adopting a global perspective when making decisions about where to source raw materials, manufacture, and sell their products or services. This has the effect of "decoupling" the firm from the factor endowments of a country. Raw materials, components, machinery, and many services are now available to firms in most countries on increasingly comparable terms. The success of a firm is thus less and less dependent on endowments of basic factors in its home country.

With the trend toward globalization of industry, it is tempting to think that the individual country is no longer important to the international success of its firms, or even that countries have become irrelevant to international competition. Results from the 10-nation study, as well as from our study of Canadian competitiveness, strongly suggest that this view is mistaken. Leading international competitors in a given industry are often located in the same country and often in the same city or region. The positions of countries in international competition tend to be surprisingly stable, stretching over several decades or even longer. This suggests that competitive advantage is created and sustained through a highly localized process, and that the attributes of particular countries *do* shape patterns of competitive success.

The Diamond of National Advantage

What is needed is a new paradigm that presents a consistent and holistic explanatory framework. This paradigm must explain several empirical facts. First, no one country is competitive in all or most industries; rather, countries are competitive in particular industries and industry segments. Second, each country exhibits distinct patterns of international competitive success and failure. Third, countries tend to succeed in clusters of industries rather than in isolated industries, and the pattern of competitive clusters differs markedly from country to country.

The principal conclusion from the 10-nation study is that sustained international competitive advantage results from ongoing improvement and innovation, not from static advantages. Here, innovation is defined very broadly, to encompass technology and the full spectrum of activities relevant to competing in the marketplace. Creating competitive advantage requires that its sources be relentlessly upgraded and broadened.

Against this backdrop, the critical questions then become: What is it about a country that supports high and rising levels of productivity in individual industries? In what ways does a country provide a dynamic environment for its firms? How do countries differ in the competitive environment created for their industries? The results of the 10-nation study suggest that the answer to these questions lies in four broad attributes of a country that, individually and as a system, constitute the "diamond of national advantage." This can be thought of as the playing field that each country establishes for its industries and companies (see Exhibit 3). The four attributes are:

• *Factor conditions.* The country's position in basic factors of production such as labour, land, natural resources, and infrastructure. Also included are highly specialized and advanced pools of skills, technology, and infrastructure tailored to meet the needs of particular industries.

EXHIBIT 3   National Determinants of Competitive Advantage: "The Diamond"

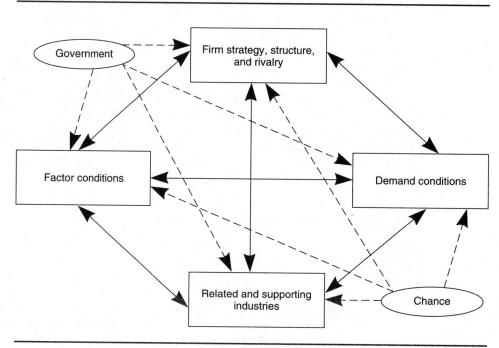

- *Demand conditions.* The nature of home-market demand for the output of local industries. Particularly important is the presence of sophisticated and demanding local customers who pressure firms to innovate and whose needs anticipate needs elsewhere.
- *Related and supporting industries.* The presence (or absence) in the country of supplier industries and other related industries that are internationally competitive. This determinant includes local suppliers of specialized inputs (e.g., machinery, components, and services) that are integral to innovation in the industry, as well as innovative local companies in industries related by technology, skills, or customers.
- *Firm strategy, structure, and rivalry.* The conditions in the country affecting how companies are created, organized, and managed, as well as the nature of domestic rivalry.

Two additional variables, government and chance, also influence the national competitive environment in important ways. *Government policy* is best understood by examining how it has an impact on each of the four determinants of competitive advantage included in the diamond. The role of government is analyzed by looking at its effects on factor creation and the goals and behaviour of individuals and firms, its role as a buyer of goods and services, and its influence on the competitive environment through competition policies, regulation, and government ownership of enterprises.

Chance events are developments outside of the control of the country's government and its firms, but which affect the competitive environment. Examples include breakthroughs in basic technologies; external political, economic and legal developments; and international war and conflict. Chance events can create opportunities for a country's firms to acquire or strengthen competitive advantage.

The Diamond as a System

Each of the four determinants of competitiveness influences the capacity of a country's industry to innovate and upgrade. Together they constitute a dynamic system that is more important than its parts.

The ability to benefit from one attribute in the diamond depends on the state of the others. The presence of sophisticated and demanding buyers, for example, will not result in advanced products or production processes unless the quality of human resources enables firms to respond to buyer needs. There must also be a climate that supports sustained investment to fund the development of these products and processes. At the broadest level, weaknesses in any one determinant will constrain an industry's potential for advancement and upgrading.

The four determinants are also mutually reinforcing. For example, the development of specialized supporting industries tends to increase the supply of specialized factors that also benefit an industry. Vigorous domestic rivalry also stimulates the development of unique pools of specialized factors. This is particularly likely if the rivals are all located in one city or region.

The diamond also bears centrally on a country's ability to attract mobile factors of production, a final form of mutual reinforcement. Mobile factors, particularly ideas and highly skilled individuals, are becoming increasingly important to international competitiveness. Mobile factors tend to be drawn to the location where they can achieve the greatest productivity, because that is where they can obtain the highest returns. The same features that make a country an attractive home base also help it attract mobile factors.

Advantages in the entire diamond may not be necessary for competitive advantage in low-skill or inherently resource-dependent industries. Firms may also be able to penetrate the standardized, lower technology segments of more advanced industries without broad advantages in the diamond. In such instances, basic factor costs may be decisive. Competitive advantage in more sophisticated industries and industry segments, on the other hand, rarely results from strength in a single determinant. Sustained success in these industries and segments usually requires the interaction of favourable conditions in several of the determinants and at least parity in the others.

Geographic concentration also elevates and magnifies the interaction of the four determinants. It enhances the pressure from local rivalry and the frequency of spin-offs, works to stimulate and raise the sophistication of local customers, stimulates the formation of related and supporting industries, triggers greater local investment in specialized factor creation, and provides a magnet for mobile factors.

These same forces explain another important finding of the 10-nation study with particular relevance to Canada. There is often a marked disparity between the economic success of regions within countries. The striking difference between the industrial success of northern and southern Italy, northern and southern Germany, and eastern and central Canada are three such examples.

One manifestation of the systemic nature of the determinants is in the phenomenon of clustering. Clusters involve supplier industries, customer industries, and related industries that are all competitive. Such clusters are characteristic of every advanced economy—American entertainment, German chemicals, Japanese electronics, Danish foods. Countries tend to be successful in clusters of linked industries. It is rare that an isolated industry or firm achieves international success.

Clusters grow and transform themselves through spin-offs and diversification of firms into upstream, downstream, and related industries and activities. The fields where several clusters overlap are often fertile grounds for new business formation. In Japan, for example, the interstices among electronics and new materials are spawning new competitive strengths in fields as diverse as robotics and displays.

Vital clusters of industries are often at the heart of a country's economic development, and especially its capacity to innovate. As suggested by the earlier trade analysis, however, the creation of more dynamic industry clusters represents a major challenge facing the Canadian economy.

Applying the Diamond in a Canadian Context

In applying this framework to Canada, four features of the Canadian economy must be addressed: the prominence of natural resource industries in Canada's exports, the role of rivalry in the relatively small Canadian market, the high degree of foreign ownership of Canadian industry, and the effects of Canada's location next to the huge U.S. market.

1. *Natural resources.* Canada's economy, and especially its export economy, is heavily based on natural resources. Some argue that resource industries are inherently less desirable than manufacturing or "high-tech" industries. This logic is flawed. There is nothing inherently undesirable about resource-based industries, provided they support high levels of productivity and productivity growth. Such industries can make a country wealthy if its resource position is highly favourable, as has been the case for Canada during most of its history. If resource-based industries continually upgrade their sophistication through improvements in their processes and products, competitive positions can be sustained and productivity growth assured. In many resource-based

economies, however, resource abundance contributes to a set of policies, attitudes, and institutions that reduce incentives to upgrade and make it difficult to move beyond the factor-driven stage of development. This can leave resource-based economies vulnerable to adverse shifts in technology, markets, and international competition. The key test we must apply in appraising Canada's resource-based industries is their record in upgrading competitive advantage and their capacity for upgrading in the future.

2. *Domestic rivalry.* Domestic rivalry is critical to innovation and to the development of competitive advantage. Yet some commentators contend that Canada's relatively small market precludes the coexistence of strong Canadian-based rivals. Others argue that the proximity of the United States—and thus of U.S.-based competition in the form of imports of American goods—can compensate for limited rivalry at home. Previous research, however, has shown that vigorous domestic rivalry encourages international success not just in large countries, but also in small and mid-sized economies such as Denmark, Sweden, Switzerland, and Taiwan. The number of local firms needed for effective local competition will vary by industry, depending on economies of scale and other factors. In every country studied in the 10-nation research, some firms were found that had achieved a measure of international success without the benefit of local rivalry. Sometimes government policy has limited local competition in virtually all countries (as in telecommunications). Local rivalry may also be less important to competitive advantage in pure commodity businesses in which advantage derives from factor costs rather than innovation. However, the great preponderance of evidence suggests that local rivalry plays a powerful role in competitive advantage. Weak domestic rivalry in many industries in Canada, then, will tend to diminish the odds of achieving sustained international success.

3. *Foreign investment.* There are three main types of foreign investment. Factor-sourcing investment typically seeks access to a country's natural resources, labour, or other basic factors. Foreign firms making such investments have their home bases outside of the host country. Market access foreign investment arises when companies are required—for example, by tariffs or government regulations—to develop a presence in a country in order to gain access to its domestic market. In these cases, too, the home base remains in the country of the parent firm. Most foreign investments in Canada have been motivated by a desire to source Canadian resources or gain access to the Canadian market.

The third, and most beneficial, type of foreign investment is that which establishes or acquires a home base for a particular business or business unit in the host country. In these cases, the management and other core activities are located in the host country, which signals that that country possesses true international competitive advantage in the industry. The home base is where the firm normally contributes the most to the local economy in a particular industry, by establishing the most productive jobs, investing in specialized factor creation, acting as a sophisticated buyer for other local industries as well as a sophisticated related and supporting firm for other local industries as well as a sophisticated related and supporting firm for other industries, and helping to create a vibrant local competitive milieu.

Canada has witnessed a good deal of debate on the issue of foreign investment and its impact on the country's economy. Much of this debate has been wide of the mark. We believe that in most circumstances, a country is better off with foreign investment than without it. And Canada, in our view, has been a net beneficiary. Foreign companies bring to the host country capital, skills, and technology—all of which boost productivity. Yet the pattern of foreign activities in Canada also signals circumstances that create vulnerabilities for the future. Though there are exceptions, few foreign-controlled firms have made Canada a home base for product lines.

As competition becomes more global and trade and investment barriers fall, the location of firm activities will reflect true economic advantage. The key challenge then is to create the conditions under which foreign—and Canadian—firms will *want* to locate home bases, and perform sophisticated activities, in Canada.

4. *The importance of Canadian diamonds given North American and global competition.* Canada and the United States share a lengthy, easily permeable border as well as many social and cultural attributes. Why, then, should we focus our attention on the Canadian diamond? Wouldn't it make more sense to look at the larger North American diamond, and ask how Canadian firms can take advantage of circumstances in the United States to achieve competitive success? The most basic reason to be concerned about the Canadian diamond is that Canada's standard of living largely depends on the activities that take place in Canada. The location of the most productive economic activities, especially home base activities, is determined by the health of the Canadian diamond in any given industry compared to other locations. And while there are many similarities between Canada and the United States, there are also significant differences—in institutions, trading patterns, tax policies, customer behaviour, economic structure, and labour force composition, among other areas. It is these differences that serve to create distinctive Canadian diamonds in industries. Although the Canada–United States Free Trade Agreement is likely to lessen some of the differences between the two countries, it will also magnify the competitive impact of those that remain.

Competitive advantage tends to be highly localized within countries. Locations differ in the environment they provide for innovation and upgrading. Proximity to customers, suppliers, rivals, and sources of specialized factors is crucial to the innovation process. The geographic locus of competitive advantage can cross national borders. In the case of Canada, the relevant arena of competitive advantage for a particular industry may encompass adjacent parts of the United States. In addition, it makes sense for Canadian firms to reach into the U.S. diamond to strengthen their competitive position or overcome weaknesses in the Canadian diamond—for example, by selling to and getting feedback from more sophisticated American customers. But Canadian firms can only take advantage of the U.S. diamond selectively. Basic factors and demand are easiest to access. In contrast, industry-specific infrastructure, a highly skilled workforce, and certain types of supplier and customer relationships are difficult for a country's firms—including Canada's—to source at a distance.

In short, there is no single North American diamond in industries which allows us to ignore Canadian circumstances. Our attention must therefore be directed to the strength of Canadian determinants.

DIRECTIONS FOR CHANGE

The Comfortable Insularity of the Old Order

The preceding section presents a picture of an economic system that had served Canada well in many respects but leaves the economy ill-equipped for the future. This old economic order was an internally consistent system in which the determinants were mutually consistent and reinforcing. This makes change exceedingly difficult.

Canada's abundant factor resources have been the bedrock of the economy. In many cases, these resources allowed Canadian firms to be profitable by exporting relatively unprocessed commodities rather than through upgrading. Strategies based on basic factor advantages often limited the demand for advanced technology. This in turn constrained investment in R&D and demand for highly skilled employees, which was reflected in enrolment patterns in universities and in the nature of educational programs. The virtual absence of leading-edge related and supporting industries inhibited another possible source of technology.

These tendencies spilled over into other sectors of the economy where Canada did not have such advantages. Many firms, insulated from external and internal rivalry, were content to exploit the profitable home market. The rate of innovation was slow. What emerged was a tendency to administer existing wealth rather than to invest vigorously to create new wealth.

Canada's wealth also provided little incentive for labour, management, and government to work together to improve national competitiveness. Significant chasms now exist between the three constituencies and within government itself. The relationship between labour and management has often been confrontational. At the same time, management has seldom treated labour as partners. Labour and government have also not worked well together, with labour often taking on an adversarial role with respect to many aspects of economic policy, while governments' relations with their own workforce have also sometimes been strained.

Canadian companies have sought government assistance in export promotion, investment in specialized infrastructure, government procurement, and other forms of support. They rarely have cooperated, however, with governments in areas that have important impacts on international competitiveness, such as R&D, training, and education. The federal and provincial governments have struggled over roles and mandates. This has led to conflicting and overlapping programs that have worked to the detriment of the economy.

These attitudes and behaviours reflect the old competitiveness paradigm. Business acted as if economic rents would go on forever and moved to exploit the sheltered Canadian market. Labour acted as if jobs and high and rising wages could be taken for granted, because business profits were high and secure. Governments held the view that ample resources would continue to exist to fund social needs.

Government's Overall Effect on the Old Economic Order

Government's proper role is to challenge and raise the sights of industry by improving the quality of the inputs that firms draw upon, and creating a competitive context that promotes upgrading. Effective government policies create an environment which stimulates companies to gain competitive advantage, rather than involving government directly in the process.

As we have discussed, government policies in Canada have often not measured up. Those policies that have most hampered competitiveness in the Canadian economy can be grouped into a small number of major themes that are outgrowths of the old economic order.

1. *Insulation from external and internal competition.* Historically, considerable effort has been directed at insulating the Canadian economy from external pressures by protecting firms from international competition and safeguarding national autonomy. Similarly, weak competition policies were a natural outgrowth of the view that companies had to be large to compete with foreign firms.

2. *Forestalling the need for upgrading.* Canadian government policies have often sought to remove the need for upgrading rather than encourage it. Artificially constrained factor input costs—in industries as diverse as transportation, hydroelectric power, and agriculture—lessen pressures for upgrading and reflect a static, cost-based conception of competition. In fact, it could be argued that the current Canadian preoccupation with bringing down exchange rates is a reflection of the same mindset.

3. *Direct intervention instead of business action.* Canadian governments have had a strong tendency to intervene directly in competition rather than stimulate upgrading by industry itself. In many policy areas, particularly in science and technology, and education and training, private sector participation has not been well leveraged. Direct intervention in the form of subsidies and bailouts has also been a prominent feature of the Canadian economic landscape.

4. *Programs to distribute wealth and improve welfare needlessly undermine the economy.* There is a strongly held belief in Canada that all citizens have a right to essential services such as health care and education, a minimum standard of living maintained by social welfare programs, and the opportunity to be employed. Yet the implementation of programs has often proven counterproductive. Canada's commitment to employment has frequently been used to justify protective strategies that preserve jobs in the short term but simultaneously distort rivalry and delay necessary adjustment. In addition, the effectiveness of the substantial resources devoted to the task of narrowing regional economic disparities has often been undermined by programs which emphasize diversification rather than building on regional strengths.

5. *Conflicting government policies and objectives.* No one level of government in Canada controls a full set of variables in any given policy area, which complicates the process of policy development and implementation. A high level of policy coordination is necessary to make Canada's decentralized system work, but such coordination has been lacking. For example, in labour market programs, the provinces set and enforce employment standards, while the federal government maintains responsibility for training and unemployment compensation. Furthering Canada's science and technology capabilities has also been hampered by a lack of coordination between federal and provincial research bodies. Jurisdictional overlap has often added a layer of complexity and compounded the level of uncertainty that firms face in anticipating changes in the business environment.

Forces of Change

As we have seen in our discussion of the determinants of competitive advantage, the Canadian economy is coming under increasing external pressures. Forces of change are disintegrating the old order. New competitive realities—including globalization of production, finance and markets, accelerating technological change, lower tariffs worldwide, and free trade between Canada and the United States (and perhaps Mexico)—call for a more dynamic and flexible set of responses than those typical of the old Canadian order. Canada's future competitiveness, therefore, must be driven by a new paradigm, based on productivity and innovation.

Major structural adjustment in Canada is inevitable. The question is whether the adjustment is positive or whether it leads to an erosion in the standard of living. Also at issue is how long and painful the restructuring process will be, even if business, labour, and government move in the right direction. How long will it take for Canada to transform itself from the old paradigm to a new one? And how much will it cost?

As external pressures are increasing, Canadian firms are beginning to experience greater internal pressures. This is due partly to a number of government policies that are increasingly oriented toward providing a more challenging competitive domestic environment, and partly as a result of positive initiatives taken by firms themselves.

At the federal level, positive government steps include the recently strengthened competition laws, privatization of crown corporations, and efforts to deregulate industries, including energy and transportation. Government is also beginning to employ policies that encourage, and even pressure, firms to upgrade. Tax reform has reduced past distortions, and generous R&D incentives are in place. Increasing the private sector's commitment to training is at the heart of the federal government's new Labour Force Development Strategy. Reform of unemployment insurance has improved incentives to upgrade skills and return to the workforce, though more must be done. In the area of science and technology, a rising number of government programs are being oriented to priorities driven by the private sector.

In response to the significant external and internal pressures facing the economy, we have also seen signs of positive change in a number of industries studied, including industries in the resource sector. For example, Inco has taken significant steps to upgrade its mineral extraction and smelting technologies and improve labour-management relations. A number of companies in the pulp and paper sector are beginning modernization programs. Other firms have begun to reposition their activities in light of intensified competition by becoming more focused and effective producers.

Systemic Barriers to Change

With increasing external pressures and some positive internal initiatives, one might be tempted to believe that Canada's weaknesses will be corrected naturally. However, the vestiges of the old economic order in Canada have imposed significant barriers to upgrading. These barriers are systemic, not isolated. They reside in policies, institutions, and attitudes that permeate the economy. The challenge is heightened by the fact that the diamond is an interdependent system, in which the weakest link constrains progress.

While some necessary steps are being taken, the current extent of change is inadequate. Our analysis of the determinants of competitive advantage in Canada revealed both tangible and intangible barriers to upgrading. Though each industry has a unique diamond, the strength of which is driven by features specific to that industry, virtually all industries we have examined are affected by at least some of these barriers.

Canada's workforce is not well equipped for upgrading and change. The basic skill levels of many citizens are inadequate, in spite of high per capita spending on education. Shortages exist or are looming in skill- and technology-related occupations. Specialized skill development is lagging due to poor vocational apprenticeship training and weak links between educational institutions and industry. Finally, company investments in training are low compared to other industrialized countries.

Canada's R&D infrastructure is not well aligned with requirements for upgrading. Too much R&D spending takes place through government laboratories. The links between publicly funded research institutes and industry are poorly developed. The supply of highly qualified personnel may be inadequate for future research needs.

The level of sophistication of Canadian home demand also works against upgrading. Weak related and supporting industries, as well as inadequate cluster development, constrain innovation and new business formation in Canada. The lack of Canadian process equipment manufacturers is particularly striking and contributes to the weakness in process technology development and adoption in this country.

Firm strategies and structure and the extent of local rivalry in Canada have done little to enhance domestic productivity. Too many Canadian firms continue to maintain an insular focus, concentrated almost exclusively on the domestic market. Finally, a number of Canada's "safety net" programs continue to diminish personal incentives to upgrade skills.

In many ways, however, the most significant barriers to upgrading are attitudinal. Too often, the old mindsets are still in place in business, labour, and government. Canadians still see competitiveness in terms of the old paradigm, which points to inappropriate responses to the current difficulties.

Threats to Canadian Industries

The forces we have described in general terms can be translated into specific threats in the broad categories of Canadian industries identified earlier. These individual threats differ from group to group, though their underlying causes and implications are similar.

Resource-Based Industries

Given its abundant factor endowments, Canada's heavy emphasis on resources is not surprising. Yet the sustainability of these industries' competitive advantage is in question. Depletion of resources is a threat to both renewable resource industries, such as fisheries, where a number of factors can upset projected equilibrium levels, and nonrenewable resource industries, where new sites are often more remote and therefore more expensive to exploit.

Canada's biggest problem is likely the emergence of lower cost competitors. Basic factor advantages are increasingly replicated by countries such as Venezuela in aluminum or Brazil in pulp and paper. Apart from the resource costs themselves, Canada does not generally have strong cost positions in activities that are driven by labour rates, productivity, or the age and efficiency of capital stock. In these areas, Canada has often failed to make the necessary investments, such as upgrading process technology to increase the efficiencies in production, that would yield a stronger position. Unless Canada upgrades its resource-based industries, it will be trapped in segments where investments tend to be inflexible and where its marginal costs are higher than major competitors'.

Market Access-Based Industries

Many of Canada's market access-based industries, initially spawned to overcome high tariff barriers, are seriously threatened by the increasingly open trading environment. As trade barriers continue to fall, market access no longer requires a major production base in Canada. Many firms are now in the process of reconfiguring their North American and, in some cases, global operations. Some have made decisions to move production out of Canada, taking with them not only jobs but also valuable skills and expertise.

One particularly unattractive aspect of many Canadian industry diamonds is interprovincial barriers to trade: By moving to the United States, firms may encounter virtually no penalty in terms of access to other Canadian provinces, given present trade barriers between provinces. Clearly, if effective barriers remain, firms that choose to stay in Canada are unlikely to invest as much in upgrading their existing domestic facilities than if these barriers were removed.

Innovation-Driven Industries

Canada's innovation-driven industries are tangible proof that Canada can achieve an innovation-driven economy. Yet these industries may also be at risk. Firms that have prospered in spite of weak Canadian clusters may find this weakness increasingly eroding their competitiveness. Firms in such industries may move their home bases outside of Canada to take advantage of more favourable diamonds elsewhere. Even those Canadian industries within strong clusters are at risk because of systemic barriers to upgrading discussed earlier.

Moving to a New Order

We believe Canada is at an economic turning point. Its old economic order is outmoded and in the process of being dismantled. Canadians can respond in one of two ways. One path is to cling to the old order and actively resist the process of change. The other is to continue building on recent economic reforms and seek to further the process of systemic adjustment in the economy. We are convinced that this second path will better ensure Canada's continued prosperity in the fast-changing global economy. Moving to a new economic order will be uncomfortable for many and actively resisted by some. Inevitably, it will involve short-run costs. Yet we are persuaded that these costs are less than might be supposed. It is not that Canadian business and government must spend more, but that they must act and spend differently. More importantly, however, the shift to a new economic order will require a different mindset on the part of government, business, labour, and many individual citizens, one which recognizes and adopts a new paradigm of competitiveness.

The mandate of this study has been to diagnose the state of competitiveness in Canadian industry and highlight key priorities for change. We have not sought to generate detailed policy recommendations. The task of fashioning specific policies and responses must fall to Canadian policymakers and private sector leaders themselves. The final part of this study seeks to provide some guidance by outlining a new economic vision for firms, labour, and governments. We begin, however, by briefly reviewing Canada's major economic strengths.

Strengths to Build On

As it faces a shifting competitive environment, Canada is in the favourable position of having a solid foundation on which to build. In particular, Canada is in many respects better placed to respond to changing global competition than other resource-rich countries such as Australia and New Zealand. Canada has a large export sector that accounts for more than one quarter of GDP and represents a significant share of world trade. It also enjoys preferred access to the world's largest and richest economy, the United States. Canada has a large, diversified natural resource base and ranks among the world's leaders in a range of renewable and nonrenewable resources. It also benefits from having a relatively young and well-educated labour force.

Many Canadian firms have proven that they can compete in global industries. Canada's success in a number of highly contested global industries—including telecommunications, consulting engineering, and nickel—illustrates the intrinsic potential for continued prosperity. Canadian firms have proven that they can compete on the basis of innovation. Northern Telecom, CAE Electronics, Inco, and Canstar are a few examples of firms examined in our research which are at the leading edge of technological sophistication in their industries. They have built and sustained internationally competitive positions through a commitment to R&D and technology adoption. They have created and drawn upon strengths in their home diamonds to achieve international success. Innovation and upgrading are at the core of their business strategies.

There is, in short, a foundation in place in Canada that should allow more firms and industries to achieve sustained advantage in international competition. Canadian industry enjoys a good basic infrastructure, a core of university and other research capability, and an educated human resource base with demonstrated potential. The challenge is to redirect government policies and company strategies to develop and build upon these strengths. Free trade will play a positive role here. With the advent of the Canada-United States Free Trade Agreement, Canadian firms can increasingly benefit from proximity and ready access to the U.S. market. The United States represents not only a significant and growing export market but also a source of products, technology, and ideas. Free trade will hasten the process by which the Canadian economy specializes in those areas where it performs best, thereby boosting productivity. At the same time, Canadian firms will be able to tap selectively into stronger U.S. diamonds to overcome weaknesses in Canada's competitive context in areas such as home demand conditions and related and supporting industries—although, as we have stressed, this is not a panacea.

Elements of an Economic Vision

We believe that a new vision for the Canadian economy is needed, one in which Canada's natural resource abundance is fully exploited, in which firms and governments focus on creating advanced skills and technology, in which sophisticated home demand drives more firms to create advanced products and processes, in which many more Canadian firms compete globally, and in which competition provides a key stimulus for continual upgrading. This does not mean that Canadian firms must compete in different industries than they do today. But it does suggest that they will have to compete in different ways. Firms in Canada need to employ different and more effective strategies, rely on more advanced methods and technologies, and migrate into more sophisticated segments of their industries. In cases where industries cannot be upgraded, resources should flow to more productive uses.

While many specific steps are necessary to raise productivity and improve the dynamism of the economy, we believe that a new economic vision for Canada is best defined in terms of a small number of overarching imperatives:

• *Become an innovation-driven economy.* Innovation—in its broadest sense—is the critical requirement for economic upgrading and increased prosperity. Canadian enterprises in all sectors must move to develop innovation-based advantages. This includes firms in nontraded service industries as well as in the traded sector. Governments must align their policies to support this strategic objective.

• *Increase the sophistication of the natural resource sector.* Resource-based industries have been and will remain a mainstay of Canada's economy. But threats exist to the sustainability of Canada's position in many resource-based industries—threats such as declining real commodity prices, the emergence of low-cost foreign suppliers, and technologically driven changes in end-markets. In the future, Canadian resource producers will be under unprecedented pressure to increase productivity, use more sophisticated technology and specialized skills, and develop more sophisticated and differentiated products.

• *Tackle barriers to upgrading throughout the economy.* Eliminating barriers to upgrading productivity must be a priority for firms and governments.

Strategies to develop more advanced and specialized factors must be implemented. Incentives must be shifted, wherever possible, to encourage a greater focus on work, investment, and skill building.

• *Build on Canada's regional strengths.* Many government policies in Canada have put a higher priority on economic diversification than on competitive advantage. A different concept of regional and industrial development is needed, one that focuses on building industry clusters where they already have established or nascent strengths.

• *Move quickly and decisively to achieve complete free trade with Canada.* The fruits of greater specialization will not be fully realized unless Canada becomes a true single market. Competitiveness in a variety of industries has been hindered by the existence of internal nontariff barriers to trade, investment, and labour mobility. These have worked against the development of sufficient scale in some industries and dulled the rivalry necessary to achieve competitive advantage. It is encouraging that the federal government's recent proposals for constitutional reform promise to move toward internal free trade and a strengthening of the Canadian economic union.

• *Transform foreign subsidiaries into home bases.* Given its high levels of foreign investment and large number of branch plants (especially in manufacturing industries), transforming foreign subsidiaries into home bases is one of the most critical challenges facing Canada in the 1990s. Branch plants whose sole raison d'être has been to serve the Canadian market will relocate if their productivity does not match or exceed operations elsewhere. Multinationals will make choices about where to make investments in new skills, technologies, and product lines according to whether or not the Canadian environment is conducive to innovation and productivity growth.

• *Create and maintain a supportive and stable macroeconomic climate.* Finally, sound macroeconomic policies are central to any vision of a competitive, dynamic Canadian economy. Fiscal, monetary, tax, and regulatory policies should all be geared to attaining low inflation, balanced and manageable public finances, and a stable overall economic climate. This will result in a lower cost of capital, encourage investment, and neutralize the tendency for companies to be distracted by exchange rates and interest rates instead of concentrating on the true underpinnings of long-term competitiveness.

Implications for Canadian Firms

Business, labour, governments, and other public sector institutions must all play a role in responding to these imperatives. A particularly heavy responsibility, however, falls on companies and their managers. Firms, not governments, are on the front lines of international competition. Forced to compete in a more global, open, and fast-changing environment, Canadian firms must focus on setting strategies that will allow them to create and sustain competitive advantage. They should move now to reexamine their strategies, not wait for government or outside forces to intervene. While each Canadian industry will present different challenges, many firms will need to take steps in several important areas.

Assess the Canadian Diamond

Canadian firms must begin by understanding their competitive position by product area as well as how their Canadian home bases create competitive advantages and disadvantages. In analyzing their competitive position, the most formidable international competitors in an industry should be the key reference points. Internationally successful firms, as well as the national diamonds in which they are based, provide the benchmarks against which Canadian conditions must be assessed. Canadian companies should be addressing the following questions:

- *The boundaries of the home diamond.* What are the geographic boundaries of the "home" diamond? Does it appear to cross the border with the United States and, if so, what are the key differences for firms operating on either side?
- *Sustainability of basic factor advantages.* How sustainable are Canadian advantages in raw materials, electricity, or other natural endowments? To what extent does the firm rely on explicit or implicit subsidies rather than real factor advantages? How are evolving international trade rules and foreign circumstances likely to alter existing advantages?
- *Quality of human resources.* How does Canada compare in terms of specialized skills relevant to the firm's industry? Are Canadian workers as well trained and well motivated as their foreign counterparts?
- *Technology access.* Where does Canada stand in specialized technologies related to the industry? Are there research institutes or programs in Canada that will assist Canadian firms to innovate?
- *Infrastructure access.* How supportive is Canada's basic and specialized infrastructure in terms of the requirements for competitive advantage in the firm's industry? How does Canada compare with other countries?
- *Canadian demand for sophistication.* Is Canadian demand for the firm's products/services sophisticated? Does it anticipate international needs?
- *Supplier access.* Compared to foreign rivals, does the Canadian firm have better or inferior access to local suppliers in important technologies?
- *Related industries.* What are the related industries that will most influence industry competition? What strengths does Canada have in these industries?
- *Competitor diamonds.* Who are the most significant foreign competitors in the industry? What is the state of their diamonds?
- *Potential entrants.* Who are the emerging potential entrants? What is their cost position? How dependent are they on low-cost natural resources, inexpensive labour, or government support?

• *Capacity for differentiation.* What are the sources of differentiation relative to rival firms? Are there products or segments in which the Canadian firm is more innovative?

Move toward Innovation-Driven Advantages

Many Canadian firms have long pursued static, cost-based strategies in which they produce "me-too" products and depend on factor costs or pure scale to provide advantages. A large number of such firms are now under pressure from foreign rivals with more efficient processes or cheaper basic factors. To respond to these challenges, firms need to compete in more sophisticated ways. A broader, more dynamic view of cost makes sense for many firms. More investments must be channeled into efficient and innovative processes to increase productivity. Firms facing low-cost foreign competitors may need to reorient their strategies from producing unprocessed and semiprocessed products (where competition is necessarily based on cost) to more highly processed and differentiated products in related segments.

Focus on Areas of True Competitive Advantage

After looking at these issues and questions, many Canadian firms will conclude that they should adopt more focused strategies. In a world of soft economic competition and tariff protection, the proliferation of product lines and businesses may have made sense. The new imperative is to focus on those product lines, market segments, and businesses where Canadian firms can achieve sustainable advantage. Often, this will call for a rationalization of product lines and a concentration on lines that draw on unique competitive strengths. A number of firms in Canada have begun this process. GE Canada, for instance, has narrowed its Canadian product line and increased production of selected products to supply other GE operations worldwide. Similarly, Culinar, a Quebec-based consumer snack food producer, has moved to reduce the breadth of its core product line, divest weaker peripheral businesses, and focus on areas of advantage.

In addition to rationalizing product lines, many businesses will need to reevaluate their degree of vertical integration and exit from products where vertical integration does not provide advantage vis-à-vis rivals. For some companies, a reevaluation of growth-through-diversification strategies will also be required. In a world of more open trade and tougher competition, a greater focus on core businesses will make sense for most firms.

Upgrade the Canadian Diamond

Upgrading the Canadian diamond takes on special importance as firms move toward more sophisticated business strategies. Canadian firms need to act in several areas:

• *Increase investment in specialized human resource development.* Like any asset, employees at all levels require investment to keep them up-to-date.

In an environment characterized by more open competition, Canadian firms will have to rely more on advanced skills and improved labour force productivity and less on traditional basic factor advantages.

• *Forge closer ties with educational institutions.* Canadian firms must take a more pro-active approach if they want educational institutions to produce employees with both the general and specialized skills required for competitiveness. Canadian business, like its counterparts in Germany and several other countries, should be providing more direct input into course development at universities, colleges, and technical institutes. Business in Canada should be looking at ways to enhance the status of community colleges to ensure they are not viewed as "second-best" alternatives. Firms should also actively promote and participate in more cooperative educational programs where students work part-time or alternate periods of work and schooling. More businesses are becoming involved with co-op programs. For example, Inco entered into a partnership with Cambrian College in Sudbury to develop an innovative 48-week course that combines academic studies with training at Inco.

• *Improve technology development and adoption.* Firms should also be playing a more active role in ensuring that work conducted at university research institutes or centres and government laboratories is commercially relevant. Many successful firms contract out a great deal of their basic research and perform applied and developmental research in-house. Unfortunately, Canada has few specialized "centres of excellence" within its universities or community colleges where leading-edge research takes place, where the world's best professors come to teach, and where students are attracted from around the world. Firms should consider jointly funding and influencing the research conducted in such centres through trade associations, with related industries, and with government.

• *Transform trade associations into factor-creating mechanisms.* For the small- and mid-sized enterprises that dominate in many sectors of the Canadian economy, the need to upgrade in the areas of human resources and technology development and adoption may appear to pose daunting challenges. Cooperative ventures can be a fruitful path to upgrading factor capabilities for such companies. For example, firms can expand technical assistance and provide more funds to trade associations to develop training programs relevant to their industry. They can support the development of training consortia in which labour and government may participate as partners to industry—as has recently taken place in the electrical/electronics industry. Trade associations can also be a critical liaison between industry and educational institutes in helping to ensure the relevance of curricula discussed above. Finally, in the area of technology development and adoption, trade associations can also represent a valuable clearing house for dissemination of precompetitive research into common areas of concern such as the environment.

• *Nurture Canadian supplier industries.* The absence of dynamic clusters of competitive industries in Canada has been detrimental to innovation. Many firms have sourced abroad, while others have backward-integrated to compensate for the lack of indigenous supporting industries. Canadian companies should be taking steps to strengthen domestic supplier industries. Encouraging domestic suppliers, through local sourcing and the transferring of technology and skills, has become integral to the strategies of prominent Canadian companies such as IBM Canada and Nova Corporation.

• *Strive to develop and serve demanding Canadian buyers.* Firms should strive to serve the most sophisticated and demanding buyers in their home market. Selling to demanding local buyers will strengthen their ability to compete in global markets.

• *Establish links with Canadian-based firms in related industries.* Related industries are those linked to an industry by common technologies, distribution channels, skills, or customers. Canadian firms should strive to develop links with Canadian-based firms in related industries in order to increase technical interchange and information flows in a variety of areas.

• *Develop labour-management relations centered on productivity.* To improve productivity, many Canadian firms will have to adopt less authoritarian approaches to workforce management and a broader view of employees' potential to contribute to firm goals. Labour should be treated as a partner, not an adversary. Employees should be rewarded for productivity growth but should also expect to share the pain in periods of economic adversity.

• *Rely more on performance-related compensation.* In structuring compensation schemes, Canadian companies should move toward making both individual and company performance a significant part of remuneration at all levels.

Adopt More Global Strategies

More than 70 percent of Canadian manufacturers do not serve any export markets, and the majority of those that do export sell solely to the United States. Canada's reliance on the United States as an export market has grown over the past decade, at a time when globalization of many industries has increased. Given a more open global trade and business environment, firms in Canada need to develop global strategies if they are to compete successfully against foreign rivals in many industries. Competing globally means competing beyond North America. First and foremost, it means penetrating foreign markets both through trade and, ultimately, foreign investment. To succeed in international markets, Canadian firms must move more aggressively to satisfy the needs of foreign buyers and establish foreign sales and service channels. They must have the patience to make the investments necessary to build foreign market positions. Northern Telecom's recent acquisition of STC, a U.K.-based supplier of switches and transmission equipment, should enhance Northern's ability to sell into the post-1992 European market.

Competing globally can bring many advantages aside from increased sales. No country has a unique advantage in all the determinants of competitive advantage. Firms can selectively tap into sources of advantage in foreign diamonds, both to compensate for deficiencies at home and to exploit unique characteristics abroad. Canadian firms will benefit by serving the most sophisticated and demanding buyers in foreign countries. Given the ease of access to the U.S. market and the cultural similarities between the two countries, Canadian companies have an unusual ability to benefit from American buyers. The essential foundations for innovation must be present in the home base, however.

Define a North American or Global Mandate

Many foreign-owned or -controlled subsidiaries in Canada are today faced with urgent questions about their future role. Foreign subsidiaries in the manufacturing sector tend to be the firms with the broadest product lines, which overlap with those of subsidiaries in other countries. They also face the need to conform to their parents' global strategy. The potential consequences of a weak Canadian diamond are particularly acute for these firms given the ease and speed with which Canadian operations can be downsized and operations in other countries reconfigured to compensate.

Canadian subsidiaries must try to define a new role that is consistent with the evolving nature of the global strategies being pursued by many of the world's most advanced multinationals. This role is to have the Canadian operation become a North American or global headquarters for a particular product line or business segment in order to exploit particular advantages and strengths in the Canadian diamond. A number of foreign firms operating in Canada have moved in this direction. IBM Canada, for example, has the worldwide mandate for hardware power supplies. Hewlett-Packard Canada's Edmonton-based Idacom division manufactures computer-based protocol analyzers for the worldwide market, while its Calgary operation has the world mandate for supervisory control and data acquisition software. Campbell Soup is reconfiguring its Canadian operations to fit a North American manufacturing strategy. Canada is taking responsibility for a series of small-batch, specialty product lines that are especially well suited to the small yet flexible Canadian plants. The British firm ICI, after taking full control of its Canadian subsidiary ICI Canada, located the world headquarters for its industrial explosives business in Canada.

Redefine the Relationship with Government

Canadian firms must reevaluate their expectations of government and place different demands on government than in the past. First, they should insist that government activity not substitute for business initiative. Second, they should no longer look to government to provide traditional forms of assistance—subsidies, artificial cost structures, lax regulations, guaranteed procurement. Third, Canadian firms should pressure government to contribute to competitiveness through the provision of high-quality infrastructure, advanced factor creation, and appropriate incentives. Government-assisted R&D centres and training programs, for example, can be significant assets for firms. More generally, Canadian firms should promote government policies that promise to improve the home diamond in the industry or industries in which they compete.

Implications for Labour

With some 37 percent of the labour force unionized, organized labour in Canada plays a significant role in the country's economy as well as in a host of individual industries (especially in the resource and manufacturing sectors). Unions also exercise influence by adopting strategies and objectives that affect workplace relations in the broader private sector. The attitudes, policies, and approaches of organized labour can either help or hinder competitiveness. Far-sighted union leaders understand that efforts to increase productivity, upgrade skills, and facilitate shifts into more sophisticated jobs are the best guarantee of good wages in the long term.

In the old Canadian economic order, breakdowns in labour-management relations generally carried little cost. Large resource rents were there to be divided. Market protection and weak rivalry allowed cost increases to be passed on. Companies could prosper without paying much attention to their workforce. Finding themselves in a comfortable competitive environment, many companies accepted wage demands unconnected to productivity performance and tolerated work practices that impeded innovation. These behaviours and attitudes no longer fit the new competitive realities facing Canadian industry. New approaches to labour-management relations are needed. For organized labour, several implications follow from this:

• *Focus on productivity.* Canadian unions have sometimes been hostile to the imperative of productivity improvement, seeing it as a threat to jobs or a veiled attempt to reduce wages and benefits. To varying degrees, they have resisted developments geared to achieving higher productivity—such as workforce reorganization, multiskilling, and compensation systems more closely tied to performance. Today, more than ever before, the future viability of many Canadian industries and firms depends on their success in upgrading productivity. Unions can make an important contribution by assisting firms to identify and remove obstacles to productivity improvement by pressing for job enhancement and flexibility and by supporting advancement based on training and merit.

• *Skills upgrading.* Broadening and increasing workers' skills should be a central objective of labour. In recent years, there have been encouraging signs that unions have come to accept the inevitability of technological change and the necessary skills upgrading that accompanies it. Most of the onus for developing a "training culture" within Canadian business, however, must fall on managers, not workers or their unions.

• *More cooperative labour-management relations.* Shifts in production technologies and increasing competition call for a deeper reevaluation of the traditional labour-management framework. A more collaborative approach is essential. For their part, unions should embrace opportunities to participate in firm planning and encourage more information exchange. If Canadian industry is to compete successfully in the future, labour must move beyond its traditional and deeply rooted inclination to see management as the "opposing team."

Implications for Governments

Both the 10-nation study and our Canadian research have demonstrated that government can improve or detract from national competitive advantage. The question is not whether government should have a role, but what that role should be. Government's role in shaping competitiveness is inherently partial. Government policies in a particular area will generally fail unless they work in tandem with other determinants of competitive advantage. Government policy should be directed to building the skills, research infrastructure, and other inputs on which all firms draw. Through regulations, tax legislation, competition policies, and policies in other areas, government should seek to fashion an environment that supports upgrading and productivity growth. In this section, we summarize the broad implications of our findings for Canadian policymakers. We begin by outlining several general principles for sound policy and then focus on a number of specific areas in which changes are needed.

Some General Principles

Canadian governments should be guided by a limited number of principles as they seek to develop policies to assist Canadian industries and companies achieve international competitive success:

1. *Encourage adjustment and upgrading.* Competitive success grows out of dynamism, not static advantages such as cheap labour or subsidized input costs. Too often, government policy reflects a static mindset. In the next several years, many industries in Canada will be forced to restructure and refocus—rationalizing product lines, exiting from peripheral businesses, shifting away from some industries and segments and toward others. Government should facilitate these adjustments, not stand in the way. This will involve a government commitment to retraining, building infrastructure appropriate to changed circumstances, and providing an overall environment conducive to restructuring.

2. *Minimize direct interventions.* Direct interventions in the economy often have unfortunate consequences. Ineffective use of expenditures results in wasted resources. In addition, direct intervention frequently leads to an

unhealthy dependence on government by industry. Federal and provincial governments should be using indirect means rather than direct interventions to promote competitiveness. Indirect policies encompass programs designed to improve infrastructure and human resources, as well as economic policies that encourage investment and upgrading.

3. *Rely on incentives instead of grants.* Subsidies and grants to specific firms rarely translate into durable competitive advantage. There is little evidence that governments can successfully "pick winners" by targeting support to particular enterprises. Broader incentives that encourage individuals and firms to upgrade skills, or that create advanced factor pools and improved infrastructure, are more effective policy tools.

4. *Reengineer social policies.* In the long run, competitiveness and social goals tend to be mutually reinforcing. More productive industries lead to a stronger national economy, which in turn is better able to meet diverse social policy objectives. At the same time, an effective social infrastructure helps to underpin economic success. The design of social programs can have profound and often unanticipated consequences for the economy. In New Zealand, for example, a noncontributory pension scheme reduced national savings, while the structure of social assistance payments encouraged young people to drop out of school and militated against skill upgrading. Aggregate social spending in Canada is not out of line compared to most other industrialized countries. However, to create an attractive environment for competitive advantage, it is crucial that social goals be pursued in a way that does not sacrifice incentives, upgrading, and productivity growth. Consideration must be given to redesigning social programs that do not meet this test.

5. *Improve intergovernmental policy coordination.* Government imposes an increasingly heavy burden on Canada's economy. This burden is magnified by inadequate coordination of federal and provincial government policies in areas such as economic management, tax policy, training, education, the environment, and procurement. Canadians today are paying a high price to maintain elaborate bureaucracies at both the federal and provincial levels, yet are not receiving the benefits of either strong central control or effective decentralized decision making. The ultimate structure of a potentially reformed Canadian confederation is now under active discussion. This subject lies outside the scope of our study. However, we are convinced that improving Canada's international competitiveness will necessitate a substantially greater degree of collaboration and coordination between Ottawa and the provinces than has been typical in the past.

6. *Maintain an open policy toward foreign investment.* We strongly believe that efforts to restrict foreign investment in Canada, or to legislate foreign company behaviour, should be avoided. Except in rare cases, foreign investment contributes to the economy through new products, processes, assets, and skills that boost productivity. A substantial body of Canadian research supports this view. Foreign-owned companies are often more efficient and more technologically advanced than domestic firms; many invest as much, if

not more, in R&D as their Canadian counterparts. However, while Canada is better off with foreign investment than without it, the existing pattern of foreign activity in the economy reflects weaknesses that are cause for concern. Because of deficiencies in Canadian industry diamonds, foreign operations in Canada are too often limited to sourcing raw materials or performing the minimum activities needed to gain access to the local market. An important objective of government economic policy must be to improve the Canadian economic environment so that foreign companies will, over time, change and broaden the nature of their Canadian activities.

7. *Promote a sound and stable macroeconomic environment to complement other initiatives.* While a stable macroeconomic environment assists in achieving international competitiveness, it does not create or ensure it. Devaluing Canada's currency also does not provide a long-term solution to the country's underlying competitiveness problems. There is, however, little doubt about the types of macroeconomic goals that governments should be setting in order to support competitiveness: low inflation, which works to lower the real cost of capital; a high rate of national saving; and balanced public sector finances. The size of government deficits, and the rapid growth of government debt which has resulted from many years of large deficits, is perhaps the most critical macroeconomic problem facing Canada today. Chronic public sector deficits contribute to higher inflation, interest rates, and taxes. Determined action to reduce government deficits is imperative if Canada is to compete successfully through the 1990s and beyond.

Priorities in Specific Policy Areas: Factor Conditions

The number of government policies that affect the competitiveness of a country's industries and firms is almost limitless. Based on our Canadian research, we have identified some specific priorities for improvement in each part of the Canadian diamond. Because Canadian competitiveness has been mainly rooted in factor advantages, government policies bearing on factor conditions are particularly important.

Investment in Education and Specialized Skills.   Upgrading human resources will be critical to Canadian firms' ability to become more competitive. Canada has a relatively well-educated workforce, but its education and training systems have failed to respond adequately to the challenges posed by the contemporary global economy. Ensuring that the education system does a better job imparting basic skills is one priority. Improving and expanding private sector training is another. Governments should be considering new initiatives in several areas:

• *Provide more training for the unemployed.* Recent moves by the federal government to direct a larger share of labour market program funding to training the unemployed are a promising beginning, but more must be done to shift from passive income support to "active" labour market programs that encourage adjustment and skill upgrading.

• *Promote private sector training.* Canadian firms, in general, spend significantly less on workforce training than their counterparts in other industrialized countries. Governments should consider providing incentives to stimulate more training. One option might be to give UI premium rebates to firms that undertake training (possibly targeted at small and mid-sized firms). Another option would be to develop tax exemptions or credits to encourage training.

• *Set high national educational standards.* Canada's relatively generous spending on education has not translated into superior performance. Canada is virtually alone among advanced countries in having no national education standards of any kind. In other countries, such standards are an important ingredient in fostering high achievement. National standards are not inconsistent with a decentralized education system. In Germany, for instance, national standards coexist with an education system administered by the states, not the central government. A national standard need not require a full-fledged national system for testing, provided an appropriate level of intergovernmental cooperation exists. Provincial governments should move quickly to collaborate in developing agreed standards and testing mechanisms.

• *Put more emphasis on practical curricula and science skills.* Compared to other countries examined in our research, Canada has relatively few scientists, engineers, and technical workers in its labour force. Evidence points to declining interest in the sciences among elementary and high school students, declining enrollment in trade and vocational programs at the postsecondary level, and flat or falling enrollment in college-based technology-oriented programs. School curricula should be redesigned to put more emphasis on science, mathematics, and technology disciplines.

• *Expand apprenticeship programs and update curricula.* Many apprenticeship programs in Canada suffer from limited access, lack of standardized certification criteria, and high drop-out rates. Cooperative efforts on the part of governments, industry, and labour to update apprenticeship programs and extend such training into more occupations are urgently needed if Canada is to expand its pool of highly skilled workers.

• *Work more closely with trade associations.* As discussed above, trade associations represent a potentially high leverage mechanism for upgrading Canadian factors, particularly in the areas of education and training. Governments at all levels should seek to work more closely with these associations to strengthen factor conditions.

• *Promote cooperative education.* Cooperative education programs have proven to be an excellent vehicle for linking education to the workplace and for facilitating the transition from school to the labour force. Participation in these programs should be broadened.

• *Align university funding to support competitiveness.* As currently structured, government funding mechanisms for universities may not adequately underwrite the cost differentials that exist between science- and technology-related courses and other fields of study. Governments should reevaluate existing funding mechanisms and take steps to ensure that adequate resources are available for programs directly linked to competitiveness. Provincial governments should also reexamine the appropriate role of tuition in the overall university funding mix and the potential for school autonomy in setting tuition fees. The privatisation of some programs or even institutions should be seriously considered.

More Focused Technology Development and Faster Adoption.   Technology development and adoption are areas where Canada suffers from significant weaknesses. The problem lies more with the private sector than with government, however. Stimulating more research and development and faster adoption of technology in the private sector must be a priority objective of government. Among the specific steps we recommended are the following:

• *Improve coordination of government R&D programs.* Our research revealed a number of areas where excessive fragmentation of government expenditures has limited the effectiveness of science and technology programs. Duplication of research between universities and government labs is also of concern given the overall scarcity of government resources. Expenditures and research efforts in federal and provincial government research organizations must be better coordinated and tied more closely to university research activities.

• *Forge stronger links among government laboratories, provincial organizations, universities, and the private sector.* Government policy on science and technology has attached a high priority to advancing science and to training qualified personnel. While these goals are important, in the future, government policy in this area should put a greater emphasis on fostering more intimate linkages with industry.

• *Increase the proportion of government-funded R&D performed in the private sector.* While government R&D spending has increasingly emphasized private sector and university performance, federal laboratories still accounted for 55 percent of government expenditures of $2.7 billion in 1990, while provincial laboratories accounted for 41 percent of provincial government expenditures of $664 million. Given the funding issues which currently exist within the university system in terms of science and technology infrastructure, as well as the issues of ensuring commercial relevance and technology diffusion associated with government labs, we believe governments at the federal and provincial levels should continue to reduce the proportion of their funds spent internally, in addition to increasing the linkages with industry with respect to the activities that remain.

• *Encourage greater specialization among universities.* Current government policies and funding mechanisms often discourage specialization among Canadian universities. To create the specialized skills and other advanced factors necessary to achieve competitive advantage, more specialization in university programs and research activities should be encouraged.

• *Expand information available on intellectual property.* Intellectual property laws, and the information infrastructure that supports them, play an important role in fostering technology diffusion. The federal government should move rapidly to complete the automation of the patent search process.

Increase the Pace of Regulatory Reform in Infrastructure Sectors.   Regulatory reform in Canada has generally lagged the pace set in the United States. This has resulted in higher service costs to Canadian producers of many goods and services. Canada should continue to move ahead with regulatory reforms in key infrastructure areas such as transportation and communications. In addition, the federal and provincial governments should renew efforts to achieve a greater degree of harmonization of policies that restrict interprovincial competition and rationalization in areas such as trucking.

Strengthen Resource Conservation and Renewal Policies.   Effective natural resource conservation is vital to sustaining the competitiveness of resource-based industries. Canada's record to date has been mixed, although improvements are evident in areas such as forest replantation. With close to half of Canada's goods sector exports dependent on natural resources, governments must ensure that their resource policies promote long-term conservation, not short-term exploitation.

Priorities in Specific Policy Areas

Demand Conditions

Governments have a significant impact on a country's home demand conditions. Their leverage over demand is greatest in the areas of government procurement, regulation of product safety and standards, and environmental standards. The aim of government policy should be to encourage home demand that is early and sophisticated and that anticipates international needs and trends.

Restructure Government Procurement.   The effectiveness of government procurement policy in spurring innovation and competitive advantage in Canada has been undermined by several factors: blurred policy objectives, provincial government restrictions on out-of-province bidding, and a common preference for off-the-shelf products. Only infrequently have governments acted as a sophisticated buyer and sought to pressure Canadian companies to upgrade or created an early market for new products. While some progress in reforming procurement practices has been made in recent years, further efforts are required:

• *Encourage more open competition for government contracts.* Discriminatory purchasing practices, especially at the provincial level, have resulted in significant economic costs. All governments should strive to ensure that competition is open to out-of-province and out-of-country bidders.

• *Use challenging performance specifications.* Use of "make to blueprint" design specifications still appears to be widespread in government procurement in Canada. Wherever possible, governments should move toward performance-based specifications in order to encourage suppliers to develop and proliferate innovative products and processes.

Adopt Stringent and Forward-Looking Regulatory Standards.   Strict, anticipatory regulatory standards can be a potent force for spurring upgrading in industry, provided they are designed and administered effectively. Strict product quality and safety standards pressure firms to improve products in ways that are eventually demanded by international markets. High regulatory standards in areas such as construction, telecommunications, and transportation can stimulate early and sophisticated home demand. Tough standards for energy efficiency and environmental impact trigger innovations in products and processes that are highly valued elsewhere. In all of these areas, governments in Canada should be continuing to move toward more stringent standards and regulations.

Priorities in Specific Policy Areas: Related and Supporting Industries

Our research has found that the presence of home-based related and supporting industries is often critical in stimulating and facilitating innovation and productivity growth. The lack of depth and breadth in most Canadian industry clusters represents a significant weakness as the country and its industries seek to respond to a new competitive environment. Canadian government policy in areas such as regional and industrial development has frequently worked against the objective of building strong, geographically concentrated clusters. Government policies should be tailored to meet the following guidelines:

• *Ensure that programs and policies in all areas are consistent with the development of stronger industry clusters.* Governments should critically examine the full range of policies to determine whether these policies support the growth of clusters.

• *Employ policies that build on existing regional strengths.* The presence of an industry or cluster in a region is generally a sign that some competitive advantage already exists. Government policies should be geared to enhancing clusters rather than—as has so often been the case in Canada—subsidizing existing, inefficient industries and activities or trying to create industries unrelated to local economic strengths.

• *Focus on promoting the development of specialized factors.* The most effective way for governments to reinforce cluster development is to focus on investments that assist in creating specialized factors such as technical institutes, training centres, and other infrastructure related to the needs of specific

industries. Importantly, many of the policies and programs that most effectively promote specialized factors are provincial or local in origin.

Priorities in Specific Policy Areas: Firm Strategy, Structure, and Rivalry

Governments can strengthen the competitiveness of their industries by fostering a stable economic environment and creating incentives for investment,
skill upgrading, and risk-taking, and by ensuring that a healthy degree of
competition prevails in the home market.

**Create Stronger Individual and Corporate Incentives for Investment and Up-
grading.**   Through tax policies and its actions in other policy areas, government helps to structure the incentives for individuals to work, save, and invest
in skill building. Government policies also influence the goals and strategies
of firms. To strengthen this important determinant of competitive advantage,
governments in Canada should be looking at initiatives such as the following:

• *Reengineer "safety net" programs to ensure they are well targeted to those
in need and provide appropriate incentives.* Some existing social programs
should be restructured so that clear incentives always exist for individuals to
work and improve skills. In particular, consideration should be given to reforming social assistance programs to allow recipients to keep a greater portion
of earnings from employment, thereby encouraging them to participate in the
labour force and upgrade their skills.

• *Encourage stronger linkages between performance and compensation.*
Canada currently trails a number of competitor countries in linking compensation to productivity or firm performance at both the managerial and worker
levels. Governments can assist in promoting compensation linked to performance through its policies toward its own workforce and also by encouraging
appropriate behaviour in the private sector. Providing further incentives for
employees to invest in their companies would be one way to strengthen
linkages between pay and performance in the private sector.

• *Provide more favourable tax treatment for long-term equity investment.*
To increase its international competitiveness, Canada must invest heavily in
training, technology, machinery, and equipment. Yet the payoff from such
investments is often realized only over the long term. There is concern in
Canada (and the United States) that investors—individual, corporate, and
institutional—are often guided by a shorter-term outlook. Current tax policy
may contribute to a short-term view. While the tax treatment of capital gains
in Canada is somewhat more favourable than that in the United States, this
is largely offset by higher marginal tax rates. In addition, a number of other
countries have introduced measures specifically designed to encourage long-
term investment. We believe that Canada should also be exploring ways to
restructure capital gains taxation in order to increase incentives for long-term
investment in productive assets.

Extend Efforts to Increase Rivalry.   Canada has made significant strides in recent years toward instituting policies that enhance domestic rivalry. Freer trade, deregulation, and the modernization of competition laws are all important steps that have moved the country in the right direction. Now the federal and provincial governments must make an extraordinary effort to eliminate interprovincial barriers as expeditiously as possible. The federal government's recent constitutional initiative should provide a useful impetus to achieve progress in this field.

Move Aggressively to Restore a Favourable Macroeconomic Environment.
All levels of government must share in the burden of bringing deficits and debt under much better control, by reevaluating spending programs and increasing the effectiveness of dollars spent. The underlying philosophy of the federal government's recent proposals, contained in its report *Canadian Federalism and Economic Union,* which calls for increased fiscal coordination among the federal and provincial governments, is a sound one and the proposals deserve serious consideration. Finally, despite recent proposals by some, devaluing Canada's currency is not a long-term solution to Canada's competitiveness problems, even if it might temporarily improve the competitive position of some Canadian industries.

Implications for Canadian Citizens

Perhaps the most important factor in Canada's ability to move forward is the attitudes and the mindset of individual Canadians. Unless individual citizens can accept and internalize the new reality, positive programs will be undermined. Canadians must better understand the foundations of their past prosperity and the fact that the comfortable old order is disintegrating. They must also recognize that the sources of Canadian competitiveness are at risk. Most importantly, Canadians must understand that they cannot return to the old order. Instead of looking longingly at the past, Canadians must adopt the new paradigm for what will determine future Canadian competitiveness. They must respond to this new paradigm in their roles as employees, as managers, as voters, and as members of their communities.

SUSTAINABLE COMPETITIVE ADVANTAGE—WHAT IT IS, WHAT IT ISN'T

Kevin P. Coyne

> I shall not today attempt to define the kinds of material to be embraced within that shorthand description; and perhaps I could never succeed in intelligibly doing so. But I know it when I see it.
>
> Supreme Court Justice Potter Stewart
> (*Jacobellis v. State of Ohio*)

Although it was pornography, not sustainable competitive advantage, that the late Justice Stewart doubted his ability to define, his remark neatly characterizes the current state of thinking about the latter subject as well. Explicitly or implicitly, sustainable competitive advantage (SCA) has long occupied a central place in strategic thinking. Witness the widely accepted definition of competitive strategy as "an integrated set of actions that produce a sustainable advantage over competitors."[1] But exactly what constitutes sustainable competitive advantage is a question rarely asked. Most corporate strategists are content to apply Justice Stewart's test; they know an SCA when they see it—or so they assume.

But perhaps an SCA is not always so easy to identify. In developing its liquid hand soap, Minnetonka, Inc., focused its efforts on building an advantage that was easily copied later. In the wristwatch market, Texas Instruments attempted to exploit an advantage over its competitors that turned out to be unimportant to target consumers. RCA built barriers to competition in the vacuum tube market in the 1950s only to find these barriers irrelevant when

---

[1] *Competitive strategy,* as the term is used in this article, is exclusively concerned with defeating competitors and achieving dominance in a product/market segment. It is thus—in concept, and usually in practice—a subset of business strategy, which addresses the broader goal of maximizing the wealth of shareholders.

Source: Reprinted with permission from *Business Horizons* (January–February 1986). Copyright © 1986, by the Foundation for the School of Business at Indiana University.

transistors and semiconductors were born. CB radio producers built capacity to fill a demand that later evaporated. In each case, the companies failed to see in advance that, for one reason or another, they lacked a sustainable competitive advantage.

Perhaps it is because the meaning of "sustainable competitive advantage" is superficially self-evident that virtually no effort has been made to define it explicitly. After all, it can be argued that the dictionary's definitions of the three words bring forth the heart of the concept. But every strategist needs to discover whether an SCA is actually or potentially present, and if so, what its implications are for competitive and business strategy.

Therefore, this article will describe a number of established strategic concepts and build on them to develop a clear and explicit concept of SCA.

Specifically, we will examine:

• The conditions for SCA.

When does a producer have a competitive advantage? How can the strategist test whether such an advantage is sustainable?

• Some implications of SCA for strategy.

Does having SCA guarantee success? Can a producer succeed without an SCA? Should a producer always pursue an SCA?

Conditions for SCA

Any producer who sells his goods or services at a profit undeniably enjoys a competitive advantage with those customers who choose to buy from him instead of his competitors, though these competitors may be superior in size, strength, product quality, or distribution power. Some advantages, however, are obviously worth more than others. A competitive advantage is meaningful in strategy only when three distinct conditions are met:

1. Customers perceive a consistent difference in important attributes between the producer's product or service and those of his competitors.
2. That difference is the direct consequence of a capability gap between the producer and his competitors.
3. Both the difference in important attributes and the capability gap can be expected to endure over time.

In earlier strategy work, these conditions have been jointly embedded in the concepts of "key factors for success" (KFS), "degrees of freedom," and "lower costs or higher value to the customer." In the interest of clarity, however, they deserve separate consideration.

Differentiation in Important Attributes

Obviously, competitive advantage results from differentiation among competitors—but not just any differentiation. For a producer to enjoy a competitive advantage in a product/market segment, the difference or differences between him and his competitors must be felt in the marketplace: that is, they must be reflected in some *product/delivery attribute* that is a *key buying criterion* for the market. And the product must be differentiated enough to win the loyalty of a significant set of buyers; it must have a *footprint in the market*.

Product/Delivery Attribute

Customers rarely base their choice of a product or service on internal characteristics of the producer that are not reflected in a perceived product or delivery difference. Indeed, they usually neither know nor care about those characteristics. Almost invariably, the most important contact between the customer and the producer is the marketplace—the "strategic triangle" where the producer meets his customers and competitors. It is here that the competitive contest for the scarce resource, the sales dollar, is directly engaged.

Just as differences among animal species that are unrelated to scarce resources do not contribute to the survival of the fittest, so producer differences that do not affect the market do not influence the competitive process. Differences among competitors in plant locations, raw material choices, labor policies, and the like matter only when those differences translate into product/delivery attributes that influence the customers' choice of where to spend their sales dollars.

"Product/delivery attributes" include not only such familiar elements as price, quality, aesthetics, and functionality, but also broader attributes such as availability, consumer awareness, visibility, and after-sales service. Anything that affects customers' perceptions of the product or service, its usefulness to them, and their access to it is a product/delivery attribute. Anything that does not affect these perceptions is not.

Having lower costs, for example, may well result in significantly higher margins. But this *business* advantage will become a *competitive* advantage only if and when the producer directly or indirectly recycles the additional profits into product/delivery attributes such as price, product quality, advertising, or additional capacity that increases availability. Only then is the producer's competitive position enhanced. Two examples illustrate this point.

1. For years, the "excess" profits of a major packaged goods company—the low-cost producer in its industry—have been siphoned off by its corporate parent for reinvestment in other subsidiaries. The packaged goods subsidiary has therefore been no more able to take initiatives or respond to competitive threats than if it did not produce those excess profits. Thus, business advantage

may exist, but competitive advantage is lacking. If risk-adjusted returns available from investments in other business exceed those of additional investment in the packaged goods subsidiary, the corporate parent may be making the best business decisions. However, the packaged goods subsidiary has gained no competitive advantage from its superior position.

2. The corporate parent of a newly acquired, relatively high-cost producer in an industrial products market has decided to aggressively expand its subsidiary. This expansion is potentially at the expense of the current market leader, an independent company occupying the low-cost position in the industry. The resources that the new parent is willing to invest are far larger than the incremental profits generated by the market leader's lower costs. Because the new subsidiary can invest more than the market leader in product design, product quality, distribution, and so forth, it is the subsidiary that has, or soon will have, the competitive advantage.

In short, it is the application, not just the generation, of greater resources that is required for *competitive* advantage.

Key Buying Criterion

Every product has numerous attributes that competitors can use to differentiate themselves to gain some degree of advantage. To be strategically significant, however, an advantage must be based on positive differentiation of an attribute that is a *key buying criterion* for a particular market segment and is not offset by a negative differentiation in any other key buying criterion. In the end, competitive advantage is the result of all net differences in important product/delivery attributes, not just one factor such as price or quality. Differences in other, less important attributes may be helpful at the margin, but they are not strategically significant.

Key buying criteria vary, of course, by industry and even by market segment. In fact, because market segments differ in their choice of key buying criteria, a particular product may have a competitive advantage in some segments while being at a disadvantage in others. Price aside, the elaborate technical features that professional photographers prize in Hasselblad cameras would baffle and discourage most of the casual users who make up the mass market.

In any one product/market segment, however, only a very few criteria are likely to be important enough to serve as the basis for a meaningful competitive advantage. These criteria are likely to be basic—that is, central to the concept of the product or service itself, as opposed to "add-ons" or "features." For example, in the tubular steel industry, there are just two key product/delivery attributes: a single measure of quality (third-party testing reject rate) and local availability on the day required by the customer's drilling schedule.

Texas Instruments (TI) apparently did not fully understand the importance of differentiation along key buying criteria when it entered the wristwatch market. Its strategy was to build upon its ability to drive down costs—and therefore prices (the products attribute)—beyond the point where competitors could respond. But this competitive strategy, which had worked in electronic components, failed in wristwatches because price, past a certain point, was no longer a key buying criterion: customers cared more about aesthetics. TI had surpassed all of its competitors in an attribute that did not matter in the marketplace.

"Footprint in the Market"

To contribute to an SCA, the differences in product/delivery attributes must command the attention and loyalty of a substantial customer base; in other words, they must produce a "footprint in the market" of significant breadth and depth.

Breadth.   How many customers are attracted to the product above all others by the difference in product attributes? What volume do these customers purchase?

Depth.   How strong a preference has this difference generated? Would minor changes in the balance of attributes cause the customers to switch?

Breadth and depth are usually associated in marketing circles with the concept of "branding." Branding can indeed be a source of competitive advantage, as shown by Perrier's spectacular advantage in a commodity as prosaic as bottled mineral water.

But the importance of breadth and depth are not limited to branding strategies. Even a producer who is pursuing a low-price strategy must ensure that his lower price will cause customers to choose his product and that changes in nonprice attributes by competitors would be unlikely to lure them away.

Durable Differentiation

Positive differentiation in key product/delivery attributes is essential to competitive advantage. However, a differentiation that can be readily erased does not by itself confer a meaningful advantage. Competitive advantages described in such terms as "faster delivery" or "superior product quality" are illusory if competitors can erase the differentiation at will.

For example, Minnetonka, Inc., created a new market niche with "Softsoap." As a result, its stock price more than doubled. Before long, however, 50 different brands of liquid soap, some selling for a fifth of Softsoap's price, appeared on the market. As a result, Minnetonka saw its earnings fall to zero and its stock price decline by 75 percent.

An advantage is durable only if competitors cannot readily imitate the producer's superior product/delivery attributes. In other words, a gap in the *capability* underlying the differentiation must separate the producer from his competitors; otherwise no meaningful competitive advantage exists. (Conversely, of course, no meaningful advantage can arise from a capability gap that does not produce an important difference in product/delivery attributes.)

Understanding the capability gap, then, is basic to determining whether a competitive advantage actually exists. For example, an attribute such as faster delivery does not constitute a real competitive advantage unless it is based on a capability gap such as may exist if the company has a much bigger truck fleet than its competitors can afford to maintain. Higher product quality does not in itself constitute a competitive advantage. But unique access to intrinsically superior raw materials that enable the producer to deliver a better quality product may well do so.

A capability gap exists when the function responsible for the differentiated product/delivery attribute is one that only the producer in question can perform, or one that competitors (given their particular limitations) could do only with maximum effort. So defined, capability gaps fall into four categories.

1. **Business system gaps** result from the ability to perform individual functions more effectively than competitors and from the inability of competitors to easily follow suit. For example, differences in labour union work rules can constitute a capability gap resulting in superior production capability. Superior engineering or technical skills may create a capability gap leading to greater precision or reliability in the finished product.

2. **Position gaps** result from prior decisions, actions, and circumstances. Reputation, consumer awareness and trust, and order backlogs, which can represent important capability gaps, are often the legacy of an earlier management generation. Thus, current competitive advantage may be the consequence of a past facilities location decision. BHP, the large Australian steel maker, enjoys important production efficiencies because it is the only producer to have located its smelter adjacent to its iron ore source, eliminating expensive iron ore transportation costs.

3. **Regulatory/legal gaps** result from government's limiting the competitors who can perform certain activities, or the degree to which they can perform those activities. Patents, operating licenses, import quotas, and consumer safety laws can all open important capability gaps among competitors. For example, Ciba-Geigy's patent on a low-cost herbicide allowed it to dominate certain segments of the agricultural chemical market for years.

4. **Organization or managerial quality gaps** result from an organization's ability consistently to innovate and adapt more quickly and effectively than its competitors. For example, in industries like computers or financial services, where the competitive environment is shifting rapidly, this flexibility may be

the single most important capability gap. In other industries, the key capability gap may be an ability to out-innovate competitors, keeping them always on the defensive.

Note that only the first category, business system gaps, covers actions that are currently under the control of the producer. Frustrating as it may be to the strategist, competitive advantage or disadvantage is often the result of factors he or she is in no position to alter in the short term.

The broad concept of a capability gap becomes useful only when we succeed in closely specifying a producer's *actual* capability gap over competitors in a *particular* situation. Analysts can detect the existence of a capability gap by examining broad functions in the business system, but they must then go further and determine the root cause of superior performance in that function.

Individual capability gaps between competitors are very specific. There must be a precise reason why one producer can outperform another, or there is no competitive advantage. The capability gap consists of specific, often physical, differences. It is likely to be prosaic and measurable, not intangible. Abstract terms, such as "higher labor productivity" or "technological leadership," often serve as useful shorthand, but they are too general for precise analysis. Moreover, they implicitly equate capability gaps with marginal performance superiority, rather than with discrete differences—such as specific work rule differences or technical resources capacity—that are not easily imitated.

For example, if marginal performance superiority constituted competitive advantage, one would expect "focus" competitors—those who have no capability advantage but excel in serving a particular niche through sheer concentration of effort—to win over more general competitors who decide to invade that niche. But as American Motors learned when Detroit's "Big Three" began producing small cars, and as some regional banks are learning as money center banks enter their markets, "trying harder" is no substitute for the possession of unique capabilities.

Only by understanding specific differences in capability can the strategist accurately determine and measure the actions that competitors must take to eliminate the gap and the obstacles and costs to them of doing so.

Lasting Advantage (Sustainability)

If a meaningful advantage is a function of a positive difference in important attributes based on an underlying capability gap, then the sustainability of the competitive advantage is simply a function of the durability of both the attributes and the gap.

There is not much value in an advantage in product/delivery attributes that do not retain their importance over time. Manufacturers of CB radios, video games, and designer jeans saw their revenues decline and their financial losses mount not because their competitors did anything to erode their capability advantages, but because most of their customers simply no longer valued those products enough to pay the price. In each case, industry participants believed that they had benefited from a permanent shift in consumer preferences and began to invest accordingly. In each case they were wrong.

Whether consumers will continue to demand a product over time, and how they can be influenced to prefer certain product attributes over time, are essentially marketing issues, subject to normal marketing analytical techniques. How basic is the customer need that the product meets? How central to its function or availability is the attribute in each question? These may be the key questions to ask in this connection.

The sustainability of competitive advantage is also a function of the durability of the capability gap that created the attractive attribute. In fact, the most important condition for sustainability is that existing and potential competitors either cannot or will not take the actions required to close the gap. If competitors can and will fill the gap, the advantage is by definition not sustainable.

Obviously, a capability gap that competitors are unable to close is preferable to one that relies on some restraint. Unfortunately, a producer cannot choose whether a particular capability gap meets the former or the latter condition.

Consider the two cases more closely.

Case 1

Competitors cannot fill the gap. This situation occurs when the capability itself is protected by specific entry and mobility barriers such as an important product patent or unique access to a key raw material (for example, DeBeer's Consolidated Mines). In a Case 1 situation, sustainability is assured at least until the barrier is eroded or eliminated (converting the situation to Case 2). Barriers can erode or be eliminated over time, unless they are inherent in the nature of the business.[2]

A more significant danger to Case 1 advantages, however, probably lies not in the gradual erosion of barriers, but in the possibility that competitors may leapfrog the barriers by a new game strategy.

For example, the introduction of the transistor in 1955 did nothing to erode the barriers that RCA had created in vacuum tubes; it simply made RCA's leadership irrelevant. Therefore, although sustainability can be estimated by (1) considering all the changes (environmental forces or competitor actions) that could erode the barriers, and (2) assessing the probabilities of

---

[2] For example, if the business is a "natural monopoly." A natural monopoly exists where either (1) economies of scale cause marginal costs to decline past the point where production volume equals market demand (that is, where the most efficient economic system is to have only one producer); or (2) the social costs of installing duplicate production/distribution systems outweigh the benefits, a situation usually leading to the establishment of a legal monopoly by government fiat.

their occurrence over a specified time horizon, there will, of course, always be uncertainty in the estimate.

Case 2

Competitors could close the capability gap but refrain from doing so. This situation might occur for any one of four reasons.

a. Inadequate Potential.   A simple calculation may show competitors that the costs of closing the gap would exceed the benefits, even if the possessor of the advantage did not retaliate.

For example, the danger of cannibalizing existing products may preclude effective response. MCI, Sprint, and others were able to create the low-price segment of the U.S. long-distance telephone market largely because AT&T did not choose to respond directly for some time. Most likely it considered that the cost of cutting prices for 100 percent of its customers in order to retain the 1 to 2 percent in the low-price segment was simply too high, and that only when the segment grew to sufficient size would a response become worthwhile.

Other examples of situations where a payoff is not worth the required investment include investing in capacity to achieve "economies of scale" when the capacity required to achieve the required economy exceeds the likely additional demand in the industry; and labor work rules, where the additional compensation demanded by the union in return for such changes would more than offset the potential savings.

The inadequate-potential situation represents a sustainable advantage because the "end game" has already been reached: there are no rational strategic countermoves for competitors to take until conditions change.

b. Corresponding Disadvantage.   Competitors may believe that acting to close the capability gap will open gaps elsewhere (in this or other market segments) that will more than offset the value of closing this one.

For example, a "niche" competitor relies on this factor to protect him against larger competitors, who (or so he hopes) will reckon that an effective attack on his niche advantage would divert resources (including management time) needed elsewhere, destroy the integrity of their own broader product lines (opening gaps in other segments), or create some other gap.

A "corresponding disadvantage" situation constitutes at least a temporarily sustainable advantage, because for the moment an "end game" has been reached. However, as the attractiveness of competitors' other markets changes, so does their estimate of whether a corresponding disadvantage is present in the niche (as American Motors learned to its cost). In addition, competitors will always be searching for ways to fill the capability gap without creating offsetting gaps. Only if the creation of offsetting gaps is an automatic and inevitable consequence of any such action will the producer's advantage be assured of sustainability in the long run.

c. Fear of Reprisal.   Even though it initially would appear worth doing so, competitors may refrain from filling the capability gap for fear of retaliatory action by the producer. The sustainability of the producer's existing advantage depends, in this case, on the competitors' continuing to exercise voluntary restraint, accepting in effect the producer's position in this market segment.

For example, Japanese steel makers voluntarily refrain from increasing their U.S. market share for fear that American producers can and will persuade the U.S. government to take harsh protectionist measures.

"Fear of reprisal" is probably among the most common strategic situations in business, but it must be considered unstable over time, as competitor's situations and managements shift.

d. Management Inertia.   Finally, there are cases where competitors would benefit from closing the capability gap but fail to do so, either because management has incorrectly assessed the situation or because it lacks the will, the ability, or the energy to take the required action.

For example, Honda's success in dominating the British motorcycle industry is generally attributed to Norton Villiers Triumph's failure to respond to a clear competitive threat until too late.

Psychologists tell us that managers will implement real change only when their discomfort with the status quo exceeds the perceived personal cost of taking the indicated action. This may well explain why competitors often tolerate a performance gap that they could profitably act to close. But it is risky for a producer to rely for long on the weakness or inertia of competitors' management to protect a competitive advantage; by definition, the end game has not been reached.

In all four cases, how long competitors will tolerate capability gaps they are capable of closing depends largely on the relationship between the value of the advantage created by the gap and the cost (to each competitor) of closing it. The worse the cost-to-benefit ratio, the longer the advantage is likely to be sustainable, because greater changes in the environment are required before value would exceed cost. Coupled with an informed view of the rate of environmental change in the industry, this ratio thus allows the analyst to estimate sustainability.

SCA and Strategy

The classic definition of competitive strategy as "an integrated set of actions designed to create a sustainable advantage over competitors" might suggest that possessing an SCA is synonymous with business success—that those producers who have an SCA are guaranteed winners, and that those competitors who lack one should simply exit the business to avoid financial disaster.

This apparently reasonable conclusion is, however, incorrect. Although an SCA is a powerful tool in creating a successful business strategy, it is not the only key ingredient. In fact:

1. Possessing an SCA does not guarantee financial success.
2. Producers can succeed even when competitors possess an SCA.
3. Pursuing an SCA can sometimes conflict with sound business strategy.

Losing with an SCA

Although an SCA will help a producer to achieve, over time, higher returns than his competitors, there are at least three circumstances where its possessor can fail financially:

1. If the market sector is not viable. In many cases (including most new product introductions), the minimum achievable cost of producing and selling a particular product or service exceeds its value to the customer. In this situation, an SCA will not guarantee the survival of its possessor; it will tend merely to ensure that his competitors will fare even worse.

2. If the producer has severe operational problems. An SCA can allow management the luxury of focusing more fully on achieving operational excellence, but thousands of companies have failed for operational, rather than strategic, reasons.

3. If competitors inflict tactical damage. An SCA rarely puts a producer completely beyond the reach of competitor actions such as price cuts and "buying" market share, which may be unrelated to the SCA itself. A producer will be particularly vulnerable to such competitive tactics if the SCA is not very important, either because the depth of the "footprint" described earlier is shallow or because the gap in capability is minor.

In these cases, producers must select their actions very carefully. Actions that can and will be imitated may result only in intensified competitive rivalry. And, where the producer's advantage is unimportant, he will have little cushion against the competitive repercussions. For example, recent airline pricing policies and "frequent flyer" programs have done nothing to contribute to the long-term profitability or competitive positions of their originators. Unimaginative direct cost-reduction efforts (cutting overhead or staffs, for example) may improve profitability in the short term. But if competitors can and will imitate these efforts, the only long-run effect may be to raise the general level of misery throughout the industry.

Competing against an SCA

By definition, not all producers can possess an SCA in a given product/market segment. Other competitors face the prospects of competing (at least for some time) from a handicapped position. Under certain circumstances, however, it is still possible for some to succeed.

Rapidly growing markets constitute one such situation. As long as real market growth over a given period exceeds the additional capacity advantaged competitors can bring on line during that time (due to organizational constraints, risk aversion, and so forth), even competitors can thrive. For example, the booming market for microcomputer software over the past five years has enabled many weak competitors to grow rich. Only when market growth slows or the advantaged competitors increase the rate at which they can grow will true competition begin and the impact of an SCA make itself felt.

In markets where true competition for scarce sales dollars is taking place, the number of disadvantaged competitors who can succeed, the degree to which they can prosper, and the conditions under which they can prosper will vary, depending on the value of the advantage held by the "number-one" competitor.

If the number-one competitor has only a shallow or unimportant advantage, many disadvantaged competitors can prosper for long periods. As noted earlier, each competitor is unique. When all attributes are considered, each will have a competitive advantage in serving some customers. The disadvantaged competitors are more likely to receive lower returns than the number-one producer, but they certainly may be viable.

If the number-one competitor has an important advantage in a given product/market segment, some theorists assert that over the long run there will be only one viable competitor. Others may remain in the segment, but they will be plagued by losses and/or very inadequate returns. If there are six different ways to achieve a major advantage, this reasoning runs, then the market will split into six segments, each ruled by a different competitor, who uniquely excels in the attribute most valued by the customers in that segment.

Be that as it may, in practice other strong competitors may also profitably exist alongside Number One under two conditions:

1. *If the number-one producer's advantage is limited by a finite capacity* that is significantly less than the size of the market; that is, he may expand further, but will not retain his advantage on the incremental capacity. Obstacles to continued advantaged expansion are common: limited access to superior raw materials, finite capacity in low-cost plants, prohibitive transportation costs beyond certain distances. Antitrust laws also tend to act as barriers to expansion beyond a level by number-one competitors.

2. *If the size of the individual competitors is small* relative to the size of the market. In this case, a number of strong competitors can expand for many years without directly competing with each other, by taking share from weak competitors rather than each other.

Weak competitors, of course, are likely to fare badly when competition is intense and the depth of the advantage enjoyed by others is great. Their choices are:

1. To leave the business.
2. To endure the situation until the advantage is eroded.
3. To seek to create a new advantage.

If a weak competitor chooses to pursue a new advantage, then he must ensure that it will be preemptive, or that competitors will not notice his move and will fail to respond until he has consolidated his position. Otherwise, his action is virtually certain to be copied and the intended advantage erased.

Pursuing the Wrong SCA

Although its attainment is the goal of *competitive* strategy, sustainable competitive advantage is not an end in itself but a means to an end. The corporation is not in business to beat its competitors, but to create wealth for its shareholders. Thus, actions that contribute to SCA but detract from creating shareholder wealth may be good strategy in the competitive sense but bad strategy for the corporation. Consider two examples.

1. Low-cost capacity additions in the absence of increased industry demand. Adding low-cost capacity and recycling the additional profits into product/delivery attributes that attract enough customers to fill that capacity is usually a sound business strategy. However, as industry cost curve analysis has demonstrated, if the capacity addition is not accompanied by increases in industry demand, the effect may well be to displace the high-cost, but previously viable, marginal producer. When this happens, prices in the industry will fall to the level of the costs of the new marginal producer, costs which by definition are lower than the costs of the former marginal producer. Thus, the profit per unit sold of all participants will be reduced.

Depending on the cost structure of the industry, the declines in the profit per unit sold can be dramatic (for example, if all the remaining producers have similar costs). In this case, even the producer who added the new capacity will face declining profitability on his preexisting capacity; in extreme cases his total profit on new and old capacity may fall below the profit he had previously earned on the old capacity alone. While gaining share and eliminating a competitor (good competitive strategy), he has invested *more* to profit *less* (bad business strategy).

2. Aggressive learning-curve pricing strategies that sacrifice too much current profit. Under these strategies, prices are reduced at least as fast as costs in order to buy market share and drive out competitors. The assumption is that the future payoff from market dominance will more than offset the costs of acquiring it. The value of new business, however, is likely to be very sensitive to the precise relationship between prices and costs. This is true particularly in the early stages of the learning curve, when the absolute levels of prices, costs, and margins are relatively high and the profit consequences

are therefore greater for any given volume. Especially in high-tech industries such as electronics, where the lifetime of technologies is short, the long-term value of the market share bought by overly aggressive learning-curve strategies can be less than the profit eliminated in the early stages by pricing too close to costs.

The framework for SCA proposed in this article is far from complete. Its treatment of product/delivery attributes and capability gaps (notably organizational strength) is impressionistic rather than detailed. It leaves other aspects of the topic (for example, the sustainability of competitive advantage at the corporate level) unexplored.

But a major concern of the business unit strategist is to determine whether the enterprise (or a competitor's) possesses or is in a position to capture an SCA, and, if so, to examine its strategic implications. The conditions for SCA and the implications of SCA for strategy that have been proposed provide an initial framework for these tasks.

From Warning to Crisis: A Turnaround Primer

P. Scott Scherrer

Long before a business fails, warning signals start flashing. But managers often don't notice the red lights, or even ignore them. When they finally do acknowledge something's amiss, some managers will treat the problem as a temporary phenomenon, putting out the fire but not remedying the hazard.

With a bit of education, however, managers can train themselves to perk up and recognize the bad signs, whether they are activated from within the organization or from the outside. Once managers learn the signals, they also can differentiate between the various stages of organizational decline. No matter what phase a company is in, managers need to act—fast.

Following is a turnaround primer that identifies warning signals, categorizes decline phases, and provides a framework to help managers reverse the direction of an organization that may well be on its way to hell in a handbasket.

External Influences

Many managers believe a downward trend will dissipate when bad news from the outside improves. The external elements that cause them trouble range from increased competition to legal/political vacillations (see Exhibit 1).

Among these external, uncontrollable elements are market changes, customer preference changes, foreign competition, capital market movements, legal precedents, and the political climate. Since all businesses in an industry are similarly affected by external elements, each business survives these changes only because of the ability of its management. Some businesses come through external changes with increased market share and profitability; others fail.

Source: Reprinted with permission of publisher, from *Management Review,* September 1988. Copyright © 1988, American Management Association, New York. All rights reserved.

Exhibit 1   Nine External Warning Signals

1. Economic growth activity gives management an indication of the economic climate and influences expansion plans.
2. Credit availability and money-market activity are barometers of trends in commercial and investment banking that will alter the cost of funds.
3. Capital market activity gives a clear signal to management of investor attitudes toward any given industry and the state of the business climate.
4. Business population characteristics show the numbers of businesses entering and exiting any given industry, signaling market expansion and contraction and the degree of competition within the industry.
5. Price-level changes indicate the rate of inflation and impact production considerations.
6. Changes in the competitive structure of the marketplace affect products, pricing, and marketing/distribution.
7. Breakthrough technology also causes changes in products, marketing/distribution, and production.
8. Cultural/social changes alter consumer preferences or the conditions under which a product can be sold.
9. Legal/political changes can adversely affect the marketplace or have an impact on the production, sale, and distribution of a product.

A major problem with the uncontrollable elements is their interaction with each other. A cultural/social change, for example, can result in a legal/political change. This, in turn, can affect the economic environment, leading to a shift in technological developments. The rate of technological development affects the status of the competition, which in turn influences the cultural/social environment, and the circle is complete. What managers often do not realize is that they can create a similar chain reaction within their businesses to combat the external elements. Foresight and flexibility will help management safeguard against uncontrollable elements, using tactics such as promotion, education of the consumer, accelerated research and development, product improvements or elimination, changing expansion plans, changing markets, and changing channels of distribution.

Consider the tobacco companies. They have known for many years about the external changes taking place in their industry—most importantly, the discovery of smoking's serious health hazards. They have been affected by cultural/social and legal/political changes for the past several decades, and recently experienced severe tests in the court system. To offset declining product sales, they developed new products, such as smokeless tobaccos. They also invested in new businesses: RJR Nabisco, Miller Beer, and other consumer products companies that would use established channels of distribution to gain competitive advantage. The tobacco producers understood the early warning signals of the external, uncontrollable elements and acted to offset them. The ability to cope with external, uncontrollable elements requires that management plans for the unexpected and implements that plan when the unexpected occurs.

Internal Elements

Only 20 percent of business failures are caused by external elements. The other 80 percent are the result of mishandled internal elements. Management is the force that drives the internal functions of finance, production, and marketing/distribution, and yet these elements are at the root of the majority of business failures.

When management does not recognize the internal signals of decline, it pretends that slowdowns are caused by external elements. A shortage of cash is often attributed to poor collections or lack of sales. In fact, the shortage of cash is usually a signal pointing to a deeper problem buried within the firm's management and accounting information systems. It may be that the firm is selling its products or services at a price that does not cover the variable costs of making the product or service. The firm may not have calculated contribution margins, actual product costs, and the direct cost of sales to determine the amount of profitability in the product or service.

Like external forces, the internal elements can interact with each other, and any one of the internal, controllable elements may spark a decline. Production techniques can become antiquated. Marketing/distribution can be in the wrong market with the wrong product. Finance can be unaware that the financial requirements of the other departments have changed. (Poor information flow between departments is another signal of decline.)

Coping with Internal Elements

Management often does not use the managerial tools at its disposal to control internal forces. Many managers do not utilize cash projections, but are only aware of balance sheets and income statements. The heart of any company is the synergy developed between the efficient operations of its various departments. The pulse beat for that synergy is the financial statements. Businesses should run on budgets and cash projections. Budgets are the foundation of financial statements, which reflect the success or failure of the business. For many businesses; however, budgets are mystery stories couched in scenarios that allow managers to hedge their positions. Managers create budgets that cannot be wrong, and consequently they cannot be accurate.

Balance sheets may show adequate working capital even when a company is in decline. When the balance sheet is overly burdened with inventory and accounts receivable that are inaccurate, obsolete, or uncollectable, a company is in trouble. The manager should know the status of accounts receivable. If they are increasing on the financial statements, is it because sales are increasing or collections are slow? If inventory is increasing, is it because sales are increasing or collections are slow? If inventory is increasing, is it because sales have decreased and production has not? Managers can reduce a firm's reliance on banks by increasing accounts receivable collections, reducing inventory, and paying accounts payable within the discount period to avoid penalties.

Internal elements require constant monitoring. Since management may be unable to understand the dynamic nature of the internal elements, it is not surprising that declines go unnoticed.

Management often doesn't understand its relationships with stakeholders—the people who work for, live near, invest in, or are affected by a company. Customer service, for example, is often a low priority. In most businesses, 80 percent of sales come from 20 percent of customers. Often the cost of servicing a customer and the cost of a sale are unknown. Customers are not classified into categories to determine the most favorable customers to the business. Management may perceive that the best customers are those who order the most, although these may be the same people who pay the slowest. In many companies, channels of information—from customers, competition, employees, vendors, and other managers—are not open. Without this information, the business cannot adapt to change. Information and the ability to react to it are the most powerful weapons a business has against decline.

Early Internal Warning Signals

Danger signals can be used by management to begin an internal corporate renewal. There are distinct phases of decline, and the danger signals vary within the stages (see Exhibit 2). Not all of the symptoms of decline will appear; there is sufficient cause to worry if some of them occur.

Also, internal warning signals take on different meaning depending on the company's growth rate. In stabilized companies, managers may continue

---

EXHIBIT 2   Common Danger Signals and the Stages in Which They Occur

Early decline
Shortage of cash.
Strained liquidity.
Reduced working capital.
Stretched accounts payable.
Late accounts receivable.
Reduction of ROI by 20 to 30%.
Flat sales.
Several quarters of losses.
Increased employee absenteeism.
Increased employee accidents.
Increased customer complaints (product quality, delivery, back orders, stock-outs).
Late financial and management information.

Mid-term decline
Increasing inventory.
Decreasing sales.
Decreasing margins.
Increasing expenses.
Increasing advances from banks.

Exhibit 2   *(Concluded)*

Additional requests for consideration from banks.
Late and unreliable financial and management information.
Eroding customer confidence.
Accelerating accounts payable from vendors.
Overdrafts at the bank.
Delayed accounts receivable from opportunistic customers.
Violation of loan covenants.
Bank used to cover payroll.

Late decline
Little attention paid to decreasing profit.
Staff is cut back without analyzing cause of problems.
Overdrawn bank account substituted for a line of credit.
Cash crisis.
Accounts payable are 60 to 90 days late.
Accounts receivable are more than 90 days late.
Sales decline further.
Employee morale is extremely low.
Company credibility is eroding.
Inventory turnover has decreased excessively.
Supplier restrictions are initiated.
Fewer reports to bank are submitted.
Auditors qualify opinions.
Checks bounce.
Credit is offset.
Accounts receivable continue to age.
Margins decrease further.
Sales volume decreases further.
Uncollectable receivables increase.
No liquidity.
Working capital is depleted.
Lack of funds for payroll.
Ineffective management.
Attempts to convince lenders that company is viable and liquidation is not necessary.

Signals that can occur in any stage
Decreased capital utilization.
Decreased market share in key product line(s).
Increased overhead costs.
Increased management and employee turnover.
Salaries and benefits growing faster than productivity and profits.
Increased management layers.
Losing market share to competition, which is not keeping up with marketplace changes.
Management in conflict with company goals and objectives.
Direction of management and company are different.
Sales forecasts predict company can sell its way out of difficulty.
Poor internal accounting.
Credit advances to customers who do not pay on time.
Nonseasonal borrowing.
Sudden overdrafts.
Increased trade inquiries.

to manage as if the growth will continue in the near future. When plans are not modified to address the new situation, the business courts trouble. Many companies religiously draft strategic plans. All too often, however, the plans are carved in granite and are not adaptable to changing situations. When shifts occur (internal, external, or both), the business is unable to cope with them, and instead continues to follow its strategic plan. Managers believe the strategic plan represents the very best of their creative abilities, and therefore are loathe to deviate from it. The strategic plan becomes part of the problem, rather than the solution.

Financial Predictors

Many financial ratios are tip-offs to a downturn, but management often considers them accounting busywork and pays no heed. Five ratios useful throughout all phases of decline and the turnaround process are:

1. Working capital to total assets.
2. Retained earnings to total assets.
3. Earnings before interest and taxes (EBIT) to total assets.
4. Market value of equity to book value to total debt.
5. Sales to total assets.

These ratios are especially useful when they are used for at least three years. The business will begin to establish a pattern within the ratios, and deviations from the pattern can be corrected quickly. More mature businesses have long histories, and the ratios should have reached a point where they are consistent annually. A deviation is as good as a red flag.

The ratios noted by turnaround managers generate a picture of the company. They indicate the ability of the business to survive on its own. When they are extremely low, it is time to approach the bank for bridge capital. The bank will not be willing to have any further involvement unless the plan for the turnaround is valid and based on the business's actual ability to support itself after the turnaround.

Double Decline

Often a company suffers a decline thanks to a combination of internal and external elements. Some common signals when both forces are at work include:

- Management by exception rather than flexible planning.
- Delegation without inspection, control, feedback, or reinforcement.
- Vertical organization chart, with little if any interaction between departments.

- Managers with responsibility for more than five direct reports.
- Employees with more than one boss.
- Broken chain of command.
- Overreliance on management by objectives.
- Senior managers' abuse of perks.
- Marketing the wrong products.
- Marketing in the wrong markets.
- Inadequate research and development.
- Inappropriate channels of distribution.
- Unresponsive financial information systems.
- Loss of competitive advantage.
- Changing technology.
- Regulatory changes.
- Inadequate understanding of customers' needs.
- Allowing one department or business function to dominate and dictate the mission, goals, and objectives of the business.

Crazy Eddie, Inc., is an example of a company that has suffered from both internal and external problems. Internally, there were too many layers of management, excessive wages, corporate waste, cost overruns, employee morale problems, and information flow deficiencies. The company had almost every signal of decline.

Externally, new competitors entered the market. Since Crazy Eddie's had damaged its relationships with appliance suppliers, it could not receive the necessary merchandise to compete. The company is now undergoing a turnaround; part of the strategy is to cut costs and payroll by a minimum of $25 million. There is also a slump in the company's markets, so revenue has decreased. The internal elements were changed by laying off unnecessary managers, reducing wages, adding a profit-sharing plan, settling the lawsuits on corporate waste, reducing costs, and adding a computer system to prevent selling items below cost. The external elements are being addressed by rebuilding relationships with suppliers, banks, and consumers.

The Turnaround Process

Turnaround managers bring order to chaos, which usually means they must take control of every function in the business. They create budgets from the bottom up and strictly enforce accountability. They analyze products and markets to determine which have the most profitability. Those that generate losses are terminated quickly and permanently, regardless of the company's relationship with the customer or product. The turnaround manager cuts costs, increases the business's adaptability, and saves the profitable products and markets. Actual costs replace standard costing, and product contribution margins are used to determine which products contribute the most to the fixed costs of the business. Cash flow reports are used continually; at first they may be used daily, then weekly, then monthly, and finally semiannually. The reports are used in developing the operating plan. The time line and the amount of cash flowing in will determine how the business can survive.

The classifications of customers and the aging of accounts receivable determine which customers are profitable. The business may have many customers with repeat orders, but they all may be delinquent in paying their accounts. The business cannot afford to carry them any longer. Reviewing accounts receivable is an essential task of turnaround managers. They decide which customers to keep and which to pursue for more business.

Get Everyone Involved

Banks, vendors, customers, employees, boards of directors, and others affected by the decline of the business need to be made part of the solution. Banks and boards of directors are usually the parties that suggest the use of a turnaround manager. Normally, by the time they notice a problem exists, the situation is approaching crisis proportions. This is a common situation because bank executives and boards tend to be chiefly concerned with balance sheets and income statements driven, despite the fact that healthy looking balance sheets and income statements can disguise many problems. Bank managers and board members do not visit the business and review operations. They do not walk the plant floor and talk with employees. They do not review basic financial information, such as accounts receivable and payable. They only learn about employee morale, customer service, equipment condition, and other on-site situations from a report generated by management.

Trade vendors also need to be included in the situation. They are the business's lifeline to its suppliers. When payments to them are delinquent, the business is in jeopardy of losing its supply line. Management may argue that it can find other suppliers, but unless the underlying problem causing delinquent payments is addressed, suppliers will evaporate along with the company's credit. New suppliers require credit references, and changing suppliers has substantial switching costs. The new supplier has to produce or acquire the supplies requested, schedule deliveries, and obtain payments. As the business adds new suppliers, the bank will receive credit report requests. This is another signal of decline.

Employee participation is essential in the turnaround process. Turnarounds often require asking for pay concessions. Hours on the job and working conditions may be affected. When employees are part of the restructuring plan, they tend to accept painful concessions with more ease. When the restructuring is complete, management should consider itself indebted to these people and should reward them financially.

SRC, a leveraged buyout from International Harvester, is an example of a turnaround where employee participation was the key ingredient for success. In 1979, the company was losing $2 million per year on sales of $26 million. In 1983, 13 employees of International Harvester bought SRC. They developed a detailed reporting system and a full-blown, daily cash flow statement. In 1986, sales reached $42 million. Net operating income increased to 11 percent and the debt-to-equity ratio has been reduced from 89-to-1 to 5.1-to-1. The appraised value of a share in the company's stock ownership has increased from 10 cents to $8.45. Absenteeism and serious workplace accidents have almost disappeared. The company attributes the turnaround to allowing employees to reach their highest potential.

To facilitate a turnaround, union cooperation is essential. It also can greatly influence morale. A turnaround can be accomplished despite the unions, but may require drastic steps such as bankruptcy or massive layoffs. Concessions regarding pay rate, hours, working conditions, raises, vacations, accumulated sick leave, and benefits will be granted only when the union is convinced that the company can survive. That this is possible is indicated by the arrival of the turnaround manager and by the turnaround plan. The cooperation of the other stakeholders also places pressure on the union to cooperate.

Customers must also be taken into account during the turnaround, but businesses in decline tend to forsake customer service. Quality control diminishes, which causes more order returns. This adds expenses to an already strained financial condition. Orders are taken and delivery dates missed, causing loss of credibility with the customers. The inventory, which was a main part of the balance sheet, becomes obsolete and therefore not usable to meet the current demands of the customers. The end result is the loss of the customer base.

Types of Turnarounds and Strategies

A turnaround can take several forms. It can be *strategic* if the business needs to be redefined because of changing markets and products. In the General Nutrition turnaround, for example, the company moved away from its core of vitamins and specialty health foods to the much wider category of health in general. The stores needed items that would make people come to them rather than grocery stores. The company searched for new products and new lines. Brookstone, the specialty gadget store, inspired many of the changes made at General Nutrition. Prior to the turnaround, the stock had plummeted from a high of 29⅝ to a low of 3⅞.

An *operational* turnaround involves changing a business's operations, which could include cost cutting, revenue generating, and asset reduction. In the case of General Nutrition, the turnaround was also focused on the operations of the business. (It is very common for turnarounds to be mounted on several fronts and combine strategies.) At General Nutrition, the management team was strengthened and the company divided into three distinct segments: retailing, manufacturing, and specialty services.

Another example of an operational turnaround is Black and Decker. The company had more than 200 different motor sizes. It had split consumer and professional tools into two separate groups that seldom communicated with each other. This made it easy for the competition to find niches where Black and Decker did not make tools. To remedy the situation, the company organized plants around motor sizes, reduced product variations, and streamlined manufacturing. The number of plants was reduced from 25 to 19. Excess capacity utilization increased by 75 percent. In addition, the company began producing new products to meet consumer demand.

The *financial* turnaround restructures the financial operations of a business. The object is to utilize the financial strength of the businesses as an asset. ITT, for example, divested itself of 23 businesses for almost $1.5 billion and increased return on equity from 8 percent in 1979 to 12 percent in 1987. Management slashed expenses by abandoning its lavish lifestyle, renting out full floors at its Park Avenue headquarters, and cutting the work force by two-thirds.

Each different type of turnaround may focus on a particular strategy. These include:

- *Revenue generating.* Management tries to increase sales, advertising, and markets while decreasing prices.
- *Product/Markets refocusing.* Managers analyze products and markets to determine their profitability. Customers are analyzed to determine the nature of their purchases, payment history, and ability to purchase more. Channels of distribution are analyzed to determine their effectiveness. Products are analyzed further to determine their saleability, contribution margins, actual cost of production, cost of sale, cost of distribution, manufacturing efficiency, inventory carrying costs, and cost of customer service. Businesses may have reached the limits of their growth in products and markets, in which case they need to analyze potential moves into other product and market areas.
- *Cost cutting.* Managers reduce adminstrative costs, R&D, and marketing.
- *Asset reduction.* Management removes unnecessary assets that usually look nice on the balance sheet but actually produce only costs of maintenance and no revenue stream.
- The combination of any of the above.

Using the correct strategy is part of the art of successfully turning around a company. As the turnaround progresses, the strategy may change. Cost cutting may be superseded by revenue generating, and so forth. Strategies may be combined and used in various sequences, but using an inappropriate strategy can be a terminal error. Here are four pointers to choosing the correct strategy:

- Mature businesses should use retrenchment and efficiency strategies, not product/marketing refocusing.
- Businesses with low capacity utilization should pursue cost-cutting strategies.
- Businesses with high capacity utilization should also pursue cost-cutting strategies.
- Businesses with high market share should pursue revenue-generating strategies and product/market refocusing.

The time frame for a turnaround varies depending upon the business, industry, market, severity of the crisis, cooperation of stakeholders, and turnaround manager. A business that has been in decline for several years cannot expect to be renewed quickly. Its reputation for low credibility will have permeated all of its stakeholders and will take some time to reverse. A business that recognizes signals of decline in the early stage can be renewed more quickly.

In general, turnarounds occur in five stages:

1. Evaluation of the situation, which can take from one week to three months.
2. Creating a plan, which can take from one to six months.
3. Implementation of the plan, which can take from six months to one year.
4. Stabilization of the business, which can take from six months to one year.
5. Return to growth of the business, which can take from one to two years.

Astute managers constantly monitor the health of their businesses and act on the warning signals. Often, managers can see the signals but need outside help to cure the problem. The need to address decline and failure is obvious. The waste of corporate assets and employees' talents that can stem from managerial ignorance can be astronomical. This waste can be minimized if management can notice and address decline in its early stages.

FORGING ALLIANCES IN MEXICO

Dennis Stevens
Paul Beamish

Although firms from all over the industrialized world are discovering that Mexico is an increasingly attractive production site and consumer market, many Canadian companies continue to view the Mexican market with caution. Our message—get on with it before the best opportunities have passed you by.

Canadian firms can prosper in Mexico, but, as is common when entering any culturally different market, firms often need to link with a local partner to succeed. There is, however, a limited supply of quality partners available. North American Free Trade Agreement (NAFTA) will present the Canadian firm with the opportunity to be viewed as a priority partner, but this advantage will not last forever. Europeans, Japanese and Americans are moving into Mexico. Canadians can either use their current advantage now or be prepared to join a long queue later.

Our Research

We wanted to learn something about how Canadian companies are doing business in Mexico, with the objective of preparing a set of guidelines for others to follow. We used a three-stage process:

Stage I—We first visited Mexico and met with Canadian and Mexican business people to define the issues and to make contacts.

Stage II—Returning to Canada, we mailed a questionnaire to 30 Canadian companies thought to be doing business in Mexico. We received 14 completed responses.

Canadian Companies That Completed Questionnaire
1. BCE Telecom International, Montreal
2. Bovar Engineering Products, Western Research, Calgary
8. Glenayre Electronics Ltd., Toronto
9. Mitel Corporation, Kanata
10. GWN Systems Inc.

Source: Previously published in Business Quarterly. Used with permission.

3. Custom Trim Ltd., Kitchener

4. ABC Group, Rexdale

5. Connaught Laboratories Limited, Willowdale

6. HydMech Saws Ltd., Vancouver

7. Bombardier Inc., Montreal

11. Orchid Automation, Cambridge

12. Bionaire International, Inc.

13. Canadian Airlines International Limited, Calgary

14. Moore International Division, Latin America and Pacific, Toronto

Stage III—We visited Mexico again, this time conducting structured interviews with the top person in each of six Canadian subsidiaries or divisions, and with senior representatives of six Mexican firms that do business with Canadian companies in Mexico.

Local Partnership or Contact is Essential

From our interviews and survey, it became evident that whatever form a Canadian company's entry took, it was in almost all cases undertaken with a Mexican partner or contact. According to Alejandro Espejo Bartra, the general director of an alliance between BCE Telecom International and Grupo IUSA of Mexico, establishing a long-term foothold in Mexico requires an alliance with a local company, or at least a strong contact. Of course, the telecommunication service industry is a special situation in which entry by a foreign company without a local partner is impossible. Although Canadian business people can impart some very valuable business practices to Mexico, notes Bartra, they are very unfamiliar with the way in which business in that country actually operates. He says there are differences that one can read or be told about, but the only way to truly learn and understand the difference is to experience it. This difficulty can be circumvented by connecting with local Mexicans who know the environment and the way industry actually operates there.

The significance of linking up with local know-how is made apparent by a combination of two main factors of doing business in Mexico: the role of personal relationships, and the impact of cultural differences.

Personal Relationships and Trust Play a Key Role

Most respondents to our questionnaire survey suggested that Mexicans not only make a habit of mixing business with pleasure, they depend on it. The Mexican businessmen contacted identified the tendency of American and

Canadian business people to jump into business matters too quickly. Whereas Canadians may find socializing and talking about personal matters before getting down to business a waste of time, Mexican business people view it very differently. As one Mexican executive pointed out:

> "How better and more efficiently can I get a feel for the type of person I'm going to be doing business with? To us the most important factor in anybody we deal with is the level to which we can trust each other. Talking freely about non-business matters with my business associates allows me to identify with them, bringing down barriers. Establishing this level of trust allows us to work more quickly and effectively."

Canadian companies currently in Mexico concur, and overwhelmingly view establishing trust as very important to doing business with Mexicans.

Business Culture and Practices Differ

The difficulty of establishing trust is compounded by Canadians' inability to speak Spanish, lack of knowledge of the Mexican culture, image of being an outsider, and awkwardness in manoeuvring through a very different business environment. As the export manager of Iko Canada put it, "If they can't understand you, how do you expect them to trust you?"

Canadian Firms Have an Edge

Canadian companies do have an advantage over their U.S. counterparts. In a number of interviews Mexicans expressed a preference to doing business with Canadians because the two tend to be more compatible with each other—a view reflected by both Canadian and Mexican executives. One of the executives who was instrumental in the formation of BCE Telecom International's joint venture in Mexico, for example, stated that Canadians are politically and culturally more acceptable.

Other executives said that there is an affinity for Canadians in Mexico, mainly because we are not American. For example, Dr. Jaime Alonso Gomez of ITESM in Monterrey believes that Canadians generally have a more sensitive style than Americans, due in part to the fact that Canadians have always been a more outward looking trading nation than the U.S., and for this, Canadians are highly respected. Another reason relates to NAFTA; some Mexicans want a counterbalance to the power and weight of the U.S.

Now especially, there is a window of opportunity for Canadian companies to firm up a quality alliance or partnership in Mexico because (a) the market is opening up in business areas in which Canada has competitive strengths, and (b) Canadian firms now hold a relationship advantage that could enable them to effectively implement an early entry with the best partners.

Several Options Open

Which entry option a Canadian company chooses depends on the particular dynamics of its own industry both in Canada and in Mexico, as well as the needs and internal capabilities of the specific company. Canadian companies can choose from a wide number of potential modes of entry: direct export, licensing, royalty agreement, fully owned subsidiaries, partly owned subsidiaries, agents, representatives, distributors and dealers, joint ventures, strategic alliances, local partnerships, and supply commitments. A Canadian company's individual situation will dictate the approach that is chosen, taking into account factors such as: the company's objective in entering Mexico, transferability of technology, risk tolerance of the company, the product or service for sale, timing requirements, and management capabilities.

Of the companies contacted in our study, 82% had begun with committed representation in Mexico, either through joint venture (38%), acquisition (19%), own sales force (6%), or dedicated representation (25%). The rest (12%) used independent distributors. Since entering Mexico, over 50% of the respondents have established their own sales force separately or as an extension to their original alliances.

There is no clear pattern in the data that would indicate the general effectiveness of any one of these methods; there is mixed success in all of them. "The trick is to find the right people whichever way you decide to go," says Paul St. Amour of the Trade Commission at the Canadian Embassy in Mexico City, who also stressed the importance of meeting often with these people face-to-face to build confidence in both directions.

Forging Relationships Presents Challenges and Costs

The survey indicated that establishing the initial contact to find proper representation or a partner was not very difficult, and the expenses associated with establishing it were relatively low, ranging from $10,000 to $15,000. Some contacts charged a commission on future sales. Related expenses included travel expenses, the cost of a trade show booth, entertainment, and agent finder fees. Once a contact was made, securing good representation or an appropriate business relationship was only slightly more difficult.

Because of these contacts, language was initially not seen as a major barrier, but all companies were serious about dealing with the language issue once their entry was up and running. Most respondents stated that they translated all their literature, manuals, and packaging, and then hired local staff or transferred Spanish-speaking staff from home to Mexico. Many respondents said they learned Spanish themselves.

The time and cost to actually develop the business in Mexico was quite varied. Time from initiation of contact to first shipment ranged from three months to five years; most companies were able to get products moving within six to 12 months, however. Total development costs ranged from $40,000 to $700,000. The need for product modifications and adaptation was seen as being minimal; translation was usually the extent of modification. Time and cost were affected by other factors such as the complexity of the business or of the particular deal, and the willingness of each party to make it work. Proper evaluation of the proposed relationship can save a new entrant a lot of time, money and frustrations.

Finding the Right Partner or Alliance Important

"Coming to the conclusion that having a local partner is the way to go, is the easiest part of a critical process," explained one Canadian executive. "Determining who or what the partner should be is the real challenge."

The first step in starting a search for a partner is to outline exactly what your company is hoping to get from it. As well, you should make an assessment of what your company is able and willing to offer, and what benefits will be perceived by a potential Mexican partner. According to the Canadian government publication, *Partnering for Success,* a well-structured partnership offers concrete benefits to both sides, often translating the synergy gained into a competitive advantage that will help the partnership to survive today's global marketplace. The publication suggests that:

- If each company focuses on what it does and knows best, they will both more likely succeed.
- If the partners share the risk, they will minimize the consequences of failure.
- Partnering extends each side's capabilities into new areas.
- Ideas and resources can be pooled to help both sides keep pace with change.
- Even small firms can use partnering to take advantage of economies of scale, and achieves the critical mass needed for success.
- Through a partner a company can approach several markets simultaneously.
- Partnering can provide a firm with technology, capital, or market access that it might not be able to afford or achieve on its own.

Task Easier if Partners Complementary

A local partner should complement a company's capabilities, providing the expertise, insights, and contacts that can propel the two to further heights. With this in mind, the task becomes clearer; you should focus on identifying companies that:

1. Are compatible and complementary with yours in terms of business activities and capabilities.
2. Have a corporate and management style that you can work with.
3. Are willing to commit to the relationship the energy that your firm is prepared to commit.

Almost half the respondents to our survey initiated their search using publicly available sources of contacts such as trade shows, trade missions, and the Canadian embassy. The larger companies tended to have the Canadian government more directly involved in the process than the smaller firms. Most executives praised the efforts of the staff of the Canadian Embassy in Mexico, and consider their service very helpful and necessary.

The Canadian embassy is not always able to take companies by the hand through the process. This is especially true now, given the sheer volume of business visitors it receives—4,528 in 1992, up from 190 in 1989. For this reason, some Canadian companies rely on their contacts or professional consultants to make introductions and guide them through the lengthy process. To be effective in building a relationship and to avoid costly problems in the future, this introduction process should be extensive.

Consultants may work with clients early on in the process to develop a customized entry strategy, usually providing a report on the dynamics and stage of development of their clients' industry in Mexico, and an assessment of the potential of their products or service there. Once the most appropriate mode of entry is determined, the consultants may provide a search and screen service to identify potential alliances.

At this point, consultants that are knowledgable about how business is conducted on both sides of the potential alliance can take on the role of an agent and act as a buffer between the two parties. If both parties are guided through a process that is new to them, the probability of achieving successful meetings and negotiations is increased.

Referring to the search and screen process that can be offered, one international partnering consultant we interviewed stressed the importance of making sure that the consultants themselves have a valuable alliance in Mexico. He went on to describe the extent of corporate concentration in Mexico as having only "a few *grupos* that are considered to be part of the gang that represents an important network of contacts within industry and government. Getting inside this circle of power is very advantageous for any company that is serious about entering the Mexican market."

Canadians Need to Adapt

Once companies have established themselves with their selected Mexican partners, they are finally faced with the even greater challenge of making it work. Canadians need to adapt the way they approach many aspects of their management style, from conducting meetings to budgeting. Face-to-face communication is extremely important. Here are some of the differences:

1. **Meetings.** Piero Comel of the French firm GEC Alsthom, which is the holding company controlling ALCATEL and which recently acquired Canada Wire & Cable Ltd., explains:

"Relationship building is an ongoing process; it is believed in Mexico that good friends do good business, and this is evident in the meetings that take place here, which are often in social environments such as a restaurant. This manifests itself into the development of a mutual respect between the business associates."

This mutual respect between business associates is consistent with what one executive referred to as the pride factor. According to Lyn McDiarmid of Mitel, saving face is the most important part of a meeting. In Mexico, there is never a confrontation between business associates, and everyone is always polite.

2. **Decision-making process.** The survey revealed that Mexican buying patterns were generally similar to those in Canada. This was not the case when it came to big ticket items, however, where the decision-making process is very different. Subordinates generally have little authority because corporate culture tends to be very hierarchical. This top-down structure of authority causes the decision-making process to be slow, making the time and cost to close a sale involving large capital purchases quite high.

3. **The *mañana* syndrome.** "Things have their own rhythm in Mexico," comments Manuel Lopes of Bombardier. In the interviews, most of the respondents indicated that getting things done quickly and on time in Mexico was a challenge. When asked about their own Mexican employees, however, the response was mixed. Some executives said that they find employees tend not to take the initiative; others said that workers are eager to learn and work very hard.

The stereotype foreigners typically have about Mexican workers is no longer valid. The working population is young and enthusiastic, and ready to learn. Management-level employees also tend to be rather young and, in many cases, work long, hard hours. Some Canadian companies are more effective in bringing out these positive qualities than are others.

A combination of authority, flexibility, and patience is essential to manage Mexican workers. Adapting to their ways is important. It was expressed by a number of Canadian executives that Mexicans tend to manage Mexicans better than foreigners do, and for this reason they suggest hiring locals as much as possible for most levels of the organization. Canadian companies must be ready to adapt, according to Mitel's Lyn McDiarmid, "It is essential that you adapt your own North American values and ideals to the Mexican business culture. Never, never try to change Mexican employees and partners to your way of life."

Doug Clark on Mexican Business People and Their Ways:

"As in all Latin American countries, building relationships is critical. Business follows relationships and trust. Personal attention is very critical. Patience is essential—they do think differently, they act differently. All Latin countries are different; Mexicans in particular are a little like the Japanese—sometimes YES means NO, sometimes NO means YES, and often means MAYBE. The body language—you have got to understand the clues. They hate offending you so they won't disagree with you. You can ask for confirmation of something "Do you understand this?" and they will say "yes." Five minutes later it's painfully obvious they didn't understand you and didn't want to offend you.

"Time has a different meaning [when arranging meetings]. They will start late but will go on forever–that happens often.

"A lot of Mexican business executives will speak English and they are very good. That's great at the beginning when you come and you don't know Spanish, but it does become an obstacle, a burden. You become an outsider, because you can't get inside that way; and it is not the way to sustain a long term business relationship."

Doug Clark, Director General
Northern Telecom Mexico

The Next Step

Many Canadian companies are attracted to Mexico because of their expectation of the impact of NAFTA. Other companies interviewed stated they entered Mexico regardless of NAFTA; they went to Mexico because they viewed it as a strategic market opportunity and because business was good. Over half of the survey respondents said they are pleased with their performance there, and about three-quarters are at least satisfied. Interestingly, most view the potential impact of NAFTA as either irrelevant or slightly positive.

Many firms see their move into Mexico as the first step into Latin America. Mexico is viewed as the natural hub and gateway to the countries south of it that are following Mexico's tracks to economic reform. Mexico has already solidified free trade agreements with other Latin American countries. The strategy of Canadian companies making Mexico their Latin American beachhead makes much sense, because it is probable that their trained Mexican managers will be better equipped, socially and culturally, for these markets. Although there are significant differences within Latin America, there are also some important similarities and ties with Mexican culture, including language, that would make expansion from Mexico into these countries easier.

This finding is consistent with the overall theme of this study, and the action agenda that has surfaced from all the participating companies and individuals. First, if Mexico has been on your company's back burner, now is a good time to move it forward. Second, begin seeking a partner for some form of alliance. If there are strategic reasons for avoiding a joint venture, then at least begin building significant local market knowledge. Third, respect the cultural differences you will inevitably encounter. The Canadian firms that have already succeeded in Mexico have established a tradition of respect the Mexicans have welcomed and on which the new Canadian entrant can capitalize.

THE RIGHT ATTITUDE FOR INTERNATIONAL SUCCESS

Companies that want to be more successful global players require executives with the right attitude toward foreign cultures

Jonathan L. Calof
Paul W. Beamish

International Business Success: Most companies need it, the federal government wants more firms to have it, and managers are trying to figure out how to get it. For many Canadian companies, survival depends on enhancing international success, and while there are many factors that influence such success, one of the most important is management's international business attitude. The impact of attitudes on international performance is so great that some theorists have suggested that future international management research should focus almost exclusively on it.

We studied, in 38 Canadian multinational corporations, the relationship between centricity (defined as a person's attitude towards foreign cultures) and international performance. The results point to a more than 100 percent difference in international sales for what is called geocentric organizations over companies with other attitudes. This is a difference that can not be ignored.

Understanding Centricity

Decisions such as what mode to use (joint venture, wholly owned subsidiary, sales branch, or export), who to hire to run subsidiaries, and whether to adapt a product for export markets are basic international strategy decisions. Making the wrong choice can hinder international success. According to many of the executives interviewed as part of this study, assumptions about host-country market and cultural differences drive these decisions and contribute to the resulting performance. This is centricity.

Source: Previously published in Business Quarterly. Used with permission.

Everyone has a centric profile—or dominant attitude—toward foreign cultures. Do you think that the Canadian way of conducting business is superior to other business practices? Do you believe that when in a foreign country, you should do as the locals do? Who would you hire to run a foreign subsidiary? Your answers to these questions will reveal much about your centricity and may also help explain your company's performance internationally.

The attitude typology of centricity was developed in 1969 by Wharton's Howard Perlmutter, who initially identified three orientations toward foreign cultures—*ethnocentric* (home-country oriented), *polycentric* (host-country oriented) and *geocentric* (world oriented). These attitudes refer to how the executives view foreign cultures in terms of which cultures are thought to be superior and the complexity of the cultures. The attitudes are so important, they have been incorporated into most international business textbooks and heralded by academics and practitioners alike. Here is a description of the three centricities:

1. *Ethnocentrism* refers to an attitude towards foreign cultures whereby employees and practices within the foreign market are believed to be inferior to those of the domestic market. Home-country people are perceived to be more capable, or more reliable than foreign personnel. Ethnocentric attitudes are reflected in a bias toward the development of human resource, finance, marketing, and production policies that reflect the home-country policies. For example, prospective managers for a foreign subsidiary are likely to be selected on the basis of their compatibility with the parent country, such as having work experience in the parent's country. Here are two comments we heard that indicate an ethnocentric attitude:

> "When I took over the operation, the U.K. plant was totally controlled from Canada. The old management felt that the British personnel were relatively incompetent and had to have everything spelled out for them."
>
> > Executive of a Canadian
> > manufacturing firm

(The executive went on to say that he gave the U.K. plant more autonomy, with spectacular results. Sales doubled in three years, and now the U.K. research and new products are in demand in Canada.)

> "We tried it the North American way in Mexico and it didn't work."
>
> > Executive of a Canadian
> > technology-based company

Ethnocentrism does not bring with it a desire for either global coordination or local responsiveness. Rather, decision makers are biased toward strategic choices suited to the domestic market. Each foreign country is treated as if it is the same as the headquarters country—an attitude that might be appropriate if markets are virtually identical to the headquarters market.

In general, however, ethnocentrism should be less effective than other approaches because by definition it sacrifices local responsiveness, and assumes that the home country way of doing business is the best. Ethnocentric biases could result in perceptions of the environment that are generally inconsistent with either the local or the global environment. Consequently, strategic choices may also be inconsistent with the overall global environment, and performance may suffer.

2. *Polycentrism* is the attitude that cultures of various countries are different, that foreigners are difficult to understand and should be left alone as long as their work is profitable. In justifying a decision, headquarters executives of such a company might say, "When in Rome, do as the Romans do . . . let the Romans do it their way." This confusion about the foreign culture leads to a bias toward human resource, finance, marketing, and production policies that reflect the local country practices. For example, polycentric decision makers are likely to let each overseas office decide sales discount policies and hiring policies without any coordination among other countries or corporate headquarters. Here are two quotations that show a polycentric attitude. In both cases, the executive quoted believed that major cultural differences require that host-country personnel manage host-country production facilities.

> "You must let local managers run the operations . . . culturally they know how institutions work and how the government works."
>
> Executive of a Canadian
> technology-based company

> "I never want to own a subsidiary outside of North America. You need local people, who are financially committed to the venture and understand the local culture and language."
>
> Executive of a Canadian
> furniture manufacturer

A variation on polycentrism is regiocentrism. Regiocentric decision makers perceive that certain similarities exist between different countries within a geographic region, and adopt policies and procedures consistent with this belief. For example, they might believe that a single production facility may be used to serve the Belgian, French, U.K., and Italian markets because they are all European.

Polycentric decision makers are biased towards strategic choices that maximize local responsiveness. This preference results in each country or region having its own strategy and organization. These decisions limit international performance for several reasons:

   a. Benefits of global coordination such as the development of economies of scale are not realized.
   b. Learning that occurred in one geographic region is not applied in another.
   c. Treating each market as unique may lead to the duplication of facilities.

One of the executives in our study summed up the problem with this approach when he reported on how his technology-based company had once had plants in several European countries. Management had decided that local cultural and business differences necessitated a separate plant in each country. "Looking back, we never should have had so many production facilities. It is not economically viable," he said.

3. *Geocentrism* is the attitude that there are global similarities in both cultures and markets. Unlike the ethnocentric attitude in which domestic personnel and practices are thought to be superior, and polycentric attitudes for which cultural superiority is thought to rest with host-country or host-region personnel and practices, geocentric attitudes do not assume either local or domestic practices to be superior. Geocentric attitudes are biased toward human resource, finance, marketing, and production policies that try to balance local practices and global practices. The emphasis is on having the appropriate policies and people. For example, a geocentric decision maker would recommend a worldwide pricing policy that would be adjusted for local or regional conditions.

Geocentric decision makers, in their attempt to adopt policies that reflect both global commonalities and local differences, get the best of both worlds. The advantages of global coordination, such as economies of scale and shared learning, are realized, as are some of the advantages of being locally responsive. The attitudes of the executives drive the selection of systems, procedures, strategy, and structure. Not surprisingly, cultivating geocentric attitudes eventually leads to the development of a geocentric organization.

Centricity Affects Actions Taken

Centricity need not impact the desire to engage in international activities. Managers of any profile can equally view international activities as being important to the firm and actively seek international opportunities. Centricity colors executives' perceptions, however, influencing their assessment of several important external environment variables such as the capabilities of foreign personnel. In turn, these attitudes reflect management's preferences on how to develop international organizations. They can impact the choice of strategies and the method for their implementation, such as choice of structures and systems and hiring decisions. Further, if these attitudes do not reflect the actual environment, they could result in strategic and operating decisions that hamper international performance.

Study Results Revealing

Our study assessed the centricity of the senior executives who made international decisions by asking them questions about how they thought critical international decisions should be made. We found 15 percent of the respondents were ethnocentric, 44 percent polycentric, and 41 percent geocentric. We also examined critical decisions on capital expenditures, pricing, dividend policy, product selection and design, production planning and control, quality control, marketing and selling policies and programs, purchasing and supplier choice, financial systems and accounting procedures, and the selection, promotion, and compensation of subsidiary executives. From this information we could assess the centricity of the organization. Unsurprisingly, and due in part to the firms in this study being mainly medium-sized, we found that senior executives' centricity was the same as organization centricity. For all the companies in this study, ethnocentric organizations were run by ethnocentric senior managers, and so forth.

But, whether looking at the success of the individual strategic decision or at the overall international performance of the firm, significant differences in performance were clear among geocentric, ethnocentric, and polycentric firms. The most dramatic difference was with overall international performance. Export intensity (international sales/total sales) was 27 percent for ethnocentric firms, 54 percent for polycentric firms, and 68 percent for geocentric firms. Further, when looking at the overall level of international sales, geocentric firms had on average $66 million in export sales compared to $47 million for polycentric and $32 million for ethnocentric firms. Ethnocentric, polycentric, and geocentric firms were all of similar size; no significant differences were found in either total sales or number of employees, implying that the differences in international sales and intensity did not arise because of the size of the firm. Rather, attitudes—centricity—emerged as the dominant factor differentiating performance.

We concluded that higher levels of performance were associated with firms that were geocentric in their orientation. Do these results mean that geocentrism causes superior performance? Not necessarily. But several executives indicated that a change in attitude was a precursor for increased international revenues. One executive recounted how failures in Australian and U.K. subsidiaries arose from running them in an ethnocentric fashion. He noted that a change in senior management led to an operating policy that stressed "hiring good local managers and then equipping them with technical advisers from the parent company." Further, the company also adopted a mixed control approach, wherein subsidiaries and headquarters jointly set goals, but operating control rested solely in the hands of subsidiary managers. "We are evolving" said the executive of this company, "and our new approach has helped us grow internationally." In our research, we found many such examples of a change toward a geocentric approach, followed by improved international performance.

Developing the Geocentric Organization

The dramatic difference in the performance of ethnocentric firms compared to that of geocentric firms should not be surprising in that every conceivable international business decision and the subsequent success of the decision are affected by centricity. Further, the procedures, structure, and systems of the organization shape the context in which both strategic and operating decisions are made. Therefore, if geocentrism more accurately reflects the international operating environment, having geocentric attitudes among key managers and having a geocentric organization should lead to higher levels of international performance.

Here is a three-stage process for developing a geocentric organization:

The Centricity Change Process

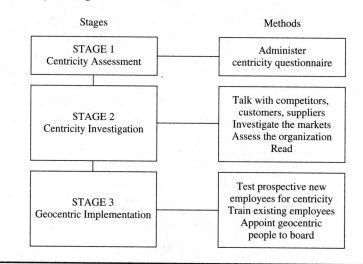

Stage 1—Assessment

Start by assessing the attitudes of executives and the orientation of key policies, procedures, and structure. Who do you hire to run foreign subsidiaries! How do you adapt products and services to foreign markets? How are prices set? In the accompanying box is a short centricity questionnaire designed to help identify the centricity of a firm's attitudes, systems, structure, procedures, and policies.

For the following decision areas, please indicate which of the three decision approaches described above is being followed by your company, and which approach you believe should be followed. Place a 1, 2, or 3 in each box.

Decisions Made	How Decisions are Currently Being Made	How decisions Should be Made
1. Capital expenditures	[ ]	[ ]
2. Pricing	[ ]	[ ]

Decisions Made	How Decisions are Currently Being Made	How decisions Should be Made
3. Dividend policy	[ ]	[ ]
4. Product selection or design	[ ]	[ ]
5. Production planning and control	[ ]	[ ]
6. Quality control	[ ]	[ ]
7. Marketing and sales policies and programs	[ ]	[ ]
8. Purchasing and choice of suppliers	[ ]	[ ]
9. Financial systems and accounting procedures	[ ]	[ ]
10. Selection, promotion, and compensation of subsidiary executives	[ ]	[ ]

Total number of:

Ethnocentric responses (number of 1s)	[ ]	[ ]
Polycentric responses (number of 2s)	[ ]	[ ]
Geocentric responses (number of 3s)	[ ]	[ ]

Your centric classification will correspond to the category with the maximum number of responses. Don't worry if you are not consistent in all decision areas. While more than one type of centricity may be evident in the firm's processes, one will dominate. It may make good business sense to have some decisions made geocentrically and others polycentrically. A detailed assessment of your systems, procedures, policies, structure, and attitudes with your strategy and markets will help determine what approaches are appropriate.

But be forewarned, a more accurate centric assessment is much more complex than a one-page self-evaluation. For example, one of Perlmutter's original centricity questionnaires was approximately 50 pages long. Further, Perlmutter refers to five different centric classifications, whereas the short form uses only three.

Short-Form Centricity Assessment

This form will help to identify the decision orientation of the firm and its top management group. There are different approaches to decision making for building or operating a firm internationally. These can be described as follows:

1) **Ethnocentric:** All major decisions are made either in Canada, by Canadian personnel, or overseas by Canadian nationals who manage the subsidiary. Canadian standards, procedures, and objectives are used for making the decision. Overseas offices use the Canadian systems, processes, and products with little or no modification.

2) **Polycentric:** All major decisions are tailored to suit the local (host-country) market. In general, decisions are made in the local office, by host-country personnel using their own standards, procedures, and objectives. Limited liaison is required between the host-country office and the Canadian corporate office. It is possible to have different products, procedures, and prices in each market. A variation on a polycentric decision orientation is regiocentric. Under this approach, all major decisions are tailored to suit the regional market. In general, decisions are made at the regional level, such as Europe or Asia, by regional personnel using regional standards, procedures, and objectives. Limited liaison occurs between the regional office and the Canadian corporate office. It is possible to have different products, procedures, and prices in each region.

3) **Geocentric:** All major decisions are made centrally, and managed to satisfy global needs as

efficiently as possible on a global basis. Substantial coordination exists between local offices, regional offices, and company headquarters. Either there are uniform pricing policies and products throughout the world, or all major decisions are made through collaboration among local, regional, and Canadian offices. The focus is on global systems, procedures, and objectives. Allowances are made for local and regional differences. For example, local and regional offices could modify the global policies and procedures in light of local differences.

The short form combines regiocentrism and polycentrism because of their similarity, and does not distinguish between different types of geocentrism. The short form is a good starting point for most organizations, however.

Fundamentally, in a centricity assessment exercise you are trying to identify the centric profile of the senior executives who are making the critical international decisions, and the overall centricity of the organization. This exercise establishes the context under which your international operations are being run. Ideally, your firm will have both geocentric attitudes and a geocentric organization.

Stage 2—Investigation

Stage 1 should identify which executives, procedures, policies, and systems are not geocentric. The next step is to decide whether any of the nongeocentric elements of your organization should be changed. Centricity theorists have found that while an organization's overall profile should be geocentric, the entire organization, that is, all policies and procedures, may not be geocentric. There may be distinct differences between foreign countries that require the implementation of more polycentric procedures. For example, it may make sense to have all pricing decisions made at the country level. To help in the investigation stage, talk to competitors, suppliers, and government trade officials, and read material on international business. These are all useful measures for assessing which approach is most appropriate.

Stage 3—Implementation

If after the investigation stage it is concluded that the approach being followed can be improved, actions should be taken to change it. At a basic level, this step involves changing attitudes—a very difficult process and one that people strongly resist. When faced with information that is contrary to their attitudes, many individuals will choose to ignore or minimize the importance of this information, and will change only when overwhelming evidence has been produced. There are, however, several methods for developing more geocentric attitudes.

How the Study was Done

Thirty-eight firms, all Canadian owned and located in Ontario, participated in our study. They represented a broad range of industries, with electronics/electrical predominant. Most firms had some form of foreign direct investment: 100 percent had sales branches, 52 percent were involved in joint ventures, and 70 percent had wholly owned production subsidiaries. Firms were selling their products in an average of 27 countries and had been involved in international activities for 21 years. All 38 firms exported to the U.S., and 79 percent had sales in the U.K. Average sales were $99 million, with international sales averaging $53 million.

To classify the firms into centric classifications, a variety of approaches were used including a centricity questionnaire, executive self-assessment, and interviewer assessment. To identify the centricity attitudes of the executives making critical international decisions, executives were asked to identify which approach (geocentric, ethnocentric, or polycentric) best described how they thought critical international strategy decisions should be made. This approach enabled us to identify the centricity of the key international executives. In addition, to identify the centricity of the organization, an examination was made of how critical decisions were actually made. In particular, the following decision areas were studied: capital expenditures, pricing, dividend policy, product selection and design, production planning and control, quality control, marketing and sales policies and programs, purchasing and choice of suppliers, financial systems and accounting procedures, and the selection, promotion, and compensation of subsidiary executives. An assessment was made of the extent to which these decisions were being made in an ethnocentric, polycentric, or regiocentric manner.

Cultivating Geocentric Attitudes

If you are convinced that success internationally is an important part of your firm's future, you can achieve this partly through hiring decisions. When potential recruits are being interviewed, test for both functional skills and geocentric attitudes. Organizations can look for employees who have a high probability of already having geocentric attitudes. Individuals who have worked outside the country, attended university or college in a country other than their birth country, graduated from an international educational program, speak more than one language, took international business courses, or participated in an international exchange program are more likely to have geocentric attitudes.

To determine what the centric orientation is of prospective new employees, an attitude-testing procedure can be used. It is useful to apply the testing to all employees—not just those who are being hired for an international business position—because these other employees may eventually fill an international role within the company, and be making decisions with indirect international implications.

The hiring process can help infuse geocentric attitudes in the organization, but will not change centricity overnight. The full benefit of a new geocentric hire may not be felt until either a critical mass has been achieved or until the individual geocentric employee is in a position of influence.

International assignments are an effective way to help employees develop geocentric attitudes. By being exposed to foreign cultures daily, employees have a chance to challenge and develop their international attitudes. Existing executives can also be sent on international training courses, another way to develop geocentric attitudes.

A simple training mechanism lies in reading habits. Reading magazines, newspapers, and other literature (including historical) from foreign countries helps in the development of geocentric attitudes.

Another approach that can be used to infuse geocentrism into organizations is to appoint individuals with geocentric attitudes to the board of directors. Since it is the directors who will be assessing business decisions, geocentric attitudes at this level will filter into business decisions. Several companies in our study attributed their international success to having a geocentric board. "The best investment a firm can make is in having an international board. It's more important to have international [board] experience than product experience," claimed one manufacturing executive in explaining his firm's international success.

Geocentric Firms More Successful

Developing a geocentric organization is a complex task. Questions that challenge their existing attitude may have to be asked of managers. For true learning to occur, management should be willing to accept that their underlying attitudes about international business may require revision. If they believed that, "When in Rome, do as the Romans do," or "All _____ are lazy," they must be prepared to have these attitudes challenged and possibly proven to be inappropriate.

Most firms can survive being ethnocentric or polycentric. Most of the non-geocentric firms in our study had foreign subsidiaries, they exported to multiple countries, and had been exporting for several years. But, the evidence is strong that geocentric firms are more successful in the global marketplace.

SECTION

III

CASES

AER LINGUS—ATS (A)

On July 15, 1985, Denis Hanrahan was flying from Dublin to Toronto, as he had many times over the past 11 months, to meet with Klaus Woerner. Klaus was owner and president of a robotics firm, Automation Tooling Systems (ATS), based in Kitchener, Ontario. Hanrahan's job was to expand the "non-airline" activities of Aer Lingus, and ATS was a company in which he wanted to acquire an equity position.

The negotiations between Denis and Klaus had been friendly but protracted, and it appeared that they were finally nearing an end. The deal, which both sides had agreed to orally, was that Aer Lingus would purchase 75 percent of the shares of ATS and that Klaus would stay on and manage the company. The price that he would receive for his shares would depend on the earnings of ATS in the years ending September 30, 1985 and 1986. If ATS met the profit forecast that Klaus had prepared for it, he would receive a total of $4.6 million in cash and retain a 25 percent interest in the company.

Aer Lingus

Aer Lingus was the Irish international airline, wholly owned by the Irish government. As shown in Exhibit 1, Aer Lingus, like many airlines, had difficulty producing a consistently high level of earnings. The early 1980s in particular were not good years for the airline (nor for any other), and only

Case material of The University of Western Ontario School of Business Administration is prepared as a basis for classroom discussion. This case was prepared by Peter Killing, associate professor. Copyright © 1989, The University of Western Ontario, and the IMEDE Management Development Institute, Lausanne, Switzerland.

EXHIBIT 1   Aer Lingus Financial Results—Years Ending March 31 (Millions of Irish Pounds)

	1985		1984		1983		1982		1981	
	Revenue	*Profit*	*Revenue*	*Profit*	*Revenue*	*Profit*	*Revenue*	*Profit*	*Revenue*	*Profit*
Air transport	281	0.5	270	1.4	244	(2.7)	218	(11.2)	164	(15.9)
Ancillary operations										
Airline related	110	12.7	82	11.1	66	9.0	62	8.6	47	7.5
Hotel and Leisure	79	11.7	82	7.7	82	6.0	71	7.8	54	7.7
Financial and Commercial	33	5.4	24	4.5	11	3.6	8	2.0	6	1.3
Net profit after head office expenses, interest, tax*	11.6		4.9		(2.5)		(9.2)		(13.6)	

NOTE: In 1985 the group total assets stood at Ł285 million. A breakdown of assets employed in each business area was not publicly reported.
* The company earned a positive net profit in each of the four years preceding 1981.
CDN Dollars per Irish Pound
1981: 1.90
1982: 1.75
1983: 1.54
1984: 1.41
1985: 1.44

the consistent profitability of the group's hotels, airline-related businesses (maintenance and overhaul of the other firm's aircraft, training of flight crews, and so on), and financial and commercial businesses kept the company's overall losses in check.

A small group of managers under the leadership of Gerry Dempsey were responsible for managing and expanding Aer Lingus's nonairline activities. Hanrahan, second in command, commented:

> We all recognize that the airline business is a cyclical one, and our goal is to create a stable base of earnings which will see the airline safely through the bottom of the cycles. We have been successful so far so we don't know if the government would bail us out if we did make continued heavy losses, and we don't want to have to find out! The mission of our "ancillary activities" is to increase the group's reported earnings and to strengthen its balance sheet.

The financial and commercial results shown in Exhibit 1 include a data processing firm, an insurance company, a helicopter company, a hospital management firm, a land development company, and a 25 percent interest in GPA, formerly Guiness Peat Aviation. Many of these firms, with the exception of the hotels, were founded by former Aer Lingus employees. Although most of the companies were performing well, the undoubted star was GPA. A manager explained:

> In 1975 or so, Tony Ryan, our New York station manager, was transferred back to Ireland and asked to lease out a 747 which we did not need for the winter. In

looking at the leasing market, he thought he saw a very good business opportunity, and he convinced us and a related British company to each put up 45 percent of the capital requried to start an aircraft leasing company. He kept the remaining 10 percent. As things have developed, he was certainly right about the opportunity. In the 10 intervening years, we have received almost 20 million Irish pounds from that business, and our initial investment was only 2.2 million! We still own 25 percent of the company, and now have firms like Air Canada and the General Electric Credit Corporation as partners. GPA is one of *the* Irish success stories of the past decade.

The Move into Robotics

In 1983 Denis Hanrahan began an informal search for a new area of investment which could provide healthy financial returns to Aer Lingus for at least the next decade. By January 1984, he had concluded that robotics was an extremely interesting field. Robots had been used in Japan since the 1960s, but were not adopted in Europe and the United States until the late 1970s. Many analysts expected a robotics boom, with growth rates as high as 30 percent per annum, as Western firms strove to catch up.

Although robot manufacturing appeared to Denis to be an overcrowded field, he was excited about the possibility of becoming a developer of the ancillary technology and components that were required by firms wanting to install robot-based flexible manufacturing assembly lines. His figures suggested that the market value of ancillary systems was at least equal to the value of the robots themselves. Although the volume of business being done in this new area was impossible to quantify with any degree of precision, it appeared to be growing quickly and offer high margins. There were as yet no major companies in the business.

Denis described Aer Lingus' initial entry into the field:

> The first company we looked at was in the United Kingdom. We fairly quickly decided that it was too big, too sexy, and considering its size, depended too heavily on a single supplier of robots. One thing you have to watch out for in this business is guys in very classy suits who know more about doing deals and driving for the initial public offering which is going to make them rich than they do about robotics. It turned out that we were right about that company, as it went bankrupt afterwards.
>
> The company we did buy was Airstead International Systems of the United Kingdom. This is a very small company, much smaller than ATS, but it has the rights to distribute Seiko robots in England. Seiko, in addition to producing products such as watches and Epson computer printers, is a prominent robot manufacturer that was doing very well in some fast growing niches.

After the acquisition of Airstead, Aer Lingus dispatched an analyst to North America to examine six companies that Seiko had identified as the most promising North American robotics systems firms. On August 15, Denis received a telex containing a thumbnail sketch of ATS, indicating that it was the best of the three firms the analyst had seen to date and was worth a closer look. On August 28, Denis was in Kitchener for his first meeting with Klaus Woerner.

Klaus Woerner and ATS

Born in Germany in 1940, Klaus Woerner emigrated to Canada at age 20 after serving an apprenticeship in the tool and die business. He subsequently worked for a variety of manufacturing firms in Canada but, tired of the "hierarchies and rigidities of large corporations," founded ATS in 1978. The new company was not successful, however, until Klaus turned it away from manufacturing and into systems work. The move into robotics was made in late 1981.

By the summer of 1984, ATS had grown to employ 44 people, including 26 tool makers, 15 hardware and software designers, and 3 in sales and administration. Denis was encouraged to see that Klaus was a technically oriented "hands-on" manager whose elegant and creative solutions to systems problems played a major role in the company's success. Klaus, Denis observed, was more at home on the shop floor than talking to accountants, bankers, or lawyers. In his summary of their first meeting, Denis made the following points:

1. Mr. Woerner was an easy individual to get along with, though I would anticipate that he is used to getting his own way. He is the key decision maker in the company, although he does solicit the opinions of his senior colleagues.

2. The company currently turns over approximately $3.5 million per year and expects to double its sales this year after a number of years of relatively slow growth. Woerner reports a current backlog of $3 million.

3. The major financial problem with the business is that there is a significant working capital requirement. I have heard a rule of thumb that suggests 40 percent of turnover is required in this business, but Klaus thought that was far too high. The practical problem is that the final payment of 30 percent of systems cost tends to be delayed for several months after completion of the work while fine tuning is being performed.

4. Mr. Woerner recently came very close to selling ATS to Berton Industries,[1] a major Canadian corporation in the automotive components business. One hundred percent of ATS was to be acquired and, depending on results, it would have been valued at $3 to $4 million. Woerner got very concerned, however, at what he perceived to be the inordinate length of time being taken in detailed negotiations and at the aggressive attitude of the other party's attorneys. In addition, Berton would not give him any assurances about future investment in ATS and apparently Woerner learned that plans had been made to move ATS to another location without any consultation with him. When the president of Berton then ignored Woerner's request that a number of written commitments be made within one week, the deal was off.

---

[1] Disguised name

5. Mr. Woerner's proposal was that Aer Lingus would get 50 percent of the company for an undetermined amount and that 50 percent of this money would be left in the company and that he would take out 50 percent. I indicated to him that 50 percent would probably be the minimum share that we would require and it could be that we would want considerably more. However, any deal that we would do would be structured in such a way that he and his key people would be committed to staying with the company. He had no difficulty with this point and conceded that he was not wedded to the 50:50 formula, which was clearly an ideal going-in position from his point of view.

6. On balance, I found ATS to be very impressive. Although operating in cramped facilities, it does appear to have a real technical depth and undoubtedly has an established customer base. The company appears to be an appropriate size to take over since it is neither too small as to be extraordinarily risky nor so big as to be extraordinarily expensive.

The meeting ended with the two men agreeing to continue discussions and to try to reach a gentlemen's agreement reasonably quickly rather than getting bogged down in protracted technical or legal discussions. Woerner promised to send some financial information as soon as he could get it put together, although he warned that his business plan should not be taken unduly literally as "these things are more exercises than necessarily forecasts of reality."

Subsequent Meetings

Over the next six months, Hanrahan held a number of meetings with Woerner, bringing with him on occasion Gerry Dempsey and Larry Stanley, another of Aer Lingus's ancillary business managers. Both men subsequently supported Denis' view that ATS would be a good acquisition. This positive feedback was also strengthened by comments from Seiko's North American sales manager, who stated that in 10 years ATS would be "one of the top three robot systems integrators firms in North America" if it grew to its potential. The meetings with Klaus also yielded more information about his expectations and the operations of ATS. The following excerpts are taken from Hanrahan's notes and comments on various meetings, all of which were held in Kitchener or Toronto.

Meeting of November 6

Present: G. P. Dempsey, Denis Hanrahan, Klaus Woerner, and Peter Jones,[2] who was Woerner's personal financial adviser and company accountant.

---

[2] Disguised name

1. Woerner outlined his expectations for growth of the automation and robotics industry and for ATS. It seems clear that they have not done very much forward planning. . . . Woerner quoted Laura Conigliaro of Prudential-Bache as suggesting growth from $250 million in 1984 to $1 billion by 1987, but these figures were not very convincing since they relate to the total industry rather than to the subsegment in which ATS is involved.

2. Woerner related that he expected ATS revenues to total $4 million for the year ending September 1984, $6 million for 1985 (rather than the $5 million he had earlier been projecting), and to reach $10 million in three years' time. He believed that growth to $10 million could be financed through a combination of retained earnings and bank debt.

3. Northern Telecom (a major Canadian multinational firm) apparently accounts for approximately 40 percent of ATS revenues. Woerner indicated that this proportion would fall to one third in 1985 due to the growth of ATS. He stated strongly that in spite of the company's high dependence on Northern Telecom, he could, if necessary, survive a total loss of Northern's business by falling back on traditional nonflexible production line work ("hard" automation). However, he expressed the view that Northern Telecom could not break the relationship with him since they were dependent on ATS for maintenance and software updates.

4. There was an extensive discussion on the subject of control. Woerner's recent negotiations with Berton left him very uneasy about the behaviour of large corporations, and he again expressed his strong preference for a 50:50 partnership. Dempsey responded that our whole approach to subsidiaries was to work in partnership with the management of them and that this approach was not altered whether the shareholding was 2 percent, 50 percent, or 99 percent. Woerner appeared to implicitly accept that we might go to 75 percent or higher of the equity as long as we were concerned only with issues such as overall earnings and growth rather than the detailed operating practices involved. Dempsey suggested that Woerner should write to us in simple nonlegal terms outlining those issues upon which he believed he would require assurance from us. Woerner accepted this suggestion.

5. Woerner also expressed concern that his was a small company and in danger of being "trampled on" by Aer Lingus. While he was happy enough with the people he currently knew in Aer Lingus, he felt that these individuals could change and he could thus find himself exposed to changes of policy or personality. Dempsey responded that we could not fully reassure him on this issue. We had now had a wide range of relationships with subsidiaries over a long period of time and as this had not occurred historically, he saw no reason why it should happen in the future.

6. There were no specific discussions on the matter of price. Dempsey stated on a number of occasions that it was purposeless to discuss price until the financials were available and had been reviewed. Woerner concurred.

EXHIBIT 2   ATS Financial Statements (Canadian $000)

	1980	1981	1982	1983	1984
Sales	332	765	1,210	1,753	4,168
Cost of sales	187	491	902	1,450	3,197
Gross margin	145	274	308	303	971
Overheads	58	127	188	243	451
Operating profit	87	147	120	60	520
Interest	2	10	20	26	71
Tax	11	22	4	-0-	18
Net profit	74	115	96	34	431
Balance sheets					
Assets					
Fixed assets	106	211	308	390	517
Current assets	113	282	384	457	1,300
Current liabilities	(35)	(129)	(209)	(252)	(390)
Working capital	78	153	175	205	910
	184	364	483	595	1,427
Funded by					
Share capital	1	6	5	3	3
Revenue reserves	79	114	177	(160)	164
Shareholder's funds	80	120	182	(157)	167
Loan capital	104	244	301	752	1,260
	184	364	483	595	1,427

---

7. The meeting ended on a positive and progressive note. It was agreed that we would appoint Peat Marwick to review the affairs of ATS and they would contact Jones as necessary. It was also agreed that Jones would shortly produce a three-year forecast for ATS.

Meeting of January 10

The next meeting between Klaus and Denis included Bill Harcourt[3] of Peat Marwick Mitchell. During this meeting, the ATS financial statements and projections (see Exhibits 2 and 3) were given to Denis. These were to have been sent to Ireland several weeks earlier.

Denis learned during this meeting that Klaus had not written the promised letter concerning his specific issues of concern because he preferred to discuss them face to face. Further discussion ensued during which Klaus reiterated his general unease at the prospect of being controlled and repeated his desire for a 50:50 deal. While still not raising any specific concerns, Klaus repeatedly referred to the Berton deal and how lucky he was to have avoided it. Denis commented after the meeting:

---

[3] Disguised name

EXHIBIT 3   Projected ATS Financial Statements (Canadian $000)

	1985	1986	1987	1988
Sales	8,000	11,000	14,000	17,000
Cost of sales	5,920	8,360	10,920	13,260
Gross margin	2,080	2,640	3,080	3,740
Overheads	1,040	1,430	1,750	2,210
Operating profit	1,040	1,210	1,330	1,530
Interest	70	120	200	300
Tax	427	480	497	541
Net profit	543	610	633	689
Dividends (projected)	-0-	-0-	250	300

Projected Balance Sheets	1984	1985	1986	1987	1988
Assets					
Fixed assets	517	680	1,030	1,310	1,860
Development				1,000	1,000
Current assets	1,300	2,417	4,904	5,740	6,580
Current liabilities	(390)	(760)	(1,720)	(1,886)	(2,260)
Working capital	910	1,657	3,184	3,854	4,320
	1,427	2,337	4,214	6,164	7,180
Funded by					
Share capital	3	750	2,000	2,300	2,700
Revenue reserves	164	707	1,317	1,701	2,090
Shareholder's funds	167	1,457	3,317	4,001	3,790
Loan capital	1,260	800	897	2,163	3,390
	1,427	2,337	4,214	6,164	7,180

Note: These projections were prepared by Klaus Woerner and Peter Jones.

All of this was territory that we had covered several times previously with him and we essentially just covered it again. It was clear that as the discussion progressed, Klaus began to get more comfortable and his fears began to recede. I have no doubt that after I depart from Canada he begins to get uneasy again at the unknown. He reiterated that he was quite comfortable working with Mr. Dempsey or myself but that he could naturally have no assurance that we would be around forever.

In the earlier part of the meeting when Klaus was appearing very reluctant, Bill Harcourt asked him directly if he, in fact, wanted to sell ATS. Klaus replied that he didn't really want to—he had devoted all of this time in the last few years in building up the company and wished to continue to do so in the future—but because ATS would not be producing large amounts of cash in the short term he had no choice. He believes that ATS can and must grow very rapidly to forestall the competition—the opportunities are there and if ATS does not take advantage of them, someone else will. In this vein, he mentioned that he had just revised his estimate of the current year's sales from $6 million to $9 million.

The other reason that Klaus feels that he has to sell ATS is that important customers like Northern Telecom are nervous of becoming too dependent on him, as long as he does not have a major corporate backer. Klaus told us in the meeting that Northern had in fact deliberately cut back their orders to him for this reason, and we independently checked that this was indeed the case.

The meeting ended on a very friendly note with Denis again encouraging Klaus to make up a list of his specific concerns so that they could be addressed, and Klaus inviting Bill Harcourt to visit the ATS plant before the next meeting so that he could develop a better understanding of what they were doing.

Meetings of January 24 and February 20

The meetings of January 24 and February 20 were devoted to discussions of a deal whereby Aer Lingus would acquire 75 percent of ATS stock, with Klaus Woerner holding the remaining 25 percent. At the January 24 meeting, Klaus appeared to accept the idea that he would sell the 75 percent of the company but, apparently as a result of his earlier negotiations with Berton, was adamant that ATS was worth at least $6 million. In the February 20 meeting, Denis finally agreed that ATS could be worth $6 million if the company met Klaus' new projections for it (Exhibit 4) but at the moment it was not. As a consequence, Denis proposed that the amount paid to Klaus should depend on the company's performance in 1985 and 1986. The details,

EXHIBIT 4   Revised Income Projections (Canadian $000)

	1985	1986	1987	1988
Sales	8,000	14,000	20,000	30,000
Gross margin	2,080 (26%)	3,360 (24%)	4,400 (22%)	6,000 (20%)
General and administration See Schedule 2	862	1,190	1,578	2,159
Income	1,218	2,170	2,822	3,841
Profit sharing	120	217	282	384
Pre-tax income	1,098	1,953	2,540	3,457
Tax @45%	494	879	1,143	1,556
After-tax income	604	1,074	1,397	1,901

Note: These revisions were dated February 20, 1985. They were prepared by Klaus Woerner, working with Bill Harcourt.

spelled out in a letter from Denis to Klaus following the February meeting were as follows:

1. We propose that a valuation be established for ATS as of September 30, 1986. This valuation will be calculated by taking 3.5 times the pre-tax income for the fiscal year ended September 30, 1985, and adding to it 3.5 times the incremental pre-tax income earned in the fiscal year ending September 1986. By incremental income here I mean the excess of pre-tax income in fiscal 1986 over that earned in fiscal 1985.

2. In determining pre-tax income, research and development costs shall be charged at a rate contained in your financial projections or at a higher rate if so incurred. Profit sharing to employees shall be charged at 10 percent of pre-tax income before profit sharing or such higher rate as may be incurred. In addition, we would require the company to maintain a key-man insurance policy on yourself in the amount of $5 million and the cost of such coverage would be borne as a charge before striking pre-tax income.

3. On the basis of the pre-tax income figures outlined above, the company would have a total of $6,835,000 as of September 30, 1986.

4. Under the above formula, the maximum value that we would be prepared to put on ATS would be $7 million even if the results are better than projected.

5. It is our view that the company is in need of significant additional funds to allow it to develop to the sales and income levels in your projections. Accordingly, we are willing to inject $2 million into ATS for agreed working capital and investment use in the form of a secured debt with a 10 percent interest rate. It would be our intention to make available $750,000 at time of closing, $750,000 at time of completion of the 1985 audit, and the remaining $500,000 as needed by the company on an agreed basis during 1986.

It would be our intention that this loan would be used to purchase treasury stock from ATS at the end of 1986 using the valuation for the company as established by the formula outlined above. In other words, if the company was valued at $6,835,000, the $2 million loan would convert to give us 22.6 percent of the enlarged equity in the company. The attraction of this arrangement from your point of view is that it provides you with the money now to grow but that the shares are ultimately purchased in ATS at the valuation achieved in 1986 rather than at a current valuation.

Depending upon the ultimate valuation of the company, the percentage of its enlarged equity that would be bought by the $2 million referred to above would vary. It would then be our intention to purchase, directly from you, existing shares held by you in ATS such as would give us 75 percent of the then enlarged equity of the company. In the example quoted above, we would need to purchase 67 percent of your shareholding to give us a total of 75 percent of the enlarged equity. Using the value above, this would cost $4.6 million. In other words, what you would receive would be $4.6 million in cash plus 25 percent interest in the $2 million injected by us, for a total of $5.1 million, which is 75 percent of $6,835,000. We propose that you would be paid for these shares as follows: on closing $500,000;

in March 1986 and March 1987, further payments of $500,000; in March 1988 and March 1989 further payments of $1 million each; the balance payable on March 1990. To the degree that the final value of the company is larger or smaller than the $6,835,000 figure, the above payments would be prorated.

Moving Forward

On March 16, Bill Harcourt phoned Denis to report that he had met with Klaus subsequent to the February 22 meeting. Denis recalled the discussion:

> Apparently Klaus was initially very unhappy with the limit of $7 million that we put on the company, although he is now willing to live with it and in fact has become very positive about a deal with Aer Lingus. He appears to have overcome his hesitancy and concern at another party becoming the majority shareholder of ATS. This may be due to the fact that he has taken advice from a friend named Bob Tivey who is the retired president of Monarch Canada.[4] Some minor improvements are required, however.
>
> One of these is that Klaus wants us to increase the $500,000 coming to him on closing so that he can pay employee bonuses—these will come out of his own pocket—and have more for himself. He also wants us to pay interest on the portion of the purchase paid which remains unpaid until the earn-out is completed. Finally, he would like a personal contract which will last five years, and include a good salary plus a bonus that is 2 percent of pre-tax earnings, and a car.
>
> Other news included the fact that Klaus is in the process of hiring a financial person and is considering a second-year registered industrial accountancy student. Bill suggested that he discuss this matter in some detail with us, as it might be advisable to opt for a more high-powered person. Bill also told me that Klaus was facing an immediate decision with respect to new premises for ATS—the major question being whether the company should rent or buy. The purchase cost will be close to $1 million.

Shortly after this phone call, Denis received a letter from Klaus which began, "I wish to advise you that I am prepared to accept the proposal as outlined . . . subject to the following changes." As expected, the most important of the requested changes were an increased initial payment, the payment of interest on the unpaid portion of the purchase price, and a five-year employment contract.

After some negotiation, Aer Lingus agreed to increase its initial payment to allow Klaus to pay employee bonuses and to increase the initial funds going to his own pocket by approximately 50 percent, which was less than what he had requested, but was deemed satisfactory.

In early April, Klaus traveled to Ireland for a meeting with the chief executive of Aer Lingus, and later that month the Aer Lingus board approved

---

[4] Disguised name

the purchase of a 75 percent shareholding of ATS on the terms which had been agreed with Klaus.

At the end of April, Denis was once again in Kitchener, where he and Klaus held a most amicable meeting. Denis learned that Klaus and Bob Tivey had prepared a new business plan which they had used to obtain an increase in the ATS credit line. Also, Klaus had decided to proceed with the acquisition, his only objection being that eight board meetings a year was too many. Denis concluded his notes on the meeting with the following:

> We discussed at length the need for ATS management to develop credibility with me and for me to develop credibility on ATS subjects in Dublin, which he seemed to accept. All in all, the discussions were satisfactory and straightforward and have put to rest a significant number of my fears concerning Mr. Woerner's independence and his unwillingness to accommodate the requirements of a major corporate shareholder. In my view, he will accept direction provided that the direction is fast placed and is seen by him as being responsive to ATS's needs.

Due to some apparent foot dragging on the part of Klaus' lawyers and intervening vacations, it was July before Denis arrived in Kitchener to review the drafts of the sale contracts and bring the deal to a conclusion.

The Meeting of July 16

Klaus attended this meeting with Ron Jutras, his new financial controller (who had been hired without consultation with Aer Lingus), and Bob Tivey, who was acting as a consultant to Klaus. Denis recalled the meeting as follows:

> They opened the meeting by tabling a number of requirements which they said were critical to the deal going ahead. These were
>
> 1. A reluctance to hand over control to us before the valuation date of September 1986.
> 2. A five-year guaranteed contract for Klaus, with a 10-year period before we can force him out of share ownership.
> 3. A degree of protection against the possibility that one-off costs may depress 1986 earnings—specifically a *minimum* buy-out price of $6 million!
>
> I was very distressed to find such a total about face on something that we had agreed three months earlier, and when faced with this, Klaus acknowledged that he was changing his mind, but said that he could not afford the possibility of one bad year depressing his buy-out price. As for the contract length, Klaus was very emotional when the possibility of anything shorter than a five-year contract was raised.
>
> The question facing me as I sat in that meeting was how to react. Was it time to give up on this long and apparently fruitless process, or should I continue—and if so, how?

ALCAN ALUMINUM LTD. (CONDENSED)

Alcan is determined to be the most innovative diversified aluminum company in the world. To achieve this position, Alcan will be one global, customer-oriented enterprise committed to excellence and lowest cost in its chosen aluminum businesses, with significant resources devoted to building an array of new businesses with superior growth and profit potential. In the 1990s Alcan will outperform the S&P 400.

In the spring of 1986, David Culver, president and CEO of Alcan Aluminum Ltd, a Montreal-based multinational, was reviewing the above draft of a new mission statement he had been working on for the company (see Appendix A for detailed discussion). Culver had spent the previous months consulting with various managers about the statement, which he felt was nothing less than a "call to arms." The statement crystalized the company's new strategy, which Culver had foreshadowed in the annual shareholders' meeting in 1984. While the company had published a statement of its purpose, objectives, and policies in 1978, it was not as sharply focused as the new mission statement drafted by Culver with the input of a few key senior managers. In particular, the new statement contained a clear financial objective for the 1990s, and Culver wondered what it would take to achieve it.

BACKGROUND

Alcan had just come through a particularly difficult year, suffering an unprecedented $180 million loss in 1985, even higher than the $58 million loss experi-

Source: This case was prepared from published records by Professor Mark C. Baetz, School of Business and Economics, Wilfrid Laurier University. It was prepared as a basis for class discussion rather than to illustrate either effective or ineffective handling of an administrative situation. Revised January 1992. Copyright © 1992, Mark C. Baetz.

enced in the major 1981–82 recession, which had represented the first loss in 50 years (see Exhibit 1 for selected financial information). The 1985 loss position was a result of a special charge of $252 million after tax. Approximately one-half of this charge reflected a write-down in the value of Alcan's bauxite and alumina assets and most of the other half reflected the cost of a companywide program to reduce management levels and the number of employees. In fact, numbers had been reduced by 3,100 since the end of 1984.

Culver was considering a one-week conference in June 1986 involving Alcan's top 70 managers from around the world. Like Culver, many of these managers had spent most of their working lives with Alcan. The conference would be at a secluded hotel in Quebec and its purpose would be to review the draft mission statement which had been prepared. Culver felt such a conference could be an exercise in common understanding as a prelude to coordinated action. Through plenary sessions and 10-person work groups, all conference delegates would have an opportunity to help set Alcan's course for the future. Culver, a 61-year-old Harvard MBA from the 1940s who in 1979 became the third CEO of Alcan, was well aware that the conference he was considering had no precedent in the long history of Alcan.

Production of Aluminum and Alcan's Position in 1986

Producing 1 metric ton of aluminum requires 4 or 5 tons of bauxite, which is one of the most abundant metals in the earth's crust. Bauxite comes from tropical or subtropical regions particularly in the Caribbean, West Africa, and Australia. The bauxite is chemically refined into about 2 metric tons of alumina, which is then treated at the smelter using an electrolytic process that consumes between 14,000 and 18,500 kilowatt-hours of electricity. Other metals can then be added to the molten aluminum metal to make aluminum alloys which are then cast into various ingot shapes and sizes, depending on the way the ingot is then to be fabricated.

There were a number of rigidities built into bauxite and alumina production. First, it took several years—between five and six—to build an alumina plant. Second, in order to capture economies of scale, large plants needed to be built; in the 1980s, alumina plants could cost more than $1 billion (U.S.), requiring in some cases consortium approaches. Finally, alumina plants could not be used for other purposes, and, in fact, each plant was locked into certain grades of bauxite.

As of 1986, Alcan's bauxite and alumina operations were expected to provide a geographically diversified supply base sufficient for all the company's smelters and other commitments for more than 50 years. Most of the aluminum required for Alcan's smelter operations came from the company's plants in Canada, Ireland, and Jamaica and from related companies in Australia. Bauxite for Alcan's Canadian and Irish alumina plants was purchased mainly from a related mining company in Brazil and a mining company in Guinea in which

EXHIBIT 1   Selected Financial Information for Alcan Aluminum Ltd.

Information by Geographic Areas	Location	1985	1984	1983
Sales and operating revenues to third parties (millions of U.S. $)	Canada	$ 921	$1,004	$1,003
	United States	1,957	1,576	1,358
	Latin America	339	349	298
	Europe	1,756	1,683	1,766
	Pacific	664	709	627
	All other	81	146	126
	Total	5,718	5,467	5,208
	Sales	5,511	5,272	4,969
	Operating revenues	207	195	239
	Total	$5,718	$5,467	$5,208
Net income (Loss)	Canada	$ (41)	$ 141	$ 105
	United States	14	17	24
	Latin America	20	39	(11)
	Europe	(7)	51	26
	Pacific	(13)	33	(28)
	All other	—	6	(4)
	Consolidation eliminations*	(153)†	(34)	(39)
	Total	$ (180)	$ 253	$ 73
Totals assets at 31 December	Canada	$2,476	$2,785	$2,582
	United States	1,110	999	802
	Latin America	705	716	697
	Europe	1,829	1,469	1,652
	Pacific	821	842	845
	All other	268	324	400
	Consolidation eliminations*	(348)	(445)	(378)
	Total	$6,861	$6,690	$6,600
Capital expenditures	Canada	$ 152	$ 194	$ 127
	United States	136	45	34
	Latin America	57	37	48
	Europe	161	35	96
	Pacific	61	98	64
	All other	30	18	13
	Total	$ 597	$ 427	$ 382
Average number of employees (thousands)	Canada	17	18	19
	United States	7	5	5
	Latin America	10	10	9
	Europe	20	20	22
	Pacific	14	14	13
	All other	2	3	3
	Total	70	70	71

* Represents intersubsidiary transactions.
† Includes provision against investments in bauxite and alumina operations.

EXHIBIT 1   Principal Products *(continued)*

Fabricated products: Since 1982, the company's shipments of fabricated products have increased steadily at an annual average rate of 13 percent, to reach a total of 1,340,000 tonnes in 1985. Over half of this increase has been due to mergers and acquisitions in the United Kingdom and the United States while the balance reflects higher shipments by existing Alcan operations, particularly in the United States. Gross margins on fabricated products decline in 1985 by 24 percent to $437 per tonne from $577 in 1984, compared with $424 in 1983.

Ingot products: In 1985, shipments increased to a record 878,000 tonnes. Increased sales were made principally in the United States and the Far East. Closely following trends in spot metal prices, Alcan's average realizations for ingot products decline by 35 percent from their cyclical peak in the first quarter of 1984 to the fourth quarter of 1985, which was 8 percent lower than the year earlier quarter. Despite steady cost reductions, margins on ingot products averaged $42 per tonne in 1985, as against $293 in 1984 and $200 in 1983.

Other products: In 1985, sales of other products total $813 million. The decline in 1985 was due primarily to lower revenues from sales of alumina. Other major contributions to revenues in this category were provided by sales of other metals, particularly stainless steel, magnesium and nickel, and by nonaluminum building products, industrial chemicals, and bauxite.

Operating revenues: In 1985, operating revenues were $207 million, compared to $195 million in 1984 and $239 million in 1983. Tolling (processing of products for third parties for a fee) and sales of surplus power from Canadian and British generating plants, constituted 70 percent of total revenues in this category. The third major component was revenues from third-party ocean freight operations.

Other income: These revenues, consisting principally of foreign exchange items and interest income, totaled $113 million in 1985, $109 million in 1984, and $97 million in 1983.

Revenues by Product
1985 (millions of U.S. $)

		1985	1984	1983	1982	1981
36.4%	Flat-rolled products	2,123	2,024	1,826	1,522	1,760
17.9%	Extruded, rolled, drawn	1,042	1,126	996	934	1,067
9.5%	Other fabricated	554	418	373	353	323
	Total fabricated	3,719	3,568	3,195	2,809	3,150
16.8%	Ingot products	979	817	975	867	789
13.9%	Other products	813	887	799	677	793
5.5%	Operating revenues and other income	320	304	336	356	321

Gross Profit by Product
1985 (millions of U.S. $)

		1985	1984	1983	1982	1981
65.8%	Total fabricated products (integrated)	586	700	497	398	627
4.2%	Ingot products	37	169	146	40	166
10.8%	Other products	96	101	85	68	125
19.2%	Operating revenues and other income	171	162	160	153	132

(continued)

Exhibit 1   **Principal Markets** *(concluded)*

Containers and packaging: The increase in consolidated sales to this market was largely due to the acquisition of assets from Arco, which strengthened the company's position in the United States as a supplier of sheet products, especially for beverage containers, and enabled it to enter the foil market for packaging in the United States. Approximately half of the company's total sales for containers and packaging were made in the United States, while one quarter were in Europe, where there is close cooperation among German, British, and Swiss operations in the foil packaging market.

While penetration of aluminum of the U.S. beverage can market is almost complete, efforts continue to develop this market elsewhere. In Canada, the consumption of aluminum for beer cans doubled during 1985, helping to increase the company's shipments to this market. In Germany, the company has been involved in pilot recycling projects to demonstrate some of the benefits from using aluminum for beverage containers, particularly with regards to the disposal of household waste.

Transport: The decline in sales to this market in 1985 was shared by all geographic regions. Approximately 80% of the company's sales were made by German, U.S., British, and Canadian operations. Largely due to the acquisition of assets from Arco, sales to the U.S. automotive industry of fin stock for radiators and air conditioners grew strongly.

Electrical: The United States and Canada accounted for over half of consolidated sales to this market, and declines in these two countries contributed to a reduction in the total. A new wire and cable plant at Shawinigan, Quebec, commenced partial operation in 1985 and will be fully operational in 1986.

Building and Construction: Increased sales in Europe to this market helped to offset reductions elsewhere. Operations in Europe and North America each accounted for approximately 40 percent of total sales. In Europe aluminum applications for building and construction are mostly in the form of extrusions, while in North America the company's sales to this market are made up largely of sheet products, including steel and vinyl, as well as aluminum.

Other markets: The company's sales to the international market for ingot products rose strongly, particularly in the United States and the Far East, and accounted for 17.8 percent of consolidated sales to all markets. The company also sells bauxite, alumina, and other raw materials used to produce aluminum. Sales of other metals and industrial chemicals increased during the year.

Scales by Market
1985 (millions of U.S. $)

		1985	*1984*
20.2%	Containers and packaging	1113	1009
6.7%	Transport	368	432
8.9%	Electrical	490	552
21.0%	Building and construction	1160	1223
43.2%	Other	2380	2056

Source: All information in Exhibit 1 comes from Alcan Aluminum Ltd., *Annual Report*, 1985.

the company had a minority equity interest. Subsidiaries with smelters in Brazil and India had their own bauxite mining and alumina production facilities.

Alcan owned 17 primary aluminum smelters with a total annual rated capacity of 1.8 million tonnes. Six of these smelters were in Canada: five in Quebec (807,000 tonnes of capacity) and one in British Columbia (268,000 tonnes of capacity). The remaining smelters which were owned either directly or indirectly were in seven other countries.

In Canada, Alcan's smelters obtained virtually all of their power from the company-owned hydroelectric generating plants. These plants were all constructed by 1959. Some of the surplus power from these plants was sold under contract. The power for Alcan's smelters outside Canada was supplied by various sources. The English smelter operated under its own coal-fired plants, those in Australia and India purchased power under long-term contracts from government-owned electric utilities, and those in Brazil and Scotland obtained power from both owned hydroelectric generating plants and outside sources. The German smelter was supplied by a local power authority, and the U.S. smelter purchased power under long-term contract from a financially troubled generating cooperative.

Like many producers of primary aluminum, Alcan was involved in supplying semifabricated and finished products. (There were also many independent fabricators). In 1986 Alcan was the largest domestic manufacturer of fabricated aluminum products in many countries including Canada, Brazil, India, New Zealand, and the United Kingdom (see Exhibit 1 for more details on the various products and markets served).

As of 1986, Alcan had bauxite holdings in 7 countries, refined alumina in 7 countries, smelted primary alumina in 8 countries, fabricated aluminum in more than 20 countries, and had sales outlets in more than 100 countries. In addition, the company had research laboratories in Kingston, Ontario; Banbury, England; and Arvida (Jonquiere), Quebec.

History of Alcan's Ownership Structure

In 1901, the Aluminum Company of America (Alcoa) launched a Canadian subsidiary under the name of Northern Aluminum to develop smelting facilities at Shawinigan, Quebec, on the St. Maurice River. As a result of this move, Canada entered the aluminum-producing ingot market 15 years after the United States and Europe first began to produce this versatile metal.

By 1925 Alcoa had smelters in Canada, Italy, and Norway, fabricating plants in England and Germany, and bauxite mines in Yugoslavia and Guyana. Alcoa decided to transfer all the foreign businesses to a new Canadian holding company, Aluminum Ltd., with its former Canadian subsidiary, now renamed the Aluminum Company of Canada (Alcan), being the largest member. Alcoa handed one share in the new company to the Alcoa shareholders for each three they held in Alcoa.

Setting up Alcan solved a personal problem for Arthur Vining Davis. As Alcoa's chairman, he was looking for a new president, and both E. K. Davis, his younger brother, and Roy Hunt, son of a founder, were qualified for the position. He appointed Davis president of Alcan and Hunt president of Alcoa. In 1947, E. K. Davis retired and his son, Nathanael Davis, was appointed president at age 32. In 1979, after 32 years as CEO, Davis retired from active management duties. He remained as chairman of the board until he retired in March 1986.

Although ownership of the Alcan shares had dispersed when Nathanael Davis was appointed president, the U.S. Justice Department believed that Alcan and Alcoa were too intimately connected. In 1950, a judge gave the major shareholders 10 years to sell off their holdings in either Alcan or Alcoa. All but E. K. Davis sold their shares in Alcan.

History of Alcan's Development

In the early 1920s, Alcoa and Northern had set out to develop the power potential of the Saguenay River in Quebec. A new smelter was opened in 1926 at the town of Arvida, named after the then president of Alcoa using the first two letters in each name, Arthur Vining Davis. Nathanael Davis explained the choice of the Saguenay as follows:

> The Saguenay attracted the Americans because of its combination of hydroelectric power and good logistics on deep water. To produce aluminum, you have to bring a tremendous lot of raw materials to the power. Power in the middle of Canada would have been far less attractive than power on deep water; and the Saguenay was a deep-water port.
>
> At the time, too, Canadian-made aluminum would have had preferential tariffs in Commonwealth countries.
>
> There was probably even more to it than that. I suspect that the risk of other foreign interests moving in led Alcoa to say, "We'd better stake out a position in Canada." The French producers were interested. That power stood there waiting for a user.[1]

Fabrication of aluminum also started at the same time as smelting. A small rod, wire, and cable mill was built beside the original Shawinigan smelter in 1902. Sheet foil and casting followed at several locations.

World War II brought quick growth to the aluminum industry and after a short postwar slump, aluminum became widely used in household items, as well as in paints, cars, and airplanes due to its superior properties of strength and lightness. Much of the use of aluminum came as a result of substitution for other products. For example, aluminum replaced wood and steel in windows and copper in electrical cables.

In the early 1950s, Alcan built the Kitimat hydro and smelting facilities in British Columbia, 400 miles north of Vancouver. The only access to the site was by air or sea. At Kitimat, Alcan was faced with the challenge of creating a whole new community based upon one industry in a remote area with a harsh climate. It also had to construct a deep-water port. With $450 million worth of smelters and generators, Kitimat represented the largest private enterprise undertaking in Canadian history. It was also the world's second largest smelter; the world's largest was Alcan's facility at Arvida.

---

[1] *Executive,* November 1979.

In the early 1950s, while Alcan's rivals stepped up fabrication to go after the U.S. postwar markets, Alcan basically stuck to its strategy of being the "producer's producer." Alcan's strategy of continuing to produce ingots for fabrication by others meant that they were taking on debt to invest in major hydro and smelting projects. Alcan paid for this nonconformity in the late 1950s when plunging ingot prices caught the company with a high debt load. Up until 1957, the demand for aluminum grew steadily, but in that year it fell sharply. This brought to an end the seller's market that the producing industry had been experiencing, and in 1959 Alcan was forced to temporarily close 34 percent of its Canadian smelting capacity. From 1947 to 1957, the average annual price increase was 6 percent. However, from 1957 to 1972, the industry experienced no price increases. The beginning of this buyer's market occurred three years after the Kitimat operation came on stream. Nathanael Davis commented on Kitimat as follows:

> The [Kitimat] decision built up over years of investigation. . . . With the benefit of hindsight we can see that we miscalculated on cost and in timing. The remoteness factor had been completely misjudged. At the time it put a terrible strain on the company. It ran over budget very significantly and for many years was fairly unproductive.[2]

Revisions to Alcan's Strategy

Too much capacity and declining demand forced the directors of Alcan to revise their strategic direction. Alcan was to forward integrate and to stop being a "producer's producer." This decision committed Alcan to capital expenditures of over $1 billion to develop fabrication plants worldwide. Nathanael Davis explained the significance of this decision as follows:

> It takes a long time to see trends and make a major change in a business such as this. It might take a year or 18 months to make the decision and then you really can't get anything going under five years, so you want to be pretty sure of your ground before you start. All our projects take a lot of capital, and once you start you don't turn back. Like a ship you can change course only fairly slowly.[3]

Between 1955 and 1970, Alcan established new fabrication operations in more than 20 countries. In fact, the company changed from being largely a supplier of primary aluminum to being largely a supplier of fabricated products. In the United States, a market representing one-half of the total world market, Alcan teamed up in 1965 with three independent fabricators to build a mill in Oswego, New York. Eventually the independents' share was bought out, but the U.S. subsidiary did not turn a profit until 1973. However, it became the fourth largest U.S. fabricator with 1978 sales of more than $1 billion.

---

[2] *Executive,* December 1979.

[3] Ibid.

Future efforts at entry into the United States met with resistance. In 1976, Alcan's efforts to buy the Revere Copper and Brass Company's aluminum smelter were stopped by the antitrust regulators. Because Alcan was one of the major players in a concentrated industry, the regulators felt they should not pick up a facility from a smaller company, even though Alcan believed they would have added to competition by strengthening a weak facility. Alcan decided not to pursue the acquisition because of the risks associated with a legal battle.

Alcan in the 1980s

Later, in 1984, Alcan again encountered resistance to its expansion plans in the United States when it attempted to buy the aluminum assets of Atlantic Richfield Co. (Arco) of Los Angeles. Arco, like many major oil companies that diversified into metals in the 1970s, had become disillusioned with aluminum and found profits hard to come by. U.S. antitrust officials objected to Alcan's desire to buy Arco's ultramodern $450 million rolling mill in Logan County, Kentucky, which produced the aluminum sheet used in beverage cans. Regulators said the purchase of the plant would double Alcan's 7 percent share of the $3.4 billion U.S. market for the product. After 11 months of negotiations, Alcan's lawyers worked out a compromise with the regulators. For $500 million, Alcan would purchase 40 percent of the Kentucky rolling mill, along with 100 percent of Arco's Kentucky-based smelter, two other rolling mills, two foil-producing plants in the United States, and finally Arco's 25 percent interest in an Irish alumina factory. Before the deal was concluded, one report commented on what Alcan's strategy would have been if U.S. antitrust officials were to completely veto the acquisition as they had done in the case of Revere Copper and Brass:

> Alcan President and Chief Executive, David Culver makes it clear that another veto will not deter Alcan from expanding south of the Canadian border. "No one's ever stopped us from building a new plant in the U.S.," he says. Adds a former Alcan executive: "They need a facility in the U.S. If they don't buy it from Arco, they're going to build it." Such grit illustrates the change at Alcan under Culver, who became the first Canadian to head Alcan. Before that, Americans held the top job, and—in part because they did not want to raise Canadian hackles—made few bold moves, creating Alcan's long-held reputation for being a "gentleman's club." Says former Alcan executive, Manley S. Schultz: "Visitors said you could fire a cannon in headquarters at five after five and not worry about hurting anybody." No longer. "They're extremely aggressive now," says a rival.[4]

Alcan's aggressiveness was revealed during the recession of the early 1980s, when the company decided to reduce its production much less than its competitors. This move was a break from Alcan's traditional approach to

---

[4] *Business Week,* August 27, 1984, pp. 95–96.

downturns of cutting production at least as much as competitors. Alcan's new strategy was seen as a major blunder by many Wall Street metals analysts and by Alcan's competitors, who saw Alcan's operating rate as exacerbating a price collapse that made the recession worse for all producers, including Alcan.

Two major economic factors important to Alcan were energy and transportation costs. While Alcan had always benefited from low electricity costs, it also had to contend with high transportation costs of both raw materials to its smelters and aluminum ingot to the marketplace; it was hauling bauxite and alumina from the Southern Hemisphere to its Canadian smelters, and then shipping finished or semifinished products to places as distant as the Far East. While the cost of transportation may offset Alcan's edge in electricity in the past, the two energy price surges in the 1970s clearly put the company among the world's lowest cost producers. A media report in 1983 explained Alcan's position as follows:

> Alcan's power advantage now more than makes up for its shipping-cost penalties. . . . In the last five years the weighted-average electricity costs for smelters in the non-Communist world has doubled from 0.9 cent to 1.8 cents per kwh. As a result, electricity costs now account for about 25 percent, or $300, of the average price of producing a metric ton of aluminum. But the price of power from Alcan's Canadian hydroelectric stations, all of which were built before 1960, has risen hardly at all. It is now just 0.3 cent per kwh, one-sixth of the industry average.
>
> Electricity costs Alcan about $50 per metric ton of aluminum. Japan, at the opposite extreme with power from oil-fired generators, faces a cost of 6 cents per kwh, or $990 per metric ton of aluminum. Not surprisingly, most of Japan's smelting capacity is idle and the country is importing most of its aluminum. In the U.S. the Bonneville Power Administration recently jacked up the price it charges aluminum smelters in the Northwestern to 2.6 cents, or about $430 per metric ton. . . . Hydropower gives Alcan a peculiar disincentive to cut back in lean times. While other producers' costs vary according to how much electricity they use, Alcan's power costs are fixed. . . . The company lacks a ready market for any surplus (electricity from its hydroelectric plants). "If we shut down our smelters, we go to bed with the electricity that's liberated," says Murray Lester, Alcan's director of energy resources. "If the whole industry had to wind down to the last 2 million tons, and the invisible hand of Adam Smith were working, we'd be the last to go."
>
> High production levels also appear to be part of a company campaign to win labor peace. While its U.S. competitors worked without major disruptions during the 1970s, Alcan was hit with two big strikes, both in years of rising demand. It has been keeping employment relatively high despite the recession and has refrained from fully opening a brand-new $500-million non-union smelter in Quebec until business improves. "We've tried to maintain our team," Culver says.[5]

Another key part of Alcan's strategy was to ensure that Alcan's shipments of primary aluminum to third parties (i.e., shipments other than to Alcan's

---

[5] *Fortune,* February 21, 1983, p. 126.

own fabricating plants) would not fall below 25 percent of total smelter output. This compared to the U.S. companies that reduced third-party shipments of primary aluminum to 20 percent or less of total shipments. The two major U.S. companies—Alcoa and Reynolds—produced ingot almost exclusively for use in their own fabricating plants. The main rationale for the Alcan strategy was its continuing anticipated power cost advantage in smelting. However, ingots were clearly in a commodity market subject to huge cyclical swings.

Environment in the Mid-1980s

By 1985, Alcan was facing lower world prices for ingot and excess smelter capacity. This was caused by restarts in 1983–84 of previously mothballed smelters, as well as by government-owned aluminum producers outside North America, who ignored low prices and maintained high production levels to protect jobs. Alcan's top managers concluded that the company's economic environment had changed radically. As part of its response to this situation, Alcan adopted a cost-cutting and rationalization program. In addition to cutbacks in the number of production workers, Alcan postponed construction of a major smelter in Laterriere, Quebec, pared investment in Latin America, sold marginal fabricating plants around the world, and withdrew from Africa. It also recognized the impaired economic value of its bauxite and alumina assets arising from significant excess of world production capacity in those areas and took a write-down of these assets in 1985 of approximately $200 million before tax. It also set out to reduce the number of levels of management and rationalize and reduce employee numbers throughout the company, including its head office.

Another response of the company to the environment of the mid-1980s was to increase and redirect R&D expenditures, particularly in the areas of product innovation and exploration (i.e., seeking out entirely new business areas). Alcan's R&D projects included a series of low-density aluminum lithium alloys for aircraft sheet, an integrated manufacturing process for aluminum-structured motor cars, a prototype high-performance light-weight freight rail car, and a revolutionary new packaging system for cooking frozen foods in microwave ovens.

Despite the increase in R&D expenditures, Alcan's efforts remained smaller than competitors, notably Alcoa, which spent $120 million on R&D in 1985 while Alcan spent $77 million. Earlier, in 1979, Davis described Alcan's R&D efforts as follows:

> In some processes we're leaders but we can't be leaders in everything. Alcoa will lead in certain fields and another company will lead in another field. We're making an effort to have a better interchange of technology, for example with our Japanese associated companies.[6]

---

[6] *Executive*, December 1979.

In 1984, Alcan's chief scientific officer, Hugh Wynne-Edwards, had described the significance of R&D at Alcan as follows:

> Culver has given us a mandate to be on the cutting edge of technological change. We're in a horse race with the rest of the industry and with manufacturers of other materials. Everybody is trying to out-innovate the other guy.[7]

The president of Alcoa provided the following perspective on the industry's R&D efforts:

> After aluminum replaced steel in the U.S. beverage can market in the 1970s, we somehow let ourselves think that we'd found every practical use for aluminum. Lately, we've realized that aluminum is still a wonder metal and that we have many more mountains to climb.[8]

Despite the various internal efforts by Alcan to deal with lower prices and excess capacity, some observers concluded that the prospects for Alcan heavily depended on uncontrollable external forces. As one analyst even noted: "Alcan is at the mercy of events beyond its control."[9]

The next section covers some of the external forces which were affecting Alcan's prospects.

Competitive Forces

One of the most important structural changes in the aluminum industry to affect Alcan was the increase in the number of competitors. The number of non-Communist aluminum producers grew from 16 in 1950 to more than 80 by 1986, including a number of oil-fired plants in OPEC countries. The dominance of an oligopoly of companies—including Alcan, Alcoa, Reynolds, Kaiser, Pechiney, and Alusuisse—that once controlled up to 80 percent of non-Communist capacity was being undermined.

By the 1980s, a number of the new competitors, lacking a marketing network, turned to middlemen such as metal traders. One metals trader, Marc Rich, controlled a million metric tonnes, the equivalent of half of Alcan's output. Rich reportedly made annual profits in the 1980s of up to $150 million (U.S.) pretax on aluminum-related activities.

Most of Alcan's biggest competitors moved or planned to move their activities downstream, devoting more attention and money to higher value-added activities or diversifying. For example, Alcoa, in an effort to be known as a materials company rather than an aluminum company, hoped to reduce its dependence on aluminum from 85 percent of its sales to 50 percent by 1995. To fulfill this strategy, the company purchased fibre optics, ceramics, and plastic packaging ventures.

---

[7] *Canadian Business,* January 1984, p. 16.

[8] Ibid.

[9] MacLean's, July 8, 1985.

One reason for the increase in the number of competitors was that more and more governments, particularly in developing countries, built smelters to create jobs and to earn foreign currency. By 1986, state-owned aluminum producers accounted for about a third of world smelting capacity, up from less than 6 percent in the early 1960s. One observer noted: "Aluminum has changed from an orderly, stable business controlled by more or less like-minded, profit-oriented players into a more chaotic free market."[10]

Impact of Government

Part of Alcan's operations in Quebec almost became state owned. During the 1960s, Rene Levesque, the energy minister in the Liberal government of Jean Lesage, persuaded his colleagues that it would be in the public interest to gather Quebec's hydro resources under the umbrella of a state-owned enterprise. As it turned out, Levesque nationalized 11 utilities and power distribution companies but exempted Alcan's power plants. Some observers saw this as a recognition that Alcan's contribution to Quebec as an aluminum exporter was important and valuable. Nevertheless, the Quebec government took other actions which affected Alcan's competitive government. In attempting to fulfill its goal of making Quebec an international centre of aluminum production, the Quebec government in 1963 encouraged Reynolds Metals Co. of Richmond, Virginia, to come to Quebec. Reynolds established a wire and cable fabricating plant in Charlevoix and a smelter in Baie Comeau. Similarly, in 1986, Pechiney, a state-owned French metal and chemical conglomerate, encouraged by the Quebec government with favourable power rates, started up a smelter at Becancour on the St. Lawrence River. In this latter case, the Quebec government took a 25 percent equity interest.

Although Alcan had always aimed to retain some emphasis on primary aluminum production, there was on-going pressure on the company by the Quebec government to integrate forward. The government was anxious to see levels of employment maintained. As one former Quebec industry minister noted: "If Alcan rationalized in the primary activity, it must invest in secondary and tertiary activity."

In responding to the pressures, Alcan argued that fabricating plants needed to be close to markets. Nevertheless, Alcan had made investments in Quebec for the fabrication of some commodity products such as coiled sheet and wire bar. These investments employed about 10 percent of Alcan's Quebec work force, which in 1986 amounted to about 10,000 people.

Despite the political pressures, the thrust of Alcan's strategy in Quebec was clearly primary production. One observer provided the following analysis in 1983 of Alcan's relations with the Quebec government:

> Alcan's vitality and political sensitivity have made it extremely popular in Quebec. Provinces that balk at its plans for expansion and exploitation of hydroelectricity

---

[10] *Fortune*, February 21, 1983, p. 128.

have found, to their peril, that Alcan can always come home to Quebec to find room to grow. In 1982 in Manitoba, when politicians began to argue over the merits of an Alcan smelter operation, Alcan cancelled its feasibility studies and promptly exercised an option on 2,000 more acres of land in the Saguenay. As a result about $2 billion worth of modernization will take place there over the next two decades. . . . That is touted by the company and the provincial government alike as proof of the viability of investing in Quebec. In fact, Alcan remains one of the few companies investing money in the province.[11]

Although Alcan may have had generally positive experiences with the Quebec government, this was not always the case with other governments. For example, in 1971, the government of Guyana nationalized Demerarra Bauxite Company, a subsidiary of Alcan. In Norway, Alcan had another frustrating experience with government as described by Davis:

> Norway, with all its hydroelectric power, seemed a very sound place for us. Our company there had very close commercial relationships with a fully owned government company. We provided all its aluminum oxide and took metal in return on a barter basis. So then we thought, "Why not put the two companies together on a 50–50 basis?"
>
> That worked pretty well for a few years but then the government's philosophies and objectives and our objectives started to go in different directions. . . . The outcome was that we sold them half our interest. After a few more years we both agreed that the government's objectives and ours were not identical. The government needed to maintain employment in the remote fjords. We were private enterprise-oriented. So we finally sold them the second half.[12]

Davis described the general pressures of government on the company in the following way:

> There is constant pressure, not only in Quebec but in Canada, in Norway, in every country we go into; they all feel that, if we don't carry the product one step further locally, then we're not doing right by the host government. This is always a bit of a battle.
>
> But if it's carried too far you could start doing things that are silly and just won't work. These are things that are a little hard for the politician to accept.[13]

Other government-controlled factors affecting Alcan's competitive position were currency and investment controls, withholding taxes, and changes in import duties and restrictions.

Slower Growth

Another external force affecting Alcan was a slowdown in the rate of growth of demand. Annual growth in world demand had slowed from 8 percent in

---

[11] *MacLean's,* April 4, 1979.
[12] *Executive,* December 1979.
[13] Ibid.

the early 1970s to less than 2 percent by the 1980s. In fact, during the recession in the early 1980s, there was a significant fall in demand and prices, particularly in North America and Europe.

One cause of lower overall growth was increased product sophistication, which meant the reduction in size, gauge, and weight of aluminum materials. Culver estimated that because of lighter, thinner, and stronger versions of existing products in the canning, automotive, and general extrusion markets, aluminum sales in 1983 in the Western world were at least 1 million tonnes a year less than would have been made for the same output of finished product in the mid-70s. Another important factor was significant growth in the recycling of aluminum scrap, primarily in the beverage can area. Culver estimated that this had reduced primary aluminum demand by a further 1 million tonnes a year from the level that would have been required in the mid-70s for the same number of finished units.

Substitute products were another cause of the overall decline in demand growth for aluminum. For example, vinyl had damaged the aluminum siding business, and plastics, benefiting from low oil prices, represented a growing threat. New types of oven-proof cardboard moved into the food packaging market. Another cause of the decline in demand was the lack of product innovation. Critics claimed that the industry's last major product innovation was the aluminum can.

The slowdown in demand growth affected prices. Before the 1981–82 recession, ingot spot prices touched $1 a pound, but after a peak in 1983, prices plummeted in 1986 to 52.8 cents a pound. Price movements also became more exaggerated beginning in 1978 when the London Metal Exchange (LME) started trading aluminum contracts. One Alcan manager described the effect of the LME as follows: "The LME reflects a game of paper rather than physical metal. As a result, prices for aluminum have become more volatile."

Alcan's Strategy and Strengths

As Culver considered the new mission statement and the various pressures on the company, he reviewed the five elements of Alcan's strategy he had outlined to shareholders in 1984:

1. Dispersal and sufficiency in our raw material base of bauxite and alumina.
2. Enlargement of our smelter base only where we have our own power, or can expand incrementally, together with a 30-year modernization programme for our Quebec smelter system.
3. Selective growth in fabricating, including finished product businesses which support upstream strengths.
4. Development and application of market-related technology in both existing and new fields.

5. Selective investment in nonaluminum sectors related to our
strengths.

Along with the strategy, Culver also reviewed the company strengths as
he described them to shareholders in 1983:

> Alcan's strengths are people, power, and internationality. . . . Alcan people,
> individually and collectively, represent an enormous wealth of skills and experi-
> ence, operating in a decentralized organization in many countries of the world.
>
> Alcan's owned Canadian power position is an undoubted advantage, but one
> which is needed in our production of primary aluminum, to offset the logistical
> disadvantages of the distance of our Canadian smelters from both their raw
> material sources, and their major markets.
>
> Our hydroelectric assets are the result of past investment decisions that were
> both imaginative and risky, and some of which preempted for many years Alcan's
> ability to develop in other directions. The benefit of those decisions is, however,
> increasingly clear and valuable.
>
> Our third major strength, internationality, is also one which is becoming more
> valuable with time. As the economic geography of both the supply and the demand
> side of the industry changes, Alcan's ability to deal with the political dimensions,
> to manage the finances, the technology transfer, and the market development in
> a truly international industry, is a vital strength.

The June Conference

In contemplating the idea of a June conference to discuss his drafted mission
statement, Culver wondered what kind of role the conference and mission
statement could or should play in the overall strategic planning process of the
company. Under Nathanael Davis, the planning process could be described
as reactive. The various subsidiaries around the world submitted annually
their plans for the next two years and these were used by head office to
allocate scarce resources (usually capital and metal). There were also long-
term "strategic plans" where head office asked: "What are your ambitions
for the next 7 to 10 years?" These provided the background for the approval
of major projects which could dominate the company's capital spending and
financing activities for a period of years. In describing Alcan's strategic planning horizon, and the company's future, Nathanael Davis commented in 1979
as follows:

> It's unreasonable to try to look too far ahead. Over a 10- or 15-year span I see
> the company continuing to grow very much along the same general lines as in
> the past. We do have opportunities. The demand for aluminum may not grow
> quite as rapidly as it has—it was extraordinarily rapid growth—and our plans are
> based on a more modest growth rate. Aluminum is a very useful material that
> continues to have a good future and our company is fortunate in having the basic
> materials needed to let us compete effectively over the next decade or longer.

However, we have to keep exploring new technological opportunities to reduce the cost of production and develop new ways of production. Aluminum was long considered a growth industry in financial terms. Profits were growing year by year and aluminum stocks were selling at 20 times earnings. It's no longer considered a growth industry by the financial fraternity; it's considered "cyclical." But in terms of volume it had continued to be a growth industry. Indeed, volume may have been our problem. We produced too much and didn't make a proper return on our investment. Now we're doing much better. . . .

This industry went through many, many years of very low returns. It helped the market of course because aluminum was being sold at very low prices. But the true challenge ahead is to maintain our improved earnings.[14]

With Culver's new mission statement, Alcan's strategic planning process could be seen as more proactive and participative, that is, the senior managers of the company would have an opportunity to help set the company's spending priorities and earnings target, recognizing the constraints and challenges faced by each part of the Alcan Group. The ensuing central decision making would then be in the context of a set of priorities which the CEO had adopted after full discussion.

One issue with the new mission statement was how it might be linked to the statement of Alcan's purpose, objectives, and policies (Appendix B), first published in June 1978. Nathanael Davis, chairman and CEO at that time, explained in the foreword that the statement was for distribution to all Alcan employees in all countries to strengthen their awareness of the basic general principles and policies which had guided the conduct of Alcan's business over the years. This document had emerged from consultation and participation of approximately 200 Alcan managers around the world. The statement was also distributed to Alcan's shareholders and was made available to others on an unrestricted basis.

The statement was reprinted without change in September 1984. In this reprinting, Culver added a foreword which indicated that the 1978 statement had stood the test of time. However, in 1986, Culver felt a new element would have to be added to the "purpose" section of the 1984 statement to make it consistent with the new mission statement. This element would state that the company would concentrate on those chosen aluminum activities in which the company expected to achieve an acceptable rate of return, as well as investment in other businesses, related to company strengths, with better long-term growth and earning prospects. Amending the 1984 statement would require a third printing of the statement.

One issue for Culver with the new mission statement was the likelihood of Alcan outperforming the Standard & Poor's 400[15] in the 1900s. Culver, who beneficially owned 36,500 Alcan shares (trading between 39⅞ and 48⅜ in the

---

[14] Ibid.

[15] Standard & Poor's is a financial index based on the return on equity of 400 industrial companies.

first quarter of 1986 on the Toronto Stock Exchange) and 13,300 shares subject
to options, was aware of criticism of the company's past strategies. One report
in 1984 noted:

> The world's major aluminum producers have long envied Alcan Aluminum Ltd.
> of Montreal its energy self-sufficiency. Until recently they have worked hard
> to streamline their plants in order to prevent Alcan—the industry's low-cost
> producer—from pricing them out of the market. Lately, however, the big U.S.
> producers have abandoned their attempt to beat Alcan at its own game. Instead
> they're responding to new and bigger threats: increased Third World production,
> the substitution of plastic and other materials for aluminum, and recycling. Ironi-
> cally, they may be better able to cope with these challenges than Alcan, which,
> some critics suspect, has been blinded by its sizable energy advantage to the need
> to find new uses for the metal and not just cheaper ways to make it.
>
>   As long as aluminum was a commodity business—in which all players sold
> pretty much the same products and competed mostly on price—the low-cost
> producer stood to gain the most. But these days the aluminum industry is becoming
> heavily oriented toward marketing as well as research and development. . . .
> Alcoa and Reynolds Metals Co. of Richmond, Va., the No. 2 U.S. producer, have
> ordered their R&D labs to emphasize new-product innovations over cheaper
> production methods. . . But the main factor responsible for altering the way
> most producers think is recycling. Recycling is both the boon and bane of the
> industry. "Aluminum wouldn't be a contender for all these new applications if it
> weren't for its very high recyclability," says Culver. But Culver concedes that
> recycling has one dreadful and obvious drawback: it reduces demand for the stuff
> in the first place. Some 56 percent of all U.S. beverage cans are now recycled;[16]
> the metal salvaged is equal to the annual tonnage of three large smelters. And if
> such catchy recycling efforts as Alcoa's "Cangaroo," a vending machine in reverse
> that pays for used cans, become widespread, the impact on raw-ingot producers
> such as Alcan could be severe. . . . Recycling is good news for such firms as
> Reynolds, which depends on used cans and other scrap for a quarter of its annual
> production. The capital investment required to produce a kilogram of aluminum
> from recycled materials is about one-tenth the investment needed for a kilogram
> of primary aluminum. Refining recycled aluminum also saves 95 percent of the
> energy used in producing primary aluminum; this has helped close the power gap
> between Reynolds and Alcan. "We're not looking to the auto industry only for
> the increased aluminum that we hope to sell to it," says a Reynolds spokesperson,
> "but also for the huge scrap value an aluminum vehicle would have. We're begin-
> ning to think of cars as very large cans."
>
>   . . . With aluminum demand likely to crawl along (growing at 4 percent per
> year, at best, for the next several years), observers feel that the only place to be
> is in semifinished-product manufacturing. And despite Alcan's heavy commitment
> to R&D, some feel it isn't moving far enough, fast enough. . . . It's the old
> Canadian problem of getting caught in the transition from a traditional resource-
> based company to a competitor selling value-added products in the global market.
> "Alcan still envisions itself as having a mission to be the raw-ingot supplier to

---

[16] The can market represented nearly 20 percent of total aluminum consumption.

the world," says Stewart Spector, an aluminum analyst with Tsai-Spector Research Associates Inc. of New York. "But the world is rapidly changing, and Alcan will be in serious trouble if it doesn't produce more exclusively for its own plants and cast off the role of being a producer's producer."[17]

Despite the criticism of Alcan, it still represented one of Canada's most formidable Canadian-controlled multinational enterprises. Nevertheless, given the long history and size of Alcan, Culver recognized that setting the company in any kind of new path would require a Herculean effort.

APPENDIX A
DRAFT OF MISSION STATEMENT

The Statement is nothing less than a call to arms. It will act as a catalyst for change within the Company. In due course the effects of the action taken as a result of the Statement should touch everyone in the Company. The succinct, strongly worded Mission Statement sums up what Alcan intends to become and how it will get there.

[Following is a sentence-by-sentence review of the new Mission Statement with commentary by Culver about each key word.]

Alcan is **determined** to be the most **innovative diversified** aluminum company in the world.

Determined "The strongest possible commitment to change. Having averaged 9 percent ROE over 30 years and having developed an Alcan style and culture (much of which we are proud of and wish to keep) that has tolerated this mediocre performance, determination is required."

Innovative "This word should be accepted as applying both to our chosen aluminum business and to our new businesses. It does not only mean product and process innovation, which are vital, but also means a new look at the way we solve all our business problems.

"The result of innovation can create some excitement. A reduction in receivables; an increase in recovery; getting by with fewer bodies, etc.—excitement is made of that stuff, just as it is made of new discoveries successfully brought to market. Flawless implementation breeds excitement and excitement breeds flawless implementation. There is excitement in being acknowledged as the most successful aluminum investment. There is excitement in demonstrating how a global enterprise can excel even if based on a commodity!"

Diversified "Aluminum—the metal—is and remains great and growing. It has the qualities that other metals seek and it lends itself to modern living and modern demands for more value to the customer per ton of metal used. We are learning to sell it the way we did after the Second World War. Yes—we intend to be the most exciting *diversified* aluminum company, but not because there is anything wrong with the metal itself! The reason for diversification is the manner in which man has organized himself

---

[17] *Canadian Business,* January 1984, pp. 16, 19, 20.

to make and sell aluminum. What used to be a restricted number of integrated producers has rapidly become a large number of non-integrated producers. This de-coupling of a commodity-based industry has happened before. It changes who our competitors are. It will have much the same impact on our industry as de-regulation has had on the U.S. airlines. All of this restricts Alcan's future ability to achieve earnings growth. We could respond by downsizing—and staying within—our aluminum business. We might achieve a 14 percent ROE on the much smaller business. But we cannot achieve 14 percent ROE plus sustainable growth in earnings per share without diversification."

To achieve this position, Alcan will be **one, global, customer enterprise** committed to **excellence and lowest cost** in its aluminum businesses, with **significant resources** devoted to an **array** of new businesses with superior growth and profit.

One "Splitting Alcan into two pieces with two pieces would not accomplish our aim of changing Alcan. While there will always be different cultures in Alcan, we must strive for cooperation, mutual understanding and respect between them. In this way we will have a sense of *one* Alcan and not a divided Alcan."

Global "Alcan early on accepted the reality of the global economy. We are increasingly adjusting ourselves to that reality. Some of our best existing businesses are already 'global.'

"We should not confuse the above with the recent departures of Alcan from certain countries. There is no conflict between thinking globally and withdrawing from certain countries where our existing aluminum businesses are not meeting—and seem unlikely to meet—our profitability targets. Alcan never intended 'global' to mean presence in each country for the *sake* of presence."

Customer-oriented enterprise "There is a big difference between *knowing* that we exist to give services and value to our customers, and *living* that way. Those three words are in the Mission Statement to act as a *constant reminder*."

Excellence and lowest cost "An average of 9 percent over 30 years is not the ROE of a business that is characterized by excellence or uniqueness. To break out of that rut requires the total dedication and commitment of everyone in Alcan to achieving excellence and lowest cost in our cost-driven businesses. In some of our chosen aluminum businesses, as well as in our new businesses, we can also achieve high added value through uniqueness, but, even in these, it is important to have the lowest competitive costs."

Chosen "This is a key word in the Mission Statement. Whereas in the past Alcan fought hard (and expensively!) to grow and to gain market share across a broad spectrum of the global aluminum market, we are now only interested in those specific parts of the total market where we can achieve a minimum of 14 percent ROE. To accomplish this, Alcan will reshape its aluminum activities, concentrating its efforts on the businesses chosen for their sustainable competitive advantage, which should be able to meet the target return on a regular basis. Businesses which show no credible promise of reaching those targets will be sold, or, if that is not possible, closed down."

Significant resources "We mean business—no blowing hot and cold—no stop/go. The status quo is not acceptable. To outperform the S&P 400 in the 1990s, and to provide our shareholders with earnings growth as well as a good ROE, will require significant and sustained diversification effort. This effort will comprise a combination of many small experiments and some big bold moves."

Array "The route we are taking to outperform the S&P 400 in our diversified aluminum business will be to institute a number of small experiments and a small number of big bold moves. The former requires the acceptance of an admittedly wasteful growth culture in an atmosphere wherein efficiency takes a back seat to experimentation. The latter (big bold moves) requires management courage, an iron will and flawless analysis. There will be some 'market pull' companies as well as some 'technology push' companies. Because these two separate cultures must coexist within one management, that management must be 'bi-cultural.' "There will be many more starters than finishers."

In the 1990s Alcan will **outperform** the S&P 400.

Outperform "For our performance to be acceptable to our shareholders and also attractive to our investors, we need to outperform the S&P 400 over the business cycle, both in terms of ROE *and* sustained growth in earnings per share. It is the latter requirement which dictates our moves into new businesses."

APPENDIX B
ALCAN, ITS PURPOSE, OBJECTIVES, AND POLICIES 1978

Alcan's Purpose.   Alcan's purpose is to utilize profitably the risk capital voluntarily invested by the shareholders as a financial base to create productive facilities, employment, and skills devoted to the production and distribution of aluminum and related products to the public on an international scale. This purpose is based on the following convictions:

1. That aluminum possesses superior properties for a large number of uses, is derived from raw materials which are abundant, and, by combining lightness in weight and ease of recycling, incorporates qualities of energy conservation superior to many other materials;

2. That responsible, competitive, private enterprise is the most efficient system for producing and making aluminum available to the public at large. We believe that the role is complementary to the responsibility of governments to develop their own priorities and goals, to set legal and taxation frameworks for corporate enterprises within their jurisdictions, and thus to share in the economic benefits of industrialization;

3. That partnerships with national and local governments are on occasion appropriate, provided that our business objectives and their development aspirations are compatible.

Alcan's Objectives.   Recognizing that the conduct and effectiveness of an organization is highly dependent upon the quality of the people who comprise it, Alcan's ability to fulfill its purpose and to serve the following interdependent objectives is seen to require a complement of able employees who place a high value not only on the interests of the Company but also on the interests of other individuals and entities with whom they relate both inside and outside Alcan.

These objectives are:

1. To operate at a level of profitability which will ensure the long-term economic viability of the Company by providing a return on the shareholders' investment which

---

Note: Alcan's "Policies" are not reprinted in this appendix.

compares favourably with other industries of similar capital intensity and risk and will enable the Company to attract capital adequate to support its growth;

2. To maintain an organization of able and committed individuals in the many countries in which we operate and to provide opportunities for growth and advancement both nationally and internationally.;

3. To strive for a level of operating, technical, and marketing excellence which will ensure a strong competitive position in the various markets which we serve;

4. To recognize and seek to balance the interests of our shareholders, employees, customers, suppliers, and governments and the public at large, while achieving Alcan's business objectives, taking into account the differing social, economic, and environmental aspirations of the countries and communities in which we operate;

5. To maintain high standards of integrity in the conduct of all phases of our business.

CASE

3

BOMBARDIER INC.

In early March 1989, Barry Olivella, Bombardier's Vice President of Planning and Acquisitions, and his 28-person team had been at Short Brothers (Shorts) for three days and were well into the job of evaluating the company's operations. In late July 1988, Her Majesty's Government (HMG) had announced that the Belfast aerospace manufacturer would be returned to the private sector. Of the 11 firms that submitted preliminary proposals, Bombardier was one of three invited to participate in the due diligence process. With the 1986 acquisition of Canadair, Bombardier had catapulted itself into the aerospace business, and acquiring Shorts would give Bombardier the critical mass to become a significant industry player. But Olivella wondered whether the company's problems were too large and too fundamental. He had to make a recommendation to Laurent Beaudoin, Bombardier's CEO, at the end of the week.

Bombardier's History

Bombardier was a publicly traded company that was 60 percent owned by the Bombardier family. Based in Montreal, the company manufactured recreational vehicles, transportation equipment, and aerospace products, and provided inventory financing services for its distributors and dealers. In 1988, these activities generated a net income of $68.3 million on sales of $1.4 billion. Exhibit 1 shows that this was a several-fold increase over the company's position just a few years previously. Additional financial information is contained in Exhibit 2. Each of Bombardier's four industrial groups was responsi-

This case was prepared by Joyce Miller under the supervision of Professor J. Peter Killing for the sole purpose of providing material for class discussion at the Western Business School. Copyright 1993 © The University of Western Ontario

314

EXHIBIT 1 Bombardier Inc.:

FINANCIAL HISTORY
1983–89
Operations Summary
(millions of dollars)

	Years Ended January 31						
	1983	*1984*	*1985*	*1986*	*1987*	*1988*	*1989*
Sales by Continuing Industry Segments							
Transportation equipment	$193.8	$148.0	$221.3	$312.1	$403.6	$ 492.9	$ 347.3
Motorized coinsumer products	128.5	113.6	145.7	171.9	206.3	240.7	274.3
Aerospace	—	—	—	—	287.6*	554.7	630.7
Defence	90.5	132.8	33.7	64.7	92.0*	100.8	143.9
Total	412.8	394.4	400.7	548.7	989.5	1389.1	1396.2
Income (Loss) by Continuing Industry Segments							
Transportation equipment	14.8	25.8	30.1	20.2	32.1	48.0	46.9
Motorized consumer products	(13.8)	(13.3)	6.1	2.9	7.1	12.4	14.0
Aerospace	—	—	—	—	15.4*	39.7	34.8
Defence	8.7	15.3	3.5	2.5	0.4*	0.6	7.4
Financial services	1.9	1.3	0.9	1.4	(0.8)	2.1	5.7
Total	11.6	29.1	40.6	27.0	54.2	102.8	108.8
Income Taxes	5.2	11.4	16.2	10.8	11.4	23.8	19.9
Income from continuing operations	6.4	17.7	24.4	16.2	42.8	79.0	88.9
Income (loss) from discontinued operations	(0.3)	(11.4)	(14.3)	(0.1)	3.3	(12.2)	(20.6)
Net income	6.1	6.3	10.1	16.1	46.1	66.8	68.3

*Five months for the Aerospace segment and the Surveillance Systems and Military Aircraft divisions.
Source: Annual Reports

ble for its own operations and for long-term and short-term growth and profit. Almost 80 percent of sales were made in markets outside Canada.

The organization traced its beginnings back to 1942 and J. Armand Bombardier's invention of a tracked vehicle to carry passengers and cargo on snowbound roads in rural areas. Its transformation into a personal snowmobile, named Ski-Doo,® gave rise to a new sport and a new industry. In 1974, Bombardier began its diversification into mass transit by winning a contract to supply the Montreal Urban Community with subway cars. Bombardier subsequently delivered subway cars to New York and Mexico City, double-decker, self-propelled commuter cars to Chicago, light rail vehicles to Portland

---

® Registered Trademark of Bombardier

EXHIBIT 2   Bombardier Inc.:
Consolidated Balance Sheet (in millions of dollars)

	For the Years Ended January 31		
	1989	*1988*	*1987*
Assets			
Current Assets			
Cash and term deposits	$150.0	$109.9	$161.3
Accounts receivable	174.0	119.1	144.6
Inventories	220.2	247.3	114.9
Prepaid expenses	9.9	8.9	12.9
	554.1	485.2	433.7
Full Assets			
Land, buildings, equipment and other	638.1	450.2	401.4
Accumulated depreciation	378.2	251.3	221.0
	259.9	198.9	180.4
Investments and other assets	57.4	69.1	54.5
	$871.4	$753.2	$668.6
Liabilities			
Current Liabilities			
Accounts payable and accrued liabilities	$328.3	$297.2	$251.2
Income taxes	5.7	1.3	4.9
Long-term debt due within one year	5.4	5.1	5.8
	339.4	303.6	261.9
Long-term debt	70.6	65.4	74.1
Provision for severance pay and pension costs	41.6	9.5	8.2
Minority interest	12.9	—	—
Share capital	246.1	244.7	243.1
Retained earnings	160.8	130.0	81.3
	406.9	374.7	324.4
	$871.4	$753.2	$668.6

Source: Annual Reports

(Oregon), and push-pull commuter train cars to several northeastern U.S. states.

These projects were made feasible through the acquisition of key proven technologies, including the Budd and Pullman vehicle designs and the PeopleMover® and monorail systems developed by Walt Disney Company. These technologies added significantly to the company's range of production and gave Bombardier a clear edge in the North American mass transit market. As a result of a 1987 agreement with GEC Alsthom, Bombardier had also obtained the lead role in the marketing and manufacturing of TGV for North America. The TGV is the 300 kph high-speed French train that revolutionized mass transit in Europe. At least 20 corridors in Canada and the United States had potential for TGV lines.

In 1986, Bombardier took a 45 percent interest in the stock of BN Constructions Ferroviaires et Metalliques SA, a Belgian manufacturer of rolling stock. This was increased to 90.6 percent in 1988. BN gave Bombardier a critical foothold in the Western European mass transit market. Analysts estimated that the replacement market in Europe was worth $4 to $5 billion annually. BN was part of a consortium bidding for the Paris-London-Brussels TGV project and it was also part of a group vying for the production of shuttle trains for the tunnel link across the English Channel. BN operated three rail equipment plants in Belgium. Barry Olivella, Bombardier's VP of Planning and Acquisitions, remarked:

> When many firms make acquisitions, they spread out their resources too thinly. The reason we can expand quickly and control what we're doing is that we make sure we acquire good management, at the working levels and at the middle and senior management levels. We don't do things merely because strategically they make sense; they have to make economic sense too.

By early 1989, Bombardier held a 30 percent share of the transit equipment market in North America. The company produced a range of vehicles to meet urban, commuter, and intercity transportation needs. Although the transportation segment was Bombardier's profit engine, the company saw enormous potential in the aerospace sector.

The Move into Aerospace

In August 1986, Bombardier took a major step into the aerospace industry and virtually doubled its turnover to almost $1 billion with the acquisition of money-losing Canadair, Canada's foremost airframe manufacturer, from the Canadian federal government. Bombardier paid $120 million in cash together with a stream of royalty payments potentially totalling $173 million over a 20-year period. The government had earlier relieved Canadair of $1.2 billion of its $1.35 billion debt load, effectively absorbing the considerable development costs of a revolutionary, wide-body executive jet named Challenger.®

At the time of the acquisition, Canadair had 4,600 employees on its payroll and operated four plants in the Montreal area, including the main manufacturing and assembly plant at the Cartierville Airport. Since its formation in 1944, Canadair had built over 4,000 civil and military aircraft and produced components for defence contractors and aircraft manufacturers like Boeing, Lockheed, and McDonnell Douglas. Its CL-215 waterbomber, designed to fight forest fires, was world renowed. When Bombardier became Canadair's new owner, the company had delivered 126 Challengers and had another 11 firm orders booked.

Donald Lowe, an experienced executive who had built his reputation through what he called "change situations," took over the presidency of Canadair and reported directly to Laurent Beaudoin, Bombardier's CEO. Lowe's mandate was to get the new subsidiary, which had a highly centralized management structure, operating to its full potential. Lowe remarked:

> When we took over Canadair, one of the objectives we had was to force the decision making down into the organization where it belonged. We did this by divisionalizing the company into business units with their own responsibility for profit or losses. The guy at the top of the unit is the decision maker. We monitor his progress and he has to operate within certain policy guidelines, but he basically goes and does his business.

At the same time, Lowe's strategy was to broaden Canadair's operating base and make it less reliant on the Challenger jet. In October 1986, Canadair was awarded a controversial 20-year, $1.17 billion maintenance contract to provide technical support for the Canadian Forces CF-18 fighter aircraft. Canadair subsequently obtained contracts from the French and German governments to design and manufacture unmanned CL 289 airborne surveillance systems, so-called "drones," to gather intelligence on the battlefield. Canadair was also selected by France's Aerospatiale, and later by British Aerospace, to develop and/or manufacture major components for the Airbus A330/340 program. The Airbus programs were funded by several European aerospace manufacturers, backed by their governments, in an effort to develop a family of aircraft to compete with Boeing's product line. This was just one example of the trend in the industry to pool resources for technological development.

In August 1988, Bombardier decided to put $14 million into an advanced design study for a Regional Jet® based on the proven technology of the Challenger business jet. The Canadian government contributed $6.8 million towards the study in the form of a repayable loan. A decision on going ahead was expected by the end of the year.

The Regional Jet Project

The Regional Jet would be a "stretched" version of the Challenger. The Regional Jet would be a quiet aircraft with a 50-seat capacity, a speed of 850 kph, a 1,600 km range, and a U.S. $14 million price tag. Studies showed that passengers suffered discomfort travelling on slower, noisier turboprop aircraft on flights with a duration of over 1.5 hours. Bombardier believed that its Regional Jet would fill a niche in the market that would be worth $15 billion by the turn of the century. Company officials forecast worldwide demand for regional jets at 1,000 units over the next 10 years. Airlines were expected to purchase the Regional Jet to carry regional and commuter passengers directly to their destinations, to bypass congested airport hubs, and to utilize longer routes with thin passenger traffic.

Developing a regional jet would be a major step forward for Bombardier in the aerospace area. It would involve a major expansion of the company's activities in the medium term and would employ as many as 3,000 people by 1994–95, at which time the peak production level of 48 aircraft per year was expected to be reached.

Under existing aerospace support programs Bombardier believed it would be able to obtain repayable assistance of up to $86 million through federal and provincial programmes, to develop the Regional Jet. If the project were launched in the spring of 1989, the Regional Jet would be ready for delivery in mid-1992. Bombardier estimated it could bring its Regional Jet to market for about $250 million, well below half of what it would cost a competitor to build a completely new aircraft. There were currently no aircraft within this category, although Boeing's de Havilland division was considering adding a 70-seat Dash 8 to its turboprop line-up. It was also rumoured that the Brazilian manufacturer, Embraer, might announce a competing aircraft, but its earliest delivery would be mid-1993. Another possible direct competitor was Short Brothers' FJX. At this point, the FJX was in a preliminary design stage, but there was a lot of uncertainty about the project as a consequence of the British government's plan to privatize the company.

Short Brothers

In late July 1988, Peter Viggers, the Under-Secretary of State for Northern Ireland, announced that Short Brothers would be returned to the private sector. Although HMG preferred to sell the company as a whole, Viggers indicated that the sale of different parts of the business to separate interests would not be ruled out. Roy McNulty, Shorts' Managing Director, recalled:

> Viggers made the announcement without even advising us beforehand, and he defended the decision by saying that privatization had initially been proposed in 1984. Many people felt that the process started off being badly handled and believed the company suffered serious damage because of it. Right through to early 1989, trade union members were doing joint demonstrations with Harland & Wolff and the Electricity Commission, and they had launched a campaign, entitled 'Keep Northern Ireland in Full Employment.'
>
> The first thing I did was set up a Privatization Steering Committee to meet weekly and put together a plan to address the government, the workforce, and the community, as well as to develop an Information Memorandum with Kleinwort-Benson, HMG's financial advisor. We were very conscious of the need to manage this process, both inside and outside of the company. I didn't think that Shorts had to be a helpless pawn in privatization. We decided to take every opportunity to influence the process, including the possibility of making our preference for a particular owner known, if it came to that. We put together eight objectives for privatization (see Exhibit 3) and emphasized it was fundamental that the company not be broken up. Eventually, we got the unions to embrace these eight points and to work with management to prepare submissions for Parliament.

EXHIBIT 3   Bombardier Inc.:
Shorts' Key Objectives for Privatization

---

1. Maintaining the Company as a single unit.
2. Retaining the Short Brothers name.
3. Continuing as an integrated design and production unit in Northern Ireland.
4. Securing a major input of funds to give Shorts a proper capital structure for its future.
5. Proceeding with the modernization and re-equipment of Shorts so that we can compete on an equal footing with other aerospace companies worldwide.
6. Securing participation in a new civil aircraft project to replace the SD3 series when it eventually stops selling at an economical level some years hence.
7. Ensuring a continuing commitment to develop the business in Northern Ireland.
8. Retaining and increasing customer confidence.

Source: Shorts' Privatization Newsletter, March 1989.

The prospectus issued by Kleinwort-Benson on January 10, 1989, provided an overview of Shorts' activities and capabilities. Interested parties were asked to submit preliminary proposals by early February. No actual costing was involved at this point. HMG asked prospective purchasers to outline their aerospace activities and interest in the FJX project, the reason for acquiring Shorts, and what assurances they would be prepared to give regarding the future of Shorts' headquarters, R&D programmes, and its manufacturing base in Northern Ireland. Only a handful of the 40 expressions of interest in Shorts were seen as credible.

HMG judged that Messerschmitt-Bolkow-Blohm (MBB), a large German aircraft company and a partner in the Airbus consortium, was serious about acquiring Shorts. It built aerostructures for 150+ seat jets in connection with the Airbus program, had recently acquired Dannier, a turboprop manufacturer, and planned to enter the smaller jet aircraft category with the announcement of its MPC75 regional propfan. However, MBB dropped out before the due diligence process because of the upheaval it was undergoing in its acquisition by Daimler-Benz.

Britain's General Electric Company (GEC) and Fokker, a Dutch aircraft company, initially tendered separate indicative bids, which they subsequently combined. Although some people viewed this as an unlikely alliance, joining forces did enable the consortium to get on HMG's short list. Fokker was motivated by the need to protect its supply of wing sets. Shorts, which was struggling to produce wing sets on time, was its only supplier of these structures, and Fokker would have seen privatization as disruptive and a threat to its entire operation. On its own, Fokker would not have had the capacity to absorb Shorts, which was about the same size. GEC was interested primarily in Shorts' missile business, which some referred to as the company's "crown jewel." Given that GEC was a potential rival to Shorts' Startstreak missile project, HMG knew that the company would have a lot of sensitivity about opening its books to this particular competitor.

In addition to gaining a critical mass in the aerospace business, Bombardier, the only other serious contender, was interested in acquiring Shorts to strengthen its presence in Europe. Bombardier already knew something of Shorts from earlier discussions about mutual interests in producing a regional jet. In the end, Bombardier had decided to develop the Regional Jet on its own, and Shorts had continued to search for partners to work on its FJX project. Shorts believed that it was possible that in partnership with another firm's resources and assistance, the FJX could be developed as a head-on competitor to Bombardier's aircraft.

Barry Olivella had spearheaded Bombardier's acquisition activities since advising Laurent Beaudoin in connection with the Canadian acquisition and joining the company in March 1987. Over the years, Bombardier had acquired numerous technologies and successfully brought several organizations into its fold. Olivella reflected:

> The timing of Bombardier's move into aerospace was largely opportunity driven, and within two years, we had Canadair operating very profitably. As a consequence, I think we know something about the aerospace business and I think we know something about turning companies around. Of course, acquiring Shorts would be a more complex situation because the financial restructuring—getting rid of the debt, injecting equity, making the necessary write-offs and provisions for losses—would have to be done at the same time. In the case of Canadair, this restructuring was completed before its privatization. HMG is willing to partially fund the restructuring and facility upgrading, but its level of commitment will be determined within the bidding process.

From the prospectus alone, Olivella found it difficult to determine the source of Shorts' losses, although he suspected that the aircraft division was in trouble and that the company was losing money on the Tucano military trainer project as well as on the Fokker contract. Also, there was some question about the risk and feasibility of the FJX project. Nonetheless, the company was competent in the production of aircraft and components and even had composites capabilities that were superior to those of Canadair. As well, Shorts had developed critical know-how in the use of advanced composites to increase the strength and reduce the weight of aerostructures. However, the company had ancient equipment, much of it World War II vintage, and its facilities were scattered across many buildings and locations.

Another challenge was how to deal with the random terrorism carried out by the Irish Republican Army (IRA). Because of its high profile operation and ownership of the Belfast Harbour Airport, Shorts might someday find itself the target of IRA campaigns. Although the violence was regularly reported in the media, most residents claimed it did not affect their daily lives. Nevertheless, security costs would likely be relatively high compared to other industrial areas. As well, Shorts was currently at the centre of controversy over alleged anti-Catholic hiring practices, a controversy that stemmed primarily from the geographic location of the company's main facility in East Belfast and the demographic history of that area.

The Due Diligence Process

In early March 1989, Barry Olivella took a 28-person team to Northern Ireland to evaluate Shorts' operations. The GEC/Fokker group would be going through the same process in the following week. Kleinwort-Benson was present during these sessions to monitor the situation on behalf of HMG, to ensure that the process yielded the information required and to see that both parties were treated fairly. Although HMG expected the bidders to ask for certain warranties and indemnities, the government was intent on making a clean break in the privatization.

Olivella's plan was to review each of Shorts' divisions in depth and assess the company's resources, strengths, weaknesses, risks, potential, strategic position, and the possible synergies with Bombardier. After spending three days in Belfast, Olivella made several observations:

> Shorts is clearly part of the British scientific community and its people are plugged into leading edge defense research. The company is an established supplier to the UK Ministry of Defense, Rolls-Royce, British Aerospace, and Boeing, the latter two of which are also major Canadair customers. In addition, Shorts is a risk-sharing partner in Fokker's F100 wing programme and designs and manufactures nacelles (engine coverings and mountings) for the V2500 engine fitted to the Airbus A320 and the British Aerospace 146. This is an area where Canadair has no involvement. In fact, Shorts is arguably Europe's foremost manufacturer of nacelles. There could be some distinct possibilities here. Also, Shorts has an enormous engineering capability and we could look at having them do some of the design and manufacturing for the Regional Jet, possibly the fuselage or the wing.
>
> Shorts has a good marketing organization headed by Deputy Managing Director Alex Roberts, who is the driving force behind the FJX, with worldwide coverage. They've got 75 people working in the area and connections with all the major airlines. The fact that they can sell an ugly, unpressurized aircraft like the SD330/360 series into the commuter market indicates some considerable capability. What really is concerning me is the fact that the large losses are not all behind Shorts. They are losing money on virtually everything they do, and much of the work is under long-term contracts.

For the most part, Olivella's team was staggered by what they saw at Shorts. One person remarked:

> It's hard to comprehend and describe the condition of the facilities. It's so different from what you'd expect from a modern aircraft manufacturer. Most of their buildings are from the 1940s and are badly in need of repair (see Exhibit 4). The main factories are built on reclaimed land and there are a lot of foundation problems that make it difficult to use the assembly tooling effectively. Until recently, the social facilities were a disaster. The cafeteria is a typical war-time canteen and the washrooms are indescribable. In the past year, though, there have been some major renovations here.
>
> The composites and metal bonding facilities are cramped together, and the equipment is ancient. The missiles and composite areas are an exception. Some

of the company's equipment and technologies in these areas are actually quite impressive, with state-of-the-art capability in electronics, microelectronics, and small parts machining. Moreover, the Engineering Group is strong. They just need some direction. They've got nothing to work with; they need a proper working environment. Upgrading Shorts' facilitites would require £200 to £250 million. It would take four to five years to complete, and it would be on a scale virtually never seen in the aerospace industry.

I couldn't believe that Shorts could make some of the highly specialized aircraft parts with their equipment. The maintenance and operating people must have a lot of skill. They can deliver a product that meets the specs even though the machines they're using aren't designed to produce the required tolerances. One operator joked that if smoking was banned, the whole place would have been shut down long ago. He used cigarettes for packing during boring to make sure a piece came in at the proper angle. The British machine tool industry has all but disappeared over the years, and Shorts is maintaining 30 to 40-year-old equipment itself. People are not only making their own spare parts; they're replacing key bits of the system. This isn't just pieces of metal; it's electronics too. Shorts is an expert at doing this.

But the company is behind on many of its programmes because of chronic and acute shortages of parts for final assembly. The manufacturing systems and controls are generally poor. Projects are a scramble and chase to get out the door. The situation looks out of control. The Fokker wing contract, the mainstay of the aerostructures division, looks like a nightmare. It's based on a well-proven 1960s design, but is made up of 14,000 parts! The company has had some real delivery problems in the past on this. They were delivering 25 wing sets, when the demand was for 67. Last year, they produced 39. Right now, Shorts is trying to keep up by having 200 people at Fokker in Amsterdam install the wing control mechanisms and anything else that didn't get put on in Northern Ireland before the wing was shipped.

Olivella noted that over the past months and throughout the due diligence process, the seven unions representing the companies had initiated strikes, walkouts, and overtime bans in a protest over new working practices, which Shorts was insisting on. A trade unionist conveyed some of his concerns:

Why, when there is so much opposition to privatization, is the Government determined to destroy the Province's already unsteady economy, which could happen in the event of privatization? . . . If privatization is the best thing for the long-term future of Northern Ireland's economy and the future of the workforce, why the need for such strong-arm tactics? Why deceive the people of Belfast and Northern Ireland? When the livelihood of so many, all over the Province, depends on the engineering industry, and if the workforce is reduced or Shorts closes, what future is there for the young people and school-leavers?

In general, Olivella felt that the workforce was qualified and experienced although extensive retraining would be required as modernization proceeded. The median age was 38 years and employees averaged 10.5 years of service. Olivella elaborated:

Northern Ireland has a strong tradition of young men going into technical and mechanical apprenticeships and the universities have strong engineering faculties. As the only aerospace manufacturer in the Province, Shorts has no problem attracting new graduates. With 900 engineers on the premises, they have a tremendous capability. However, being the only game in town has its drawbacks. People don't move jobs a lot, and it can be extremely difficult to attract mid-career talent. People typically won't immigrate to Northern Ireland unless they have family there. As a consequence, you don't get the cross-fertilization effect that is so common in the North American aerospace industry where people are constantly on the move between companies.

Jackie McCune, who worked in Shorts' Communications area, offered her view of the situation:

There are overtones for anyone coming into Northern Ireland. Belfast has a west-east political divide. Shorts is located in the east in the predominantly Protestant area. For many years, people didn't venture across the city, and a short travel threshold still lingers. The company is under constant scrutiny from the Fair Employment Agency because the majority of employees are Protestant. Shorts is really a victim of historical circumstance in the current charges of anti-Catholic hiring.

McCune's boss, Tom Russell, noted that the company had undergone some significant changes since Roy McNulty had taken over as Managing Director from his predecessor, Sir Philip Foreman, in April 1988. He commented:

This used to be a highly centralized operation. The former Managing Director had his finger in every pie and on every pulse. There was no desire to push decisions down.

McNulty recognized the benefits of decentralization and the need for more open communication. He introduced team briefing and actively sought the views of senior management about the company's structure and culture. We were coming down the road on getting people to focus on what needed to be done. In late 1988, he invited questions from the workforce about privatization, and they fairly flooded in. Roy McNulty and Brian Carlin, the Resources Director, put a lot of effort into answering them in a newsletter to all employees.

We are pretty comfortable with what we're seeing from Bombardier. They've come in here with sensitivity and professionalism. It's obvious they've been through this process before. They seem to be serious about acquiring Shorts to run as an ongoing business. This isn't just about killing off competition to the RJ, and Bombardier doesn't come across as an asset-stripper. Of course, we are aware that the various suitors could be posturing simply to acquire us.

Based on what he had seen so far, Olivella believed that Bombardier could work with Shorts' existing management group:

They appear to have an understanding of the problems they are facing, and they seem to like us. I like the look of Roy McNulty. He knows what is going on in the business and he has the respect of the management team. He recognizes there is a need to reduce costs by at least 25 percent, and I feel he has the basic capability to reorganize with Bombardier's assistance and direction. However, there are still some areas where we need to do more homework and, in particular, to get a handle on where the company is on its contracts.

Olivella's Summation

Laurent Beaudoin, Bombardier's CEO, expected a full report from the due diligence team at the end of the week and a recommendation from Olivella about how to proceed in the event that the Bombardier senior management team reached a consensus to proceed toward acquisition of Shorts. Olivella remarked:

> We're not looking for efficiency savings as a result of the acquisition; the savings would have to come through a programme of modernization. Synergies with Canadair are fairly elusive except where we could combine participation in things like the Paris Air Show. What we're really looking at is turning Shorts around.
>
> I have concerns about the peculiar style of local violence in Northern Ireland, but we should be able to live with the situation as it has never affected Shorts directly and the people there seem to be able to carry on regardless.
>
> I think Bombardier has the financial resources to do the acquisition, but there are few other spare resources around and certainly not senior aerospace people. We could explain Bombardier's philosophy and way of operating and introduce some new production, technical, and financial control systems, but it would essentially be left to the management that's in place at Shorts to put together and carry out a strategic plan. If we go ahead, it would have to be conditional upon arranging funding from HMG to write off the debt, pay for some of the modernization, and look after the losses that are projected for the next four years or so for each of the contracts and programmes currently under way.
>
> The writing is on the wall that the Shorts 360 aircraft program will have to be phased out, but at the present time, we don't know of another complete aircraft program to replace it.

CANADIAN TIRE CORPORATION (CONDENSED)

In November 1981 Dean Muncaster, president and CEO of the Canadian Tire Corporation (CTC), was assessing the position he should take with respect to the takeover of White Stores, Inc., which was headquartered in Wichita Falls, Texas. Since 1977 CTC had been looking for an opportunity to expand to the United States and preferably into the Sunbelt states. For a price that was not to exceed $45 million (U.S.) pending a year-end audit, CTC would acquire White's 81 retail stores, 4 warehouses, trucking fleet, and access to more than 425 independent dealer-owned stores centered in Texas, Louisiana, Oklahoma, and 11 other states. It was now up to Dean Muncaster to decide if he should recommend to the board that Canadian Tire proceed with the purchase.

History of Canadian Tire

In 1922, two brothers, Alfred and John Billes, invested $1,900 and formed Hamilton Tire and Garage Ltd. in Hamilton, Ontario. They dealt primarily in automobile parts and servicing. The firm, renamed Canadian Tire, grew quickly and in 1927 had three stores in Toronto. During the 1930s, the company started supplying other automobile parts and service centres in Ontario. Prior to World War II, six stores existed in Ontario.

The Billes family demonstrated significant innovation during their early years, a trademark that remained as one of the cornerstones to the firm's

---

This case was written primarily from published sources by Mark C. Baetz and Ralph Troschke, School of Business and Economics, Wilfrid Laurier University. Copyright © 1986 by Mark C. Baetz; condensed, 1989.

success. For instance, the first CTC store on Yonge Street in Toronto in 1937 had stockroom clerks on roller skates moving parts to the sales counter for faster customer service time. CTC adopted computer-aided accounting and inventory control procedures as early as 1963. Throughout the 1970s, CTC built one of the most modern distribution networks in the country, utilizing the latest technology in warehousing and inventory control.

By the end of 1981 the firm had grown to 348 retail stores and 83 gasoline stations. The product line had been expanded to include hardware products, lawn-care products, sporting goods, and small household appliances. Internationally, CTC had purchased a 36 percent controlling interest in McEwan's Ltd. of Australia in 1979.

Much of the success of CTC was attributed by some observers to the leadership of Dean Muncaster, age 48, who had been involved with CTC since he was 12 years old. Muncaster had worked in his father's store in Sudbury during the summers while attending the University of Western Ontario and Northwestern. In 1957 he was hired by Canadian Tire as a financial analyst. Approximately two years later, he left Canadian Tire in Toronto and returned to Sudbury to be the manager of the Sudbury dealership held by his father. He returned to Toronto in 1961 as a vice president and became president in 1966. During his presidency, CTC's sales rose from $100 million to over $1.3 billion (1981), and after-tax net income reached $51.4 million or $4.05 per share. He was well liked and respected by CTC's dealer network and by Canadian financial experts.

Muncaster was faced with managing three divergent groups while steering CTC. The three groups were, first, Alfred Billes and his family; second, the heirs of John Billes headed by John's son, Dick; and, third, the dealer network. The two factions of the Billes family collectively controlled 60.8 percent of the voting shares in the corporation (representing only 8.5 percent of all outstanding shares) and were not always in agreement with one another. For example, Muncaster's decision to enter the Australian market was heavily contested between the two family groups, with Dick Billes in favour and Alfred Billes in opposition. The decision left its scars.

The Billes family was active in the corporation. They managed several stores and held directorships on the board. Their influence was not always evident to the general public as they shunned the limelight and the media.

The Canadian Tire Success Formula

CTC was extremely successful due to the corporation's emphasis on the dealer-run network, advantages incurred from its highly modernized distribution system, and a marketing program that clearly established its desired image in the minds of the consumers. The dealer-manager network was the cornerstone to CTC's success and essential in an understanding of corporate values and strategies.

The dealer-run stores were a type of franchise operation. CTC usually owned the building (87 percent of the time) and acted as the central buyer, distributor, national advertiser, and dealer recruiter. The dealer ran the store as his own business. He would buy all of his goods from CTC (approximately 6,000 of 32,000 products were mandatory), and most operational decisions (for example, personnel, local advertising, and so forth) were his to make. CTC wanted to blend the entrepreneurial spirit with that of a corporate manager. It was hoped that this arrangement would provide individual dealers with enough incentive to turn their stores into a success. The dealers did not have to pay franchise fees but had to invest a minimum of $50,000 into their location. They were free to reap as much profit as they could from their stores.

The corporation was very careful in its selection of prospective dealers. The ability to invest at least $50,000 was not the only criterion. Exhaustive examinations and interviews were utilized to trim the 1,000–1,200 applicants down to the final 50 trainees. The trainees spent three months of in-class training followed by six months of in-store training before posting to a store. Corporate support was always available after the training period on any retailing issue, and dealer-support group meetings were numerous. The system worked so well, in fact, that virtually no dealer failure was encountered by CTC.

The desire for revenues and profits was instilled through the dealer-run network. The advanced distribution system ensured that the parent corporation managed its costs to make its own profit. As well, by having the right merchandise in the right store at the right time, the system ensured customer satisfaction. The key ingredients in this distribution system were three fully automated one-storied warehouses (one in Edmonton and two in Toronto) that utilized robotics, conveyor belts, and computerized cataloguing of parts. The inventory levels of the warehouses, as well as those of individual retail operators, were monitored by computers. Reorder points of the retail and wholesale levels were automatically triggered on a nightly basis. This ensured a maximum delivery time of two days to retail outlets.

The result of CTC's advanced distribution system, from a customer's point of view, was constant availability and selection of thousands of products that CTC carried. This became a trademark of the firm. Inventories were also reduced, increasing CTC's inventory turnover and decreasing its carrying charges. This made profitability easier to attain for CTC and its retailers.

The constant availability and broad selection of numerous products were part of an image that CTC had built for itself through an effective marketing campaign. Consumers also came to know Canadian Tire as a retail outlet offering value with a reputation for low price. This was especially important during 1981 as inflation, interest rates, and unemployment all rose. The value-low price appeal attracted a lot of people who had turned into "do-it-yourselfers" during this period. The average purchase at a Canadian Tire store was $15, and these purchases were said to be interest-rate-proof as they were small "must" expenditures. While the average purchase seemed low, CTC would see approximately 2 million customers per week according to Muncaster.

The typical customer found it difficult to enter the store and buy just one item. Due to the firm's low prices and broad product lines, it was not uncommon to witness the typical customer filling up a shopping basket with various products.

Muncaster identified several additional key factors to CTC's success: (1) CTC became known as a place for "more than just tires," a theme employed in its advertising. Traditionally, 80 percent of CTC's customers had been male, but by 1981, the split was almost even. (2) To lure customers back to the store, the firm employed "Canadian Tire money," which was a form of discount coupons given to customers after each cash purchase. (3) Twice per year, 7 million catalogues listing the entire CTC product line were published and distributed to households across Canada.

These factors led to unusually high growth rates and startling financial successes for CTC. Exhibit 1 highlights the performance of the corporation during this period of high growth and image development. Walter Hachborn, general manager of Home Hardware Stores Ltd., CTC's major Canadian competitor, explained the success of CTC in the following way: "Canadian Tire has succeeded because of excellent marketing and superior merchandising combined with the fact that they were the first to fill a void in the Canadian retailing market. They happened to come along at the right time and place."

Suppliers to CTC were also impressed with CTC operations. One supplier noted: "We've been impressed by the energy levels exhibited by the CTC head office when negotiating contracts, and although they have pushed the cost of advertising our product in their catalogue on to us, we consider their organization as top-notch."

Despite the phenomenal growth, it was apparent to Muncaster and other senior CTC executives that CTC growth could not be sustained indefinitely. Since 1977 CTC had been following a master plan prepared by Muncaster for future growth. The strategy in 1977 was to blanket the Canadian market by expanding into British Columbia, as yet untapped, and by establishing retail outlets in any community or suburban area that could support a regular-size CTC store. It was estimated in 1980 that 65 percent of Canadians lived within 15 minutes of a Canadian Tire store, and it was felt that by 1985, the maximum penetration of 400 stores would be reached.

The strategy also called for growth into other countries and markets with an English language/cultural component as well as a similar economic base. The Australian entry had taken place in 1979, and the United States was earmarked for entry in 1981. Carrying the CTC concept into these countries was not expected to be difficult, and consumer acceptance was anticipated to be high.

The need to expand was foremost in the mind of Muncaster. Without further expansion, an adverse impact on operating performance was anticipated. Expansion in British Columbia was well under way by 1981, and CTC had attempted to diversify somewhat by getting into gasoline stations and a small automobile engine remanufacturing plant for resale of the engines at its stores. These developments merely held off the inevitable total market saturation by CTC.

The Australian venture into McEwan's, a hardware chain, was intended to allow CTC to enter Australia to gain a foothold, then to expand its opera-

EXHIBIT 1   Four-Year Review of Performance (dollars in thousands except per share amounts)

	1981	1980	1979	1978	1977
Comparative Income Statement					
Gross operating revenue	$1,340,764	$1,057,536	$935,753	$798,717	$718,114
Pre-tax income	100,432	72,240	69,583	53,938	52,240
Taxes on income	48,966	34,513	33,070	25,163	23,750
Income before extraordinary gain	51,466	37,727	36,513	28,775	28,490
Extraordinary gain	2,212	901	2,195	694	1,000
Net income	53,678	38,628	38,708	29,469	29,490
Cash dividends	9,936	8,487	7,017	10,435	5,800
Income retained and reinvested	43,742	30,141	31,691	19,034	23,690
Comparative Balance Sheet					
Current assets		435,183	343,372	312,831	277,894
Investments		44,151	49,371	1,823	1,014
Net property and equipment		266,854	244,496	235,989	218,209
Other assets		2,213	2,582	3,620	4,026
Total assets		748,401	639,821	554,263	501,143
Current liabilities		279,451	211,903	165,040	134,511
Long-term debt		136,387	136,361	138,377	142,317
Deferred income taxes		3,599	3,822	3,382	1,512
Shareholder's equity		328,964	287,753	247,464	222,803
Per Share Data					
Income before extraordinary gain	4.05	3.07	3.07	2.49	2.50
Net income	4.22	3.14	3.26	2.55	2.59
Dividends	.78	.69	.59	.90	.51
Shareholder's equity	30.44	26.75	24.20	21.40	19.59
Statistics at Year-End					
Number of associate stores		333	319	314	314
Number of gasoline stations		71	64	62	61
Number of Class A shareholders		8,665	9,310	10,435	10,035
Number of common shareholders		1,252	1,315	1,450	1,417

Source: For years 1977–80: Canadian Tire annual report, 1980; for 1981; Estimated.

tions and to conquer Australia as Canada was conquered. The Australian venture was a small one, involving only a $2.2 million investment for a 36 percent interest. However, McEwan's suffered losses of $1,837,000 (Canadian) in 1980 and $548,000 in 1981. While performance was improving, CTC was disappointed. The Foreign Investment Review Board of Australia had also made it clear that it would prohibit CTC from acquiring a greater than 50 percent share in the Australian firm. CTC decided to sell off the investment in 1982 and use the funds of the sale toward the costs of an entry into the United States.

The Australian experience put some pressure on the president of CTC to seek out a successful expansion opportunity whereby the firm could parachute its Canadian success formula and reap large rewards. The original timetable called for an expansion to the U.S. market. Muncaster had favored the Sunbelt states as they had exhibited the fastest growth in populations and incomes. Demographic trends from 1973 to 1981 definitely pointed to this area of the United States as a ripening market. Some disagreement existed in CTC management, as some favoured expansion to the northeast, where climatic conditions and automobile models tended to parallel those of the Canadian market more closely.

American/Sunbelt Retail Market Considerations

In its analysis of the Sunbelt area, CTC managers felt that no competitors had a stranglehold on the things that CTC did well. Given the successes in Canada which CTC had enjoyed even when the retailing was on a decline, the general consensus among the management in Toronto was that the Sunbelt market was a "sure-fire success." Long-term demographic studies were undertaken, and a heavy reliance was placed on their favourable findings (see Exhibit 2).

EXHIBIT 2   Sample Demographics for Texas

---

1. Texas was the second-largest state in retail sales.
2. Houston was the eighth and Dallas was the ninth in terms of ranking the size of metropolitan statistical areas.
3. Dallas was expected to increase by 12.9 percent in population from 1980 to 1984; Houston by 14.2 percent; the U.S. average was only 5.2 percent.
4. Mean income (1977):

Dallas	$19,443
Houston	18,340
New York	16,714
U.S. average	17,137

It was noted that only six major competitors existed for Canadian Tire in the Texas and Sunbelt markets: Sears Roebuck, Montgomery Ward, K mart, Builders Square, Home Depot, and Handy Dan. The first three competitors did, however, carry a lot of clout within the market. For example, Sears was heavily involved in auto parts and services, and it was not unusual for Sears to have 16 or more auto bays as opposed to 5–6 at White's. Wal-Mart, a potential entrant to this market and a major U.S. retailing force, had chosen at this point in time to forgo expansion into the major metropolitan areas in the state of Texas.

On a television documentary, one prominent retail market analyst in Houston described the market characteristics of the United States and, in particular, the Sunbelt states, as follows:

1. In any U.S. market, three markets were at work: a national one, a regional one, and one based on local climate.

2. Retailing in the United States, and more so in the Sunbelt, was highly competitive and dynamic (the rate of change was far greater than in Canada).

3. The Sunbelt market was witnessing an ever-increasing number of retail entrants who were scrambling to get into very specific market niches.

4. Corporate image and advertising had to be slanted to two very different groups: the English- and the Spanish-speaking populations.

5. Promotional campaigns should take into account a high degree of illiteracy and a variety of racial problems (for example, white versus black, white versus Mexican, Mexican versus black).

6. The impact of revenues flowing from oil after 1973 had created a "gold rush" where even poorly run businesses could make money. New people were arriving every day.

7. Every neighbourhood in this area varied due to its ethnic composition.

8. Shopping malls predominated since most consumers preferred one-stop shopping.

9. Sunbelt consumers were sophisticated, however, and would visit a variety of shops (usually specialty stores) within one mall to accomplish their shopping needs.

10. Stores in the United States tended to be far larger, especially department stores, where 25,000 square feet would be considered a small area.

11. The U.S. consumer enjoyed a wide option of shopping choices (for example, it would have been typical to see 40 brands of an automotive product available on one shelf).

12. Older downtown areas were considered marginal and these "strip centres" tended to cater to the neighbourhood traffic.

13. Hardware and sporting goods stores in Texas were a rarity as every major store sold this kind of merchandise.

14. Some observers considered the Houston area as the toughest market in the United States.

15. Consumers needed to identify with a firm's message (that is, a reason for its existence) in order for it to survive and prosper.

White Stores, Inc.

The White Stores were held by Household International Ltd. of Chicago, which was one of the largest retailers in the United States. At approximately $150 million (U.S.) in annual sales, White's represented only 4 percent of Household's revenues. It was an insignificant holding to this large firm and thus received very little attention from its owners.

Although White's was losing money, CTC felt that if the price was low enough, it could refurbish the units and have them take on a CTC philosophy and market appeal. It was felt that a time frame of two or three years would be necessary before White's could break even and start to contribute to corporate profits. It was felt that the added top management attention and CTC's successful Canadian strategy could turn this firm around and represent a springboard for further U.S. expansion.

With White's, CTC would be acquiring 81 retail outlets, access to supply 425 independent dealer-owned stores, and four warehouses. The chain of stores covered Texas (the majority), Louisiana, New Mexico, and Oklahoma as well as 10 other states. Approximately half of the White-owned outlets were on leased properties, while all of the real estate (that is, land and buildings) of the other half were owned by White Stores. The price tag of a maximum of $45 million (U.S.) seemed reasonable to CTC executives when compared to recent costs of $2.5 million per store to establish new outlets in British Columbia. Exhibit 3 shows a proposed financing scheme for the acquisition.

CTC saw other positive factors in the purchase option. The White Stores name was long established, and therefore CTC assumed the name would be a source of loyalty and brand recognition. White's had a store size (approximately 25,000 square feet) that was similar to that of the typical CTC store. As well, like CTC, White's had only a few brands for their products. In general, White Stores did many of the same things that CTC did: automotive service and parts sales; and other broad product lines were available which were similar to CTC except that White's carried furniture as well. This probably would be dropped if the purchase was made. Plenty of warehouse capacity existed. It was estimated that the four warehouses could conduct two to

EXHIBIT 3   Purchase of White Stores—Financing (Canadian dollars in thousands)

Net working capital to be acquired		$ 12,134
Property and equipment, including capitalized leases and leasehold interest	$35,658	
Long-term portion of capital lease obligations	(287)	35,371
Other assets		208
Net assets to be acquired		$ 47,713
The effect on consolidated working capital is:		
Use of working capital:		
Payment on closing		$ 15,904
Promissory note due December 31, 1982		10,603
		26,507
Working capital to be acquired		(12,134)
Net use of working capital		$ 14,373

three times their existing volumes without any further capital. The current warehouse utilization rate varied between 30 and 50 percent. The infrastructure for expansion, therefore, was in place.

There were some concerns with an acquisition of White Stores. The locations of many of the stores were not in prime commercial or retail areas but, rather, in local neighborhoods. In some of these neighbourhoods, the people were Mexican and could not read or understand English. CTC proposed to gradually relocate these by establishing a greater concentration of stores in prime retail space in the lucrative Dallas–Forth Worth market. Further, the 81 stores owned by White Stores were not dealer operated but company owned and operated. CTC felt that this would have to change and become a number one priority in terms of introducing its philosophy and corporate objectives. Although CTC would prefer a dealer network to replicate the strategy in Canada, some of the states containing White Stores locations prohibited exclusive distributor-dealer relationships because of antitrust legislation. Finally, most of the stores were in desperate need of refurbishing. A lot of the outlets were 20 to 30 years old and looked it. CTC did not feel that this would be a problem as it had anticipated having to pour up to an additional $100 million (U.S.) over the following 2½ years into the project.

Other Options

Other growth options had been tossed around CTC's corporate office in Toronto. One option being considered was to access the U.S. market by building a new chain from the ground up and, therefore, not be confined by an existing organization's limitations and problems. However, costs and the time commitment to establish a major foothold made this a difficult option to pursue. Another option was to search out an acquisition in the nearby northeastern U.S. states. One CTC executive who favoured this option noted: "We should expand to a market that is similar to our own—with the same climate, the same autos, and the same kind of products. A place that is close enough, that if there is a problem we can do something about it." But this meant ignoring the fastest-growing segment of the United States, namely, the Sunbelt. A third option involved oil and gas opportunities in Canada. The existing Liberal government in Ottawa heavily favoured Canadian involvement in this industrial sector. The difficulty here was a lack of expertise on the part of CTC's management in this field. A fourth option was vertical integration. The manufacture of CTC products would require a massive capital investment into a field where CTC again had little expertise, and production runs for only CTC dealers would not always prove economical. Furthermore, due to CTC's large size, it already controlled a fair amount of power in distribution channels and could, therefore, already influence prices to some extent. Finally, CTC could turn to real estate sales. The firm had already engaged in some of this type of business and had made a small amount of money at it. Interest rates, however, were disturbingly high and unstable. Furthermore, the risk involved in a massive venture of this nature might not have been acceptable to CTC shareholders.

Muncaster had a difficult decision ahead of him. Growth in Canada for CTC would peak in approximately three to four years, so the groundwork for a new growth spurt would have to be laid down shortly. Shareholders would not react favourably to a flattening out of earnings per share after 1985. The White Stores acquisition would involve a major refurbishing program to bring the White Stores up to par, and this would create a temporary short-term drain on CTC's earnings.

The Turnaround Strategy

As the president and executive vice president of CTC more closely examined White Stores, they agreed on the following turnaround strategy if they were to acquire White's:

• There would be an aggressive renovation schedule at a cost of $100 million (U.S.) to be completed by the end of 1983. Up to 22 stores would be closed at any one time for up to two months for the renovation.

• CTC dealers would be brought in to run some of the stores with a goal of 81 dealer-run stores by the end of 1983.

• The merchandise mix (currently at 23,000 items) would be phased in gradually. (See Exhibit 4 for existing mix and other information on the typical store.)

• More money would be spent on advertising than was spent by the

---

EXHIBIT 4   Typical White's Store/White's Auto Centre

Typical store size in square feet (excluding auto bays):	
Gross area	24,000 sq. ft.
Selling area	14,000
Percent selling area to gross area	58%
Number of auto service bays	5–6
Store focus and sales mix:	
Auto	10—50%
Hardware	15–20
Lawn and garden	15
Sporting goods	15
Housewares	10
Electronics, miscellaneous	5
Percentage of products under promotion discounts	50
Typical inventory (at cost)	U.S. $900,000
Number of products carried	22,000
Final retail gross margin	16–22%
Store sales per year (breakeven point)	U.S. $2.5 million

---

average U.S. retailer in order to develop a clear image. The predominant form of advertising would be flyers.

• The White Stores name would be retained to take advantage of existing customer loyalty.

• In order to gain market share and increase store traffic, White's would use loss leaders.

• In order to help dealers finance their inventories, credit would be given quite freely, although at the prevailing interest rates. If a dealer could not afford a shipment of goods, the price to the dealer would be lowered and the difference added to the notes payable to White's.

• No additional capital would be required to upgrade warehousing facilities since the four warehouses were remaining at 30–35 percent capacity.

• The independent dealer network would be reduced from the existing 425 to 300 stores by cutting off the outlying dealers.

Muncaster summarized the strategy: "We plan to change their [White's] merchandise offering substantially. . . . We believe the appeal will be in a merchandise offering which you see in a Canadian Tire Store." With this strategy, CTC expected White's to break even by the third year.

CARON FURNITURE LTEE.

On May 20, 1987, Yves Richard, president of Caron Furniture Ltee. of St. Jean, Quebec, was assessing Caron's future U.S. export strategy. Caron, one of Canada's larger producers of wood office furniture, currently exported its products via a six-person company sales force and 11 manufacturers' representatives, who in turn serviced 1,700 dealers in the United States. Two options for the U.S. market were being considered: status quo or increased direct investment in showrooms and company sales staff. If the second option was chosen, Richard would have to decide on both the level of investment and the geographic focus. The larger question that loomed was the role the U.S. market should play in Caron's future.

To describe the context in which Richard had to make this decision, information about the North American furniture industry and the history of Caron Furniture Ltee. will be first presented.

The North American Office Furniture Industry

From 1982 to 1985 North American office furniture production increased at an annual rate of 18.7 percent, going from $5.6 to $9.8 billion (Exhibit 1). Growth slowed in 1986, with U.S. production increasing by only 4.4 percent. A 3 percent increase was projected for 1987. Demand for medium-price office furniture was forecasted to grow between 7 percent and 16 percent annually over the next decade.

This case was prepared by Jonathan Calof, under the direction of Professor Paul Beamish. Certain names have been disguised; however, essential relationships are maintained. Copyright © 1988, The University of Western Ontario.

EXHIBIT 1   The North American Office Furniture Market and North American Furniture Production (1982–1987)

	(Cdn $ millions)			
	1982	*1983*	*1984*	*1985*
Canada				
Wood/other	$ 204	$ 323	$ 379	$ 482
Metal	313	256	321	363
Total Canada	517	579	700	845
United States				
Wood	1,414	1,592	1,942	2,290
Metal	3,687	4,639	5,640	6,684
Total United States	5,101	6,231	7,582	8,974
Total North America	$5,618	$6,810	$8,282	$9,819

	Selected Furniture Production Segments (Cdn $ millions)*					
	1982	*1983*	*1984*	*1985*	*1986*	*1987 (est.)*
Chairs						
Wood Canada	14	14	16	22	39	31
Wood United States*	351	432	540	612	711	788
Metal Canada	79	75	85	96	104	140
Metal United States	870	955	1,231	1,537	1,734	1,866
Exports Canada	28	24	23	28	32	38
Desks						
Wood Canada	46	55	65	80	92	111
Wood United States	314	347	435	468	531	573
Metal Canada	29	30	30	32	34	35
Metal United States	251	252	350	360	405	437
Exports Canada	19	25	39	50	48	52

* 1986 and 1987 U.S. figures are estimates, based on 12 years average annual growth. Exchange rate as of December 31 used to convert U.S. sales to Canadian dollars.

Source: *Statistics Canada* 35:006 Quarterly Shipments, Office Furniture Industry. U.S. Commerce Department 85-9633, 87-7411, 83-18541, Office Furniture Industry.

The North American office furniture industry was highly competitive and fragmented, with some 700 office furniture manufacturers in the United States and 160 in Canada vying for market share. The acknowledged market leader in 1987 was Steelcase with a 21 percent market share in the United States and extensive sales in Canada. Steelcase was a privately held company, with 1986 sales of $1.4 billion (U.S.). Their primary product lines were metal office furniture, storage units, and office systems. Steelcase also produced wood office furniture. Their products were distributed through a wide North American distribution system which included 550 dealers in the United States. Steelcase prided itself on its delivery system which it claimed was 99.5 percent on schedule.

The number two firm, with a 7 percent market share in the United States, was Herman Miller. In 1986, its sales were $531.6 million, with net income of $37.8 million. Like Steelcase, Herman Miller produced both wood and steel products. Known for its marketing innovativeness, Herman Miller had within the past year announced numerous sales incentives including five-year product warranties, trade-in allowances of up to 100 percent, guaranteed delivery dates, and an Office Pavilion dealership program; which provided incentives such as service and management support to dealers in certain locations who enter into partial exclusivity agreements with Herman Miller. As well, Herman Miller planned to hire people for the pavilions who would call on and service small and medium-size businesses.

The office furniture market was composed of two distinct segments: wood and metal. Metal furniture utilised mass-production technologies and was targeted to a broad market. Competition was primarily on the basis of price. In 1985, metal office furniture sales were $7 billion (Exhibit 1), 71 percent of total office furniture sales. Metal sales had increased by 14.5 percent annually over the past 13 years.

Wood furniture was generally targeted to executives and professionals. In 1985, wood furniture production totaled $2.8 billion. Sales of wood office furniture, which 20 years ago had accounted for one-fifth of the office furniture market, accounted for 28 percent in 1985 and were expected to increase by 15.8 percent annually over the next 10 years—a rate greater than that of metal. In 1987, wood office furniture production was expected to reach $3.6 billion.

Between 1982 and 1985, many companies in the wood office furniture industry experienced strong gains in both sales and earnings as a result of increased demand and increased production efficiency. Shipments per employee increased by 39 percent in the United States, while in Canada it increased by 13 percent (Exhibit 2). In 1984, the profit margins for the largest U.S. wood manufacturers averaged 10.6 percent.

Wood furniture was usually produced using either batch or job shop technologies. Competition was along the lines of product quality, price, and design. The nature of the product yielded somewhat limited opportunities for automation; thus, capital entry barriers were rather low. This resulted in a proliferation of small firms: over 77 percent of all firms employed less than 50 people. However, due to distribution dynamics which favoured larger, more established firms, sales were somewhat concentrated. In Canada, five firms accounted for 38 percent of all production activity, while in the United States, eight firms accounted for 40 percent. The major U.S. markets were located in the Eastern United States (Exhibit 3), while in Canada major markets were in Ontario and Quebec (Exhibit 4). Approximately 67 percent of Caron's Canadian sales were in Quebec.

The office furniture market can be further subdivided into the following product categories: chairs, desks, tables, filing and storage units, office systems/

EXHIBIT 2   North American Wood Furniture Market (Miscellaneous Statistics; 1983–1985)

U.S. Industry (wood)	U.S. $ millions		
	1983	*1984*	*1985*
Shipment value	$1,167	$1,478	$1,505
Materials	473.4	586.7	557.4
Total payroll	324.0	406.6	410.5
Production payroll	212.1	272.4	270.0
Employment—000 workers	20.8	24.8	23.7
Production—000 workers	16.6	19.6	18.5
Materials/dollar sale	.406	.397	.370
Payroll/dollar sales	.182	.184	.179
Sales/employee—Cdn $000	69.8	78.8	88.8

Canadian Industry (nonmetal)	Cdn $ millions*		
	1983	*1984*	*1985*
Shipment value	$256.0	$321.2	$363.3
Materials	108.4	136.4	149.4
Total payroll	68.9	87.2	101.9
Production payroll	50.0	64.1	73.6
Employment—000 workers	3.6	4.2	4.8
Production—000 workers	2.8	3.5	4.0
Materials/dollar sale	.423	.425	.411
Payroll/dollar sales	.195	.200	.202
Sales/employee—Cdn $000	71.3	76.1	75.0

* Exchange rate as of July 31 was used for conversion.

Source: *Predicast* 1987. *Statistics Canada* Cansim matrix 5477–Nonwood Office Furniture Firms.

panels, and panel components. Caron's main product lines were wooden chairs and wooden desks, which accounted for 80 percent of sales. In 1987, total North American wooden chair production was expected to reach $819 million (Cdn), while wooden desk production was forecast to be $684 million (Exhibit 1).

Wooden Office Furniture Industry: Competition and Distribution

Office furniture firms can be divided into three size classes: large (greater than 500 employees and sales greater than $50 million), medium (100 to 500 employees and sales up to $50 million), and small (less than 100 employees). In 1985, there were approximately 15 large firms in the United States and one in Canada. These large firms had diversified product lines, with products at multiple price points. As well, they generally diversified either into other industries (e.g., Kimball also produced pianos) or into both the metal and

EXHIBIT 3 Top Markets in the United States

City and State or Province	Sales (Cdn $000s)*
New York, New York	$156,039
Chicago and area, Illinois	121,661
Houston and area, Texas	58,191
Detroit/Ann Arbor, Michigan	56,313
Dallas/Fort Worth, Texas	53,664
Washington, D.C.	49,372
Cleveland/Akron, Ohio	40,094
Minneapolis/St. Paul, Minnesota	38,635
Atlanta, Georgia	35,895
St. Louis, Missouri	34,663
Seattle/Tacoma, Washington	35,048
Cleveland, Ohio	29,522
Denver/Boulder, Colorado	29,420
Baltimore, Maryland	28,464
Miami and area, Florida	27,447
Denver, Colorado	26,657
Seattle, Washington	26,097
Milwaukee/Racine, Wisconsin	23,174
Cincinnati/Hamilton	22,727
Kansas City, Kansas	22,174
Phoenix, Arizona	21,864
Portland, Oregon	18,508
New Orleans, Louisiana	18,175
Columbus, Ohio	17,595
Indianapolis, Indiana	16,345
Ontario, Canada	49,142
Quebec, Canada	22,850

* Exchange rate as of December 31, 1985, used to convert sales to Canadian dollars. U.S. sales are for 1985; Canadian sales are for 1986.

Source: NOPA study, 1986.

EXHIBIT 4 1983–1987 Canadian Wood Office-Furniture Market (Shipments of Wooden Chairs and Desks within Selected Markets; Cdn $000s)

Province or Region	1983	1984	1985	1986	1987 (est.)
British Columbia	$ 3,566	$ 4,128	$ 8,841	$ 7,814	$ 7,520
Alberta	4,516	3,936	4,719	6,958	5,844
Saskatchewan	1,096	1,067	1,220	2,022	—
Manitoba	—	1,107	1,424	1,084	2,247
Ontario	—	23,825	26,232	35,477	39,908
Quebec	11,136	12,834	15,282	22,850	28,401
Atlantic	2,149	2,009	2,261	3,853	3,185

Source: *Statistics Canada* 35:006 Quarterly Shipments, Office Furniture Industry. Figures, 80–85% of industry production.

wooden segments of the furniture market. Large firms had national distribution systems and sophisticated marketing and production systems. Due to the high overheads associated with these systems, the large firms' products were usually high priced. A few of the large firms (Herman Miller and Steelcase) were recognized as being among the 100 best-managed firms in the United States.

Large firms distributed their products through the largest and most established dealers. Their size allowed them to exercise significant clout over the distributors and it was not unusual for them to pressure dealers into reducing the number of competitive products which they carried. In recent years, the larger firms had been purchasing medium and small firms as one means of expanding production capacity, line breadth, and line depth.

There were approximately 47 medium-size firms in the United States and 8 in Canada, including Caron. These medium-size firms often concentrated on regional markets close to their manufacturing facilities and distributed their products primarily through independent agents. In recent years many of these firms had started to purchase showrooms and hire their own sales reps.

Small firms usually focused on narrow product lines and relied on economies of specialization. These firms were the most numerous in the industry.

Historically, office furniture was pushed through the dealer channels by the manufacturer. This had started to change. Over the past few years up to 50 percent of sales arose from designers/specifiers and the end-user requesting specific types, brands and models of furniture—thereby pulling sales through the system. In choosing office furniture, designers usually sought (in order) product aesthetics, construction quality, delivery, and price. Caron had a sales rep in Montreal whose sole job was to contact and service both designer/specifiers and corporations. Although there had been some change in traditional distribution patterns, finding good dealers and then developing and maintaining relationships with them continued to be important. Dealer quality covered a wide spectrum. Quality of a dealer primarily reflected the volume of product moved. To attract top dealers, firms were required to offer, in order of importance, competitive price/price discounts, better than average delivery, good product aesthetics, and quality construction. In addition, it was important that the manufacturer provided showroom support (where the dealer could show customers the manufacturer's products), broad product lines, the ability to service dealers and troubleshoot their problems—and for regional dealers—the ability to offer services to their entire geographic target market.

While dealers, designers, and end-users had different product attribute needs, delivery speed and reliability had begun to emerge as one of the most important attributes for all of them.

In Canada, Caron had exclusively used "A" dealers, while in the United States, Caron's dealers fell into the "B" category (based on the ABC quality classification system). Caron was trying to break into A dealers in the United States; however, this was proving to be difficult, as there were many high-quality producers who had long-term relationships with the A dealers. As well, the high quality of the large firms' products and their clout resulted in their domination of the class A dealers. As a result, many of the medium-size manufacturers were forced to distribute their product through the B dealers.

Company History

Caron was a privately owned company that had been in the wooden furniture business for over 40 years. It was founded in St. Jean in 1935 by Andre Caron to produce and sell wooden residential furniture. During World War II, Caron dropped their residential furniture line and concentrated on producing office furniture for the war effort. The resultant increased volume continued into the early 1950s. The bubble burst when metal office furniture was introduced. Within a few years, metal office furniture captured 75 percent of the market. As a result, Caron's sales dropped in half and profits virtually disappeared. Caron management felt that part of the decline in profits arose from poor labour productivity. In answer to this problem, a piecework incentive program was successfully introduced in 1966. Prior to the incentives, it took 360 minutes to upholster a particular executive chair; after the system was introduced, it took only 86 minutes.

In 1968 Caron weathered its second major crisis. The Canadian government switched to metal furniture, thereby depriving Caron of its single most important source of revenue. Caron responded by upgrading its focus on the business market. This required a reorientation of the firm's marketing and design efforts. The reorientation appeared to succeed. During the 1970s, volume increased: sales in 1970 were $1.2 million, and by 1980 they had reached $10 million. During this period, Caron began exporting to the United States.

Coping with Growth

The increased demand for the firm's products became too great to be handled by Caron's 100-person workforce in its old plant on Lavalle Street in St. Jean. In 1980, Caron purchased another furniture plant in neighbouring St. Therese, Quebec.

In 1982, at the suggestion of some of its U.S. representatives, Caron entered the desk market. Caron management felt that the complementary nature of the product in terms of the core market and core production skills made desks a natural extension to the product line. Within three to four years, Caron had one of the largest market shares in the Canadian wood office-desk market.

To cope with increased volume pressure, Caron leased space at the back of a facility on Outremont Drive in St. Jean in 1984. Six months later, the entire facility was bought outright. This served as the new headquarters for Caron as well as its central shipping facility.

With the increased marketing efforts and a broader line, sales doubled between 1980 and 1985, going from $10 to $21 million. As well, the number of product lines increased beyond tables and chairs to include executive and secretarial desks with matching office cabinetry, conference tables, and office systems in order to provide an integrated office line. There were now three plants instead of one, and sales to the United States now accounted for over 40 percent of the firm's volume. The increased complexity of rapid growth during this period made it difficult for the senior managers to operate as they had in the past. Products were shipped late and customer complaints increased. Caron was developing a reputation in the United States for poor delivery, and inventory inaccuracies resulted in production bottlenecks, which in turn led to a mass of partially finished product cluttering up the factories. By 1985, these factors contributed to a deterioration in profits.

Management realised that there were problems. These included management and control system design, and differences in the core skills and processes required to produce the different products. For example, while it was not a problem for a wooden chair to have scratches as most of the frame would be covered with upholstery, the slightest imperfection on a table or desk surface was readily apparent and led to customer complaints.

In response to these problems, Caron changed plant layouts and production processes and modified the organization structure. Caron maintained their functional form, but during this growth period added several new positions. At the senior level, Caron created a vice president, production, position. This executive was responsible for plant operations and for the newly formed engineering and quality control departments. Under the treasurer, several new departments were formed, including inventory control, purchasing, and scheduling (Exhibit 5). Prior to the organizational change these activities were handled in an informal manner by Yves Richard and the plant managers. The modifications resulted in a tripling of the administration staff.

Delivery and production problems were addressed by investment in a computerized manufacturing planning system (MRP II) which was fully integrated by late 1986.

Once delivery systems were improved, Caron developed a quick-ship program that promised a two-week turnaround for 25 percent of Caron's product line with limited product options. For example, although there were over 2,000 choices of material for upholstering chairs (excluding customer material) only 30 fabric choices were offered on the quick-shipment program. By early 1987, quick-shipment sales accounted for 40 percent of all chair and 60 percent of all desk sales.

With MRP II in place and improved inventory systems, inventory accuracy increased to 95 percent, and production times were reduced for most products. In addition, delivery reliability increased so that 75 percent of the orders were

EXHIBIT 5   Caron Furniture Ltee. Organization Chart (March 31, 1987)

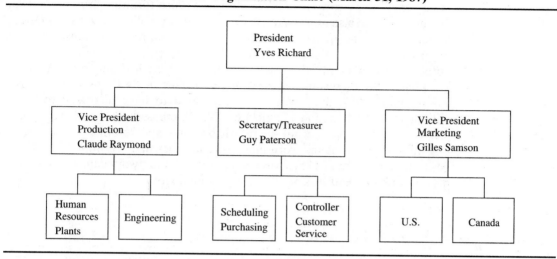

EXHIBIT 6   Caron Furniture Ltee. (Selected Financial Information; Cdn $000s)

Sales	1983	1984	1985	1986	1987 (est.)
Canadian sales	$ 7,735	$10,201	$11,594	$13,582	$16,496
U.S. sales	5,575	7,902	9,286	9,871	11,235
Total sales	13,332	18,103	20,880	23,050	27,731
Fixed expenses*	3,393	5,085	6,936	8,716	10,763
Increase in sales (percent)	31.3	36.0	15.3	12.2	18.3
Current assets/current liabilities	3.7	1.9	2.2	1.9	1.8
Assets/liabilities	4.4	2.3	2.8	2.6	2.7
Debt to equity (percent)	4.7	26.8	20.6	17.1	12.9
Staff (numbers)	229	338	346	361	378

* Some of the fixed cost is allocated to the cost of goods sold. The gross margin (38%—in case) excludes other variable costs of transporation, duty, sales discounts and commissions.

Source: Company records.

now shipped on time, up from 40 percent; quick-shipment orders were now 98 percent on time.

By the end of 1986, many of Caron's problems had either been solved or were in the process of being solved. Customer complaints had decreased dramatically, delivery time had been reduced, and sales were a record—over $23 million.

For 1987, Caron's 378 employees were expected to generate $28 million in sales, making Caron one of the larger wood office-furniture firms in Canada. Productivity had also improved due to a combination of increased automation, the success of the quality circle program, and improved in-house training programs. However, the adoption of a more complex organization structure, purchase of new plants, the MRP II system, and the high marketing costs in the United States resulted in dramatic increases in fixed costs. In the five years ending 1987, fixed costs were estimated to have increased to $10.8 million from $3.4 million (Exhibit 6). This increased the breakeven point and contributed to a decline in return on sales and return on investment. Organizational problems were emerging; in particular, coordination of the desk, chair, and systems lines was becoming increasingly difficult. The addition of a new metal chair was adding to the complexity.

Involvement in the United States

In 1976, with the domestic market flourishing, consultants were hired to prepare a study of the U.S. wood office-furniture market and suggest the appropriate distribution strategy. They reported that the U.S. market was a viable outlet for Caron, and that the most appropriate form of distribution was through independent representatives. The consultants provided Caron with a list of representatives in the United States. Agents were then appointed throughout much of the United States. It was decided that Caron would manufacture the furniture in its Canadian plant and then ship the product to the United States. Caron entered the market with its existing products of chairs and tables and utilised the same pricing structure that it had in Canada. These prices were comparable to those charged by other U.S. furniture manufacturers.

In 1982, Caron increased its U.S. investment by leasing a showroom facility in Chicago and hiring a regional manager and salesman for Chicago. At the same time, they introduced their new desk line to the U.S. market.

By 1984, U.S. sales increased to $7.9 million (Cdn)—44 percent of sales (Exhibit 6). Caron reevaluated their U.S. distribution strategy and decided to increase their investment in the United States—sales managers were hired for New York and Atlanta.

By 1985, the increased volume in both Canada and the United States had placed a great strain on Caron's resources. Several problems emerged within the United States; there were spotty delivery schedules and product complaints, difficulties in being able to manage the independent agents, and problems in agent reliability. To address the problem of agent reliability, Caron continued to replace weaker agents with either new agents or company salesmen.

By the end of 1986, U.S. sales had reached $9.9 million—42 percent of all Caron sales. At this level of sales and continued growth appearing likely,

EXHIBIT 7   Caron Furniture Ltee. (Distribution Arrangements for 1982–1987)

	1983	1984	1985	1986	1987	1988 (est.)
Canadian agents	7	7	7	7	7	7
U.S. agents	16	15	16	15	11	9
Canadian salesmen	3	3	4	4	7	7
U.S. salesmen	0	2	2	3	6	8
Canadian dealers	400	400	375	350	325	315
U.S. dealers	3,500	4,000	3,500	2,700	1,700	1,200

Caron modified their structure to recognize the importance of the United States. Caron split marketing into Canadian and U.S. divisions and in early 1987 appointed a U.S. national manager, Gerard Thompson, who would spearhead future movements within the United States. Within a few months, Thompson had identified what he perceived to be three major weaknesses in the U.S. operation:

1. *Too many dealers.* By the end of 1986, Caron was servicing over 2,700 dealers. One of the largest firms in the United States had 225 dealers throughout the entire country. The large number of dealers strained delivery systems and spread both salesmen and agents too thinly.

2. *Too broad a geographical focus.* The current organization could not effectively cope with a national operation.

3. *Desk design.* Although Caron products were competitive on price and quality, some additional elements such as line enlarging and additional finishes were needed for the U.S. market.

Caron dealt quickly with Thompson's concerns. Involvement in California and in Phoenix, St. Louis, and other West Coast markets was substantially decreased by not replacing unproductive agents. Company salesmen were added in Florida and in Minneapolis and New York. As well, Caron was considering adding more salesmen in Chicago, and the number of dealers was reduced from 2,700 to 1,700 (Exhibit 7). Reactions to desk-design concerns were slower to materialize, as Caron was trying to determine what product characteristics were generally required.

Caron Organization and Management Philosophy

Caron's ownership rested in the hands of a holding company owned by Yves Richard and assorted trusts held by members of the Caron family. The firm was principally run by Richard and three senior executives (Claude Raymond, vice president–production; Gilles Samson, vice president—marketing; and

Guy Paterson, secretary/treasurer). All of the top management team were chartered accountants and none had experience in the office-furniture industry prior to joining Caron (Exhibit 8), but together they had over 50 years service with the company. Richard considered that having a background in the furniture business was often less important than having good management skills.

Most strategic decisions were made centrally by Richard. Caron had centralized most aspects of the business including purchasing, engineering, quality control, customer relations, and scheduling. However, they were increasingly giving the plant operating autonomy.

One of Richard's primary concerns was for the welfare of Caron's employees. For example, Caron maintained a no-layoff policy. To maintain this policy, Caron cross-trained employees and had in the past kept workers employed at painting the factory or improving the grounds rather than laying them off when demand was too low to keep the plants operating. Caron had also

---

EXHIBIT 8   Caron Furniture Ltee. (Senior Management–Biography)

Yves Richard (President)
Age: 55
Joined company: 1966
Credentials: Honours, Business Administration, University of Western Ontario
             Chartered Accountant designation
Prior work experience: Accounting firm

Gilles Samson (V.P., Marketing)
Age: 42
Joined company: 1973
Credentials: Law degree, C.A., Quebec (1973)
Prior work experience: General, as a lawyer and as an accountant

Claude Raymond (V.P., Production)
Age: 34
Joined company: 1977
Credentials: Honours, Business, McGill (1975)
             Chartered Accountant designation (1977)
Prior work experience: General, as an accountant

Guy Paterson (Secretary/Treasurer)
Age: 40
Joined company: 1980
Credentials: Chartered Accountant designation (1973)
Prior work experience: Two years in construction and work as an accountant

Gerard Thompson (National Manager, United States)
Joined company: 1987
Credentials: Business degree, University of Michigan
Prior work experience: Salesman within the U.S. furniture industry. Worked for
  Hauserman, Herman Miller, and Steelcase

instituted both profit sharing and stock ownership plans. These personnel philosophies helped create an informal work atmosphere at Caron and was in part responsible for good employee morale and a generally low turnover rate.

Production

Caron was known in Canada as a producer of high-quality, medium- to high-priced office furniture. Caron maintained a unique mix of human and physical resources from which they developed the ability, somewhat unique in the industry, to work with solid wood.

The importance of product quality led Caron to minimize dependence on outside suppliers for important inputs; 67 percent of all Caron inputs, such as veneer, lumber milling, and wood bending were produced internally. Besides quality, this provided Caron with benefits such as guaranteed supply and lower costs. Few firms in the Canadian industry had integrated to this degree.

Caron's product line included about 60 series of chairs, most of which were upholstered, a dozen series of lounge chairs and sofas, eight types of small tables, conference tables, five series of desks, and office systems (panels). Caron prided itself on offering a broad product line. For example, each desk line had 25 to 30 different basic models. For any model, customers could choose from two wood types and eight finishes. There were 2,000 different table configurations. For chairs, Caron offered over 2,100 types of upholstery, or customers could provide their own material for upholstery.

Production of high-quality wood furniture was difficult. It required experienced craftsmen and consistently high-quality inputs; both were hard to obtain. Getting skilled workers was difficult. However, Caron's reputation for its excellent working environment attracted applicants. In-house training programs were designed to ensure that skill levels were maintained even if fully qualified applicants could not be found. Training ran from six months to over a year, depending on the employees' expertise and the skill requirements of the position.

Difficulty in securing high-quality wood arose from the "living" nature of the inputs. For example, wood could shrink or grow during processing, contained knots, and there could be significant color variations even with the same type of wood. Since there was so much variability with wood, no industry-quality standards or predefined quality levels existed. As a result, input quality was based on supplier quality standards. The importance of final product quality led Caron to establish their own quality standards for wood colouring, knots, and so on.

The production system was built around making the maximum use of piecework methods. For example, batches of chairs or small tables were produced for "white inventory," or storage as completely assembled but unfinished frames. In this way, lots of 50 to 600 units could be scheduled through the plant independent of customer orders. The batches of parts were moved from station to station on trolleys. Employees worked on batches in efficient, repetitive patterns and were paid on the basis of pieces completed. The frames were then stored until orders were received which called for the specific frame style. The unfinished frames were then moved through the finishing operation, then the upholstery shop (if required), and finally to the shipping department where it would be shipped to the Outremont plant. There the entire client order was gathered.

The piecework system, workflow layout, vertical integration, and especially the product mix resulted in Caron having one of the lowest rates of direct labour and material costs as a percentage of total direct costs of any Canadian furniture manufacturer, and rates which were competitive with U.S. firms.

Caron's production systems and procedures allowed the company to cope with the increased volumes; however, problems still remained. A plant inspection revealed jobs which were one to three months behind promised delivery dates. As well, stock-outs of materials had occurred.

The Current Situation

On May 20, Richard convened a management group meeting to discuss U.S. market options.

Yves Richard: "As impressive as our past growth has been, it has been below our growth objective of 26 percent. If we are to attain our objectives and improve profitability, we might have to make changes in our products, prices, distribution arrangements, and markets. The issue that I am bringing forward today is the role that the U.S. market should play in Caron's future."

Gerard Thompson: "The U.S. market is our best source for future growth. We are already one of the largest and best-known firms in Canada, so growth in Canada might be somewhat limited, but in the United States, we are barely scratching the surface. However, if we are to be a significant presence in terms of gaining a meaningful market share, then we will have to commit more resources to it. At a minimum, I need to replace some agents with our own sales force. Although agents connect with dealers, some of them are not committed enough to our products and we cannot really manage them."

Gilles Samson: "I would tend to agree with Gerard. Our experience has been that where agents were replaced with company sales reps and showrooms, sales have subsequently increased. For example, over the past five years two salesmen were added in Chicago and additional showroom space was purchased. During that time, sales increased by 552 percent. Although part of the increase might have arisen from other factors such as better personnel, more marketing support, or even improved economic environments, some of it was definitely, attributable to the change in our sales approach.''

Richard: "But what's this going to cost us?''

Samson: "As near as Gerard and I can figure it in U.S. dollars, a sales rep will cost us $30,000—50,000 a year plus 3 percent commission. Showroom costs are hard to estimate, but for New York it would be $250,000 (U.S.) per year, while in Chicago it would be $200,000 per year. Add in another $200,000 for leasehold improvements, $150,000 for showroom furniture, $30,000 for administration, and another $20,000—30,000 for salesman-related expenses.''

Richard: "That's rather steep, Gilles. Depending on the extent of our commitment to the United States, the costs could run well into the millions. Besides, as it now stands, although we have been putting more company sales reps into the United States, sales have increased by 20.3 percent per year over the past five years, while Canadian sales have been increasing by 22.6 percent. This might indicate that there is in fact more room for sales growth in Canada. Maybe we should put more resources into Canada and leave the U.S. market as is?''

Thompson: "The cost might seem steep, but if we use our own sales force we will save the 8 percent commissions that the agents charge us. Last year alone this amounted to $875,000.''

Samson: "As for the total cost, if we increase our investment in the United States, I would not recommend blanketing the entire country with sales reps, agents, and showrooms. Any investment should be limited to the largest potential markets. In fact, over the past two years, we have been reducing our geographic scope to the point that by next year I hope to be limited to the northeastern and north central United States. In line with this focus, showrooms would only be required in what we feel are our major markets. As well, replacing unproductive agents with our own salesmen is the direction we have been heading over the past year, and I would like to see it speed up [Exhibit 7].''

Thompson: "My current focus is on Chicago and New York City as they are two of the top markets in North America. I would like large showrooms in each.''

Richard: "There is another issue which we should look at. Assuming that the U.S. market materializes for us, do we have the production capacity to cope with the increased volume? It's taken us three years to develop systems for coping with our current volume.''

Claude Raymond: "We are hitting capacity constraints in all our plants. But I think that with a change in plant layouts, shifting plant product mixes, and improving some of the production processes, we can add about 30 percent capacity to the Lavalle Street plant and 50 percent to the St. Therese plant. Additional equipment requirements would be minor, but we would need more personnel. As well, I would like to see the Outremont plant's role expanded to include panel and workwall production. The cost for this would be approximately $3 million over four years. The net effect of all these changes would be to increase our capacity to over $60 million. Alternatively, if volume increased dramatically, we could subcontract out some of the less important work or purchase another facility. As for getting more skilled labour, St. Jean College is expanding its wood-working program, so within the next year we will have access to trained craftsmen."

Richard: "What can we expect by way of competitive reaction if we start capturing more market share in the States?"

Samson: "Although the U.S. market is significantly more competitive than the Canadian market, I don't expect much reaction from major competitors as we are not looking to take away much of their business. We are going to go through B dealers, not the major competitors' A dealers, and we are only trying to skim a bit of the market so we are not going to be a major threat to anyone, yet."

Richard: "Is there anything else that any of you would like to add?"

Samson: "The United States is our biggest source of profits; we charge a similar price for the products, but it is in U.S. dollars, and our only incremental cost besides marketing expenses is a 3.8 percent tariff into the States since our customers pay for shipping. In 1986, the gross profit as a percentage of sales for U.S. operations was 30 percent higher than that for Canadian sales. Most of the incremental profit arose from a 32 percent exchange rate differential. When you consider that our total gross profit last year was 38 percent of sales, you can see how much of an impact the United States has on our operations. Only an improvement of the Canadian dollar vis-à-vis the American dollar can change this. Meanwhile our Canadian market is nicely protected for two reasons: (1) we have an excellent reputation with dealers and designers, who are committed to Caron; and (2) with a 15 percent Canadian tariff for wood office furniture, it is difficult for U.S. firms to export their products into Canada. However, in the event of free trade, this second source of protection will be eliminated. In a worst case scenario—with free trade and a strengthened Canadian dollar—we will be in the throes of the most competitive situation that Caron has ever faced. In all likelihood, our margins throughout North America will be reduced. Within this context, the more competitive we are in the United States, the more competitive we will be under either free trade or an improvement in the exchange rate. This might argue for rethinking our U.S. strategy in order to strengthen ourselves for future competition."

Richard: "Exchange rate fluctuations concern me. If the rate had not changed at all over the past five years, we would have lost $1,500,000 from our pretax profits. For each 1 cent increase in the value of the Canadian dollar, we lose $100,000 from our bottom line."

Raymond: "Free trade and exchange rate fluctuations are only part of the competitive threat. The Canadian market is going to be more competitive within the next few years as some of our U.S. competitors are starting up operations in Canada."

Thompson: "I don't know if we really have a choice. The U.S. market is getting more and more competitive, with many firms offering dealers and designers a lot of service support. In my view, having our own showrooms and sales force is the price of being in the game—without them our growth will be limited."

Richard: "I think that I have all the information I need. Unless I hear from any of you with additional information in the interim, I will get back to you next week with my recommendation."

COOPER CANADA LTD. (CONDENSED)

In late 1982 CCM Canada, a manufacturer of bicycles, skates, and hockey equipment, was put into receivership and the business put up for sale. While CCM's competitors had noted the company's accumulating problems with some satisfaction and relief, they were now faced with new questions: Who would acquire the assets of CCM? What would be the impact on the competitive structure of the industry?

In the meantime, the CCM receiver was pressing for action. John Cooper, vice chairman of Cooper Canada Ltd., one of the interested competitors, described the situation:

> Our people visited the CCM plant and offices last week and they had no sooner returned than the receiver called wanting to know how soon we could make a bid. He said that speed is critical because he expects other bids at any moment and that the creditors want action since CCM's situation worsens every day. We will have to act fast . . . we have a meeting set for next Monday to make an offer if we want to. It is too bad we are under such time pressure but that's the way this deal is.

Cooper was interested only in the skate and hockey equipment part of the CCM business. Here, some elements of the fit between Cooper and CCM's winter goods business were obvious. Cooper could completely outfit a hockey player except for sweaters and skates. CCM's skate line was still one of the most respected in the business. The value of CCM's competing lines of hockey sticks and protective equipment, however, was less clear. The bicycle line was of no interest, but Cooper had made arrangements with another prospective

---

This case was prepared by Professor Donald H. Thain. Copyright © 1985 by The University of Western Ontario.

buyer to pick up this part of the CCM operation in a joint bid. The question facing Cooper management, under time pressure, was whether they wished to proceed with their side of a bid and, if so, with what price and conditions.

The Skate and Hockey Equipment Industry

There were four basic product lines in the industry: skates, protective equipment (e.g., helmets, gloves, pads), sticks, and apparel. Cooper management estimated the industry's 1981 value of shipments for these lines was as follows:

	($000)
Ice skates	$78,000
Hockey equipment	31,500
Hockey sticks	29,000
Apparel	27,000

The overall demand for hockey-related products had grown slowly in the 1970s and little or no growth was expected in the 1980s. Population trends in the prime hockey-playing age groups were not favourable, and participation rates were under pressure. A major problem with participation was the increasing cost of equipping a player: from $100 to $200 for beginners (including used equipment) and up to $1,500 for a professional.

The rapidly changing technology of hockey equipment was one reason for the high cost of equipment. Product innovation was driving toward lighter, safer, and more comfortable gear. As a 1982 article in the Maple Leaf Gardens program described it:

> Space-age hockey equipment is speeding up the game and cutting down on injuries. Technological breakthroughs are sending the NHL where it has never gone before—to lighter, cooler, stronger, tighter-fitting one-piece body protection; aluminum or fibreglass and plastic laminated sticks; and zircon-guarded, carbon-bladed skates encased in ballistic and nylon-wrapped boots.
>
> Leaf trainer Danny Lemelin thinks skates have "changed most dramatically" in the past few years. He points out that most are 4 ounces lighter because of the plastic blade holder and nylon boot. This space-age equipment has speeded up the game and cut down on injuries. And, it's made the felt-and-fibre shin, shoulder, elbow, and pant pads, one-piece ash sticks, and leather tube skates, so popular only a decade ago, obsolete. . .
>
> The evolution turned revolution in NHL gear is the by-product of by-products. New foams, plastics, nylon, and fiberglass (many invented in Korea during the fifties to keep fighting forces warm and protected) have made things "lighter and stronger," says one long-time equipment manufacturer. All these new inventions have been developed to conform to the game of hockey.

Canadian brands had established an international reputation for product excellence, and exports of hockey equipment had increased from $20 million in 1971 to $41.5 million in 1980. Skates represented the largest export product. The United States was the largest market, but Scandinavia and western Europe were also strong. Japan and Australia were newly developing markets.

The market shares of the major competitors in the industry by-product line are given in Exhibit 1. The skate business was dominated by three firms: Warrington Industries Ltd. (with three brands—Bauer, Lange, and Micron), CCM, and Daoust. Cooper was the primary company in hockey equipment. The stick business was shared by half a dozen significant competitors, of which the largest was Sherwood-Drolet. Cooper and Sport Maska were the two most significant competitors in apparel. A brief description of the companies that Cooper considered interested and capable of bidding for CCM is given in the appendix.

EXHIBIT 1   Products and Estimated Percent Market Shares of Major Competitors in the Canadian Hockey Equipment Market, 1981

Company	Skates	Hockey Equipment	Sticks	Apparel
Cooper		69%	7%	31%
Canadien		7	12	
CCM	25%	7	6	
D & R		7		
Jofa		3		
Koho		2.5	10.5	
Sherwood			25	
Victoriaville			11	
Louisville			6.5	
Titan			11	
Maska				42
Bernard				11
Sandow				10
Bauer*	33			
Lange*	5			
Micron*	13			
Daoust	17			
Orbit	5			
Roos	1			
Ridell	1			
Others		4.5	11	6
	100%	100%	100%	100%
($000,000s)	$78	$31.5	$29	$27

* Brands of Warrington Industries Ltd.
Source: Rough estimates by Cooper product managers.

Skates

The demand for skates in Canada had for several years fluctuated between 1 million and 1.3 million pairs. There were two basic types of skate boots, sewn and molded. Leather had been the first boot material and was still used in most high-quality, high-priced skates. Over 90 percent of NHL players wore leather skates. However, in the 1970s molded boots had entered the market and the low-priced market in particular had become competitive with leather-booted skates.

Information on the total Canadian hockey-skate market and the shares of major competitors segmented by sewn and molded boots is presented in Exhibit 2. Hockey skates could also be segmented by price point as follows:

Range	Retail Price	1982 Estimated Share (units)
High	More than $200	15%
Medium	$120–$180	20%
Low	Less than $90	65%

Industry observers noted that the high- and low-end market shares were increasing and the medium range decreasing. The breakdown of CCM's total unit skate sales in the high-, medium-, and low-price ranges was approximately 60 percent, 25 percent, and 15 percent, respectively, and that of Bauer, the largest brand, was thought to be 20 percent, 30 percent, and 50 percent, respectively.

Skate blades were another factor in the market. They were available from three sources in Canada. The largest manufacturer, the St. Lawrence Company of Montreal, sold mainly to CCM and Daoust, Canpro Ltd., owned by Warrington, sold mainly to Bauer, Micron, and Lange. CCM manufactured their own Tuuk blades and sold some to other skate makers. While blade technology had changed significantly in the late 1970s with the introduction of plastic mounts to replace tubes, the major current change was the trend back to carbon steel, from the newer stainless steel.

Hockey Equipment

Hockey equipment included all items on the list shown in Exhibit 3, which also shows the range of typical retail prices. Continuous research and development was necessary to ensure that these items provided maximum protection and comfort. Cooper dominated the market with a 69 percent share.

Sticks

The composition of sticks was continually changing. What had started out as a one-piece blade and handle developed into a two-piece solid-wood handle

EXHIBIT 2   Canadian Hockey Skate Production (000s of pairs)

Year	Sewn	Molded	Total
1977	1,050	50	1,100
1978	775	150	925
1979	1,050	250	1,300
1980	850	300	1,150
1981	970	400	1,370
1982 (forecast)	750	300	1,050
1983 (forecast)	900	350	1,250

1982 Factory Sales and Market Shares of Leading Competitors (000s of pairs)

	Sewn		Molded		Total		Sales		$ Average of Total
	Pairs	%	Pairs	%	Pairs	%	($000)	%	
Bauer	305	42.9%	50	13.7%	355	32.9%	$20,265	35.4%	$57.08
Micron	—	—	185	50.5	185	17.2	8,690	15.2	46.97
Lange	—	—	100	27.3	100	9.3	3,280	5.8	32.80
Daoust	205	28.7	—	—	205	19.0	9,780	17.0	47.70
CCM	147	20.6	6	1.6	153	14.2	12,050	21.0	78.76
Orbit	55	7.8	25	6.8	80	7.4	3,205	5.6	40.06
	712	100%	366	100%	1,078	100%	$57,270	100%	$53.13

1982 Hockey Skate Sales by Geographic Market (000s of pairs)

Manufacturer	Canada	U.S.A.	Europe	Far East	Total
Canadian	785	23	67	15	1,105
Non-Canadian	—	312	233	25	570
Totals	785	550	300	40	1,675

Source: Estimates based on industry information and casewriter's estimates.

EXHIBIT 3   Price Ranges for Hockey Equipment

	Typical Retail Price Range	
Item	Mens	Boys
Pants	$40–$130	$30–$60
Gloves	50–140	25–70
Helmet	27–45	27–45
Cooperall	115–125	98
Shin pads	20–75	20–75
Elbow pads	19–50	7–25
Shoulder pads	25–70	14–40

and blade, and later a laminated handle and curved blade with fibreglass reinforcement. The most recent development was an aluminum handle with a replaceable wooden blade. Changes were intended to improve strength and passing and shooting accuracy. Sherwood-Drolet led in this market with a 25 percent share.

Apparel

Differences in prices of sweaters and socks were due basically to the material used in the product. The most popular sweater materials were polyester and cotton knits because of their strength and lightness. Designs of sweaters were fairly standard, with lettering and cresting done separately. Socks were a standard product with little differentiation. Sport Maska controlled 42 percent of this market because of its quality product, excellent distribution, and good rapport with dealers.

Distribution

Skates and hockey equipment were sold in a wide range of retail outlets, including specialty, independent, department, discount, chain, and catalogue stores. Although specific numbers were not available, the split of business between these outlets followed a common retail pattern. The specialty independents and chains dominated in the higher-priced items where product knowledge and service were essential. The mass merchandisers were dominant in the lower-priced product areas.

In Canada the most common route from manufacturer to retailer was through distributors who used sales agents. Manufacturers wanted agents who would represent their product aggressively, seek out new orders, and provide them with market feedback. Usually these agents either were, or had been, actively involved in sports. However, since the agents sold multiple lines, it was difficult to control their activities and level and mix of sales. Most companies used a sales force of 10 to 12 reps to cover most of Canada. A few small companies utilized wholesalers to supplement their sales force.

Retail outlets had experienced little real growth in sales and were finding themselves with increasing inventories. Therefore, retailers started carrying shallower stocks, ordering more frequently, and relying on manufacturers or distributors to provide back-up inventories. This trend meant that bargaining power had shifted from the manufacturers to the retailers, who were trying to gain volume discounts and delivery advantages by reducing the number of suppliers.

Promotion

Three types of promotion were used: company and product promotion, media advertising, and trade show participation. Product and image promotion seemed to be the most effective avenue for stimulating sales. Because professional players set industry trends, it was important to get popular players to use and endorse products. To recruit these players, professional "detail men" from sports equipment manufacturers were assigned to players to make sure their equipment fit perfectly and that the player was loyal to the brand. It was also important to get as many players as possible wearing the products so that the brand name would enjoy good exposure during televised games. Therefore, the detail men also tried to work through team trainers to supply most of the team with the brand. While some competitors used financial incentives to push a product, Cooper relied on high-quality, fast service in fitting and repairs and intensive sales efforts, and was not involved with special deals or endorsement contracts.

Media advertising was primarily confined to the larger firms. Print advertising in the concentrated population areas was the most common approach.

Trade shows significantly influenced retail buyers. Many sales took place at the shows, bookings were made for orders, and sales were made on follow-up calls by sales reps. The Canadian Sporting Goods Association organized two shows annually.

Cooper Canada

In 1946, Jack Cooper left Eaton's to join General Leather Goods Ltd., as its first and, until 1951, only salesperson. Subsequently, Cooper and Cecil Weeks bought out the company's original owner and changed the name to Cooper-Weeks. In 1954, Cooper acquired Cecil Weeks' interest, and the company became the exclusive Canadian manufacturer of Buxton Leather goods. In the following years, the company grew through internal development and acquisitions to encompass a wide range of leather and sporting goods products. In 1970, the company changed its name to Cooper Canada Ltd. and went public. By 1981, revenues were almost $63 million, but Cooper experienced its first loss in years. Cooper management expected a return to profitability in 1982 in spite of a recession and high interest rates. Financial statements for Cooper Canada from 1977 through 1981 are presented in Exhibits 4 and 5.

In 1982 Cooper was engaged in two major lines of business; sporting goods (hockey equipment, apparel, golf bags, baseball gloves, inflated goods, etc.) and leather goods and finishing (wallets, carrying bags, etc.). The relative scale and performance of these businesses is illustrated in Exhibit 6. Cooper also had a significant sales and distribution operation in the United States as indicated by the geographic segmentation of the business in Exhibit 6.

Management Goals

Jack Cooper, "the chief," and his two sons, John and Don,[1] owned 82 percent of the company's outstanding common stock. Jack Cooper, who retained

---

[1] Don, who had managed the leather goods division for several years, left the company in 1980 and started a women's sportswear retailing company. He remained a director.

EXHIBIT 4   Consolidated Statement of Income and Retained Earnings, Years Ended December 31, ($000s)

	1981	1980	1979	1978	1977
Net Sales	$62,827	$62,183	$55,810	$49,429	$42,803
Less: Operating costs	57,049	55,901	51,844	44,364	38,538
Net before Depreciation, etc.	5,778	6,282	3,966	5,064	4,265
Less: Deprec. & amortization	724	746	748	626	609
Long-term debt interest	1,905	934	1,022	929	778
Other interest	2,933	2,866	2,068	1,138	941
Add: Foreign exchange gain	(105)	369	(107)	216	173
Earnings, discontinued operation	929	—	—	—	—
Less: Income taxes					
Current	14	176	20	525	518
Deferred	208	48	454	21	58
Net Income, Operations	818	1,977	455	2,039	1,650
Add: Extraordinary item	(1,543)	76	—	—	—
Net Income	(725)	2,053	455	2,039	1,650
Shares Outstanding					
Common ($000s)	1,486	1,483	1,483	1,404	1,388
Net income per share	(0.49)	1.38	0.31	1.45	1.18

voting control, was chairman and chief executive officer and Henry Nolting was president and chief operating officer. They worked closely together, meeting for frequent discussions daily. The company's organization is shown in Exhibit 7.

Management's immediate concerns were to increase sales and margins; to implement a badly needed information system; to strengthen and control activities in marketing, production, and finance; to reduce short-term bank debt and high-interest expenses; to bring the leather goods division from a loss to a profit; and to iron out troublesome technical and production problems in J. B. Foam, a manufacturer of plastic foam pads and products that had recently been purchased and moved to Cooper's Toronto plant.

Long-term goals called for further development of sporting goods to increase growth and utilize the great strengths of the Cooper name. Additions to the product line were sought through new-product development and/or acquisition. Cooper was also developing more export markets for its sporting goods products.

Performance

Growth had always been foremost among Jack Cooper's goals. Sales had increased continuously since 1969, except in 1975. However, earnings had fluctuated widely over the same period. Earnings dropped in 1979 because of

EXHIBIT 5   Consolidated Balance Sheet as at December 31 ($000s)

	1981	1980	1979	1978	1977
Assets					
Current					
Short-term bank deposit	—	$ 1,790	—	$ 22	$ 95
Accounts receivable	$ 9,726	10,625	$10,315	9,185	8,340
Inventories:					
Raw materials	6,177	8,792	13,064	5,675	5,535
Work in process	1,593	1,758	1,817	1,006	1,379
Finished goods	15,954	11,669	10,530	10,937	10,839
Prepaid expenses, etc.	580	691	545	886	630
	34,030	35,325	39,271	27,714	26,897
Fixed assets at cost					
Buildings	6,179	6,145	6,145	6,117	6,078
Machines, equipment, etc.	4,191	4,521	4,171	3,354	3,174
Dies, moulds, etc.	235	567	619	435	284
Land	91	91	91	90	90
Less: Accumulated depreciation	5,351	5,104	4,518	4,000	3,712
	5,345	6,220	6,508	5,998	5,914
Investment in nonconsolidated subsidiaries	1,122	—	—	—	—
Deferred income taxes	373	581	533	—	—
	40,870	42,126	46,312	33,713	32,889
Liabilities					
Current					
Bank indebtedness	10,373	15,853	17,423	8,283	6,955
Accounts payable	3,463	3,380	6,380	3,153	3,576
Income and other taxes payable	1,002	695	641	352	314
Long-term debt due	16	233	603	1,134	1,059
	14,854	20,161	25,047	12,924	11,905
Long-term debt					
Bank loans	9,000	4,000	5,375	5,875	6,900
10% sinking funds debs. due 1990	1,582	1,892	1,920	2,053	2,148
6.5% mortgage, due 1992	248	265	273	291	280
Notes payable to shareholders	—	125	437	504	—
Less amount due 1 yr.	16	233	603	1,134	1,059
Deferred taxes	—	—	—	418	397
Shareholders' Equity					
Capital Stock					
Common	3,403	3,392	3,392	2,764	2,716
Retained Earnings	11,799	12,524	10,471	10,016	9,600
	$40,870	$42,126	$46,312	$33,713	$32,889

EXHIBIT 6   Cooper Canada Revenues and Profits by Business Segment, 1981 ($000s)

	Industry Segments			Geographic Segments		
	Sporting Goods	*Leather Goods & Finishing*	*Total*	*Canada*	*United States*	*Total*
Revenue	$46,913	$16,076	62,827	$57,122	$11,321	$62,827
Operating profit	7,434	1,678	8,939	7,823	1,289	8,939
Identifiable assets	28,703	8,001	40,870*	30,403	6,301	40,870*

* Includes corporate assets of $4,549.

EXHIBIT 7   Organization Chart

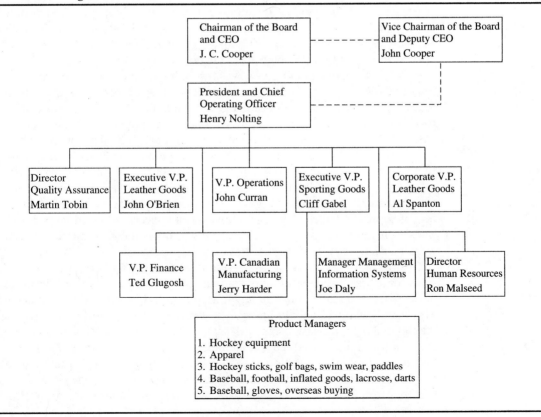

problems in absorbing the purchase of Winnwell Sports. And in 1981, high interest rates, the recession, and the disposal of Cooper's unsuccessful production operations in Barbados all hurt the bottom line. However, interim 1982 figures indicated much stronger performance. Although there was little growth in sales, the tight inventory and cost controls implemented by Henry Nolting had helped to increase earnings.

Marketing

Cooper products covered a wide range of quality and price points. In hockey equipment, for example, the Cooper line ranged from high-end items, used by top professional teams around the world, to medium-low for the beginning player. In baseball equipment and supplies, the quality and price covered a medium-high to low range, appealing to younger and more experienced players, but not professionals.

Hockey equipment was the company's major line and future growth area. To keep its competitive edge, Cooper employed eight people to work full time on product development, with a priority on hockey products. The aim was product leadership, giving athletes the best effectiveness and protection. An example of the product development work was Cooper's latest product, the Cooperall, an elasticized body garment which held all the protective pads in place. Cooperalls represented a major innovation and had given Cooper a clear lead on competitors who were currently trying to copy the product.

Distribution of Cooper goods was through its 25-person sales force, which provided the most extensive national coverage of any company in the industry. Sales reps were organized on a geographic basis and were paid on a salary-plus-bonus-minus-expenses system, with no upper limit on bonuses. The total customer base was around 1,600. Because Cooper and CCM had been competitive across a wide product line and Cooper accounts usually sold Bauer skates, significant overlap of Cooper and CCM accounts was not extensive. Sales were distributed equally throughout the East, Ontario, and the West. National coverage by its own sales force gave Cooper an advantage over its competitors, few of whom had such coverage. However, a concern was that 90 percent of sales were made to 20 percent of accounts and almost 40 percent of sales were made to only 20 major customers.

Cliff Gabel, executive vice president, sporting goods, reported that the sales force was enthusiastic about adding skates to their line. While no one in the Cooper organization had any in-depth experience in the skate business, Mr. Gabel, who was widely known and highly respected in the industry, had maintained a good relationship with several key marketing managers at CCM, some of whom were now retired. He believed that one man in particular, who had an outstanding reputation as perhaps the "best skate man around," would welcome the opportunity to help Cooper take over and manage CCM should the opportunity arise. A respected and now retired manager from the Bauer

Company who was a good friend of John Cooper was also thought to be available.

Cooper was the largest national advertiser in the sporting goods industry and had won awards for the quality of its television and print ads. The latest campaign had featured the Cooperall and was aided during the 1982 Stanley Cup telecasts.

Manufacturing and Distribution

Cooper had two manufacturing facilities. A plant in west Toronto did the bulk of the work but an older woodworking plant in Cambridge produced hockey sticks, baseball bats, and canoe paddles. Each facility manufactured hundreds of separate products that involved thousands of parts, requiring control procedures that were complex and numerous.

There was an excess of relatively expensive manufacturing space in the Toronto plant because it was built larger than necessary in 1976. In addition, several products, previously produced in Canada, had since been contracted to offshore manufacturers at lower costs. These manufacturers were primarily in the Orient and did contract work for most of Cooper's competitors. As a result, Cooper's designs were widely and easily copied by the other companies.

In distribution, Cooper chose to act as a "stockhouse," filling as many customer orders as possible on request. Speedy response was a major factor in maintaining customer loyalty. Cooper had a policy of providing a fill rate of 90 percent in nonpeak seasons and 80 percent in peak seasons. This required substantial working capital, as Cooper's line encompassed over 12,000 stock-keeping units (SKUs). The sporting goods division carried 65 percent to 80 percent of the total company inventory. Sporting goods' finished goods inventory reached as high as $18 million each April for deliveries of fall lines. A company objective was to reduce year-end inventories from $23.7 million in 1981 to a more manageable $18 million by the end of 1982. One manager indicated that a recent reduction in the past company policy of producing 120 percent of forecast sales to a level of 100 percent of forecast sales would be a major factor in reducing inventory.

Information Systems

A monthly report of sales and gross profit for each SKU and product line was available to each product manager. Quarterly reports provided by cost accounting attempted to determine actual margins realized by each division on each product line. Product managers were also provided with a report on the inventory of each SKU. Product managers were expected to make decisions on pricing and provide input on production levels based on the information provided by these reports.

Product managers were evaluated on the basis of sales, market share, and product margins. The market share was expected to be maintained or increased to achieve sales growth. Product line margins were compared to the company average. However, a major argument of the department and product managers, particularly for leather goods, was that allocated overheads were not fair or accurate. The cost accounting department had struggled with this problem for years.

Financing

A bank operating loan and other term loans were the company's major sources of financing. Banking services for Canada were provided by the Canadian Imperial Bank of Commerce (CIBC) and for Cooper International by Marine Midland Bank of Buffalo, New York. The CIBC provided an operating loan to a maximum line of $16 million at ¼ percent above prime and a term loan at ¾ percent above prime to be paid in $1 million per year installments in the first five years and $2 million per year thereafter. The bank prime rate was currently 12 percent, but had been as high as 20 percent in mid-1982.

A combination of high working capital requirements and high interest rates in the early 1980s had prompted Cooper to seek to minimize capital expenditures without adversely affecting manufacturing or productivity. The payback requirement approval of capital expenditures was 2.5 years or better. Typical annual capital expenditures were additions of new dyes and molds and the purchase of manufacturing equipment.

CCM

Incorporated in 1899 as the Canadian Cycle and Motor Company, CCM was Canada's oldest sporting goods manufacturer. Over its history, CCM had been engaged in three separate businesses: bicycles; automobiles; and skates, hockey sticks, and equipment.

The skate business was entered in 1905 to even out the seasonal sales and production of bicycles. Originally CCM manufactured high-quality blades and riveted them to the best available boots purchased from George Tackaberry of Brandon, Manitoba, to make the skates used by virtually all professional and high-level amateur hockey players. Later, to fill out the line, it purchased lower-quality boots from two small shoe companies in Quebec and its hockey equipment from other manufacturers. By 1967, all winter goods were manufactured by the company in what was then a large, modern, efficient plant, in St. Jean, Quebec.

Through industry-leading product innovation, CCM became the world's premier hockey skate manufacturer. For years, customers in Europe equated Canada with hockey and hockey with CCM.

Performance

Starting in 1961, CCM went through an unfortunate series of ownership and management changes. This resulted at various times in serious labour problems, inadequate attention to marketing and distribution, and to a general deterioration of the company's reputation for quality and service. Despite sales growth in recent years, profitability had been erratic and in 1982 devastatingly poor, since an operating loss of $4.3 million was expected.

The company's financial position, as at September 30, 1982, was summarized by the interim receiver as follows:

> CCM owes two secured creditors $33 million—the Royal Bank $28 million and the Enterprise Development Board $5 million—while the liquidation value of the company is $11.6 million less than its total debts of $41 million.
>
> Preferred creditors are owed $1.2 million and product liability claims amount to almost $13 million—$12 million of which rests on the resolution of a New York civil suit lodged by a hockey player who suffered an injury while wearing a CCM helmet.

The financial information available to Cooper on CCM's winter goods operation is presented in Exhibits 8 and 9.

Marketing

CCM's world-class strength was in leather skates. Like other leading skate manufacturers, CCM concentrated heavily on supplying skates to professional players because they were the trend setters. Three special pro detail men were employed to sell and service these players, who were often given custom-fitted skates free of charge.

Up to the mid-seventies, when it began to slide, CCM's share of the Canadian and worldwide hockey skate markets had been approximately 60 percent, 30 percent, and 20 percent of the high-, medium-, and low-priced markets, respectively. Because of its domination of the top end of the market, "Supertack," its long-established premium brand name, was better known around the world than CCM. Although skate sales were the largest contributor to fixed costs, they declined from 68 percent of winter goods sales in 1980 to 58 percent in 1982. At the same time, protective equipment sales roughly doubled from 14 percent to 26 percent, with gross margins of 24 percent. Total gross margin as a percent of sales decreased from 27.8 percent in 1980 to 26.6 percent in 1982.

Distribution

From 1945 to 1982, CCM's dealer network had shrunk from 2,500 to 1,500 and its sales force from 21 to 12. All dealers sold the total CCM line but spent most of their time on winter goods. Up to 1970, the sales reps had been paid salary plus car and expenses and had been encouraged to service dealers and

EXHIBIT 8   CCM Inc. Winter Goods Operations ($000s)

| | Actual Year Ended | | | | | | Projected Year Ending Dec. 31/83 | |
	Sept. 30/80		Sept. 30/81		Sept. 30/82			
Sales								
Skates	$17,148		$16,530		$14,304		$16,500	
Sticks	1,413		2,307		1,445		2,000	
Helmets	1,774		1,814		1,714		2,000	
Protective	3,681		5,047		6,455		6,000	
Sundries	1,250		838		787		1,000	
	$25,266		$26,536		$24,705		$27,500	
Gross Margins		%		%		%		%
Skates	$5,985	35.0	$5,604	34.0	$4,577	32.0	$5,940	36.0
Sticks	(230)	(16.3)	(30)	(1.3)	(267)	(18.5)	—	—
Helmets	415	23.4	424	23.4	492	28.7	600	30.0
Protective	482	13.1	934	18.5	1,556	24.1	1,350	22.5
Sundries	381	30.5	262	31.3	215	27.3	300	30.0
	$7,033	27.8	$7,194	27.1	$6,573	26.6	$8,190	29.8
Expenses								
Selling							$1,291	
Administration							661	
Warehouse and distribution			(not available)				1,086	
Financial							618	
							$3,656	
Net before income taxes							$4,534	

Sources: 1980–82 from audited financial statements; 1983 projections estimated by CCM management.

customers. However, industry sources reported that by 1982, the sales reps were strictly on a commission basis and, pressured to get orders through as many dealers as possible, spent little time on service.

Although CCM's reputation for service was suffering, its reputation for quality had been maintained fairly well. A quick survey of a few present or past CCM dealers in November 1982 indicated that approximately one-third said they would never carry CCM again; one-third would consider carrying CCM again if they could be assured of delivery and service; and one-third would stick with CCM through thick and thin because they were enthusiastic about the product and the name.

Manufacturing

Early in November, Henry Nolting, president, and Jerry Harder, vice president of manufacturing of Cooper Canada, Ltd., visited CCM's winter goods plant

EXHIBIT 9   Summary of CCM Winter Goods Assets (at cost) October 29, 1982 ($000s)

Inventories		
Finished goods		
Skates	$1,861	
Sticks	407	
Helmets	264	
Protective	1,476	
Sundries	349	
		$ 4,357
Raw material		
Skates	1,264	
Protective	798	
Blades	1,604	
		3,666
Work in process		
Skates	216	
Sticks	250	
Protective	234	
Blades	25	
		725
		$ 8,748
Fixed assets		
St. Jean	1,200	
Hudson	70	
Nylite	867	
		$ 2,137
Total		$10,885

Source: CCM management estimates.

in St. Jean. The following are excerpts from their reports on the visit:

> The woodworking facility is not modern, looks somewhat like ours as far as equipment and machinery are concerned, and it is not surprising that they do not turn a profit in that part of their operation. The roof in the stick-making facility is leaking and that part of their plant is badly maintained.
>
> The protective equipment manufacturing has nothing in it which we do not know, there is nothing innovative being done and, as far as I am concerned, it is worth very little.
>
> The skate manufacturing operation seems reasonable despite the fact that there are no great innovations. The boot-making part is something which is easily transferable to our location. Jerry feels he would like to have it and can run it. The whole layout seems relatively simple but modern enough and efficient. The equipment is not new but in good repair.

The existing machine shop is old and dirty and there is nothing in it which I would like to buy. They have, at present, approximately 100 people working, but cleaning up work in process. The people are very slow; they seem to be puzzled, unenthusiastic and listless.

There seems to be a lot of old stock in the finished goods warehouse.

The major lasting machines are leased from United Shoe Machinery which is normal in this trade. They say they have 3,000 plus pairs of lasts (many are specials for individual players) at about $25 per pair. The lasts I saw were in very good repair.

The R&D department has two employees. They have had tremendous problems with their Propacs (copies of Cooperall) and are constantly trying to improve the product. They are working very closely with the Quebec Nordiques in perfecting this product. They have never done any helmet-related work at that facility.

We think their sporting goods division lost approximately $.5 million each year, in 1980 and 1981, sharing equally in the total company loss of $4.3 million at end of September 1982.

The offices are in terrible condition. They are old and in an unbelievable mess.

The president's assessment of the situation is that somebody will buy the assets and he feels that they might go for book value. His opinion is that nobody could pick it up for less.

Not counting raw material storage, we would need at least 25,000 sq. ft., which excludes cutting, to accommodate the skate-making operation. This is equal to 42 of our present 600 sq. ft. bays. To give you another perspective, this area would be slightly larger than the whole area now devoted to apparel. Because of the size, we would have to do major relocations of our existing floors (in Toronto plant). Also, we must be careful of the existing electrical supplies—I would make a cautious estimate of a $25,000 rewiring charge.

Organization

As a result of natural attrition and dim prospects, the CCM organization had shrunk to skeleton status. While it was reportedly limping along, many of the best and most experienced managers had either retired or moved on to better opportunities.

Deciding to Bid

In reviewing a list of possible bidders for CCM (see Appendix), John Cooper felt that the strongest competitive threats would be Warrington and Sport Maska. Both companies had strong management teams, well-established distribution systems, and adequate financial strength. In addition, both companies were Canadian-owned and would not face possible delay and veto of their offer by the Foreign Investment Review Agency. Of further concern was the realization that the St. Jean plant represented up to 200 politically sensitive jobs and that the Quebec government might become involved directly or indirectly in the proceedings. Immediate decisions and actions were essential, however, if Cooper wanted to acquire CCM. Two questions puzzled John Cooper: "If we don't buy CCM, who will? And how will it affect our business?"

APPENDIX
COMPETITORS IN THE SKATE AND HOCKEY EQUIPMENT INDUSTRY

There were many manufacturers of hockey equipment, helmets, skates, and sticks in Canada. There were seven businesses that Cooper management considered capable and perhaps interested in the CCM winter goods assets.

1. *Canadian Hockey Industries.* CHI was a small company that made high-quality hockey sticks. Its use of fibreglass technology and other materials such as graphite, plastics, laminates, and aluminum had resulted in the most unique stick line in the market. It also marketed a full line of hockey equipment, including a helmet, but no skates or apparel.

Located in Drummondville, Quebec, it had sales of $10 million in 1981, which had been growing rapidly for the past five years. In the factory it employed approximately 120 workers. It was owned by Amer Industries, a Finnish company that also owned Koho.

2. *Koho.* Koho was owned by Amer Industries Finland, and shared marketing, distribution, and some hockey stick manufacturing with Canadian Hockey Industries. It was thought to be the largest hockey stick manufacturer in the world. It also manufactured and marketed hockey equipment and helmets, but no skates or apparel.

Koho had sales of approximately $14 million from about 800 or 900 dealers, serviced by six or seven commission agents who primarily sold Koho and Canadian. Major accounts included large department stores (e.g., Eatons, Simpsons, and Sears), sporting goods chains such as Collegiate Sports, and other stores such as Canadian Tire.

Sticks were manufactured in the Canadian plant in Quebec; sticks and some hockey equipment were manufactured in Finland, and some hockey equipment was purchased in the Orient.

Koho's organization in Canada was headed by a sales manager who reported to a president for North America. The United States also had a sales manager who reported to the North American president. This president reported to the head office of Amer, a very large and profitable Finnish corporation that was involved with shipbuilding, steel, food, and tobacco.

3. *Jofa.* A Volvo-owned company, Jofa manufactured and marketed hockey equipment, hockey sticks, and skates, but not apparel. It had one factory in Sherbrooke, Quebec, and others in Sweden. The rest of its products were purchased in the Orient.

Sales of $10 million were achieved through 700 to 800 dealers and approximately seven commissioned sales agents. Major accounts included large department stores and sporting goods stores and Canadian Tire.

The organization of the company was thin, with one director of marketing responsible for all of North America. Supporting him was a sales manager and a small number of commissioned sales agents.

4. *Sherwood-Drolet.* Sherwood-Drolet was a Quebec company, 80 percent owned by an American firm, ATO Inc. ATO was the world's largest integrated producer of fire protection equipment and also owned Rawlings and Adirondack sporting goods in the United States.

Sherwood, a producer of high-quality hockey sticks, had been an industry leader in sales and in the introduction of new materials and production processes. It had one of the most automated plants in the industry, enabling it to produce large volumes of sticks of consistent quality. In 1981 its share of the Canadian market was 25 percent.

Sales of approximately $15 million came from approximately 600 dealers. The company's direct sales were aided by 10 sales agents who sold to 300 dealers.

5. *Hillerich and Bradsby.* Hillerich and Bradsby's head office and manufacturing facility were located in Wallaceburg, Ontario. The company was a wholly owned subsidiary of H & B, Louisville, Kentucky, the world's top baseball bat manufacturer. Besides producing the Louisville hockey stick and being a market leader in brightly coloured goalie sticks, it was making aggressive inroads into the baseball glove and accessory markets. It had also earned a good name for itself in manufacturing golf clubs that were sold primarily through club professionals. The plant employed 62 people.

Sales in 1981 were about $6 million. H & B's distribution system included warehouses in Richmond, B.C.; Dorval, Quebec; Winnipeg, Manitoba; and Concord, Ontario. The sales were achieved primarily by commission sales agents through approximately 400 dealers. Management was reportedly very strong.

6. *Warrington Industries.* Warrington produced Bauer, Micron, and Lange skates. Bauer had been in the skate business for many years and was CCM's major competitor. This Canadian-owned company was located in Kitchener, Ontario, and produced only skates and shoes. It employed 400 in the skate business and 150 in the shoe business.

Sales of approximately $30 million were generated by 12 to 15 agents through a dealership of 1,200 stores. Warrington was in turn owned by Cemp Investments, a firm representing the interests of the Bronfman family.

7. *Sport Maska.* Maska was a high-quality hockey-jersey manufacturer. Good distribution resulted in Maska being exclusive suppliers to the NHL. Besides hockey jerseys and apparel, its business consisted of spring and summer ball uniforms and apparel, soccer jerseys, and leisure wear. The plant in St. Hyacinthe, Quebec, employed approximately 175 people.

Sales in Canada were achieved by approximately nine commissioned agents through 1,200 to 1,500 dealers across Canada. The agents did not carry Maska exclusively. It was distributed coast to coast across the United States through the use of commission agents. Recently, Maska had purchased Sandow, another Canadian athletic apparel company, and had consolidated the manufacturing into its own plant.

Sport Maska was a private company that appeared to be profitable and to have a strong equity base. Industry sources felt that the management team, directed by president Denny Coter, was strong and had good depth.

CURRIE CONSTRUCTION LIMITED (A)

In May 1984, Martin Cook, president of Currie Construction Limited, a British Columbia–based road construction and maintenance firm, was contemplating U.S. market entry. Having investigated the opportunity to establish an operation in Houston, Texas, Cook now needed to make his decision.

The B.C. Road Construction and Maintenance Industry

The construction and maintenance of Canada's highways and roads fell under the jurisdiction of the provincial and municipal governments. In British Columbia, for example, the primary government funding agency responsible for the construction and maintenance of the major transportation structures (i.e., highways, roads, bridges) was the Department of Transportation (DOT). As well, each municipal government (e.g., city of Victoria) was also responsible for constructing and maintaining certain roadways in its respective jurisdiction.

The president of the B.C. Road Builders Association, which represented more than 60 road construction/maintenance companies in British Columbia, expressed in a press release his concern about the lack of funding. He noted serious concern about the condition of highways, roads, and bridges on which usage was continually on the increase, while provincial funding for both new construction and maintenance work on the existing system had decreased over the past decade. This view was supported in a series of other recently published reports stating that over half of British Columbia's paved municipal road systems needed either resurfacing or reconstruction over the next five years. This would require over $1.0 billion. As well, one third of the bridges in British Columbia were in need of replacement or rehabilitation within the next five years at an estimated cost of over $150 million. In spite of this real threat to B.C.'s infrastructure, government officials would probably not increase funding significantly within the period.

Competition in the road construction industry was fierce. Exhibit 1 presents market share data and contract value for all road construction work awarded by DOT in 1984. This was only for new construction work awarded by DOT and excluded work tendered by the municipal governments. The industry was fragmented among many competitors.

A tendering process was used by both the DOT and municipal governments to award work to contractors. A tender document was broken down into specific stages where a cost was assigned for each stage (i.e., stage 1—survey stake out, stage 2—shrubbery removal, stage 3—direct excavation). A unit cost was attached to each stage so that if a cost overrun occurred that was beyond the control of the contractor, then DOT would pay the contractor for the overrun. A contract was awarded on a lowest cost basis among those contractors who prepared a tender for a specific job. There was no limitation on the number of jobs a contractor could bid for as long as the company was qualified (i.e., total dollar value of work the company could do per year) and the qualification associated with each tender call (i.e., assets of company) was

EXHIBIT 1   1984 Market Share Ranking (DOT)*

	Total Contracts 195	**Total Value $197,799,506**	**Total Tonnes 1,259,373**	
Rank	*Contractor*	*Contracts*	*Dollar Value*	*Market Percentage*
1	ARC Holdings Ltd.	13	37,152,682	18.78
2	TCN Construction	4	18,973,518	9.59
3	Arvac Construction	4	11,738,241	5.93
4	Jean Ltd.	2	10,007,533	5.06
5	Pey Ltd.	2	7,028,088	3.55
6	Atlas Construction Ltd.	1	6,482,646	3.28
7	RAC Paving	7	6,394,994	3.23
8	Dunn Construction	8	5,876,584	2.97
9	Alden Ltd.	5	5,438,526	2.75
10	Currie Construction	4	5,333,212	2.70
11	Gant Paving Ltd.	1	5,069,375	2.56
12	Lyee Construction Ltd.	3	4,921,515	2.49
13	Rant Construction Ltd.	8	4,815,610	2.43
14	Rome Construction Ltd.	3	4,543,044	2.30
15	Ram Brothers Construction	1	4,100,067	2.07

* Figures are disguised.

satisfied. As a result, in British Columbia often as many as 10 companies bid on one job at a time, thus making it extremely difficult to gain market share.

In order to stay profitable, construction companies had a number of options. The first was to invest in new unproven technology (e.g., recycling) in order to become the leader in this field in developing the B.C. market. This option involved a large amount of risk because DOT and the road construction industry were cautious of new technology claims. The second option was to invest in costly capital equipment. This was critical in this labour-intensive industry because equipment breakdowns were a major reason for cost overruns on a job. A third option was to integrate vertically backwards into the commercial end of the industry. This involved owning an asphalt production plant and/or a sand and gravel operation. Large amounts of money were required as well as a strategic decision to compete in a related industry. The fourth option was to compete in markets other than British Columbia (i.e., the United States, Ontario, Alberta). With this option, the firm risked an incomplete understanding of the market, the competitors, and the customer (i.e., government agencies responsible for road construction/maintenance have varying specifications and methods of doing business in each province or state). The final option was to diversify into an unrelated industry (e.g., concrete, housing, or transportation). This option also involved a great deal of risk because of market unfamiliarity and the large amounts of capital required.

Background Information on Martin Cook

Cook graduated from the University of Manitoba with a bachelor of science degree in 1960 and immediately accepted a job as an asphalt engineer with Shell Canada Limited (SCL). It was in the asphalt division that Cook established a working relationship with David Thomas that would have a significant effect on both their future careers within SCL. By the mid-1960s, Cook was elevated to the position of asphalt sales manager for Western Canada. Not totally satisfied with the constraints of a large corporation, he turned down two excellent promotional opportunities within SCL.

In 1970, Cook and Thomas discussed the possibility of entering into business together in the asphalt-related products market. The business would supply road asphalt and other oil-based by-products to the consumer. On January 1, 1971, Cook and Thomas left SCL and formed a company called Costal Asphalt Limited (Costal). They each contributed their personal savings of $15,000 into this company. As Cook said: "When we left Shell we did not know where we were going. We had to first find a place to set up our plant and then find the necessary financing. However, we knew we had a good idea."

Development of Costal Limited

Cook and Thomas approached the B.C. Development Corporation and the Federal Department of Regional and Industrial Expansion (DRIE) for financial support for Costal. They were turned down because their proposal was determined to be infeasible. The banks also would not provide any financing because Cook and Thomas had no personal assets for use as collateral. However, they were able to get financial support from Mark Currie and Evan Clarry, owners of Currie Construction Limited. The deal was structured so that Currie Construction owned 51 percent of Costal and Cook and Thomas 49 percent. After payment of a $100,000 loan to Currie and Clarry, the equity position would become 50 percent Currie, 25 percent Cook, and 25 percent Thomas. It took one and one-half years to repay the original $100,000 loan.

In 1973, Costal entered into a joint venture with an investor (Jake Garner) to purchase profitable road construction company, A.A. McLeod Construction Limited (McLeod), in the Queen Charlotte area in British Columbia. Garner was responsible for the day-to-day operations and management of the firm.

From 1973 to 1976, Cook and Thomas concentrated primarily on expanding Costal operations by opening up terminals in Calgary and Edmonton. McLeod continued to be profitable under Garner's direction.

Costal's success to this point was attributed mainly to the dedication of Cook and Thomas. It was not unusual for either partner to work seven days a week, 15 hours a day. During this period, Cook's responsibilities included answering the phone, pouring 425°F asphaltic product into 25 kg containers in the shop, and taking care of financial matters as well as "pounding the pavement to drum up business." This hard work paid off for Cook and Thomas: Costal was profitable from its inception. Over this period, their management skills and business know-how increased enormously.

In 1976, Cook and Thomas wanted to further vertically integrate forward. They attempted to purchase a profitable road construction company in Victoria (similar in size to McLeod), but the deal fell through. At the same time, Currie Construction was offered for sale. Currie and Clarry had received a serious offer from a British-based company to purchase Currie; however, they desired to sell it to Canadian investors if they could be found. Cook and Thomas saw this as an excellent opportunity to become fully integrated in the road construction industry in British Columbia. Because Currie was a major customer for Costal product, a change of ownership could jeopardize this account. Also, the purchase of Currie by another firm could have a negative effect on Costal's operations since Currie owned 50 percent of Costal. Up to this time, Currie and Clarry were silent partners in Costal; they never interfered with the management of Costal, and McLeod and the valuable long-term assets on Currie's balance sheet.

Currie Construction Limited

Currie Construction was one of the oldest and largest road maintenance and construction companies based in British Columbia. Its history dated back to 1919 when Eugene Boyle built the foundations upon which Currie would grow and prosper for the next 60 years. During that time, Currie participated in building such large projects as the Trans Canada Highway and the Alaskan Highway. The company enjoyed enormous success in the 50s and 60s when governments were spending huge amounts of money to build Canada's transportation infrastructure. However, during the late 1960s and early 1970s, Canada's infrastructure was nearing completion and the industry was shifting away from new construction of road systems to reconstruction and maintenance of the existing road networks.

Cook and Thomas decided that with the purchase of Currie Construction, Cook would leave Costal and become president of Currie. There was too much at stake to allow someone else to run the company for them; this was a major acquisition that could cause the collapse of everything they had achieved to date if not managed properly.

On November 15, 1976, Cook took over total control of Currie's operations. During the negotiations to purchase Currie for $10.6 million, Currie had indicated that he expected Currie to make a profit of $1 million for the fiscal year (ending March 31) of 1977. However, much to Cook's surprise, Currie experienced a net operating loss of $1.3 million instead.

Despite the poor performance in 1976, Cook believed that Currie was still a good deal. The company owned valuable pieces of real estate (e.g., two golf courses) whose potential value was enormous. As well, Currie owned and operated asphalt production plants in key strategic locations in the province and owned valuable land north of Vancouver that contained large amounts of aggregate used in the construction process and in the asphalt production plants. Having an asphalt supply was extremely important in the road construction business.

Cook identified some critical problems with Currie's operations initially. A glaring problem was that they were still competing heavily in the highway road construction segment of the market, yet they were losing money. Currie had failed to recognize that the market was undergoing a change from new highway construction to reconstruction and road maintenance. Road construction placed much greater emphasis on earth moving (excavating, drilling, blasting) than road maintenance, where the emphasis was more on grinding and recycling. In addition, Currie's equipment was old and tended to break down. This led to cost overruns and reduced profit margins on all jobs.

Another problem was that Currie was an old company which had old ways of doing business. The majority of the senior-level management had been with the company for over 20 years; in fact, a lot of them had started out as equipment operators and worked their way up into management. Currie lacked fresh "blood" in the organization, the environment was changing dramatically, and management was not able to realize this or keep up with it.

The employees of Currie were very dedicated and loyal to the company. A great majority were immigrants who had worked for Currie for many years. However, Cook noticed that some of the older employees had become comfortable and complacent with their positions and hence their motivation had dropped. As Cook stated: "We had a lot of old employees who were getting late in their years and did not have too much drive. It was imperative that we get their productivity to increase dramatically."

For the next three years, Cook concentrated on restructuring the organization in terms of personnel and operations. The key was to identify those people in management who were able to make the quantum leap from the "old school" to the "new school." Those who were not able to adapt had to retire. Also, Currie had to reorient itself in the market by making the transition from the heavy construction end of the business to the road maintenance end where the profit margins were higher.

By 1980, Cook felt that he had moulded Currie into a more aggressive and stronger competitor in the road construction market. He had removed all the older management that could not adapt to Currie's new environment and, as a result, the senior management staff was much leaner and more aggressive. Secondly, Cook hired two key people to the management staff: one brought valuable experience to the commercial side of the business and the other to the equipment operations area. Finally, Cook had rationalized the operations in some areas and expanded efforts in other areas.

Cook identified six key strategic decisions that were made:

1. Entered into a joint venture operation with a successful and experienced sand and gravel company to develop Currie's 500 acres of gravel deposits north of Vancouver.

2. Made a commitment to become the leader in the pavement maintenance market in British Columbia. This required investing in technology that was new to the industry such as recycling, road surface scarifying, and pavement profiling. Recycling was a process whereby the existing pavement surface was removed (i.e., by grinding machines or by using back hoes to completely tear it up) and used along with virgin aggregate to form a new recycled mix of asphalt. The new mix was then relaid on the roadway using the usual procedures. This process required additional equipment installed in the asphalt production plant. Pavements profiling was a process whereby a machine (i.e., a grinder) with a large rotating drum containing carbide teeth planed the surface of the road to various depths. The material removed from the road could be used in a recycled asphaltic mixture or it could be used as a subgrade material in another project. This process was used to remove surface distress appearing in the pavement. As well, it corrected the pavement profile to allow for proper drainage and to correct curb heights. Road surface scarifying was a process in which a machine heated up the pavement and removed the surface distress. The removed material was treated with an emulsion to rejuvenate its properties and then relaid.

3. Increased Currie's presence in the road calcium segment of the market. Calcium was sprayed on dirt roads to control the amount of dust.

4. Obtained operating authority to transport petroleum products (for Currie and commercially) in Alberta and several surrounding northern U.S. states.

5. Rationalized Currie's operations in Burnaby, moving away from road construction and concentrating on supplying materials (i.e., asphalt and aggregate) and carrying out winter operations (i.e., snow removal and sanding).

6. Purchased a road surfacing company in Alberta. This made Currie one of the dominant firms in this market.

These changes had a positive effect on Currie's income statement. Exhibit 2 presents a financial summary of Currie's performance from 1977 to 1984. Since 1979, Currie had been a profitable company.

A major burden upon Currie's profitability was the interest owing on the $10.0 million loan. The original plan was to repay the bank the entire debt by 1982. However, this was based on an initial interest rate of 8.5 percent, which was adjusted for inflation in the following years. In the early 80s interest rates reached highs of 20 to 25 percent. Consequently, Currie was not able to make any interest payments until 1983. Cook was able to get the bank to agree to capitalize the interest payments over that time.

In 1980, Currie was able to sell some property in order to pay off some of the outstanding debt. As well, the company seemed to be going in the right direction and, as Cook stated: "We were able to see faintly the light at the end of the tunnel."

The Proposed Houston Division

In the summer of 1983, Cook had business dealings with Brad Carlyle. Carlyle worked for a pipeline construction company in the Calgary area. Prior to this job, he worked in Houston supervising the completion of a rapid transit system. In December 1983, Carlyle arranged to have lunch with Cook. Over lunch, Carlyle told Cook about the opportunities that he saw in the Houston market. Carlyle knew that Currie was looking to expand its operations and he felt

EXHIBIT 2   Currie Paving Limited
Financial Summary (Yearly) ($000)

Year	Current Assets	Current Liabilities	Long-Term Debt (LTD)	L.T.D. Interest	Revenue	Net Income	Fixed Asset Purchases
March 77*	5,481	4,537	8,974	—	6,899	(1,370)	573
March 78	6,006	5,646	9,725	901	22,380	2,124	—
March 79	6,029	4,323	11,918	1,390	21,159	153	1,337
March 80	5,114	3,970	10,501	1,631	23,433	3,719	1,136
March 81	5,063	2,864	10,280	1,954	23,267	1,025	1,995
March 82	10,478	7,051	11,028	2,095	29,784	2,169	2,082
February 83	9,289	3,588	12,955	2,105	34,702	1,144	1,695
February 84	12,983	8,145	6,827	1,663	40,921	740	2,309

* 1977 values for an eight-month period.

that the Houston market was one area that Currie should seriously consider. Currie Construction had previously only worked in the United States as a subcontractor on several road rehabilitation projects.

Carlyle indicated to Cook that he wanted to return to Houston. He believed that he was capable of developing a successful division in this market for Currie. Carlyle had made some valuable contacts within both the government and the construction industry that would be very beneficial. As well, he knew the market and the way it functioned. Cook was impressed with Carlyle's enthusiasm and his belief in the Houston market. Although Carlyle did not have a civil engineering background and was not totally comfortable with road construction techniques, Cook had full confidence in his ability to learn on the job. Cook indicated that he would get back to Carlyle very soon.

As a result of this meeting, Cook and Thomas decided that it would be worthwhile to spend a few days in the Houston market in order to get a better feeling for its potential. None of Currie's senior management people had experience in this market. In mid-January 1984, Cook, Thomas, and Carlyle spent three days in Houston meeting with Department of Transportation officials and touring the area. During this brief stay, a large amount of positive information was gathered about the prospects of entering this market. The DOT officials were excited about Currie entering the market because a recent combines investigation found that a large number of the old established road construction firms were guilty of price fixing and collusion. As a result, they were barred from bidding work for one to two years.

Texas was also experiencing a tremendous amount of growth, and government officials realized that improvements to the infrastructure were required to ensure this growth. As a result, the government had made it a priority to upgrade the highways, bridges, and roadways throughout the state. Cook and Thomas were astonished at the amount of money budgeted to infrastructure upgrading. It was approximately $700 million (U.S.) a year, roughly 4.5 times more than the amount allocated by the DOT in British Columbia.

Even more enticing about this market was the fewer number of competitors compared with the competition in British Columbia. The average number of contractors bidding per job was approximately four.

Further discussion regarding the Houston market took place between Cook, Thomas, and Carlyle. More visits to Houston followed.

The main reason to enter this market according to Cook was because "it offered an opportunity to get better utilization out of our specialized machinery. Instead of having our grinding machines and scarifiers sit idle during the winter months, we could find work for them in Houston. There were no grinders at all in this area of the United States and no one had become involved in recycling."

Cook's orientation for the Houston market was to concentrate primarily on the road maintenance activities of pavement grinding and scarifying operations where Currie was strongest. It was thought that by going in small, Currie could get a better understanding of the market, make some key contacts in government, and develop a good reputation within the industry by doing quality work. Because the road maintenance techniques which Currie possessed were more advanced than those in use in Texas, the company realized it would take a little time to demonstrate their merits to the key government contacts. Currie planned eventually to reproduce its B.C. operations in Texas, where there were no companies totally vertically integrated. Once Currie was established in Texas, it would be able to compete in the nearby surrounding states: Florida, Georgia, North and South Carolina, Tennessee, Alabama, and Louisiana.

The proposed organization chart for the Houston operations is presented in Exhibit 3. Carlyle would report directly to Cook on all matters concerning operations. If the entry took place, Cook planned to spend time overseeing the move to Houston. However, after operations were running, Cook did not plan on spending much time in Houston because Currie did not have much slack in the management ranks. The existing people were all so extended that U.S. entry would have to be delayed if Brad Carlyle, or someone like him from outside existing management, was not available.

EXHIBIT 3   Proposed Organization Chart: Houston, 1984

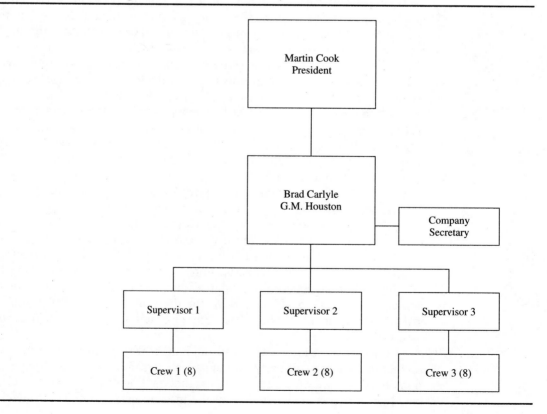

EXHIBIT 4   Currie Construction Ltd.
Cost Analysis for Period Ended

	Cost for Month		Cost To Date		Cost to Complete		Forecasted Final		Planned*		Variance
	Unit	*Cost*	*Unit*	*Cost*	*Unit*	*Cost*	*Unit*	*Cost*	*Unit*	*Cost*	
100–*Contract costs*											
110–*Construction costs*											
198–*Cost of operations*											
200–*Traffic Control*											
Quantity											
Man hours											
Labour											
Man hours											
Supervisor											
Permanent materials											
Other construction costs											
Equipment											
Totals											
210–*Erosion control*											
Quantity											
Man hours											
Labour											
Permanent material											
Other construction costs											
Equipment											
Totals											
220–*Lump sum construction*											
Quantity											
Man hours											
Labour											
Permanent material											
Other construction costs											
Equipment											
Hired equipment and operator											
Hired equipped/operated											
Minority business enterprises											
Totals											

* Equals original bid cost

Subsequent Thinking

Although Currie's primary strength was in road maintenance, the decision was made to get involved in the road construction end of the business if Currie entered this market. There were two reasons for this strategy. The first was to generate some cash flow in order to cover the operating expenses until the grinding and scarifying operations picked up. Secondly, according to information provided by Carlyle, the market appeared to be made of gold; it offered easy access to abnormal profits.

Although little public data were available, the competition in this market was primarily family-owned companies. These firms were cash rich and were not accustomed to much competition. As Cook described them, "They are a bunch of old-time southern contractors who are financially very strong and wealthy, primarily from the price fixing that had occurred." One additional key player in the market was ARRON, a subsidiary of Petro Oil, one of the largest corporations in the United States.

If they proceeded, Cook and Carlyle decided that Currie would buy new equipment since abnormal profits seemed to be present. While Currie would normally lease and/or rent equipment for new operation initially in order to minimize investment in a new market, this would reduce profit margins slightly. It was felt that Currie could be competitive and easily make even more than 4 percent net profit on revenue with new equipment.

Carlyle felt there would be no problem locating supervisors and equipment operators. Due to the large population growth occurring in the southern states and the minor influence of labour unions, Carlyle felt he would be able to hire blue-collar employees at about half the wage rate that Currie was paying its employees in British Columbia. Carlyle would be responsible for hiring all the blue-collar employees; however, he would require Cook's approval in hiring supervisors.

If Currie decided to enter this market, the Houston subsidiary would utilize Currie's existing centralized control systems. In 1982, Currie had paid $15,000 and invested a further $70,000 for a fully integrated job costing/receivable/ledger cost reporting and accounting system which was one of the most comprehensive of any firm in the industry. For each of the 200 active accounts that Currie was working on, it received a monthly cost analysis (see Exhibit 4, for example). This allowed the company to see costs broken down by subcategory on each job for the current month, to date, to complete, and forecasted final—all versus the original plan. For *any* given job, it might be several years before all of the relevant costs had been accounted for and the accounts closed off.

With this background, Cook realized that if he were to enter the U.S. market at all in the next few years, he would have to decide soon.

DELTA AGROCHEMICALS, INC.

Based in Denver, Colorado, Consolidated Western Holdings (CWH) was a large Fortune 500 listed industrial company. From its beginning in the 1940s as an oil and gas venture, CWH had steadily expanded its oil operations and had diversified through acquisition to become a major participant in the chemical industry. The company also owned and managed coal mining operations around the world and had acquired a collection of small, but growing, high-technology, energy-related businesses in the United States.

CWH's chemical business consisted of four divisions, each run as an autonomous profit centre. The smallest and newest of these was the Western Biotechnology ("Westec") business, managed by John Finlayson. In May 1991, however, Finlayson was considering moving to Delta Agrochemicals ("DeltaAg"), a much larger sister division in the agricultural chemicals business. Finlayson knew the senior managers of DeltaAg well, as he had been a member of the division's internal management board since the mid-1980s.

Because of his success in building Westec, Finlayson was widely reviewed as a competent manager, and he was sure that if he asked for a transfer to DeltaAg, it would be approved. Although the move would not be a promotion, Finlayson thought that the change would be an interesting one as DeltaAg faced a number of major issues. He added, "I now have someone here who can run Westec with only minor consultation with me, and I am spending so much time working on DeltaAg issues that I think I might as well move over there full time." DeltaAg's head office was about two kilometres from Westec's. Both were located in St. Louis, Missouri.

This case was prepared by Professor J. Peter Killing with the assistance of Joyce Miller for the sole purpose of providing material for class discussion at the Western Business School. Copyright 1991 © The University of Western Ontario.

The Agrochemicals Business

Agrochemical companies discovered, developed, registered, and sold products for controlling pests (insecticides), plant diseases (fungicides), and weeds (herbicides). Traditionally, it had been a high-growth, high-margin business, and gross margins in the 60 percent range were not uncommon. By the 1990s, however, industry profit was eroding as costs skyrocketed and growth flattened. In many countries, the industry was not able to increase its prices sufficiently to offset cost inflation. Moreover, the food supply in the developed world was broadly in surplus, and arable land was being taken out of production. At the same time, mounting public concern about the environmental effects of agrochemicals was delaying registration of new products. Over the long term, no more than 1 to 2 percent growth per annum was expected in existing markets.

Some industry observers felt that there was strong market potential in centrally planned and developing countries, but the question was when and where such growth would occur. Hot spots like South East Asia looked very promising, but Eastern European countries were problematic. In terms of crops, it was widely believed that wheat production was likely to decline, while rice and maize, for example, would increase. Eighty percent of the world agrochemicals market was believed to be found in less than 20 countries.

Overall, the market for agrochemical products was highly fragmented, with more than 40 separate product categories each worth more than $100 million. Herbicides, for example, were sold for approximately 10 different crops, including cotton, rice, maize, soya beans, sugar cane, sugar beets, and so on. Within any of these general crop areas were a variety of individual product categories. In the maize segment, for example, there were separate herbicide products available to: (1) kill grass before it emerged; (2) kill grass after it emerged; (3) kill broad-leafed weeds before they emerged; and (4) kill broad-leafed weeds after they emerged. Delta had products in most, but not all, of these product categories.

Expectations were that the fight for market share would continue to intensify. All major companies were spending heavily on research and development. The key to success was to find new "active ingredients" with novel effects for controlling pests, diseases, or weeds, and then to get these to the market ahead of the competition. It was, however, a long and expensive process. Gestation periods of 7 to 10 years were not uncommon as companies took their new products through toxicology tests, metabolism tests, studies of crop residue, environmental impact assessments, and so on. Detailed field studies had to be performed before a product could be offered for sale in an individual country and this was both time-consuming and expensive in most major markets. The registration process could cost up to $50 million per product, and of course, it cost the same whether the product turned out to be a world beater or a lacklustre "me too" offering.

A further hurdle facing agricultural chemical producers was the 1988 American legislation, that required products (which had been introduced when registration standards were less stringent) to be re-registered, at great cost. The result was that poorly performing old products were taken off the market. For companies like DeltaAg, however, which had a range of successful older products, re-registration was an expensive necessity. Other countries were expected to follow the American lead.

Delta Agrochemicals, Inc.

With almost $2.5 billion in sales in 1990, DeltaAg had a 14 percent share of the world agrochemical market. The company's product line, which consisted of more than 2,000 individual chemical formulations, was built on 35 to 40 active ingredients, 7 or 8 of which accounted for 80 percent of sales. The company manufactured its active ingredients in a few key plants in North America and Europe, and shipped them to more than 50 formulation plants around the world where final formulation, packaging, and labelling took place. DeltaAg's products were sold in more than 100 countries, and the company had its own selling organization in 45 countries. DeltaAg's largest markets were the United States, Canada, and France.

In the mid-1960s, shortly after CWH acquired DeltaAg, the company developed a "blockbuster" weed killer, Melinor, which sold well in many markets around the world and fuelled the company's growth for the next 10 years. Then in the late 1970s, DeltaAg acquired a mid-sized French company and a British firm which specialized in insecticides. These acquisitions, combined with strong market growth, brought DeltaAg's sales volume to approximately $1.4 billion by the mid-1980s. In 1988, DeltaAg purchased the agrochemical division of another major American company, which was particularly strong in corn and wheat protection. In addition to growth by acquisition, DeltaAg had been introducing new products at a record rate. George Hill, DeltaAg's research director, commented:

> We spent a decade looking for another blockbuster like Melinor, without success, and then changed our strategy to go for incremental development of existing products. This worked extremely well and by the early 1980s, we were introducing two new products per year, which is remarkable by industry standards. As late as 1979, Melinor accounted for 80 percent of the company's gross margin; thanks to our new products, it is now down around 10 to 15 percent.
>
> We are currently spending about $300 million on research and development. The budget is split into three equal parts—one-third for invention, one-third for the development and registration of new products, and one-third for the reformulation and re-registration of existing products.

1988—Strategic and Organizational Changes

In 1988, DeltaAg underwent a major strategy review. Under the direction of Alan Jemison, who had been the president of DeltaAg for five years, the management team set an objective of becoming the "world's leading agricultural chemical company." Profitability targets were established: the immediate goal was a 16 percent operating profit to sales ratio (compared with 10 percent in 1987) and by 1997, the return on assets was to reach 36 percent, approximately double the 1987 figure. Growth would be at a rate 50 percent greater than the market. All of these objectives were considered ambitious but achievable, and in the words of the strategy document, they would require "increasingly selective decisions aimed at steering all activities towards the areas of highest reward."

As a first step in implementing the new strategy, countries were divided into six categories, with a different DeltaAg objective established for each. These objectives ranged from "defend dominant position" to "improve market share rapidly." At the same time, three broad product categories were created, namely: "products of key strategic importance," "high-price, high-margin specialties," and products with "commercial or technical limitations." Again, different objectives were set for the products in each category.

The 1988 strategy was accompanied by organizational changes. Cost-savings reductions were made in the St. Louis head office, particularly in the marketing areas. About 80 of St. Louis' 600 employees were laid off. In addition, a new vice presidential layer of management was added (see Exhibit 1) in order to free up the senior vice presidents to concentrate on the long-term future of the business. An employee commented:

> We tried to create a common culture in the business and to heal some of the wounds caused by the 1988 reorganization. We got everyone at St. Louis into groups and worked with them to identify the key success factors in the business and their role in delivering them. We thought that ideas would flow back and forth and people would talk about where they were and where they wanted to be as an organization. There was a lot of cynicism, however, and it became clear that the vice presidents had not really bought into the exercise. The president, who was committed, was reluctant to push the others very hard because the groups said 'this exercise is about trust—so trust us.' The end result was that some people signed on, but a lot did not.

1991—Another Look at the Organization

By early 1991, it was clear that the previous year had not been a financial success for DeltaAg. Virtually all measures of profitability had fallen from previous years, and as shown in Exhibit 2, all were far below budget. David Jans, the Vice President of Finance for DeltaAg, explained the situation:

> The 1988 strategy looked great on paper, but we never implemented it. Since then, we have built in even more fixed costs—probably hitting a billion in 1990. Last year we delivered to CWH only 50 percent of the cash that they were

EXHIBIT 1   Partial Organization Chart

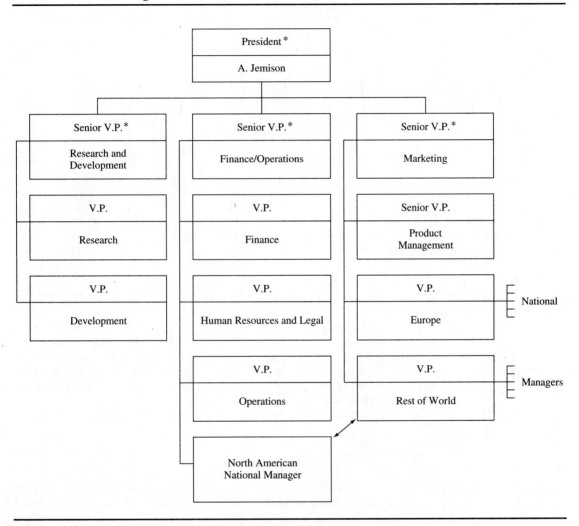

---

* These four executives plus John Finlayson comprised the Delta Agrochemicals, Inc. management board, responsible for overseeing the company's activities.

expecting! It does not take a genius to figure out that our absolute priority now has to be to cut costs. We cannot go before CWH management this summer without a cost cutting plan already being implemented.

At the instigation of John Finlayson, we recently looked at cutting the number of active ingredients that we produce by 50 percent and selling through distributors in about half of the 45 or so countries in which we currently maintain company operations. At the outset this looked very attractive, because like most organizations we make 80 percent of our total gross margin with 20 percent of our products

EXHIBIT 2   Financial Performance
(millions of dollars)

	1986	1987	1988	1989	Actual 1990	Budget 1990
Sales	1350	1610	2160	2452	2485	2570
Gross Margin	665	815	1195	1360	1392	1445
Percent of Sales	49%	51%	55%	55%	56%	56%
R&D, Sales, Administration	548	564	830	942	1000	980
Depreciation	32	36	60	70	82	80
Other	4	20	26	24	40	28
Operating Profit	81	195	279	324	270	357
Cash Flow						
Operating Profit	81	195	279	324	270	357
Depreciation	32	36	60	70	82	80
Capital Investment	(114)	(74)	(128)	(176)	(152)	(152)
Acquisition Reorganization			(30)			
Working Capital Changes	(48)	28	(22)	(145)	(42)	42
Cash to Consolidated Western Holdings	(49)	185	159	73	158	327

and in about 20 percent of our markets. However, the study was very disappointing. Our country managers indicated that they could not cut their number of employees very much if they dropped their worst selling products. And we would not be able to save much on the production side either. The net result was that eliminating the bottom half of our product line and markets served would actually reduce our return on capital.

But we still need to do something. Corporate is not happy with us.

In early 1991, Delta Ag management instituted a 13 percent cost cut across the board. All departments were to comply. Also, John Finlayson was asked to begin a study of the organization to see how it could be streamlined. He believed that DeltaAg needed lower costs, fewer people doing more rewarding jobs, clearer accountabilities, and better coordination between the functional departments in St. Louis. He explained:

We need to change this organization to get rid of the duplication and cross-functional boundaries. My approach is to begin trying to determine exactly what transactions are necessary to the successful functioning of the organization. Once we know that, we will be in a position to decide how to organize, and we will know where we can cut, and where we cannot.

To do this, I have set up two task forces. One is to examine the product supply chain within the company, and the other is to study the new production introduction chain. These are both lateral processes that cut across the functional departments. Each task force is to identify the key interactions and figure out how they could be performed more efficiently—I am sure that there is room for great improvement. I may also set up a group to look at the role of head office here in St. Louis vis-à-vis the national organizations around the world. They say that we collect too much information from them, and do nothing with it. They also complain that we exercise too much control over their strategies. Are they right? We need to find out the minimum required to manage this company, not the "nice to have." Let's push decision making down to the lowest possible level, stop the second guessing, and make decisions only once.

We do not have the kind of performance measures you'd expect in a company this well established. Personal reward and pain have to be more direct.

An employee who had been working in the development department at St. Louis for two years (after spending four years in another part of CWH) applauded the organizational review. She commented:

My job is to help get the technical resources in this company applied to real world projects where they are needed most—for the product areas that I cover. I am a coordinator—I have no direct power—and to be successful, I have to influence people in different parts of the organization to work together. Working up the hierarchy is not effective because I don't get a quick enough response, and often the information that does come back is not useful. It seems like there are eternal gripes between the people who make things and the people who sell things. There are endless circles going up and nothing going across. For the past 18 months, I have been trying to get $80,000 of formulation time devoted to a product that could give us an immediate $10 million return in the market. I can't get the time, and I can't figure out why not. Right now, the project is in limbo and I've run out of options to move it forward. It's unbelievably frustrating.

The 1991 Strategy Review

CWH'S management system called for a comprehensive strategy review of each of its businesses every third year. DeltaAg's review was due in the summer of 1991, and in April, Alan Jemison called a management meeting to discuss the DeltaAg submission. After the meeting, he commented:

This strategy review is a major event and I hope we can take advantage of it. There is no doubt that the business needs to be more profitable—even if that means making it smaller. We should probably cut the product line a little and step out of some markets. We also need to change our R&D strategy to concentrate on fewer, larger product developments. Our strategy of incrementalism has worked well, but with the rising cost of registration, it is getting too expensive to maintain. Finally, we need to devolve headquarters functions to the national companies—we must learn to stop doing things for them. The trouble is that a lot of our people here don't feel right unless they are out in the field selling something.

My challenge is to get people to buy into the strategy-making process—to take it seriously. I will be retiring in 24 months and no one knows whether my successor will be appointed from inside DeltaAg or from another part of CWH. There is a lot of speculation, and not enough emphasis on improving the business.

I do not believe that we need to change the organization. We have had a lot of organizational changes, and we now need stability. I hear people saying that we need to get rid of the vice presidential layer—I don't think so. What we do need is to turn the managers at the top of this company into a team—a committed team with a common objective.

Other senior DeltaAg executives commented on the situation facing the businesses in 1991.

Senior Vice President of Research and Development

This is a technically driven business, and the success of any company in it depends on its ability to create new, high-margin, active ingredients. In the short term, we could cut our research spending and it would improve the bottom line—but we would be giving away our future. We need to preserve our research skills, and work toward developing more significant new products. At the moment, we have too many marginal products and too many marginal territories. What we need to do is identify the key product/territory combinations and focus on them.

Vice President of Human Resources

I came from the chemicals subsidiary of an American oil company to join this business in 1990. I see my role as being a change agent. This business is too complex, and people seem to revel in its complexity. Managers make their careers here by winning arguments. A decision is the starting point for a debate rather than a move to action. I heard that Alan once gave a clear instruction that a product under development was to be cancelled. When this happened the researchers began to work on it secretly, and even introduced it to the market a few years later. It failed.

To take this organization forward we need to do two things:

1. We need to create horizontal business processes that will increase communication between the functional areas. As well, we need a flatter organization. The middle level and junior employees see this vice presidential layer and it drives them crazy. Until senior management gets its act together, they say, why should we behave any differently?
2. We need to reduce the number of products that we produce and markets that we serve. We need to create the mix that will produce the most cash in the short term, and growth for the longer term.

Senior Vice President of Marketing

I have discussed the situation with my vice presidents and we agree that we should not cut back our product line or reduce our territorial coverage. Our customers need our full line, and every product that we sell makes money. There is no point in throwing away gross margin. Of course, we can improve our efficiency, and we are already doing this.

We have moved from 18 operating units in Europe down to 8, and we're looking at a plan that would bring us down to only three formulation plants for the whole region.

To increase profitability, we need to reduce fixed manufacturing costs. We are using a lot of old manufacturing equipment that requires a lot of maintenance. We could get some of our formulation manufacturing done by outside companies—it certainly would be cheaper and we would not need these far-flung plants all over the world.

Vice President of Operations

In the mid-1980s, at the insistence of CWH senior management, we introduced MRP 2 into this business, and it has made a tremendous difference. Our manufacturing performance has increased dramatically over the past few years.

If our priority is to cut costs, we need to look first at cutting back our research. Research has two major laboratories, one in California and the other in the U.K. that came with one of the acquisitions. That British lab is costing in the neighbourhood of $75 million per year. I believe that we should shut it down and fold its operations into our U.S. operation. British researchers are difficult to control, and the British management team has a tendency to use the lab for their own pet projects; they're also duplicating some of the work that we are doing here.

We also need to reduce the complexity of the business. In spite of what the marketing people say, we do have too many marginal products and too many marginal territories.

John Finlayson's Decision

At the end of May 1991, John Finlayson was reviewing his situation. He felt that he could not continue to manage Westec and spend so much time working on DeltaAg issues. It was time to make a decision.

I have to move one way or the other. I am concerned that without my full-time presence in DeltaAg, some of the things that we are doing, like the task forces, will not have any impact. I am already worried that they are losing their way and are just going through the motions. Whether I join the company or not, I think that we should create a vice president of planning position and give that person the job of managing the change that has to happen. Everyone else is just too busy to give it the time it needs.

The other thing that makes me think that I should move into DeltaAg is the impending strategy review. Alan sent me a draft of their first attempt at a strategy and I found it too conservative—too much business as usual. In the past week, I have put together something stronger—what I call a focused strategy. It clearly separates our winning territories and products, and specifies different levels of service for them than for our more marginal products and areas. I've shown it to a few people in DeltaAg and they seem to like it. Some say it is obvious and what we are already doing—but no one has said it does not make sense.

On a personal level, I don't think that Alan has strong feelings either way about the possibility of my moving over there. We have discussed it, and it's pretty clear that the decision is mine to make. I might be able to move into one of the senior vice president spots, or perhaps we could create a new one.

FIRST FIDELITY BANCORPORATION (A)

In April 1990, Don Parcells, recently appointed Head of Corporate Operations and Systems at First Fidelity Bancorporation (FFB), New Jersey, was considering ways to improve the productivity of the bank's Operations and Systems departments. As he sat down to ponder his organizational restructuring and operational consolidation he wondered which of the three main options he should use to effect the change. FFB could use the internal systems department resources, an information systems consulting company, or a new method for operating Information Systems departments—outsourcing. He knew how important cost effective, innovative information technology was to the bank's competitive position. Whichever path FFB were to proceed down, he knew he had better identify the risks and the benefits expected. Considering the faltering economy and the FFB president's desire for a lean organization within 18 months, Parcells realized that a decision would have to be made quickly.

United States Banking Industry

The structure of the United States (U.S.) banking industry was characterized by small local and regional banks serving local customers. Except for a few of the larger, money-centre banks, services varied widely by bank and by branch. A customer could not receive the same set of services in multiple locations, and electronic interconnection was cumbersome. This industry structure had developed in response to historically restrictive legislation that had limited interstate banking and the products that banks were able to offer.

Barbara L. Marcolin and Kerry McLellan prepared this case with the assistance of Professor Paul Beamish solely to provide material for class discussion. Copyright © 1992 The University of Western Ontario.

These restrictions, as well as antitrust legislation, had limited the growth potential of individual firms in the industry.

During the past 20 years there had been a gradual easing of banking regulations. Many of the restrictions confining banking activities had been removed, enabling banks to expand their product offerings and geographic scope. The standard growth pattern that emerged involved friendly acquisitions with the acquired banks being organized under a holding company structure. In general, these acquired banks continued to operate autonomously with little consolidation of bank operations or systems. This led to incompatibility between the banks' systems and limited efficiencies within the holding company structure. Despite these problems, banks within the industry continued to amalgamate at a fairly fast pace.

Recently, there were pressures which prompted a shift from this historical pattern. Pressure was growing within the U.S. Congress to develop a global banking strategy and to allow greater financial sector consolidation. Further, there was a growing market demand for transparent banking; both commercial and personal customers wanted consolidated bank access for interstate transactions. Although the legislative barriers to consolidation were decreasing, the recent failure of the savings and loan institutions had introduced a countervailing pressure for more regulation. In response to this financial disaster, the government had tightened banking regulations, particularly those concerning the reporting of financial information. The government also developed more stringent guidelines for reviewing the asset quality and operating procedures of all financial institutions. It appeared that all bank functions would soon be subjected to more careful scrutiny with assets being more thoroughly reviewed, new products more closely examined, and acquisitions and financial performance more attentively monitored.

History of FFB

First Fidelity was established in 1812 as the State Bank of Newark, and grew gradually during its first 150 years. However, the last 30 years had witnessed many changes caused by reorganization, acquisitions, and mergers. The introduction of new state-wide bank holding laws in the late 1960s was a major force for change. In 1969, the bank was reorganized under a holding company structure. This enabled First Fidelity to become increasingly involved in business beyond its historical boundaries of Newark, New Jersey.

Capitalizing on the new bank holding laws, major expansion occurred in the 1980s when several banks were brought under the holding company's control. During this expansion period, the company's name was changed to reflect its increased dimensions; it became the First Fidelity Bancorporation (FFB). The acquisition of a healthy savings bank in 1986 had reinforced the innovative, aggressive posture of FFB. It was the first time a financially strong savings bank had been acquired by a commercial bank holding company.

Although the holding company was expanding rapidly, each acquired bank continued to operate as an independent unit with FFB reporting the consolidated financial statements.

In 1988, FFB continued its strategy of expanding into contiguous geographic regions when it merged with another holding company, Fidelcor Inc., which had a similar history of growth and acquisition in the Philadelphia area. Bringing these banks under the FFB umbrella gave the bank access to new business products such as Trust and International Banking, and also enabled FFB to serve New Jersey customers in the neighbouring state with these acquisitions. FFB was poised to respond to the call for standardized products in a larger geographic region for commercial and retail customers.

In the late 1980s, FFB experienced a period of lacklustre performance. The stock price had dropped well below its book value, making it an attractive takeover target. The bank's operating efficiency was ranked 44th of the top 50 U.S. banks. The asset quality of the Philadelphia and Newark banks surfaced as a problem after the 1988 merger and the company was forced to write off a large portion of these assets in 1989. In an attempt to strengthen FFB's position in the industry, the old management team was replaced in February 1990.

The new Chairman and Chief Executive Officer, Tony Terracciano, immediately announced three new executive vice president positions. Don Parcells, one of the new executive vice presidents, was given responsibility for operations and systems.

Parcells' past experience in both the international and domestic operations of several larger banks made him particularly well qualified for this position. His association with Terracciano began in the mid-1970s when Terracciano, then Chief of Staff for international affairs at Chase Manhattan Bank, asked him to assume responsibility for the bank's European operations area. This job was challenging as the situation was chaotic and costs were out of control. Parcells successfully turned around the Operations Department and within two years had the area functioning at top efficiency. This experience allowed him to develop the skills needed to successfully implement major operational restructuring.

Following his European success, Parcells accepted a position with another major U.S. bank. Eventually, as head of international operations, he integrated the U.S. branch operations with their international counterparts. These experiences in consolidation and integration prepared Parcells for his current challenge at FFB.

FFB Today

In April 1990, FFB was the holding company for eight independent banks representing 500 branches and $28 billion in assets. FFB was ranked as one of the top 25 super regional banks in the U.S. The holding company acted as the corporate integrating level, while the operating banks were autonomous, decentralized units. Each operating bank had a president and vice presidents responsible for the major business units (Exhibit 1).

Little progress had been made in consolidating services or banking activities. However, by April 1990, several initiatives had begun. Treasury operations for two banks were now the responsibility of one person. Furthermore, the physical processing sites for check activities were being consolidated into fewer operational units which provided services to numerous branches. In addition, all Trust operations were now under the control of central management. Plans were also being developed to consolidate additional functions such as installment loan and customer services, and mortgage processing under one structure with services provided to other banks. Some progress was being made in the consolidation of physical systems. However, each bank was still processed as a stand-alone entity with its own software application set.

These pockets of centralized management were integrated into the decentralized holding company structure through the cumbersome decision-making process that existed. Committees had been used to coordinate activities, because direct-line authority only existed at the FFB CEO level. This coordinating mechanism consumed significant management time and resources that could be better spent on more fundamental operational problems. However, consolidation efforts were hampered because no corporatewide plan for operational activities or computer architecture existed to guide future development and restructuring efforts.

Overview of Operations and Systems

The operations and systems within the banks included all the major activities required to support the daily banking transactions. Each was critical to the functioning and performance of that bank, and both were intricately linked to each other in a complex network of activitites. Operations involved a number of back office activities that supported the processing of transactions and services. Typically, these functions were labour-intensive and included activities such as encoding, exception processing, proofing, clearing, mortgage servicing, lock box services, and trust activities.

Management Information Systems (MIS) within the bank involved three major activities: system development, relationship management, and data processing. The latter activity was most closely tied to the bank operations. Commonly referred to as "the systems," data processing involved the data centre activities where application systems processed the daily transactions including mortgage, loan, deposit, and commercial services.

Whether an activity was defined as an operation or a system varied from function to function and, for some business procedures, was best defined as a combination of both. Check processing, for example, involved many steps from capturing the check data to processing it and finally to clearing the funds between banks. The line between operational and systems activities was often

EXHIBIT 1   FFB Current Operational Structure

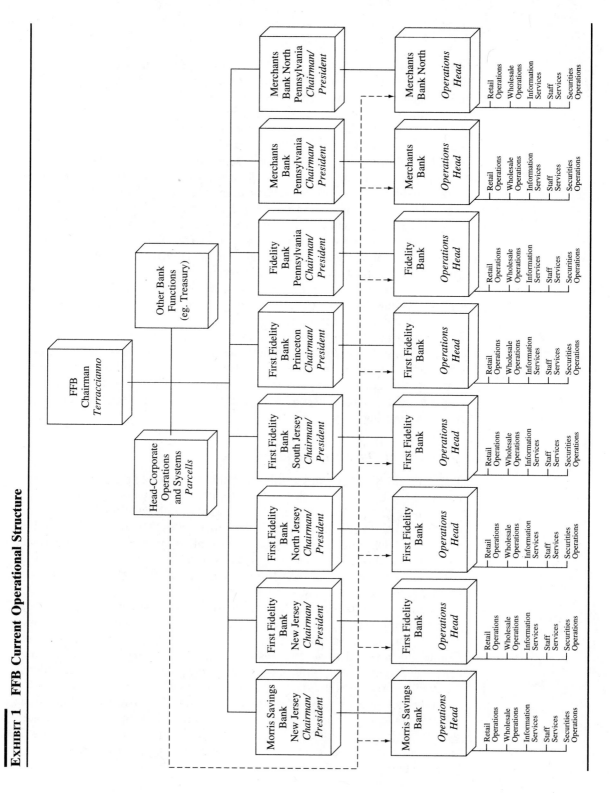

EXHIBIT 2   Banking Services

Commodity-Type Functions	*Stand-Alone Products*
• Courier and messenger services	• Lock box
• Mail processing	• Credit card
• Printing and reproduction	• Corporate trust
• Physical security	• Estate banking trust and personal trust
• Automated teller machine switching	• Stock transfer
• Network management	• Custody services
• Coin and currency	• Check processing
• Facilities services	
• Data processing operations	
• Mortgage servicing	

---

blurred. In general, systems were used to support major business functions or product offerings, and were critical to these operations.

Banking services could be separated into two distinct groups: commodity-type functions and stand-alone products (Exhibit 2). Commodity-type functions were those activities that were transparent to the customer. Changes to these functions would not affect customer perceptions, as long as the services were presented in a similar manner. This limited the strategic and marketing risks associated with consolidating these functions. Stand-alone products were those activities that were used directly by the customer, and thus changes to these activities would be seen by the marketplace. Given the high visibility of these products, proposal changes would have to be given careful consideration. Since the strategic fit of these products was not yet determined, the firm's strategic positioning would dictate how these products were handled.

Making changes to custom stand-alone products was a difficult process. The major functional and business unit groups usually defended their territory with aggressive actions, resulting in many compromises across banks so that customers could maintain their individualized services. Though two banks might be using the same operating procedures or computer systems, they might have tailored them in specific ways to meet local demands. These differences caused several difficulties across the banks. Each branch scheduled statement printouts based on their own demands and produced statement printouts with individualized messages. Systems efficiencies were impossible to achieve within the present structure. It was not uncommon to have bank branches offering different interest rates at the same time! Corporate customers who dealt with a few branches were not pleased with these discrepancies. If this situation persisted, there could be negative ramifications for marketing and customer services. Although FFB looked like a larger bank, it had realized few of the potential efficiencies or benefits.

Senior management was aware of the problems inherent in FFB's holding company structure and recognized the need for systems integration and operational consolidation. Although rapid and drastic modifications were needed, there were built-in cultural impediments to change. Many of the bank presidents and employees had developed within one bank and strongly identified with its local area. If operating procedures or systems were to be changed, these employees would have to expand the scope of their loyalty to encompass the institution as a whole. FFB had initiated a lengthy process of education and negotiation to accomplish this goal.

Pressure for Rapid Change

FFB was under pressure to develop standardized products, global banking capability, and improved efficiency. Consolidation appeared to be the only way FFB could respond to these pressures, as well as the need to improve the reporting and management control information required to run a firm as large as FFB. Better controls were also needed to respond to governmental regulatory bodies who were becoming more stringent regarding asset quality and capital requirements. The government was vigorously enforcing these requirements against other banks, and management figured it would be 18 months at the most before the focus shifted to FFB.

From the beginning, it was clear that drastic consolidation action was needed within this firmly set 18-month time frame. The time pressure led to the realization that only two options were available: make the bank as efficient as possible and sell it; or consolidate and grow. The general feeling was that the business had the capacity to support growth. As Parcells recalls:

> With all the problems, there were some interesting aspects. We had over 500 branches in the most densely populated state in the country, with the second highest per capita income. We had one of the lowest funding costs of almost any bank in the U.S. and, if run efficiently, it could make a lot of money. If you make money, you can get your share price up and then make acquisitions in a market which was fairly depressed. We felt that if we could get better faster than some of the others, then we would have a window of opportunity to grow.

With the determination to fix up the business, management set forth to review the situation. Three problems emerged in the early analysis. First, the economy was heading into a recession. Second, the asset quality was beginning to deteriorate as the economy worsened. The commercial real estate market which was beginning to soften would need increased reserve requirements and would put a strain on working capital. Although working capital was not an immediate problem, steps would have to be taken to improve credit policies and to reduce potential drains. This could not be done quickly, and, in fact, might not have an effect for several years. Third, productivity had to be improved and expenses had to be cut. The unconsolidated operational structure represented significantly higher costs than comparable banks in the industry. In March 1990, a 10 percent arbitrary cut of operating expenses and staff was made across the organization. This action was intended to save $95 million that year and an estimated $125 million in subsequent years (see financial statements in Exhibit 3). Management recognized that significant further cuts

Exhibit 3   FFB Financial Statements

Consolidated Income Statement 1989 ($000)

Total interest income	2,677,777		
Total interest expense	1,693,312		
Net interest income		984,465	
Provision for possible credit losses		200,254	
Net income after loss provision		784,211	
Trust income	77,624		
Other income (e.g., service charges, security transactions)	272,626		
Total non-interest income		350,250	
Total income			1,134,461
Total non-interest expenses (e.g., salaries & benefits, equipment)			945,797
Income before taxes			188,664
Income taxes			28,616
Net income			160,048

Consolidated Balance Sheet
as of December 31, 1989 ($000)

Assets			
Cash	1,685,068		
Interest-bearing time deposits	80,801		
Investment securities	7,937,379[1]		
Total loans and leases		19,243,024	
Other assets		1,781,543	
Total Assets			30,727,815
Liabilities			
Total deposits	22,872,460		
Short-term borrowing	4,509,198		
Other liabilities	1,000,753		
Long-term deposits	780,438		
Total Liabilities		29,162,849	
Preferred stock	157,271		
Common stock	58,492		
Surplus	663,398		
Retained earnings	685,805		
Total common stakeholders' equity	1,407,695		
Total stakeholders' equity		1,564,966	
Total liabilities and stakeholder equity			30,727,815

[1] Market value 1990: $6,707,209

would be more difficult to make, and any subsequent cost savings would only come through the difficult task of organizational rationalization and consolidation. There was little the bank could do to reverse the recession, but it could address the other two problems. Management immediately began reviewing asset quality and taking appropriate actions. Parcells' responsibility was to address the productivity and expense issue.

Information Gathering to Reach a Decision

Parcells undertook an immediate review of the back office operations and systems to determine what potential savings could be realized. An experienced consultant was hired to help identify a new structure for operations and systems, to calculate the estimated savings, and to itemize the rationalization steps.

Senior management considered every possible option for a new corporate structure. Each of these alternatives was evaluated against an explicit set of criteria:

- Cost effectiveness
- Responsiveness to business needs
- Responsiveness to individual bank needs
- Ability to standardize product and service offerings
- Ability to support outsourcing options
- Ability to support acquisitions
- Service/quality orientation/incentives

The structural options that were considered ranged from keeping the current structure to realigning operations management centralized by bank, centralized by function, centralized by business, centralized by a hybrid of function and business, or organized as a service company. The consultant discussed the key features of each of these options in his report to Parcells, as shown in Exhibit 4. Each of these options could be compared against the strategic objectives. Clearly, the latter two options supported more of the proposed criteria, and of these, the centralized hybrid structure seemed the most logical at the time. This structure would allow FFB to gain the benefits from the functions and businesses of the lowest cost operating structure, the greatest standardization of products and services, the greatest flexibility, and the future support for assimilating acquisitions. While FFB would still be poised to move into a service corporation structure if desired, it seemed the centralized hybrid structure would be an intermediary step in any case. Accordingly, the proposed high-level operations structure divided this organization into five major functions and businesses: retail operations, wholesale operations, information services, staff services, and securities operations (Exhibit 5). These new departments would replace the independent bank operations.

EXHIBIT 4   Evaluation of Possible Structures

	Dedicated Bank Operations	Centralized By Bank	Centralized By Function	Centralized By Business	Centralized Hybrid	Services Company
Cost Effectiveness	○	◐	●	◐	●	●
Responsiveness to Business Needs	◐	◐	○	●	◐	◐
Responsiveness to Bank Needs	●	◐	○	◐	◐	◐
Standardized Product and Service	○	○	●	●	●	●
Flexibility for Outsourcing	◐	◐	●	○	●	●
Ability to Support Acquisitions	○	○	●	●	●	●
Services and Quality Orientation	●	●	○	◐	◐	●

● - Fully support
○ - Does not support

Source: Consultant's report and FFB Board of Directors' presentation

Together, Parcells and the consultant determined that a consolidated oganization would offer significant savings over the current organizational structure. The annual savings from an operational consolidation were determined to be more than $65 million, which would be incremental to the 10 percent arbitrary cut already made. Together, the cuts represented a 20 percent reduction of the $1 billion expense base, and would contribute directly to the bottom line. The problem was determining how to get these incremental savings within the time frame available.

The rationalization of operations meant that all commodity-type functions would be reviewed against market opportunities. Since the functions were transparent to the customer, they presented few obstacles if changed. It appeared that most functions could be purchased at a lower cost than could be done within FFB, and thus should be contracted out.

The rationalization of systems meant that a common set of applications had to be found, and one data centre had to be assembled. This would require the consolidation of the physical data centres including renovating and ex-

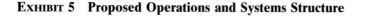

EXHIBIT 5   Proposed Operations and Systems Structure

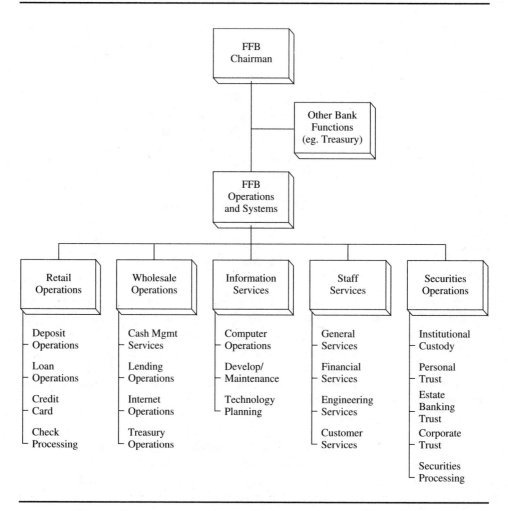

panding an existing site, moving all hardware, restructuring the communications network, and phasing out other sites. A few capture and encoding sites (possibly 2 and 5, respectively) for check processing and commercial loan operations would be used as logistics dictated. Currently, there were data processing operations in each bank, and eight capture and 18 encoding stations. The software applications would have to be standardized to establish a common application platform upon which marketing could build new products. This would involve the rationalization of 260+ applications down to approximately 60. Though most application packages processed similar functions within the banks, they had been acquired from different vendors. Few banks used the same commercial package and, unfortunately, when common applications did exist, they were tailored to the local bank and were, therefore, not compatible with other sites. The final task would be to convert all banks to this common application platform. The banks would have to standardize all products and services, convert existing data and files, and train staff in the new procedures.

The consolidation plans did not include all of the MIS department. Systems development and, to a lesser extent, the IS-user relationship management activities would continue to operate as an independent, decentralized department. Since systems development activities were so critical to bank products and marketing services, FFB would be able to control this department, yet keep it focused on individual bank needs and market forces. The combination of consolidating data processing while retaining the old systems development process promised to give FFB better strategic control in the future, and lower costs now.

Rationalization Options

Since systems were vitally important to the bank's operations, Parcells knew the rationalization and consolidation had to be done well and fit with the bank's new strategic direction. He saw three options available: the rationalization could be done in-house, by consultants, or through an outsourcing agreement. Each of these options had to be considered in terms of its fit with the organizational objectives.

Criteria

It was important to management that the employees be treated well. Any solutions had to include comparable pay and benefits for existing staff. In terms of time frame, the job had to be done in 18 months. No other time frame was acceptable. The group had to have the capacity to do the job in terms of staff numbers and appropriate skill levels. Also, the applications had to be taken from the existing software packages currently used by the eight banks. Many packages were the best commercial products available, and were already designed to fit FFB's banking environment.

If an outside vendor were to become involved, additional criteria would have to be met. First, the contract would have to be for a fixed price over a 10-year period. Second, the vendor's experience and track record would play an important role in determining the best candidate. Third, both resources and their quality would be considered. Finally, the vendor's commitment to the business would be of the utmost importance.

Any savings to be realized by involving a third party would have to be compared to the projected $65 million savings made possible by rationalizing the Operations and Systems departments in-house. "Comparing to any other standard," Parcells observed, "would be absurd!" The discussions would also include identifying additional savings beyond the internal review.

Options

Internal

The first option was to achieve the operations and systems consolidation with the internal staff and resources. Some efforts were already being made to centralize operations and systems (e.g., trust and check processing); however, these were relatively superficial reporting changes or simple sharing of physical hardware. Such minor changes were not of the magnitude being considered by upper management. Were the job to be done in-house, current staff would have to undergo a fundamental change in their thinking about consolidation. While upper management foresaw the need for fundamental change to operations and systems, the banks and department heads were more inwardly focused on their respective domain. For instance, the current IS head did not understand the magnitude of upper management's consolidation plans. He had spent $102 million in 1989, and, while "consolidating," had proposed to spend $112 million on systems in 1990. This conflicted with Parcells' evaluation of an $80 million consolidation budget with savings from reduced staff, software and hardware maintenance, professional fees, telecommunications expenses, and hardware leases.

In addition to reorienting the current staff, FFB would have to hire up to 100 temporary people with the requisite skills to complete the job. Perhaps three to five months would be required to hire and educate these people about the FFB environment and where it was going. While hiring and educating staff introduced another layer of complexity to the project management task, this would be temporary.

After reviewing the Information Systems department consolidation estimates, Parcells was concerned that the internal resources required to complete the project in-house could not be mustered within the preferred 18-month time frame. The shortest estimate for completing the consolidation project was about three years. This estimate, of course, was only tentative as the IS staff had never attempted a conversion of this magnitude before, and could not be sure how quickly things would progress.

Parcells also considered whether a third-party vendor could ensure that the rationalization was completed on time. There were many third-party vendors who were willing to provide assistance in consolidating the bank's operations and systems. These vendors ranged from consultants who would offer advice on the process to outsourcing companies who would take over the data centre operations and system development.

Consultants

The consultants were large firms which specialized in information systems applications and generally had developed expertise in outsourcing activities.

For a fee, these firms would come into an organization and offer advice on the planning and implementation of the systems solutions. These consultants brought both a broad perspective of the information technology (IT) options and many narrowly focused, specialized skills to the client's organization. This broad IT perspective enabled the consultant to consider all configuration alternatives and to apply more creative solutions in design and implementation. The narrowly focused, specialized skills provided efficiency in the systems development activities and provided technical sophistication.

As an example, Arthur Andersen, one of the top firms in this business, would be a suitable candidate to review FFB's consolidation efforts. Andersen had considerable experience with applications in the financial services industry, and had conducted outsourcing activities in the United Kingdom, and to a lesser extent in the North American market. Arthur Andersen was anxious to build upon their existing track record. Arguably such an interest might be used as a lever to get them to moderate their costs, which were viewed as quite expensive by FFB at the time. Most other consultant organizations had similar benefits and risks.

Outsourcing

Outsourcing involved the provision of services to an organization by a third-party vendor. From a quick review of the marketplace, FFB had identified several outsourcing vendors who offered the range of outsourcing approaches from service bureau to private label. (See Exhibit 6 for further background on outsourcing.) Of these vendors (Exhibit 7), the ones that offered a wide range of services were the most likely candidates. These included Systematics, M&I Data Services (M&I), Electronic Data Services (EDS), International Business Machines (IBM), Mellon Financial Services Corp. (Mellon), and Perot Syscorp. As Parcells reviewed the consultant's report, he focused on the general characteristics of these firms.

First, the firms seemed to be focused on different outsourcing market segments. Two firms, Mellon and M&I, predominantly pursued service bureau activities and used proprietary software applications. In contrast, EDS, Perot, and IBM pursued private label activities and offered non-proprietary software applications. Systematics appeared to be strongly entrenched in the private-label/proprietary software application outsourcing business. Although companies might offer other services, these market positions represented the main outsourcing strategy for each vendor.

Second, these vendors had different track records in the private-label outsourcing business. Systematics and EDS were industry leaders with vast experience serving financial institutions. Respectively, these two firms generated $230 and $700 million in revenue during 1989. As a relative newcomer to this business, IBM was serving five financial institutions with outsourcing-related services. However, this experience represented a limited range of activities. Likewise, Perot Syscorp had gained very little experience in the two years it had been in business even though its corporate staff had been recruited

---
Exhibit 6   Background on Outsourcing

In the late 1980s, outsourcing was applied to information processing activities, but had existed for many years in various forms. Service bureau support had been around since the 1960s and represented one of the earliest forms of outsourcing activities. A service bureau was a vendor who processed data transactions from a remote site on a prearranged schedule. The computer processing time would be allocated to clients depending on their demands. In the 1980s, facilities management became another popular form of outsourcing. A vendor would run systems and provide operational support on the client's premises. The next type of outsourcing became known as private label. The vendor would provide all computer services in support of a function or business from a facility which it managed. It usually involved the vendor taking over the client's physical data centre facilities and operating them as part of the vendor's business. In addition, vendors offered both proprietary and non-proprietary applications for the operation of these data processing facilities. Proprietary private label vendors would convert all applications to their software and run the business from this basis. Non-proprietary private label vendors would take over and manage the client's application architecture in the data centre.

By 1990, the scope of outsourcing had expanded and become a complex and varied activity. The companies which engaged in this activity used words like strategic rationale, strategic partnership, vision, and commitment. This approach went beyond the off-loading of an inefficiently run operation. It reflected a perspective which sought a strategic partnership with the outsourcing vendor. First, the employees were transferred to the vendor's organization and became employees of that firm. The partnership, if successful, was characterized by cooperation on both sides and a striving toward discovering business opportunities. This was different from the supplier/buyer relationship of other "outsourcing" options. As a buyer, the client would only get a specific service within well-defined bounds which, when completed, would terminate the relationship. Outsourcing relied upon a shared vision and a long-term commitment to the partnership which guided the relationship through day-to-day conflicts. Ideally, both parties focused on the same goals, and if the company succeeded, the outsourcing vendor succeeded.

Many financial sector firms were taking a renewed interest in outsourcing for several reasons. There had been a dramatic increase in mergers and acquisitions, straining internal management resources when integrating these new entities. This strain could sometimes be alleviated by purchasing the required resources. The outsourcing vendor offered leverage through technical resources, infrastructure, software investment, and technology. The client usually gained access to a technology platform and experienced personnel which were unavailable to them before. Since additional resources would accelerate conversion and consolidation, firms would sometimes realize any savings sooner. Further, outsourcing could provide significant cost savings, notwithstanding the vendor's need for profitability! It introduced economies of scale and overcame inefficiencies that would not have been realized without the vendor's participation. Also, outsourcing could facilitate operational consolidation by acting as a catalyst for change. Not only could outsourcing propel change, but it sometimes did so at a guaranteed price, reducing some of the company's financial risk during the rationalization. This commitment would increase the probability of success. Outsourcing sometimes generated revenue improvements. The banks could increase the probability of success. Outsourcing sometimes generated revenue improvements. The banks could increase revenue by offering integrated state-of-the-art services demanded by commercial and retail customers. Finally, outsourcing was more available within the marketplace from a wider range of vendors who were flexible in their approach. This created a willingness on behalf of the vendors to bundle or unbundle the services as required and, consequently, produced more opportunities to fit this service to the company's needs. Against these potential benefits, however, were some definite costs to the bank, not least of which was potential loss of control over a piece of its operation.

EXHIBIT 7   Vendor Market Positioning

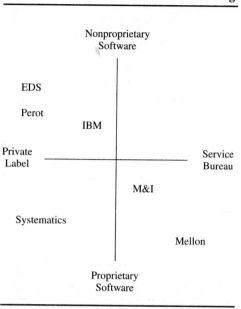

from EDS. M&I and Mellon had not participated in the private-label outsourcing business.

A fundamental concern was how outsourcing could help in the Operations and Systems department's restructuring and consolidation. If the bank were to proceed with the outsourcing option, many factors would have to be considered: Which activities should be outsourced? What services were available in the market? How would the bank maintain control over its information technology resources? What would be the nature of the relationship with the outsourcing vendor: partner or supplier?

Conclusion

As Don Parcells reviewed the three main options, he realized that he needed to be very clear on the advantages and disadvantages of each. While some of the costs and benefits were certain to occur, others were "promised" or potential. Whichever option was chosen would represent a very significant allocation of resources.

FISHERY PRODUCTS INTERNATIONAL

In late January 1989, Vic Young, chief executive officer of Fishery Products International (FPI), was considering the future of their new venture in Japan. Following several years of research and development, FPI had launched 11 value-added products in Japan in February 1988, and sales to date had exceeded all expectations. Despite this early success, questions had been raised about FPI's future involvement in Japan, particularly in the light of the dramatically reduced fishing quotas that had just been announced by the Canadian government. As he reviewed an internal report on the profitability of the new venture, Young realized that the company had to decide if it should stay in the Japanese market.

The Canadian East Coast Fishing Industry

There are two main sectors in the east coast fishery: the inshore and the offshore. The inshore fishery is based on independent fishermen who supply fish on a daily basis to primary processing plants. These fishermen own and operate small to medium-size vessels that fish close to the shore. The offshore fishery is serviced by large company-owned trawlers (up to and including factory freezer trawlers), which fish further from shore for periods up to 10 days before returning to unload their catches.

This case was prepared by R. William Blake and Diane M. Hogan, Faculty of Business Administration, Memorial University of Newfoundland, with the assistance of Louise Handrigan Jones. It is intended as the basis for classroom discussion rather than to illustrate either effective or ineffective handling of an administrative situation. This case was made possible in part by financial assistance from External Affairs and International Trade Canada. © R. William Blake, 1991.

Under the terms of the Northwest Atlantic Fishery Organization (NAFO) convention, the waters off Canada's Atlantic coast are divided into three divisions and 16 individual zones. The government of Canada, as part of its management plan for the Atlantic fishery, uses an enterprise allocation system under which each zone is given an annual allocation, or quota, of fish by species that can be caught during the fishing season.

Three main fish species groupings are used in the allocation system: groundfish including cod, flounder, sole, and redfish; pelagics made up of capelin, mackerel, and salmon; and the shellfish group of crab, shrimp, and lobster. The quota system is subdivided into allocations for the inshore and offshore fishery, with the offshore quota further subdivided into allocations for the various fishing companies.

In the early 1980s, the fishing industry off the east coast of Canada was in a dismal state. Poor fishery management practices, an increase in the number of plant closures, and escalating labour unrest had led to a sharp increase in the number of government bailouts.

As consumer tastes and diets changed, the market had increasingly been demanding a high-quality fish product. The east coast fishery had been slow to respond to this trend and, despite access to the world's greatest fishing grounds and projections of a continuing increase in cod stocks, had been having difficulty increasing its sales in the Canadian market.

To address these issues, the Atlantic Canada Fisheries Restructuring Act was adopted in November of 1983. This act authorized the minister of fisheries to invest in, and provide financial assistance for, the restructuring of the Atlantic fishery. One of the mandates the government set for the restructuring was that, following the stabilization of the Atlantic fishing industry, it was to move from government control back to the private sector.

In the restructuring, two of the larger independent companies, National Sea Products and Fishery Products, were chosen as the vehicles to create an economically viable and competitive industry. In December of 1984, Fishery Products became the basis for the formation of Fishery Products International Ltd. This new company was formed from 12 individual companies that had been involved in the fishing industry off the Atlantic coast of Canada. In 1986, Fishery Products International was given the largest allocation of fish off the east coast of Canada (Exhibit 1).

Fishery Products International (FPI)

Prior to creation of FPI, Fishery Products operated six primary processing plants and one small secondary processing plant in Atlantic Canada. After the merger, FPI, from its head office in St. John's, Newfoundland, undertook a major modernization program. Marginal plants were closed and a program of intensive capital investment in processing plants and trawler equipment was implemented. Fourteen of FPI's inshore plants were targeted for sale to

EXHIBIT 1   Groundfish Allocations (in thousands of tonnes)

Species		1986	1987	1988	1989
Cod	Inshore	326.7	320.6	309.7	306.9
	Offshore	192.5	193.1	213.7	150.1
FPI quotas		84.6	82.1	86.3	68.0
Percentage of TAC caught		88%	81%	85%	
Haddock	Inshore	19.2	19.2	14.3	11.6
	Offshore	18.0	8.3	10.6	11.5
FPI quotas		1.6	1.6	1.7	4.0
Percentage of TAC caught		94%	3%	4%	
Redfish	Inshore	20.6	22.1	19.7	24.9
	Offshore	119.2	121.2	121.2	108.1
FPI quotas		27.2	26.9	23.7	23.4
Percentage of TAC caught		54%	8%	9%	
American plaice	Inshore	18.9	17.4	17.4	16.4
	Offshore	59.0	53.4	46.5	37.9
FPI quotas		53.9	47.3	38.7	33.0
Percentage of TAC caught		61%	29%	25%	
Yellowtail	Inshore	—	—	—	—
	Offshore	17.6	17.6	17.6	7.8
FPI quotas		13.2	13.1	13.1	4.3
Percentage of TAC caught		80%	13%	10%	
Witch	Inshore	3.0	3.0	2.5	2.5
	Offshore	9.8	9.7	8.1	8.1
FPI quotas		7.7	7.6	6.3	6.3
Percentage of TAC caught		39%	4%	5%	
Flounder	Inshore	5.4	6.4	5.4	6.6
	Offshore	8.4	7.3	8.3	7.1
FPI quotas		0.6	0.5	0.5	0.4
Percentage of TAC caught		53%	0.1%	0.2%	
Greenland halibut (turbot)	Inshore	41.6	45.5	47.2	47.2
	Offshore	30.7	38.7	38.7	28.7
FPI quotas		17.1	17.1	12.0	15.9
Percentage of TAC caught		22%	2.2%	0.6%	
Pollock	Inshore	20.0	23.0	24.5	25.5
	Offshore	20.0	21.5	23.8	22.8
FPI quotas		0.3	0.3	0.6	0.5
Percentage of TAC caught		108%	0.4%	0.5%	

Note: Inshore—vessels less than 100 feet; offshore—vessels larger than 100 feet.
TAC—Total allowable catch.

independent processors, leaving FPI to own and operate 16 primary and 3 secondary processing plants[1] (Exhibit 2).

To service their plants, FPI operated 58 company-owned trawlers that harvested over 260 million pounds of cod, flounder, sole, perch, haddock, and turbot annually. The company also purchased crab, shrimp, capelin, and herring from some 2,500 independent inshore fishermen in Newfoundland. FPI had traditionally not fully harvested its quotas of underutilized species, such as redfish (ocean perch) and turbot. Redfish was not as lucrative in its markets as Atlantic cod, and Canadian companies lacked the deep-water-harvesting technology to fully utilize the turbot quotas.

Under the restructuring, FPI became a vertically integrated seafood company, catching and processing fish, developing new seafood products, and marketing them in the international marketplace. Through this process, FPI emerged as a major international player, with sales of $260 million, and a loss of $35 million, in 1984, its first year of operation. Although the company recorded another loss in 1985, it reported healthy profits of $46 million and $58 million in 1986 and 1987, respectively (Exhibit 3). In 1987, Canada accounted for 16 percent of FPI's sales; the United States, 77.6 percent; and other countries (Europe, Australia, and Japan), 6.7 percent.

FPI's approach to the market differed from country to country. FPI was the largest foreign supplier of frozen seafood to the United States and supplied the value-added component of that market from two secondary processing plants in Massachusetts through a subsidiary company, Fishery Products, Inc.

In Europe, FPI principally supplied fish blocks to other processors and finished products to food service companies, using sales offices which employed local people with specific market knowledge in sales and distribution. These subsidiaries were located in West Germany (Fishery Products GmbH) and Great Britain (Fishery Products of Canada Ltd.). The market in Europe was fiercely competitive and Canadian value-added products were subject to high tariffs which made it difficult for them to compete. Marketing and all other related activities for the European operations were handled by headquarters in St. John's.

Prior to the restructuring of the industry, independent fishing companies had placed less emphasis on quality than on increasing the catch. In the light of forecasts of shifting consumer preferences toward higher-quality products, FPI management realized that the company needed to catch and process fish more effectively. The company also needed higher-quality fish for many of the new products being produced in its secondary processing plants.

---

[1] Primary processing involves the conversion of raw fish into fillets or blocks for sale as an end product or for transfer for secondary processing. A "block" is an international standard and consists of 16.5 pounds of fish which has been processed and frozen in a freezing frame of exact dimensions. Forty percent of FPI's cod was processed into block, and half of this block was sold to other processors. Secondary processing plants are devoted to the production of value-added finished products, such as fish burgers, fish sticks, and frozen fish dinners for use by the end customer.

Exhibit 2   FPI Plant Locations

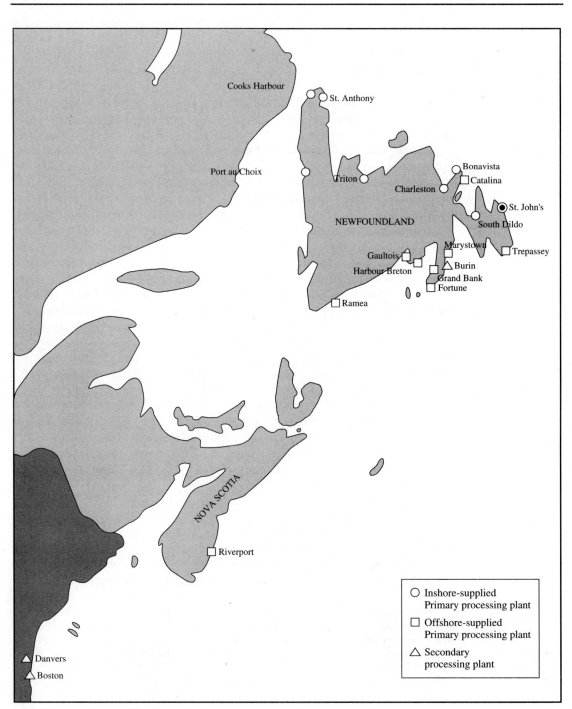

- ○ Inshore-supplied
  Primary processing plant
- □ Offshore-supplied
  Primary processing plant
- △ Secondary
  processing plant

EXHIBIT 3   Fishery Products International
Summary of Financial Statement
(thousands of dollars)

	1988	1987	1986	1985
Sales	366,611	395,705	388,664	298,182
Net income (loss)	16,755	57,963	46,596	(20,160)
Cash flow[a]	29,275	71,298	56,731	(8,357)
Working capital	99,467	94,035	55,404	41,192
Long-term debt	38,593	17,487	14,471	24,531
Segmented Information				
Sales				
Canada[b]	338,328	367,051	354,149	252,111
Intercompany[c]	(272,563)	(317,055)	(300,661)	(205,047)
	65,765	49,996	53,488	47,064
United States	264,263	314,342	304,490	231,282
Other[d]	36,583	31,367	30,686	19,836
	366,611	395,705	388,664	298,182
Profit (loss)[e]				
Canada	16,969	58,951	44,757	(15,396)
United States	1,097	7,001	3,945	(4,831)
Other	300	37	(52)	67
	18,366	65,989	48,650	(20,160)
Identified Assets				
Canada	281,662	286,416	238,485	208,516
United States	50,009	56,029	42,085	50,726
Other	9,409	4,626	3,212	5,060
Intercompany accounts	(31,931)	(68,815)	(59,730)	(62,924)
	309,149	278,256	224,052	200,376

Note: [a] Cash flow from operations before net changes in noncash working capital balances.

[b] Canadian sales include sales to customers in the United States and other geographic regions.

[c] Transfer pricing: Intercompany sales are at market prices less commissions.

[d] Other includes sales to Europe, Australia, and Japan. Sales to Japan were $3 million of capelin product only.

[e] Profit (loss): Profit is income before provision for profit sharing, income taxes, and extraordinary items.

Improved quality was to be achieved through a capitalization program and an increasing emphasis on quality control. FPI had invested heavily in its fleet and processing facilities. To complement this capitalization program, and to increase productivity and motivation, it had also invested heavily in its workforce. This had been accomplished through the implementation of such programs as employee ownership, the use of an FPI newsletter, and employee of the month awards. The company adopted the motto, "Excellence through people, productivity, and profits." It was realized that attempts to increase quality had to be reflected in the employees' attitude, and the employees slowly began to realize that, if they could not produce a higher-quality fish product, their jobs could be lost.

FPI management had become increasingly concerned about the company's financial vulnerability to fluctuations in the exchange rate of the American dollar. Over 75 percent of FPI's sales were in the United States, and management was looking for ways to reduce their relations on this market. An integral part of the new strategy was to diversify into new markets and to place an increased emphasis on secondary processing.

Fishery Products' expertise prior to the creation of FPI (1984) had been in the supply of both raw and finished products to the food service industry with little emphasis placed on retail sales. The new emphasis on research and development of new value-added products had led to several Canadian awards for innovative products.

To meet its corporate goal of increasing emphasis in the area of secondary processing, FPI had developed a world-class secondary processing capability in its plant in Burin, Newfoundland. The newly modified plant, which reopened in June of 1987, had the capacity to process 15 million pounds of finished product per year. Given the fact that the Canadian market would not immediately utilize the new plant's capacity, part of the company's strategy included steps to explore the Japanese market.

The Japanese Seafood Market

The market development division of FPI had continued the collection of information about the Japanese market that had been started by Fishery Products. As part of their ongoing analysis of the potential of the Japanese marketplace, a team from FPI, including Randy Bishop, director of international marketing sales, participated in a government-sponsored trade mission to Japan in late 1985. During this mission, FPI's representatives learned about the characteristics of the Japanese marketplace and had the opportunity to meet with various seafood marketers. Upon returning to Canada and reviewing their findings, the team concluded that, despite the fact that FPI had been exporting unprocessed capelin, squid, and cod to Japan for years, it knew very little about the Japanese domestic market.

The FPI research found that, on a per capita basis, Japan had the highest fish consumption in the world at 68 kilograms per year as compared to the United States at 7.2 kilograms and Canada at 7 kilograms. Because local resources were insufficient to meet the high demand for fish, Japanese fishing companies used factory freezer trawlers outfitted to fish, freeze, and store while operating worldwide. Historically, Japan had been a major fishing nation, harvesting in excess of 15 percent of the total world fish catch and exporting far more than it imported. Recently, however, the increasingly restrictive policies of many nations had limited access to their fishing grounds, and Japan had become a fish-importing nation (Exhibit 4).

Exhibit 4   Fish Consumption in Japan (in thousands of metric tons)

	1965	*1970*	*1975*	*1980*	*1984*	*1986**
Production	5547	6857	7522	7421	7352	—
Imports	109	294	752	1027	1746	2300
Exports	618	791	755	817	624	—
Apparent domestic consumption	5048	6356	7549	7666	8251	8600
Imports as a % of total market	2.1	4.6	9.9	13.3	21.1	26.7

Note: * = Estimated consumption.

Since World War II, Japan had used very restrictive import policies as a way of developing its economy. Approximately 20 percent of Japanese imports were finished goods, compared to 50 percent for the United States and 40 percent for the European Economic Community. In the fishing industry, a focus on the importation of raw product allowed Japan to continue to utilize the massive fish processing infrastructure developed when it was a major fishing nation.

In recent years, Japan, as a member of the General Agreement on Trades and Tariffs (GATT), had been working at reducing both tariff and nontariff barriers. Despite this trend, companies still found it difficult to enter the Japanese market as government regulations and nontariff barriers were used as deterrents. The quality control standards applied to imports were examples of such nontariff barriers. The FPI team realized during their investigation that there was no central governing body in Japan that it could access to determine product standards. Although there had been a movement to central-ize these standards, the process was very slow.

The retail market for frozen seafood in Japan in the large chain grocery stores alone was worth Cdn $1.3 billion annually; in the three major regions of Tokyo, Osaka, and Nagoya, there were 40 of these chains with approxi-mately 2,000 stores. The rest of the retail market, which represented approxi-mately 30 percent of the seafood market, was split among the food sections of department stores and convenience stores with approximately one store per 68 people in the country. Each of these stores had very small sections devoted to frozen food, and there was tremendous competition among brands.

The introduction of new food products in Japan is done very methodically with new releases occurring primarily in February and October. As many as 2,000 new entries will be released each time, of which approximately 300 would be in the frozen food category, the sector FPI would be entering. The success rate for new products was approximately 15 percent, and, in general, new products faced a very short product life cycle, often less than two years.

The Japanese consumer demands high-quality foods and seeks a wide variety of choice in products; as Randy Bishop noted, "the Japanese eat with their eyes." Portion size had to be uniform and be composed of top-quality fish. This would have considerable ramifications for FPI if it decided to enter the market with value-added products. FPI felt that many current top products (as classified by North American and European standards) would not pass the Japanese quality standards for importation.

Japan was becoming more westernized in its tastes and placed a high demand and value on imported products. Once a foreign product was adopted in the domestic market, it usually commanded a high price. Despite the high demand for imported products, FPI realized that the Japanese had very distinct tastes. It was common knowledge that companies such as Nestle and Heinz had entered the Japanese domestic market with their standard products and failed. The experience of such companies had earned Japan the reputation of being a very difficult market to enter successfully.

The distribution network in Japan reflected many characteristics of a hierarchical and closed society. A greatly simplified version of a Japanese distribution chain is provided in Exhibit 5. Imports of raw materials were handled by large trading companies through their import/export divisions. Foreign companies wishing to sell value-added products to the Japanese domestic market would have to do so through the domestic marketing division of the trading company. Given the nature of the trading companies, the

EXHIBIT 5   Simplified Diagram of the Japanese Distribution Chain for Imported FPI Value-Added Products

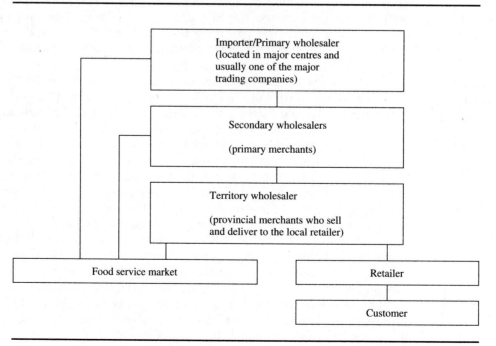

import/export division and the domestic marketing division were independent operations. Even though FPI had been exporting raw materials to Japan for years, it had no contacts in the domestic marketing division and, therefore, no access to the domestic retail market or the larger food service market. From its research, FPI realized that the sale of imported value-added fish products was essentially unknown in these markets.

In addition to increased Japanese demand for foreign products and the potential size of the Japanese market, FPI was encouraged by two other factors: the change in value of the Japanese currency and the Japanese fish consumption pattern. In 1982, the Canadian dollar was worth close to 200 yen, but by 1987 the exchange rate was approximately 100 yen to the dollar (Exhibit 6). This would allow FPI to set prices on its products that would be attractive to the Japanese consumer and generate returns equivalent to its sales in other markets. In terms of consumption, the Japanese were keenly interested not only in cod and sole, but in species such as redfish and capelin,

Exhibit 6   Average Quarterly Exchange Rate 1980–89 (Japanese yen to Canadian dollar)

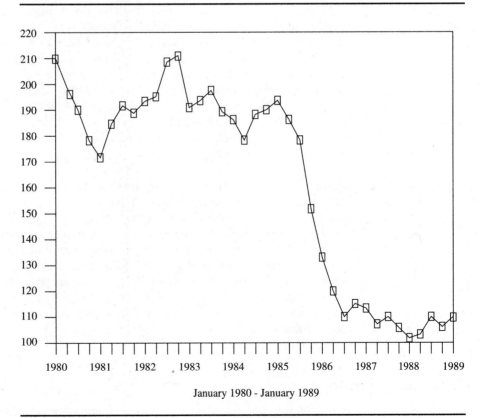

January 1980 - January 1989

EXHIBIT 7   Japanese Fish Imports by Major Suppliers

	1985 U.S. $ (millions)	% Share	Ranking 1985	Ranking 1983	Ranking 1981
United States	915.0	18.5	1	1	1
Korea	688.4	13.9	2	2	2
Taiwan	578.4	11.7	3	3	3
Canada	269.7	5.5	4	6	8
India	232.7	4.7	5	4	4
Indonesia	226.2	4.6	6	5	5
Australia	198.8	4.0	7	7	7

neither of which played a significant part in the North American diet. Exports of fish products from Canada had increased significantly in recent years as Japan actively sought supplies to satisfy its domestic demands (Exhibit 7). This fact was of particular interest to FPI since the quotas for these species were not being fully utilized (Exhibit 1).

The Japanese were very uncomfortable doing business with individuals that they had not known for extended periods of time. They desired to develop "ningen kankei," a sense or feeling of good human relations, before they established any relationship (business or otherwise). Even if FPI was able to establish such relationships, it was recognized that the Japanese would require a high degree of personal contact in order to maintain the relationship. Because of the hierarchical nature of the Japanese culture, these relationships would have to be between individuals at equal levels in the organization (i.e., a Canadian vice president of marketing would not be able to establish such a relationship with a CEO of a Japanese company).

FPI's experience to date had not taught it to deal with the subtleties of negotiation in Japan. In the past, they had sold capelin, squid, and cod to the Japanese, and more recently they had also been selling some redfish, an underutilized species. If FPI wished to sell excess catches of raw fish, this was done by placing a phone call to the import/export division of a Japanese trading company. FPI management had no experience in negotiating contracts in Japan, although they were aware that Japanese consensus style of negotiating was very different from the North American style. If FPI decided to enter Japan with its value-added products, it would entail significantly more management involvement, money, and long-term commitment to the development of the market.

The Entry Strategy

In considering possible strategies for the Japanese market, three alternatives were considered. The first was for FPI to maintain the status quo by continuing exports of raw materials. This alternative was attractive as the Japanese demand for raw materials was high, the infrastructure was available to process this material, and the price that could be commanded for quality fish would be favourable. Second, FPI could set up an independent sales office in Japan to market its products while maintaining corporate control. The third alternative was to develop a cooperative venture with an existing Japanese seafood marketing company to allow FPI value-added products to be exported to the Japanese market.

After reviewing the alternatives, top management decided to seek an arrangement with one of the larger Japanese seafood marketing firms dealing in both the food service and retail markets. The decision was based on the belief that, despite a lower return on investment, this approach would allow it to penetrate the market more quickly than would be possible if it attempted to set up its own operations in Japan. Through 1986, FPI actively researched Japanese seafood marketing companies, including Toyo, Nippon Su, and Nichiro, in an attempt to identify a potential partner. The analysis led FPI to approach Nichiro Gyogyo Kaisha (Nichiro), the third largest of the seafood marketing companies, with a proposal for them to market FPI's value-added products in the Japanese domestic market. Nichiro was one of the five Japanese companies purchasing ocean perch and capelin from FPI and was hoping to get exclusive access to FPI's quota for these underutilized species.

After the preliminary meetings of corporate representatives, the CEOs of the two companies met in Boston in September 1986 and agreed that some type of arrangement would be mutually beneficial. The details of the arrangement were to be left to the marketing departments of the companies to complete.

In order to further assess the Japanese market potential, FPI requested that Nichiro provide detailed information on the Japanese distribution system and consumer needs. In addition, a team from FPI, headed by Randy Bishop, made three trips (two lasting a week to 10 days, the other three weeks) to Japan over the following year to become more familiar with the Japanese market and to define the parameters of the agreement. As well, the domestic marketing team from Nichiro visited the FPI plants in Burin, Newfoundland, and Danvers, Massachusetts, to aid in its evaluation of the FPI operations.

In June 1987, Vic Young, CEO of FPI, and Junzo Sasaki, CEO of Nichiro, signed a formal agreement. It was agreed that Nichiro would market FPI's value-added products in Japan and that FPI would provide Nichiro with exclusive access to the purchase of raw fish species traditionally supplied by FPI to the Japanese market.

Development of Product Specifications

In the summer of 1987, FPI's corporate R&D department headed by Nancy Wilson began to develop products for potential release in the Japanese market. In order to maximize effectiveness, research and development into new products was conducted by teams from both partners. The initial contact between the R&D representatives from FPI and Nichiro was a week-long meeting to address product issues, specifications, and consumer demands. Nichiro had advised FPI that a February release date was much preferable to October in the Japanese market. The teams met frequently through the summer in Newfoundland and, although FPI was not obligated by their agreement with Nichiro to produce a specific number of products, eventually 20 were developed for possible release with new Nichiro products in February of 1988. Nichiro typically introduced between 40 and 50 of their own new products at a time.

FPI's first efforts were aimed at producing a bread coating mix specifically for products for the Japanese market. The Japanese deep-fry at lower temperatures than North Americans, a factor which had to be addressed in developing breaded and battered products. FPI already produced breaded products, but the standard coating used did not meet the Japanese requirement of a crunchy look with a soft bite. FPI's initial efforts to develop a new batter to meet Japanese standards were unsuccessful, and it was not until late October 1987 that a suitable coating was developed that met both the needs of the Japanese consumer and FPI production requirements and abilities. Of the 11 products eventually included in the final release, 7 were breaded products.

Packaging requirements presented a number of problems. Japanese package sizes, which averaged 180 grams and contained portion sizes of 20 to 40 grams each, were much smaller than the 300-gram packages FPI was currently producing for its North American and European markets. Product packaging also caused concern as FPI planned to maintain its use of cardboard, a type of packaging that was uncommon in the Japanese marketplace. During the fall of 1987, there was a shortage of cardboard in Canada, which further complicated the production of appropriate packaging. FPI also wanted to ensure that the FPI logo and the Canadian flag were prominent on the package itself. The design of the package was made more difficult because the products to be released in February 1988 were not chosen until October 1987.

Although initial product development was done at FPI's head office, sample production runs were performed at the Burin plant (a four-hour drive from St. John's) to assess the capability of equipment and determine productivity standards. It was also critical to determine whether the stringent Japanese quality standards could be met. The initial sample production runs had reject rates as high as 30 percent, due largely to the Japanese tolerance level of approximately 3 percent on portion sizes compared to a North American standard of approximately 10 percent. All of the rejects from the sample run for the Japanese market would have been considered first quality in the American or European markets.

Concurrent with product development, FPI's marketing department was attempting to determine a pricing strategy for the products to be marketed in Japan. This was complicated by the fact that, although production costing could normally be accurately estimated, the Japanese product would be subject

EXHIBIT 8   FPI Japan—Value-Added Contribution Plan 1988

	Price $/lb.	Direct Cost	Total Cost	Contribution $/lb.
Retail Market				
Item				
Cod nuggets	2.88	1.97	2.32	0.56
Cod strips	2.84	2.02	2.35	0.49
Sole dinner	2.67	2.18	2.50	0.17
Food Service Market				
Cod nuggets	2.38	1.58	1.91	0.43
Cod sticks	2.42	1.55	1.96	0.46
Scotch sole	2.22	1.86	2.15	0.07
Sole boat	2.72	2.39	2.71	0.01
Sole portion	2.72	2.61	2.89	(0.17)
Fresh-formed sole	2.15	1.51	1.91	0.24
Cod wedge 50 g.	2.23	1.56	1.91	0.31
Cod wedge 65 g.	2.21	1.52	1.87	0.34

Note: Cod block raw material costed at U.S. $1.50 rate vs. current price of $1.30.
Direct cost of raw fish based on transfer price.

to Japanese quality control standards, the impact of which was impossible to accurately estimate until full-scale production was under way. Moreover, the pricing estimates were to be based on positioning the product as unique and premium in the market, rather than simply on the cost of production. Although contributions appeared to be highest for the cod-based products, cod was relatively unknown to the Japanese consumer. Sole (or flatfish) was well known, and liked, and it was hoped that sole-based products could be used as a part of a "pull" strategy to market the cod products (Exhibit 8).

Most of FPI's previous experience had been in negotiating sales to the food service industry rather than the retail market. It did produce some "house brand" retail packages, but this would be the first significant retail market outside North America that FPI had entered. Japan was perceived as a growth market, particularly for frozen products, although the potential for FPI products in the Japanese market was unknown. Given a per capita fish consumption of 68 kilograms, it was not unrealistic to believe that this market could absorb more of the increased capacity of the Burin plant over time. Conscious of the market potential, FPI priced the product without detailed cost information.

The Burin Plant

When FPI was created in 1984, the Burin plant was redundant to the needs of the new organization. Although it had once been a productive primary processing plant, it had not been well maintained. However, federal and provincial government money was available to help the community of Burin, and the decision was made to renovate the plant. Because there was inadequate secondary processing capacity in Canada, some value-added products were being imported from the United States at considerable cost. Accordingly, the decision was made to convert the plant to secondary processing. After the renovations, the Burin plant would be able to supply value-added products to the Canadian and international markets. In June 1986, the plant was closed, and renovations to turn it into a state-of-the-art secondary processing facility began. When the renovations were completed in June 1987, staff were recalled and production resumed. During the first two months, production and productivity were low as the plant geared up and the plant workers were trained on the new equipment and production lines, but by October 1987, all 108 people on the seniority list had been recalled.

FPI had contributed approximately $7.3 million of the $11.3 million cost of the Burin plant renovation. While some major equipment, including the deep fryer and cold storage facility, was retained, new equipment, including extensive conveyor equipment, two spiral freezers, and breading lines, was also installed. The renovation increased the plant's capability to process and freeze finished products from 5 million pounds to 15 million pounds annually.

Through the summer and early fall of 1987, R&D efforts at Burin were intensified as products were developed for the Japanese market. In test production runs, wastage of fish continued to be high, as much as 10 percent on certain products, due mainly to products not being shaped properly. It was recognized that until the Burin plant could install additional specialized equipment, part of the processing for some of the Japanese products would have to be transferred to the Danvers plant, since Danvers possessed the only prototype of an acceptable cutting machine in existence.

Staff at the Burin plant were well aware of the importance corporate headquarters was placing upon the new products they were producing. This was illustrated in late 1987 when the decision was made to ship sole, which was then in short supply, to Burin for processing for the Japanese market, rather than supplying traditional customers in the United States. With the pressure to produce a quality product, extra staff had been placed on the breading lines, and the number of quality control personnel was increased. The workers were not accustomed to such strict standards; however, they realized that it was important to produce a quality product, or their jobs and the future of the plant would be jeopardized.

By far the greatest pressure was felt by the management team who had to ensure the coordination of activities so that everything was available in time for production. Because partial processing for some products had to be temporarily carried out at Danvers, management spent considerable time scheduling and coordinating the transfer of fish to the United States, working it into the production schedule at the Danvers plant, and transporting back to Burin for final processing. It was not unusual for the Burin plant to be waiting on a shipment of semiprocessed fish from Danvers and/or packaging materials from Toronto to allow the daily production schedule to be established. There was a considerable amount of time pressure as well, given Nichiro's advice to aim for a February release date.

There was considerable pressure on the Burin workers and management to keep to production schedules and produce a top-quality product which met the stringent Japanese quality control standards. During the production stage, three quality control specialists from Nichiro worked at the plant on a full-time basis alongside FPI's quality control employees. The groups provided constant feedback to the workers in relation to the control standards.

The first consignments of the 11 products produced at Burin for the February launch into the Japanese market were completed in December and shipped immediately to allow for the six-week lead time. The Burin plant planned to ship products twice a month via Halifax to Japan. Demand for the product was not yet known and neither Nichiro nor FPI was able to predict if these products would be accepted by the Japanese consumer.

With the first shipment of products to Japan completed, management undertook a general assessment of Burin operations, including the production for the Japanese market, and concluded that the plant would have to invest in capital equipment, including the installation of a microwave tempering and block-pressing system, to improve overall productivity. With respect to the Japanese product, Burin management questioned if some of the products currently being produced could be made profitable at the negotiated prices, even with additional equipment.

Release of Products in Japan

The release of value-added products for the Japanese domestic market took place in February 1988 with a press conference and a reception and display of products in Tokyo, jointly hosted by Young and Sasaki. This was followed by similar promotions in six additional cities in Japan during February. All of the products were well received and one, sea strips, was noted by many to be the best product to be produced in the frozen seafood class in the previous 10 years. Demand for the products in Japan through the first six months after the release date was strong.

Review of the Japanese Product Line

A detailed financial review of the Japanese venture was conducted in September 1988 (Exhibit 9). The sales of value-added product to the Japanese market for the period from the February release date to September 3, 1988, were over $4 million, more than one-third of the estimated total sales to Japan for that year and significantly higher than expected.

EXHIBIT 9   FPI Japan—Sales Analysis of Value-Added Products to September 3, 1988

Product	Pounds (000's)	Canadian Dollars (000's)
Retail market		
Nuggets	306.1	$ 830
Sea strips (cod)	324.9	925
Sea dinner (sole)	286.8	765
Total retail	917.8	$2,520
Food service		
Nuggets	99.4	233
Fish sticks	59.4	158
Scotch sole	52.4	116
Fresh formed	140.2	302
Sole boat	190.4	517
Cod boat	31.8	89
Cod loin	24.1	69
Sole portion	104.3	284
Total food service	702.0	$1,770
Total value-added	1,620.0	$4,290

Note: The date of September 3 corresponds to Nichiro's fiscal year. FPI uses the calendar year.

A contentious issue was the pricing of the raw materials used in the finished product. FPI treated Burin as a profit centre and used open market prices to determine the transfer price charged by its primary production plants to Burin. If, for example, one pound of cod cost $1 on the open market, that was the transfer price used, irrespective of the actual production cost, which might be as low as $.65. Utilizing this cost accounting approach, FPI had determined that certain of the products produced for the Japanese market were marginally profitable or unprofitable for Burin at the prices negotiated in the original arrangements (Exhibit 8). FPI's management knew, however, that when an alternate system of cost allocation was used, some of those products were profitable because production costs were lower than market prices. Despite the oversupply of cod in the market and the resulting buildup in inventory, the determination of the profitability of the Japanese products continued to be based on market pricing.

Management at the Burin plant knew that, although their existing equipment could freeze up to 15 million pounds of fish annually, they could not produce that amount of packaged finished product, particularly for the retail market. With the purchase of $640,000 worth of specialized equipment, Burin would be able to improve its overall productivity, including productivity on the Japanese line and operate independently of the Danvers plant. That investment was expected to yield an annual saving of $195,000 based solely on the projected volumes of sales for 1989 for established Nichiro products.

Because of the innovative nature and high quality of the FPI products, they had been positioned in the premium price range. Although the products had proven to be popular, the fact that the Japanese consumer did not seem to be able to differentiate between premium Atlantic cod and Alaskan pollock, which was being sold for 25 percent less in the ultracompetitive Japanese retail market, had caused some concern.

Conclusion

FPI had made a significant commitment to the Japanese venture and was developing an in-house expertise that would allow it to continue in that market. Although the company realized it was capable of developing products for the Japanese domestic market, it was unsure what its strategy should be, given that not all of its products were profitable. Although the corporate R&D department of FPI continued to research additional new products, the company needed to forecast its long-term opportunity in the Japanese market. The per capita consumption of 68 kilograms of fish was very inviting, but the market share that FPI could realistically hope to achieve was unknown.

On January 30, 1989, the Canadian government announced new fish quotas and allocations, based on research which had shown a major depletion in the cod stock (Exhibit 1). The situation was considered serious, and fisheries experts predicted that further cuts would be necessary in subsequent years. The quota reduction hit FPI hard, and virtually overnight, cod moved from a position of oversupply to undersupply. FPI now had to consider whether it might not be wiser to market its limited resource in traditional markets, rather than attempt to maintain the company's presence in Japan. Foreign exchange markets were also causing some concern. The yen, which had moved from 200 to the dollar to as low as 99 to the dollar in January 1988, had reversed the downward trend. In January 1989, it stood at 109 yen to the dollar, and experts were predicting further increases. Because the prices had been negotiated in Canadian dollars, Nichiro was absorbing the resulting costs, but it was unclear how long they would continue to do so, or what the future financial implications might be for FPI.

As Young again reviewed the report from Randy Bishop, he acknowledged that, although sales to Japan were higher than FPI had anticipated, this had not been achieved without strain on the company. FPI was growing rapidly; in 1986 and 1987, profit had been $22,330,000 and $31,004,000, respectively. Although the company had been successful in Japan, the nature of that market would require the on-going development of new and innovative products and a commitment to the venture which might call for a disproportionate amount of management time. Nichiro was already pushing for the development of new products for October 1989. With currency exchange fluctuations, and a major drop in quotas, Young wondered what the strategy should be for the Japanese market and how it fit with the future growth and direction of FPI.

CASE

THE GE ENERGY MANAGEMENT INITIATIVE (A)

In August 1992, Raj Bhatt, Business Development Manager for GE Canada, met with executives from GE Supply, a U.S.-based distribution arm of GE. The purpose of the meeting was to discuss new business opportunities in Energy Efficiency, an industry that focused on the reduction of energy usage through the installation of energy-efficient technologies. Bhatt had recently gained pre-qualification for GE Canada to bid in a $1 billion program to install energy-efficient technologies in all federal government buildings. He was confident that GE's expertise in lighting, motors, appliances, and financing was sufficient to win at least some of the contracts. Furthermore, he saw the program as a stepping stone to building a new GE business to service the Energy Efficiency needs of a range of clients.

The GE Supply executives informed Bhatt that they had already established a position in the U.S. Energy Efficiency industry, through a joint venture with a new Energy Service Company (ESCo), and had retained the services of a full-time consultant to develop the business. They were interested in the Federal Buildings program that Bhatt had been working on, but felt that it would be more efficiently run through a division of GE Supply, rather than as a locally managed Canadian venture. The meeting posed a dilemma for Bhatt. He was encouraged by the level of interest that already existed for Energy Efficiency within GE, but at the same time held certain misgivings about folding the Federal Buildings program into GE Supply's nascent business. Specifically, he was concerned that a lot of interesting Energy Efficiency opportunities existed in Canada which a U.S.-focused business would not be in a position to exploit. Bhatt left the meeting uncertain how to proceed.

This case was prepared by Julian Birkinshaw and Professor Nick Fry for the sole purpose of providing material for class discussion at the Western Business School. Copyright 1994 © The University of Western Ontario.

General Electric (GE)

GE, with $60 billion in revenues in 1991, was among the top ten industrial corporations in the world. From the early days of Thomas Edison, it had grown to be a diversified 54-business corporation by the early eighties. With 400,000 employees and a very strong corporate planning division, it exemplified the traditional strategic planning-oriented corporation of the 1970s.

In 1980, Jack Welch, the incoming CEO, made a series of sweeping changes. The corporate planning department was eliminated, layers of management were eliminated, and the concepts of empowerment and customer focus became the new drivers behind GE's activities. Of the 54 businesses that Welch inherited, some were sold and others were amalgamated, leaving just 13. Welch's stated position was that the major criterion for holding onto a business was that it was number one or number two worldwide in its chosen industry.

The corporate structure under Welch was simplified and decentralised. Each division was autonomous, and was further subdivided into a number of operating companies. The head office for each division was in the U.S., but on average, 25 percent of GE's revenues came from its non-U.S. operations. International operations, including Canada, were structured under the Vice Chairman, International Operations, but operating authority was held by the relevant division of GE. Thus, the lighting plant in Oakville, Ontario, reported to GE Lighting in Cleveland, Ohio, with only a secondary line of reporting through GE Canada.

Welch was committed to creating a more open and candid management style at GE. A central thrust of this commitment was the "Work-Out" program, which he described as follows:

> The ultimate objective of Work-Out is clear. We want 300,000 people with different family aspirations, different financial goals, to share directly in this company's vision, the decision-making process, and the rewards. We want to build a more stimulating environment, a more creative environment, a freer work atmosphere, with incentives tied directly to what people do. (*Harvard Business Review,* Sept 1989: 112–120)

Through a series of workshops and facilitated sessions, Work-Out's objective was to challenge the accepted practice at every level in every business. Work-Out sessions had already realized large cost savings by identifying non-essential practices that had gone undetected for years, but equally important, they had created a new level of creativity and enthusiasm among employees.

GE Canada

GE Canada was the international subsidiary of GE with the longest standing, with operations in 12 of the company's 13 businesses. In the 1970s, GE Canada operated as a "miniature replica" of its parent company: all functions were represented in Canada, and typically a full line of products was made, primarily for the Canadian market but with some exporting possibilities. The Canadian CEO was fully responsible for the profits of the Canadian operating divisions, and separate financial statements were prepared (GE held a 92 percent stake in GE Canada).

In the eighties, Jack Welch embarked on a major structural change to GE's North American business. Consistent with the increasingly global business environment that was taking shape, Welch recognized that maintaining separate country organizations could not be justified. Instead, an integrated organizational model emerged that became known as "direct-connect."[1] Essentially, this meant creating 13 strategic business units, and organizing them according to the global demands of the business rather than national interests. Typically, the general manager's role was eliminated in Canada, so that business leaders or functional managers reported directly to their business headquarters in the U.S., rather than through the Canadian organization. For example, the marketing manager for GE Lighting's Canadian operations reported directly to the GE Lighting marketing manager in Cleveland, Ohio. Profit responsibility was held by the global business unit. This arrangement ensured that business activities were effectively coordinated on a global basis. It also furthered Welch's objective of removing layers of management and empowering employees.

Matthew Meyer, CEO of GE Canada, had a vastly different role from his predecessors. With all operations reporting straight to their U.S. divisional bosses, Meyer was directly responsible only for the activities of a very small number of employees. He had vice presidents in finance, environmental affairs, legal, human resources, and government affairs. These managers were responsible for all the uniquely Canadian issues that cropped up, such as new legislation, tax accounting, government grants, and so on. In addition, there was a small business development group, consisting of three managers. Traditionally, this group had been involved in feasibility studies and new market development for the business units in Canada. Following the shift to a "direct-connect" structure, the role had become primarily one of looking for opportunities to leverage the strengths of Canadian activities on a global basis. They were also concerned with identifying new business opportunities in Canada. Bhatt, one of the business development managers, explained:

> Canada is a relatively small marketplace. Consequently, most U.S.-based business leaders have a limited awareness of the opportunities here because they have either a U.S. or a global focus. The role of business development is to attempt to identify investment or market opportunities here that they might find valuable.

---

[1] The integration process was smoothed by the buyout of minority shareholders in GE Canada in 1989. The 1989 Free Trade Agreement further streamlined the change.

EXHIBIT 1   GE Structure (North America)

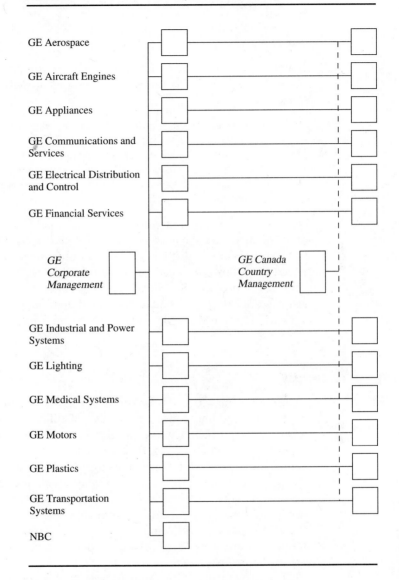

GE Aerospace

GE Aircraft Engines

GE Appliances

GE Communications and Services

GE Electrical Distribution and Control

GE Financial Services

GE Corporate Management

GE Canada Country Management

GE Industrial and Power Systems

GE Lighting

GE Medical Systems

GE Motors

GE Plastics

GE Transportation Systems

NBC

There was some discussion among business development managers over the extent to which they should actively "sell" business opportunities to the GE businesses. Some felt that a proactive strategy of promoting Canadian opportunities was appropriate; others preferred to investigate only those cases where business development's involvement had been solicited. The recent decision to promote the VP, Business Development, but not replace him, added further to the uncertainty over the group's role.

Raj Bhatt

Bhatt was only 29. He had worked at GE for just one year, following a successful period at Northern Telecom and an MBA at the University of Western Ontario.

> Business development is quite a challenging experience. There are lots of good opportunities in Canada, but it is sometimes difficult to achieve the level of interest and buy-in necessary to attract the appropriate attention. The Oakville lighting plant, a global manufacturing mandate, is a planned $144 million investment and is certainly our biggest success so far, but there have been a lot of ideas that failed to materialize.

The business development manager typically held that post for only two years, after which he or she was expected to take a line position in one of the businesses. Bhatt had been given a number of attractive options, but had turned them down because he was afraid that his involvement was critical to a number of projects. Specifically, he was concerned that the energy efficiency business opportunity he had championed up to now would die because no one else had the knowledge of, or the enthusiasm for, that particular opportunity.

Energy Efficiency

Energy efficiency covered the multitude of ways that energy usage could be optimised, including conservation, use of efficient appliances, and off-peak usage. Energy efficiency was originally conceived in the early 1970s as a response to rising oil prices. It recently saw a resurgence due to the environmental movement and the increasing need for cost competitiveness in the late eighties. Although strongly motivated by public opinion and government pressure, energy efficiency initiatives were usually sponsored by the energy supply utilities. They recognized that they could more effectively keep their investment down by reducing demand than by building expensive new power stations. There were also obvious benefits to consumers (in reduced costs) and to the environment.

The growth in utility-sponsored programs for energy efficiency was responsible for the formation of many Energy Service Companies (ESCos). These companies aimed to meet the demands and needs of their customers by utilizing these programs. Under the most common arrangement (called a performance contract), the ESCo would install energy-efficient technologies at no upfront cost to the client. The costs would be recouped from the savings realized. Such an arrangement could be very lucrative, but the ESCo bore all the risk in the event that the promised savings never materialized.

The ESCo Industry in Canada

The Canadian ESCo industry was among the most advanced in the world. Both federal and provincial governments had active energy-management programs to promote "green" issues, and had targeted energy efficiency as a critical industry. Ontario Hydro and Quebec Hydro had budgets for energy efficiency of $800 million and $300 million, respectively, in comparison to the CDN$1.5 billion budget for all U.S. utilities combined.

As a result of the utilities' involvement, the Canadian ESCo industry was growing very rapidly; 1989 revenues of $20 million had grown to $100 million by 1992, and one estimate put the total market potential in the billions of dollars. Three major segments could be identified, each accounting for approximately one-third of the total volume. They were *Commercial,* which consisted primarily of office buildings, hospitals, and other public buildings; *Industrial,* which consisted of factories and production plants; and *Residential,* which consisted of single-family dwellings. So far the commercial sector had been the most rewarding to ESCos, largely due to the similarities between (for example) one hospital and another. Industrial also had potential, but required knowledge of the specific process technology used in each case.

Over the past decade, the ESCo industry in Canada had experienced mixed fortunes, as companies struggled to understand the dynamics of the market. Lack of technical and risk management experience, flawed contracts, lack of financial strength and energy price collapses had all led to very low levels of profitability among major players. The recent upsurge of interest in energy efficiency, however, had the industry onto a more steady footing. Furthermore, a shake-out had occurred, leaving between 5 and 10 serious competitors in Canada.

ESCo Strategies

ESCos saw themselves as undertaking three useful functions with commercial and industrial customers. First, they could undertake energy audits of client sites and advise what forms of energy management were most appropriate. Second, they could engineer and provide access to a wide range of energy-efficient technologies that would normally be hard to get hold of. Third, they could install new energy-efficient equipment, under a performance contract or similar arrangement. In the Canadian industry, there were several hundred consulting engineers that participated in energy audits, but only seven "full-service" ESCos that undertook all three functions.

Of the three functions, programs such as performance contracting offered the greatest potential return to ESCos, but also the highest degree of risk. Following an installation, it took between five and ten years before the financial benefits were realized. ESCos were paid at the time of installation by their financing partners, who recovered their costs over the lifetime of the project, but in the event that the project was badly estimated, the shortfall in revenue would have to be made up by the ESCo. Access to capital at a reasonable cost was thus critical. Some ESCos had parent companies with deep pockets. The audit and supply functions, while less lucrative, were important elements of the ESCO's business because they established legitimacy in the eyes of the customer. Many commercial clients were extremely sceptical of the estimated energy savings provided by ESCos, but if they agreed to an energy audit, there was a greater likelihood they could be sold on the merits of an installation. The credibility of the guarantee provided by the ESCo was thus of great importance.

The GE Energy Management Initiative

The Initial Opportunity

As GE Business Development Manager, Raj Bhatt received a communication from the federal government inviting ESCos to seek to be prequalified for the implementation of performance contracts in 50,000 federal buildings in Canada. The program had a potential total value of $1 billion, which was to be split into a number of smaller contracts. Bhatt was struck by the potential fit between GE's areas of expertise and the requirements of the program. ESCos had to be able to provide energy-efficient lighting, motors, and controls and provide financing for the project; GE was a leading supplier of many of the required products and had a large financing division. Unlike rival firms that would have to form consortia between electrical and financing companies, GE could do many things in-house.

Bhatt submitted a proposal for the Federal Buildings program and, along with a number of other consortia, achieved "prequalification," meaning the right to bid on subsequent contracts that fell under the Federal Buildings umbrella. This success underlined the magnitude of the opportunity that GE was facing in the ESCo industry. Rather than limiting GE's involvement to the one-off Federal Buildings program, Bhatt thought there was potential for an ongoing GE business to meet the expected surge in demand for energy management services. He began to think through the best way of proceeding.

The GE Canada Executive Meeting

Bhatt's first move was to meet with the GE Canada executive group and get their reaction to his idea for an Energy Management Business. Attending were Matthew Meyer, Chairman & CEO, Mike Kozinsky, VP Finance, and Scott Larwood, VP Government Relations. Larwood had already been heavily involved in the Federal Buildings program and was in favour of Bhatt's proposal.

> *Bhatt:* GE Canada is very well positioned to start an Energy
> Management business. We have a broader range of relevant products

and services than any other ESCo, and the Ontario and Quebec Hydro programs are among the most advanced in the world.

Kozinsky (Finance): But this is a systems business. We have never been very good at systems implementation.

Bhatt: I realize that we may have to find partners. We are working with a small ESCo on the Federal Buildings project which will do all the installation work. We can identify suitable future partners as things progress.

Kozinsky: But what is our experience in being a prime contractor? This seems to be very different from any business we have been involved with before.

Larwood (Government Relations): That's not quite true. The Apparatus Technical Service (ATS) business in Power Systems manages service contracts, and there is a lot of project experience in the States.

Meyer (CEO): But there seems to be a considerable risk here. What happens if we pull down a load of asbestos when we're changing a lighting system? GE is an obvious target for legal action.

Kozinsky: And you stated earlier that there is some downside financial risk if the performance contract does not yield the expected savings.

Bhatt: True, but the estimates are conservative. The overall financial projections are very promising, and involve very little up-front cost. Apart from the salaries of three or four employees, most costs are on a contract-by-contract basis.

Meyer: Have you given any thought as to how this business would fit into the GE structure?

Bhatt: One of the strengths of GE Canada is that it already taps into all the different businesses. I would like to see the Energy Management business based in Canada, and drawing from the other GE businesses as required.

Bhatt received a lot of questioning and cautioning on various aspects of the proposal, but there was consensus at the end that the project was worth pursuing. Meyer recommended that Bhatt investigate the level of interest in the U.S. businesses and at the corporate level before any formal proposal was put together.

The GE Supply Opportunity

In discussion with U.S. colleagues, Bhatt discovered that three U.S. divisions were attempting to establish their own ESCo-like initiatives. Two of them were at about the same stage of development as Bhatt. The third, GE Supply, was more advanced. They had been working with an ESCo for a number of months, and had retained a well-connected consultant to advise them. Up to now, the ESCo had assumed all the risk, with GE providing their name, their products, and some servicing expertise, but the division was planning to create a joint venture with the ESCo in the near future.

On hearing about the GE Supply initiative, Bhatt went to Connecticut to visit the GE Supply executives to discuss their respective plans. Present at the meeting were Bhatt, Doug Taylor, CEO of GE Supply, and Fred Allen, manager of the Energy Management business.

> *Taylor (CEO):* Last week we signed a formal alliance agreement with Wetherwell Inc. to run for 18 months. We are now actively looking for contracts.
>
> *Allen (Energy Management):* But the U.S. market requires some education. How is the market in Canada?
>
> *Bhatt:* There is a very promising opportunity that we are working on right now. Basically, the federal government is looking for bidders on a $1 billion program, and we have already gained pre-qualification.
>
> *Allen:* That beats anything we've got down here. I think there could be some real opportunities for us to work together. We have gained quite a lot of experience over the past 12 months, and combined with your market, we could have a winning combination.
>
> *Bhatt:* I am certainly interested in exploring opportunities. How do you see a Canadian Energy Management business fitting with your business?
>
> *Taylor:* We could manage the Canadian business out of our office here.
>
> *Bhatt:* That causes me some concern. The business relies on close coordination with utilities and government bodies, and a strong local presence would definitely be necessary. I must admit, we considered that management of at least part of the business should be in Canada. The opportunities in Canada are unmatched.
>
> *Taylor:* Well, there is some strength to your argument, but I don't see why this business should not fit the normal model.

Bhatt had some misgivings when the meeting came to a close. The business depended on close ties with government bodies, provincial utilities, and local contractors to be really successful, and he felt that these would be lost if there was not a strong Canadian presence. Under the "direct-connect" system, he felt that would be more difficult to achieve.

THE HERITAGE GROUP, INC. (CONDENSED)

In October 1985, Henry Beben (pronounced "Beeben"), president and chief operating officer of The Heritage Group, Inc., was preparing for a meeting with Fred Schneider, chairman of the board and CEO. The Heritage Group, one of Canada's largest food processing corporations, had plunged from record earnings in the second half of fiscal 1984 to a first-ever overall loss for fiscal 1985. In his annual address to shareholders in April 1985, Beben assessed the situation as follows:

> This is bitterly disappointing and exasperating. I feel like the little Dutch boy who put his finger in the dike. We solve one problem and another one appears. . . . Five years ago I thought the process [of making a successful transition to a national food products company] would have been finished by now. Now, I'm loathe to predict how long it could take.

Despite his remarks at the annual meeting, Beben recognized he needed to develop a plan for turning things around at Heritage. In the upcoming meeting with Fred Schneider, he planned to present such a plan.

Company Background

In the spring of 1890, John Metz Schneider of Kitchener, Ontario, made sausage in his basement and sold it door to door. After two years, J. M., as he was commonly known, quit his factory job and with $200 in savings went into business for himself.

This case was prepared by Professor Mark C. Baetz with the assistance of Ms. Louise Carroll as a basis for class discussion rather than to illustrate either effective or ineffective handling of an administrative situation.

The initial business was a family operation. Pork sausage was made according to a family homemade recipe. J. M.'s early insistence on quality resulted in steady demand for his sausage products, and his philosophy about quality became a company creed: "Don't use it if you would not eat it yourself or serve it to your family."

Following a strategy emphasizing quality products, the Schneider business enjoyed steady growth and expansion for the next five decades. The company's product lines were broadened during the 1930s to include beef cattle, poultry, eggs, butter, and cheese. In the 1940s, as part of an on-going philosophy of practicality and frugality, production space was built and used as office space until needed for production. J. M. Schneider died in 1942 at the age of 83.

In the 1950s, the company located its cremery and cheese production in Wellesley, Ontario, just outside Kitchener, and numerous building and renovation projects continued at the main operation. The 1960s were big expansion years: payroll, customer orders, and internal data reporting needs were handled by computer and data processing equipment; the product line now covered upward of 350 different products; a half-million-dollar primary sewage treatment plant was completed; and expansion of the largely regional market area was encouraged by forays into Quebec and the Maritimes.

In 1965, the company went public and offered shares of stock to prospective buyers outside of the company's employees. In April 1969, Schneider common and preferred shares were listed on the Toronto Stock Exchange for the first time. A stock purchase plan was also set up at the same time for employees.

Members of the Schneider family maintained a controlling number of company voting shares with 70 percent of the common voting shares and 27 percent of nonvoting shares. Of the 70 percent voting shares, 53.7 percent were held by three of the Schneiders (Fred, 21 percent; Herb, 16.5 percent; and Howard, 16.2 percent). Nonvoting shares represented 85 percent of the publicly raised cash invested in the company. Most of these shares were widely held by financial institutions and small investors.

As of 1985, three members of the third generation of the Schneider family held senior management positions: Fred Schneider, chairman of the board and CEO of the Heritage Group, Inc.; Herb Schneider, vice-president, personnel and public relations; and Howard Schneider, vice-president and director of research and development. All three were members of the board of directors.

Relations with the Employees and the Community

A section of "J. M. Schneider, Inc.—A Company History" written in 1985 described the company's relations with its employees:

> The company has always prided itself in treating the employees as members of a large family . . .
>
> In 1944, the Schneider Employees Association was certified by the Ontario Government. The company and the union continue to experience amicable

relations. . . . A form of profit sharing was introduced in 1917 for all employees, but [because corporate profits became an increasingly smaller percentage of the total wages paid] the plan was discontinued in 1975.

As far as basic business philosophy is concerned, there is little reason to tamper with an approach which has led to development of an organization that has won: the respect and loyalty of its employees; a high regard for its integrity and efficiency in service among those who do business with it, and a "Famous for Quality" reputation for the products which it offers to its customers.

One top manager who had been with the company for many years described the corporate culture:

All through the evolution of the company, there has been a family orientation. Not only has the Schneider family played a vital role, but many non-Schneider families with two, three, and four generations of service are employees. A preference has been given to hire individuals related to existing employees. In many ways it is a "corporation of families." If an employee becomes a problem, family members will go after him! It is really a paternalistic culture.

The Meat Packing and Processing Industry

The meat packing and processing industry transformed livestock, mainly cattle and hogs, into such customer products as sausage and other variety meats. Competition in the meat packing industry was intense. Meat packing was a very low-margin, high-volume business where cost controls were critical. The difference between profit and loss was very small. The squeeze on profitability in the meat packing industry was a result of the following:

1. Retail margins were in the 1 to 2 percent range. Unprocessed meat was considered a commodity and, as a result, the meat packer had little influence on price. However, brand loyalty could be created among consumers of processed meats and, therefore, a degree of control could be regained by manufacturers of processed meat products. Nevertheless, major meat packers such as Heritage were also faced with increasingly powerful customers; beginning in the 1970s, the food chains began acquiring the independent stores, and the independent stores formed buying groups, so that by the 1980s, there were only two to four major buyers of processed meat in any particular region in Canada.

2. Raw materials represented 65 to 80 percent of cost of sales. The sale price for hogs (Schneider's most important raw material) was determined on the basis of grade. Beef cattle sales prices were determined on a live weight basis, a process which introduced some uncertainty for the packer: overestimating the quality or yield of the carcass resulted in reduced profits. Generally the supply and price for raw materials such as hogs and beef cattle was very volatile.

3. Wages paid out to labour represented the second largest cost item at 10 to 20 percent of sales. In the early 1980s, Canadian rates were about $3 per hour above the falling U.S. rate; this represented a differential of almost $5 when fringe benefits were considered. Although the U.S. had imposed countervail duties of 4–5 cents per pound for live hogs to offset Canadian support programs, the border between the United States and Canada was relatively open for the movement of livestock and meat. This made it important that wage rates remained comparable between the two countries after taking into account the exchange rate.

In the 1980s, a nationwide rationalization was taking place in the industry. Despite a rash of plant closings, it was reported in 1984 that the industry still had twice the capacity it needed. Furthermore, even when major packers such as Canada Packers and Burns suffered from labour disruptions, there was little impact on overall industry production because independent packers were able to expand production and fill the demand, sometimes using nonunion labour.

Another concern to meat packers was the existence of marketing boards. Prices were up to 80 percent higher for commodities in Canada controlled by marketing boards which controlled both production and price. Commodities controlled by such boards included eggs, chicken, turkey, and milk. However, products such as pork were controlled by marketing boards without supply management or price controls, and prices for pork products were in some cases lower in Canada than in the United States.

J. M. Schneider, Inc.—National Expansion

In the 1950s, Schneider Corporation made its first attempt at geographic expansion by purchasing a Winnipeg meat packing plant. After the acquisition turned out to be a disaster, the plant was sold. The experience "bloodied our nose," according to Fred Schneider and "made later expansion much more difficult." Nevertheless, primarily through geographic expansion of the product line through the 1970s, J. M. Schneider became a national, rather than solely a regional, meat processor. Supporting the national expansion were a number of acquisitions, some of which were unsuccessful. For example, the company suffered losses approaching $1 million on acquisitions involving dry groceries, frozen food, canned meats, and dry sausage. Because of the losses, these operations were closed in 1975.

During the 1970s, the development of an efficient distribution system consisting of warehouses in Winnipeg and Vancouver, a combination of both company and common carriers, and a number of supplier plants, contributed to the company's progress. However, toward the mid-70s, Schneider slowed its rapid expansion and focused on developing new products and on improving its market position. By stressing sales to the food service market (i.e., hospitals, restaurants, and institutions), Schneider was quick to respond to market trends which indicated that this market was the fastest growing segment in the industry.

During the 1970s, J. M. Schneider, Inc. achieved record sales and profits. Between 1970 and 1979, the company increased its sales from $79.3 million to $374.4 million, an average annual increase of 19.0 percent. Over the same time frame, net earnings increased from $1.4 million to $7.5 million, representing an average increase in profits of 20.6 percent per annum. Despite growing sales and profits, the company suffered at times from declining returns on investment. For example, in 1978, return on capital employed dropped to 16.75 percent from 20.54 percent. The average return over the previous 10 years (1969–78) was 20.73 percent. In order to halt the falling rates of return, capital expenditures on a Vancouver distribution centre were postponed, cost-cutting measures were taken, and part of the outstanding Class B preferred shares were bought back. This quick action, combined with improvements to internal management systems (e.g., upgrade of cost accounting systems, new customer service, and raw material control systems) enabled an increase in the return on capital employed to 23.49 percent in fiscal 1979. Overall, Schneider had been regarded as Canada's most profitable meat processor since 1971. Furthermore, it achieved this status with an extremely conservative debt-equity ratio of 0.24:1.

Schneider's performance in the 1970s was all the more significant when considered in the context of the overall industry. The raw materials situation was characterized by frequent shortages and high prices. Changes in consumer economics and preferences meant a decrease in meat consumption, a trend which showed no signs of reversing. In addition, the general economy was poor, resulting in record inflation rates and restrictive government measures (e.g., the Anti-Inflation Board). Despite all this, Schneider grew rapidly in terms of volume of products sold, number of specific product lines offered, capital expansion, and staff size. Not only did it perform well but it resisted the temptation to lower its quality or to cut its prices; the company explicitly recognized that consumers wanted food products of consistently high quality. In 1981, Beben described part of the strategy of the company and results:

> Others in the business thought Schneider was making a mistake by centralizing its meat processing in Kitchener by building a world-scale plant and delivering its production nationally. But the company has found that despite rising energy prices, the economies of scale made possible at the plant more than offset transportation costs and there is nothing on the horizon that suggests this will not continue to be the case. The energy costs of operating a packaging plant are high too.
>
> From being a regional food processor operating basically in the Ontario market 10 years ago, the company has become a major force on the national scene.

Fred Schneider described in 1981 other aspects of Schneider's strategy during the 1970s to which the company's success could be attributed:

> We improved our ability as a marketing company. In particular we improved our selling to the chain stores. . . . At the supermarket, and chain buying level, in addition to a name for quality, you also need the reputation of being able to work

with these people successfully, to help them in turn market successfully. You work with them on the kind of deals they require to build volume; you do the kind of things they need done to make sure that the product is rotated properly on the shelves and that it looks good.

[In terms of product mix] we have never put a strong emphasis on the fresh product side of our sales. Unlike traditional packers, we try to cut and slaughter to the market requirements, buying extra cuts when we need them. So we have tended to look on the more perishable side of our product line in a more limited way and have kept that fairly regional.

As we've striven to become national in scope, we have made great strides in increasing the shelf-life of most of our products through better sanitation and better processes in general. . . . This has been, as much as anything, responsible for our ability to market on a national basis from one centralized plant.

In terms of new product introduction, our record of success has been fairly good. (Each year new products account for about 4 percent of the company's business.) Ten or 15 years ago we went to the product management system of marketing, borrowing from the Procter & Gamble approach. We've applied that system as well as we can in meat packing.

We've always had a very strong new product development department. Currently [1981] it involves 12 or more people, which is probably higher than other companies of comparable size. They work solely with the marketing people, the product managers, through committees on new products.

We make effective use of a consumer panel to make sure we don't make many blunders. However, it's something that you have to continually work at. It's very easy for a meat packer to forget he's in the business of satisfying consumer needs.

Despite the success of the national expansion, the company was concerned that its reliance on the meat segment of the food dollar made it vulnerable. By the close of the decade, J. M. Schneider, Inc., considered itself a food-oriented company and not merely a meat processing organization. With this shift in thinking came the realization that continued growth would require diversification into areas with more dynamic growth than the conventional meat lines. With future growth opportunities in mind in 1979, the chairman of the board, Fred P. Schneider, announced the formation of a new corporate planning group. The group was headed by Beben, senior vice president, corporate development, and its function was to "plan and guide the company into a more balanced product and market grouping and to seek out opportunities for diversification and expansion into food areas other than meat."

The Heritage Group, Inc.—Diversification

Amid great controversy and debate, in 1980, J. M. Schneider, Inc., changed its name to The Heritage Group, Inc. The retired, elder family members felt the Schneider name should stay at the top because the name had become synonymous with quality over the decades. However, 95 percent of the shareholders voted in favour of authorizing the name change and moving the

Heritage Group head office to leased space in Waterloo, a few miles away from the Schneider meat division in Kitchener. One manager noted: "It was hoped that physically separating the head office from the meat division would facilitate diversification."

The Heritage Group, Inc., was to act as an "umbrella" corporation under which a group of related, but independent, companies would operate. It would oversee and coordinate the activities of the affiliated companies. The rationale behind the name change included the desire to separate the Schneider name, which was almost exclusively linked to quality meat products, from future forays into other food products. As Beben noted: "We've been promoting J. M. as a master butcher for years. We'd be bending the truth in saying he's a master baker. . . . [Furthermore] consumer research concluded people would resent seeing the image of J. M. Schneider extended to products unrelated to his original butcher shop." It was felt therefore that the name change provided the corporation with the means to grow through product diversification and acquisition. The name change was also regarded as a move to protect one of the company's most valuable assets—the Schneider name—in the event of poor market reception of new product lines. Meat operations were to continue under the subsidiary company name of J. M. Schneider, Inc.

Beben, the major force behind the company's diversification thrust, described the corporate strategy for the 80s as an effort to become Canada's number-one food processor. This goal was expected to be accomplished in two ways: (1) by diversifying to reduce the Heritage Group's dependence on meat and (2) by developing minority interests in suppliers and in areas where the Heritage Group currently lacked expertise. In short, Heritage was looking for opportunities in which the corporation's strengths could be applied to new markets.

Fred Schneider described the rationale and possibilities for diversification:

> We felt we had more or less reached the end of the road for expansion in our traditional processed meat lines. We are either number one or number two in wieners, bologna, and other products right across the country. Once you get to that point it's difficult and very expensive to achieve higher penetrations.
>
> So to continue with the rapid growth we have had, it seemed we would have to branch out and it was logical to do that in areas of food where we have a double advantage. We have marketing experience in working with chain stores and in the food service market as well, so we can use that knowledge and expertise to good effect. In addition, we can use the facilities and knowledge we have in distributing frozen and refrigerated products on a national basis. We have spent a good deal of money and taken a lot of trouble to develop the system which we have in place to do just that.
>
> Using those two advantages, we felt we should get into other areas of food where there was room to grow and where we could use that same frozen distribution system.

Heritage moved quickly in its bid to diversify. In 1980, the corporation held two wholly owned subsidiary companies: J. M. Schneider, Inc., the meat subsidiary, and National Consolidated Food Brands, Inc. (Natco), the newly formed grocery division. By 1981, it had acquired F. G. Bradley, Inc., a major manufacturer and marketer of processed meat products in the food service business. Link Services, Inc., was also established that year; it was responsible for providing transportation and distribution services to all Heritage companies. Finally, in 1984, Heritage established Portage Trade Development to expand the corporation's export trade opportunities.

Each of the five subsidiary companies operated as independent tax-paying corporate entities with a president and slate of officers. Each subsidiary company had its own support services such as computer systems and accounting. The Heritage Group, Inc., was to provide corporate functions along the lines of setting strategic objectives, helping to plan and coordinate the operating objectives of the subsidiary companies, developing business outside the existing businesses, monitoring performance, and obtaining and allocating investment dollars. Heritage was also to provide a personnel function. Each of the subsidiary companies will now be described in greater detail.

J. M. Schneider, Inc.

This company's mandate remained unchanged, that is, Schneider was left to pursue its leadership position in the meat industry. However, the emphasis in the 1980s was threefold: (1) new products which met changing consumer lifestyles and preferences (e.g., the introduction of lite products in 1981), (2) improvements in quality assurance practices (e.g., a shelf-life goal on all products of at least 60 days), and (3) improvements in the company's capacity to deliver products quickly. (This emphasis on distribution ultimately led to the establishment of a distribution subsidiary company, Link Services.)

To minimize the effects of anticipated increased costs in raw materials, supply, and labour, a number of measures were implemented including cost-cutting programs, improved production techniques, increased market penetration, expanded market areas, and the maintenance of a national pricing system. In fact, as the decade unfolded, it became increasingly apparent that the challenge of becoming more competitive in the 80s was to control costs; by 1982, Schneider recognized that efficiency and cost effectiveness were vital and increased efforts to control costs and penetrate markets.

Schneider's volume and profit objectives went unmet after an initial 11 percent increase in sales in 1980. Although prices were raised, prohibitive raw material and labour costs were increasingly responsible for the company's inability to increase its margins. Nevertheless, the increase in profits at J. M. Schneider, Inc., was the primary factor in the doubling of earnings at Heritage from 1982 to 1983, and while other Heritage subsidiaries were losing money, J. M. Schneider remained profitable. According to one top manager, "Reinvesting the profits of J. M. Schneider into other divisions of the company which were losing money had a demoralizing impact on the Schneider employee group."

In terms of facility locations, by 1985, J. M. Schneider, Inc., had a manufacturing plant and distribution centre in Vancouver, a distribution centre in Calgary, two plants and a distribution centre in Winnipeg, the main plant and distribution centre in Kitchener, and a poultry operation in Ayr, Ontario.

In terms of organizational structure, J. M. Schneider had basically a functional organization with vice presidents of human resources, R&D, manufacturing, sales and marketing, plus a controller. In 1983, an executive vice president position was added to groom a new president when long-time president Ken Murray announced his intention to retire.

National Consolidated Food Brands, Inc. (Natco)

Natco began operations in April 1980. Its mandate was to "apply existing corporate strengths to the development of grocery, dairy, and frozen food products." It would draw on the Schneider expertise in such areas as data processing, cost control systems, finance, and distribution of refrigerated products. Natco intended to accomplish its mandate with the development of new and existing products and the acquisition of companies producing complementary products. According to Beben, the decision was made to buy an interest in supplier companies where possible because "if we were to duplicate these facilities, it would take longer and a lot of money." Following this strategy, interests of up to 100 percent were acquired in the following companies: Winchester Cheese (processed cheese), Millbank Cheese and Butter Co. (specialty and cheddar cheese), Dorset Foods (frozen sausage rolls and quiche), and Mother Jackson's Open Kitchens (fruit and meat pies).

Natco's marketing strategy consisted of a quick response to market trends and the innovative development of new products. When Natco was first established, it inherited the Schneider cheese line. Because cheese was considered a "dairy" rather than "meat" item, it was purchased and handled by departments different from meat within retail grocery operations. Therefore, Schneider's cheese products did not always get the marketing attention they deserved. Natco planned to make cheese one of its marketing priorities.

Natco's initial product lines included cheese, shortening, lard, margarine, and Grandma Martin's frozen pastries (tarts, pie shells, quiche). Seven sales reps were employed to secure product listings from the grocery and dairy buyers of major retailers; however, until 1982, the company relied on the Schneider sales force to handle details at the store level, to sell to independents, and to sell Natco products to medium-size and smaller accounts. As the Natco line grew, the Natco direct sales force also grew. One top manager explained the rationale for segregating the grocery and meat sales forces:

> Grocery products are purchased by different buyers from meat products. In addition, with grocery, you can plan your promotional program months ahead but with meat products, program planning does not go beyond a few weeks.

Natco was expected to boost sales to 25 percent of the total Heritage Group sales in 5 to 10 years. During its first full year of operation, Natco had sales of $39 million and earnings were $187,000.

In terms of market development, product listings grew steadily from 225 in 1980 to 875 in 1982. By 1984, Natco had developed manufacturing self-sufficiency and had expanded its direct sales force. But while sales growth was encouraging, earnings were modest, attributed to high start-up costs, particularly advertising and promotional costs associated with new products. Despite the modest earnings, Beben was proudest of the Natco subsidiary, which he described as "the shining light within the corporation." One investment analyst supported this view by noting in 1980: "Schneider's expansion into the highly profitable frozen-grocery-product market is well timed and should result in accelerated growth over the coming decade."

In terms of organizational structure, Natco first started off with a general manager, director of sales, and office administrator/accountant. Natco's equity interests in Winchester Cheese, Mother Jackson's, and Dorset Foods were controlled through individual boards of directors with no direct operating responsibilities for each of these businesses. In 1983, the head of Natco was given the title of president, and the office administrator became controller. Beben assumed leadership of Natco for two years until a president was chosen.

F. G. Bradley, Inc.

In February 1981, F. G. Bradley, Inc., was acquired for approximately $12 million, making it Heritage's first major acquisition. With sales approaching $120 million and a workforce of 500, Bradley supplied the high-growth food service sector with quality portioned fresh meat products. It was the largest supplier to the fast food chain sector of the market. Bradley contributed three manufacturing plants to the corporation—one each in Toronto, Edmonton, and Winnipeg—thereby opening new markets to both Schneider and Natco.

Various top managers justified the Bradley purchase by noting: (1) it gives access to a larger share of the food service markets, (2) Bradley products will find new markets because of links to the larger Heritage distribution network, (3) Heritage plans to expand Bradley's product line by adapting Heritage lines in meat retail and grocery retail, (4) because Bradley is beef oriented, it will open the door to diversification of Heritage's pork-dominated commodity base, and (5) the acquisition changes the perception that Schneider is not an important part of the food service business.

While Bradley was expected to gain access to Heritage's strengths in the areas of systems, data processing, finance, and some areas of administration and access to other Heritage group products, no change was anticipated in Bradley's marketing and operating concepts. Some of these concepts were different from other Heritage products; for example, while J. M. Schneider always followed a premium-priced strategy, Bradley was not a premium-priced company, due in part to the nature of the food service business. Fred Schneider described in 1981 the key success factors in the food service business in general:

> To be successful in the food service business, price is extremely critical and brand means very little. What counts in food service is how well you can formulate and prepare and process a product to meet the requirements of that particular customer

at a price he's willing to pay. There it's loyalty with the trade that you're after. With the hospitality and institutional trade, you have to get a reputation for service, for value, for price.

Growth goals for Bradley were to expand market share with more products in existing markets and with new products in new and existing markets. Projected sales and earnings increases were $24 million and 4.5 percent, respectively, for its first year under the Heritage umbrella. At the time of acquisition, Bradley was experiencing losses.

Bradley failed to meet sales and profit objectives in 1982 and 1983. This poor performance was attributed to a general market decline during the economic recession and to inherited operating deficiencies which took longer to correct than originally estimated. The greatest ongoing problem was unsatisfactory margins. Beben felt the performance of Bradley was especially disappointing because it was a major acquisition that "ended up much poorer than expected." Bradley also suffered from high management turnover. This turnover exacerbated the deficiencies of Bradley's reporting systems. Nevertheless, in conjunction with the Link subsidiary, Bradley lowered costs considerably with a new on-line order entry system and an inventory reporting system. By 1984, Bradley was contributing positively to the earnings of Heritage.

It was originally expected that the J. M. Schneider food service business would be integrated into Bradley. This integration was intended to give a single focus to food service and to increase volume to Bradley to help overcome Bradley's losses. By 1985, this integration had not occurred because of concerns that the Schneider food service business would be lost if it was folded into the Bradley division. In fact, some Schneider processed meat food service business in the west was transferred to Bradley, and within 18 months this business was lost. Bradley's sales force was used to selling fresh red meat and did not feel comfortable selling processed meat. Ultimately, the two food service businesses were kept separate, which meant that two sales forces competed against each other, sometimes selling the same products to the same customer but using different pricing strategies.

In terms of organizational structure, there was a complete reorganization at Bradley in 1982. When Bradley was bought, it had three profit centres—Toronto, Winnipeg, and Edmonton—each with a general manager reporting to the president in Toronto. This was changed to a functional organization. There was now a president, a senior vice president, and four vice presidents: controller, sales and marketing, corporate development and personnel, operations and distribution. Beben assumed the presidency of Bradley until 1985 when a president was appointed.

Link Services, Inc.

Link Services, Inc., was established as a subsidiary company to integrate and provide complete transportation and distribution services for all of the Heritage Group companies. It was set up as a corporate function to be used and paid for by the other subsidiary companies. One of the advantages of Link was that each company would know its exact distribution costs. In addition, Link Services fulfilled three major services: warehousing, administrative services, and transportation.

Progress toward the integration of services was quickly made. Link worked closely with individual companies so that by 1984 it was handling and transporting all Heritage company products. In a number of instances, Link was instrumental in providing new market opportunities for Heritage products. Link's trucks, a combination of owned and common carriers, carried products from all companies to several destinations, a cost-effective measure achieved through rationalization. Finally, Link's administrative services included order processing, order filling, inventory control, and management information reporting. It also worked with companies to develop tailored systems which fulfilled individual system needs and requirements. Link was a corporate service and therefore reported to the senior vice president, corporate services, who reported to the chairman of the board.

Portage Trade Development

Portage was established in 1983. Its mandate was to expand the corporation's export trade opportunities. To this end and in cooperation with its sister companies, Portage selected a variety of existing products which it felt would appeal to foreign markets. By the end of its first year of operation, Portage had made progress into the Caribbean and the United States. Initial orders from the latter were minimal and as a result, Portage had to rely on Link services to process and deliver smaller quantities. In 1984, Portage recognized that the regional character of the U.S. markets would require different marketing techniques and possibly different products if it were to promote higher volume sales. Therefore, Portage was reassessing its market and product strategy to the United States in an effort to identify new opportunities. The general manager of Portage reported to the president of Heritage Group.

The Current Situation

Beben joined J. M. Schneider, Inc., in 1969, and in 1973 he was appointed vice president marketing, J. M. Schneider Limited, and was elected to the board of directors. Fred Schneider described Beben as "instrumental" in turning Schneider into a national company during the 1970s. According to Schneider, a lot of the growth in the 1970s "could be credited to Henry's aggressiveness." As senior vice president of corporate development and the head of the corporate planning group, Beben was also instrumental in the corporation's diversification strategy which led to the establishment of The Heritage Group, Inc., in 1980. In addition to his responsibilities to the corporate entity, Beben assumed the presidencies of both Natco and F. G. Bradley when they were established. In 1981, he became the executive vice president and chief operating officer for The Heritage Group. Two years later, "in recognition of the high level of his management skills and continuing contribution to the growth of the corporation," Beben was appointed president and chief operating officer.

As a management team, Fred Schneider and Henry Beben were a contrast in styles. Schneider was a "mild-mannered and soft-spoken" person who described his management style as "that of a delegator who likes to keep channels of communication open and be visible both in the office and in the plant." He admitted to not being involved in the business community as he should be. He described himself "as a person who is most comfortable with my personal friends" and one who dislikes large parties. He noted further: "I avoid the limelight. That's the part of the job I like the least."

In contrast, Beben was in the limelight a great deal. Various reports described him as "aggressive," "entrepreneurial," and "immaculately tailored." Beben was the focus of most of the attention that surrounded the company's strategy for the 80s. He was credited with the change in corporate image from a "conservative, traditional company" to a high-growth, dynamic company in tune with major trends in the marketplace. The Heritage Group, with Beben's guidance, was gearing to become a significant player on the world stage in the food industry. Financial analysts and the investment community saw Beben as "the guy who is going to make things happen" at Heritage and characterized the company as "a conservative long-term investment but not one for an investor seeking quick returns." Beben did not object to this description and in fact admitted, "We did not make this [diversification] decision to look good in the short term, but to make good in the long term and to protect our shareholders' interests in the long term." One analyst recommended the purchase of Heritage shares in 1980 because of the company's "strong financial position, strong operating base, national distribution network, and expanding horizons into growing lucrative markets."

Despite corporate enthusiasm and endorsements from the financial community, The Heritage Group's performance since the diversification strategy was adopted had been less than satisfactory (Exhibit 1). Net earnings per share dropped significantly in 1981 to $.73 from the 1980 figure of $2.55; although the EPS had largely recovered by 1984, earnings as a percentage of sales were not commensurate with sales increases. The company failed to maintain or even regain its earnings levels of the 70s and only the Schneider subsidiary was contributing significantly to corporate profits. As the results of the Heritage Group faltered, the senior corporate officers became more involved in the operating decisions of the subsidiary companies.

Employers became increasingly concerned about the rationale for the Heritage Group concept, and this resulted in some strain in management-labour relations. In August 1982, 140 angry poultry workers at the Kitchener plant phoned in sick to protest what they felt was an unsatisfactory contract settlement which gave meat workers raises of $1.25 an hour compared to 50 cents for poultry workers. One report in 1982 put the dispute in the

EXHIBIT 1 The Heritage Group, Inc.: Ten-Year Statistical Review, Seven-Year Selected Ratios ($000 except where noted)

	1985	1984	1983	1982	1981	1980	1979	1978	1977	1976
Sales	$648,598	$645,558	$590,074	$581,071	$539,364	$391,637	$374,374	$324,675	$262,834	$254,970
Earnings										
Earnings before income taxes and extraordinary items	2,841	10,011	9,494	5,125	3,304	11,535	12,164	7,766	7,544	7,865
Income taxes	832	4,245	4,222	2,238	1,382	4,844	4,620	3,079	2,944	3,288
Earnings before extraordinary items	2,009	5,766	5,272	2,887	1,922	6,691	7,544	4,687	4,600	4,577
As percent of sales	.31	.89	.89	.50	.36	1.71	2.02	1.44	1.75	1.80
Net earnings (loss)	(2,036)	5,766	5,272	2,887	1,922	6,691	7,544	4,687	4,600	3,579
Net earnings (loss) as percent of sales	(.31)	.89	.89	.50	.36	1.71	2.02	1.44	1.75	1.40
Dividends paid	1,167	1,167	1,167	1,162	1,390	1,258	1,088	1,011	824	756
Capital expenditures	6,983	5,254	5,741	3,329	8,486	6,406	4,104	9,389	11,030	5,377
Depreciation and amortization	7,072	5,960	5,978	5,861	5,129	4,725	4,476	3,674	2,652	2,567
Salaries, wages, and employee benefits	126,791	128,316	108,508	100,515	88,924	71,004	61,538	56,501	47,747	42,084
Average number of employees	3,971	3,970	3,827	3,817	3,880	3,327	3,131	3,009	2,874	2,676
Working capital	22,786	24,336	22,487	22,333	18,816	23,842	22,304	17,286	18,984	12,774
Working capital ratio	1.41	1.49	1.51	1.62	1.42	1.89	2.11	1.92	2.44	1.95
Total assets	143,814	136,811	126,867	119,715	126,692	95,537	83,627	76,275	65,057	50,917
Shareholders' equity at end of year	58,780	61,983	57,384	53,279	51,300	50,766	45,364	40,118	36,361	32,287
Percent return on equity at beginning of year	(3.28)	10.05	9.90	5.62	3.79	14.75	18.80	12.89	14.25	12.01
Per share statistics, in dollars										
Earnings before extraordinary items	.76	2.17	1.99	1.10	.73	2.55	2.78	1.73	1.70	1.70
Net earnings (loss)	(.77)	2.17	1.99	1.10	.73	2.55	2.78	1.73	1.70	1.33
Dividends paid	.44	.44	.44	.44	.53	.48	.40	.37	.31	.28
Equity at end of year	22.17	23.38	21.64	20.10	19.56	19.36	17.29	14.77	13.47	11.98
Selected Ratios										
Long-term debt/shareholders' equity	.43	.31	.40	.45	.48	.24	.28			
Total debt/assets	.59	.55	.55	.56	.60	.46	.46			
Inventory/turnover (times)	14.1	14.8	16.7	18.1	17.0	16.2	19.1			
Inventory/Working Capital	2.0	1.8	1.6	1.4	1.7	1.0	.88			

following context:

> Poultry workers and union spokesmen said labour relations at the plant have soured in the last few years, most notably since the creation two years ago of Heritage Group, Inc. They said that instead of being employees of a proud family company, they feel they have become cogs in an impersonal and profit-conscious corporation.
>
> Employee spokesmen said they felt further alienated this summer during contract talks, when management wanted an agreement containing wage gains of less than the industry pattern. The union said efforts to negotiate this summer were "hampered" by Heritage Group announcements in July of a wage freeze and 6 percent pay ceiling for salary personnel.
>
> The company's self-imposed salary cuts came in the face of a profit crunch brought on partly by its aggressive expansion into grocery products and the hotel-restaurant trade.

The company's office workers also felt the company was becoming more impersonal by making decisions without their involvement. Following a unilateral announcement in 1982 by the Heritage corporate office that there would be pay curbs and an increase in prices in the cafeteria, the office workers felt it was "time to protect themselves" and filed for certification with the Ontario Labour Relations Board.

For the first time in the firm's history, there were work disruptions. In 1983, the United Food and Commercial Workers' Union struck the Winnipeg plant. In 1984, the Retail, Wholesale and Department Store Union struck the Winchester plant, and later in the same year a strike was narrowly avoided at the Kitchener plant. Furthermore, in 1984 slowdowns and work-to-rule campaigns prevented the company from picking up market share from strike-prone Canada Packers and Burns. The Schneider Employees' Association struck the Ayr plant in 1985.

A communication program including a 25-minute film was developed in early 1984 to explain to employees and customers the development of the Heritage Group and its subsidiary companies. Nevertheless, Heritage management found itself on the defensive at the 1984 annual meeting of shareholders (see Appendix A for excerpts of Beben's remarks at this meeting).

The faltering performance surprised company observers. One investment analyst noted:

> We are mystified by [these] results as they seem to belie the improving industry and Company trends. . . . As far as industry conditions are concerned, there has been an improving trend in capacity (there is still too much but far less than previously), an apparent end to spiraling labour rates (which have seen Heritage's labour costs rise from 16.5 percent of total costs in 1981 to 20 percent last year), restrictions on hog exports to the United States (which should reduce raw material prices here and permit margin expansion) and, finally, less aggressive pricing by industry leader, Canada Packers (which should also help on the margin front). . . . Internally, Heritage has finally put F. G. Bradley into the black and continues to record improving results from Natco.

In his address to the shareholders on April 24, 1985, Beben reviewed the performance of the various subsidiary companies and then cited a number of factors that continued to contribute to Heritage's lackluster performance including the cost of raw materials, the decline in consumption in meat products, and the steady increase in labour costs (see Appendix B for excerpts of remarks). The local newspaper, the *Kitchener-Waterloo Record,* reported on the annual meeting and on community reaction to Beben's remarks. Headlines in the weeks following the meeting in various newspapers ranged from "Schneider's staff faces tough times" and "Heritage Group finds transition difficult" to "Workers plan Schneider rally" and "Workers angered by 'pay back' comments." Most of the reports concentrated on the part of the address which focused on the role of the employees.

Heritage employees took exception to Beben's remarks and staged a rally outside the J. M. Schneider plant in Kitchener "to send a message to senior management." According to one media report, "Many workers believed the rally is aimed directly at Henry Beben." A statement released at the rally warned, "If the company keeps putting negative pressure on us, the result will be negative pressure from us." Workers rebutted Beben's remarks about their lack of generosity with reminders that employees had accepted a 22-month wage freeze (which was still in effect), that workers had accepted casual labour in the plants, and that production was up. Employees felt that instead of criticizing their workers, management should be thanking them for the sacrifices they have already made.

Beben's Concerns

Beben felt that his remarks were appropriate given the current corporate situation. His comments were directed at all employees, both management and those covered by a collective agreement with the firm. The tension arose from the fact that his statements had been reported out of context. Nonetheless, Beben realized that he would need the cooperation of the employees in order to improve Heritage's overall performance. He wondered what else he could do to ensure better returns.

APPENDIX A
EXCERPTS OF BEBEN'S REMARKS AT 1984 ANNUAL
MEETING OF SHAREHOLDERS

The most pressing questions, I suspect, on the lips of many people in this audience are "What has happened to our corporation over the past four and one half years?" "Why have the financial results deteriorated so significantly from our 1979 high?"

What have been our responses to this situation? Many and varied.

We have stayed the course. We continue to believe in our strategic direction. We have not and will not give up our share of the market. We have worked hard at streamlining and making our operations as efficient as possible.

We have strengthened communications with all of our employees so that we all better understand the circumstances facing us.

The results of all these efforts are a matter of public record, a decrease of profits in 1980 followed by an even larger decrease in 1981 and some recovery in 1982 and 1983. The first half of 1984, however, is most disconcerting to your management. We will have to work very hard for the remainder of the year to meet or beat last year's results.

One of our major problems is apparently being in an industry where profit has no meaning or motivation. Unless and until this attitude changes, things will be difficult.

In light of this fact, it will be incumbent upon all of our employees to be extremely cognizant of current circumstance and of our cost structure so that we may be able to produce significantly better results than many of our competitors and it is against this benchmark that we should, as management, judge ourselves . . .

We've had a long and favourable relationship with our employees at J. M. Schneider in Kitchener and have been able to give them a most respectable and secure standard of living . . .

In other parts of our corporation we have found, however, that reason and even generosity have failed and this gives rise to much concern. It appears to us that there is uneven access to the minds of our employees and that in many instances good dialogue is impossible.

We have all asked what is wrong with labour relations in Canada. Our view, in part, is that even the most enlightened employer is at a disadvantage in communicating ideas and concerns to his employees. A new equilibrium is necessary if a spirit of labour-management cooperation is to be started and fostered . . . Our lawmakers have the prime responsibility for beginning the process . . .

APPENDIX B
EXCERPTS OF BEBEN'S REMARKS AT 1985 ANNUAL MEETING OF SHAREHOLDERS

Déjà vu seems like an appropriate comment to make as I begin these remarks . . . Certainly at the end of the last fiscal year and the beginning of this current year, there was every reason to be optimistic about our future results. Yet here we stand in just about the identical position of a year ago.

This is bitterly disappointing and exasperating to your management, particularly, since we feel that fundamental changes have been made that are definite improvements over past practice . . .

In J. M. Schneider's case there is no doubt that some circumstances difficult to control have contributed to their poor first-half results. In January and February, because of a marketing board decision we were losing 30–40¢ per pound on broiler chickens . . . In addition, we continue to see declining consumption in many of our key product categories.

Given the situation as it is, it's hard to be overly optimistic about Schneider's prospects for the remainder of the year . . . The task at hand will be to be more proactive in anticipating the required changes in order to maintain current contributions and future prospects. I suspect that many of the adjustments management will have to make will prove to be unpopular. However, it must be understood that they will be absolutely necessary in order to maintain the viability of the company.

I'm certain that it hasn't escaped your attention that our new companies (NATCO, Portage) seem to have picked up momentum and are progressing satisfactorily while the two mature organizations (J. M. Schneider, F. G. Bradley) are experiencing difficulties. These troubles are, in significant part, caused by outside influences that we predicted would occur several years ago. Part of our problem has been that our own people have found it hard to adapt to these fast-changing realities. Some of them simply don't want to believe them even now. This corporation has prided itself on its human relations over many decades. Indeed, it has been exceedingly generous with its employees. I believe, as an employee, that it is now time to begin to pay back to the company some of that generosity as we struggle to come to grips with our changing world. If we display understanding, cooperation, enthusiasm, and willingness to work harder, then the crisis will pass and we will go on to become the truly great company that we can and should be. On the other hand, if we show recalcitrance, sullenness, greed, and idleness, then we doom our collective futures. I believe this company and its employees are far too good to allow that to happen . . .

In closing, your management is committed to make whatever changes are necessary to protect the investment of the shareholders and the future of the employees in these trying times. I believe we will succeed.

13

Hydro-Quebec and the Great Whale Project

In February 1992, managers at Hydro-Quebec were concerned about the possible cancellation of a major contract to export electricity to the New York Power Authority (NYPA). The agreement, which was set to run for 21 years and was worth $17 billion in revenue, formed the backbone of a massive effort by Hydro-Quebec to further expand electrical generation in the north of the province. While a contract had been signed more than two years earlier, it was still subject to confirmation by both parties. At the request of NYPA, the original ratification deadline of November 30, 1991, had already been extended by one year. Now, political pressures from environmental groups in the United States, along with reduced demand forecasts for Northeast U.S. power needs, were causing New York State officials to consider terminating the deal.

For Hydro-Quebec, cancellation of the contract would have a severe impact on the economics of the project named after the Great Whale River, a major waterway in northern Quebec. Managers at Hydro-Quebec realized that a decision by the government-owned utility to halt the development could also have far-reaching effects on Quebec's economy, as well as an adverse influence on the province's economic leverage in ongoing Canadian constitutional talks. A decision to proceed would carry its own economic risks; namely, whether the massive amounts of electricity generated could be sold at a price that would cover both fixed and variable costs. In addressing the trade-offs, managers at Hydro-Quebec realized that fixed costs were influenced in part by the nature and extent of concessions offered to expedite construction. How to proceed was anything but clear.

This case was prepared by Professor Allen J. Morrison and Detlev Nitsch for the sole purpose of providing material for class discussion at The Western Business School. Copyright 1993 © The University of Western Ontario and The American Graduate School of International Management.

Hydro-Quebec and James Bay

Hydro-Quebec was created in 1944 by the Quebec parliament as a government-owned utility. Under its charter of incorporation, Hydro-Quebec's mandate was to provide energy to industrial and commercial enterprises, as well as to Quebec citizens through municipal distributors. With the backing of the province, Hydro-Quebec took control over essentially all electrical generation in the province, thereby streamlining production, eliminating redundancies, and encouraging the development of new sources of power generation.

In the late 1960s, Hydro-Quebec officials became increasingly convinced of the huge potential of the province's northern regions for hydroelectric power generation. Shaped by ice-age glaciers, northern Quebec was covered with thousands of lakes and fast-running rivers. Advocates of commercializing the hydroelectric potential of the region argued that every day millions of potential kilowatt-hours of electrical energy flowed out to sea. The energy potential from the James Bay region of the province was regarded as particularly high. If the James Bay region were fully developed, estimates of its power generation topped 30,000 megawatts (MW) at peak production.

Set against this generating potential was the growing demand for electricity in Quebec and the Northeast United States. Throughout the 1970s, Quebec and Northeast U.S. electrical energy demand was predicted to rise at an average annual rate of over 7 percent. The growth forecast for the 1984 to 1993 period was considerably less, at 2.7 percent for the United States and 3.1 percent for Canada. However, even this more modest rate of growth would require huge increases in generating capacity over the next decade. The cost and pollution associated with coal and oil-fired generators, together with the growing opposition to nuclear power, convinced Hydro-Quebec officials that demand for cost-effective and clean hydroelectric power would remain buoyant for the foreseeable future.

On July 14, 1971, the James Bay Development Corporation (JBDC) was organized by the government of Quebec. JBDC's initial capitalization of $100 million was underwritten by the province of Quebec. Hydro-Quebec held 51 percent of JBDC's shares and was given authority to begin development work on a 150,000-square-mile region east of James Bay. On December 21, 1972, James Bay Energy Corporation (JBEC) was established to complement JBDC. This new organization was capitalized with CDN$1 billion, 70 percent of which was underwritten by Hydro-Quebec. With large sums of capital at their disposal, engineers planned to dam a number of major rivers, flooding much of the 150,000-square-mile project area.

The region affected was enormous—equivalent in size to the entire Northeast United States, including New York, New Jersey, Pennsylvania, and all of New England. The area lay to the east of James Bay, at the south end of Hudson Bay, extending almost to Labrador. The southern boundary of the project was the 49th parallel—approximately the latitude of Paris, France, and just north of Seattle, Washington. The 55th parallel marked the project's northern border—the latitude of Copenhagen, Denmark, or the tip of the Alaska peninsula. The annual temperature in this rugged region averaged slightly below freezing. Because the only means of access to most of the region was by chartered float planes, the area remained isolated from population centers hundreds of miles further south. Only a handful of non-aboriginal Canadians had ever lived in or even visited the region. Exhibit 1 presents a general overview of the geography of the region.

Opposition from Native Groups

The announcement of extensive development plans for the James Bay region caught many aboriginal people by surprise. Approximately 10,000 native Cree Indians and 5,000 Inuit inhabited the area. To these groups, the extensive flooding that would result from the project spelled the destruction of the habitat for such wildlife as moose, caribou, beaver, owls, geese, and a variety of fish, including salmon and Arctic char. The majority of aboriginals earned at least part of their livelihoods from hunting and fishing and, not surprisingly, they worried that the James Bay project represented a serious threat to their way of life.

Both the Inuit and Cree had been in the James Bay region long before European explorers first arrived in the 16th century. Since first interacting with settlers, the aboriginals' relationship with them had always been strained. Despite assurances from generations of first European and later North American governments that their culture would be protected, the economic potential of resource-rich northern Quebec led to increasing industrialization of the region. By the early 1970s, mines, pulp mills, and other resource-intensive industries established operations in what had been native hunting areas in northern Quebec. This was often done, especially in the early days, with little or no regard for the fate of either the natural environment or the lives of aboriginals.

While the Cree and Inuit had different base languages and generally lived apart, they shared many similarities in their lifestyles and cultures. Both groups shared a reverence for the land and a value system centered around the family unit, with no real central authority. Individually, both the Cree and Inuit were often described as nonassertive and reluctant to become involved in others' affairs. Most native beliefs were alien to the predominant North American culture, which emphasized self-aggrandizement and material consumption. Aboriginal people felt a reverence for nature's gifts and believed that animals and other elements of their natural environment should be treated with respect and dignity. While the Cree and Inuit acknowledged the abstract principle of land ownership, hunters used land belonging to someone else as frequently as their own, with boundaries between areas typically loosely defined. To most native hunters it was not so much geographic boundaries but animal movements that determined where one should place trap lines or catch fish.

EXHIBIT 1   Area Affected by the Great Whale Project

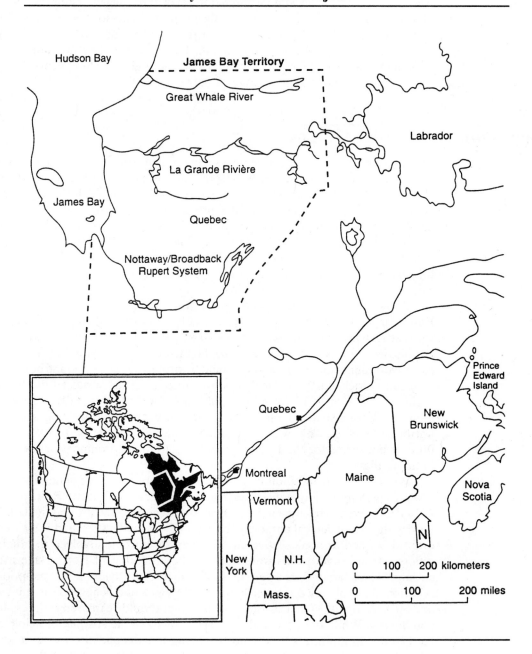

When forced to live under transplanted European laws and customs, many aboriginal people underwent changes to their lifestyles that frequently resulted in social problems for their communities. The transition from being self-sufficient hunters to wage-earners was difficult. Accusations of racial prejudice and exploitation of native workers were frequent. Native Cree and Inuit often complained that they were the last hired for the worst jobs and that they would be the first let go in the event of a layoff. The results of these and other social difficulties had contributed to high rates of alcoholism, drug abuse, suicide, and crime in native populations.

Citing these problems, native leaders began in the late 1960s to increasingly reject the notion of cultural assimilation as unworkable and unconscionable. Not surprisingly, Hydro-Quebec's initiatives to develop James Bay led to legal challenges on the grounds that the rights of the aboriginal people to the land had not been considered. Native leaders sought to put a halt to the entire project on the basis of a 1912 statute, which, they argued, affirmed their exclusive rights over the entire James Bay region.

Through the ensuing legal process, Cree and Inuit concerns came to be taken seriously by Hydro-Quebec. In November 1975, an agreement was successfully negotiated between both aboriginal groups and the federal government. The resulting James Bay and Northern Quebec Agreement (JBNQA) provided formal reserves for both groups—2,000 square miles for the Inuit and 3,250 square miles for the Cree—as well as exclusive hunting, fishing, and trapping rights over an additional 25,000 and 35,000 square miles, respectively (see Exhibit 2 for a map illustrating these reserves). In addition, both groups received cash compensation in the amount of $225 million (approximately $18,750 per person) over 20 years, and a voice in future environmental assessments relating to James Bay development. As part of the JBNQA, the government of Quebec also extended to Cree and Inuit groups limited self-government authority related to the administration of social services and education.

The Growth of Hydro-Quebec

When this agreement had been signed with native groups, the development of James Bay proceeded at a rapid pace. After having secured additional debt financing, primarily through the bond market, Hydro-Quebec began operating the first power plant of James Bay Phase I in 1979. Located on the La Grande River, it provided 666 MW of power for transmission to customers in Quebec, New York, and New England. Two more massive stations were completed in 1985, bringing an end to James Bay Phase I. Total generating capacity for Phase I was approximately 10,000 MW. In 1991, Hydro-Quebec's total installed capacity, including both its hydroelectric and thermal generating plants, was approximately 26,800 MW.

EXHIBIT 2   Cree and Inuit Reserves

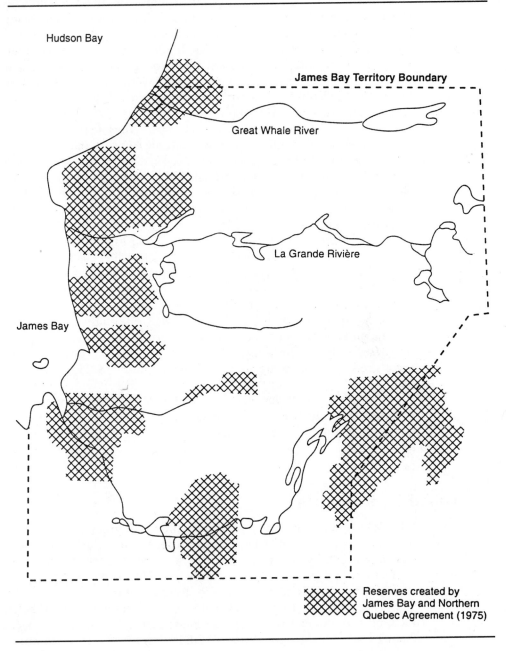

Hudson Bay

James Bay Territory Boundary

Great Whale River

La Grande Rivière

James Bay

⊠⊠⊠⊠ Reserves created by
James Bay and Northern
Quebec Agreement (1975)

By the end of 1991, Hydro-Quebec's assets had grown to $41.85 billion, making it the 12th-largest utility company in the world. Of these assets, approximately $9.40 billion was represented by stockholders' equity. It was estimated that heavy borrowing made the utility one of the single largest holders of U.S. denominated debt in the industrialized world. In the spring of 1992, Standard & Poor's rated the utility a AA-credit risk. Despite a relatively heavy debt load, the utility remained highly profitable. In 1991, revenues were $6.28 billion and profits were $760 million, an increase in profits of 88.1 percent over 1990. Of the 500 largest global service companies ranked by *Fortune,* Hydro-Quebec was rated number 14 in terms of return on revenues. The utility employed 20,000 people directly, with thousands more employed in related construction, investment, and support industries. It was estimated that direct and indirect employment related to Hydro-Quebec totalled over 80,000, or about 2 percent of Quebec's workforce. Financial statements for the utility are reported in Exhibit 3.

Critics argued that Hydro-Quebec's high profitability was at least in part a function of lucrative contracts the utility was able to negotiate with power companies in the United States. Hydro-Quebec's rate structure had recently led to controversy when it was reported through leaks in the Quebec press that the NYPA was paying four times the rate for electricity imports than some magnesium and aluminum smelters in the province were charged and

---

EXHIBIT 3 **Financial Results: Hydro Quebec (in millions of Canadian dollars)**

	Income Statement			
	1989	*1990*	*1991*	*1992**
Total revenue	5,559	5,885	6,284	6,916
Expenditures	2,759	3,047	3,183	3,702
Income before interest and exchange loss	2,800	2,838	3,101	3,214
Interest and exchange loss	2,235	2,434	2,341	2,514
Net income	565	404	760	700

* Projected.

	Balance Sheet		
	1989	*1990*	*1991*
Total assets	33,873	36,684	41,851
Long-term debt	21,957	24,072	28,111
Shareholders' equity	8,233	8,637	9,397

Source: Company annual reports.

about twice the rate that Quebec consumers were paying. Hydro-Quebec argued that it was simply using competitive pricing to entice businesses into remote and underdeveloped regions of the province, not unlike tax concessions and other inducements offered to companies elsewhere. It also pointed out that contracts signed with heavy power users in the province were often risk-sharing contracts under which the price per kilowatt-hour was pegged to the price of the user's end product (usually on the commodity markets). The utility argued that to criticize the system at a time when commodity prices happened to be very low was misleading and politically motivated.

At the same time, some economists accused Hydro-Quebec of using low domestic electricity rates to artificially inflate demand for electricity in the province, thereby justifying further grandiose expansion plans. Despite these negative points of view, Hydro-Quebec was still a leader in North America in terms of providing competitive rates for residential users, as shown in Exhibit 4.

Role of Hydro-Quebec in Quebec Nationalism

Critics of Hydro-Quebec's ambitious expansion plans looked beyond economics to find political motives in the development of James Bay. While legally independent from the provincial government, Hydro-Quebec was often accused of being a tool of the government. The relationship was clearly encouraged by the location of the provincial premier's Montréal office, which was inside Hydro-Quebec's headquarters building. To the critics of Hydro-Quebec, James Bay served a pivotal role in the broader plans of some Quebecers for greater economic and political independence from the rest of Canada.

Since Canada's creation in 1867, Quebec stood apart from other provinces, not only for the predominant use of the French language but also for its unique legal system, distinct culture, and separate educational system that focused much more explicitly on language and religious issues. Maintaining Quebec's uniqueness in the face of an ever-shrinking population was the principal concern of a rising group of Quebec nationalists. They saw Quebec's French heritage being increasingly overwhelmed by the predominantly English-speaking majority in Canada. In 1976, the Parti Québecois was elected

EXHIBIT 4   Average Costs for Residential Consumers for 1,000 KW-Hour Consumption per Month, Sales Tax Excluded, 1991

Montréal	$ 54.81
New York	144.58
Boston	114.73
Toronto	77.55
Vancouver	56.55

Source: Hydro-Quebec 1991 annual report.

to govern the province on a platform that many felt was explicitly separatist. Once in power, the new government made substantial changes to provincial legislation governing language and education laws with the objective of promoting the use of French in all facts of life in Quebec. While a referendum in Quebec supporting total independence from English Canada failed, many in Quebec remained suspicious of the other provinces and contemptuous of federal institutions.

Deeply worried about the impact of Quebec nationalism on national unity, the federal government throughout much of the 1970s and 1980s moved to make membership in the Canadian federation as attractive as possible for Quebecers. National policies promoting bilingualism were passed, substantial grants were offered to the people of Quebec as well as to the Quebec government, and massive new programs were begun to provide regulatory and monetary support for culturally sensitive industries. While to a degree placating Quebecers, such largesse caused some anglophones in the rest of Canada to view Quebec with disdain.

In the early 1990s, Quebec separatism was again in the forefront in the wake of a failed attempt to bring the province into a revised constitutional framework with the rest of the country. The "Meech Lake Accord," drafted in 1986 by Canadian Prime Minister Brian Mulroney, would have provided official recognition of Quebec's special status within confederation. However, its ratification in 1990 was blocked by some of the provincial premiers, as well as by native groups who worried that a new constitution would result in their disenfranchisement. The failure of Meech Lake once again made secession an attractive option to many Quebecers.

By early 1992, with Quebec now governed by a Liberal government under the leadership of Robert Bourassa, the future status of the province in Canada remained uncertain. However, a healthy Hydro-Quebec was certain to strengthen Bourassa's hand in renewed constitutional discussions, since low-cost electrical energy was a powerful tool in attracting industry, promoting exports, and sustaining the economy. A strong, export-oriented economy would add credibility to threats for separation that could translate into concessions from the federal government and other provinces. If accommodation could not be reached and separation resulted, then Hydro-Quebec would play a critical role in the industrial policy of the new country.

James Bay II: The Development of Great Whale

In March 1989, Hydro-Quebec announced plans to begin the second phase of the James Bay hydroelectric development project. At this time, approximately 30 percent of the total hydroelectrical energy potential of James Bay had been developed. James Bay II was designed to exploit the generating capacity of three river systems in the region: La Grande and the Grande Baleine (Great Whale) rivers as well as the Nottaway-Broadback-Rupert

(NBR) system. The headwaters of these rivers were between 800 and 1,200 feet above sea level and flowed through a system of lakes and minor rivers to the Hudson Bay basin. The plan was to develop these systems sequentially, with the first stage harnessing the Great Whale river.

Great Whale's total generating capacity was estimated at 3,168 MW, or about 12 percent of Hydro-Quebec's total capacity in 1991. Plans for the Great Whale complex called for the construction of five dams and 126 dikes, creating four reservoirs used to feed three generating stations. Five rivers were to be diverted, 400 square miles of wilderness flooded, and 4,200 acres of forest removed to make room for 400 miles of roads and two small airstrips. A major independent association of Quebec engineers estimated that approximately 1.5 percent of the land habitats of the region would be directly affected as a result of Great Whale. Hydro-Quebec engineers estimated that only 0.16 percent of land habitats would actually be flooded. The total cost for Great Whale was estimated at $13.1 billion. Construction was originally slated to begin in 1991, with completion scheduled for 1999. Supporters of the development argued that, by 1998, Quebec would face an energy deficit if no new sources of electricity were developed.

Shortly after announcing plans to begin work on Great Whale, Hydro-Quebec and the NYPA signed a contract worth $17 billion, committing 1,000 MW of generating capacity to NYPA for 21 years. Under the terms of the agreement, the contract was to be ratified by November 30, 1991, with exports beginning in 1995. Despite the enormous size of the deal, Hydro-Quebec estimated that growing provincial demand for electricity would account for at least 90 percent of the utility's total output over the duration of the NYPA contract. Total electricity exports from Quebec had been less than 10 percent of production over the past several years, with about half that amount going to the United States and the rest to neighboring provinces in Canada. At the end of 1991, Hydro-Quebec had interconnections with neighboring systems that gave it the capacity to export 2,675 MW to New York, 2,300 MW to New England, and 2,512 MW to the Canadian provinces of Ontario and New Brunswick. Not all of this capacity was used and, because of shared transmission installations, Hydro-Quebec's total simultaneous export capacity was limited to 6,337 MW.

By committing the equivalent of 30 percent of Great Whale's capacity to NYPA, Hydro-Quebec would not only add to its U.S. denominated revenue but would see its profitability potentially rise. By the year 2000, it was estimated that Hydro-Quebec's total export commitments including NYPA would represent 7.5 percent of revenues and 28 percent of profits. Cash flow and the security associated with a NYPA contract would enable Hydro-Quebec to service much of the massive debt it would have to secure to finance construction. By locking in these revenues, Hydro-Quebec would also enhance investor confidence in its other bond issues, keeping interest and underwriting expenses at a minimum.

Concerns of the Aboriginal People

Already uncomfortable with the disruptions brought about by James Bay I, the aboriginal people in the region worried that massive additional changes to the landscape would irreversibly affect the complex interrelationships of flora and fauna in the area. A related concern was that the flooding of areas not currently under water would release bacteria that would transform the abundant but innocuous mercury in the rocks into deadly methyl mercury, a known toxin that caused disease and death in humans. Among other ecological effects, caribou calving grounds would be shifted, James Bay's beluga whale populations threatened, and the habitats of many other species altered in unpredictable ways. There was also a possibility that the climate of the region might be changed because of the much increased surface area of the proposed reservoir systems. Evidence from Russia—where efforts to divert water from the Aral Sea had produced an ecological disaster—showed that environmental engineering could go terribly wrong.

The Campaign to Beach Great Whale

When Hydro-Quebec announced its intention to pursue the Great Whale project, the utility argued that the JBNQA gave it authority to proceed without the consent of aboriginal groups. The Inuit, believing that the project was thus inevitable, argued for additional concessions from the utility. As part of these concessions, the Inuit demanded financial compensation from the Quebec government as well as concurrent talks on native self-government. It was hoped that money generated from a new James Bay II settlement would provide a greater degree of independence for the Inuit, making full autonomy an attractive option.

The actions of Hydro-Quebec provoked a much angrier reaction from the Cree, who vowed to fight the Great Whale project on all fronts. Many Cree leaders wondered how they could ever benefit from Great Whale, arguing that they would lose their hunting and fishing grounds "so that Americans can plug in their blowdryers." Matthew Coon-Come, leader of the Grand Council of the Cree, asserted that the Cree might resort to civil disobedience by lying down in front of earth moving equipment to stop the project. In May 1989, a lawsuit was launched by the Cree challenging Quebec's right to exclude the federal government from an environmental review of the project. By bringing the federal government into the equation, the Cree hoped Great Whale would get bogged down in endless delays as the national and provincial governments fought it out over issues of jurisdiction and sovereignty.

At the same time, the Cree, with the encouragement of the Inuit, mounted a major public relations campaign designed to raise public awareness about Great Whale's (and James Bay as a whole) environmental impact. Their often emotional message focused on the negative effects of the project, while claiming that its economic viability was, at best, questionable. In support of this effort, they retained the world's largest public-relations firm, Hill & Knowlton, Inc. For fees reported to have exceeded $230,000, Hill & Knowlton helped gather public opinion data, produce videos, and provide media training for Cree leaders.

The efforts of the Cree first made headlines when they organized a voyage in a traditional canoe/kayak called Odeyak. This trip, begun in March 1990, culminated with a handful of native leaders paddling into New York City's harbor on Earth Day, April 22. The Cree were subsequently invited to make speeches at Cornell, Columbia, and New York universities. Immediate grass-roots support for the cause came from environmental groups in the United States, as well as student activists on campuses throughout the Northeast region. The press appeared overwhelmingly sympathetic to the native view-point. Negative articles appeared in a wide variety of publications, including *Time,* the *Boston Globe Magazine,* and *Penthouse.* Government officials in Quebec denounced the articles, saying they contained exaggerations, inaccuracies, and errors. It was felt that complete disregard for the positive aspects of the Great Whale project presented a distorted and unfair view.

In New York City, two highly organized groups calling themselves the James Bay Defense Coalition and PROTECT were created to encourage New Yorkers to begin letter-writing campaigns to elected municipal officials. Other groups were formed, including No Thank Q Hydro-Quebec, which claimed to have been instrumental in blocking an additional $4.1 billion power sale to Maine. Another group called the New England Coalition for Energy Efficiency and Environment became highly critical of Vermont for taking the easy way out by also agreeing to buy Quebec's power.

In August 1991, NYPA asked for and was granted a one-year extension on the no-penalty escape clause in its contract. According to Richard Flynn, NYPA's chairman, the agency was already reevaluating its anticipated power needs, in light of revised demand forecasts. As a result of the ongoing recession and improved conservation measures, NYPA had reduced its annual growth rate estimates from 1.5 percent in the mid-1980s to 0.6 percent in 1991. In arguing for the extension, chairman Flynn also cautioned that Hydro-Quebec should not use the NYPA contract to create a false sense of urgency about the Great Whale project and that it could not justify taking short cuts in assessing the environmental impact of the project. Within days, Quebec Environment Minister Pierre Paradis reversed his previous decision and announced that a global environmental assessment would be conducted. Such an assessment could take up to two years to complete.

In September 1991, a Canadian federal judge ruled in favor of the Cree in their outstanding lawsuit against the government of Quebec. The judge argued that the JBNQA fell under the jurisdiction of both the federal and provincial governments and that both levels of government were required by law to provide environmental assessments of the project. Plans were immediately announced by the federal government to establish an environmental review committee that guaranteed prominent positions for Cree and Inuit representatives. Quebec announced that it would appeal the judge's ruling and hinted that it might ignore a federal assessment in determining whether or not to go ahead.

The delay in ratifying the contract did not put a stop to the public-relations campaign. Three "Ban the Dam Jam for James Bay" rock concerts were held during the week of October 7, 1991, featuring well-known musicians, such as Bruce Cockburn, Dan Fogelberg, Roseanne Cash, Jackson Browne, and James Taylor. These concerts raised close to $300,000 in support of the natives' cause. Two cyclist groups also toured Vermont and New York to spread word of the project's negative aspects to villagers in those states. At Hampshire College, students from Boston, Hartford, New York City, and Newark watched a performance incorporating a slide show, songs, and speeches about ecology. A new protest group called Dam No was created at the end of the evening.

On October 21, 1991, the crusade reached its climax with a Greenpeace-sponsored full-page advertisement in the *New York Times*. Environmental groups, including the Friends of the Earth, the Humane Society of the United States, the Sierra Club, and the National Audubon Society, as well as native-rights groups signed the ad, identifying themselves collectively as The James Bay Coalition. In paying for the ad, Greenpeace vowed to make Great Whale a major campaign issue if New York Governor Mario Cuomo were ever to run for President. In response to mounting political pressure, Governor Cuomo asserted that he would not let himself be manipulated by special-interest environmental groups. Similar statements of defense were offered by Vermont Governor Howard Deans.

Despite these assertions, it was becoming increasingly apparent that the negative campaigning was having a major impact. In testimony before a committee of the New York state legislature on November 15, 1991, assemblyman William Hoyt argued that the state's review process must take into account the environmental impact on the Great Whale region, not just New York, to ensure that ". . . we are not participating in the creation of a major environmental disaster." New York Mayor David Dinkins, while visiting Montreal for an international mayors' conference, offered his official support to the Cree and Inuit, arguing that "environmental rights and human rights go together." In Vermont, State Senator Elisabeth Ready and Burlington Mayor Peter Clavell began to actively campaign against importing energy from Quebec.

Some observers argued that the inflammatory and sensational tone of the public-relations campaign would eventually hurt the credibility of the environmentalists. Denunciations were provided by the Quebec government as well as several smaller environmental groups. The Greenpeace ad in particular was criticized for impeding a serious and credible evaluation of Quebec's energy policies in general and the Great Whale project in particular. Even the Audubon Society's chief scientist, Dr. Jan Bayea, while remaining firm in his opposition to Great Whale, admitted that the project's opponents had made "embarrassingly misleading" statements about it.

Throughout most of the campaign to discredit the Great Whale project, Hydro-Quebec's policy had been to avoid debating the issues in public. While some observers interpreted this silence as arrogance, many managers at Hydro-Quebec thought that the utility's financial track record, its importance to Quebec's economic future, and the commercial merits of Great Whale would ultimately act to overwhelm the accumulation of negative popular opinion. This strategy did not appear to be working, however, and three days after the Greenpeace ad, Hydro-Quebec placed its own full-page ad in the *New York Times* rebutting the arguments made by the environmentalists. The major points made by Hydro-Quebec included:

- That hydroelectric power was inherently cleaner and safer than the alternatives of nuclear or fossil-fueled generators.
- That over $500 million in cash compensation had been paid out to aboriginal people (as of November 1991) under the JBNQA and other agreements.
- That, as a result of James Bay I, the Cree population was growing at a rate faster than the Quebec population as a whole—the infant mortality rate had been cut in half, and life expectancy had been increased by 50 percent—clearly the net effect of James Bay I on native health was positive.
- That, as a result of its reforestation efforts, and the apparent health of the ecosystem, the James Bay caribou population had tripled since the early 1970s, and fish and bird populations had stabilized.
- That these were the same activists who had supported anti-fur campaigns who were now insisting on the aboriginal peoples' rights to pursue their traditional way of life, which depended, in part, on the fur trade.

February 1992

By February 1992, the public-relations campaign had slowed and management at Hydro-Quebec had more time to reflect on whether to proceed with Great Whale. There was a growing recognition that Hydro-Quebec had been too slow in reacting to the environmentalists south of the border. Many had felt that a pro-development campaign would only stir up the rhetoric and end up being counter-productive. The situation evoked memories of European and U.S. activists' opposition to the Canadian seal hunt in the 1960s and 1970s, all but shutting down that industry. Managers at Hydro-Quebec wondered about the appropriate limits to national sovereignty as well as the rights of special-interest groups and governments to determine the outcome of these matters in a free market economy.

In reviewing its alternatives, Hydro-Quebec faced several different courses of action. Some argued that Hydro-Quebec should simply go it alone and begin work on Great Whale at the earliest possible moment. Under this scenario, the utility would have to approach the provincial government to underwrite potential losses should NYPA cancel the contract. The utility could argue that NYPA represented less than 3 percent of Hydro-Quebec's electricity production and that, even if this business were lost, NYPA would be back just as soon as the controversy had died down and demand for energy began to rise. And if they never came back, the province would need the energy itself by the time Great Whale was on stream. Any energy not exported could be used to attract foreign businesses to the province at subsidized rates.

By February 1992, there had been no ruling on Quebec's appeal of the verdict requiring the involvement of both the provincial and federal governments in an environmental assessment of Great Whale. Quebec had publicly supported an environmental review and could not back away now. It could, however, carry out its own independent review and ensure that it was completed well in advance of any federal assessment. Once a favorable provincial review had been prepared, construction would commence, thus pre-empting the federal government from taking any action. The federal government had backed off similar confrontations in the past and might not want to risk national unity over this issue. Indeed, Canadian prime minister Brian Mulroney had come to the defense of the Great Whale project in a confrontation with a member of the European parliament during a Francophone Summit in November 1991. In an emotional presentation, Mulroney had argued that the European Community had no right to meddle in the internal economic affairs of Canada. How could Mulroney, himself a native Quebecer, now move to stop Great Whale?

Despite the appeal to go it alone, a number of top managers at Hydro-Quebec thought that a combination of patience and good management would eventually win over both the environmentalists and the NYPA. It was too much of a financial gamble to act unilaterally. Hydro-Quebec was one of the world's largest U.S. dollar borrowers. Of its total $29.7 billion debt, $8.4 billion was in U.S. currency, and a large proportion of the contemplated $9.5 billion debt to finance Great Whale would also be in U.S. dollars. (See Exhibit 5 for a breakdown of debt by currency.) Some observers argued that the negative publicity generated from an orchestrated "go it alone" strategy would ensure that NYPA would never sign a contract. A decision by NYPA to pull out would also make it much more difficult for Hydro-Quebec to service its existing debt. Bond rating agencies already had the utility on credit watches; if its rating were downgraded, the resulting higher interest rates and tougher underwriting terms for new issues would reduce the possibility of profitability from planned expansion projects. In addition, the lack of U.S. dollar revenue would significantly increase Hydro-Quebec's exposure to the risks of exchange rate fluctua-

---

EXHIBIT 5   Breakdown of Debt by Currency

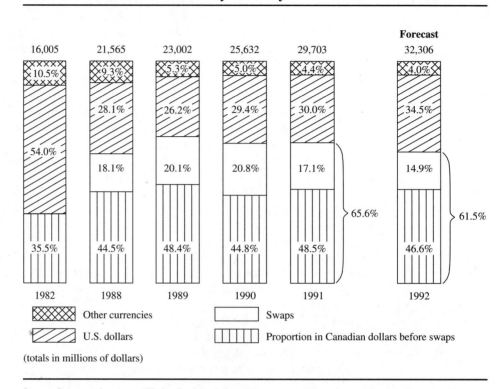

(totals in millions of dollars)

Legend:
- Other currencies
- U.S. dollars
- Swaps
- Proportion in Canadian dollars before swaps

Source: Company document, "Hydro-Quebec: A Sound Investment," Financing and Treasury Branch, 1991.

---

tions. Its U.S. debt was not hedged because of expected offsets in revenue of the same currency; without this revenue, it would be at the mercy of foreign exchange markets.

It was becoming increasingly clear that, without the full backing of the provincial government, Great Whale could seriously undermine the financial integrity of Hydro-Quebec. Taxes in Quebec were already among the highest in North America, thus limiting the government's ability to act as a guarantor. A move to load the province with debt for a money-losing mega-project risked being interpreted as a blatantly political act that would jeopardize both the credibility of the government in power as well as the ability of the province to raise funds for other purposes.

It seemed that no matter which direction management turned, it faced significant opposition. And yet time was running out. In just nine months—and perhaps less—NYPA would commit to a course of action that would dramatically impact on Hydro-Quebec's future. With its enormous size, many wondered how Hydro-Quebec had lost so much control over its own future. Perhaps there was still time to act.

HYBRID—SKYLAKE

In early October 1987, Mr. Julien Den Tandt, President of Hybrid Turkeys Inc. of Kitchener, Ontario, received a telex on behalf of Tianjin Skylake Foodstuffs Corp. Ltd. (hereafter Skylake) in Tianjin, The People's Republic of China. Skylake was the seventh partner-member of the world's largest independent turkey marketing cooperative, Norbest Inc. of Salt Lake City, Utah. The telex from Tianjin requested that Hybrid lower the price of the turkey breeding stock they were proposing to provide to the cooperative in China through a 10-year agreement.

This request posed a problem for Mr. Den Tandt. Unlike the practices of some foreign companies, Hybrid had not inflated their original asking price. In fact, their quoted price was now slightly below current market levels. Furthermore, the contract value (Cdn.[1] $50–$100 thousand a year) was not sufficiently large that any further slack could be squeezed out of the selling price.

Hybrid management had to decide whether to refuse a price change, make a further concession, or abandon their attempts at trying to do business in China.

In order to place this decision in context, the sections which follow will first set out a brief history of Hybrid and the nature of its business, review China's economic and technological environment, review the history of Norbest's involvement in China, and review Skylake negotiations with Hybrid between February and September 1987.

This case was prepared by Paul W. Beamish, School of Business Administration, University of Western Ontario, London, Canada, and Jiping Zhang, School of Economic Management, Qinghua University, Beijing, People's Republic of China. Funding was provided by the Economic Development Institute of The World Bank. Copyright © 1989, Paul W. Beamish.

[1] Exchange Rate in October 1987 was U.S.$1.00 = Cdn $1.40 = Rmb 3.05.

History of Hybrid

In 1953, Milo and Ross Shantz of Kitchener, Ontario, began raising commercial turkeys on their farm. During the next 13 years as the business grew they integrated backward through the purchase of a hatchery and forward through the purchase of a processing plant. In 1958, they decided to begin producing hatching eggs. Until that time they had purchased one-day-old turkeys (called poults), and raised them until they were market weight.

By 1962, the Shantz's commitment to the turkey business had grown to the extent that they decided to get into breeding. At that time, they were supplying turkeys from their farm to a killing plant which was having difficulty acquiring a certain type and size of bird. In order to satisfy the killing plant's needs, the Shantz's began doing some selection and breeding on their own. From this beginning the business grew quite rapidly, due in part to their development of a unique, smaller bird (which they called the Diamond White) which met the market needs.

During these early years, the name of the organization changed several times, but by 1970 the present name was in place. Almost from the beginning, Hybrid exported its breeding stock to other countries.

Although Hybrid operated production farms, their principal status rested on their expertise as a primary breeder. (See Exhibit 1 for a description of the major stages in the turkey business.)

Primary breeders produced hatching eggs and poults for breeding. With a heavy emphasis on research, the objective of primary breeders was to develop and market breeding stock which met certain characteristics. Depending on the particular market used, turkeys might be bred to satisfy a large range of requirements. These included:

Size and weight (some markets preferred small turkeys, others medium or large).

Exhibit 1   Major Stages in Turkey Business

Stages	Principal Function(s)	Examples of Firms in Industry
1. Primary breeder	Produce hatching eggs for breeding	Hybrid Nicholas B.U.T.
2. Multipliers/hatcheries	Produce hatching eggs	Coldsprings Farms
3. Farmers	Grow the birds	Coldsprings Farms Many independents
4. Processors	Kill; prepare for retail sale	Coldsprings Farms Pand H
5. Retailer/stores	Sale to consumer	Schneiders
6. Consumer purchase	Consumption	—

Note: Governments and larger companies were increasingly becoming vertically integrated.

Egg production (number produced during the 24-week laying period).

Fertility and reproductive performance (turkey hens produced eggs—as many as five or six per week—when they were between 30 and 54 weeks old).

Hatchability (not all eggs hatched. Hatch rates ranging from 70–90 percent, depending on conditions, were considered acceptable within the industry.)

Fat content; skeletal potential to increase the portion of breast meat.

Feed conversion (the amount of weight they would gain from a given amount of feed before processing; birds would normally be processed when they were between 12 and 24 weeks old).

Leg strength (leg problems were at their worst just before the bird went to market—males could weigh as much as 35 kilograms).

Disease control and health status (with respect to bio-security, in the event of a disease outbreak, a whole flock might have to be destroyed or the farm might be unable to sell the eggs).

Growth rate (speed at which birds would reach final weight).

Adaptability to seasonal variations (for example, heat hurts egg production), geographic location, and feed ingredient availability.

Genetic consistency.

Turkey breeders might sell either eggs or poults with the price for each depending on such things as the sex of the bird, distance being shipped, and the genetic purity of the stock of birds.

The least expensive turkey stock sold was eggs for commercial meat. In 1987, commercial stock-eggs sold for roughly $0.55 each. If, as was often the case, the customer wished to purchase poults of a particular sex, the price would increase to compensate for losses from the hatch rate and number of opposite sex birds (off-sex) which sometimes could not be used.

More expensive than commercial eggs and poults—and the primary product sold by such firms as Hybrid—were what was called Parent Stock (PS). These would be a particular genetic cross which the purchaser could use as the basis for breeding large quantities of commercial birds. Parent Stock, as the name suggests, were the previous generation to the commercial stock. Parent Stock eggs shipped a long distance might sell for approximately U.S.$2–$2.50 each. Parent Stock poults of a particular sex might be two and one-half times higher in price.

While it was theoretically possible for a commercial farmer to continue breeding beyond one generation with the Parent Stock purchased, in practical terms the results were ultimately disastrous. It was very important that farmers regularly replaced with fresh *unrelated* breeding stock. For this reason, primary breeders—who maintained a variety of genetic lines—did tend to receive fairly regular business from farmers and multipliers. As Exhibit 2 illustrates, however, the amount of Parent Stock a farmer might require was significantly smaller than the number of commercial turkeys which would ultimately result.

EXHIBIT 2   Egg to Turkey Conversion Example

This is a hypothetical and simplified example to illustrate the general relationship between the number of parent stock eggs which a breeder might need to supply to a commercial turkey farmer who wished to market 500,000 turkeys a year. *All* ratios provided are rough approximations, and would be affected by a wide number of considerations.

22,220	Parent Stock eggs would be shipped.
−6,666	Eggs (30%) which would either not hatch or not live beyond one day.
15,554	Poults
−8,088	Poults (i.e., 52%) would be males (toms).
	Since toms cannot lay eggs, most of these poults (the off-sex desired) would be allowed to grow to market size. A small number (one-tenth the number of hens) would be kept for artificial insemination.
7,466	Available female poults.
−448	Hens (6%) which will die or be rejected for a variety of reasons before reaching the reproductive age of approximately 30 weeks.
7,018	Hens "in lay."
×95	Number of eggs which *each* hen will produce during the breeding cycle.
666,710	Total number of commercial eggs laid.
−166,678	Eggs (25%) which would either not hatch or not live.
500,032	Commercial turkeys available for market.

Very infrequently, a primary breeder might consider sharing what was called Grandparent Stock. These were the parents of the Parent Stock and possessed all of the necessary genetic makeup to permit the purchaser to produce Parent Stock on his own. In the sale of Grandparent Stock, both the male and female side of the female line and the male and female side of the male line would be provided.

The breeding technology was not easy to either develop or maintain. Over the period 1957–80 literally hundreds of primary breeders had left the business, to the extent that by 1983, three firms dominated. These were (a) Nicholas, a California-based firm which was generally conceded to have in excess of 50 percent of the market, (b) British United Turkeys (BUT), and (c) Hybrid. Throughout the industry, there was a constant demand for efficiency, which tended to keep industrywide profits low.

During the 1950s, farmers and organizations with as few as 500 breeding hens were calling themselves breeders. Over the next two decades, nearly all of them left the business. The reason for the high attrition among breeders was the great difficulty in establishing a successful breeding operation. To be a successful breeder required (a) access to a wide gene pool of the different blood lines, (b) large investment in specialized facilities, and (c) a great deal of know-how and experience.

As Hybrid's business grew more complex, it became impossible for a single person to handle the selection process. Thus, while one person was responsible for all of Hybrid's turkey selection from 1962 to 1980, a "genetic team" was subsequently appointed to manage this function.

Hybrid's success attracted the interest of Euribrid, B.V. of Holland and in late 1981 they acquired 100 percent of Hybrid. Euribrid was owned by Hendrix International B.V. in the Netherlands, which was in turn controlled by British Petroleum Nutrition Holdings B.V. With the acquisition, Euribrid left the existing management in place. Euribrid management understood the breeding business and appreciated the long-term view that was required. Den Tandt, for example, had found Euribrid to be generally supportive of his plans.

China's Economic and Technical Environment

The "open-door" policy initiated by the Chinese government in 1978 continued to gain momentum in China through the mid-1980s. In a desire to modernize and acquire foreign technology, the State Economic Commission in 1983 began encouraging Chinese enterprises to spend more of China's accumulated foreign exchange reserves. In 1984 imports rose by 29 percent and in 1985 by a further 46 percent. These funds went for such things as consumer goods, raw materials, and parts. By late 1985, the government realized that it had lost control of spending and took the major step of cutting off foreign exchange. Many contracts which had been signed could not be implemented, assembly lines which used imported materials and parts were shut down, and the government began asking joint ventures to balance their foreign exchange requirements themselves.

In September 1985, the seventh Five Year National Economic Development Plan was passed. It outlined the development orientation and focal points of China's future technology imports. It specified that technology imports would be expanded, and focused on supporting exports and products which generated foreign exchange. As well, emphasis should be given to energy, transportation, communications, raw materials for building construction, machinery, and electronics industries. It was also to continue acquiring technology for the renovation of existing industries. Priority was to be given to the acquisition of production know-how for processing technology, manufacturing technology, and administration expertise. Finally, attention would be placed on digesting, absorbing, applying, and innovating using the acquired foreign advanced technology.

Among the sectors targeted for first-time import of technology were feedstuffs, printing, and agriculture and husbandry. China had quarantine agreements for transferring turkey to the P.R.C. with the United States (since May 1984), Canada (since March 1985), the United Kingdom, Denmark, Australia, France, and the Netherlands.

By 1986, general government procedures were in place to implement the import of technology. In the first step, the proposed project had to be approved. Major participants involved in this process of approval were:

Local government (bigger projects had to go to the relevant ministry).

Bureau of the relevant industry.

Banks (the China Construction Bank for capital goods investment lending, the China Industry and Commercial Bank for current capital lending, the Bank of China for foreign exchange lending).

The Bureau of Taxation and the Bureau or Ministry of Foreign Economic Relations and Trade (MOFERT).

After the project proposal was approved, the enterprise could then start their preparation formally for the project. The money primarily came from the government, and the amount was planned. Only the state-owned banks were intended to lend money to the project.

The second step in the process was a feasibility study. The feasibility study had to be approved formally and more agencies were involved.

The third step was negotiation and contract signing. In actual practice, negotiation would often go before the completion of the feasibility studies.

Detailed design examination and approval of the design was typically separate from the commercial negotiations.

During the whole process, although many agencies and individuals were involved, there was no clear decision maker. Generally speaking, the government's (local or central) planning commission and economic commission had more power than other agencies. But anyone's objection could delay the formal decision.

Background on Norbest

Norbest Inc. was a turkey marketing cooperative which consisted of seven member associations representing hundreds of individual turkey growers. Organized in 1930, Norbest had grown rapidly and established a brand image that represented premium quality turkey products to consumers throughout the United States, and many foreign countries. Their processing plants were strategically located, providing easy access to major terminal markets.

All but one of their member associations were owned and operated by the local turkey growers. Each local association selected one member to serve on the Norbest Board of Directors. The board of directors established the policies that determined the direction of Norbest. This board also appointed the officers of Norbest, who carried out the policies and procedures of the organization. The seven member associations were all located in the United States, with the exception of Skylake in China.

In 1986, Norbest marketed 245 million pounds (111.4 million kilograms) of ready-to-cook-weight turkey, out of total U.S. consumption of slightly over 3 billion pounds. Norbest was the fourth largest producer/marketer in the United States.

Practically all of Norbest's tonnage came from member plants. They occasionally marketed some turkeys and turkey products on an agency basis from several nonmember plants when the need arose to balance their member's marketing program, and meet their customer's needs. In 1986 they marketed outside purchases totaling 32 million pounds.

The marketing and service fee charged by Norbest was established by the Norbest Board of Directors and generally averaged 2¼ percent of sales. When the turkeys were sold, the marketing and service fee, freight, and any other agreed upon charges were deducted from the sales price, and the balance of the net proceeds were remitted back to the association. Each local association had the responsibility of establishing its own processing charges and pooling and payment method from the members.

Some of the items covered by the Norbest marketing and service fee were:

The use of the Norbest premium label, as well as other Norbest owned copyrights and labels.

The use of Norbest advertising and promotional programs.

The use of a Norbest customer base which included many premier distributors in the United States. Their international customers were growing rapidly due to their increased emphasis in export trade.

Norbest had a 50 percent share in the Far Eastern market, including a leading position in Hong Kong, Singapore, and Japan. They anticipated greater penetration in selected foreign markets in the succeeding months.

Norbest furnished technical assistance to their member plants in the areas of processing, quality assurance programs, USDA inspection and grading matters, label approval, residue programs, etc. They also furnished assistance on all other regulatory matters.

Market intelligence.

The ability to provide additional assistance in areas of cooperative law, financial consulting, distribution, warehousing, plant construction or renovation, etc.

Background in Pacific Rim

Norbest's involvement in the Pacific Rim market began in 1977 through an independent company which imported Norbest products from the USA, and resold and distributed it in Japan. Because Japan was a somewhat unique market, and Norbest's U.S. plants were prone not to produce specialty items, an impetus developed for the creation of a production facility to serve that market.

Another incentive to pursue a cooperative effort was the European turkey industry's penetration of the Pacific Rim market. In Europe, the production of turkeys and turkey products was heavily subsidized by the various governments. American producers, even through a marketing cooperative like Norbest, could not hope to compete in the Pacific Rim unless they produced there.

In 1984, U.S. President Reagan hosted a reciprocal banquet for senior Chinese officials at which turkey was served. Turkey was not a product familiar to most Chinese. Shortly thereafter Norbest was approached to explore a cooperative effort with China in a venture of "mutual interest for both partners." A senior Norbest executive visited China for the first time. In 1985, he returned to initiate negotiations regarding a facility. Norbest was directed by the central government to consider two possible locations. They quickly focused on Tianjin because the other city did not have port facilities. With over 8 million inhabitants, Tianjin was among the four largest cities in China.

By having a Chinese company as a full member of the cooperative, Norbest felt the savings in transportation, feed, and labor costs would be substantial and provide a competitive cost advantage. They hoped the Tianjin plant would enjoy low production costs, and provide products which could be tailored specifically to the Pacific Rim markets.

While the Chinese had originally thought Norbest would participate in an equity joint venture, Norbest preferred a cooperative venture. In September 1987, an agreement was signed for the design and construction of a fully integrated turkey processing operation in the municipality of Tianjin. The agreement called for the establishment of a facility capable of producing roughly 500,000 commercial turkeys for export markets a year. This translated to roughly 7 million pounds (3.2 million kilograms) live weight capacity. When processed, 7 million pounds would provide roughly 5.5 million pounds of eviscerated product (bone in) or 3 million pounds of raw meat. Average market commodity prices in the United States for young turkeys (i.e., 10- to 12-pound hens and 20- to 22-pound toms) were approximately US$0.58 per pound in 1987, down from $0.72–$0.76 per pound in 1985 and 1986.

The operation was called the Tianjin Skylake Foodstuffs Co., Ltd. Skylake was an independent company formed by China, and a full partner-member of the Norbest turkey marketing cooperative. There was no up-front financial cost to Skylake to join.

The partners in Tianjin Skylake Foodstuffs Co., Ltd. were:

1. Tianjin Municipal Husbandry and Industrial Commercial Corporation (TMHICC), a subsidiary of the Tianjin Municipal Bureau of Animal Husbandry.

2. Tianjin Economic–Technological Development Area Industrial Investment Company (TEDAIIC), a subsidiary of the Commission of the Tianjin Economic–Technological Development Area (TEDA).

3. China Bank Tianjin International Trust Consulting Company (CBTITCC), a subsidiary of China Bank's Tianjin Branch.

4. Tianjin Municipal Economic Development Company (TMEDC), a subsidiary of the Tianjin Municipal Bureau of the Foreign Economic Relations & Trade (TMBFERT).

5. Hong Kong Tian Fat Industry and Commerce Co., Ltd.

Skylake was located in Tianjin Economic–Technological Development Area, the special economic zone of Tianjin. The government of Tianjin municipality had opened this special area to attract foreign investment. Foreign investors were given favorable concessions to invest in this area including tax deductions, more freedom to export, separate customs, more freedom to decide wages, and more freedom to hire and fire employees.

The five partners of Skylake were joined together as an equity joint-venture. As the foreign equity from the Hong Kong partner was less than 25 percent of the total equity, Skylake was identified as a cooperative venture. ("At least 25 percent foreign equity" was required in China–foreign joint ventures in order to gain favorable conditions.) Nonetheless, Skylake received approval for special treatment as a China–foreign joint venture because it planned to build in the Special Economic Zone and because one of the members was based in Hong Kong.

The four Chinese partners were all subsidiaries of government agencies. Each partner contributed essential factors: TMHICC contributed professional personnel—managers and technicians who were experts at poultry raising; CBTITCC's participation made the local foreign exchange borrowing easier; and TEDA and TMBFERT provided administrative power.

Skylake was designated to operate the facility with technical and marketing support from Norbest. This would include breeding, hatching, growing, feed mill operations and the processing of whole birds and turkey products.

Norbest would market the turkeys and turkey products from the Tianjin plant throughout the Pacific Rim nations. At the time, Norbest had three sales offices in Japan. The output from Tianjin would, in the short term, be exported to a Japanese food processing company. In order to export, the plant would have to meet U.S. Department of Agriculture (USDA) approval. An official of China Skylake would have full membership on the Norbest board of directors.

An agreement between Norbest and Chinese agriculture and commerce officials was signed in Tianjin in April 1987. Norbest helped select a business manager and other specialists to coordinate the Chinese turkey production project. While the Chinese felt the cost of hiring a U.S. general manager was high, they agreed to go along with it, at least in the short term. Additionally, the cooperative provided marketing expertise for the sale and distribution of Tianjin plant products, first for export and eventually for marketing whole turkeys and turkey products in China itself.

Norbest also provided assistance in finding the lowest cost modern equipment available and alternative financing for the project. Technical specialists to ensure quality control would be selected by Norbest.

Hybrid's Involvement with Skylake

As part of their arrangement with Skylake, Norbest was responsible for advising Skylake on which turkey breed they felt would be most appropriate to acquire for use in the Pacific Rim market. From the beginning, Norbest had recommended that Skylake at least initially consider one of Hybrid Turkey's breeds, since it appeared to be most suited to the particular market needs. Nonetheless it remained for Skylake and Hybrid to determine if a mutually satisfactory arrangement could be negotiated.

The transfer of turkey breeding technology to Tianjin was, in strictly financial terms, only a small part of Skylake's total operating costs. Nonetheless many would argue that acquiring and implementing the appropriate breeding technology could be the single most important influence on whether the new operation would be ultimately successful.

By 1987, Hybrid had grown in terms of sales (Cdn. $10–$15 million a year), profitability, number of export markets served, reputation (it received a Government of Canada Export Award in 1987), organizational size, number of breeder farms in operation (14), and investment in facilities ($1.5 million in 1987). Yet, it was still awaiting its first major sale and transfer of turkey breeding technology to China. Although Hybrid managers had been devoting considerable resources to the China market since 1980 and had come close to signing a contract in 1984 with another group, no contracts had yet been implemented.

Hybrid first became aware from Norbest of the possible establishment of a turkey operation in Tianjin in late 1985. In June 1986, Hybrid's parent company, Euribrid, participated in an agribusiness exhibition in Shanghai. At the exhibition, Mrs. Sonja Jong, Euribrid's China-based and Mandarin-speaking representative, met Mr. Wang Zhi Jiang and Mr. Tang Xuemeng of the Tianjin Animal Husbandry Bureau. They requested information on turkeys.

When Mrs. Jong met with them again in Tianjin in September 1986, they expressed some surprise at receiving information on turkeys directly from Hybrid (they were not aware of the ownership links between Euribrid and Hybrid), but did indicate they wished to have further discussions.

In November 1986, Mrs. Jong represented Euribrid at an agricultural exhibition in Canton. There she met Mr. Liu Cheng Zhi of Tianjin Municipal Husbandry Industry Commerce Corporation, who indicated that at least on a technical basis, the Hybrid package was being favorably received.

In January 1987, a five-person Skylake delegation visited Norbest and various equipment suppliers in the United States over a two-week period. On January 30, Skylake and Norbest signed the Memorandum of Understanding which ultimately led to their September agreement. During the Skylake delegation's visit to Norbest, a group of Hybrid managers were able to explain in detail the elements of the package they were proposing to provide.

Following a subsequent request for more information, in late February Hybrid telexed Skylake in Tianjin to confirm the volumes and types of bird they proposed to sell. When the response to this and several other telexes were not immediately forthcoming, Hybrid asked Mrs. Jong for help. Mrs. Jong immediately responded, "Chinese only write/telex when it is absolutely necessary. English is a difficult language for them." No more communication followed for another two weeks, at which point Hybrid received a telex requesting more information from Tang Xuemeng, Deputy Director of the Foreign Economics Relations Department. A six-page telex was sent to him three weeks later by Hybrid.

By mid-April, it increasingly appeared that Hybrid would receive the contract from Skylake (see Appendix for the draft agreement). However, there were really two parts to the proposed agreement between Hybrid and Skylake. The first related to the number, quality, and price of the eggs. The Hybrid managers' understanding was that this had been resolved by April.

The other element of the agreement was the support system that Hybrid was advocating Skylake adopt. Although *not* part of the proposed cooperative agreement, in order to improve the prospects of the Hybrid stock flourishing in China, Hybrid management was adamant that a number of steps be followed. Hybrid was not prepared to proceed unless these steps were followed. These included:

> All birds to be grown *in confinement.*
>
> Distance between hatchery, processing plant, and/or farms—*minimum 1 kilometer.*
>
> Distance between barns on farms—*minimum 15 meters.*
>
> Have employees *live off* farms.
>
> Insulate all barns and hatchery—R18 on walls, R36 in ceiling—*no exposed rafters.*
>
> Put *plastic under all cement floors* to prevent condensation.
>
> Have *shower in facilities with clothes and shoe change* for all areas.
>
> All feed to be *pelleted.*
>
> *Incinerators* for all dead birds.
>
> *Stand-by power* to cover power failures.
>
> Follow strict biosecurity.
>
> Two persons to come to Canada to train, beginning April 1988.

It was not always clear to Skylake how important it was to follow in China the many suggestions which Hybrid provided. For example, in late April, Sonja Jong sent a telex to Hybrid indicating that Skylake managers felt Hybrid standards were high. They asked if they could get minimum requirements for the poult housing in order to keep investment as low as possible.

Mrs. Jong asked Hybrid: "Do you want to give these minimum conditions under which a poult can still grow and produce well, or shall I write him, warning him that he will lose money if he tries to cut investment this way? (As a friend I can do that.) I don't know how important the housing environment is for turkeys, but please keep in mind that if you give minimum conditions, the poults probably will not get more than that."

Two days later Mrs. Jong received the following telex from Hybrid. "In order to be successful and meet Hybrid standards for growth, production, and health, we strongly recommend that our standards be followed. If they are not maintained, lower weights, higher feed conversions, and less profitability will be experienced. If this project is becoming too expensive, maybe the size of it could be scaled down."

From February to August 1987, Skylake management raised numerous questions which, following either telex or direct communications, were satisfactorily resolved. With so much progress having been made, it was with surprise that Mrs. Jong received in Beijing the direct request from the Assistant Director of Skylake for an unspecified better price. At the beginning of October, Mrs. Jong immediately telexed Mr. Den Tandt in Canada and passed on the Skylake request.

Appendix
Draft Agreement

On Long-Term Cooperation in Production

BETWEEN:
HYBRID TURKEYS INC. a company incorporated under the laws of the Province of Ontario, Canada
hereinafter referred to as "HYBRID"

OF THE FIRST PART

and

TIANJIN SKYLAKE FOODSTUFFS CORP. LTD.,
address: TIANJIN ECONOMIC–TECHNOLOGICAL DEVELOPMENT AREA (TEDA)
hereinafter referred to as "SKYLAKE"

OF THE SECOND PART

WHEREAS Hybrid is a renowned primary breeder of turkeys, delivering product worldwide, with annual production of purelines, grandparent stock, Parent Stock, hatching eggs, and one-day-old poults for commercial production.

WHEREAS Skylake is a center for turkey production, and

WHEREAS Hybrid intends to cooperate with Skylake on a long-term basis in the production in CHINA, of Parent Stock (day-old), hatching eggs, and day-old final product.

AND WHEREAS Skylake wishes to accept and promote current state-of-the-art Hybrid technology, the objective being to increase its total production.

Article I

In the agreement, the following definitions shall have the same meaning as are respectively assigned to them, and will exclude all other meanings:

1.1 *Parent Stock*—will be Hybrid Type 2200 Heavy Medium female and male line poults or eggs.

1.2 *Hatching Eggs*—will represent the finished product of parent stock.

1.3 *One-Day-Old Final Product*—will represent the finished product of hatching eggs.

1.4 *Technical Information*—will mean information instructions and technological solutions in the area of production and maintenance of buildings which Hybrid will provide for Skylake so that Skylake can attain Hybrid's standard in its own production facilities.

Article II

Aim of Agreement

2.1 Hybrid and Skylake plan to cooperate in a program of long-term production with the following objectives:

To supply Skylake with Hybrid products.

To supply technical expertise to Skylake in order to raise Parent Stock and final product, using Hybrid's current state-of-the-art technology.

To establish Skylake production for both Export and Domestic consumption of final product turkey meat.

Article III

Subject of Agreement

3.1 The program consists of the delivery of Parent Stock eggs.

3.2 *Warranties*—Hybrid warrants that all eggs delivered against this Agreement will be accompanied by a Health Certificate issued by the Canada Department of Agriculture and agreed upon between the Canada Department of Agriculture and the People's Republic of China.

If Chinese Veterinary Authorities prohibit the importation from the exporting country due to reasons of disease, execution of this contract shall be delayed until such time as product is certified disease-free.

3.3 *Guarantees*—Airline insurance is not available. Hybrid Turkeys Inc. guarantees compensation for losses for C & F shipments, provided the following procedures are strictly followed by the purchaser.

a. Your driver must not leave the premises at the airport of final destination until a thorough inspection has been made inside each egg case. If damage has occurred, make a note of the exact number of eggs lost during transit on all copies of the airline's delivery receipt. This receipt must then be signed by an airline official. A copy of this receipt must be sent to Hybrid Turkeys Inc. in Canada immediately.

b. Advise Hybrid of losses immediately that day by telex, telephone, or fax.

In the event of losses, failure by the purchaser to follow the above guidelines upon receipt of shipment will result in vendor's inability to file and attempt to settle any claims on your behalf with the airlines.

Hybrid Turkeys Inc. guarantees true fertility of eggs to be minimum 85 percent, based on 100 eggs to be set and candled at 10 days in Kitchener, Canada, results to be telexed to Skylake. Depending on hatching capabilities, we would anticipate 70 to 75 percent hatch of total eggs.

Article IV

Technical Cooperation for Development and Promotion of Production

4.1 Hybrid and Skylake will cooperate in sharing information in the following areas on an ongoing basis:

Technology and production procedure.

Quality control.

Protection of flock and buildings.

Exchange of information innovation and technical and technology procedure.

Periodic visits by Hybrid and Skylake representatives for training purposes.

Article V

5.1 *Technical Services*—Hybrid will provide advice and make recommendations concerning:

Husbandry of parent stock and final product turkeys.

Parent Stock replacement scheduling and selection.

Specifications for buildings and equipment.

Artificial insemination.

Broody control programs.

Hatching egg handling.

Incubation and hatching technology.

Feeding and nutrition.

Disease prevention and control.

The price includes a maximum of two visits from Hybrid personnel in the first year to aid in original project development, and, thereafter, on an as needed basis, maximum one visit per year, Hybrid agrees that throughout the term of this contract, it will accept the visit of groups of two people from Skylake from time to time for technical training in Canada.

Detailed schedule as follows:
a. From Hybrid to Skylake: Each visit to consist of a maximum of two people for approximately two weeks per visit.
b. From Skylake to Hybrid: First Year: (i) Two people for maximum two weeks, for official visit; (ii) Two people for two to three months for technical training visit.

For the remainder of the contract, two people for a period of time to be agreed upon for each visit.

For all the above-mentioned visits, transportation costs will be paid by the visiting party, reasonable food and lodging will be covered by the host company.

Most visits other than the above can be made; however, in this case all expenses are to be covered by visiting party.

5.2 *Utilization of Off-Sex*—Under no circumstances *can* or *should* the off-sex birds be used for breeding purposes.

Article VI

Prices and Payment

6.1 Skylake authorizes China National Animal Breeding Stock Import and Export Corp. (CABS) to negotiate on its behalf prices and payment terms.

Hybrid and CABS will determine unit prices and product volumes for each business year.

Preliminary contract discussions will commence by May 1st and be concluded on or before September 15th for business during the following calendar year. Beginning in 1988, Hybrid Turkeys Inc. will supply Heavy Medium Parent Stock eggs at the following C and F prices* (U.S. currency):

	Female	*Male*
1988	xxx each	xxx each

Article VII

Confirmation, Coming into Force, and Duration of the Agreement

7.1 This Agreement will come into force upon signing by both parties.

7.2 This Agreement will remain in force for a period of 10 (ten) years. Hybrid and Skylake will meet two years before the Agreement expires to discuss future cooperation.

Article VIII

Force Majeure

8.1 For the purpose of this Agreement, Force Majeure is defined as acts of God, fire, explosion, floods, earthquake, sabotage, breakdown of machinery, disease in flock, delays en route, uprising, riot, war, including civil war, strike, lockout, policies or restrictions of Governments, including restrictions of export and other licenses and generally any contingencies whatsoever beyond the control of the parties and those causes which cannot be eliminated. The party affected by a force majeure incident shall notify the other party immediately.

---

* Prices deleted from case for competitive reasons.

If, during the term of this contract, a force majeure occurs and as a result thereof, this contract, or any part of it, cannot be performed, the party affected by the force majeure incident shall not be held liable by the other party.

If a force majeure incident occurs and either party cannot perform as specified herein, the party prevented from so performing shall resume full performance of this contract upon termination of the force majeure incident. Failure of either party to resume performance as stated herein, shall give to the other party the option to terminate this contract for cause.

Article IX

Exclusivity

9.1 Because Hybrid agrees to transfer to Skylake state-of-the-art technology relating to this contract free of charge, Skylake agrees that during the term of this Agreement, Hybrid will be their sole supplier of turkey breeding stock and final product poults or eggs.

9.2 Hybrid agrees to inform Skylake of any detailed discussions with other potential clients in the People's Republic of China, prior to same taking place.

Transfer of Rights and Liabilities under this Agreement

9.3 The Agreement is binding for both parties. This Agreement may be inherited, that is, transferred to another party, on condition the other party under this Agreement agrees.

Article X

Arbitration

10.1 Should any dispute occur, Hybrid and Skylake will endeavor to settle it in a friendly manner. If this proves impossible, the final decision will be brought to Arbitration of the Foreign Economic and Trade Arbitration Commission of the China Council for the Promotion of International Trade, Beijing, pursuant to its rules of procedures.

Article XI

Industrial Property

11.1 Hybrid and Skylake agree to safekeep all business secrets and production information for the duration of this Agreement and during the renewal of the same.

11.2 Trademarks shall mean any names or designations under which the turkey breeds developed by Hybrid are sold, whether or not such name or designation is registered in Canada or elsewhere.

Skylake agrees not to use the name "Hybrid" or any trademark of Hybrid as part of its business or corporate name without prior consent from Hybrid.

It is understood that the use of the name "Hybrid" as part of the description of the breeders sold hereunder, shall not constitute a contravention of this Agreement.

Skylake agrees to assist Hybrid in all trademark registration within China.

Upon termination of this Agreement, Skylake shall discontinue any usage of the Hybrid's trademarks whatsoever.

Article XII

Communication

12.1 All information under this Agreement will be communicated in writing and dispatched airmail to the following addresses, or in some other manner as advised by the parties.

HYBRID TURKEYS INC.   TIANJIN SKYLAKE FOODSTUFFS CO.
9 CENTENNIAL DRIVE TIANJIN ECONOMIC–TECHNOLOGICAL
KITCHENER, ONTARIO   DEVELOPMENT AREA (TEDA)
N2B 3E9   TLX: 23263 TEDA CN
CANADA

Article XIII

Publicity

13.1 Both parties may give statements on the existence of this Agreement. However, before doing so, one party will consult the other.

Entity of Contract

13.2 This Agreement represents a complete agreement between the parties. There may be no other Agreement or understanding, either written or verbal between them. Every amendment, either in full or in part, may be made only in writing.

Descriptive Titles

13.3 Under this Agreement, descriptive titles are given only to simplify things and may not be interpreted as restricting or influencing in any way the meaning of any of the articles.

Copies and Valid Text

13.4 This Agreement is made up in six (6) identical copies in English.* Each party will receive three (3) copies.

---

* Six identical copies were also prepared in Chinese.

IKEA Canada Ltd.—1986 (Condensed)

Founded as a mail-order business in rural Sweden in 1943, IKEA had grown to more than $1 billion (U.S.) in sales and 70 retail outlets by 1985, and was considered by many to be one of the best-run furniture operations in the world. Although only 14 percent of IKEA's sales were outside Europe, the company's fastest growth was occurring in North America.

Success, however, brought imitators, and in mid-1986 Bjorn Bayley and Anders Berglund, the senior managers of IKEA's North American operations, were examining a just-published Sears Canada catalogue, which contained a new 20-page section called "Elements." This section bore a striking resemblance to the format of an IKEA Canada catalogue (see Exhibits 1 and 2 for sample pages), and the furniture being offered was similar to IKEA's knocked-down, self-assembled line in which different "elements" could be ordered by the customer to create particular designs. Bayley and Berglund wondered how serious Sears was about its new initiative, and what, if anything, IKEA should do in response.

The Canadian Furniture Market

Canadian consumption of furniture totaled more than $2 billion in 1985, an average of well over $600 per household. Imports accounted for approximately 18 percent of this total, half of which originated in the United States. The duties on furniture imported into Canada were approximately 15 percent.

Furniture was sold to Canadian consumers through three types of stores: independents, specialty chains, and department stores. Although the independents held a 70 percent market share, this figure was declining due to their

---

This case was written by Professor Paul W. Beamish. Condensed by Peter Killing. Copyright © 1988, The University of Western Ontario.

EXHIBIT 1 Sample Page from IKEA Catalogue (1985)

GUTE 126/6

GUTE 126/10

GUTE 87/8

GUTE 87/4

$98

GUTE 49/6

GUTE 49/2

GUTE 126/6

$130

GUTE 87/4

GUTE. EIGHTEEN DIFFERENT CHESTS OF DRAWERS TO FIT IN ALMOST ANYWHERE.

GUTE chests of drawers ●möbelfakta White lacquered or pine veneered particleboard, natural or nutbrown stained. W80 cm, D40 cm. QA.
49/2. 2 drawers. H49 cm. White **$94**. Natural or nutbrown **$98**.
49/6. 6 drawers. H49 cm. White **$115**. Natural or nutbrown **$125**.
87/4. 4 drawers. H87 cm. White **$130**. Natural or nutbrown **$145**.

87/8. 8 drawers. H87 cm. White **$170**. Natural or nutbrown **$185**.
126/6. 6 drawers. H126 cm. White **$175**.
Natural or nutbrown **$195**.
126/10. 10 drawers. H126 cm. White **$215**.
Natural or nutbrown **$225**.

EXHIBIT 2 Sample Page from Sears Catalogue (1986)

Dressers and chests whose quality and practicality are inherent—
in the colors and sizes you want. Assemble them yourself with ease.

Your choice of clear knot-free pine veneer over non-warp platewood core
or White baked-on European-quality low gloss enamel on a platewood core.

3 Drawer Units. 38 cm deep, 54 cm high (15 x 21¼").	4 Drawer Units. 38 cm deep, 69 cm high (15 x 27¼").	6 Drawer Units. 38 cm deep, 99 cm high (15 x 39")
Wide. 75 cm wide (29½").	Wide. 75 cm wide (29½").	Wide. 75 cm wide (29½").
012 065 012 DLT – *Pine* Each.139.98	012 065 011 DLT – *Pine* Each.159.98	012 065 010 DLTJ – *Pine* Each.219.98
012 065 002 DLT – *White* Each.139.98	012 065 001 DLT – *White* Each.159.98	012 065 000 DLTJ – *White* Each.219.98
Narrow. 50 cm wide (19½").	Narrow. 50 cm wide (19½").	Narrow. 50 cm wide (19½").
012 065 015 DLT – *Pine* Each.119.98	012 065 014 DLT – *Pine* Each.139.98	012 065 013 DLT – *Pine* Each.189.98
012 065 005 DLT – *White* Each.119.98	012 065 004 DLT – *White* Each.139.98	012 065 003 DLT – *White* Each.189.98

inability to compete with the chains in terms of advertising, purchasing power, management sophistication, and sales support. The average sales per square metre in 1985 for furniture stores of all three types was $1,666 (the figure was $2,606 for stores which also sold appliances) and the average cost of goods sold was 64.5 percent.

While the major department stores such as Eaton's and Sears tended to carry traditional furniture lines close to the middle of the price/quality range, chains and independents operated from one end of the spectrum to the other. At the upper end of the market, specialty chains attempted to differentiate themselves by offering unique product lines, superior service, and a specialized shopping atmosphere.

The lower end of the market, on the other hand, was dominated by furniture warehouses that spent heavily on advertising, and offered lower price, less service, and less emphasis on a fancy image. The warehouses usually kept a larger inventory of furniture on hand than the department stores but expected customers to pick up their purchases. Over half the warehouse sales involved promotional financing arrangements, including delayed payments, extended terms, and so on. The major firms in this group, both of whom sold furniture and appliances, were The Brick and Leon's. The Brick had annual sales of $240 million from 15 Canadian stores, and was rapidly expanding from its Western Canada base. With 30 additional stores in California under the Furnishings 2000 name, The Brick intended to become the largest furniture retailing company in the world. Leon's had annual sales of $160 million from 14 stores, and was growing rapidly from its Ontario base. These 14 stores were operated under a variety of names. Leon's also franchised its name in smaller cities in Canada. For part of their merchandise requirements, The Brick and Leon's often negotiated with manufacturers for exclusive products, styles, and fabrics and imported from the United States, Europe, and the Far East. Although both firms had had problems earlier with entry to the U.S. market, each intended on expanding there.

Most furniture retailers in Canada purchased their products from Canadian manufacturers after examining new designs and models at trade shows. There were approximately 1,400 Canadian furniture manufacturers, mostly located in Ontario and Quebec. Typically, these firms were small (78 percent of Canadian furniture plants employed less than 50 people), undercapitalized, and minimally automated. One industry executive quipped that one of the most significant technological developments for the industry had been the advent of the staple gun.

Canadian-produced furniture typically followed American and European styling. It was generally of adequate to excellent quality but was often more costly to produce. The reason for high Canadian costs was believed to be a combination of short manufacturing runs and high raw material, labour, and distribution costs. In an attempt to reduce costs, a few of the larger manufacturers such as Kroehler had vertically integrated—purchasing sawmills, fabric warehouses, fibreboard, and wood frame plants—but such practices were very much the exception in the industry.

The IKEA Formula

IKEA's approach to business was fundamentally different from that of the traditional Canadian retailers. The company focused exclusively on what it called "quick assembly" furniture, which consumers carried from the store in flat packages and assembled at home. This furniture was primarily pine, had a clean European design look to it, and was priced at 15 percent below the lowest prices for traditional furniture. Its major appeal appeared to be to young families, singles, and frequent movers, who were looking for well-designed items that were economically priced and created instant impact.

According to company executives, IKEA was successful because of its revolutionary approach to the most important aspects of the business: product design, procurement, store operations, marketing, and management philosophy, which stressed flexibility and market orientation rather than long-range strategy. Each of these items is discussed in turn.

Product Design

IKEA's European designers, not the company's suppliers, were responsible for the design of most of the furniture and accessories in IKEA's product line, which totaled 15,000 items. The heart of the company's design capability was a 50-person Swedish workshop, which produced prototypes of new items of furniture and smaller components such as "an ingenious little snap lock for table legs which makes a table stronger and cheaper at the same time" and a "clever little screw attachment which allows for the assembly of a pin back chair in five minutes." IKEA's designers were very cost conscious, and were constantly working to lower costs in ways that were not critical to the consumer. The quality of a work top, for example, would be superior to the quality of the back of a bookshelf, which would never be seen. "Low price with a meaning" was the theme.

Although it was not impossible to copyright a particular design or process, IKEA's philosophy was "if somebody steals a model from us we do not bring a lawsuit, because a lawsuit is always negative. We solve the problem by making a new model that is even better."

Procurement

IKEA's early success in Sweden had so threatened traditional European furniture retailers that they had promised to boycott any major supplier that shipped products to the upstart firm. As a result IKEA had no choice but to go to the smaller suppliers. Since these suppliers had limited resources, IKEA began assuming responsibility for the purchase of raw materials, packaging materials, storage, specialized equipment and machinery, and engineering. What began as a necessity soon became a cornerstone of IKEA's competitive strategy, and by 1986 the firm had nearly 100 production engineers working as purchasers.

Together with IKEA's designers, these engineers assisted suppliers in every way they could to help them lower costs, dealing with everything from the introduction of new technology to the alteration of the dimensions of a shipping carton.

Although IKEA sometimes leased equipment and made loans to its suppliers, the firm was adamant that it would not enter the furniture manufacturing business itself. In fact, to avoid control over (and responsibility for) its suppliers, the company had a policy of limiting its purchases to 50 percent of a supplier's capacity. Many products were obtained from multiple suppliers, and frequently suppliers produced only a single standardized component or input to the final product. Unfinished pine shelves, for example, were obtained directly from sawmills; cabinet doors were purchased from door factories; and cushions came from textile mills.

In total, IKEA purchased goods from 1,500 suppliers located in 40 countries. About 52 percent of the company's purchases were from Scandinavia, 21 percent from other countries of Western Europe, 20 percent from Eastern Europe, and 7 percent elsewhere.

Store Operations

IKEA stores were usually large one- or two-storey buildings situated in relatively inexpensive stand-alone locations, neither in prime downtown sites nor in shopping malls. Most stores were surrounded by a large parking lot, adorned with billboards explaining IKEA's delivery policy, product guarantee, and the existence of a coffee shop and/or restaurant.

On entering a store, the customer was immediately made aware of the children's play area (a room filled with hollow multicoloured balls), a video room for older children, and a receptionist with copies of IKEA catalogues, a metric conversion guide, index cards for detailing purchases, and a store guide. The latter, supplemented by prominent signs, indicated that the store contained lockers and benches for shoppers, a first aid area, restrooms, strollers and a baby care area, an "as-is" department (no returns permitted), numerous checkouts, suggestion boxes, and, in many cases, a restaurant. All major credit cards were accepted.

Traffic flow in most IKEA stores was guided so as to pass by almost all of the merchandise in the store, which was displayed as it would look in the home, complete with all accessories. Throughout a store, employees could be identified by their bright red IKEA shirts. Part-time employees wore yellow shirts which read "Temporary Help—Please Don't Ask Me Any Hard Questions." The use of sales floor staff was minimal. The IKEA view was that "salesmen are expensive, and can also be irritating. IKEA leaves you to shop in peace."

While IKEA stores were all characterized by their self-serve, self-wrapping, self-transport, and self-assembly operations, the company's philosophy was that each new store would incorporate the latest ideas in use in any of its existing stores. The most recent trend in some countries was an IKEA Contract Sales section, which provided a delivery, invoicing, and assembly service for commercial customers.

Marketing

IKEA's promotional activities were intended to educate the consumer public on the benefits of the IKEA concept and build traffic by attracting new buyers and encouraging repeat visits from existing customers. The primary promotional vehicle was the annual IKEA catalogue, which was selectively mailed out to prime target customers, which in the Toronto area, for instance, had the following characteristics:

- Income $35,000+.
- Own condominium or townhouse.
- University degree.
- White collar.
- Primary age group 35–44.
- Secondary age group 25–34.
- Husband/wife both work.
- Two children.
- Movers.

With minor variations, this "upscale" profile was typical of IKEA's target customers in Europe and North America. In Canada, IKEA management acknowledged the target market, but felt that in fact the IKEA concept appealed to a much wider group of consumers.

IKEA also spent heavily on magazine advertisements, which were noted for their humorous, slightly off-beat approach. In Canada, IKEA spent $2.5 million to print 3.6 million catalogues, $2 million on magazine advertising, and $1.5 million on other forms of promotion in 1984.

Management Philosophy

The philosophy of Ingvar Kamprad, the founder of IKEA, was "to create a better everyday life for the majority of people." In practice, this creed meant that IKEA was dedicated to offering, and continuing to offer, the lowest prices possible on good quality furniture, so that IKEA products were available to as many people as possible. Fred Andersson, the head of IKEA's corporate product-planning group stated, "Unlike other companies, we are not fascinated with what we produce—we make what our customers want." Generally, IKEA management felt that no other company could match IKEA's combination of quality and price across the full width of the product line.

IKEA also made a concerted effort to stay "close to its customers," and it was not unusual for the general manager of IKEA Canada, for instance, to personally telephone customers who had made complaints or suggestions. Each week an employee newsletter detailed all customer comments and indicated how management felt they should be dealt with.

Another guiding philosophy of the firm was that growth would be in "small bites." The growth objective in Canada, for instance, had been to increase sales and profits by 20 percent per year, but care was taken to sequence store openings so that managerial and financial resources would not be strained.

Internally, the company's philosophy was stated as "freedom, with responsibility," which meant that IKEA's managers typically operated with a good deal of autonomy. The Canadian operation, for instance, received little in the way of explicit suggestions from head office, even in the one year when the budget was not met. The Canadian management team traveled to head office as a group only once every several years. As Bjorn Bayley explained, "We are a very informal management team and try to have everyone who works for us believe that they have the freedom to do their job in the best way possible. It's almost impossible to push the philosophy down to the cashier level, but we try."

IKEA in Canada

IKEA's formula had worked well in Canada. Under the direction of a four-person management team, which included two Swedes, the company had grown from a single store in 1976 to nine stores totaling 75,000 square metres and, as shown in Exhibit 3, predicted 1986 sales of more than $140 million. The sales of IKEA Canada had exceeded budget in all but one of the past five years, and usually by a wide margin. Net profits were approximately 5 percent of sales. Profit and loss statements for 1983 and 1984, the only financial statements available, are presented in Exhibit 4.

IKEA Canada carried just less than half of the company's total product line. Individual items were chosen on the basis of what management thought would sell in Canada, and if IKEA could not beat a competitor's price by 10–15 percent on a particular item, it was dropped. Most of the goods sold in the Canadian stores were supplied from central warehouses in Sweden. To coordinate this process, a five-person stock supply department in Vancouver provided Sweden with a three-year forecast of Canada's needs, and placed major orders twice a year. Actual volumes were expected to be within 10 percent of the forecast level. As Bayley noted, "You needed a gambler in the stock supply job."

Individual stores were expected to maintain 13.5 weeks of inventory on hand (10.5 weeks in the store and 3 weeks in transit) and could order from the central warehouse in Montreal, or, if a product was not in stock in Montreal, direct from Sweden. Shipments from Sweden took six to eight weeks to arrive, from Montreal two to three weeks. In practice, about 50 percent of the product arriving at a store arrived via each route.

EXHIBIT 3   IKEA Canada Sales (by store, including mail order; Cdn. $000s)

	1981	1982	1983 (Actual)	1984	1985	1986 (Forecast)	Mail* Order (%)
Vancouver	$12,122	$11,824	$12,885	$19,636	$ 19,240	$25,500	6.8%
Calgary	7,379	8,550	7,420	7,848	9,220	11,500	8.6
Ottawa	5,730	6,914	8,352	9,015	10,119	12,500	1.8
Montreal			8,617	12,623	15,109	22,000†	2.2
Halifax	3,634	4,257	4,474	6,504	7,351	9,000	22.9
Toronto	11,231	13,191	16,249	18,318	22,673	30,500	1.8
Edmonton	6,506	7,474	8,075	8,743	9,986	16,000	15.4
Quebec City		5,057	8,284	9,027	10,037	12,000	6.1
Victoria					2,808	3,500	
Total	$46,602	$57,267	$74,356	$91,714	$106,543	$142,500	6.7%

* 1984 most recent data available.

† Projected growth due to store size expansion.

IKEA's success in Canada meant that the firm was often hard pressed to keep the best-selling items in stock. (Twenty percent of the firm's present line constituted 80 percent of sales volume.) At any given time in Canada, IKEA stores might have 300 items out of stock, either because actual sales deviated significantly from forecasts or because suppliers could not meet their delivery promises. While management estimated that 75 percent of customers were willing to wait for IKEA products in a stockout situation, the company nevertheless began a deliberate policy of developing Canadian suppliers for high-demand items, even if this meant paying a slight premium. In 1984, the stock control group purchased $57 million worth of goods on IKEA's behalf, $12 million of which was from 30 Canadian suppliers, up from $7 million the previous year.

As indicated in Exhibit 3, IKEA Canada sold products, rather reluctantly, by mail order to customers who preferred not to visit the stores. A senior manager explained: "To date we have engaged in defensive mail orders—only when the customer really wants it and the order is large enough. The separate handling, breaking down of orders, and repackaging required for mail orders would be too expensive and go against the economies-through-volume approach of IKEA. Profit margins of mail order business tend to be half that of a store operation. There are more sales returns in shipping, particularly because of damages, which can reach 4 percent of shipments. It is difficult to know where to draw the market boundaries for a mail-order business. We don't want to substitute mail-order customers for store visitors."

In 1986, the management team which had brought success to IKEA's Canadian operations was breaking up. Bjorn Bayley, who had come to Canada in 1978, was slotted to move to Philadelphia to spearhead IKEA's entry into the U.S. market, which had begun in June 1985 with a single store. With early sales running at a level twice as high as the company had predicted, Bayley

EXHIBIT 4   Statement of Earnings and Retained Earnings (year ended August 31, 1984, with comparative figures for 1983)

	1984	1983
Sales	$92,185,188	$74,185,691
Cost of merchandise sold	49,836,889	38,085,173
Gross profit	42,348,299	36,100,518
General, administrative, and selling expenses	28,016,473	23,626,727
Operating profit before the undernoted	14,331,826	12,473,791
Depreciation and amortization	1,113,879	1,066,286
Franchise amortization	257,490	257,490
Franchise fee	2,765,558	2,225,571
	4,136,927	3,549,347
Earnings from operations	10,194,899	8,924,444
Rental income	769,719	815,683
Less rental expense	245,803	258,296
	523,916	557,387
Interest expense	2,453,116	3,042,471
Less other income	438,683	65,757
	2,014,433	2,976,714
Earnings before income taxes	8,704,382	6,505,117
Income taxes		
Current	3,789,773	2,716,645
Deferred	(70,400)	175,500
	3,719,373	2,892,145
Net earnings for the year	4,985,009	3,612,972
Retained earnings, beginning of year	5,501,612	1,888,640
Retained earnings, end of year	$10,486,621	$ 5,501,612

Source: Consumer and Corporate Affairs, Canada.

expected to be busy and was taking Mike McDonald, the controller, and Mike McMullen, the personnel director, with him. Anders Berglund, who, like Bayley, was a long-time IKEA employee and had been in Canada since 1979, was scheduled to take over the Canadian operation. Berglund would report through Bayley to IKEA's North American sales director, who was located in Europe.

New Competition

IKEA's success in Canada had not gone unnoticed. IDOMO was a well-established Toronto-based competitor, and Sears Canada was a new entrant.

IDOMO.   Like IKEA, IDOMO sold knocked-down furniture that customers were required to assemble at home. IDOMO offered a somewhat narrower selection than IKEA but emphasized teak furniture to a much greater extent. With stores in Hamilton, Mississauga (across from IKEA), Toronto, and Montreal, IDOMO appeared to have capitalized on excess demand that IKEA had developed but was not able to service.

The products and prices offered in both the 96-page IDOMO and 144-page IKEA catalogues were similar, with IKEA's prices slightly lower. Prices in the IKEA catalogue were in effect for a year. IDOMO reserved the right to make adjustments to prices and specifications. A mail-order telephone number in Toronto was provided in the IDOMO catalogue. Of late, IDOMO had begun to employ an increased amount of television advertising. IDOMO purchased goods from around the world and operated a number of their own Canadian factories. Their primary source of goods was Denmark.

Sears.   The newest entrant in the Canadian knocked-down furniture segment was Sears Canada, a wholly owned subsidiary of Sears Roebuck of Chicago and, with $3.8 billion in annual revenues, one of Canada's largest merchandising operations. Sears operated 75 department stores in Canada, selling a wide range (700 merchandise lines comprising 100,000 stock-keeping units) of medium-price and quality goods. Sears Canada also ran a major catalogue operation, which distributed 12 annual catalogues to approximately 4 million Canadian families. Customers could place catalogue orders by mail, by telephone, or in person through one of the company's 1,500 catalogue sales units, which were spread throughout the country.

A quick check by Bayley and Berglund revealed that Sears' Elements line was being sold only in Canada and only through the major Sears catalogues. Elements products were not for sale, nor could they be viewed, in Sears stores. In the Fall-Winter catalogue that they examined, which was over 700 pages in length, the Elements line was given 20 pages. Although Sears appeared to offer the same "type" of products as IKEA, there was a narrower selection within each category. Prices for Elements' products seemed almost identical to IKEA prices. One distinct difference between the catalogues was the much greater emphasis IKEA placed on presenting a large number of coordinated settings and room designs.

At least some of the suppliers of the Elements line were Swedish, although it did not appear that IKEA and Sears had any suppliers in common. The IKEA executives knew that Sears was generally able to exert a great deal of influence over its suppliers, usually obtaining prices at least equal to and often below those of its competitors, because of the huge volumes purchased. Sears also worked closely with its suppliers in marketing, research, design and development, production standards, and production planning. Unlike IKEA, Sears tended to purchase completed units. Many lines of merchandise were manufactured with features exclusive to Sears and were sold under its private brand names. There was a 75 percent buying overlap for the catalogue and store and about a 90 percent overlap between regions on store purchases.

Like any Sears' product, Elements furniture could be charged to a Sears charge card. Delivery of catalogue items generally took about two weeks, and for a small extra charge catalogue orders would be delivered right to the consumer's home in a Sears truck. If a catalogue item was out of stock, Sears policy was either to tell the customer if and when the product would be available, or to substitute an item of equal or greater value. If goods proved defective (10% of Sears Roebuck mail-order furniture purchasers had received damaged or broken furniture), Sears provided home pick-up and replacement and was willing, for a fee, to install goods, provide parts, and do repairs as products aged. Sears emphasized that it serviced what it sold, and guaranteed everthing that it sold—"satisfaction guaranteed or money refunded." In its advertising, which included all forms of media, Sears stressed its "hassle-free returns" and asked customers to "take a look at the services we offer . . . they'll bring you peace of mind, long after the bill is paid."

In their assessment of Sears Canada, Bayley and Berglund recognized that the company seemed to be going through something of a revival. Using the rallying cry that a "new" Sears was being created, Sears executives (the Canadian firm had 10 vice presidents) had experimented with new store lay-outs, pruned the product line, and improved customer service for catalogue orders. Richard Sharpe, the chairman of Sears Canada, personally addressed as many as 12,000 employees per year, and the company received 3,000 suggestions from employees annually. Perhaps as a result of these initiatives, and a cut in work force from 65,000 to 50,000 over a several-year period, Sears Canada posted its best-ever results in 1985.

Conclusion

With the limited data they had on Sears, IKEA management recognized their comparison of the two companies would be incomplete. Nonetheless, a decision regarding the Sears competitive threat was required. Any solution would have to reflect Kamprad's philosophy: "Expensive solutions to problems are often signs of mediocrity. We have no interest in a solution until we know what it costs."

KOLAPORE, INC. (CONDENSED)

In January 1986, Mr. Adriaan Demmers, president and sole employee of Kolapore, Inc., a firm based in Guelph, Ontario, specializing in the importation, processing, and sale of high-quality souvenir spoons, was becoming increasingly frustrated with the pace at which his business was developing. Over a two-year period, Demmers had taken his idea of importing souvenir spoons from Holland to Canada to annual sales of nearly $30,000. He believed the potential existed for well over $100,000 in Canadian sales plus exports to the United States. This success to date had been a strain, however, on Demmers's limited financial resources and had not provided any compensation for the long hours invested. Demmers was beginning to question if he was ever going to have the major breakthrough which he had always believed was "just around the corner."

Recently, Demmers had accepted a full-time position with another firm in an unrelated business. While Demmers realized that he could continue to operate Kolapore, Inc., on a part-time basis, he wondered if he should "face reality" and simply fold up the business or try to sell it. Alternately, Demmers could not occasionally help wondering if he should be devoting himself full-time to Kolapore.

Background

In February/March 1984, Demmers conducted a feasibility study of starting a business to market souvenir spoons. His idea was to offer a high-quality product depicting landmarks, historic buildings, and other unique symbols of the area in which the spoons were to be sold.

This case was prepared by Professor Paul W. Beamish. Copyright © 1986 by Paul W. Beamish. (Condensed, 1992)

There were numerous spoons on the market, but most tended to be for Canada or Ontario rather than local sites of interest and were generally poorly made and not visually appealing. There were few quality spoons, and the ones that did exist were priced in the $15–$40 range.

Sources of spoons were examined and quotations were received from firms in Canada, the United States, and the Netherlands (Holland). The search process for a country from which to source the spoons was a limited one and was settled quickly, thanks to Demmers's Dutch heritage, the existence of a well-recognized group of silversmiths in Schoonhoven, plus a particular company which already had over 40 Canadian specific dies and lower prices.

Demmers felt the key factors for success were good quality product, using designs of local landmarks, and an eye-catching display. He felt displays should be located in a prominent position in retail stores because souvenir spoons are often bought on impulse.

As part of his feasibility study, Demmers conducted a market analysis (including customer and retailer surveys), a competitive analysis (both manufacturers and distributors), and developed an import plan, marketing plan, and financial projections (including projected break-even and cash flows). Excerpts from this study follow.

Market Analysis

The market for souvenir spoons consists of several overlapping groups—primarily tourists and the gift market. There are also groups interested in spoons for more specialized purposes such as church groups, service clubs, associations, and others. These are very specialized and for special occasions.

A random telephone survey conducted in March 1984 of 50 people in Guelph revealed that 78 percent owned souvenir spoons. Forty-six percent of those people had purchased the spoons themselves, while 54 percent had received them as gifts. In total, almost 25 percent of the people in the sample collected souvenir spoons or had a rack on which to hang them. Retailers indicated that sales occurred primarily during the summer months and at Christmas time. Twelve retail outlets were visited to obtain information regarding quality, sales, and prices. Background on a selection of these retailers is summarized in Appendix A.

There was a high awareness of souvenir spoons in the market, but the product quality was generally at the low end of the market. For example, rough edges on the bowls were common, and the crests on the spoons were often crooked. In fact, one manufacturer's spoon had a picture of Kitchener City Hall which was out of focus and off-center. (Terms concerning souvenir spoons are explained in Appendix B.)

A limited variety of spoons was often available, and few of the spoons were of local points of interest even though these were the spoons that were most in demand. One retailer noted that of a total of 140 spoons sold in 1983, 106 were one variety, a spoon with a relief design in plastic of a Conestoga wagon. This was the only unique spoon Demmers found in the area "other than the cheap picture spoons."

There was no advertising for souvenir spoons due to the nature of the product and the lack of identification with a particular brand.

Souvenir spoons appeared to be a low priority in many producing companies, with little marketing effort made to push the products. Even the packaging was of poor quality; often, boxes were not supplied for gift wrapping.

The sale of spoons was viewed as seasonal by some retailers. Point-of-purchase displays were removed once the summer rush was over in many instances.

Spoons were not prominently displayed in most stores, yet they are largely an impulse item. In several stores, they were kept in drawers and only taken out when requested.

Competitive Analysis

Souvenir spoons essentially serve two customer functions: as gifts or commemoratives. They can be used as gifts for family, friends, or special occasions such as Christmas. They can also serve as a commemorative token of having visited somewhere or for a special anniversary (for example, the Province of Ontario's 200th anniversary). They can be either functional (used for coffee or teaspoons) or may be used for decorative purposes (hung in a spoon rack or put in a cabinet).

Competition comes from all other gift items and all other souvenir items in approximately the same price range.

Demmers identified 11 companies that distributed souvenir spoons in the Southwestern Ontario area and gathered what data he could—much of it anecdotal—on each. This process had provided encouragement for Demmers to proceed. Background on these suppliers is summarized in Appendix C.

Southwestern Ontario contained a number of large urban areas, including Toronto (over 2 million people), Hamilton/Burlington, Kitchener/Waterloo, and London, with over 300,000 people in each—plus many smaller cities, such as Guelph. Guelph was located roughly in the centre of the triangle formed by Toronto, Waterloo, and Burlington and was within an hour's drive of each.

Importing

To import goods into Canada on a regular basis in amounts over $800, an importer number was required. This was available from Revenue Canada, Customs and Excise. Requirements for customs were an advise notice from the shipper and a customs invoice. These were available in office supply stores. A customs tariff number and commodity code were also required to complete the customs B3 form.

Souvenir spoons of either sterling silver or silver plate were listed in the customs tariff under number 42902-1. The Netherlands has Most Favoured Nation status, so the duty was 20.3 percent. On top of the cost of the merchandise (excluding transportation and insurance but including duty), there was a further 10 percent excise tax and 10 percent federal sales tax.

A customs broker could be hired to look after the clearing of goods through customs. Rates were approximately $41 plus $3.60 for every $1,000 of value, duty included.

Insurance on a shipment of less than $10,000 costs a fixed fee of about $150 with insurance brokers. This can be reduced if insurance is taken on a yearly basis, based on the expected value of imports over the year. Freight forwarders charge approximately $2 per kilo regardless of the total weight of the shipment.

The importing can be easily handled without help on small shipments such as spoons. The product can be sent by airmail and insured with the post office. It can also be sent to a small city like Guelph rather than Toronto, and this avoids the busy Toronto customs office and possible delays of several days. The customs office in Guelph can easily clear the goods the same day they arrive.

Marketing Plan

Product. The proposed souvenir spoons would be a high-quality product with detailed dies made to give them a relief design far superior to any competitive spoons (except for those retailing in the $30 range). These spoons are available in silver plate and alpacca, which makes them similar to jewellery.

Designs would be of specific points of interest. In the Kitchener-Waterloo area, for example, possible subjects would include Seagram Museum, Schneider House, Doon Pioneer Village, university crests, and city crests. Kitchener-Waterloo would be printed under the picture, also in relief in the metal, along with the title of the particular picture.

Price Points.

$2.25	—Metropolitan Supplies: nickel-plated.
$4.50–$6.00	—Breadner Manufacturing: rhodium-plated and silver-plated. Candis Enterprises. Gazelle Importers.
$7.00–$8.00	—Oneida or Commemorative: simple designs with engraved insignia. Appear to be made of a silver alloy.
$10.00–$14.00	—Proposed price range for retail.

> *a.* Quality comparable to $30.00 spoons, but silver content is lower.
> *b.* Detailed designs of local landmarks.
> *c.* Variety of 6–10 spoons in each market.

$30.00 and up—Breadner

> *a.* Sterling silver.
> *b.* Fine workmanship.
> *c.* Very limited variety of designs.

Place. Because souvenir spoons are purchased on impulse, locations with high traffic are essential. Jewellery stores and gift stores in malls and tourist areas are probably most suitable in this respect.

Due to the price range proposed and the quality of the merchandise, the quality and image of the store has to be appropriate. This would eliminate discount jewellery stores and cheap souvenir shops for the aforementioned reasons. Secondly, it would not please higher-end retailers if the same spoons were sold for less in the same area and would likely restrict distribution in the appropriate channels.

Jewellery stores are perceived by many people as selling expensive, luxury items that are not part of one's everyday needs. For this reason, it would be helpful for these stores to have a window display.

Promotion. Each retail location will carry a minimum product line of six varieties of spoons: one with a Canadian theme, one with a provincial theme, and at least four spoons with designs of local landmarks or points of interest.

The packaging will be suitable for gift wrapping, so will likely consist of a small box with a clear plastic cover.

Each retail location will have an oak countertop display rack. There will be a relatively high cost to the displays initially, but they will attract attention and convey the quality of the spoons. Different sizes can be made depending on the number of spoons for a particular market.

Because souvenir spoons are primarily an impulse purchase, location in the store is important and should be near the entrance or have a window display. This is something which can be controlled only by persuading the retailer that this would increase the turnover and consequently his profits.

EXHIBIT 1   Forecast Variable Costs and Margins of Spoons

	Alpacca	*Silver Plate*
Quote by Dutch manufacturer (Zilverfabriek) (in guilders) 1 guilder = $.43 Cdn.	2.20 guilders	3.10 guilders
Factory cost in $Cdn.	$0.95	$1.33
Duty @ 20.3 percent	.19	.27
Cost, duty included	$1.14	$1.60
Federal sales tax @ 9 percent	.10	.14
Federal excise tax @ 10 percent	.11	.16
Freight and insurance	.10	.10
Cost	$1.45	$2.00
Contribution margin	$2.05 to $3.55	$1.50 to $3.00
Cost to retailer	3.50 to 5.00	3.50 to 5.00
Retailer markup	3.50 to 5.00	3.50 to 5.00
Retail price	7.00 to 10.00*	7.00 to 10.00

* These prices are lower than originally forecast due to Demmers's recognition that a $10 to $14 retail price was too high.

EXHIBIT 2   Forecast Breakeven

Distribution costs (transportation)	$ 4,000
Rent expense (work from home)	—
Salary	15,000
Office supply costs (including telephone)	1,000
Inventory costs	1,000
Merchandising expenses (displays and boxes)	3,000
Investment in dies (10 @ $125 each)	1,250
Total fixed costs	$25,250

$25,250/$1.50 = 16,833 spoons
$25,250/$2.05 = 12,317 spoons
$25,250/$3.00 = 8,416 spoons

EXHIBIT 3   Forecast Cash Flow, May–August 1984

	May	*June*	*July*	*August*
Cash	$3,000	$ (750)	$1,000	$ 7,500
Disbursements:				
Moulds	1,250	—	—	—
Purchases	—	7,250	—	7,250
Promotion expenses	2,000	1,000	—	—
Car expenses	500	500	500	500
Total disbursements	3,750	8,750	500	7,750
Net cash	(750)	(9,500)	500	(250)
Receipts:				
Accounts receivable	—	10,500	7,000	10,500
Cash balance (to be borrowed)	$ (750)	$ 1,000	$7,500	$10,250

Note: Terms n/30.

Finance

Contribution margin per spoon has been calculated using the most conservative numbers and at a wholesale price of $3.50. Typically, retailers would mark prices up to 100 percent (see Exhibit 1). The contribution margins worked out to $2.05 on alpacca spoons and $1.50 on silver-plated spoons.

The breakeven, assuming costs of $25,250 per year and a contribution margin of $2.05, would be sales volume of 12,317 spoons with sales value of $43,110 (see Exhibit 2). Assuming the spoons would be introduced in the Ontario market and distribution obtained in 100 retail locations, this means sales of 124 spoons per store.

Upon graduating from a university business school in April 1984, Demmers planned to devote his efforts to Kolapore. He felt that while there could be a short-term financial drain, his cash balance would be positive at the end of the second month of operation (see Exhibit 3).

Subsequent Events

Soon after graduating in April, it became clear to Demmers that Kolapore was not going to realize forecast sales of $28,000 by September 1984. Due to delays in getting shipments from Holland and difficulty in obtaining distributions in Canada, sales were only $1,830 over the summer. A number of assumptions in the original feasibility study (as described in the first section) had proven incorrect:

1. The number of dies ultimately required (each of which costs $125) was not going to be 10 but closer to 50.
2. The federal sales tax rate had increased to 10 percent from 9 percent.
3. Duty was payable on the dies themselves as well as on the spoons at the rate of 20.3 percent excise tax plus federal sales tax.
4. Delivery time for new dies was closer to six months than the forecast 10–12 weeks (the artist had been ill for several months). Several orders were cancelled during this period as a result.
5. Packaging costs per spoon were closer to 32 cents per unit than the estimated 10 cents.
6. Distribution had been difficult because the large chain stores which dominated the market all had established suppliers.
7. The target market was not nearly as upscale as originally envisioned. Although Kolapore's spoons were readily identifiable as being of superior quality, most customers would only pay a maximum of $7–$8 retail for any spoon. Demmers had estimated the total Canadian souvenir spoon market at about $1.5 million annually. Within that, a very small portion was for sterling silver (where Demmers could not compete), about $450,000 was at the $7 retail price point where Demmers was selling (some of his competitors were promoting similar or poorer-quality spoons at the same price), with the balance of the market reserved for lower-priced/lower-quality spoons.

The goal of 100 stores by September 1984 was still a long way off.

Demmers had also discovered that the chain stores plan all their buying from 6 to 12 months in advance. Because many of the spoons he had designed did not arrive until September 1984, this meant that he had missed much of the tourist season (and nearly all of the Christmas market).

On the positive side, the Dutch guilder had depreciated relative to the Canadian dollar. In September 1984, it cost Canadian $0.39 for 1 guilder rather than $0.43 as forecast. In addition, delivery times for spoons from existing dies required three to four weeks rather than the expected four to six weeks, and the cost of display cases was only about $16 each. These were made of plastic rather than the originally envisioned oak.

Although Kolapore was showing a negative cash balance at the end of August 1984 (see Exhibit 4), sales began to improve in September (see Exhibit 5), growing to nearly $16,000 by the end of the first full year of operation (see Exhibits 6 and 7 for financial statements). A financial loss of $1,800 was

EXHIBIT 4   Actual Cash Flow, 1984

	May	*June*	*July*	*August*
Cash	$2,600	$1,000	$ 950	$ 530
Disbursements:				
Purchases	1,000	550	870	1,460
Expenses	1,000	80	300	300
Total disbursements	2,000	630	1,170	1,760
Net cash	600	370	(220)	(1,230)
Receipts:				
Accounts receivable	400	580	750	1,100
Cash balance	$1,000	$ 950	$ 530	$ (130)

EXHIBIT 5   Actual Sales, 1984–1985

May	$ 400
June	580
July	750
August	1,100
September	2,600
October	2,540
November	1,500
December	1,400
January–March	4,923

incurred for the first year of operation, and this took no account of the countless hours Demmers had invested. Since the business was not yet self-supporting, in September 1984 Demmers had begun to look for other sources of income.

Between September 1984 and January 1986, Demmers worked for five months in a fibreglass factory, acquired a house in Guelph in which he was able to live and to rent out rooms, sold Bruce Trail calendars on a commission basis, worked at organizing and selling several ski tours (which did not take place), and opened an ice-cream store in a regional resort area (Wasaga Beach). Due to a low volume of traffic, this latter venture in the summer of 1985 resulted in an $8,000 loss. In the fall of 1985, Demmers accepted a position as production manager for a weekly newspaper in Guelph.

By this time, Demmers was selling direct to retailers in 20 towns and cities in Ontario and through five chains: Simpsons and United Cigar Stores and, to a much smaller extent, Eaton's, Birks, and Best Wishes. Other chains such as The Bay, Sears, and Woolco had been approached but so far without success. Demmers was hoping to find the time so that he could approach the

---

EXHIBIT 6   **Kolapore, Inc.**
Balance Sheet
As of March 31, 1985
(Unaudited—See Notice to Reader)

Assets
Current assets:

Cash	$1,708
Accounts receivable	1,763
Inventory	2,873
Total current assets	6,344
Incorporation expense	466
Total assets	$6,810

Liabilities
Current liabilities:

Accounts payable and accruals	$268
Due to shareholder (note 2, Table 7)	8,342
Total liabilities	8,610

Shareholders' Equity

Retained earnings (deficit)	(1,800)
Total liabilities and shareholders' equity	$6,810

Note: Notice to reader: These financial statements have been compiled solely for tax purposes. I have not audited, reviewed, or otherwise attempted to verify their accuracy or completeness.
Guelph, Ontario
May 2, 1985   Chartered Accountant

---

buyers at K mart, Zeller's, Consumer's Distributing, Robinson's, Woodwards, and others.

Kolapore spoons were sold in Simpsons stores from Windsor, Ontario, to Halifax, Nova Scotia, and in 18 United Cigar Store locations in southern Ontario. Four months after Demmers's first delivery to the chain outlets in the summer of 1985, about half the stores were sold out of Kolapore spoons. Neither chain would reorder stock part way through the year.

To sell direct in some of the smaller cities, Demmers's practice had been to drive or walk through the main shopping areas, stopping at jewellery stores or other likely retail outlets. If he was unable to meet with the store owner, he would usually leave a sample and a letter with some information (see Exhibit 8 for a copy of the letter). Demmers's experience had been that unless he personally met with the right person—which sometimes took three or more visits—no sales would occur. When he was able to meet with the owner, his success rate was over 70 percent. To sell direct in larger centres such as Toronto (where he had 40 customers), Demmers had focused his efforts on hotel gift shops. Having established these customers, he could now visit all 40 customers in Toronto personally in two to three days.

EXHIBIT 7   **Kolapore, Inc.**
Statement of Income
Year Ended March 31, 1985
(Unaudited—See Notice to Reader)

Sales		$15,793
Cost of sales:		
Inventory at beginning of year	—	
Purchases	8,453	
Duty and freight	2,288	
Dies	3,034	
	13,775	
Less: Inventory at end of year	2,873	
Cost of sales		10,902
Gross profit		4,891
Expenses:		
Office	657	
Samples	582	
Auto expenses	1,137	
Car allowance	3,900	
Bank interest and charges	139	
Advertising	26	
Accounting	250	
Total expenses		6,691
Net profit (loss) for the year		$(1,800)

Notes: 1. Significant accounting policies:
Kolapore, Inc., is a company incorporated under the laws of Ontario on April 6, 1984, and is primarily engaged in the importing and selling of souvenir spoons.
The accounting policies are in accordance with generally accepted accounting principles.
Inventory is valued at lower of cost or net realizable value.
Incorporation expense is not amortized.
2. Due to shareholder is noninterest-bearing and payable on demand.

By year-end, Demmers had access to a pool of 89 Canadian-specific dies. Demmers's supplier in Holland had 46 dies in stock which another Canadian from Western Canada had had designed. Spoons based on these dies were no longer being sold anywhere as far as Demmers could tell.

For the most part, Demmers was selling spoons based on his own designs. (For those spoons which Demmers had had designed, he had exclusive rights in Canada). In less than two years, he had 43 more dies made up (see Exhibit 9 for a complete list). In some cases, Demmers had asked a particular company/ group to pay the cost of the dies; in others, such as for universities, he had built the die cost into his price for the first shipment; while in others he had simply gone ahead on his own with the hope that he could achieve sufficient sales to justify the investment.

There was a wide variability in the sales level associated with each spoon. Sales from his best-seller—the Toronto skyline (which depicted major buildings and the CN Tower)—were about 1,000 spoons a year. Demmers's second-

EXHIBIT 8   Kolapore, Inc., Letter of Introduction

Kolapore, Inc.
P.O. Box 361
Guelph, Ontario
N1H 6K5

Dear

    Kolapore, Inc., would like to offer you the opportunity to have your own design on a spoon made up in metal relief, for example, a logo, coat of arms, crest, building, or whatever you would like.

    There is always a large market for souvenir spoons of unique design and high quality. Kolapore Collection Spoons fit this category extremely well and are priced very competitively.

    The spoons are available in silver plate at $3.50 per spoon. This price includes a gift box, federal sales tax, and shipping.

    The minimum order is 100 spoons to get a new design made up, and there is also a one-time die charge of $125.00 to help offset the cost of making the new die. Delivery time is approximately three months if a die has to be made up; subsequent orders will take four to six weeks.

    The dies for Kolapore Collection Spoons are made by master craftsmen in Schoonhoven, Holland, the silversmith capital of the world. The spoons themselves are made in Canada. As a result, the quality of the spoons is exceptional and recognized by the consumer at a glance.

    I trust that this is sufficient information. I look forward to hearing from you. If you have any questions or concerns, please don't hesitate to contact me. Thank you for your time and consideration.

Sincerely,

Adriaan Demmers
President

---

best-selling spoon in Toronto was 300 units of Casa Loma. (For a list of the major tourist sites in Toronto, see Exhibit 10.) This spoon had quickly sold out on site in 10 days. (However, the buyer had been unwilling to order more part way through the year.) Spoons with other Toronto designs were selling less than 50 units a year.

By December 1985, inventories had increased and Kolapore, Inc., was still showing a small loss (see Exhibit 11). Any gains from changes in the rate of import duty on spoons (20.3 percent in 1984 to 18.4 percent in 1986) had been negated by changes in federal sales tax (9 percent in 1984 to 11 percent

EXHIBIT 9   Kolapore Collection Spoons—Designs Available

Canada:
Deer
Elk
Caribou
Cougar
Mountain goat
Moose
Bighorn sheep
Grizzly bear
Salmon
Coast Indian
Indian
Coat of arms
Mountie
Maple leaf

Province of Ontario:
✔Trillium
✔Windsor, Ambassador Bridge
✔Sarnia, Bluewater Bridge
✔Chatham, St. Joseph's Church
✔London, Storybook Gardens
✔Woodstock, Old Town Hall
✔Stratford, swan
✔Kitchener, Schneider Haus
✔Waterloo, The Seagram Museum
✔Waterloo County, Mennonite horse and buggy
✔Elora, Mill Street
✔Guelph, Church of Our Lady
✔Guelph, Credit Union
✔Guelph, St. Joseph's Hospital
✔Kitchener-Waterloo, Oktoberfest
✔Hamilton, Dundurn Castle
✔St. Catharines, Old Court House
✔Niagara Falls, Falls, Brock Monument, and Maid of the Mist
✔Acton, Leathertown (hide with buildings)
✔Toronto, skyline
✔Toronto, City Hall
✔Toronto, St. Lawrence Hall
✔Toronto, Casa Loma
✔Kingston, City Hall
✔Ottawa, Parliament buildings
✔Collingwood, Town Hall
✔Owen Sound, City crest

University and community college crests/coats of arms:
✔Wilfrid Laurier
✔Waterloo
✔Carleton
✔Guelph

✔York
✔Western
✔Windsor
✔McMaster
✔Brock
✔Fanshawe
✔Humber

Province of Quebec:
Montreal, skyline
Montreal, Olympic Stadium

Province of Nova Scotia:
Bluenose (schooner)

Yukon Territory:
Coat of arms
Gold panner

Province of British Columbia:
Coat of arms
Prince George
Victoria, Parliament buildings
Victoria, lamp post
Victoria, Empress Hotel
Nanaimo, Bastion
Dogwood (flower)
Totem pole
Kermode Terrace
Smithers
Northlander Rogers Pass, bear
Northlander Rogers Pass, house
Kelowna, The Ogopogo
Okanagan, The Ogopogo
Vancouver, Grouse Mountain/skyride/chalet
Vancouver, Grouse Mountain skyride
Vancouver, Grouse Mountain skyride/cabin
Vancouver, Cleveland Dam
Vancouver, The Lions
Vancouver, The Lions Gate Bridge

Province of Alberta:
Banff, Mount Norquay
Banff, Mount Rundle
Banff, Banff Springs Hotel
Calgary, bronco rider
Edmonton, Klondike Mike
Wild Rose (flower)
Oil derrick
Jasper
Jasper sky tram

Note: Check mark denotes those made up on Demmers's initiative.

EXHIBIT 10   Some Major Tourist Sites in Toronto

1. Metro Zoo
2. CN Tower
3. Casa Loma
4. Royal Ontario Museum (ROM)
5. Black Creek Pioneer Village
6. Art Gallery of Ontario (AGO)
7. Canada's Wonderland
8. Ontario Place
9. The Ontario Science Centre

EXHIBIT 11   Kolapore, Inc.
Statement of Income
Eight Months* Ending November 30, 1985
(Unaudited)

Sales	$21,000
Cost of sales:	
Inventory at beginning of year	2,873
Purchases	12,000
Duty and freight	3,500
Dies	1,950
	20,323
Less: Inventory at end of year	5,000
Cost of sales	15,323
Gross profit	5,677
Expenses	6,500
Net profit (loss) for the year to date	$(823)

* Annual sales expected to be $30,000.

---

in 1986) and exchange rates. The fluctuating Dutch guilder was at a two-year high relative to the Canadian dollar. From a March 1984 value of Cdn. $0.43, the guilder had declined to $0.36 in February 1985 and climbed to $0.50 by December 1985. Partially due to these exchange fluctuations, during the past eight months, Demmers had also arranged for the spoons to be silver-plated at a cost of 40 cents each in Ontario. This had resulted in a savings of 15 cents a spoon (which varied with the exchange rate). More significantly, because many spoons were purchased as souvenirs of Canada, by adding sufficient value by silver plating in Canada, the imported product no longer had to be legally stamped, "Made in Holland." In fact, the packaging could now be marked "Made in Canada." Demmers was quite optimistic regarding the implications of this change because a number of potential store buyers had rejected his line because it did not say "Made in Canada." Demmers's supplier was upset, however, with the change.

Meanwhile, the feedback he was receiving from many of his customers was positive—in most cases they were selling more of his spoons than any other brand. Some customers, in fact, had enquired about other products. Since he had so far not experienced any competitive reactions to his spoons, Demmers was thinking of investigating the possibility of adding ashtrays, letter openers, key chains, lapel pins, and bottle openers to the product line in 1986—if he stayed in business. Each one of these products could have a crest attached to it. These crests would be the same as those used on the spoons and would thus utilize the dies to a greater extent. The landed costs per metal crest from the same supplier would be 85 cents. Demmers contemplated attaching these crests himself onto products supplied by Canadian manufacturers. However, initial investigations had revealed no obvious economical second product line.

Demmers also planned to phase out alpacca imports—all products would now be silver plated. In fact, Demmers was also wondering if he should acquire the equipment and materials in order to do this silver plating and polishing himself.

With no lack of ideas, many of the original frustrations nonetheless remained. The buyers at major chains such as Eaton's and Simpsons had changed once again, and because they did not use an automatic reorder system, new appointments had to be arranged. This was as difficult as ever. Also, Demmers still had not been able to draw anything from the firm for his efforts. These factors, coupled with his lack of cash and the demands of his new full-time position, had left Demmers uncertain as to what he should do next. With the spring buying season approaching—when Demmers would normally visit potential buyers—he realized that his decision regarding the future of Kolapore could not be postponed much longer.

APPENDIX A:
SURVEY OF SPOONS CARRIED BY LOCAL RETAILERS IN GUELPH AND KITCHENER-WATERLOO REGION

A Taste of Europe—Delicatessen & Gift Store
                Guelph Eaton Centre
    A selection of spoons from Holland with Dutch designs.
    One with the Canadian coat of arms which looked good.
    Rhodium-plated spoons—$5.98 per spoon.
    Well displayed at front of store.
Eaton's—Guelph Eaton Centre
    Breadner spoons with maple leaf or Canadian flag and "Guelph"
       stamped in the bowl.

Rhodium-plated—$4.98.

No display and hard to find.

Pequenot Jewellers—Wyndham Street, Guelph

Carry Candis spoons, which look cheap and do not sell very well. $4.98.

Poorly displayed.

Smith & Son, Jewellers—Wyndham Street, Guelph

Do not carry souvenir spoons because they are not in line with the store's image. They often get requests for them.

Franks Jewellers—King Street, Waterloo

Carry Breadner spoons with the Waterloo coat of arms.

Rhodium-plated spoons—$4.50 per spoon.

Not on display but kept in drawer.

Sell less than 12 per year.

Copper Creek—Waterloo Square Mall, Waterloo

Candis spoons—$5.00 each.

Birks—King Centre, Kitchener

Carry Oneida and Breadner spoons.

Rhodium-plated spoons for $5.98.

Onedia spoons were $8.95 and looked like a silver alloy.

Sterling silver Breadner spoons for $31.95.

Displayed in a spoon rack, looked good.

Birks regency spoons with crest of each province, $12.50.

Eaton's—Market Square, Kitchener

Breadner spoons, two types for Canada only.

Rhodium-plated—$4.98 each.

Young's Jewellers—King Street, Kitchener

Rhodium-plated Breadner spoons, $4.50 each.

Walters Jewellers

Against chain policy to carry souvenir spoons because of poor quality and low turnover.

Peoples Jewellers

Do not carry souvenir spoons.

Engels Gift Shop—King Street, Kitchener

Carry Breadner, Oneida, Gazelle, and Metropolitan.

Altogether about 20 varieties.

Well displayed near entrance of store; prices range from $2.25 for Metropolitan spoons to $7.98 for Oneida spoons.

Saleslady said they sell hundreds every year, mostly in the summer.

APPENDIX B:
TERMS CONCERNING SOUVENIR SPOONS

Crest: Emblem, either metal, plastic, or enamel, that is affixed to a standard spoon.

Picture spoon: Spoon with a picture under plastic which is heat moulded to the spoon.

Relief design: Spoon with an engraving or picture which is moulded into the metal of the spoon.

Enamel: Opaque substance similar to glass in composition.

Plated: Thin layer of metal put on by electrolysis.

Rhodium-plated: Shiny "jeweller's metal" which does not tarnish (no silver content).

Silver-plated: Silver covering on another metal (such as steel).

Sterling silver: Alloy of 92.5 percent silver and 8.5 percent copper, nickel, and zinc.

Alpacca: Alloy of 82 percent copper and 18 percent nickel.

APPENDIX C:
SOUVENIR SPOON SUPPLIERS

Name	Location	Retail Price Points	Notes
Breadner	Hull, Quebec	$4.50–$6.00 ($32.00 for Sterling)	National distribution (including catalogue). Have basic design with different crests glued on. Lots of manufacturing capability.
Candis	Willowdale, Ont.	$4.00–$6.50	Good distribution. Have wide selection but quality toward lower end.
Metropolitan	Toronto, Ont.	$1.00–$4.00	Natural distribution includes other souvenirs and novelty items. Low-end spoons.
Gazelle	Grimsby, Ont.	$6.00	Previously imported from Holland. Ontario and Canada general designs. Quality same as Breadner's low end.
Oneida	Niagara Falls, Ont.	$8.00	U.S. subsidiary. High quality but little variety.
Commemorative	Ottawa, Ont.	$7.00–$9.00	Have three basic designs (supplied by Oneida). Often deal with clubs for whom they make up custom spoons.
Parsons-Steiner	Toronto, Ont.	$2.00–$6.00	Lower quality. (Appear to be cast iron with a decal attached.)
Boma	Vancouver, B.C.	$10.00–$20.00	High-quality pewter spoons.
Aalco	Vancouver, B.C.	$2.50–$3.00	National distributor with 300 three-dimensional models of spoons. Also carry numerous other souvenir items.
Souvenir	Downsview, Ont.	$3.00	Operate across North America. Have standardized spoons with crests attached. Have a wide complementary product line.

LAKELAND MINING CORP.

In late 1992, Samuel Firestone, a member of the board of directors of Lakeland Mining Corp., had to make a delicate and difficult decision. He had witnessed extraordinary tension develop between Lakeland's CEO, Peter Sevko, and its chairman, Philip Scott. The personal conflict had forced Scott to contemplate submitting his resignation as chairman. Firestone believed Scott to be an able chairman, one who had run Lakeland's board effectively, and had thought that most if not all directors felt the same way. However, recent events suggested that Sevko's friends on the board had persuaded two influential directors that Scott's position as chairman was untenable. In total, roughly half the board now appeared to believe that the chairman could no longer carry out his job effectively. Although Firestone was not at all convinced that Scott's resignation was in the long-term best interests of the shareholders, he realized that this conflict was seriously diminishing the effective functioning of the board. Cordial discussion between the CEO and chairman had ceased, and the resultant tension was beginning to affect all board members. Firestone had to decide whom he was going to support: Scott, a long-time associate and in his view, a first-rate chairman; or Sevko, the CEO who was instrumental in making Lakeland profitable and competitive.

Lakeland Mining Corp.—Company Background

In 1983, Lakeland Mining Corp. was owned and controlled by Bofred Investment Ltd., a privately held investment company with extensive worldwide holdings in oil and gas, mining, and several manufacturing industries. Its

Jonathon D. Kovacheff prepared this case with the assistance of David S. R. Leighton and funded by the NCMRD solely to provide material for class discussion. Copyright © 1994 The University of Western Ontario.

mining investments employed 3,000 people and assets totalled $600,000,000. Corporate headquarters were situated in Toronto, Ontario, but most of Lakeland's reserves were located in Canada's northern territories.

Bofred Investment was 100 percent owned and controlled by brothers Fred and Boris Bloom. Both were primarily investment specialists, with only a limited interest in or understanding of the mining industry. Consequently, they took a hands-off approach when it came to managing their mining interests and left the bulk of that work to Lakeland's long-time chairman/CEO, Milton Howser. A geologist by trade, Howser was very comfortable running the mining business while leaving the investment and corporate governance decisions to the Bloom brothers.

In 1983, the Lakeland board consisted of eight individuals, all long-time friends and associates of the Blooms. The Blooms used their board largely as an 'advisory' committee, one which was intended to provide Lakeland with expertise regarding investment opportunities in mining. Since there were no minority shareholders, the board did not involve itself with reviewing CEO and corporate performance, or discuss corporate strategy other than in the mining business. Directors were selected because of their expertise in mining, not as managers or experts in corporate governance.

In late 1984, the board and the Blooms came to the decision that they could make a substantial profit by going public with Lakeland shares. The company was profitable and Howser had been doing a good "hands-on" job of running the company. However, Howser's title as chairman was in name only. He never presided over a board meeting and knew very little about corporate governance. Therefore, the board's first move before going public was to place a high-profile individual from the private sector in the chairman's seat and to make Howser president and CEO.

Thus, in early 1985, Philip Scott, 38, was appointed as the new chairman of the company. Scott was a graduate in business and in law with considerable practical experience in family business. He seemed the ideal candidate for the job.

In March 1985, the bulk of Lakeland's preferred and common shares were sold to the public, with the idea that the company would become a widely held corporation. In fact, the Blooms were able to divest themselves of all their shares within two years. Many of the buyers were large institutions, including public and private sector pension funds and several large mutual funds. During this time, the board composition changed dramatically. The old advisory board was transformed into a formal board staffed with individuals who had experience serving on boards of publicly traded companies. Milt Howser continued as president and CEO.

During Philip Scott's first three years as chairman, Lakeland grew substantially. The company was doing so well that by 1989, production of base metals had increased by 30 percent while gold production had tripled.

However, after the share issue, Scott gradually came to the conclusion that Howser was not comfortable making decisions as the leader of a publicly traded company. Howser, it seemed, felt much more at ease when he had to report to only two owners. He wasn't comfortable dealing with the needs of minority shareholders or with a board of directors. In December of 1988, after discussion with Scott and the rest of the board, Howser tendered his resignation. The board was now required to hire a CEO. After considering several candidates, the board decided that Peter Sevko, a current board member, would become the new CEO.

Peter Sevko—CEO of Lakeland Mining

In January 1989, Peter Sevko began his job as president and CEO of Lakeland. A trained engineer and MBA, Sevko had considerable experience in the oil industry. He had a reputation as a first-rate deal maker who was aggressive, smart, and competent. The son of poor immigrants, Sevko had always considered himself to be a "self-made man," one whose success depended on working long hours and putting the company before family and friends. He was not beyond bullying and manipulation and was in many respects a very tough CEO. He had very little time for any individual who, in his words, was "born with a silver spoon in his mouth." He had been a strong and forceful board member, and his business credentials as CEO of a smaller independent were excellent. The board thought he was the ideal man to run Lakeland.

Sevko wasted no time making changes at Lakeland. He began his tenure as CEO by "cleaning house." He fired and replaced several executives he described as incompetent, and increased company assets by several acquisitions. With these acquisitions, Sevko had increased Lakeland's total assets to over $3 billion.

Within two years of taking over as CEO, Sevko had proven himself an excellent deal maker and exemplary performer. Share value was sharply up, and the board was very pleased with Lakeland's overall performance. In fact, the company had done so well that its performance had been highlighted in several national periodicals (see Exhibit 1 for a five-year financial performance table).

Philip Scott—Chairman of the Board

Philip Scott was the son of a prominent Ontario businessman who had been active in federal politics. He had been educated at some of North America's finest institutions and after graduating with a BA in business and a law degree, had joined the family business. During this time he became closely associated with a leading political party.

His appointment as chairman of Lakeland in 1985 had represented a considerable personal challenge. As a first-time chairman, Scott's initial years on the job had been filled with learning experiences. He did extensive reading

Exhibit 1　Five-Year Summary of Financial Information
(millions of dollars except per share amounts)

	Financial Position				
	1991	*1990*	*1989*	*1988*	*1987*
Cash	$ —	$ —	$ 7.3	$ 47.3	$ 73.6
Working capital	(36.0)	(64.6)	25.6	54.2	98.4
Property and equipment	3,618.5	3,478.6	3,096.0	1,802.1	934.3
Total assets	3.985.2	3,765.5	3,246.9	1,743.4	1,154.2
Long-term debt	1,549.6	1,354.3	1,298.9	604.7	45.0
Deferred revenue and other liabilities	191.3	15.7	21.7	1.7	66.1
Shareholder equity	2,267.8	2,523.3	1,987.3	1,287.4	1,009.6
Revenue	961.1	1,004.8	665.4	346.7	352.1
Royalty expense	(178.2)	(192.5)	(102.5)	(60.1)	(75.6)
Operating expense	(255.3)	(212.2)	(156.6)	(107.6)	(78.9)
Depreciation	(366.2)	(296.4)	(222.3)	(132.0)	(89.9)
General and administrative	(101.4)	(72.5)	(59.3)	(44.7)	(33.0)
Interest	(112.7)	(121.3)	(62.1)	(30.0)	(0.3)
Deferred income taxes	(1.8)	(48.0)	—	—	(32.7)
Capital and other taxes	(16.1)	(21.6)	(10.2)	(3.3)	(1.2)
Earnings before extra items	(67.4)	42.4	22.3	(25.6)	39.9
	—	—	76.8	—	27.9
Extraordinary items	(67.4)	42.4	99.1	(25.6)	67.8
Earnings	—	(5.1)	(16.5)	(16.5)	(16.5)
Dividends					
Average shares					
- basic	181.9	175.3	149.3	113.0	67.2
- diluted	210.6	205.3	171.8	154.7	101.3
Earnings per share	($ 1.02)	$ .63	$ 1.92	$ 1.23	$ 2.28
Cash flow per share					
- basic	$ 4.23	$ 6.18	$ 5.12	$ 2.52	$ 6.45
- diluted	4.21	6.00	4.68	2.52	5.40

in the area of corporate governance and studied the boardroom behaviour of several of the more senior Lakeland board members.

By 1988, Scott believed he had become a more experienced and effective chairman. He took a more proactive role in managing the affairs of the corporation and the board. For instance, Scott was actively involved in selecting new board members and corporate executives. Also, he continuously and objectively monitored CEO and individual director performance and was always consulted by management whenever strategic plans were initiated.

Although he felt the board was effective already, he decided to implement several initiatives to further improve board performance. He believed that a forum was needed in which board members and company executives could meet periodically to review the board's performance and to discuss the more complicated corporate governance and strategic issues affecting Lakeland.

Scott did not see the regular quarterly board meetings as the appropriate forum for these discussions. Therefore, he organized an annual weekend retreat where directors were encouraged to communicate frankly with one another and to discuss possible solutions to important corporate problems. The two-day retreat was structured so that one day was spent discussing the company's corporate strategy and planning, and the other was spent discussing governance-related issues.

Scott felt that the second day of the retreat became the real focal point of the weekend as it was used to educate board members on a number of important board-related issues. The day began with the corporate legal counsel's review of relevant legal and legislative issues regarding such issues as environmental legislation and director liability. Next, directors were encouraged to put forward their concerns regarding the manner in which board meetings were run. They were asked to present suggestions as to how to improve the effectiveness or efficiency of the meetings. Scott also felt it was very important to determine whether each member was getting a chance to express himself or herself during board meetings. Therefore, he elicited advice about the improvement of board communication.

If time permitted, Scott would summarize any new scholarly work on corporate governance. Often, a discussion followed his summary of the work. Every second year, board committee chairmen would reconsider their mandates. All board members were invited to discuss ways in which the two existing committees could be improved and whether to constitute new committees (see Exhibit 2 for committee membership). Members were also encouraged to discuss issues such as director selection and recruitment. As a direct result of these discussions, selection of new directors was to become more formal and systematic.

Other Key Lakeland Board Members—1990

By 1990, several Lakeland directors were playing more prominent roles during and between board meetings. Because of a combination of broad business experience and knowledge, or their close association with the CEO or chairman, these individuals carried considerably more weight than did other directors. The directors who had considerable influence on the board due to their experience and expertise were Steven Smith, Tom McCoy, Frank Jones, Samuel Firestone, and Lee Coxon (see Exhibit 2).

Steve Smith, 52 years of age and a lawyer, had been president of Smith Minerals Co. Ltd., and had become a director when his company had been acquired by Lakeland. He was a highly "political" and charming individual who had befriended Sevko soon after his own appointment to the Lakeland board in early 1989. Tom McCoy, 61, was a very experienced management consultant who added a considerable know-how to the Lakeland board. He was a knowledgeable director who had been appointed to Lakeland's board

EXHIBIT 2   Directors (1992)

The name, age, municipality of residence, position held with Lakeland, date of appointment, and principal occupation of each of the directors are set forth below:

Name, Age, and Municipality of Residence	*Position Held with Lakeland*	*Date of Appointment to Board*	*Principal Occupation*
Philip C. Scott* (45) Toronto, Ont.	Chairman and Director	February 10, 1985	President Sun Management
Frank G. Jones* (55) Toronto, Ont.	Director	May 30, 1985	President Sapphire Inc.
Thomas B. McCoy* (61) Calgary, Alt.	Director	January 20, 1986	Management consultant
Peter H. Sevko (52) Toronto, Ont.	President, CEO and Director	January 2, 1987	President and CEO Lakeland Mining Corp.
Lee Coxon** (64) Oakville, Ont.	Director	October 23, 1986	President Time Management
Steven W. Smith** (52) Toronto, Ont.	Director	March 14, 1989	President and CEO Smith Minerals
Mary P. Chapman (53) Toronto, Ont.	Director	May 17, 1990	Dean Business Admin. Univ. of Toronto
Samuel Firestone (60) Toronto, Ont.	Director	November 23, 1987	Chairman Realcorp. Ltd.
Anthony Brier (56) Calgary, Alt.	Director	May 14, 1990	President Investco Ltd.
Lyle Walkerton (51) Toronto, Ont.	Director	May 14, 1990	Director Lyle Securities
Paul S. Twibble (60) St. Catharines, Ont.	Director	June 12, 1991	Independent management consultant
Peter W. Munch (48) London, Ont.	Director	June 12, 1991	CEO Mace Electric Ltd.

* Member of Executive Committee
** Member of Audit Committee

in 1986 because of his previous involvement with several mining ventures. McCoy enjoyed Smith's company. The two became good friends and, together, developed a close relationship with the CEO, frequently golfing or going on vacation together.

Jones, Firestone, and Coxon were all senior business leaders with considerable board experience. Of these three, Frank Jones, age 55, had the longest tenure on the board, having been appointed in 1985. In 1987, Sam Firestone, age 60, had been recruited by Scott to serve on the board. At age 64, Lee Coxon was the oldest director on Lakeland's board and had served as a member since 1986. These directors, and especially Firestone, did not build particularly close personal relationships with senior company executives or the CEO. They assumed that evaluation of corporate and, therefore, executive performance would be more valid if not complicated by close personal friendships. Therefore, they kept a "safe" personal distance from management, preferring to deal with them at arm's length. Nevertheless, all three maintained good but professional working relationships with both Sevko and Scott.

Philip Scott and Peter Sevko—1991

Following the public issue of shares, Scott and Sevko developed a productive and congenial working relationship. As Scott told Firestone in late 1988, "While Peter and I have never been the best of friends, we often meet to discuss corporate objectives and problems, and have been able to communicate effectively. There seems to be a mutual respect for each other. We understand our respective roles in the corporate structure: the CEO initiates corporate policy and runs the day-to-day operations of the company, while I evaluate overall corporate strategy and maintain the integrity of the board. All things considered, we seem to work well together."

However, around Thanksgiving of 1991 all this seemed to change. Sevko was "riding high" after a very positive *Globe and Mail* article had been written about him and the company. The article suggested that Sevko was the prime reason for a dramatic rise in Lakeland stock value. In fact, when Sevko took over in 1989 the stock was selling at $15.50 a share. As of late 1991, the stock was trading at $33.

Around this time, Scott approached Samuel Firestone after a board meeting and asked to speak with him in private. Scott seemed nonplussed. He told Firestone,

> Sevko's opinion of me seems to have changed dramatically over the last few months. He's made several unilateral decisions that have really altered our relationship. He has stopped phoning or communicating with me in any way and, at the same time he stopped submitting his expenses for my approval. He's always submitted his expenses to me, as we both thought that was the best way to maintain a semblance of accountability. He must be really ticked off about the concern I showed over an extravagant expense bill he submitted. Who wouldn't have been upset with *one* dinner that's going to cost the company nearly $700!
>
> I should've known something was up when Frank Jones pulled me aside last month and told me that he had picked up a few signals about the changing attitude of our CEO. While Frank shared those with me, in my excitement about the progress of Lakeland and the performance of our president, frankly I disregarded this advice and defended Sevko. My first sign should have been the announcement that Sevko had been appointed as a director of Fraser Development Ltd. without

the knowledge of anybody on the board. Although there's no company policy against our CEO sitting on other boards, it's important for me know how and where Sevko is spending his time. He should at least have told someone about it. That was a harbinger of things to come.

The latest issue to arise concerns my own expenses. Sevko had his secretary, Kathy, call me about one of my expenses. To date he had given no impression that he reviewed and approved my expenses. I explained to Kathy that there was a process in place whereby my expenses are paid and then reviewed in detail by the audit committee at the end of the year. Her reply was that Peter reviews them. Rather than persisting with her, as she is obviously taking direction from Peter, I let this matter stand down and hope that the audit committee will clarify the issue of expense approval.

I am also wondering whether Peter is unhappy with the recognition he is receiving from the board. After his first year, we rewarded him with a $60,000 cash bonus. That summer his salary was increased by more than 15 percent, and for that reason there was no cash bonus at the end of the year, which by coincidence seems to correspond to his recent change of attitude. He has been awarded substantial stock options, and while Peter has exercised his first three grants of options, for what must be a before tax gain of at least $2.1 million, financial reward through stock options is evidently not the same as specific recognition by the board for outstanding performance.

Firestone listened carefully, and he and Scott chatted about some other corporate business before concluding their meeting.

In early 1992, after several months of having only cursory contact with Sevko, Scott decided that he had had enough of the "cold-shoulder" treatment. He confronted the CEO in his office and asked, "So what exactly is your problem?" According to Scott, Sevko just unloaded. He vociferously told the chairman:

I don't think I can work with you any longer. The company and I have outgrown you. You're just a lightweight who likes being chairman for ego gratification. You love the fluff and perks; the fancy meals and clothes and trips. You know nothing about running a corporation and even less about the mining business. The only reason you even have this job is because you come from a powerful family with all the right connections. You were born with a silver spoon in your mouth and have no idea how much effort it takes to run this company. You're starting to get in my way and I'm becoming more interested in applying for your job every day.

Sevko's outburst represented an intense personal attack, with no reference being made to professional incompatibility or strategic conflicts.

Scott was stunned. After speaking individually with several directors, he went to the other executive committee members (i.e., Frank Jones and Tom McCoy) and to Samuel Firestone to explain what had happened, and to get some advice as to how to respond. He asked them whether they had trouble with him as chairman. He was unequivocally endorsed by all three directors. Scott then stated that if the board believed that he was truly a "lightweight" then, "I'll leave as chairman."

After hearing Scott's account of the confrontation, Firestone realized something constructive had to be done. He approached McCoy and Jones and explained that, in his view, allowing this kind of situation to fester would be terrible for the company. Firestone and McCoy endorsed Jones's suggestion that a special committee be appointed to review corporate governance at Lakeland, and a presentation of committee findings be made at the annual summer retreat. Other board members were not to be told that such a committee was being formed.

Firestone advanced the group's proposal to Scott. The chairman considered their suggestion and, not without some serious reservations, finally agreed that a special committee should be formed. Thus, an "informal" special committee reviewing corporate governance was struck with Samuel Firestone, Frank Jones, and Lee Coxon as members.

Special Events Leading to Scott's Proposed Resignation

March 1992—The special committee reviewing corporate governance asked both the chairman and CEO to write memos outlining individual views on their current difficulties. Sevko refused to comply, saying only that he needed a "bigger company guy" than Scott. He was not willing to expand on this. Scott, on the other hand, complied and explained his views in a detailed memo.

May 1992—After consulting with Sevko, the committee told Scott that the CEO did not want to have anything to do with him. Scott was told to "stay out of the CEO's way" because Sevko wanted no more than superficial interaction to take place between the two men.

June 1992—The board went on its annual retreat. The special committee met with both men and told them that they had to work out their differences. Unfortunately, Sevko was not willing to meet with Scott to discuss their problems. In fact, although he started to submit his expenses to the chairman again, he carried on as though the special committee had never been struck. Sevko was condescending to Scott at board meetings, interrupting often and not listening to his opinions. He never spoke directly to him and refused to relate information concerning meetings with important corporate clients. In all ways, the CEO responded as if the chairman were irrelevant.

August 1992—By late summer 1992, Scott had chaired several annual shareholder meetings and was quite cognizant of the proper protocol. At each of these meetings Scott addressed the shareholders first, by speaking globally about the company and its objectives. He would then introduce the CEO. Then, after the CEO had finished talking more specifically about the company, the chairman would return to answer any questions from the floor.

However, this year things were different. After completing his presentation, Sevko told the audience that the CEO would be answering all questions concerning Lakeland's performance this year. Scott and several board members were appalled. Only then had he realized that unlike all preceding annual meetings, he had not been provided with a microphone from which he could answer any questions addressed to him. He perceived this as a deliberate attack on his authority. Without discussion or board approval, the CEO was taking over the responsibilities of the chairman.

September 1992—Lee Coxon submitted his resignation from the board. Although Coxon did not formally state his reasons, Firestone knew that he was resigning because he was totally discouraged about the direction in which Lakeland and its board had been going. He did not want to be part of such a destructive process and felt powerless to stop it. Firestone was beginning to feel the same way.

The board was faced with the task of finding a replacement for an extremely competent outside director. The problem was, however, Lakeland did not have a formal recruiting or selection process in place. Lakeland did not have a nominating committee and director selection had always been the responsibility of the executive committee. Philip Scott, Frank Jones, and Tom McCoy sat on this committee.

Sevko did not want the presently constituted executive committee to have a say in the selection of new directors. More importantly, he did not want Scott to have any say in the selection of Coxon's replacement because he had been very unhappy when Scott had recruited Firestone in 1987. Sevko thought Firestone was becoming far too "proactive" as a director. In the CEO's view, Firestone was starting to get involved in too many issues that were none of his business, including paying far too much attention to his relationship with Scott. On the other hand, in Scott's view, Firestone was a very competent and ethical director who was carrying out his responsibilities to enhance shareholder value.

The issue, therefore, became who was going to have control over the nominating process. The chairman was fearful that if the CEO became too involved, he would be able to "stack" the board with his friends. Scott did not think that directors should be exclusively or even largely selected by the CEO because any director so chosen would have difficulty making truly independent judgments about the CEO's decisions. In fact, the two individuals that Sevko suggested for the vacant position were, in Scott's opinion, highly undesirable and of dubious reputation. Neither had any board experience or knew anything about the mining industry. Sevko, he believed, wanted them on the board so that he wouldn't have to worry about board support, something which he felt should be automatic. Scott didn't want them on the board because he thought that neither could add lustre to the company's reputation or evaluate objectively Sevko's performance as CEO.

Therefore, at the fall executive committee meeting attended by Scott, McCoy, and Jones, the chairman asserted that it was time for Lakeland to put a proper selection procedure into place. He suggested that the most reasonable way to do so was to form a nominating committee with the mandate to recruit and nominate individuals for selection to the board. He went on to state that neither the CEO nor the chairman should be allowed to sit on the new committee so as to minimize pressure to select friends or supporters of either individual.

The next day, after hearing of Scott's proposal, Sevko hit the roof. He let both Jones and McCoy know in no uncertain terms that he would not accept the formation of a nominating committee unless he was a member. When Jones and McCoy did not push him on the matter, the whole idea of a nominating committee was dropped.

Consequently, the executive committee and the CEO, without informing Scott of their intentions, began the search for a new director. The chairman was still a member of the executive committee, but Jones, McCoy, and the CEO had decided to exclude him from the process.

Late September 1992—The chairman was told that Sevko was very upset with him. Sevko had discovered that, in the spring, Scott had gone independently to other board members in order to discuss the difficulties the two were having. The CEO reportedly took this action as a personal insult and was going to make Scott "pay for it."

At the same time, McCoy and Smith had been selected to sit on another board. Smith was very close to Sevko and showed the same disregard for the chairman. Smith knew that to get Scott replaced he would have to convince executive committee members, McCoy and Jones, that Scott was not worthy of their backing. Therefore, while attending these other board meetings, Smith told McCoy that if the chairman wasn't fired, Sevko was going to resign. McCoy was in a quandary. He had always supported the chairman and believed he was doing a first-rate job. But Smith was persuasive and was his friend. And Sevko was very important to the company. McCoy was very reluctantly convinced that his support of the CEO was more important. McCoy agreed that, forced to make this choice, the chairman would have to go.

October 1992—Smith knew that convincing McCoy was not enough. He had to persuade Jones, the other executive committee member, that Scott should be asked to leave. Jones was not as easily convinced as McCoy, as he had always supported Scott's work as chairman and was a close friend of neither Smith nor Sevko. In order to convince Jones, Smith explained that the chairman and Sevko were barely speaking, and this was neither conducive for a well functioning board nor in the long-term best interest of the company. After much deliberation, Jones agreed and decided to support Smith's position.

November 1992—Scott had been considering his role and position in the company for several months. He realized that his hold on the chairmanship was tenuous at best. The CEO had been successful at usurping the chairman's role on several occasions. Scott had also learned that Steve Smith was working behind the scenes in support of Sevko's position. He decided to call a board meeting for November 23, 1992, so that he could speak to each director individually to discern where each stood on the issue of his chairmanship. He approached Samuel Firestone to enlist his support. He told Firestone that he was especially interested in speaking with Frank Jones, as he did not as yet know Jones's position.

After a dinner attended by all directors, held the night before the formal meeting, Firestone, Scott, and Jones informally met to discuss the important governance crisis at Lakeland. Scott and Firestone were shocked to discover how adamantly Jones supported Sevko. No matter how hard Scott tried, he could not get Jones to waver in his backing of the CEO. After speaking to several other members, Scott saw how effective Smith had been in garnering support for Sevko. Scott also discovered that the CEO had told Jones that he would resign if Scott stayed on as chairman. After counting heads, Scott discovered that only four directors supported him, while four were decidedly against him, and two had apparently not yet determined their attitudes.

Scott realized that his position as chairman was in serious jeopardy. He had never realized that Sevko and Smith had been lobbying against him with such vehemence. He knew that if the situation continued any longer, Lakeland would suffer.

The next day, Scott decided to outline a proposition to Firestone. He proposed to submit his resignation as chairman in exchange for the formation of a proper nominating committee. Scott also suggested that the nominating committee control the selection and appraisal of directors, chairman, and CEO, and that the CEO should not be a member of the committee.

Samuel Firestone had to make a difficult decision. As a member of the board of directors of Lakeland, he had witnessed the tension develop between Peter Sevko and Philip Scott. Firestone believed in Scott's ability to run the board effectively and did not believe it was in the company's best interest or the long-term interests of the shareholders to accept the chairman's resignation. He also realized that Scott's mandate as chairman was dubious and his hold on the position tenuous. Some directors now believed that the chairman could no longer carry out his job effectively. He understood only too well that the personal conflict between the two most important company officers was deeply affecting the effective functioning of the board.

However, his main concern involved Scott's final proposal to exchange his resignation for a nominating committee. Without Firestone's support, the proposal was doomed to fail. But Firestone did not know whether supporting such a swap was a sound management decision. He had to think through his options and decide what he was going to do.

MAGNA
INTERNATIONAL
AND NAFTA

"Government must attract successful business people with a social conscience who have the capability and commitment to improve the living standards for all citizens."

Frank Stronach, *CEO of Magna International,* on his decision to run for the Canadian Parliament in 1988

"To be in business, your first mandate is to make money, and money has no heart, soul, conscience, homeland."

Frank Stronach, *Chairman of Magna International,* quoted in *Newsday* August 7, 1992

"We're a Canadian company with a European heritage," said Fred Jaekel, President and Chief Operating Officer of Cosma International, the second largest of Magna International's four Automotive Systems Groups.

> Most of Magna's plants are in Ontario. Half our General Managers are originally from Germany or Austria. But the geography of the auto industry is changing. As a supplier to the industry, we need to make sure we understand these changes and make the right investments—without repeating the mistakes we made in the 1980s.

Like Magna's chairman Frank Stronach, Fred Jaekel was a tool and die maker by trade. Although he grew up in Argentina, Jaekel was born in

Copyright © 1994 by the Sloan School of Management, MIT. This case was prepared by Tony Frost, Doctoral Candidate, International Management, and Ann Frost, Doctoral Candidate, Industrial Relations, both Sloan School of Management, MIT. It is intended for classroom use and may be reproduced without permission. Financial support was provided by the Business Fund for Canadian Studies in the U.S., and is gratefully acknowledged. Thanks to Rose Batt, Mauro Guillen, Don Lessard, Gil Preuss, and Eleanor Westney for valuable comments.

Germany and had returned there at the age of 19 to undertake an apprenticeship. Several years later a vacation brought him to Canada and he decided to stay.

Now an 11-year veteran of Magna, Jaekel and several executives at Cosma were meeting to discuss the preparation of their long-term business plan, "Year 2000: Paving the Road." A central item on the agenda was the recent signing of the North American Free Trade Agreement (NAFTA) by the governments of Canada, the United States, and Mexico. In the wake of the heated political battles that had eventually led to NAFTA's ratification in the three countries, Jaekel's team was trying to understand what the agreement meant for Cosma, which specialized in steel stampings for automotive frames and parts.

Would the further integration of 85 million Mexican consumers into the regional economy provide a key source of long-term growth? Would Mexican wage rates, in some cases less than one-tenth of those in the U.S. and Canada, spur a massive southward shift in production by Cosma's customers and competitors? And how would other changes brought about by NAFTA—in local content rules, for example—affect the industry and Cosma's growth strategy? Answers to these questions would form an important part of Cosma's business plan that Jaekel was due to present to Frank Stronach and Magna's executive management. The first task was to sketch out Cosma's most realistic alternative strategies. From there, Jaekel would have to decide on a course of action that would carry Cosma through to the turn of the century.

Magna International

Origins and Growth

In 1954, Frank Stronach, Magna International's mercurial and charismatic chairman, arrived in Canada from his native Austria with little more than his skills as a tool and die maker. Three years later, at the age of 25, Stronach founded the company that would eventually make him a wealthy man, using a Cdn.$2,000 bank overdraft to buy a few basic tools. Over the next three decades, the company grew at an exceptional pace, driven by the energies of the young, competitive, and entrepreneurial group of expatriate Austrian and German tool and die makers Stronach attracted to work with him.

By 1992, the company had developed a reputation as one of the premier suppliers of automotive components and systems in North America, ranking fourth in auto parts sales behind only the components divisions of GM and Ford, and Du Pont Automotive. Its 68 plants produced over 5,000 different parts (the broadest range of any independent supplier in the industry), employed 15,000 people, and generated over Cdn.$2.4 billion in sales. Exhibit 1 summarizes Magna's financial performance since 1984.

EXHIBIT 1   Magna Financial Review 1984–1993 (Millions of Cdn$)

	1992	*1991*	*1990*	*1989*	*1988*	*1987*	*1986*	*1985*	*1984*
Operations Data									
Sales	2,359	2,017	1,927	1,924	1,459	1,152	1028	690	494
Cost of goods sold	1,885	1,622	1,567	1,535	1,133	886	789	524	370
SG&A	156	154	203	204	179	125	101	74	45
Interest expense	50	82	86	73	50	28	15	4	5
Taxes	50	27	24	23	13	28	39	30	26
Net income	98	17	(224)	34	20	40	47	38	29
Balances									
Current assets	500	486	740	601	550	356	293	258	177
Fixed assets	752	841	918	1101	1000	881	590	359	180
Current liabilities	407	472	1363	545	496	298	225	194	97
Long-term debt	81	381	NA	589	518	370	280	104	97
Convertible	165	201	NA	96	98	100			
Shareholders equity	590	268	231	464	446	449	346	295	149
Other Information									
Employees	14,500	15,000	16,900	17,500	15,000	12,000	10,300	7,500	5,800
% Sales from Canadian operations	67	70	75	80	81	86	85	86	88
Sales per NA auto produced (Can$)	190	173	NA	NA	NA	NA	66	44	38
Number of divisions	68	71	112	126	120	107	85	70	NA

Organization

Frank Stronach's personal stamp was visible on virtually every aspect of Magna's operations, from the technical sophistication of the company's products and manufacturing processes to the extreme decentralization of its organizational structure. Stronach had even given a name to the set of ideas that guided his approach to business: Fair Enterprise. Enshrined in Magna's Corporate Constitution (Exhibit 2), Fair Enterprise aimed to motivate employees—both workers and managers—through equity and profit-sharing incentives, at the same time that it kept greed in check by limiting management's share of company profits to a fixed 6 percent and allocating up to 2 percent to charities and societal institutions. Central to Stronach's philosophy were the principles of individual autonomy and entrepreneurialism, both of which were encouraged through an organizational structure that kept divisions small (most were less than 200 employees) and pushed responsibility and accountability to the lowest possible level.

Each of the company's 68 plants—known as *divisions* inside Magna—was separately incorporated and run as a profit center by a General Manager (GM) who was rewarded based on divisional performance. Within broad company guidelines, GMs had discretion over most aspects of their business, from hiring and pay standards to decisions about which contracts the division

---

EXHIBIT 2   Magna's Corporate Constitution

Board of Directors
Magna believes that outside directors provide independent counsel and discipline. A majority
of Magna's Board of Directors will be outsiders.

Employee Equity and Profit Participation
Ten percent of Magna's profit before tax will be allocated to employees. These funds will be
used for the purchase of Magna shares in trust for employees and for cash distributions to
employees, recognizing both performance and length of service.

Shareholder Profit Participation
Magna will distribute, on average, 20 percent of its annual net profit to shareholders.

Management Profit Participation
In order to obtain a long-term contractual commitment from management, the Company
provides a compensation arrangement which, in addition to a base salary comparable to
industry standards, allows for the distribution to corporate management of up to 6 percent
of Magna's profit before tax.

Research and Technology Development
Magna will allocate 7 percent of its profit before tax for research and technology development
to ensure long-term viability of the Company.

Social Responsibility
The Company will contribute a maximum of 2 percent of its profit before tax to charitable,
cultural, educational, and political institutions to support the basic fabric of society.

Minimum Profit Performance
Management has an obligation to produce a profit. If Magna does not generate a minimum
after-tax return of 4 percent on share capital for two consecutive years, Class A
shareholders, voting as a Class, will have the right to elect additional directors.

Major Investments
In the event that more than 20 percent of Magna's equity is to be committed to a new
unrelated business, Class A and Class B shareholders will have the right to approve such an
investment with each class voting separately.

Constitutional Amendments
Any change to Magna's Corporate Constitution will require the approval of the Class A and
Class B shareholders with each class voting separately.

---

would compete for. The decentralized structure and the small unit size not
only fostered interpersonal communication and a sense of ownership among
employees, but it also encouraged competition between Magna's divisions.

Magna's divisions were clustered into four "Automotive Systems Groups"
according to their technical and product specializations: Atoma (doors, interi-
ors, and electronics); Cosma (metal stamping, rust proofing, and sunroofs);
Decoma (plastics and trim); and Tesma (engines and transmissions). Exhibit
3 provides a list of the four groups' product lines. Each group had its own

EXHIBIT 3 Magna's Product Lines by Automotive System Group

Seating Systems

Modular Seat Assemblies
Seat Adjusters
Seat Frames
Seat Risers
Headrest & Armrest Supports
Release Handles
Molded Seat Cushions
Integrated Child Safety Seat

Panel Systems

Interior Panels
Wood and Polyurethane Substrates
Sunroof Sunshades

Electronics

Interior Lamp Assemblies
Switch Plate Assemblies
Integrated Alarm and Control Modules
ICAM
Audible Alarms
Printed Circuit Board Assemblies
PRNDL—Modules
Switches
ABS-Coil Assemblies
Fuel Sender Assemblies

Door Systems

Door Hinges Stamped, Cast and Profile
Door, Hood & Deck Latches
Door Checkers
Release Cables
Door Strikers
Mirror Assemblies
Manual/Power and Breakaway
Cable and Padded Remote Mirrors
Mirror Remote Controls
Window Regulators
Manual, Power and Cable

Hardware

Modular Door Assemblies
Fuel Filler Doors
Pedal Assemblies
Parking Brake Assemblies
Shift Selectors
Headlamp Assemblies
Vehicle Emblems
Stamped Parts

Chassis Stampings

Crossmember Assemblies
Engine Compartment Panels
Floor Pans
Radiator Supports
Shock Towers
Transmission Supports

General Stampings

Armrest Supports
Seat Belt Anchor Plates
Instrument Panel Supports

Bumper Stampings

Aluminum Impact Bars
High-Tensile Steel Impact Beams
Stamped and Roll-Formed Bumper Beams

Engine and Brake Related Stampings

Oil Strainers
Oil Pans
Heat Shields
Water Pumps
Brake Backing Plates
Master Cylinder Vacuum Shells

Body Sheet Metal

Body Side Assemblies
Door Assemblies
Hood & Deck Assemblies
Roof Panels
Rear Quarter Panels
Medium/Large Stamping Dies

Sunroofs

Large Stamping Dies
Electric Sliding and Tilting
Electric Spoiler
Manual Sliding
Pop Up

Finishing

E-Coating

Decoma Plastics

Complete Bumper Systems
Vertical and Horizontal Body Panels
Hard Tops and Roof Systems
Complete Body Dress-Up Kits
Airdams
Body Cladding
Clear Hard-Coated Glazing Panels

Grilles
Headlamp Lenses
Rocker Panels
Spoilers
Bumper Beams
Energy Absorbers
Acrylic Backlites

Decoma Trim

Complete Body Trim Systems
Body Front, Rear and Side Mouldings
Bright Metal Mouldings
Bumper Guards
Co-Extruded PVC and EPDM Mouldings
Door/Window Channels
Fuel Tank Straps

Headlamp Bezels
Headlamp Retainers
Rocker Panel Mouldings
Scuff Plates
Tail Light Bezels
Wheel House Opening Mouldings
Roof Drip Mouldings
Dynamic Sealing Systems

Engine

Air Conditioning Clutch Rotor Assemblies
Automatic Belt Tensioners
Engine Timing Belt Tensioners and Sprockets
Flywheels
Heat Shields
Idler Pulleys
Aluminum Pulleys
Alternator Pulleys

Timing Gears
Oil Pickup Tubes
Plastic Pulleys
Poly-V Pulleys
Starter Ring Gears
Timing Chain Covers
Torsional Isolators/ Decouplers
Torsional Vibration Dampers
Water Pump Accessories

Transmission

Clutch Housings and Hubs
Clutch Pistons
Stamped Covers and Housings

Systems

Automatic Belt Tensioner Systems
Front End Accessory Drive Systems
Timing Belt Systems
Clutch Pack Assemblies

Other Products

Aluminum Die Castings
Collapsible Drive Shafts
Fine Blanked Components

technical sales force and product development engineers located in Detroit, as well as its own management team, all of whom provided technical and commercial guidance to the divisions. Group sales engineers also had dotted line responsibility to corporate marketing to ensure a coordinated approach to Magna's customers and to provide headquarters with important information about industry trends and changes in OEMs'[1] product and process strategies.

Staff at Magna's corporate headquarters was also kept to a bare bones minimum, again reflecting Stronach's philosophy and the company's steadfast aversion to bureaucracy: only about 70 people, mostly in legal, accounting, and human resource functions, worked out of Magna's headquarters in Ontario. There were also about a dozen executives at corporate headquarters who coordinated activities across groups, raised and allocated capital, and analyzed industry trends and growth opportunities. The long-term and strategic plans developed by the executive management team were utilized by the groups in the development of their own business plans. Recently, the company had also established a centralized purchasing function to leverage Magna's corporatewide buying power. A purchasing director negotiated pricing agreements with suppliers of commodities such as steel, plastics, and lubricating oils, the terms of which were made available to each of the divisions, regardless of its size, input requirements, or location.

Human Resources

Magna employed a range of skilled and semi-skilled employees within its divisions. Each division typically employed two or three engineers who solved problems on the shop floor and interfaced with group engineers in Detroit over design and quality issues. Magna placed a great deal of emphasis on shop floor quality and productivity, and virtually all of its GMs and AGMs had at one time worked on the production line at a Magna division. Many GMs and AGMs were, in fact, skilled tool and die makers, and it was well understood that the path to management lay in the acquisition and development of solid technical skills. In 1991, the company employed over 1,600 skilled tradespeople, and an additional 300 were completing apprenticeships as tool and die makers in various Magna divisions.

Operators of the actual machines used on the shop floor came from diverse backgrounds and were generally less skilled, although Magna trained many of these workers in continuous improvement techniques such as SPC and team problem solving. Average hourly wage rates for shop floor employees were around U.S.$10 in 1992. In addition to the Corporate Constitution, Magna had also developed an Employee Charter of Rights, which laid out a set of principles regarding safety, training and assistance, and employment equity that Magna strove to uphold. These principles were supported in prac-

---

[1] OEM stands for *original equipment manufacturers,* and refers to auto assemblers, such as the Big Three, Toyota, and BMW.

tice by a number of different programs and procedures, such as a toll-free hotline that could be used by employees to lodge complaints, and a grievance process that provided for a binding vote by a panel of workers and management—with workers forming the panel majority.

Magna's human resource practices, along with its extremely decentralized structure, served an additional purpose: they helped to preserve the company's non-union status. Magna believed small divisions were less tempting targets for union organizing, and, further, that they fostered the development of close personal relationships between employees and management, an outcome that significantly reduced the likelihood of successful union organizing drives.

Strategy

Magna positioned itself as a full-line supplier to the automotive industry. Through its four systems groups, the company claimed it had the capability to develop an entire car from concept to clay model to full prototype. In 1989, *Automotive News* even reported that Magna was designing *and* assembling small lots of Lamborghinis for Chrysler, which had taken over the marque in the mid-1980s. Although several Magna executives saw design and development of niche cars as a potential growth area, the bulk of Magna's business came from supplying integrated modules and systems—bumper systems, seating systems, vehicle frames—to OEMs.

Central to the company's strategy was an emphasis on innovation, which provided a critical source of competitive differentiation. Several of Magna's product innovations, such as its integrated child safety seat (co-developed with Chrysler), door intrusion beams, and electronic sunroof, had enabled Magna to carve out distinct and lucrative product niches. Magna further prided itself on numerous process innovations that had led to greater production efficiencies, higher quality, and even entirely new products. One such innovation, known as polyurethane vacuum molding, provided a method of fabricating car seats that eliminated cutting, sewing, and gluing, thus providing a major reduction in labor costs over traditional cut-and-sew methods. The company attributed much of its innovativeness to its organizational structure and culture, which encouraged and rewarded ideas from the shop floor.

Perhaps equally important to Magna's strategy was its careful targeting of OEM product lines. Dennis Bausch, Senior Vice President of Marketing and Strategic Planning, explained:

> It's the old 80:20 rule. In North America, the top 10 selling vehicles account for about 25 percent of total automobile production. What we try to do is pick those winners. Right now, 50 percent of our sales come from parts we produce for the 10 best sellers.

Bausch continued:

> We average about Cdn.$190 worth of parts for every vehicle produced in North America, but on cars like the Ford Taurus, Cadillac Seville, and Jeep Grand

Cherokee we do a lot better than that. We've got over Cdn.$1,000 of parts on the Chrysler Minivan and over Cdn.$700 on the new Chrysler LH—those are key models for us. We're building our presence with the Japanese, too: right now, transplants only account for about 5 percent of our sales, but we've made good inroads on models like Toyota Camry and Honda Accord.

Bausch's analysis began by looking at forecasts and trends for various segments of the industry, both cars (compact, midsize, luxury) and light trucks (sport utility, full size, minivans). The next step was to analyze the potential of particular "body types"—for example, Taurus/Sable—within these segments. Bausch looked at the OEM's estimates for each of the body types as a starting point, but then did his own analysis using data from consultants and other industry experts.

> What we look for first is volume—that's got to be there. Our contracts stipulate that we've got to have enough capacity to meet the OEM's forecast, so if we don't think they're going to hit their sales numbers on a particular model, we've got to factor in the cost of excess capacity when we're putting together a bid.
>
> After volume, we look at the expected margin on the car. If the OEM has good margin, it's likely there will be less margin pressure on us. Chrysler makes over $6,000(U.S.) on each minivan. We do all right on that model, too. The other factor is the life cycle of the model. Taurus is in its eighth year. That means less development outlays and fewer start-ups and die changes.

Once the demand for each body type had been estimated, Bausch then looked at the capabilities Magna had to add to that car: Could it do the plastic body panels required by the design? Did the car require intrusion beams, one of Magna's technical specialties? Did one or more divisions have the capacity to take on this business? Were they located close enough to the OEM's production facility to be competitive on transportation costs and delivery standards? Was it business that was "strategic"—leading to future business or to new and promising areas of technology? Based on this analysis, Bausch categorized OEM request for proposals into three categories—red, yellow, and green—signaling the level of effort divisions should expend in obtaining a particular piece of business.

Magna's Experience in the 1980s

By 1980 Magna had grown from its roots as a small tool making shop to a Cdn.$180m parts supplier with over 40 divisions in Canada and the United States. Over the course of the next decade, the number of divisions mushroomed to 126, sales reached Cdn.$1.9 billion, and the company invested over Cdn.$1 billion in new facilities, real estate, equipment, and technology. Consistent with its culture and operating structure, Magna's expansion proceeded on a highly decentralized basis.

Top management's guidance was even more hands-off than usual after April 1988, when Frank Stronach stepped down as CEO of Magna to run for the Canadian parliament in that year's federal election. Stronach set out to convince voters that his Fair Enterprise system was "perhaps the most important chapter in Western industrial society in many years" and he predicted it would "have an enormous bearing on the future structure of corporations [and] law making." Political insiders speculated that Stronach was a top candidate for Minister of Industry if the Liberal party he was running for were elected.

Although pro-free trade by nature, Stronach nonetheless came down against the impending Canada-U.S. Free Trade Agreement (FTA), arguing that the country was ill prepared for an open trading relationship with the much larger United States, especially without an industrial policy to facilitate Canadian adjustment. In the end, Stronach, along with the anti-FTA Liberal Party, lost the election.

Returning to Magna in the Fall of 1989, Stronach soon discovered that the company he had founded more than 30 years before had taken a rapid turn for the worse. The competitiveness problems of the Big Three—which accounted for the vast majority of Magna's business—and the general downturn in the North American automotive market had taken a heavy toll on Magna's bottom line. At the same time, a number of Magna's new facilities had not yet come fully on-line, causing the company to operate at low capacity levels. Diversification into non-auto parts businesses such as magazine publishing and radio stations also distracted the company's attention and proved a large financial drain.

In 1990, Magna found itself in the red for the first time. That year the company lost Cdn.$224 million—more than it had earned in the previous 10 years combined. Worse, the company's expansion had been financed largely through debt, especially after the 1987 stock market crash, and the combination of operating losses and high interest payments plunged the company into default on virtually all of its outstanding loans.

What followed was a drastic restructuring as Magna worked with its customers and creditors to repair its operational and financial woes. The company's plan called for a return to its core auto parts business. Employment dropped from a high of 17,500 in 1989 to 15,000 in 1992, by which time the company had streamlined its operations to 68 divisions—40 in Canada, 20 in the United States, and an additional 8 overseas. On the finance side, Magna's major focus was its debt problem, and it set the ambitious objective of eliminating its long-term debt by the end of 1994. Future growth would be financed by equity or out of cash flow from operations.

By the end of 1992, Magna appeared to have regained its momentum. *Ward's Auto World,* an influential trade journal, called Magna's recovery the "comeback of the year" in the auto parts industry. Graham Orr, Senior Vice President of Corporate Development and Investor Relations, summed up Magna's situation:

> What we're focused on now is bottom-line-oriented growth. Before we were totally focused on growth. The key question for us is what investments to pursue—in products, customers, geographic markets—to ensure disciplined growth. We made

mistakes in the 80s because we didn't do strategic planning. Now we're putting the process of strategic planning into place. This time we'll look very carefully before we leap.

The Automotive Industry

The Competitiveness Crisis of the 1980s

Over the 15-year period from the late 1970s to the early 1990s, the North American automobile industry experienced sweeping changes in market structure, production methods, and buyer-supplier relations. Long the dominant force in the worldwide production of automobiles, U.S. assemblers had seen their share of the North American market fall from over 97 percent in the late 1960s to around 60 percent by 1991. In a period of just under 15 years, Japanese auto makers collectively increased their share to more than 30 percent of the North American market.

The penetration of the North American market by the Japanese producers was initially accomplished through the export of small, competitively priced vehicles that proved reliable over the long haul. Having established a reputation for quality and value with entry-level vehicles, the Japanese producers gradually moved up market toward the more lucrative mid-size and luxury car segments. Through a superior organizational model,[2] Japanese auto makers were able to design vehicles that consumers demanded, bring them to market faster, with fewer defects, and at a lower cost than their American competitors.

By the early 1980s, however, the competitiveness crisis of the Big Three had produced a political backlash against the Japanese auto producers. This resulted, initially, in attempts to limit Japanese penetration of the North American market through the 1981 "voluntary restraint agreement" between the U.S. and Japan and four years later through "voluntary export restraints" initiated by the Japanese. These trends toward protectionism, along with the appreciation of the yen, were instrumental in moving Japanese producers to establish assembly operations in North America—the so-called "transplants." Led by Honda in 1982 with its Marysville, Ohio, plant, the Japanese were producing over 1.5 million vehicles in 10 plants in the United States and Canada less than a decade later—more than 20 percent of total North American production. The inflow of direct investment by the Japanese automobile producers also led to a second wave of investment, this time by Japanese parts suppliers, who were operating more than 300 plants in the United States and Canada by 1992.

By the late 1980s there were signs that many of the principles of lean production were beginning to diffuse to the Big Three. Through joint ventures

---

[2] The hallmarks of this model—often referred to as "lean production"—include design for manufacturability, the use of teams of multiskilled workers, flexible machinery, the absence of buffering inventory (just-in-time delivery), and the dedication to continuous improvement in quality, efficiency, and cost.

with the Japanese, visits to Japanese production facilities, and the intense scrutiny given to the Japanese transplants by journalists, consultants, and academics, the Big Three appeared to be slowly learning and adopting techniques such as statistical process control, just-in-time delivery, total quality management, concurrent engineering, and design for manufacturability. With time these changes in the way cars were designed and produced began to have visible effects, both in the quality ratings received by new American models, and, most importantly, in the marketplace. In 1992, an American car, the Ford Taurus, regained the title of top-selling passenger vehicle, edging out the Honda Accord, which had taken the title the previous few years. In 1992, for the first time in over a decade, the Japanese share of the U.S. market actually declined, dropping 3 percent, while the Big Three's share rose by 11.5 percent.

For North American automotive suppliers such as Magna, the restructuring of the Big Three also brought major changes in the way they conducted their businesses. Not only were suppliers required to learn and adopt the techniques of lean production in their own factories; in many cases they faced a fundamental transformation of their traditional relationships with the OEMs. By the early 1990s, these changes were having dramatic effects on the structure and operation of the North American automobile parts industry.

The Changing Buyer-Supplier Relationship

Perhaps the biggest change in the buyer-supplier relationship was the movement to outsourcing by the OEMs. Under the old mass production system, many of the nearly 10,000 parts contained in a car were designed and produced in-house by the Big Three. In contrast, under the emerging system, responsibility for entire subsystems, from design and engineering to just-in-time delivery, was being transferred to outside suppliers. Components were also increasingly being sourced from a single supplier, a major break with traditional sourcing practices in the North American industry. In 1992, Magna estimated that fully ¾ of its revenues came from parts on which it was the sole supplier. The objectives of the new sourcing strategies—reduced cycle times, improved quality, and decreased costs—were basic to the competitive recovery of the Big Three.

The movement to subsystem sourcing from single suppliers led directly to the consolidation of the auto parts industry and the emergence of "tiers" of suppliers. First-tier suppliers were the elite cadre of suppliers such as Magna that contracted directly with the OEMs. In addition to their engineering and production responsibilities, first-tier suppliers also served as integrators, managing networks of second- and third-tier subcontractors who supplied them with components for the subsystem that would eventually be delivered to the OEM. The OEMs chose their first-tier suppliers for their track record in meeting cost, technical, quality, and delivery standards as well as their ability and willingness to adopt the new practices associated with lean production. The financial stability of the supplier was also an important consideration in achieving first-tier status, since single sourcing of major vehicle subsystems created potential vulnerabilities for the OEMs.

Although the industry shakeout had caused the number of North American parts suppliers to decline by an estimated 35 percent in the decade of the 1980s, there were still more than 2,000 companies involved in the industry by the early 1990s. The vast majority were second- and third-tier suppliers, generally small companies that tended either to specialize in a narrow range of products for the auto industry or to produce a wider variety of products for several industries, including autos. Magna's direct competitors in the first tier could be classified into three main groups: parts divisions of the OEMs themselves, including GM's Automotive Components Group, Ford's Automotive Components Group, and Chrysler's Acustar; automotive divisions of large, diversified companies such as Du Pont, ITT, Rockwell, and TRW; and specialized parts suppliers such as Budd, A. O. Smith, and Robert Bosch.

Beyond the structural changes that were sweeping the parts industry as a result of the changing sourcing strategies of the OEMs, a new set of practices also governed the relationship between the OEM and the first-tier supplier. Not surprisingly, many of these practices were variants of the Japanese model of buyer-supplier relations that were believed to have contributed so greatly to the competitive success of the Japanese.

Chrysler's launch of its new LH models was illustrative of the direction buyer-supplier relations in the auto industry appeared to be headed. Approximately two years before production was scheduled to begin, Chrysler selected its suppliers for the LH. Whereas under the old mass production system the car might have had over 1,000 parts and materials suppliers, Chrysler had contracted with only 230 suppliers for the LH. Although most of the suppliers were responsible for the total design of the system they were producing, Chrysler engineers on the LH team worked with engineers from the parts suppliers to ensure that finished subsystems were tightly integrated with the rest of the design and could be efficiently assembled by workers on the production line. Additional goals were also pursued through this common effort: reductions in the number of parts in each subsystem, decreased component weight, and efficient material usage.

In the case of Magna and several of the other major parts suppliers, location of technical facilities near Chrysler's LH headquarters at Auburn Hill, Michigan, facilitated close interaction between supplier and OEM engineers. In other cases, parts engineers worked out of LH headquarters for the design phase of the project, or Chrysler temporarily transferred key individuals to suppliers' technical facilities.

For each of the components, Chrysler set "target prices" based on value analysis it conducted prior to production. Chrysler then worked with the supplier to meet these cost targets. In addition to the initial target price, Chrysler negotiated annual price reductions in the 3 to 5 percent range for each of the components, reflecting an estimate of the cost reductions achievable through experience effects. Chrysler also provided incentives for suppliers to exceed their cost targets in the form of additional content in the subsystem or gain sharing.

On the LH, as in virtually all Big Three models in production by the early 1990s, primary responsibility for component quality rested with the suppliers. Parts inspection by OEMs was greatly reduced or eliminated altogether. Virtually all first-tier suppliers had implemented SPC on their production lines, and many had moved toward team-based assembly, job rotation, and multi-skilling of shop floor employees. The OEMs had also launched grading systems for their suppliers that rated supplier performance along a wide spectrum of quality metrics, usually over an extended period of time. Some had even initiated programs to improve their suppliers' production processes directly by sending specially trained teams to suppliers' production sites.

The same concern for quality and cost was also driving first-tier suppliers to work with second- and third-tier suppliers to implement many of the same practices. In many cases, first-tier suppliers were acquiring suppliers of key components to ensure that the capability for complete subsystems was in-house and to prevent supply disruptions due to inefficient or financially troubled suppliers. Changes originated by the OEMs were thus having ripple effects throughout the industry value chain.

The responsibility of the parts supplier did not end with production of the subsystem. An integral part of the movement toward lean production was delivery of the subsystem just-in-time and, increasingly for parts incorporating trim and color options, in-sequence.[3] For Magna, which supplied front and rear fascias, exterior moldings, and side panel and floor pan stampings on the LH, just-in-time and in-sequence delivery were facilitated by the location of its stamping division, which was only 10 miles from Chrysler's LH assembly plant in Bramalea, Ontario. During the ramp-up to full production, suppliers such as Magna frequently placed engineers in the OEM's production facility to ensure that their parts were meeting the quality and delivery standards of the new production system. Having suppliers' engineers on-site ensured that problems could be more easily identified, traced back to their source, and remedied. On the LH, suppliers of complex subsystems continued to provide onsite engineers to Chrysler a year after production had begun.

North American Economic Integration

Politics had long played an important role in shaping the geography of the North American automobile industry. Canada and Mexico were locations for automobile production largely as a result of government policies that required

---

[3] In-sequence delivery refers to the practice of delivering parts to the assembly line that match the requirements of individual vehicles. For example, if the interior colors on the next three vehicles on the line are blue, black, blue, then the supplier of seats for that model was expected to arrange delivery such that the seats arrived to the line in the same sequence—blue, then black, then blue.

companies to produce locally in exchange for market access. However, despite the heavy hand of government, trade in autos and auto parts remained relatively unfettered by protectionist barriers compared to sectors such as agriculture, textiles and apparel, and steel. At the onset of NAFTA negotiations, automotive products constituted the single largest component of trade between each of the three NAFTA countries, accounting for about ⅓ of total Canada-U.S. trade and about ⅙ of U.S.-Mexico trade.

Integration of the North American automobile market was achieved through three distinct phases of intergovernmental bargaining: the 1965 Canada-U.S. Auto Pact, the 1988 Canada-U.S. Free Trade Agreement, and the 1992 North American Free Trade Agreement.

The 1965 Auto Pact

In response to an escalating trade dispute between the U.S. and Canada over Canadian export subsidies, governments of the two countries negotiated the Auto Pact, which eliminated tariffs on autos and parts produced with at least 50 percent local content. Although the Auto Pact effectively created an integrated market for autos and parts, the agreement also contained several Canadian safeguards designed to ensure autos would continue to be produced in Canada. The most important of these provisions was the production-to-sales ratio test, which required companies to produce in Canada autos or parts worth at least ¾ of their Canadian sales. Companies that met this requirement would qualify for duty-free status on their exports to Canada, even on goods originating from third countries such as Mexico or Japan.

The 1988 Canada-U.S. Free Trade Agreement

In 1988, Canada and the U.S. negotiated a comprehensive free trade agreement (FTA) designed to secure and extend open trade between the world's two largest trading partners. The Canada-U.S. agreement was also the direct precursor to, and model for, NAFTA, which added Mexico to the bilateral free trade zone. In the auto sector, the 1988 agreement included provisions designed to relieve tensions that had emerged as a result of changes in the worldwide automobile industry since the negotiation of the Auto Pact. Inside the industry, the FTA became known as "Auto Pact Plus."

The most important feature of the FTA pertaining to autos was the freeze placed on new participants to the Auto Pact, a measure that resulted in the exclusion of Japanese producers, all of whom had elected not to join the Auto Pact prior to 1988 because of the onerous Canadian production requirement. The freeze on membership, along with the elimination of Canadian export-based duty drawbacks,[4] ensured that non-Auto Pact producers would pay at

---

[4] In the early 1970s, Canada began a policy of remitting duty to non-Auto Pact producers who exported goods manufactured in Canada. This "parallel benefits" policy was an important factor in inducing investment into Canada by non-North American auto assemblers such as Honda, Toyota, Suzuki, and Hyundai; it was also a major source of tension in the trade relations between the two countries.

least some duty on vehicles or parts imported into the region. Prior to the agreement, the Big Three were alarmed that Japanese producers could export vehicles or parts to Canada duty-free under the drawback scheme, while using their Canadian production facilities to export vehicles to the large U.S. market under the duty-free provision of the Auto Pact. After passage of the FTA, Japanese cars produced in Canada could only be exported duty-free to the U.S. if they met the 50 percent North American content requirement. Many industry observers believed these changes had significantly reduced the attractiveness of Canada as a location for transplants.

The other significant change brought about by the FTA concerned the basis for calculating the 50 percent North American content requirement needed for duty-free status. Prior to the agreement, parts manufacturers had lobbied for a 65 percent local content requirement as a way of increasing North American sourcing by OEMs. Instead, the FTA imposed a tougher standard by which the existing 50 percent would be calculated: only labor and direct processing costs—factory costs—would be included, not advertising or overhead costs. This change was believed to have increased domestic sourcing by OEMs, especially transplant producers who still imported a large number of parts.

NAFTA

The addition of Mexico to the Canada-U.S. FTA introduced a fundamentally new dynamic into the North American political economy. In the U.S. and Canada, the uncertainty about NAFTA's consequences—it was the first free trade agreement between large developed and developing nations during the postwar period—led to fears that the industrial core of each country's economy would be lost to Mexico due to low wages and lax enforcement of labor and environmental standards.[5]

In November 1993, after one of the most fiercely contested battles in the history of U.S. trade politics, NAFTA was finally ratified by the U.S. Congress. From Tuktoyaktuk to Tapachula, more than 360 million people would be linked together in the world's largest free trade area.[6]

Auto sector provisions under NAFTA reflected the complex configuration of interests involved in the negotiations. Exhibit 4 provides a summary of the main features of the agreement pertaining to autos.

---

[5] Different economic models produced widely disparate forecasts of NAFTA's impact on trade flows, economic growth, employment gains and losses, and wage rates in each country. For example, projections about the impact of NAFTA on Mexican employment ranged from a net loss of 158,000 jobs to a net gain of 1,464,000 jobs, depending on the assumptions contained in the model (Source: Institute for International Economics).

[6] In 1989, the EC and EFTA countries *together* were home to 358 million people. The European project is not technically a free trade area. Formed in 1958 as a customs union with a common external tariff, the EC (now the EU) had recently embarked on a much more ambitious process of economic union.

Exhibit 4   NAFTA Provisions Pertaining to the Automotive Sector

	United States		Canada		Mexico	
	Now	*NAFTA*	*Now*	*NAFTA*	*Now*	*NAFTA*
Tariffs						
Cars	2.5%	0% by 1994	9.2%	4.6% to 0% by 2004	20%	10% to 0% by 2004
Light trucks	25%	10% to 0% by 1999	9.2%	4.6% to 0% by 1999	20%	10% to 0% by 1999
Other trucks	25%	25% to 0% by 2004	9.2%	9.2% to 0% by 2004	20%	20% to 0% by 2004
Parts	3 to 6%	0% for some parts; 5- or 10-year elimination CDN-U.S. FTA schedule for Canada	9.2%	9.2; Will match Mex. offer CDN-U.S. FTA schedule for U.S.	10–15%	75% of parts to 0% by 1999; remainder to 0% by 2004
Import Quotas	None	Light vehicles: none	Light vehicles: none		*Now:* <15% of domestic production	*NAFTA:* None by 1994
		Heavy vehicles: none	Heavy vehicles: none		*Now:* Equivalent to local content	*NAFTA:* None by 1994
Trade Balancing	None		None		*Now:* No deficit; $1.75 of exports for $1 of imports	*NAFTA:* $.80–$.55 of exports for $1 of imports; None by 1994
Local Content	None		None		*Now:* 36% of total domestic production plus net exports 1992 level or declining % (starting at 34%), whichever lower	*NAFTA:* none by 1994
Manufacturing Requirement	None		None		*Now:* Required	*NAFTA:* None by 2004
Equity Restriction	None		None		*Now:* <40% foreign equity in parts	*NAFTA:* 49% by 1994; none by 1999
Care Rules	*NAFTA:* Mexican production counts as domestic fleet		None		*Now:* <40% foreign equity in parts	*NAFTA:* 49% by 1994; none by 1999

Perhaps the most important objective of the Big Three was improved access to the Mexican consumer market, which at the time of the NAFTA negotiations was the fastest growing automobile market in the world. Liberalization of the Mexican market was ensured through three NAFTA provisions: (1) an immediate halving of Mexico's 20 percent tariff on autos and light trucks, and a 10-year phase-out of the remaining tariff; (2) a 10-year phase-out of Mexico's requirement that vehicles sold in Mexico contain 36 percent domestic content; and (3) an immediate reduction in Mexico's trade balancing requirement from $2 of automotive exports for every dollar's worth of imports, to 80 cents, and to zero by 2004. The automotive industry hailed this last provision as "the single most significant accomplishment of the NAFTA automotive negotiations."

The gradual phase-out of tariff and non-tariff barriers was designed, in part, to ensure that the budding Mexican parts industry would not be wiped out by immediate exposure to international competition, a key Mexican objective. Still, some analysts were predicting that as many as 80 percent of Mexican parts companies would be forced to exit the market as a result of NAFTA.[7] Many Mexican suppliers were scrambling to form alliances with their U.S. and Canadian counterparts as a way of obtaining badly needed capital and technology.

The terms of the transition also reflected one of the Big Three's major priorities, namely to ensure that Mexico could not easily be used as an "export platform" to the U.S. market by foreign producers. The gradual phase-out clearly benefited producers with established Mexican facilities, primarily Chrysler, Ford, and General Motors, as well as Nissan and Volkswagen, since new entrants were required to establish sourcing relationships with Mexican suppliers just as the established OEMs had done. NAFTA ensured that there were no "late-mover advantages" conferred on companies such as Toyota and Honda that had yet to establish Mexican production facilities.

North American parts suppliers also stood to gain by several NAFTA provisions, especially the increase in the North American content requirement from 50 percent to 62.5 percent over an eight-year period. Furthermore, the method of calculating local content was again changed to a system that effectively created a more onerous requirement for assemblers: rather than counting a part as 100 percent regional if its domestic content exceeded 50 percent as under the FTA (the so-called "roll-up" method), under NAFTA the value-added of 69 key components (e.g., engines, transmissions, bumpers) would be traced and counted according to their actual percentage of domestic or foreign content. Japanese producers, who were on record as calling the auto provisions of the agreement "a giant step in the wrong direction," were expected to have the most difficulty meeting the new content requirements.

---

[7] Kay G. Husbands, "Strategic Alliances in the Mexican Auto Parts Industry," IMVP Working Paper, MIT, 1993.

Cosma's Response to NAFTA

Cosma's Business

Fred Jaekel had been C.O.O. of Cosma since 1991, four years after the group was created in a reorganization that brought together Magna's metal stamping and assembly capabilities under the management of one group. Since the reorganization, Cosma had positioned itself as a supplier of complete body components and systems to OEMs, with capabilities spanning the range from design to tooling to production. By 1992, Cosma had sales of Can$781 million and was one of the largest, most complete stamping companies in North America. Its presses, ranging from 60 to 3,500 tons, could produce virtually any body part made of sheet steel: engine compartments, bumpers, hoods, and body panels, for example. Cosma's ability to design and construct its own die making tools was a capability that had long been an integral part of Magna's competitive thrust.

Cosma operated 19 divisions in the U.S. and Canada: 12 in southern Ontario and 7 in the U.S. (5 in Iowa, 1 in Maryland, and 1 in Tennessee). In addition, the group had a design and engineering center in Detroit, where teams of engineers worked with OEMs to create drawings, feasibility studies, working prototypes, and full-scale testing programs for new products. Cosma had also recently opened Magna's first Mexican division, a stamping facility servicing the VW assembly plant in Puebla.[8] Jaekel himself had managed the start-up of the Mexican facility. In 1993 Cosma was also constructing a new plant in Greensville, South Carolina, to supply frames just-in-time to the new BMW assembly facility that was slated to open the following year.

The stamping business was highly capital intensive. Labor accounted for about 9.5 percent of Cosma's costs. The dies and presses used in Cosma's stamping facilities were among the most complex and expensive tools in the industrialized world: even the slightest deviation was enough to tear or melt the part being stamped. Servicing and maintenance of the presses was thus a critical factor in ensuring component quality and machine up-time. In addition to high capital costs, stamping operations also required large inputs of raw materials, especially steel, which comprised 50 percent of Cosma's costs. Because of Cosma's focus on body systems, much of the steel it used was of automotive grade, one of the most stringent grades on the market and only available from large, integrated steel makers such as U.S. Steel or Canada's Dofasco. The major steel makers were also increasingly providing stampers with important value-added services such as computer simulations that compared weight and stress tolerances of parts using alternative steel specifications.

---

[8] A Magna division in Europe had previously designed and developed the tools for the Golf platform that VW had now decided to produce in Mexico. VW had encouraged Magna to open a Mexican division to supply parts for the VW Puebla factory.

EXHIBIT 5   Cost of Automobile Production, USA and Mexico

	USA	Mexico
Labor*	$700	$140
Parts and subassemblies	$7,750	$8,000
Component shipping costs	$75	$600
Finished vehicle shipping	$225	$400
Inventory costs	$20	$40
Total	$8,770	$9,180

All figures in U.S. dollars.

* Assumes 20 hours of labor per U.S.-made car, 30 hours per Mexican-made car.

The Impact of Mexico

Cosma's executive team had agreed to divide the preparation of their business plan into several parts. Because of Jaekel's firsthand experience in Mexico, he chose to tackle the question of what effect, if any, NAFTA was likely to have on Cosma's future strategy, operations, and growth plans. Returning to his office, Jaekel pulled out a report prepared by Magna's executive management on NAFTA, as well as a report he had obtained from the U.S. Government's Office of Technology Assessment (OTA).[9]

The OTA report had an especially interesting chapter on the likely impact of NAFTA on the auto and auto parts industry. Two tables, in particular, caught Jaekel's eye, the first a comparison of production costs in Mexico and the U.S. for auto assemblers, and the second a similar comparison for parts suppliers to the industry—in the OTA's example, suppliers of wire harnesses. These are reproduced in Exhibits 5 and 6.

According to the OTA, Mexican wages in the auto industry ranged from a low of about U.S.$2 per hour for the assembly of wire harnesses, which typically took place in maquilladoras, to a high of about U.S.$5 per hour for assembly operations at Big Three facilities. Jaekel recalled that his own costs in Mexico were closer to the OEMs'. However, despite Mexico's low wage costs, Jaekel had encountered several difficulties setting up Cosma's stamping facility there. Engineers and other skilled employees had to be transferred to Mexico—some temporarily, some for an extended period of time. Equipment downtime had also been a problem, since few of the press and machine tool vendors that supplied Cosma had a service network that extended to Mexico, and Mexican workers had not yet developed the skills to adequately maintain the equipment. A company like Cosma, whose customers suffered losses of hundreds of thousands of dollars an hour when their just-in-time delivery

---

[9] *Pulling Together or Pulling Apart* (Washington, DC: Office of Technology Assessment, 1992).

Exhibit 6   Cost of Wiring Harness Production, USA and Mexico

Assembly Cost (40 minutes):	
Mexico (Maquilladora plant[10])	$1–2
United States	
Big Three internal supplier (@ $35/hour)	$23
Unionized supplier (@ $26/hour)	$17
Non-union supplier (@ $18/hour)	$12
Added shipping costs for Mexican assembly	$7
Extra inventory costs for Mexican production	$.50
Mexican Cost Advantage	$2.50–14.50

---

schedules were interrupted, stood to lose contracts if it were the cause of customers' downtime.

Jaekel also knew that Mexican steel makers were unable to provide the automotive grade steel necessary for most of his stamping operations, a situation that was unlikely to change in the near future, even with NAFTA. Fortunately for Cosma, prices in the steel market were soft enough that they had been able to negotiate a deal with Dofasco to supply the Puebla facility from southern Ontario without additional transportation costs. How long this agreement would last was unclear, however. Finally, there were the added costs and difficulties associated with Mexico's notoriously poor infrastructure. The shipment of supplies and finished goods into, and out of, Mexico would increase Cosma's transportation costs and would greatly increase the likelihood of damaged goods.

The major question in Jaekel's mind was what the OEMs would do as a result of NAFTA: would they relocate existing capacity to Mexico? or simply add capacity there? which models were likely to be produced in Mexico? and in what volumes?

According to both the OTA and Magna's internal report, the future of the Mexican automotive industry looked bright in 1993. In addition to the eight assembly plants already in Mexico (see Exhibit 7), several new investments had recently been announced. Ford was expected to invest U.S.$700 million to expand its Chihuahua engine plant for production of Escort and Tracer engines by 1994. GM was planning a new assembly facility for building up to 200,000 light trucks annually. Chrysler had plans for a new large facility in northern Mexico. Nissan was spending U.S.$1 billion to expand its current facilities to build 120,000 (and eventually 150,000 to 200,000) Sentras per year for export to Japan and South America. VW Mexico had also begun to expand its capacity from 250,000 vehicles per year to 350,000 to 400,000 units per year by 1994.

---

[10] Maquilladoras are foreign-owned plants located on the Mexican-U.S. border. Inputs for production are imported tariff free; all output is exported.

EXHIBIT 7   Auto Assembly Plants in Mexico

Company	Location	Models	Annual Capacity
Ford	Cuautitlan		
	Cars	Tempo/Topaz; Thunderbird	60,000
	Trucks	F Series; B200; P350	50,000
	Hermosillo	Escort/Tracer	160,000
General Motors	Ramos Arizpe	Century/Cavalier/Cutlass	100,000
	Mexico City	Suburban; Blazer; Pickups	60,000
Chrysler	Toluca	LeBaron; New Yorker; Shadow/ Sundance; Acclaim/Spirit	120,000
	Lago Alberto	Ramcharger; D Series Pickups	50,000
Nissan	Cuernevaca		
	Cars	Sentra	80,000
	Trucks	Pickups; vans	50,000
Volkswagen	Puebla		
	Cars	Beetle; Golf; Jetta	200,000
	Trucks	Pickups; vans	15,000

Source: *Pulling Together or Pulling Apart* (Washington, DC: Office of Technology Assessment, 1992).

In addition to these relatively concrete plans published in the trade press, there were other less definite pieces of information circulating about the future of the automobile industry in Mexico. Foreign parts suppliers were expected to invest as much as U.S.$4.2 billion between 1992 and 1996. Many economists were predicting rapid growth of the Mexican consumer market over the next decade as Mexican standards of living rose, creating increased demand for autos, which in 1990 alone had grown by 17 percent.

Industry analysts also pointed to the potential migration of small car production from Canada and the United States to Mexico, an outcome that was facilitated in part by NAFTA's provision allowing OEMs to count their Mexican production as "domestic" for the purposes of fuel efficiency (CAFE) regulations. Examples of models that were thought likely to migrate to Mexico included the Ford Tracer and the Pontiac LeMans, which GM was currently producing in Korea. The Big Three had always struggled to make money on small cars, and it was thought that a combination of low Mexican wages and labor-intensive production technology might prove an advantage for the production of small cars. The same logic led some observers to predict that Mexico would become a prime location for producing niche vehicles, those with a short expected life span, limited market penetration, but high margins.

Despite these press releases and industry rumors, Jaekel was not yet convinced that the path to profitability for the OEMs ran to Mexico. First there was the excess capacity that had long plagued the Big Three's North

American operations. Also, Jaekel knew that for every Mexican success story, such as Ford's Hermosillo plant and GM's Ramos Arizpe plant, both of which were world class in terms of quality and productivity, there was a failure. He had firsthand knowledge of VW's problems in Mexico: the company was forced to delay start-up of its Puebla facility for over a year while it battled strikes and undertook a massive training program so that its Mexican workers could produce Golfs at the quality levels required for sale to the North American market. The OTA data, too, seemed to indicate little cost advantage for OEMs in Mexico, although Jaekel recalled having seen other reports that pegged the bottom line advantage to producing in Mexico at between 4 and 10 percent.

The Impact of Local Content Rules

Jaekel turned next to the second set of potential opportunities he saw stemming from NAFTA, namely increased North American investment by foreign OEMs. Jaekel knew that the higher local content requirement under NAFTA and the new method by which it was calculated would create difficulties for many of the Japanese transplants. Most would be forced to increase their local sourcing, a trend Jaekel believed was likely to continue regardless of NAFTA's fate in the U.S. Congress. Political pressures and the rising yen were creating inexorable pressures in that direction.

Most of the Japanese OEMs had, in fact, publicly stated their intentions to increase their purchases from North American suppliers. In late 1991, for example, Toyota announced it would increase its U.S. purchases by 40 percent to U.S.$5 billion annually beginning in 1994. At the same time Nissan had announced that it would also increase U.S. purchases by 40 percent during the next few years. Honda, too, although it had already increased its U.S. purchases in 1991, pledged to reach U.S.$4.5 billion in domestic purchases by 1994. Finally, Mazda announced it would double its U.S. purchases by 1994, up to U.S.$3 billion from U.S.$1.43 billion in 1990.

Jaekel believed Cosma was well positioned to capture a greater share of the business from Japanese OEMs. Many of the Japanese suppliers that had followed the transplants to North America were known to be struggling. Most were unable to obtain significant business from the Big Three, and many had also experienced difficulties adapting their managerial practices to the new business environment. Moreover, Cosma had recently won several sizable contracts with Japanese OEMs, and was gradually establishing its reputation with the Japanese as an innovative supplier of high-quality components. In 1992, several of Cosma's divisions had won quality awards from the Japanese OEMs, including Toyota's prestigious Grand Slam Award.

Another potentially important development was the inflow of investment from Europe. The European automobile makers were building North American production facilities for a number of different reasons. Not only were they coming to ensure market access under NAFTA; they were also seeking lower labor costs and direct experience operating a lean production system, something that had proved difficult to implement in Europe.

Cosma had already leveraged its European links to land the contract to supply BMW's new South Carolina plant with complete framing systems. Mercedes, too, had recently announced that it would build a new production facility in Alabama, and Audi was thought to be considering a similar move. Jaekel believed Cosma also had an excellent chance of supplying these new facilities.

"Year 2000: Paving the Road"

Fred Jaekel's deadline was fast approaching and he had now digested the contents of the two reports. NAFTA, he reflected, seemed to offer a lot of different avenues for growth. But what, exactly, was the strategic vision he would put forward in Cosma's long-term business plan? Jaekel knew he needed to come up with a specific set of recommendations and be clear about the assumptions that underlay them. If there was one lesson Magna had learned from its experience in the 1980s it was to make sure that its investment plans were focused, strategic, and represented the best use of company resources.

Jaekel also knew there was still one stone he had left unturned. He turned in his chair toward the scale model of a Magna-designed niche car that sat on his desk. He reached forward and pushed a speed dial button on his office phone. Two rings later Frank Stronach was on the line.

"Hello, Frank? Ya, it's Fred," Jaekel said, still with a trace of German accent.

"NAFTA—What do ya think?"

METROPOL BASE-FORT SECURITY GROUP

Pat Haney, president of Metropol Base-Fort Security Group (Metropol), was sitting in his office contemplating the future direction of his company. Metropol, a leading Canadian security firm whose services included the provision of uniformed security guards, mobile security patrols, polygraph testing, insurance and criminal investigations, and a broad range of specialized services, was faced with a number of challenges that threatened its future profitability. "Increasing competition, especially from large multinationals such as Pinkertons, is further reducing already low industry margins," offered Pat. He was also concerned about Metropol's reliance on the commodity-like security guard business for 90 percent of its revenue. "We have to find some way to meaningfully differentiate our services from those of our competitors," Pat observed. "That is essential if we are to achieve the kind of growth we desire."

Company Background

Metropol was founded in 1952 by George Whitbread, a former RCMP officer. In 1975, Whitbread sold the company to former Manitoba premier Duff Roblin. Haney came aboard in 1976 to run the Winnipeg operation, which was then 80 percent of Metropol's business. In the late 1970s and early 1980s, Metropol expanded into Saskatchewan and Alberta. In 1984, it took over the leading Alberta security firm, Base-Fort Security Group, Inc. Pat believed

This case was written by Stephen S. Tax under the supervision of Professor W. S. Good. Copyright @ 1988 by the Case Development Program, Faculty of Management, University of Manitoba. Support for the development of this case was provided by the Canadian Studies Program, Secretary of State, Government of Canada.

this move offered economies of scale and helped to make Metropol a national company. Of Metropol's $30 million in 1985 revenues, 70 percent were in Western Canada. Offices were maintained in all four western provinces as well as in the Northwest Territories, Quebec, and Newfoundland.

The Security Industry

Security products and services were purchased by individuals and businesses as a means of reducing the risk of loss or damage to their assets. The amount of security purchased depended upon individual risk preferences, their perception of the degree of risk involved, and the value of the assets to be protected. Security, therefore, was very much an intangible product subject to individual evaluation.

The industry offered such services as unarmed uniformed security guards, mobile patrols, investigations, consulting and education, as well as hardware products such as alarms, fences, locks, safes, and electronic surveillance devices (ESDs) and monitoring equipment. Most companies purchased a package combining various services and hardware systems. "It would not make much sense to have 50 television monitors and only one person watching them," Pat pointed out, "nor would it be wise to have 50 security guards roaming around a building which had no locks on the doors."

There were a number of factors which contributed to the competitive nature of the security industry. All a firm needed to enter the business was to open an office. Start-up costs were minimal and no accreditation was required by the company or its employees. Clients considered the cost of switching from one firm to another quite low so the business often went to the lowest-cost provider. Most customers really did not understand the difference in services provided by the various competitors in the security business, which made differentiation very difficult. Pat found in studying the financial statements of the large multinational security firms that most security companies earned pre-tax profit margins of about 4 percent on gross sales.

The 1985 security guard and private investigation markets in Canada were worth about $400 million retail. ESDs and other types of hardware added close to another $400 million to this figure at retail prices.

Growth was expected to continue in the security field for a variety of reasons including a general increase in the level of risk around the world, the rising cost of insurance, economic growth, technological innovation that created new security problems, and an increasing sophistication amongst security system purchasers. The ESD and security guard segments were expected to outpace basic hardware sales growth (Exhibit 1).

On the negative side was the industry's poor reputation for the quality and reliability of its services. This perception threatened to limit growth and provide an opportunity for new competitors to enter the market.

Exhibit 1   Forecasted Market Growth for Security Guard and Private Investigation Services, Electronic Security Devices (ESDs), and Hardware Products in the United States, 1958–1995*

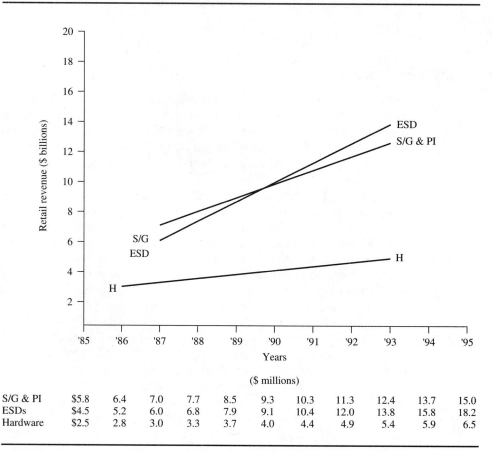

	'85	'86	'87	'88	'89	'90	'91	'92	'93	'94	'95
	($ millions)										
S/G & PI	$5.8	6.4	7.0	7.7	8.5	9.3	10.3	11.3	12.4	13.7	15.0
ESDs	$4.5	5.2	6.0	6.8	7.9	9.1	10.4	12.0	13.8	15.8	18.2
Hardware	$2.5	2.8	3.0	3.3	3.7	4.0	4.4	4.9	5.4	5.9	6.5

* The Canadian growth rate for each type of service/product was expected to be similar to the U.S. pattern.
Source: Metropol Research.

Competition

Metropol's competition came in both a direct and indirect form from a variety of competitors. "We compete with other firms who primarily offer security guard services as well as a number of companies that provide substitute products and services," observed Pat.

There were hundreds of security guard businesses in Canada, ranging in size from one or two ex-policemen operating out of a basement to large multinational firms such as Pinkertons, Burns, and Wackenhut. Metropol was the third largest firm in the country with a 7 percent market share

(Exhibit 2). It was the leading firm in Western Canada with a 25 percent share of that market.

Hardware products served as the foundation of a good security system. While items such as fencing, lighting, alarms, safes, and locks were to some extent complementary to the security guard business, they also competed with it—firms could substitute some proportion of either their security guard or hardware expenditures for the other.

Insurance had long been a favorite substitute for security and other loss prevention services. Business spent more on insurance than all forms of security products combined. However, falling interest rates, a series of major disasters around the world, and a trend to more generous damage awards by the courts were making insurance a more expensive alternative. Faced with higher premiums, lower limits, and higher deductibles, businesses were likely to consider spending more on loss-prevention products and services.

The various levels of government also provided some basic protection services to companies (fire, police, etc.). However, their services were geared more to personal than business protection. These government services tended to set the base level of risk in a community. Tight budgets were not permitting these services to keep pace with the growth in crime and the increase in the value of corporate assets. This provided the private security business with an opportunity to fill the void.

Businesses were spending almost as much for ESDs and related services as for security guard services. There were a number of different ESD products, ranging from small electronic gadgets to the very popular central station monitoring systems. ESDs were the fastest-growing segment of the security industry. The principal attribute of these products was that they provided

---

EXHIBIT 2   The Largest Security Guard Companies Operating in Canada Ranked by Market Share

Company Name	Canadian Revenue ($ millions)	Employees	Market Share
1 Pinkertons	$ 50	4,600	12.5%
2 Burns	30	4,500	7.5
3 Metropol Base-Fort	30	2,000	7.0
4 Wackenhut	12	2,000	3.0
5 Canadian Protection	12	1,700	3.0
6 Barnes	12	1,500	3.0
7 Phillips	10	1,200	2.5
Canada total	$400	40,000*	100%

* In-house guards could raise this figure by as much as 100 percent. However, a better estimate would be 50 to 60 percent, as in-house accounts use more full-time staff. This means that there are more than 60,000 people working as guards or private investigators at any time. Further, with turnover at close to 100 percent annually, there are over 100,000 people working in this field over the course of a year.

Source: Metropol Research.

accurate and reliable information to whomever was responsible for responding to a problem situation. Thus, to a large extent, these products were really productivity tools that enhanced the performance of security guards, the fire department, and/or the police force. They did tend to reduce the amount of security guard service needed. Some security-conscious firms with large-scale security needs hired their own internal (in-house) specialists. In most cases, they would also hire guards from companies like Metropol to do the actual patrolling.

The primary basis of competition in the security business was price. However, this was as much the fault of small, poorly managed firms and large multinationals trying to purchase market share as it was a fundamental characteristic of the industry. "I've seen companies bid under cost," observed Pat, "and they did not necessarily know they were doing it. It is a very unprofessional business in that sense. If you offer superior service and give a customer what he wants, in most cases you don't have to offer the lowest price. Just recently the Air Canada Data Centre job went to the highest bidder. Lowering your price is very easy but not the way to succeed in this business." However, since price was a key factor in getting jobs, cost control became crucial if profits were to be made. Pre-tax margins of 4 to 8 percent quickly disappeared if unanticipated costs occurred.

Market Segments

The market for security products and services could be segmented in a variety of ways, such as by type of service, type of business, geographic location, sensitivity to security needs, government versus private companies, and occasional versus continuous needs. Metropol segmented their customers and the rest of the market, using a combination of the above bases, as outlined below and in Exhibit 3.

Large Security-Conscious Organizations (Private and Public).   The common feature among these companies was that they had the potential for heavy losses if security was breached. They typically had high-value assets, such as computers or other high-tech equipment, or valuable proprietary information, as in the case of research and development firms. These buyers were usually quite knowledgeable about security and rated quality over price. This group included firms in both local urban and remote, rural locations.

Organizations for Whom Security Was a Low Priority.   This group was dominated by local companies, commercial property management companies, and branches of firms that were headquartered elsewhere. They were less knowledgeable about security and tended to have limited security programs. They were price sensitive and principally utilized low-cost security guards.

EXHIBIT 3   Security-Guard Service Market Segmentation by Gross Margins and Guard Wages

---

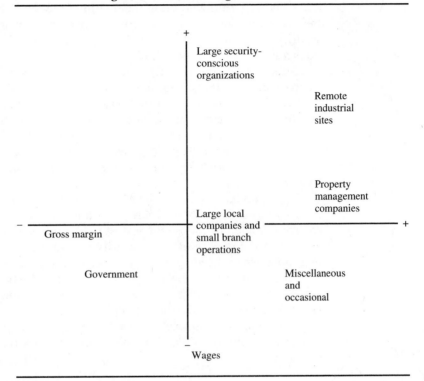

Government Organizations.   Government organizations (nonhospital) typically awarded contracts based on a tendered price for a predetermined period of time, usually one to two years. The price for these contracts was commonly in the vicinity of the minimum wage plus 5 percent.

Occasional Services.   These included anything from sporting or entertainment events to social or emergency services. For example, this might include seasonal contracts, as with a CFL or NHL sports team, or one-time affairs. Wages paid to the security personnel were usually quite low, but profit margins to the firm were above average.

Buyer Behavior

The buyer of security services was commonly in the stronger position. This resulted from a multitude of firms offering what buyers perceived to be largely undifferentiated products and services, and sellers trying to win business by providing the lowest price. Further, the cost of switching suppliers was low because of the customers' perceived similarity of their services. It was also quite simple for firms to bring the security function in-house if they believed they could achieve substantial cost savings or other improvements in their security programs. In addition, some buyers tended to give security considerations a low priority in their budgeting.

Firms purchasing security products and services had three levels of decisions to make: (1) a general policy on the role and risk-cost framework that security would play in their firm, (2) a decision regarding the types of products and services to be purchased, and (3) the selection of suppliers.

Each decision level involved new groups or individuals within the organization. Policy decisions were generally made at the senior executive level while the product/service and supplier decisions tended to be made at the local level.

Most purchases were straight tender purchases based on a sealed bidding process. Firms with whom security was a low priority, and most government agencies, tended to choose the lowest bidder. Companies who took a greater interest in the quality of their security program considered attributes other than price when deciding upon their security supplier.

As part of a study on the security industry, Metropol surveyed buyers' ratings of the importance of several factors in choosing a security firm. They also had buyers rate Metropol's performance on those performance factors. Among the most significant decision-making criteria identified were consistency and reliability, availability of service representatives, and price. Metropol

---

EXHIBIT 4   Customer Decision-Making Criteria—Survey Results

How important are the following attributes to you when making a decision on security services?

	Not Important				Very Important	Average Score
	1	*2*	*3*	*4*	*5*	
Consistency and reliability	—	—	—	3	14	4.824
Quality of service representatives	—	—	—	5	12	4.706
Price competitiveness	—	—	3	8	6	4.176
Company reputation	1	1	—	7	8	4.176
Emergency services	—	2	4	7	4	3.765
Full range of products and services	—	4	2	6	5	3.706
Consulting services	—	6	6	3	2	3.059
National coverage	4	4	6	2	—	2.375

Note: The survey was a convenience sample of Metropol customers.
Source: Metropol Research.

scored highest on the quality of their representatives and the customers' view of the firm's reputation (Exhibits 4 and 5).

Metropol

Metropol organized its operations on a regional (provincial) basis. The Manitoba headquarters developed a centralized policy and operating guidelines procedure that was instituted in all offices. While sales representatives dealt with the day-to-day needs of customers, top management was involved in making sales presentations to large accounts.

Services

Despite Metropol's variety of services, supplying unarmed, uniformed security guards accounted for most of their revenue. Their sales revenue breakdown by service type was

Security guards	90%
Mobile security checks	8
Other (investigation, polygraph testing, retail services, consulting, and education)	2
	100%

Providing security guard services involved more than just sending guards to industrial or office sites. Metropol had to train, pay, uniform, and insure

Exhibit 5   Customer Decision-Making Criteria—Survey Results

How would you rate Metropol Security on the following attributes?

	Poor 1	Fair 2	Sat. 3	Good 4	Excellent 5	Average Score
Consistency and reliability	1	1	5	7	3	3.588
Quality of service representatives	—	2	—	11	4	4.000
Price competitiveness	—	1	4	10	2	3.765
Company reputation	—	—	2	10	5	4.176
Emergency services	1	1	6	7	3	3.556
Full range of products and services	1	2	7	6	1	3.235
Consulting services	—	4	5	5	2	2.944
National coverage	1	—	7	3	—	3.091

the guards. They also had to supervise and dispatch their people as well as provide reports to their clients.

"We have attempted to provide greater value to our customers than our competitors have," stated Pat. "For example, we have a 24-hour dispatch service while all the other firms use an answering service. There is a $100,000 (annual) difference in cost, but we can respond much faster to any situation. Some customers will say they just consider price in their purchase decision but end up liking and buying the extra service."

Metropol also gave their guards special training on the procedures to follow in the case of such emergencies as bomb threats, hostage takings, and fire evacuations. Again, this was an attempt to differentiate their services from those of other security guard companies.

The mobile security business was contracted out to local firms. This market was not considered to be a growth area, and Metropol did not invest a great deal of resources in it.

Investigative and polygraph services were contracted out to a couple of ex-RCMP officers. Metropol had maintained these investigators on its staff at one time but found that demand for these services was not great enough to justify having the high-salaried people as full-time employees.

Education programs were another means Metropol used to create added value and increase switching costs for their customers. Pat explained, "We give seminars on such topics as 'The Protection of Proprietary Information' for our clients and even invite some companies we don't currently serve. We want our clients to realize that if they switch security firms they will be losing something of value."

Metropol did not sell hardware products such as fences, alarms, and locks. However, it could arrange the purchase of such equipment for their clients. It was presently considering working in conjunction with a systems engineer so the company would be able to provide a total security package to their customers.

Costs

Metropol divided its costs into two groups, direct and administrative. A typical job had the following cost characteristics:

Direct costs	83–86%
Selling and administrative costs	8–9%
Pre-tax profit margin	4–7%

Given the above figures, cost control was a key success factor for Metropol and the security industry in general. Metropol's margins were, in fact, higher than the industry average of approximately 4 percent. "We use a job-costing process," volunteered Pat. "Every pay period (two weeks) we look at what we made on each job. We consider and analyze every expense item very closely to see if there was any deviation from what was budgeted."

Direct costs included wages, uniforms, bonding, transportation, and supervision. Metropol did a good job of keeping its costs as low or lower than its competitors despite offering a higher level of service. Some of this was a result of economies of scale in purchasing such items as uniforms, achieved because of their comparatively large size. The company also did a superior job in collecting their outstanding receivables within a two-week period.

Pricing

Prices were determined by identifying the direct costs associated with a job, allowing for a contribution to selling and administrative overhead and providing for a profit margin. Consideration was also given to any particular reason there may be for pricing a bid either particularly high or low. "We once bid at very close to our direct cost for a job in a town where we had no competition in order to discourage other firms from entering that market," noted Pat. He also suggested that it was important to anticipate competitors' likely pricing strategy when bidding on a job as well as recognizing that some projects had greater potential for cost overruns.

Promotion

Metropol individually identified the companies in each of their trading areas that were potential clients and concentrated their promotional efforts on that group. In Manitoba, this "club" amounted to about 500 firms.

Once these firms were identified, strategies were developed to either sell to those potential accounts which presently had no security service or to become the logical alternative for those businesses who were using competitive services. "We want to put pressure on these incumbent firms to perform," explained Pat.

Metropol used, among other things, their educational seminars to stress to their clients that they offered superior service. At times, firms using competing security companies were invited as a means of encouraging them to switch to Metropol.

Employees

Metropol employed almost 2,000 people, 1,900 of whom were security guards and 100 who were selling, administrative, or management personnel.

Security guards came principally from three backgrounds: (1) young people (18–25) who could not find other work, (2) older people (50–65) looking for a second career, or (3) ex-military or police personnel who liked the quasi-military nature of the job.

Annual employee turnover in the security guard industry was very high, estimated to be in the vicinity of 100 percent. Metropol's turnover rate was in the same range. Reasons for the high level included a combination of low wages, generally boring work, and a lack of motivation or support from senior management.

"We have some employees who have been with the company for 15 years," Pat pointed out. "However, the wages we pay are based on our billing rate which often only allows for minimum wages to be paid to our employees." Intense competition and clients who wanted to pay a bare minimum for security guard services forced companies to pay their guards the legal minimum wage. This caused high turnover rates which, evidently, did not bother some clients. Other customers, concerned with employee turnover, specified a higher minimum wage rate which the security company had to pay its guards. Pat liked this attitude because it allowed him to pay his people a higher wage and still be competitive.

Metropol's supervisors and customer service representatives (salespeople) did a good job servicing their accounts and handling any crisis that arose. They helped maintain Metropol's reputation as a competent and reliable security company despite the generally poor reputation of the industry.

The Future

Pat turned his attention to the future. He believed that the way business was conducted in the security guard industry would not significantly change in the near future. He did expect the business to become somewhat more professional with guards being trained in formal, standardized programs. The pressure on profit margins was expected to continue and perhaps even intensify as the larger, multinational firms fought for market share and smaller independents struggled for survival. Pat was thinking about how he could use Metropol's present position and reputation in the security guard sector to expand into more profitable segments of the industry or improve the company's general standing within the guard sector. Some of the opportunities he was considering included

- Geographic expansion.
- A focused strategy.
- Expanding the range of security products and services offered by the company.
- Diversification into other service areas outside the security field.
- Serving the consumer home-security market.

Geographic Expansion.   "To be a national company in Canada you need a presence in Southern Ontario," observed Pat. Even though many companies' security needs were handled at the local level, there was considerable potential for a national accounts program. To be involved in providing a national service, a company had to be active in the Toronto area, where most national companies' security decisions were made. In addition, the Ontario market offered substantial local business. Pat explained, "We handle Northern Telecom's security guard needs throughout Western Canada, but not in Ontario. Northern Telecom has three times the business volume there as it does in all of the western provinces combined."

There were three ways Metropol could enter the Ontario market: (1) by purchasing a local security firm; (2) through merging with another company, or (3) bidding on contracts in Ontario and opening up an office once a contract was obtained.

Pat believed that the merger method was the most appealing since it offered the potential for increased profits with virtually no additional cash investment. He had discussed the possibility with two firms that had head offices in Ontario and were also minor competitors in the Winnipeg, Edmonton, Calgary, and Vancouver markets. The western offices of the merged firm could be closed down, and the business operated under the Metropol name. "The gross margin on their western contracts would go right to the bottom line," suggested Pat, "because all the current Metropol offices could meet their administrative needs and absorb any incremental expenses."

A restricting factor in this strategy was Metropol's limited product/service line. To provide a "complete" security package for any company on a national basis, it was necessary to offer the hardware and ESD packages in addition to the security guards.

A Focused Strategy.   This alternative was really a continuation of Metropol's current strategy. Following this approach, Metropol's principal objective would be to become the fastest-growing security guard firm in Western Canada, with the highest profit margin and return on equity, the lowest employee turnover, and the most satisfied customers in the business of providing contract, unarmed security personnel. This strategy required an increased emphasis on developing a formal marketing program and increasing the value added of Metropol's security guard and support services. Tighter control of costs and employee motivation would be critical success factors as would be the need to carefully segment the market and identify the most profitable clients.

The strategy would be designed to match the distinct competencies and resources of Metropol with the needs of the marketplace. Pat believed that while the strategy "sounded good," it would be very difficult to implement. "Even if you offer the highest quality service you might not get the job," he offered. "Too many contracts, particularly those involving the government sector and crown corporations, are based solely on price, and simply supplying a higher service level in the provision of security guards is not likely to change that."

Expansion of Security Products and Services.   From the customer's point of view, there was an advantage to having one firm coordinate and provide the complete security coverage required by his business; the security system was more effective and efficient. If the customer had to contract with different firms for guards, fences, locks, lights, alarms, and ESDs, there was likely to be a lot of overlap and, in some cases, gaps in the overall system. Also, it was likely to be more expensive. Pat considered an investment in the production of hardware equipment much too costly, given his firm's limited resources, but he was investigating the possibility of arranging a deal with a large multinational distributor of security hardware and ESD products.

Pat explained, "We would like to have an exclusive relationship whereby they [large multinationals] would provide us, at wholesale, with all the hardware and ESD equipment we needed on a private label basis (Metropol brand) and they would train our people. We could offer them our monitoring services and access to new markets." Metropol would package the system, which would include hardware, software, and people in whatever mix its clients needed. The products would be sold to the client or leased on a five-year arrangement.

The expanded product-line strategy would deliver significant benefits to Metropol. Hardware and ESD equipment offered better margins than security guard services and, in some cases, were subject to becoming obsolete. This provided opportunities to sell upgraded systems. For example, television monitoring devices had already gone through several generations of change despite their relatively recent entry into the security product mix. Service contracts to maintain the equipment would provide another source of additional revenue. Finally, the need of these systems for close monitoring and servicing increased the dependence of the customer on Metropol. This higher dependence meant that switching costs for the customer were much higher than with security guard services. This would be especially true if the equipment was leased for a five-year period.

Diversification into Other Service Areas.   This alternative would capitalize on Metropol's skills in hiring people for contract-type jobs and administering a payroll. Their current product line could be expanded to include one or all of the following additional services, which could be provided on a contractual basis: secretarial services, nursing care, janitorial services, or landscaping services. The commercial sector would continue to be their primary target market.

Several years ago Metropol got into the commercial cleaning business with poor results. "Businesses such as janitorial and landscaping services are beyond our particular expertise," revealed Pat. "However, we are looking at providing people and handling the payroll for temporary clerical or nursing services. In those cases, we would be taking our established skills to another market." Pat cited Drake International's experience as evidence that the strategy could work. That company went from providing temporary help to the provision of security guards.

The Consumer Market.   Another alternative for Metropol would be to expand into the consumer market for security products and services. The major products of interest to residential customers were locks, supplementary lighting, fences, mobile home checks, house sitting, and alarm systems. This segment was growing more slowly than the business sector, but still offered substantial opportunity.

Pat was currently exploring Metropol's opportunities as a franchisor of home alarm systems to the numerous small Canadian alarm system dealers. "We would become the Century 21 of the alarm business," Pat suggested.

The alarm business in Canada was made up of a large number of small independent dealers and a few large multinationals. The "small guys" would buy their alarms from wholesalers in small lots which precluded much discounting. They also had to contract out their alarm monitoring to their competition, the large multinationals, because they could not afford the central station monitoring equipment. In most cases, advertising and financing of installations for customers was too expensive to be carried out on a significant basis.

Pat thought a Metropol alarm franchise offered a number of important strategic advantages to independent alarm dealers: (1) by arranging with a large alarm manufacturer to produce a private label Metropol brand alarm line, they could pass on volume discounts to their dealers, (2) franchises would have the Metropol name behind them, (3) co-op advertising would provide greater exposure, (4) an arrangement for consumer financing could be established, and (5) Metropol would set up a central monitoring system.

Consideration was also being given to making locksmiths subdealers of Metropol alarm systems. "Normally a customer must call a locksmith and an alarm specialist to secure his home," suggested Pat. "It would be more effective, especially from a selling perspective, if the locksmith could do both."

Conclusion

Pat realized that the alternatives he was considering were not merely incremental changes in Metropol's strategy. In fact, each option represented a distinct direction for the firm's future development. "We have to define our business mission more specifically," Pat thought to himself. "Then we can choose and implement the strategy that best suits that mission."

MR. JAX FASHION INC.

It was 6:30 a.m., Monday, January 16, 1989. Dawn had not yet broken on the Vancouver skyline, and Louis Eisman, President of Mr. Jax Fashion Inc., was sitting at his desk pondering opportunities for future growth. Growth had been an important objective for Eisman and the other principal shareholder, Joseph Segal. Initially, the company had focused on the professional/career women's dresses, suits, and coordinates market, but by 1986 it had virtually saturated its ability to grow within this market segment in Canada. Growth was then sought through the acquisition of four companies: a woolen textile mill and three apparel manufacturing companies. The result of this decade-long expansion was a company that had become the sixth largest apparel manufacturer in Canada.

In the future, Eisman felt continued growth would require a different approach. A good option appeared to be expansion into the U.S. market. Strong growth was forecast in the women's career/professional market, Mr. Jax's principal market segment, and the recently ratified Free Trade Agreement (FTA) provided an excellent low tariff environment for expansion into the U.S. Yet, Eisman wanted to ensure the appropriate growth strategy was selected. He was confident that if the right approach was taken, Mr. Jax could become a major international apparel company by the end of the next decade.

The Industry

The apparel industry was divided into a variety of market segments based upon gender, type of garment, and price points. Based on price points, the women's segments ranged from low-priced unexceptional to runway fashion segments. Low-priced segments competed on a low-cost manufacturing capability, while the higher quality segments tended to compete on design and marketing capabilities. Companies in the higher priced segments often subcontracted out manufacturing.

The professional/career women's segment ranged from the medium to medium-high price points. During the late 1970s and early 1980s, this segment had experienced strong growth due to the demographic growth in career-oriented, professional women. In the U.S., it had grown by 50 percent annually during the first half of the 1980s, but had slowed to about 20 percent in 1988. Experts predicted that by the mid-1990s, growth would drop to the rate of GNP growth. The U.S. professional/career women's segment was estimated to be $2 billion in 1988. The Canadian market was estimated to be one-tenth this size and growth was expected to emulate the U.S. market. Yet, the exact timing of the slowing of growth was difficult to predict because of extreme cyclicality in the fashion industry. During difficult economic times, women tended to delay purchases, particularly in the mid-priced, fashionable market sectors. Then during times of economic prosperity, women who would not otherwise be able to afford fashionable items tended to have more resources to devote to these items.

Competition

Some of the more prominent Canada-based companies competing in the professional/career women's segment included the following:

Jones New York of Canada

Jones New York of Canada, a marketing subsidiary of a U.S.-based fashion company, was thought to share the leadership position with Mr. Jax in the Canadian professional/career women's market. The company focused exclusively on marketing clothes to this market segment. Manufacturing was contracted out to Asian companies.

The Monaco Group

The Monaco Group had become a major Canadian designer and retailer of men's and women's fashions during the 1980s. By 1988, the company had sales of $21 million and a rate of return on capital of over 20 percent. The company designed their own fashion lines, which were merchandised through their own retail outlets as well as major department stores. Manufacturing was contracted out to Asian companies. Recently, the company had been purchased by Dylex Inc., a large Canada-based retail conglomerate with 2,000 retail apparel stores located in both Canada and the U.S.

Nygard International Ltd.

Nygard International Ltd., with revenues of over $200 million, was Canada's largest apparel manufacturer. Approximately one-third of their sales and production were located in the U.S. This company had historically focused on lower priced clothing, but they had hired away Mr. Jax's former designer to create the Peter Nygard Signature Collection, a fashion line aimed at the professional/career women's market. This new line had been out for only six months, and sales were rumored to be moderate.

Additional competition in this Canadian segment included a wide variety of U.S. and European imports. These companies generally manufactured garments in Asia and marketed them in Canada through independent Canadian sales agents. Historically, most had concentrated their marketing resources on the rapidly growing U.S. market, yet many had captured a significant share of the Canadian market based upon strong international brand recognition. Prominent U.S.-based competition included the following companies:

Liz Claiborne

Liz Claiborne, as the originator of the professional/career women's fashion look, had utilized their first-mover advantage to build a dominant position in this segment. This company, started in 1976, grew tremendously during the late 1970s and early 1980s, and by 1988 they had sales in excess of U.S.$1.2 billion, or nearly two-thirds of the market. Claiborne generally competed on price and brand recognition, a strategy copied by many of the larger companies which had begun to compete in this segment. To keep prices low, Claiborne contracted out manufacturing to low-cost manufacturers, 85 percent of which were Asian. The company's large size allowed them to wield considerable influence over these manufacturing relationships. Recently, the company had diversified into retailing.

J.H. Collectibles

J.H. Collectibles, a Milwaukee-based company with sales of U.S.$200 million, had one of the more unique strategies in this segment. They produced slightly upscale products which emphasized an English country-sporting look. Using facilities in Wisconsin and Missouri, they were the only company to both manufacture all of their products in-house and to produce all of them in the U.S. In addition to providing stronger quality control, this strategy enabled J.H. Collectibles to provide very fast delivery service in the U.S. Limiting distribution of their product to strong market regions and retailers also enabled them to maintain production at levels estimated to be at or near their plants' capacities.

Jones of New York

Jones of New York, the parent company of Jones New York of Canada, was a major competitor in the U.S. market. In fact, the majority of their U.S.$200 million in sales was derived from this market.

Evan-Picone

Evan-Picone was a U.S.-based apparel designer and marketer which had become very successful in the slightly older professional/career women's market. This company also contracted out their manufacturing function, and had annual sales in excess of U.S.$200 million.

In addition, there were a myriad of other apparel designers, marketers, and manufacturers competing in this segment. They included such companies as Christian Dior, Kasper, Pendleton, Carole Little, Susan Bristol, J. G. Hooke, Ellen Tracy, Anne Klein II, Perry Ellis, Adrienne Vittadini, Tahari, Harve Bernard, Norma Kamali, Philippe Adec, Gianni Sport, Regina Porter, and Herman Geist.

Profitability in this segment had been excellent. According to data from annual reports and financial analyst reports, Liz Claiborne led profitability in the apparel industry with a five-year average return on equity of 56 percent and a 12-month return of 45 percent; J.H. Collectibles had averaged over 40 percent return on equity during the last five years. This compared to an average return on equity in the overall apparel industry of 12.5 percent in the U.S., and 16 percent in Canada during the past five years.

Distribution

The selection and maintenance of retail distribution channels had become a very important consideration for apparel manufacturers in the 1980s. The retail industry had gone through a particularly bad year in 1988, although the professional/career women's segment had been relatively profitable. Overall demand had declined, and retail analysts were predicting revenue increases of only one to two percent in 1989, which paled beside the six to seven percent growth experienced in the mid-1980s. The consensus was that high interest rates and inflation, as well as somewhat stagnant demand levels, were suppressing overall profitability.

Although initially considered a mild downturn, recent market indicators suggested that this downward trend was relatively stable and long lasting. Industry analysts had begun to suspect that permanent market changes might be occurring. With baby boomers reaching their childbearing years, further constraints on disposable income might result as this group's consumption patterns reflected increasing emphasis on purchases of homes, or the decision by many women to permanently or temporarily leave the workforce to raise their children. In addition, the effects of rampant growth in the number of retail outlets during the 1980s were beginning to take their toll. Vicious competition had been eroding margins at the retailer level, and the industry appeared to be moving into a period of consolidation. As a result of these developments, a shift in power from the designers to the retailers appeared to be under way.

To counter the retailers' increasing power, some apparel designers had been vertically integrating into retailing. The attractiveness of this option was based on controlling the downstream distribution channel activities, and thus enabling an apparel company to aggressively pursue increased market share. The principal components for success in the retail apparel industry were location, brand awareness, and superior purchasing skills. The apparel companies which had integrated successfully into retailing were the more market-oriented firms such as Benetton and Esprit.

The Free Trade Agreement

Historically, developed nations had protected their textile and clothing industries through the imposition of relatively high tariffs and import quotas. Tariffs for apparel imported into Canada averaged 24.5 percent, and into the U.S., 22.5 percent. Tariffs for worsted woolen fabrics, one of the principal ingredients for Mr. Jax's products, were 40 percent into Canada, and 22.5 percent into the U.S. Import quotas were used to further limit the ability of developing country manufacturers to import into either country. Despite these obstacles, Canadian apparel imports had grown from 20 percent to 30 percent of total shipments during the 1980s, most of which came from developing countries. Shipments into Canada from the U.S. represented an estimated $200 million in 1988, while Canadian manufacturers exported approximately $70 million to the U.S.

The FTA would alter trade restrictions in North America considerably. Over the next ten years, all clothing and textile tariffs between the two countries would be eliminated, but stringent "rules of origin" would apply. To qualify, goods not only had to be manufactured in North America, but they also had to utilize raw materials (i.e., yarn, in the case of textiles, and fabric, in the case of apparel) manufactured in North America. Unfortunately, these "rules of origin" favoured U.S. apparel manufacturers as 85 percent of the textiles they used were sourced in the U.S., while Canadian manufacturers utilized mostly imported textiles. To ameliorate this disadvantage, a clause was appended to the agreement which allowed Canadians to export $500 million worth of apparel annually into the U.S. that was exempt from the "rules of origin" but would have a 50 percent Canadian value-added content. There was much speculation as to how this exemption would be allocated when, in approximately five years, exports were projected to exceed the exemption limit. Experts expected that the companies successfully demonstrating their ability to export into the U.S. would have first rights to these exceptions.

Many industry experts had contemplated the consequences of the FTA. There was some agreement that in the short term the FTA would most severely impact the lower priced apparel segments in Canada because of the economies of scale which existed in the U.S. market (i.e., the average U.S. apparel manufacturer was ten times larger than its Canadian counterpart). Yet, long-term prospects for all segments were restrained because the industry was slowly being pressured by the Canadian government to become internationally competitive. The question was when international negotiations would eliminate more of the protection afforded to the industry. It was with this concern in mind that Eisman had been continuously pushing the company to become a major international fashion designer and manufacturer.

Overall, Eisman considered the FTA a mixed blessing. Competition in Canada would increase moderately over time, but he felt that the lower tariff rates and the company's high-quality, in-house woolen mill presented a wonderful opportunity for potential expansion into the U.S. market.

Mr. Jax Fashions

In 1979, a venture capital company owned by Joseph Segal acquired a sleepy Vancouver-based apparel manufacturer having $3 million in sales, 70 percent of which was in men's wear. Segal immediately recruited Louis Eisman, a well-known women's fashion executive, who proceeded to drop the men's clothing line, and aggressively refocus the company on the career/professional women's market segment.

Eisman appreciated the importance of fashion, and for the first three years he designed all of the new lines. In 1982, he recruited an up-and-coming young Canadian fashion designer, yet he continued to influence the direction of designs considerably. He travelled to Europe for approximately two months annually to review European trends and procure quality fabrics appropriate for the upcoming season. He personally reviewed all designs. The combined women's fashion knowledge and designing abilities provided Mr. Jax with a high-quality, classically designed product which differentiated it from most other Canadian competition. In 1989, the designer resigned, and Eisman recruited a New York-based fashion designer, Ron Leal. Leal had excellent experience in several large U.S. design houses and, unlike the previous designer, he brought considerable U.S. market experience and presence.

Eisman's energy and drive were also critical in establishing the merchandising and distribution network. He personally developed relationships with many of the major retailers. He hired and developed sales agents, in-house sales staff, and in 1983, recruited Jackie Clabon, who subsequently became Vice President–Marketing and Sales. The sales staff were considered to be some of the best in the industry. Clabon's extensive Canadian sales and merchandising experience, combined with Eisman's design and marketing strength, provided Mr. Jax with considerable ability in these critical activities.

Initially, acceptance by Eastern fashion buyers was cool. The fashion "establishment" was highly skeptical of this new Vancouver-based apparel designer and manufacturer. Thus, Eisman focused on smaller independent retail stores, which were more easily swayed in their purchasing decisions. As Mr. Jax gained a reputation for high quality, classical design, and excellent service, larger retail chains started to place orders. By 1988, Mr. Jax's products were sold in over 400 department and specialty stores across Canada. Major customers included The Bay, Eaton's, Holt Renfrew, and Simpson's, and, although initial marketing efforts had been aimed at the smaller retailer, the majority of Mr. Jax's sales were now to the larger retail chains. The apparel lines were sold through a combination of sales agents and in-house salespersons. Ontario and Quebec accounted for 72 percent of sales. In addition, two retail stores had recently been established in Vancouver and Seattle; the Vancouver store was very profitable, but the Seattle store was very unprofitable. Industry observers had suggested a number of factors to explain the two stores' performance differences. These factors included increased competition in U.S. metropolitan areas due to increased market density, lower levels of regulation and other entry barriers, greater product selection, and more timely fashion trend shifts compared to the Canadian market, which often exhibited lags in fashion developments of six months or more. Mr. Jax also had a local presence in Vancouver, which was believed to have helped their store by way of reputation, ancillary promotions, and easier access to skilled resources.

Many industry experts felt that Mr. Jax's product line success could be attributed directly to Eisman. He was known for his energy and brashness, as well as his creativity and knowledge of the women's fashion market. In his prior merchandising and marketing experience, he had developed an intuitive skill for the capricious women's apparel market. This industry was often considered to be one of instinct rather than rationality. Eisman was particularly good at design, merchandising, and marketing (Exhibit 1). He worked very closely with these departments, often getting involved in the smallest details. As Eisman said, "It is the details that make the difference in our business." Although Eisman concentrated a great deal of his time and effort on these functions, he also attempted to provide guidance to production. The production function had been important in providing the service advantage, particularly in terms of delivery time, which Mr. Jax held over imports. By 1988, Mr. Jax's professional/career women's fashion lines accounted for $25 million in revenues and $3 million in net income (Exhibit 2).

Diversification through Acquisitions

In 1986, Segal and Eisman took Mr. Jax public, raising in excess of $17 million although they both retained one-third of equity ownership. The newly raised capital was used to diversify growth through the acquisition of four semi-related companies.

Surrey Classics Manufacturing Ltd.

Surrey Classics Manufacturing Ltd., a family-owned, Vancouver-based firm, was purchased for $2 million in 1986. This company was principally a manufacturer of lower priced women's apparel and coats. The acquisition was initially made with the objective of keeping the company an autonomous unit. However, the previous owner and his management team adapted poorly to their position within the Mr. Jax organization, and, upon expiration of their noncompetition clauses, they resigned and started a competing company. Unfortunately, sales began to decline rapidly because of this new competition and the absence of managerial talent. To stem the losses, a variety of designers

**EXHIBIT 1   Mr. Jax Fashion's President Helping in a
Promotional Photo Session**

were hired under contract. However, Surrey's poor cash flow could not support the required promotional campaigns and the new fashion lines fared poorly, resulting in mounting operating losses.

In late 1988, Eisman reassigned Mr. Jax's Vice President–Finance as interim manager of Surrey Classics. As Eisman stated, "The company needed a manager who knew the financial priorities in the industry and could maximize the effectiveness of the company's productive capacity." Several administrative functions were transferred to Mr. Jax, including design, pattern making, sizing, and scaling operations. Marketing and production continued to be independent operations housed in a leased facility just outside of Vancouver. Surrey Classics now produced a diversified product line which included Highland Queen, a licensed older women's line of woolen apparel, and Jaki Petite, a Mr. Jax fashion line patterned for smaller women. During this turnaround, Eisman himself provided the required industry-specific management skills, which demanded a considerable amount of his time and attention. Eisman kept in daily contact and was involved in most major decisions. During this time Surrey's revenues had declined from $12 million in 1986 to $10.8 million in 1988, and net income had dropped from $100,000 in 1986 to a loss of approximately $2 million in 1988. Eisman felt that in the next two years

EXHIBIT 2 Mr. Jax Fashion Inc. Financial Statements

	1981	*1982*	*1983*	*1984*	*1985*	*1986*	*1987* *9 months*	*1988*
Sales	4,592	4,315	5,472	7,666	13,018	24,705	53,391	72,027
Cost of sales	2,875	2,803	3,404	4,797	7,885	14,667	38,165	49,558
Gross profit	1,717	1,512	2,068	2,869	5,133	10,038	15,226	22,469
Selling & gen. admin.	1,172	1,117	1,458	1,898	2,434	4,530	9,071	18,175
Income from operations	545	395	610	971	2,699	5,508	6,155	4,294
Other income	22	25	25	10	16	564	418	117
Loss from discontinued operation								(554)
Income before taxes	567	420	635	981	2,715	6,072	6,573	3,857
Income taxes–								
Current	150	194	285	432	1,251	2,874	2,746	1,825
Deferred	47	2	(5)	28	24	57	245	(195)
Net income	370	224	355	521	1,440	3,141	3,582	2,227
Share price range: Low						$7.5	$8	$7.5
High						$11	$18	$14

Income Statement (000s)

Note: In 1987, the accounting year end was changed from February 1988 to November 1987. This made the 1987 accounting year nine months in duration.

Exhibit 2   (Concluded)

Balance Sheet (000s)

	1981	1982	1983	1984	1985	1986	1987	1988
Assets								
Current Assets								
Short-term investments	—	—	—	—	—	5,027	1,794	495
Accounts receivable	709	874	961	1,697	2,974	6,430	16,133	14,923
Inventories	464	474	684	736	1,431	3,026	15,431	16,914
Prepaid expenses	11	15	20	22	201	398	404	293
Income taxes recoverable	—	—	—	—	—	—	—	1,074
Prop., Plant & Equip.	318	349	424	572	795	4,042	7,789	13,645
Other Assets	—	—	—	—	—	273	526	513
Total Assets	1,502	1,712	2,089	3,027	5,401	22,196	42,077	47,857
Liabilities								
Current Liabilities								
Bank indebtedness	129	356	114	351	579	575	1,788	4,729
Accounts payable	490	435	678	963	1,494	3,100	4,893	6,934
Income taxes payable	126	58	86	153	809	1,047	546	
Deferred Taxes	84	86	81	109	133	217	462	267
Shareholder Equity								
Share equity	127	7	13	5	4	12,252	26,577	26,577
Retained earnings	546	770	1,125	1,446	2,347	5,005	7,811	9,350
Total liabilities	1,502	1,712	2,097	3,027	5,401	22,196	42,077	47,857

Note: Years 1981–84 were estimated from change in financial position statements.

Surrey's operations would have to be further rationalized into Mr. Jax's to save on overhead costs.

West Coast Woolen Mills Ltd.

West Coast Woolen Mills Ltd. was a 40-year-old, family-owned, Vancouver-based worsted woolen mill. Mr. Jax acquired the company for $2.2 million in 1987. Eisman was able to retain most of the previous management, all of whom had skills quite unique to the industry. West Coast marketed fabric to customers across Canada. In 1986, its sales were $5 million, profits were nil, and its estimated capacity was $10 million annually. The company was the smallest of three worsted woolen mills in Canada, and in the U.S. there were about 18 worsted woolen manufacturers, several being divisions of the world's largest textile manufacturing companies.

Both Mr. Jax and West Coast had mutually benefitted from this acquisition. The affiliation allowed Mr. Jax to obtain control of fabric production scheduling, design, and quality. In particular, Mr. Jax had been able to significantly reduce order lead times for fabric produced at this subsidiary, although the effects of this on West Coast had not been studied. West Coast benefitted from increased capital funding which allowed it to invest in new equipment and technology, both important attributes in such a capital-intensive industry. These investments supported the company's long-term stategic objective of becoming the highest quality, most design-conscious worsted woolen mill in North America. This objective had already been reached in Canada.

Mr. Jax was presently fulfilling 30 percent to 40 percent of its textile demands through West Coast. The remainder was being sourced in Europe. By 1988, West Coast's revenues were $6.5 million and profitability was at the break-even point.

Olympic Pant and Sportswear Co. Ltd. and Canadian Sportswear Co. Ltd.

Mr. Jax acquired Olympic Pant and Sportswear Co. Ltd. and Canadian Sportswear Co. Ltd. both privately owned companies, in 1987 for $18.3 million. The former management, excluding owners, was retained in both of these Winnipeg-based companies.

Olympic manufactured lower priced men's and boys' pants and outerwear as well as some women's sportswear. Canadian Sportswear manufactured low-priced women's and girls' outerwear and coats. Canadian Sportswear was also a certified apparel supplier to the Canadian Armed Forces, and, although these types of sales made up a minority of their revenue base, such a certification provided the company with a small but protected market niche. The disparity in target markets and locations between these companies and Mr. Jax dictated that they operate largely independently. The expected synergies were limited to a few corporate administrative functions such as finance and systems management.

Combined revenues for these companies had declined from $35 million in 1986 to $30 million in 1988. Both of these companies had remained profitable during this period, although profits had declined. In 1988, combined net income was $1.2 million. Management blamed declining revenues on increased competition and a shortage of management because of the previous owners' retirement.

The Corporation's Present Situation

Diversification had provided the company with excellent growth, but it had also created problems. The most serious was the lack of management control over the now diversified structure (Exhibit 3). By 1988, it had become quite clear that without the entrepreneurial control and drive of the previous owners, the companies were not as successful as they had been prior to their acquisition. Therefore, in late 1988, Eisman recruited a new CFO, Judith Madill, to coordinate a corporate reorganization experience, but had limited operating experience in an entrepreneurial environment such as the fashion industry. Madill

EXHIBIT 3 Mr. Jax Fashion's Organization Chart

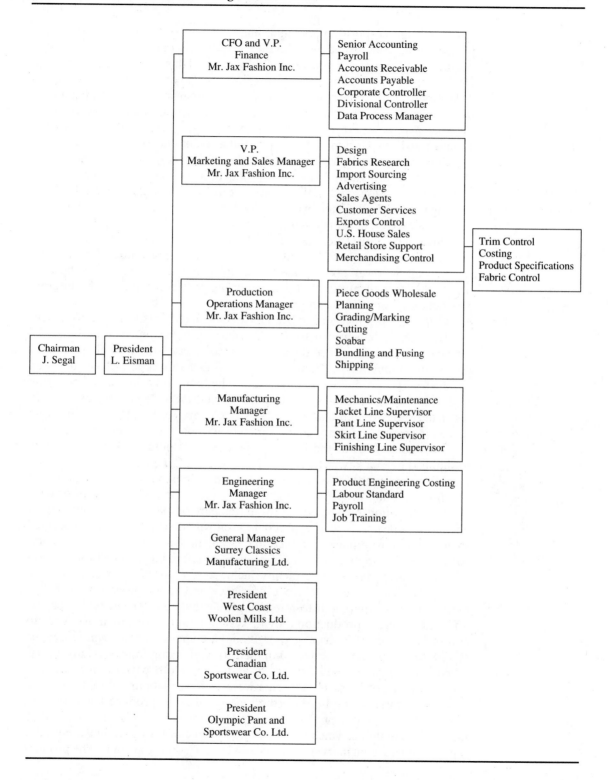

suggested that corporate personnel, financial, and systems management departments be established to integrate and aid in the management of the subsidiaries. Eisman was not completely convinced this was the right approach. He had always maintained that one of Mr. Jax's competitive strengths was its flexibility and rapid response time. He thought increased administrative overhead would restrict this entrepreneurial ability, and that extra costs would severely restrict future expansion opportunities. Thus, he had limited the administrative expansion to two industrial accountants for the next year.

Consolidation was also occurring in the existing organization. Eisman was trying to recruit a vice president of production. Mr. Jax had never officially had such a position, and, unfortunately, recruiting a suitable candidate was proving to be difficult. There were relatively few experienced apparel manufacturing executives in North America. Furthermore, Vancouver was not an attractive place for fashion executives because it, not being a fashion centre, would isolate him or her from future employment opportunities. Higher salaries as well as lower taxes tended to keep qualified individuals in the U.S. Yet, a manager of production was badly needed to coordinate the internal production consolidation program.

Originally, production had been located in an old 22,000-square-foot facility. By 1986, it had grown to 48,000 square feet located in four buildings throughout Vancouver. Production flow encompassed the typical apparel industry operational tasks (Exhibit 4). However, the division of tasks between buildings made production planning and scheduling very difficult. Production problems slowly accumulated between 1986 and 1988. The problems not only restricted capacity, but also caused customer service to deteriorate from an excellent shipment rate of approximately 95 percent of orders to recently being sometimes below the industry average of 75 percent. Mr. Jax's ability to ship had been a key to their growth strategy in Canada. Normally, apparel manufacturers met between 70 percent and 80 percent of their orders, but Mr. Jax had built a reputation for shipping more than 90 percent of orders.

Consolidation had begun in the latter part of 1987. An old building in downtown Vancouver was acquired and renovated. The facility incorporated some of the most modern production equipment available. In total, the company had spent approximately $3.5 million on upgrading production technology. Equipment in the new facility included a $220,000 Gerber automatic cloth cutting machine to improve efficiency and reduce waste; $300,000 of modern sewing equipment to improve productivity and production capacity; a $200,000 Gerber production moving system to automatically move work to appropriate work stations as required; and a computerized design assistance system to integrate the above equipment (i.e., tracking in-process inventory, scheduling, planning, and arranging, and sizing cloth patterns for cutting). The objectives of these investments were to lower labour content, improve production capacity, and reduce the time required to produce a garment.

In the last quarter of 1988, Mr. Jax had moved into this new head office facility. The building, which was renovated by one of Italy's leading architects, represented a design marvel with its skylights and soaring atriums. The produc-

EXHIBIT 4 Mr. Jax Fashion's Production Flow Chart

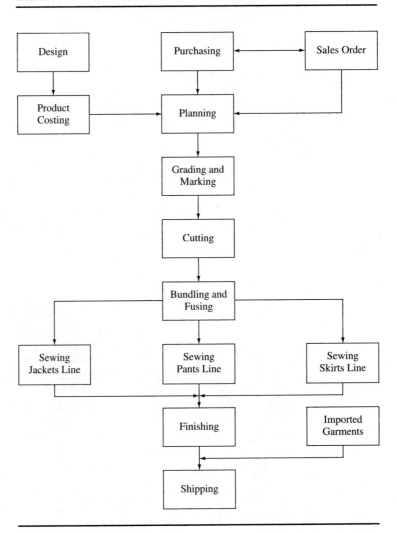

tion department had just recently settled into its expansive space. However, the move had not gone without incident. The equipment operators had difficulties adapting to the new machines. Most of the workers had become accustomed to the repetitive tasks required of the old technology. The new equipment was forcing them to retrain themselves and required additional effort—something that was not appreciated by many of the workers. In addition, the largely Asian workforce had difficulty understanding retraining instructions because English was their second language.

To further facilitate the implementation of the consolidation program, an apparel production consultant had been hired. The consultant was using time-motion studies to reorganize and improve task efficiency and effectiveness. An example of a problem which had resulted from the move was the need for integration between overall production planning, task assignment, worker remuneration, and the new Gerber production moving system. If these elements were not integrated, the new system would in fact slow production. Unfortunately, this integration had not been considered until after the move, and the machine subsequently had to be removed until adjustments were made. The adjustments required converting workers from a salary base to a piece rate pay scale. The consultants were training all the workers to convert to piece rate work, and to operate the necessary equipment in the most efficient manner. Three workers were being trained per week. The conversion was expected to take two years.

Despite these ongoing problems, production appeared to be improving, and operational activities were now organized and coordinated with some degree of efficiency. Eisman was hopeful that production would gain the upper hand in the fight to remedy scheduling problems within the next six months.

Opportunities for Future Growth

Despite problems such as those detailed above, Mr. Jax's revenues and profits had grown by 1,500 percent and 500 percent, respectively, over the past eight years. Furthermore, Eisman was extremely positive about further growth opportunities in the U.S. market. During the past two years, Eisman had tested the Dallas and New York markets. Local sales agents had carried the Mr. Jax fashion line, and 1988 revenues had grown to U.S.$1 million, the majority of which had come from Dallas. Follow-up research revealed that retail purchasers liked the "classical European styling combined with the North American flair."

This initial success had been inspiring, but it had also exposed Eisman to the difficulties of entering the highly competitive U.S. market. In particular, attaining good sales representation and excellent service, both of which were demanded by U.S. retailers, would be difficult. Securing first-class sales representation required having either a strong market presence or a promising promotional program. In addition, Mr. Jax had found U.S. retailers to be extremely onerous in their service demands. These demands were generally a result of the more competitive retail environment. Demands were particularly stringent for smaller apparel suppliers because of their nominal selling power. These demands ranged from very low wholesale prices to extremely fast order-filling and re-stocking requirements. Eisman recognized that Mr. Jax would have to establish a focused, coordinated, and aggressive marketing campaign to achieve its desired objectives in this market.

Eisman had studied two alternate approaches to entering the U.S. market. One approach involved establishing a retailing chain, while the other involved starting a U.S.-based wholesale distribution subsidiary responsible for managing the aggressive promotional and sales campaign required.

Establishing a retail chain would require both new capital and skills. Capital costs, including leasehold improvements and inventory, would be initially very high, and an administrative infrastructure as well as a distribution and product inventorying system would have to be developed. Yet, starting a retail chain did have benefits. The retail approach would provide controllability, visibility, and rapid market penetration. It was the approach taken by many of the aggressive apparel companies in the women's professional/career market segment, such as Liz Claiborne, Benetton, and Esprit. Furthermore, Mr. Jax's marketing strength fit well with this approach. It was estimated that the initial capital required would be about $10 million to open the first 30 stores, and then cost $300,000 per outlet thereafter. Sales revenues would grow to between $300,000 and $750,000 per outlet, depending upon the location, after two to five years. Operating margins on apparel stores averaged slightly less than 10 percent. Experts felt that within five years the company could possibly open 45 outlets; five the first year, and ten each year thereafter. In summary, this option would entail the greatest financial risk, but it would also have the greatest potential return.

The alternative approach was to establish a U.S. distribution subsidiary. This alternative would require capital and more of the same skills the company had developed in Canada. In general, the company would have to set up one or more showrooms throughout the U.S. The location of the showrooms would be critical to the approach eventually implemented. Exhibit 5 illustrates regional apparel buying patterns in North America.

A wholesale distribution approach could be carried out in one of two ways: either on a regional or national basis. A regional approach would involve focusing on the smaller regional retail stores. These stores tended to attract less competitive attention because of the higher sales expense-to-revenue ratio inherent in servicing these accounts. The approach required the new distributor to provide good-quality fashion lines, and service the accounts in a better manner than established suppliers. An advantage to this approach was that regional retailers demanded fewer and smaller price concessions compared to the larger national chains. The obstacles to this approach included the large sales force required and the superior service capability. Even though Mr. Jax had utilized this strategy successfully in Canada, success was not assured in the U.S. because of the very competitive environment. These factors made this approach both difficult to implement and slow relative to other approaches. Experts estimated fixed costs to average $1 million annually per region, of which 75 percent would be advertising and 25 percent other promotional costs. Additional operating costs would consist of sales commissions (7 percent of sales) and administrative overhead costs (see below). Revenues would be dependent upon many factors, but an initial annual growth rate of $1 million annually within each region was considered attainable over the next five years. In summary, this approach would minimize Mr. Jax's risk exposure, but it would also minimize the short-term opportunities.

The national approach was also a viable option. The greatest challenge in a national strategy would be the difficulty in penetrating well-established

EXHIBIT 5   North American Apparel Consumption by Region

Source: U.S. and Canadian governments.

buyer/seller relationships. Floor space was expensive, and national chains and department stores tended to buy conservatively, sticking with the more reputable suppliers who they knew could produce a saleable product and service large orders. They also tended to demand low prices and rapid reorder terms. In summary, the national approach provided significant entry barriers, but it also provided the greatest potential for market share growth. Clearly, if economies of scale and competitive advantage in the larger North American context was the desired goal, this had to be the eventual strategy.

The principal costs of this approach would be the advertising and promotional expenses. National apparel companies had advertising expenditures of many millions of dollars. In discussions with Eisman, industry advertising executives had recommended an advertising expenditure of between $3 and

$5 million annually in the first three years and then, if successful, increasing it by $1 million annually in the next two successive years. Additional operating costs would be required for sales commissions (7 percent of sales) and administrative overhead (see below). The results of this approach were very uncertain and two outcomes were possible. If the approach was successful, Eisman expected that one or two accounts grossing $1 to $2 million annually could be captured in the first two years. Eisman then felt the sales would expand to about $5 million in the third year, and increase by $5 million annually for the next two successive years. However, if the expected quality, design, or service requirements were not sustained, sales would probably decline in the third year to that of the first year and then virtually disappear thereafter.

Both the national and regional approaches would require an infrastructure. Depending upon the approach taken, the head office could be located in a number of places. If a national approach was taken, Mr. Jax would have to locate in one of the major U.S. apparel centres (e.g., New York or California). Eisman estimated that the national approach would require a full-time director of U.S. operations immediately, while the regional approach could delay this hiring until required. Such a managing director would require extensive previous experience in the industry, and be both capable and compatible with Mr. Jax's marketing, operating, and strategic approach. To ensure top-quality candidates, Eisman felt that a signing bonus of at least $100,000 would have to be offered. The remuneration would be tied to sales growth and volume, but a continued minimum salary guarantee might be necessary until the sales reached some minimum volume. In addition, a full-time sales manager would be required. Eisman estimated that the subsidiary's administrative overhead expense would be $500,000 if a regional approach was taken, versus $1 million for a national approach in both cases. These overhead costs would then escalate by approximately $0.5 million annually for the first five years.

Eisman had now studied the U.S. growth options for more than six months. He felt a decision had to be made very soon; otherwise the company would forgo the window of opportunity which existed. The new FTA environment and the growth in the professional/career women's market segment were strong incentives, and delaying a decision would only increase the costs as well as the possibility of failure. Eisman realized the decision was critical to the company's evolution toward its ultimate goal of becoming a major international fashion company. The challenge was deciding which approach to take, as well as the sequencing and timing of the subsequent actions.

NEILSON
INTERNATIONAL
IN MEXICO

In January 1993, Howard Bateman, Vice President of International Operations for Neilson International, a division of William Neilson Limited, was assessing a recent proposal from Sabritas, a division of Pepsico Foods in Mexico, to launch, Neilson's brands in the Mexican market. Neilson, a leading producer of high-quality confectionery products, had grown to achieve a leadership position in the Canadian market and was currently producing Canada's top-selling chocolate bar, "Crispy Crunch." In the world chocolate bar market, however, Neilson was dwarfed by major players such as M&M/Mars, Hershey/Lowney, and Nestlé/Rowntree. Recognizing their position as a smaller player with fewer resources, in a stagnant domestic market, Neilson in 1990 formed its International Division to develop competitive strategies for their exporting efforts.

Recent attempts to expand into several foreign markets, including the United States, had taught them some valuable lessons. Although it was now evident that they had world-class products to offer to global markets, their competitive performance was being constrained by limited resources. Pepsico's joint branding proposal would allow greater market penetration than Neilson could afford. But, at what cost?

Given the decision to pursue international opportunities more aggressively, Bateman's biggest challenge was to determine the distributor relationships Neilson should pursue in order to become a global competitor.

The Chocolate Confectionery Industry[1]

The "confectionery" industry consisted of the "sugar" segment, including all types of sugar confectionery, chewing gum, and the "chocolate" segment,

---

This case was prepared under the supervision of Professors P. W. Beamish and C. B. Johnston by Gayle Duncan and Shari Ann Wortel. Copyright © 1995 The University of Western Ontario Western Business School Case 9-95-G003.

[1] Some information in this section was derived from James C. Ellert, J. Peter Killing, and Dana Hyde, "Nestlé-Rowntree (A)," in *Business Policy, A Canadian Casebook,* (eds.) Joseph N. Fry *et al.* (Prentice Hall Canada Inc., 1992), pp. 655–667.

which included chocolates and other cocoa-based products. Most large chocolate operations were dedicated to two major products—boxed chocolates and bar chocolates—which represented nearly 50 percent of the confectionery industry by volume.

Competition from imports was significant with the majority of products (39 percent) coming from the United States. European countries, such as Switzerland, Germany, the United Kingdom, and Belgium, were also major sources of confectionery, especially for premium products such as boxed chocolates. (See Exhibit 1 for a profile of chocolate-exporting countries.) In order to maintain production volumes and to relieve the burden of fixed costs on operations, Canadian manufacturers used excess capacity to produce goods for exporting. Although nearly all of these products were traditionally exported to the United States, in the early nineties the world market had become increasingly more attractive.

Firms in the confectionery industry competed on the basis of brand-name products, product quality, and cost of production. Although Canadian producers had the advantage of being able to purchase sugar at the usually lower world price, savings were offset by the higher prices for dairy ingredients used in products manufactured for domestic consumption. Other commodity ingredients, often experiencing widely fluctuating prices, caused significant variations in manufacturing costs. Producers were reluctant to raise their prices due to the highly elastic demand for chocolate. Consequently, they sometimes reformatted or reformulated their products through size or ingredient changes to sustain margins. Three major product types were manufactured for domestic and export sales:

Blocks   These products are molded blocks of chocolate that are sold by weight and manufactured in a variety of flavours, with or without additional ingredients such as fruit or nuts. Block chocolate was sold primarily in grocery outlets or directly to confectionery manufacturers. (Examples: baking chocolate, Hershey's Chocolate Bar, Suchard's Toblerone.)

Boxed   These products included a variety of bite-sized sweets and were generally regarded
Chocolates as "gift" or "occasion" purchases. Sales in grocery outlets tended to be more seasonal than for other chocolate products, with 80 percent sold at Christmas and Easter. Sales in other outlets remained steady year round. (Examples: Cadbury's Milk Tray, Rowntree's Black Magic and After Eights.)

Countlines These were chocolate-covered products sold by count rather than by weight, and were generally referred to by consumers as "chocolate bars." The products varied widely in size, shape, weight, and composition, and had a wider distribution than the other two product types. Most countlines were sold through non-grocery outlets such as convenience and drug stores. (Examples: Neilson's Crispy Crunch, Nestlé-Rowntree's Coffee Crisp, M&M/Mars' Snickers, and Hershey/Lowney's Oh Henry!)

Exhibit 1   World Chocolate Exports (Value as % of Total): 1990

	1987	*1988*	*1989*	*1990*
Africa	x1.5	x1.0	x1.1	x0.7
Americas	8.1	9.1	9.2	x9.1
LAIC[1]	2.1	1.9	1.4	x1.4
CACM[2]	0.1	x0.1	x0.1	x0.1
Asia	2.5	3.2	3.4	2.9
Middle East	x0.5	x0.5	x0.7	x0.4
Europe	86.4	85.0	84.2	85.4
EEC (12)[3]	73.3	71.8	71.3	73.5
EFTA[4]	12.5	12.7	12.1	11.5
Oceania	x1.5	1.8	x2.1	x1.8

Figures denoted with an "x" are provisional or estimated.
Adapted from: The United Nations' "International Trade Statistics Yearbook," Vol. II, 1990.
[1] LAIC = Latin American Industrialists Association.
[2] CACM = Central American Common Market.
[3] EEC (12) = The twelve nations of the European Economic Community.
[4] EFTA = European Free Trade Association.

Sweet chocolate was the basic semi-finished product used in the manufacture of block, countline, and boxed chocolate products. Average costs of sweet chocolate for a representative portfolio of all three product types could be broken down as follows:

Raw material	35%
Packaging	10
Production	20
Distribution	5
Marketing/sales	20
Trading profit	10
Total	100% (of manufacturer's selling price)

For countline products, raw material costs were proportionately lower because a smaller amount of cocoa was used.

In value terms, more chocolate was consumed than any other manufactured food product in the world. In the late eighties, the world's eight major markets (representing over 60 percent of the total world chocolate market) consumed nearly 3 million tonnes with a retail value close to $20 billion. During the 1980s countline was the fastest growing segment, with close to 50 percent of the world chocolate market by volume and an average annual rate of growth of 7 percent. An increasing trend towards indulgence in snack and "comfort" foods strongly suggested that future growth would remain strong.

Competitive Environment

In 1993, chocolate producers in the world included: M&M/Mars, Hershey Foods, Cadbury-Schweppes, Jacobs Suchard, Nestlé-Rowntree, United Biscuits, Ferrero, Nabisco, and George Weston Ltd. (Neilson). Chocolate represented varying proportions of these manufacturers' total sales.

For the most part, it was difficult to sustain competitive advantages in manufacturing or product features due to a lack of proprietary technology. There was also limited potential for new product development since the basic ingredients in countline product manufacturing could only be blended in a limited variety of combinations. This forced an emphasis on competition through distribution and advertising.

Product promotion played a critical role in establishing brand-name recognition. Demand was typified by high-impulse and discretionary purchasing behaviour. Since consumers, generally, had a selection of at least three or four favourite brands from which to choose, the biggest challenge facing producers was to create the brand awareness necessary to break into these menus. In recognition of the wide selection of competing brands and the broad range of snack food substitutes available, expenditures for media and trade promotions were considerable. For example, Canadian chocolate bar makers spent more than $30 million for advertising in Canada in 1992, mostly on television. This was often a barrier to entry for smaller producers.

Major Competitors

M&M/Mars

As the world leader in chocolate confectionery, M&M/Mars dominated the countline sector, particularly in North America and Europe, with such famous global brands as Snickers, M&Ms, and Milky Way. However, in Canada in 1992, M&M/Mars held fourth place with an 18.7 percent market share of single bars. (Exhibits 2 and 3 compare Canadian market positions for major competitors.)

M&M/Mars' strategy was to produce high-quality products which were simple to manufacture and which allowed for high-volume, automated production processes. They supported their products with heavy advertising and aggressive sales, focusing marketing efforts on strengthening their global brands.

Exhibit 2   Single Bars Canadian Market Share: 1991–1992

Manufacturer	1992 (%)	1991 (%)
Neilson	28.1	29.4
Nestlé/Rowntree	26.9	26.2
Hershey/Lowney	21.6	21.9
M&M/Mars	18.7	19.0
Others	4.7	3.5

Source: Neilson News—Issue #1, 1993.

Exhibit 3   Top Single Bars in Canada: 1991–1992

Top Single Bars	Manufacturer	1992	1991
Crispy Crunch	Neilson	1	1
Coffee Crisp	Nestlé/Rowntree	2	3
Kit Kat	Nestlé/Rowntree	3	2
Mars Bar	M&M/Mars	4	4
Caramilk	Cadbury Schweppes	5	6
Oh Henry!	Hershey/Lowney	6	5
Smarties	Nestlé/Rowntree	7	7
Peanut Butter Cups	Hershey/Lowney	8	8
Mr. Big	Neilson	9	11
Aero	Hershey/Lowney	10	10
Snickers	M&M/Mars	11	9
Crunchie	Cadbury Schweppes	12	12

Source: Neilson News—Issue #1, 1993.

Hershey/Lowney

Hershey's strength in North America was in the block chocolate category in which it held the leading market position. Hershey also supplied export markets in Asia, Australia, Sweden, and Mexico from their chocolate production facilities in Pennsylvania. In Canada in 1992, Hershey held third place in the countline segment with a 21.6 percent share of the market.

Hershey's strategy was to reduce exposure to volatile cocoa prices by diversifying within the confectionery and snack businesses. By 1987, only 45 percent of Hershey's sales came from products with 70 percent or more chocolate content. This was down from 80 percent in 1963.

Cadbury Schweppes

Cadbury was a major world name in chocolate, with a portfolio of brands such as Dairy Milk, Creme Eggs, and Crunchie. Although its main business was in the United Kingdom, it was also a strong competitor in major markets such as Australia and South Africa.

Cadbury Schweppes diversified its product line and expanded into new geographic markets throughout the 1980s. In 1987, Cadbury International sold the Canadian distribution rights for their chocolate products to William Neilson Ltd. Only in Canada were the Cadbury brands incorporated into the Neilson confectionery division under the name Neilson/Cadbury. In 1988, Cadbury sold its U.S. operations to Hershey.

Nestlé-Rowntree

In 1991, chocolate and confectionery comprised 16 percent of Nestlé SFr 50.5 billion revenue, up sharply from only 8 percent in 1987. (In January 1993, 1SFr = Cdn.$0.88 = U.S. $0.69.) This was largely a result of their move into the countline sector through the acquisition in 1988 of Rowntree PLC, a leading British manufacturer with strong global brands such as Kit Kat, After Eights, and Smarties. In 1990, they also added Baby Ruth and Butterfinger to their portfolio, both "Top 20" brands in the U.S. Considering these recent heavy investments to acquire global brands and expertise, it was clear that Nestlé-Rowntree intended to remain a significant player in growing global markets.

Neilson

Company History

William Neilson Ltd. was founded in 1893, when the Neilson family began selling milk and home-made ice cream to the Toronto market. By 1905 they had erected a house and factory at 277 Gladstone Ave., from which they shipped ice cream as far west as Winnipeg and as far east as Quebec City. Chocolate bar production was initiated to offset the decreased demand for ice cream during the colder winter months and as a way of retaining the skilled labour pool. By 1914, the company was producing 1 million pounds of ice cream and 500,000 pounds of chocolate per year.

William Neilson died in 1915, and the business was handed down to his son Morden, who had been involved since its inception. Between 1924 and 1934, the "Jersey Milk," "Crispy Crunch," and "Malted Milk" bars were introduced. Upon the death of Morden Neilson in 1947, the company was sold to George Weston Foods for $4.5 million.

By 1974, "Crispy Crunch" was the number one selling bar in Canada. In 1977, "Mr. Big" was introduced and became the number one teen bar by 1986. By 1991, the Neilson dairy operations had been moved to a separate location and the ice cream division had been sold to Ault Foods. The Gladstone location continued to be used to manufacture Neilson chocolate and confectionery.

Bateman explained that Neilson's efforts under the direction of the new president, Arthur Soler, had become more competitive in the domestic market over the past three years, through improved customer service and retail merchandising. Significant improvements had already been made in Administration and Operations. All of these initiatives had assisted in reversing decades of consumer share erosion. As a result, Neilson was now in a position to defend its share of the domestic market and to develop an international business that would enhance shareholder value. (Exhibit 4 outlines the Canadian chocolate confectionery market.)

Neilson's Exporting Efforts

Initial export efforts prior to 1990 were contracted to a local export broker—Grenadier International. The original company objective was to determine "what could be done in foreign markets" using only working capital resources and avoiding capital investments in equipment or new markets.

Through careful selection of markets on the basis of distributor interest, Grenadier's export manager, Scott Begg, had begun the slow process of introducing Neilson brands into the Far East. The results were impressive. Orders were secured for containers of "Mr, Big" and "Crispy Crunch" countlines from local distributors in Korea, Taiwan, and Japan. "Canadian Classics" boxed chocolates were developed for the vast Japanese gift ("Omiyagi") market. Total 1993 sales to these markets were projected to be $1.6 million.

For each of these markets, Neilson retained the responsibility for packaging design and product formulation. While distributors offered suggestions as to how products could be improved to suit local tastes, they were not formally obliged to do so. To secure distribution in Taiwan, Neilson had agreed to launch the "Mr. Big" bar under the distributor's private brand name "Bang Bang," which was expected to generate a favourable impression with consum-

Exhibit 4   Canadian Confectionery Market—1993

	$ (millions)	(%)
Total Confectionery Category	$1,301.4	100.0
Gum	296.5	22.8
Box chocolates	159.7	12.3
Cough drops	77.0	5.9
Rolled candy	61.3	4.7
Bagged chocolates	30.3	2.3
Easter eggs	22.0	1.7
Valentines	9.4	0.7
Lunch pack	3.6	0.3
Countline chocolate bars	641.6	49.3
Total chocolate bar market growth	+8%	

Source: Neilson Marketing Department Estimates.

ers. Although sales were strong, Bateman realized that since consumer loyalty was linked to brand names, the brand equity being generated for "Bang Bang," ultimately, would belong to the distributor. This put the distributor in a powerful position from which they were able to place significant downward pressure on operating margins.

Market Evaluation Study

In response to these successful early exporting efforts, Bateman began exploring the possible launch of Neilson brands into the United States (discussed later). With limited working capital and numerous export opportunities, it became obvious to the International Division that some kind of formal strategy was required to evaluate and to compare these new markets.

Accordingly, a set of weighted criteria was developed during the summer of 1992 to evaluate countries that were being considered by the International Division. (See Exhibit 5 for a profile of the world's major chocolate importers). The study was intended to provide a standard means of evaluating potential markets. Resources could then be allocated among those markets that promised long-term incremental growth and those which were strictly opportunistic. While the revenues from opportunistic markets would contribute to the fixed costs of domestic production, the long-term efforts could be pursued for more strategic reasons. By the end of the summer, the study had been applied to 13 international markets, including the United States. (See Exhibit 6 for a summary of this study).

Meanwhile, Grenadier had added Hong Kong/China, Singapore, and New Zealand to Neilson's portfolio of export markets, and Bateman had contracted

---

EXHIBIT 5   World Chocolate Imports (Value as % of Total): 1990

	1987	1988	1989	1990
Africa	x0.7	x0.7	x0.7	x0.7
Americas	x15.6	x15.0	x13.9	x13.2
LAIC[1]	0.2	0.4	1.1	x1.3
CACM[2]	x0.1	x0.1	x0.1	x0.1
Asia	11.7	x13.9	x15.6	x12.9
Middle East	x3.5	x3.3	x3.9	x2.8
Europe	70.8	68.9	67.7	71.4
EEC (12)[3]	61.1	59.5	57.7	59.3
EFTA[4]	9.3	9.0	8.9	8.4
Oceania	x1.3	x1.7	x2.1	x1.8

Figures denoted with an "x" are provisional or estimated.

Adapted from: The United Nations' "International Trade Statistics Yearbook," Vol. II, 1990.

[1] LAIC = Latin American Industrialists Association.

[2] CACM = Central American Common Market.

[3] EEC (12) = The twelve nations of the European Economic Community.

[4] EFTA = European Free Trade Association.

EXHIBIT 6 Summary of Criteria for Market Study (1992)

Criteria	Weight	Australia	China	Hong Kong	Indonesia	Japan	Korea	Malaysia	New Zealand	Singapore	Taiwan	Mexico	EEC	USA
* U.S. countline	-	4	4	4	4	4	4	4	4	4	4	4	4	4
1. Candybar economics	30	20	20	30	20	20	28	20	15	25	15	20	10	10
2. Target market	22	12.5	14	13	15.5	19	15	10	7	9.5	12.5	21	22	22
3. **Competitor dynamics**	20	12	15	8	7.5	11	13.5	10	12	14.5	12	11	20	6.5
4. Distribution access	10	9	4	4	3.5	5	6	6.5	9	3.5	7.5	9.5	9	9
5. Industry economics	9	2.5	3.5	6	5.5	2	5	2.5	7	4.5	3	3.5	3.5	4.5
6. Product fit	8	7	6	6	6	3	7.5	7.5	7.5	8	4	8	5	8
7. Payback	5	4	4	1	2.5	4	5	2.5	4	2	2	5	2	1
8. Country dynamics	5	5	1	4	3	5	3.5	4.5	4.5	5	4	3	2	4
Total	**109**	**72**	**67.5**	**72**	**63.5**	**69**	**83.5**	**63.5**	**66**	**72**	**60**	**81**	**73.5**	**65**

Competitor Dynamics	Score	Mexico
Financial success of other exports	0-8	5
Nature(passivity) of competition	0-6	2.5
Brand image (versus price) positioning	0-6	3.5
Score/20	/20	11

Due to Neilson/Cadbury's limited resources, it was not feasible to launch the first western-style brands into new markets. The basic minimum criteria for a given market, therefore, was the presence of major Western industry players (ie: Mars or Hershey). Countries were then measured on the basis of eight criteria that were weighted by the International Group according to their perceived importance as determinants of a successful market entry. (See above table). Each criterion was then subdivided into several elements as defined by the International Group, which allocated the total weighted score accordingly. (See table, right).

This illustration depicts a single criteria, subdivided and scored for Mexico.

Source: Company records.

592

EXHIBIT 7   Neilson Export Markets—1993

Agent (Commission)	Country	Brands
Grenadier International	Taiwan	Bang Bang
	Japan	Canadian Classics, Mr. Big
		Mr. Big, Crispy Crunch
	Korea	Mr. Big, Crispy Crunch
	Hong Kong/China	Mr. Big, Crispy Crunch, Canadian Classics
	Singapore	Mr. Big, Crispy Crunch
CANCON Corp. Ltd.	Saudi Arabia	Mr. Big, Crispy Crunch, Malted Milk
	Bahrain	Mr. Big, Crispy Crunch, Malted Milk
	U.A.E.	Mr. Big, Crispy Crunch, Malted Milk
	Kuwait	Mr. Big, Crispy Crunch, Malted Milk
Neilson International	Mexico	Mr. Big, Crispy Crunch, Malted Milk
	U.S.A.	Mr. Big, Crispy Crunch, Malted Milk

Source: Company records.

a second local broker, CANCON Corp. Ltd, to initiate sales to the Middle East. By the end of 1992, the International Division comprised nine people who had achieved penetration of 11 countries for export sales (see Exhibit 7 for a description of these markets).

The U.S. Experience

In 1991, the American chocolate confectionery market was worth U.S.$5.1 billion wholesale. Neilson had wanted to sneak into this vast market with the intention of quietly selling off excess capacity. However, as Bateman explained, the quiet U.S. launch became a Canadian celebration:

> Next thing we knew, there were bands in the streets, Neilson t-shirts and baseball caps, and newspaper articles and T.V. specials describing our big U.S. launch!

The publicity greatly increased the pressure to succeed. After careful consideration, Pro Set, a collectible trading card manufacturer and marketer, was selected as a distributor. This relationship developed into a joint venture by which the Neilson Import Division was later appointed distributor of the Pro Set cards in Canada. With an internal sales management team, full distribution and invoicing infrastructures and a 45-broker national sales network, Pro Set seemed ideally suited to diversify into confectionery products.

Unfortunately, Pro Set quickly proved to be an inadequate partner in this venture. Although they had access to the right outlets, the confectionery selling task differed significantly from card sales. Confectionery items demanded more sensitive product handling and a greater amount of sales effort by the Pro Set representatives who were used to carrying a self-promoting line.

To compound these difficulties, Pro Set sales plummeted as the trading-card market became oversaturated. Trapped by intense cash flow problems and increasing fixed costs, Pro Set filed for Chapter 11 bankruptcy, leaving Neilson with huge inventory losses and a customer base that associated them with their defunct distributor. Although it was tempting to attribute the U.S. failure to inappropriate partner selection, the U.S. had also ranked poorly relative to other markets in the criteria study that had just been completed that summer. In addition to their distribution problems, Neilson was at a serious disadvantage due to intense competition from the major industry players in the form of advertising expenditures, trade promotions, and brand proliferation. Faced with duties and a higher cost of production, Neilson was unable to maintain price competitiveness.

The International Division was now faced with the task of internalizing distribution in the U.S., including sales management, broker contact, warehousing, shipping, and collections. Neilson managed to reestablish a limited presence in the American market using several local brokers to target profitable niches. For example, they placed strong emphasis on vending machine sales to increase product trial with minimal advertising. Since consumer purchasing patterns demanded product variety in vending machines. Neilson's presence in this segment was not considered threatening by major competitors.

In the autumn of 1992, as the International Division made the changes necessary to salvage past efforts in the U.S., several options for entering the Mexican confectionery market were also being considered.

Mexico

Neilson made the decision to enter the Mexican market late in 1992, prompted by the investigations of the parent company, Weston Foods Ltd., into possible market opportunities which would emerge as a result of the North American Free Trade Agreement (NAFTA). Mexico was an attractive market which scored very high in the market evaluation study. Due to their favourable demographics (50 percent of the population was within the target age group), Mexico offered huge potential for countline sales. The rapid adoption of American tastes resulted in an increasing demand for U.S. snack foods. With only a limited number of competitors, the untapped demand afforded a window of opportunity for smaller players to enter the market.

Working through the Ontario Ministry of Agriculture and Food (OMAF), Neilson found two potential independent distributors:

Grupo Corvi a Mexican food manufacturer, operated seven plants and had an extensive sales force reaching local wholesalers. They also had access to a convoluted infrastructure which indirectly supplied an estimated 100,000 street vendor stands or kiosks (known as "tientas") representing nearly 70 percent of the Mexican confectionery market. (This informal segment was usually overlooked by marketing research services and competitors alike.) Grupo Corvi currently had no American- or European-style countline products.

Grupo Hajj   a Mexican distributor with some experience in confectionery, offered access to only a small number of retail stores. This limited network made Grupo Hajj relatively unattractive when compared to other distributors. Like Grupo Corvi, this local firm dealt exclusively in Mexican pesos, historically a volatile currency. (In January 1993, 1 peso = Cdn.$0.41.)

While considering these distributors, Neilson was approached by Sabritas, the snack food division of Pepsico Foods in Mexico, who felt that there was a strategic fit between their organizations. Although Sabritas had no previous experience handling chocolate confectionery, they had for six years been seeking a product line to round out their portfolio. They were currently each week supplying Frito-Lay type snacks directly to 450,000 retail stores and tientas. (The trade referred to such extensive customer networks as "numeric distribution".) After listening to the initial proposal, Neilson agreed to give Sabritas three months to conduct research into the Mexican market.

Although the research revealed strong market potential for the Neilson products, Bateman felt that pricing at 2 pesos (at parity with other American-style brands) would not provide any competitive advantage. Sabritas agreed that a 1-peso product, downsized to 40 grams from a Canadian and U.S. standard of 50 to 60 grams, would provide an attractive strategy to offer "imported chocolate at Mexican prices."

Proposing a deal significantly different from the relationships offered by the two Mexican distributors, Sabritas intended to market the "Mr. Big," "Crispy Crunch," and "Malted Milk" bars as the first brands in the "Milch" product line. "Milch" was a fictitious word in Spanish, created and owned by Sabritas, and thought to denote goodness and health due to its similarity to the word "milk." Sabritas would offer Neilson 50 percent ownership of the Milch name, in exchange for 50 percent of Neilson's brand names, both of which would appear on each bar. As part of the joint branding agreement, Sabritas would assume all responsibility for advertising, promotion, distribution, and merchandising. The joint ownership of the brand names would provide Sabritas with brand equity in exchange for building brand awareness through heavy investments in marketing. By delegating responsibility for all marketing efforts to Sabritas, Neilson would be able to compete on a scale not affordable by Canadian standards.

Under the proposal, all "Milch" chocolate bars would be produced in Canada by Neilson. Neilson would be the exclusive supplier. Ownership of the bars would pass to Sabritas once the finished goods had been shipped. Sabritas in turn would be responsible for all sales to final consumers. Sabritas would be the exclusive distributor. Consumer prices could not be changed without the mutual agreement of Neilson and Sabritas.

Issues

Bateman reflected upon the decision he now faced for the Mexican market. The speed with which Sabritas could help them gain market penetration, their competitive advertising budget, and their "store door access" to nearly a half million retailers were attractive advantages offered by this joint venture proposal. But what were the implications of omitting the Neilson name from their popular chocolate bars? Would they be exposed to problems like those encountered in Taiwan with the "Bang Bang" launch, especially considering the strength and size of Pepsico Foods?

The alternative was to keep the Neilson name and to launch their brands independently, using one of the national distributors. Unfortunately, limited resources meant that Neilson would develop its presence much more slowly. With countline demand in Mexico growing at 30 percent per year, could they afford to delay? Scott Begg had indicated that early entry was critical in burgeoning markets, since establishing market presence and gaining share were less difficult when undertaken before the major players had dominated the market and "defined the rules of play."

Bateman also questioned their traditional means of evaluating potential markets. Were the criteria considered in the market evaluation study really the key success factors, or were the competitive advantages offered through ventures with distributors more important? If partnerships were necessary, should Neilson continue to rely on independent, national distributors who were interested in adding Neilson brands to their portfolio, or should they pursue strategic partnerships similar to the Sabritas opportunity instead? No matter which distributor was chosen, product quality and handling were of paramount importance. Every chocolate bar reaching consumers, especially first-time buyers, must be of the same freshness and quality as those distributed to Canadian consumers. How could this type of control best be achieved?

NEWFOUNDLAND AND LABRADOR COMPUTER SERVICES LIMITED (B)

In March 1991, the President of Newfoundland and Labrador Computer Services Limited (NLCS) was reflecting on the report of the consulting company that had been retained by the NLCS Board of Directors since June 1990, to undertake a role and mandate review of the organization.

The concerns of the president and of the board, which led them to retain the consultants, are described in the Newfoundland and Labrador Computer Services Limited (A) case. Now that the consultants had delivered their report, the president knew that he would have to make recommendations to the board at its next meeting. NLCS could not continue to try to be all things to all people, and the president's recommendations would include a strategy for the future for NLCS and an action plan for implementing changes.

The Company

NLCS is a crown corporation established in 1969 to provide data processing and other computer services in the province of Newfoundland and Labrador. NLCS' major clients, which also constitute its board of directors, are the Government of Newfoundland and Labrador, Memorial University of Newfoundland, Newfoundland and Labrador Hydro, and Newfoundland Medical Care Commission. NLCS is established in its own building in close proximity

This case was written by Dr. M. D. Skipton with Dr. R. K. Gupta, Faculty of Business Adminstration, Memorial University of Newfoundland. It was made possible with the cooperation of NLCS. The case is written as a basis for class discussion rather than to illustrate either effective or ineffective handling of a management situation. Copyright © 1994 M. D. Skipton and R. K. Gupta.

to the seat of the provincial government, the Confederation Building, in St. John's. It is the largest computing and information technology services establishment in Newfoundland and Labrador.

NLCS is responsible for operating in a business-like manner and generates all of its revenues from billing its clients for services it provides. NLCS has not directly competed with the private sector in the province because NLCS, being a large crown corporation with assured government and public-sector clients, would be seen as unfair competition. However, NLCS has from time to time provided services (e.g., microfiche services) to the private sector that were not otherwise available in the province.

Since its establishment in 1969, the range of services offered by NLCS has expanded to include the following:

- Computer operations
- Information centre services
- EDP consulting
- Applications development
- Programming training and education
- Application software packages
- End-user software packages
- Microcomputer support
- Data entry
- Specialised services, e.g., microfiche
- Optical character recognition and plotting

The company is responsible for funding its own capital requirements. In December 1988, an Amdahl 5890 computer was acquired and installed, giving a 50 percent increase in computing capacity over the previous Amdahl 5880 system.

In the fiscal year ended March 31, 1991, total revenue was approximately $20 million, with a net income of approximately $1 million. In 1991, revenue was obtained as follows:

By source:	Provincial government	77%
	Memorial University	10
	Crown corporations	11
	Other	2
By type:	Computer	38%
	Systems development	21
	Production support	12
	Other	29

Further selected financial data for fiscal years 1990 and 1991 are given in Exhibit 1.

EXHIBIT 1   Newfoundland and Labrador Computer Services Ltd.
Balance Sheets as at March 31, 1991 (and 1990)

	1991	1990
Assets		
Current		
Cash	$ 1,796,219	$ 190,335
Accounts receivable	3,246,098	3,206,532
Prepaid expenses and supplies	604,533	618,279
Current portion of investment in leased assets	563,384	332,944
Total current assets	6,210,234	4,348,090
Fixed assets	4,146,280	4,467,938
Deferred charges	351,771	351,533
Investment in leased assets	163,840	422,812
Total assets	$10,872,125	$9,590,373
Liabilities		
Current		
Accounts payable and accrued liabilities	$ 2,230,450	$1,403,025
Deferred revenue	624,527	724,646
Current portion of long-term debt	442,504	437,290
Total current liabilities	3,297,481	2,564,961
Long-term debt	2,052,703	2,495,207
Total liabilities	5,350,184	5,060,168
Shareholders' Equity		
Share capital	2,500,300	2,500,300
Retained earnings	3,021,641	2,029,905
	5,521,941	4,530,205
Total liabilities and shareholders' equity	$10,872.125	$9,590,373

Statement of Income and Retained Earnings
For the Year Ended March 31, 1991 (and 1990)

	1991	1990
Operating revenue	$20,614,339	$19,254,763
Operating Expenses	18,292,448	16,857,677
Operating income	2,321,951	2,397,086
Depreciation and amortization	1,034,172	1,020,782
Interest on long-term debt	322,102	415,959
Interest and bank charges	6,380	39,153
Gain on disposal of fixed assets	(32,439)	(18,252)
Net income for the year	991,736	939,444
Retained earnings, beginning of the year	2,029,905	1,090,461
Retained earnings, end of the year	$ 3,021,641	$ 2,029,905

EXHIBIT 1   (*Continued*)
Schedule of Operating Revenue and Expenses
For the Year Ended March 31, 1991 (and 1990)

	1991	1990
Computer time	$ 7,786,530	$ 7,624,723
Systems and programming	6,877,116	5,760,989
Data preparation	336,102	343,170
Production control and file charges	2,146,226	2,337,588
Other	3,468,425	3,188,293
	$20,614,399	$19,254,763
Operating expenses		
Salaries	$ 9,854,535	$ 8,795,398
Fringe benefits	946,796	1,180,566
Rent-computer equipment	4,954,296	4,747,189
Rent-office equipment	16,920	12,875
Data processing operating supplies	326,539	336,296
Stationery and office supplies	85,569	73,047
Moving and delivery charges	8,720	11,674
Repairs and maintenance	1,117,903	936,775
Travelling	112,706	84,351
Telephone and telegrams	118,731	106,988
Light and power	187,975	180,343
Staff and training	194,623	141,207
Insurance	22,276	15,047
Advertising and publicity	18,671	18,932
Membership and subscriptions	30,670	28,532
General	108,068	113,917
Research and development	34,651	54,950
Professional fees	152,800	19,590
	$18,292,448	$16,857,677

NLCS has for a number of years adopted an organization structure which reflects its three main areas of service:

- Operations
- Development
- Consulting and training

The organization chart of the company is shown in Exhibit 2. The company employs approximately 220 full-time individuals.

Consultants' Report

The remainder of this case study consists of summary information from the consultants' report on the future role and mandate of NLCS. Abbreviations used are as follows: Information Technology = IT; Information Systems = IS.

EXHIBIT 1 *(Concluded)*
Statement of Changes in Financial Position
For the Year Ended March 31, 1991 (and 1990)

	1991	*1990*
Cash provided by (used in)		
Operating activities		
Net income	$ 991,736	$ 939,444
Add items not requiring (generating) cash		
Depreciation and amortization	1,034,172	1,020,782
Gain on disposal of fixed assets	(32,439)	(18,252)
	1,993,469	1,941,974
Net change in non-cash working capital	701,486	378,917
	2,694,955	2,320,891
Investing activities		
Additions to fixed assets, net of proceeds of disposition	(495,674)	(474,682)
Decrease (increase) in investment in leased assets	28,532	(232,670)
Increase in deferred charges and other assets	(184,639)	(316,518)
Financing activities		
Decrease in long-term debt	(437,290)	(490,892)
Increase in cash for the year	1,605,884	806,129
Cash (bank indebtedness) beginning of the year	190,335	(615,794)
Cash, end of the year	$1,796,219	$ 190,335

Emerging Customer and Market Trends

General Trends

The IT/IS field is driven by technology that is developing and changing at an accelerating pace. The changes in IT to date have brought large changes in the organization and execution of information processing, and more changes are expected for the future.

The cost of information processing has been decreasing at an increasing rate. Computer designers and engineers have mastered the art of manufacturing very large-scale integrated (VLSI) circuits on microchips. These enable very large amounts of processing power at relatively low prices. (Currently, processing power is measured in millions of instructions per second, or MIPS; and soon will go to billions of instructions per second, or BIPS.)

Major advances in telecommunications using fibre optics enable greater amounts and faster rates of information transmission. This allows various computers to be interconnected, leading to distributed processing, information networks with shared databases, and mobile and remote computing. Most of

Exhibit 2   Organization Chart, March 1991

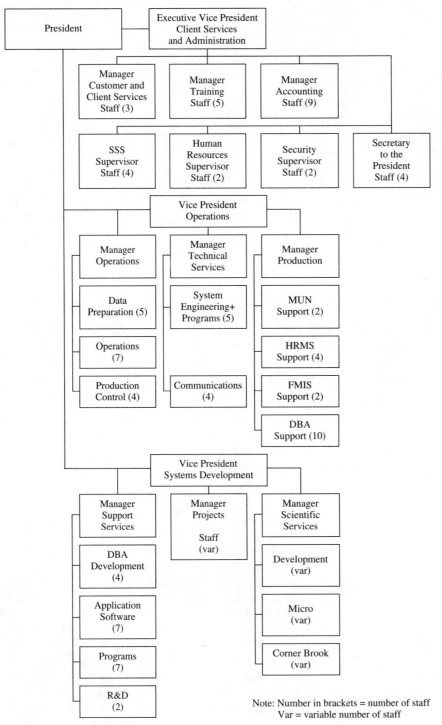

Note: Number in brackets = number of staff
Var = variable number of staff

the industrialized nations are embarking on very high bandwidth communication networks operating at very high speeds (billion bits per second). These will facilitate the strengthening of client networks and stand-alone systems, but to take full advantage of the communications technology, powerful server machines may be required.

Technological advances will enable powerful workstations within networks to act as servers to various client machines. These servers will not be much bigger than today's desktop computers. These servers will work as file servers and gateways to databases, act as a depository of organizational data storage, and control the utilisation of printers and other peripherals. Many of the functions of today's mainframes might be taken over by servers and networks.

Significant advances in vision and pattern recognition will enable better computer graphics leading to higher level representations and simulations.

Many organizations are shedding their central EDP departments based on mainframes. Instead, they are either utilizing client/server network architecture, e.g., Pillsbury, or contracting out the central EDP function, e.g., Kodak. Companies such as IBM and Arthur Andersen claim that they can carry out the EDP task more effectively and more efficiently. Even though the unit price for computing power is falling at an increasing rate, the price of keeping up with information technology advances is increasing because of the rapid rate of technological development. Another factor driving up EDP costs is that the cost of technical experts needed to design and operate EDP systems is still climbing fairly steeply.

Conclusions from information provided by the Association for Computing in Government (ACIG) are that NLCS clients' evolving IT needs and requirements and their demands for services are likely to be in line with emerging trends in the industry as a whole. They are not likely to be significantly different in the future from the situation being experienced and anticipated in government and industry IT circles throughout North America. Generally, user involvement and their control of information systems development is expected to increase, so that the user organization manages the process while suppliers such as NLCS provide technical and systems expertise.

Larger organizations, not least NLCS' government department customers, are likely to realise that related data gathered by different departments can be usefully combined and analysed. Systems integration across departments will then be demanded. User organizations will likely develop a need for more assistance and support in implementing and maintaining their information systems, due to inevitable increases in systems complexity. Standards and quality assurance will become ever more important as user organizations and the IT industry move towards systems integration.

In the future, therefore, it is increasingly likely that large organizations will seek economies and greater effectiveness through adopting centralized/decentralised information systems strategies. These strategies will mean reverting to one or two central service bureaus for control of hardware and software costs, while decentralising much of their IT staff throughout their organizations to place information systems people as close as possible to the users.

On the supply side, the total user cost of decentralised computer systems may be expected to rapidly increase as micro- and minicomputers become more sophisticated, and as suppliers look to software license fees as their major source of revenue in order to offset relatively declining hardware profits.

NLCS' Clients and Their Changing Requirements

All of NLCS' government and public-sector clients are under heavy budgetary and political pressures to reduce the costs of their operations and to shift work to the private sector. In addition, political pressures will cause departments to become increasingly decentralized as government tries to become closer to the people in the regions of the province and puts increasing emphasis on regional economic development.

Public and industry demand for access to government databases is expected to increase as individuals become more aware that these government databases exist. However, protecting the privacy of information will continue to be a sensitive issue.

Existing NLCS mainframe business is based on large-scale applications, i.e., government accounts payable and revenue applications, payrolls, confidential medical and personnel records, motor vehicle registrations, etc. These applications and the resulting mainframe business are likely to continue, but pressure from client departments to reduce NLCS' service charges will inevitably increase. However, even though NLCS' charges and therefore costs for these services must decrease in the future, existing core (now mainframe) applications will need ongoing enhancement, restoration, and replacement due to the combination of hardware and software obsolescence, changing client needs, and IT/IS developments.

None of NLCS' clients is able to be specific at this time about anticipated future needs for NLCS services. Only two clients have developed their own IT strategic plans. However, as yet, the provincial government has no comprehensive IT/IS policy or plan. Even though they had recognised the need for a plan, some clients have not considered approaching NLCS for help in their IT/IS and support planning.

Even so, since 1990, government departments have been allowed or even encouraged to establish their own information systems groups, with their own staffs. Government has also been moving to encourage private sector competition for its own IT systems and services. For example, the provincial government, in co-operation with the federal Atlantic Canada Opportunities Agency (ACOA), recently established a provincewide, computer-based information network, the ACOA/Enterprise Network. Existing NLCS government and public-sector clients can be expected to increasingly contract out to other private-sector suppliers. NLCS' existing clients, especially government departments, are likely to further develop their own IT/IS staffs, thereby reducing and changing the nature of their dependence on NLCS. IT/IS strategic planning developments by clients, especially government clients, will likely increase, although these clients in carrying out this planning will likely require technology and systems advisory and consulting assistance from NLCS.

Clients are now starting to "own" their systems, especially microcomputers and networks, rather than rely completely on NLCS to design and/or provide them. Moreover, client departments are now themselves developing computing and IT/IS expertise and are themselves buying computers and building systems and networks. Many of these systems and networks are not being analysed and designed to NLCS standards, and many users of microcomputers in client organizations are unaware of the basic data processing rules of file backup, security, transferability, documentation, etc. However, when individuals in client departments encounter problems, they are turning to NLCS for assistance. As the provincial government's IT "expert," NLCS is expected to be able to offer immediate resolution of any problems its clients may encounter.

In addition, some clients are purchasing their own minicomputer systems, and strong interest in obtaining minicomputer application support, processing, and consulting was mentioned by several NLCS clients. It is possible that clients' own minicomputers could become a likely threat to NLCS' mainframe services for administrative and financial computing.

Generally, the increasing rate of IT change in software developments will make computer access and use easier, but will increase the complexity of software development and maintenance. As an IT supplier, NLCS will be expected by customers to possess up-to-date and increasingly specialised knowledge on as many fronts as it is prepared to accept. Clients will be impatient for quick results from NLCS, in advising them and in solving their problems. Many client departments have already expressed concerns about the currency, breadth, depth, availability, and suitability of NLCS' IT and IS expertise and resources.

Provincial Government Information Systems Policies

The government of Newfoundland and Labrador now spends well over $30 million per year directly on IT. This figure does not include indirect costs or the many costs that can be influenced positively by effective information systems and the use of IT generally. Since its establishment in 1969, NLCS has been regarded as the government's provider of computer services. Although Cabinet Minutes referring to NLCS have not specifically required that all government departments and agencies obtain their IT services from NLCS, this practice has been followed. Reinforcing this has been Treasury Board's insistence in the past that government departments use NLCS rather than incur possible duplication and other extra costs by developing independent computer systems and staffs.

However, since mid-1990, Treasury Board has itself been actively exploring a policy option whereby NLCS would continue to provide mainframe data processing services to government departmental and agency clients, but would compete with qualified private-sector suppliers for provision of minicomputer, microcomputer, and related IT/IS and data communications services, including applications development. In line with this, government departments have been allowed to establish their own IT/IS groups.

More recently, it has become evident that Treasury Board has several responsibilities in government for IT systems activities. These are suggested to include:

- Determining government policy relative to information systems activities, i.e., planning, standards, security, procurement, etc., and expenditures.
- Identifying and determining responsibility for corporate data and common systems, e.g., financial, land, payroll, and human resources; and for government technology architecture, e.g., DOS-based, UNIX-based, etc.
- Establishing minimum guidelines, content, and process for development and maintenance of departmental IT strategic plans.
- Reviewing and approving departmental information systems plans and expenditure proposals.
- Monitoring the financial aspects of departmental and government information systems activities.

Some consensus on the role and responsibilities of Treasury Board with regard to government and departmental information systems is needed so as to provide a framework against which any NLCS' responsibilities can be defined. Although Treasury Board has a role in determining policy, and reviewing, approving, and monitoring the implementation of policy throughout the branches of government whose budgets are controlled by it, the implementation of policy in each department is its own responsibility.

None of the client interviews carried out by the consultants revealed the existence of any global information technology or systems strategy or policies for the government of Newfoundland. However, Treasury Board, through its Organization and Management (O&M) group, has since late 1990 been defining its role and responsibilities for strategic information systems policy and planning.

Treasury Board is expected shortly to take the initiative in developing, adopting, and implementing an overall governmental IT/IS policy. As the agency with by far the widest involvement in government IT from an operational and planning perspective, NLCS could usefully advise Treasury Board on the content, direction, and applicability of this policy. Currently, Treasury Board perceives that duplication exists in the way its O&M group and NLCS support application development steering committees for client departments.

In the future, Treasury Board is likely to take the role of assisting government departments in developing their IT/IS strategic plans. NLCS may then be expected to provide technical advice upon request to departments in their IT strategic planning. The intention seems to be that NLCS should not be both strategic advisor and service provider.

Based on its experience, NLCS may be viewed by the government as a central resource in the development of a global policy on IT. Such an involvement could also be advantageous to government, as NLCS' effectiveness in implementing the systems would be strengthened by the understanding it gains in the policy development process. Also, NLCS can contribute to achieving the government's economic development objectives, as they apply to the provincial IT industry, through its potential for working with the private sector.

Issues to be addressed in IT/IS strategic planning would include:

- Standards for departmental IT and information systems strategic plans
- Responsibility for corporate data and common systems.
- Standards for government technology architecture, i.e., hardware platforms, operating systems, applications software, etc.
- Systems development standards and methodologies, including documentation, tools, techniques, etc.
- Standards for departmental systems
- Organization arrangements, i.e., roles, responsibilities, relationships, classifications, staffing

Ideally, any global IT/IS policy developed by Treasury Board should provide specific direction with respect to corporate or common or shared data/applications, and general guidelines with regard to departmental systems. Exhibit 3 illustrates possible relationships between data and applications.

The government's global IT/IS policy may also go a step further by defining the responsibility of departments with regard to NLCS as a supplier. For certain applications such as major data processing and management requirements that have strategic significance to government, departments may be required to use NLCS. However, on requirements of significance only to an

EXHIBIT 3   Relationships between Data and Applications

| | Applications | |
Data	Common	Unique
Common	Corporate (e.g., payroll)	Shared data (e.g., GIS) (data definition standards)
Unique	Common systems (e.g., accounts payable) (system selection standards)	Departmental systems (development and documentation standards)

individual department, it could be required to invite competing proposals from other, private-sector suppliers, as well as from NLCS.

The implication for NLCS is that the provincial government, its largest customer, is acting to bring in departmental and private sector competition in computing services and information systems. Its clients will increasingly have much more freedom to select other suppliers for their computing and IT needs.

A recent example of what is happening now is the establishment of the ACOA/Enterprise Network. This Network will, by 1994, interconnect regional and branch offices of Enterprise Newfoundland and Labrador Corporation (ENLC), a crown corporation which is the provincial government's agency for regional economic development, and up to 50 "telecentres" around the province. The total cost of establishing this Network is approximately $14 million over three years.

The control of the Network's information technology direction and development resides with ENLC, although an NLCS employee has been given leave to act as the project manager and other NLCS employees are working on the project. Open tenders for carrying out the project's technical aspects were invited from the private sector by ENLC. For the first time, the private sector became heavily involved with a major IT project for government.

Provincial Government Telecommunications

The Government of Newfoundland and Labrador currently spends in excess of $7 million per year on voice and data communications. Major voice communications include both local services and interexchange services, i.e., Message Toll Service (MTS) and Wide Area Telephone Services (WATS) lines, most of which are provided by Newfoundland Telephone. Ninety-three percent of the province's expenditures are for voice and mobile communications services, co-ordinated by the Department of Works, Services and Transportation. All new lines and moves of existing equipment are arranged by the Department and the work is done by Newfoundland Telephone Company. Data communications services are arranged by NLCS.

A 1989 consultant study indicated that substantial savings on voice telecommunications costs could be realised through more effective management of telecommunications usage. This could be through the substitution of dedicated facilities for many of the MTS and WATS services being used by the various departments, and through the planning, implementation, and operation of an interexchange voice network and the eventual integration of voice and data services on a single digital network. The integration of the provincial government's voice and data networks on common digital facilities would require NLCS' involvement, because NLCS currently manages the data network.

As a result of this 1989 study, the Department of Works, Services and Transportation will likely assume responsibility for all telecommunications services, i.e., voice, data, and image, required by the provincial government. The current proposal is that some other organization will manage these services under contract to the Department. Among the telecommunications responsibilities which this contractor could be asked to assume are the following items:

- Local service order processing and administration, i.e., fulfillment of requests for moves, changes, and adds of telephone service. (Local services order processing and administration has been handled for some time by the Department of Works, Services and Transportation, and it is difficult to envisage how any organization managing government telecommunications under contract could recover its costs for providing this service.)
- Interexchange voice network planning, implementation, and operation.
- Rates design, billing, and collections for use of the interexchange voice network.
- Integration of the interexchange voice network with NLCS' existing data communications network.
- Specification and purchasing of PBXs.
- Mobile services planning, implementation, and operation. (The Department of Works, Services and Transportation currently manages this service. Although this service is presently in a state of change, it involves a different technology and any serious savings as a result of inclusion with interexchange voice and data services are not anticipated.)
- Client advisory committee establishment and administration.

The organization that is awarded the telecommunications management contract will need to charge a fee sufficient to cover the costs of hiring the appropriate additional professional and support staff and of providing additional training for certain current staff as required.

Whether rates would be volume and distance sensitive, or only volume sensitive, and whether they should be route sensitive or not, will underlie design of an appropriate rate structure. This will require a knowledge of all operating costs, and traffic volume forecasts. As the telecommunications manager organization is to be the operator of the network and will have the data required for billings, it could prepare the billings, and bill on behalf of the Department of Works, Services and Transportation, which would do the collections.

Specification and purchasing of PBXs is likely to be a short-term requirement until terminal interconnection is implemented. However, as the preparation of specifications for a PBX requires a study of user requirements, it is not a simple matter. It is likely that departments requiring assistance in PBX specification, preparation of requests for proposals, and evaluation of bids for supply of PBXs, will contract directly with the telecommunications manager organization, which would charge a full-cost consulting fee for this service.

If the government of Newfoundland and Labrador is to undertake to own and operate its own integrated voice and data telecommunications network, it will be important to provide for the interaction of users with those responsible for operating the network. A client advisory committee would be established, logically chaired by the Department of Works, Services and Transportation, in its role as the supervisor of the telecommunications management contract.

It is likely that Treasury Board will be advising the provincial government on its policy regarding the telecommunications manager organization. Newfoundland Telephone Company would clearly be able to undertake this role, but government may prefer to have another company as the manager.

Regional Industrial and Economic Development

The provincial Economic Recovery Commission has expressed concern that the province is missing out on federal government initiatives that could lead to the development or enhancement of the IT industry in Newfoundland.

NLCS could explore initiatives with the private sector, such as joint ventures. One possibility is for NLCS to take the lead in consortia with Newfoundland-based private-sector IT companies to try to obtain out-of-province federal/provincial government and other public- or private-sector IT/IS contracts. Second, NLCS could become a supplier to private-sector companies; for example, it could sell backshift processing capacity for remarketing. Third, NLCS could sell direct to the private sector, services that it has developed and which are not otherwise available in Newfoundland and Labrador—for example, magnetic image character reading (MICR) or high-volume printing.

If economic policy or related government plans call for NLCS, as a crown corporation, to undertake initiatives with the private sector that are not self-funding, any such initiatives could be organized as self-contained programs. The government could be requested to allocate program funding to NLCS for this purpose, so as to avoid creating a burden that would be carried by NLCS' other clients and activities. For example, NLCS could be used as an agency to help attract IT business to the province by offering services to the private sector. It may be appropriate for government to subsidise these services, and NLCS could make an application for a subsidy on the basis that these services would not otherwise be available from within the private sector.

Through the provision of IT and information systems services, NLCS offers the government the potential to attract private sector activity that is not primarily directed at IT. For example, on a commercial basis NLCS could conceivably find a market for its services among oil companies involved in offshore oilfield exploration and in development of the Hibernia field, or generally among major engineering firms. Again, these services would have to be not otherwise available from the province's private sector.

A final possibility is that NLCS itself could be privatised by the provincial government, although this would be a political decision out of the control of the NLCS' Board of Directors.

Client/User Perspectives

Clients depend on NLCS as their primary advisor and resource for their IT requirements and services. They spoke glowingly of the calibre of the NLCS' response to their problems, NLCS' commitment, attitude, and the quality of the final deliverables. Clients also shared the view that preserving NLCS mainframe capability is a necessity for the future. However, many clients had only a partial appreciation of the range of NLCS' capabilities and expertise.

Clients repeatedly and consistently praised the quality of work done by NLCS but there is a gap between client expectations and the service(s) that are being provided by NLCS. Environmental causes for this gap are rapidly growing client sophistication and local and national competitive comparisons. Some general factors perceived by clients to be under the control of NLCS and adversely affecting their perceptions of service are:

- delays and long completion times for projects

- weakness in cost estimates, i.e., cost overruns

- bias towards mainframe solutions

- high processing costs

- their inability to understand billings from NLCS

- difficulty in obtaining timely estimates of next year's costs, for budget preparation

One of the strongest messages from clients is that NLCS does not take the initiative to suggest new ideas to them. Clients may be able to appreciate that this is because NLCS always has more requests for service than it can handle, but this does not change client perceptions that they are not getting the advice and support that they want from NLCS. For example, in the case of the geographic information system (GIS) for the Department of Forestry and Agriculture, it has been said that the expertise has been gained almost exclusively at the Department's initiative and expense and that NLCS has done little to gather experience in other GIS solutions or to extend its GIS involvement significantly beyond Forestry.

Particular concern has also been expressed about the role of NLCS' Senior Systems Consultants (SSCs). The SSC is perceived by Treasury Board as central to ensuring that NLCS truly understands the client's business and serves that business appropriately, and Treasury Board believes that the SSCs primary role in the future should be as account manager, to serve as the central and continuous liaison person for the client within NLCS.

Clients also provided "second-hand" knowledge of some past situations which had not turned out satisfactorily for others and where NLCS was blamed, and they admitted to some negative feelings due to this.

Information Technology Directions

The pace of change in information technology continues to quicken and NLCS and its clients are being forced to make IS development methodology and software decisions in a constantly developing and changing IT environment. These decisions will have significant cost and other implications for years to come. Some of the concerns for NLCS and its technologies are described below.

Multiple Platform Architectures

Concerning its mainframe processing business and technical capabilities, NLCS has a strong and enviable position in the province. Its expertise relative to microcomputers, software, networks, and systems is growing. However, NLCS currently has no knowledge or expertise regarding mid-range or mini-computers, and their corresponding software, networks, and systems. If the solutions of the future will span all of the hardware platforms, NLCS must change accordingly.

However, changes in customer orientation to information technology and increased competition lead to the very difficult practical question for IT suppliers of which hardware platform(s) to specialize in, i.e., mainframe, minicomputer, or microcomputer. This is of particular concern at the present time when trends in technology and effective computer resource management are moving towards integration of these platforms to most effectively meet user needs.

Database Management Systems

For many years, IDMS/R has been the database management system (DBMS) used by NLCS for mainframe application systems, and the company's skills with IDMS are very strong. However, the industry standard DBMSs have now evolved to become truly relational and are now Standard Query Language based—for example, IBM's DB2, and ORACLE. IDMS/R, being one of the more mature DBMSs, is not truly relational and is becoming obsolete. Many IBM mainframe owners are gradually migrating their IDMS-based environments to relational DBMS environments, DB2 being the most widely chosen system at this time. NLCS has also become aware that the company that markets and supports IDMS in Canada has recently encountered business difficulties, and the vendor of an application software package used by one of NLCS' clients has recently decided to drop support of its IDMS version.

If NLCS is to move from IDMS to DB2, a number of problems would occur during the changeover. Parallel running of IDMS and DB2 systems during conversion would require significant time and resources. NLCS would need to invest and train (and likely hire) technical support and application development staff with DB2 expertise, while continuing to support staff capabilities in IDMS/R. NLCS would have to justify the costs of conversion when clients would not realise any immediate significant functional improvements, but would only be provided with a more secure technological platform for enhancements to applications systems. At the same time, however, clients are also becoming free to move to their own micro- or mini-computer based systems, to construct their own databases, and to perhaps take over database management work previously performed by NLCS.

Systems Development Productivity Tools and Methodologies

NLCS is moving to systems development methodologies such as SDM/Structured and SDM/70. NLCS has been gradually migrating to a computer-assisted software engineering (CASE)-oriented environment through adopting fourth-generation languages, e.g., SAS and FOCUS. CASE tools also apply to micro-computer-based software.

Early generation CASE tools like EXCELERATOR are being used by NLCS today. Research and experimentation with next-generation CASE tools are also taking place. Recently, a set of structured development approaches, which are the theoretical basis of most CASE tools today, has been installed. However, progress in this area is sporadic, as the resources assigned to these research and development activities are often diverted to revenue-generating client work. These diversions mean that the time frames for research, selection, and adoption of more productive software development tools are extended.

CASE tools will be an important consideration for NLCS if or when existing IDMS applications systems are converted to another DBMS such as DB2, as mentioned above. The industry is working on re-engineering tools which would reverse-engineer an IDMS application and its databases to first principles and then re-engineer them, using CASE tools, as a DB2 application supporting DB2 databases. These re-engineering tools are probably at least two years away from introduction.

To optimise the positive impact of development productivity gains from CASE tools, systems development and project management methodologies must be highly integrated. However, the current state of the art for integrated CASE is that it is still developing. The most successful CASE tool supplier at present can claim only 200 or so sites where its products have been fully adapted and integrated with its clients' systems development organizations.

Expanding Networks

NLCS currently manages a data communications network of more than 1,400 terminals connected to its mainframe and serving users across the island of Newfoundland. The final major technological area which will challenge NLCS over the coming years is the support of more decentralised client needs with (or within) an expanded yet more integrated telecommunications network. However, NLCS' skills in data communications are sound and improving.

NLCS clients, especially government departments, are now rapidly developing microcomputer-based application systems that are currently almost all stand-alone. Several departments also have minicomputers which again are not usually integrated into networks. Many government departments are regionally dispersed and have many stand-alone systems applications in their regional offices, as well as terminals connected to the NLCS mainframe through its communications network.

If current trends continue, NLCS will face an increasing demand for data sharing between computers on and off a data communications network, within and between client departments and with the public. The initial demand may be satisfied through telecommunications-based solutions using file transfer. As demand increases, shared databases on the network must gradually be built to eliminate file redundancy and conversion. The implications for NLCS will include the need for a much higher level of local area network (LAN) skills than exists in the company today, and the development of knowledge, skills, and expertise in related voice/data transmission and imaging technologies.

However, individuals with IT systems and software skills and expertise are in short supply and are difficult to recruit, expecially in Newfoundland and Labrador. In finding and retaining these individuals in the future, NLCS is likely to be competing with its own clients and with private-sector IT suppliers.

Functional Concerns, Issues, and Possibilities for the Future

Marketing and Client Service

NLCS, in common with other IT suppliers, is facing a developing "tyranny" of client expectations as the technology explodes. Perhaps a program of regular client visits is necessary, and NLCS could explore the feasibility of a "one-stop shopping" approach, including a more comprehensive client help-desk with call tracking. More client involvement could be developed through seeking regular feedback on NLCS' performance, asking clients for their needs, and establishing client support and user groups. Increasing customer involvement in applications development is to be expected and may be encouraged by NLCS, perhaps in conjunction with increasing use of CASE tools. However, NLCS will need to consider saying no to requests for services that it knows it cannot meet without increasing net costs.

A higher proportion of work could be carried out by NLCS staff in client offices, so that they are closer to the clients. The transfer of responsibility for new systems from those in NLCS who developed the system to those in client departments who will operate the system could be streamlined and made more effective.

NLCS could enter into service level agreements with clients, based on a client services planning and contracting program. This could include controlling the use of subsidised services and moves towards elimination of non-revenue-producing services. NLCS could try to repatriate to clients those services that can be effectively performed by clients' staffs—for example, production control and data entry. A reduction in mainframe processing rates, to bring them more in line with actual costs as the prices of other services are increased to reflect their actual costs, could improve client understanding of the costs of different services.

NLCS administrative systems that create client frustration, for example, the billing system and the telephone message system, can be improved. Along with this, reinforcing client satisfaction could be emphasized as an objective in all NLCS staff training and development. In order to more effectively resolve client problems and satisfy client needs, NLCS employees could be empowered to make more decisions, including those having financial implications. Employee recognition and rewards could be designed to reflect client satisfaction objectives.

NLCS must learn to operate in a true staff support mode, giving clients the power and skills to exercise control over their systems, and hence to achieve effective ownership of their systems. While this support mode starts at the application development stage and earlier, it must flow through to operations and NLCS administrative functions including billing.

The consultants have prepared a draft mission statement for NLCS (see Exhibit 4). Also, the consultants have suggested the customers and services that NLCS can aim to provide in the future (Exhibit 5), and those IT services that NLCS should consciously exclude from its future service offerings (Exhibit 6).

Data Communications and Telecommunications

The NLCS operated fibre optic data communications link uses leased lines and services from Newfoundland Telephone, and the service costs approximately $500,000 annually for the operation of a network of approximately 1,400 terminals throughout the province. Technological developments will make it more feasible for users of data and information throughout the province to communicate with each other—telecommunications will play a key role in regional development efforts in the province. For NLCS, a critical aspect will be the role of telecommunications in supporting the information technologies, networks, and systems which NLCS will be expected to provide.

Cost Effectiveness

A restructured, comprehensive "help desk" could improve quality of client service while reducing NLCS staff time taken up in resolving enquiries and problems from clients.

NLCS could acquire application development productivity tools and tailor these tools (including their respective development methodologies) to the

---

EXHIBIT 4 Draft Mission Statement
Newfoundland and Labrador Computer Services Limited

We provide public organizations in Newfoundland and Labrador with a comprehensive range of high-quality information technology services. We have built our approach to doing business on a strong commitment to these few key goals, values, and principles:

Excellent in client service and satisfaction. NLCS will develop and use excellent marketing skills, explicitly manage client expectations and satisfaction through client service planning and contracting, and provide honest and objective advice to clients about their choices.

Affordable and competitive costs of services. NLCS will be a commercially viable organization but not a profit maximiser. The principal economic benefits of competitive pricing and cost effectiveness will be passed onto the organization's clients. Cost effectiveness of services will include the concept of quality, which will continue to be a key organization value.

Facilitation of clients' ability to use information technology effectively and independently. Services will be provided in a manner that builds client expertise and emphasises the training and development of client staff.

Technical expertise and leadership. NLCS clients will consistently find that NLCS understands the major contemporary technologies and platforms or is readily able to access state-of-the-art technical information that is relevant to clients. While NLCS cannot be state-of-the-art in every area of information technology, it should be perceptively advanced from the majority of its clients and actively foster the introduction of up-to-date technology.

Contribution to the province's IT industry and resources. NLCS will contribute in two major ways. First, as an excellent employer of IT people who want to develop and sustain a successful personal career within Newfoundland and Labrador. Second, as a facilitator of private-sector development in information technology as a partner, contractor, consultant, client, or joint venture partner.

Support of overall provincial government goals and policies. NLCS will consciously approach the delivery of services with government objectives in mind. For example, if the government is moving towards development or decentralization of its services, NLCS would search for innovative means of supporting that overall direction.

---

needs of individual clients. For example, SDM/70 and similar tools and methodologies are more complex than necessary for some client needs, and, consequently, more costly. Clients could make the decision, on a fully informed basis, as to whether a simpler tool will be sufficient for their specific needs.

Any realignment of mainframe rates, with accompanying increases in prices of other services, both reflecting actual costs, could focus attention on cost management. Maintenance services can be rationalised, separating out and charging clients for those aspects of maintenance that are really follow-on application development work. A simplified billing system could reduce NLCS billing and follow-up costs (in addition to improving client understanding and satisfaction.)

To reduce operational costs further, automation can be introduced. For example, mainframe operating software can be acquired to reduce the need for human intervention in those functions that can be automated. The nature

EXHIBIT 5   Consultants' Suggested Service Offerings for the Future

Service Descriptions	Large Government Departments	Small Government Departments	Boards and Agencies	Crown Corporations	Other Public Sector	Not for Profit	Private Sector
Mainframe processing	X	X	X	X	X	X	X
Telecommunications	X	X	X	X	X	X	
Application development and support	X	X	X	X	X	X	
Network services	X	X	X	X	X	X	X
Mini-computer processing and consulting	X	X	X	X	X	X	
Systems consulting	X	X	X	X	X	X	
Management education and seminars	X	X	X	X	X	X	X
Facilities management	X	X	X	X	X	X	X
Staff secondment	X	X	X	X	X	X	
Project management services	X	X	X	X	X	X	X
Backup site services	X	X	X	X	X	X	X
Disaster recovery services	X	X	X	X	X	X	X
Records management	X	X	X	X	X	X	
Office automation	X	X	X	X	X	X	
Electronic office systems	X	X	X	X			
Public enquiry services							X
Private-sector initiatives	X	X	X	X	X	X	X
Printing services (laser, MICR)	X	X	X	X	X	X	X

EXHIBIT 6   Consultants' Suggested Service Offerings to Be Excluded in the Future

Service Descriptions	Large Government Departments	Small Government Departments	Boards and Agencies	Crown Corporations	Other Public Sector	Not for Profit	Private Sector
Systems staff training	X	X	X	X			
Research and development	X	X	X	X	X	X	
Micro-computer selection, application support, vendor software	X	X					
Information centre	X	X	X	X	X	X	
Data packaging and sales	X	X	X	X		X	X
Software sales	X	X	X	X	X	X	
Package development and sales	X	X	X	X	X	X	X
Information technology legal services	X	X	X	X			

and extent of backshift services provided can be rationalised in order to reduce overtime and standby charges that are currently taken for granted. Some existing NLCS functions (for example, courier services) may be contracted out at lower costs.

Technological Credibility

NLCS is not perceived by clients as being sufficiently technically competent in all areas of IT/IS. Although NLCS should not be trying to be an IT/IS encyclopedia, it is essential that clients come to recognise the expertise that NLCS has in its selected areas of service.

To develop this recognition, NLCS can:

- take the initiative to bring new systems opportunities to clients' attention;
- take the initiative to reduce its costs and, therefore, the prices of the services it provides to clients;
- broadcast its successes to the entire client population;
- establish client user and support groups;
- take the time to "show and tell" clients what NLCS is doing, whenever the opportunity presents itself;
- sponsor client seminars on new developments in IT; and
- invest more heavily in technical training for its own development and operations professionals.

Organization Structure and Culture

In its current organization structure, NLCS has two groups of database specialists and two groups of application development project staff. Facilities management personnel report in two separate departments of NLCS. Consideration could be given in each of these three areas to streamlining and bringing together similar functions, which could result in more cost-effective co-ordination and service to clients.

The organization's management depth requires attention to empower staff at all levels and to plan for retirements in the next five to eight years among its senior management group. The span of control at the top of the organization is relatively small—only three vice presidents report to the president. At present, NLCS does not have strong management depth either in terms of skills or levels of management expertise, although it has considerable supervisory depth. Increasing this span of control could result in a higher level of authority being given to project managers and other front-line supervisors.

It may be that organization restructuring also offers opportunities for reduction in NLCS' operating costs and for increases in operational effectiveness. For example, the number of data entry staff could be reduced, and

EXHIBIT 7 Organization Chart Proposed by Consultants

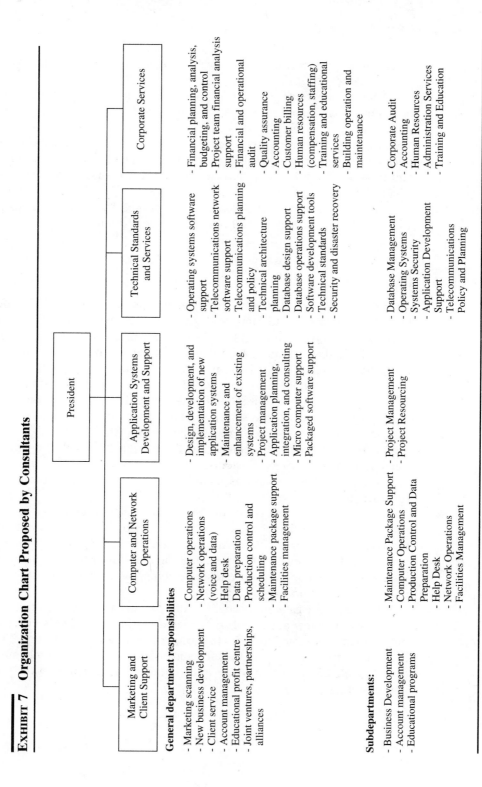

President

| Marketing and Client Support | Computer and Network Operations | Application Systems Development and Support | Technical Standards and Services | Corporate Services |

General department responsibilities

Marketing and Client Support
- Marketing scanning
- New business development
- Client service
- Account management
- Educational profit centre
- Joint ventures, partnerships, alliances

Computer and Network Operations
- Computer operations
- Network operations (voice and data)
- Help desk
- Data preparation
- Production control and scheduling
- Maintenance package support
- Facilities management

Application Systems Development and Support
- Design, development, and implementation of new application systems
- Maintenance and enhancement of existing systems
- Project management
- Application planning, integration, and consulting
- Micro computer support
- Packaged software support

Technical Standards and Services
- Operating systems software support
- Telecommunications network software support
- Telecommunications planning and policy
- Technical architecture planning
- Database design support
- Database operations support
- Software development tools
- Technical standards
- Security and disaster recovery

Corporate Services
- Financial planning, analysis, budgeting, and control
- Project team financial analysis support
- Financial and operational audit
- Quality assurance
- Accounting
- Customer billing
- Human resources (compensation, staffing)
- Training and educational services
- Building operation and maintenance

Subdepartments:

- Business Development
- Account management
- Educational programs

- Maintenance Package Support
- Computer Operations
- Production Control and Data Preparation
- Help Desk
- Network Operations
- Facilities Management

- Project Management
- Project Resourcing

- Database Management
- Operating Systems
- Systems Security
- Application Development Support
- Telecommunications Policy and Planning

- Corporate Audit
- Accounting
- Human Resources
- Administration Services
- Training and Education

a reporting level between executive management and the front line could be eliminated.

Achievement of any strategy for the future will require that NLCS possess or acquire a particular set of organization skills. The mind-set of the organization must change from that of a mainframe-centred service bureau in a protected market to one of a competitive supplier of IT services. NLCS needs to change from thinking of self-preservation to thinking of client preservation, and to behave in a less bureaucratic fashion if it wishes to be responsive to clients' needs.

An organization structure has been proposed by the consultants in the Role and Mandate review, and this is given in Exhibit 7.

Back in the Office

The president knew that the two utility companies in the province, Newfoundland Telephone Co. Ltd. and Newfoundland Light & Power Co. Ltd., are likely to be major competitors in the future. Currently, NLCS provides and manages the data communications network for the provincial government, while Newfoundland Telephone provides all voice communications through Wide Area Telephone Services and Message Toll Services lines. However, Newfoundland Telephone is in the business of data communications also, and it provides these services to some very large users, such as banks, credit card customer centers, etc. The company has partnership with and is majority owned by Bell Canada, a communications industry group. Newfoundland Telephone owns Paragon Systems, a company which is active in providing microcomputer-based solutions, including hardware, local area networks, and software, to several government departments.

Newfoundland Light & Power also possesses data communications expertise, obtained from managing its electricity distribution system. Furthermore, the controlled deregulation of the communications industry by the federal government has allowed Newfoundland Light & Power to enter into partnership with a new long-distance telephone company, Unitel. Thus, it also could provide competition to NLCS.

As the northeast wind brought in the weather from the Atlantic and the sleet began to blow against his office windows, the president's vision of the outside world became blurred. He thought this an appropriate signal to now begin to sharpen his vision of the future in order to formulate his recommendations for NLCS' future strategy and organization and his action plan for implementing changes.

Northern Telecom Japan, Inc.

In late May of 1988, Howard Garvey, the newly appointed president of Northern Telecom Japan, Inc. (NTJI), was reviewing the financial projections for the subsidiary's next three years of operation. After two months of studying the operations of the company, Garvey was planning to address a committee, consisting of the presidents of all the Northern Telecom (NT) companies, regarding the current state of NTJI. In his presentation, he would have to either accept the current three-year operating plan or present his proposed revisions. If he accepted the plan, he would be responsible for delivering the forecasted results. If he rejected the plan, he would have to explain why his forecasts differed from those of his predecessors.

With the meeting scheduled to be held in Toronto, Canada, in a month, Garvey decided to review the projections in light of what he had seen during his first six weeks in Japan.

The Telecommunications Industry

The decade of the 80s brought about major changes in the telecommunications industry. Of the approximately 30 major telecommunications manufacturers

This case was prepared by Christopher Lane under the supervision of Professor C. B. Johnston for the sole purpose of providing material for class discussion at the Western Business School. Funding for this case was provided by the Pacific 2000 programme operated by the Department of External Affairs, Government of Canada. Certain names and other identifying information may have been disguised to protect confidentiality. It is not intended to illustrate either effective or ineffective handling of a managerial situation. Any reproduction, in any form, of the material in this case is prohibited except with the written consent of the School. Copyright 1992 © The University of Western Ontario.

that had existed in the late 70s, only 15 remained in 1988. The impetus for this change was the rising cost of research required to remain a competitor in this industry. Digital switching, existing only in the minds of engineers at the turn of the decade, had become a necessity for doing business. By 1988, the estimated cost of developing a state-of-the-art digital central office switch was $1 billion.

With the need for greater research dollars came the need for volume. Companies could no longer exist by relying on their national markets alone. Some analysts, extrapolating this trend into the future, were predicting that by the year 2000 only 5 of the current 15 companies would remain, as any one company would need at least a 10 percent share of the world market to continue to compete. Exhibit 1 lists the top eight telecommunications manufacturers in 1988.

By 1988, the major thrust in the industry was on the development of ISDN systems. ISDN was an internationally agreed-upon protocol for an integrated service digital network, a network that would support the simultaneous transmission of data, voice, and image. ISDN technology united the computer, telephone, and television into one network and could eventually devolve these three devices into one.

Northern Telecom

NT first began manufacturing telecommunications instruments in Canada in 1884. The company, then named Northern Electric, began operations as the Canadian subsidiary of the U.S.–based manufacturing giant Western Electric. In 1956, the U.S. Department of Justice passed the AT&T Consent Decree, which forced American Telephone and Telegraph (AT&T) to sever all relationships with firms outside of the United States. The purpose of this action was to prevent the American giant from using its monopoly in the United States to compete unfairly in the rest of the world. Western Electric, as the manufacturing arm of AT&T, was forced to sever its relationship with Northern Electric in the same way that AT&T was forced to sever its relationship

---

EXHIBIT 1   The Top Eight Manufacturers of Telecommunications Equipment—1988 (revenues in U.S.$ billions)

1	Alcatel	France	$11.5*
2	AT&T	United States	$11.3
3	Siemens	West Germany	$10.8
4	NEC	Japan	$ 6.5
5	Northern Telecom	Canada	$ 5.2
6	LM Ericsson	Sweden	$ 4.2
7	Hitachi	Japan	$ 3.4
8	Fujitsu	Japan	$ 2.9

* The chart shows only revenues attributed to telecommunications sales. Sales for each company may be significantly higher.

with Bell Canada. With this action, NT became a wholly owned subsidiary of Bell Canada.

Historically, both Bell Canada and NT had relied on their parent's research facility, Bell Labs, to keep them at the forefront of the industry. With these relationships now severed, the long-term survival of NT, as a producer of telecommunications equipment, became contingent upon the development of its own research facility. In 1959, NT established an internal research and development division which specialized in designing products for the Canadian market. In 1971, the division was spun off into a jointly owned subsidiary of both NT and Bell. The new company, named Bell Northern Research (BNR), provided research and development for both Bell Canada and NT.

The tricorporate structure provided an ideal environment for the growth of all three companies. Bell Canada, operating as a monopoly in the provinces of Ontario and Quebec,[1] worked closely with BNR and NT to develop the equipment needed to meet its future requirements. While Bell Canada served as the operating telecommunications company (telco) specialist, and BNR as the development specialist, NT provided the manufacturing and marketing expertise.

By the mid-70s, it had become apparent that research and development expenses required to keep NT at the forefront of the telecommunications industry would require revenues greater than those available in Canada alone. NT had to decide to become a small niche player in the industry or to expand its operations globally. In 1976, NT management set themselves an ambitious goal. In an attempt to increase their share of the U.S. market, they focused their research on digital technologies with the hope of becoming the first telecommunications company in the world to offer a complete digital switching system. They thought success in this endeavour would help to springboard them into the world market.[2] In 1976, NT invited executives from North American telephone operating companies to a conference in Disney World, Florida. The Canadian company's announcement that the age of the "Digital World" had arrived through NT's development of the first truly digital switches started the major thrust toward digital switching in North America.

In the early 80s, the U.S. Department of Justice ruled that AT&T would have to be broken up in order to promote greater competition within the U.S. telephone market. In 1984, Judge Green announced the Modification of Final Judgment, which ruled specifically how AT&T would be divided, and ordered that the 22 Bell subsidiaries be grouped together to form seven independent, regional telcos.

This event provided NT with an unprecedented opportunity for growth in the U.S. market. Many of the engineers within these newly formed companies were familiar with the benefits offered by digital switching and were

---

[1] The provinces of Ontario and Quebec accounted for 68 percent of the population and roughly 80 percent of the Canadian telecommunications market.

[2] For a more detailed account of this decision, please refer to Western Business School Case 9-83-4031 (REV 10/85), "Northern Telecom (A)".

anxious to begin incorporating this technology into their networks. With these companies now free to purchase their equipment from any supplier, not just from AT&T–owned Western Electric, NT was able to make substantial inroads.

By the beginning of 1988, NT had become the world's leading supplier of fully digital telecommunications systems, with sales of $4.85 billion.[3] Bell Canada remained the majority shareholder with a 53 percent holding, while the remaining shares were traded on the New York, Toronto, London, and Tokyo exchanges. On a geographic basis, revenues were derived as follows: 62 percent from Northern Telecom, Inc. (NTI), the U.S. subsidiary; 33 percent from Northern Telecom Canada Ltd.; and 5 percent from Northern Telecom World Trade Corp., the umbrella company which oversaw all international subsidiaries, including Japan. (See Exhibit 2 for the consolidated financial statements.) NT was positioned as the fifth largest telecommunications manufacturer in the world with a 6.5 percent share of the global market for telecommunications equipment and related services. NT operated 41 manufacturing facilities worldwide. Of these, 24 were located in Canada, 13 in the United States, 2 in Malaysia, 1 in the Republic of Ireland, and 1 in France. Research was conducted at 24 of these plants as well as at 10 BNR labs including 4 in Canada, 5 in the United States, and 1 in the United Kingdom.

On the technological front, NT was well positioned for competing in the upcoming decade, and NT maintained its lead in ISDN development with a successful test of more than 20 business, government, and residential applications during a trial in Phoenix, Arizona. In addition, NT's SuperNode software technology, which allowed software modules to be added as needed, provided the most powerful and flexible digital switches in the business.

The management of the company chose 1988 to announce to its employees and shareholders Vision 2000, outlining NT's ambitious goal of becoming the world's leading supplier of telecommunications equipment by the year 2000 (see Exhibit 3).

The Japanese Market

The Japanese, impressed by the technological developments that had occurred at Bell Labs in the United States, had modeled their domestic telephone company after AT&T. Their version, Nippon Telegraph and Telephone (NTT), had been established as a government-owned monopoly with the mandate of providing domestic telecommunications services throughout Japan. Another government-owned company, Kokusai Denshin Denwa (KDD), provided all international long-distance service. NTT's research facility worked very closely with the Ministry of International Trade and Industry,

---

[3] All dollar figures in this case are U.S. denominated.

EXHIBIT 2	**Consolidated Financial Statements of Northern Telecom Limited**

For the Year Ended December 31 ($U.S. millions)

Earnings and Related Data	*1984*	*1985*	*1986*	*1987*
Revenues	3,374.0	4,262.9	4,383.6	4,853.5
Cost of revenues	2,074.1	2,708.9	2,730.5	2,895.8
Selling, general, and administrative expense	603.2	701.9	764.6	917.8
Research and development expense	333.1	430.0	474.6	587.5
Depreciation	162.8	203.3	247.3	264.1
Provision for income taxes	120.8	132.8	127.9	141.5
Earnings before extraordinary items	255.8	299.2	313.2	347.2
Net earnings applicable to common shares	243.2	273.8	286.8	328.8
Earnings per common share ($) before extraordinary items	1.06	1.18	1.23	1.39
Dividends per share ($)	0.16	0.18	0.20	0.23
Financial position at December 31				
Working capital	859.0	933.9	1,188.7	570.7
Plant and equipment (at cost)	1,458.0	1,737.5	1,975.2	2,345.6
Accumulated depreciation	591.5	672.4	877.3	1084.2
Total assets	3,072.9	3,490.0	3,961.1	4,869.0
Long-term debt	100.2	107.6	101.0	224.8
Redeemable retractable preferred shares	293.6	277.5	281.0	153.9
Redeemable preferred shares	—	73.3	73.3	73.3
Common shareholders' equity	1379.8	164.6	1894.9	2333.3
Return on common shareholders' equity	19%	18.3%	16.3%	15.6%
Capital expenditures	437.3	457.3	303.8	416.7
Employees at December 31	46,993	46,549	46,202	48,778

Source: Northern Telecom Ltd. Annual Report, 1987.

operating more as a national research center than as a corporate research facility. Jointly sponsored research conducted at the lab was largely responsible for helping Japan catch up to the United States in semiconductor technologies.

Unlike AT&T in the United States, NTT did not have any manufacturing facilities. Instead, it relied on four major Japanese suppliers, Nippon Electric Company (NEC), Hitachi, Oki, and Fujitsu, to manufacture its equipment. The "big four" worked closely with NTT researchers to jointly design all of the switches for the Japanese telecommunications network. Under this arrangement, each of them manufactured identical equipment and received roughly a 25 percent share of NTT's business. Through these relationships, Japan was able to build and support a significant manufacturing base for telecommunications equipment.

In 1982, an ad hoc commission of administrative reform was set up by the Japanese government to study ways of introducing competition into the

---

EXHIBIT 3   Vision 2000: The Challenge of Leadership

Between now and the year 2000, the global market for telecommunications equipment and associated services is going to explode—from about $75 billion in 1987, to approximately $300 billion, a growth rate unmatched by any other industry.

Northern Telecom's own growth will be equally dramatic. It will be based on the steps we are taking now to ensure the achievements of Vision 2000—our goal of leadership in the worldwide telecommunications marketplace into the next century.

The global information network has already become one of the world's most effective means of increasing productivity. From the remote oil fields of The People's Republic of China, to the financial institutions of the United Kingdom, to the high-tech innovators of California's Silicon Valley, communications provides the advantages for competitive success and improved quality of life.

This is recognized by enlightened governments around the world, which have singled out telecommunications as a major priority for development and modernization.

Traditional voice services and rapidly increasing requirements for data transmission are outstripping the ability of existing networks to meet the competitive pressures of global business needs and the growing demands of society. At the same time, new technologies and new generations of equipment are creating additional demands for services previously only dreamed of.

While new products, services, and technologies are propelling the growth of telecommunications worldwide, we are focusing on markets where the opportunity is greatest. Beyond North America, we are concentrating on such markets as Australia, China, France, Japan, New Zealand, West Germany, and the United Kingdom, where deregulation and growth are creating market opportunities that have already led to strategic sales of our products. In these seven countries alone, the market will grow from $20 billion to $100 billion by the year 2000.

We expect our business outside North America to rise to about 15 percent of our total revenues in the early 1990s and continue to increase through the rest of that decade.

Northern Telecom's vision of the year 2000 involves a number of imperatives. It means continually generating sustainable advantages over our competitors through excellence in creating value for our customers, which in turn enhances their growth and profitability.

It requires our corporation to be global in reach and thinking, while showing flexibility, sensitivity, and good corporate citizenship in diverse markets.

And it demands that Northern Telecom deliver products and systems of the highest quality and reliability, on time, tailored to the varying needs of our customers. We must also provide the highest level of service in the industry.

The conditions of leadership are clear. In a fiercely competitive international marketplace, leadership will go to that corporation with the clearest global vision, the fastest response, the capability, and the commitment to satisfy the ever-more complex market requirements of the future.

Northern Telecom intends to be that corporation.

Source: Northern Telecom Ltd. Annual Report, 1987.

Japanese telecommunications system. In 1985, the committee released a report calling for deregulation of the entire telecommunications industry and the privatization of government-owned NTT. One of the most important results of the report was the establishment of the new common carriers (NCCs). The NCCs were firms that would be licensed to compete in both the domestic and international long-distance telephone markets in a manner similar to Sprint and MCI in the United States. October 1, 1989, was the date set for the beginning of service by the NCCs.

The NCCs presented an opportunity for foreign telecommunications equipment suppliers, as many of these new firms were building their own networks from scratch. Furthermore, these companies didn't have existing relationships with the domestic suppliers and were looking outside of Japan to see how they could gain a competitive advantage over the existing NTT/ KDD networks.

In 1988, the Japanese telecommunications market, estimated at $25 billion, was the third largest in the world and one of the fastest growing. The three main segments that made up this market were telcos, corporations, and households.

Telcos

Telcos, providing the network for telecommunications, had needs ranging from wiring and optical fibre to large-scale switching equipment, from underwater cables to satellite or microwave transmission equipment. Sales to telcos were usually made through tenders, often called four to five years in advance of the required installation date. (See the appendix for an explanation of NTT's procurement process.)

Success in this market required not only state-of-the-art hardware but also an extensive service organization. Highly trained servicemen and an inventory of spare parts had to be kept within easy access of all areas of the network, since any problems had to be fixed within hours. In 1988, sales to telcos represented 50 percent of the total Japanese telecommunications market. Sales to NTT represented roughly 90 percent of this segment.

Corporations

As the networking and communications needs of companies grew throughout the 80s, so did the market for private branch exchanges (PBXs). A PBX is the brain of a corporate phone system. It allows companies with only a few outside lines to provide phone service to all of their employees, thus reducing overall telephone costs. PBXs had become increasingly more sophisticated and complex over the years by offering facilities such as voice mail, automatic callback, and direct-inward dialing. Sales of PBX systems were usually made through a tender process.

One factor that distinguished the Japanese market from other world markets, however, was the existence of Keiretsus. A Keiretsu was a group of firms loosely connected through part ownership. (See "A Note on The Japanese Keiretsu," Western Business School Case 9-92-G008, for more information.) These firms had a tendency to purchase equipment from within their group whenever possible. With the big four Japanese competitors all firmly entrenched in their own Keiretsus, the size of the market that was left for NT to compete in was questionable.

Households

In Japan, most individuals purchased their own telephones rather than renting them from NTT. Phones were sold through three primary distribution outlets: department stores, electronics specialty chain stores, and numerous large and small independent electronics stores. Along with the big four, many of Japan's leading consumer electronics companies also manufactured telephones. The resulting market was extremely competitive. (See Exhibit 4 for market data.) Competition among producers tended to occur along three dimensions: product-features, design, and price. In the spirit of "kaizen,"[4] phones were being continually introduced with new features. Many of the best-selling phones were heavily advertised.

---

[4] *Kaizen* is a Japanese word used to describe the Japanese philosophy of continuous incremental improvement.

EXHIBIT 4   Telephone and PBX Sales in Japan in 1988

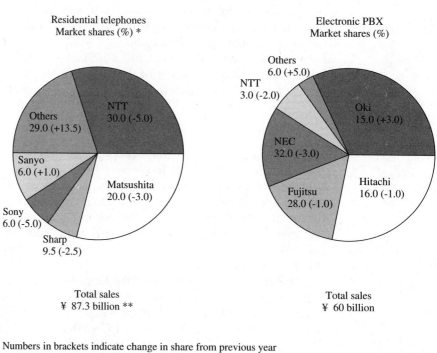

Residential telephones
Market shares (%) *

Others 29.0 (+13.5)
NTT 30.0 (-5.0)
Sanyo 6.0 (+1.0)
Sony 6.0 (-5.0)
Sharp 9.5 (-2.5)
Matsushita 20.0 (-3.0)

Total sales
¥ 87.3 billion **

Electronic PBX
Market shares (%)

Others 6.0 (+5.0)
NTT 3.0 (-2.0)
NEC 32.0 (-3.0)
Fujitsu 28.0 (-1.0)
Oki 15.0 (+3.0)
Hitachi 16.0 (-1.0)

Total sales
¥ 60 billion

Numbers in brackets indicate change in share from previous year
** 125 Japanese Yen ▪ $1.00 U.S. (1988)

Source: *Information & Communications in Japan.* Tokyo: InfoCom Research Inc., 1990, p 171.

The Competition

There were numerous competitors in the Japanese telecommunications market (see Exhibit 5). However, NT faced only four primary domestic competitors in selling to NTT.

EXHIBIT 5   Competition in the Japanese Telecommunications Markets

Company	Telephone Sets	PBXs	Digital Switches
Alphone Co., Ltd.	X		
Alcatel NV	X	X	X
Anritsu Corporation	X		
Iwasaki Tsushiniki Co. Ltd.	X	X	
AT&T International Japan	X	X	X
Oidenki Co., Ltd.		X	
Oki Electric Industry Co. Ltd.	X	X	X
Kanda Tsushin Kogyo	X		
Canon, Inc.	X	X	
Kyushu Matsushita	X		
Kenwood Corporation	X		
International Electronics	X		
Sun Telephone Co.	X		
Sanyo Electric Co. Ltd.	X	X	
Siemens K.K.	X		X
Sharp Corporation	X	X	
Shinwa Tsushinki	X		
Sony Corporation	X		
Taiei Manufacturing Ltd.		X	X
Taiko Electric	X	X	X
Takachiho Ltd.	X		
Takamizawa Electric Co.		X	
Omron Electronics Co.	X	X	
Tamura Electric Works Ltd.	X		
Toshiba Corporation	X	X	
Nakayo Telecommunications Ltd.	X	X	X
Nitsuko Corp.	X	X	
NEC Corporation	X	X	X
Victory Company of Japan	X		
Northern Telecom	X	X	X
Pioneer Electronic Corp.	X		
Hitachi Ltd.	X	X	X
Fujitsu Ltd.	X	X	X
Matsushita Corporation Ltd.	X	X	
Mitsubishi Electric Corporation	X	X	
Ricoh Co. Ltd.	X		

Source: *Information & Communications in Japan.* Tokyo: InfoCom Research, Inc., March 1990, pp. 173–178.

Nippon Electric Company

NEC, the fourth largest telecommunications producer in the world, reported overall revenues of $22 billion in 1988. The company was organized into four divisions:

1. Communications systems and equipment.
2. Computer and industrial electronic systems.
3. Electronic devices.
4. Home electronic products.

Communications systems and equipment contributed 28 percent of the overall revenue. NEC was well known for the high quality of its hardware. However, adding advanced features to NEC's product was difficult because the company's software was less flexible than NT's.

Hitachi

With revenues of $40 billion in 1988, Hitachi was the largest overall company of the four competitors. A huge Keiretsu in itself, its product range extended from nuclear power plants to semiconductors. The company was divided into five principal business groups:

1. Power systems and equipment.
2. Consumer products.
3. Information and communication systems and electronic devices.
4. Industrial machinery and plants.
5. Wire and cable and chemicals.

The information and communication systems and electronic devices division encompassed businesses from computers to semiconductors and telecommunications equipment. This division accounted for 33 percent of revenues in 1988. Hitachi was ranked as the seventh largest telecommunications manufacturer in 1988.

In 1987, the company opened a subsidiary to produce PBX units in the United States.

Fujitsu

Fujitsu, IBM's most aggressive worldwide competitor in the mainframe computer market, was divided into four primary business groups:

1. Computers and data processing.
2. Telecommunications.
3. Semiconductors.
4. Components.

Telecommunications represented 12.5 percent of the company's $16 billion in revenue in 1988. The company was strong in all areas of the telecommunications business from fibre optic cable to digital switching equipment. In March 1988, the company released an ISDN system linking computers, word processors, and networks into one package.

Internationally, Fujitsu had formed an alliance with General Electric in the United States to manufacture and market PBX systems.

Oki

Oki, the smallest of the big four Japanese suppliers, was strong internationally in cellular telephones and fax machines. Revenues in 1988 amounted to $3.6 billion with 26.9 percent of this amount resulting from sales of telecommunications systems. The company was divided into three principal groups:

1. Telecommunications systems.
2. Information processing systems.
3. Electronic devices.

Northern Telecom Japan, Inc.

In the early 80s, NT initiated a program whereby senior managers were sent as ambassadors to various telecommunications markets around the world. These managers met with potential customers and assessed the prospects of the market from NT's perspective. Japan, at that time representing the third largest telecommunications market in the world, was selected early as one of the countries to be visited. In 1982, Edward Fitzgerald, president of Northern Telecom Limited, went to Japan as NT's ambassador.

Fitzgerald, although not an expert in doing business in Japan, knew that the Japanese loved baseball as much or more than most Americans. Having owned the Milwaukee Brewers at one point, he was well connected in baseball circles and shared their enthusiasm for the sport. Thinking that it might help, he asked his good friend Bowie Kuhn, the ex-commissioner of major league baseball in the United States, to join him for the trip.

Through Kuhn's connections with Japanese baseball officials and those officials' connections in Japanese business circles, Fitzgerald was able to get a letter of introduction to Dr. Shinto, the president of NTT. Through a combination of his personality, his baseball stories, many gifts of Inuit carvings, and his sincerity in wishing to do business in Japan, he was able to win the respect of his Japanese counterparts, thus laying the groundwork for building NT's relationship with NTT.

While in Japan, Fitzgerald employed the services of a well-known Japanese businessman/consultant to look into NTT's operations and various government and legal issues. The work of the consultant uncovered two significant facts for NT. First, NTT needed to replace a significant number of small community dial office systems in the rural areas of its network. Second, the recent trade friction between the United States and Japan was making the Japanese government very uncomfortable. It seemed very plausible that NTT as a government-regulated monopoly would feel pressure to open up to foreign suppliers, especially to those from the United States.

Armed with this information, NT, acting through its American subsidiary, NTI, prepared an unsolicited proposal for NTT to supply the Japanese company with NT's DMS-10, the world's first fully digital switching system. With a capacity of up to 10,000 lines, the DMS-10 was ideally suited for use as a community dial office. The bid to NTT was made in 1982. At the same time, NT established an office in Japan with the arrival of a single expatriate. Although the bid to NTT was well received, it did not immediately translate into a direct order.

In 1983, NT committed itself to the Japanese market with the legal registration of NTJI. In the latter part of the year, NT received an invitation from NTT to participate in a competitive bid for a single emergency switching system. This switch, which was to be mounted in a trailer, would be used to provide emergency switching capability if an earthquake or other type of disaster left a community without telephone service. Coincidentally, the specifications for this switch were very similar to those of NT's DMS-10. The slightly modified DMS-10 was named the KS-2, and NT succeeded in beating the competition to become the first foreign telecommunications company to supply to NTT. Although the one-time sale represented less than $400,000, the associated benefits for NT were far greater. The sale allowed NT to learn more about NTT, its needs, and its methods of doing business. At the same time, the opportunity for NTT to evaluate NT's quality and technology helped to strengthen the relationship that had been developing over time.

In 1984, NTT announced a competitive tender to replace a large number of rural electromechanical community switching exchanges. A decision by NT to bid for this tender would have to include a commitment to establish a full-service network in Japan, as the vendor was required to provide ongoing servicing of the equipment. NT, believing in the long-term potential of the Japanese market, entered a bid, once again featuring the DMS-10.

Designing flexible software systems was one area where North American producers had a competitive advantage over their Japanese rivals. A feature of NT's proposal extended to NTT the right to modify the software operating system of the switch for the purpose of developing market-specific feature applications. This arrangement required NT to provide NTT with documentation on its operating software. AT&T, also bidding on this contract, was reluctant to include this right, fearing that NTT might divulge this information to the four domestic manufacturers.

NT management, after assessing the long-term opportunity of doing business with NTT, determined that the risk was minimal, as the software programs within the switch were reaching maturity. More importantly, however, they wanted to develop a relationship between NT and NTT which was based on reciprocal trust.

On May 19, 1986, Northern's bid was selected by NTT and NT was committed to building and maintaining a subsidiary in Japan capable of installing and servicing 1,500,000 lines over a five-year period, beginning in late 1988. The contract was worth $250 million for NTJI.

The Penetration Strategy

With the establishment of NTJI, NT was committing to a long-term strategy of becoming a supplier of its full line of switching equipment to NTT. Because this relationship would take time to develop, a short-term penetration strategy was also developed for attacking the two other main segments of the Japanese telecommunications market: telephones and PBX units.

Telephones

NTJI entered the Japanese telephone market in 1984 with the launch of its Contempra model, an upscale "designer" telephone set. Initial sales were encouraging, as the Contempra filled a niche at the top of the market. Unfortunately, when this product was introduced into the middle segment of the market, NT found that the competition was extremely severe. Without the volume of the more standard telephone sets to support the administrative overhead, NT realized that the telephone segment provided little opportunity for profit. As a consequence, efforts were withdrawn on marketing these products.

PBX Unit: The SL-1

NTJI's disappointment in the telephone set segment of the market was not a complete surprise to upper management in Northern Telecom Ltd., as NTI, the U.S. subsidiary, was also experiencing similar stiff competition. What upper management did not anticipate, however, were the problems that NTJI experienced in trying to sell its PBX systems in Japan. The SL-1, NT's digital PBX system, was the world's best-selling PBX system. Because of its successful sales throughout North America, NT had expected that the SL-1 would be a success in Japan as well. When actual sales fell considerably short of forecasts, management decided to investigate.

Examination of this issue highlighted a multitude of miscalculations in NT's marketing approach. First, NT had seriously underestimated the strength of the domestic competition and their Keiretsu relationships. Second, NTJI had not studied how Japanese companies actually used their phone systems and therefore did not realize that its product did not meet the basic needs of the Japanese corporation. To the Japanese, direct access dialing was not a desirable feature, as every call to the company should be answered and greeted by the company's receptionist. She would then call ahead to check if the person was in before either transferring the call or taking a message.

Consequently, NT's highly advanced product offered little advantage to the Japanese customer. Third, the product was being marketed at a premium price. On average, NT's system was priced 20 percent higher than the local competition's product. Finally, all of the promotional materials for the SL-1 were in English, and the product was being sold through a distributor who had been given insufficient product training. Needless to say, the relationship between NT and the distributor became very strained.

Despite the problems encountered in the telephone set and PBX markets, NTJI continued its efforts into the telco market, and in January of 1988, signed an agreement with International Digital Communications (IDC), one of the newly sanctioned NCCs, to provide the switching equipment needed to run their network. IDC chose NT's DMS-250 tandem switching system and DMS-300 international gateway switch. This decision was influenced by NT's previous success in selling these switches to MCI and Sprint in the United States, as NT supplied 50 percent of MCI's and 100 percent of Sprint's switching equipment. IDC was licensed to begin operations on October 1, 1989, and NT was committed to installing a complete network to be ready by that date.

By early 1988, NTJI had grown to employ 87 full-time employees. Of these, roughly 40 were expatriates from NTI and the remaining were local Japanese.

Howard Garvey

Howard Garvey joined NT in 1955 as an installer. He worked his way through the Canadian organization, and after 18 years of service, was appointed assistant to the vice president, sales, of NTI, the U.S. subsidiary. In 1978, he was appointed NTI's first national account manager and subsequently generated the first $50 million supply contract in the United States. In March of 1982, he was appointed vice president, sales, with responsibility for AT&T and the Bell operating companies. This promotion coincided with the beginning of the thrust to market digital systems to the Bell system in the United States, accounting for just under $100 million of NTI's sales.

By 1988, sales in his division were exceeding $1.2 billion, and Garvey was recognized as one of the key people instrumental in achieving NT's success in penetrating the U.S. market. In March of that year, Desmond Hudson, the president of Northern Telecom World Trade (NTWT), asked Garvey if he would do in Japan what he had done so well in the United States. Garvey accepted a three-year posting and was told he had until July to learn all he could about Japan. Shortly afterwards, Fitzgerald, the chairman and CEO of Northern Telecom Limited, upon returning from a trip to Japan, prompted Hudson to accelerate Garvey's assignment. A few weeks later, in April of 1988, Garvey arrived in Japan as president of NTJI.

Garvey's Impressions of NTJI

In commenting on NTJI, Garvey pointed out that:

> In January of 1988, the chairman and several other key executives within Northern Telecom took stock of where the company was in respect to the Japanese market. We had a major contract with NTT to install 1,500,000 lines worth $250,000,000. We had a major contract with IDC with a date staring us in the face that not only meant part of our future but also IDC's future was at stake. If that thing went down then we were dead in Japan. We also had an unprecedented opportunity over here, as we were moving into a new marketplace with the NCCs.

When they reviewed the NTJI operation, they noticed that there were an increasing number of bypasses around NTJI. The customers, apprehensive about the local organization's ability to service their needs, often dealt directly with North America. It was concluded that the situation required a change in the management of NTJI.

> Because of my background and experience in increasing our market share in the United States, into the Bell system in particular, and because there was such a similarity between the structures of AT&T in North America and NTT in Japan, I was given the opportunity to come and see what needed to be done to make sure that we didn't jeopardize the opportunity that was facing us.

During April and May, Garvey examined the operations of NTJI in an effort to find areas upon which he could improve. The following were his observations:

> The organization that existed in Japan was essentially being run from the United States. Executives in NTI, proud of their accomplishment as one of the few American companies that had successfully broken into the Japanese market, had not been proactive in developing NTJI into a stand-alone subsidiary. There was a sense that NTI owned NTJI and the practice was that representatives of NTI were continually flying over to Japan to interact with various NTT officials.
>
> As a result, NTJI was still heavily dependent on the United States. This created within Japan an organization very limited in technical, marketing, and management skills, even though the organization had been in Japan for over four years.
>
> There were people in the local management group that were not compatible with Japanese customers. As an example, there was a fellow that was in charge of service, the leading edge in your customer relationship, with a domineering attitude based upon years in the U.S. military . . . he didn't fit very well.
>
> There was a heavy ex-pat presence and that relates back to the dependency on the United States. The ex-pats of course could go back to the United States for anything they wanted. Over and above that, there was no support infrastructure within the Japanese organization. The company was growing with minimum sense of direction, and a complementary management hierarchy was lacking within the company.
>
> Another major shortcoming was that the organization that existed in Japan was facing the United States. In other words, the organization was plugged into the organizational structure that existed in NTI in the United States, into a market-

ing group in the United States, into a service group in the United States, into a technical support group in the United States, without consideration of turning around and facing the customer and adapting to their organization.

As a result of the existing organization in Japan, engineers in some divisions within NTT would have to interface with two or three different divisions within NTJI (see Exhibit 6). For example, members of NTT's software engineering centre would have to regularly contact people in NTJI's Design, Design Follow-up, and

EXHIBIT 6   An Example of Structural Problems in NTJI

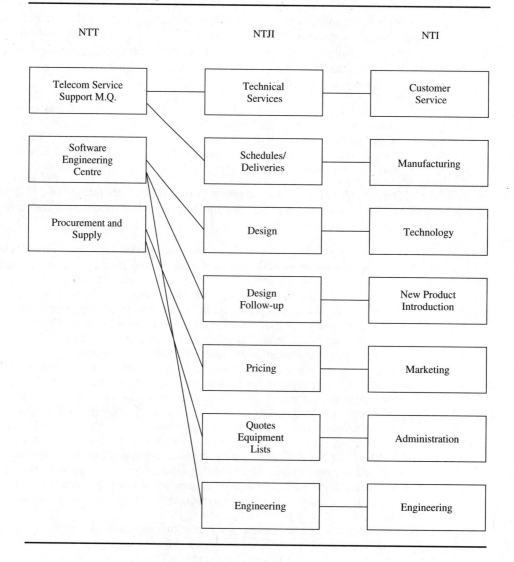

Engineering divisions. Even more troublesome, though, managers of NTT regional centres, who managed the outlying areas of NTT's network, would at times have to interface with almost every division within NTJI. This presented great problems for the regional manager, who inevitably called the wrong person within NTJI and spent the rest of the day playing telephone tag with various people before finding the right person to solve his problem.

When we talk about how to succeed in business, we hear more and more these days that you'd better be aware of your customer's needs. You can't have your back to the customer as NTJI did here. The company was structured to do business more conveniently with the United States than with our customers.

An additional problem within the company at the time was that there was a lack of business discipline. For example, local purchasing went virtually uncontrolled. The existing approval system was very loosely monitored. In fact, almost anyone could travel anywhere with minimal approvals.

Because of these factors, there existed a great deal of client apprehension. Customers didn't see any effective marketing, technical, or management support within NTJI. They were justifiably concerned about how NTJI was going to meet the obligations that it had here in Japan, as the company appeared to be run from the other side of the world.

There was also a perceptible split between the ex-pats and the nationals, and I again refer back to trying to do business in Japan and facing the customer. It was to the point where there was minimal reciprocal dialogue between the national employees and the ex-pats. Unfortunately, the ex-pats were predominantly in management positions in NTJI, and many decisions were made without any discussion or involvement with the Japanese employees. They were usually in the situation of "do as we tell you, we know best." Of course, that cost us an awful lot of employee discontent. It carried over into the recognition that we had to start growing some local experienced talent, but our reputation presented further difficulties in trying to recruit people.

There was an inadequate definition of responsibilities within the organization. The nationals particularly did not know what their jobs were. They took day-to-day directions from the ex-pats. Their responsibilities changed because the ex-pats were able to go to any individual, regardless of what his job was, and say "do this" or "go here." It was very unsettling for them. There was a definite lack of definition of responsibilities, and little sense of belonging to NTJI for the national employees.

Lastly, there was a serious lack of focus on where we were going in NTJI. For example, many of the people required for the installation and maintenance of NTT's contract for DMS-10s had not yet been hired or trained. The company's objectives in Japan and how they were going to be achieved were not communicated well to the employee population.

The Financial Projections

In late May of 1988, Garvey was reviewing the current operating projections for NTJI (see Exhibit 7). He was aware of several developments that had occurred since the original projections had been made in January 1988.

EXHIBIT 7 NTJI Financial Projections
For the Year Ended December 31 (in U.S.$ millions)

	1988				Totals		
	Q1	*Q2*	*Q3*	*Q4*	*1988*	*1989*	*1990*
Orders					43	126	173
Sales	2.1	2.3	3.0	9.1	16.5	75	130
Earnings					(6)	3	9
Headcount					136	196	232

First, NT had received an order from NTT for a single DMS-200. The order was the first central office switch sold to NTT by a non-Japanese vendor. It was commissioned by NTT to be used as an overflow switch to handle the surge in telephone traffic that occurred every year following "golden week."[5] In previous years, NTT had come under severe criticism as its network became jammed with calls and many people could not get through. The DMS-200–based system, to be installed in November of 1989, would eventually contribute $20–30 million in revenue. However, it would also require a similar sized investment in development costs by NT to adapt the DMS-200 to work within the Japanese public network and to develop the necessary supply infrastructure.

Second, it appeared that additional development costs would have to be incurred to modify NT's DMS-250 and DMS-300 for the IDC network. Garvey estimated the costs of these modifications within a range of $10–20 million.

Furthermore, Garvey had the benefit of being able to compare the first quarter's actual results against the projections. Revenues for the first quarter were slightly lower than projections and costs were slightly higher. From his earlier assessment of the company, he calculated that the forecast seriously underestimated the costs of product development, servicing, and support that companies like NTT demanded. Garvey estimated that over the next two years, an additional $5 million would be needed for increased technical support from the United States, and at least $2 million would be needed for training local personnel.

With these factors in mind, Garvey began planning his presentation for the executive committee.

---

[5] "Golden week," falling in April, is so named because it contains three public holidays within the span of seven days. Many Japanese companies close for the entire week, making this a very popular time for Japanese people to travel.

APPENDIX
NTT's PROCUREMENT PROCESS

Outline of Procedures

Based on the policy of "open, fair, and nondiscriminatory" procurement, NTT procures products required to operate its business following competitive procedures.

At NTT, procurement procedures are divided into five different categories according to the nature of the products to be procured. These are Track I, II, III and II-A and III-A.

When NTT purchases or hires any products in excess of 130,000 SDR per year (equivalent to 24 million yen[6] for FY 1988), the products are procured according to one of the above-mentioned procedures.

Track I covers the procedures for the procurement of specific products offered to GATT by NTT as items which fall under the "Agreement on Government Procurement." NTT selects suppliers by public tender in conformity with GATT[7] rules.

Track II, III, and Track II-A, III-A cover the procedures for the procurement of products other than those specified for Track I. In addition, NTT procurement procedures are transparent and nondiscriminatory in compliance with the spirit of GATT.

What Is a Track?

Track I.   Track I covers the procedures for the procurement of specific products offered to GATT by NTT as items which fall under the "Agreement on Government Procurement."

As a general rule, NTT issues a public announcement in *Kampo* (the Japanese official gazette) when purchasing Track I products, and product suppliers are selected by tender. Tenders are conducted periodically. Usually, the period is one or two years.

There are two types of Track I tender. One type is the open tender, where tenders are submitted by anyone who desires to participate in the tender, and successful tenderers are selected upon evaluation following tender opening. The other type is the selective tender; for this type of tender, anyone who desires to participate in the tender is required to pass prequalification. Notice of prequalification is provided publicly in advance of the tender notice. Those applicants who have passed the prequalification are eligible to participate in Selective Tender.

Tracks II and III.   Tracks II and III cover the procedures for initial procurement of new products other than those procured through Track I.

Track II covers the procedures for initial procurement of such new products produced on a commercial basis or that can be used as is or with minor modification.

---

[6] 125 Japanese Yen = $1.00 U.S. (1988).

[7] GATT: General Agreement on Tariffs and Trade.

Source: "Guide to NTT Procurement Procedures," published by NTT.

NTT selects applicants offering the most attractive proposals to NTT as suppliers for Track II products based on the results of the evaluation of the proposals submitted by the applicants following the instructions provided in the public notice.

Track III covers the procedures for procurement of products that are not produced on a commercial basis and that need to be newly developed. Joint development partners are selected from among the applicants submitting application documents following the instructions provided in the public notice. Joint development partners may be requested to manufacture a prototype for testing to confirm function and performance of the newly developed product.

Track II-A and III-A.   Track II-A and III-A cover the procedures for repeat procurement of the same products already procured previously through Track II and Track III procurement. Track II-A & III-A procedures are also applied to new applicants who have not been qualified but who desire to supply such products. NTT, at all times, welcomes proposals from new applicants. When a new applicant is judged to be superior to a qualified supplier, NTT will also award a contract to such superior applicant as a newly selected supplier.

Products Procured by NTT

NTT procures various categories of products as required to provide telecommunication services:

1. Switching equipment
2. Transmission equipment.
3. Radio equipment.
4. Data communication equipment.
5. Power supply equipment.
6. Customer equipment.
7. Cables.
8. Others (i.e., office equipment, vehicles, etc.).

Of the products listed above, those that fall under the category of Track I procurement are as follows:

1. Equipment and materials for plants (i.e., vehicles, poles, modems, computers, facsimiles, etc.).
2. Paper and other products for office use including clothing.
3. Equipment for research and development.
4. Equipment for training.
5. Equipment for medical use.

Flow chart diagrams of all procurement procedures were attached to the original document.

A NOTE ON THE MALAYSIAN PEWTER INDUSTRY

May 3rd, 1994, was another hot and humid afternoon in Kuala Lumpur (KL), the capital city of Malaysia. About 5 km from the city, several busloads of tourists arrived at the largest pewter factory in Malaysia, reputedly the largest in the world. The factory, operated by Royal Selangor International Sdn Bhd[1] (RSI), was a major attraction for foreign visitors to KL. At RSI, the pewter alloy was handcrafted into high-quality, aesthetic products such as decorative household utensils, giftware items, and souvenirs. They were sold under the brand name of Royal Selangor pewter (RS pewter).

At the conclusion of the short factory tour, visitors at the RSI facility were given the opportunity to make purchases from among the many products in the showroom. A few visitors, seeing the crowds and knowing that pewter was made mostly of locally abundant tin, could not help wondering whether investment opportunities existed in the Malaysian pewter industry. For them, at issue was the need to assess how attractive the industry was, and whether export opportunities existed.

Historical Perspectives of the Industry

Pewter is an alloy of tin. During the Middle Ages, the composition of pewter ranged from 65 to 75 percent tin, 20 to 30 percent lead, and small amounts

---

R. Azimah Ainuddin prepared this case under the supervision of Professor Paul Beamish. Copyright 1994 The University of Western Ontario, Western Business School Case 9-94-M014.
[1] Sdn Bhd is an abbreviation for Sendirian Berhad, which means Private Limited.

of copper. English pewter was then considered the finest pewter as it contained 75 percent tin and only 2 to 3 percent lead.

The lead content in the pewter alloy caused pewter items to tarnish easily, giving it an unappealing appearance. Lead could also separate easily from the alloy to contaminate drinks or food contained in pewter containers such as beer mugs, plates, and bowls. The toxic nature of lead caused alarm among pewter consumers and subsequently affected the demand for pewter utensils.

In the 1770s, English pewterers invented a new pewter alloy, named Britannia metal, which contained tin, copper, and antimony as a replacement for lead. This alloy then became the standard pewter alloy. High-quality pewter was set to contain 84 percent tin with variable amounts of antimony and copper. Since tin was abundant in Malaysia, Malaysian pewter was able to exceed the standard by producing finer quality pewter with 97 percent tin and very small amounts of copper and antimony. Tin used in Malaysian pewter is refined (Malaysian) Straits Tin, which is 99.85 percent pure. Although the tin content determined the quality of pewter, copper and antimony had to be added to make tin, a soft and brittle metal, harder and malleable.

The use of pewter dated back to at least the time of the Roman Empire. Artifacts found in ancient Egyptian tombs indicated the existence of pewter since 1300 B.C. The use of pewter utensils had flourished during medieval Europe. Although these utensils were used initially by the richer households to replace wood and coarse pottery, pewter had then become the most common material suitable for daily use by most households. Some of the most common utensils made of pewter were tankards, plates, bowls, dishes, flagons, and spoons.

At that time, pewter guilds were formed to ensure the credibility of the pewterer and his products. The guilds regulated the quality of metal used, checked on prices and wages, and organized apprenticeships. An apprenticeship could last for at least seven years before the apprentice could become a pewterer and set up his own business. A pewterer usually used marks called touches or touchmarks to identify the maker and to guarantee the quality of his work. Pewter guilds were known to have been established in Germany, Sweden, France, and England. In the 1980s, the guilds were replaced by new organizations such as the Association of British Pewter Craftsmen, the Gutegemeinschaft Zinngart of Germany, and the Belgian Pewter Association. In North America, the American Pewter Guild was founded in 1958 to actively promote trade in the region.[2]

By the end of the 17th century, throughout Europe and America, pewter's popularity as tableware began to decline steadily as new materials such as glass, porcelain, and good-quality earthenware became more favoured. While most pewter items had simple and dull designs, the new materials were more

---

[2] Brett, Vanessa. 1981. Phaidon guide to pewter. Lausanne: Elsevier Publishing.

appealing with their brightly coloured and decorative designs. Nevertheless, the pewter industry persisted and pewterers began to manufacture pewter items for decorative purposes.

Pewter also had a history of use in Japan when it was introduced into the country from China over 1,000 years ago. This was evidenced by a 1,200 year-old pewter piece currently displayed at an ancient treasure house at Nara Prefecture in Japan. During the early days, pewter was a highly valued material used for making utensils for the nobility in the imperial courts. In particular, pewterware was used to keep sake (Japanese wine) warm. The tin content was believed to "soften" the flavour of the wine and this practice is common even today among those with a refined sense of taste. A similar belief was prevalent among the German pewter users who said that beer tasted better when drunk from a pewter mug.

The Industry in Malaysia

The pewter industry began during the 19th century when Malaysia (then known as Malaya) was ruled by the British. The British had exploited the large tin resources in the country to meet the demand for tin by British industries. Over the years, as the tin industry expanded, Malaysia became the world's largest tin producer. In 1960, the country's annual tin production peaked at 70,000 tonnes and employed approximately 40,000 people.

Apart from the abundance of the raw tin for the foreign pewter industry, there was also a small demand from England for finished pewter products (particularly pewter tankards, wine goblets, and flower vases). The local demand for pewter was almost negligible since the use of pewter was not in the tradition of the local population. In addition, pewter was not highly regarded because it was made mostly of tin, a cheap and abundant local resource in the country. As such, interest in pewter-making was non-existent. As well, the skills in pewter-making had always been confined to the pewterer and passed down to family members. Thus, the pewter industry could not easily expand.

Among the first pewterers who capitalized on the small demand for Malaysian pewter was an immigrant pewtersmith from China who set up a pewter business in the tin-rich state of Selangor. The Chinese had used pewter items such as incense burners and joss-stick holders, but these were limited mostly to ceremonial purposes. The business, established in 1885, was later known as Selangor Pewter Sdn Bhd and today, as Royal Selangor International (RSI). It became the leading pewter company in the country, synonymous with the Malaysian pewter industry. In 1993, RSI captured 75 percent of the Malaysian market and was one of the largest pewter manufacturers in the world.

When the British rule ended in 1957, there was continued demand for Malaysian pewter from the former British residents. Consequently, local pewter companies began exporting their products to England. As these companies gained experience in the export market, they started to explore other markets in Europe where traditionally there was a strong demand for pewter. By the 1970s, the pewter industry in Malaysia was export driven and local companies were producing quality pewter products that met the tastes and preferences of their customers overseas. Locally, pewter was positioned as a high-end gift item.

In 1985, the Malaysian economy was hit by a recession caused by its excessive dependence on the export of commodities such as tin, rubber, and palm oil. A 10-year Industrial Master Plan was implemented to diversify into the manufacturing sector.

Several industries were identified for development via a pragmatic foreign investment policy. Consequently, there was an influx of foreign companies and expatriates to the country, which led to increased demand for pewter products. In 1987, increased living standards and purchasing power among the local population after the recession further boosted the demand for pewter gifts and souvenirs.

The rapid growth of the Malaysian economy in the late 1980s could not, however, overcome the consistent deficits in the country's balance of payments. In 1990, the government undertook programmes to develop the tourism industry in Malaysia. A "Visit Malaysia Year" campaign in 1990 resulted in a marked increase of tourist arrivals to the country. Tourists had since become a major market for the pewter industry in Malaysia. Tourists were attracted to Malaysian pewter souvenirs because pewter was considered a national heritage and a local handicraft.

In 1993, the retail sales of pewter in Malaysia were estimated at about RM40 million[3] (equal to approximately US$16 million). Although there was an increase in the local demand, there were only six Malaysian companies known to be actively involved in the manufacture of pewter. This included a recent entrant to the industry, JS Pewter Sdn Bhd (JS). The excess demand had encouraged new entrants to the industry, but their presence was short-lived. The owner of JS explained:

> At least two other companies established in KL in 1992 had left the industry. Although these companies were knowledgeable about the market, they lacked the skills in pewter-making. Basically, pewter-making is still a handicraft industry which requires skilful hands to ensure high-quality products. In addition, new pewter companies must be able to produce products that are comparable in quality to that of RS pewter and subsequently compete on price. Although buyers tend to be price sensitive, sometimes they are not willing to give up on quality for a small difference in price.

Exhibit 1 describes the processes involved in making pewter.

---

[3] The Malaysian currency is the Ringgit Malaysia (RM). On December 31, 1993, US$1 = RM2.73.

EXHIBIT 1   The Methods of Making Pewter

There are two main methods of making pewter: casting and spinning. Cast pewter was usually preferred to spun pewter because cast pewter was made from molten pewter and was thought to be of the best quality. Spun pewter, made from thin pewter sheets, was light and considered to be of lower quality. However, spun pewter was easier to mass produce than cast pewter and was gaining in popularity as improvements in quality, designs, and finishes were made.

Casting

The two methods of casting commonly used in the Malaysian pewter industry were die casting and casting by centrifugal force in a rubber mold. The traditional method of pewter-making in Europe was die casting, using a gun-metal (bronze) mold. Pewter companies in Malaysia had instead used steel molds in casting pewter.

In die casting, a pewter maker poured molten pewter from a ladle into a pre-heated steel mold. The mold was held at an angle and molten pewter was ladled into the mold and the pewter maker slowly held the mold upright as it was filled. This technique required skill and experience to know exactly at which angle to hold the mold as the molten pewter was poured. This was to ensure that the molten pewter flowed smoothly to obtain a smooth hardened pewter with minimal rough edges.

Although the casting was done by hand, the process took only a few seconds as the molten pewter inside the mold solidified within seconds. The hardened pewter was removed from the steel cast and rough edges were scraped before the pewter was ready for polishing. Polishing removed a layer of pewter oxide left on the surface and was usually done using a fine-grade sandpaper or against a buffing wheel. The pewter was rotated on a lathe as the craftsman peeled off the thin coating on the pewter. This process required steady hands as a sharp steel blade was used to peel off the coating while it was rotated.

The different parts of a pewter product were cast separately, polished, and then joined by soldering. These pieces included appendages such as handles, spouts, or hinges to be attached to a pewter mug or pitcher. Soldering pewter was especially difficult because of its low melting point. Thus, this process required skill and experience to ensure that neat joints were made. In a well-soldered piece, the joints were almost invisible to the naked eye. The final product was then polished with a soft flannel and with a dried stone leaf (a wild tropical leaf with fine, abrasive texture) to achieve a satin sheen. Other finishes included shiny, sandblast, and stained or antique.

Major pewter companies included a quality control check as the final stage of the production process. Items that did not pass the quality check were melted down into the molten mass.

Another casting technique used in pewter-making in Malaysia was centrifugal casting. This method used two halves of a flat circular mold which were clamped together. The upper half of the mold had a central hole from which channels ran into cavities which were to be filled with molten pewter. The mold was rotated at very high speed on a turntable as molten pewter was poured in. A few seconds later the pewter hardened and was removed from the mold. This technique had the advantage of using the less expensive rubber mold but its use was limited to the production of small items such as figurines and keychains. Large and hollow-ware items such as vases and mugs could not be produced by this technique.

Spinning

In this process, a circular pewter alloy sheet was placed in a lathe, pressure was exerted by a spinning tool, and the pewter was forced into the required shape. This method required a skilled craftsman to model the metal as it was spun but it was a more efficient method than die casting, particularly in making hollow cylindrical items such as vases, tumblers, and pitchers. The spun product was finished on the lathe or given a satin or polished finish by high-speed polishing using a greased mop. A different mop was used for each type of finish. Compared to casting, the spinning method was faster and more efficient, and was used to make the cheapest pewter mugs.

The Product

Malaysian pewter companies offered a wide selection of pewter products. In 1993, RSI produced more than 1,000 different items ranging from designer pewter collections to pewter sets and small pewter souvenirs.

The aesthetic value of pewter seemed to be a very important factor in determining the success of a product. Thus, it was common for pewter companies to employ in-house designers to create new designs and refine the existing ones. RSI employed a team of 15 designers to design the company's standard and custom-made products. Investments were also made in engaging well-known designers in other industries such as jewellery and fashion apparel to design pewter collections.

In the early 1970s, RSI began to penetrate foreign markets in a planned and aggressive fashion. It took a multidomestic approach in terms of the design of its pewter products. The company developed designs that suited the tastes and preferences of the market within a specific country. For example, wine goblets of the Roemer design were produced for the German market and Oxford-styled goblets for the Australian market. In recent years, although RSI continued to produce pewter designs according to cultural tastes, such as the sake sets for the Japanese and the four seasons oriental design for the Chinese, these products were marketed on a global basis.

RSI was very aggressive in the development of new product designs with at least four new product lines being introduced each year. In January 1993, RSI introduced a collection of figurines based on the mythical fantasy of unicorns and sorcerers which was launched in Australia, Hong Kong, and Singapore. About three months later, the Meridian Collection comprised of a shaving kit crafted from pewter with a combination of leather and sailcloth was launched. Shortly after that, a range of pewter desk accessories known as the "corporate jungle," featuring letter openers, book ends, and business card holders with animal designs, was introduced. Another product line introduced within the year was a collection created by a controversial fashion designer from Japan, Junko Koshino. In this collection, pewter plates, picture frames, and trays were finished with a wood-grain pattern which appeared simple, yet was considered a dramatic innovation using pewter.

Large capital investments in design and product development were beyond the financial capability of the other local companies. Occasionally, these companies would capitalize on RSI's designs and produce a similar range of products, and subsequently, compete on price. Others catered to special orders and custom-made designs. A pewterer commented, "A pewter company could take advantage of a new product design for at most, six months. Designs can easily be copied by the other companies and vice versa. Unless some new form of technology was used for a particular design of a pewter item, a company could not sustain its advantage based solely on a particular design for a very long period of time."

In response to the demand for pewter souvenirs, the local pewter companies turned to designs reflecting Malaysian culture in the form of local landmarks, people in traditional dresses, and various scenes of Malaysian life. These designs were inscribed on the flat surface of a pewter plate, keychain, or the handle of a letter opener. There were also pewter figurines of Malaysian people, and local landmarks and scenes carved out of pewter.

Pewter Substitutes

A major and continuing challenge faced by Malaysian pewter companies was the threat of substitute products. In place of pewter gifts, a customer had a wide range of gift products ranging from handcrafted jewellery to textiles, electronic gadgets, ceramics, crystal, porcelain, wood-based products, glassware, and earthenware products. Within the fabricated metal product category, pewter had to compete with silver, brass, and even gold and gold-plated products.

Pewter as a Malaysian souvenir was only one of many Malaysian handicrafts which reflected the local culture and national heritage of the country. Malaysian batik, a fabric handpainted with attractive designs, appealed to many tourists. Batik prices ranged widely, due in part to the fabric used. Batik could be made from relatively cheap cotton material or the best quality Italian, Chinese, or Korean silk. These batik materials were sewn into traditional dresses, shirts, ties, handkerchiefs, and purses.

On a global perspective, another potential pewter substitute was a pewter-look-alike alloy made of statesmetal, which was used by companies in the USA to produce souvenir and gift items. Some of these items, which went under the name Armetelle, looked like pewter, but were much more scratch resistant. One company, Carson Industries, Inc., produced about 100 different items, and the product range appeared to be quite similar to the range of pewter products offered by most pewter companies. There were letter openers, picture frames, candle holders, wind chimes, and even art nouveau design trays made of this pewter-like alloy. These items were available in gift outlets that carried various other giftware products. At a glance, both retailers and customers could easily be fooled by these products because they looked very much like pewter since they were given a stained, antique finish.

The Pewter Market

The Malaysian market for pewter consisted of several groups—corporate purchasers, tourists, and the gift market. Corporate purchasers included private companies, government departments, associations, sports and recreation clubs, and non-profit organizations. Engraved pewter plates were popular among corporate purchasers as gifts for foreign visitors and long-serving employees, while pewter trophies were common as prizes in competitive events.

Increased prosperity among Malaysian companies led to increased demand for high-end gift items. There was a tendency for these companies to give high-end gifts and souvenirs to their valued customers. For example, at the launch of a new car model in the local market, the local distributor of a Japanese automobile company switched from plastic to pewter keychain souvenirs for its new car purchasers.

To meet the demand from corporate purchasers, prompt delivery, quality, and competitive prices seemed to be the key success factors. As the leader in the market, RSI had set the industry standard for quality and price of pewter products. RSI was also an efficient producer and paid particular attention to prompt delivery. For a May 1993 special order, RSI formed a special team to run additional shifts for several days to meet the delivery of an order of 7,000 tankards within eight days. Smaller companies that offered competitive prices but were not able to deliver on time would not pose much competition to RSI.

Another major market segment in the Malaysian pewter market consisted of tourists and foreign visitors (participants in international conferences and sporting events, and corporate guests). This segment was characterized by impulse buying, although there were some foreign purchasers who had planned their purchase prior to their visit to Malaysia. It was common for foreign visitors to request a visit to the pewter factory or a pewter outlet to make their purchase. They seemed to possess awareness of the product from sources within their own country. Such visitors usually ended up making large purchases, which sometimes required the pewter company to make special shipments back to their home country.

Although there were some items which seemed to be a bargain when bought in Malaysia, the price difference of others was not significantly large (see Exhibit 2 for a comparison of RSI's prices in Malaysia and prices of similar items in Canada). Nevertheless, there was a wider selection of items in the RSI's showrooms in Malaysia compared to the very limited range of RS pewter displayed in gift shops overseas.

Generally, tourists preferred low- to medium-priced pewter souvenirs with cultural motifs to commemorate their visit to Malaysia. Such items were also favourites among Malaysians who purchased pewter as gifts for foreign friends and acquaintances. Among the local population, pewter was positioned as high-end gifts and was popular for special occasions—birthdays, weddings, and anniversaries. Favourite items were vases, picture frames, potpourri containers, and jewellery boxes.

The Export Market

Since the 1960s, the export market had been a major market for Malaysian pewter companies. The most common markets among these companies were

EXHIBIT 2   RSI's Retail Prices in Malaysia and Canada for Selected Items (in Cdn$)

Product	Prices in Malaysia	Prices in Canada
Erik Magnusson Collection		
Candlestand	34.00	39.00
Bowl (small)	120.00	125.00
Large coffee pot	207.00	275.00
Gerald Benney Collection		
Bowl (5.75 cm high)	37.00	45.00
Coffee pot (122 cl)	235.00	275.00
Tankard, mirror finish (45 cl)	46.00	85.00
Water goblet (23 cl)	30.00	45.00
Hip flask (9.5 cl)	44.00	55.00
Sugar bowl (9.5 cm high)	55.00	85.00
Vase (15 cm high)	22.00	28.00
Vase (20 cm high)	27.00	35.00
Picture frame	22.00	32.00

Source: Royal Selangor, Retail Price Lists.

Singapore, Japan, Australia, and the USA. RSI exported about 60 percent of its production directly to 20 countries and about 15 percent more was exported indirectly through foreign visitors.

Although the pewter industry was not identified as one of the priority industries for development under the Industrial Master Plan, a pewter company could enjoy many privileges provided to any manufacturing concern. These privileges were in the form of tax allowances for capital expenditure in the expansion of a production facility or in R&D activities.

Additional incentives were available for companies that exported and promoted their products overseas. Incentives in the form of tax deductions were given to companies that incurred expenses for overseas advertising, market research in foreign countries, maintenance of sales offices, and participation in trade or industrial exhibitions. The availability of such incentives, coupled with the high demand for pewter in foreign countries, had encouraged Malaysian pewter companies to emphasize the export market.

Another factor that induced Malaysian companies to export was the reduced tariff rates resulting from most favoured nation (MFN) status. Consequently, Malaysian pewter was more competitive in certain foreign markets than pewter from countries that did not enjoy the MFN privilege. However, in markets such as Canada, Malaysian pewter would be less competitive than pewter imports from the USA. Even before the implementation of NAFTA, the import duty for American pewter was only 9.1 percent compared to 10.2 percent imposed on Malaysian pewter imports.

RSI had established sales offices in its major foreign markets while the smaller companies like JS would usually sell their products on a free-on-board basis. The importer would take the responsibility to make arrangements to ship the products into a particular country and bear the costs of freight and handling and the insurance charges. An importer from Canada explained:

> The easiest way to import 500 pieces of Christmas ornaments, each weighing 20 grams and priced at Cdn.$4, from a pewter company in Malaysia is to appoint a broker who makes further arrangements with an agent in Malaysia. The agent picks up the package from the Malaysian producer and has it transported to Canada either by sea or by air. Shipment by sea will take about three and one-half weeks to reach Vancouver but only five days to reach Toronto by air. The costs involved to transport it by air include Cdn.$75 for freight and handling charges in Kuala Lumpur, Cdn.$55 for airport terminal handling in Toronto, Cdn.$80 for customs clearance charges, Cdn.$204 for import duty based on a rate of 10.2 percent of Cdn.$2,000, and the federal 7 percent Goods and Services Tax charge, which is added to all goods sold in Canada.

Marketing Practices

Pricing

As the leader in the Malaysian pewter industry, RSI set the prices of Malaysian pewter. RSI's products were sold at standard prices throughout the country to maintain the perception of high quality and to ensure that retailers did not undercut prices or give unnecessary discounts. The other pewter companies based their pricing on RSI's prices, and subsequently priced slightly lower to ensure a share in the market. This pricing strategy guaranteed their continued existence in the industry. While RSI enjoyed large mark-ups, the smaller companies were willing to accept smaller profit margins. RSI's keychain with Malaysian cultural motifs was retail priced at RM20 while JS's wholesale price was RM10 and retail price was RM15. The cost of producing such an item was estimated at only RM6.

In the export markets, RSI's prices had to be competitive in view of the large variety of products offered by local pewter companies as well as those from other foreign companies. For example, in Canada, an RS pewter photo frame was retail priced at Cdn.$31.95 compared to an equivalent item with almost similar design made by Seagull, retail priced at Cdn.$33.95. However, an almost similar pewter item made in Korea was retail priced at only Cdn.$24.95.

A retailer commented,

> Pewter is now produced in many countries and not limited to tin-producing countries. In fact, there are pewter companies in Belgium that operate tin mines in African countries to supply the raw material to their manufacturing facilities in Belgium. In addition, customers are not too particular about the pewter brand. For example, a customer looking for a letter opener made of pewter would settle

for one that was made in Thailand with an antique finish priced at Cdn.$29.95 rather than RSI's shiny letter opener displayed in a nice wooden box priced at Cdn.$39.95.

Distribution

RSI had established more than 40 pewter showrooms in the major cities and main towns throughout Malaysia. These places were the best markets because of the large concentration of government departments, institutions, private companies, and tourist attractions. These showrooms were equipped with engraving facilities, and RSI employees conducted pewter-making demonstrations for tourists.

At the showrooms, the pewter items were displayed on open racks where customers were able to take a closer look at the design and material. Once a customer decided on an item he/she wished to buy, a brand new item was presented to the customer. Most customers were amazed to see the difference between the item on display and the fresh new item in the box. Due to constant handling by various customers, the pewter on display on open racks tended to lose its lustre and shine unless fingerprints were wiped off immediately. In fact, a special cleaning agent was available for the long-term maintenance of pewter.

In places within Malaysia where RSI had not established its own showroom, the company appointed more than 250 authorized retailers, particularly giftware outlets and book stores, to carry its products. In such outlets, pewter brands other than RS pewter were also available. In these outlets, buyers were able to compare RSI's products with those of the other pewter companies. In comparing the products, price-conscious buyers who were not too concerned over brand image would usually settle for products other than RS pewter.

In foreign markets, RSI had established its own representative offices and outlets in Australia, Singapore, Hong Kong, Japan, Switzerland, and Denmark. There were about 2,500 agents and distributors of RS pewter overseas. Currently, many international exclusive shops carried RSI's products. They included Harrods in London, Ilum Bolighus in Denmark, Birks of Canada, Myer of Australia, and Mitsukoshi of Japan. The other Malaysian pewter companies had also ventured into foreign markets in their own small way, mainly through foreign agents.

There was a significant advantage for pewter companies that established their own retail outlets or distributed their products through appointed retailers which sold exclusively the products of a particular pewter company. While competition could be increasingly intense when pewter of competing companies was displayed side by side, the shelf space available for each company was also very limited. These companies were not able to provide a wide selection of their products. On the contrary, a retail shop would be able to accommodate a larger shelf space to display the products of only one particular company that had appointed it as the retailer for a specific location.

Promotion

To obtain international exposure, it was common for pewter companies to participate actively in trade shows and exhibitions, particularly in international gift fairs. Numerous fairs were held in major cities all over the world throughout the year. These fairs were the Toronto Gift Fair, the Birmingham Fair, Formland Fair in Denmark, the Frankfurt International Gift Fair, and the Sydney Gift Fair. Fairs provided new and existing companies with the opportunity to promote their products to leading retailers in the giftware industry.

RSI had made heavy investments in export promotion by consistent participation in international trade fairs. For the last 10 years, RSI maintained a permanent stand at the spring and autumn international fairs in Frankfurt; this meant paying an annual rental for about 10 days of use in a year when the fair was on. As one RSI manager had said, "This seemed like a very expensive investment but we were able to enhance our image as a serious exporter to international business people. These fairs had acted as a springboard for our new products."

Participation in trade shows and exhibitions also helped companies to evaluate their own positions in the industry. Pewter companies took advantage of these occasions to keep up with the designs of their competitors and to seek new ideas in designing their own products. Since a design was not company specific, pewter companies could easily imitate the designs of each other's best-selling items.

In the 1970s, in view of the positioning of pewter as high-end gifts and souvenirs, RSI decided to invest in the design of a suitable package to accompany the image of the product it contained. The other Malaysian companies were quite content to use ordinary boxes and simple plastic sleeves to package their smaller products. Usually, the cost of packaging was included in the price of most pewter items.

The Malaysian Pewter Companies

Besides RSI, the largest pewter company in Malaysia, there were four other pewter companies that sold pewter under their own specific brands. These companies were Penang Pewter & Metal Arts Sdn Bhd (Penang pewter), Oriental Pewter Sdn Bhd (Oriental pewter), Zatfee (M) Sdn Bhd (Tumasek pewter), and Selex Corporation (Selwin pewter), a subsidiary of RSI. JS, a new pewter company in Malaysia, sold generic pewter which was used for custom-made products for marketing agents or individual orders.

Apart from RSI, the other Malaysian companies were niche players and were less well-known among the Malaysians. They had established their own markets within the locality where they operated. Penang Pewter and Oriental Pewter catered to markets in the northern states of Peninsular Malaysia (Penang and Perak), JS in Melaka, and Zatfee and Selex in KL and Selangor. These companies had also ventured into the export markets. The following segment describes RSI as the leader in the industry, depicts JS as the new entrant, and provides brief accounts of some of the other Malaysian pewter companies.

Royal Selangor International

RSI, established more than 100 years ago, operated as a family business with a paid-up capital of RM16 million. The company had grown dramatically in the late 1980s. In 1988, RSI's profits doubled from RM1.0 million in 1987 to RM2.2 million in 1988. The number doubled again in 1989 when profits jumped to RM4.9 million. In the following years, growth averaged about 14 percent.

RSI was a major consumer of local tin, using about 250 metric tons of the commodity annually. RSI produced its own pewter alloy by melting tin ingots and adding copper and antimony to the molten metal. In 1993, the Malaysian tin industry experienced a dramatic decline when its annual tin production dropped to 10,000 tonnes and employment in the tin industry slipped to only 2,300 people. Although RSI was a major consumer of tin, the decline in the tin industry would not significantly affect the profitability of the company. RSI's manager commented, "Even if the tin output in Malaysia had declined, tin is readily available from the international commodity market. Furthermore, our products are many times value-added. Thus, the price of the commodity has no direct effect on our costs."

RSI had positioned itself in the market as a producer of high-quality pewter products. In 1991, the company was conferred the use of "Royal" in its name by the ruler of the State of Selangor, where RSI was established. According to RSI's manager, the name change from Selangor to Royal Selangor was a move towards exclusivity. RSI predicted that over the next 12 years, more than 12 million pieces of its pewter items would be exported to various parts of the world, accounting for about 60 percent of the company's total production.

RSI's products were sold in more than 20 countries and were particularly successful in Europe, Canada, Australia, and Hong Kong. RSI had won several international awards for the design and quality of its products and its innovative packaging. Locally, RSI enhanced its image by winning non-pewter-related awards such as Best Employer of the Handicapped Award, given by the Ministry of Welfare Services, Malaysia, in 1982 and 1985.

In 1993, RSI employed about 1,000 workers in its pewter factory. The workers were highly skilled in performing specific tasks such as casting the molten pewter, soldering parts of an item together, and creating hammered finishes on pewter mugs. While RSI operated a modern factory, traditional methods of craftsmanship were retained where most of the individual tasks were done by hand.

Industry observers commented that as an established pewter company, RSI had invested large amounts of money in training its craftsmen in specific skills. While this was to ensure that these workers became more productive as they became more skilful, such specialization served two other important purposes. First, specialization helped to deter new entrants. Craftsmen specializing in casting would not be skilful in the other aspects of pewter making. Thus, it would be difficult for them to take advantage of their skills and entrepreneurial spirit to set up their own pewter business. This had prevented the entry of new competitors into the industry.

Secondly, since there were very few pewter companies, RSI could further ensure its leadership by maintaining a strong bargaining power with its skilled workers. These workers were skilful in a particular craft which had very limited use in other industries. Thus, their mobility was limited to jobs in other pewter companies which might not be able to offer better deals.

JS Pewter

JS was established in January 1993 by C. Y. Tay and his two brothers. Tay's brothers were former employees of RSI. They were employed as factory workers for more than 10 years and had acquired the skills of pewter-making.

JS had a paid-up capital of RM100,000. During the first year of operation the company incurred a loss but Tay was positive that JS would be able to recover its losses this year. Tay attributed the losses to JS's lack of experience in the industry. He said "Last year, we were still new and had to sell cheap and provide better terms to our customers. We are slowly gaining their trust and when we get ourselves established, only then can we seek for better deals."

Upon entering the industry, JS had positioned itself as a niche player by catering to small corporate and special orders. Tay believed that JS was filling a gap in the industry by taking jobs which RSI would have turned down.

> JS was willing to accept small orders of even less than 100 pieces, which RSI would not be willing to fill. We were not competing for the same business as RSI. Our target customers were those who could not afford RSI's products and were not particular about the RSI brand. We used RSI's price for a similar item as a guide and priced our products 30 to 40 percent lower.

JS operated a factory in Melaka, about 200 km from its sales office in KL. The factory was a rented shop measuring 20 feet by 50 feet. Rental and energy charges amounted to about RM2,000 per month. Other overheads included insurance premiums, and capital investments on a casting machine costing about RM50,000. JS did not produce its own pewter alloy but purchased pewter bars from local metal-based companies. In 1994, the price of a pewter bar containing 97 percent tin, weighing 4 kg, was RM72. Tay said that the price of pewter bars had not changed much since he ventured into the business.

JS used the less expensive rubber mold production process. Since JS catered to specific orders, the rubber mold could be discarded once an order had been fulfilled. Rubber molds were cheaper but their application was limited to the production of figurines and smaller items such as key holders. JS charged RM300 for the cost of making a mold for an order of less than 500 pieces. JS had not ventured into the production of large and hollow items such as mugs and vases, which required the use of steel molds.

JS employed 10 workers who were paid a monthly salary of RM300 to RM400, depending on their skills and experience. The factory operated daily from nine to five, six days a week. During busy periods, JS had to pay overtime at more than double the daily wage of the workers. On average, a worker earned up to RM500 to RM600 per month on overtime. Tay said:

> We have only 10 workers and our factory is still very small to cope with large orders. Although we would like to take advantage of scale economies by filling large orders for few clients, it would be too risky to be dependent on a few large orders. At this stage, we are trying to develop a wide customer base and gain experience in producing a wide range of products.

JS also employed two sales personnel: one to handle sales in KL, the other to establish markets in Melaka. Melaka was a major tourist attraction known for its historical sites including the remains of a Portuguese fortress and buildings of Dutch architecture, preserved to retain the state's heritage. In 1994, Melaka had also joined in the country's pace of industrialization and undertook various activities to woo local and foreign investors to the state. By the end of 1993, rents in Melaka had increased 100 percent and employment in the low-income sectors such as construction had to depend on immigrants mainly from Indonesia, the Philippines, and Bangladesh.

Other Malaysian Pewter Companies

Penang Pewter & Metal Arts was one of the better known pewter companies. The company catered to markets in Penang, an island off the northern coast of Peninsular Malaysia. Penang, known as the Pearl of the Orient, was a major tourist attraction in Malaysia because of its beaches. In recent years, the state had developed industrial parks to attract foreign investment which further boosted the demand for pewter in the area. Locally, Penang was the major geographical market for Penang pewter although the products were readily available in gift outlets in major cities, particularly KL. With a complement of about 100 workers, the company produced a wide range of pewterware which was exported to markets such as Australia, Singapore, Japan, and USA.

Zatfee produced a wide range of pewter under the brand name of Tumasek pewter, which was exported to Canada, USA, and Japan. The company had expanded gradually from 90 employees in 1987 to 200 in 1993. In 1993, the company increased its global market penetration by entering new markets such as Australia, Hong Kong, Korea, New Zealand, and Singapore. Zatfee's annual turnover of RM1.5 million in 1987 had grown to RM6.5 million in 1993.

Oriental Pewter was located in Perak, formerly another tin-rich state in Malaysia. With a workforce of about 100 employees, the company produced modern and unique pewterware which was exported to Canada, New Zealand, Singapore, Australia, UK, and Japan.

Global Competition

The export market had always been the thrust of the Malaysian pewter industry. However, in recent years, the world market had become increasingly competitive with the emergence of pewter companies even in countries where tin was an unknown metal. For example, the pewter industry had flourished in Sweden, and pewter was manufactured in Korea, Taiwan, and Belgium. (Exhibit 3 gives a list of countries known to have tin deposits.)

Pewter companies had initiated the establishment of pewter-making concerns in Taiwan and Korea to take advantage of the relatively cheap and skilled labour in these countries. Thailand and Indonesia seemed to have the potential for the establishment of a competitive pewter industry in view of the presence of large tin deposits and a cheap workforce. Pewter was at present manufactured in Thailand while PT Tambang Timah, an Indonesian tin producer, was planning to set up a pewter plant which would consume at least half of its tin supplies for the production of high value-added pewter products. (See Exhibit 4 for hourly compensations of the workforce in fabricated metal industries in selected countries.)

In Sweden, the pewter industry began about 150 years ago. At present, there was a strong market demand, particularly for pewter trophies. Prizes

EXHIBIT 3   Estimates of Tin Deposits in Selected Countries

Country	1987–1990 Average (in tonnes)
Australia	8,000
Brazil	31,500
Canada	3,500
Germany	3,900
Indonesia	10,700
Malaysia	32,800
Portugal	100
South Africa	1,400
Thailand	16,000
United Kingdom	4,000

Source: IMD & World Economic Forum, The World Competitiveness Report, 1992.

EXHIBIT 4   Hourly Compensation in Fabricated Metal Products: 1990

Country	U.S.$
Belgium	15.07
Brazil	1.12
Canada	15.90
Germany	19.88
Korea	3.94
Portugal	2.90
South Africa	3.05
Sweden	20.31
Taiwan	3.80
United Kingdom	11.84
United States	14.98

Source: IMD & World Economic Forum, The World Competitiveness Report 1992.

Note: The hourly compensation in Indonesia, Malaysia, and Thailand was estimated at U.S.$1.60, U.S.$3.30, and U.S.$3, respectively.

for most sporting events such as yachting, skiing, ice hockey, and swimming were made of pewter, and Swedish sportsmen were known to have built a collection of pewter trophies. Other pewterware produced by the Swedish pewter companies included household items, jewellery, and gifts.

Scandiapresent was the largest pewter manufacturer in Sweden and was noted for its antique finished pewter. Another company was Arktis Smedgen, formed in 1980 and employing four craftsmen; it produced a range of pewterware with engraved patterns. AB Harryda Adelmetallsmide produced the Harryda Tenn pewter products such as tankards, bowls, and goblets with a shiny finish.

Other pewter companies in Sweden included AB Koppar & Tennsmide, Jokkmok Tenn AB Sigurd Ahman, Metallum AB, and several other companies which mostly operated as small concerns employing four to eight craftsmen. Metallum AB in Stockholm, set up in 1988, produced small pewter gifts and jewellery; it was also the agent in Sweden for the supply of pewter sheets and ingots from a UK supplier, George Johnson & Company (Birmingham) Limited.

In the UK, where the pewter industry had a long history, there was a high concentration of pewter companies in Sheffield. Of 14 pewter manufacturers in the UK, two were located in London, three in Birmingham, one in Glasgow, and the rest in Sheffield. Sheffield pewter, noted for its highly polished and hammered finishes, was distributed in large retail outlets as an exclusive product, usually displayed in glass cases. The product line was, however, quite narrow, limited to tankards, mugs, and hipflasks.

Canada was one of the countries that produced pewter and had quite a large retail market. In 1994, Seagull Pewter and Silversmiths Ltd (Seagull)

EXHIBIT 5   Seagull Pewterers & Silversmiths Limited (Seagull)

Seagull, located in Pugwash, Nova Scotia, was established in 1979 by a husband and wife team, John Caraberis and Bonnie Bond, who were seeking a more peaceful lifestyle and a less expensive place to live. In a town with a population of 1,000 people, they expanded their original basement operation to a 6,000-sq.-ft. factory 10 years later. Their business line had developed from silver and pewter jewellery to pewter giftware. Currently, Seagull produced 1,000 different items and was constantly adding new products and refining existing ones.

Seagull employed 100 pewter makers, designers, and sales representatives. The company had a wide product line of pewter giftware ranging from picture frames, letter openers, and mugs to a large selection of Christmas ornaments. The Caraberis' ranked their company's pewter line as the broadest in North America.

The business was booming at Seagull, and for most of the year, the workers worked two separate shifts (10-hour days, four days a week). Several methods were employed to produce different pewter products. Jewellery was hand-made from twisted pewter wire and thin pewter plates. Seagull's hollow-ware was made by spinning while a majority of its other items were made in rubber casts. In rubber casting, original items were designed and several copies of the models were made by hand. These models were then used to make several thousand rubber molds. The company used over 400 molds a week and each mold lasted for between 100 and 200 casts.

Seagull was very aggressive in promoting its products and claimed to have a total of 10,000 accounts spread across every state and province in North America. The accounts included independent retail shops, tourist shops, country and craft shops, and jewellery stores. Aggressive selling was undertaken by Seagull's 12 sales representatives and strengthened by dozens of other giftware distributors. In 1988, the U.S. accounted for about 70 percent of Seagull's total sales and the company was looking for opportunities in Australia, Japan, and Europe, particularly Germany.

In the Canadian market, Seagull would appoint an exclusive retailer who carried only Seagull pewter together with a range of giftware, except pewter from other companies. Seagull pewter would occupy a corner of the retail gift outlet where a wide selection of the pewter items was displayed in open racks. Customers were able to handle the product without having to seek assistance from the salesperson. Items purchased were taken off the rack and packed in boxes or plastic sleeves for the smaller items. Seagull's pewter bookmark was retailed at Cdn.$7, a keychain at Cdn.$13, a photo frame at Cdn.$34, and a Christmas ornament at Cdn.$8.

For the past several years, Seagull had invested heavily in giftware design to ensure that its product line was current, comprehensive, and consumer-oriented. "Given the giftware industry which typically launches two product lines a year, that can be hectic. The development of new products does not require new technology but is very demanding and takes a lot of work and money," said Caraberis.

The owners of Seagull Pewter had also attributed the company's success to their active participation in trade shows. Seagull attended and displayed its products at 40 to 50 shows throughout North America each year, at show locations such as Boston, Washington DC, New York, Dallas, Kansas City, Toronto, Montreal, Edmonton, and Halifax. "We're a little more rigorous in getting out there in the marketplace for a small business. You've got to be there to build up your reputation, to build up your clientele," explained Caraberis.

was one of the most successful Canadian pewter companies. Exhibit 5 gives a brief description of Seagull to provide an insight into the operations of a pewter company in a foreign country. Seagull had recently grown rapidly to become one of the top ten pewter manufacturers in North America and represented major competition to the Malaysian pewter companies in the global market.

There were at least eight other Canadian pewter manufacturers. They were located in Nova Scotia (Amos Pewterers), Newfoundland, Quebec (Val David's pewter), New Brunswick (Aitkens Pewter), Ontario (Morton-Parker Ltd), Alberta, and British Columbia (Boma Manufacturing Ltd). Currently, in the Canadian market, the products of Malaysian pewter companies such as Tumasek pewter, Oriental pewter, RS pewter, and Selwin pewter faced intense competition from the local and foreign pewter companies.

To understand the global nature of supply on the retail side, the experience in Stratford, Ontario, is illustrative. Stratford was a small town with a major tourist attraction in Canada due to its Shakespearean Festival. In Stratford, only The Touchmark Shop carried RS pewter and Selwin pewter. Although RS pewter and Selwin pewter were among Touchmark's best-selling items, there was intense competition from pewter made in Brazil (John Sommers pewter), Thailand, Belgium (Riskin pewter), and England (Sheffield pewter), and the locally produced pewter, particularly Boma pewter and Lindsay Claire pewter. A salesperson at Touchmark commented, "Pewter was an impulse item; thus, customers looked for items that had appealing designs and were reasonably priced. Only customers who had prior knowledge of pewter were conscious of pewter brands and their country of origin."

Seagull pewter was sold exclusively at three large gift shops in Stratford: Bradshaws, La Crafe, and Christmas and Country Gift Shop. Bradshaws, however, had on display a very small selection of pewter made in Korea and Metzke pewter from the USA. Since these shops did not carry pewter of other manufacturers, Seagull pewter occupied a relatively large shelf space and purchasers could not make a spontaneous comparison in terms of product design and price with competitors' products.

Touchmark was reported to have sold more than Cdn.$500 worth of pewter per month during the summer season. On the contrary, at about the same time, the retailer of a large gift shop in Kitchener complained that the pewter items were selling more slowly than the rest of the other gifts such as crystal, silver, and porcelain. As a result, the shop had a limited range of products, mainly Riskin pewter and John Sommers pewter from Brazil.

Future Outlook

Based on the current situation in the pewter industry in Malaysia, RSI's leadership in the industry was indisputable and was expected to remain so for the next decade at least. RSI had been a family-owned business and there were no immediate plans for the company to go public. Such a strategy shielded the company from acquisition threats and leakages of trade secrets. Although RSI had conquered a major share of the Malaysian pewter market, RSI together with the other Malaysian pewter companies faced a major challenge from existing and emerging pewter companies all over the world. At issue for the new entrants was whether they could compete globally by emphasizing efficient production and targeting the low- to medium-priced giftware market segment. But was this realistic? And overall, was this an attractive industry for investment?

A Note on the U.S. Cable TV Industry

"They want a recommendation in a week." Carol Dixon looked again at the last line of the urgent message she had just received through the intercompany electronic mail system. It was March 11, 1994. She had worked at Pigot, da Silva (a medium-sized New York investment bank) for five years, after receiving an MBA from a prestigious Canadian business school. During this time, Dixon had conducted many detailed industry studies for Pigot, da Silva's clients, but had rarely received a request of this magnitude.

"Our client is considering whether to make an offer to Rogers Communications for Maclean Hunter's U.S. cable assets," the message from Dixon's boss began.

> Acquiring a cable company is a way for them to diversify. Consequently, they don't know how to put a value on the Maclean Hunter cable business. They do know what Rogers paid, but they need us to go beyond the obvious—anyone can analyze the financial statements. I want you to prepare a report that tells them what factors will be of most importance in deciding the value of the U.S. cable TV industry of the future. Then suggest an appropriate price and cash flow multiple for the Maclean Hunter assets. Confidentiality is important, and as always, time is of the essence.

CATV Operations

Cable television (CATV) systems originated in the early days of television when many smaller and remote communities could not receive television

Douglas Reid prepared this case under the supervision of Professor Paul Beamish and with the assistance of Professor John Banks of Wilfrid Laurier University. Copyright © 1995 The University of Western Ontario, Western Business School Case 9-95-G005.

broadcast signals with simple home antennas. By the late 1960s, CATV systems had spread to many communities in the U.S. where broadcast signals were not easily received, including parts of major cities where signal reflections and shadowing by large buildings interfered with signal reception quality.

The advent of satellite-based signal transmission created the present-day CATV industry since it led to the creation of a wide range of new channels that bypassed and competed with traditional broadcast networks. In addition, rulings by the U.S. Supreme Court legalized the provision of pay-TV services such as Home Box Office. The CATV operators added new channels that served specialized subscriber niches with dedicated news, music, and sports broadcasts. By 1990, the Cable Facts Book listed more than 100 such channels in operation, including 10 pay-TV and 10 pay-per-view services. Since then, the number of these services has grown, and specialty channels such as ESPN and CNN have become key sources of entertainment and information.

The explosion of new channels resulted in rapid growth in demand for cable services. Exhibit 1 shows the growth that occurred in the industry in selected years from 1976 to 1993. The coaxial cables of CATV operators passed approximately 95 percent of homes in the U.S.,[1] and by the end of 1993, the industry served 56.3 million subscribers or 62 percent of American homes. About 90 percent of these homes received more than 30 channels. As a result of this ready availability of service, plus the predominance of television as an entertainment medium, cable operators generated total industry revenues in 1993 of $22.8 billion. Average cable company operating margins were 46 percent[2] and the size of an average monthly bill sent to a cable subscriber in 1993 was $33.84.

To receive a satellite channel, a cable operator needed to install a receiving antenna and other headend equipment and to pay a fee to the satellite program provider. In most communities there were three principal categories of programming, each with a different fee structure:

Basic Programming: This category included all the channels that cable subscribers received by paying a basic monthly fee. The basic package included the signals of the major broadcast networks, which were essentially free to the cable operator who also carried the advertising that was associated with them. The cable operators paid a monthly fee to receive each satellite channel, usually $0.20 to $0.25 per subscriber. However, the satellite networks and the cable operators also sold advertising time in competition with the networks. These revenues were $3 billion in 1993.

Pay Channels: For an additional monthly fee, which averaged $5.70 in

---

[1] Cable systems passed by many homes that chose not to subscribe to cable. The "passed by" figure is thus a measure of a CATV carrier's potential market, since only homes passed by cable service could ever subscribe to it.

[2] All amounts are in U.S. dollars, unless indicated otherwise. At the time of the case, U.S. $1 = CDN$1.3643.

EXHIBIT 1   History of Cable and Pay-TV Subscribers and Revenues

Averages for Year	Basic Subscribers (mil.)	% Change
1976	11.0	—
1981	21.5	22.9
1986	38.2	7.6
1991	52.6	4.1
1992	54.3	3.3
1993	56.3	3.7

At Year End	Homes Passed (mil.)	Basic Subscribers (mil.)	Full Pays (mil.)	Mini Pays (mil.)	Pay-TV Homes (mil.)	Basic Subscribers as % of Homes Passed	Full-Paying Subscribers as % of Basic
1976	23.1	11.8	1.0	—	n/a	51.1	8.5
1981	41.8	23.0	15.5	—	13.8	55.0	67.4
1986	69.4	39.7	32.1	—	20.7	57.2	80.9
1991	88.4	53.4	39.9	3.2	24.0	60.4	74.7
1992	90.6	55.2	40.7	3.7	24.7	60.9	73.7
1993	92.9	57.4	41.5	4.8	26.4	61.8	72.3

Year	Basic Revenues (mil.)	Pay-TV Revenue (mil.)	PPV Revenue (mil.)	Home Shopping Revenues (mil.)	Install Revenue (mil.)	Ad Revenue (mil.)	Misc. Revenue (mil.)	Revenues from Sources (mil.)	Total Revenues per Subscribers Per Month	% Change
1976	$ 851	$ 65	n/a	n/a	$ 13	n/a	$ 3	$ 932	$ 7.06	—
1981	2,061	1,317	n/a	n/a	67	$ 17	173	3,656	14.17	16.7
1986	4,891	3,872	$ 37	$ 23.0	253	192	472	10,144	22.13	5.5
1991	11,414	4,943	378	81.0	269	721	951	19,463	30.86	4.8
1992	12,433	4,980	404	90.0	278	852	1,004	21,044	32.30	4.6
1993	13,552*	4,633	512	128.4	289	984	1,123	22,863	33.84	4.8

All amounts are U.S.$.

* Weighted average basic rate of $20.06 per month used to calculate full year revenues, representing eight months of unregulated basic rates, and four months of the FCC rolled-back rate.

Reprinted with permission of Paul Kagan Associates, Inc., Carmel, CA, from *Cable TV Investor,* March 31, 1994.

1993, subscribers could receive a pay channel using a set-top decoder or through "traps" between the tap on the feeder cable and the drop to the subscriber's residence. There were only a small number of these channels, and they all offered movies as their chief programming fare. Typically, a cable system would pay 50 percent of the monthly subscriber fees to the satellite network for pay channels. The satellite system would, in turn, pay half of what it received to the owners of the program rights. To offer a full schedule, a pay channel needed to show 300 movies per year. Although 80 percent or more of subscribers to basic services opted for at least one pay channel, a continuing problem for CATV operators was subscriber "churn," a situation that occurred when a subscriber dropped the subscription to one channel and switched to another (usually because of the kinds of movies that were available).

Pay-per-view (PPV) channels: PPV channels were a more recent innovation, and as such, they were not available to a large percentage of U.S. cable subscribers. PPV channels required subscribers to pay for each program they viewed either by credit card or by telephoning in an order (the fee would be added to their cable bill). PPV rates were similar to the rental price of a movie (approximately $3 to $4). Once placed, an order could not be cancelled. A subscriber wishing to order PPV programming had to have an addressable set-top decoder box attached to his or her television. This box cost $100 to $150, and a rental fee for the decoder box was built into a subscriber's monthly bill. PPV had been successful only with major athletic events such as heavyweight boxing. Estimated CATV revenues for PPV in 1993 were $512 million, an increase of more than 25 percent over the previous year. During the 1990s, the average home in those cable service areas supporting PPV ordered 3.5 PPV features each year.

CATV operators were concerned that delays in receiving hit movies were harming cable revenues. They claimed they needed to show movies before the movies had reached video stores. For that to happen, the distribution system would have to change. Movie distribution was tightly controlled by the studios that owned movie rights. Each year between 300 and 400 movies were produced; only 20 to 25 would ever become major box office successes. To maximize their returns, the studios normally launched a movie in stages. First, exhibition would occur in theatres, accompanied by an intensive domestic and international promotional campaign. At this point, individual theatre admission would cost from $7 to $8 per patron. When theatre revenues slowed, the studios permitted distribution through video stores. Video rental charges were in the range of $3 to $5, but could be seen by a large number of people during the rental period. After six weeks or so of video store distribution, movies were made available to PPV, and then to pay channels (meaning that the customer incurred no additional cost beyond the cost of the pay service), and, eventually, were released to major network broadcasters which distributed the signal free of charge to viewers.

Cable Television System Technology

A cable television company distributed television signals to customers that resided within its service area through a network of cables. A typical cable distribution system was designed to transmit the same information, one way, to many locations and required a considerable amount of capital. However, most of the signal distribution equipment was readily available in competitive markets within the U.S. and was only somewhat differentiable on performance.

Support wire and system electronics were imported from Taiwan, Mexico, and other countries, but were not considered to offer differentiable performance.

The architecture of a CATV system began with the headend, which received video signals from transmission sources such as satellites, or from a super-trunk line connected to another headend. Main lines, called trunks, then carried the signals into a community. The length of a trunk was limited by the number of amplifiers needed to boost television signals since these signals weakened due to losses in the cable. Each amplifier in an analog cable system introduced a slight signal distortion, and the effect was cumulative. Feeder lines branched off the trunks. Each feeder line typically served 200 to 400 homes. Individual homes were connected to the feeder line by drops (see Figure 1 for a typical cable system configuration). This "tree and branch" configuration was a very economical way of distributing the same information to many subscribers. New cable systems were estimated to cost approximately $300 per subscriber, with feeder lines and drops accounting for more than 75 percent of the cost. However, this amount varied between cable systems according to the density of the market served, the total size of the installed system, and the proportion of aerial to underground cable in each system's design. Some analysts estimated that the cost breakdown for a new cable system plant was as follows: headend (6 percent); trunk network (19 percent); feeder or distribution network (55 percent); subscriber drop and house wiring (20 percent).

Cable operators have traditionally rebuilt their plant approximately every 10 to 15 years and upgraded electronics every 7 years. Most large CATV systems were built in the early 1980s. They used coaxial cable to distribute signals from the headend to the home. The measure of the carrying capacity of a cable system was bandwidth—more bandwidth meant that more signals

FIGURE 1   Tree and Branch Cable System Configuration

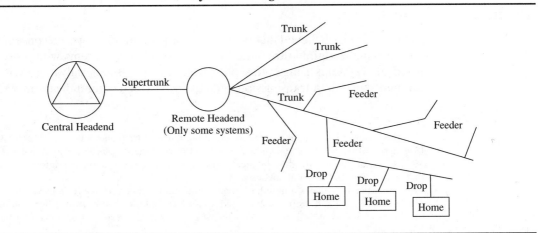

could be carried. Most early cable systems had the capacity to provide 35 channels using P1 cable, which had a bandwidth of several hundred Megahertz[3] (MHz). Next-generation systems began using P3 cable, which had a bandwidth of 750 MHz and offered up to 55 channels, but the electronic components in the cable system only had a capacity of 330 MHz. In the late 1980s, new cable plant installations and rebuilds began using P3 cable to offer subscribers 110 channels.

During the 1990s, most cable systems started to upgrade their trunks to optical fibre, which had a higher bandwidth than amplified coaxial cable. On systems extensions and rebuilds, many cable companies assumed that the additional cost of installing optical fibre instead of coaxial cable would be small even though the total cost of an upgrade was between $12,000 and $15,000 per above-ground mile. A study by the Federal Communications Commission (FCC) estimated that the cost of building a new, fibre-based CATV network would be approximately $424 per home, or an annualized cost of $137 when the household penetration was 60 percent.[4]

Approximately 80 percent of the U.S. CATV network was above ground. Suburban areas often had far more buried cable than urban areas. Underground upgrade costs were estimated to cost 40 percent more than aerial systems, although upgrade costs for small "all concrete" areas in the downtown core of cities such as Chicago or Detroit could total upwards of $100,000 per mile. However, the cost of upgrades was readily measured on a per-subscriber basis. Thus, the population density of a carrier's served area had an important influence on the value of the carrier's system. Analysts and carriers assumed a density of 20 homes passed per mile in rural areas, 80 homes passed per mile in suburban areas, and several hundred homes passed per mile in urban areas. When a cable system was sold, the cost of upgrades or rebuilds was usually subtracted from the cash flow multiple to arrive at a selling price.

Technology Trends

Industry experts believed that plant investment in the 1990s would concentrate on replacing traditional tree-and-branch coaxial cable systems with more sophisticated systems using optical fibre cable, which was generally more suitable for high-speed data transmission and advanced video communications. When

---

[3] The bandwidth of a system is measured in the range of frequencies that it can carry. One Megahertz (Mhz) represents a bandwidth of 1,000 Hertz. One Gigahertz (Ghz) equals 1,000 Mhz. The wider the bandwidth, the greater the number of signals (amount of information) that can be transmitted simultaneously.

[4] This estimate assumes a fibre backbone architecture with a fibre feeder segment and coaxial distribution and drop segments, and it also included the cost of a video headend to provide 64 channels of distributed video and of addressable converters at 60 percent of the households.

combined with switching capabilities as the headend and digital signal compression, this configuration could distribute a wide range of new services including video-on-demand and certain telephone-like services.

Experts forecasted that these new systems would become popular because the main trunk cable leading from the headend contained a number of fibre strands, each of which could itself serve as a trunk. These individual trunk fibres could be split off, in star fashion, to different parts of a CATV carrier's service area and each could run for considerably longer distances than could coaxial cable. Short feeder lines would then be deployed into communities. Each feeder line might be connected to fewer than 150 homes. By partitioning the system, a cable operator could divide an operating area into a collection of clusters and be able to segment program offerings accordingly. It was considered theoretically possible to segment program offerings and commercials to the level of the individual household.

Cable systems were also expected to evolve in a series of stages. At first, fibre backbone systems would be installed to reduce maintenance costs and to improve the quality and reliability of the video signal. Systems would continue to use analog transmission until the demand for bandwidth prompted an upgrade to digital technology. Then a digital compression overlay would be added, further increasing carrying capacity. Approximately 80 digitally compressed channels would be located in the 600 MHz to 1 GHz frequency range and provide new services. In the lower frequency ranges, 70 analog channels would carry normal programming. It was expected that these hybrid systems would evolve to all-digital systems over time. America's largest CATV company, TCI, announced that it planned to offer digital compression and 500 channels by the end of 1996.

The movement of CATV companies towards using compressed digital signals was driven by the prospect of new revenues, although the cost of conversion was expected to be significant as components throughout the cable system would require upgrading. However, by upgrading to carry digital signals, an operator could probably avoid the cost of replacing coaxial feeders and drops with optical fibre, as coaxial cable's bandwidth was expected to be adequate to handle bandwidth demands in the foreseeable future.

The National Cable Television Association estimated that the CATV industry would spend more than $18 billion in the years 1994–2004 for upgrades to plant and equipment, with more than 60 percent of the existing CATV systems slated to be rebuilt. All of the trunk and most of the feeder lines scheduled for construction during this period were expected to use optical fibre.

Industry Market Structure and Regulation

CATV operated in a highly regulated environment in which the FCC had the ultimate authority to set rules and standards. In cable's early days, the FCC was concerned that CATV networks remain independent of both telephone companies and large broadcast networks. Thus, the FCC prohibited both types of companies from owning cable systems in their operating areas.

The FCC began regulating rates at the time of cable's inception. Since cable companies operated as legal monopolies within their service areas, the FCC felt that rate regulation was needed to counterbalance the CATV operator's potential to overcharge or under-service a market. Another force behind industry regulation was the apparent absence of readily available substitutes. At the time the FCC established a regulatory framework for CATV, there were insufficient alternatives available to customers who desired clear signal reception and a large number of viewing choices. Consequently, the FCC did not consider it possible for customers to switch CATV service providers and used regulation as a means of ensuring that CATV carriers focused on delivering promised service at reasonable prices.

A main objective of the 1984 Cable Communications Policy Act was to decentralize much of the control of the cable industry to the municipal level and to give CATV operators more freedom to set rates. Municipalities were empowered to grant franchises for terms of between 5 and 15 years. Most municipalities preferred shorter terms so as to improve the accountability of CATV operators.

Obtaining a franchise involved navigating a lengthy, cumbersome process involving competitive bidding and often, aggressive lobbying. A bidder's local reputation and experience in other communities were significant factors in winning franchises. Prospective franchise holders had to submit detailed tenders that described the number and type of channels that would be offered, make guarantees about signal quality, planned system extensions and improvements, and the franchise fee they would pay. Such fees ranged between 3 and 5 percent of revenues. Municipalities frequently insisted that cable operators make time available to local groups for community programming.

If the cable franchisee lived up to the terms of the agreement, the Act provided some level of legal protection so that the franchise could not be arbitrarily withdrawn at renewal time. However, competitive bidding for franchises at renewal time was common and the winner was usually expected to make major investments to upgrade a system to meet the demands of the municipality. Common subscriber complaints were related to the quality of the video signal, the number of system outages experienced, and the number and type of channels offered. It was generally felt in the industry that subscribers were virtually powerless to demand new services until it was close to franchise renewal time.

Recent court rulings had found that local franchises could no longer be offered on an exclusive basis. As a result, by 1991 approximately 50 cities had competing cable systems, twice as many as in 1989. In competitive situations, a second system would "overbuild" the first by installing cables along the same route or right-of-way as the first system. When overbuilding occurred, it usually preceded intense competition between the rivals in price, advertising, service give-aways, and service expansion.

In the 1990s, rates were essentially deregulated, except for those covering some rural areas. The rationale was that CATV was no longer a natural monopoly, that other forms of entertainment were broadly available and they acted to keep cable rates competitive, that customers had a choice of whether or not to subscribe, and that customers had a choice between service providers. However, the FCC retained a broad power to order rate rollbacks. Exhibit 2 shows how cable rates evolved between 1976 and 1993.

During the 1980s, many cable companies were acquired by other, larger operators. Some systems were selling for upwards of $2,500 per subscriber. This was considerably higher than the average system's undepreciated book value of plant and equipment of approximately $465 per subscriber. These larger companies were called MSOs (multiple systems operators) because they operated several cable systems that were usually not geographically adjacent and thus were not run as a single system from a signal distribution standpoint. Exhibit 3 lists the top cable MSOs in the U.S.

MSOs benefited in significant ways from industry consolidation. First, it was easier to raise money to fund system upgrades and expansions. Second, an MSO had greater bargaining power in dealing with satellite program providers and could offer more to attract potential advertising revenue. Scale economies were possible in administration, government relations, and franchise negotiations. As a result, the larger MSOs had cash flows often in excess of 50 percent of revenues. However, cumulative industry debt was high. Most of the larger MSOs had diversified into other areas of entertainment or information distribution within the U.S. and internationally.

Exhibit 2 Cable Rates

Year	Basic Cable Rate	% Change	Full-Pay-TV Rate	Mini-Pay-TV Rate	Total Pay-TV Rate % Change
1976	$ 6.45	—	$ 7.71	—	—
1981	7.99	3.9	8.92	—	3.5
1986	10.67	9.7	10.31	—	0.6
1991	18.10	7.9	10.27	$1.50	(0.3)
1992	19.08	5.4	10.17	1.50	(0.8)
1993	19.39*	1.6	9.11	2.75	1.6

* Weighted average basic rate of $20.06 per month used to calculate full year revenues, representing eight months of unregulated basic rates, and four months of the FCC rolled-back rate.

Reprinted with permission of Paul Kagan Associates, Inc., Carmel, CA., from *Cable TV Investor,* March 31, 1994.

EXHIBIT 3   Top 50 Cable System Operators as of December 31, 1993

Company	Basic Subscribers (000)	Expanded Basic (000)	Pay Units (000)	Mini Pay (000)	Homes Passed (000)	Percentage Ratios Basic/Homes Passed	Pay/Basic	Pay/Homes Passed
1. Tele-Comm. Inc. (1, 2, e)	10,406	9,288	6,362	3,704	17,425	59.7	61.1	36.5
2. Time Warner Cable (3)	7,215	2,141	4,558		12,012	60.1	63.2	37.9
3. Continental Cablevision (4)	3,149		2,615		5,637	55.9	83.1	46.4
4. Comcast Cable (2, 5)	2,648		1,812		4,219	62.8	68.4	42.9
5. Cablevision Systems	2,148		3,940		3,563	60.3	183.4	110.6
6. Cox Cable Communications	1,784	1,754	1,206	42	2,838	62.9	67.6	42.5
7. Newhouse Broadcasting	1,384	560	1,009	22	1,940	71.3	72.9	52.0
8. Cablevision Ind. (e)	1,328		697		1,957	67.9	52.5	35.6
9. Times Mirror Cable	1,274	1,230	703		2,069	61.6	55.2	34.0
10. Jones Spacelink	1,263	1,198	1,031	3	2,163	58.4	81.6	47.6
11. Adelphia Communications	1,244	27	555		1,758	70.8	44.6	31.6
12. Viacom	1,094	1,065	718	53	1,730	63.3	65.6	41.5
13. Sammons Communications	1,072	1,036	607		1,592	67.4	56.6	38.1
14. Falcon Cable TV	1,055	183	369	8	1,287	81.9	35.0	28.6
15. Century Communications (e)	945		539		1,653	57.2	57.0	32.6
16. Crown Media	857	484	518		1,572	54.5	60.4	33.0
17. Colony Communications	787		467		1,222	64.4	59.3	38.2
18. TeleCable Corporation	717	583	647		992	72.2	90.3	65.2
19. Scripps Howard	702	702	600		1,159	60.5	85.5	51.7
20. Lenfest Communications (6, 7)	658	646	500		1,025	64.2	76.0	48.8
21. InterMedia Ptrs. (6) #	632		386		1,030	61.4	61.0	37.5
22. KBLCOM (8)	605	513	488		1,198	50.5	80.7	40.7
23. TKR Cable (2, 6)	602		496		898	67.1	82.4	55.3
24. Prime Cable	557	435	475		1,190	46.9	85.3	40.0
25. Post-Newsweek Cable	482	442	279	22	693	69.6	57.9	40.3
26. TCA Cable (e)	473	283	241	4	645	73.5	50.9	37.4
27. Wometco Cable Corporation	452	444	268		783	57.7	59.4	34.3
28. Tele-Media	426	42	156		611	69.8	36.5	25.5
29. Maclean Hunter	425		378		751	56.6	89.0	50.3
30. Multimedia Cablevision	417	394	323		694	60.1	77.4	46.5
31. Rifkin & Associates	380		219		536	70.9	57.5	40.8

No.	Company							
32.	Triax Communications	370		193		562	65.8	52.0	34.2
33.	Western Communications (e)	323		149		434	74.6	46.0	34.3
34.	C-TEC	258	247	176		417	62.0	68.2	42.3
35.	Columbia International (6)	249		193	10	399	62.6	77.2	48.4
36.	Service Electric	242		80		342	70.7	33.1	23.4
37.	SBC Media Ventures (9)	233	226	195	40	395	59.0	83.8	49.5
38.	Greater Media	227	218	198		373	60.7	87.4	53.1
39.	Harron Communications	223	174	150	4	330	67.5	67.2	45.4
40.	Media General	220	201	164	24	324	68.1	74.5	50.7
41.	U.S. Cable Corporation	209	198	119		348	60.0	57.1	34.3
42.	MultiVision	208	74	153		357	58.4	73.2	42.7
43.	Garden State Cable	192		152		284	67.7	79.3	53.7
44.	Sutton Capital Association	183	176	171		273	67.0	93.2	62.5
45.	Armstrong Utilities	181		97		229	79.2	53.5	42.3
46.	Bresnan Communications*, #	174	167	85	24	267	65.0	49.2	32.0
47.	Simmons Communications	169	163	64	1	243	69.6	38.1	26.5
48.	Northland Communications	158	155	44		214	73.8	28.0	20.7
49.	Summit Comm. Group	157	150	93		235	66.9	59.3	39.6
50.	Blade Communications	149	148	88		237	62.7	59.4	37.2

1 TCI counts include 100 percent of UA partnerships (13 percent owned by TCI) but do not include 80 percent BRESNAN, 70 percent TKR Cable I, II, and III. Liberty spin-off interests or international holdings. Net owned basic subscribers number 10,701,000; total gross TCI owned/affiliated basic subscribers total 15,206,000.

2 Includes STORER split-off subscribers: TCI-609,000; Comcast-927,500; TKR-265,788.

3 Time-Warner Cable counts include: 100 percent Paragon, 937,715 basic subscribers (50 percent owned); 100 percent of other affiliated systems, 400,000.

4 Continental counts include 34 percent of Insight (52nd largest cable company).

5 Pro rata 40 percent Garden State Cablevision (76,888), Comcast subscriber count would be 2,724,888.

6 Partially owned by Liberty Media: TKR 50 percent; Lenfest 50 percent; Intermedia 3 percent; Columbia 30 percent; and other various percentages of non-listed cable holdings. Total Liberty net subscribers: 938,580.

7 Lenfest counts reflect 40 percent equity in Garden State Cable (43rd largest cable operator).

8 Paragon (50 percent owned by Houston Industries) included at 100 percent in Time-Warner count. Pro rata 50 percent Paragon, Houston Industries has 1,073,451 subscribers, ranking it as the 14th largest operator.

9 SBC Ventures is Southwestern Bell's cable operating company-acquisition of Hauser Communications complete by 12/31.

Count reflects a recent sale or acquisition.
* Owned in part by TCI.
e Estimate by Paul Kagan Associates.

Reprinted with permission of Paul Kagan Associates, Inc., Carmel, CA., from Cable TV Investor, March 31, 1994.

Future Services

Most analysts believed that CATV was a mature product in the markets it served. Future growth was expected to come from a range of enhanced services:

• *Pay per view:* This service was still unavailable in most parts of the U.S., but availability was expected to grow steadily.

• *Enhanced pay per view (EPPV):* The additional channels needed to offer EPPV could be obtained by upgrading the amplifiers on the system to take advantage of the full capacity of coaxial cable (up to 150 channels). Such new equipment was not expected to cost more than $150 per subscriber.

• *Impulse pay per view (IPPV):* IPPV was an enhancement that would make it possible for customers to place PPV orders closer to airtime. Digital signals were not required, but they would make IPPV function more efficiently. IPPV would normally be installed along with EPPV, but the stand-alone installation cost was expected to be $20 per subscriber.

• *High-Definition TV (HDTV):* This service would require CATV companies to add digital capabilities to the existing coaxial cable network. The set-top decoder needed to convert digital signals was expected to cost approximately $450 at the time of introduction, although it was widely believed that the $250 threshold would be the level at which most operators would earn an adequate return on their investment. The cost of the digital converter was expected to account for between 60 and 70 percent of the total investment required to introduce HDTV as measured on a per-subscriber basis. However, the lack of an agreement on a common HDTV standard meant that this service was not expected to generate much revenue in the medium term.

• *Video on Demand (VOD):* This system was expected to offer customers an opportunity to order any one of a range of available videotapes for immediate viewing. It was highly likely that VOD would require the installation of a sophisticated new network with additional bandwidth, incorporating optical fibre from the headend to the feeder, plus switching and digital compression to handle the demand and bandwidth requirements of such a service. The cost of an upgrade has been estimated by industry experts to be approximately $1,350 per subscriber ($400 for fibre to the feeder, $500 for switching, $450 for digital compression and conversion). One CATV operator had conducted a study of VOD and discovered that customers would purchase an average of 2.5 movies per month, at $3 to $4 per showing, selected from an available play list of 80 movies.

VOD service would compete against the $15 billion video rental business, but as executives in the video rental business knew, most of these annual revenues were earned on rentals of older titles (not on rentals of current movies) and increasingly, on rentals of sophisticated video games. Video rental company executives believed that VOD would be viable at the earliest by 2002–2004, and even then, would only be capable of offering 100 movies on-line at any one time. However, Blockbuster Entertainment Corporation, a leading U.S. video rental chain, had announced plans to develop a VOD service in conjunction with Viacom, a cable company, and, eventually had plans to merge with Viacom.

• *Telephony:* Industry executives believed that the U.S. Congress would soon pass legislation allowing CATV companies to offer local exchange telephone service within their cable service areas. Cable companies would then be able to offer local telephone services, most likely at a discount to prevailing telephone company rates, although it was expected that there would be no extraordinary prohibitions preventing the telephone companies from lowering their rates to forestall customer churn. In return, telephone companies would be permitted greater freedom to offer video services, including television signals, over their lines. It was not clear what additional expenditure CATV companies would need to make to offer local exchange telephone service, although the experience of some U.K. cable companies involved in telephony since January 1991, was expected to be quite valuable in helping estimate capital requirements. More than 300,000 British households depended on their cable carriers for telephone service, and some of these carriers were owned by U.S. CATV networks. Many U.S. cable companies planned to rebuild their plant to handle local telephone calls and data transmission. Fibre optic feeder cable was being installed down to blocks of 300 houses on almost all new construction.

• *Catalog Shopping:* Mail-order catalog shopping in the U.S. was a $70 billion business in 1993, although only a small fraction of the overall $2.1 trillion spent at all U.S. retail locations. More than $200 million alone was sold to consumers who placed orders through modems which connected them to on-line databases. Via cable, catalog shopping was expected to present customers with "virtual" catalogs, which could be updated rapidly. Orders could be placed using touchpads connected to a cable converter or via the telephone.

Catalog shopping offered customers two main benefits: cost savings and convenience. Since the costs of intermediate distribution outlets would be eliminated, it would be possible for home shopping services to be profitable on low margins, below the 8 to 10 percent usually earned by the most aggressive price competitor, warehouse clubs. One area where home shopping was felt to have strong potential was grocery purchasing, which was consistently identified in studies as the type of shopping least liked by Americans. Conceivably, cable operators offering home grocery shopping services could charge food manufacturers a stocking fee to feature their products in a virtual supermarket catalog. One analyst estimated that sales of $100 billion through cable could be possible 10 years after the introduction of a catalog shopping service.

• *Other Information Services:* The American public was beginning to become increasingly interested in a set of information services, including electronic mail and remote database access, that was being referred to as the "information highway." Because of the bandwidth requirements for data transfer, cable television networks could conceivably serve to connect subscribers with data resources stored in remote computers. However, such access would likely be routed from the headend to the remote site using telephone lines or through a private data transmission service. Some level of upgrade to the cable network would be required to make interactive communications possible, although it would be difficult to estimate the cost of the necessary hardware and software. However, once in place, an interactive network would make it possible for a broad range of applications to be offered by cable carriers, including burglar and fire alarm services and remote home energy management.

Competition

Other than industry rivals, CATV operators experienced little competition for video direct access to households. One exception that was expected to become more important was direct broadcast satellite (DBS). Viewers who purchased a DBS system could receive signals directly using a satellite receiving dish. Although widely used in Europe and Japan, DBS was not popular in the U.S. except in those areas where conventional cable service was not available. Where cable was available, it was almost always less expensive than DBS. In cities, it was often impractical to use DBS given the size of satellite dish that was required.

However, new DBS technology was threatening to make satellite broadcasting more competitive. A new company owned by MSOs planned to launch a satellite network that would deliver 80 channels of service to customers anywhere in the U.S. when it was scheduled to begin service in June 1994. Moreover, the satellite dish needed to receive television signals from a satellite would be only a few feet in diameter—considerably smaller than the dishes used to date. However, DBS had one critical flaw—it did not have enough bandwidth to offer video-on-demand service. Nevertheless, it did present a viable alternative to CATV although the price of hardware (estimated to be $700 to $800 for a satellite receiver and decoder) meant that customers would incur significant switching costs if they ceased relying on their local CATV operators for signals.

Other potential competitors included the local telephone operating companies, including the Regional Bell Operating Companies (RBOCs). The RBOCs held more than 75 percent of the local exchange service market in the U.S. They were individually quite large and had combined 1993 revenues of more than $84 billion.

The telephone companies had lobbied vigorously in Washington to be allowed to be freed from restrictions set down in federal law, FCC rulings, and in the 1984 "Consent Decree" that had broken up AT&T and established the RBOCs as seven independent regulated companies to serve local calling needs. In the early 1990s, regulations had been relaxed somewhat to permit the telephone companies to offer information services such as home banking and shopping. In October 1991, the FCC issued a Notice of Proposed Rule that would allow local telephone companies to carry "video dial tone." This meant they could carry video programs provided by third parties, but would not be allowed to select or edit programs themselves.

Traditionally, telephony used twisted pair copper wire to carry signals in two directions. But twisted pair had a relatively small bandwidth (since voice telephony could be delivered using as little as 6 MHz). This meant that the telephone companies would have to use a different system to transmit video signals, especially if they chose to offer interactive services. A new technology was proposed by Bellcore (the RBOC standards-setting and technology planning company) called Asymmetrical Digital Subscriber Loop (ADSL). ADSL promised to provide one digital video channel to each subscriber's home using the existing twisted pair telephone line. The subscriber could switch this channel at the TV set to select a program. The signal would be of VCR-grade quality, and while this was not up to the level of signal quality provided by a good CATV carrier, it did present a viable alternative to cable. Moreover, the RBOCs already had an installation and customer service infrastructure in place, along with extensive expertise in both operating addressable networks and providing services that relied on switching technology. While the deployment of ADSL would require a considerable capital expenditure on the part of the RBOCs, estimated at $750 to $1,500 per subscriber, it seemed certain that they would offer cable service in selected markets within a few years.

RBOCs could also offer video on demand (VOD) but only at costs per subscriber that were higher than those for comparable CATV-based services since the RBOCs would need to install optical fibre lines with big bandwidths right to each customer's home. Deploying fibre to the home was estimated to cost between $2,000 and $3,000 per subscriber, although the RBOCs could use combinations of fibre and coaxial cable to reduce their costs. Upgrading the switches in the telephone system to handle multimedia products was expected to add another $500 per subscriber, but it was believed that these costs would drop as technologies improved. While the RBOCs appeared to be uncompetitive in VOD service, it was expected that they planned to install additional VOD-like capabilities to provide customers with other services such as improved video conferencing. The business savings associated with the successful introduction of multimedia services to business telephone customers could result in system growth and increased volume, making VOD a more economic proposition due to the realization of potential scope economy effects.

On August 24, 1993, a federal judge in Virginia struck down sections of the Cable Act that prevented telephone companies from operating cable systems in their local market. This decision had the effect of making cable companies potential targets for acquisition by RBOCs, especially as RBOC revenues were growing at only 2 to 3 percent each year. On October 13, 1993, Bell Atlantic announced its acquisition of 100 percent of TCI, America's largest cable operator, in the country's largest such transaction ($32.6 billion).

This was equivalent to 11.75 times the annualized latest three-month cash flow for TCI, or an estimated $2,350 per subscriber. Less than two months later, Canada's BCE Telecom International announced that it had acquired 30 percent of Jones Intercable as its first step in taking complete ownership of the company in a deal that was to be completed over eight years, and at an estimated cost of $2,089 per subscriber.

At least one CATV CEO was reported as saying that the RBOCs wanted to enter other areas of service, including cable, to protect their own local telephone service franchise from competition. Such competition could come from CATV companies if regulatory barriers were lowered and additional capital investments were made by these companies to provide telephone service. Most cable companies had spare bandwith and, with the introduction first of digital compression and then of optical fibre cable, the additional capacity needed for telephony would be readily available. Some CATV executives even felt that the RBOCs were also interested in acquiring CATV networks outside their own operating areas, and then, using these acquisitions to offer local telephone service and, thus, competing with other RBOCs.

Maclean Hunter Cable

The Offer

At the end of 1993, Maclean Hunter Cable was the 29th largest operating cable company in the U.S. Maclean Hunter Cable was part of Maclean Hunter Ltd., a Canadian cable and publishing firm which had, on February 2, 1994, received an unsolicited offer from Rogers Communications Inc. to purchase all its shares. On February 11, the Rogers board announced they would offer Cdn.$17 a share plus a right to receive a payment if Rogers sold Maclean Hunter's U.S. cable operations for more than Cdn.$1.5 billion. The deadline for acceptance of this offer was March 15. The Maclean Hunter board rejected this offer, claiming it to be insufficient. After prolonged negotiations, Rogers and Maclean Hunter announced on March 8 that a take-over deal had been concluded. Rogers would pay Cdn.$17.50 for Maclean Hunter shares, and shareholders would lose any right to claim a portion of the proceeds from the sale of the U.S. cable assets. The total value of the take-over was Cdn.$3.1 billion, including bridge financing of Cdn.$2 billion. Rogers had indicated that it would sell Maclean Hunter's U.S. cable assets to repay Cdn.$1.5 billion of the loan. The estimated cost of these cable assets to Rogers was Cdn.$1,082 million (Cdn.$2,192 per subscriber), or 11 times the cable assets' cash flow. See Exhibit 4 for a valuation of each company's main lines of business.

History and Cable Background

During the 1980s, there was intense competition for cable franchises within the U.S. The rivalry was so strong that this period was often referred to as

---

EXHIBIT 4 Maclean Hunter/Rogers Business Valuation

Assets	*1994 Cash Flow (Cdn$ millions)*	*Cash Flow Multiple*	*Value (Cdn$ millions)*
Maclean Hunter			
Cable	$229	10.7x	$2,450
Periodicals	16	9.5	152
Business Forms	55	9.0	495
Newspapers	21	10.5	221
Broadcast	9	9.5	86
Communications Services	6	8.0	48
Subtotal/Average	$336	10.3x	$3,452
Net Debt			(187)
Private Market Value		(Cdn$)	3,265
Fully Diluted Shares		(millions)	179.0
Private Market Value/Share		(Cdn$)	$18.24
Rogers Communications			
Cable	$228	9.5x	$2,736
Cellular	377*	14.0	5,278
Radio	12	8.0	96
Long Distance	31*	25.0	775
Subtotal/Average	$708	12.5x	$8,885
21% of Canadian Satellite Communications			35
25% of Teleglobe			123
80% of Cantel Paging			49
Canadian Home Shopping Network			20
Total Assets			$9,112
Net Debt			(1,846)
Private Market Value		(Cdn$)	$7,266
Fully Diluted Shares		(millions)	202.1
Private Market Value/Share		(Cdn$)	$35.95

* Calculated using present values of 1996 cash flows, discounted at 10%.

Reprinted with permission of Paul Kagan Associates, Inc., Carmel, CA., from *Cable TV Investor,* February 28, 1994.

"the franchise wars." Two factors contributed to the rivalrous climate. First, a number of very large U.S. media conglomerates had realized the enormous financial potential of the cable business and decided to gain entry by applying their resources to the task of winning franchises. Second, the number of major urban areas without cable service had diminished considerably. It was felt by 1983 and 1984 that all of the most attractive franchises had been awarded. This type of shortage helped increase the value of existing franchises, including those held by Maclean Hunter.

Despite the risks and costs that the company faced as a result of shifts in the competitive environment, Maclean Hunter remained intent on expanding its American CATV holdings in the 1980s, partly because it had reached the limits of growth in the smaller Canadian market. Then, average penetration in the U.S. market was only 45 percent of homes passed, meaning that significant system expansion was still possible. As well, the regulatory climate in the U.S. had shifted towards market-based mechanisms. Ancillary services were often lightly regulated. The proliferation of channels further fragmented the U.S. market, meaning that advertisers had to rely increasingly on cable to deliver their messages to target audiences.

Maclean Hunter made every effort to capitalize on its strengths during the 1980s. It decided to pursue new opportunities through the franchising route rather than engage in acquisitions (an increasingly popular tactic among U.S. cable operators) because it felt that managing cable systems was a firm-specific advantage. To benefit from this advantage, Maclean Hunter had to build its own system from the ground up. The acquisition route was also unattractive because the company found the asking price of existing systems excessive in view of weak fundamentals. The asking price of 7 to 10 times cash flow was too high, since most acquisition targets required a significant investment to bring them up to Maclean Hunter's standards.

The company's strategy was to build state-of-the-art systems so that subscribers could be assured of receiving new services as they were developed. The basic cable package was continually expanded, and arrangements made with the programmers of the latest and best pay-TV services so they could be offered to customers at attractive rates. Considerable attention was given to local origination programming and strong local management teams were given a high degree of autonomy to respond to local market needs. These policies cemented Maclean Hunter's reputation as a leading cable operator.

The company continued to focus its efforts on winning suburban systems. Not only did Maclean Hunter find the bidding process to be less costly than in the cities, but believed that suburban franchises offered advantages that urban franchises did not. For instance, some suburban franchises had a population density that was on par with those in nearby cities. Since building a state-of-the-art plant in suburban locations could be done more rapidly and at a lower cost than an upgrade within a city, a suburban cable system could be activated sooner. This had the effect of more rapidly generating cash, a consideration that was of prime importance to a financially conservative company like Maclean Hunter. The company also found that suburban communities were more homogeneous, meaning that programming requirements were simpler and less expensive. Eventually, Maclean Hunter began bidding for franchises in a number of U.S. cities, rather than concentrating on building up contiguous systems. The primary reason was the need for additional revenue, and Maclean Hunter accepted the need to manage each system as a separate entity.

The increasing cost of bidding, and the lack of attractive new franchises forced the company to rethink its strategy in the early 1980s. Maclean Hunter decided to expand through acquisition. However, it had no early success following this strategy because competitors were often willing to pay more for franchises, reasoning that regardless of their acquisition cost, they represented reliable investments. Maclean Hunter made three key strategic changes: first, while the company had avoided "new concept" investments because of the low probability of payback, it decided to invest in bringing some new concepts to market based on the idea that research and development activities would give the company experience and open up areas of prospective new growth; second, Maclean Hunter was now prepared to accept an ownership stake of less than 50 percent so long as it had effective control; third, guidelines for acceptable rates of return on new investments, and the yardstick for measurement of existing operations where appropriate, were increased from 12 percent to 15 percent after tax, for normal "low-risk" situations. This change had a particularly important effect on cable television operations, as management would have to become more rigorous in enforcing financial discipline and optimizing operations. At the same time, they encouraged investments in innovation that likely would not have been supported in the past. The balance of the 1980s saw Maclean Hunter concentrate on optimizing its existing network systems and expanding into Florida via its acquisition of Selkirk Communications, a Canadian firm with cable operations in that state.

At the time of the Rogers acquisition, Maclean Hunter had 425,000 subscribers in New Jersey, Michigan, and Florida. The company was considered to be one of the leading cable operators in the U.S., offering its customers a wide variety of channels delivered through technologically advanced distribution systems. Moreover, the company's U.S. operations were profitable and relations with municipalities were for the most part harmonious. However, some industry analysts felt that the company's U.S. cable operations had not been upgraded sufficiently to justify a high cash flow multiple if sold.

The FCC and Rate Roll-Backs

On May 3, 1993, the FCC released a 475-page manual implementing the Cable Act of October 3, 1992. This Act was intended to force cable companies that had been overcharging customers to reduce their rates and was rooted in a congressional drive to re-regulate cable television as part of a four-year effort to curb escalating cable charges. The FCC published cable rate benchmarks and new reporting that required operators to provide the FCC with extensive information about rate-setting procedures, and it also ordered the cable companies to roll back rates by $2 per month per subscriber beginning in September 1993. Rates were frozen at the new lower level. Further rate increases would be tied to changes in a GNP-fixed-weight price index plus some portion of a CATV operator's expenses.

The effect of the roll-back on the U.S. cable industry was to immediately reduce forecast revenues by an estimated $2 billion. For an average operator, this roll-back would reduce revenues by 7.4 percent, cash flow by 15.7 percent, and cash flow margin by more than 4 percent (from 46.5 percent to 42.3

percent). The cost of FCC compliance monitoring, estimated by the FCC Chairman at $28 million, would be passed on to the industry through a supplemental assessment. One of the effects of the roll-back was to reduce the amount of cash that had been used to expand the broadband network and to offer more programming.

On February 22, 1994, the FCC unanimously voted to reduce rates a further 7 percent. The FCC Chairman, Reed Hundt, indicated that the combined rollbacks would affect 90 percent of all cable systems and save consumers $3 billion. In effect, operators were required to reduce their September 1992 rates by 17 percent and then compare these rates to new FCC benchmarks. Systems whose rates were below the new benchmark after making the 17 percent deduction were entitled to a phased implementation of rate reductions following an FCC cost study. A typical cost study took a year to complete. Small cable operators (those with less than 15,000 subscribers) also qualified for phased roll-backs. Basic cable service would be permitted to earn a maximum ROA of 11.5 percent. One effect of this decision was to end the merger plans between Bell Atlantic and TCI. Industry executives were concerned that FCC rate unpredictability would make it difficult to properly value cable holdings in the future.

Carol Dixon's Evaluation

After reviewing published analysts reports (selected comments are given in Exhibit 5) and after conducting her own background research, Dixon reached some tentative conclusions about the direction of the cable industry in the U.S. These are summarized in Exhibit 6.

As she saw it, setting a final price involved weighing uncertainty as well as considering the potential consequences of the acquiring firm's strategy. Key uncertainties included:

• *Standards:* Despite an abundance of discussion about new services such as video-on-demand, there were no accepted technical standards in existence that would permit the industry to move beyond the concept stage. Dixon worried that the U.S. Congress was considering a bill that would set a deadline for industry to establish standards because if the deadline was not met, then the FCC could make standards decisions that the industry would have to live with for a long time. Many interests wanted a say in setting standards: the telephone companies and database operators saw standards as a way to steer the future of the industry to naturally favour their key competencies. Other interests, including Microsoft, Apple, and General Instrument (suppliers of set-top descramblers and other in-home cable equipment) wanted the industry to set its own standards, but wanted to keep some technological breakthroughs private, thereby limiting the number of open standards that could be readily

EXHIBIT 5   Selected Cable Analysts' Comments, March 1994

". . . Trophy cable properties will sell at 12x cash flow multiples, or $2,800 to $3,000 per subscriber, but systems tied to regulated revenues will only get 8x to 10x if they're lucky."

". . . The multiple isn't 12x cash flow and it isn't likely to be 12x for a while."

"I anticipate that smaller systems will sell for 7x to 8x cash flows . . . but sooner or later re-regulation will only be a bad memory."

". . . Telephony is now what will drive system values."

". . . Look at the trends, the numbers are coming back up and there won't be much on sale for some time."

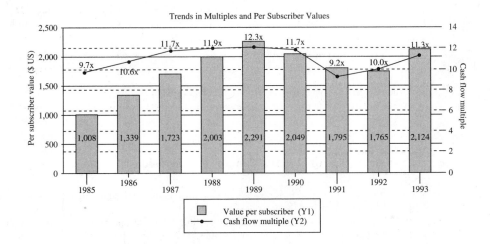

Trends in Multiples and Per Subscriber Values

"While the cable companies' low and non-investment-grade ratings will improve if they merge with the telephone companies, remember that the telcos' ratings will be hurt by any kind of merger activity. And the new rating for the merged companies won't necessarily be the average of the two partners."

"Competition will be a bigger driver in helping determine values and creditworthiness. The government seems to be moving toward deploying two broadband communications networks into the home. This means there'll be lots of opportunities to offer high-growth, high-margin services. Both cable and telephone companies will have to learn to compete hard."

"Cash flow multiples are used to compare cable companies because they make it possible to perform a consistent comparison between companies, regardless of where they operate. Since cable companies are so capital intensive, using cash flow multiples makes some sense, and it's consistent with the way that utilities are measured everywhere. But this industry is becoming more competitive, and it's getting that way because of technology. When I look at a company in the future, yes, I'm going to worry about net free cash flow[5] but I'm also going to look at cash flow adequacy,[6] debt-to-earnings before interest, taxes, depreciation, and cash flow coverage of cash interest obligations."

"Earnings before interest, taxes, and depreciation. And cash flow, of course."

EXHIBIT 5   *(Concluded)*

"Government will change this industry, and I'm not sure it'll be for the better. Competition between telcos and cable companies could be a big departure from the way things have been done in the past, where the telcos and cable companies ran their business behind a lot of shelter from the market."

"Cable companies have always been evaluated using cash flow measures, and I don't see any reason to change. What's most important for me will be net free cash flow and the right cash flow adequacy ratio."

"To me, it's unlikely that the cable industry will generate any kind of significant revenues from telephony for the next three years. Even then, does anybody seriously expect the RBOCs to sit back and watch their market being nibbled away?"

"Where's the value? In content, of course. Think about it: who'd you rather own—Disney or CBS? Carriers will become commodities within ten years, just wait for technology to level the playing field."

Reprinted with permission of Paul Kagan Associates, Inc., Carmel CA, from Cable TV Investor, March 31, 1994.

[5] Defined as cash flow after interest, taxes, and capital expenditures.

[6] Annual net free cash flow relative to the average scheduled debt maturity over the next five years.

EXHIBIT 6   **Carol Dixon's Tentative Conclusions**

Cable TV distribution architecture is evolving into digitally switched regional hubs, just like those that exist in the telephone network.

    This regional hub strategy is making it possible for cable operators to consider whether they should connect headends in various cities. This could lead to territory swaps with other operators, but also produce scale economies. As low-cost providers, the realigned cable companies could become effective competitors for local telephone access.

    To become full-service networks for both residential and commercial customers, cable TV operators must consider strategies that include alliances with long-distance carriers. They may be able to bypass local loop telephone service altogether.

    The demand for more programming will lead to an expansion in the number of channels that an MSO must offer. If 150 channels becomes the norm, MSOs must shift to either fibre or higher bandwidth-capable coaxial cable. This observation is supported by the current construction/rebuild plans of most MSOs. A hybrid fibre-coax network is the low-cost solution for broadcast-dominated video services.

    Re-regulation of cable rates will ultimately harm the consumer as well as make it difficult for firms to raise money on Wall Street to expand their networks and services.

    Competition from alternative providers (e.g., RBOCs, DBS, etc.) will change the monopolistic nature of the cable industry. The big question then becomes: is the existing CATV management capable of handling the transition to a competitive environment?

    The new world of cable TV means that a new value chain will have to be created. Smart players will forge linkages through alliances or joint ventures with others, so as to dominate those parts of the value chain with greatest profit potential and to diversify market, competitive, and regulatory risk.

---

emulated. The delay in confirming standards also served to introduce uncertainty about the future, since the costs of new technologies kept changing and would remain largely indeterminate until careful designs based on new standards had been completed and production volumes for new equipment became known.

• *Alliances:* While cable signals were sent via hardware, consumer acceptance of new services was going to be decided by the quality of the interface presented by each cable operator. Therefore, many executives in the CATV industry felt that the presence or absence of existing or prospective alliances with software companies would have a long-term effect on a CATV company's ability to build a customer base for new, enhanced services.

• *Open Access:* Dixon's key concern centred around mandated access to the cable network. Would legislation oblige networks to carry any and all traffic according to published rate schedules (especially important for data, telephony, and some entertainment services) or could the cable carrier decide what it would carry and at what price? The answer to this question would determine where the cable carriers would be positioned on the emerging "info-tainment" industry value chain.

• *Content:* Owners of rights to video productions received approximately 25 percent of revenues for movie channels. Would that remain constant or change in the future? With more and more of America's entertainment companies becoming owned by Japanese investors, could access to the critical resource of cable TV content ever become a bargaining chip in some future international negotiation over standards or in an important equipment supply contract?

• *Market:* The market for many new services was only hypothesized, or at best substantiated based on a few small market trials. Consequently, Dixon wondered about customer behaviour in the future: would new services persuade customers to spend more time in front of their televisions than they did in early 1994?

• *Video on Demand:* Most people who watched the industry thought that VOD could supplant video rental companies as the preferred distribution channel to satisfy American demand for movie entertainment. That, thought Dixon, would certainly depend on the CATV operators ability to offer VOD at prices which were competitive to those charged by video rental stores. Moreover, would the owners of the movies be content to let control of their secondary distribution channel (i.e., after in-theatre screening) become concentrated in the hands of the cable companies? She also wondered what effect the initial limited movie selection would have on customer acceptance of the technology, and hence, on VOD revenues.

• *The FCC:* The long-term intentions of this agency were not clear. While re-regulation of cable rates seemed to Dixon to be bad economics but, perhaps, good politics, she knew that FCC intervention in price-setting would introduce a random, uncertain element into investors' thinking. That would lower the share price since future revenue streams became less reliable, and, therefore, the effect on the cost of capital could only be bad.

Dixon also though that two key questions of strategy had to enter into a proper determination of a price for the Maclean Hunter assets.

    • *Alliances:* A cable company should consider forging an alliance with a long distance carrier such as AT&T, MCI, or Sprint. The cable carrier could provide a way to bypass the RBOC that delivered local loop telephone service and in so doing, create a possibility for making a small profit on long-distance calling. Alternatively, the cable company could explore an alliance or joint venture with the RBOC in its service area, which could lead to scale and scope efficiencies as far as billing, repair, and customer service were concerned. As well, an integrated company would have a wealth of information about the buying habits of customers, meaning that micro-marketing or mass customization initiatives could become viable.

    • *Bundling:* Could a cable carrier find a way to offer a bundle of high-value services at low cost? An example that had been discussed for the West Coast involved bundling cable, Home Box Office (a specialty movie channel), and a new home energy management service from Pacific Gas & Electric.

    • *Rogers Communications:* Rogers had shouldered a huge debt load in order to buy Maclean Hunter Ltd. While Dixon knew that Rogers would not dispose of Maclean Hunter's U.S. cable assets without seeking to maximize proceeds from the sale, she also understood that Rogers was under pressure to pay down their borrowings. As well, it was widely known in the industry that Rogers had no real interest in operating Maclean Hunter's cable franchises, and as a result, it was believed that Rogers was anxious to find a suitable buyer. Dixon wondered whether these twin pressures could work for her client in any subsequent negotiations over price.

But the most important question in Carol Dixon's view was identifying the new value chain for the cable industry produced by rapid technological change and steady deregulation. Once that was clear, then she could make a price and cash flow multiple recommendation for the Maclean Hunter assets.

PRINCE EDWARD ISLAND PRESERVE CO.

In August 1991, Bruce MacNaughton, president of Prince Edward Island Preserve Co. Ltd. (P.E.I. Preserves), was contemplating future expansion. Two cities were of particular interest: Toronto and Tokyo. At issue was whether consumers in either or both markets should be pursued, and if so, how. The choices available for achieving further growth included mail order, distributors, and company-controlled stores.

Background

Prince Edward Island Preserve Co. was a manufacturing company located in New Glasglow, Prince Edward Island (P.E.I.), which produced and marketed specialty food products. The company founder and majority shareholder, Bruce MacNaughton, had realized that an opportunity existed to present P.E.I. strawberries as a world-class food product and to introduce the finished product to an "up-scale" specialty market. With total sales in the coming year expected to exceed $1.0 million for the first time, MacNaughton had made good on the opportunity he had perceived years earlier. It had not been easy, however.

MacNaughton arrived in P.E.I. from Moncton, New Brunswick, in 1978. Without a job, he slept on the beach for much of that first summer. Over the

This case was prepared by Professor Paul W. Beamish for the sole purpose of providing material for class discussion at the Western Business School. It is not intended to illustrate either effective or ineffective handling of a managerial situation. Any reproduction, in any form, of the material in this case is prohibited except with the written consent of the School. This case was funded in part by a grant from Foreign Affairs, Canada. Copyright 1991 © The University of Western Ontario.

next few years, he worked in commission sales, waited tables in restaurants, and then moved to Toronto. There he studied to become a chef at George Brown Community College. After working in the restaurant trade for several years, he found a job with Preserves by Amelia in Toronto. After six months, he returned to P.E.I., where he opened a restaurant. The restaurant was not successful, and MacNaughton lost the $25,000 stake he had accumulated. With nothing left but 100 kg of strawberries, Bruce decided to make these into preserves in order to have gifts for Christmas 1984. Early the following year, P.E.I. Preserves was founded.

The products produced by the company were priced and packaged for the gift/gourmet and specialty food markets. The primary purchasers of these products were conscious of quality and were seeking a product which they considered tasteful and natural. P.E.I. Preserves felt their product met this standard of quality at a price that made it attractive to all segments of the marketplace.

Over the next few years as the business grew, improvements were made to the building in New Glasgow. The sense of style which was characteristic of the company was evident from the beginning in its attractive layout and design.

In 1989, the company diversified and opened The Perfect Cup, a small restaurant in P.E.I.'s capital city of Charlottetown. This restaurant continued the theme of quality, specializing in wholesome, homemade food featuring the products manufactured by the company. The success of this operation led to the opening in 1990 of a small tea room at the New Glasgow location. Both of these locations showcased the products manufactured by the P.E.I. Preserve Co.

In August 1991, the company opened a small (22 sq. metre) retail branch in the CP Prince Edward Hotel. MacNaughton hoped this locale would expand visibility in the local and national marketplace, and serve as an off-season sales office. P.E.I. Preserves had been given very favourable lease arrangements (well below the normal $275 per month for space this size), and the location would require minimal financial investment. As Exhibit 1 suggests, the company had experienced steady growth in its scope of operations.

Exhibit 1   P.E.I. Preserve Operations

	Year Opened				
Operation	*1985*	*1989*	*1990*	*1991*	*1992 Projected*
New Glasgow—manufacturing and retail	X	X	X	X	X
Charlottetown—restaurant (Perfect Cup)		X	X	X	X
New Glasgow—restaurant (Tea Room)			X	X	X
Charlottetown—retail (CP Hotel)				X	X
Toronto or Tokyo?					X

Marketplace

Prince Edward Island was Canada's smallest province, both in size and population. Located in the Gulf of St. Lawrence, it was separated from Nova Scotia and New Brunswick by the Northumberland Strait. The various levels of government were the major employer in P.E.I. Many people in P.E.I. worked seasonally, in either farming (especially potato), fishing, or tourism. During the peak tourist months of July and August, the island population would swell dramatically from its base of 125,000. P.E.I.'s half million annual visitors came "home" to enjoy the long sandy beaches, picturesque scenery, lobster dinners, arguably the best-tasting strawberries in the world, and slower pace of life. P.E.I. was best known in Canada and elsewhere for the books, movies, and (current) television series about Lucy Maud Montgomery's turn-of-the-century literary creation, *Anne of Green Gables*.

P.E.I. Preserves felt they were competing in a worldwide market. Their visitors were from all over the world and in 1991, they expected the numbers to exceed 100,000 in the New Glasgow location alone. New Glasgow (population 200) was located in a rural setting equidistant (15 km) from Charlottetown and P.E.I.'s best known North Shore beaches. In their mailings, they planned to continue to promote Prince Edward Island as "Canada's Garden Province" and the "little jewel it was in everyone's heart!" They had benefited, and would continue to benefit, from that image.

Marketing

Products

The company had developed numerous products since its inception. These included many original varieties of preserves as well as honey, vinegar, mustard, and tea (repackaged). (Exhibit 2 contains a 1990 price list, ordering instructions, and a product picture used for mail order purposes.) The company had also added to the appeal of these products by offering gift packs composed of different products and packaging. With over 80 items, it felt that it had achieved a diverse product line and efforts in developing new product lines were expected to decrease in the future. Approximately three quarters of total retail sales (including wholesale and mail order) came from the products the company made itself. Of these, three quarters were jam preserves.

With the success of P.E.I. Preserves, imitation was inevitable. In recent years, several other small firms in P.E.I. had begun to retail specialty preserves. Another company which produced preserves in Ontario emphasized the Green Gables tie-in on its labels.

Price

P.E.I. Preserves were not competing with "low-end" products and felt their price reinforced their customers' perception of quality. The 11 types of jam

EXHIBIT 2 P.E.I. Preserves Mail Order Catalogue

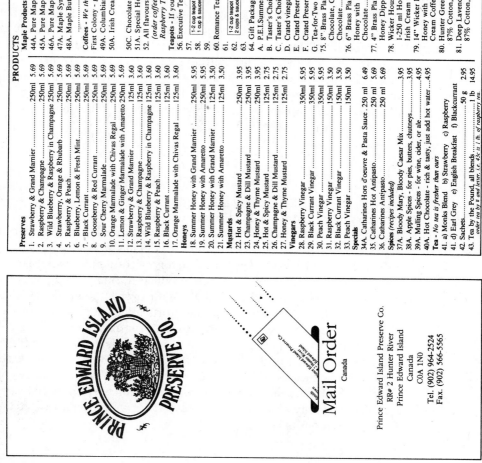

PRODUCTS

Preserves

1. Strawberry & Grand Marnier	250ml	5.69
2. Raspberry & Champagne	250ml	5.69
3. Wild Blueberry & Raspberry in Champagne	250ml	5.69
4. Strawberry, Orange & Rhubarb	250ml	5.69
5. Raspberry & Peach	250ml	5.69
6. Blueberry, Lemon & Fresh Mint	250ml	5.69
7. Black Currant	250ml	5.69
8. Gooseberry & Red Currant	250ml	5.69
9. Sour Cherry Marmalade	250ml	5.69
10. Orange Marmalade with Chivas Regal	250ml	5.69
11. Lemon & Ginger Marmalade with Amaretto	250ml	5.69
12. Strawberry & Grand Marnier	125ml	3.60
13. Raspberry & Champagne	125ml	3.60
14. Wild Blueberry & Raspberry in Champagne	125ml	3.60
15. Raspberry & Peach	125ml	3.60
16. Black Currant	125ml	3.60
17. Orange Marmalade with Chivas Regal	125ml	3.60

Honeys

18. Summer Honey with Grand Marnier	250ml	5.95
19. Summer Honey with Amaretto	250ml	5.95
20. Summer Honey with Grand Marnier	125ml	3.50
21. Summer Honey with Amaretto	125ml	3.50

Mustards

22. Hot & Spicy Mustard	250ml	3.95
23. Champagne & Dill Mustard	250ml	3.95
24. Honey & Thyme Mustard	125ml	2.75
25. Hot & Spicy Mustard	125ml	2.75
26. Champagne & Dill Mustard	125ml	2.75
27. Honey & Thyme Mustard	125ml	2.75

Vinegars

28. Raspberry Vinegar	350ml	5.95
29. Black Currant Vinegar	350ml	5.95
30. Peach Vinegar	350ml	5.95
31. Raspberry Vinegar	150ml	3.50
32. Black Currant Vinegar	150ml	3.50
33. Peach Vinegar	150ml	3.50

Specials

34A. Catharines Hors d'oeuvre & Pasta Sauce	250 ml	6.49
35. Catharines Hot Antipasto	250 ml	5.69
36. Catharines Antipasto	250 ml	5.69

Spices *(recipes included)*

37A. Bloody Mary, Bloody Caesar Mix	3.95
38A. Apple Spices - for pies, butters, chutneys	3.95
39A. Mulling Spices - for wine, cider, or ale	4.95
40A. Hot Chocolate - rich & tasty, just add hot water	4.95

Tea - *No tea is fresher than ours*
41. a) Monks Blend b) Strawberry c) Raspberry
41. d) Earl Grey e) English Breakfast f) Blackcurrant

42. Sachets	50 g	2.95
43. Tea by the Pound, all blends	1 lb	14.95

order tea by # and letter, i.e. 43c is 1 lb. of raspberry tea.

Maple Products

44A. Pure Maple Syrup	100 ml	3.95
45A. Pure Maple Syrup	250 ml	5.95
46A. Pure Maple Syrup	500 ml	10.95
47A. Maple Syrup with Light Rum	250 ml	5.95
48A. Maple Butter, excellent on pancakes, toast or baking	250 ml	5.95

Coffees - *We think this is the best coffee available*
First Colony - ground coffee, available 8 oz. and 2 oz.

49A. Columbian Supremo	8 oz.	6.49
50A. Irish Cream 50B. Swiss Chocolate Almond		
50C. Chocolate Raspberry Truffle	8 oz.	6.49
51A. Special House Blend	8 oz.	6.49
52. All flavours available in 2 oz. packs	2 oz.	2.25

(order coffee by # and letter, i.e. 52C is a 2 oz Chocolate Raspberry Truffle)

Teapots - If you've had tea with us, these are the ones!

56. Executive Tea set Black with Sterling Silver		49.95
57.	Sky Blue with Sterling Silver	49.95
58.	Fern Green with Gold Inlay	49.95
59.	Rust with Gold Inlay	49.95
60. Romance Tea set Black with Sterling Silver		59.95
61.	Sky Blue with Sterling Silver	59.95
62.	Fern Green with Gold Inlay	59.95
63.	Rust with Gold Inlay	59.95

1-2 cup teapot, 1 cup & saucer
1-2 cup teapot, 2 cups & saucers

Gift Packages - We pack all for long journeys!

64. P.E.I.Summer House		24.99
A. Taster's Choice Duo.	2-125 ml Preserves Crated	8.25
B. Taster's Choice Trio.	2-125 ml Preserves, 1-125 Honey Crated	11.95
C. Crated vinegars	2-150ml Fruit Vinegars Crated	7.49
D. Crated Preserves (2 jars)	250 ml size	12.49
E. Crated Preserves (3 jars)	250 ml size	17.95
F. Tea-for-Two -	1-125 ml Preserves, Tea, 1-125 ml Honey	11.95
75. 8" Brass Planter - filled with Swiss Chocolate, Hot Chocolate, Chocolate Coffee and more		23.99
76. 6" Brass Planter - 1-125 ml Preserve, 1-125 ml Honey with Liqueur, Honey Dipper and Chocolate		16.50
77. 4" Brass Planter - 125 ml Honey with Liqueur and Honey Dipper		10.95
78. Wicker House - 2-250 ml Preserves with Liqueur, 1-250 ml Honey with Liqueur, 100 ml Maple Syrup, Irish Cream Coffee, Strawberry Tea		39.95
79. 14" Wicker Hamper - 1-125 ml Preserve, 1-125 ml Honey with Liqueur, 1 Raspberry Tea, 1 Irish Cream Coffee, Honey Dipper		32.95
80. Hunter Green S M L XL Sweatshirt		29.95
87% Cotton, 13% Poly, Preshrunk		
81. Deep Lavender S M L XL Sweatshirt		29.95
87% Cotton, 13% Poly, Preshrunk		

PRINCE EDWARD ISLAND PRESERVE CO.

Mail Order
Canada

Prince Edward Island Preserve Co.
RR# 2 Hunter River
Prince Edward Island
Canada
C0A 1N0
Tel. (902) 964-2524
Fax. (902) 566-5565

EXHIBIT 2 (Continued)

Shipping cost per Address

Value of Order	*Shipping Cost
$ 0. - $30.	5.00
$31. - $40.	6.00
$41. - $55.	7.00
$56. - $65.	8.00
$66. - $75.	9.00
$76. - $100.	10.00
$101. & over	5% of order

All packages are packed well for shipping. We use double strength corrugated boxes and finish the packages with a heavy brown paper wrap.

*Please note that if the postage cost is less than the amount charged to you, we then will charge you the least amount. That is why we prefer if you paid by credit card. Thank you, Bruce.

Gift Wrapping
$3.50 per package

Using the appropriate gift wrap for the season, we'll give your package that little extra. We can supply a small card with your salutation, or if you send us your card with your order, we will include it.

Gift Packaging
Friends, we have many packaging ideas, too many for our catalogue. If you wish us to do up a basket in a certain price range, or any special order for that matter just give us a call, fax or mail in your request. We are here for you!

Method of Payment

☐ MasterCard ☐ Visa

CREDIT CARD NUMBER
[ ][ ][ ][ ] [ ][ ][ ][ ] [ ][ ][ ][ ] [ ][ ][ ][ ]

Cardholder Name _____
Please Print

mo./___ yr.___
Expiry Date

We require a signature _____

---

① SOLD TO: ☐ Mr. ☐ Mrs. ☐ Ms.

Name _____ Please Print

Address _____

City _____ Prov _____ PostalCode _____
May we have your phone number in case of a question about your order?

Home ( ) _____ Work ( ) _____

Send to me at the above address.
Ship to arrive: ☐ Now ☐ Christmas ☐ Other.........

Prod.#	Quantity	Price Each	Gift Wrap	Total Price
			3.50 ☐	
			3.50 ☐	
			3.50 ☐	
			3.50 ☐	
			3.50 ☐	
			3.50 ☐	
			3.50 ☐	
			Shipping	
			Total Cost	

② Send to: ☐ Mr. ☐ Mrs. ☐ Ms. ☐ Firm

Name _____ Please Print

Address _____

City _____ Prov. _____ Postal _____
Greetings from: _____
Ship to arrive: ☐ Now ☐ Christmas ☐ Other.........

Prod.#	Quantity	Price Each	Gift Wrap	Total Price
			3.50 ☐	
			3.50 ☐	
			3.50 ☐	
			3.50 ☐	
			3.50 ☐	
			3.50 ☐	
			3.50 ☐	
			Shipping	
			Total Cost	

Dear Shopper,

If you have visited our store recently, and wish to purchase an item which is not on this list, please feel free to do so.

On a separate sheet of paper, write a description of the item to the best of your ability, and we will do our best to satisfy your request.

sincerely,

Bruce MacNaughton

For *FAST* delivery call:
(9:00 am to 5:00 pm A.S.T.)

(902) 964-2524
Fax (902) 566-5565

*Prices subject to change without notice.

Exhibit 2 *(Concluded)*

preserves retailed for $5.89 for a 250 ml jar, significantly more than any grocery store product. However, grocery stores did not offer jam products made with such a high fruit content and with champagne, liqueur, or whisky.

In mid-1991, the company introduced a 10 percent increase in price (to $5.89) and, to date, had not received any negative reaction from customers. The food products were not subject to the 7 percent national goods and services tax or P.E.I.'s 10 percent provincial sales tax, an advantage over other gift products which the company would be stressing.

Promotion

Product promotion had been focused in two areas—personal contact with the consumer and catalogue distribution. Visitors to the New Glasgow location (approximately 80,000 in 1990) were enthusiastic upon meeting Bruce, "resplendent in the family kilt," reciting history and generally providing live entertainment. Bruce and the other staff members realized the value of this "island touch" and strove to ensure that all visitors to New Glasgow left with both a positive feeling and purchased products.

Visitors were also encouraged to visit the New Glasgow location through a cooperative scheme whereby other specialty retailers provided a coupon for a free cup of coffee or tea at P.E.I. Preserves. In 1991, roughly 2,000 of these coupons were redeemed.

Approximately 5,000 people received their mail-order catalogue annually. They had experienced an order rate of 7.5 percent with the average order being $66. They hoped to devote more time and effort to their mail-order business in an effort to extend their marketing and production period. For 1991–92, the order rate was expected to increase by as much as 15 percent because the catalogue was to be mailed two weeks earlier than in the previous year. The catalogues cost $1 each to print and mail.

In addition to mail order, the company operated with an ad hoc group of wholesale distributors. These wholesalers were divided between Nova Scotia, Ontario, and other locations. For orders as small as $150, buyers could purchase from the wholesalers' price list. Wholesale prices were on average 60 percent of the retail/mail order price. Total wholesale trade for the coming year was projected at $150,000 but had been higher in the past.

Danamar Imports was a Toronto-based specialty food store supplier which had previously provided P.E.I. Preserves to hundreds of specialty food stores in Ontario. Danamar had annually ordered $80,000 worth of P.E.I. Preserves at 30 percent below the wholesale price. This arrangement was amicably discontinued in 1990 by MacNaughton due to uncertainty about whether he was profiting from this contract. P.E.I. Preserves had a list of the specialty stores which Danamar had previously supplied and was planning to contact them directly in late 1991.

Over the past few years, the company had received numerous enquiries for quotations on large-scale shipments. Mitsubishi had asked for a price on a container load of preserves. Airlines and hotels were interested in obtaining preserves in 28 or 30 gram single-service bottles. One hotel chain, for example, had expressed interest in purchasing 3,000,000 bottles if the cost could be kept under $0.40 per unit. (Bruce had not proceeded due to the need to purchase $65,000 worth of bottling equipment and uncertainty about his production costs.) This same hotel chain had more recently been assessing the ecological implications of the packaging waste which would be created with the use of so many small bottles. They were now weighing the hygiene implications of serving jam out of multicustomer-use larger containers in their restaurants. They had asked MacNaughton to quote on $300,000 worth of jam in two-litre bottles.

Financial

The company had enjoyed a remarkable rate of growth since its inception. Sales volumes had increased in each of the six years of operations, from an initial level of $30,000 to 1990's total of $785,000. These sales were made up of $478,000 from retail sales (including mail order) of what they manufactured and/or distributed, and $307,000 from the restaurants (the Tea Room in New Glasgow, and Perfect Cup Restaurant in Charlottetown.) Exhibits 3 and 4 provide income statements from these operations, while Exhibit 5 contains a consolidated balance sheet.

This growth, although indicative of the success of the product, has also created its share of problems. Typical of many small businesses which experience such rapid growth, the company had not secured financing suitable to its needs. This, coupled with the seasonal nature of the manufacturing operation, had caused numerous periods of severe cash shortages. From Bruce's perspective, the company's banker (Bank of Nova Scotia) had not been as supportive as it might have been. (The bank manager in Charlottetown had last visited the facility three years ago.) Bruce felt the solution to the problem of cash shortages was the issuance of preferred shares. "An infusion of 'long-term' working capital, at a relatively low rate of interest, will provide a stable financial base for the future," he said.

At this time, MacNaughton was attempting to provide a sound financial base for the continued operation of the company. He had decided to offer a preferred share issue in the amount of $100,000. These shares would bear interest at the rate of 8 percent cumulative and would be nonvoting, nonparticipating. He anticipated that the sale of these shares would be complete by December 31, 1991. In the interim, he required a line of credit in the amount of $100,000, which he requested to be guaranteed by the Prince Edward Island Development Agency.

EXHIBIT 3	**P.E.I. Preserve Co. Ltd. (Manufacturing and Retail)**

Statement of Earnings and Retained Earnings
Year Ended January 31, 1991
(unaudited)

	1991	*1990*
Sales	$478,406	$425,588
Cost of sales	217,550	186,890
Gross Margin	260,856	238,698
Expenses		
Advertising and promotional items	20,632	6,324
Automobile	7,832	3,540
Doubtful accounts	1,261	—
Depreciation and amortization	11,589	12,818
Dues and fees	1,246	2,025
Electricity	7,937	4,951
Heat	4,096	4,433
Insurance	2,426	1,780
Interest and bank charges	5,667	17,482
Interest on long-term debt	23,562	9,219
Management salary	29,515	32,600
Office and supplies	12,176	10,412
Professional fees	19,672	10,816
Property tax	879	621
Rent	—	975
Repairs and maintenance	6,876	9,168
Salaries and wages	70,132	96,386
Telephone and facsimile	5,284	5,549
Trade shows	18,588	12,946
	249,370	242,045
Earnings (loss) from manufacturing operation	11,486	(3,347)
Management fees	—	7,250
Loss from restaurant operations—Schedule 2	3,368	—
Earnings before income taxes	8,118	3,903
Income taxes	181	1,273
Net earnings	7,937	2,630
Retained earnings, beginning of year	9,290	6,660
Retained earnings, end of year	$ 17,227	$ 9,290

EXHIBIT 4   **P.E.I. Preserve Co. Ltd.**
Schedule of Restaurant Operations
(Charlottetown and New Glasgow)
Year Ended January 31, 1991
(unaudited)

	Schedule 2
	1991
Sales	$306,427
Cost of sales	
Purchases and freight	122,719
Inventory, end of year	11,864
	110,855
Salaries and wages for food preparation	42,883
	153,738
Gross margin	152,689
Expenses	
Advertising	2,927
Depreciation	6,219
Electricity	4,897
Equipment lease	857
Insurance	389
Interest and bank charges	1,584
Interest on long-term debt	2,190
Office and supplies	2,864
Propane	2,717
Rent	22,431
Repairs and maintenance	3,930
Salaries and wages for service	90,590
Supplies	12,765
Telephone	1,697
	156,057
Loss from restaurant operations	$ 3,368

Projected sales for the year ended January 31, 1992 were

New Glasgow Restaurant	$ 110,000
Charlottetown Restaurant	265,000
Retail (New Glasgow)	360,000
Wholesale (New Glasgow)	150,000
Mail order (New Glasgow)	50,000
Retail (Charlottetown)	75,000
Total	$1,010,000

EXHIBIT 5	**P.E.I. Preserve Co. Ltd.**

Balance Sheet
As at January 31, 1991
(unaudited)

	1991	1990
Current assets		
Cash	$ 5,942	$ 592
Accounts receivable		
Trade	12,573	6,511
Investment tax credit	1,645	2,856
Other	13,349	35,816
Inventory	96,062	85,974
Prepaid expenses	2,664	6,990
	132,235	138,739
Grant receivable	2,800	1,374
Property, plant, and equipment	280,809	162,143
Recipes and trade name, at cost	10,000	10,000
	$425,844	$312,256
Current liabilities		
Bank indebtedness	$ 2,031	$ 9,483
Operating and other loans	54,478	79,000
Accounts payable and accrued liabilities	64,143	32,113
Current portion of long-term debt	23,657	14,704
	144,309	135,300
Long-term debt	97,825	99,679
Deferred government assistance	54,810	—
Payable to shareholder, noninterest bearing, no set terms		
of repayment	43,373	49,687
	340,317	284,666
Shareholders' equity		
Share capital	55,000	5,000
Contributed surplus	13,300	13,300
Retained earnings	17,227	9,290
	85,527	27,590
	$425,844	$312,256

Operations

Preserve production took place on site, in an area visible through glass windows from the retail floor. Many visitors, in fact, would videotape operations during their visit to the New Glasgow store, or would watch the process while tasting the broad selection of sample products freely available.

Production took place on a batch basis. Ample production capacity existed for the $30,000 main kettle used to cook the preserves. Preserves were made five months a year, on a single-shift, five-day-per-week basis. Even then, the main kettle was in use only 50 percent of the time.

Only top-quality fruit was purchased. As much as possible, P.E.I. raw materials were used. For a short period the fruit could be frozen until time for processing.

The production process was labour intensive. Bruce was considering the feasibility of moving to an incentive-based salary system to increase productivity and control costs. Because a decorative cloth fringe was tied over the lid of each bottle, bottling could not be completely automated. A detailed production cost analysis had recently been completed. While there were some minor differences due to ingredients, the variable costs averaged $1.25 per 250 ml bottle. This was made up of ingredients ($.56), labour ($.28), and packaging $.20/bottle, $.11/lid, $.03/label, and $.07/fabric and ribbon).

Restaurant operations were the source of many of Bruce's headaches. The New Glasgow restaurant had evolved over time from offering dessert and coffee/tea to its present status where it was also open for meals all day.

Management

During the peak summer period, P.E.I. Preserves employed 45 people among the restaurants, manufacturing area, and retail locations. Of these, five were managerial positions (see Exhibit 6). The company was considered a good place to work, with high morale and limited turnover. Nonetheless, most employees (including some management) were with the company on a seasonal basis. This was a concern to MacNaughton, who felt that if he could provide year-round employment, he would be able to attract and keep the best-quality staff.

Carol Rombough was an effective assistant general manager and book-keeper. Maureen Dickieson handled production with little input required from Bruce. Kathy MacPherson was in the process of providing, for the first time, accurate cost information. Natalie Leblanc was managing the new retail outlet in Charlottetown, and assisting on some of the more proactive marketing initiatives Bruce was considering.

Bruce felt that the company had survived on the basis of word of mouth. Few follow-up calls on mail order had ever been done. Bruce did not enjoy participating in trade shows—even though he received regular solicitations for them from across North America. In 1992, he planned to participate in four *retail* shows, all of them in or close to P.E.I.

Bruce hoped to be able eventually to hire a sales/marketing manager but could not yet afford $30,000 for the necessary salary.

The key manager continued to be MacNaughton. He described himself as "a fair person to deal with, but shrewd when it comes to purchasing. However, I like to spend enough money to ensure that what we do—we do right." Financial and managerial constraints meant that Bruce felt stretched

---
EXHIBIT 6   Key Executives

President and general manager—Bruce MacNaughton, Age 35

Experience: Seventeen years of "front line" involvement with the public in various capacities.

Seven years of managing and promoting Prince Edward Island Preserve Co. Ltd.

Past director of the Canadian Specialty Food Association.

Responsibilities: To develop and oversee the short-, mid-, and long-term goals of the company.

To develop and maintain quality products for the marketplace.

To oversee the management of personnel.

To develop and maintain customer relations at both the wholesale and retail level.

To develop and maintain harmonious relations with government and the banking community.

Assistant general manager—Carol Rombough, Age 44

Experience: Twenty years as owner/operator of a manufacturing business.

Product marketing at both the wholesale and retail level.

Personnel management.

Bookkeeping in a manufacturing environment.

Three years with the Prince Edward Island Preserve Co. Ltd.

Responsibilities: All bookkeeping functions (i.e., accounts receivable, accounts payable, payroll).

Staff management—scheduling and hiring.

Customer relations.

Production manager—Maureen Dickieson, Age 29

Experience: Seven years of production experience in the dairy industry.

Three years with the Prince Edward Island Preserve Co. Ltd.

Responsibilities: Oversee and participate in all production.

Planning and scheduling production.

Requisition of supplies.

Consultant—Kathy MacPherson, Certified General Accountant, Age 37

Experience: Eight years as a small business owner/manager.

Eight years in financial planning and management.

Reponsibilities: To implement an improved system of product costing.

To assist in the development of internal controls.

To compile monthly internal financial statements.

To provide assistance and/or advise as required by management.

Store Manager—Natalie LeBlanc, Age 33

Experience: Fifteen years in retail.

Responsibilities: To manage the retail store in the CP Hotel.

Assist with mail-order business.

Marketing duties as assigned.

("I haven't had a vacation in years") and unable to pursue all of the ideas he had for developing the business.

The Japanese Consumer

MacNaughton's interest in the possibility of reaching the Tokyo consumer had been formed from two factors: the large number of Japanese visitors to P.E.I. Preserves, and the fact that the largest export shipment the company had ever made had been to Japan. MacNaughton had never visited Japan, although he had been encouraged by Canadian federal government trade representatives to participate in food and gift shows in Japan. He was debating whether he should visit Japan during the coming year. Most of the information he had on Japan had been collected for him by a friend.

Japan was Canada's second most important source of foreign tourists. In 1990, there were 474,000 Japanese visitors to Canada, a figure which was expected to rise to 1,000,000 by 1995. Most Japanese visitors entered through the Vancouver or Toronto airports. Within Canada, the most popular destination was the Rocky Mountains (in Banff, Alberta, numerous stores catered specifically to Japanese consumers). Nearly 15,000 Japanese visited P.E.I. each year. Excluding airfare, these visitors to Canada spent an estimated $314 million, the highest per capita amount from any country.

The Japanese fascination with Prince Edward Island could be traced to the popularity of *Anne of Green Gables*. The Japanese translation of this and other books in the same series had been available for many years. However, the adoption of the book as required reading in the Japanese school system since the 1950s had resulted in widespread awareness and affection for "Anne with red hair" *and* P.E.I.

The high level of spending by Japanese tourists was due to a multitude of factors: the amount of disposable income available to them, one of the world's highest per person duty-free allowances (200,000 yen), and gift-giving traditions in the country. Gift-giving and entertainment expenses at the corporate level are enormous in Japan. In 1990, corporate entertainment expenses were almost ¥5 trillion, more than triple the U.S. level of ¥1.4 trillion. Corporate gift giving, while focused at both year-end (seibo) and the summer (chugen), in fact, occurred throughout the year.

Gift giving at the personal level was also widespread. The amount spent would vary depending on one's relationship with the recipient; however, one of the most common price points used by Japanese retailers for gift giving was offering choices for under ¥2000.

The Japanese Jam Market

Japanese annual consumption of jam was approximately 80,000 tons. Imports made up 6 to 9 percent of consumption, with higher grade products (¥470 or

---

EXHIBIT 7   Jam Distribution Channel in Japan

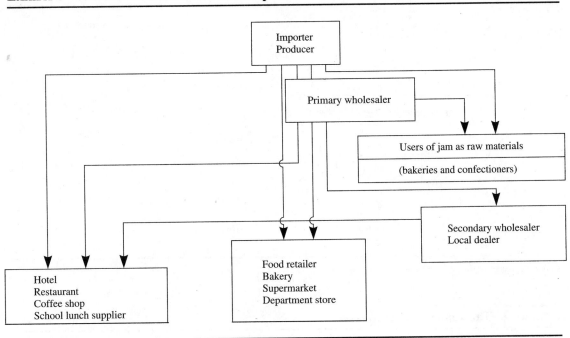

Source: Access to Japan's Import Market, *Tradescope,* June 1989.

---

more per kilo wholesale CIF) making up a third of this total. Several dozen firms imported jam and utilized a mix of distribution channels (see Exhibit 7). Prices varied, in part, according to the type of channel structure used. Exhibit 8 provides a common structure. Import duties for jams were high—averaging about 28 percent. Despite such a high tariff barrier, some firms had been successful in exporting to Japan. Excerpts from a report on how to access Japan's jam market successfully are contained in Exhibit 9.

Canadian World

In spring 1990, P.E.I. Preserves received its biggest ever export order; $50,000 worth of product was ordered (FOB New Glasgow) for ultimate shipment to Ashibetsu, on the northern Japanese island of Hokkaido. These products were to be offered for sale at Canadian World, a new theme park scheduled to open in July 1990.

In 1981, Japan's first theme park was built outside Tokyo. Called Tokyo Disneyland, in 1989 it had an annual revenue of $815 million, 14.7 million visitors, and profits of $119 million. Not surprisingly, this success has spawned

---

EXHIBIT 8   Example of Price Markups in Japan

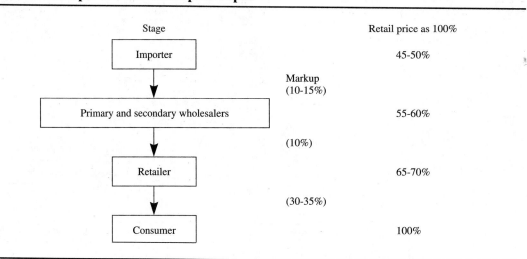

	Stage	Retail price as 100%
	Importer	45-50%
Markup (10-15%)		
	Primary and secondary wholesalers	55-60%
(10%)		
	Retailer	65-70%
(30-35%)		
	Consumer	100%

Source: Access to Japan's Import Market, *Tradescope,* June 1989.

EXHIBIT 9   The Japanese Jam Market

To expand sales of imported jam or to enter the Japanese market for the first time, it is necessary to develop products after precise study of the market's needs. Importers who are making efforts to tailor their products to the Japanese market have been successfully expanding their sales by 10 percent each year. Based on the analysis of successful cases of imported jam, the following factors may be considered very important.

Diversification of consumer preferences: Strawberry jam occupies about 50 percent of the total demand for jam and its share is continuing to rise. Simultaneously, more and more varieties of jam are being introduced.

Low sugar content: European exporters have successfully exported low-sugar jam that meets the needs of the Japanese market. Jam with a sugar content of less than 65 percent occupies a share of 65–70 percent of the market on a volume basis.

Smaller containers: Foreign manufacturers who stick to packaging products in large-sized containers (650g, 440g, 250g), even though their products are designed for household use, have been failing to expand their sales. On the other hand, foreign manufacturers who have developed products in smaller containers (14g, 30g, 42g) specifically for the Japanese market have achieved successful results.

Fashionable items: Contents and quantity are not the only important aspects of jam. The shape and material quality of the containers and their caps, label design, and product name can also influence sales. It is also important that the label not be damaged in any way.

Development of gift items: Sets of various types of imported jams are popular as gift items. For example, there are sets of 10 kinds of jam in 40g mini-jars (retail price ¥2,000) sold as gift sets.

Selection of distribution channel: Since general trading companies, specialty importers, and jam manufacturers each have their own established distribution channels, the selection of the most appropriate channel is of the utmost importance.

Source: Access to Japan's Market Import, *Tradescope,* June 1989.

a theme park industry in Japan. Over the past decade, 20 parks with wide-ranging themes have opened. Another 16 were expected to open in 1991–92.

The idea to construct a theme park about Canada was conceived by a Japanese advertising agency hired by the Ashibetsu city council to stop the city's declining economy. The city's population had decreased from 75,000 in 1958 to 26,000 in 1984, due principally to mine closures.

With capital investment of ¥750,000,000, construction started in mid-1989 on 48 of the 156 available hectares. The finished site included six restaurants, 18 souvenir stores, 16 exhibit event halls, an outdoor stage with 12,000 seats, and 20 hectares planted in herbs and lavender.

The theme of Canadian World was less a mosaic of Canada than it was a park devoted to the world of Anne of Green Gables. The entrance to the Canadian World was a replica of Kensingston Station in P.E.I. The north gateway was Brightriver Station, where Anne first met with Matthew. There was a full-scale copy of the Green Gables house, Orwell School where you could actually learn English like Anne did, and so forth. Canadian World employed 55 full-time and 330 part-time staff. This included a high school girl from P.E.I. who played Anne—complete with (dyed) red hair—dressed in Victorian period costume.

In late August 1991, Canadian World still had a lot of P.E.I. Preserves' products for sale. Lower than expected sales could be traced to a variety of problems. First, overall attendance at Canadian World had been 205,000 in the first year, significantly lower than the expected 300,000. Second, the product was priced higher than many competitive offerings. For reasons unknown to Canadian World staff, the product sold for 10 percent more than expected (¥1200 versus ¥1086).

Wholesale price in P.E.I.	$3.50
Freight ($4.20/kilo, P.E.I. to Hokkaido)	.80
Duty (28% of wholesale price + freight)	1.20
Landed cost in Japan	5.50
Importer's margin (15%)	.83
Price to primary wholesaler	6.33
Wholesaler margin (10%)	.63
Price to retailer	6.96
Canadian World markup (30%)	2.09
Expected retail price	$9.05
Exchange (Cdn. $1.00 = 120 yen)	¥1086

Third, the product mix chosen by the Japanese buyers appeared to be inappropriate. While it was difficult to locate any of the company's remaining strawberry preserves in the various Canadian World outlets which carried it, other products had not moved at all. Canadian World personnel did not have a tracking system for product-by-product sales. Fourth, the company's gift packs were not always appropriately sized or priced. One suggestion had been to package the preserves in cardboard gift boxes of three large (250 ml) or five small (125 ml) bottles for eventual sale for under ¥2000.

An increasing portion of all of the gifts being sold at Canadian World were, in fact, being made in Japan. Japanese sourcing was common due to the high Japanese duties on imports, the transportation costs from Canada, and the unfamiliarity of Canadian companies with Japanese consumer preferences.

The Tokyo Market

With 10 million residents, Tokyo was the largest city in Japan and one of the most crowded cities anywhere. Thirty million people lived within 50 km of Tokyo's Imperial Palace. As the economic centre of the nation, Tokyo also had the most expensive land in the world—U.S. $150,000 per square meter in the city centre. Retail space in one of Tokyo's major shopping districts would cost $75–$160 per square metre or $1,600–$3,400 per month for a shop equivalent in size to that in the CP Prince Edward Hotel. Prices in the Ginza were even higher. In addition to basic rent, all locations required a deposit (guarantee money which would be repaid when the tenant gave up the lease) of at least $25,000. Half of the locations available in a recent survey also charged administrative/maintenance fees (5–12 percent of rent), while in about one third of the locations a "reward" (gift) was paid by tenants to the owner at the time the contract was signed. For a small site, it might amount to $10–15,000.

The Toronto Market

With 3 million people, Toronto was Canada's largest city and economic centre. It contained the country's busiest airport (15 million people used it each year) and was a popular destination for tourists. Each year, roughly 20 million people visited Toronto for business or vacation.

MacNaughton's interest in Toronto was due to its size, the local awareness of P.E.I., and the high perceived potential volume of sales. The company did not have a sales agent in Toronto.

The Toronto market was well served by mass market and specialty jam producers at all price points. Numerous domestic and imported products were available. Prices started as low as $1 (or less) for a 250 ml bottle of high sugar, low fruit product. Prices increased to $2.00–$2.50 for higher fruit, natural brands, and increased again to $3.00–$3.50 for many of the popular branded imports. The highest-priced products, such as P.E.I. Preserves, were characterized by even higher fruit content, highest-quality ingredients, and a broader selection of product offerings.

The specialty domestic producers were from various provinces and tended to have limited distribution areas. The specialty imports were frequently from France or England. The Canadian tariff on imports was 15 percent for most countries. From the United States, it was 10.5 percent and declining.

The cost of retail space in Toronto varied according to location but was slightly lower than that in Tokyo. The cost of renting 22 square metres would be $100 per square metre per month (plus common area charges and taxes of $15 per square metre per month) in a major suburban shopping mall, and somewhat higher in the downtown core. Retail staff salaries were similar in Toronto and Tokyo, both of which were higher than those paid in P.E.I.

Future Directions

MacNaughton was the first to acknowledge that, while the business had been "built on gut and emotion, rather than analysis," this was insufficient for the future. The challenge was to determine the direction and timing of the desired change.

RAYMARK
TECHNOLOGIES INC.

Raymark Technologies Inc. (Raymark) had just completed another extremely successful year. Founded in 1976, Raymark, an Ottawa, Ontario-based company that produced hardware and software interfaces for industrial control equipment, had grown from 15 employees in 1983 to 425 employees and sales of almost $50 million in 1993. Nevertheless, in April 1994, Steve Thomas, founder and President of Raymark, was not entirely sure if the current structure of the partnership with Sentor Equipment (Sentor) was in the best long-term interests for the firm. There was little question that the relationship with Sentor was a major part of Raymark's success. However, Raymark was no longer a struggling young firm in search of markets and customers. Several acquisitions in recent years had allowed Raymark to lessen its dependence on Sentor as a customer, although sales to Sentor still represented 75 percent of total Raymark sales. The question now facing Thomas was what shape the relationship should take in future years. Perhaps, Thomas thought, it was time to restructure the 10-year-old agreement between Sentor and Raymark.

Raymark Technologies

Raymark was a world leader in products used for a range of applications as diverse as semiconductor manufacturing, airline baggage handling, integrated building control, retail point-of-sale terminals, blood analysis machines, and industrial process control for a variety of industries including brewing, food processing, and hazardous chemical disposal.

The firm was founded in 1976 by Steve Thomas. After earning a doctorate in Engineering Physics from the University of Toronto and working for several

---

This case was prepared by Andrew Inkpen for the sole purpose of providing material for class discussion. Copyright 1995 © Andrew Inkpen.

years as a consulting engineer, Thomas decided to start his own business. Using microprocessors, Raymark was able to enter the industrial control market. With Steve Thomas as the creative force at Raymark, the firm created new computer alternatives to the traditional push-button control market.

From the outset, Raymark developed products able to facilitate the exchange of information between computers and direct manufacturing processes. Using innovative graphics and communication devices, manufacturing processes could be monitored and controlled. The company's monitors, computers, and realtime software were used to simplify the interface between people and their control systems by providing easy ways for users to effectively interact with computer-controlled machines and processes. A continuing objective was the modification of the controls to make them even more sensitive and sophisticated. In recent years, this had led Raymark into the manufacturing of sensors for robotic hands.

Raymark management viewed the firm as both a software and a hardware firm, and for many products Raymark's software and hardware skills were equally important. For example, Raymark manufactured a line of touch control systems that incorporated a touch screen computer with high-quality graphics capabilities. The product was housed in a rugged case impervious to chemicals and cleaning solutions. The computer was a complete PC that operated in a DOS and Microsoft Windows environment. Standard off-the-shelf software development tools could be used to create unique applications. The product could be customized with a variety of different-colored cases, buttons, and function keys. Raymark utilized advanced computer-aided design and simulation tools to design and manufacture the touch-screen computers in Raymark in-house facilities.

Underlying the success at Raymark was a corporate culture dedicated to innovation. Steve Thomas was largely responsible for the innovative spirit in his talented employees. As a business press article emphasized, constant innovation drove the culture of Raymark:

> Like so many other firms making leading-edge products, Thomas understands the innovative treadmill Raymark walks. A high-tech item has a short life cycle. A company must redemonstrate its ingenuity about every year and a half. But, risky product development expenditures eat up revenues. For example, half of Raymark's payroll goes for developmental work. According to Thomas, one can't simply keep the faith that new ideas will bear fruit.

The Industrial Controls Industry

Considered a mature market in the mid-1980s, technological advances in computer hardware and software were driving the industrial controls industry in many new directions. Industrial controls were found in virtually every manufacturing location and increasingly, in a range of service industries. At their most basic, controls were used to start, regulate, stop, and protect electric motors. Other industry controls were used in factory floor applications requiring logic, data transfer, machine diagnostics, computer interfacing, and distributed control. The automation of many industrial processes was facilitated by the use of sophisticated control devices.

The traditional control market covered such products as starters, controls for adjustable speed drives, motor control centers, mechanical positioning sensors, and relays. In many industries, these traditional products had been replaced by electronic and computer-based controls using operator interfaces (such as those produced by Raymark). Computer-based controls with enormous information-gathering and processing capabilities could be used in large-scale industrial control environments in which hundreds of variables had to be continuously controlled. These type of controls eliminated the use of conventional application-specific and general industrial controls.

With the changes in the technological nature of industrial controls there has been a consolidation in the controls industry in the United States. The largest companies included Allen-Bradley, Sentor, Texas Instruments, and Eaton. Each of these companies was spending large sums of money on the development of in-house computer expertise. Competition from firms in Japan, the United Kingdom, Germany, and Switzerland was also increasing.

The Sentor-Raymark Partnership

The relationship between Sentor and Raymark began in the early 1980s. At that time, Raymark was a struggling young high tech company with plenty of ideas and initiative, little capital, and few products. The company had only 15 customers, minimal infrastructure, and was relying on sales representatives and distributors to market its products.

Sentor, a firm with $1.6 billion in sales in 1994, was based in Rochester, Michigan, a Detroit suburb. Sentor was a leading firm in the industrial controls industry with sales channels throughout the world. More than 30 percent of Sentor sales were exports. Sentor was founded in 1921 as a manufacturer of electric motors and electric motor parts. In 1994, Sentor offered specialized control and automation expertise for virtually every industry. Sentor produced more than 250,000 control products and variations. Sentor was an industry leader in plant floor automation, with a focus on helping customers become more competitive through increased manufacturing flexibility. Some of Sentor's automation and control product categories were programmable controls, communications networks, sensing and motor control devices, machine vision, and computer numerical control systems.

In 1982, a large automation equipment and industrial controls manufacturer, Sterling Automation (Sterling), developed an innovative computerized technology for operating and controlling equipment. Sentor, a direct competitor of Sterling, had not yet developed a similar technology for its products.

Without this operator interface technology and as rapid developments in microprocessors began to occur, Sentor was in danger of being leapfrogged in technology by its competitors.

Sentor's industrial automation group decided it could not take the time to develop new operator interface technology in-house. Sentor management began discussions with a number of outside firms to supply operator interface hardware and software. Steve Thomas heard through the grapevine that Sentor was looking for a partner and was able to get Raymark on the short list of potential Sentor suppliers. Sentor's objective in soliciting bids was to find a supplier to carry them for a few years until the technology could be developed in-house.

Raymark was selected as the firm to develop and supply the products to Sentor. After a year of negotiating, an agreement between Sentor and Raymark was signed in November 1983. The deal had two parts. One part was a commercial agreement for Raymark to supply a line of human-machine interface products to Sentor. Under the agreement, Raymark designed and manufactured products that were brand labelled by Sentor and sold as if they were Sentor's own products. These products were designed specifically to the requirements of Sentor customers. For example, in 1986 Raymark developed a family of intelligent plant floor terminals with integrated touch screens that were more functional and cost effective than controls with push buttons and indicators. Raymark also manufactured a set of realtime software products that integrated process control, data management, and graphical operator interface for industrial personal computers. Raymark had been able to maintain its innovative lead in control products that could perform a very wide variety of graphics and depended on the development of both software and hardware devices.

Sentor used many Raymark products as integral elements of its industrial control systems. For products distributed by Sentor, Raymark relied largely on Sentor to keep them up-to-date on customer and market developments. With the exception of a few visits to large Sentor customers in conjunction with Sentor marketing personnel, Sentor preferred that Raymark not interact directly with Sentor customers. While Raymark was free to sell to Sentor competitors outside the United States, the firm had never done so. Recently, with Sentor's permission, Raymark had started selling to a U.S.-based competitor of Sentor. The product involved was not directly competitive with the products sold to Sentor.

The deal provided Sentor with exclusive U.S. rights to certain Raymark products. Raymark was prohibited from selling the specified products to any Sentor competitors in the United States. Raymark was free to sell these products to customers outside the United States. The commercial agreement was initially for five years. After five years, each party to the agreement would have the right to end the agreement 90 days before the end of the Raymark fiscal year. As of early 1994, the commercial agreement was still in place.

Sentor's Purchase of Raymark Stock

The second part of the Sentor agreement involved Sentor acquiring 25 percent of Raymark stock for $1.5 million. After Sentor's purchase, there were four Raymark shareholders, each with a one-quarter interest. Not long after the Sentor agreement was signed, the other two shareholders were bought out by Thomas and Sentor. Since Thomas had little capital, payment to the two shareholders was via Raymark earnings. This left two Raymark shareholders, each with 50 percent equity: Thomas Holdings Inc., a company wholly owned by Steve Thomas, and Sentor.

Although the ownership was equal between Thomas and Sentor, voting on the board of directors was not. When Steve Thomas founded Raymark, he opted not to use a lawyer. Instead, he used a $15 "do-it-yourself" articles of incorporation. In these articles, the president had an extra vote on the board of directors. As president of Raymark, Thomas retained the extra vote. The articles of incorporation clearly specified the decisions that could be made at the board level and those to be voted on by shareholders. Decisions on new share issues, stock options, and major sales of shares had to be voted on by shareholders. Decisions involving product lines, marketing, corporate acquisitions, and capital expansions were to be made at the board level.

Within Raymark, the deal with Sentor was not seen as a case of "do a deal with Sentor or die." The partnership was viewed as a means of getting a channel to North American and worldwide markets with a high-quality firm. Sentor controlled as much as 40 percent of the U.S. and Canadian markets. Thomas had looked at other options and this looked like the best one. As far as Thomas was concerned, the critical piece missing in Raymark's strategy was a way to the market. The products and technology were in place; Sentor provided market access. A relationship with a well-known and highly respected company like Sentor provided Raymark with instant credibility. In a sense, it was a way for Thomas to buy market share. The deal also forced Raymark to develop new management processes and systems, without which Raymark would have been unable to meet Sentor's very strict customer expectations.

Sentor's objectives in forming the relationship were very straightforward. Sentor needed an inexpensive visual interface that was competitive with other products on the market. Since the product was not going to be developed in-house, at least initially, an outside supplier was required. The commercial agreement with Raymark guaranteed supply and its noncompetition clause meant that Raymark would have to work very closely with Sentor.

R&D and Innovation at Raymark

Raymark products often had life cycles of less than two years. Although some products remained installed for up to 10 years, a continual process of improvement resulting in automatic obsolescence was under way in the industrial controls industry. Consequently, the creation of new products and the improvement of existing products was critical for Raymark. As evidence of the emphasis on innovation, Raymark allocated 15 percent of sales revenue to research and development. Of the 86 people in the R&D group, more than half were software engineers or computer scientists. As Thomas explained, "This company has grown because we are committed to the development of new products. We reinvest our money and develop new products. So far, we have managed to grow steadily and it has worked very well."

For Raymark, labor empowerment was a central feature of the business. All employees were treated as part of a team. Raymark had a single cafeteria where everybody ate together, including Thomas and other senior managers. Thomas described his ideas about empowerment and the Raymark corporate culture:

> High-tech companies require a certain kind of culture. If we do something which interferes with that culture, Raymark will not be successful and we will lose our best people. We need highly responsive teams that can work closely together.
>
> Raymark has annual awards of excellence [The reception room walls were decorated with photographs of employees receiving awards of excellence.] The objective of the awards is to recognize people who have done outstanding things. Everyone at Raymark is eligible for an award. The awards are peer judged and moderated by the Raymark VPs. We don't want to sprinkle favors and reward our favorites. We want people to be judged as outstanding by their colleagues.
>
> Under various categories, peer committees decide who has done an outstanding job. We then hand out about $10,000 worth of cash bonuses to the winners. In my opinion, people deserve to be recognized and that is the culture we have tried to build at Raymark. After the winners have been chosen, the results are released to the media because people thrive on recognition.

Personnel turnover at Raymark was very low, averaging about 2 percent per year. At the management level, the same team had been in place for almost 10 years. In contrast, the Sentor managers interacting with Raymark changed regularly. According to a senior manager at Raymark, credit for the durability of the Raymark management team must be given to Thomas:

> He is a very bright person with a high IQ. He has excellent management skills and is an excellent person to work for. Even though he is very smart and capable, he is willing to use outsiders for help when necessary.

Raymark Performance

Prior to signing the agreement with Sentor, Raymark's sales were less than $1 million per year. In 1984, sales jumped to just under $3 million. Sales reached $10 million in 1989 and almost $50 million in 1993. Of this total, 15 percent could be attributed to software and the remainder to hardware. In 1994, sales were expected to reach $67 million. Average sales growth over the past 10 years was 28 percent. Almost 75 percent of Raymark sales were through Sentor channels, down from 100 percent a few years earlier.

The end user value of Raymark's 1993 sales was approximately $100 million. Almost 90 percent of the end users of Raymark products were located outside Canada. As Thomas explained, "We are competing with firms that are primarily located in the United States. Therefore, we have to compete with U.S. cost structures. And, we have to be careful that our cost structures stay in line."

Raymark's main facility in Ottawa was 92,000 square feet and two additional 18,000-square-foot areas were leased in Ottawa. Negotiations were under way to build a new 150,000 plant beside the existing plant.

Acquisitions

In 1992, Raymark acquired a division of an electronics firm based in Boston. This division was established as a subsidiary of Raymark called Raysys Inc. The division manufactured a complementary line of control products and had a solid base of domestic and international customers. Because the products sold by this new division would not be sold to Sentor, they were considered outside the Sentor–Raymark commercial agreement. Sentor management did not support this acquisition and voted against it at a Raymark board meeting. For the first time, Thomas exercised his majority vote on the board and the acquisition was made at a cost of $10 million, supported in part by a low-interest loan from the Ontario government.

In early 1994, Raymark purchased a business from a firm based in Chicago. After investing more than $15 million in the business, the Chicago firm decided to exit the business and sold it for $1.5 million. When the business was purchased, there were about 30 employees; after a few months Raymark had built the business up to 75 employees. The business manufactured components used in custom products and computer screens. This business provided Raymark with the opportunity to expand into new markets and strengthen its technological expertise. With the acquisition, Raymark acquired state-of-the-art equipment, several patented processes, and a highly qualified team of designers and manufacturing personnel. This new business was also set up as a Raymark subsidiary. Management in Chicago had a small minority interest in this division.

In both acquisitions, Raymark wasted little time in making its decision. According to Dan Wilson, Raymark's finance VP, one of the reasons the acquisitions were quickly and successfully executed is that "Raymark has faster lawyers than some of their competitors—that is one of our strategic competences."

The products in the new divisions, and other products not sold through Sentor channels, were marketed in various ways. Some products were sold directly to end-users, OEMs, and systems integrators. Geographic regional manufacturers' representatives were also used and in Europe, independent dealers were used for several products. At trade shows, Raymark products were shown at both a Raymark booth and at Sentor exhibits. Raymark and its divisions had 41 people involved in sales, marketing, and publications. The marketing personnel regularly interacted with Raymark R&D people.

Sentor and Raymark

The relationship with Sentor had lasted more than 10 years, which was quite unusual for Sentor. When Sentor made equity investments in small firms, one of two things usually happened. One, if Sentor was satisfied with the relationship and saw some strategic value in continuing it, Sentor would buy out the smaller firm and fold the company into the Sentor organization. Two, Sentor often ended its relationships after a few years because of conflict between the partners or because the original goals of the relationship were not achieved. By lasting ten years, the Raymark–Sentor relationship was unusual and a survivor.

Dan Wilson referred to the relationship with Sentor as a strategic partnership that benefitted both sides. Sentor was by far Raymark's largest customer. To a large degree, Raymark relied on Sentor for its market intelligence. The Sentor relationship provided additional purchasing leverage for Raymark and internationally, Raymark was able to capitalize on its relationship with a large, well-known firm like Sentor.

The relationship was beneficial to Raymark in other ways. For example, in 1986 Raymark was developing a new product line. Development costs were expected to run into the millions of dollars. Raymark management were seriously concerned that the company might exhaust its liquidity and be forced to lay off staff. After discussing the situation with Sentor, Sentor agreed to buy some products to help Raymark's cash flow. As a result, the new product line was successfully developed and no layoffs were necessary.

A primary concern for Raymark was that when Sentor saw a product or part of the business becoming lucrative or "strategic," Sentor tended to act like a Raymark competitor rather than a partner. In 1988, Sentor established its industrial computer and communications group to manufacture industrial computers and develop operator interface software for IBM personal computers. In the early 1990s, Sentor set up two engineering teams with the explicit goal of outdesigning Raymark.

> One team was going to design us out of one product and the other team was going to design us out of another product. That would be the bulk of our product line. They spent about $50 million but we kept coming out with products faster. Finally, they gave up and eliminated the teams.

Despite Sentor's inability to replicate Raymark's products successfully, Raymark management were convinced that Sentor continued to view their relationship with Raymark as a stopgap measure. Wilson described Sentor objectives:

> We were a temporary fix for Sentor. We would come in until Sentor could do it right and use their massive technology to displace us. They are working on products that could put us out of the market. We were a two-year fix. But, every two years we have become another two-year fix. Our goal is to stay forever with our two-year mandate.

Wilson identified some other negative aspects of the relationship:

• Changes in both partners' managements created significant time demands in managing the relationship.

• Sentor's size sometimes resulted in conflicting messages. "Lower level staff want one thing and upper levels want something else. All sorts of different people have to be kept happy at the different levels."

• Politics on both sides was sometimes difficult to deal with.

• The cultures of the two companies were very different, sometimes leading to inconsistent expectations in the two companies.

• Raymark management often felt as if the firm were being treated as a subsidiary of Sentor rather than a partner.

• The relationship created some strategic marketing constraints for Raymark.

• It was sometimes hard to get good business opportunities from Sentor because Sentor had their own engineering software groups also looking for new products.

Clearly, the partnersip with Sentor had played an important role in Raymark's success. But, would the partnership payoff be as great in the future? Wilson described the dilemma facing Raymark:

> We would like to have our cake and eat it, too. We want to keep our sales to Sentor and expand our non-Sentor business. We think the partnership is pretty solid but Sentor would prefer that we concentrate on them and they have made that clear to us. They were not very happy when we purchased the Raysys business. We know, because Sentor has told us that if they can develop the same technology in-house, they will get rid of the commercial agreement with Raymark. A Sentor VP described our relationship like this: Raymark is like a minnow swimming around a whale. One day the whale will flip its tail and squash the minnow.

RUSSKI ADVENTURES

On July 15, 1991, Guy Crevasse and Andrei Kakov, the two major partners in Russki Adventures (Russki), contemplated their next move. They had spent the last year and a half exploring the possibility of starting a helicopter skiing operation in the USSR. Their plan was to bring clients from Europe, North America, and Japan to a remote location in the USSR to ski the vast areas of secluded mountain terrain made accessible by the use of helicopters and the recent business opportunities offered by *glasnost*.

During the exploration process, Crevasse and Kakov had visited a number of potential locations in the USSR, including the Caucasus Mountains near the Black Sea, and the Tien Shen and Pamir ranges north of Pakistan in the republics of Kazakistan and Tadzhikistan, respectively. After close inspection of the three areas, and consideration of many issues, the partners had decided upon the Caucasus region.

After almost two years of planning and research, the thought of making a solid commitment weighed heavily on their minds. Their first option was to accept the partnership offer with Extreme Dreams, a French company that had started a small ski operation in the Caucasus Mountains during the 1991 season. Their second option was to enter a partnership with the USSR's Trade Union DFSO and a Russian mountaineer, and establish their own venture in a Caucasus Moutains area made available to them by a Soviet government agency. Their final option was to wait, save their money, and not proceed with the venture at this time.

The Partners

Andrei Kakov, 27, was born in Russia. His family emigrated to Italy and then to Canada when he was 17 years old. After completing an undergraduate degree in economics at the University of Toronto, he worked with Sebaco for two years before enrolling in 1989 in the Master's of Business Administration (MBA) program at the University of Western Ontario (Western). Sebaco was a Canadian-Soviet joint venture that, since 1980, had been facilitating business ventures in the Soviet Union by acting as a liaison between the foreign firms and the different levels of Soviet government and industry. This job gave Kakov extensive contacts in the Soviet Union and in many of the firms, such as McDonald's and PepsiCo, which were doing business in the Soviet Union. Kakov was fluent in Russian, Italian, English, and Japanese.

Guy Crevasse, 28, had an extensive ski racing career which began at a young age and culminated in the World Cup with the Canadian National Ski Team. His skiing career took him to many countries in Europe, North America, and South America. During his travels, he learned to speak French, Italian, and some German. After retiring from competitive ski racing in 1984, Crevasse remained active in the ski industry as a member of the Canadian Ski Coaches Federation. He led the University of Western Ontario Varsity Ski Team to four consecutive Can-Am titles as a racer/coach while pursuing an undergraduate degree at Western. Before returning to Western to complete an MBA, Crevasse worked for Motorola, Inc., in its sales and marketing departments, where he worked on key accounts, set up product distribution channels, and developed product programs with original equipment manufacturers in the automobile industry. Crevasse had also worked with a ski resort planning and development firm on a number of different projects.

Overview of the Skiing and Helicopter Skiing Industries

Development of the Ski Resort Industry

In 1990, the worldwide ski market was estimated at 40 million skiers. The great boom period was in the 1960s and 1970s when growth ran between 10 and 20 percent annually. However, the growth stagnation which began during the 1980s was expected to continue during the 1990s. Some of this decline was attributable to increased competition for vacationers' time, the rapidly rising real costs of skiing, and baby-boom effects. The only growth segment was female skiers, who represented 65 percent of all new skiers. The total revenue generated by ski resorts in the United States for 1990 was estimated at $1.5 billion. This figure did not include any hotel or accommodation figures.

Prior to World War II, most skiing took place in Europe. Since there were no ski lifts, most skiing was essentially unmarked wilderness skiing, requiring participants who enjoyed the thrill of a downhill run to spend most of their time climbing. There were no slope-grooming machines and few slopes cut especially for skiing.

The development of ski lifts revolutionized the sport, increased the accessibility to many previously inaccessible areas, and led to the development of ski resorts. After the skiing market matured, competition for skiers intensified and resort operators shifted their efforts away from the risk sport focus toward vacation and entertainment. In order to service this new market and to recover their large capital investments, the large resorts had developed mass market strategies and modified the runs and the facilities to make them safer and easier to ski in order to serve a greater number of customers.

Introduction of Helicopter Skiing

This change in focus left the more adventurous skiing segments unsatisfied. For many, the search for new slopes and virgin snow was always a goal. The rapid rise in the popularity of skiing after World War II, increased demand on existing ski facilities, and thus competition for the best snow and hills became more intense. Those who wanted to experience the joys of powder skiing in virgin areas were forced to either get up earlier to ski the good snow before the masses got to it or hike for hours from the top of ski areas to find new areas close to existing cut ski runs. Hiking to unmarked areas was tiring, time-consuming, and more dangerous because of the exposure to crevasses and avalanches.

This desire to ski in unlimited powder snow and new terrain away from the crowds eventually led to the development of the helicopter skiing industry. The commonly held conception was that powder skiing was the champagne of all skiing, and helicopter skiing was the Dom Perignon. The first helicopter operations began in Canada. From the beginning of the industry in 1961, Canadian operations have been typically regarded as the premium product in the helicopter skiing industry for many reasons, including the wild, untamed mountains in the western regions. For many skiers worldwide, a trip to a Western Canadian heliski operation is their "mecca."

Operators used helicopters as a means of accessing vast tracts of wilderness areas which were used solely by one operator through a lease arrangement with the governments, forest services, or regional authorities. The average area leased for skiing was 2,000–3,000 square thousand kilometres in size, with 100–150 runs. Due to the high costs in buying, operating, maintaining, and insuring a helicopter, the vast majority of operators leased their machines on an as-needed basis with rates based on hours of flight time.

In the 1970s and early 1980s, the helicopter skiing industry was concentrated among a few players. During 1990–1991, the number of adventure/ wilderness skiing operators increased from 41 to over 77. The industry could be divided between those operations that provided day-trips from existing alpine resorts (day-trippers) and those operations that offered week-long trips (destination-location).

By 1991, the entire global market for both day-trippers and destination-location was estimated to be just over 23,000 skiers per year with the latter group representing roughly 12,000–15,000 skiers. Wilderness skiing represented the largest area of growth within the ski industry in the 1970s and 1980s. Market growth in the 1980s was 15 percent per year. Only capacity limitations had restrained growth. The addictive nature of helicopter skiing was illustrated by the fact that repeat customers accounted for over 75 percent of clients annually. The conservative estimate of total margin available to the destination-location skiing industry (before selling and administration costs) was U.S.$12.4 million in 1990. Exhibit 1 gives typical industry margin figures per skier for heliskiing.

From a cost standpoint, efficient management of the helicopter operations was essential. Exhibit 2 provides a larger list of industry key success factors.

Combination of Resort and Helicopter Skiing

The number of resorts operating day facilities doubled in 1990. Competition in the industry increased for a number of reasons. Many new competitors entered because of the low cost of entry (about $25,000), low exit barriers, the significant market growth, and the rewarding margin in the industry. The major growth worldwide came mainly from the day operations at existing areas, as they attempted to meet the needs for adventure and skiing from their clientele. The major concentration of helicopter operators was in Canada; however, competition was increasing internationally. Industry representatives thought that such growth was good because it would help increase the popularity of helicopter skiing and introduce more people to the sport.

In Canada, where helicopter skiing originated, the situation was somewhat different. Out of the 20 wilderness skiing operations in Canada in 1991, only two were tied to resorts. However, for the rest of the world, roughly 80 percent of all the operations were located and tied closely to existing ski operations.

EXHIBIT 1   Helicopter Skiing Margin per Skier Week (North America)

Price		$3,500	100%
Costs:	Helicopter*	1,260	36
	Food and lodging	900	26
	Guides	100	3
	Total operating costs	$2,260	65%
	Total margin	$1,240	35%

* Helicopter costs were semi-variable, but were based largely on a variable basis (in-flight hours). The fixed nature of helicopter costs arose through minimum flying hours requirements and the rate negotiations (better rates were charged to customers with higher usage). On average, a helicopter skier used seven hours of helicopter time during a one-week trip. A typical all-in rate for a 12-person helicopter was $1,800 per flying hour. Hence, the above figure of $1,260 was calculated assuming full capacity of the helicopter using the following: $1,800 per hour for 7 hours for 10 skiers + pilot + guide.

Exhibit 2   Helicopter Skiing Industry Key Success Factors

Factors within management control
- Establishing a safe operation and reliable reputation.
- Developing great skiing operations.
- Attracting and keeping customers with minimal marketing costs.
- Obtaining repeat business through operation's excellence.
- Providing professional and sociable guides.
- Obtaining operating permits from government.
- Managing relationships with environmentalists.

Location factors
- Accessible destinations by air travel.
- Available emergency and medical support.
- Favourable weather conditions (i.e., annual snowfall, humidity, altitude).
- Appropriate daily temperature, sunshine, daylight time.
- Suitable terrain.
- Quality food and lodging.

Both Crevasse and Kakov realized that there were opportunities to create partnerships or agreements with existing resorts to serve as an outlet for their helicopter skiing demand.

Russki's Research of the Heliski Industry

Profile of the Skier

The research that the Russki group had completed revealed some important facts. Most helicopter skiers were wealthy, independent, professional males of North American or European origin. Increasingly, the Japanese skiers were joining the ranks. The vast majority of the skiers were in their late 30s to mid-60s in age. For them, helicopter skiing provided an escape from the high pace of their professional lives. These people, who were financially secure with lots of disposable income, were well educated and had done a great many things. Helicopter skiing was a good fit with their calculated risk-taker image. Exhibit 3 describes a typical customer. It was not unusual for the skiing "addict" to exceed 100,000 vertical feet of skiing in a week. A premium was then charged to the skier.

Buyers tend to buy in groups rather than as individuals. They typically had some form of close association, such as membership in a common profession or club. In most cases, trips were planned a year in advance.

Geographically, helicopter skiers could be grouped into three segments: Japan, North America (United States and Canada), and Europe. In 1991, they represented 10 percent, 40 percent (30 percent and 10 percent), and 50 percent of the market, respectively. There were unique features associated with each

EXHIBIT 3   **Description of a Typical Helicopter Skiing Addict**

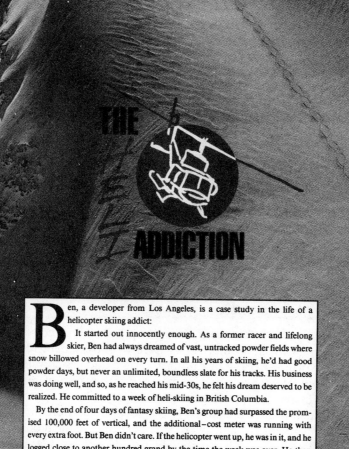

THE HELI ADDICTION

en, a developer from Los Angeles, is a case study in the life of a helicopter skiing addict:

It started out innocently enough. As a former racer and lifelong skier, Ben had always dreamed of vast, untracked powder fields where snow billowed overhead on every turn. In all his years of skiing, he'd had good powder days, but never an unlimited, boundless slate for his tracks. His business was doing well, and so, as he reached his mid-30s, he felt his dream deserved to be realized. He committed to a week of heli-skiing in British Columbia.

By the end of four days of fantasy skiing, Ben's group had surpassed the promised 100,000 feet of vertical, and the additional–cost meter was running with every extra foot. But Ben didn't care. If the helicopter went up, he was in it, and he logged close to another hundred grand by the time the week was over. He then committed to another week the following year.

"My wife is going to kill me," he said to himself, "but this skiing, so far from any other human, so wild and untamed and pure, is worth it."

Is helicopter skiing that big a deal? Is it worth the dent in your bank account, the risk of the addiction that snared Ben? Well, take a good, *loooong* look at the photo on this page.

Are there any doubts?

Source: *Powder, The Skier's Magazine*, November 1990.

segment, and Crevasse and Kakov knew that all marketing plans would need to be tailored specifically to each segment. In general, they felt that the European and North American customers placed more emphasis on the adventure, were less risk adverse, and had a propensity to try new things.

Analysis of the Competition

Crevasse and Kakov had thought that more detailed information on their competitors would help answer some of their questions. During the winter of 1991, they conducted a complete physical inspection of skiing and business facilities of many helicopter skiing operations. As a result of the research, Russski determined that the following companies were very significant: Rocky Mountain Helisports (RMH), Cariboo Snowtours, and Heliski India. RMH and Cariboo Snowtours were industry leaders, and Heliski India was another new entrant trying to establish itself in the market. A close analysis had provided Crevasse and Kakov with some encouraging information.

Rocky Mountain Helisports, the first operation to offer helicopter skiing, was started in 1965 in Canada by Gunther Pistler, a German immigrant and the "inventor" of helicopter skiing. In 1991, his operation, servicing 6,000 skiers, represented roughly 40–50 percent of the worldwide destination-location market. He followed a strategy which cloned small operating units at seven different sites in the interior of British Columbia. RMH's strategy was designed to offer a product that catered to a variety of different skier abilities and skiing experiences. The company serviced all segments that could afford the $4,000 price of admission, including introducing less-able skiers to the experience of helicopter skiing. Compared with the revenue of traditional Canadian ski resorts, such as Whistler Resorts in British Columbia, RMH's gross revenue for the 1990 season was larger than any resort in Canada at over $21 million. RMH, which had developed a loyal following of customers in North America and Europe, enjoyed a significant competitive advantage because of proprietary client lists, a loyal consumer base, and economies of scale due to its large size.

Cariboo Snowtours, the second largest operation in the world, was established by another German immigrant, Fritz Mogler, at Blue River, British Columbia. In 1991, Cariboo Snowtours served over 2,000 skiers, a number which represented roughly 18 percent of the market. Mogler developed a strategy of one megaoperation and enjoyed economies of scale in the operations area. Similar to RMH, Cariboo Snowtours had a loyal following from North America and Europe and catered to a variety of skiing abilities and price levels.

Heliski India was a new entrant to the helicopter skiing business. In 1990, the first year of operation, the company serviced 30 skiers in a three-week period, increasing to 120 skiers during the 1991 season. Heliski India followed a more exclusive and adventurous strategy aimed at the experienced helicopter skiing enthusiast. To cover the high costs and low volume, the operation charged $5,500.

EXHIBIT 4   Russki's 1991 Projections*: Profit Dynamics of Typical RMH Operation

Revenues				
Ski season duration—Peak	20 wks			
—Regular	0 wks			
Total season duration	20 wks			
Revenue per skier—Peak		$ 3500		
Weekly group size (10 skiers + 1 guide × 4)	44 people			
Total season regular revenue (3,500 × 40 skiers × 20 wks)			$2,800,000	
Revenue from skiers exceeding 100,000 vertical feet (10%)			280,000	
Total revenue				$3,080,000
Expenses				
Variable: 9 nights lodging/person/night		$ 80	$ 720	
9 days meals/person/day		50	450	
Total variable cost/person/week			$ 1170	
Total annual variable costs (20 wks × 44 × $1,170)				$1,029,600
Contribution margin				$2,050,400
Fixed:				
Helicopter cost/weekly basis (20-week season)		$ 50,000	$1,000,000	
Guides—1 guide per 10 skiers @ $50,000 per guide/year	4 guides		$ 200,000	
Support staff—5 employees @ $20,000 per employee			$ 100,000	
Promotional			$ 250,000	
Total direct fixed costs				$1,550,000
Total margin				$ 500,400
(Revenue—Direct variable costs × Direct fixed costs)				
Annual overhead—Communication		$ 20,000		
—Staff travel		50,000		
—Office branch		20,000		
—Office North America		100,000		
—Insurance @ $5/day/person		50,000		
Total overhead				$ 240,000
Operating profit				$ 260,400
Number of operations	7			
Total operating profit				$1,822,800

* These projected statements were best guesstimates based on discussions with a wide range of industry experts, managers, and investors.

Russki estimated margins and profit dynamics for these three operations. Exhibit 4 contains the projection for RMH. These projected statements were best guesstimates based on discussions with a wide range of industry experts, managers, and investors. Cariboo Snowtour's total profit was estimated as slightly over $2 million, while Heliski India was projected to turn a small profit. Crevasse and Kakov found these figures very encouraging.

Land Usage and Environmental Concerns in the Industry

The helicopter skiing industry was facing some land use issues which were tough on many operators, but which also created new opportunities on which

Russki wanted to capitalize. Of particular concern to many helicopter skiing operations, especially European, were pressures from environmentalists who were concerned that noise from helicopters could adversely affect wildlife habitat and start avalanches.

As a result, severe downsizing or complete shutdown of existing European operations had recently occurred, leaving only eight helicopter skiing operations in continental Europe in 1991. The one Swiss and one Austrian operation were under pressure to close, and a 1992 season for the latter was already doubtful. The six small operations in Italy, which worked in conjunction with existing ski areas, were basically the only helicopter skiing available in Western Europe. Flying for skiing in France was illegal due to environmentalists' concerns about a negative impact on the limited areas in the Alps. In Sweden, a few companies operated with a shorter season due to the high latitude and provided less expensive daily services for visitors who skied within the existing lift systems, but week-long packages were not part of their program.

The North American industry had not been exposed to the same environmental and limited area constraints as the European, mainly because of the vast size of the mountain ranges and good relationships with all interested parties. The American operators, who were associated mostly with the large ski areas, had good working relationships with the forest services, which controlled the areas and issued the working permits.

Canadian operators received their permits from the Ministry of Lands and Forests and the provincial governments. Helicopter skiing had been encouraged because of its ability to bring money into the regions. Due to the vast size of the Canadian mountain ranges and the limited competition for the land use, pressure on the operators in any form had been minimal or nonexistent.

Crevasse and Kakov realized that the environmental and capacity constraints in Europe provided helicopter skiing operators worldwide with significant opportunities. Thus far, it had been mainly the North American operators who had capitalized on this situation, and Russki wanted to find a way to capture unsatisfied demand.

Russian Environment

The Political Environment

Crevasse and Kakov knew that starting a venture in the Soviet Union at this time would be complex. The political situation was very unstable in July 1991, and most expert predictions were not encouraging, including the possibility that the Soviet Union might not exist in the near future. There was a major power struggle going on: the hardliners, most of whom were from the old guard of the Communist party, were trying to hang on to power; and others, such as Russian President Boris Yeltsin, wanted sweeping democratic changes. The new buzz word on the streets was not *glasnost* or *peristroika*, but *razgosudarstvo*, which refers to the breakup of the Soviet state. Secession pressures from many of the republics such as the Baltics tested the metal of the political leaders, *peristroika*, and the strength of the union itself.

On a regional basis, the future status of some of the regions and republics where the physical conditions met the requirements for helicopter skiing, such as Georgia and Kazakhistan, was unknown. However, Crevasse and Kakov were encouraged by the fact that experts predicted that no matter what the state of the whole union, Russia would remain intact and continue to function as a unit. This was one of the many reasons why the Russian Republic was selected for the potential initial location.

The Economic Environment

The economy of the Soviet Union was in dire straits. Confusion, lack of focus, and compromise were crippling the process of change from a government-controlled economy to a market-based one. Real gross domestic product was projected to drop anywhere from 3 to 11 percent or more in 1991. Soviet President Mikhail Gorbachev had been given authority to overhaul the economy. However, what changes he would initiate, and whether he still had the support and power to see the process through to completion, were questionable.

Therefore, developing a helicopter skiing operation in the Soviet Union presented Russki with a difficult business environment. Marshall Goldman, director of Harvard's Russian Research Centre, summed up part of the dilemma facing any new venture in the Soviet Union at this time:

> For those entrepreneurs who think chaos is an ideal environment, this is a perfect time, but for others it is a scary time. The society is collapsing. The company—both the marketing portion and the planning and administrative sector—is a shambles.

Russki's research indicated that only 20 percent of the 1,300 joint ventures signed since 1987 were operational because of currency exchange problems, bureaucratic delays, and lack of legal framework to make agreements. Also, it had been very hard for the few operational ventures to realize a return on their investment. In 1991, any business in the Soviet Union had to be viewed with a long-term bias in mind. The big question for many businesses was getting hard currency out of Soviet ventures because there was no international market for the Soviet currency, the ruble. Those who were operating business ventures in the Soviet Union suggested to Russki that it was not an area for the fainthearted to tread. PlanEcon's Keith Crane advised that "even after the agreement has been signed it can be very difficult to get down to specifics and venture into working entities. It took McDonald's 14 years to do it." Due to the political and economic realities of the Soviet environment, firms were making deals with republics, with city agencies, directly with Soviet firms or factories, and sometimes with all of them. More and more frequently, firms had to go to the enterprise level to find the right people and partners. Additionally, foreign firms found the business environment difficult because the concept of business that Westerners had was very different from the one that the Soviets had after 70 years of a controlled Marxist economy. The addition of cultural differences made for a demanding business climate. Russki thought long and hard about the fact that doing business in the Soviet Union had never been easy. In 1991, as the nation wrestled with the gargantuan task of restructuring the country, most firms were finding it more confusing than ever. No road map or blueprint for business development existed.

In addition, without the significant financial resources of a highly capitalized firm that could overlook short-term profits for long-term gains, Crevasse and Kakov realized they would be in a more exposed position if they decided to go ahead with the venture. Political unrest or civil war in the Soviet Union, especially in Russia, could destroy their business and investment. Without a steady supply of repeat and new customers, the venture would be finished as an on-going concern. They knew that credibility from an existing operation or established name would make the task of attracting customers to an uncertain environment easier but, in a time of crisis, would guarantee nothing.

The Opportunities

Despite all the negatives, Crevasse and Kakov thought that helicopter skiing in the Soviet Union would be developed on a large scale in the next few years for a number of reasons. The sport was experiencing tremendous growth, environmental pressures were great in Europe, and capacity at all of the good locations was already stretched.

Therefore, a current opportunity existed in the industry. The partners speculated about how fast they could proceed with their business plan and whether they were exposing themselves to too much risk for the return. Would the opportunity still exist in a couple of years? Could a business of this nature function with the future of the Soviet Union being so unstable? The complete answer to these questions was unknown. Crevasse and Kakov felt as if they were doing a case back at business school where someone had left out half the case facts. Regardless, this was a real-life situation, and a decision had to be made on the knowledge available.

After looking closely at their competition and the general environment, they concluded that, despite the instability in the Soviet environment, there were a number of strong points that suggested that they might be able to make a venture of this nature work. On a positive note, the Canadian prime minister, Brian Mulroney, had recently signed the Foreign Investment Protection agreement to ensure stability of Canadian ventures in the USSR. Also encouraging to entrepreneurs wanting to enter the Soviet Union was the new law that allowed for full ownership of Soviet subsidiaries by foreign firms. Experts suggested that these agreements would be honoured by whatever form of government was in place.

The critical factor in the minds of the Russki partners was the fact that they would be taking in all revenue in hard currency. Thus, the absence of profit repatriation risk decreased this business exposure dramatically. Russki would operate all of the sales and administrative tasks outside of the Soviet Union and as a result, all of its revenues would be collected in the West in hard currency, thereby eliminating the currency risk completely. This was a position that would be envied by any firm attempting to do business in the Soviet Union. Also, Russki was attractive to all levels of government because the venture would bring desperately needed hard currency into the country.

Mt. Elbrus, the highest peak in Europe and the Caucasus mountain region, was where Russki had options to locate. It was well known throughout Europe and its high altitudes and warm climate offered ideal skiing conditions. Because a strong allegiance already existed between the European customers and the Canadian operators, Russki's Canadian background would sit well with customers. In addition, Russki would deliver comparative cost advantage for the Europeans in a Soviet operation, as shown in Exhibit 5, even if Russki charged similar costs for a week of skiing.

The uniqueness of the region and mystique of Russia offered an interesting alternative for tourism. Russia had a 2,000-year history and a rich culture which was reflected in the traditions of the local people and the architecture. Furthermore, the Black Sea area, which was close to the Caucasus Mountains, had been used as a resort area for centuries. The dramatic changes during the early 1990s in the Soviet Union and Eastern Europe had resulted in tremendous interest in these areas.

EXHIBIT 5   Cost Comparison by Geographic Location

North America
Costs for customer to go Heliskiing in North America from different geographic locations

Origin of skier	Trip	Transportation	Total
Japan	$4,000	$2,500	$6,500
Europe	$4,000	$2,000	$6,000
North America	$4,000	$ 750	$4,750

Russia
Cost for customers to go Heliskiing in Russia from different geographic locations

Origin of skier	Trip	Transportation	Total
Japan	$4,000	$2,000	$6,000
Europe	$4,000	$1,000	$5,000
North America	$4,000	$2,500	$6,500

Conclusion: This comparative analysis of all-in costs to the consumer shows that the Russian operation offers a 20 percent cost advantage to the European customers.

Since Russki already had the money required for start-up, the company could move quickly without having to take time to raise the capital. The low cost of leasing Soviet helicopters, pilot salaries, service, and fuel as compared with North America was a distinct advantage, and one of the original attractions of Russia. Negotiations with the Russians had shown that this cost advantage was obtainable. The high costs of helicopter operations represented the largest part of the operating costs in helicopter skiing. Lower helicopter costs in Russia would result in cost savings in the range of 50 percent or more in this expense relative to North American competitors.

The Russki management team was strong. Both men were business-school trained individuals with international work experience, language skills, and ski industry background. Additional hard-to-copy assets, including access to the "Crazy Canucks" (a World Cup ski team) and European ski stars as guest guides and Soviet knowledge, would be tough for anyone to match in the short term.

Positioning and Marketing of Russki Adventures

Positioning and Pricing

The Russki team had considered two positioning strategies, a high and low pricing strategy. A premium pricing and service strategy like that of Heliski India at around U.S.$6,000 would require superior service in every aspect of the operation. The lower-priced strategy at $3,500 to $4,000 was $500 below the $4,000 to $4,500 U.S. pricing of Canadian operators like RMH for the initial season. The second positioning strategy would be designed to target a larger market and concentrate on building market share during the first few years, allowing more time and flexibility to move down the learning curve.

Even with parallel pricing of U.S.$4,000, the "all in" (as shown in Exhibit 5) would give a cost advantage to the European and Japanese customers. Crevasse and Kakov knew that this situation would help challenge customers' traditional allegiance to the Canadian operators.

Based on a "best-guess scenario," profit models for the two pricing strategies using conservative sales levels are shown in Exhibits 6 and 7. Though the higher-priced strategy was more lucrative, Crevasse and Kakov felt that they had a higher capacity to execute the lower-price strategy during the first few years of operations regardless of which partner they chose. They were not sure that they could meet the sales volume for the premium strategy as shown in Exhibit 7, regardless of the realization of savings from use of Russian helicopters. (In the unlikely event that the projected helicopter saving could not be realized, the discounted cash flow in Exhibit 6 dropped from $526,613 to $293, and in Exhibit 7 from $597,926 to $194,484.)

These estimates were extremely conservative. One helicopter could service 44 people per week (four groups of 10 skiers and one guide). All

EXHIBIT 6   Profit Dynamics Low Price Strategy with Low Helicopter Costs

	Year 1	Year 2	Year 3	Year 4	Year 5
Revenues					
Total season duration	10 weeks	15 weeks	15 weeks	20 weeks	20 weeks
Revenue per skier—peak	$ 4,000	$ 4,000	$ 4,000	$ 4,000	$ 4,000
Weekly group size	10	15	20	25	25
Total season revenue	$400,000	$900,000	$1,200,000	$2,000,000	$2,000,000
Expenses					
Total variable cost	$100,000	$225,000	$ 300,000	$ 500,000	$ 500,000
(variable cost/skier @ $1,000)					
Contribution margin	$300,000	$675,000	$ 900,000	$1,500,000	$1,500,000
Fixed					
Helicopter cost (assumes Soviet costs of $10,000/week	$100,000	$150,000	$ 150,000	$ 200,000	$ 200,000
Guides—1 guide per 10 skiers @ $50,000 per guide/year	$ 50,000	$ 75,000	$ 100,000	$ 125,000	$ 125,000
Soviet staff—3 employees @ $5,000 per employee	$ 15,000	$ 15,000	$ 15,000	$ 15,000	$ 15,000
Promotional	$100,000	$100,000	$ 100,000	$ 100,000	$ 100,000
Total direct fixed costs	$265,000	$340,000	$ 365,000	$ 440,000	$ 440,000
Total margin (revenues–direct variable costs–direct fixed costs)	$ 35,000	$335,000	$ 535,000	$1,060,000	$1,060,000
Total overhead	$ 35,000	$115,000	$ 115,000	$ 115,000	$ 115,000
Operating profit	–0–	$220,000	$ 420,000	$ 945,000	$ 945,000

	Year 0	Year 1	Year 2	Year 3	Year 4	Year 5
Investment	$−230,000					
Operating profit		–0–	$220,000	$ 420,000	$ 945,000	$ 945,000
N.A. partner's share: 100%		–0–	$220,000	$ 420,000	$ 945,000	$ 945,000
Taxes @ 30% profit	$−230,000	–0–	$154,000	$ 294,000	$ 661,500	$ 661,500
DCF Year 1–5 PV @ 20.00%		$526,613				
IRR		71.86%				

projections for the profit dynamics were made with the number of skiers per week below capacity. In addition, the first two years were estimated using 10 and 15 skiers, respectively. In subsequent years, the number of skiers was increased, but never to full capacity, in order to keep estimates conservative. Russki realized that operating at or close to capacity on a weekly basis would increase its efficiency and returns dramatically.

Russki also built in an additional $250 in the variable costs per skier per week for contingent expenses such as the cost of importing all foodstuffs.

If Russki proceeded with the lower-priced approach, it would position its product just below the industry standard at $4,000 initially. The intent would

EXHIBIT 7   Profit Dynamics Premium Price Strategy with Low Helicopter Costs

	Year 1	Year 2	Year 3	Year 4	Year 5
Revenues					
Total season duration	5 weeks	10 weeks	10 weeks	20 weeks	20 weeks
Revenue per skier—peak	$ 6,000	$ 6,000	$ 6,000	$ 6,000	$ 6,000
Weekly group size	10	10	15	15	20
Total season revenue	$300,000	$600,000	$900,000	$1,800,000	$2,400,000
Expenses					
Total variable cost	$ 50,000	$100,000	$150,000	$ 300,000	$ 400,000
(variable cost/skier @ $1,000)					
Contribution margin	$250,000	$500,000	$750,000	$1,500,000	$2,000,000
Fixed					
Helicopter cost (assumes Soviet costs of $10,000/week	$ 50,000	$100,000	$100,000	$ 200,000	$ 200,000
Guides—1 guide per 10 skiers @ $50,000 per guide/year	$ 50,000	$ 50,000	$ 75,000	$ 75,000	$ 100,000
Soviet staff—3 employees @ $5,000 per employee	$ 15,000	$ 15,000	$ 15,000	$ 15,000	$ 15,000
Promotional	$100,000	$100,000	$100,000	$ 100,000	$ 100,000
Total direct fixed costs	$215,000	$265,000	$290,000	$ 390,000	$ 415,000
Total margin (revenues–direct variable costs–direct fixed costs)	$ 35,000	$235,000	$460,000	$1,110,000	$1,585,000
Total overhead	$ 35,000	$115,000	$115,000	$ 115,000	$ 115,000
Operating profit	–0–	$120,000	$345,000	$ 995,000	$1,470,000

	Year 0	Year 1	Year 2	Year 3	Year 4	Year 5
Investment	$−230,000					
Operating profit		–0–	$120,000	$345,000	$ 995,000	$1,470,000
N.A. partner's share: 100%		–0–	$120,000	$345,000	$ 995,000	$1,470,000
Taxes @ 30% profit	$−230,000	–0–	$ 84,000	$241,500	$ 696,500	$1,029,000
DCF Year 1–5 PV @ 20.00%		$597,926				
IRR	70.78%					

be to attack the market as the Japanese automobile manufacturers had done when entering into the North American luxury car market.

Crevasse and Kakov were encouraged by the numbers because the conservative sales estimates using the low-price positioning strategy would allow them to generate a profit in the second year of operations if they could realize the projected savings with Russian helicopters. However, if they didn't, the strategy would still show a profit in the third year. They thought that the return on their investment would be sufficient as far as the internal rate of return was concerned, but they wondered whether the risk of the Soviet environment should increase their demands even more.

Product

Crevasse and Kakov planned to model the Russki product after the RMH operation, which was the best in the industry, by evaluating what RMH had built and improving on its processes. Although Russki wanted very much to differentiate itself from the rest of the industry, the partners were not sure how far they could go within the constraints of the Soviet environment.

Geographic Distribution

Although Russki would focus on the European and North American markets, the former segment was most important. Both Crevasse and Kakov realized that they would need a strong European operation in marketing and sales if they were going to capitalize on the opportunity available. Developing these functions quickly, especially in Europe, which was not their home turf, was a major concern. They had to decide on the best sales and marketing channels immediately and set them up as soon as possible if they decided to go ahead with the venture.

Promotion

Due to the small size of the target market and promotion budgets, the new company would have to make sure that the promotional dollars spent were directed effectively. Russki would do this by direct mail, personal selling by the owners, travel agents, and free tour incentives to trip organizers and guides. Long-term word of mouth would be the best promotional tool, but it had to be supplemented especially in the start-up phase of the business.

Additionally, Crevasse and Kakov planned to increase the value to customers by inviting business and political speakers to participate in the skiing activities with the groups in return for their speaking services. Celebrity skiers, such as Canadian Olympic bronze medallist and World Cup champion Steve Podborski, would be used as customer attractions. As outlined in Exhibit 8, they budgeted $100,000 for promotional expenses.

Exhibit 8 Marketing Promotion Budget—Year 1

Information nights with cocktails @ $1,000/night @ 20 cities	$ 20,000
Travel expenses	10,000
Trip discounts (1 free trip in 10 to groups)	25,000
Direct mail	5,000
Brochures	5,000
Commissions	15,000
Celebrity	20,000
	$100,000

Labour

Where possible, Russki planned to employ Russians and make sure that they received excellent training and compensation, thereby adding authenticity to the customers' experience. Providing local employment would also ensure the Canadian company's existence and create positive relations with the authorities.

Currency

Through Kakov's contacts, Russki had worked out a deal to purchase excess rubles from a couple of foreign firms which were already operating in the Soviet Union but which were experiencing profit repatriation problems. Russki would pay for as many things as possible with soft currency.

The Partnership Dilemma

During the exploration period, Crevasse and Kakov had well over a dozen offers from groups and individuals to either form partnerships or provide services and access to facilities and natural resources. They even had offers from people who wanted them to invest millions to build full-scale alpine resorts. Many of the offers were easy to dismiss because these groups did not have the ability to deliver what they promised or their skill sets did not meet the needs of Russki. Crevasse and Kakov's inspection and site evaluation helped them to determine further the best opportunities and to evaluate firsthand whether the site and potential partner were realistic. This research gave Russki a couple of excellent but very distinct partnership possibilities. They knew that both options had trade-offs.

Extreme Dreams

A partnership with the Extreme Dreams group had some definite strengths. This French company, located in Chamonix, an alpine town in the French Alps, had been running the premier guiding service in and around Mont Blanc, the highest peak in the Alps, for 11 years. Chamonix was the "avant-garde" for alpinists in Europe and one of the top alpine centres in the world. Extreme Dreams had a 5,000-person client list, mostly European but with some North American names.

What Extreme Dreams had was the operational expertise Russki needed to acquire in order to run the helicopter skiing and guiding side of the business. However, they lacked experience in the key functional areas of business. During the 1991 winter season, it had run a three-week operation servicing 50 skiers in the Elbrus region in the Caucasus Mountains. The Soviet partner facilitated an arrangement with a small resort villa in the area. The facilities, which had just been upgraded during the summer, now met Western standards.

The French company had invested roughly U.S.$100,000, and although it did not have a capital shortage, the partnership agreement that was outlined would require Russki to inject the same amount of capital into the business. The firm would be incorporated in the United States and the share split would be equal amounts of 45 percent of the stock with 10 percent left over for future employee purchase. The Soviet partner, a government organization that helped facilitate the land use agreements and permits, would be paid a set fee for yearly exclusive use of the land.

However, Extreme Dreams lacked experience in the key functional areas of business. Possibly, this situation could be rectified by the partnership agreement whereby the management team would consist of three members. Marc Testut, president of Extreme Dreams, would be in charge of all operations. Guy Crevasse would act as president for the first two years and his areas of expertise would be sales and marketing. Andrei Kakov would be chief financial officer and responsible for Soviet relations.

Extreme Dreams had overcome the lack of some foodstuffs by importing on a weekly basis products not securely attainable in Russia. These additional costs were built into the variable cost in projected financial statements. Russki would do the same if it did not choose Extreme Dreams as a partner.

Trade Union DFSO

The other potential partnership had its strengths as well. The partnership would be with the All-Union Council of Trade Union DFSO, and with a mountaineer named Yuri Golodov, one of the USSR's best-known mountaineers, who had agreed to be part of the management team. Golodov, who had been bringing mountaineers from all over the world to parts of the Soviet Union for many years, possessed valuable expertise and knowledge of the Caucasus area. One of his tasks would be coordination of travel logistics for Soviet clientele. Sergei Oganezovich, chief of the mountaineering department, had made available to Russki the exclusive rights to over 4,000 square kilometres in the Caucasus Mountain Range about 50 kilometres from the area awarded to Extreme Dreams. A small user fee per skier would be paid to the trade organization in return for exclusive helicopter access to the area.

A profit-sharing agreement with Golodov, which would allow him to purchase shares in Russki and share in the profits, was agreed to in principle by Russki, the Trade Union DFSO, and Golodov. Under this agreement, Crevasse and Kakov would remain in control of the major portion of the shares. Capital requirements for this option would be in the $230,000 range over the first two years. The two Canadians would perform essentially the same roles as those proposed in the Extreme Dreams agreement. If Crevasse and Kakov selected this option, they would need to bring in a head guide, preferably European, to run the skiing operations. On a positive note, a small resort centre that met the standards required by Western travelers had been selected for accommodations in the area.

As far as medical care in case of accidents, both locations were within an hour of a major city and hospital. Less than an hour was well under the industry norm. In addition, all staff were required to take a comprehensive first aid course.

After discussions with many business ventures in the Soviet Union and with Extreme Dreams, Russski concluded that having the ability to pay for goods and services with hard currency would be a real asset if the situation were critical. Russski would use hard currency, where necessary, to ensure that the level of service was up to the standard required by an operation of this nature.

Crevasse and Kakov knew that selecting a compatible and productive partner would be a great benefit in this tough environment. Yet they had to remember that a partnership would not guarantee customer support for this venture in the Soviet environment or that the USSR would remain stable enough to function as an on-going concern.

The Decision

Crevasse and Kakov knew that it would take some time for the business to grow to the level of full capacity. They were willing to do whatever it took to make ends meet during the early years of the business. Because helicopter skiing was a seasonal business, they realized that they would need to find a supplementary source of income during the off-season, especially in the start-up phase.

However, they also were confident that, if they could find a way to make their plan work, they could be the ones to capitalize on the growing market. The Soviet Union had the right physical conditions for helicopter skiing, but the business environment would present difficulties. Moreover, the two partners were aware that starting a venture of this nature at any time was not an easy task. Starting it in the present state of the Soviet Union during a recession would only complicate their task further. Yet the timing was right for a new venture in the industry and, in general, they were encouraged by the potential of the business.

Crevasse and Kakov had to let all parties involved know of their decision by the end of the week. If they decided to go ahead with the venture, they had to move quickly if they wanted to be operational in the 1992 season. That night they had to decide if they would proceed, who they would select as partners if they went ahead, and how they would go. It was going to be a late night.

SCOTCH-BRITE 3M

In June 1990, the 3M operating committee met in world headquarters in St. Paul, Minnesota, to consider a proposal to rationalize the North American production and distribution of SCOTCH-BRITE hand scouring pads. Due to increased consumer demand, the decision had been made to upgrade the equipment which converted the jumbo-sized rolls into consumer and industrial-sized packages and quantities. At issue was where this upgraded processing equipment would be located.

Currently, most of the conversion took place in Alexandria, Minnesota, from jumbo rolls supplied from Perth, Ontario. The Alexandria facility then shipped finished goods to eight distribution centres around the United States (see Exhibit 1).

The Canadian division of 3M was now proposing that all production and distribution for SCOTCH-BRITE hand pads take place from Perth. This would mean that $4 million in new equipment would go to Perth, the current SCOTCH-BRITE workforce in Alexandria would be shifted to different responsibilities, and Perth would now ship directly to the various distribution centres (see Exhibit 2). This proposal to grant a regional product mandate to

This case was prepared by Professor Paul W. Beamish for the sole purpose of providing material for class discussion at the Western Business School. Copyright 1993 © The University of Western Ontario and The Ontario Premier's Council on Economic Renewal. Western Business School Case 9-93-G003.

EXHIBIT 1   Present SCOTCH-BRITE Product Flowchart

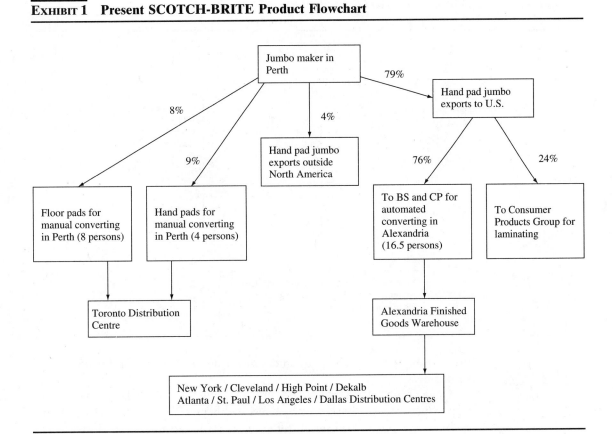

Perth had not gone unopposed. The Alexandria plant felt it would be preferable to place the new converting equipment in their facility, and to maintain
the existing relationship with Perth.

3M Background

3M was a multinational enterprise with 80,000 employees, subsidiaries, and
operations in 50 countries, and worldwide annual sales in excess of U.S.$10
billion. During the past decade, 3M's outside-the-U.S. (OUS) sales had
climbed from about one-third to nearly one-half of total sales. This growth
was a result of a conscious strategy of global expansion. The company was
organized into four divisions: Industrial and Consumer, Electronic and Information Technologies, Life Sciences, and Graphic Technologies.

Among the more familiar products were SCOTCH brand transparent
tapes, magnetic tapes, cassettes, and cartridges. Abrasives and adhesives were

Exhibit 2   Proposed SCOTCH-BRITE Product Flowchart
(All Hand Pad)

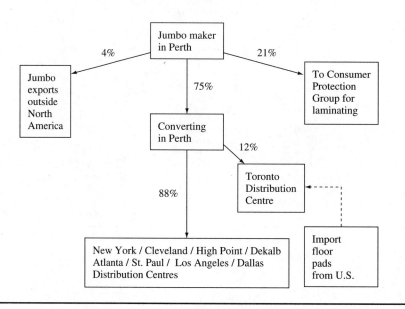

early products of the company and still formed a very important portion of the business.

Developing other technologies and applying them to make problem-solving products was the basis on which 3M had been able to grow. So many new products were produced on an on-going basis that 25 percent of any year's sales were of products that did not exist five years before.

Like its parent company, 3M Canada Inc. was a highly diversified company which manufactured thousands of different products for industry, business, the professions, and the consumer. The head office and main plant were located in London, Ontario, with sales and service centres across the country. 3M Canada was established as part of the newly founded International Division in 1951. Additional subsidiaries were set up at that time in Australia, Brazil, France, West Germany, Mexico, and the United Kingdom. 3M Canada employed about 2,000 people. In addition to operations in London and Perth, the company had manufacturing plants in Toronto, Havelock, and Simcoe, Ontario, and Morden, Manitoba. Canada was the sixth largest of 3M's subsidiaries.

With the exception of two or three people from the worldwide organization, everyone working for 3M Canada was Canadian. The Canadian subsidiary annually lost 10 to 15 people to the worldwide organization. Although a high proportion of the professional management group in Canada had a career goal to work in the worldwide organization at some stage, this was not a requirement. For example, several managers at the plant manager level and above had indicated a preference to stay in Canada despite offers within the worldwide organization.

The Canadian subsidiary, under the direction of its president Jeffery McCormick, was expected to generate sales growth and to produce an operating income on Canadian sales. Increasingly, emphasis was being placed on achieving certain target market share levels.

Within Canada, the 25 individual business units were split among eight groups, each of which operated as a profit centre. Variability existed in each with respect to the amount of divisional input from the United States.

The headquarters perception of the competencies of the Canadian subsidiary varied according to the business and functional area. For example, Canadian manufacturing and engineering had a solid reputation for getting things done.

In terms of research, Canada specialized in three somewhat narrow areas. These dealt with polymer chemistry, materials science, and electro-mechanical telecommunications. Several dozen scientists pursued research in these areas within Canadian laboratories.

The Canadian subsidiary did not have a critical mass in R&D for all the technologies necessary to support SCOTCH-BRITE. In addition, it was not deemed feasible to move (or build) a pilot plant to Canada for SCOTCH-BRITE testing purposes since pilot plants tended to serve a multitude of products.

Partly as a consequence of the 1988 Canada–U.S. Free Trade Agreement, the overall level of company harmonization between the two countries had risen. Some U.S. divisions were asking for more direct control over their businesses in Canada. The Canadian president needed to deal with these issues and to develop the necessary organizational response.

The Canadian subsidiary had placed a lot of importance on building intercompany sales. Over 20 percent of its sales were of this type, and further increases were intended.

3M Canada sales in 1990 were over $500 million while after-tax earnings were in the range of 10 percent (see Exhibits 3 and 4 for financial statements).

The Perth SCOTCH-BRITE Plant

The $5 million Perth plant went into operation in 1981, employing 22 people. The plant covered 36,000 square feet on a 78-acre site and was the first Canadian production facility for this product line. It was built to supplement the jumbo output of Alexandria, which was nearing capacity. The plant was designed with sufficient capacity to produce enough hand pads and floor pads to eliminate imports, but with exports in mind. In 1981, the Canadian duty on shipments from the U.S. to Canada was 13.5 percent, while shipments from Canada could enter the U.S. duty free.

EXHIBIT 3   3M Canada Inc.
Consolidated Statement of Earnings and Retained Earnings for the Year Ended
October 31, 1989

	1989 ($000s)	1988 ($000s)
Revenue		
Net sales*	$561,406	$516,663
Other income	8,823	3,536
	570,229	520,199
Costs and expenses		
Costs of goods sold and other expenses	451,298	412,826
Depreciation and amortization	16,908	15,921
Interest	312	239
Research and development	1,876	2,010
	470,394	430,996
	99,835	89,203
Provision for income taxes	41,636	38,339
Net earnings for the year	58,199	50,864
Retained earnings—beginning of year	215,960	185,496
	274,159	236,360
Dividends	28,046	20,400
Retained earnings—end of year	246,113	215,960
* Includes Net Sales to Parent and Affiliated Companies	106,773	89,709

Over the next decade, the plant was expanded several times, and employment grew to 80 people. Throughout this period, the plant exclusively produced "SCOTCH-BRITE." SCOTCH-BRITE was a profitable, growing product line in a core business area. The total scouring pad market in which SCOTCH-BRITE competed was estimated to be $60 million in the U.S. and nearly $5 million in Canada.

SCOTCH-BRITE material was a web of non-woven nylon or polyester fibres impregnated throughout with abrasive particles. The result was a pad, disk, or wheel used to scour, clean, polish, or finish materials such as wood, metal, plastic, and many other surfaces.

As SCOTCH-BRITE material wears down, it exposes more abrasives so that it continues to be effective all through its life. Because it is made of synthetic fibre it does not rust or stain. Some types of SCOTCH-BRITE have a sponge backing so that both scouring and washing can be done with the one product. Other versions of this material have integral backing pads and handles made of strong plastic to enable the user to scour and clean flat surfaces and corners with ease.

EXHIBIT 4 3M Canada Inc.
Consolidated Balance Sheet as at October 31, 1989

	Assets	
	1989 *($000s)*	*1988* *($000s)*
Current Assets		
Interest bearing term deposits	$ 66,998	$ 52,896
Accounts receivable	73,524	69,631
Amounts due from affiliated companies	18,050	13,670
Other receivables and prepaid expenses	5,472	4,592
Inventories		
Finished goods and work in process	67,833	63,745
Raw materials and supplies	9,321	10,601
	241,198	215,153
Fixed Assets		
Property, plant and equipment—at cost	180,848	164,313
Less accumulated depreciation	85,764	76,676
Other Assets	9,590	8,856
	345,872	312,628

	Liabilities	
Current Liabilities		
Accounts payable—trade	21,600	18,388
Amounts due to affiliated companies	18,427	17,985
Income taxes payable	9,394	12,437
Deferred payments	1,437	1,422
Other liabilities	20,832	18,367
	71,690	68,599
Deferred Income Taxes	14,669	14,669
	86,359	83,268

	Shareholder's Equity	
Capital Stock		
Authorized—Unlimited shares		
Issued and fully paid—14,600 shares	13,400	13,400
Retained Earnings	246,113	215,960
	259,513	229,360
	345,872	312,628

SCOTCH-BRITE products were made in sheet, roll, and wheel shapes, and used in a wide variety of applications in the metal-working, woodworking, and plastics industries, as well as in the hotel and restaurant trade, and the home.

Floor and carpet cleaning companies, schools, hospitals, and building maintenance personnel used a wide variety of SCOTCH-BRITE disks and pads for floor maintenance. Other smaller hand-held pads were used for cleaning painted surfaces such as door frames, stairs, walls, sinks, and tile surfaces. SCOTCH-BRITE products were used in hotels and restaurants for griddle and grill cleaning, deep fat fryer scouring, and for carpet and floor maintenance. Several types of SCOTCH-BRITE products were available for home use. These ranged from a gentle version designed for cleaning tubs, sinks, tile, and even fine china, to a rugged scouring pad with a built-in handle for scouring barbecue grills.

The Perth Proposal

During the 1980s as the Perth plant grew in size and experience, its reputation as a workforce with a demonstrated ability to work effectively began to develop. With increased confidence came a desire to assume new challenges. An obvious area for potential development would be to take on more of the SCOTCH-BRITE value-added function in Perth, rather than to ship semi-finished goods to the United States.

In the mid-80s, the Perth managers advocated that they should now supply finished goods to the U.S. for certain mandated products. The SCOTCH-BRITE manufacturing director during this period opposed this approach. He claimed that nothing would be saved as all the finished goods would have to be sent to Alexandria anyway, for consolidation and distribution to the customer.

The U.S.-based manufacturing director also argued that mandating products could reduce the utilization of the larger, more expensive maker at Alexandria, which would increase the unit burden costs on other products there. During this period, the Perth maker operated as the swing maker with utilization cycling in order to keep the Alexandria maker fully loaded.

With a change in management came a willingness to take a fresh look at the situation. The new manager, Andy Burns, insisted that a more complete analysis of all the delivered costs be provided. To that end, a study was initiated in December 1989 to determine the cost of converting and packaging SCOTCH-BRITE hand pads in Perth, rather than shipping jumbo to Alexandria for converting and packaging.

The task force struck in Canada was led by Len Weston, the Perth Plant Manager. Procedurally, any proposal would first go to Gary Boles, Manufacturing Director for Canada, and Gord Prentice, Executive Vice President of Manufacturing for Canada. Once their agreement had been obtained, the

Perth plant manager would continue to champion the project through the 3M hierarchy, although people such as Prentice would facilitate the process.

The proposal would next go to the Building Service and Cleaning Products (BS + CP) division for review and agreement. If successful, the proposal would then be sent back to Canadian engineering to develop an Authority For (capital) Expenditure, or AFE. It would then be routed through senior Canadian management and U.S. division and group levels. The final stage was for the AFE to go to the Operating committee at the sector level for assessment. See Exhibits 5 and 6 for partial organization charts for 3M Worldwide International.

The Perth proposal acknowledged that Alexandria was a competently managed plant and that putting the new equipment in either location would reduce costs from their current levels. At issue was where the greater cost savings would be generated. The Perth proposal argued that these would occur in Perth (see Exhibit 7) through a combination of reduced freight and storage costs, and faster and more efficient manufacturing. The Perth proposal's overall approach was to emphasize what was best for shareholders on the basis of total delivered costs.

Overall employment needs were expected to increase by eight in Canada yet decline by at least double that in Alexandria (see Table 1).

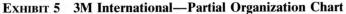

EXHIBIT 5   3M International—Partial Organization Chart

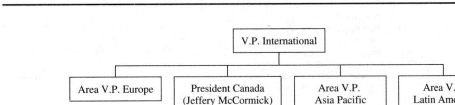
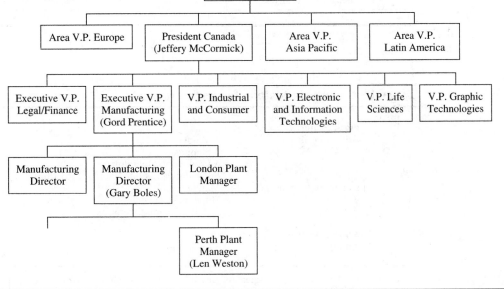

EXHIBIT 6   3M Worldwide—Partial Organization Chart

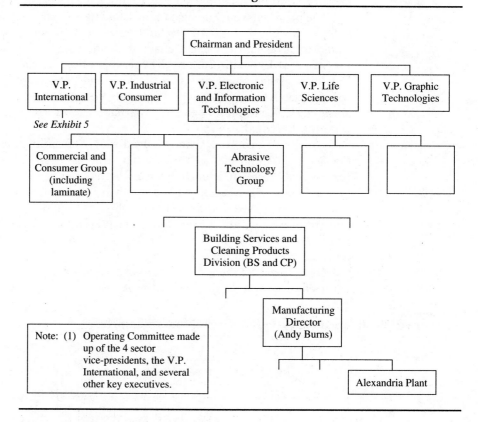

Note: (1) Operating Committee made up of the 4 sector vice-presidents, the V.P. International, and several other key executives.

TABLE 1   Changes in Staffing for Each Proposal

Perth Proposal

Add in Perth	1 Maintenance
	3 Shippers
	4 Production Operators*
Total	8 Persons @ Labour Rate U.S.$13.18/hr
Delete in Alexandria	Maintenance?
	Shipping/Receiving?
	16.5 Production Operators

Alexandria Proposal

Add in Alexandria	6 Operators @ $15.43

* In addition, 8 persons in floor pad manual conversion, and 4 persons in hand pad manual conversion would now be shifted to hand pad automated conversion in Perth.

EXHIBIT 7   Sample Unit Cost Comparison (U.S. Dollars per Case)

	Current Alexandria Operation	*Upgraded Cutter Alexandria*	*Upgraded Cutter Perth*
Jumbo cost ex Perth	$ 6.20	$ 6.20	$ 6.20
Jumbo freight to Alexandria	$ 0.70	$ 0.70	—
Jumbo storage	$ 0.70	$ 0.70	$ 0.05
Jumbo burden absorption	—	—	($ 0.20)[1]
Input cost to converting	$ 7.60	$ 7.60	$ 6.05
Converting waste	$ 0.95	$ 0.65	$ 0.45
Converting labour	$ 1.35	$ 0.30	$ 0.15[2]
Variable converting overhead	$ 0.60	$ 0.45	$ 0.30
Fixed converting overhead	$ 1.00	$ 0.55	$ 0.85[3]
Packaging supplies	$ 1.20	$ 1.20	$ 1.20
Fin goods whse/mat hand	$ 0.45	$ 0.45	$ 0.25
Fin goods direct charges	$ 1.15	$ 1.15	$ 0.90
Cost including converting	$14.30	$12.35	$10.10
Freight to branch	$ 0.90	$ 0.90	$ 1.05
Cost delivered to branch	$15.20	$13.25	$11.15

[1] Volume savings through equipment usage.

[2] Lower than Alexandria due to faster equipment speed and smaller production teams.

[3] Higher than Alexandria due to larger investment in equipment.

Source: Perth Proposal

Some of the modest employment increases in Canada could be traced to the fact that the small amount of manual converting in Perth would now be automated. It had been viable to convert a small quantity of hand pads in Canada, even manually, when shipping costs and duties were factored in.

The biggest reason for the small number of proposed new hires in Canada was the plan to discontinue floor pad manual converting in Perth and to shift those operators to the automated hand pad area. The initial response to this in Canada, in several quarters, had been less than enthusiastic.

The Canadian floor pad business manager felt that he might now have to pay a premium if purchasing from the U.S. As well, he was concerned that some of his customers might notice a difference in performance. He felt the manually converted floor pads from Perth were of a slightly higher quality than the automatically converted ones from Hutchison, Minnesota. The Canadian business manager had built a higher market share for 3M floor pads in Canada than his U.S. counterparts, and he did not wish to see this jeopardized.

A shift from floor pad manual converting to hand pad automated converting would also have immediate implications for the operators. Currently, most of the manual floor pad (and hand pad) jobs were on a one-shift (day) basis. A second, evening shift was sometimes required, but no one worked the midnight-to-morning shift. With automation, all operators would now need to work a three-shift rotation in order to maximize machine utilization. In a non-union plant, with a 10-year tradition of day jobs in converting, and with a no-lay-off policy, this could be an emotional issue. The task of selling it to the operators would fall to Weston.

The Alexandria Response

The Alexandria response was less a proposal, and more a reaction to the Perth initiative. A variety of concerns, some old and some new, were raised.

- First, the increased production volume in Canada and the resultant re-exports to the United States would cause an increased vulnerability to currency fluctuations.
- Second, lengthening the supply distance would make it more difficult to guarantee delivery to U.S. customers.
- Third, the Perth plant would now need to be interfaced with the 3M-USA computer-based materials management system in order to have effective transportation. This would require the Canadian information technology group to work with the logistics people in order to develop a program which would allow for cross-border integration of information.
- Fourth, cost of shipping finished goods to the branches would increase in both Perth *and* Alexandria. In Perth it would be due to the smaller volumes, and increased distances associated with shipping a single product line. In Alexandria it would now take longer to make up a truckload without the hand pads.
- Fifth, since SCOTCH-BRITE converting was already well established in Alexandria, and there would be savings wherever the new equipment was located, it was safer to keep it where the manufacturing experience already existed rather than to rely on optimistic projections from Perth.

Conclusion

In part, due to the distances involved, regional production mandates on various products had been granted as early as the 1970s by 3M in Europe. SCOTCH-BRITE, in fact, was already also being produced in Europe, Asia, and Mexico. However, unlike these other production mandates, the Perth proposal was to supply the core U.S. market. For the operating committee, the decision would come down to how much confidence they had in the Perth proposal.

SID'S SUNFLOWER SEEDS LTD.

Introduction

In late 1988, Issy Steen, president and owner of Sid's Sunflower Seeds (Sid's) of Regina, Saskatchewan, sat down to assess the results and progress for the year. The assessment was particularly important as Steen had made a major move during the year by signing, in March 1988, an agreement that made Sid's the "official supplier of sunflower seed of Major League Baseball."

Steen had regarded the agreement as a great opportunity but after signing the agreement, he became concerned about certain implications of the decision, such as the need to expand the plant and the availability of raw materials. Steen had to decide how to deal with these concerns, and perhaps even whether he should attempt to withdraw from the agreement.

Company History

Sid's Sunflower Seeds was established in 1938 by Sid Bercovich, who saw an opportunity to capitalize on the growing popularity of sunflower seeds. Bercovich established a small production line in his garage and an office in his house. Sid's manufactured and sold one product: roasted and salted sunflower seeds in the shell. All selling and distribution functions were personally undertaken by Bercovich. This limited growth and initially restricted distribution to Regina.

This case was written by C. Brooke Dobni of the University of Saskatchewan as a basis for class discussion rather than to illustrate either effective or ineffective handling of an administrative problem. Some of the financial and other data has been disguised to protect the integrity of the business. Copyright Brooke Dobni.

The post–World War II affluent society and demographics fostered snack and confectionary foods. The market for pet foods also expanded over this period. Bercovich broadened his company's distribution to Saskatoon, Saskatchewan, and points in between with all of the selling still done personally, by Bercovich, or through word of mouth. Orders were filled on an "as available" basis. This nonaggressive approach to marketing and customer service resulted in small but stable growth. Eventually, the business was moved from Bercovich's garage to an older but larger facility in northeast Regina, which allowed for increased storage of raw materials and finished goods.

By the end of 1973, gross sales reached $300,000. Sales were seasonal, peaking in the summer months. During peak production periods, Sid's employed over 50 people. All processing and packaging was done manually from one seed roaster and one packaging line. Seeds were packaged in popcorn-like paper bags and came in two sizes, 200 and 500 grams. After a bag was filled, it was then stapled shut and placed in boxes for shipment.

Market penetration was still confined to Saskatchewan. There was very little competition for sunflower seeds in Saskatchewan, and Bercovich had no desire to expand geographically. Any increase in sales was generally developed and not acquired from the competition.

In 1974, Issy Steen purchased Sid's from Bercovich, who lived in the same apartment building as Steen. By this time, the plant was old and dilapidated. The only significant piece of equipment was the seed roaster. The transition of ownership was also strained by the fact that Bercovich had wanted to back out of the deal at the last minute. Steen refused, so Bercovich pulled all of the corporate records prior to the transfer and refused to introduce Steen to the production process. Steen knew absolutely nothing about the business or related markets and within weeks of the sale, all 50 of the production staff refused to return to work because Steen would not agree to an employment contract. Steen recounts:

> I did not know who I was selling to or who I was buying raw materials from or even how to manage the production process. What I did know, however, was that I had no staff and that the demand for the product appeared overwhelming, so I rolled up my sleeves and began to roast sunflower seeds. I literally destroyed thousands of pounds of seeds before I got the hang of it. Fortunately for me, it was the slow part of the season.

Steen did not make any changes to the production process in 1974. Instead, he wanted to learn more about the business before making any major decisions. He was able to hire new staff in time for the peak season. Even at a rate of one package per minute, production was still a problem as Steen could not meet the demand and his facilities could not accommodate more workers. In fact, Steen estimated that he could only fill one third of his orders.

In 1975, Steen purchased some production and packaging equipment in efforts to increase production efficiency, and soon production outpaced sales.

As well, he was able to reduce his staff, allowing him to significantly increase his margins. The next logical step for Sid's was to expand its market presence. For the first time in the company's history, this meant going beyond Saskatchewan's borders.

Throughout the late 1970s and 1980s, Steen continued to improve production efficiency and geographically expand markets through brokers in the northwestern United States, Australia, Europe, the Pacific Rim, and Scandinavian countries. (For market breakdown, see Exhibit 1.) He also broadened the product line to include pumpkin seeds and hulled sunflower seeds. By 1988, Sid's sold more sunflower seeds than any other company in Canada, employed 19 people, and had five seed roasters and an automated production process. In 1988, Sid's sold nearly 3 million kilograms of sunflower seeds.

Sid's built a reputation for product taste and quality. Sid's offered a product that was less salty than competitors and presented it as a nut as

---

EXHIBIT 1   Sid's Sales Breakdown by Percentage—Geographic

With MLB Market Penetration (1990–1995 projected)

	1974	1978	1982	1986	1990	1991	1992	1993	1994	1995
Western Canada	100	100	97	92	85	80	70	64	53	40
Eastern Canada*	0	0	0	0	5	7	10	12	15	18
United States†	0	0	2	4	4	6	10	13	18	24
Australia, New Zealand, and Europe‡	0	0	1	4	6	6	8	8	8	8
Pacific Rim§	0	0	0	0	0	1	2	3	6	10
Total kilograms processed‖	680	1,181	1,772	2,500	3,540	4,000	4,700	5,400	6,600	8,600

Without MLB Market Penetration

	1974	1978	1982	1986	1990	1991	1992	1993	1994	1995
Western Canada	100	100	97	92	87	83	81	75	71	65
Eastern Canada*	0	0	0	0	3	5	6	8	12	15
United States	0	0	2	4	4	5	5	6	6	8
Australia, New Zealand, and Europe†	0	0	1	4	6	6	6	8	8	8
Pacific Rim	0	0	0	0	0	1	2	3	3	4
Total kilograms processed‖	680	1,181	1,772	2,500	3,250	3,700	4,100	4,400	4,800	5,200

* Put product into Eastern Canada in 1989 on a test basis.

† The percentage of Sid's sunflower seed sales will increase as Steen signs on more baseball stadiums in the United States.

‡ Sid's sells bulk seeds (roasted, salted, but not packaged) to Europe. The seeds are packaged by a producer in Europe and sold under another label. Sid's would like to deemphasize this practice and replace it with their own packaged product.

§ Sid's is attempting to capitalize on the popularity of baseball in Japan and Korea. Steen is hoping that the major league baseball logo will help him to do this. By 1995, Sid's hopes to have a strong presence in this market.

‖ Total kilograms of all confectionery product processed by Sid's. This includes hulled and dehulled sunflower seeds (bulk and packaged), and pumpkin seeds.

opposed to a seed. According to Steen, the production process (particularly roasting and salting), combined with an entrepreneurial spirit, was the secret to the company's longevity and success. This corporate philosophy remained apparent, and the production process was a proprietary secret.

The Sunflower Seed Industry

The Product and Market

The cultivation and eating of seeds originated in Europe and was brought to North America by early settlers. By 1988, the sunflower was grown mainly for the production of edible oils, though demand for non-oilseed varieties had also grown rapidly. Production of non-oilseed sunflower seeds in the United States and Canada had increased from 24,000 tonnes in 1973 to 276,000 tonnes in 1988, an average annual growth rate of about 17 percent. This was grown in 310,000 hectares concentrated in the midwestern United States and the warmer growing areas of Canada.

About 50 percent of the non-oilseed production was used for confectionary, primarily in two forms. The largest seed (usually 15–25 percent of the non-oilseed crop) was separated, roasted, and packaged whole (i.e., hulled), and sold in the same way as roasted peanuts in the shell. The remainder was dehulled, and the kernels used for confectionaries or in confectionary products, often appearing in roasted form in competition with other packaged shelled nuts. The fraction of the smallest seed (15–20 percent of the non-oilseed crop) was used in the rations for birds and seed-eating pets. Although raw sunflower seed could be stored for an indefinite period of time under the right conditions, it was important to secure top-quality seed to meet production requirements. Unavailability of the proper sizes of seed was often a limiting factor when determining production mix (i.e., hulled versus dehulled).

Food and snack processors bought sunflower seed either from the growers directly by contract or from a seed broker. In order to ensure raw material supply, most processors contracted production for the year, with contracts established in early April just prior to planting. Contracting provided both growers and processors with a predetermined price for specific production levels. However, the amount produced could not be guaranteed due to a number of uncontrollable factors such as weather and insects. Since raw material supply was critical to processors, most spread the risk by contracting with growers in different growing areas.

Human consumption of sunflower seeds in the shell was rather seasonal and often confined to the outdoors. The biggest consumers of sunflower seeds were sports enthusiasts, particularly baseball and football fans, where watching the game and eating seeds had long been considered a "natural" tradition. This tradition contributed to the seasonality of the products. This pattern was slowly changing as market development efforts for sunflower seeds were being directed at more and alternate season sports in the United States.

The status of sunflower seeds as a consumer product was described by Aaron Steen (Issy's brother and sales manager) as follows:

> Sunflower seeds, like other snack foods, are an impulse purchase item. A consumer rarely goes to a store with the intention of buying sunflower seeds. Rather, he or she will notice the product while shopping and then throw it in their basket. This is why product recognition and brand loyalty is important. For example, if they have had Sid's seeds before, say at a sporting event, and enjoyed them, hopefully they will choose our product over the competition the next time they are in the store. Shelf space and displays in strategic positions in as many stores as possible translates into three key marketing variables we rely on: exposure, recognition, and availability. We know our efforts are paying off when retailers tell us that consumers specifically asked for our product when it was not on the shelf.

Distribution and Competition

Confection goods always experienced a great deal of competition, especially as North America's demand for snack foods increased. Securing and retaining shelf space in grocery and convenience stores was tantamount to establishing a competitive edge.

Sunflower seeds had traditionally been considered an add-on to the snack food product lines of potato chips and nuts. This resulted from the seasonality of sales and the lack of effort directed toward market development. Further, sunflower seeds were often only one of a number of products that were processed and marketed by a single company. For example, companies like Old Dutch, Hostess-Frito Lay, and Nutty Club produced and marketed potato chips, pistachios, peanuts, and related products in addition to sunflower seeds. As a result, sunflower seeds were relatively obscure in Eastern Canada and points in the United States.

In Western Canada, confectionary sunflower seeds were considered to be a stand-alone product. This could be credited to the marketing efforts of Sid's and Tasty Flavour. Both Sid's and Tasty Flavour processed and marketed sunflower seeds as their primary product and distributed directly to the retailers without the use of middlemen. Both had embarked on major marketing campaigns in the early 1980s in Western Canada that were directed toward consumer awareness and new market development. As a result of their activity, the consumption of sunflower seeds in Western Canada increased significantly, although this market appeared to be approaching saturation. Both Sid's and Tasty's emphasized the necessity to develop new markets.

Sid's was highly dependent on this Western Canadian market with 83 percent of its sales in this area and only 3 percent in Eastern Canada, 4 percent in the United States, and 6 percent offshore. However, it did hold a dominant position in Western Canada with estimated market shares of 70 percent in British Columbia, 75 percent in Alberta, and 83 percent in Saskatchewan.

Sid's major competition in North America included the following:

Tasty Flavour.   Tasty was Sid's major competitor in Western Canada. Based out of Winnipeg, Tasty's initially concentrated on the Manitoba market where in 1988 it held an estimated 80 percent market share versus Sid's 10 percent. In 1982, in response to Sid's entry into Manitoba, Tasty began to expand its marketing and distribution efforts outside of Manitoba. Although their efforts had not been as concentrated and aggressive as Sid's, their market share had shown moderate increases in Saskatchewan, Alberta, British Columbia, and Eastern Canada. Of all the competition, Tasty's product was most closely positioned to Sid's, emphasizing freshness and quality. Sunflower seeds represented 85 percent of Tasty's revenues.

Old Dutch.   Old Dutch offered both hulled and dehulled sunflower seeds as a part of their broad product line. The company tended to concentrate on the densely populated Eastern Canadian market. However, their advantages in distribution (using company truck jobbers with sunflower seeds being an extension of their potato chip and nut product line) allowed them to develop markets in Western Canada by supplying more remote areas and capitalizing on existing distribution channels. Old Dutch also benefited from strong brand recognition.

Hostess-Frito Lay.   As a division of General Foods Canada, Inc., Hostess-Frito Lay offered a diversified product line. It focused its activities on Eastern Canada. Like Old Dutch, Hostess seeds were an extension of their potato chip product line. Hostess also took advantage of a comprehensive distribution network, providing them with a competitive advantage, particularly in Eastern Canada.

Other.   Humpty Dumpty, Johnson Nut, Nutty Club, Trophy Nut, Opechee, and David and Sons all offered sunflower seeds as an add-on to potato chips, nuts, and other confection items. These competitors were heavily concentrated in Eastern Canada and the United States while their market presence in Western Canada was minimal due to the lack of population density in the west.

Sid's competition, with the exception of Tasty Flavour, possessed a competitive advantage in their ability to distribute product more effectively and at a lower cost per kilogram. As an add-on product to their mainline confectionary products such as potato chips and nuts, promotion and distribution costs were rationalized. Moreover, competition such as Old Dutch, Hostess-Frito Lay, and Johnson Nut had established shelf space in most stores. Incremental shelf space costs for these companies would be lower than what Sid's would have to pay.

Sid's Operations

Management

The Sid's management group worked informally with a minimum of structure and control. (Exhibit 2 reviews the backgrounds and responsibilities of the top management group.) The team did what had to be done, often covering for each other. In fact, it was not an unusual sight to see Issy or Aaron Steen load a last-minute order for shipment. All of the managers were pressed by the requirements of everyday business. Priority was given to "putting out fires," which often preoccupied one's day. The installation of an information system in late 1986 smoothed out operations, particularly since the plant and the head office were separated.

Marketing

Marketing duties were split between Issy and Aaron Steen. Issy concentrated on identifying and developing growth opportunities in new markets. Aaron was responsible for product line marketing and the maintenance of current accounts. As well, Aaron developed new accounts in existing markets as

---

EXHIBIT 2   Backgrounds and Responsibilities of Top Management Group, Sid's Sunflower Seeds (1974) Ltd.

Issy Steen, Owner/President—Age 42
Degree in Sociology/Psychology—University of Manitoba 1967. Between 1968 and 1974, managed the head office for a family chain of eight restaurants. Purchased Sid's Sunflower Seeds in 1974 and then concentrated his efforts on the general management of this organization. Responsibilities also included contracting of seeds and other major purchases.

Aaron Steen, Sales Manager—Age 35
Joined Sid's Sunflower Seeds in 1986. Prior to coming to Sid's, had worked as a sales representative for Hershey Canada, Inc., a major confectionery company for 12 years. In the last four years of employment with Hershey, was sales manager for Manitoba and Saskatchewan. At Sid's, concentrated on servicing existing accounts and further developing markets in territories where Sid's was already established. Also assumed general management responsibilities when Issy was away for extended periods.

Jerry Cheslok, Controller—Age 48
Bachelor of Administration degree from the University of Regina and a Chartered Accountant (CA) designation. Prior to joining Sid's in 1984, worked for 11 years as a credit officer for SEDCO. At Sid's, responsible for all accounting and credit functions and monitoring relationships with outsiders such as banks and government agencies.

Henry Veenstra—Age 58
Has been production manager with Sid's for over 20 years. At Sid's, responsible for production scheduling, production, maintenance, minor purchases, shipping, and receiving.

---

the opportunities arose. Surprisingly, Aaron Steen knew very little of Issy's developmental efforts.

Sid's employed eight sales representatives (two in British Columbia, two in Alberta, three in Saskatchewan, and one in Manitoba). These reps, who reported to Aaron Steen, made regularly scheduled calls and faxed orders back to the plant on a daily basis. They were paid a wage plus commission, giving them incentive to develop new accounts in their respective territories. Recently, market growth in Western Canada had been slowing, and it appeared that the market was approaching saturation.

Sid's marketing philosophy was to market their product to anybody, anywhere provided that a sufficient return could be made without jeopardizing existing accounts. Aaron summed up the market strategy as follows:

> Our target market is anyone with teeth—right from the day that they get them to the day that they lose them. Our product has no legal, cultural, or political barriers; the only thing that we have to be concerned about is getting the product to the customer's place, on time, in a fresh state, and at a cost that will allow us to remain competitive. All product is shipped FOB to the account's doorstep.
>
> We also have to be very careful not to oversell as we do not want to be in the position of having to ration shipments. This could prove devastating to our reputation, especially since the market has become quite competitive.
>
> We are also attempting to capitalize on the health food craze. Within the past two or three years, we have begun to offer roasted, no-salt, hulled, and dehulled sunflower seeds. This, combined with the already low levels of cholesterol associated with seeds, allows us to market it as a health food where necessary. Seeds are great for people who are overweight but like to snack or for people who have just quit smoking and have the sensation to eat.

A key element in Sid's overall marketing program was packaging. In 1976, Sid's converted to a bright red plasticized and laminated foil package that kept the product fresh for up to nine months and added visual appeal with its bright colours. Since the product could sit for some time in the client's stock, freshness had to be guaranteed upon consumer purchase.

Sid's also differentiated its product through price. Their prices were higher across the board, but they were able to maintain this differential by relying on other competitive advantages. Originally, this price differential was necessary to cover higher than average distribution costs. Luckily, it inferred higher product quality, allowing Sid's to be referred to as the "cadillac of sunflower seeds."

Until 1988, Issy had single-handedly developed all of the company's export markets and identified other feasible growth opportunities. The development of new markets had always preoccupied Steen:

> It is costly and difficult to develop new markets. One has to determine how much effort to expend on such tasks. Remember our business relies on volume. When we identify new opportunities, we have to look at areas that will promote volume.

When we go into a new market, we have no guarantee that our product will be accepted, or if it is, that the anticipated volume will be guaranteed. We've been burned in the past and that's been costly.

In the continuing effort to develop new markets, Sid's looked to Eastern Canada and the United States. Previous market entry efforts in Eastern Canada were marginally successful, but Sid's was unable to maintain a presence due to excessive costs or other nonmitigating factors. Steen felt that Sid's required a competitive advantage that would allow the organization to sustain a market presence—something that would further differentiate his product from that of the competition. As market growth in Western Canada slowed, the issue of new market development would become even more important. Issy elaborated:

> Trying to get a product established in an already competitive market is both costly and time-consuming. In Eastern Canada, we simply could not compete against the economies of scale possessed by our competition. At that time, nobody there had heard of Sid's sunflower seeds and likely nobody cared. We did an observation study of our product in Fortinos Supermarkets in Toronto. People looked at our product, and even picked it up, but then put it back down in favour of a well-known competitor's product. Quite simply, we did not possess the recognition or loyalty that we enjoyed in the West. Television would have been a natural in an entry campaign, but producing a television commercial would have cost $25,000 or more. Then, of course, air time must be added to this. This would blow our entire advertising and promotional budget. What would that do to our other marketing initiatives?

Promotion

Although Sid's did not develop an explicit marketing plan, the company spent approximately 10 percent of annual revenues on advertising and promotion. At the retail level, campaigns were often aimed at the promotion of eating seeds and outdoor activities. For example, in some of their better retail accounts, a promotion campaign included a canoe and tent giveaway. The instore static display had two mannequins portraying campers in front of a tent with a canoe filled with bags of Sid's sunflower seeds. With each purchase of a bag of seeds, customers were able to enter their names for a draw to win the canoe and tent. Other promotion activities included sunflower seed giveaways, joint promotions with other products such as Coca-Cola, contests, couponing, other static displays, and print and radio media. Sid's also sponsored a number of sporting events and teams, such as little league baseball tournaments and baseball teams. Many of these activities were done on a test basis and carried a high price tag. After completion of any one campaign, the management team would sit down and attempt to quantify the costs versus the benefits.

Distribution

Sid's emphasized getting the product to the customer on time, in the quantities ordered, and as cheaply as possible. Sid's did not employ truck jobbers, but rather utilized the common carrier system. Under this system, Aaron spent much of his time "tracking" when a shipment became lost in transit.

To reduce shipping costs of less than truckload shipments, Sid's leased a warehouse in Vancouver, British Columbia. Truckload lots were shipped to this warehouse where they were broken down and distributed to various accounts. All of the B.C. accounts and some international accounts were serviced out of this warehouse. All other orders were shipped from the Regina warehouse. Distribution was seen as one area that needed improvement if they were to remain competitive in markets outside of Western Canada.

Sid's took particular pride in being able to deliver their product on time and in the amounts ordered. According to Issy:

> This type of customer service is the basis for our repeat purchases. If the customer can count on us, we can count on them. Not only that, our reputation has been the foundation for much new business. We get calls from all over Western Canada asking if we can immediately supply an order—an order that another producer has failed to supply. Naturally, we jump at the opportunity, providing it will not jeopardize existing accounts. Much of our new business often comes at the expense of a competitor. Once we get a new account, we do our best not to lose it.

Production

Sid's operated an 8,000-square-foot production facility in Regina, Saskatchewan. Raw material was delivered to the plant by the semitrailer load. Once delivered, the raw material was screened and then stored in one of two silos on site. Raw material storage capacity was 30,000 kilograms. There was no room at the production site to build more storage silos, and large capital expenditures would be required to accommodate roof storage.

From bulk storage, the product passed through two more screening areas and one sieve area. Sid's attempted to rid the product of all foreign matter (sticks, rocks, and stems) and ensure proper seed size before roasting. After this process was complete, the seed was stored in clean holding.

Roasting and salting took place on one of five roasting lines. Three lines were dedicated to hulled and unhulled sunflower seeds to be salted. One line was dedicated to pumpkin seeds to be salted while one line processed product that was not to be salted. Sunflower seeds were roasted for approximately 30 minutes at 180 degrees celsius. Salt flour was added while roasting took place. Thus, there were only two raw materials required for production, seeds and salt. From the roaster lines, the product passed through a final screening process before entering one of three packaging lines. Each line was capable of packaging in excess of 60 bags per minute. The product was packaged, boxed, and loaded in a Sid's truck and shipped across town to their office and

EXHIBIT 3   Sid's Sunflower Seeds, Production Mix 1988

Product	% Production
Hulled sunflower seed	75%
Dehulled sunflower seed	10
Pumpkin seed	13
Bird seed	2

		Package Size					
Production Breakdown	*% Prod.*	*45 g*	*65 g*	*150 g*	*350 g*	*900 g*	*Bulk 50 lb.*
Hulled sunflower seeds roasted, and salted	72	X	X	X	X	X	X
Hulled sunflower seeds roasted, no salt	3	X	X	X	X	X	X
Dehulled sunflower seeds roasted, and salted	8	X	X				
Dehulled sunflower seeds roasted, no salt	2	X	X				
Pumpkin seed	13	X	X	X			X
Bird seed	2						X

warehouse. Orders to wholesalers and retailers were filled from the warehouse building and carried by independent truckers. During peak season (April to October), product was processed and shipped daily.

Maximum plant capacity of the existing Regina plant was 5.5 million kilograms annually. This would be realized on three 8-hour shifts, seven days per week (with one portion of a shift being allocated to maintenance). Ideal plant capacity was 4.5 million kilograms annually. The production mix package size for 1988 is presented in Exhibit 3. A percentage breakdown of cost of goods manufactured is presented in Exhibit 4.

Issy Steen had gone a long way to improve the efficiency of the production process. By automating functions and increasing the capacity of equipment, he had decreased production staff from 50 people per shift in 1974 to 6 in 1988, while increasing output from 50 packages per minute in 1974 to 180 per minute in 1988. Obviously, this had decreased the production cost per unit dramatically.

Inventory

During the spring and summer months, scheduled deliveries of raw material arrived at the plant two to three times per week. In the slower winter months, one trailer load per week was received. Sunflower and pumpkin seeds in a raw state can be inventoried for an indefinite period given the right conditions. A major concern was securing the proper size seed at peak production times, which may require holding more inventory than desired at any given time.

All raw inventory (primarily seed product and salt) were stored at the

Exhibit 4   Sid's Sunflower Seeds, Cost of Goods Manufactured Breakdown (percentage basis averaged over a year)

Raw material	
Seeds	28
Salt	2
Freight	
In	12
Out	18
Wages	19
Overhead (including electricity)	21
	100

production facility. On a daily basis, finished goods were trucked to the 12,000-square-foot warehouse where the corporate office was also located. In the peak production season, the plant had only enough capacity to store three days' worth of raw material. As a result, coordination of raw material deliveries was of primary importance.

Contracting

All of the sunflower seeds used by Sid's were grown under contract. Every April Steen hooked up his camper trailer to his car and headed to the United States to meet with growers and negotiate contracts. Almost all of the product used by Sid's came from Kansas, Wyoming, and Colorado. To reduce the risk associated with crop failure, Steen established contracts with numerous growers in diverse growing regions and because yields could not be guaranteed, he often contracted for amounts greater than the estimated annual requirements. Only in extenuating circumstances did Steen go to the farmgate to purchase raw material. According to Steen, the price one pays for raw material in any one year can mean the difference between profit and loss, especially in years of poor yields, where demand for material often exceeds supply. Contracts were established FOB the grower, a long-standing industry standard.

Finance and Administration

Given its size, the relative simplicity of its operations, and the informal management structure, the company did not have an elaborate management information system. Although limited use was made of the reports that the management information system was capable of generating, a monthly report of sales by product line and area was made available to each manager. Versions of these reports were then filtered to sales reps and production personnel. Quarterly reports, compiled manually by accounting, attempted to determine actual margins by product line.

EXHIBIT 5   SID'S SUNFLOWER SEEDS (1974) LTD.
Income Statements
Years Ended September 30
($000s)

	1988	*1986*	*1982*	*1978*	*1974*	*1973*
Sales:						
Product	2,136	1,656	1,102	735	406	300
Other	3	3	4	2	—	—
Total sales	2,139	1,659	1,106	737	406	300
Cost of goods sold:						
Direct labour	252	194	127	91	55	42
Direct material	397	305	201	145	89	70
Overhead	278	214	140	101	61	47
Freight	397	306	201	144	87	64
Depreciation	75	61	50	38	12	6
Other	82	66	45	30	6	2
Total cost of goods sold	1,481	1,146	764	549	310	231
Gross profit:	658	513	342	188	96	69
Selling and administrative:						
Wages and fringe	200	180	124	80	45	40
Advertising and	260	175	115	75	27	10
promotion	60	44	29	15	6	4
Expenses	520	399	268	170	78	54
Financial:						
Interest and financial	42	42	50	35	13	—
Other*	—	—	100	—	—	—
	42	42	150	35	13	—
Earnings (loss) before taxes	96	72	(76)	(17)	5	15
Provision for taxes	21.8	10.8	—	—	1.2	3.7
Net income (loss)	74.1	61.2	(76)	(17)	3.8	11.3

* The expense in 1982 can be attributed to an investment by Sid's that failed.

With the exception of a few bad years, the company had been consistently, though not exceptionally, profitable (Exhibit 5). As a result, by the end of fiscal year 1988, net worth was $377,800 and all loan obligations were secured and readily serviceable (Exhibit 6).

Sid's employed a very tough credit policy which helped to limit bad debts. Thirty percent of Sid's customers were well-established national wholesalers representing 70 percent of the company's business. New accounts were screened carefully and often were required to pay COD until credibility could be established. Credit terms were net 30 days with no incentive for early payment. Often, however, it seemed that even the best accounts stretched payments beyond 60 days.

Exhibit 6   SID'S SUNFLOWER SEEDS (1974) LTD.
Balance Sheet (1973–1988)
As of September 30

	1988	1986	1982	1978	1974	1973
Assets						
Cash	5,025	3,000	150	150	1,000	500
Accounts receivable	281,749	258,009	175,200	105,751	58,421	40,052
Other current assets	20,351	15,272	1,100	9,872	4,500	–0–
Inventory	250,100	190,350	142,600	89,720	42,100	19,100
Total current assets	557,225	466,631	319,070	205,493	106,021	59,652
Fixed assets	452,350	409,000	310,050	300,192	93,005	100,110
Total assets	1,009,575	875,631	629,120	505,685	199,026	159,762
Liabilities						
Operating loan	153,500	150,000	105,650	71,125	42,120	25,001
Accounts payable	269,269	233,296	136,552	89,747	53,354	50,900
Other current liabilities	33,052	26,756	39,200	12,651	3,052	1,250
Total current liabilities	455,821	410,052	281,402	173,523	98,526	77,151
Term loans	175,950	220,025	244,592	260,000	70,500	0
Total liabilities	631,771	630,077	525,994	433,523	169,026	77,151
Share capital	60,000	60,000	30,000	30,000	30,000	1,500
Retained earnings	317,804	185,554	73,176	42,162	–0–	81,111
Total equity	377,804	245,554	103,176	72,162	30,000	82,611
Total liabilities and owner's equity	1,009,575	875,631	629,170	505,685	199,026	159,762

Sid's utilized a $150,000 revolving bank line of credit to finance receivables and inventories. Outstanding term debt had been used for both capital and noncapital purposes. It consisted of commercial bank debt as well as agreements with government agencies, the Federal Business Development Bank (FBDB), and the Saskatchewan Economic Development Corporation (SEDCO).

Strategic Planning

Goals, objectives, and strategies were not documented or communicated to employees. Issy felt that the organization was small enough that a formal planning process was still not necessary.

> We have limited resources, both in time and human factors, to formalize this process. I know what I want this company to do over the next five years and how to achieve it. That's good enough for me and so far it's worked for us.

One common goal shared by the organization was that of growth; however, the means to achieve this growth was not totally consistent.

Formal planning sessions were limited in scope and held on an ad hoc basis. Issy and Aaron Steen and Jerry Cheslok periodically sat down to analyse accounts in respect to promotion efforts. Changes in promotional strategies were made as necessary.

Issy had a number of reasons for not articulating his strategies. These reasons ranged from industry competitiveness to not wanting to freeze the organization. He was also aware of the dangers associated with not formalizing the organization's strategies. As he said, "If I got struck down by a truck tomorrow, the future plans for Sid's would go with me."

Issy's goals remained quite simple. He wanted the company to remain the number-one producer of seeds in Canada and continue to grow on an incremental basis by exploiting new marketing opportunities. He also wanted the company to continue its growth by expanding its market presence in Eastern Canada and the United States. The idea of building on a reputation of over 50 years while remaining a family-owned and -operated business remained first and foremost in Issy's future plans for Sid's. At the same time, Issy was also very loyal to the city of Regina. He and his wife had lived there for over 20 years, and he felt that both the city and province had been good to him and his business.

The Major League Baseball Agreement

Background

The opportunity to obtain the endorsement of major league baseball came about quite accidentally. Several months after a trade show in New York in May 1987, Issy was contacted by Bart Lewis of the Licensing Corporation of America (LCA). He said that he had enjoyed product samples Issy had sent him and he suggested that sunflower seeds would be ideal for a new promotion that the LCA and Major League Baseball (MLB) were working on. They wanted to change the image of baseball by getting players to switch from chewing tobacco to an alternative product. Lewis asked if Sid's would like to negotiate for the rights to become the official supplier of sunflower seeds to MLB. Steen agreed almost immediately since he saw it as a vehicle for breaking into the eastern market.

The factor underlying MLB's interest was concern with the use of chewing tobacco by players. Chewing tobacco is moist, flavoured tobacco that is chewed instead of smoked. This tobacco is very addictive as the nicotine is highly concentrated. Use of chewing tobacco had been directly linked to mouth, tongue, and lip cancer as well as to chronic halitosis and severely discoloured teeth. Four out of 10 players in MLB used chewing tobacco. In 1988, C. Everett Koop, then Surgeon General of the United States, reported that the use of chewing tobacco had reached epidemic proportions, that over 2 million Americans under the age of 15 were regular users. Since many MLB players were role models for young Americans, the league decided to take positive action to eradicate the use of chewing tobacco. Stopping short of banning its use altogether, these efforts included designating baseball stars such as Nolan Ryan of the Texas Rangers to go on television and speak out against its use to encouraging players to find alternate products to occupy their habits. MLB hoped that sunflower seeds would be one product to provide the natural replacement, allowing the players to set a new example for America's youth.

The Agreement

Sid's and the LCA agreed to terms and signed an agreement in March of 1988. The initial agreement was for five years with a mutually agreed option of renewal for an additional five years. During the agreement period, the LCA could not enter into similar negotiations with competing firms.

The agreement gave Sid's the exclusive right to use the major league baseball logo on packaging and all other advertising and promotion activities. Further, it allowed Sid's to represent their product as the official sunflower seed of MLB. In return, Sid's had to supply sunflower seeds free of charge to players in dugout and clubhouse areas and pay a royalty of $.04 to the LCA on each bag of sunflower seeds sold in major league baseball cities. Any benefits that accrued outside of MLB cities as a result of this agreement would be a bonus to Sid's and of no interest to the LCA. The LCA would in turn pay a royalty to MLB to be divided amongst the 26 teams.

This agreement did not automatically secure concession space in major league baseball stadiums, nor did it exclude the competition from attempting to gain entry to these stadiums. Negotiations, marketing, and promotion efforts to gain entry to each stadium was up to Sid's. After careful consideration, Issy felt that these issues could be mitigated by the very fact that Sid's would be recognized as the official supplier. The potential long-term benefits, in Steen's estimation, appeared to outweigh the short-term costs.

One concern of the LCA was that Sid's maximize its distribution efforts to include all 26 MLB stadiums as soon as possible. Bart Lewis explained:

> Naturally we want to maximize our royalties and get as many players as possible eating seeds. We are in business like anyone else. Initially, Sid's wanted to negotiate for the rights team by team, beginning with the two teams in Canada. I said that this was not acceptable, so we came to an agreement which resulted in Issy taking an option on all 26 teams. He will attempt to penetrate all 26 stadiums and teams by 1995. In 1993, we will review the progress to date before we agree to a renewal. If progress is being made, we will renew.
>
> On several occasions, Issy has made it clear to me that this is a rather aggressive schedule and his concerns about his company's ability to supply are well founded. But we both agreed that the benefits inherent in this opportunity were too significant to overlook. Given Issy's entrepreneurial spirit, we are confident that he can achieve the goals that have been set.

Stadium by Stadium

Stadiums that were homes to MLB teams varied in respect to concession operating policies. For example, in the Toronto Skydome scheduled to open in June 1989, the concessions were to be owned by the Skydome Corporation, which had rigid policies concerning product listing. The Skydome Corporation required a $5 million exclusive listing and partnership fee just to get product into concessions. In contrast, in Olympic Stadium where the Montreal Expos played and owned the concession rights, new products could be listed with no up-front fees. Of the 24 teams in the United States, 12 of the stadium concession rights were owned by the occupying team (see Exhibit 7). It was much easier to penetrate stadiums that had team-owned concessions. In the case where concessions were not team owned, Sid's had to negotiate with both the team and stadium concessionaires.

EXHIBIT 7   Sid's Sunflower Seeds—Major League Baseball Stadiums

Stadium	Home of (and Division)	Location	Team-Owned Concession
Exhibition Stadium/Skydome*	Toronto Blue Jays (ALE)	Toronto, Ont.	Yes/No
Olympic Stadium	Montreal Expos (NLE)	Montreal, Que.	Yes
Shea Stadium	New York Mets (NLE)	New York, NY	Yes
Yankee Stadium	New York Yankees (ALE)	New York, NY	Yes
Fenway Park	Boston Red Sox (ALE)	Boston, Mass.	No
Memorial Stadium	Baltimore Orioles (ALE)	Baltimore, Md.	Yes
Astrodome	Houston Astros (NLW)	Houston, Tex.	No
Tiger Stadium	Detroit Tigers (ALE)	Detroit, Mich.	Yes
County Stadium	Milwaukee Brewers (ALE)	Milwaukee, Wis.	Yes
Comiskey Park	Chicago White Sox (ALW)	Chicago, Ill.	No
Wrigley Field	Chicago Cubs (NLE)	Chicago, Ill.	Yes
Oakland-Alameda County Coliseum	Oakland Athletics (ALW)	Oakland, Calif.	No
Anaheim Stadium	California Angels (ALW)	Anaheim, Calif.	No
Candlestick Park	San Francisco Giants (NLW)	San Francisco, Calif.	No
Dodger Stadium	Los Angeles Dodgers (NLW)	Los Angeles, Calif.	Yes
Kingdome	Seattle Mariners (ALW)	Seattle, Wash.	No
Arlington Stadium	Texas Rangers (ALW)	Arlington, Tex.	Yes
San Diego Stadium	San Diego Padres (NLW)	San Diego, Calif.	No
Hubert Humphrey Metrodome	Minnesota Twins (ALW)	Minneapolis, Minn.	No
Municipal Stadium	Cleveland Indians (ALE)	Cleveland, Ohio	Yes
Royals Stadium	Kansas City Royals (ALW)	Kansas City, Mo.	Yes
Three Rivers Stadium	Pittsburgh Pirates (NLE)	Pittsburgh, Penn.	No
Veteran's Stadium	Philadelphia Phillies (NLE)	Philadelphia, Pa.	No
Busch Memorial Stadium	St. Louis Cardinals (NLE)	St. Louis, Mo.	Yes
Riverfront Stadium	Cincinnati Reds (NLW)	Cincinnati, Ohio	No
Atlanta-Fulton County Stadium	Atlanta Braves (NLW)	Atlanta, Ga.	Yes

Note: Key: ALE—American League East   ALW—American League West
NLE—National League East   NLW—National League West

* The Toronto Blue Jays planned to move to the Toronto Skydome in mid-season.

Soon after signing the agreement with LCA, Steen set out to exercise the options and began negotiating with the Toronto Blue Jays and the Montreal Expos. By the season's end, Sid's was successful in getting their product into Exhibition Stadium and Olympic Stadium. Steen estimated that his company spent $25,000 per stadium to sponsor a Sid's night and another $25,000 in related advertising and promotion expenses. Sid's effort in these two stadiums appeared to be successful. In Montreal alone, the ratio of a bag of seeds per fan increased from 1 to 1,110 up to 1 to 200 by season's end. With the Blue Jays moving to the Skydome, Issy concluded Sid's would not be able to get their product into the concessions because of the prohibitive listing cost.

The stadiums that Sid's could penetrate would be costly. Steen estimated that he would have to spend between $50,000 and $75,000 per stadium for initial endorsement advertising and promotion expenses. He felt that this would be a one-time cost in efforts to establish the product and the name in the ball park. This cost would be exclusive of listing fees, where they were imposed by the concession owners.

Central to Steen's entry strategy was the ability to get key players and personnel of respective teams to act as official Sid's spokesmen and endorse the product. He had done this successfully in Toronto and Montreal where Dave Stieb (starting pitcher for Toronto) and Buck Rogers (manager of the Expos) endorsed the product and undertook promotional activities. Issy remarked:

> Buck Rogers has a box of seeds in the Expos dugout. Before each game, he will go to the opponent's dugout and hand out bags to players and coaches. On one occasion, during a game, he noticed Tommy Lasorda, manager of the Los Angeles Dodgers, eating a competitor's seeds. Between innings Rogers walked over to the

---

EXHIBIT 8   Sid's Sunflower Seeds—Total Production in Kilograms (Actual and Projected 1974–1995)

With MLB Penetration

	1974	1978	1982	1986	1990	1991	1992	1993	1994	1995
Kilograms (000) with MLB	680	1,181	1,772	2,500	3,540	4,000	4,700	5,400	6,600	8,600
Manufacturer's level cents/kilogram	.59	.62	.62	.66	.69	.69	.70	.72	.72	.74

Without MLB Penetration

	1974	1978	1982	1986	1990	1991	1992	1993	1994	1995
Kilograms (000) without MLB	680	1,181	1,772	2,500	3,250	3,700	4,100	4,400	4,800	5,200
Manufacturer's level cents/kilogram	.59	.62	.62	.66	.69	.69	.70	.72	.72	.74

Note: Total kilograms of all production; hulled and dehulled sunflower seeds, pumpkin seed, and birdseed.

Los Angeles dugout and offered him a bag of Sid's. Lasorda took them. This is what I pay Buck Rogers to do.

Steen also hoped that promotion activities inside the park would lead to spin-offs outside the park:

> Over 30 million plus fans would be exposed to our product in Shea Stadium. Those fans become consumers when they go back home into their retail stores. It is our hope that they would request and buy Sid's seeds. We would actually be able to make some money, not so much in the stadiums as we will in retail and corner stores and supermarkets in the outlying suburbs around the stadium. Another challenge is to make Sid's seeds available in these stores.

EXHIBIT 9   SID'S SUNFLOWER SEEDS (1974) LTD.
Projected Income Statement 1990–1995
Years Ended September 30
($000's)
with MLB Penetration

	1990	1991	1992	1993	1994	1995
Sales:						
Product	2,446	2,760	3,290	3,888	4,752	6,364
Other	3	5	1	1	10	15
Total sales	2,449	2,765	3,291	3,889	4,762	6,379
Cost of goods sold:						
Direct labour	279	326	388	458	559	747
Direct materials	443	517	614	727	884	1,181
Overhead	308	360	428	507	617	825
Freight	438	512	610	723	880	1,177
Depreciation	75	95	115	200	250	300
Other	82	100	110	120	130	150
Total cost of goods sold	1,625	1,910	2,265	2,735	3,320	4,380
Gross profit	824	855	1,026	1,154	1,442	1,999
Selling and administrative:						
Wages and fringe	220	250	300	325	350	375
Advertising and promotion	350	525	600	650	700	900
Expenses	80	100	100	100	120	140
	650	875	1,000	1,075	1,170	1,415
Financial:						
Interest and financial	45	45	180	180	160	110
Other*	40	—	—	—	—	70
	85	45	180	180	160	180
Earnings (loss) before taxes	89	(65)	(154)	(101)	112	404
Provision for taxes	20.2	—	—	—	—	21.8
Net income (loss)	68.8	(65)	(154)	(101)	112	382

* Projected shareholder bonuses and income from operations used for expansionary purposes.
Assumes expansion of plant in Regina (1992).

Future Direction—The Next Five Years

Steen and his management were optimistic about the future, particularly as it concerned growth potential. Steen felt that the MLB logo opened the door for tremendous growth opportunities in the United States and the Pacific Rim. Further, it would provide him with the competitive edge required to break away from the competition in Eastern Canada and the United States. This growth was consistent with Steen's preferences to grow in foreign markets.

It was also clear to Steen that both he and his company were feeling stretched. Some significant changes would have to be made to allow Sid's to capitalize on future opportunities. As background to the necessary analysis, Steen developed sales estimates with and without the MLB agreement (Exhibit

EXHIBIT 10   SID's SUNFLOWER SEEDS (1974) LTD.
Projected Income Statement 1990–1995
Years Ended September 30
($000's)
without MLB Penetration

	1990	1991	1992	1993	1994	1995
Sales:						
Product	2,250	2,250	2,870	3,160	3,456	3,848
Other	3	3	4	5	6	6
Total sales	2,253	2,553	2,874	3,165	3,462	3,854
Cost of goods sold:						
Direct labour	265	303	334	366	390	442
Direct materials	420	482	530	580	619	700
Overhead	293	335	369	404	432	488
Freight	415	477	525	576	614	695
Depreciation	75	95	115	130	145	150
Other	82	85	85	90	90	95
Total cost of goods sold	1,550	1,777	1,958	2,146	2,290	2,570
Gross profit	703	776	916	1,019	1,172	1,284
Selling and administrative:						
Wages and fringe	220	230	300	300	320	320
Advertising and promotion	280	325	350	400	450	550
Expenses	80	80	90	90	100	100
	580	635	740	790	870	970
Financial:						
Interest and financial	40	40	40	38	36	33
Other*	40	40	40	60	60	60
Total other expenses	80	80	80	98	96	93
Earnings (loss) before taxes	43	61	96	131	206	221
Provision for taxes	9.4	13.4	21.8	28.8	47.9	53.7
Net income (loss)	33.6	47.6	74.2	102.2	158.1	167.3

* Projected shareholder bonuses.

EXHIBIT 11 **Sid's Sunflower Seeds—State-of-the-Art Processing Facility (Location, Costs, and Financing Options)**

The cost, sources, and application of funds for a new production facility. Costs are expressed in 1992 Canadian dollars.

	Western Canada	Eastern Canada	Midwest United States
Item			
Land	$ 0*	$ 250,000	$ 200,000
Infrastructure	300,000	350,000	250,000
Building	1,500,000	1,750,000	1,200,000
Equipment	1,000,000	1,000,000	750,000
Environmental assessment	30,000	30,000	0
Contingency (@ 10%)	283,000	338,000	240,000
	$3,113,000	$3,718,000	$2,640,000
Source of funding (Potential):			
Equity	500,000	500,000	250,000
Debt			
Interest bearing[†]	1,000,000	3,118,000	790,000
Noninterest bearing[‡]	1,513,000	0	1,000,000
Income from operations	100,000	100,000	100,000
Grant[§]	0	0	500,000
	$3,113,000	$3,718,000	$2,640,000

* Would be built on existing land owned by Sid's.

[†] Projected interest rate average of 12 percent on debt in Western and Eastern Canada. Debt would consist of a combination of bank debt and government institutional funding. Effective interest rate in the United States would be 10 percent.

[‡] In Western Canada, assumes interest-free Western Diversification Program (WDP) repayable contribution. (WDP was a federal government program aimed at assisting firms with a Western Canada location to penetrate new markets.) In the United States, assumes state industrial revenue bond economic development and relocation assistance (provided Sid's purchases land, constructs a building, and creates jobs in state).

[§] One-time relocation grant.

8) and their impact on earnings (Exhibits 9 and 10). Further, feeling that the expansion of production capacity would eventually be necessary, he had asked Jerry Cheslok to prepare some cost estimates and financing options for several alternative locations. (See Exhibit 11.) Government assistance was available for financing a new plant. While Sid's had used government programs to develop contacts in the United States and Japanese markets, the company had been generally reluctant to access government funding programs for international market development because of time delays and the restricting conditions attached to the disbursement of funds.

SIGMA-ALDRICH[1]

The agenda for the February 1992 meeting of the Board of Directors of Sigma-Aldrich called for a report by the Nominating Committee. The report would recommend the list of proposed directors to be submitted to the shareholders at its annual meeting in May. In some ways it was reminiscent of a similar meeting a year earlier; once again the role of Dr. Alfred Bader, one of the founders of the company, was to be decided. In 1991, the question had been whether Bader would remain as Chairman of the company; in 1992, the question was whether he would remain a director. A lot had happened in the interim.

The February 1991 Board Meeting

On Monday, February 18, 1991, Dr. Tom Cori, President and CEO of Sigma-Aldrich, phoned the Chairman, Dr. Alfred Bader, in Milwaukee, and told him to get an early flight to St. Louis so that he could meet Don Brandin, chairman of the Board's Compensation Committee at 6:00 PM. Brandin wanted to discuss Dr. Bader's proposed retirement from the Board this May. The Board was scheduled to meet for cocktails at 6:15 PM, followed by dinner at 7:00; this was the typical, informal routine for the evening before the Board held its business meetings.

The schedule for the 19th called for a meeting of the Compensation Committee at 8:00 AM, followed by a meeting of the Nomination Committee at 8:30 AM. The membership on the two committees was the same except that Tom Cori also sat on the Nomination Committee. The Audit Committee was

---

[1] This case was prepared by P. Bruce Buchan, as the basis for class discussion. Comments by Garnet Garven of the Western Business School on an earlier draft were most helpful.

to meet at 8:45 AM and the full Board at 9:15. Except for the Nomination Committee, only outside directors served on these committees.

The responsibility of the Compensation Committee was to review all areas of executive compensation and advancement. Don Brandin, chairman of the committee, had talked with Dr. Bader as far back as November suggesting that he should be thinking about retirement now that he was 65. He also indicated the company was anxious to avoid the kind of problem it had run into with Dan Broida, the previous chairman, who had fought against retirement until forced to do so in 1980 at the age of 67.

Bader did not believe there was any basis for comparing his situation with Broida's. Whereas Broida had been very autocratic and unwilling to share authority with anyone, he, Bader, had been willing to turn the CEO's position over to Tom Cori in 1983. As Chairman, he had focused most of his efforts on the vital liaison work with the company's suppliers and customers, promoting the company and its products. He believed that the liaison had been a key success factor in the strategy, which saw Aldrich and then Sigma-Aldrich dominate their segment of the specialty chemical industry. Tom Cori's strength was in dealing with the internal dynamics of the organization, especially Sigma, since that was the division in which he had made his mark. In addition, as CEO, Bader had given Cori his full backing in all of the important decisions affecting the company. He never interfered with Cori's decisions as CEO. He believed that Tom Cori was immensely able and hard working but was concerned by certain aspects of his managerial style. One financial analyst described Cori as having a "rough edge" in his treatment of people: "it takes a certain kind of person to work for him." Possibly this was one reason why management ranks at the top of Sigma-Aldrich were very thin, an aspect which troubled Bader. Bader had expressed these concerns to Brandin (and to Cori) and told him that he would be willing to step down as Chairman and assume the title of honorary chairman, or some such title, as soon as Tom came up with someone to take over as President. That would be a logical and quite normal order of progression among the ranks of the senior officers.

The Compensation Committee disagreed. It believed that Bader was at retirement age and should go gracefully. The time had come to recognize Cori for his contribution to the company. Its growth, since he became CEO in 1983, had been at a compound growth rate of over 17 percent per annum. Not to recognize him with the chairmanship would be to send negative signals about the Board's confidence in Cori and its ability to handle progression at the top. Besides, it was a simple matter of equity; Cori had earned the title.

On his trip to St. Louis, Bader took with him a one-page letter addressed to Don Brandin with copies for Dr. Cori and the other members of the Compensation Committee. In the letter he made an unconditional commitment to step down as Chairman upon the election of a new president but no later than the 1992 annual meeting held in May. Bader would continue as a director and as Chairman Emeritus. He expressed the hope that, in the interval, management would designate one or more younger executives to accompany him and to pick up the valuable contacts he had made over the years.

At the 6:00 o'clock meeting Don Brandin turned the proposal down flat. He reiterated the committee's desire that Bader tender his resignation gracefully; otherwise, he simply would be forced out. During dinner, Bader distributed his written proposal to Messrs. Newman and O'Neil (Dr. Kipnis did not attend the evening reception). They confirmed, as had Dr. Kipnis's secretary, that they had indeed received the package he had sent to them explaining in detail his contribution to the company. (Appendix C summarizes the gist of the contents of that package.)

As scheduled, the Compensation Committee met at 8:00 AM on Tuesday and it was attended by both Dr. Cori and Dr. Bader. Dr. Bader, in his soft-spoken, deliberative style, carefully summarized his case one last time—his contribution to the company, the increasing profitability of the Aldrich division relative to Sigma's, the thinness of management at the top as well as the need for the Board itself to play a more active role in learning what was going on in the company. He then left them to their deliberations.

The Audit Committee meeting was cancelled and the regular meeting of the Board, chaired by Dr. Bader, started at approximately 9:30 AM. The Compensation Committee remained unanimous in its recommendation that Dr. Bader should resign on May 7. Despite their efforts to get Dr. Bader to resign gracefully and to become the Chairman Emeritus, he had refused. Therefore, no further action was to be taken until the annual meeting in May, at which time Dr. Bader would be forced to resign.

Dr. Bader requested a short recess to take counsel with his close friend and fellow director Marvin Klitsner. The cause was lost. Dr. Bader returned to the meeting and said he would tender his resignation as Chairman and become the Chairman Emeritus, while remaining a director.

The Compensation Committee immediately reconvened and asked Dr. Bader to attend. He was invited to continue his activities with the company and to work out the details with Dr. Cori, which he did later in the day.

The Board reconvened and Dr. Harvey, Executive Vice President and Chief Operating Officer, who had come up through the Aldrich wing of the company, gave a glowing speech attesting to Bader's skills as a great "deal maker" and how much he had contributed to the company.

And so the Chairmanship was passed at the company's annual meeting on May 7, 1991. Dr. Bader became Chairman Emeritus and Dr. Cori became Chairman, President, and CEO.

The August 1991 Board Meeting

At the August meeting of the Board, the company's second quarter earnings were released and several of the officers (in accordance with SEC regulations) indicated their intention to dispose of a small portion of their stock in the company. On the return flight home to Milwaukee, Alfred Bader casually asked Marvin about selling stock options. His son Daniel had told him a bit about it the other day and said it was a good way of locking in the price of stock at a figure above the current trading price. Marvin agreed and said he had personally been selling options for some time. On Thursday, August 15th, Alfred phoned his stock broker, and had him sell 100 options (for 10,000 shares) on his Sigma-Aldrich stock. On August 14th the stock had closed at $43¼ and on the 15th the price for $45 January options was $2⅝. Bader was committed to a large contribution of money and shares to his University, and by selling the options he guaranteed a sure $26,875 beyond the value of the 10,000 shares.

On November 15, 1991, Dr. Bader and his family were to be special guests of Queen's University. It marked the 50th anniversary of his enrolment at the university. A teen-aged, Austrian Jew, just released from an internment camp outside of Montreal, Queen's was the only university, out of three to which he had applied, which would taken him in at that late date. He obtained undergraduate degrees in engineering, chemistry, and history, and a M.Sc. in chemistry. He continued his doctoral studies in chemistry at Harvard, completing his work there in 1949. His first job was as a research chemist with Pittsburgh Plate and Glass, in its paint laboratory in Milwaukee.

Shortly after joining PPG's laboratory, Bader recommended that a small division within PPG be set up to make and sell specialty chemicals. As a research chemist he had suffered the frustration of waiting for Eastman Kodak to deliver a chemical he needed to complete his experiments. Kodak was more interested in filling large orders rather than small, sporadic orders for specialty chemicals placed by the research laboratories. The proposal was turned down. However, there would be no objection if he started his own enterprise on his own time, provided it did not interfere with his work with PPG.

Bader had the knowledge of chemistry and chemical processes and the desire to capitalize on the opportunity. He lacked the legal knowledge necessary to launch the business enterprise but this was supplied by a local Milwaukee lawyer. Each put up $250 in order to provide the minimum capital requirements, and the company was incorporated on August 17, 1951.

The first product the fledgling company marketed was a chemical Bader had learned to make in the lab of Professor A.F. McKay while studying for his M.Sc. degree. First year sales were only $1,705, rose to $5,400 in the second year, and in the third year sales almost tripled to $15,000. When PPG decided, in 1954, to move its Milwaukee laboratory to Springdale, near Pittsburgh, Bader decided to stay in Milwaukee. He liked the city and it was worth the risk to devote full time to the fledgling enterprise.

Sales more than doubled to $34,000 in the fourth year. However, Bader was now devoting all of his time to the company, putting in long hours every day, while the other partner was, if anything, spending more time in his law practice. The disproportionate contribution to the success of the company, compared with the equal ownership, did not seem fair to Bader. He gave his partner, therefore, three alternatives, all of which would have led to either the dissolution of the partnership or Bader gaining 70 percent control. The lawyer did not like any of the alternatives but eventually, and with great bitterness, sold all his share to Bader for $15,000. He never spoke to Bader again.

Aldrich's Strategy

The target market was clearly defined from the very start: chemists in research labs who needed specialty chemicals to carry out their research. The products usually played a small, but very vital part in the activities of the laboratory. Although the chemical might be expensive on a unit basis, the number of units required was so small that the actual cost was insignificant relative to the overall cost of the experiment. However, the product had to be of reliable quality, not necessarily perfect, but good, and it had to be available quickly. Given the relatively small unit sales, it was obvious that Aldrich would have to expand its product line and its customer base.

To purchase the necessary products, Bader had to travel outside of Milwaukee. The potential suppliers were any of the laboratories in the world and some of the best laboratories were located in Germany, England, and Switzerland. Bader was fluent in German and English and also spoke passable French. He began canvassing laboratories throughout the United States and Europe. As a research chemist he could talk their language, recognize who were the top producers, what were their needs, what were their problems, and always—how could he help them in their work?

It was a relatively easy matter to identify the commercial and academic research laboratories and to communicate with them. A simple catalog was sufficient to identify Aldrich's product line. By 1965, the company cataloged over 9,000 different chemicals with its best-selling chemical accounting for no more than 2 percent of its total sales and no other chemical accounting for as much as 1 percent of its total sales. The company's customers included many substantial industries throughout the world, the federal government, universities, and laboratories doing medical research. The federal government's laboratories accounted for less than 10 percent of the company's sales, and no private concern accounted for as much as 5 percent of sales. Regionally, 80 percent of the sales were in the United States, 10 percent west of the Rockies, and 45 percent each in the Midwest and the east. Foreign sales were distributed across 20 countries, usually through foreign agents.

By 1965, the company manufactured approximately 15 percent of its sales, (up from only 5 percent in 1960), purchased approximately 10 percent from a German affiliate (EGA), and purchased the rest from many different sources, none of which supplied more than 10 percent. Approximately 50 percent of the chemicals offered for sale by the company were acquired outside the United States.

The company's strategy was to manufacture only those products which it could not purchase advantageously from other sources. Even when it did initiate new chemicals in its own facilities, it would farm these out to other producers whenever it was economical to do so. No company, not even Eastman Kodak, could afford to build production facilities which would ensure adequate supplies of the thousands of rare chemicals used sparingly. But individual labs could devote part of their facilities to making one or two products for their own use and the marginal cost of producing a few extra kilos for Aldrich was negligible. To ensure product quality, the company maintained its own analytical laboratories to check the chemical analysis and purity of all products sold.

Bader personally visited laboratories throughout the world in order to locate reliable sources of the specialty chemicals which were the backbone of the product line. He selected the chemists who staffed the company's laboratories and kept close contact with all of the employees in the office and those who handled the shipping and receiving.

In order to ensure product quality, to develop new products (an aspect which could not be entirely ignored), and continue the dialogue with his research customers, he created an organization in which leading scientists played a key role. By 1965, there were 125 people in the organization of whom 34 were graduate chemists with no less than nine holding Ph.D. degrees in chemistry. To process the orders effectively, there were 34 office employees and 49 in shipping, receiving, and sales, while eight were involved in maintenance, plant engineering, and other miscellaneous functions. All but nine employees were located in Milwaukee.

In 1965, a decade after Bader decided to devote full time to his specialty chemical company, revenues had increased from $34,000 to over $2,000,000. Bader's salary, which in 1955 had been $6,000 (provided he did not cash any of his cheques during the first six months), was over $34,000 in 1965. Profits were increasing rapidly as well, reaching almost $200,000 in 1965, and profit margins were some 20 percent before taxes. By 1974 (the last year before the merger) sales were over $11,000,000 and profits almost $3,000,000.

In 1965 it owned two buildings with almost 100,000 square feet of floor space. It also leased about 12,000 square feet in New Jersey in order to expedite shipments to its eastern customers. By 1974 it had added another 110,000 square feet of floor space with two new buildings, on three acres of land, located about half a mile from its existing facilities. The New Jersey warehouse was also expanded and new computers were installed in Milwaukee and in its subsidiary in England. The expansion was completely financed out of earnings and the company's very conservative balance sheet remained virtually free of long-term debt.

The Board of Directors, Aldrich Chemicals 1965–74

Between 1961 and 1974 there were 11 persons who served on the Board, at one time or another. The two most enduring members were Alfred Bader and his closest friend, confidant, and business and legal advisor Marvin

Klitsner. Until 1968, Klitsner was the only person who could be described as an "outside" director, in the narrow definition of the term, i.e., not an employee of the company. The other insiders through 1967 were Helen Bader, Alfred's wife who was also the company's Treasurer, John Biel, Vice President and Director of Research, and William Buth, Vice President and Director of Operations.

Biel was an internationally recognized medicinal chemist. Well connected in the American Chemical Society, he set up a number of research contracts and attracted some highly qualified chemists to the company. He was considered by Bader to be the most technically able person in the company. The relationship between the two was not always easy and in 1968 Biel left the company. Bader, who was admittedly tight-fisted, especially during the early years of the company, kept a close eye on expenditures, and it did not sit well with Biel, for example, when Bader questioned a salary increase Biel gave his secretary.

Buth, also a chemist, made his contribution in organizing the company's order processing system, setting up, for example, the company's advanced computer systems for inventory control and shipping. However, before the merger, he, too, left the company, partly because of the close scrutiny Bader kept on operations, often asking two different people to check out whether tasks had been carried out. For Bader, it was simply a matter of attending to details, while for Buth it must have seemed more like a lack of trust.

In 1968, the size of the Board increased to seven from five. The president of the investment firm which handled the sale of Aldrich shares to the public, and the president of Ventron Corporation, a manufacturer of inorganic chemicals with which Aldrich had had a joint venture, were added. Mr. R. N. Emanuel, a close personal friend of Bader, and president of Aldrich's distributor in England, replaced Mrs. Bader in 1969, and Mr. B. E. Edelstein, Vice President and Secretary, took Biel's slot on the Board. Edelstein, who was a patent lawyer, but also had a degree in chemistry, had been hired in 1962 and was quite good at soothing ruffled feathers when Bader's impatience to get things done got people upset.

By 1970, the Board was very much less an "inside" Board but the "outsiders" had very strong links with the company in a direct business sense. They were knowledgeable about the company and/or the industry. Bader, majority shareholder and chief executive officer of the company, had complete control over the composition of the Board and obviously felt most comfortable with people with whom he had done business and who had a personal interest in the company.

In 1971–72, the last appointments before the merger, Dr. H. C. Brown and J. McGaffey, were added to the Board in place of Bickel and Lauenstein. (One of the reasons Lauenstein left the Aldrich Board was the low pay Bader gave to outside directors.) Dr. Brown, a member of the faculty at Purdue and a renowned chemist, had developed a process which permitted the production of hundreds of compounds by hydroboration. Aldrich bought exclusive right to Brown's patents and set up a wholly owned subsidiary (Aldrich-Boranes Inc.) to produce the products. Brown was invited to be a member of the Aldrich Board. J. McGaffey was a lawyer with M. Klitsner's law firm, and was also appointed Assistant Secretary of Aldrich, to provide the necessary legal advice the company increasingly needed.

The Merger with Sigma-International

By the early seventies Bader began to see the advantages of a still bigger operation, especially from the financial market's perspective. The growth of the company had been dramatic but it was still a comparatively small company and therefore did not have wide appeal on the financial market. Taking the company public in 1965 had not generated the interest among the investing community that he had hoped for. One way of achieving the desired growth could be through a merger and one company which had caught his eye was Sigma-International, almost a clone of Aldrich except that its market was biochemistry (as opposed to organic chemistry). Bader's first, informal approach to Sigma in the late sixties was rebuffed almost out of hand, by its president Dan Broida. But by 1974, Aldrich's track record had continued its impressive performance and Sigma (which first offered some of its stock to the public in 1972, with somewhat limited success), also began to appreciate the advantages of a merger with Aldrich.

The two merged in 1975, forming Sigma-Aldrich, with the Sigma shareholders receiving two-thirds of the shares in the new company and the Aldrich shareholders one-third. The division of ownership reflected the relative contribution of the two companies according to sales and profits. Combined net sales in 1975 were $43 million, and profits, before taxes, $11 million. Each company received four positions on the Board of Directors.

Sales and profits of the new company simply continued the dramatic upward trajectory which had been the hallmark of the individual firms. By 1985, sales had reached $215 million, and profits $53 million, a compound annual growth rate of over 17 percent. The growth continued dramatically, but the basic elements of the strategy did not change. In 1976, the company had 18,200 products in its catalogs and of these it purchased 68 percent with no one supplier accounting for 10 percent of the company's purchases. In 1991, the company had 56,000 products in its catalog and of these it purchased 59 percent with no one supplier accounting for 10 percent of the company's purchases. Its primary sales instrument was its catalog of which, in 1976, it distributed 225,000 copies, and in 1991 the number of copies distributed was 2,700,000. In 1976, it had 20,000 customers, with no single customer accounting for as much as 5 percent of net sales and in 1991, it had 117,000 customers with no single customer accounting for as much as 1 percent of net sales.

The essence of the strategy was to supply specialized chemicals, of high quality, to research and diagnostic laboratories and get the product out to the customer within 24 hours of receipt of the order. If anything, Aldrich's quality and promptness standards improved, although the quality requirements of its customers, generally, were not as high as Sigma's. Since there was very little overlap of the companies' customers (Sigma's largely in the life sciences, i.e., hospitals, medical laboratories, and the biochemical departments of universities and Aldrich's in the organic chemical departments of universities and the research and development laboratories of chemical and pharmaceutical companies), each continued to run relatively autonomously.

Dan Broida, founder and President of Sigma International, became the chairman, and Alfred Bader the President, of the combined enterprise Sigma-Aldrich. No one was designated the CEO. This relationship continued until Broida retired in 1980, whereupon Bader became Chairman and CEO, and Tom Cori, who had been president of the Sigma division, became president and chief operating officer. There was a suggestion that Cori be named Chairman/CEO but it was defeated.

Cori had been a vice president of Sigma-Aldrich since the merger, and was promoted to President of Sigma in July of 1976 (succeeding D. Broida in that capacity). Cori's rise through the ranks was quite exceptional, having joined Sigma in 1970 as a production chemist, fresh out of Washington University (Missouri) with a Ph.D. in biochemistry. He came by his interest in chemistry legitimately, his parents having won the Nobel prize in Chemistry in 1947 for their work on carbohydrate metabolism and enzymes. Although Aaron Fischer (second only to Broida in Sigma International) had not played a direct role in bringing Cori into the company, he had been a neighbor and friend of his parents and took a special interest in Cori's career at Sigma.

In 1983, Cori became the CEO while Bader retained his position as Chairman of the Board. Aaron Fischer, who turned 70 in 1977, became an emeritus director but continued to play an active role in the company.

The Board of Directors, Sigma-Aldrich 1975–85

Immediately following the merger of Sigma and Aldrich, the board consisted of eight directors, four each from Sigma and Aldrich. The Aldrich directors, chosen by Bader, were A. Bader, H. C. Brown, R. Emanuel and M. Klitsner. Brown's appointment to the board was not renewed in 1978 and, somewhat ironically, the following year he received the Nobel prize in chemistry.

The Sigma directors were D. Broida, A. Fischer, J. W. Sandweiss, and S. J. Weinberg. Broida was the principal founder of Sigma International. A. Fischer had hired Broida, fresh out of college in 1936, into the small consulting firm which Fischer and his brother had started in 1934. Sigma was started in the early 1950s under the umbrella of the consulting firm, but was created almost entirely through the initiative of Dan Broida. Fischer joined Sigma on a full-time basis in 1959, and played an active role as a senior officer of the company, bringing to bear his financial, organizational, and planning

EXHIBIT 1   Aldrich Financial Highlights 1961–1974
A. Bader, President and CEO

Aldrich Financial Highlights 1961–1974										
A. Bader, President and CEO										
Year	Net Revenues	Earnings before Taxes								
1961	$826,272	$222,034								
1962	$999,484	$313,177								
1963	$1,203,513	$271,334								
1964	$1,701,782	$354,586								
1965	$2,064,875	$372,700								
1966	$2,639,492	$543,124								
1967	$3,426,525	$853,876								
1968	$4,020,164	$882,903								
1969	$4,681,767	$1,117,381								
1970	$5,858,462	$1,345,141								
1971	$6,041,818	$1,399,997								
1972	$6,560,791	$1,549,646								
1973	$8,583,853	$1,960,475								
1974	$11,277,647	$2,827,272								

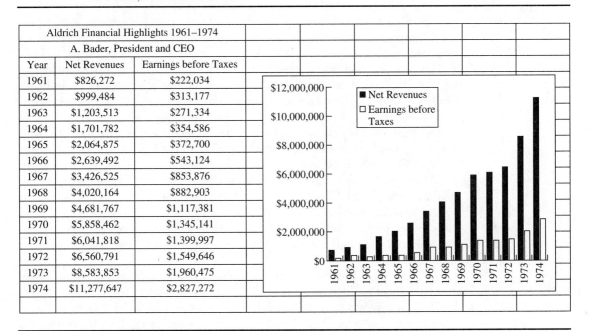

EXHIBIT 2   Sigma-Aldrich Financial Highlights 1974–1979
D. Broida, Chairman, A. Bader President

Sigma-Aldrich Financial Highlights 1974–1979						
D. Brolda, Chairman, A. Bader, President						
Year	Net Revenues	Earnings before Taxes				
1974	$38,506,000	$9,800,000				
1975	$42,979,000	$10,936,000				
1976	$46,197,000	$11,945,000				
1977	$54,803,000	$14,065,000				
1978	$67,838,000	$17,330,000				
1979	$86,675,000	$20,345,000				

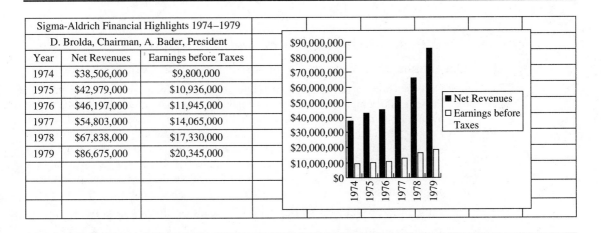

skills. J. W. Sandweiss was a partner in a St. Louis law firm which provided legal services to Sigma. S. J. Weinberg was a partner in Goldman Sachs & Co. Investment Bankers, the company which had taken Sigma public in 1972.

The Sigma-Aldrich board was increased by two in 1977 when D. N. Brandin, Chairman of the Board of Boatmen's Bancshares, Inc., a Bank Holding Company, and T. Cori joined.

The merged board was dominated by insiders who were also large shareholders. The board performed its "monitoring" and "approving" role but it also served as a "deciding board" if there was a problem which was of concern to both companies. For example, it voted to sell Sigma products to a large Aldrich customer which had previously been blacklisted by Broida. The decision was in the best interest of Sigma-Aldrich and Broida was the only director to vote against the proposal.

Although Bader retained the title of Chairman of the Board, Cori, from the time he became CEO, performed most of the Chairman's duties (determining the agenda and deciding on the board's membership). Bader would normally defer to Cori on major policy issues. Unity of command was not in question and the company continued to flourish under Cori's guidance (see Exhibit 3).

In 1985, Cori prepared a re-organization plan which envisaged a larger board and increased representation by "outside" directors. It is significant that Bader was not consulted during the preparation of this plan nor was there any mention of Bader's name in this report even though he was the Chairman of the Board at the time and was to remain Chairman for another six years. By 1991, when Cori became Chairman, as well as President and CEO, the board had increased to 12 (including the emeritus director), and of the 12, six had been appointed by Cori since becoming CEO. Only Bader and Klitsner remained from the original Aldrich board, although David Harvey, who had come up through the Emanuel side of Aldrich, had been a member of the board since 1981 and succeeded Cori as the Chief Operating Officer of Sigma-Aldrich in 1983.

The Director Recruiting Process under Tom Cori

One outside director described his first meeting with Cori:

> Cori had done a fair amount of relatively good homework, searching through Fortune 500 companies, looking at names . . . One day out of the blue he called me up, I had never heard of him and he told me he wanted to come and see me. I asked why and he didn't want to tell me why. I made a guess, but I thought it was strange that he didn't want to tell me why and he came and saw me and I kind of liked him . . . He was clearly an aggressive CEO type guy [and he was looking for someone who] had experience in large businesses or experience in acquisitions or experiences in growing businesses significantly.

This director went on to describe his views on boards in general:

> They are living things and they don't always come together. How people got on the board, and what they think they were put on the board for is important. And

EXHIBIT 3   Sigma-Aldrich Financial Highlights 1980–1982
A. Bader Chairman and CEO, T. C. Cori, President and COO

Sigma-Aldrich Financial Highlights 1980–1982		
A. Bader, Chairman and CEO, T.C. Corl, President and COO		
Year	Net Revenues	Earnings before Taxes
1980	$104,932,000	$23,425,000
1981	$123,009,000	$27,431,000
1982	$136,012,000	$30,244,000
Sigma-Aldrich Financial Highlights 1983–1992		
T.C. Corl, President and CEO, A. Bader Chairman		
Year	Net Revenues	Earnings before Taxes
1983	$150,592,000	$34,838,000
1984	$179,529,000	$43,602,000
1985	$214,848,000	$52,821,000
1986	$253,097,000	$62,326,000
1987	$304,858,000	$72,222,000
1988	$375,282,000	$88,522,000
1989	$441,099,000	$99,872,000
1990	$529,103,000	$110,028,000
1991	$589,371,000	$123,878,000
1992	$654,406,000	$147,312,000

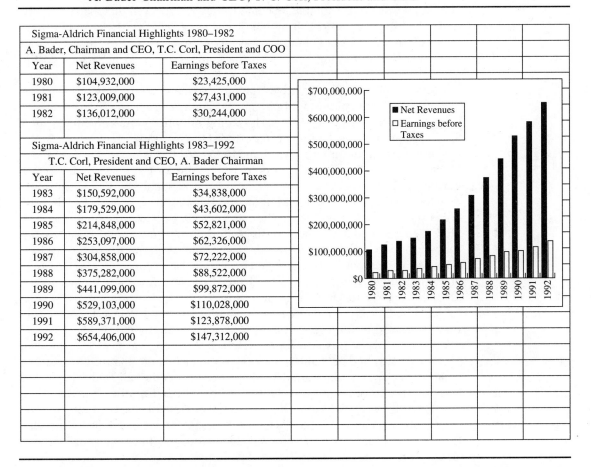

getting the board to come together and be willing to have a few good fights, on an equal basis, and get rid of egos. Getting rid of egos is a very important part of getting value out of the board. It's not easy to get a bunch of high-powered guys—who are, in their own right, successful and important to some extent—to be prepared to look at the issues of another entity without getting their egos in the act. It can screw things up considerably when they do.

The November 1991 Board Meeting

The regular board meeting was scheduled for Tuesday, November 12th, with the usual dinner meeting on the 11th. Dr. Bader met with Dr. Cori and they drafted the terms of Bader's assignment for the coming year. Earlier, Cori had told him that he would receive no compensation, other than expenses, and if that was not acceptable he could simply resign from the board. In 1991, Bader had received a consulting fee of just over $90,000. Bader didn't think Cori's offer was fair but the money was inconsequential to him; the important thing was his continuing work with the company and so he agreed to the terms without a fuss.

Marvin Klitsner, during the evening of November 11th, advised Dr. Cori that he had been selling options on his Sigma-Aldrich stock and had just learned that, as of May 1, 1991, such trading of options had come under new SEC regulations, and had to be reported. On November 12th, while Bader was still in St. Louis, a letter was hand delivered to his personal secretary in Milwaukee. The letter had been prepared by one of the lawyers at Foley & Lardner (M. Klitsner's law firm and Bader's personal law firm) explaining they had just learned through Marvin, and Bader's stock broker, Bill Schield, of his sale of options on Sigma-Aldrich stock. It went on to explain the new SEC regulations that applied to his trading in options and also enclosed a copy of the SEC disclosure forms for him to sign. It also outlined the implications and alternative courses of action he might wish to consider. Upon reading the letter Bader immediately signed the disclosure form and sent it to the SEC with a copy to Dr. Cori in St. Louis.

On Wednesday, November 13th, while preparing to leave for Kingston, Bader received a call from Dr. Cori, who was obviously angry. He indicated that David Harvey was also on the line (hence there was a witness to what was being said) and he wanted to know whether he and Marvin Klitsner had been selling options on Sigma-Aldrich stock, "in concert." Bader explained he had, on one occasion, last August, 15th, sold 100 options but there had been no collusion with Marvin; his transaction was simply part of a contribution he was going to make to Queen's University. He had learned, just yesterday, that such transactions now required disclosure and the requisite form was already on its way to the SEC with a copy to Dr. Cori. Cori closed the conversation indicating he was turning the matter over to the company's lawyers.

November 15, 1991, was scheduled to be a busy day for Bader and he had just finished his lecture in the chemistry department when a call came for him from Tom Cori in St. Louis. Bader took Cori's call and in the brief phone conversation Cori, in his rather blunt, direct manner, advised Bader that he had to see him as soon as possible; he would not say why. Since Bader was flying directly to England from Canada, Cori said they should meet at the Russel Hotel in London, the following Wednesday at 1:00 PM.

Cori's call disturbed Bader and when he found a free moment between lectures he got in touch with his legal advisor at Foley & Lardner to double check the seriousness of the stock option sale. He was assured that it was a very minor infraction of the new regulations, and the only thing he technically had done wrong was to file his declaration late. The company would have to declare this on its next proxy statement, but it was unlikely that the SEC would consider it even worth a slap on the hand.

The London Meeting, November 20, 1991

Alfred Bader walked slowly, but deliberately, through the entrance of the Russell Square Hotel located in the Bloomsbury district of London. The rich, wood panelling and the elegantly appointed lobby went largely unnoticed. This was a bit unusual for the man who had gained a world reputation as an art collector. Today his mind was on the business at hand; except that he really did not know what was at hand! Probably it had to do with the acquisition of the English company they had been contemplating. Then he spotted Cori waiting in the lobby and was a bit surprised to see that he had brought along David Harvey, the company's Chief Operating Officer, and the man Bader had promoted through the upper echelons of Aldrich. Tom hadn't mentioned that David was coming. The board would be upset if they both had come over on the same plane. They spotted him and immediately approached. Their facial expression was stolid, formal.

If the air in the elevator was chilly, it turned absolutely frigid as soon as they entered Cori's room. Cori got right to the point.

There was no room on the Board for anyone who would "bet against the company," and selling options was just that, a bet against the company; it indicated that he had some doubts about how well the company would perform. The board questioned his judgment and was unanimous in its request for his resignation.

Here was a letter of resignation for him to sign.

Bader was stunned. If selling 100 options (for 10,000 shares) was a bet against the company, what was the retention of the other 3.7 million shares which he owned?

How could anyone think for a moment he would ever bet against his own company? The sale of the call options had simply been part of his planned gift of 10,000 shares to Queen's. He had never sold a single share in Sigma-Aldrich. The only shares he had disposed of had been given to various universities throughout North America and Europe.

> *Bader:* "Had Tom explained the reason for his sale of stock options to the Board members?"
> *Cori:* "Yes!"
> This was preposterous; it couldn't be happening. Surely, David Harvey wouldn't have voted against him.
> *Bader:* "Would you, David?"
> *Harvey:* "Yes, the vote was unanimous."
> He believed Bader should resign gracefully; everyone had to retire sooner or later.

Bader: "What about my pending work at Aldrich?"

Cori: "They would just have to learn to get along without him."

Bader: "What about the lectures and laboratory visits scheduled over the next few weeks?"

Cori: "Do as you wish but we want you packed and out of your office by the end of the year!"

But he wouldn't get back to Milwaukee until December 23rd, and with the Christmas holidays . . .!

Cori: "We will be reasonable."

Bader: "What about Marvin?"

Cori: "He would be dealt with, too."

Bader: "That wouldn't be fair while he was in the hospital to undergo heart surgery!"

What should he do?

APPENDIX A
SIGMA-ALDRICH DIRECTORS-1991

Bader A. R. (67), Founder, President, Aldrich Chemicals (1951–1974). President, Sigma-Aldrich (1975–1979). Chairman & CEO (1980–1983). Chairman (1984–1990). Compensation, 1990, as Chairman, $180,000. Did not participate in Stock Bonus Plan. Shares owned: 3,660,430 (7.4% of outstanding shares). B.Sc., B.A., M.Sc. (Queen's), M.A., Ph.D. (Harvard). Six honorary degrees from universities in U.S.A., Canada, U.K.

Brandin D. N. (70), Retired (1989) Chairman of the Board and Chief Executive Officer of Boatman's Bancshares, Inc., bank holding company, St. Louis, Missouri. Director from 1977 to February 1985 and from November 1985 to present; also a director of EAC Corporation and Laclede Gas Company. Shares owned: 8,000.

Cori C. T. (55), President and CEO of company (1990). Joined Sigma 1970, as production chemist. Vice President, Sigma (1975). President of Sigma (1976–1980). President and COO, Sigma-Aldrich (1980–1983). President and CEO (1983–1990). Director since 1977. Compensation, 1990, as President & CEO, $998,168 ($470,000, salary component, $528,168, through stock bonus plan). Shares owned: 123,900. B.Sc., U. of Wisconsin (1959), Ph.D., Washington University (Missouri) (1969).

Fischer A. (84), Director Emeritus. Chemical engineer, one of founders of Midwest Consultants, 1934. Midwest became the parent company for Sigma Chemical Company, which was formed following WWII. He and his family held a large number of shares in Sigma and then in Sigma-Aldrich (15.8 percent) but reduced their holdings significantly in 1985 in a special public offering.

Harvey D. R. (53), Executive Vice President and Chief Operating Officer (COO) since 1983. President of Aldrich, May 1981–January 1987. Director since 1981. B.A., M.A., D.Phil. (Chemistry), Oxford. Compensation, 1990, as Executive V.P. and COO, $670,725 ($330,000, salary component: $340,725, through stock bonus plan). Shares owned: 75,620.

Kipnis D. M. (64), Chairman, Department of Medicine, Washington University School of Medicine, St. Louis, Missouri; Director since 1984. Shares owned: 4,300.

Klitsner M. E. (73), Lawyer, director since 1975. Former director of Aldrich, close personal friend, confidant, and advisor to A. Bader for over 35 years. Shares beneficially owned: 3,096,156 (includes 1,482,928 shares held as co-trustee for parties not related to Mr. Klitsner, over which Mr. Klitsner has shared voting and investment power, and 1,540,928 shares held as co-personal representative of an estate over which Mr. Klitsner has shared voting and investment power (net balance 72,300).

Newman A. E. (47), Chairman of the Board, Edison Brothers Stores, Inc., specialty fashion retailer, St. Louis, Missouri, since April 1987. Prior to that time he was Executive Vice President of Edison Brothers Stores, Inc. Director of Sigma-Aldrich since 1989; also director of Edison Brothers Stores, Inc. and Boatmen's Bancshares, Inc. Shares owned: 2,000.

O'Neil W. C., Jr. (57), Chairman of the Board, President, and Chief Executive Officer, ClinTrials, Inc., a clinical trials management company, Nashville, Tennessee, since November 1989; prior to that time he was Chairman of the Board and President and Chief Executive Officer of International Clinical Laboratories, Inc., from Sept. 1977 until June 1988. Director of Sigma-Aldrich since 1987; also director of Atrix Laboratories, Inc. Shares owned: 2,000.

Sandweiss J. W. (67), Lawyer, director since 1975. Shares beneficially owned: 368,416. Includes 361,416 shares held as co-trustee for a party not related to Mr. Sandweiss, over which Mr. Sandweiss has shared voting and investment power (net balance 7,000).

Urban T. N., Jr. (57), Chairman of the Board and President, Pioneer Hi-Bred International, Inc., developer and producer of hybrid corn and other seeds, Des Moines, Iowa. Elected to the Board by the Directors of Sigma-Aldrich on November 13, 1990; also a director of pioneer Hi-Bred International, Inc., and Equitable Companies of Iowa. Shares owned: none.

Weinberg S. J., Jr. (68), Limited Partner, The Goldman Sachs Group. Director since 1975; also director of Eagle-Picher Industries, Inc., R. H. Macy & Co., Inc., and Tejon Ranch Company. Shares beneficially owned: 27,600; includes 9,600 shares held by Mr. Weinberg as co-trustee of a charitable foundation, over which Mr. Weinberg has shared voting and investment power, but does not include shares which may be held by Goldman, Sachs & Co., in the course of maintaining an over-the-counter market in the Company's common stock.

APPENDIX B
STRUCTURE OF THE BOARD OF DIRECTORS—1990

Composition: The Board consisted of 12 members although one of these, A. Fischer, was an honorary director. As an honorary director his name did not appear on the proxy statement's list of nominees for election to the Board. He received all Board material and was eligible to attend all Board meetings.

Structure: The Board had three committees which functioned throughout the year; the Audit Committee, the Compensation Committee, and the Nominating Committee.

The Audit Committee (Klitsner, Sandweiss, Weinberg) recommends a public accounting firm to be retained for the coming year, reviews the work to be done by such firm, and reviews and analyzes the financial results of the company. It met three times during 1990.

The Nominating Committee (Cori, Kipnis, Brandin, Newman, O'Neil) recommends nominees to the Board of Directors, held one meeting during the year.

The Compensation Committee (Brandin, Newman, O'Neil, Kipnis) reviews all areas of executive compensation and advancement within the company. The committee held three meetings in 1990.

The company's compensation plan is made up of two parts: a salary component and an incentive stock bonus plan.

The salary component: at the end of each fiscal year, the Committee reviews with Dr. Cori and approves, with any modifications it deems appropriate, an annual salary plan for the Company's executive officers (including Dr. Cori).

The Incentive component: the Incentive Stock Bonus Plan was developed in 1978 and its size is determined by the percentage increase in the company's pre-tax operating income.

Golden Parachutes: in the event a change of control should occur in the company, and the employment of the four executive officers terminated these officers were guaranteed, under the bonus plan, 69,078 shares and approximately $1,100,000, plus a salary component totalling $2,562,500.

Compensation for directors: directors who were not employed or retained as legal counsel by the company are compensated by an annual fee of $10,000, and receive $1,500 for each directors' or committee meeting attended and reimbursement of their travel expenses.

The Board met six times during 1990, the Audit committee met three times, the Compensation Committee held three meetings, and the Nominating Committee held one meeting. Most committee meetings are scheduled for the same day as regular Board meetings.

APPENDIX C
MAJOR ACTIVITIES OF A. BADER, CHAIRMAN OF SIGMA-ALDRICH AND FOUNDER OF THE ALDRICH CHEMICAL COMPANY.

His responsibilities required that he travel about half of the time, about four months in Europe and two in the United States, concentrating on:

1. **Acquisition of new products,** both for Sigma and Aldrich, since they were vital to the company's future growth. In 1990, he had devoted special attention to products from East Germany and Czechoslovakia and Hungary. He visited many established suppliers and ordered those products which were new to them and to Sigma-Aldrich.

2. **Contact with academics** in North America and Europe. Ninety percent of the world's best research was done by 10 percent of the academics, and he tried to visit these each year to get their suggestions for new products which were new to them and to the company.

3. **Recruitment of scientists.** During his travels, professors would tell him about some of the really able chemists who were about to graduate. The last two Ph.D.s hired by Aldrich, and several at Sigma-Poole, had joined through such referrals.

4. **Bulk purchases.** Many of the company's best sellers were based on purchase contracts which were not routine, and required delicate, personal negotiations.

5. **The *Aldrichimica Acta*,** which had become the best chemical house organ in the world, and was distributed to 250,000 scientists around the world, had been started by him, and most of the papers were submitted through him. He still retained responsibility for its layout.

6. **Advertisements.** Aldrich advertised in about 10 international scientific journals and many of the suggestions came from and were written by him.

7. **Contact with subsidiaries.** He visited most of the subsidiaries each year, and spoke to the company's German and English companies several times a week, usually to coordinate purchases.

8. **The Alfred Bader Library of Rare Chemicals.** This was a collection of about 50,000 research samples acquired from professors around the world. Sales, handled by two people, were substantial and profitable.

9. **Lectures.** He presented about 80 lectures per year mainly on the history of the company and of chemistry.

10. **Public Relations.** He personally funded a number of awards and many scholarships and prizes in the United States, Canada, and Britain. His and his wife's personal gifts had exceeded $600,000 in 1990 alone, but because of his position as Chairman these gifts would have been identified with Sigma-Aldrich.

TETRA PAK, INC.

In November 1990, Tetra Pak, Inc.'s Environmental Steering Committee, comprised of the president and CEO, the vice president marketing/environment, the vice president finance, the corporate communications manager, and the manager environmental affairs, met to review the company's communications campaign which had been established during the previous fall. The members of the committee were particularly interested in determining whether the campaign had been successful over the past year and what the company needed to do in the future.

A year earlier, Tetra Pak, Inc., of Aurora, Ontario, had obtained consent from the head office in Lausanne, Switzerland, to officially pursue the possibility of recycling its drink boxes. This action was taken to respond to growing Canadian public concern about the contribution of nonrecyclable, nonrefillable packages to solid waste landfill sites. To address these concerns, a manager environmental affairs was hired and, in conjunction with Superwood Ontario Limited, a method of recycling juice boxes by mixing them with plastics to manufacture plastic lumber was implemented. Tetra Pak also carried out an aggressive multifaceted communications campaign, targeting the general public, Tetra Pak customers, the government, and the media. Although the campaign attracted attention to the recyclability of juice boxes, its main objective was to highlight the benefits of the package and its minimal impact on the environment.

This case was prepared by Jennifer McNaughton and Fred Chan under the supervision of John S. Hulland of the Western Business School and by Mark Baetz, with the assistance of Peter Kelly, both of Wilfrid Laurier University. Copyright 1992 © The University of Western Ontario and Wilfrid Laurier University.

The Company

Tetra Pak, Inc. (hereafter Tetra Pak), was the wholly owned Canadian subsidiary of Swiss-based Tetra Pak Rausing SA (hereafter TPR), which was founded in 1951 by Dr. Ruben Rausing, a Swedish scientist. From a small Swedish company with one research facility in Sweden, TPR grew into a highly successful multinational corporation based in Lausanne, Switzerland. Its products were sold in 108 countries around the world. Operations included specialized research facilities in 7 countries and production plants in 30 countries.

In the 1940s, Dr. Rausing developed a new kind of food package that would lock in the nutritional value of perishable beverages without the need for refrigeration or preservatives. His packages were lighter and more compact than existing containers, required fewer resources to manufacture and transport, and generated less waste after their use. Dr. Rausing's vision continued to motivate his company. TPR had remained 100 percent family-owned since its inception and was managed by Dr. Rausing's sons. The company expected 1991 revenues of more than $5 billion from sales of about 60 million cartons around the world.

TPR obtained its first overseas patent in Canada in 1958. It enjoyed great success with its Canadian entry product, a single-serve coffee cream carton in the shape of a tetrahedron. In the mid 1970s, it set up a sales office near Toronto in order to increase its sales efforts in Canada. In 1985, the company decided to invest roughly $25 million in a state-of-the-art production facility in Aurora, Ontario, just north of Toronto.

In terms of its administration, TPR was a lean organization. The president and CEO of the Canadian subsidiary reported to a senior executive in Switzerland. Tetra Pak had extensive autonomy over its day-to-day operations, with the exception of major capital and operating expenditures. It employed approximately 240 employees across Canada. In Aurora, there were people involved in technical service, production, research and development, and sales administration. In addition, there were sales offices in Vancouver and Montreal.

The Product

TPR's sole business was the manufacture of packaging systems for liquid food products. Research efforts examining packaging for semisolid food such as soup and cheese were under way. However, TPR did not intend to look beyond the food industry for packaging business. For example, it would not consider shampoos, bleaches, and motor oils.

The major product manufactured by the company was the Tetra Brik Aseptic (TBA) carton (commonly known as a juice box). The carton was made of a layer of paper (about 75 percent of the package), four layers of food-grade polyethylene plastic (about 20 percent), and a microthin layer of aluminum (about 5 percent), which was sandwiched between the polyethylene plastic.

The juice box maintained a high level of nutrition and flavour protection while ensuring safety to consumers. These benefits had persuaded many consumers to switch containers. For example, in September 1986, the Institute of Cardiology in Montreal switched from cans to drink boxes for the fruit juice supplied to its new heart recipients. Juice boxes ensured maximum hygiene during the recovery period and were considered easier and safer to use than cans.

The juice box's benefits, both as a product and in terms of its impact on the environment, had been confirmed by various independent studies (Exhibit 1). The first study, which described the marketplace in Germany, was done in 1984–1985 by a Swedish consulting firm. The Netherlands Organization for Applied Scientific Research conducted a similar study in 1990. It examined the same parameters considered in the first study but used Dutch data. Deloitte & Touche Management Consultants of North York, Ontario, had undertaken a Canadian study. Results were expected by the summer of 1991.

Production

The packaging cartons (both TBA and nonaseptic) were produced worldwide in seven sizes of varying shapes. Tetra Pak manufactured 250 ml and 1 L boxes and was one of several plants supplying these sizes to TPR's worldwide markets. In late 1990, it was additionally assigned responsibility for the 125 ml carton. Sizes not produced in Canada were imported from plants in other countries to service Canadian customers.

Customers worked closely with Tetra Pak to design the packaging artwork. Tetra Pak then printed the design on offset printing presses. The printed paper was laminated with layers of polyethylene and a microthin layer of aluminum. End-products were then delivered to the customers as rolls of "laminated paper." Due to economies of scale, the minimum purchase order quantity had been set at 250,000 boxes.

The process of sterilizing the paper, filling the packages with liquid food, and then folding the packages into boxes took place at the customers' premises. The juice box was aseptic because the product was sterilized with hydrogen peroxide and the sterilized liquid filling occurred with no air contact. The machines which performed this process cost approximately $1 million each and were leased to customers by Tetra Pak. This allowed Tetra Pak to ensure that regular maintenance was performed and that the high-quality standards of the machines were maintained. In 1990, approximately 25 Canadian customers leased these machines. They sold surplus production time to an additional 50 to 60 customers whose volumes did not justify their own capital investment.

EXHIBIT 1   The Inside Story

Outside and in, Tetra Brik cartons were designed to ensure optimum flavour and nutrition protection for a variety of liquid foods, and to use minimal amounts of materials and energy.

The end result is a unique package that reduces demands on the environment.

- Most Tetra Brik paper comes from forests where the growth rate is greater than the fell rate. A renewable resource, paper composes 75 percent of Tetra Brik cartons and uses little or no chlorine in the bleaching process.
- Tetra Brik paper uses 1.5 times less water in the manufacturing process than refillable glass bottles, and 2.5 times less than nonrefillable glass bottles.
- A micro-thin layer of aluminum, about 5 percent of the total, provides an impenetrable barrier against air, light, and bacteria.
- There's less aluminum in a Tetra Brik carton than the lightest of any screw-on bottle cap.
- The small amount of aluminum in a Tetra Brik carton saves more energy than is required to make it, because it allows liquid food to be shipped and stored without refrigeration.
- Pure, food grade polyethylene plastic makes up 20 percent of all Tetra Brik cartons. In all, Tetra Pak cartons seal in the best food quality possible.

A Clean-Air Approach to Packaging
- Manufacturing Tetra Brik cartons creates less air and water pollution than most other kinds of packaging.
- Tetra Brik users indicate that these cartons require half the energy costs to manufacture and deliver products to market than other packaging.
- Tetra Brik cartons comprise less than 3 percent of the total weight of the product. A 1-litre glass bottle comprises 30 percent or more of the product's total weight.

- In June 1989, The Institute of Food Technologists in the United States recognized aseptic packaging as the most significant food science innovation in the past 50 years. The reasons cited were outstanding levels of nutrition and flavour protection, and consumer safety.

Going the Distance for Less
- Less than two standard semitrailers can transport a million unfilled 1-litre Tetra Brik cartons. 52 semi-trailers are needed to haul a million unfilled litre-size glass jars or bottles.
- Filled Tetra Brik cartons take up to 30 percent less energy to ship than glass bottles.
- Tetra Brik cartons produce 12 times less waste than glass bottles for equal product shipments (taking into account Canada's 25 percent recycling rate for glass bottles).

Tetra Brik Cartons are Recyclable
- Tetra Pak packaging recycles into many useful products including sole shoes, mats, and a durable lumber substitute called "Superwood."
- In June 1990 Tetra Brik cartons were collected for the first time in curbside Blue Box containers in Markham, Ontario.
- Tetra Pak plans to extend recycling programs for drinking boxes into Vancouver and Montreal by the end of 1990, and eventually across all of Canada.

Already, Tetra Pak is minimizing its effect on the environment by greatly reducing its environmental demands during manufacturing and shipping.

Now that it is recyclable, this modern packaging miracle will come full circle in meeting consumers' needs and those of the environment.

Tetra Pak's major customers were major juice and fruit beverage producers. Tetra Pak had operated under stringent internal environmental policies since inception. The company purchased its raw materials (paper, foil, polyethylene granules, and ink) from suppliers which it believed utilized the "best available technology" to ensure minimum impact on the environment. Tetra Pak used nonsolvent organic inks which were cured by electron beam in the offset printing process, again to minimize emissions to the atmosphere.

Sales

Tetra Pak dominated the drink box industry in Canada, with a major share of the approximately 1 billion carton annual market. Combibloc, Inc., was the only other supplier of juice boxes in Canada.

Tetra Pak faced significant secondary competition from glass bottles, cans, gable-top cartons, plastic bottles, polyethylene pouches, and plastic jugs. In 1990, respective shares of these container suppliers for the ready-to-serve juice/drink and nectar market were estimated to be (1) juice boxes, 35 percent; (2) glass bottles, 15 percent; (3) gable-top cartons, 15 percent; (4) plastic bottles, 15 percent; (5) cans, 15 percent; and (6) other, 5 percent.

Events Leading up to November 1989

TPR had not felt a need to actively pursue the possibility of recycling its juice boxes. To a great extent, this view was influenced by the fact that incineration for energy recovery (electricity and steam heat) was a widely accepted method of solid waste disposal in Europe. Fifty to 70 percent of solid waste in Sweden, France, and Germany was incinerated. Landfill sites were not a viable alternative given the population density of European countries.

In Canada, however, there was growing concern over incineration. For example, a 35- to 40-year-old incinerator plant in Toronto, Ontario, had been closed down in 1988 as a result of public outcry against its smoke and other toxic emissions. In this instance, the plant was old and had not been well maintained. New incineration facilities, such as Victoria Hospital's Energy from Waste Plant in London, Ontario, employed sophisticated equipment and stringent emission control technologies. Nonetheless, the public image of incinerators had already been irreversibly damaged by earlier events (Exhibit 2).

Furthermore, there was increasing public concern over capacity problems at landfill sites which were attributed to one-way packaging materials. Between 1991 and 1994, Ontario faced the loss of about 45 percent of its annual landfill capacity. Pollution Probe and other environmental organizations, which echoed "green movements" in Germany, Austria, and Belgium, advocated the use of refillable containers over one-way containers and recycling over incineration. However, such groups did not always take a consistent position. For example, in 1988, Pollution Probe in the United Kingdom issued the original "Green Consumer Guide" in which it stated that Tetra Pak cartons were close-packing, light, and save space and therefore economize on fuel in transport. Pollution Probe in Canada issued a Canadian version in 1989 listing "5 Bad Packages," with Tetra Pak heading the list. When this discrepancy was pointed out to Pollution Probe in Canada, their response was that the two organizations were separate and distinct.

Exhibit 2   NDP Facing 'Environment Test' from Antipollution Activists

NDP
Transition to Power
11 days to Oct. 1

Pollution Probe says the first 18 months of Rae government will indicate how much is going to be done.

**By Gordon Sanderson
and Rob McKenzie**
The London Free Press*

TORONTO—Pollution Probe has set a tough timetable for the new NDP government to deliver on its promise of an environmental cleanup.

"We're looking at the first 18 months as a real test of how much is going to be done," the coalition's Janine Ferretti said Wednesday at Queen's Park. "We will fight for the adoption of the new government's environmental blueprint for Ontario."

INCINERATOR BAN: Among other things, the watchdog group is calling for an immediate ban on new garbage incinerators and, within a year, a plan to shut down existing incinerators, including Victoria Hospital's three-year-old, $32-million energy-from-waste plant, where the bulk of London's household garbage is burned.

Hospital spokesman John Finney said the incinerator is equipped with "state-of-the-art pollution control equipment" and complies with strict rules on pollution. He said it also reduces the hospital's energy bill, freeing up dollars for health care.

Last December, Westminster (nearby London) sued the hospital and London because the city was dumping fly ash from the incinerator at a city-owned landfill in Westminster. Federal tests indicated excesses of toxic metals such as cadmium and lead in the ash.

The hospital stopped dumping the ash in March and began shipping it to a waste company near Sarnia. Westminster dropped the portion of its suit against the hospital and is "not actively pursuing" the portion against the city, says Mayor Dave Murray.

BAN SUPPORTED: Ferretti said Pollution Probe was encouraged by Rae's responses during the election campaign to a questionnaire on the environment.

Rae supported an immediate ban on municipal garbage incineration and endorsed the view that incinerators undermine efforts to reduce waste. (The Liberal government ended the dumping of incinerator fly ash in municipal landfills as of Sept. 1.)

* September 20, 1990. Reprinted by permission.

The theme "reduce, reuse, and recycle" was well advertised via radio and newspaper. Notwithstanding the many benefits of the juice box, it became a prime target for environmentalists. Elementary school teachers were writing to parents, asking them not to include juice boxes in their children's lunches. This posed a serious threat to the survival of Tetra Pak. Consequently, Tetra Pak felt strong pressures to respond.

Given the movement toward recycling in Canada, the executives of the company felt that, until juice boxes could be recycled, it would not be possible to effectively convince the Canadian public that Tetra Pak cartons were "environmentally benign." An innovative recycling approach (which involved recycling mixed plastic waste to produce durable synthetic lumber material) developed by Advanced Recycling Technology Ltd. of Belgium, had been available since 1987. Patents to the technology and the equipment had subsequently been transferred to Superwood International (based in Dublin, Ireland), who, in turn, had licensed Superwood franchises around the world. Superwood Ontario Limited of Mississauga, Ontario, obtained its license in 1989. Tetra Pak, working closely with Superwood International in Ireland, determined that juice boxes, as well as the wrap and straws, could be used as a raw material for this plastic lumber. The juice boxes blended well into the process, and physical testing showed that the incorporation of the paper and aluminum fibres gave the lumber improved strength and stiffness.

Given this development, Tetra Pak requested approval from its head office to sanction the possibility of recycling its products. Approval to "do whatever was deemed necessary" was granted in November 1989. Tetra Pak began by providing financial and technical assistance to Superwood Ontario Ltd., which opened its doors on June 1, 1990. The Ontario and federal government each provided about $200,000 in grants to Superwood. The grants were made available by the Waste Reduction Branch of the Ontario Ministry of the Environment under the Industrial Waste Diversion Program and the federal Department of Industry, Science and Technology under a program to encourage new recycling technologies. Second, the company engaged in an expensive, multifaceted communications campaign to promote its carton's recyclability and minimal environmental impact. In the longer term, some Tetra Pak managers hoped to convince relevant stakeholders that incineration of its packages to create energy was the optimal waste management solution so that recycling would be unnecessary as in many other countries.

Superwood Ontario Limited

Superwood was the result of an innovative plastic extrusion technology. The process combined mixed plastic waste from consumer and industrial sources to produce plastic lumber which could replace wood in a variety of useful applications. At full capacity, Superwood Ontario Limited could process over 3,200 (metric) tonnes of mixed plastic and juice boxes per year. Superwood was a strong, durable, and waterproof material which could be used to produce a variety of products, including picnic tables, park benches, curb stops, planter boxes, and retaining walls.

Several Toronto-area pools had adopted Superwood for benches and storage areas. A mall opening in Scarborough in February 1991 was planning to use 400 curb stops manufactured from Superwood, as well as 48 benches and approximately 100 planter boxes. If acceptance of Superwood continued to grow, environmental concerns regarding juice boxes might be reduced. However, the markets for such recycled products were undeveloped and only a maximum of 15 percent of the volume of the final product contained Tetra Pak materials. The company was working to find a production technology which would incorporate a higher degree of its own material.

Municipal Collection

Of the 27 million tonnes of solid waste produced by Canadians, less than 12,000 tonnes consisted of juice boxes. Because of this low volume, Tetra Pak could not be expected to operate a collection system for its cartons. Instead, the company had to convince municipalities, who were legally responsible for solid waste management, to include juice boxes as part of the plastic stream in their Blue Box programs. The rough breakdown of recyclable materials collected in 1990 was newspapers, 75 percent; glass, 10 percent; steel, 10 percent; and PET/plastics, 5 percent.

The Blue Box collection system had been created under the auspices of a unique business–government cooperative arrangement. In 1985, Ontario Multi-Material Recycling, Inc. (OMMRI), an association of the soft drink industry and its container and container material suppliers, reached an agreement with the Ontario government whereby the costs of the Blue Box program would be shared and nonrefillable containers would be permitted using an initial sales ratio of 60/40 nonrefillable to refillable. The ratio would change to 70/30 when a 50 percent recycling ratio was achieved. Over the period 1986 to 1989, the costs of the Blue Box program were shared as follows: (1) OMMRI, one third of capital costs and some of the promotional costs (OMMRI contributed $20 million over the four-year period); (2) provincial government, one third of capital costs and a declining ratio of operating costs (from 50 percent to zero); (3) municipalities, one third of capital costs and operating costs not covered by the province. In 1989, the Blue Box system was acclaimed by the United Nations Environment Program and the Ontario Ministry of Environment; the Recycling Council of Ontario and OMMRI were jointly presented with the UN's Environment Award. In the spring of 1990, because of provincial government desires to broaden private sector involvement in waste reduction activities, a new agreement was reached involving more industry groups to expand the Blue Box program. Under the new agreement, six industry sectors agreed to provide $45 million over the five years, 1990 to 1994, to help fund the system which had a mandate to extend the Blue Box network to reach 80 percent of Ontario households and expand the range of materials collected. There was some concern that if provincial governments did not continue to subsidize the Blue Box program, the municipalities would pull out of the program. Overall, it was estimated by Pollution Probe that the soft drink industry was savingup to $80 million annually by being allowed to use nonrefillable containers.[1]

It was not easy to sell municipalities on the idea of collecting juice boxes as part of the Blue Box program. Many did not have the ability to sort or bale the materials nor the capacity to warehouse them once collected. Others simply expressed no interest in the concept. Several municipalities were also reassessing their existing recycling programs. Superwood had three arguments to use in attempting to include juice boxes in municipal recycling programs: (1) significant volumes of materials are diverted from landfills, (2) no sorting of plastics into different types and sorts is necessary, and (3) a guaranteed market exists given that Superwood will sign a contract to buy all their baled postconsumer waste at $60/tonne for a specified period of time.

---

[1] *Financial Times of Canada,* February 3, 1992, p. 1.

Tetra Pak's first success with the Blue Box Program occurred in Markham, Ontario. In June 1990, coinciding with the opening of Superwood, the town of Markham announced that it would expand a pilot program to include all mixed plastics and, for the first time in Canada and the world, juice boxes. Only those boxes bearing the triangular "Tetra Pak" logo would be accepted. In light of the success of the pilot, the municipality was collecting juice boxes from over 40,000 Markham homes by the fall of 1990. The municipality of Lindsay, Ontario, followed in early October, 1990.

The Eco Logo

In 1988, the federal government announced a new environmental labeling program to help consumers recognize products deemed least harmful to the environment. A black and white maple leaf, made of three intertwined doves, and known as the Eco Logo, was the government's "environmental seal of approval." A 16-member Environmental Choice Board was created to decide whether to give Eco Logos for various product categories and if so, to establish criteria for deciding if an applicant could be licensed (for three years) to use the Eco Logo. The Canadian Standards Association administered the testing. The program was patterned after similar efforts in other countries, particularly the Blue Angel symbol developed in Germany in the late 1970s.

Soon after the Eco Logo program was announced, Tetra Pak made inquiries about using the Eco Logo. Government officials were impressed with the energy efficiency and reduction characteristics of Tetra Pak's product, but stated that politically, granting permission to use the logo would not be appropriate, since the product could not be recycled. However, Superwood applied and had been given permission to use the Eco Logo. By the fall of 1990, 26 products had won the right to display the logo, but it was suspected that many more products would be approved. The federal government was planning a multimillion-dollar advertising program to give such products a marketing advantage over competitors.

Manager-Environmental Affairs

In addition to the efforts described above, Tetra Pak's president created a new position, manager environmental affairs, in January 1990. This individual reported to the vice president, marketing/environment, and was given full authority by the Environmental Steering Committee to deal with issues within his or her mandate. This individual's responsibilities included (1) researching new technologies to validate the company's sustainable development efforts, (2) establishing internal recycling programs, (3) developing markets for recycled materials, (4) reducing plant emissions and energy consumption, and (5) responding to concerns of a technical nature from the public, government, and so on. The individual selected for this position possessed a doctoral degree in chemistry and had relevant work experience in the United States and Canada in the management of environmental affairs and government relations.

A National Packaging Protocol

In 1989, in response to demands from consumer groups, environmentalists, and various levels of government, the Canadian Council of Ministers of the Environment (federal and provincial ministers of the environment) decided to explore the feasibility of developing national policies aimed at reducing the amount of waste entering landfill sites. A task force was commissioned, composed of representatives from all relevant stakeholder groups, including the packaging industry, to develop a set of "guiding principles" to achieve the goal of minimizing landfill waste.

During the task force consultations, Tetra Pak strongly recommended that before any further policy development occurred, more research should be conducted to determine the relative environmental impacts of various disposable, recyclable, and refillable containers. The company also made the following points:

1. A "waste efficiency audit" of different packaging systems should be conducted to examine the amount of material used (weight, volume) to deliver an equivalent amount of product. For example, a European study found that a 1-litre Tetra Pak aseptic carton generated 27 grams of waste, as compared to 338 grams for an equivalent volume nonrefillable glass container.

2. An "environmental impact audit" should be conducted to examine the amount of raw materials, water, and energy consumed in producing different types of packages, as well as the amount of pollution created.

3. Municipal officials in Ontario were concerned that the 25 percent interim and 50 percent final reduction goals of the Ontario government for landfill waste, to be achieved by 1992 and 2000, respectively, were too ambitious and unrealistic, particularly in view of the negative stance the provincial government had taken toward municipal incineration. The provincial government provided little financial support to municipalities to meet the reduction targets and to help fund programs like Blue Box collection. As a result, the municipalities were pushing for the return of a bottle deposit system and a ban on all nonreusable or nonrecyclable packages. However, retailers and packaging companies were generally opposed to any form of deposit system.

4. A voluntary set of guidelines, incorporating a monitoring mechanism to ensure reduction targets were met, would be preferred to government-imposed regulations.

Overall, Tetra Pak recommended that reduction be established as the first priority of any waste management strategy. While recycling should be viewed as an important component to reduce the volume of waste diverted to landfills, Tetra Pak felt the packaging industry should be encouraged to develop new technologies and preserve existing ones (such as aseptic cartons), which achieved reductions in the amount of inputs used to produce packaging material.

The final text for the National Packaging Protocol was endorsed in early 1990. The protocol was based on the "3R hierarchy": reduce, reuse, and recycle. Recovery options, such as energy from waste (EFW) and incineration were not encompassed or envisioned in the protocol. The adoption of a 3R hierarchy placed companies like Tetra Pak at a severe disadvantage, inasmuch as aspetic containers were not reusable or easily recyclable, and it was not possible to further reduce the volume of raw material inputs used in manufacturing the container, since such reductions had been incorporated into the original package design. Specific across-the-board waste reduction targets were established in the protocol as follows: Packaging sent for disposal shall be cut to at least 80 percent of the 1988 level by the end of 1992, 65 percent of the 1988 level by the end of 1996, and 50 percent of the 1988 level by the end of 2000.

An independent auditor was appointed to determine the appropriate 1988 base figure for each type of packing material sent to landfills, in order to monitor compliance with these targets. The initial base figure for Tetra Pak had been set at 12,000 tonnes.[2] Given the relatively light weight of the aseptic carton, this 1988 base figure for Tetra Pak was extremely low for the number of litres distributed by that amount of packaging material, even when compared to packages that could be recycled (see Exhibit 3). Tetra Pak was concerned that its own base figure of 12,000 tonnes would have to be reduced by 50 percent, but learned from the Packaging Task Force that the 50 percent reduction target was intended to be an across-the-board target rather than a target to be applied equally to each product. In any case, compliance with the targets was entirely voluntary, although various levels of government throughout Canada threatened to implement regulations and even ban products or increase taxes if specified reductions were not achieved voluntarily.

While the National Packaging Protocol could conceivably ensure a consistent approach to regulations for packaging across Canada, different provinces were in fact considering different regulatory approaches. Some provinces were inclined to adopt deposit refillable systems, where industry would be told what to do, while other provinces were considering a "product stewardship model" involving industry self-regulation. The product stewardship model was considered by some observers to be more mature because industry would be responsible for regulating itself, but also more dangerous given the challenges of enforcement and the uncertainty about what financial and other commitments would be made by each company.

---

[2] Disguised figure to protect confidentiality.

EXHIBIT 3   Over 500,000 Tonnes of Landfill Saved

- Between 1982 and 1989 inclusive, Tetra Pak sold packaging for a total of approximately 1.6 billion litres of liquid food, using 62,000 tonnes of packaging material (all of which went to landfill).
- If the same volume had been sold in 1.36-L and 284-ml steel cans, the net landfill would have been about 130,000 tonnes (with 50 percent recycling included in the calculations).
- If the same volume had been sold in 1-L and 284-ml glass bottles, total landfill would have been about 625,000 tonnes (with 25 recycling included in the calculations).
- The difference in landfill additions between Tetra Pak packaging and glass (563,000 tonnes) is roughly equal to the total amount of landfill produced annually by a city the size of Ottawa.
- Had the same 1.6 billion litres been sold in refillable bottles, making 13 round trips (the average in Europe is 7), the amount of landfill produced by glass bottles would have been about the same as that produced by beverage boxes, but with the added disadvantage of more fossil fuels used in transporting these heavy containers back and forth and more energy used in heating wash water.

These are the assumptions upon which the above comparisons were made:

Weights		*TBA* Volume (1982—1989 inclusive)*	
1-L TBA carton	31.4g	784 million litres	(1-L family size)
1-L glass bottle	400 g	<u>853.5 million litres</u>	(250-ml single serve)
1.36-L steel can	166g	1637.5 million litres total	
250-mL TBA carton	11g		
284-mL glass bottle	173g		
284-mL steel can	55g		

Recycling rates (national average)
TBA: 0% (TBA recycling began in 1990)
Glass: 25%
Steel: 50%

---

* TBA refers to Tetra Brik Aseptic cartons.

Other Tetra Pak Initiatives

Tetra Pak addressed the issue of minimizing the environmental impact of the company's products through a number of initiatives:

1. In Canada, the company provided financial and technical assistance to Superwood, which produced synthetic wood products using, in part, Tetra Pak juice boxes. However, in 1990, the amount of waste diverted to the three plastic lumber companies operating in Canada was small (representing a total of 2,000 tonnes per annum) and synthetic wood, being new to Canada, had a very small market.

2. Pilot programs began on a limited scale in the United States, Germany, and Spain to "repulp" used Tetra Pak cartons. Repulping was a recycling process commonly employed in paper mills whereby wastepaper was shredded, mixed with water in a pulper, and then remanufactured into new paper. Tetra Pak cartons could be repulped in a normal repulping unit outfitted with

specially designed screens to remove aluminum and polyethylene particles. These particles could then be recycled along with waste plastics into plastic lumber.

3. In 1990, a pilot project had been launched in Germany to produce chipboard composed entirely of aseptic carbon waste. The end product had many of the physical properties of wood and, because of the plastic content, could be thermoformed by placing it in a mould and applying heat. To be economically viable, a chipboard plant required a reliable feedstock supply of approximately 100,000 tonnes per year, which far exceeded the amount of drinking carton waste generated in the Canadian market (12,000 tonnes per annum).

4. A number of extrusion applications were explored. In the extrusion process, aseptic cartons were shredded, heated, and, in some instances, mixed with other inputs to produce a number of different products. Using extrusion, fuel pellets could be produced from cartons to be burned in industrial boilers and cement kilns. These pellets were cheaper than coal and burned cleanly, but tended to cause uneven temperature levels and slagging in boilers, hindering market development efforts. Pallet spacers could also be made using extrusion technology. These spacers were widely used by a variety of industrial firms, including Tetra Pak. However, the end product was heavier than conventional wood pallets.

5. Tetra Pak signed a development contract with BTI of Germany to refine a method of manufacturing low-density rigid board using drink cartons. These boards could be used in products such as wallboard and acoustic panels.

6. Tetra Pak had been able to dramatically reduce the volumes of its own plant waste.

7. In Canada, Tetra Pak funded research to explore the development of other processes which could use aseptic carton waste. These included the use of cartons to replace various quantities of wood chips in the manufacture of medium-density fibreboard (used extensively in the construction and furniture industries).

The 1990 Communications Campaign

Tetra Pak structured its 1990 communications campaign around three major target groups: the general public, the company's customers and suppliers, and various levels of government. The overall objectives were to change the perception that laminated plastics could not be recycled and to reinforce the environmental advantage of juice boxes in terms of reductions in waste, energy consumption, and use of raw materials.

General Public

For years, school boards had encouraged students to make nutritious lunch choices in packages that did not break and were safe to use. Juice and milk in Tetra Pak drink boxes seemed to be an obvious choice for many families. However, teachers and parents had developed a negative impression of juice boxes based upon misinformation about their environmental impact.

To kick off the awareness campaign, Tetra Pak worked with a major advertising agency to develop a full-page print ad (Exhibit 4) which appeared in newspapers within Eastern Canada in August and September 1990. The ad stated that the juice box was "a package of environmental solutions" and highlighted reduction of waste, raw materials, air pollution, and energy, as well as the carton's recyclability. Similar advertisements appeared in *Chatelaine, Canadian Living,* and *Macleans* magazines and in several teachers' journals.

With the assistance of a major British Columbia–based advertising firm, Tetra Pak also developed a full colour newspaper insert titled "The Juice Box Story," which appeared in all dailies and some weeklies across Canada during the fall of 1990. Tetra Pak's "very efficient package" (combining the best technology and materials, minimal energy use, minimal landfill impact, and recyclability) was emphasized. Flyers were also distributed to residents whenever their city or municipality began to accept drink boxes in their Blue Box program.

Customers and Suppliers

Tetra Pak took a different approach with its business partners. The company felt it was crucial that its customers and suppliers understood that Tetra Pak was taking a proactive role in managing issues of sustainable development. In early October 1990, Tetra Pak developed the following "Ten-Point Program" for its customers and suppliers: (1) theme: "Good for you, good for the earth," (2) publicity, (3) advertising (consumer/trade), (4) in store campaign ("shelf talkers"), (5) consumer promotions, (6) educators' program (school kits), (7) recycling (Superwood), (8) government relations, (9) cooperative programs, (10) establishment of the Canadian Beverage Box Council (an association of aseptic packagers, i.e., Tetra Pak, Combibloc, and their customers).

By November, the program had been communicated, via presentations by senior management, to Tetra Pak's major customers. Feedback was positive, with the general message being "we're glad you're doing something." Tetra Pak also encouraged its customers to be proactive by including "environmental messages" as part of their package design. The company's interaction with its suppliers was still at a preliminary stage.

Government

During his previous work, the manager environmental affairs had established excellent connections with federal and provincial government officials and various committees across Canada. He maintained regular contact with these organizations in his new role at Tetra Pak. For example, Tetra Pak had

EXHIBIT 4   Example of Advertising

THIS IS
A BOX OF SOLUTIONS

The juice box is a package of environmental solutions.
Reduced waste. A juice box is 97% beverage, only 3% packaging. Litre for litre, that's ten times less packaging than glass bottles.
Reduced raw materials. Juice boxes use less raw materials than glass bottles. And 75% of those raw materials come from renewable resources.
Reduced energy. Filled juice boxes are compact and fit together like building blocks with no wasted space, saving energy when storing and shipping them.

Reduced air pollution. Empty juice boxes are light weight and are shipped in compact rolls to food manufacturers for filling. A million empty one-litre packages can be carried in 2 semi-trailers, compared to *50 semi-trailers* for that many one-litre glass bottles.
Recycling. Juice boxes are starting to be recycled. Over 500 Canadian schools already have juice box recycling bins. And some municipalities are leading the way by accepting juice boxes in their regular Blue Box programs.
The right choice. Juice boxes

reduce waste, reduce energy use, and conserve resources. They're one of the most healthy and nutritious ways to package liquid food. For these reasons, in 1989, the Institute of Food Technologists named them the most important food science innovation in 50 years.

Juice boxes *are* an environmental solution. For your family, and for your future.

Good for you.
Good for the earth.

For more facts on juice boxes and the environment, call **1·800·263·2228**
or write Tetra Pak Inc., 200 Vandorf Road, Aurora, Ontario L4G 3G8

enjoyed a strong relationship with the Ontario Liberal government, actively participating in committees such as the Ontario Recycling Advisory Council, which represented various business and environmental groups and municipalities. In 1990, a senior manager of Tetra Pak also joined the board of directors of OMMRI.

The company recognized the importance of communicating with government groups on an on-going basis. Recent experiences in the United States had demonstrated the costs of not communicating adequately with government. For example, the state of Maine passed legislation in 1989 which banned the sale of any beverage in aseptic cartons. At that time, aseptic packaging manufacturers were not active in packaging ban lobbying battles. The plastics industry and local retailers did most of the lobbying because plastic packaging was the main target of restrictive bills at that time. The legislators decided that, because they could neither be recycled or reused, aseptic cartons would not fit in with their new law expanding the bottle deposit system to all noncarbonated beverages. Throughout 1989 and 1990, 12 other states either considered some form of multimaterial container bans or formed task forces to look at issues involving multimaterial packaging.

Responding to this threat, aseptic carton makers in the United States, Tetra Pak, and Combibloc formed the Aseptic Packaging Council (APC) and hired a public affairs firm to represent their interests in state capitals. APC started research on recycling pilot programs in early 1990, and by setting up recycling programs, was successful in its lobbying efforts to prevent proposed multimaterial container bans in several states. The APC continued to lobby Maine legislators to lift the aseptic carton ban temporarily in order to facilitate an APC-sponsored pilot-recycling program. Tetra Pak managers in Canada were not involved in APC.

From Tetra Pak's view, the regulatory environment in Canada was both fluid and complex. As a result, the company hired a government relations consulting firm to keep the company informed about what was happening at both the federal and provincial government levels, since each province had to be viewed as a "separate challenge." The consulting firm was not hired to lobby on Tetra Pak's behalf but to gather information about what options the governments were considering, the individuals involved and their backgrounds, and the "key influence" on each government. The consulting firm also provided Tetra Pak with an objective view and periodically gave advice to the company about possible alliances.

To assist Tetra Pak in communicating its message to governments in Canada, a 12-minute video entitled "A Balanced Environment" was developed with the help of a major public relations firm (see Exhibit 5). The show was initially used in a presentation to the British Columbia government which was considering deposit legislation. Tetra Pak planned to use the show in similar presentations to other provincial governments, the federal government, and a variety of other groups in the educational and recycling fields.

EXHIBIT 5   Communication Video: "A Balanced Environment"

"All of us are in a balancing act between what consumers want and what the environment can take; between what we produce and what we are left with. All packaging is very much under the microscope from an environmental point of view and there is a lot of misinformation out there in the marketplace. We don't have a crisis; we have an opportunity to get a head start on what we throw away. We must reduce by taking less out of the environment when a product is made and when economically and environmentally feasible, we must recycle by putting less back in the environment when the product is consumed. So consumers like to focus on recycle but we've got to be sure that in fostering recycling we don't defeat source reduction. Reduce and recycle—for a truly balanced environment we must strive to do both."

The next segment of the video described the composition of the Tetra Pak aseptic carton.

In the next segment of the video, different individuals representing the Institute of Food Technologists, National Research Council, American Management Association, and Tetra Pak commented on the benefits of the Tetra Pak (TP) carton. An "environmental summary" concluded this segment of the video by flashing the following four points: (1) "No hot water washing/detergents." (The viewer was expected to be aware that reusing glass bottles required hot water washing—which required energy—and the use of detergents—which created water pollution; however, the Tetra Pak carton was never, and could never be, refilled, primarily because health authorities prohibited refilling packages consisting of semipermeable materials, such as paper, wood, and plastic.) (2) "Less aluminum—than screw-on caps." (This point was meant to address concerns that aluminum should not be thrown away but should be recycled.) (3) "Lower energy consumption." (The video noted: "The environmental impact of any package is fundamentally in the areas of energy use, nonrenewable resource use and solid waste creation. When you reduce the weight of a package you reduce the energy required because you reduce the materials.") (4) "Reduced fuel and exhaust emissions." (The video noted: "52 semitransport trailers are needed to transport 1 million empty glass or metal containers. Tetra Pak cartons are shipped in compact rolls. One million cartons require less than two semitrailers reducing fuel consumption and exhaust emissions by over 26 times.) The end of this segment of the video noted: "Tetra Pak environmental policy sums up these facts and figures: To provide *cost effective* packaging systems for liquid food that maximize product *quality and safety* and simultaneously *minimize effects on the environment*" (underlined words were emphasized).

The final segment of the video dealt with the recycling issue and noted the following: "As consumers, we all make choices about the products we consume and their waste. When that waste is an empty Tetra Pak carton, we have two choices: throw it out or recycle it. In either case, because the carton is made with less material in the beginning, there is less waste. The first and best way of dealing with solid waste is to not create it at all—what is called source reduction. . . . Litre for litre, Tetra Pak cartons produce as little as one-tenth the landfill produced by today's glass bottles and that's after subtracting the bottles that are recycled. Caps and labels off glass bottles are not usually recycled and even they can weigh up to one third of the whole aseptic package. . . . If we achieved our goal of source reduction to a very high degree, recycling would essentially disappear because there wouldn't be enough material around to recycle."

The segment concluded by describing how Tetra Pak cartons were being recycled into "excellent" particle board and synthetic lumber. It was noted that "the first production plant is in Germany," and "Blue Box collection of TP cartons has already begun in parts of southern Ontario and TP is working to expand this across Canada. . . . A study by the Grocery Product Manufacturers of Canada states that almost 7 of 10 Canadians are willing to participate in a curbside recycling program.")

The video concluded as follows: "Because it reduces and is now recyclable, we're convinced the Tetra Brik aseptic package is a responsible and environmentally sound package. We will cooperate with government, industry partners, and consumers to make it even better. That's our commitment to a world insisting on healthy products and a healthy environment."

Tetra Pak also developed another 12-minute video entitled "A Box Called Tyler" to educate students about the possible recyclability of the juice box in light of the increasing trend toward "garbageless lunch" programs. In these programs, students were discouraged from bringing nonreusable and nonrecyclable packages for lunch. In addition to the video, the company initiated a pilot school recycling program to collect Tetra Pak packages from the school board in the region of York north of Toronto. Student committees were formed to take responsibility for collecting the packages, and Tetra Pak took responsibility for providing the necessary equipment and collecting and delivering the packages to Superwood for recycling. From this program, the company hoped to gain information about the costs, logistics, and attitudes of school boards, teachers, and children. The Environmental Committee of the Toronto School Board reviewed the program and decided not to participate.

In general, Tetra Pak's approach was "to make itself very available" to participate in packaging or environment-related events or conferences. The company's attitude was that these presented opportunities to communicate accurate messages about the environmental impact of juice boxes.

November 1990

In November 1990, one year after the initiation of their communications campaign, the Environmental Steering Committee felt it was time to review their progress to date. The committee's general feeling was that the communications campaign was "good, but not good enough" and, therefore, members considered changes Tetra Pak could make. To date, advertising efforts had focused on print. The committee wondered if other methods/media should be considered and whether the message should be changed. Members believed that it might be possible for Tetra Pak to do something else to enhance public education and awareness.

Tetra Pak had received some encouraging feedback regarding the newspaper advertisements and inserts. A toll-free telephone number had been established to handle inquiries from the public regarding information in Tetra Pak advertisements. Over 2,000 calls were recorded, more than 85 percent of them positive. However, many people had the perception that Tetra Pak was promoting recyclability, even though the company knew that its product was not being recycled in many municipalities. They complained that the claims meant little to them personally until their communities began to accept juice boxes as part of their local Blue Box programs. Tetra Pak's explanations that municipalities had the prerogative to determine which materials would be recycled and that municipalities often were slow to implement collection programs seemed to fall on deaf ears.

During pre-election speeches, the newly elected NDP government in the province of Ontario had pledged to ban the use of juice boxes (Exhibit 6).

EXHIBIT 6   NDP's Promise to Outlaw Beverage Boxes 'Shocking'

By John Fox
Financial Post

The pre-election pledge of a senior Ontario New Democrat to ban the use of boxes as beverage containers because they are difficult to recycle is "shocking and shortsighted," says a spokesman for **Tetra Pak Inc.,** the product's maker.

Ruth Grier, a senior NDP MPP rumored to be headed for the environment portfolio in premier-elect Bob Rae's cabinet, promised the ban during a public debate in Toronto a week before her party's election win.

Many environmentalists don't like the containers—used to package everything from wine to milk shakes—because they are not reusable and contain a combination of plastic, paper and aluminum that makes them hard to recycle.

A spokesman for Grier said she would have no comment on the fate of the boxes until after a cabinet has been appointed.

Jaan Koel, a spokesman for the Aurora, Ont. company Tetra Pak, a wholly owned subsidiary of Swiss-based Tetra Pak Rausing SA, said Grier's opposition to drinking boxes is based on "purely a surface evaluation of the situation" and not on "solid, factual information."

He said the company, with sales of 920 million boxes a year in Canada worth $100 million—and 35 percent to 40 percent of sales in Ontario—is launching a recycling program in Lindsay, Ont. and Markham, Ont. in October. Householders will be asked to separate drinking boxes and other plastics from their blue boxes for collection and sale to Superwood Ontario Ltd. of Mississauga, Ont., which will turn them into plastic lumber.

Superwood is also in negotiations with recycling officials in Vancouver and Montreal. Koel said it may take several years to expand the program to the entire Ontario blue box system.

In the meantime, critics of the drinking boxes ignore their environmental and economic advantage, he said.

He said the lightweight packages offer huge savings in transportation costs and the environmental impacts of burning fossil fuels. For example, two million empty drinking boxes can be shipped in two tractor trailers. The same number of empty glass or metal containers would require 52 trucks, Koel said.

Because they are more compact than bottles or cans, he added, they also contribute less to the province's overflowing garbage dumps.

---

* September 18, 1990.
Reprinted by permission.

The Environmental Steering Committee was uncertain about the impact this would have on the company's business, as policies had not yet been established regarding environmental issues. However, the company was concerned about the role that the new government might play in helping or hindering its activities.

UNIVERSITY HOSPITAL—1987

Finding a better way.[1]

In the fall of 1987, University Hospital (UH) had just completed, with the assistance of outside consultants, an extensive strategy review culminating in a formal strategic plan. The original stimulus for the plan had been to better understand the growth patterns and potential of the hospital's services in order to forecast the need for and justify a significant expansion of the hospital's facilities. However, the final document had gone beyond this original intention, raising questions about the hospital's "service portfolio" and its future potential.

The strategic plan had seven key recommendations (see Exhibit 1), several of which represented significant departures from past practice. As part of the planning process, the hospital's services had been put into different categories, a portfolio approach, with apparent implications for future emphasis and resource allocation. As one UH vice president commented:

> The plan has forced us to establish some priorities for our different services. Not everything we do is, or will be, world class, and the plan will help us allocate our increasingly scarce resources, capital, and operating funds, toward our premier services.

---

[1] UH's motto; attributed to Thomas Edison.

This case was prepared by Mary Crossan, Research Assistant, and Rod White, Associate Professor, for the sole purpose of providing material for class discussion at the Western Business School. Certain names and other identifying information may have been disguised to protect confidentiality. It is not intended to illustrate either effective or ineffective handling of a managerial situation. Any reproduction, in any form, of the material in this case is prohibited except with the written consent of the School. Copyright 1989 © The University of Western Ontario.

Exhibit 1   Key Recommendations from the Strategic Plan

Recommendation #1: Pursue a Service Cluster Product Line Development Approach
Product line management is a system that organizes management accountability and operations around discrete service or product lines. Service clusters are those groups of services that are provided to distinct market segments. By shifting management focus to product line development, hospitals can increase their market share by improving the efficiency of their services and by tailoring services to specific market needs.

Recommendation #2: Adopt an Appropriate Bed Complement for UH in the 1990s
To facilitate the implementation of a service cluster or product line concept for University Hospital, it will be essential to adopt an appropriate bed complement (for each service).

Recommendation #3: Address Facility Considerations through a Medical Mall Implementation Strategy
The purpose of the medical mall is multifold:

• It compartmentalizes functions and services to allow an optimum level of capital expense by type of service.
• It targets and controls traffic by patient type while ensuring convenience and accessibility.
• It provides a "one-stop" location for multiple levels of inpatient and outpatient support services.

Recommendation #4: Pursue a Networking Strategy as Part of the Role of Tertiary Care
Pursuit of a networking strategy asserts that the role of University Hospital in tertiary care should represent a "hub" within the Canadian and international health care system. As such, options have been developed to ensure University Hospital is able to accept patients who need to be "stepped-up" from community hospitals and outpatient settings and also to "step down" patients who no longer require UH's intensity of services.

Recommendation #5: Adopt a Diversification Strategy
To encourage management to investigate which type of integration makes most sense for UH given its tertiary nature and commitment to research and education. Diversification efforts can be adopted by an institution in basically three ways, through vertical integration, horizontal integration, or geographic dispersion.

Recommendation #6: Implement an Organizational Enhancement Strategy
Due to the complexity and dynamic nature of University Hospital, ongoing strategic planning and administrative support and leadership will be essential. The recommended organizational enhancement strategy has, as its focus, to

• Pursue process planning and implementation by adopting an ongoing planning cycle.
• Assign responsibility/authority for successful ongoing strategic planning.
• Address management/medical staff succession.
• Exploit the benefits of University Hospital's relationship with Health Corporation of America (HCA).

At the heart of this strategy is the need to formalize and integrate current planning mechanisms into an ongoing process.

Recommendation #7: Continue an Aggressive Financial Strategy: Preserve/Enhance Financial Resources
The objectives of this recommendation are twofold:

• To enhance financial resources.
• To preserve financial resources.

Further, the plan recommended organizing business units around these "service clusters" (or product lines), and continuing the planning process as an ongoing, in-house activity. As Pat Blewett, president and CEO of UH, reviewed the report and its recommendations, he was satisfied with both the process and the results. Blewett was widely recognized as a highly positive, entrepreneurial type of administrator willing to try new ideas and promote innovative services. Results had been impressive. New services had contributed substantially to UH's growth and cash flow. However, the facility was straining within its existing physical space. In addition, UH, like other hospitals in the province of Ontario, had to cope with increasing budgetary pressures from the Ministry of Health, while demand for all services continued to grow. Blewett hoped the recommendations from the strategic plan would allow the hospital to deal with these issues while maintaining the institution's innovative and entrepreneurial spirit.

Background

While a separate institution, UH was part of a larger health sciences complex of the University of Western Ontario. UH had been an educational and research, as well as a health care delivery, facility since opening in 1972. It was the newest of the three major acute care hospitals in London, Ontario, a community of about 300,000 in southwestern Ontario. UH was established, owned, and operated by the London Health Association (LHA).

Founded in 1909, the LHA's activities had changed dramatically over the years. Originally, it had operated a tuberculosis sanatorium on the outskirts of the city. As the number of tuberculosis patients declined, the LHA made plans to diversify into chest diseases and purchased property adjacent to the university for a new hospital. However, in the decade of the 1960s, the university was growing rapidly, especially in the health sciences, and wanted a full-fledged teaching/research hospital attached to the university. The LHA was persuaded to undertake this more ambitious task but stipulated that their institution would remain administratively separate from the university.

Planning for the new facility began in 1966. An innovative spirit was evident from the outset. Hospitals tend to be very traditional institutions, but the planning group, in its efforts to create an outstanding medical facility, were willing to deviate from conventional practices. The UH motto, "Finding a better way," was applied to facilities design, organizational practice, as well as patient care and research activities. Using a philosophy of form follows function, the hospital layout was guided by an analysis of function. The result was revolutionary with physicians' offices, research areas, inpatient and outpatient departments, and teaching space all on the same floor. Essentially, each of the floors operated as a specialized minihospital sharing support services within a larger hospital setting. UH's deviation from accepted hospital practices were wide ranging from the use of noise-deadening carpeted floors, a hospital blasphemy at the time, to the decentralized organizational structure with an unconventional division of tasks.

The Health Care Environment

Canada's health care system was one of the most comprehensive in the world, providing equal access to all Canadians. The publicly funded system was the responsibility of the provincial governments, although a substantial portion of the funding came from the federal level by way of transfer payments. In Ontario, the Ministry of Health (MOH) was the department concerned with hospitals. Health care costs accounted for 32 percent of the province's $32 billion budget, the single largest category of expenditure with the most rapid growth. As a result, the province was becoming increasingly active in its efforts to contain these costs. Examples included the banning of extra billing by doctors, cuts in the number of medical residency positions, and provision for the MOH to take over any hospital in a deficit position.

Health care funding had evolved in a piecemeal fashion into an extremely complex and often ambiguous system. Basically, the MOH contracted with the hospitals to provide services, in an approved plant, at an approved ("global") budget. Further, the ministry expected each hospital to show an excess of revenue over expenses sufficient to provide for a reasonable accumulation of funds for future capital requirements. Program, service reductions, or bed closures which related directly to patient care required the agreement of the ministry. However, under pressure to balance budgets, some hospitals were reducing services without the formal agreement of the ministry. Using a universal formula based largely on history, the ministry arrived at a hospital's global operating budget. Most MOH revenues were *not* directly tied to actual expenditures or the provision of services. New programs could be initiated by the hospital, but incremental capital and/or operating costs had to be incorporated into the existing global funding base. Additional funds were forthcoming only if approved by the ministry.

In the approval of new programs, district health councils had a prominent voice. They provided the forum for ensuring that changes met the health care needs of the *local* community. The Thames Valley District Health Council (TVDHC) was responsible for the 18 hospitals in the London area. New program proposals submitted to TVDHC were very diverse, ranging from a $400,000 request from UH for a four-bed epilepsy unit, to Victoria Hospital's $94 million expansion request. Evaluating programs on a regional basis, based on local community need, did not allow much consideration of the type of care provided or the referral base they served. UH frequently went outside this process, appealing directly to the ministry, or failing that, by funding projects from their own accumulated surplus.

The government's influence upon hospitals extended well beyond the control of global operating budgets and new programs. It also affected the supply of nurses, residents, and physicians by controlling the number of available positions in nursing and medical schools, by influencing the certification of immigrants, and by limiting the number of hospital residency positions funded. The MOH had recently reduced, provincewide, the number of medical residency positions for physicians doing postgraduate specialty training. Essentially, medical residents learned a specialty while providing patient care in a hospital, freeing physicians to do teaching, research, and other activities. Reduction in residency positions created a gap in the provision of service in larger, teaching hospitals and would ultimately lead to a decline in the number of indigenously trained medical specialists and researchers.

Pressures on the health care system were increasing. Because of an aging population, demand for basic services was expected to increase into the 21st century. Further, increasingly sophisticated and expensive new medical technologies not only improved existing services but also developed new treatments for previously untreatable illnesses; all at a cost, however. While gross measures of productivity, like patient days in hospital per procedure, had been improving, the increasing sophistication of treatments appeared to be increasing costs at a faster rate than offsetting gains in productivity. Further, most gains in productivity came about by requiring fewer personnel to do the same tasks, rather than reducing the number of tasks. The increasing stresses and turnover that naturally resulted were present in all hospital health care professionals but especially evident in the exodus from the nursing profession. Although not as severe in the London area, it was estimated 600 to 800 beds in Toronto hospitals were closed because of a lack of nursing staff. Shortages of staff existed in other areas, like occupational and physical therapists, radiologists, and pharmacists.

The province's basic approach to managing demand (and costs) appeared to be by limiting supply. As a result, waiting lists were growing, especially for elective procedures. Certain serious, but not immediately life-threatening, conditions had waiting lists for treatment of six months to a year and were getting longer.

Social and political expectations also put pressures on the system. Universal, free access to a health care system offering equal, high-quality care to all had become a societal expectation and a political sacred cow. Politically acceptable ideas for fundamentally restructuring the industry were not obvious. There was no apparent way to reconcile increasing demand and costs with the governmental funding likely to be available. As a result, many observers felt that the health care system was out of control. And the ministry was under tremendous pressure to control costs and account for its expenditures, while at the same time providing more, new, and enhanced services. Without an overall approach to the health care situation, it was not clear how the ministry would allocate funds in the future. Choices between high technology, expensive procedures, like heart transplantation and intensive care for premature infants, and basic care for the aged were difficult to make and politically sensitive.

University Hospital

UH was a well-designed and maintained facility. It was located in north London, Ontario. Rising from a three-floor service podium, each of its seven tower floors was divided into two basic components—one an inpatient area, the other an outpatient, office, research, and teaching area. Each inpatient area, except paediatrics, had a corresponding outpatient department for initial assessment and follow-up, and the performance of minor procedures. UH had 463 inpatient beds with an average occupancy rate of over 90 percent, which effectively meant 100 percent utilization. The occupancy rate and number of beds had been fairly constant over the past few years. Although space was severely constrained within the hospital, there was a land bank available for future expansion.

In the past, UH had employed some creative solutions to its problem of space constraints. Services had been reviewed to determine whether they could be more effectively provided in one of the other London hospitals, or, as in the case of the Occupational Health Centre, whether they could be better served in an off-site location. Some specialization had already occurred within the city. For example, since another major acute-care hospital specialized in maternity, UH did not duplicate this service. However, UH did have an in-vitro fertilization programme (popularly known as test-tube babies). In a major move during 1986, the Robarts Research Institute (RRI) was opened adjacent to UH. A separate but affiliated institution with its own board, the RRI specialized in heart and stroke research. Moving researchers from UH to this new facility helped to alleviate, at least temporarily, some of the hospital's space pressures. The five-floor, 69,000-square-foot institute housed 35 labs. By the end of 1987, it was expected 80 RRI researchers would be active in conducting basic research into stroke and aging, heart and circulation, and immunological disorders relating to transplantations.

UH housed some of the latest medical technology. For example, a magnetic resonance imaging (MRI) machine costing $3 million was added in 1986. One of the most powerful machines in Canada, the MRI provided unparalleled images of all body organs. Interestingly, neither funding for the total capital cost nor the majority of the ongoing operating costs for this advanced technology instrument was assumed by the ministry. However, this had not deterred Blewett, and UH was considering other high technology equipment like a $3 million gamma knife which would enable neurosurgeons to operate without having to cut the skin surface.

Mission and Strategy

UH's mission involved three core activities: research, teaching, and patient care. And in this way it did not differ from other university-affiliated teaching hospitals. What made it more unique was the emphasis on innovative, leading-edge research. Clinical and teaching activities were expected to reflect and reinforce this focus. This strategy had implications for UH's product/market scope and its service portfolio.

Product/Market Scope

UH attempted to serve the needs of three related, but different markets: teaching, research, and the health care needs of the community. Local community and basic teaching needs generally required a broad base of standard services. On the other hand, research needs argued for focus and specialization of products offered with a physician's clinical activities related to their research and necessarily drawing from a large patient referral base.

With three different markets, service focus was not easy to achieve. The initial design of UH had included only a small emergency service because another hospital in the city specialized in trauma. However, in response to local community pressure, a larger emergency department was incorporated. Balancing the product/service portfolio under increasing space constraints, funding pressure, and demand for basic health care services was becoming ever more challenging.

Overall, UH's mix of cases had a high proportion of acute cases, very ill patients requiring high levels of care. UH had approximately 1 percent of the approved hospital beds in Ontario, as well as 1 percent of discharges and patient days in acute-care public hospitals. However, when broken down by the acuity/difficulty of the procedure, UH's tertiary focus was clear (see Exhibit 2).

Geographically, 81 percent of UH's admitted patients came from the primary service area of southwestern Ontario, with one third of all patients originating from the hospital's primary service area of Middlesex County. Fifteen percent of all patients came from the secondary service area, which consisted of all parts of Ontario outside the primary region. The remaining 4 percent of patients came from outside the province of Ontario. However, because these cases tended to be more acute than the norm, they accounted for a disproportionate share of patient days, approximately 6 percent, and an even larger proportion of revenues. Exhibit 3 provides a breakdown of current patient origin by service. For the future, the strategic plan had identified transplantation, in-vitro fertilization, neurosciences, diabetes, cardiology/cardiovascular surgery, epilepsy, orthopaedics/sport injury, and occupational health care as services with high, out-of-province potential.

To help manage the service/product portfolio, the strategic plan called for the following designation of products: *premier product lines* were designated on the basis of the world-class, cutting-edge nature of the service; *intermediate product lines* represented those services that were approaching premier status

EXHIBIT 2   Market Share of Ontario Patients by Acuity*

Level I: Primary	0.7%	8,092
Level II: Secondary	1.4	2,616
Level III: Tertiary	4.2	2,783
Examples: Heart transplant	66.0	31
Liver transplant	30.8	175
Kidney transplant	27.0	71
Craniotomy (age > 18 yrs)	15.7	388

* As classified by a scheme developed in the United States designed to reflect intensity of nursing care required.

Exhibit 3   Patient Origin by Service—1986 (percent)

| | | Origin | | |
| | | | Tertiary | |
Service	Primary (S-W Ont.)	Secondary (Remainder of Ont.)	Canada (except Ont.)	International
Cardiology	71.9	22.3	3.9	1.9
Cardiovascular and thoracic surgery	61.4	28.8	7.8	2.1
Chest diseases	88.1	10.8	0.6	0.5
Dentistry	89.1	10.8	0.0	0.1
Endocrinology	83.2	15.4	0.0	1.5
Gastroenterology	80.1	15.7	2.5	1.0
General surgery	87.5	11.1	0.6	0.8
Gynaecology	70.9	24.4	3.8	1.0
Haematology	92.2	6.8	0.0	1.0
Immunology	90.0	10.0	0.0	0.0
Internal medicine, infectious diseases	85.6	10.1	0.2	2.0
Nephrology	76.8	20.4	0.2	2.5
Neurology	70.0	26.2	2.4	1.4
Neurosurgery	42.6	36.3	2.4	18.6
Ophthalmology	75.9	23.7	0.0	0.4
Orthopaedic surgery	85.6	13.4	0.3	0.7
Otolaryngology	92.2	7.0	0.4	0.0
Paediatrics	42.6	45.0	0.0	12.4
Plastic surgery	86.8	12.4	0.2	0.6
Psychiatry	91.0	6.7	0.3	2.0
Rheumatology	91.9	7.7	0.0	0.4
Urology	92.9	7.1	0.0	0.0

Source: UH Strategic Plan.

or that stood alone as a service entity; *service support clusters* were services that supported the intermediate and premier product lines; *ambulatory/emergency services* included outpatient clinics, emergency services, and regional joint venture arrangements; and *diversification/collaboration ventures* were stand-alone services that generated revenue for UH. The services for premier and intermediate categories are listed in Exhibit 4. A more detailed profile of the premier product lines is provided in Appendix A.

Product Innovation

Developing new and improved leading-edge treatments for health problems was a key element of UH's mission relating to research and teaching. And while the institution, over its relatively brief history, had participated in a number of medical innovations, this success did not appear attributable to formal planning. Rather new programs and services developed at UH in a

---
EXHIBIT 4   Services by Strategic Category

Premier product lines

- Cardiology/Cardiovascular Surgery
  - Arrythmia Investigation and Surgery
  - VAD
- Clinical Neurosurgical Sciences (Neurology/Neurosurgery)
  - Epilepsy Unit
  - Stroke Investigation
  - Multiple Sclerosis
  - Aneurysm Surgery
- Multiple Organ Transplant Centre (Adult and Paediatric)

Kidney	Pancreas
Liver	Small bowel
Heart	Bone marrow
Heart/lung	Whole joint and bone
Other	

- Reproductive Biology
  - IVF Clinic

Intermediate Product Lines

• Chest Diseases	• Dentistry
• Endocrinology/Metabolism	• Gastroenterology
• General Internal Medicine	• General Surgery
• Haematology	• Immunology
• Nephrology—Dialysis unit	• Ophthalmology
• Orthopaedic Surgery	• Otolaryngology
• Paediatrics	• Plastic/Reconstructive Surgery
• Physical Medicine and Rehabilitation	• Psychiatry
• Rheumatology	• Urology

---

seemingly ad hoc fashion. As Ken Stuart, the vice president medical observed, "New services happen because of individuals. They just grow. There is some targeted research, but it is not the route of most (activities) because it would stifle people's ideas. They need to fiddle with things and be able to fail." The development of the Epilepsy Unit, outlined in Appendix B, describes an example of this process.

Blewett commented on the development of new programs at UH.

The fact that the hospital is so small—everyone knows everyone—I can get around. Everyone knows what's going on in the hospital. . . . People just drop in to see me. Someone will come down and tell me that they've found a real winner and they just have to have him/her, and so we go out and get them. There's always room for one more; we find a way to say yes.

When it impacts other resources, Diane [Stewart, executive vice president] becomes involved. She says it's easy for me to agree, but her people have to pick up the pieces. In order to better identify the requirements for new physicians and new programs, Diane came up with the idea of the impact analysis (a study of how new or expanded programs affected hospital staffing, supplies, and facilities). But even when the study is done, we don't use it as a reason to say no; we use it to find out what we have to do to make it happen.

Diane Stewart, the executive vice president, was sensitive to the need for continued innovation. She had stated, "We like to leave the door open to try new things. We go by the philosophy that to try and fail is at least to learn." A UH vice president commented:

> People here are well-read. When ideas break, anywhere in the world, they want them. There is a lot of compromising. But things get resolved. It just takes some time. We haven't learned the meaning of the word "no." But we're at a juncture where we may have to start saying no. We're just beginning to be (in the tight financial position), where many other hospitals have been for several years.

Revenues and Costs

UH's revenues and costs could not be neatly assigned to its major areas of activity. As shown in Exhibit 5a, in 1983, 73 percent of UH's sources of funds were a "global allocation" from the MOH; by 1987, this amount had been reduced to 70 percent. For the most part, these funds were not attached to specific activities, acuity of patients, or outcomes. Over the past few years, UH, like all other hospitals, had simply been getting an annual increase in its global allocation to offset inflation. The stipulation attached to MOH funds was that there could be no deficit.

Some small part of MOH funding was tied to activity levels. Increases in outpatient activity did, through a complex formula, eventually result in increased funding to the hospital. Further, the ministry had established a special "life support fund" to fund volume increases for specified procedures. However, this fund was capped and the number of claims by all hospitals already exceeded funds available, so only partial funding was received. The MOH also funded the clinical education of medical students and interns. This accounted for most of the $5.8 million in revenue from MOH programs (Exhibit 5a).

Approximately 30 percent of UH's revenues did not come directly from the Ministry of Health through its global funding allocation. A large percentage of these self-generated revenues originated from servicing out-of-province patients. For patients from other provinces, the MOH negotiated with the paying provinces a per diem charge for services provided. Even so, because out-of-province patients generated incremental revenues, above and beyond the global allocation, they were a very attractive market. For out-of-country patients, UH could set their own price for services provided, thereby ensuring that the full cost of providing health care was recovered. But, as shown in Exhibit 6, the out-of-province and out-of-country revenue appeared to have reached a plateau at around 14 percent of total revenue. There was also a sense the mix of this component was shifting away from out-of-country patients toward out of province.

EXHIBIT 5a   UH Statement of Revenues and Expenses
For the Year Ended March 31
($000s)

	1983	1984	1985	1986	1987
Revenue:					
MOH allocation	$47,067	$51,527	$ 56,329	$ 61,103	$ 69,502
Inpatient services	5,355	7,482	9,986	13,945	14,771
Accommodation differential	1,548	1,624	1,746	2,277	2,537
Outpatient services	1,692	2,069	2,033	2,428	3,135
MOH programs	4,908	5,083	5,405	5,503	5,811
Other revenue	3,626	3,471	4,079	4,510	4,836
	64,196	71,256	79,578	89,766	100,592
Expenses:					
Salaries and wages	35,779	39,480	43,505	47,450	53,581
Employee benefits	3,869	4,441	4,711	4,866	5,628
Supplies and other services	10,312	11,751	13,640	15,289	18,960
Ministry of Health programs	4,978	5,376	5,701	5,976	6,099
Medical supplies	3,679	3,915	4,842	5,506	6,547
Drugs	2,226	2,079	2,871	3,846	5,220
Depreciation	2,444	2,818	3,121	3,398	3,843
Bad debts	192	205	165	197	141
Interest	75	137	144	122	420
	63,554	70,202	78,699	86,650	100,439
Excess of revenue over expenses from operations	642	1,054	878	3,116	153
Add (deduct) unusual items:					
Debenture issue cost					(154)
Gain on asset sale					466
Excess of revenue over expenses	642	1,054	878	3,116	465
Operating statistics					
Inpatient days (000)	137.5	138.5	139.7	140.4	142.0
Inpatient admissions (000)	11.8	11.9	12.5	12.9	13.1
Average inpatient stay (days)	11.7	11.6	11.2	10.9	10.8
Occupancy (percent)	89.5%	89.9%	90.3%	91.0%	90.9%
Outpatient visits (000)	96.5	101.9	108.4	113.1	122.4
Total patients seen	n/a	n/a	221,090	233,688	254,001
Equivalent patient days	n/a	n/a	208,932	214,980	222,137
Bookings ahead:					
Urgent				294	584
Elective				650	724
Number of beds:					
Approved	421	424	424	428	436
Rated	451	451	451	463	463

EXHIBIT 5b   UH Balance Sheet
As of March 31
($000s)

	1983	1984	1985	1986	1987
Assets					
Integrated funds*					
Current:					
Cash and securities	$ 2,795	$ 1,580	$ 1,562	$ 1,799	$ 1,541
Accounts receivable					
Province	3,095	3,341	4,324	6,068	7,508
Other	2,299	3,119	3,742	6,394	7,006
Inventories	1,005	1,147	1,130	1,127	1,064
Prepaid expenses	101	109	99	78	100
Total current assets	9,231	9,296	10,857	15,466	17,219
Funds available to purchase plant, property, and equipment	2,099	3,701	3,086	2,764	6,800
Fixed assets:					
Property, plant, and equipment	36,884	37,873	38,511	40,325	48,223
Capital leases	173	144	141	40,249	48,114
	37,057	38,017	38,652	40,325	48,223
	48,387	51,014	52,596	58,555	72,242
Special funds*					
Cash and deposits	19	21	35	40	90
Marketable securities (cost)	4,256	5,042	5,948	7,105	7,187
Accrued interest	57	103	108	123	141
Mortgage receivable	59	56	53	49	46
Advance to integrated fund	1,264	1,004	744	734	1,775
	5,655	6,227	6,888	8,051	9,869
	54,042	57,241	59,485	66,606	82,112
Liabilities and equity					
Integrated funds					
Current:					
Account payable	2,941	4,490	4,153	5,618	6,987
Accrued charges	2,401	2,074	2,580	2,988	3,668
Current portion of leases and loans	417	401	400	260	307
Total current liabilities	5,759	6,965	7,133	8,866	10,962
Long-term					
Debentures†					5,629
Advances from special funds	1,265	1,004	744	734	1,775
Capital lease	175	141	95	18	12
	1,440	1,145	839	752	7,417
Less principal due	417	401	400	260	307
	1,023	744	439	492	7,109

	1983	1984	1985	1986	1987
Integrated equity	41,605	43,305	45,025	49,196	54,170
	$48,387	$51,014	$52,597	$58,554	$72,241
Special fund‡					
Equity	5,656	6,227	6,888	8,052	9,870
Total equity and liabilities	54,042	57,241	59,485	66,606	82,111

* Revenue and expenses relating to the day-to-day activities of the hospital are recorded in the statement of revenue and expenses and the integrated fund statement of assets. Activities relating to funds made available to the LHA under conditions specified by the donor are recorded in the special funds statement. Most of these monies were donated to the LHA prior to the establishment of the foundation.

† In February 1987, the hospital issued debentures to finance the new parking garage and attached office facility.

‡ The hospital has received the following advances from the special fund, repayable with interest:

Year	Amount	Purpose
1983	$1,264,000	New telephone system
1986	$ 250,000	Establishment of Occupational Health Centre
1987	$1,400,000	Finance MRI building

Exhibit 5c UH Statement of Changes in Equity
Year Ended March 31

	1983	1984	1985	1986	1987
Integrated funds					
Balance, beginning of year	$40,386	$41,605	$43,305	$45,025	$49,196
Add (deduct) MOH settlements	(1,114)				
	39,272	41,605	43,305	45,025	49,196
Donations and grants	1,692	646	842	1,054	4,509
Excess of revenue over expenses	641	1,054	878	3,117	465
	2,333	1,700	1,720	4,171	4,974
Balance, end of year	$41,605	$43,305	$45,025	$49,196	$54,170
Special funds					
Balance, beginning of year	$ 5,044	$ 5,651	$ 6,227	$ 6,888	$ 8,052
Add:					
Donations and bequests	1	1	11	409	835
Net investment income	606	575	650	755	983
Balance, end of year	$ 5,651	$ 6,227	$ 6,888	$ 8,052	$ 9,870
Represented by:					
Nonexpendable funds	$ 492	$ 492	$ 492	$ 492	$ 492
Expendable funds	5,139	5,734	6,396	7,560	9,378
	$ 5,651	$ 6,227	$ 6,888	$ 8,052	$ 9,870

EXHIBIT 6   University Hospital Revenue Breakdown

Fiscal Year	MOH Global Base	Other Revenue	Out-of-Province & Out-of-Country
1983	74.6%	25.4%	7.4%
1984	73.7%	26.3%	8.7%
1985	72.1%	27.9%	11.3%
1986	69.3%	30.7%	13.8%
1987	70.5%	29.5%	13.9%

Additional funds also came from the University Hospital Foundation of London and other entrepreneurial activities. The numerous fund-raising appeals by the foundation included sales of operating room greens in sizes ranging from doll-size through to a small child, and a specially produced record and music video. The foundation was a separate financial entity, and funds flowing to UH appeared as an addition to UH equity (and cash) with no effect on revenues.

Salaries, wages, and benefits made up the single largest cost category. (The base salary of medical staff, who were employees of the university, were not directly included in this number.) As a proportion of total revenues, these costs had declined marginally over the last five years. Other costs had, however, increased, in particular medical supplies and drugs. Much of this increase was due to the MOH's unwillingness to pay for certain drug therapies. For example, drugs used to prevent rejection of transplanted organs were not paid for by the MOH because the drugs were considered experimental and therefore the cost of these drugs had to be covered under the hospital's global budget. Similar funding limitations had evolved with other drugs and medical apparatus (e.g., implantable defibrillators). The boundary between clinical research and clinical practice was often difficult to draw. Research funding bodies, like the Medical Research Council, would not pay for medical procedures beyond the purely experimental stage. And often the MOH would not immediately step in and fund procedures after research grants expired.

On balance, UH had never recorded a deficit year. However, its operating surplus had been decreasing. (See Exhibit 5a.) Blewett felt the key to UH's future financial success was reduced reliance on ministry funding. (UH's reliance on ministry funding was already less than most hospitals.) UH was actively pursuing opportunities with the potential to generate funds. One recent development was the Occupational Health Centre (OHC), which opened in 1986 as a separate private, for-profit organization to provide occupational health care services to the business community. By the end of 1987, it had 30 companies with 11,000 employees as clients. However, like most start-ups, the OHC had required an initial infusion of cash and was not expected to generate net positive cash flow for several years.

EXHIBIT 7   Clinical Services with Largest Research Budgets

Service	*Amount ($000)*
Transplantation & Nephrology	$1,979
Gynaecology	1,454
Neurology	1,105
Endocrinology	923
Cardiology	678

Source: *Research Annual Compendium*; does not include the Robarts Research Institute.

Not all of the activity undertaken at UH was reflected in its financial statements and operating statistics. Research grants and many of their associated costs were not included in the hospital's statements, even though they were administered by the university and much of the activity was conducted at UH. During 1986–87, UH physicians and researchers were involved in over 200 projects with annual funding of $9.5 million. Exhibit 7 lists the services most involved in research. In an effort to capitalize on the revenue potential of the innovations developed at UH, an innovations inventory was being developed and the potential for licensing explored. It was expected this activity, if it demonstrated potential, would be spun out into a private, for-profit corporation.

Staffing and Organization

UH was a large and diverse organization employing 2,600 personnel. There were 128 medical clinicians and researchers, 70 residents, 44 interns and research fellows, 875 nursing staff, 140 paramedical, 312 technical, 214 supervisory and specialist, 444 clerical, and 379 service staff.

The relationship with UH's medical staff was especially unique. *All* UH physicians held joint appointments with UH and the university and were technically university employees. As well, they did not have a private practice outside of University Hospital. As a consequence, all patients (except those admitted through the emergency department) were referred to UH by outside physicians. At most other hospitals, physicians were not salaried employees. They had hospital privileges and spent part of their time at the hospital and the rest at their own clinics/offices, usually separate from the hospital. These physicians billed Ontario Health Insurance Plan (OHIP) directly for *all* patient care delivered. At UH, the "GFT"[2] relationship with physicians was very different. They were paid a base salary by the university. Physicians negotiated with the dean of medicine and department chairperson for salaries in excess of this base. This negotiated portion was called the "if earned" portion. UH

---

[2] Geographic full-time.

physicians were expected to make OHIP billings from clinical work inside the hospital at least up to the level of their "if earned" portion. Any additional billings were "donated" to the university and were placed into a research fund. Although arrangements varied, the physicians who contributed their billings usually had some say in the allocation of these research funds.

Because of this GFT relationship, the medical staff at UH generally developed a stronger identification and affiliation with the institution. Even so, retaining medical staff was not easy. Most could make significantly higher incomes if they gave up their teaching and research activities and devoted all their efforts to private practice. While the salary of UH physicians was competitive with similar institutions in Canada, many research hospitals in the United States were perceived to offer higher compensation and often better support for research. To further complicate matters, the available number of university positions in the medical faculty and the dollar amount of the salary had been frozen for several years. As a result, the base salary for any net new positions or salary increases were funded entirely by UH.

Structure

The physicians were by nature highly autonomous and independent. Nominally, at least, medical staff were responsible through their clinical service head (e.g., neurology) or a department head (e.g., neurosciences) to Ken Stuart, vice president medical. The role of service and department head was a part-time responsibility rotated amongst senior clinicians in the particular specialty. The heads of services and departments in the hospital, often, but not always, held parallel appointments in the Faculty of Medicine at the university.

The division of services and departments was in most instances determined by traditional professional practice. However, "product offerings," which crossed traditional departmental boundaries, were common. At UH, the only one with formal organizational recognition was the multiorgan transplant service (MOTS). It had its own medical head, manager, and budget. Other multidisciplinary units, like the Epilepsy Unit, did not have formal organizational status, even though the strategic plan recommended organizing around product lines (or business units).

In general, the hierarchy could best be described as loose and collegial. Although it varied from individual to individual, most physicians, while they might consult with their service and department heads when confronted with a problem or pursuing an opportunity, felt no requirement to do so. Typically, they dealt directly with the persons concerned. Most chiefs of services supported this laissez-faire approach, since they wanted to encourage initiative and did not wish to become overly involved in administration, coordination, and control.

At an operational level, the primary organizational difference between UH and traditional hospitals was its decentralized approach. Each floor acted as a minihospital. A triumvirate of medical, nursing, and administrative staff were responsible for the operation of their unit. In many hospitals, nurses spent much of their time doing nonnursing tasks including administrative duties like budget preparation, coordinating maintenance, and repairs, and so on. At UH, a service coordinator located on each floor handled non-nursing responsibilities for each unit and interfaced with centralized services like purchasing, housekeeping, and engineering. Whenever possible, the allied health professionals, such as psychologists, occupational therapists, and physiotherapists, were also located on the floors. In traditional hospitals, hiring, staff development, quality assurance, and staff assignment of nurses were done on a centralized basis. At UH, a nursing manager, located in each service, handled the nursing supervision responsibilities. A nursing coordinator handled the clinical guidance and supervision of the nurses.

Organizationally, service coordinators and allied health professionals reported through their respective managers to the newly created, and as yet unfilled, position of vice president patient services. Nursing reported through nursing managers to the vice president nursing. In practice, the physicians, nurses, and service coordinators on each floor formed a team which managed their floor. Ideally, integration occurred and operational issues were addressed at the floor level, only rarely referred up for resolution.

Nonmedical personnel working in centralized laboratories and services but not directly involved in patient care reported to the vice president administration. Activities dealing with financial, accounting, and information were the responsibility of the vice president finance. While final hiring decisions for nonphysician positions were decentralized to the units concerned, job description, posting, and initial screening was done in the human resources department. In addition, some employee education and health services were handled through this department. The hiring of physicians, even though technically university employees, was usually initiated within UH. Typically, service or department heads would identify desirable candidates. If the person was being hired for a new position (as opposed to a replacement), then after discussion of the physician's plans, an impact analysis would be prepared identifying the resources required. Generally, Pat Blewett was very involved in the recruitment of physicians.

UH was considered progressive in its staffing and organization, having recorded many firsts among Canadian hospitals. Over the years, they had been one of the first to introduce service coordinators, paid maternity leave, dental benefits, 12-hour shifts, job sharing, workload measurement, and productivity monitoring. The concern for employees was reflected in UH's relatively low turnover, in the 9 percent range. Exit interviews indicated very few people went to another health care job because they were dissatisfied with UH. Aside from normal attrition, the biggest reason for leaving was lack of upward job mobility, a situation caused by UH's flat structure and low turnover amongst its management.

Committees at all levels and often crossing departments were a fact of life at UH and reflected the organization's decentralized and participative approach to decision making. Diane Stewart, for example, was a member of 48 different hospital and board committees. Medical staff were also expected to be involved, as Ken Stuart explained:

> Committee work is not a physician's favourite activity. But it's important they be involved in the management of the hospital. I balance committee assignments amongst the medical staff and no one can continually refuse to do their part. This is a demand UH makes of its GFT physicians that other hospitals do not.

UH's management group had recently undergone a reorganization, reducing the number of direct reports to Pat Blewett from five to three. Now the vice president human resources and the vice president administration along with the vice presidents of patient services and nursing reported to the executive vice president, Diane Stewart (Exhibit 8). The reorganization centered control of operations around Stewart, allowing Blewett to concentrate on physicians, external relationships, and the future direction of UH.

Budgets

There were five groups that submitted budgets to administration: support services, nursing, allied health, diagnostic services, and administrative services. The annual capital and operating budgetary processes involved a lot of meetings, and give and take. As one manager described:

> The budget of each department is circulated to the other departments within our service. We have a meeting with . . . vice president administration and . . . vice president finance and all the department heads. Although the department heads are physicians, often the department managers will either accompany or represent the department head. In that meeting, we review each department's budget, questioning any items which seem out of place. The department will either remain firm on its budget, back down, or decide to postpone the expenditure to the following year. People do back down. If we can't get our collective budgets within the budget for our service, the vice presidents will either make trade-offs with the other service categories, or speak with the department heads privately to try and obtain further cuts. The majority of cuts are made in the meeting. . . . It works because the department heads are fiscally responsible, and there is a lot of trust between the departments and between the departments and administration.

Operating budgets were coordinated by the service coordinator on each floor but really driven by the plans of the medical staff. Each year, physicians were asked about their activity levels for the upcoming year; these were translated into staffing and supplies requirements, in terms of number of hours worked and the physical volume of supplies consumed. Costs were attached and the overall expense budget tabulated later by the finance department. In the last fiscal year when the overall budget was tabulated, it exceeded the estimated revenues of the hospital by over $10 million, roughly 10 percent. Ross Chapin, vice president finance, explained what happened:

> We went back to each of the clinical services and looked at their proposed level of activity. The hospital had already been operating at 100 plus percent of its

physical capacity. Most of the services had not taken this into account in preparing their plans. They had assumed more space and more patient beds would be available. Since this just wasn't going to happen, at least in the short term, we asked them to redo their budgets with more realistic space assumptions. As a result, our revenue and expense budgets came more into line.

While the activity of the medical staff drove the operating expenditures of the hospital, physicians were not in the ongoing budgetary loop. If expenditures were exceeding budget, physicians might not even be aware, and if aware had no incentive to cut expenses and reduce activity levels in order to meet budget. Aside from the number of physicians and the limits of their own time, the major constraint on expenditures was space and the availability of support services. A patient could not be admitted unless a bed was available; an outpatient procedure could not be conducted unless a consultation room was free and the needed support services (e.g., radiology, physical therapy, etc.) could be scheduled.

Because of MOH funding and space constraints, the hospital had a set number of inpatient beds. The allocation of beds amongst services was determined by a committee made up of the manager of admitting, several physicians, and chaired by the vice president medical. Since bed availability affected the activity level of the services and their physicians, this allocation was a sensitive area. Services would often lend an unused bed to another, usually adjacent, service. However, the formal reallocation of beds was done infrequently, and when done, was based on waiting lists (by service) and bed utilization rates.

New Program

While capital and operating budgets for ongoing activities originated with the managers on the floors, the medical staff usually initiated requests for *new* programs and equipment. Money to fund large outlays associated with new or expanded programs would be requested from the MOH or might be part of a special fund-raising campaign. (Private charitable foundations had made significant contributions to the Epilepsy Unit, the MOTU, and the MRI facility.) When proposals for a new program or the addition of a new physician were made, an impact analysis was undertaken. These studies detailed the resource requirement: space, support staff, supplies, and so on, of the initiative and summarized the overall financial impact. The analysis did not, however, identify the availability or source of the required resources should the initiative be pursued. As one vice president explained:

> The impact analysis might show that if we bring on a new orthopaedic surgeon, we'll need two more physical therapists (PTs). But there is no space (and probably no money) for the PTs. Quite often the physician is hired anyway, and the PTs currently on staff have to try and manage the additional work load. We *know* what a new physician will need beforehand, but we don't always ensure it's there before they come on board.

Recently a new physician had arrived after being hired and office space was not available.

EXHIBIT 8   Organization Chart

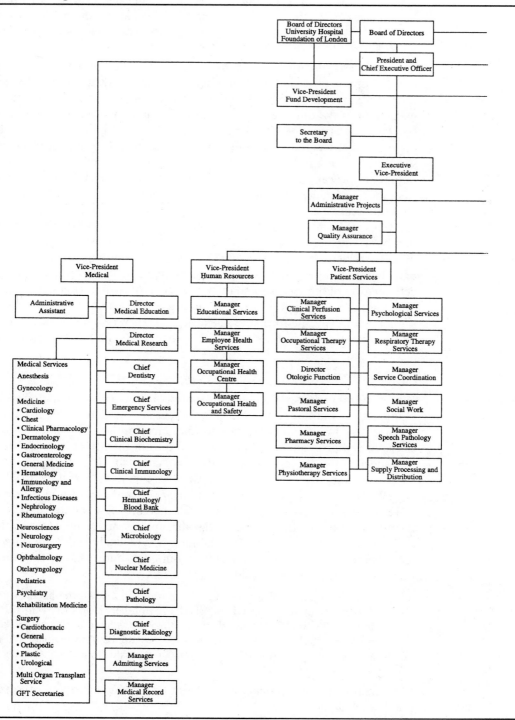

EXHIBIT 8   *(Concluded)*

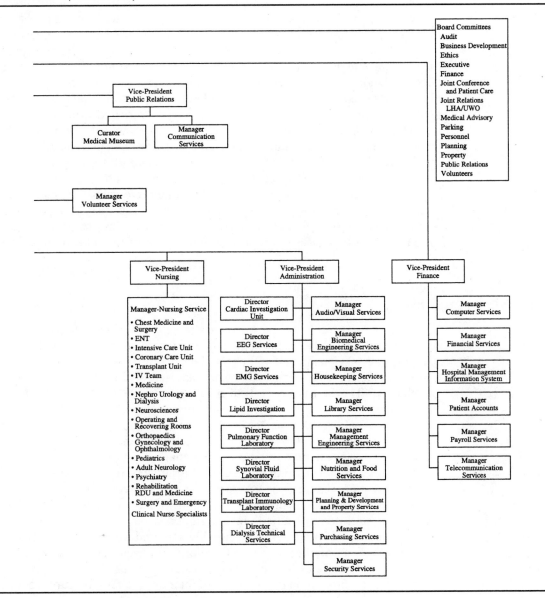

Basis for Success

UH attributed its success to several factors. A primary factor was the GFT status of the medical staff, which cultivated a high degree of loyalty and commitment to the hospital and supported the integration of excellence in teaching, research, and practice. The ability of the medical staff to attract out-of-province patients contributed to the hospital's revenues. The strong entrepreneurial orientation of management, its ability to identify and create additional sources of revenue, and a widely shared understanding of the mission of UH helped to foster commitment to the organization's goals.

Early in its development, UH had attracted physicians/researchers capable of developing major internationally recognized research and clinical programs: Doctors Drake and Barnett in neurosciences and Dr. Stiller in transplantation. These physicians and their programs had developed international recognition and generated patient referrals from all over the country and around the world.

UH's product portfolio required a delicate balance. It was natural for products to evolve and mature. As innovative procedures became more commonplace, they tended to diffuse to other hospitals. Indeed, UH contributed to this process by training physicians in these procedures (as part of their teaching mission). As a consequence, UH's patient referral base would shrink, and so too would out-of-country, out-of-province revenues from maturing service. UH required a constant inflow of innovative, internationally recognized clinical procedures in order to sustain its out-of-province referral base.

The Strategic Plan

UH did not have an internal ongoing strategic planning process. In 1985, a change occurred. UH signed an affiliation agreement with the Hospital Corporation of Canada (HCC), an affiliate of the Hospital Corporation of America (HCA), a large, publicly owned international health care company, which gave UH access to HCA strategic planning expertise. For UH's existing service portfolio, the consultants assessed underlying demand, UH's share of market, its capability base, and abilities relative to other research and teaching hospitals. They did not specifically consider MOH funding policy.

Senior management wanted a process that would enable people to buy into the emerging plan, so they conducted a series of planning sessions. The first information session was conducted in the fall of 1986, when general information about the health care environment was presented to the chiefs of services and administration. In December, a day-long retreat was held to disseminate information and to provide some education on key strategic concepts such as market share and product life cycle. In January 1987, a second retreat was held. The chiefs of services were asked to come prepared to make a presentation on the direction of their department, resource requirements, and priorities. Blewett commented on the meeting:

> The chiefs did an outstanding job. They really got into it, using business ideas to look at their services and where they are going. They were talking about market share and product life cycles. I believe it gave them a new way to think about things. Really, the chiefs were presenting to each other and they wanted to do a good job and make their best case. A lot of information sharing occurred.

In late February, the consultants' initial recommendations were presented to administration. One of the recommendations was to adopt a portfolio approach to planning. A preliminary designation of products into portfolios of premier, intermediate, and service support clusters was provided. The initial criteria used to determine premier status were: geographic "draw," "leading edge" service, consensus as a priority, and future orientation of its people. Subsequent meetings with the medical staff led to some modifications of these designations. Blewett reflected on the process of identifying the product/ service portfolio.

> I never thought we would do it. But when it came down to making the hard decisions, it didn't take that long. I give a lot of credit to the planners and to our administrative person, who kept in close contact with everyone, and made sure that concerns were taken care of. . . . The GFTs are committed to this institution, therefore it's easier to mobilize these people. . . . We also made it clear that services could move between categories, which provides some incentive.

Indeed, sport medicine had not initially been categorized as a premier service, but in the final version of the plan was placed in this category.

The final strategic plan, a 150-page document, was approved by both the Medical Advisory Committee of the hospital and by its board of directors. As Blewett reflected on the process, he was pleased with the results of the effort which had taken over a year to complete. Blewett knew many of his senior managers had applauded the direction the report had taken in providing a more solid foundation on which to make difficult resource allocation decisions. However, he was concerned the plan not be used as a reason to say "no," to stifle initiative and the emergence of new areas of excellence. He wondered how an ongoing planning process would have affected the evolution of the epilepsy unit (described in Appendix B). With this in mind, he was wondering where to go from here. How could the plan, and its recommendations, be used to help guide the hospital?

APPENDIX A
PROFILE OF PREMIER SERVICE CATEGORIES

The premier product lines fell under four categories: cardiology/cardiovascular surgery, clinical neurological sciences, multiple organ transplant, and reproductive biology. More detailed descriptions follow.

Cardiology/Cardiovascular Surgery

The two major programs in cardiology/cardiovascular surgery were arrythmia investigation and surgery and the ventricular assist device (VAD). *Arrythmia investigation* received a major breakthrough when, in 1981, the world's first heart operation was performed to correct life-threatening right ventricular dysplasia. In 1984, UH entered into a collaborative relationship with Biomedical Instrumentation, Inc., a Canadian research and development firm based near Toronto, to produce a sophisticated heart mapping device, which greatly advanced the surgical treatment of patients suffering from life-threatening heart rhythm disorders. The computer-assisted mapping system, which fit over the heart like a sock, enabled doctors to almost instantaneously locate the "electric short circuit" in the hearts of patients afflicted with cardiac arrhythmias. Physicians were then able to more easily locate and destroy the tissue which caused the patient's heart to beat abnormally.

The *ventricular assist device (VAD),* which UH began using in 1987, was functionally no different from some life-support machines, such as the heart-lung machine already in use. In assisting the heart to pump blood, the VAD was used for patients waiting for transplants, those needing help after open heart surgery, and hearts weakened after a severe heart attack. The VAD worked outside the patient's body, carrying out approximately 50 percent of the heart's work. When the patient's heart recovered sufficiently or when a donor organ became available for those who required a transplant, the pump could be disconnected without difficulty. Other than UH, there was only one other hospital in Canada using the VAD.

Clinical Neurological Sciences (CNS)

There were four major programs in CNS: the Epilepsy Unit, Stroke Investigation, Multiple Sclerosis, and Aneurysm Surgery.

The Epilepsy Unit, discussed at length in Appendix B, was one of only a few of its kind in North America. The demand for its services had extended the waiting time for a bed to over a year.

A four-bed *Investigative Stroke Unit* was established at UH in 1983 to improve the diagnosis and treatment of stroke. In 1986, UH, and The University of Western Ontario collaborated in the development of the Robarts Research Institute, which focused its efforts on stroke research.

The Multiple Sclerosis (MS) clinic at UH conducted exploratory research to study the causes and incidence of MS, a chronic degenerative disease of the central nervous system. One study involved 200 MS patients in 10 centres, coordinated by UH, to determine whether cyclosporin[3] and prednisone, either alone or in combination with repeated plasma exchange treatments could prevent further deterioration in MS patients.

Aneurysm surgery became a centre for excellence and internationally renowned early on, when in 1972, Dr. Charles Drake pioneered a technique for surgically treating a cerebral aneurysm. In October of 1979, vocalist Della Reese underwent neurosurgery at UH. She returned to London the following year to give a benefit concert to raise funds for UH.

Multiple Organ Transplant Centre

The first kidney transplant at UH was performed in 1973, followed by its first liver transplant in 1977. In 1979, UH was chosen as the first centre in North America to

---

[3] Cyclosporin was the drug originally used to minimize the body's rejection of transplanted organs. Because of its transplantation experience, UH had a considerable expertise with this drug and immunology in general.

test the antirejection drug cyclosporin A. In 1981, the first heart transplant at UH was performed. In that same year, UH became the site of the Canadian Centre for Transplant Studies. In 1984, Canada's first heart-lung transplant was performed at UH.

In 1984, the provincial government announced that they would partially fund a multiorgan transplant unit (MOTU) at UH. The 12-bed MOTU, which opened in 1987, was one of the first units of its kind in the world. With the help of leading-edge computer technology, transplant patients were closely monitored for the first signs of organ rejection. A highly specialized team of transplant experts including surgeons, physicians, nurses, technologists, and physiotherapists joined together in the MOTU to care for transplant patients.

Reproductive Biology

The primary work in reproductive biology was the in-vitro fertilization (IVF) programme. The programme was launched in 1982, with the first birth occurring in 1985. By 1987, the 100th child was born to parents who previously had been incapable of conceiving a child. The pregnancy rate was 27 percent using this method, with a birth rate of 22 percent. These results were comparable to those of well-established clinics worldwide. It was anticipated that with the combination of continually increasing experience together with basic science and clinical research interests in IVF, the success rate in the program would continue to increase. There was a two-year waiting period to participate in the program.

APPENDIX B
THE PROCESS OF INNOVATION AT UH—THE EPILEPSY UNIT

Research and service innovations had been important to UH. This appendix describes how one of these came about.

The Epilepsy Unit probably had its genesis when Dr. Warren Blume, a neurologist, joined Dr. John Girvin, a neurosurgeon at UH in 1972. Girvin had trained under a founding father in epilepsy treatment at the Montreal Neurological Institute (MNI). Blume had done postgraduate work in epilepsy and electroencephalography (EEG)[4] at the Mayo Clinic. Girvin was unique among neurosurgeons in that he had also gone on to obtain a Ph.D in neurophysiology.

In 1972, the primary treatment for epilepsy was through drug therapy. However, there were many patients whose epilepsy could not be effectively treated this way. For those patients, the only hope was a surgical procedure to remove that part of their brain which caused the epileptic seizure. This required an EEG recording of a patient's seizure to identify the focus of the problem. There were few individuals trained in the use of EEG to study epilepsy. However, Blume had this expertise. Furthermore, Girvin had the training in neurosurgery to carry out the surgical procedure. Neither physician, however, was recruited specifically to do work in epilepsy. It was an interest they both shared and developed over time.

---

[4] The mapping of electrical activity in the brain.

There were a number of factors that united Blume and Girvin, providing the impetus for the dedicated Epilepsy Unit that was eventually opened in May of 1986. One factor was the integration within UH of neurosurgery and neurology under the umbrella of neurosciences. In most hospitals, the two departments were separate, neurosurgery being part of surgery and neurology being its own service. At UH, they were integrated organizationally and located on the same floor. Many attribute this unique relationship to the leadership and friendship of Doctors Barnett and Drake, the original chiefs of neurology and neurosurgery.

In 1974, a young Italian boy and his father arrived on the doorstep of UH seeking help to control the boy's epilepsy, the precipitating factor that brought Blume and Girvin together to work on their first case experience. It was a complex case, requiring the expertise of both Blume and Girvin. The surgery was successful, and Blume and Girvin realized that by pooling their expertise, they could make a significant contribution to the field. Prior to that time, Blume's efforts had been focused on providing EEG readings for epileptic patients that would either be treated with medication or referred to the MNI for possible surgical treatment. Girvin's efforts had been directed at neurosurgery in general, having no special contact with epileptic patients.

Blume and Girvin began to draw together a team. The technique of removing part of the brain for the treatment of epilepsy was based on the fact that most human functions were duplicated in both temporal lobes of the brain. In the early days of surgical treatment of epilepsy at the MNI, there was no method of ensuring that both temporal lobes were functioning normally. As a result, in some cases where a malfunctioning temporal lobe could not duplicate the function of the part of the brain that had been removed, patients were left with serious brain dysfunction like loss of memory capacity. Later, a procedure was developed whereby neuropsychologists were able to assess the level of function of one temporal lobe, while the other temporal lobe was anaesthetized. It so happened that a neuropsychologist with this expertise was working at UWO's psychology department. She was asked to join the team. For Blume and Girvin, adding a neuropsychologist was essential to their ability to deal with more complex cases. The addition of full-time researchers also served to enhance the team's capability.

Capability was further enhanced, when in 1977, Blume and Girvin were successful in obtaining funding to purchase a computer that would facilitate the recording and reading of the EEG. This was a significant step, since to obtain funding, they positioned themselves as a regional epilepsy unit. This was the first formal recognition of their efforts as an organized endeavour. The computerized monitoring could benefit from a dedicated unit; at the time, beds and staff were still borrowed from other departments as needed. Epileptic patients were scattered around the neurosciences floor.

As the volume of patients increased, it became increasingly apparent that a unit was needed. In order to identify the focus of the brain that triggered the epileptic seizure, it was necessary to record a seizure. As a result, EEG recording rooms were tied up for several hours in the hope that a patient would have a seizure. There were a number of problems with this approach. The patient had to have a seizure while in a recording room, and the patient or technologist had to activate the recorder. It was estimated that over 50 percent of seizures were missed using this method. Furthermore, leaving the patient unattended without the benefit of medication to control their seizures was dangerous. A unit that would provide full-time monitoring in order to get the vital EEG recordings and ensure patient safety was needed.

Blume, Girvin, and the manager of EEG developed a proposal for a four-bed epilepsy unit. The beds that they had been using on an ad hoc basis were the neurosciences overflow beds which "belonged" to paediatrics. Paediatrics was located on the same floor as EEG, so when Blume, who was also a member of the department of paediatrics, heard that paediatrics was downsizing, he had approached the chief of paediatrics to negotiate for four beds. As well, the paediatric nurses, who had been responsible for the overflow beds, had become comfortable with providing care for epileptic patients, and it was agreed that they would provide continued support for the unit. Blume and Girvin approached Blewett with a plan requiring funding of $400,000 for equipment and renovations. There was no provision for an annual budget, since paediatrics was prepared to cover the nursing salaries and supplies.

Blewett and his senior management group supported the plan, and it was submitted as a new program to the TVHC for funding in February 1984. The proposal was ranked 10th, which meant it was not one of the top few submitted to the ministry for consideration. A revised proposal was resubmitted the following February. In the meantime, Blewett, Girvin, and Blume met with the assistant deputy minister of health to make a plea for funding, to no avail. They subsequently received news that the TVDHC had given the proposal a ranking of sixth. Blume and Girvin did not lose hope and were persistent in their efforts to obtain funding. After exhausting all alternatives, Blewett decided to fund it out of the hospital's operating surplus. However, compromises were made in the plans by cutting the budget back as far as possible. The board approved the allocation, and shortly thereafter, the unit was opened.

VICTORIA HEAVY EQUIPMENT LIMITED (REVISED)

Brian Walters sat back in his first-class airline seat as it broke through the clouds en route from Squamish, a small town near Vancouver, British Columbia, to Sacramento, California. As chairman of the board, majority shareholder, and chief executive officer, the 51-year-old Walters had run Victoria Heavy Equipment Limited as a closely held company for years. During this time, Victoria had become the second-largest producer of mobile cranes in the world, with 1985 sales of $100 million and exports to more than 70 countries. But in early 1986, the problem of succession was in his thoughts. His son and daughter were not yet ready to run the organization, and he personally wanted to devote more time to other interests. He wondered about the kind of person he should hire to become president. There was also a nagging thought that there might be other problems with Victoria that would have to be worked out before he eased out of his present role.

Company History

Victoria Heavy Equipment was established in 1902 in Victoria, British Columbia, to produce horse-drawn log skidders for the forest industry. The young firm showed a flair for product innovation, pioneering the development of motorized skidders and later, after diversifying into the crane business, producing the country's first commercially successful hydraulic crane controls. In spite of these innovations, the company was experiencing severe financial

---

This case was prepared by Thomas A. Poynter and Paul W. Beamish, The University of Western Ontario. Case material has been disguised; however, essential relationships are maintained. Copyright © 1986 by The University of Western Ontario. Revised, 1989.

difficulties in 1948 when it was purchased by Brian Walters, Sr., the father of the current chairman. By installing tight financial controls and paying close attention to productivity, Walters was able to turn the company around, and in the mid-1950s, he decided that Victoria would focus its attention exclusively on cranes and go after the international market.

By the time of Brian Walters, Sr.'s retirement in 1968, it was clear that the decision to concentrate on the crane business had been a good one. The company's sales and profits were growing, and Victoria cranes were beginning to do well in export markets. Walters, Sr. was succeeded as president by his brother, James, who began to exercise very close personal control over the company's operations. However, as Victoria continued to grow in size and complexity, the load on James became so great that his health began to fail. The solution was to appoint an assistant general manager, John Rivers, through whom tight supervision could be maintained while James Walters' workload was eased. This move was to no avail, however. James Walters suffered a heart attack in 1970, and Rivers became general manager. At the same time, the young Brian Walters, the current chairman and chief executive officer, became head of the U.S. operation.

When Brian Walters took responsibility for Victoria's U.S. business, the firm's American distributor was selling 30–40 cranes per year. Walters thought the company should be selling at least 150. Even worse, the orders that the American firm did get tended to come in large quantities—as many as 50 cranes in a single order—which played havoc with Victoria's production scheduling. Walters commented, "We would rather have 10 orders of 10 cranes each than a single order for 100." In 1975, when the U.S. distributor's agreement expired, Walters offered the company a five-year renewal if it would guarantee sales of 150 units per year. When the firm refused, Walters bought it, and in the first month fired 13 of the 15 employees and canceled most existing dealerships. He then set to work to rebuild—only accepting orders for 10 cranes or less. His hope was to gain a foothold and a solid reputation in the U.S. market before the big U.S. firms even noticed him.

This strategy quickly showed results, and in 1976 Walters came back to Canada. As Rivers was still general manager, there was not enough to occupy him fully, and he began traveling three or four months a year. While he was still very much a part of the company, it was not a full-time involvement.

Victoria in the 1980s

Victoria entered the 1980s with sales of approximately $50 million and by 1985, partly as a result of opening the new plant in California, had succeeded in doubling this figure. Profits reached their highest level ever in 1983 but declined somewhat over the next two years as costs rose and the rate of sales growth slowed. Financial statements are presented in Exhibits 1 and 2. The following sections describe the company and its environment in the 1980s.

EXHIBIT 1   Balance Sheet for the Years 1981–1985 ($000s Cdn.)

	1981	1982	1983	1984	1985
Assets					
Current Assets					
Accounts receivable	$ 8,328	$ 7,960	$ 9,776	$10,512	$10,951
Allowance for doubtful accounts	(293)	(310)	(287)	(297)	(316)
Inventories	21,153	24,425	24,698	25,626	27,045
Prepaid expenses	119	104	156	106	129
Total current assets	29,307	32,179	34,343	35,947	37,809
Advances to shareholders	1,300	1,300	1,300	1,300	1,300
Fixed assets:					
property, plant, and equipment	6,840	6,980	6,875	7,353	7,389
Total assets	$37,447	$40,459	$42,518	$44,600	$46,598
Liabilities and Shareholders' Equity					
Current Liabilities					
Notes payable to bank	$ 7,733	$ 8,219	$ 9,258	$10,161	$11,332
Accounts payable	9,712	11,353	10,543	10,465	10,986
Accrued expenses	1,074	1,119	1,742	1,501	1,155
Deferred income tax	419	400	396	408	345
Income tax payable	545	692	612	520	516
Current portion of longterm debt	912	891	867	888	903
Total current liabilities	20,395	22,674	23,418	23,943	25,237
Long-term debt	6,284	6,110	6,020	6,005	6,114
Total liabilities	26,679	28,784	29,438	29,948	31,351
Shareholders' Equity					
Common shares	200	290	295	390	435
Retained earnings	10,568	11,385	12,790	14,262	14,812
Total shareholders' equity	10,768	11,675	13,080	14,652	15,247
Total liabilities and share-holders' equity	$37,447	$40,459	$42,518	$44,600	$46,598

EXHIBIT 2   Income Statement for the Years 1981–1985 ($000s Cdn.)

	1981	1982	1983	1984	1985
Revenue					
Net sales	$63,386	$77,711	$86,346	$94,886	$100,943
Cost and Expenses					
Cost of sales	49,238	59,837	63,996	71,818	75,808
Selling expense	7,470	9,234	10,935	11,437	13,104
Administrative expense	2,684	3,867	5,490	5,795	7,038
Engineering expense	1,342	1,689	1,832	1,949	2,109
Gross income	2,652	3,084	4,093	3,887	2,884
Income taxes	1,081	1,281	1,630	1,505	1,254
Net income	$ 1,571	$ 1,803	$ 2,463	$ 2,382	$ 1,630

Product Line

The bulk of Victoria's crane sales in the 1980s came from a single product line, the LTM 1000, which was produced both in the company's Squamish facility (the firm had moved from Victoria to Squamish in the early 1900s) and its smaller plant in California, built in 1979. The LTM 1000 line consisted of mobile cranes of five basic sizes, averaging approximately $500,000 in price. Numerous options were available for these cranes, which could provide uncompromised on-site performance, precision lifting capabilities, fast highway travel, and effortless city driving. Because of the numerous choices available, Victoria preferred not to build them to stock. The company guaranteed 60-day delivery and "tailor-made" cranes to customer specifications. This required a large inventory of both parts and raw material.

Walters had used a great deal of ingenuity to keep Victoria in a competitive position. For example, in 1982, he learned that a company trying to move unusually long and heavy logs from a new tract of redwood trees in British Columbia was having serious problems with its existing cranes. A crane with a larger than average height and lifting capacity was required. Up to this point, for technical reasons, it had not been possible to produce a crane with the required specifications. However, Walters vowed that Victoria would develop such a crane, and six months later it had succeeded.

Although the LTM 1000 series provided almost all of Victoria's crane sales, a new crane had been introduced in 1984 after considerable expenditure on design, development, and manufacture. The $650,000 A-100 had a 70-tonne capacity and could lift loads to heights of 61 metres, a combination previously unheard of in the industry. Through the use of smooth hydraulics, even the heaviest loads could be picked up without jolts. In spite of these features, and an optional ram-operated tilt-back cab designed to alleviate the stiff necks which operators commonly developed from watching high loads, sales of the A-100 were disappointing. As a result, several of the six machines built were leased to customers at unattractive rates. The A-100 had, however, proven to be a very effective crowd attraction device at equipment shows.

Markets

There were two important segments in the crane market—custom-built cranes and standard cranes—and although the world mobile crane market was judged to be $630 million in 1985, no estimates were available as to the size of each segment. Victoria competed primarily in the custom segment, in the medium- and heavy-capacity end of the market. In the medium-capacity custom crane class, Victoria's prices were approximately 75 percent of those of its two main competitors. The gap closed as the cranes became heavier, with Victoria holding a 15 percent advantage over Washington Cranes in the heavy custom crane business. In heavy standard cranes, Victoria did not have a price advantage.

Victoria's two most important markets were Canada and the United States. The U.S. market was approximately $240 million in 1985, and Victoria's share was about 15 percent. Victoria's Sacramento plant, serving both the U.S. market and export sales involving U.S. aid and financing, produced 60 to 70 cranes per year. The Canadian market was much smaller, about $44 million in 1985, but Victoria was the dominant firm in the country, with a 60 percent share. The Squamish plant, producing 130 to 150 cranes per year, supplied both the Canadian market and all export sales not covered by the U.S. plant. There had been very little real growth in the world market since 1980.

The primary consumers in the mobile crane industry were contractors. Because the amount of equipment downtime could make the difference between showing a profit or loss on a contract, contractors were very sensitive to machine dependability as well as parts and service availability. Price was important, but it was not everything. Independent surveys suggested that Washington Cranes, Victoria's most significant competitor, offered somewhat superior service and reliability, and if Victoria attempted to sell similar equipment at prices comparable to Washington's, it would fail. As a result, Victoria tried to reduce its costs through extensive backward integration, manufacturing 85 percent of its crane components in-house, the highest percentage in the industry. This drive to reduce costs was somewhat offset, however, by the fact that much of the equipment in the Squamish plant was very old. In recent years, some of the slower and less versatile machinery had been replaced, but by 1985 only 15 percent of the machinery in the plant was new, efficient, numerically controlled equipment.

Victoria divided the world into eight marketing regions. The firm carried out little conventional advertising but did participate frequently at equipment trade shows. One of the company's most effective selling tools was its willingness to fly in prospective customers from all over the world. The company was generous with the use of first-class airline tickets. Victoria believed that the combination of its integrated plant, worker loyalty, and the single-product concentration evident in their Canadian plant produced a convinced customer. There were over 14 such visits to the British Columbia plant in 1985, including delegations from The People's Republic of China, Korea, France, and Turkey.

Competition

Victoria, as the world's second largest producer of cranes, faced competition from five major firms, all of whom were much larger and more diversified. The industry leader was the Washington Crane Company with 1985 sales of $400 million and a world market share of 50 percent. Washington had become a name synonymous around the world with heavy-duty equipment and had been able to maintain a sales growth rate of over 15 percent per annum for the past five years. It manufactured in the United States, Mexico, and Australia. Key to its operations were 100 strong dealers worldwide with over 200 outlets. Washington had almost 30 percent of Canada's crane market.

Next in size after Victoria was Texas Star, another large manufacturer whose cranes were generally smaller than Victoria's and sold through the company's extensive worldwide equipment dealerships. The next two largest competitors were both very large U.S. multinational producers whose crane lines formed a small part of their overall business. With the exception of Washington, industry observers suggested that crane sales for these latter firms had been stable (at best) for quite some time. The exception was the Japanese crane producer Toshio which had been aggressively pursuing sales worldwide and had entered the North American market recently. Sato, another Japanese firm, had started in the North American market as well. Walters commented:

> My father laid the groundwork for the success that this company has enjoyed, but it is clear that we now have some major challenges ahead of us. Washington Cranes is four times our size and I know that we are at the top of their hit list. Our Japanese competitors, Toshio and Sato, are also going to be tough. The key to our success is to remain flexible—we must not develop the same kind of organization as the big U.S. firms.

Organization

In 1979, a number of accumulating problems had ended Brian Walters' semire-tirement and brought him back into the firm full-time. Although sales were growing, Walters saw that work was piling up and things were not getting done. He believed that new cranes needed to be developed, and he wanted a profit sharing plan put in place. One of his most serious concerns was the development of middle managers. Walters commented, "We had to develop middle-level line managers—we had no depth." The root cause of these problems, Walters believed, was that the firm was overly centralized. Most of the functional managers reported to Rivers, and Rivers made most of the decisions. Walters concluded that action was necessary—"We have to change," he said. "If we want to grow further, we have to do things."

Between 1979 and 1982 Walters reorganized the firm by setting up separate operating companies and a corporate staff group. In several cases, senior operating executives were placed in staff/advisory positions, while in others, executives held positions in both operating and staff groups. Exhibit 3 illustrates Victoria's organization chart as of 1983.

By early 1984, Walters was beginning to wonder "if I had made a very bad decision." The staff groups weren't working. Rivers had been unable to accept the redistribution of power and had resigned. There was "civil war in the company." Politics and factional disputes were the rule rather than the exception. Line managers were upset by the intervention of the staff VPs of employee relations, manufacturing, and marketing. Staff personnel, on the other hand, were upset by "poor" line decisions.

As a result, the marketing and manufacturing staff functions were eradicated with the late-1985 organization restructuring illustrated in Exhibit 4. The services previously supplied by the staff groups were duplicated to varying extents inside each division.

EXHIBIT 3   Victoria Organization Structure, 1979–1983

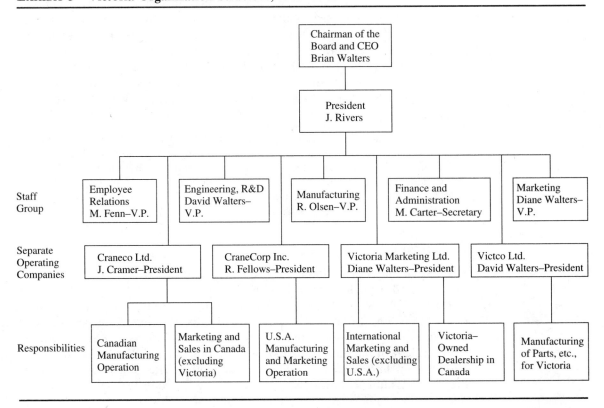

In place of most of the staff groups, an executive committee was established in 1984. Membership in this group included the president and head of all staff groups and presidents (general managers) of the four divisions. Meeting monthly, the executive committee was intended to evaluate the performance of the firm's profit and cost problems, handle mutual problems such as transfer prices, and allocate capital expenditures among the four operating divisions. Subcommittees handled subjects such as R&D and new products.

The new organization contained seven major centres for performance measurement purposes. The cost centres were

1. Engineering; R&D (reporting to Victco Ltd.).
2. International Marketing (Victoria Marketing Ltd.).
3. Corporate staff.

The major profit centres were

1. CraneCorp., Inc. (U.S. production and sales).
2. Victco Ltd. (supplying Victoria with components).

Exhibit 4   Victoria Organization Structure, Late 1985

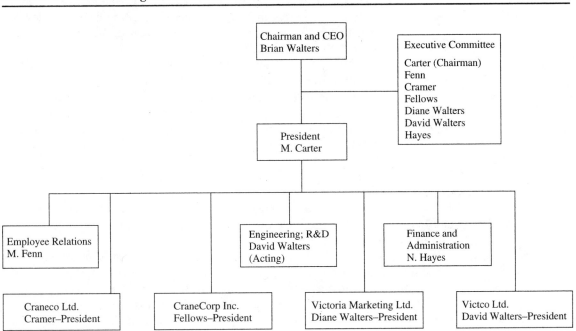

3. Craneco (Canadian production and marketing).

4. Victoria-owned Canadian sales outlets (reporting to Victoria Marketing Ltd.).

The major profit centres had considerable autonomy in their day-to-day operations and were motivated to behave as if their division were a separate, independent firm.

By mid-1985, Brian Walters had moved out of his position as president, and Michael Carter—a long-time employee close to retirement—was asked to take the position of president until a new one could be found.

Walters saw his role changing. "If I was anything, I was a bit of an entrepreneur. My job was to supply that thrust but to let people develop on their own accord. I was not concerned about things not working, but I was concerned when nothing was being done about it."

In the new organization, Walters did not sit on the executive committee. However, as chairman of the board and chief executive officer, the committee's recommendations came to him and "they tried me on six ways from Sunday." His intention was to monitor the firm's major activities rather than to set them. He did have to sit on the product development subcommittee, however, when "things were not working . . . there was conflict . . . the engineering group (engineering, R&D) had designed a whole new crane and nobody including me knew about it." Mr. McCarthy, the VP of engineering and R&D, called only five to six committee meetings. The crane his group developed was not to Walters' liking. (There had been a high turnover rate in this group, with four VPs since 1983.) Recognizing these problems, Walters brought in consultants to tackle the problems of the management information system and the definition of staff/line responsibilities.

In spite of these moves, dissatisfaction still existed within the company in 1986. The new organization had resulted in considerable dissension. Some conflict centred around the establishment of appropriately challenging budgets for each operating firm, and even more conflict had erupted over transfer pricing and allocation of capital budgets. In 1985–86, even though requested budgets were cut equally, lack of central control over spending resulted in overexpenditures by several of the profit and cost centres.

The views of staff and the operating companies' presidents varied considerably when they discussed Victoria's organizational evolution and the operation of the present structure.

Diane Walters, the president of Victoria International Marketing, liked the autonomous system because it helped to identify the true performance of sections of the company. "We had separate little buckets and could easily identify results." Furthermore, she felt that there was no loss of efficiency (due to the duplication of certain staff functions within the divisions) since there was little duplication of systems between groups so that "manufacturing won't make what marketing won't sell." Comments from other executives were as follows:

> The divisionalized system allowed me to get closer to my staff because we were a separate group.
>
> We ended up with sales and marketing expertise that was much better than if we had stayed under manufacturing.
>
> If you (run the firm) with a manufacturing-oriented organization, you could forget what people want.
>
> In a divisionalized system there was bound to be conflict between divisions, but that was not necessarily unhealthy.

Some executives saw the decentralized, semiautonomous operating company structure as a means of giving each person the opportunity to grow and develop without the hindrance of other functional executives. Most, if not all, of the operating company presidents and staff VPs were aware that decentralization brought benefits, especially in terms of the autonomy it gave them to modify existing practices. One senior executive even saw the present structure as an indicator of their basic competitive stance: "Either we centralize the structure and retract, or we stay as we are and fight with the big guys." With minimal direction supplied from Brian Walters, presidents were able to build up their staff, establish priorities and programs, and, essentially, were only held responsible for the bottom line.

Other executives believed that Victoria's structure was inappropriate. As one executive put it, "The semi-independence of the operating companies and the lack of a real leader for the firm has resulted in poor coordination of problem solving and difficulty in allocating responsibility." As an example, he noted how engineering's response to manufacturing was often slow and poorly communicated. Even worse, the executive noted, was how the priorities of different units were not synchronized. "When you manufacture just one product line all your activities are interrelated. So when one group puts new products first on a priority list while another is still working out bugs in the existing product, conflict and inefficiencies have to develop."

The opposing group argued that the present organization was more appropriate to a larger, faster-growing, and more complex company. As one senior executive put it, "We're too small to be as decentralized as we are now. All of this was done to accommodate the 'Walters kids' anyway, and it's now going to detract from profitability and growth." Another of these executives stated that rather than being a president of an operating company, he would prefer to be a general manager at the head of a functional group, reporting to a group head. "If we had the right Victoria Heavy Equipment president," he said, "we wouldn't need all these divisional presidents." Another continued,

> Right now the players (divisional presidents and staff VPs) run the company. Brian Walters gives us a shot of adrenaline four or six times a year but doesn't provide any active leadership. When Brian leaves, things stop. Instead, Brian now wants to monitor the game plan rather than set it up for others to run. As we still only have an interim president (Carter), it is the marketplace that leads us, not any strategic plan or goal.

The New President

Individual views about the appropriate characteristics of a new president were determined by what each executive thought was wrong with Victoria. Everyone realized that the new president would have to accommodate Brian Walters' presence and role in the firm and the existence of his two children in the organization. They all generally saw Brian as wanting to supply ideas and major strategies but little else.

All but one of Victoria's executives agreed that the new president should *not* get involved in day-to-day activities or in major decision making. Instead, he should "arbitrate" among the line general managers (subsidiary presidents) and staff VPs and become more of a "bureaucrat-cum-diplomat" than an aggressive leader. As another put it, "The company will drive itself; only once in a while he'll steer a little."

The 1986 Situation

Industry analysts predicted a decline of 10 percent in world crane sales—which totaled 1,200 units in 1985—and as much as a 30 percent decrease in the North American market in 1986. Victoria's sales and production levels were down. Seventy-five shop floor employees had been laid off at Squamish, bringing total employment there to 850, and similar cuts were expected in Sacramento. Worker morale was suffering as a result, and the profit sharing plan, which had been introduced in early 1985 at Walters' initiative, was not helping matters. In spite of the optimism conveyed to workers when the plan was initiated, management had announced in October that no bonus would be paid for the year. Aggravating the problem was the workforce's observation that while certain groups met their budget, others did not, hence all were penalized. This problem arose because each bonus was based on overall as well as divisional profits.

Many of the shop-floor workers and the supervisory staff were also disgruntled with the additions to the central and divisional staff groups, which had continued even while the workforce was being reduced. They felt that the paperwork these staff functions created was time-consuming and of little benefit. They noted, for example, that there were four or five times as many people in production control in 1986 as there were in 1980 for the same volume of production. In addition, they pointed out that despite all sorts of efforts on the part of a computer-assisted production control group, inventory levels were still too high.

Brian Walters commented on the 1986 situation and his view of the company's future:

> What we are seeing in 1986 is a temporary decline in the market. This does not pose a serious problem for us, and certainly does not impact on my longer term goals for this company, which are to achieve a 25 percent share of the world market by 1990, and reach sales of $250 million by 1999. We can reach these goals as long as we don't turn into one of these bureaucratic, grey-suited companies that are so common in North America. There are three keys for success in this business—a quality product, professional people, and the motivation for Victoria to be the standard of excellence in our business. This means that almost everything depends on the competence and motivation of our people. We will grow by being more entrepreneurial, more dedicated, and more flexible than our competitors. They manage only by the numbers—there is no room in those companies for an emotional plea, they won't look at sustaining losses to get into a new area, they'll turn the key on a loser . . . we look at the longer term picture.

"The hazard for Victoria," Walters said, "is that we could develop the same kind of bureaucratic, quantitatively oriented, grey-suited managers that slow down the large U.S. competitors. But that," he said, turning to his audience, "is something I'm going to watch like a hawk. We need the right people."

THE WINNIPEG SYMPHONY ORCHESTRA

"I'm in the process of putting together a five-year plan to present to our Board in three weeks' time," said Barry McArton. It was mid-January 1992, and Barry, the newly appointed executive director of the Winnipeg Symphony Orchestra, had been on the job for only a little over two weeks. In the previous few days he had been poring over market and financial data to gain understanding of both the orchestra's current position and the potential directions the organization might consider for the future. Barry had concluded that the development of his plan was not going to be an easy task, and would be made more difficult by the fact that mid-season financial results were below target. Barry continued:

> We have established a reputation for running a deficit-free operation, and that's what we had planned for the 1991–92 season. However, our mid-season results tell us that if we don't make some changes, we'll lose over $80,000 on the year. We have customer data that help explain our current problem. It suggests some very scary implications for the future as well. Over half of our audience is over 50 years of age. Within that context, four percent of our 1990–91 Pops subscribers didn't renew this season because they had died! If we are to remain a viable organization in the future, we must attract new young subscribers.

The Province of Manitoba and The City of Winnipeg

Manitoba, with a 1991 population of 1.1 million people, is the geographic east-west centre of Canada. The provincial capital, Winnipeg, with an ethni-

---

Louise Budgell prepared this case under the supervision of John Kennedy solely to provide material for class discussion. Copyright © 1994 The University of Western Ontario. Western Business School Case 9-94-A003.

cally diverse population of 650,000, was by far the dominant urban centre in the province. The next largest city, Brandon, with a population of 35,000 was located 200 km to the west. The closest city with a population over 200,000 was the Minneapolis/St. Paul metropolitan area with a population of 3.7 million, an eight-hour drive to the south. Many people viewed this geographic and cultural isolation as the primary reason for early local initiatives in developing such arts activities and organizations as the Winnipeg (School) Music Festival, the Royal Winnipeg Ballet, the Manitoba Theatre Centre, and the Winnipeg Symphony Orchestra.

By 1992, the city hosted a large number of performing arts activities. During the summer, there were music festivals almost every weekend featuring jazz, reggae, blues, and folk. This was complemented by the Fringe Festival, featuring avant-garde theatre. There was even a Children's Festival. Audiences from all over North America came to Winnipeg's "Folklorama" festival, with its international pavilions featuring ethnic dance and theatre.

The fall/winter seasons were very active as well. From September to May, Winnipegers could attend a variety of festivals, theatre, and musical events. Festivals included Oktoberfest and the Festival du Voyageur (February). Theatre was offered by five companies: the Manitoba Theatre Centre and four smaller theatre companies. Classical ballet was offered by the internationally acclaimed Royal Winnipeg Ballet; modern dance performances were given by the Contemporary Dancers and the Dance Collective. Audiences could also attend performances at the Manitoba Opera, the Winnipeg Symphony Orchestra, and several different chamber music companies and choirs.

The city size and diversity of activities in Winnipeg meant that it attracted many weekend visitors, not only from other areas in Manitoba, but from the North Dakota cities of Grand Forks and Fargo. Both cities had a population of about 70,000 and were a two-and-a-half hour and a four-hour drive from Winnipeg. Residents of both cities looked to Winnipeg for their upscale entertainment and shopping needs, and/or the opportunity to gamble at the casino in Winnipeg's luxurious Fort Garry Hotel. The casino required "nice" dress, and offered slot machines, gaming, and very high stakes betting at cards.

Provincial and city support for the arts were more generous than in many other jurisdictions in Canada. The Manitoba Ministry of Culture & Heritage allocated $7 million, 0.1 percent of the total budget, for professional performing arts organizations. The City of Winnipeg was an even stronger supporter, with 43 percent of total city grants being allocated to organizations for the performing arts.

The Winnipeg Symphony Orchestra (WSO)

The WSO was founded in 1948 as a chartered non-profit corporation operated by a voluntary board of directors. Within six seasons, under the direction of Walter Kaufmann, the WSO had grown to become one of the four leading orchestras in Canada. In 1968, the orchestra moved from its initial home in the Winnipeg Civic Auditorium to its new home, the Manitoba Centennial Concert Hall. While the orchestra prospered artistically during the 1970s, it began to run into financial difficulties. By June 1980, the WSO had run up a deficit of $720,000, with an additional $295,000 projected for the end of fiscal 1981. In July 1980, the Province of Manitoba put the orchestra into trusteeship and appointed a board of trustees to turn around WSO operations. After three years of intensive fundraising and restructuring, the WSO had paid off the accumulated debt and evolved into a self-sustaining operation with an accumulated surplus of $28,000 in June 1983. The WSO's 1992 organization chart is shown in Exhibit 1.

Since June 1983, the WSO had remained deficit-free, running accumulated surpluses ranging from $5,000 (1990) to $24,700 (1988). The WSO's recent Statement of Operations, 1992 budget, and the projected June 1992 year-end position are shown in Exhibits 2 and 3. The 1992 figures do not include financial data for a 1992 first-time event called "The New Music Festival," which was being handled with a separate budget.

Barry McArton was originally hired by the WSO as director of marketing and public relations in December 1989. Barry's prior experience included a four-year term as general manager of the Pantages Playhouse Theatre. In August 1991, Barry left the WSO for another local nonprofit organization, but returned in January 1992 as executive director after his predecessor resigned to accept a position with a major eastern Canadian arts organization.

Bramwell Tovey, the WSO's artistic director, was born and raised in England. He became acquainted with the WSO in 1983 while on a Canadian tour with the Sadler's Wells Royal Ballet. He returned several times in subsequent years as a WSO guest conductor. In 1987, attracted by the orchestra's deficit-free status and the promise that he would have considerable autonomy in determining repertoire, Mr. Tovey accepted WSO's offer to become the full-time resident artistic director.

Performance Operations

The WSO season ran from September to May. The 67-member orchestra was small compared to "world class" orchestras such as the Montreal Symphony Orchestra, which typically had 100 members or more. Each year a contract was negotiated with the orchestra for the following season that was based on the average number of "services" (e.g., a rehearsal, a performance) which the musician would provide, a weekly rate of pay, and the number of weeks in the season. For 1991–92, the agreement was for eight two-and-a-half hour services per week, a weekly base pay of $726, a 34-week season, plus two weeks paid vacation.[1]

---

[1] The salaries, overtime pay, and benefits of the 67 core orchestra members amount to approximately 90 percent of the "Talent—Orchestra" cost figure in Exhibit 3.

EXHIBIT 1   Winnipeg Symphony Orchestra 1992 Organization Chart

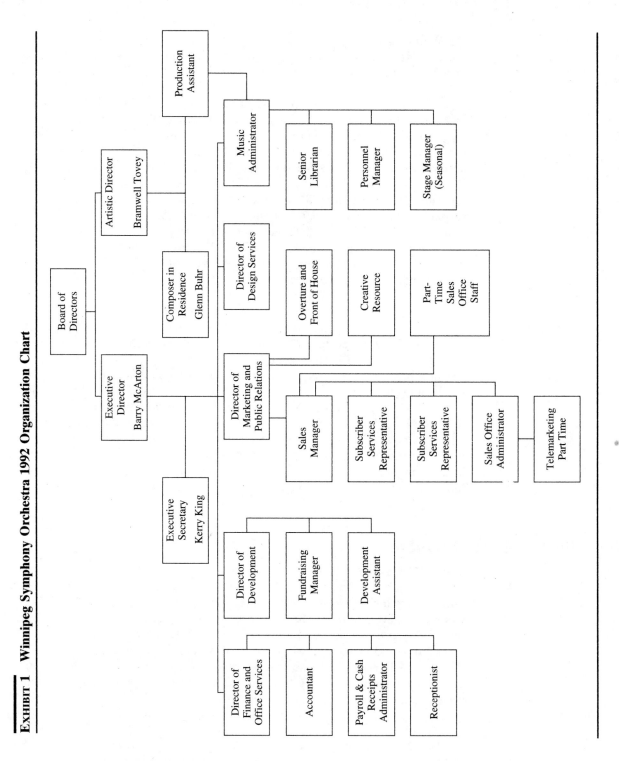

EXHIBIT 2   Revenue from Operations and Donations for the Years Ended June 30, 1990 and 1991 (Actual), 1992 Budget and Forecast Based on Results to November 30, 1991

	1990 (Actual)		1991 (Actual)		1992 (Budget)		Nov. 30 Forecast	Variance
	$000	%	$000	%	$000	%	$000	$000
Revenue from Performances								
Subscriptions	$ 981	43.1%	$1062	44.7%	$1200	45.5%	$1020	$(180)
Box office single-ticket sales	184	8.1	174	7.3	182	6.9	182	0
Supplied services (A)	450	19.8	411	17.3	451	17.1	459	8
Out-of-town concerts/tours (B)	94	4.1	110	4.6	115	4.4	114	(1)
Educational concerts	40	1.8	38	1.6	42	1.6	42	0
Non-subscription concerts (C)	174	7.6	195	8.2	209	7.9	209	0
Sponsorships	222	9.7	185	7.8	240	9.1	240	0
Program advertising	0	0.0	0	0.0	81	3.1	104	23
Other earned revenue	132	5.8	201	8.5	117	4.4	138	21
Total revenue from performances	$2277	100%	$2376	100%	$2637	100%	$2508	$(129)
Donations and Other Revenue								
Donations (D)	264	59.0	302	57.5	306	55.7	320	14
Gaming Commission (E)	88	19.6	106	20.2	115	20.9	115	0
Donations—Women's Committee	15	3.4	20	3.8	18	3.3	18	0
Special fundraising projects	80	18.0	97	18.5	110	20.0	110	0
Total donations and other revenue	$ 447	100.0%	$ 525	100%	$ 549	100%	$ 563	$ 14
Grants and Endowment Revenue								
Canada Council	}680	42.9	680	43.9	680	40.9	680	
Canada Council non-recurring			35	2.2	50	3.0	50	
Manitoba Arts Council	}575	36.3	590	38.1	610	36.7	610	
Manitoba Arts Council—Special			16	1.0	45	2.7	45	
Manitoba Arts Gaming Fund	50	3.2	—	—	—	—	—	
City of Winnipeg	149	9.4	150	9.7	155	9.3	152	(3)
Winnipeg Foundation			60	3.9	65	3.9	65	
Dept. of Communication	59	3.7	—	—	—	—	—	
Dept. of Comm.—New music	50	3.2	—	—	35	2.1	67	32
Endowment Fund Income	20	1.3	20	1.3	21	1.3	23	2
	1583	100%	1551	100%	1661	100%	1692	31
Total revenue	$4307		$4452		$4847		$4763	$ (84)

Notes: (A) Services to the Royal Winnipeg Ballet & the Manitoba Opera Association

(B) Provincial tours only; regular concerts in Brandon

(C) Music festivals

(D) From corporations

(E) Provincial lottery

EXHIBIT 3   Statement of Operations for the Years Ended June 30, 1990 and 1991 (Actual), 1992 Budget, and Forecast Based on Results to November 30, 1991

	1990 (Actual)		1991 (Actual)		1992 (Budget)			
							Nov. 30 Forecast ($000)	*Variance ($000)*
	$000	*%*	*$000*	*%*	*$000*	*%*		
Revenue from performances (Exhibit 2)	$2277	52.9%	$2376	53.4%	$2637	54.4%	$2508	$(129)
Donations and other revenue (Exhibit 2)	447	10.4	525	11.8	549	11.3	563	14
Grants and endowment revenue (Exhibit 2)	1583	36.7	1551	34.8	1661	34.3	1692	31
Total revenue	$4307	100%	$4452	100%	$4847	100%	$4763	$ (84)
Expenses								
Talent—guest artists (A)	$ 447	10.4%	$ 437	9.8%	$ 491	10.1%	$ 507	$ (16)
Talent—orchestra	2290	53.2	2416	54.3	2579	53.2	2542	37
Theatre and other prod. expenses	267	6.2	291	6.6	304	6.3	307	(3)
Administrative	532	12.3	558	12.6	614	12.7	610	4
Development and other publicity, promotion and marketing	149	3.5	149	3.3	155	3.2	155	0
Overture program			11	0.2	68	1.4	105	(37)
Subscription campaign	}621	}14.4	224	5.0	215	4.4	228	(13)
Marketing/public relations			237	5.3	289	6.0	261	28
Box office			120	2.7	124	2.6	124	0
Total expenses	$4306	100%	$4443	100%	$4839	100%	$4839	$ 0
Income from operations	1	0.0	9	0.2	8	0.2	(76)	
Major equipment purchases	8		8		7		1	
Net income (loss)	−7		1		1		(77)	
Surplus, beginning of year	12		5		6		6	
Surplus, end of year	5		6		7		(71)	

Notes: (A) When choirs are counted as single entries, the WSO had between 70 and 100 guest artists per year.

"We consider our audience radius to run from Thunder Bay in the east,[2] south into North Dakota,[3] and west to the Saskatchewan border,[4]" said Barry McArton. "In that sense, we very much have viewed ourselves as a regional orchestra."

Most of the WSO's performances were held in Centennial Concert Hall, Winnipeg's only facility for live performing arts. This hall had a seating capacity of 2,222 people. The WSO shared these facilities with the Manitoba Opera Association and the Royal Winnipeg Ballet. The WSO gave their remaining

[2] 700 kilometres
[3] 220–350 kilometres
[4] 300 kilometres

performances on occasional provincial tours and five times per year at the WestMan Centennial Auditorium in Brandon, Manitoba. This auditorium could seat 817 people. The concert series was made up of a classical series of four concerts, and one "special" that was sold on a single-ticket basis. Seven hundred and twenty-one 1991–92 subscriptions had been sold at an average price of $52.61. Single-ticket prices were $17 and $19. It was expected that the single-ticket concert would sell at least as well as the subscription concerts.

Repertoire

Mainstage Repertoire

The WSO primarily performed classical music. Subscription performances for the 1991–92 season were segmented into the following series:

- "Classics-Fanfare"—ranging from Beethoven and Mozart to Stravinsky and Shostakovich. Scheduled for Saturday evenings/Sunday afternoons.
- "Classics-Festival"—similar to the other Classics series, but with performances scheduled for Friday/Saturday evenings.
- "The Du Maurier Arts Ltd. Musically Speaking" series—"lighter" classical music ranging from Mozart to Gershwin and containing a Canadian Composers Competition Awards Concert. This series was sponsored by Du Maurier.
- "The Real Canadian Superconcerts for Kids"—classical music, music from kids' TV shows, musical plays.
- "The Seagram Pops & Family Pops"—waltzes, music from Oktoberfest, Broadway, movies, and TV shows. This series was sponsored by Seagram's.
- Special seasonal concerts and galas (Handel's Messiah at Christmas, Christmas Pops). Subscribers had "first rights" to these tickets, which were held back from non-subscribers until a month before the performance. At that time, all tickets not sold to subscribers became available at the box office for single-ticket purchasers.

These performances were all described in a 20-page colour brochure which had been mailed to 1990–91 subscribers in May 1991. Selected information from this brochure is given in Exhibit 4. Data on Winnipeg subscription sales are given in Table 1.

Each WSO concert was preceded by a pre-concert talk. Don Anderson, the WSO's creative resource person, gave this talk 45 minutes before curtain time, describing the evening's program content, the composer's style, and the historical context surrounding the composition. Coffee was served to the audience during his talk.

Exhibit 4   WSO 1991–92 Program Schedule

Series	Program Dates	Program Days/Times	Composer	Program	Soloist Instrument
Classics — Fanfare	Sept 28, 29	Sat 8 PM Sun 2 PM	Beethoven Mozart Beethoven	Fidelio Overture Oboe Concerto Choral Symphony	— Oboe Soprano, contralto, tenor, bass
	Nov 9, 10	"	Schumann Liszt Liszt Schumann	Genoveva Overture Piano Concerto Totentanz Symphony	— Piano Piano —
	Dec 14, 15	"	Mozart	3 Symphonies	—
	Feb 1, 2	"	Berlioz Mendelssohn Shostakovich	Overture Piano Concerto Symphony	— Piano —
	Mar 21, 22	"	Falla Lalo Ravel Falla	Interlude Symphonie Espagnole Pavane 3-Cornered Hat	— Violin — —
	Apr 11, 12	"	Schubert Bartok Schubert	Overture Violin Concerto Symphony	— Violin —
Classics — Festival	Oct 11, 12	Fri 8 PM Sat 8 PM	Dukas Tchaikovsky Buhr	Sorcerer's Apprentice Violin Concerto Lure of the Fallen Seraphim	— Violin —
	Nov 29, 30	"	Lutoslawski Mozart Brahms	Chain 3 Piano Concerto Piano Quartet	— Piano Piano
	Jan 17, 18	"	Max. Davies Peters Adams	Orkney Wedding Dreaming Tracks Harmonielehre	— — —
	Feb 28, 29	"	Mozart Beethoven Brahms	Impresario Overture Piano Concerto Symphony	— Piano —
	Mar 27, 28	"	Wagner R. Strauss Beethoven Hindemith	Flying Dutchman Overture Four Last Songs Ah, Perfido Suite	— — Soprano Soprano
	May 8, 9	"	Britten Buhr Stravinsky	P. Grimes Interludes Piano Concerto Petrouchka	— Piano —
Du Maurier Arts Ltd. — Musically Speaking	Oct 4	Fri 8 PM	Shostakovich Gershwin Beethoven	Overture Piano Concerto Symphony	— Piano —
	Oct 18	"	Schumann Schumann Dvorak	Manfred Overture Piano Concerto New World Symphony	— Piano —

EXHIBIT 4   *(Continued)*

Series	Program Dates	Program Days/Times	Composer	Program	Soloist Instrument
	Dec 6	"	Mozart	Cantata	—
			Mozart	Clarinet Concerto	Clarinet
			Mozart	Requiem	Soprano, mezzo soprano, tenor, bass/Winnipeg Singers Choir
	Jan 24	"	Canadian Composers Awards Concert	5 finalists' work played by the WSO	
	Feb 7	"	Kabalevsky	Overture	—
			Prokofiev	Violin Concerto	Violin
			Tchaikovsky	Symphony	—
	Apr 3	"	Delibes	Suite	—
			Ravel	Piano Concerto	Piano
			Mussorgsky	Pictures at an Exhibition	—
Superconcerts for Kids	Oct 13	Sun 2 PM, 4 PM		Symphonasaurus	Dinosaur Characters Slim Goodbody (Entertainer)
	Dec 1	"		Songs & Stories	Heather Bishop (Entertainer)
	Dec 22	"		Christmas & Hannukah Melodies	Winnipeg Singers
	Mar 1	"		Musical Play	—
	Mar 29	"		TV Theme Songs (Star Wars, Star Trek)	—
	May 10	"		Clown & Orchestra	Clown
Seagram Pops	Oct 5, 6	Sat 8 PM Sun 2 PM	Strauss and Misc. German	Waltzes, Polkas Operetta extracts	— Soprano
	Oct 19, 20	"	Weber Tchaikovsky Andersen	Dance music	—
	Nov 23	Sat 4 PM, 8 PM	Western Movies and TV Shows (Grey Cup Festival Event)	Gunfight at the OK Corral Dances with Wolves Lonesome Dove	Square dancers
	Jan 11, 12	Sat 8 PM Sun 2 PM	Mozart	Concerto for 3 Pianos	Piano Actor in Mozartian costume reading Mozart's letters
	Feb 22, 23	"	Various	Light classics Jazz Pop	— — —
	Apr 4, 5	"	Various	Broadway hits	Soprano, baritone
	May 2, 3	"	Various	Various	—

Exhibit 4 *(Concluded)*

Series	Program Dates	Program Days/Times	Composer	Program	Soloist Instrument
Special Concerts	Sept 21, 22	Sat 8 PM Sun 2 PM	Various	Selected operatic arias, ensembles, choruses	2 Sopranos 2 Mezzo-sopranos 1 Tenor 3 Baritones 2 Bass/Manitoba Opera Chorus
	Dec 7, 8	Sat 8 PM Sun 3 PM	Handel	Messiah	Soprano, mezzo soprano, tenor, bass/Mennonite Oratorio Choir
	Dec 20, 21	Fri 8 PM Sat 8 PM	Various European	Seasonal music	Winnipeg Singers
	Apr 29	Wed 8 PM	Chopin Liszt Haydn Prokofiev	Solo piano recital	Mark Zeltser, Piano

The WSO's repertoire contained a very high percentage of works composed by local and national/Canadian composers, and featured a very high percentage of local and national/Canadian soloists and conductors. A full 13 percent of the total WSO repertoire was written by Canadian composers. Of the total repertoire, 7 percent was written by Manitoban composers. WSO's "Canadian content" level was one of the highest of any Canadian orchestra, and was three times that of Ottawa's National Orchestra.

Soloists (guest artists) ranged from the internationally-acclaimed French-Canadian pianist Louis Lortie, to nationally-acclaimed Canadian singer Mark Pedrotti, to local musicians. Despite this quite impressive roster, several or-

Table 1 **1991–92 Winnipeg Subscription Sales**

1991–92 Series	No. of Subscriptions
Classics Fanfare	837
Classics Festival	471
Classics Select 6	1,153
Classics 12 concerts	783
Musically Speaking	1,173
Concerts for Kids	2,294
Seagram and Family Pops	3,688
Total	10,397

chestra musicians believed that audience size could be increased by upgrading the calibre of soloist talent.[5]

All of the children's concerts were scheduled on Sunday afternoons. All of the other Winnipeg performances took place Friday evenings, Saturday evenings, and Sunday afternoons. The Brandon concerts were always scheduled for Sunday at 2:00 PM. Audiences attending the Brandon concerts were largely Mennonites from Brandon and the surrounding farm community.

To strengthen their relationship with the Winnipeg community, the WSO often tied in WSO performances to community events. They scheduled the Seagram Pops performances around the 1991 Grey Cup football game—performances were held on Saturday to leave music fans free for Sunday's Grey Cup game, and themes from Western movies were played.

The New Music Festival

In an effort to extend the audience to include the younger age group, a plan for a week-long New Music Festival had been developed for implementation in February. The budget for this event was not yet integrated into the overall budget. The festival would be a totally new "product," a radical departure from the WSO's current offerings because it would feature contemporary orchestral and choral works composed by such international greats as John Cage and Philip Glass. The Festival would highlight Canadian composers, mainly from Manitoba. One entire evening would feature premieres by Manitoban composers, including Jim Hiscott, T. Patrick Carrabre, and Michael Matthews. Another evening would feature the world premiere of a major work by Ukrainian composer Yevhen Stankovych. Music would range from orchestral and choral works using traditional instruments to electronic and electro-acoustic scores.

To signal to the younger audience that this music was truly "their" music, the artistic director, orchestra, and audience would be casually dressed; spontaneous applause would be encouraged; and there would be dramatic "rock concert type" lighting.

A total of nine concerts had been planned. Planned pricing included a $25 single-person pass, which would enable the pass holder to attend all but the final concert. Individual tickets would range from $7 for the smaller, midweek shows, to $13–$25 for the weekend concerts.

Du Maurier had agreed to sponsor this festival (they would also take care of the graphic design, posters, and marketing), but it was unlikely their funds would cover the high costs of production equipment and crews needed to produce the special lighting and other production effects. After taking into

---

[5] North American soloist fees ranged from approximately $3,000 to $70,000 per appearance. There was widespread agreement within the business that there was very definite ticket sales response to a $50,000 artist. However, in the $12,000 to $25,000 range, many people believed that the repertoire had more impact on sales than did the artist.

account the Du Maurier support, Barry estimated that the festival would require expenditures of about $120,000. In addition to the funding issue, there remained the question of whether or not the style and content of the New Music Festival would alienate the WSO's older audience. "It's a real gamble on our part," said Barry McArton. "We really don't know how well it is going to do at the box office because we are not sure what kind of audience it will attract and just how large that audience will be. If it lives up to the potential we think is there, we could have a surplus of $5,000 to $10,000. However, if we've miscalculated the appeal, we could easily add $50,000 to $70,000 to our current projected deficit."

Educational Repertoire

The WSO offered the Shell Educational Concert Series each season to elementary school children throughout Manitoba. The series consisted of five English-language concerts and one French-language concert.[6] The concerts were virtually sold out, with over 120 different schools attending annually. Some schools travelled from as far as 350 km to see the concerts. Feedback in the form of student letters addressed to the artistic director was very positive: "I had a terrific time"; "When I grow up I want to play the violin because I love the sound of it"; and "You are the funniest conductor."

Other Repertoire

Once or twice a season, the WSO provided live music for screenings of silent movies. This was initiated in February 1990, when the WSO played Charlie Chaplin's own music for two screenings of his silent movie classic *City Lights*. A subsequent attendance survey revealed that a full 20 percent of the audience attending the screenings were not season subscribers. Realizing that these screenings were a good way to broaden their audience base, the WSO scheduled a similar event for Friday, April 5, 1991—they played Carl Davis' music to a screening of Buster Keaton's 1926 railroading comedy *The General*. This made the WSO one of very few orchestras in the world performing such fusions of silent film and music.

Pricing

Both subscription and single-ticket prices had been increasing at about five percent per year over the previous few years. Prices for the 1991–92 season are given in Exhibit 5.

---

[6] Manitoba had a large French-language community.

EXHIBIT 5 Winnipeg Symphony Orchestra 1991–92 Concert Pricing

Series	Range of Full-Price Subscription	Average Full-Price Subscription (A)	Average Subscription Price for Students and Seniors (B)	Subscription Price Per Person for Family of Four+ (C)	Subscription % Savings Over Single Ticket $/Series (D)	Subscription $ Savings Over Single Ticket $/Series (E)	Single Ticket $/Series (F)	No. of Concerts/Programs Per Series (G)	Subscription Price Per Concert (A/G) (H)	Single-Ticket Price Per Concert (Adults) (I)	Single-Ticket Price Per Concert (Students and Seniors) (J)	Average Single-Ticket Price Per Concert (K)	No. of Free Concerts for Subscribers Per Series (L)
Classics													
12 concert series (1)	$128–$244	$189	$163	—	28%	$73	$262	12	$16	$13–25	$11–23	$22	4
6 concert series (2)	71–135	104	92	—				6	17	13–25	11–23		
Du Maurier Arts Ltd.	62–118	90	75	—	34	47	137	6	15	13–25	11–23	23	3
Musically Speaking													
Superconcerts for kids	41–64	53	—	$40				6	9				
Seagram Pops	87–159	123	109	—	20	31	154	7	18	13–25	11–23	22	1
Special concerts (3)													
Opera selections (Sep 21, 22)	12–25	18	—	—				1	18				
Messiah (Dec 7, 8)	10–18	14	—	—				1	14				
Christmas Pops (Dec 20, 21)	11–21	16	—	—				1	16	13–25	11–23		
Mark Zeltser, Piano (Apr 29)	18–37	28	—	—				1	28				

Notes:
(1) 12 concerts = 6 fanfare + 6 festival concerts
(2) 6 concerts = 6 fanfare concerts or 6 festival concerts or 6 classics concerts (mix of fanfare and festival)
(3) tickets were available to subscribers only until a month before the performance; the remaining unsold tickets then became available to single-ticket purchasers

Advertising and Public Relations

The WSO advertised in the local press, on TV, and on radio. The orchestra enjoyed a good relationship with the media and was featured almost weekly in the local—and sometimes national—press that stressed their "down to earth," "unstuffy" image. This good relationship was due to systems Barry had put in place as marketing and public relations director. While in this function, Barry called the press every day and took them out to dinner frequently. He made sure that the WSO's artistic director, Bramwell Tovey, was frequently featured in their articles. Barry even got the press to feature the hockey team activities of a group of WSO orchestra musicians.

Bramwell Tovey was also a frequent speaker at local events and organizations. In 1991, Mr. Tovey spoke at a wide variety of organizations, including IBM, the Central Park Lodge seniors' home, the Cancer Centre, and the Humane Society. *The Winnipeg Free Press* named him "Music Personality of the Year."

Subcontracting Activities

Because it was Winnipeg's only symphony orchestra, the WSO contracted their services to virtually every performance of the Royal Winnipeg Ballet and the Manitoba Opera Association. They also accompanied performances of local organizations such as the Mennonite Oratorio Choir, the Mennonite Festival Choir, the Winnipeg Boys' Chorus, the O. Koshetz Ukrainian Choir, and the Dance Collective.

The WSO also supplied the musical accompaniment for all rehearsals and performances staged by national touring groups such as Les Grands Ballets Canadiens and the Native Arts Ballet.

Subcontracting activities combined with a diverse symphonic repertoire (pops, classical, modern) made the WSO a challenging place to work for orchestra members. A viola player commented, "One of the things I like the most about my job with the WSO is the diversity. We orchestra members get to play so many different types of music: classical, pops, opera, ballet. It's refreshing to switch back and forth among them."

Fundraising Operations

"The performing arts is not the business most people think it is," said Barry McArton. "They think that we are just involved in putting on artistic performances. What they don't realize is that those performances rarely pay for themselves in ticket revenues. As a result, a substantial part of our activity is devoted to raising money to keep the operation solvent."

The WSO identified five categories of support funds: grants, endowments, donations, sponsorships, and event fundraisers.

Grants

Grants are funds disbursed by the public sector. Barry, foreseeing the early 90s trend towards a permanent decline in government funding of the arts, wanted to decrease the level of public sector grants to the WSO to a maximum level of 32 percent of total revenues. Barry also realized this relatively low dependence level, together with a deficit-free operation, would be an advantage to the symphony in getting government grants. It would make the WSO appear more "deserving" of future funding in the eyes of governments compared to other Canadian orchestras, most of whom suffered from the "black hole" syndrome, i.e., they had a much higher level of dependence on government grants and still ran deficits.

The Canada Council, the agency that allocated federal grants to Canadian arts institutions, had just announced plans to conduct an in-depth review of Canadian orchestras' financial positions, repertoire content, and future strategies as the basis for evaluating the level of support they would give each orchestra. This meant that each orchestra asking for support would be required to submit a report each year containing the following information:

• *Management Statement/Acumen*—A summary of the prior season's marketing and financial performance and the overall strategic plan for the forthcoming season.

• *Canadian Content*—A listing of the prior season's and forthcoming season's Canadian conductors, soloists, and repertoire.

• *Artistic Merit and Artistic Report*—A summary of the prior season's and forthcoming season's repertoire, artistic director's and orchestra members' recent accomplishments, and funds allocated to guest artists and conductors.

Endowments

Endowments are funds that are kept in a lifetime trust for the beneficiary. The trust beneficiary can only use the interest income from the trust. The WSO's $300,000 endowment fund earned $20,000 in 1991. This was very small compared with the $5,000,000 in annual interest income received by the Pittsburgh Symphony Orchestra from endowment funds recently given to the orchestra by the Heinz corporation.

Donations and Sponsorships

Donations are given to a nonprofit performing arts organization to use as they see fit; sponsorships are tied to specific festivals or performances. WSO donors/sponsors consisted primarily of corporations, a few of which provided both sponsorship and donations.

The WSO had 12 major sponsors. The top three corporate sponsors in terms of dollar volume were Du Maurier, Seagram's, and the Bank of Montreal. Media sponsors included the CBC, MTN, CKX, and CKND television stations as well as the CBC, 1290 Fox, QX104, and CFAM radio stations. Media sponsorship entailed giving the station sponsorship of a performance in exchange for WSO airtime to advertise.

The WSO recognized the generosity of the sponsors with such activities as playing at the Winnipeg party for the Bank of Montreal's 175th anniversary.

The WSO enjoyed excellent donor/sponsor relationships due to the efforts of Charles D'Amours, the highly respected and competent director of development. However, donations had been flat for the previous few months. One of WSO's major sponsors, Seagram's, had announced a few months earlier that it would cut its support from 48 to 24 Canadian orchestras. It was common knowledge in the performing arts that the continuing recession and the permanent restructuring of Canadian companies had led to a decline in corporate donations and sponsorship of nonprofit arts organizations.

Event Fundraisers

The WSO staged special events, such as raffles, gala dinners, and special tours, to raise additional funds. For example, the WSO sold tours to their patrons for a trip to London, England, to hear the London Symphony Orchestra. The ticket price included the cost of the trip, plus a markup that the WSO funneled into their pool of operating funds.

The WSO also engaged in joint fundraising for other Winnipeg-based nonprofit organizations. In 1991, the WSO embarked on a rather unique project with the Grace Hospital Research Foundation. The WSO sold a block of 500 special concert tickets to the Grace Hospital, which then resold the tickets to their own patrons. The tickets included a fundraising dinner and concert, which was performed by the WSO. In addition to selling the Grace Hospital tickets, the WSO helped in decorating the reception hall and catering the dinner. The Grace Hospital sold tickets that included both their own and WSO's markup. This enabled both of these organizations to earn profits, which were added to their respective pools of operating funds.

Trends in Consumer Tastes and Preferences

National Trends

The recently published *Canadian Arts Consumer Profile* (CACP study) indicated that price sensitivity was the main reason consumers were attending fewer performances: recessionary times made performing arts activities too expensive. Surprisingly, the study also concluded that 53 percent of the sample between the ages of 16 and 24 had attended a traditional performing arts event in the previous six months (see Exhibit 6).

EXHIBIT 6 National Trends in Consumer Preferences for the Performing Arts

---

Demographics in Traditional versus Popular Performing Arts

	% Attending Performance within the Last 6 Months	
Age	*Traditional Concert*	*Popular Concert*
16–24	53%	76%
25–34	42	60
35–44	45	53
45–54	49	53
55–64	47	50
65+	46	36

Other Performing Arts Attended by Symphony Audiences

Event	*% Symphony Audience Attending Event*
Theatre	57%
Chamber Music	48
Ballet	45
Musicals	45

Symphony Performances Attended by Other Performing Arts Patrons

Audience	*% Audience Attending Symphonies*
Chamber/Soloists	71%
Opera	61
Ballet	43
Musicals	31

Subscription Options Wanted by Traditional Music Audiences

Feature	*% Audience Wanting Feature*
Exchange used tickets	56%
Get subscription series as a gift	55
Better subscriber discount	55
Choose only performances you want to attend	50
Earn points toward special shows	44

Source: Canadian Consumer Arts Profile, 1990–1991

The CACP study also revealed a fairly high level of audience "crossover" activity between traditional and popular performing arts activities (Exhibit 6). Audiences stated that, when listening to an orchestra play a piece of classical music, they wanted to forget their problems and feel good. They also wanted the music to have a strong emotional impact.

Fewer people were subscribing, opting instead to buy single tickets, because they wanted more choice in selecting individual performances (75 percent of CACP study respondents) and attendance dates, and because subscriptions were too expensive (67 percent of CACP study respondents). Subscribers were also frustrated that they usually could not exchange the tickets they had purchased, and were annoyed that box offices would not take back unused tickets. Some subscribers wanted "frequent attender" points toward free tickets. Others wanted to be able to purchase tickets through ATMs which would show seating plans. The top five options wanted by subscribers are rank ordered in Exhibit 6.

Canadian audiences paid an average of $151 per subscription and $23 per ticket to a symphony performance. According to the CACP study, 43 percent of subscribers would only tolerate a 5 percent increase in subscription fees; 26 percent of subscribers would tolerate a maximum increase of 10 percent.

Trends in Winnipeg

The CACP study revealed that Winnipeg enjoyed one of the highest population attendances at Canadian performing arts functions: a full 50 percent of Winnipegers attended one or more of opera, ballet, symphony, and theatre productions in the previous year. This rate was much higher than Toronto, where only 23 percent of the population attended performing arts functions. Montreal had an even lower attendance rate of 19 percent.

Issues Facing the WSO

Although WSO single-ticket sales were increasing, subscription revenues had declined for the current year. This was a puzzling disappointment to Barry. During his tenure as marketing director, he had redesigned the 1991–92 season catalogue to combine subscription series across all product "types"—pops, classics, children's concerts, special holiday recitals/concerts—in an effort to provide "one-stop shopping" for all WSO subscribers, and to encourage subscribers to purchase multiple subscription series. Subscribers also had the option of "mixing and matching" series, e.g., buying the Classics Series but trading one of these performances for one Pops Concert.

Audience survey results had also revealed customer dissatisfaction with the current offerings. With the exception of the Classics series, which were enjoying an increase in single-ticket and subscription sales, attendance was declining. The Superconcerts for Kids had experienced the largest drop in attendance of all the series offered. Audiences for the Du Maurier Musically Speaking series had been declining for the previous two years. The Pops audience was declining because the audience felt the repertoire was too repetitious. Attendance at the Brandon concerts was also declining.

Barry realized that, while other performing arts in Winnipeg were complementary to the WSO, they also represented competition for the entertainment dollar. There was strong competition as well from the city's two professional sports teams, the football Blue Bombers and the hockey Jets. Price information for these arts and sports activities is given in Exhibit 7.

Exhibit 7   Prices of Some Entertainment Competition

Event	Subscription Prices		Single Ticket Prices		No. of Events per Subscription
	Adults ($)	Students and Seniors ($)	Adults ($)	Students and Seniors ($)	
Royal Winnipeg Ballet	$35–$121	$28–$97	$10–$35	—	4
Manitoba Opera Theatre					
Tuesday evening	35–135	—	17–55	—	3
Weekend (Fri, Sat)	39–150	—	17–55	—	3
Manitoba Theatre Centre					
Wed matinees and					
previews	49–83	35–67	15–21	$12–$18	6
Mon–Thurs evenings	69–132	49–89	14–26	12–26	6
Weekend (Fri, Sat)	95–145	—	19–29	—	6
Winnipeg Blue Bombers	128–275	—	14–27	—	11
Winnipeg Jets	351–1,452	—	9–37	—	44

Barry felt that competitive pressure was increasing from the Country and Western "bars," which were opening up all around Winnipeg. These bars serve dinner, then open up the floor for line dancing (country disco where lines of people dance in synch). Staff are available to teach those patrons who don't know how to line dance. These bars are becoming very popular because they are relatively inexpensive and provided an entire social evening for just about any combination of people.

Preparing the WSO's Strategic Plan

As Barry continued his task of developing a five-year plan, he talked about his board of directors and the "boundaries" within which the orchestra currently operated. "There are two areas which the Board feels very strongly about," said Barry, "and they are highly unlikely to be moved from those positions. That's no problem at all for me because I share those perspectives.

"The first is the philosophy of fiscal responsibility with artistic excellence. The fiscal responsibility part means being deficit-free at fiscal year-end. That means that before I get to the five-year plan, I'm going to have to present a short-term plan that will get us out of our projected deficit by the end of the year. The second area where the Board takes a strong position is the role of the orchestra. They see our strength in the Manitoba community as based on the fact that we have positioned ourselves as a community-oriented arts organization. In no way should this suggest any compromise whatsoever in the quality of our activities. It does mean that we must never forget that the people we serve are the citizens of Manitoba. It is very important not only that we understand that, but that Manitobans understand that as well."

As he contemplated what alternatives he should select for further analysis,

Barry thought about the excellent relations he had built up with the artistic director, orchestra members, and administrative staff when he was marketing director. He knew these people would be essential in helping him to successfully implement his strategic plan. To give his plan a framework, Barry wrote down all the factors impacting on the WSO (see Exhibit 8). He wrote them in a circle to foster a sense of balance and to reinforce the WSO's philosophy of remaining deficit-free: for example, if a revenue-generating "point" or factor is reduced by $10,000, another revenue-generating "point" on the circle must be increased by $10,000, or a cost "point" on the circle must be decreased by $10,000.

There were some limitations on the changes that could be made to the current season. From Barry's perspective, performances for which the WSO had already advertised programs and program dates could not be cancelled. "It's not just a matter of inconveniencing those who have already purchased tickets," said Barry. "The message such a cancellation would send to the broader community would be very negative." However, there was potential

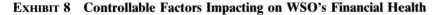

EXHIBIT 8   Controllable Factors Impacting on WSO's Financial Health

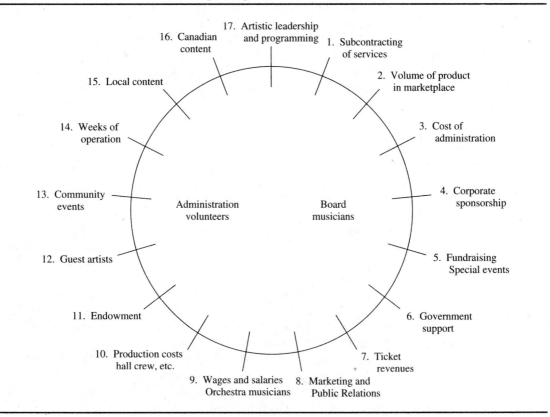

to schedule two and possibly three performances late in the season and still remain within the orchestra agreement. There also was the potential to package the remaining season programs into one or more mini-series.

"But whatever we do for the remainder of this season," said Barry, "it is very important that we don't do anything that will endanger our goal of renewing and broadening our customer base."